# THE
# BOWKER
# ANNUAL

**44th Edition • 1999**

# THE
# BOWKER
# ANNUAL

## Library and
## Book Trade Almanac™

| | | |
|---|---|---|
| *Editor* | • | Dave Bogart |
| *Consultant* | • | Julia C. Blixrud |

**R.R. Bowker®**
New Providence, New Jersey

Published by R. R. Bowker,
a unit of Cahners Business Information
Copyright © 1999 by Reed Elsevier Inc.
All rights reserved
Printed and bound in the United States of America
Bowker® is a registered trademark of Reed Elsevier Inc.
The Bowker Annual Library and Book Trade Almanac™ is a trademark of Reed
Elsevier Properties Inc., used under license.

International Standard Book Number  0–8352–4222–6
International Standard Serial Number  0068–0540
Library of Congress Catalog Card Number  55–12434

ISBN 0 - 8352 - 4222 - 6

9 780835 242226

# Contents

## International Reports

## Special Reports

# Part 2
# Legislation, Funding, and Grants

## Legislation

## Funding Programs and Grant-Making Agencies

# Part 3
# Library/Information Science
# Education, Placement, and Salaries

# Part 4
## Research and Statistics

# Part 5
## Reference Information

## Distinguished Books

# Part 6
# Directory of Organizations

## Directory of Library and Related Organizations

## Directory of Book Trade and Related Organizations

# Preface

This 44th edition of *The Bowker Annual* examines another year of challenge as the library and book trade worlds deal with the evolving complexities of the Information Age.

Both spheres are at the forefront of the age, adapting, growing, and diversifying as the pace of change steadily accelerates.

As in previous editions, we have assembled a blend of expert analysis and practical information: how things are, how things are changing, where we have been, and where we are headed.

This year's Special Reports look at four areas of concern:

- Public and school libraries are on the horns of a dilemma: Should they "filter" Internet access to protect young people from objectionable material, or does that constitute censorship? Ken Haycock, Betty Chapin, and David Bruce of the University of British Columbia closely examine the question—and possible solutions.

- How is library and information science education changing to keep pace with the times? The Kellogg-ALISE Information Professions and Education Reform (KALIPER) project is described by Joan C. Durrance, who chairs its study committee, and Karen Pettigrew, the project's principal investigator.

- In an examination of recent developments in copyright law, Robert L. Oakley of Georgetown University Law Center describes "a year in which major new legislation passed Congress, legislation that redefined the balance of rights between copyright owners and the users of copyrighted information."

- The expanding array of service demands being placed upon networks is the theme of "Networking and Cooperation in 1998," prepared by the executive directors of two major networks, Bonnie Juergens of AMIGOS and Kate Nevins of SOLINET.

Trends of the year, from apparently robust public library funding to a batch of major acquisitions among the publishing giants, are also found in Part 1 in reports by editors at *Library Journal, School Library Journal,* and *Publishers Weekly*. Next, reports from agencies and federal libraries detail their year and its accomplishments; a repeated theme is the growing role of digital information.

In Part 2, the year's legislation and regulations affecting libraries and those affecting publishing are detailed bill by bill, followed by reports from grant-making agencies and funding programs.

Professional information of all kinds for librarians is found in Part 3, including lists of scholarship and award winners, help in finding employment, and a review of the placements and salaries won by recent information science graduates.

Part 4 contains a wealth of research and statistics, from details of current research projects to tables of library acquisition expenditures and national and international book publishing data.

Reference information makes up Part 5: listings of the year's most notable books, the bestsellers, and the prize winners. There is also such basic practical information as publishers' toll-free phone numbers and explanations of how the ISBN, ISSN, and SAN systems operate.

Part 6 is an expanded directory of publishing and library organizations big and small, national and worldwide, plus a calendar of upcoming conferences, meetings, trade fairs, and other events.

It adds up to a wealth of information, and putting it all together is the work of many hands. We are grateful to those who have contributed articles, assembled statistics and reports, and responded to our requests for information. Special thanks are due Consulting Editor Julia C. Blixrud and consultant Catherine Barr.

We believe you'll find this edition of *The Bowker Annual* a valuable and handy resource. Your comments and suggestions for future editions are most welcome.

Dave Bogart  
Editor

# Part 1
# Reports from the Field

# News of the Year

## *LJ* News Report:
## Libraries Succeed at Funding Books *and* Bytes

Evan St. Lifer

Executive Editor, *Library Journal*

Armed with its highest response rate ever, *Library Journal*'s ninth annual Budget Report portends a robust 1999 for the nation's public libraries. The century that began with Andrew Carnegie's largesse, which made libraries widely available, will end with enthusiastic civic momentum carrying libraries into the next millennium. Over a span of nearly 100 years, support for libraries has endured and grown steadily, save for a few bitter bumps along the way.

### PLs Ending Century on Top

Fiscal year (FY) 1999 budget projections from the more than 530 libraries nationwide that responded to *LJ*'s Budget Report buttress the century-long trend of steady public library support. Total library budgets increased by 4.4 percent, while materials budgets and salaries jumped by 6.5 percent and 4.5 percent, respectively. The projected FY 1999 figures culminate a five-year climb in which total budgets rose by 28 percent, materials budgets by 31 percent, and salary/personnel budgets by 27 percent.

Another key indicator illustrating the aggregate fiscal health of public libraries is the continued increase of average per capita spending, which jumped from $26.08 to $26.99, in keeping with per capita's trend of increasing by nearly $1 each year for the last several years (see Table 1).

### Fate Tied to Local Taxes

Still, the exercise of trying to evaluate libraries' relative fiscal health on a regional level is next to impossible, given that their budgetary fates are tied to local property taxes and thus to the local economy. This is not to say that certain states don't place a higher priority on library service than others. Case in point: Ohio remains the standard by which all other states measure public library appropriations. Ohio libraries get anywhere from 70 percent to 90 percent of their funding from the state, which devotes 6.4 percent of its spending to public libraries.

Adapted from *Library Journal*, January 1999

Meanwhile, in neighboring Pennsylvania, libraries have been in an economic bind for years with little help from the state. On the heels of a damning 1997 report and study published by the *Philadelphia Inquirer* that detailed the exigent state of its public libraries, Pennsylvania is beginning to take steps to improve public library service statewide. Said one librarian from a rural library, "The sorry state of rural libraries [in Pennsylvania] resembles that of a Third World country."

However, the contrast in local economies is not limited to state-by-state comparisons. Neighboring communities can just as likely have economic situations—and thus library budgets—heading in opposite directions. In Texas, libraries in local towns like Sinton and Canton have foundered, while Grapevine, a larger Texas locale, has prospered due to "great economic development" taking place within its city limits. Plano is another Texas success, with its budget climbing by 17 percent in FY 1999. Several libraries in California continue to cite the passage in 1993 of the Education Revenue Augmentation Fund (ERAF)—in which state lawmakers mandated the transfer of property tax revenues from library to school coffers—as the continued cause of their fiscal ills. Other California libraries have left ERAF behind, approving referenda to replace or in some cases bolster funding lost to the measure.

## Rise of Technology Budgets

In the early 1990s, following the boom-boom 1980s, library funding mirrored the country's economic slowdown. Property values began to slide, jobs were lost, and library budgets were cut—in some cases decimated—as a result. Libraries therefore turned to their own revenue-generating devices, starting and expanding "friends" groups, launching foundations, and becoming more determined in their quest for grant money from public as well as private sources.

**Table 1 / Tracking Per Capita Funding**

Source: *Library Journal* Budget Report 1999

**Table 2 / Library Budgets for FY 1999**

| Population Served | Materials | | Salaries | | Operating Budget | |
|---|---|---|---|---|---|---|
| Fewer than 10,000 | $20,000 | NC | $69,000 | +3.0% | $121,000 | NC |
| 10,000–24,999 | 82,000 | +8.6% | 280,000 | +6.8% | 505,000 | +7.5% |
| 25,000–49,999 | 169,000 | -1.2% | 672,000 | +1.5% | 1,199,000 | +4.3% |
| 50,000–99,999 | 266,000 | +5.7% | 1,080,000 | +4.7% | 1,746,000 | +3.1% |
| 100,000–499,999 | 708,000 | +3.5% | 2,926,000 | +5.6% | 4,779,000 | +4.7% |
| 500,000–999,999 | 3,112,000 | +7.3% | 9,866,000 | +6.0% | 17,028,000 | +6.5% |
| More than 1 Million | 3,600,000 | +2.3% | 15,369,000 | -5.3% | 25,920,000 | -2.6% |
| FY 1998 vs. FY 1999 | +6.5% | | +4.5% | | +4.4% | |

Source: *Library Journal* Budget Report 1999
NC: No Change

Despite the current comforting numbers and the predominately sunny economic outlook, most libraries have long since learned that in order to maintain the essential balance between technology and books they need to seek alternative sources of income. Only through fiscal dexterity are libraries able to deliver the latest information technologies to patrons while maintaining the breadth and diversity of their collections. How else could libraries add a line item to their budget for Internet costs that accounts for anywhere from $3,000 to nearly $300,000 without cutting other critical services?

In fact, nearly 7 out of 10 librarians reported not having to "cut back in other areas" in order to handle increased technology costs. Of the 25 percent who did have to cut back, the majority cut their materials budget, while smaller numbers reported trimming staffing and hours. When asked where the money for Internet operations came from in the annual budget, 41 percent of respondents said it came from the technology/automation budget, while 25 percent reported having a separate line item. Somewhat surprisingly, 16 percent said they paid for the Internet out of their materials budget; another 9 percent used a special grant, and 3 percent spent federal money.

Librarians reported that in FY 1999 Internet-related expenditures will comprise 3.7 percent of their budgets, up from 2.9 percent in FY 1998. Over a three-year period the increase has been even more dramatic: since 1995, Internet costs as a part of the total budget have increased more than fivefold. What makes the growth rate more amazing is that in their base year, libraries spent funds on both installation and maintenance of Internet access. In the succeeding years, libraries' spending on net maintenance alone far surpassed the investment made in the base year. Holding true to last year's *LJ* budget survey, the overall average initial cost to integrate the Internet into operations was roughly $80,000. However, net maintenance costs are on the rise, with librarians reporting average annual costs of more than $60,000 in FY 1998 vs. nearly $50,000 in net operational costs in FY 1997.

## Fund-Raising Now A Staple

Fund-raising has become a staple in libraries' fiscal mix. Since 1993 fund-raising is up 228 percent, illustrating an increased need. More than two-thirds of survey respondents confirmed having a fund-raising arm, up from 62 percent in FY 1998. Even the percentage of libraries that conduct the most rudimentary fund-raising campaign increased from last year, from 48 percent to 51 percent.

Average fund-raising levels grew by about 10 percent to $151,000 in FY 1998 from $137,000 in FY 1997. Broken down by library size, libraries serving populations of fewer than 10,000 raised a median amount of $2,000 in FY 1998; from 10,000–24,999, $9,000; 25,000–49,999, $13,000; 50,000–99,999, $27,000; 100,000–499,999, $29,000; 500,000–1 million, $124,000; and more than 1 million, $1.2 million.

Further, 6 out of 10 libraries are receiving an average of $110,000 in grant money, using it for a range of initiatives including technology, books and materials, literacy projects, and staffing and hours. For those concerned that libraries are spending too much of their alternative funding on technology, the largest percentage of librarians (45 percent) reported spending their grant money not only on technology/automation but on books/materials as well.

## Spending the Technology Dollar

Given the rise of Internet implementation and maintenance costs, *LJ* sought to learn more about the way libraries spend their money. Survey respondents cited access as the prevailing Internet-related cost, amounting to 44 percent of their Internet funds. New hardware expenditures (see Table 3) took up 22 percent of Internet budgets, followed by upgrades/ maintenance (13 percent), staffing (10 percent), software (6 percent), and Web site design/management (5 percent).

Some libraries are having to account for a fairly new technology expenditure, albeit a slight one: the cost of filtering the Internet. More than 18 percent of respondents said they used a filter, at an average cost of $1,000 annually, with the smallest libraries spending an average of $18, the largest, $1,800 per year. However, it is not clear from the survey whether respondents took staff costs into account. *LJ* learned that of those libraries using filtering software, 9 out of 10 are filtering children's terminals and 4 out of 10 have installed it on terminals used by adults.

Libraries' large telecommunications bills explain their avid participation in the E-rate program, mandated by the Federal Communications Commission (FCC) under Universal Service provisions to offer discounted telecommunications rates to libraries and schools; 3 out of 4 librarians said they applied for discounted rates and expect to save an average of nearly $10,000 (for breakdowns of projected savings by library size, see Table 4).

However, fewer smaller libraries applied for telecommunications discounts. Many respondents complained that the application process was too time-consuming and complex. Since librarians who run small libraries wear many hats, they can't afford the time needed to complete the elaborate discount form, described by some as Byzantine. Nearly 8 out of 10 libraries serving populations of 50,000 or more applied for E-rate discounts, while only about 6 out of 10 serving fewer than 50,000 applied.

## Gates Foundation's Role

Any analysis of public library spending on technology would be incomplete without the inclusion of the efforts put forth by the Gates Library Foundation, which is spending $400 million in cash, software, and training to wire every public library in the nation to the Internet by the year 2002. Public libraries in several of the nation's poorest states—including Alabama, Mississippi, Kentucky, Arkansas, Louisiana, New Mexico, and West Virginia—which could not have afforded the costs associated with Internet installation and implementation, have received the necessary tools and resources to deliver Internet access to their patrons. However, significant questions loom for many of these libraries: How will they maintain their Internet services and upgrade their hardware and software once they exhaust the Gates grant money?

**Table 3  /  How Libraries Are Spending Their Internet Dollar**

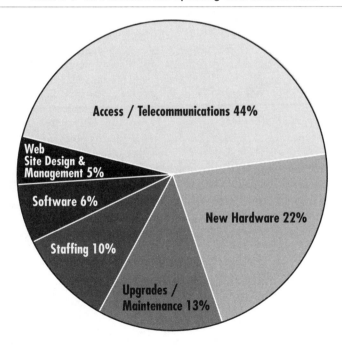

## Public Shows Support

Despite public libraries' varied economic fortunes, their strong showing once again in this year's referenda—better than 75 percent won approval—as well as the consistent number of library construction projects illustrate the public's continued enthusiastic support and willingness to invest in its public libraries.

**Table 4 / Internet Costs**

| Population Served | Initial Cost | Annual Maintenance | E-rate Savings* |
|---|---|---|---|
| Fewer Than 10,000 | $8,900 | $3,400 | $850 |
| 10,000–24,999 | 24,000 | 9,100 | 2,545 |
| 25,000–49,999 | 41,600 | 20,700 | 4,113 |
| 50,000–99,999 | 47,600 | 29,300 | 6,551 |
| 100,000–499,999 | 122,400 | 85,500 | 13,298 |
| 500,000–999,999 | 228,900 | 211,000 | 22,298 |
| More than 1 Million | 282,200 | 279,700 | 23,667 |

*The average amount libraries expect to save from telecommunications subsidies in Fiscal Year 1999

Source: *Library Journal* Budget Report 1999

# *SLJ* News Report: We're in the Money!

Renée Olson

Editor-in-chief, *School Library Journal*

Rick Margolis

News and Features Editor, *School Library Journal*

Andrea Glick

News and Features Associate Editor, *School Library Journal*

California. Chicago. Georgia. These are a few of the places that saw blessed increases in library funding in 1998. For many, it was the first time in a long time.

In a hallelujah moment, California approved a $158.5 million budget item, specifically for school libraries, in August. "To finally have a continuing source of funds to build school library collections is a dream come true," said Janet Minami, president of the California School Library Association.

One month later, in Chicago, U.S. Representative Rod Blagojevich (D-Ill.) pledged $2,140, his entire congressional pay increase, to help Chicago's struggling school libraries, prompting the school board to pony up $500,000 of its own money. That's on top of the $2 million it has allocated annually at the district level to libraries since 1996.

Back in the spring Georgia's Governor Zell Miller gave $10 million to public libraries to spend on circulating materials, 50 percent of which had to be for kids. "People went crazy," said Molly Kinney, Consultant for Children, Parents, and Family Literacy in Georgia's Department of Technical and Adult Education. "I walked in the back door [of one library] and there were boxes and boxes [of books] lined up in the hall," she said, referring to one branch where the money allowed the staff to double the size of the collection.

Now rejoice and bask in the glory of these success stories for a few moments.

Okay, time's up.

Keep in mind that in many cases, these recent increases are poor substitutes for steady library funding. California schools now have millions for library materials and equipment, but nothing new for certified librarians, who are in scarce supply.

In Chicago, as in many school districts nationwide, principals still have the discretion to not allot a single cent to their libraries. Until districts—or, better yet, states—make the decision to require stable library funding, their periodic displays of generosity are little more than hollow gestures.

Because Georgia made the $10 million available late in the fiscal year, libraries had only about four months to spend it. Librarians had no problem finding ways to use the money, but the sudden buying spurt meant that some technical services departments found themselves overwhelmed by a deluge of new materials.

Adapted from *School Library Journal*, December 1998

Still, the profession may look back fondly at a time when there actually *was* $10 million to be spent, hurriedly or not. If gloomy forecasters are correct and the eight-year-long expansion in the U.S. economy does level off, that may indeed be the case.

## The Internet Still a Dangerous Place

Congressional lawmakers were busy this year dreaming up ways to protect children from the perils of the Internet. That kept librarians and other free-speech advocates busy, too—trying to protect their customers' First Amendment rights.

One of Congress's biggest battles was fought over filters designed to block pornography on the Internet. Senator John McCain (R-Ariz.) introduced a bill requiring schools and libraries that receive the E-rate (the federal telecommunications discount) to install filters on computers used by children. In the House, Representative Ernest Istook (R-Okla.) sought to require agencies receiving federal money for computers to install filters as well.

The American Library Association (ALA) opposed both bills, saying filtering decisions should be left to local school and library boards. But the measures stayed alive until mid-October, when they were axed from the massive spending bill hammered out by the president and Congress.

Free-speech advocates had less luck preventing the passage of the Child Online Protection Act. Sponsored by Rep. Michael Oxley (R-Ohio), the new law requires commercial Web site operators to verify that users are adults before distributing material considered "harmful to minors." One way of doing this, the law says, is for sites to ask for credit-card account numbers.

Critics of the measure have dubbed it "CDA II," a reference to the Communications Decency Act struck down last year by the Supreme Court. But supporters say the latest measure is more narrowly tailored than CDA, because it applies only to commercial Web sites and uses the "harmful to minors" standard, rather than CDA's broader indecency criteria. Under the "harmful to minors" guidelines, material with "serious literary, artistic, political, or scientific value" is exempt from filtering.

Opponents, such as the American Civil Liberties Union (ACLU), have already filed suit against the new law, insisting that the measure, like CDA, will chill constitutionally protected speech. ALA was considering how the measure might affect libraries and whether to take legal action.

## Meet the Lexiles

Lexiles? They sound like a holdover from that spacy '60s sitcom *The Jetsons*, an animated send-up of the future. Actually, the futuristic comparison is not all that far-fetched. If a company called MetaMetrics has its say, Lexiles will soon play a prominent role in shaping reading instruction for eons to come.

So what's a Lexile? It's a unit of measurement that describes children's reading levels and the difficulty of reading materials. Based on factors such as sentence length and common word usage, the Lexile system rates books anywhere from 200 Lexiles (a relative snap) to 1,700 Lexiles (a potential bear).

*Make Way for Ducklings*, for example, weighs in at 750 Lexiles, while *Catcher in the Rye* is considered to be at the 1,100-Lexile level.

Per Jack Stenner, president of MetaMetrics: "One of the promises of the Lexile Framework is that targeted readers—where someone has paid attention to the student's reading level and matched it to the text—read more."

Great news? Not necessarily. Although the Lexile system is in widespread use in public schools in Florida and North Carolina, detractors claim the system is misguided and may actually restrict students' reading.

## Daniel's Dream

'Twas the night before Christmas, two years ago, when seven-year-old Daniel Swain, a precocious book lover, scripted a vision of glad tidings. Daniel wrote a letter to his local library in San Rafael, California, urging that it find a way to put books in the homes of children not fortunate enough to have books of their own. Daniel's letter prompted the library to develop a program called Books for Kids, which raises money to purchase books for children of low-income families.

More recently, four local Rotary clubs have taken up the charge, spearheading a book drive that netted approximately 10,000 books, making Daniel's dream a reality.

## Kids Think the Darnedest Things

In response to the release of Independent Counsel Kenneth Starr's report on President Clinton's relationship with former White House intern Monica Lewinsky, the American Library Association's Office for Intellectual Freedom (OIF) wondered: "Should kids be allowed to see the Starr report online?"

OIF's official opinion? "That's for parents to decide. This is an excellent example of why it's important that parents talk to their children."

Amid widespread concern that children should be shielded from the report's sexually explicit content, Linda Ellerbee, the host of a news special for children on Nickelodeon, reported a less-than-obvious discovery: the children she spoke to wanted to discuss issues relating to the president's honesty, not s-e-x.

## Classic Misunderstanding

Rewriting an American classic may be hazardous to your health. Just ask the folks at the American Association of School Librarians (AASL) and the Association of Educational Communications and Technology (AECT), who collaborated on updating their venerable guidelines for school library media centers.

Last winter, the two groups were stuck at an impasse over the final version. With the deadline rapidly approaching, ALA Editions, the guidelines' publisher, urged the two to come to an agreement. Just three months later, the first copies of the new *Information Power: Building Partnerships for Learning* (ALA, 1998), a document that strives to define school library excellence for the next millennium and sets the first student standards for information literacy, were flying off the shelves, selling briskly at ALA's Annual Conference in Washington D.C.

## Scouts' Honor

By now, you might have thought the debate over the American Library Association's 60-year-long relationship with the freckle-faced Boy Scouts of America would have been resolved. But when the California Supreme Court ruled in March 1998 that the Scouts—by virtue of being a private organization—were entitled to exclude homosexuals, atheists, and agnostics, the debate resumed.

The Association for Library Service to Children, a division of ALA, provides the Scouts with lists of recommended books they can read to earn merit badges. Because the Scouts are an exclusive club, are they still an appropriate partner for ALA? Some ALA members say yes, others disagree. A task force of the executive board was reviewing the issue.

## Privatization Verdict

Does library privatization work? Based on the experience of the Riverside County (California) Library System (RCLS), the answer is a definite maybe.

In July 1997 RCLS made dubious history when it became the nation's first library to entrust its entire operation to a private company, Library Systems and Services, Inc. (LSSI). By then the beleaguered library system had been forced to trim staff, shrink hours, and watch its budget plummet.

How has the Maryland-based company performed? To date, it has kept all of its promises: retaining librarians, beefing up hours and staff, and spending more on materials. The first-year verdict? Cautious optimism.

(Postscript: a New Jersey Superior Court judge recently nixed a similar contract between LSSI and the Jersey City Public Library. The reason? According to a report published in the October 18 *New York Times*, the judge "criticized the board for failing to allow for public discussion of the matter and for failing to properly advertise the July 14 meeting at which the contract was awarded.")

## The Magic Eight Ball

From *SLJ*'s vantage point, 1999 promises to be a year during which the publishing industry will continue to experiment with electronic ventures. Pricey electronic books, introduced at the end of 1998, may get a lukewarm reception among consumers. But the idea of portable electronic text still has merit, a view Follett Library Resources shares. The Illinois-based book distributor plans to sink upward of $1 million in 1999 into building a "cyber warehouse" capable of storing electronic text. But until there's widespread demand, we'll see publishers and book wholesalers continue to scurry to sell print through electronic channels.

It also seems likely that major reference purchases will continue to move out of individual libraries and toward statewide or large consortial agreements as more publishers put their wares on the Web and get savvy about licensing on a large scale. Four states—Missouri, New York, Rhode Island, and California—have signed agreements with Grolier for one or more of its three online encyclopedias: *Encyclopedia Americana*, *Grolier Multimedia Encyclopedia*, and *New*

*Book of Knowledge Online*, the last two covering just K–12. And at least one statewide network—the Access Colorado Library Information Network—now sees one of its roles as establishing a core electronic collection for member libraries.

This we're-in-it-together approach takes some of the fun out of collection development, especially if you don't think highly of a chosen reference title, but it can make sense in terms of efficiency and cost.

Another potential time-saver on the horizon, especially for small libraries, is the advent of the 100-percent-outsourced catalog. At least one vendor is banking that libraries will take one look at the prospect of maintaining an online catalog and say Enough! For libraries that fall into this category, the San Jose-based CASPR company will run your catalog using its Web-hosting service and update it as you add new materials to the collection, for $400 a year.

In an ideal world, such a plan might give you back your lunch hour—perhaps even your summer—for reading. And there's no need for a Magic Eight Ball to tell us there simply couldn't be a better pursuit for the last year of the millennium.

## Newsmakers

- It really does pay to have friends in high places. California's school librarians found that out in August when, after years of neglect, the state Legislature approved $158.5 million for school library materials and equipment. Credit for the windfall goes in large part to Delaine Easton, the state's Superintendent of Instruction. Easton mounted a campaign to convince Governor Pete Wilson and state lawmakers that good school libraries make a big difference in educating students. When the state found itself with a surplus, Easton's efforts paid off.

- Rudolph Giuliani, New York City's tough mayor, managed to gain a few days of warm and fuzzy publicity in February when he championed the cause of a bear. Not just any bear, mind you, but the original Winnie-the-Pooh—who since 1987 has been housed at the New York Public Library. On a visit to the library, a member of the British Parliament happened to notice Pooh—along with Kanga, Eeyore, Piglet, and Tigger—in a glass case, and decided the British-born bear and friends should be returned to England. Giuliani warned the visiting politician not to interfere with legal immigrants, the request was withdrawn, and an international incident was averted.

- Margaret McElderry was editing children's books long before many of today's librarians learned to read. So it was the end of an era last summer when Simon & Schuster announced she'd be stepping down as vice-president and publisher of her imprint, Margaret K. McElderry books. In more than 50 years as an editor, the former children's librarian worked with such admired authors as Susan Cooper, Eloise McGraw, and Helen Oxenbury. McElderry will remain at Simon & Schuster to edit a small group of writers.

- Regardless of what the judge decides in the Loudoun County, Virginia, Internet filtering case, one library trustee will still be a winner. Loudoun County Public Library installed Internet filters on all its computers—not just children's terminals—a move that promptly drew a lawsuit considered a national test case. Although the library may ultimately lose in court, the board member behind the policy, Dick Black, has used the issue to his gain: the conservative Republican was elected to the Virginia House of Delegates.

- Few people have had as great an impact on children's literature and librarianship as Lillian N. Gerhardt, *SLJ*'s editor-in-chief for the last 32 years. We said goodbye to Lillian on August 31, when she officially retired to enjoy some much-deserved leisure time. But you definitely haven't heard the last of her: She was to deliver the annual May Hill Arbuthnot lecture at San Jose (California) State University in April, and she'll also continue to make periodic contributions to the pages of *SLJ*.

- The school district says it was a routine transfer, but Cheryl Ward thinks she was punished for fighting censorship. Now the former Windsor Locks (Connecticut) Middle School librarian is suing the district, saying it violated her First Amendment rights. Ward was transferred this fall to a job teaching fifth grade after she had opposed a plan to segregate "controversial" library materials and require parental consent to read them. The superintendent proposed the new policy when a parent complained about the presence of Chris Lynch's *Iceman* (HarperCollins, 1994) on the middle school's summer reading list.

- Children's librarianship lost a towering figure this year with the death of Augusta Baker, 86. A renowned storyteller, Baker trained a generation of librarians in the storytelling art. During her 37 years at the New York Public Library, she also rose to the prestigious post of Coordinator of Children's Services. One of her greatest achievements was raising awareness of the offensive stereotypes often used to depict blacks in children's literature.

- Seattle public school students will crack open thousands of brand new library books this year, thanks to the John Stanford Book Fund. The fund was created to honor Stanford, the popular superintendent of schools and a champion of literacy, after he announced that he had leukemia. The fund met its goal of raising $500,000 in August, but checks continue to arrive, said Joel Groen of Seattle's nonprofit Alliance for Education. The biggest gift, $78,000, came from the Seattle rock group Pearl Jam.

# *PW* News Reports

## Whatever Next?

### Jim Milliot

Editor, Business and News, *Publishers Weekly*

By any measure, 1998 was a year of unprecedented deal making that will result in profound—if not yet fully understood—changes in the book-publishing industry in 1999 and beyond. The 15 largest deals last year totaled more than $11 billion and further consolidated all aspects of the industry.

The size and scope of the acquisitions "show that there are lots of companies with money interested in publishing," says industry consultant Tony Schulte. Moreover, the most aggressive players in the merger movement last year were foreign companies, prompting Tom Woll, head of Cross River Publishing Consultants, to observe that "the European investment in American publishing shows the strength of the American market compared to other areas." While some U.S. media conglomerates were eager to abandon the book industry, Woll adds, "others are more than happy to be here."

But it was more than just the amount of money involved in the transactions that made 1998 such an important year; it was the players that took part in the deals that shook the industry. It was, as one industry observer notes, "the year of the unimaginable." Adds Michael Shatzkin, president of the Ideal Logic Company, "The changes in 1998 generate more uncertainty for the industry than any changes in recent publishing history. Right now, there are more questions than answers."

While rumors that Viacom was interested in divesting Simon & Schuster were rampant in the early part of 1998, when the announcement finally came that Viacom planned to break up the nation's largest book publisher, industry members quickly realized that no company was safe from being sold. Although there was a constant buzz about what company might be sold next—HarperCollins was everyone's favorite bet—when the news came that the Newhouse family was selling the country's largest trade publisher, Random House, to Bertelsmann, the transaction, conducted largely in secret, stunned the industry. After the S&S and Random House deals, industry members could be forgiven if they felt that nothing could top those two events. In November, however, the biggest stunner of the year, especially for the trade publishing segment, occurred when Barnes & Noble announced its intention to acquire the nation's largest book wholesaler, Ingram. "Each deal was more unbelievable than the one before it," an observer says.

One of the few firm conclusions that can be made about the events of 1998 was that the big got bigger in every major publishing category, be it educational, professional, or trade. As McGraw-Hill CEO Terry McGraw told analysts at a meeting late last year, "Critical mass in the education market is more important than ever before. You need to be in all areas of the market to compete." Pearson's acquisition of the educational, professional/business, and reference divisions of Simon & Schuster gives it the size to compete in all facets of the

Adapted from *Publishers Weekly* January 4, 1999

**Major Acquisitions, 1998**

| Acquirer | Company Acquired | Price |
| --- | --- | --- |
| Amazon.com | Bookpages<br>Telebook<br>Internet Database | Total for 3 companies<br>$55 million |
| Amazon.com | Junglee Corp<br>PlanetAll | Total for 2 companies<br>$288 million |
| Bertelsmann | Random House | Estimated $1.4 billion |
| Bertelsmann | barnesandnoble.com | $200 million for 50% stake |
| Bertelsmann | Springer Verlag | $600 million for 80% stake |
| Barnes & Noble | Ingram Book Group | $600 million |
| Harcourt General | Mosby | $415 million |
| Mattel | Pleasant Company | $700 million |
| Pearson | Simon & Schuster<br>Educational and Professional/<br>Business and Reference Divisions | $4.6 billion |
| Reed Elsevier | Matthew Bender | $1.65 billion |
| Wolters Kluwer | Waverly | $374 million |
| Wolters Kluwer | Plenum Publishing | $258 million |
| Total | | $11.14 billion |

education market, which is now dominated by four companies: Pearson, McGraw-Hill, Harcourt Brace, and Houghton Mifflin.

The acquisitions made in the professional segment cemented the leadership in that category among a few companies. "Consolidation in the STM area has left fewer and fewer players," Woll notes. Professional publishers that were absorbed by larger competitors last year included Mosby, Matthew Bender, Waverly Inc., and Plenum Publishing. As a result, the dominant companies in the American professional segment consist of Wolters Kluwer, Reed Elsevier, Harcourt Brace, and the Thomson Corp.

Educational and professional companies have demonstrated that size has advantages in their respective markets. Leveraging warehousing, distribution, sales, and administrative costs across a larger product base has improved the margins of the largest educational and professional companies. Indeed, Pearson hopes to realize annual savings of $130 million annually when its integration of the S&S properties is completed.

With Random House having sales close to $2 billion, Bertelsmann will have to find the same type of savings for a trade publisher. "The question of how large a consumer publisher can be and have size work in its favor is something Bertelsmann will have to answer," notes Shatzkin. "They are in uncharted waters."

A high-ranking executive involved with integrating one of last year's major mergers explains that for the acquisition to be a success, "We will need to quickly determine who is going to do what, so we can go out and find new authors. We keep reminding ourselves that we didn't do this purchase to become experts in systems integration, but to become better publishers." Peter Adams, president of Moseley Associates, notes that blending different imprints is a delicate task. According to Adams, "The winners among the newly merged firms will be those who keep in touch with authors and with readers, in both the trade and educational areas, by nurturing good editors and marketing people."

Although the breakup of S&S and the sale of Random House were momentous events, the most important development in 1998, and the one that will have the most serious, and unpredictable, ramifications for trade publishers, was B&N's purchase of Ingram. "Len Riggio should be given the 'Shrewd Move of the Year Award' for his purchase of Ingram," Woll says. "It's an incredible maneuver that will have everyone scurrying to catch up." The B&N/Ingram marriage, however, will need to solve several questions if it is to be a success. Shatzkin notes, "B&N needs to determine if they want to use Ingram to build up their own  distribution infrastructure, or do they want Ingram to prosper as its own business? They can do both for a while, but the two are bound to come into conflict."

Shatzkin says that if B&N/Ingram want to try to convince independent booksellers that they are not sharing information with each other or that Ingram is not favoring B&N in fulfilling orders, they should establish a committee that would include booksellers. "Independent booksellers are going to need more than just words if they are going to feel comfortable dealing with Ingram," he says.

The B&N/Ingram combination, coupled with Random House's decision to phase itself out of the distribution business, should make distribution a major issue in 1999, predicts Lorraine Shanley, a principal with Market Partners International. Several publishers have already announced their intention to increase their distribution business by adding new clients, and wholesalers have promised to try to cut into Ingram's market share of the trade market. "We will have a higher retail profile in 1999," says Baker & Taylor president Jim Ulsamer.

Shatzkin asserts that B&T, Amazon.com and the Borders Group "are now strategic partners whether they know it or not. Those companies are run by creative people and I'm sure they will come up with something" to counter B&N/Ingram. An acquisition of one of those three companies by another would not shock anyone. (B&T owns an undisclosed amount of Amazon stock. According to CDA/Investnet, B&T registered to sell a total of 400,000 shares of Amazon worth more than $50 million between July and December). David Brodwin, an associate partner with Andersen Consulting, observes, "When one company gets too much power in its particular market, it is natural for its rivals to collaborate to compete against it."

One consequence of the changing distribution patterns could be an increase in returns this year. In a letter to its publisher clients, Associated Publishers Group warns that it's possible that B&N and/or Ingram could decide to clean out their inventory pipeline, which would lead to a huge wave of returns.

The B&N/Ingram combination confronts an issue that had been largely dormant in publishing: vertical integration. Although in the past some publishers owned bookstores (such as the Doubleday Book Shops and Macmillan's ownership of Brentano's), those relationships were not near the scale of B&N/Ingram or Bertelsmann's ownership of Random House plus its 50 percent ownership stake in barnesandnoble.com.

"Similar to other industries, companies that compete in one area of publishing are becoming partners in others," observes Shanley. "It can make for some strange bedfellows." Tony Schulte thinks there is more vertical integration to come, and expects B&N to take "chunks of publishers' business away by expanding their proprietary publishing program." Hiring Barbara Morgan to develop original titles "could very well be just the beginning" of a more aggressive B&N publishing operation, Schulte speculates.

Although it is uncertain where the events of 1998 will lead, most are optimistic that a stronger industry will emerge. Noting the irony that the stodgy publishing business has been in the forefront of online retailing and on-demand printing, Shanley says, "Everything that has happened gives an enormous boost to the business. The changes will catapult publishing into the 21st century from the Dark Ages." With that much time to make up, it could be a wild trip.

# No Page Like a Home Page

### Steven M. Zeitchik
Editor, *PW Daily*, Bookselling

Last fall Warner Books' catalog looked a little different from catalogs of seasons past. Alongside the blurbs, the jacket photos, and the author bios sat small yet noticeable type, not dissimilar to the movement it represented: "Web Marketing," read the copy, hinting at author chats and cyber-placements.

Greg Voynow, the new director of online marketing at Time-Warner Electronic Publishing, understood its importance. "I think it reflected the mindset that is beginning to infiltrate this company," he says. "The Internet is an efficient way to get the word out about books."

Online marketing has arrived at most medium-size and large trade publishers, who have, until recently, lagged behind micropublishers and self-published authors in this department. When small publishers discovered the Web (some as long ago as 1995, an eternity in cyber-years), large houses were either cautiously waiting to gauge the Internet's value, shrugging it off as so much geek-inspired hysteria, or both. (The Putnam half of Penguin-Putnam installed companywide e-mail only this past summer, nearly two years after self-published author Jim Donovan marketed and sold 75,000 copies of his *Handbook to a Happier Life* primarily through the Internet.)

Today, a different picture has emerged. Online-marketing departments are growing, jazzy author sites are proliferating, links are flourishing, and direct-marketing to newsgroups has become de rigueur. "I felt a switch this past summer where it became very important to have a Web component for the books on the fall lists," says Fauzia Burke, a freelance designer of author Web sites, with such clients as Grove/Atlantic and Farrar, Straus & Giroux. "This summer, it became a matter of 'No question about it.' "

But in removing one question publishers have unwittingly posed dozens of others. What to post on a Web site? How to bring people to a site, and how to keep them there? What is the ultimate goal of bringing them there anyway: branding, sales, customer service, or some strange form of 21st-century credibility that defies quantification? How to integrate online and offline marketing departments—or is segregation ultimately the best policy?

The lists run as long as a Webhead's catalog of bookmarks.

## First You Need a There, There

Web marketers of all stripes often ask how to steer surfers to sites. And, indeed, publishers often deploy considerable offline means (including print ads and author pitches) as well as online promotion (such as links and newsgroup postings) to market their marketing. But if it has dawned on houses that they need ways to bring customers there, they are also learning that, as Gertrude Stein might say, "first you need a there, there." Given that many visitors to publishers' sites come with a deliberate purpose, content becomes more than just a luxury.

Realizing this, Rough Guides took a chance. The Penguin-Putnam imprint in September announced plans to post the contents of its entire list (numbering 100 titles) on the Web. Arguably the most ambitious Internet project yet by a major publisher, its undertaking came after three years of watching sales jump by as much as 20 percent for the titles previously posted. Other publishers have similarly content-heavy sites. Times Books posted the notes of Wendy Goldman Rohm's *The Microsoft File* after critics complained of a lack of documentation in the printed version. Simon & Schuster created a site for Stephen King's *Bag of Bones* and sent the first chapter to fans by e-mail weeks before the book went on sale.

"Information sells information," says Larry Chase, an online marketing specialist who has marketed his own book, *Essential Business Tactics for the Net*, on the Net. "The more that people have access to information about your product," he notes, "the more likely it is they will buy the product."

## High Maintenance

If no limits exist to what customers will soak up, publishers' resources often impose their own constraints. Despite exponential gains in personnel, online departments remain comparatively small; Simon & Schuster currently employs 13 people, Penguin-Putnam six. (Random House, believed to have a large department, said it wished not to disclose the exact number of employees.) "A lot of people jumped into the Web and said, 'We have an infinite amount of shelf space,'" says Sorelle Braun, marketing manager at Rough Guides. "But what there is a limit to is the amount of content you can develop. A lot of the sites being developed are being scaled back because they can't be updated every day."

The future size of online departments depends, to a large degree, on other departments' perceptions. It is in this area that online departments have made the greatest strides. "Last holiday season, a lot of people in publishing noticed that Amazon.com can move books," says Ina Gottinger, director of marketing for simonsays.com, Simon & Schuster's online division. "Some editors who never touched a computer before began to notice online. We don't need to explain ourselves anymore."

At the moment, online departments' future place in the hierarchy remains unknown. One school argues that for a department to be truly effective it must exist not as an independent entity but as an extension of sales, publicity, marketing, even editorial. A day on which "online marketing" becomes an irrelevancy may not be far off.

In the meantime, size can be a mixed blessing. Publishers are finding that the heightened attention has given rise to increased pressure. "As a 13-person department, we have more resources to do what we want than a small publisher does," Gottinger says. "But we have to tie everything into offline marketing plans. I think a small publisher can be a little more offbeat and a little funkier."

While other departments warm to online's increasing role, online divisions at competing houses have taken to a cooperative strategy that embodies the democratic, information-sharing nature of ordinary Web communities (and not the proprietary approach that personifies Silicon Valley).

About a year ago, Larry Weissman, associate director of online marketing at Random House Inc., formed the Publishers Web Association. The group meets informally every month to discuss topical issues such as marketing to women and how the media can take advantage of publishers' sites. "People come together so readily and easily because even now we feel like outsiders in a very traditional business," says Greg Durham, marketing manager at simonsays and one of PWA's first members. "We can't run to other people, so we run to each other."

Lest anyone think the Internet has merely added a few jobs to publishers' rolls, houses such as Scholastic are a reminder of how the Internet's efficiency has inspired a fundamental change in houses' identity. In creating so-called destination sites—and, by extension, branding the company name—houses have uncloaked themselves to customers. Scholastic, for instance, seeks to make its site "a destination to enjoy great characters," in the words of Web site coordinator Bill Wright, and wants every reader to know the Scholastic name.

Destination sites also indicate how houses have also become more customer-service oriented than ever. Authors such as Holt's Sharon Kay Penman (*Cruel as the Grave*) routinely respond to reader comments, in another step toward the interactive utopia that mists the eyes of idealists.

The focus on customer service goes to the nub of the issue: What is the purpose of Internet marketing? The coming year may force a reevaluation. Some, however, have already begun to do so. "When we started, we never asked the question 'What is the goal of this site?' Now we're at a place where it's not just about marketing but about revenue," says one high-ranking marketer at a large publisher who asked not to be identified.

That revenue could come through many sources. Publishers such as Rough Guides have, through advertising, already generated extra cash. It could also come from more publicity for the house or for specific titles that will in turn lead to a sales spike. The Web probably isn't the place for direct sales; few publishers use it for that purpose.

Without sales, however, marketing on the Web becomes, at best, a soft science. As with traditional marketing, research doesn't yield data a number cruncher covets. To some degree, the Internet has avoided this through hit counts. But by fragmenting the market between Internet and non-Internet customers, the Internet has also complicated marketing and made it harder to ascertain efficacy.

The coming months will likely also bring a reassessment, and perhaps a switch, in houses' focus. "A tremendous amount of effort has been placed in developing sites with the thinking that 'If you build it, they will come.' But dollars could have been spent marketing authors to where buyers already are," says the anonymous executive. Marketing gurus talk about this as online's greatest challenge. "The Internet is a huge place and it's really easy to get unfocused," Chase says. "You have to ferret out the audience you need."

In the enthusiasm about the Web, big-ticket authors request—and receive—sites even when they don't work best online, while niche authors in subjects such as romance, fantasy, and even serious nonfiction get the snub. "Basically, the bigger authors' budgets are justifiable, but we're starting to learn that what makes sense for these budgets doesn't always make sense with the authors who work best on the Web," says the high-level marketer.

Publishers will continue to grope with questions of ambition as they struggle to keep expectations in check. As Voynow put it: "We're being very careful. Being online is not a panacea. It's not like Oprah."

## What Rights Have You?

### John F. Baker
#### Editorial Director, *Publishers Weekly*

The basic author contract has not changed much over the years, while technology, and even the way books can be made and distributed, has been zooming ahead. There is now, according to authors and agents, a large gray area in most contracts that fails to cover important elements like revenues from hand held e-book versions of works; the extent to which territorial rights can be abrogated by international online sales; and whether single copies produced by the on-demand process can be claimed as keeping a particular title still in print, which prevents reversion of rights to the author.

Jean Naggar, president of the Association of Authors' Representatives (AAR), says there is "rising anxiety" among the membership about the e-book question. Many agents have lately received letters from publishers, addressed to author clients, attached to a contract amendment the authors are being asked to sign, she said. Many of these amendments—which have come so far from St. Martin's Press, Simon & Schuster, Penguin Putnam, and others—have offered the authors a percentage of the net amount received by publishers from e-book sales. "But," says Naggar, "there's no indication of *what* they might receive."

AAR has now been able to establish the rough percentage of what, say, the e-book manufacturer, the bookstore, and the publisher might get on a typical e-book deal, and has sent a letter warning members to look very carefully at the amendments before letting their clients sign them. As a result of individual protests made by members (AAR cannot take collective action), two publishers have now, says Naggar, changed their policy and offered instead a percentage of the list price of the book for e-book deals.

But the battle is far from won. "It really revolves around whether an e-book version represents a licensing deal or a distribution deal, and there would be different payments according to how that is decided," said Naggar. "I feel it's a licensing deal—the publisher is not manufacturing the product, after all—and should be treated accordingly. And I'd like to see a time limit put on such a license, as in a book club or paperback licensing."

Ellen Levine, who heads AAR's contract committee, which has held several meetings on the subject lately, says that many agents believe the e-book "is a new animal altogether, and therefore should be treated in a new way, both contractually and economically." She thinks that royalties paid on publication in the new medium should be higher because the publisher has no costs. "And then, if we can agree on a royalty, how about a term for this new license?"

A question to consider, according to Levine: Does an e-book version serve to keep a book officially in print? In this area, the question ties in with the on-demand one, where agents and authors are reluctant to see the production of a handful of copies a year preventing the reversion of rights to the author, which happens automatically when a book is out of print. What will constitute a book remaining in print for these purposes?

## What Does 'In Print' Mean?

While one large publisher has let it be known that it considers even one book a year produced on demand keeps a book officially in print, Levine scoffs at that notion. "There has to be some realistic standard, and the question is whether it should be based on the number of units produced or the annual revenues." There is, however, a wide range of publisher strategies on what constitutes "in-print" status, some calling for a certain number of copies produced annually, others looking at a revenue level. (According to AAR, there is one large house where different imprints have different rules.)

Levine says some changes are beginning to appear in publisher contracts, and one big house is trying to come up with a completely new contract. In any case, she thinks that offers of percentages on net or retail on e-books do not cover the factor of lower publisher costs, "which must be taken into consideration." Some publishers, she adds, are already making recommendations, others seem to be awaiting suggestions, which the agents are working to formulate.

There are people on both sides, she says, who see the e-book as just a fad that will go away, recalling the relatively short life of the CD-ROM and the feisty contract disputes around that. Her opinion: "It doesn't feel to me as if it will go away."

Naggar agrees. "No, it won't. It's potentially as big as the invention of the printing press, or the Industrial Revolution. Contracts should be rethought completely for electronic rights; we should be looking at new definitions of the boundaries."

To that end, AAR has been sending out task forces to discuss such issues with publishers, and the Authors Guild has had a member at the association's electronics meetings. "It's going to be a major talking point in the next few months," says Naggar, adding that the group was working with BookExpo America to set up seminars at the show in Los Angeles at the end of April at which the issues were to be discussed in public.

AAR, Naggar notes, has more than 300 members, who between them represent thousands of important authors, "and I think we can have a real influence."

The territorial rights issue, particularly the anxiety among British publishers at Internet sales into the United Kingdom of books on which they hold local rights, is another concern. Naggar notes that whereas she used to make British sales of most books for which she hung onto world rights, "British publishers are now holding back."

## A Legal Viewpoint

A lawyer familiar with contracts, who has been working with agents and authors for many years, told *Publishers Weekly* he had never seen the agent community so "concerned and exercised" about an issue as the e-book and on-demand ones. "I think the speed of the development of the technology hit both sides very suddenly, last summer," he says, "and it only serves to exacerbate their relationships." He describes the publishers' attempts to get authors to sign contract amendments when they didn't really understand the issues as "sneaky." (Publishing contracts people declined to comment on the situation.)

The lawyer says his understanding of e-book rights is that they had probably already been granted under the clauses covering trade editions or electronic rights. He believes, however, that publishers are now trying to maximize their position, whereas authors and agents have only begun to try to protect their interests. He is concerned that if a precedent were set at this stage, especially if it seemed only an insignificant one, it would lock in agents and authors when the issues became more pressing and real.

"How to treat the questions of e-books and on-demand are very important issues, and they will be significant bargaining points on any new contracts," the lawyer says. He urges agents not to take anything from publishers on trust, but to "make their case" for a new payments structure. Publishers, including American ones, should be concerned, he says, about international online sales and about the potential international sale of e-book digital texts, especially if they have retained British rights. "If they can cross international lines, it's not just the authors who are going to be affected."

Richard Curtis, a former AAR head and an agent who keeps a close eye on electronic developments, is particularly interested in the e-book issue. "I don't see this as an immediate source of revenue for publishers, authors or e-book manufacturers, because at present the price of the machines is prohibitive for reaching a critical mass for the critical masses," he says, enjoying his joke. "But when the players come down to $100 or so, you have the potential for a real mass market, leading to an alternative model of publishing that would represent a major paradigm shift."

## Riding the E-Book Wave

The transformation of the publishing process from one involving paper and printing to one that consists almost entirely of electronic processes, Curtis says, "would be a most significant challenge to the role of the publisher as an intermediary between author and bookstore. That's why publishers are so concerned, and why they're clutching at such a big percentage of the rights. They can see that if there's to be a future for them they have to ride the e-book wave."

In fact, he foresees a future "author-centric universe," where they publish primarily in electronic formats, with printing of actual books done only secondarily for special markets like libraries. "This may be an offensive notion to those, like me, who love the touch, feel, and smell of books, but it's ultimately inevitable," Curtis adds.

Curtis has a succinct summary of the new situation as he sees it. "The issue is one of relevance. If traditional publishers feel they're being challenged by a publishing model that goes around them, they'll have to adapt, become more responsive to authors' needs. In fact, we all will. In fighting wars over the smaller issues, we may be losing sight of the profounder one: If authors can establish direct access with readers, what do they need publishers—or agents—for?"

A sobering thought for the 21st century nearly upon us.

# Will It Play in Paris?

## Paul Nathan

### Contributing editor, *Publishers Weekly*

Some years ago the editorial director of an Austrian publishing house for which this writer was scouting quit her job. Why? Because in order to stay in the black she found she had to buy more and more books by American authors. Finally she rebelled against what she saw as a cultural takeover.

This may have been an extreme reaction—and certainly an early one—to increasing U.S. penetration of the world literary marketplace. From today's vantage point the editorial director's objection carries an ironic twist. Now it's Americans who fear the results of takeovers by Germans.

To be sure, the two situations are not quite analogous. There's been no indication that under German ownership any U.S. publisher is being nudged to acquire translation rights in German titles. And although the German government, with the international division of the German Publishers and Booksellers Association, has opened an office in New York to promote the publication of more German literature in English translation, Americans will probably go on being less interested in books from abroad than foreigners are in ours.

Yet a change could occur; there are signs of it already as we enter the era of the Euro. At the latest Frankfurt Fair, Maria Campbell, a member of the New York scouting community, observed a growing trend: European publishers selling their forthcoming books to one another.

Hal Fessenden, handling foreign rights for Viking Penguin, is of the opinion that many of the publishers he and his colleagues deal with are finding English authors more appealing than American. "They seem to think the voices are fresher there," he says.

Be this as it may, the continuing importance of foreign rights sales to American authors, agents, and publishing houses can hardly be overestimated.

Approximately 15 percent to 20 percent of Richard Curtis Associates' revenue, for instance, now comes from foreign rights sales, made mostly by the firm's

Amy Victoria Meo and cooperating agents overseas. But for the splitting of commissions with those agents, the return would be even greater.

Other agents say the percentage of revenues from foreign rights sales might be as high as 25 percent. Rights managers at publishing houses seem less sure of the figures, but agree that many a book's profitability—or lack of it—is determined by its reception beyond our borders. Along with Hal Fessenden, Doubleday's subsidiary rights director Carol Lazare and Karen Weitzman, vice-president and director of foreign rights at Simon & Schuster, point out that foreign sales often serve the highly desirable function of helping to recoup domestic advances. Weitzman appears to speak for all in her line of work when asked if foreign rights business is more important to her company now than in the past. Her answer: "Definitely yes!"

In this time of economic turmoil the question arises: How sound are overseas markets?

Lazare finds that Germany is holding its own, while countries that had begun to show strength, such as Korea and Japan, are now "back-pedaling." Helping to compensate, she observes, "the Chinese are arriving in force."

In Linda Biagi's view, "The Asian market never was significant in terms of rights income. If you're talking about export sales of the books themselves, maybe there was a boom. Japan has been in decline for five years; there's been more activity in China than in Japan."

Biagi, director of international rights at Little, Brown, expects the repercussions on U.S. publishing from the Asian crisis to be more dramatic this year than in 1998. Britain, she believes, will be stuck in recession; Scandinavia, once thriving, will continue to slip, and Germany's political shift in recent elections is likely to exert "a damping effect." On the basis of Elisabeth Schmits's experience, Britain has become a tougher market in the past couple of years. "They're often the last to buy," says Grove Atlantic's vice-president and sub rights director. Her "best money" these days has been coming from Germany and occasionally Japan and Italy.

Brenda Segel, vice-president and director of rights, domestic and foreign, at HarperCollins, shares the common perception that Japan, Korea, Russia and some of eastern Europe are "precarious" customers.

Danny Baror, whose Baror International, acting on behalf of fellow agents, deals in foreign rights exclusively, sees Britain coming out of recession. For him it's a top market. For the most part, Baror is taking a cautious approach to Japan. With the yen at a disadvantage against the dollar, publishers there can be paying double what they paid a few years ago to meet the same asking prices. And since they have a substantial inventory awaiting publication (it can take three to four years to get a book translated and into print), purchases have declined and Baror is withholding some titles until better times.

## The Territorial Question

The issue of territoriality in the world English-language market has become a cause for concern. HarperCollins's Segel confesses to being conflicted. "I don't know how realistic it is to insist on exclusivity. I'd like it if Australia were an open market, like Singapore and New Zealand, though it would be very hard on Britain. On the other hand, I'm conservative—I believe in observing contracts." With online selling and other developments in mind, she adds, "At the same time I have to be a futurist. We can't fight what technology brings."

Likewise giving serious thought to the situation is Penguin chairman Michael Lynton, who sees the separation of markets "slowly being chipped away. The Internet accelerates the process," Lynton says, predicting "The Commonwealth will be pitted against the U.S." Rather than litigate, he believes British houses will work out arrangements to publish day-to-day with their U.S. opposite numbers.

Apropos of this forecast, agent James Vines reports that on the morning following a recent sale to Dell his British co-agent Patrick Walsh relayed offers for the book from alert London publishers. Each attached a condition: "If you can't give us Australia and New Zealand, we can't do business." There was a further warning, to the effect that if Vines can't sell them books at the same time the U.S. publisher buys them, forget it.

"One of our authors," according to Vines, "got a very good British deal. But the American edition came out first. Although it was only by five or six weeks, the British publisher felt they could have done a lot better if they'd got theirs out first. We used to just negotiate advances and royalties. It's gotten harder now— we have to pay very close attention to other factors."

## The Role of the Scouts

For a fuller appreciation of the current foreign rights picture, more notice must be taken of scouts. As they proliferate, competition among them has grown intense. Most have a spread of clients in a number of countries, and the kinds of books desired are likely to vary from client to client. "It's like being a post office," sighs Mary Anne Thompson. Germany's Droemer, she says, is interested in hearing about practically any book, but some other houses specialize more. "You've got to cover everything," Thompson concludes, "but not unload it all indiscriminately on every publisher."

Scout Maria Campbell finds that with the merging and consolidation among American publishing houses, there are fewer books to cover—making life a little less pressured for her and her staff. On the other hand, with European publishers showing increasing interest in one another's lists, there's the likelihood that they may acquire fewer titles from the U.S. Another change in her business is that its pace has quickened. "Scouting now," she says, "is like being on a daily beat for a newspaper."

Christina McInerney, who feels much has changed since she went into scouting, sensed "tremendous anxiety" at this year's Frankfurt Fair regarding the tie between Bertelsmann and Barnes & Noble. The online sales made possible without regard to international boundaries are viewed as a threat. The publisher was already thought to be in a strategic position to buy world rights and lay them off on its own companies, perhaps undercutting authors', agents', and publishers' preferences as well as whatever leverage they've had over prices paid.

## The Small-Press Position

What of the small and niche presses? How promising are their prospects overseas? Michael Bessie of Cornelia and Michael Bessie Books sees opportunities for independents who publish works of quality that the big trade houses pass up for apparent lack of bestseller potential. He points out that each year "one or two" such titles do become bestsellers and may even achieve international success.

Martin Shepard, who runs The Permanent Press with his wife Judith, reports recent sales in "unexpected places." These include Italy, Greece, Poland, and the Czech Republic.

Some American specialty publishers—among them SYBEX, which features software, hardware, Internet books, and computer games—fare unusually well beyond our borders.

When they are really struck by something still to be published and not yet validated by reviews and bestseller status, editors—wherever they are—tend to throw caution aside. By the time glowing reviews were appearing here for Atlantic Monthly Press's *Hullabaloo in the Guava Orchard* by Kiran Desai, it was already an international success. Threats of recession seemed to have evaporated in countries where publishers felt they had to have this first novel.

While big sums continue to be committed to big books at Frankfurt, the kind of bidding frenzy that erupted during earlier fairs is not so often encountered now. Still, as already noted, Frankfurt continues to exert its pull. Elisabeth Schmits indicates that when it comes to selling rights, "It's so important to meet publishers face to face there, even if they do come to New York. There's no substitute for presenting a book person to person, seeing the light in someone's eyes." A special group of American authors has cause to be happy with the foreign scene. These are novelists who happen to be even more popular abroad than in their own land. Among them are Paul Auster, Martha Grimes, Noah Gordon, Martha Cooley, and Barbara Wood. Authors of historical fiction almost always do better in Europe than here.

A particular awareness is required of those dealing in foreign rights by the globalization of the field. As Biagi puts it, "Ten years ago it was okay not to know everything that was going on in the world. Today you have to know."

# Federal Agency and Federal Library Reports

## National Technical Information Service

Technology Administration
U.S. Department of Commerce, Springfield, VA 22161
703-605-6000 or 800-553-NTIS (6847)
World Wide Web: http://www.ntis.gov

Janet E. Wooding
Writer/Editor
Marketing Communications

The National Technical Information Service (NTIS), a relatively small government organization located on the outskirts of Washington, D.C., serves as the nation's largest central source and primary disseminator of scientific, technical, engineering, and business information produced or sponsored by U.S. and international government sources. NTIS is a federal agency within the Technology Administration of the U.S. Department of Commerce.

For more than 50 years, the NTIS mission has been to operate a central point of access within the U.S. government for technical information useful to American business—information to improve the efficiency and effectiveness of the U.S. research and development enterprise, increase productivity and innovation in the United States, and increase U.S. competitiveness in the world market. NTIS is directed by statute to

- Collect technical information from both international and domestic sources
- Classify, maintain, and disseminate that information in the forms and formats most useful to NTIS customers
- Develop electronic and other new methods and media for information dissemination
- Provide information-processing services to other federal agencies
- Charge fees for its products and services that are reasonable and permit NTIS to recover its costs

The NTIS collection of approximately 3 million titles contains products available in various formats. Such information includes reports describing research conducted or sponsored by federal agencies and their contractors, statistical and business information, U.S. military publications, multimedia training programs, computer software and electronic databases developed by federal agencies, and technical reports prepared by research organizations worldwide. Approximately 100,000 new titles are indexed and added into the collection annually. NTIS maintains a permanent repository of its information products.

Customers learn of the availability of NTIS information products through a variety of ways, including the NTIS Web site, publications that index and abstract newly accessioned material, ongoing subscriptions for all reports that meet a customer's preestablished selection criteria, press releases and other media announcements, and searches of the NTIS database.

## U.S. Government Contributors

More than 200 U.S. government agencies contribute to the NTIS collection. Contributors include the National Aeronautics and Space Administration, the Environmental Protection Agency, the National Institute of Standards and Technology, the National Institutes of Health, and the Departments of Agriculture, Commerce, Defense, Energy, Health and Human Services, Interior, Labor, Treasury, Veterans Affairs, Housing and Urban Development, Education, and Transportation.

With the passage of the American Technology Preeminence Act (ATPA) of 1991 (P.L. 102-245), all federal agencies are required to submit their federally funded unclassified scientific, technical, and engineering information products to NTIS within 15 days of the date the product is made publicly available. The primary purposes of ATPA are to help U.S. industries accelerate the development of new processes and products, and to help the United States maintain a leading economically competitive position worldwide. Under ATPA, information products include technical reports, articles, papers, and books; regulations, standards, and specifications; charts, maps, and graphs; software, data collection, datafiles, and data compilations software; audio and video products; technology application assessments; training packages; and other federally owned or originated technologies. Since the passage of ATPA, the depth of NTIS's information resources has increased dramatically, and NTIS is able to provide customers with timely access to a more diverse and practical range of information.

## Worldwide Source Contributors

NTIS is a leading U.S. government agency in international technical and business information exchange. It actively acquires and distributes valuable information produced by a large number of international government departments and other organizations.

NTIS continues to negotiate agreements to improve the coverage of reports from major industrialized countries, as well as from newly industrialized countries producing advanced technologies. NTIS focuses its acquisition efforts on topics of major interest to NTIS customers.

## Online International Trade and Business Bookstore

In 1997 NTIS opened the online International Trade and Business Bookstore (http://tradecenter.ntis.gov), operated by NTIS on behalf of the Department of Commerce. This unique site brings together the world's most comprehensive collection of business and international trade information from U.S. government and nonprofit organizations. The online International Trade and Business Bookstore site helps users locate international bestsellers and industry trading standards, and also provides links to other trade-related sites. The Web site is fully implemented with secure online ordering.

The new Critic's Corner has become a popular addition to the International Trade and Business Bookstore. By regularly featuring a synopsis of a new publication from one of NTIS's partners, updates at Critic's Corner help take the guesswork out of finding information vital to the business community. The site will also feature a Partner Spotlight that will highlight a single partner and its latest products.

## National Audiovisual Center

The National Audiovisual Center (NAC) consolidates the U.S. government's collection of training programs and audio, visual, and multimedia products. Federally sponsored or produced training and educational programs are thus available to state and local governments, businesses, schools, and universities, as well as to private individuals.

NAC's collection includes approximately 9,000 active titles covering 600 subject areas from more than 200 federal agencies. Included in the collection are language training materials, occupational safety and health training materials, fire service and law enforcement training materials, drug education programs for schools and industry, travelogues, fine arts programs, and documentaries chronicling American history.

Award-winning World War II films from many of Hollywood's most celebrated directors are included in the NAC collection; John Ford's *December 7th* is one example. Another important film, *The Negro Soldier*, directed by Frank Capra and Stuart Heisler, shows the enormous contributions and sacrifices made by black Americans in the nation's armed conflicts from 1776 to 1944.

NAC has videos on such current topics of concern as ergonomics, security, workplace safety, and AIDS and other STDs. For example, *Ergonomic Programs that Work* shows how to improve work conditions in various situations, and *Computer Security* helps all computer users protect themselves and their organizations. *Emergency Response to Terrorism* helps police and EMS personnel better serve the public. *Nobody's Immune*, produced by the Walter Reed Institute of Research, Department of the Army, discusses how AIDS is contracted and the impact it has on the lives of the patient and the patient's family. *Like Any Other Employee: HIV/AIDS in the Workplace* covers appropriate health and safety precautions, laws, and insurance. *At Home with AIDS*, produced by the Veterans Administration, provides help to caregivers of HIV patients, and *1998 Guidelines for Treatment of STDs* helps doctors and clinicians provide better service.

NAC's staff is dedicated to helping customers find the multimedia program suitable for their needs. Call 703-605-6186 for assistance, or visit the NAC Web site (http://www.ntis.gov/nac) for the latest news about the center and its products.

## Federal Computer Products Center

The Federal Computer Products Center was established at NTIS to provide access to information in electronic formats. The current inventory of computer products obtained since 1990 includes more than 1,200 titles from hundreds of U.S. government agencies. Products include datafiles and software on diskette, CD-ROM, and magnetic tape, covering such topics as banking, business, the environment, health care, health statistics, science, and technology. Most of the center's products are developed or sponsored by the federal government; NTIS does, however, also announce and distribute products developed by state governments and, in a few cases, by private sector organizations.

Full descriptions of the software and data available from NTIS appear on the center's Web site at http://www.ntis.gov/fcpc.

## FedWorld

NTIS FedWorld Information Technologies has served since 1992 as the online locator service for a comprehensive inventory of information disseminated by the federal government. FedWorld assists federal agencies and the public in electronically locating federal government information—information housed within the NTIS repository as well as information that FedWorld makes accessible through an electronic gateway to other government agencies. FedWorld serves tens of thousands of customers daily.

FedWorld maximizes the potential of the Internet and the World Wide Web by offering multiple distribution channels for government agencies to disseminate information. The modes of access, the variety of documents available, and the technological expertise at FedWorld are expanding with technology. FedWorld offers the user a comprehensive central access point for searching, locating, ordering, and acquiring government and business information.

FedWorld offers simple, global access to government and business information in an efficient and cost-effective manner. To connect to FedWorld via the Internet: For World Wide Web services, point your Web browser to open URL http://www.fedworld.gov. For Internet file transfer protocol services, connect to ftp.fedworld.gov. To connect to FedWorld by modem, set modem parity to none, data bits to 8, and stop bit to 1; set terminal emulation to ANSI; set duplex to full; then set your communication software to dial FedWorld at 703-321-3339.

For more information on FedWorld, call 703-605-6585.

## NTIS on the World Wide Web

The NTIS Web site (http://www.ntis.gov) continues to evolve with enhancements to help customers quickly locate, identify, and order information they need. The site lists nearly 400,000 items, including government manuals, handbooks, computer software, electronic databases/datafiles, multimedia/training programs, CD-ROMs, and other information products added to the NTIS collection within the last ten years. The NTIS Web site is a powerful access tool for researching and pricing NTIS products. Recently, NTIS implemented direct and secure ordering via the World Wide Web. A product that can be ordered from NTIS via the Web will feature an order button on its Web page. The traditional methods for ordering NTIS products are also still an option.

Products ordered via the Web for shipment to customers outside the United States are now priced the same as those products ordered for domestic shipment. (International customers who choose to fax, mail, or phone their orders will not qualify for this special "ordered via the Web" price.) The handling fee for all international orders remains the same.

The NTIS Web site provides several search options for locating products in its vast collection. Visitors to the site can use the Search by Keyword feature to query nearly half a million product listings across all collections. For those who prefer a more structured search, the site also provides an advanced search option. This feature can be used to specify a collection and to provide more control over how search results are presented.

The NTIS Web site offers a number of subject-specific collections for such fields of interest as business, the environment, Army manuals and publications, health and safety, industry standards, military and federal specifications and standards, science and technology, databases, computer products, and audiovisuals. The What's New section focuses on the latest information in the site, including recent product announcements, the NTIS exhibit/trade show schedule, and news about other NTIS-managed Web sites such as the International Trade and Business Bookstore. A Help section assists users in navigating the site and in locating the government information they need. This section provides a guided tour, frequently asked questions, and a site map.

## Specialized Online Subscriptions

Those wishing to expand their access to subject-specific resources through use of the Internet are likely to benefit from the NTIS online options highlighted below. Online subscriptions offer quick, convenient online access to the most current information available.

### Government Research Center

The GOV.Research_Center (GRC) is a collection of well-known government-sponsored research databases available on the World Wide Web via online subscription. The following databases made available at the GOV.Research_Center by NTIS and the National Information Services Corporation (NISC) are searchable at the site utilizing NISC's powerful search engine Biblioline: the NTIS Database, Federal Research in Progress (FEDRIP), NIOSHTIC, Energy Science and Technology, AgroBase, and AGRICOLA. Databases are regularly added.

NTIS and NISC are constantly improving the content and features of GRC. Online ordering allows a user to order documents directly from the NTIS database by using a credit card or NTIS deposit account. Cross-database searching allows a user to search all databases within a subscription plan with only one search query. Soon "day-pass" access to GRC will be available for a small fee, allowing users to access the database of their choice for a limited amount of time. (Initially, the NTIS database and FEDRIP will be available through both the day-pass and subscription pricing models.)

Visit GRC at http://grc.ntis.gov for more information and to sign up for a free online trial, or call 703-605-6541.

## World News Connection

World News Connection (WNC) is an NTIS online news service accessible via the World Wide Web. WNC was developed to help individuals obtain information they could not find elsewhere, particularly in English. WNC provides English-language translations of time-sensitive news and information from thousands of non-U.S. media sources. Particularly effective in its coverage of local media, WNC enables users to identify what is really happening in a specific country or region. Compiled from speeches, television and radio broadcasts, newspaper articles, periodicals, and books, the information covers socioeconomic, political, scientific, technical, and environmental issues and events.

The information in WNC is provided to NTIS by the Foreign Broadcast Information Service (FBIS), a U.S. government agency. For more than 50 years, analysts from FBIS's domestic and overseas bureaus have monitored timely and pertinent open-source material, including "gray literature." Uniquely, WNC allows subscribers to take advantage of the intelligence-gathering experience of FBIS.

The information in WNC is obtained from the full text and summaries of newspaper articles, conference proceedings, television and radio broadcasts, periodicals, gray literature, and technical reports. WNC is updated every business day. Generally, new information is available within 48 to 72 hours of the original publication or broadcast.

Subscribers can conduct unlimited interactive searches and can set up automated searches known as profiles. When a profile is created, a search is run against WNC's latest news feed to identify articles relevant to a subscriber's topic of interest. Once the search is completed, the results are automatically sent to the subscriber's e-mail address.

For WNC pricing and subscription information, visit the Web site http://wnc.fedworld.gov.

## Worldtec

Worldtec, a foreign science and technology alert service, allows the user to browse hundreds of full-text science- and technology-related communications from U.S. embassies and international program offices throughout the world. Worldtec also incorporates science and technology information compiled from other key agencies and organizations. The content is taken from speeches, seminars and workshops, meetings, newsletters, abstracts from newspapers, periodicals, and books. Worldtec provides news coverage from 1995 to the present, and approximately 100 new articles are added to the database each month.

Worldtec sources include U.S. Department of State science and technology information; National Science Foundation reports from Asia and Europe; Technologies France; the Asian Office of Aerospace R&D Science Letter; U.S. Army Material Command Monthly Reports; Asian Technology Information Program summaries; European Office of Aviation R&D; European Space Agency press releases; Fraunhofer Gesellschaft Research News; NATO science and technology press releases; NWO News: Research from the Netherlands; the Office of Naval Research; Press Release (Austria) Seibersdorf; TNO News: Netherlands Applied Science Organization; SWOV Newsletter; and the SWOV Institute for Road Safety Research.

A subscription to Worldtec offers a central source for hard-to-find information on science- and technology-based initiatives; timely updates (Tuesday through Saturday); a system that supports secure online ordering; information that is accessible 24 hours a day; free help desk support; and affordable, flat-fee subscription pricing.

Worldtec is only available on the Web as a subscription service at http://worldtec.fedworld.gov.

### U.S. Export Administration Regulations

The U.S. Export Administration Regulations (EAR) provides exporters with the latest rules controlling the export of U.S. dual-use commodities, technology, and software. Step by step, EAR explains when an export license is necessary and when it is not, how to obtain an export license, policy changes as they are issued, new restrictions on exports to certain countries and certain types of items, and where to obtain further help.

This information is now available through NTIS in three convenient formats:

- *Online*—Offers access to new and revised regulations within 48 hours of publication in the *Federal Register*; this Web-based service also features full-search capability and provides access to the Prohibited Parties database for screening an export order prior to shipment
- *CD-ROM*—Features full-search and bookmark capability to locate specific data; allows user to print and download parts of EAR as needed (CD-ROM pricing includes four quarterly update issues) ·
- *Looseleaf*—Includes Receive EAR Base Manual plus three bulletin updates

For more information, access the EAR Web site, http://bxa.fedworld.gov.

### Davis-Bacon Wage Determination Database

Updated weekly, the Davis-Bacon Wage Determination Database contains wage determinations made by the U.S. Department of Labor under the mandate of the Davis-Bacon Act and related legislation. The department determines prevailing wage rates for construction-related occupations in most counties in the United States. All federal government construction contracts and most contracts for federally assisted construction over $2,000 must contain Davis-Bacon wage determinations.

A variety of access plans are available; for more information, access http://davisbacon.fedworld.gov.

## Additional Reference Tools

### NTIS Alerts

More than 1,600 new titles are added to the NTIS collection every week. NTIS Alerts were developed in response to requests from customers to search this new-information resource. NTIS prepares a list of search criteria that are run against all new studies and R&D reports in 16 subject areas. An NTIS Alert provides a twice-monthly information briefing service covering a wide range of technology topics. There are numerous benefits:

- Efficient, economical, and timely access to the latest U.S. government technical studies
- Concise, easy-to-read summaries
- Information not readily available from any other source
- Contributions from more than 100 countries
- Subheadings within each copy, designed to identify essential information quickly

For more information, call the NTIS Subscriptions Department at 800-363-2068 or 703-605-6060, or access the Web site http://www.ntis.gov/alerts.htm.

### Selected Research In Microfiche

Selected Research In Microfiche (SRIM) is an inexpensive, tailored information service that delivers full-text microfiche copies of technical reports. Customers choose from Standard SRIM Service, selecting one or more of the 380 existing subject areas, or Custom SRIM Service, which creates a new subject area to meet their particular needs. Custom SRIM requires a one-time fee to cover the cost of setting up a profile to retrieve only those technical reports needed. Except for this fee, the cost of Custom SRIM is the same that for Standard SRIM. Through this ongoing subscription service, customers receive microfiche copies as the reports are obtained of reports pertaining to their field of interest.

For more information on SRIM, access http://www.ntis.gov/srim.htm or call NTIS Fax Direct at 703-365-0759 and enter document code 8234. Call the NTIS Subscriptions Department at 800-363-2068 or 703-605-6060 to place an order for a SRIM subscription or to receive a free copy of the *Selected Research in Microfiche Guide*, NTISPR271LOS.

### NTIS Fax Direct

The NTIS Fax Direct service provides free information by fax on NTIS products and services, offering subject-specific listings of the most frequently requested titles, detailed product descriptions for those products, and general information on NTIS services and events. Call NTIS Fax Direct at 703-365-0759 and follow the voice prompts to receive requested information.

## NTIS Catalogs

Many of NTIS's most popular catalogs can be viewed, downloaded, or ordered at the NTIS Web site (http://www.ntis.gov/catalogs.htm). Catalogs include the following:

- *NTIS Catalog of Products* (NTISPR827LOS)
- *Catalog of Educational Multimedia Products* (NTISPR1047LOS)
- *Catalog of HCFA Information Products* (NTISPR821LOS)
- *Catalog of Multimedia and Training Products* (NTISPR1001LOS)
- *Foreign Language Training Audio and Video Courses Produced by the Federal Government* (NTISPR1002LOS)
- *Law Enforcement Training Catalog* (NTISPR1000LOS)
- *Occupational Safety and Health Audiovisual Training Programs* (NTISPR996LOS)

To receive a free catalog by mail, call the NTIS Sales Desk at 800-553-NTIS (6847) or 703-605-6000 or fax a request to 703-605-6900. Please quote the appropriate NTISPR number.

## Databases Available Via NTIS

NTIS offers several valuable research-oriented database products. To learn more about accessing the databases, visit the NTIS Web site (http://www.ntis.gov) or contact the NTIS Office of Product Management at 703-605-6515.

## NTIS

The NTIS database (listing information products acquired by NTIS since 1964) offers unparalleled bibliographic coverage of U.S. government-sponsored and worldwide government-sponsored research. It represents hundreds of billions of research dollars and covers a range of important topics including agriculture, biotechnology, business, communication, energy, engineering, the environment, health and safety, medicine, research and development, science, space, technology, and transportation.

Each year, NTIS adds approximately 100,000 new entries to the database (most include abstracts). Database summaries describe technical reports, datafiles, multimedia/training programs, and software. These titles are often unique to NTIS and generally are difficult to locate from any other source. If a user is looking for information about state-of-the-art technology, or practical and applied research, or if a user wants to learn more about available government-sponsored software, the NTIS Database is the answer. The complete NTIS database provides access to more than 2 million records.

Free 30-day trials of the NTIS database are available through the GOV.Research_Center (http://grc.ntis.gov). The NTIS database can be leased directly from NTIS, and it can also be accessed through the following commercial vendors:

| | |
|---|---|
| Cambridge Scientific Abstracts | 800-843-7751 |
| Canada Institute for Scientific and Technical Information | 800-668-1222 |
| DATA-STAR | 800-221-7754 |
| DIALOG | 800-334-2564 |
| EBSCO | 800-653-2726 |
| Manning & Napier | 800-278-5356 |
| NERAC, Inc. | (860) 872-7000 |
| NISC/NTIS | 800-363-2068 |
| Ovid Technologies, Inc. | 800-950-2035 |
| Questel-Orbit, Inc. | 800-456-7248 |
| SilverPlatter Information, Inc. | 800-343-0064 |
| STN International/CAS | 800-848-6533 |

To lease the NTIS database directly from NTIS, contact the Office of Product Management at 703-605-6515.

### Federal Research in Progress Database

As the U.S. government's central technical and scientific information service, NTIS is responsible for providing access to summaries of current and ongoing projects via the Federal Research in Progress (FEDRIP) database. FEDRIP provides advance information about the more than 150,000 research projects currently under way. The U.S. government funds billions of dollars on R&D and engineering programs annually. The ongoing research announced in FEDRIP is an important component of the technology transfer process in the United States.

FEDRIP focuses on such topics as health, physical sciences, agriculture, engineering, and life sciences. Users search FEDRIP to avoid research duplication, to locate sources of support, to identify leads in the literature, to stimulate ideas for planning, to identify gaps in areas of investigation, and to locate individuals with expertise.

### Agricultural Online Access Database

As one of the most comprehensive sources of U.S. agricultural and life sciences information, the Agricultural Online Access Database (AGRICOLA) contains bibliographic records for documents acquired by the National Agricultural Library (NAL) of the U.S. Department of Agriculture. The complete database dates from 1970 and contains more than 3.3 million citations to journal articles, monographs, theses, patents, software, audiovisual materials, and technical reports related to agriculture. AGRICOLA serves as the document locator and bibliographic control system for the NAL collection. The extensive file provides comprehensive coverage of newly acquired worldwide publications in agriculture and related fields. AGRICOLA covers the field of agriculture in the broadest sense. Subjects include agricultural economics, agricultural education, agricultural products, animal science, aquaculture, biotechnology, botany, cytology, energy, engineering, feed science, fertilizers, fibers and textiles, food and nutrition, forestry, horticulture, human ecology, human nutrition, hydrology, hydroponics, microbiology, natural resources, pesticides, physiology, plant and animal sciences, public health, rural sociology, soil sciences, veterinary medicine, and water quality.

### Agricultural Science and Technology Database

The international information system for the Agricultural Science and Technology (AGRIS) database is a cooperative system (in which more than 100 national and multinational centers take part) for collecting and disseminating information on the world's agricultural literature. References to U.S. publications covered in AGRICOLA are not included in AGRIS, and a large number of citations in AGRIS are not found in any other database. References to nonconventional literature (that is, documents not commercially available) indicate where a copy can be obtained. Anyone needing information pertaining to agriculture should use AGRIS to find citations to material from developed and developing countries around the world.

### NIOSH Certified Equipment List Database

The National Institute for Occupational Safety and Health (NIOSH) Certified Equipment List database contains comprehensive certification information on self-contained breathing apparatuses, gas masks, supplied air respirators, particulate respirators, chemical cartridges, and powered purifiers. The database is useful to such audiences as manufacturers, labor organizations, industrial hygienists, safety professionals, and emergency response personnel.

### Energy Science and Technology Database

The Energy Science and Technology database (EDB) is a multidisciplinary file containing worldwide references to basic and applied scientific and technical research literature. The information is collected for use by government managers, researchers at the national laboratories, and other research efforts sponsored by the U.S. Department of Energy, and the results of this research are available to the public. Abstracts are included for records from 1976 to the present. The database also contains the Nuclear Science Abstracts, a comprehensive index of the international nuclear science and technology literature for the period 1948–1976. Included are scientific and technical reports of the U.S. Atomic Energy Commission, the U.S. Energy Research and Development Administration and its contractors, and other agencies, universities, and industrial and research organizations. The entire Energy Science and Technology database contains more than 3 million bibliographic records.

### Immediately Dangerous to Life or Health Concentrations Database

The NIOSH Documentation for the Immediately Dangerous to Life or Health Concentrations (IDLHs) database contains air concentration values used by NIOSH as respirator selection criteria. This compilation is the rationale and source of information used by NIOSH during the original determination of 387 IDLH categories and their subsequent review and revision in 1994. Toxicologists, persons concerned with the use of respirators, industrial hygienists, persons concerned with indoor air quality, and emergency response personnel will find this product beneficial. This database enables users to compare NIOSH limits to other limits and it is an important resource for those concerned with acute chemical exposures.

### NIOSH Manual of Analytical Methods Database

The NIOSH Manual of Analytical Methods (NMAM) database is a compilation of methods for sampling and analysis of contaminants in workplace air, and in the bodily fluids of workers who are occupationally exposed to that air. These highly sensitive methods have been developed to detect the lowest concentrations as well as concentrations exceeding safe levels of exposure, as regulated by the Occupational Safety and Health Administration (OSHA) and recommended by NIOSH. The Threshold Values and Biological Exposure Indices of the American Conference of Governmental Industrial Hygienists are also cited.

### NIOSH Pocket Guide to Chemical Hazards Database

The NIOSH Pocket Guide to Chemical Hazards (NPG) database is intended as a quick and convenient source of general industrial hygiene information for workers, employers, and occupational health professionals. NPG presents key information and data in abbreviated tabular form for chemicals or substance groupings (for example, cyanides, fluorides, manganese compounds) that are found in the work environment. The industrial hygiene information found in NPG should help users recognize and control occupational chemical hazards. The information in NPG includes chemical structures or formulas, identification codes, synonyms, exposure limits, chemical and physical properties, incompatibilities and reactivities, measurement methods, recommended respirator selections, signs and symptoms of exposure, and procedures for emergency treatment. Industrial hygienists, industrial hygiene technicians, safety professionals, occupational health physicians and nurses, and hazardous-material managers will find that the database can be a versatile and indispensable tool in their work.

### NIOSHTIC Database

NIOSHTIC is a bibliographic database of literature in the field of occupational safety and health. About 160 current, English-language technical journals provide approximately 35 percent of the additions to NIOSHTIC annually. Retrospective information, some of which is from the 19th century, is also acquired and entered. NIOSH examines all aspects of adverse effects experienced by workers; thus much of the information contained in NIOSHTIC has been selected from sources that do not have a primary occupational safety and health orientation. NIOSHTIC is a beneficial resource for anyone needing information on the subject of occupational safety and health. NIOSHTIC subject coverage includes the behavioral sciences; biochemistry, physiology, and metabolism; biological hazards; chemistry; control technology; education and training; epidemiological studies of diseases/disorders; ergonomics; hazardous waste; health physics; occupational medicine; pathology and histology; safety; and toxicology.

### Registry of Toxic Effects of Chemical Substances Database

The Registry of Toxic Effects of Chemical Substances (RTECS) is a database of toxicological information compiled, maintained, and updated by NIOSH. The program is mandated by the Occupational Safety and Health Act of 1970. The original edition, known as the "Toxic Substances List," was published in 1971 and included toxicological data for approximately 5,000 chemicals. Since that time, the list has continuously grown and been updated, and its name changed to the current title. RTECS now contains more than 133,000 chemicals as NIOSH strives to fulfill the mandate to list "all known toxic substances . . . and the concentrations at which . . . toxicity is known to occur." RTECS is a compendium of data extracted from the open scientific literature, recorded in the format developed by the RTECS staff, and arranged in alphabetical order by prime chemical name. No attempt has been made to evaluate the studies cited in RTECS; the user has the responsibility of making such assessments.

## NTIS Customer Service

Automated systems keep NTIS in the customer service forefront. Electronic document storage is fully integrated with NTIS's order-taking process, which allows NTIS to provide same-day reproduction for the most recent additions to the NTIS document collection. Orders for materials in electronic storage or materials available from shelf stock are generally shipped within 24 hours. NTIS ships larger domestic order packages by express carrier with two-day delivery at no additional cost to the customer.

NTIS is taking steps to ensure the electronic products offered to its customers will be Y2K compliant; appropriate modifications, upgrades, and adjustments are being made to current NTIS operating systems. For more information on progress, access the Web site http://www.ntis.gov/y2k.htm.

## Key NTIS Contact Numbers

### Order by Phone

Sales Desk                          800-553-NTIS (6847) or 703-605-6000
8:00 A.M.–8:00 P.M. Eastern Time, Monday–Friday

Subscriptions                          800-363-2068 or 703-605-6060
8:30 A.M.–8:00 P.M. Eastern Time, Monday–Friday

TDD (hearing impaired only)                          703-487-4639
8:30 A.M.–8:00 P.M. Eastern Time, Monday–Friday

**Order by Fax**

24 hours a day, seven days a week                                    703-605-6900

To verify receipt of fax, call                                           703-605-6090
7:00 A.M.–5:00 P.M. Eastern Time, Monday–Friday

**Order by Mail**

National Technical Information Service
5285 Port Royal Road
Springfield, VA 22161

RUSH Service (available for an additional fee)              800-553-NTIS (6847)
                                                                    or 703-605-6000

Note: If requesting RUSH Service, please do not mail your order.

**Order via World Wide Web**

Direct and secure online ordering                              http://www.ntis.gov

**Order by E-Mail**

NTIS understands the concerns customers may have about security when placing
an order via the Internet. Customers can register a credit card at NTIS, thus
avoiding the need to send an account number with each order. To register, call
703-605-6070, between 7:00 A.M. and 5:00 P.M., Eastern time, Monday–Friday.
NTIS will automatically charge the credit card when an e-mail order is
processed. Order via e-mail 24 hours a day: orders@ntis.fedworld.gov.

# National Archives and Records Administration

Seventh and Pennsylvania Ave. N.W., Washington, DC 20408
202-501-5400
World Wide Web: http://www.nara.gov

Lori A. Lisowski
Assistant Director for Policy

The National Archives and Records Administration (NARA), an independent federal agency, ensures for the citizen, the public servant, the president, the Congress, and the courts ready access to essential evidence that documents the rights of American citizens, the actions of federal officials, and the national experience.

NARA is singular among the world's archives as a unified federal institution that accessions and preserves materials from all three branches of government. NARA assists federal agencies in documenting their activities, administering records management programs, scheduling records, and retiring noncurrent records to Federal Records Centers. The agency also manages the Presidential Libraries system; assists the National Historical Publications and Records Commission in its grant program for state and local records and edited publications of the papers of prominent Americans; publishes the laws, regulations, presidential documents, and other official notices of the federal government; and oversees classification and declassification policy in the federal government through the Information Security Oversight Office. NARA constituents include the federal government, a history-minded public, the media, the archival community, and a broad spectrum of professional associations and researchers in such fields as history, political science, law, library and information services, and genealogy.

The size and breadth of NARA's holdings are staggering. Together, NARA's facilities hold approximately 21.5 million cubic feet of original textual materials—more than 4 billion pieces of paper from the executive, legislative, and judicial branches of the federal government. Its multimedia collections include nearly 300,000 reels of motion picture films; more than 5 million maps, charts, and architectural drawings; more than 200,000 sound and video recordings; more than 15 million aerial photographs; more than 10 million still pictures and posters, and about 11,900 computer data sets.

## Strategic Directions

NARA's strategic priorities are laid out in *Ready Access to Essential Evidence: The Strategic Plan of the National Archives and Records Administration, 1997–2007.* NARA's essential mission, the plan declares, is to ensure, for the citizen and the public servant, the president and the Congress and the courts, ready access to essential evidence—evidence that documents the rights of citizens, the actions of federal officials, and the national experience.

Success for the agency as envisioned in the plan will mean reaching four strategic goals:

- Essential evidence will be created, identified, appropriately scheduled, and managed, for as long as needed.
- Essential evidence will be easy to access regardless of where it is or where users are, for as long as needed.
- All records will be preserved in appropriate space, for use as long as needed.
- NARA's capabilities for making changes necessary to realize its vision will continuously expand.

The plan lays out strategies for reaching these goals, sets up milestone targets for accomplishment through the next ten years, and identifies measurements for gauging progress. The targets and measurements are further delineated in NARA's Annual Performance Plans.

Copies of these plans are available on the NARA Web site at http://www.nara.gov/nara/vision or by calling the Policy and Communications Staff at 301-713-7360.

## Records and Access

### Internet

NARA's Web site offers immediate access to the NARA Archival Information Locator; the John F. Kennedy Assassination Records Collection Reference System; federal records management and holdings information; NARA publications, including the *Federal Register*; online exhibits; teaching guides; digital historical documents: links to Internet information servers maintained by Presidential Libraries; and pointers to related Internet resources.

### Electronic Access Project

The Electronic Access Project is a significant piece of NARA's electronic access strategy as outlined in the agency's strategic plan. The project has three main goals:

- Develop an electronic catalog of NARA holdings nationwide, including the holdings of the national and regional archives and Presidential Libraries
- Digitize up to 120,000 items from NARA holdings nationwide
- Upgrade NARA's public-access server capabilities

The result of the project will be tangible: a comprehensive online catalog that will provide information to citizens about NARA holdings nationwide and a core collection of digital copies of selected high-interest documents that illustrate the breadth and value of NARA's holdings and bring them directly to classrooms, public libraries, and the homes of the American people.

Although the prototype catalog contains more than 380,000 descriptions and 96,000 digital copies, it represents only a limited portion of NARA's vast holdings. It is available on the Web at http://www.nara.gov/nara/nail.html.

**Fax-on-Demand**

This is NARA's interactive fax retrieval system in which digital copies of documents are stored on the hard drive of a computer. Customers may request faxed copies of available documents at any time (24 hours a day, 7 days a week, 365 days a year) by calling 301-713-6905 from a fax machine with a handset. Except for those customers who are making long-distance calls to Fax-on-Demand, there are no other charges for using this service.

Currently available documents include brochures regarding NARA internships, NARA and federal government employment, and the semiannual Modern Archives Institute; published General Information Leaflets, other fact sheets about various NARA holdings, programs, and facilities, especially those located in Washington, D.C., College Park and Suitland, Maryland, and St. Louis, Missouri (National Personnel Records Center); instructions, forms, and vendor lists for ordering copies of records; and finding aids for some textual, audiovisual, and micrographic records.

**Online Federal Register**

The *Federal Register* is the daily newspaper of the federal government and includes proposed and final regulations, agency notices, reorganizations, and presidential legal documents. The *Federal Register* is published by the Office of the Federal Register and printed and distributed by the Government Printing Office (GPO). The two agencies also cooperate to produce the annual revisions of the *Code of Federal Regulations* (*CFR*). Free access to the full text of the electronic version of the *Federal Register* and the *CFR* is available through GPO's electronic delivery system, GPO Access, at federal depository libraries, or via the Internet. In addition to these publications, the full text of other *Federal Register* publications is available through GPO Access, including the *Weekly Compilation of Presidential Documents* and the *Public Papers of the President*, the slip laws, and the *U.S. Statutes at Large*.

# Customer Service

## Customers

Few archives serve as many customers as NARA. In fiscal year (FY) 1998 there were more than 286,000 research visits made to NARA facilities nationwide, including Presidential Libraries. At the same time, customers made approximately 819,000 requests by mail and by phone. The National Personnel Records Center in St. Louis received approximately two million requests for information from military and civilian government service records. In addition to providing research and reference services, NARA provides informative exhibits for almost 1 million people in the National Archives Rotunda in Washington, D.C., each year, and 1.5 million more visit the Presidential Library museums. NARA also serves the executive agencies of the federal government, the courts, and Congress by providing records storage, reference service, and training, advice, and guidance on many issues relating to records management. The agency's current *Customer Service Plan* and *Customer Service Performance Reports*, available free in the research rooms nationwide, list the many types of customers NARA serves and describe the agency's goals for customer service standards. These publications, available on the Internet, may also be ordered from the Product Sales Section, Room G8, National Archives and Records Administration, 700 Pennsylvania Ave. N.W., Washington, DC 20408; by toll-free telephone at 800-234-8861, or by fax at 202-501-7170.

### Customer Opinion

NARA cares about what its customers think of its service. Among the specific strategies published in the *Strategic Plan* is an explicit commitment to expanding the opportunities of NARA customers to inform NARA about information and services they need. In support of that strategy, a major survey of customers using NARA research rooms in the Washington, D.C., area was recently conducted. NARA continues to survey, hold focus groups, and meet with customers to evaluate and constantly improve services. During FY 1998 NARA joined in Vice President Gore's initiative to engage federal workers in two-way conversations with the American public on how to improve government services. NARA established a Web page as a gateway to information about Conversations with America involving our agency and for feedback from customers about what is most important to them and what NARA might do to meet their expectations. This Web site is available at http://www.nara.gov/nara/vision/convers.html.

### Centers Information Processing System (CIPS).

CIPS allows federal agencies to make electronic reference requests for records stored at a regional records services facility. CIPS improves customer service by reducing reference preparation time and cost, delivery delays, and turnaround times. Begun as a pilot project in October 1993, CIPS processed more than 950,000 electronic requests in FY 1998, and the average turnaround time has been reduced from 10–12 days to 2–3 days. NARA's service improvement allows other federal agencies to provide faster service to their public customers as well.

## Administration

NARA employs approximately 2,700 people, of whom about 2,200 are full-time permanent staff members. For FY 1998 NARA's budget was $225.3 million, with $5.5 million to support the National Historic Publications and Records Commission (NHPRC).

# United States Information Agency

Bureau of Information
Room 130, 301 Fourth St. S.W., Washington, DC 20547
202-260-1234

Bo Gilliam
Information Resource Center

The United States Information Agency (USIA), an independent organization within the executive branch, is responsible for the U.S. government's overseas information, educational exchange, and cultural programs. The work of the agency is carried out by a staff of foreign service officers assigned to U.S. missions abroad and by a professional staff of career civil servants in Washington, D.C. Known abroad as the United States Information Service (USIS), the agency has more than 200 posts in 146 countries that are grouped in six geographic areas: Africa; Western Europe; Eastern Europe and the Newly Independent States; East Asia and the Pacific; the American Republics; and North Africa, the Near East, and South Asia. Posts in these areas report to area offices in Washington, D.C.

USIA will cease to exist in its current form and will merge with the U.S. Department of State on October 1, 1999. The USIS Information Resource Centers will continue to function as they have.

## History of USIS Library Programs

Today's worldwide system of USIS Information Resource Centers evolved from a matrix of traditional library programs. First, in Latin America, came libraries associated with President Franklin Roosevelt's "Good Neighbor" program. In 1941 the coordinator of inter-American affairs, Nelson Rockefeller, contracted with the American Library Association (ALA) to establish and operate a library in Mexico City, the now-famous Biblioteca Benjamin Franklin. Under similar contracts, ALA opened and operated on behalf of the U.S. government two other libraries in Latin America: in Managua, Nicaragua (1942), and Montevideo, Uruguay (1943).

Beginning in 1942 the Office of War Information (OWI) began to establish reference libraries as part of its overseas information program. These were separate and distinct from U.S. Embassy reference libraries at the outset. Later, parts of many embassy collections were turned over to USIS libraries. The American Library in London started operations in December 1942 and officially opened in April 1943. The London library was the first overseas library directly under U.S. government control. Between 1942 and 1945 OWI established libraries in 40 more locations throughout the world. In 1945 the Department of State assumed responsibility for overseas libraries.

Shortly after World War II the U.S. Military Government began opening Information Center (Amerika Häuser) libraries and reading rooms in Germany, throughout the American Zone and in the major cities of the British and French zones. At the same time Information Center libraries were started under the auspices of the United States Forces in Austria, Japan, and Korea. The State Department assumed responsibility for these centers when civilian control was restored in each country. Nine centers came under the department's auspices in January 1949, and ten centers in Austria were added in 1950. These centers were initially transferred to the State Department and finally, on August 1, 1953, to the newly created United States Information Agency. Since that time USIS libraries and information resource centers have been opened in virtually every country with which the United States maintains diplomatic relations.

## Current Programs

Although USIS information resource centers vary significantly from country to country, all advance two mutually supportive functions:

- To provide the most current and authoritative information about official U.S. government policies
- To serve as a primary source of informed commentary on the origin, growth, and development of American social, political, economic, and cultural values and institutions

Activities of USIS libraries and information resource centers are carried out by host country staff. They provide a vital communication link between USIS posts and local audiences. A corps of 23 American information specialists provides professional guidance and define the roles of information resource centers in relation to American foreign policy objectives.

As greater emphasis is placed on current awareness and outreach services to foreign opinion leaders, USIS staff rely on direct, electronic access to the wealth of information sources in the United States. In places where information about the United States is extremely limited or virtually nonexistent, USIS information resource centers provide a balanced cross section of outstanding American contributions in the social sciences and humanities, which promote appreciation and understanding of American intellectual and cultural history, American economic and social institutions, and American political traditions. Book collections at these places usually range from 3,000 to 10,000 volumes. In countries that can support a digital environment, print collections have decreased as information resource centers rely more heavily on electronic resources.

USIA Washington continues to operate one of the federal government's most dynamic special libraries. Annually, the Information Resource Center (IRC) fields over 18,000 research and reference requests from USIA Washington staff and overseas posts. The IRC maintains a collection of 16,000 monographs, 500 journals, and extensive access to online and CD-ROM sources. USIA headquarters is also responsible for the professional development of field librarians.

## Information USA

USIA produces a CD-ROM database titled Information USA, an authoritative resource for foreign audiences seeking informed commentary on American society, culture, and political processes. By aggregating, organizing, and disseminating materials about the United States, Information USA seeks to promote better understanding of the principles and institutions that shape American values.

Information USA is designed as a CD-ROM that can be used with or without an Internet connection. Used on the Internet, Information USA provides extensive hyperlinks to selected sites and resources that provide a rich spectrum of information about the United States. Both contemporary and archived resources are included. For users who do not have access to the Internet, the CD-ROM alone provides full-text documentation on American social and political institutions and processes, simulating an Internet environment using Netscape browser software.

The online version of Information USA is accessible on the Internet through the USIA international home page (http://www.usia.gov/usia/gov/usa/infousa).

## Public Diplomacy Query Database

USIA also produces and maintains a family of databases called Public Diplomacy Query (PDQ), to index, store, and make available to USIS libraries most program and foreign policy materials acquired and produced by USIA. PDQ is available online and via CD-ROM.

## Book Programs

USIA also supports the publication of American books abroad, both in English and in translation. The agency, through its field posts abroad, works with publishers to produce a variety of translated books in the humanities and social sciences that reflect a broad range of American thought and serve to explain American life and institutions.

Through programs of book translation and through a variety of seminars, conferences, and short-term professional publishing workshops, USIA seeks to encourage respect for and adherence to international standards of intellectual property rights protection. The agency works closely on this issue both with foreign governments and with domestic and foreign nongovernment organizations.

American publishers seeking additional information about the agency's book program should direct their inquiries to Print Publications (I/TPP), Bureau of Information, USIA, 301 Fourth St. S.W., Washington, DC 20547. Foreign publishers should turn for assistance to the Public Affairs Office of the U.S. Embassy in their country.

# National Center for Education Statistics
# Library Statistics Cooperative Program

U.S. Department of Education
Office of Educational Research and Improvement
555 New Jersey Ave. N.W., Washington, DC 20208-5652

Adrienne Chute
Elementary/Secondary and Libraries Studies Division

The Library Statistics Cooperative Program is administered and funded by the National Center for Education Statistics (NCES) under the leadership of Paul Planchon, Director of the Elementary/Secondary and Libraries Studies Division. NCES regularly collects and disseminates statistical information on libraries under six surveys.* These surveys include the Public Libraries Survey, the Academic Libraries Survey, the School Library Media Centers Survey, the State Library Agencies Survey, The Federal Library and Information Centers Survey and the Library Cooperatives Survey.

The six library surveys provide the only current, comprehensive, national data on the status of libraries. They are used by federal, state, and local officials, professional associations, and local practitioners for planning, evaluation, and making policy and drawing samples for special surveys. These data are also available to researchers and educators to analyze the state of the art of librarianship and to improve its practice.

## Public Libraries

Descriptive statistics for nearly 9,000 public libraries are collected and disseminated annually through a voluntary census, the Public Libraries Survey. The survey is conducted by NCES through the Federal-State Cooperative System (FSCS) for Public Library Data. In 1998 FSCS completed its tenth data collection.

The Public Libraries Survey collects data on staffing; type of legal basis; type of geographic boundary; type of administrative structure; interlibrary relationship; type and number of service outlets; operating income and expenditures; size of collection; service measures such as reference transactions, interlibrary loans, circulation, public service hours, library visits, circulation of children's materials, and children's program attendance; and other data items. More recently, a number of technology-oriented data items have been added to the Public Libraries survey. These are

- Does the public library have access to the Internet?
- Is the Internet used by library staff only, patrons through a staff intermediary or patrons either directly or through a staff intermediary?

*Note:* Jeffrey Williams, Elaine Kroe, Rosa Fernandez, and Martha Hollins of NCES and Christina Dunn of Library Programs contributed to this article.

*The mandate of the National Center for Education Statistics to collect library statistics is included in the Improving America's Schools Act of 1994 (P.L. 103-382) under Title IV, the National Education Statistics Act of 1994.

- Number of Internet terminals
- Web address of the outlet
- Does the library provide access to electronic services?
- Number of library materials in electronic format
- Operating expenditures for library materials in electronic format
- Operating expenditures for electronic access

In general, both unit response and response to specific items in the Public Libraries Survey are very high.

The 50 states and the District of Columbia participate in data collection. Beginning in 1993 the following outlying areas joined the FSCS for Public Library data: Guam, Northern Mariannas, Palau, Puerto Rico, and the Virgin Islands. For the collection of FY 1996 data, the respondents were the nearly 9,000 public libraries, identified by state library agencies in the 50 states and the District of Columbia plus three of the outlying areas.

Data files on diskette that contain fiscal year (FY) 1995 data on about 9,000 responding libraries and identifying information about their outlets were made available in 1998. The FY 1995 data were also aggregated to state and national levels in an E.D. Tabs, an NCES publication designed to present major findings with minimal statistical analyses.

The following are highlights from *E.D. TABS Public Libraries in the United States: FY 1995*, released in August 1998:

### Number of Public Libraries and Their Service Outlets and Legal Basis

- There were 8,946 public libraries (administrative entities) in the 50 states and the District of Columbia in 1996.
- About 11 percent of the public libraries served nearly 71 percent of the population of legally served areas in the United States. Each of these public libraries had a legal service area population of 50,000 or more.
- A total of 1,480 public libraries (over 16 percent) had one or more branch library outlets, with a total of 7,124. The total number of central library outlets was 8,923. the total number of stationary outlets (central library outlets and branch library outlets) was 16,047. Nine percent of public libraries had one or more bookmobile outlets, with a total of 966.
- Nearly 54 percent of public libraries were part of a municipal government; nearly 12 percent were part of a county/parish; nearly 6 percent had multi-jurisdictional legal basis under an intergovernmental agreement; almost 11 percent were non-profit association or agency libraries; over 3 percent were part of a school district; and 8 percent were separate government units known as library districts. About 1 percent were combinations of academic/public libraries or school/public libraries. Over 6 percent reported their legal basis as "other."
- Over 80 percent of public libraries had a single direct-service outlet (an outlet that provides service directly to the public).
- Nearly 70 percent of public libraries were a member of a system, federation, or cooperative service, while over 28 percent were not. Over 2 percent served as the headquarters of a system, federation, or cooperative service.

## Income and Expenditures

- Nationwide total per capita* operating income for public libraries was $23.37. Of that, $18.26 was from local sources, $2.84 from state sources, $0.23 from federal sources, and $2.03 from other sources.
- Over 78 percent of public libraries' total operating income of about $5.9 billion came from local sources, over 12 percent from the state, 1 percent from federal sources, and almost 9 percent from other sources, such as gifts and donations, service fees and fines.
- Per capita operating income from local sources was under $3 for over 12 percent of public libraries, $3 to $14.99 for over 48 percent, and $15 to $29.99 for over 27 percent of public libraries. Per capita income from local sources was $30 or more for nearly 13 percent of libraries.
- Total operating expenditures for public libraries were over $5.5 billion in 1996. Of this, over 64 percent was expended for paid staff and over 15 percent for the library collection. The average U.S. per capita operating expenditure for public libraries was $21.98 The highest average per capita operating expenditure in the 50 states was $38.19 and the lowest was $9.42.
- Close to 38 percent of public libraries had operating expenditures of less than $50,000 in 1996; over 38 percent expended between $50,000 and $399,999; and close to 24 percent expended $400,000 or more.

## Staffing and Collections

- Public libraries had a total of 117,812 paid full-time-equivalent (FTE) staff.
- Nationwide, public libraries had over 711 million books and serial volumes in their collections or 2.8 volumes per capita. By state, the number of volumes per capita ranged from 1.5 to 5.2.
- Nationwide, public libraries had collections of over 25 million audio materials and 13 million video materials.

## Services

- Total nationwide circulation of public library materials was over 1.6 billion or 6.5 per capita. Highest statewide circulation per capita in the 50 states was 12.4 and the lowest was 2.8.
- Nationwide, over 10.5 million library materials were loaned by public libraries to other libraries.
- Total nationwide reference transactions in public libraries were over 284 million or 1.1 per capita.
- Total nationwide library visits to public libraries were over 1 billion or 4 per capita.

*Per capita figures in these highlights are based on the total unduplicated population of legal service areas in the states, not on the total population of the states. Population of the legal service area means the population of those areas in the state for which a public library has been established to offer services and from which (or on behalf of which) the library derives income, plus any areas served under contract for which the library is the primary service provider. It does not include the population of unserved areas.

**Children's Services**

- Nationwide circulation of children's materials was nearly 571 million or nearly 35 percent of total circulation. Attendance at children's programs was over 42 million.

FY 1996 FSCS data were collected in October 1997. Preliminary files were released in 1998, under FSCS's early release policy, with final release scheduled for spring 1999. FY 1997 data were collected in August 1998, with final release scheduled for late fall 1999. The FY 1998 data will be collected in July 1999, with final release scheduled for 2000.

As one way of addressing timely release of data, the Public Libraries Survey has an early release policy. In the period between data collection and final data release, preliminary data provided by states are merged and released periodically over the Internet as received by NCES. These are preliminary data subject to revision until replaced by a final fully edited data file.

The FSCS for Public Library Data is an example of the synergy that can result from combing federal/state cooperation with state-of-the-art technology. FSCS was the first national NCES data collection in which the respondents supplied the data electronically. The data can also be edited and tabulated electronically at the state and national levels through NCES-developed software. All ten FSCS data collections have been collected electronically. In addition, 20 states and one outlying area submitted their data via the Internet in 1998.

In 1992 NCES developed the first comprehensive public library universe file (PLUS) and merged it with existing software into a revised software package called DECPLUS. DECPLUS has also been used to collect identifying information on all known public libraries and their service outlets. This resource has been available for use in drawing samples for special surveys on such topics as literacy, access for the disabled, library construction, and the like. In 1998 NCES introduced WINPLUS, a Windows-based data collection software that is expected to be more user friendly than DECPLUS but also retains its key features.

NCES, in future years, hopes to make available Web-based mapping applications, a cost-adjustment calculator, Web-based custom data analysis and table generators, and a Web-based means of drawing samples for libraries of various sizes.

Efforts to improve FSCS data quality are ongoing. For example, beginning with FY 1995 data, most items with response rates below 100 percent include imputations for nonresponse. In prior years the data were based on responding libraries only. NCES has also sponsored a series of six studies on the Public Libraries survey on coverage, definitions, structure and organization, finance data, and staffing data. These studies were conducted by the Governments Division, Bureau of the Census. In 1999 Census will complete its sixth and final study, a working paper on data collection processes and technology. Over the years the clarity of FSCS definitions, software, and tables has been significantly improved.

At the state level and in the outlying areas, FSCS is administered by data coordinators, appointed by each state or outlying area's chief officer of the state library agency. FSCS is a working network. State Data Coordinators collect the requested data from public libraries and submit these data to NCES. NCES aggregates the data to provide state and national totals. An annual training conference is provided for the state data coordinators. A steering committee that represents them is active in development of the Public Libraries Survey and its data-entry software. Technical assistance to states is provided by phone and in person by state data coordinators, by NCES staff, by the Bureau of the Census, and by the National Commission on Libraries and Information Science (NCLIS). NCES also works cooperatively with NCLIS, the U.S. Department of Commerce's Bureau of the Census; the Institute for Museum and Library Services' Office of Library Programs; the Chief Officers of State Library Agencies (COSLA); the American Library Association (ALA); the U.S. Department of Education's National Institute on Postsecondary Education, Libraries, and Lifelong Learning (PLLI); and the National Library of Education. Westat, Inc. works under contract to NCES to support cooperative activities of the NCES Library Statistics Cooperative Program.

## Other Completed Public Library Data Projects

In 1998 NCES and PLLI published *How does Your Library Compare?* by Keri Bassman of the U.S. Department of Education. This Statistics in Brief categorized the almost 9,000 public libraries in the FY 1995 public libraries data set into peer groups based on size of population of the legal service area and total operating expenditures to control for variability in library size. Once libraries were assigned to peer groups based on these two variables, comparisons of service performance were made. Service performance was defined in terms of five input variables (public library service hours per year, total librarians, total ALA-MLS librarians, total number of subscriptions, and total number of books and serials) and seven output variables (library visits per capita, children's program attendance, circulation of children's materials, interlibrary loans received per 1,000 population, interlibrary loans provided, total per capita reference transactions, and total per capita circulation).

American Institutes for Research has completed a project to develop two indices of inflation for public libraries, a cost index and a price index. NCES will publish a report of the project in 1999.

Public library questions have also been included as parts of other NCES surveys. For example, in 1996 questions about frequency of use and the purposes for which households use public libraries were included on an expanded household screener for the NCES National Household Education Survey. More than 55,000 households nationwide were surveyed in such a way as to provide state- and national-level estimates on library items. A Statistics in Brief reporting the survey results was published in 1997. A CD-ROM and User's Manual was made available in July 1997.

The following are Highlights from *Statistics in Brief: Use of Public Library Services by Households in the United States: 1996*, released in July 1997.

### Public Library Use in the Past Month and Year

- About 44 percent of U.S. households included individuals who had used public library services in the month prior to the interview, and 65 percent of households had used public library services in the past year (including the past month). About one-third of households (35 percent) reported that no household members had used library services in the past year.

• When the entire past year is taken into account, households with children under 18 showed substantially higher rates of use than households without children (82 percent versus 54 percent).

**Ways of Using Public Library Services**

• The most common way of using public library services in the past month was to go to a library to borrow or drop off books or tapes (36 percent).

• Eighteen percent of households reported visiting a library for other purposes, such as a lecture or story hour or to use library equipment (the second most common form of use).

• About 14 percent of households had called a library for information during the past month.

• Only very small percentages of households reported using a computer to link to a library (4 percent), having materials mailed or delivered to their homes (2 percent), or visiting a bookmobile (2 percent).

**Purposes for Using Public Library Services**

• The highest percentage of households reported library use for enjoyment or hobbies, including borrowing books and tapes or attending activities (32 percent).

• Two other purposes for using public libraries that were commonly acknowledged by household respondents were getting information for personal use (such as information on consumer or health issues, investments, and so on; 20 percent), and using library services or materials for a school or class assignment (19 percent).

• Fewer household respondents said that household members had used public library services for the purposes of keeping up to date at a job (8 percent), getting information to help find a job (5 percent), attending a program for children (4 percent), or working with a tutor or taking a class to learn to read (1 percent).

# Other Planned Public Library Data Projects

NCES has also fostered the use and analysis of FSCS data. A Data Use Subcommittee of the FSCS Steering Committee has been addressing the analysis, dissemination, and use of FSCS data. Several analytical projects, recommended by this committee, are under way.

In 1999 Westat, Inc. will complete a trend analysis report for FY 1992–FY 1996 on 15 key variables from the Public Libraries Survey. As part of this project, FY 1992–1994 Public Libraries Survey data are being imputed for nonresponse and will be released in 1999 (FY 1995–FY1996 have already been imputed).

NCES has been exploring the potential of geographic mapping for public libraries. The goal is to develop the capability to link census demographic data with Public Libraries Survey data through geographic mapping software. Westat, Inc. has nearly completed geocoding public library service outlets nationwide and digitizing the boundaries of the almost 9,000 public library legal service area jurisdictions. These will be matched to Census Tiger files and to Public Libraries Survey data files. NCES is considering dissemination options for this resource. One option would be to make it available on the NCES Web site. Another option would be to produce a public use data file linking Public Libraries Survey data with key Census demographic variables and provide a user's guide. A technical report will describe the methods of geocoding, public library mapping, and options for keeping the project up to date.

A fast-response survey on the topic of public library programming for adults, including adults at risk is under way. The questionnaire is in development and an advisory group will make recommendations concerning the project. Westat, Inc. is conducting the survey. NCES, PLLI, and the National Library of Education are supporting and/or working on this project.

Additional information on Public Libraries data may be obtained from Adrienne Chute, Elementary/Secondary and Libraries Studies Division, National Center for Education statistics, Room 311A, 555 New Jersey Ave. N.W., Washington, DC 20208-5652 (202-219-1772).

## Academic Libraries

NCES surveyed academic libraries on a three-year cycle between 1966 and 1988. Since 1988 the Academic Libraries Survey (ALS) has been a component of the Integrated Postsecondary Education Data system (IPEDS), is on a two-year cycle, and will be continued. ALS provides data on about 3,500 academic libraries. In aggregate, these data provide an overview of the status of academic libraries nationally and statewide.

The survey collects data on the libraries in the entire universe of accredited higher education institutions and on the libraries in nonaccredited institutions with a program of four years or more. A small subset of the ALS questions is included in the IPEDS consolidated form for institutions with less than four-year programs. ALS produces descriptive statistics on academic libraries in postsecondary institutions in the 50 states, the District of Columbia, and the outlying areas.

The first release of ALS 1996 data was in November 1997 over the Internet. A universe file is also available. Several data products will follow, including an E.D. TABS and a diskette of the survey data (including the universe file).

NCES has developed IDEALS, a software package for states to use in submitting ALS data to NCES. IDEALS was used by 45 states in the collection of 1996 data.

ALS has a working group comprised of representatives of the academic library community. Its mission is to improve data quality and the timeliness of data collection, processing, and release. This network of academic library professionals works closely with state IPEDS coordinators (representatives from each state who work with NCES to coordinate the collection of IPEDS data from postsecondary institutions in each of their states). NCES also works cooperatively with ALA, NCLIS, the Association of Research Libraries, the Association of College and Research Libraries, and numerous academic libraries in the collection of ALS data. ALS collects data on total library operating expenditures, full-time-equivalent (FTE) library staff, service outlets, total volumes held at the end of the fiscal year, circulation, interlibrary loans, public service hours, gate count, reference transactions per typical week, and online services. Beginning in 1996 the libraries were also asked whether they offered the following electronic services: an electronic catalog that includes the library's holdings, electronic full-text periodicals, Internet access, library reference services by e-mail, and electronic document delivery to patron's account-address.

The following are highlights from the *E.D. TABS Academic Libraries: 1994*, released in March 1998.

### Services

- In 1993, 3,303 of the 3,639 institutions of higher education in the United States reported that they had their own academic library.
- In fiscal year 1994, general collection circulation transactions in the nation's academic libraries at institutions of higher education totaled 183.1 million. Reserve collection circulation transactions totaled 48.4 million. For general and reference circulation transactions taken together, the median circulation was 16.6 per full-time-equivalent (FTE) student*. The median total circulation ranged from 9.5 per FTE in less than four-year institutions to 31.1 in doctorate-granting institutions.
- In 1994 academic libraries provided a total of about 8.8 million interlibrary loans to other libraries (both higher education and other types of libraries) and received about 6.3 million loans.
- Overall, the largest percentage of academic libraries (43 percent) reported having 60–79 hours of service per typical week. However, 41 percent provided 80 or more public service hours per typical week. The percent of institutions providing 80 or more public service hours ranged from 6.9 percent in less than four-year institutions to 77.8 percent in doctorate-granting institutions.
- Taken together, academic libraries reported a gate count of about 17.8 million visitors per typical week (about 1.8 visits per total FTE enrollment).
- About 2.1 million reference transactions were reported in a typical week. Over the fiscal year 1994, about 487,000 presentations to groups serving about 6.1 million were reported.

### Collections

- Taken together, the nation's 3,033 academic libraries at institutions of higher education held a total of 776.4 million volumes (books, bound serials, and government documents), representing about 422.3 million unduplicated titles at the end of FY 1994.

*FTE enrollment is calculated by adding one-third of part-time enrollment to full-time enrollment. Enrollment data are from the 1993–94 IPEDS Fall Enrollment Survey.

- The median number of volumes held per FTE student was 56.9 volumes. Median volumes held ranged from 18.4 per FTE in less than four-year institutions to 111.2 in doctorate-granting institutions.
- Of the total volumes held at the end of the year, 43.3 percent (336.6 million) were held at the 125 institutions categorized under the 1994 Carnegie classification as Research I or Research II institutions. About 54.6 percent of the volumes were at those institutions classified as either Research or Doctoral in the Carnegie classification.
- In FY 1994, the median number of volumes added to collections per FTE student was 1.6. The median number added range from .6 per FTE in less than four-year institutions to 3.1 in doctorate-granting institutions.

**Staff**

- There was a total of 95,843 FTE staff working in academic libraries in 1994. Of these about 26,726 (27.9 percent) were librarians or other professional staff; 40,381 (42.1 percent) were other paid staff; 326 (0.3 percent) were contributed services staff; and 28,411 (29.6 percent) were student assistants.
- Excluding student assistants, the institutional median number of academic library FTE staff per 1,000 FTE students was 5.9. The median ranged from 3.6 in less than four-year institutions to 9.8 in doctorate-granting institutions.

**Expenditures**

- In 1994 total operating expenditures for libraries at the 3,303 institutions of higher education totaled $4.01 billion. The three largest individual expenditure items for all academic libraries were salaries and wages, $2.02 billion (50.4 percent); current serial subscription expenditures, $690.4 million (17.2 percent); and books and bound serials, $442.5 million (11.0 percent).
- The libraries of the 514 doctorate-granting institutions (15.6 percent of the total institutions) accounted for $2.496 billion, or 62.2 percent of the total operating expenditure dollars at all college and university libraries.
- In 1994 the median total operating expenditure per FTE student was $290.81 and the median for information resource expenditures was $86.15.
- The median percentage of total institutional Education & General (E&G) expenditures for academic libraries was 2.8 percent in 1994. In 1990 the median was 3.0 percent (*Academic Library Survey: 1990*, unpublished tabulation).

A descriptive report of changes in academic libraries between 1990 and 1994, *The Status of Academic Libraries in the United States: Results from the 1994 Academic Library Survey with Historical Comparisons,* was released in September 1998. A technical report assessing the coverage of academic libraries through the ALS is also under way through contract with the Governments Division of the Bureau of the Census.

Several questions about the role of academic libraries in distance education were included as part of another survey sponsored by the U.S. Department of Education's National Institute on Postsecondary Education Libraries and Lifelong Learning. the Survey on Distance Education Courses Offered by Higher Education Institutions was conducted in fall 1995 under NCES's Postsecondary Education Quick Information System (PEQIS). The following is a highlight from the resulting *Statistical Analysis Report: Distance Education in Higher Education Institutions*, released October 1997.

Access to library resources varied depending on the type of library resource. Access to an electronic link with the institution's library was available for some or all courses at 56 percent of the institutions, and cooperative agreements for students to use other libraries were available at 62 percent of institutions. Institution library staff were assigned to assist distance education students at 45 percent of the institutions, while library deposit collections were available at remote sites at 39 percent of institutions.

Additional information on academic library statistics may be obtained from Jeffrey Williams, Elementary/Secondary and Libraries Studies Division, National Center for Education Statistics, 320A, 555 New Jersey Ave. N.W., Washington, DC 20208-5652 (202-219-1362).

## School Library Media Centers

A national survey on school library media centers was conducted in school year 1993–1994, the first since school year 1985–1986. NCES plans to continue school library data collection. Surveys are planned for once every five years, with the next survey planned for 1999–2000.

NCES, with the assistance of the U.S. Bureau of the Census, conducted the School Library Media Centers Survey as part of the 1994 Schools and Staffing Survey (SASS). The sample of schools surveyed consisted of 5,000 public schools, 2,500 private schools, and the 176 Bureau of Indian Affairs (BIA) schools in the United States. This subsample was drawn from a sample of approximately 13,000 schools in the SASS. The survey consisted of two questionnaires. Data from the school library media specialist questionnaire provided a nationwide profile of the school library media specialist work force. Data from the school library media center questionnaire provided a national picture of school library staffing, collections, expenditures, technology, and services. This effort was use to assess the status of school library media centers, nationwide, and to assess the federal role in their support. Data from 1993–1994 were compared with historical data from previous surveys. The report on this survey, *School Library Media Centers 1993–1994*, was released in August 1998.

The following are highlights from the Executive Summary of this report:

- Library media centers are now almost universally available. In 1993–1994, 96 percent of all public schools and 80 percent of all private schools had library media centers. This compares with 50 percent of the public schools in 1950, and 44 percent of private schools in 1962.

- Out of 164,650 school library staff, 44 percent were state-certified library media specialists, 20 percent were other non-certified professional librarians, and 36 percent were other staff.
- Library media centers spent about $828 million in 1992–1993, including federal gifts and grants but not including salaries and wages. For public schools, after adjusting for differences between the two surveys, expenditures were $676 million (in 1993 dollars) in 1985 and $738 million in 1992–1993. Private school expenditures were $61 million (in 1993 dollars) in 1985 and $89 million in 1993.
- School libraries had 879 million book volumes in their collections at the end of the 1992–1993 school year, or a mean of 28.0 books per student. They also had 2.6 million serial subscriptions, 13.3 million tape and disk video materials, 42.5 million other audiovisual materials, 5.4 million microcomputer software items, and 314,000 CD-ROMs. For public schools, the mean number of books per pupil was 5.3 in 1958 and 17.8 in 1993.
- Two-thirds (67 percent) of schools with library media centers had at least one microcomputer that was supervised by library media center staff. Among those centers with staff-supervised computers, the mean number of computers was 8.9. Other equipment and services found at library media centers included a telephone (57 percent), one or more CD-ROMs for such uses as periodical indices and encyclopedias (41 percent), an automated circulation system (32 percent), a computer with modem (31 percent), database searching with CD-ROM (28 percent), one or more video laser disks (27 percent), an automated catalog (21 percent), a connection to the Internet (11 percent), and online database searching (9 percent).
- The total number of students using library media centers per week was 42.5 million in 1985 and 32.5 million in 1993–1994 in public schools, and 5.3 million in 1985 and 3.4 million in 1993–1994 in private schools. Over the same time period, total enrollment in public schools increased from 39.4 million to 43.5 million. The mean weekly circulation per pupil per school was 1.3 in 1993–1994 in public schools, and 0.9 in 1985 and 1.2 in 1993–1994 in private schools.
- About two-thirds (65 percent) of school head librarians were regular full-time employees at the schools in which they were surveyed, while 19 percent provided library services at more than one school, and 16 percent were employed part time.
- About half (52 percent) of school head librarians reported they earned a master's degree as their highest degree, while another 8 percent reported training beyond the master's level, either as an education specialist (7 percent) or with a doctorate or first-professional degree (1 percent).
- Head librarians generally expressed positive attitudes toward their schools, the library media centers, and their own personal roles. For example, 96 percent said students believed the library media center was a desirable place to be, 95 percent said their jobs as librarians had more advantages than disadvantages, and 89 percent said the school administration's behavior toward the library media center was supportive and encouraging.

- The median base salary of school head librarians was $30,536 during the 1993–1994 academic year, and their median annual earnings from all sources was $32,000.
- In 1993 public school districts employed 51,000 full-time-equivalent (FTE) school librarians, while another 800 FTE positions were either vacant or temporarily filled by a substitute. About 150 FTE positions were abolished or withdrawn because a suitable candidate could not be found, and 450 FTE positions were lost through layoffs at the end of the last school year.

The Bureau of the Census also completed a technical report for NCES, *Evaluation of Definitions and Analysis of Comparative Data for the School Library Statistics Program*, released in September 1998.

NCES also plans to include a few library-oriented questions on the parent and the teacher instruments of its new Early Childhood Longitudinal Study. Questions were field tested in 1997. Data collection is scheduled for 1998 and 1999, with data release scheduled for 2000.

Additional information on school library media center statistics may be obtained from Jeffrey Williams, Elementary/Secondary and Libraries Studies Division, National Center for Education Statistics, 320A, 555 New Jersey Ave. N.W., Washington, DC 20208-5652 (202-219-1362).

## Surveys on Children, Young Adults

In spring 1994, under the sponsorship of the U.S. Department of Education's Library Programs Office, NCES conducted two fast-response surveys—one on public library services and resources for children and another on public library services and resources for young adults. These surveys updated similar surveys from 1989 and 1988, respectively. The two surveys collected data directly from two different representative samples of public libraries.

The Survey on Library Services and Resources for Children in Public Libraries included questions regarding the availability of specialized staff and resources for children and the adults who live and work with them, use of available services, prevalence of cooperative activities between public libraries and other organizations serving children, and barriers to providing increased library services for children.

The Survey on Library Services and Resources for Young Adults in Public Libraries obtained information on services for young adults, use of available services, cooperation between libraries and other organizations, ways in which libraries interact with schools, and factors perceived as barriers to increasing young adult services and their use. The data from the two surveys were consolidated into one report.

The following are highlights from the report *Services and Resources for Children and Young Adults in Public Libraries (1995)*.

- Sixty percent of the 18 million people entering public libraries during a typical week in fall 1993 were youth—children and young adults.

- The percentage of libraries with children's and young adult librarians has not changed since the late 1980s. Thirty-nine percent of libraries employ a children's librarian, 11 percent have a young adult librarian, and 24 percent have a youth services specialist on staff.
- Librarians report that ethnic diversity of children and young adult patrons has increased in over 40 percent of U.S. public libraries over the last five years. Seventy-six percent of public libraries currently have children's materials and 64 percent have young adult materials in languages other than English.
- Although computer technologies are among the most heavily used children's and young adult resources in public libraries, they are also among the most scarce. Only 30 percent of public libraries reported the availability of personal computers for use by children and young adults. However, 75 percent of libraries having this resource report moderate to heavy use by young adults.
- Less than half of all public libraries (40 percent) offer group programs for infants and toddlers. These programs are more prevalent now than in 1988, when only 29 percent of libraries offered group programs for infants to two-year-olds. Eighty-six percent of libraries offer group programs, such as story times, booktalks, puppetry, and crafts, for preschool and kindergarten-age children; 79 percent of libraries offer group programs for school-age children.
- Seventy-six percent of public libraries report working with schools; 66 percent work with preschools and 56 percent with day care centers.
- While almost all libraries provide reference assistance, only about 1 in 7 libraries offer homework assistance programs for children or young adults. However, fairly large percentages of libraries with homework assistance programs report moderate to heavy use by children and young adults. Sixty-four percent report moderate to heavy use by young adults.
- Librarians report that insufficient library staff is a leading barrier to increasing services and resources for both children and young adults. Sixty-five percent of librarians consider this a moderate or major barrier to increasing services for children, and 58 percent consider lack of staff a barrier to increasing services for young adults.

Additional information on these surveys may be obtained from Edith McArthur, National Center for Education Statistics, 402K, 555 New Jersey Ave. N.W., Washington, DC 20208-5652 (202-219-1442)

## Federal Libraries and Information Centers

The Federal Libraries and Information Centers Survey was designed to obtain data on the mission and function, administrative and managerial components (e.g., staff size and expenditures), information resources (e.g., collection size), and services of federal libraries and information centers. The Federal Library Survey has been a cooperative effort between the NCES and the staff of the

Federal Library and Information Center Committee (FLICC) of the Library of Congress. The survey established a nationwide profile of federal libraries and information centers and made available the first national data on federal libraries since 1978.

The survey was pretested in 1993 and 1994 and the full-scale survey conducted in 1995. four data products resulted from this survey: an E.D. TABS with the FY 1994 data (released July 1996), the survey database (released 1996), a directory of federal libraries and information centers (released August 1997), and a *Statistical Analysis Report: The Status of Federal Libraries and Information Centers in the United States: Results from the 1994 Federal Libraries and Information Centers Survey* (released February 1998). One highlight from this report is:

> About 40 percent of responding federal libraries and information centers reported the general public among their users, and about 53 percent reported having services available to the general public.

The Bureau of the Census also competed a technical report on "Coverage Evaluation of the 1994 Federal Libraries and Information Centers Survey," released in August 1998.

Additional information on the Federal Libraries and Information Centers Survey may be obtained from Martha Hollins, Postsecondary Studies Division, National Center for Education Statistics, 315B, 555 New Jersey Ave. N.W., Washington, DC 20208-5652 (202-219-1395).

## State Library Agencies

The State Library Agencies survey began in 1994 as a cooperative effort between NCES, COSLA, and NCLIS. A state library agency is the official unit of state government charged with statewide library development and the administration of federal funds under the Library Services and Technology Act (LSTA). Increasingly, state library agencies (STLAs) have received broader legislative mandates affecting libraries of all types and are often involved in the development and operation of electronic information networks. STLAs provide important reference and information services to state government and sometimes also provide service to the general public. STLAs often administer the state library and special operations such as state archives and libraries for the blind and physically handicapped.

Annually, data are collected electronically from each state library agency through the State Library Agencies (STLA) Survey. STLA collects data on 462 items, covering the following areas: direct library services; library development services; resources assigned to allied operations such as archive and records management; organizational and governance structure within which the agency operates; electronic networking; staffing; collections; and expenditures. These data are edited electronically, but are not imputed for nonresponse. The most recent data available are for FY 1996. Two FY 1996 data products were released on the Internet through the NCES Web site: an E.D. TABS, with 27 Tables for the 50 states and the District of Columbia (also available in print), and the survey data base, including the universe file (also available on diskette).

The following are highlights from *E.D. TABS State Library Agencies, Fiscal Year 1996*, released in June 1998:

## Governance

- Nearly all state agencies (48 states and the District of Columbia) are located in the executive branch of government. Of these, over 65 percent are part of a larger agency, the most common being the state department of education. In two states, Arizona and Michigan, the agency reports to the legislature.

## Allied and Other Special Operations

- A total of 16 state library agencies reported having one or more operations. Allied operations most frequently linked with a state library are the state archives (10 states), the state records management service (11 states).
- Fifteen state agencies contract with libraries in their states to serve as resource or reference/information service centers. Eighteen state agencies operate a State Center for the Book*.

## Electronic Network Development

- In all 50 states, the state library agency plans or monitors electronic network development, 42 states operate such networks, and 46 states develop network content.
- All 50 states are involved in facilitating library access to the Internet in one or more of the following ways: training library staff or consulting in the use of the Internet; providing a subsidy for Internet participation; providing equipment needed to access the Internet; providing access to directories, databases, or online catalogs; or managing gopher/Web sites, file servers, bulletin boards, or listservs.

## Library Development Services

Services to Public Libraries

- Every state agency provides these types of services to public libraries: administration of LSCA (Library Services and Construction Act) grants, collection of library statistics, continuing education, and library planning, evaluation, and research. Nearly every state library agency provides consulting services and continuing-education programs.
- Services to public libraries provided by at least three-quarters of state agencies include administration of state aid, interlibrary loan referral services, library legislation preparation or review, literacy program support,

---

*The State Center for the Book is part of the Center for the Book program sponsored by the Library of Congress which promotes books, reading, and literacy, and is hosted or funded by the state.

reference referral services, state standards or guidelines, public relations or promotional campaigns, summer reading program support, and union list development.

- Over three-fifths of state agencies provide Online Computer Library Center (OCLC) Group Access Capability (GAC) to public libraries and statewide public relations or library promotion campaigns.
- Less common services to public libraries include accreditation of libraries, certification of librarians, cooperative purchasing of library materials, preservation/conservation services, and retrospective conversion of bibliographic records.

## Services to Academic Libraries

- At least two-thirds of state library agencies report the following services to the academic library sector: administration of LSCA Title III grants, continuing education, interlibrary loan referral services, reference referral services, and union list development.
- Less common services to academic libraries provided by state agencies include cooperative purchasing of library materials, literacy program support, preservation/conservation, retrospective conversion, and state standards or guidelines. No state agency accredits academic libraries; only Washington state certifies academic librarians.

## Services to School Library Media Centers

- Two-thirds of all state library agencies provide continuing education and interlibrary loan referral services and reference referral services to school library media centers (LMCs). Services to LMCs provided by at least half of state agencies include administration of LSCA Title III grants, consulting services, and union list development.
- Less common services to LMCs include administration of state aid, cooperative purchasing of library materials, and retrospective conversion. No state agency accredits LMCs or certifies LMC librarians.

## Services to Special Libraries

- Over two-thirds of state agencies serve special libraries* through administration of LSCA grants, consulting services, continuing education, interlibrary loan referral, reference referral, and union list development.
- Less common services to special libraries include administration of state aid, cooperative purchasing of library materials, and summer reading program support. Only Nebraska accredits special libraries and only Washington state certifies librarians of special libraries.

---

*A library in a business firm, professional association, government agency, or other organized group; a library that is maintained by a parent organization to serve a specialized clientele; or an independent library that may provide materials or services, or both, to the public, a segment of the public, or to other libraries. Scope of collections and services are limited to the subject interests of the host or parent institution. Includes libraries in state institutions.

Services to Systems

- At least three-fifths of state agencies serve library systems* through administration of LSCA grants, consulting services, continuing education, library legislation preparation or review, and library planning, evaluation, and research.
- Accreditation of systems is provided by only six states and certification of librarians by only seven states.

### Service Outlets

- State library agencies reported a total of 153 service outlets. Main or central outlets and other outlets (excluding bookmobiles) made up 47.1 percent, and bookmobiles represented 5.9 percent of the total.

### Collections

- The number of books and serial volumes held by state library agencies totaled 22.4 million, with New York accounting for the largest collection (2.4 million). Five state agencies had book and serial volumes of over one million. In other states, these collections ranged from 500,000 to one million (12 states); 200,000 to 499,999 (10 states); 100,000 to 199,999 (10 states); 50,000 to 99,999 (6 states); and 50,000 or less (6 states). The state library agency in Maryland does not maintain a collection, and the District of Columbia does not maintain a collection in its function as a state library agency.
- The number of serial subscriptions held by state library agencies totaled over 84,000, with New York holding the largest number (over 14,300). Ten state agencies reported serial subscriptions of over 2,000. In other states, these collections ranged from 1,000 to 1,999 (6 states), 500 to 999 (18 states), 100 to 499 (13 states), and under 100 (1 state).

### Staff

- The total number of budgeted full-time-equivalent (FTE) positions in state library agencies was 3,762. Librarians with ALA-MLS degrees accounted for 1,206 of these positions, or 32.1 percent of total FTE positions. Rhode Island reported the largest percentage (57.1) of ALA-MLS librarians, and Utah reported the lowest (16.3 percent).

### Income

- State library agencies reported a total income of $847.1 million in FY 1997 (83.1 percent came from state sources, 15.4 percent from federal, and 1.5 percent from other sources).

---

*A system is a group of autonomous libraries joined together by formal or informal agreements to perform various services cooperatively such as resource sharing, communications, etc. Includes multitype library systems and public library systems. Excludes multiple outlets under the same administration.

- Of state library agency income received from state sources, over $477 million (67.8 percent) was designated for state aid to libraries. Seven states had 75 percent or more of their income from state sources set aside for state aid. Georgia had the largest percentage of state library agency income set aside for state aid (97.4 percent). Six states and the District of Columbia targeted no state funds for aid to libraries. Hawaii, Iowa, South Dakota, Vermont, Washington, and the District of Columbia reported state income only for operation of the state agency.*

## Expenditures

- State library agencies reported total expenditures of over $822.2 million. The largest percentage (83.6 percent) came from state funds, followed by federal funds (15.3 percent), and other funds (1.1 percent).
- In five states, over 90 percent of total expenditures were from state sources. These states were Georgia (94.7 percent), Massachusetts (93.5 percent), Maryland (91.9 percent), New York (92 percent), and Illinois (92.4 percent). Utah had the lowest percentage of expenditures from state sources (59.2 percent), with most of its expenditures from federal sources.
- Almost 70 percent of total state library expenditures were for aid to libraries, with the largest percentages expended on individual public libraries (53.1 percent) and public library systems (16.4 percent). Most aid-to-libraries expenditures (86.2 percent) were from state sources, and 13.6 percent were from federal sources.
- Fifteen state library agencies reported expenditures for allied operations. These expenditures totaled over $24 million and represented 2.9 percent of total expenditures by state library agencies. Of states reporting allied operations expenditures, Texas reported the highest expenditure ($3.3 million) and Vermont the lowest ($398,000).†
- Twenty-seven state library agencies reported a total of over $16.7 million in grants and contracts expenditures to assist public libraries with state education reform initiatives or the National Education Goals. The area of adult literacy accounted for the largest proportion of such expenditures (47.7 percent), followed by the areas of lifelong learning (34.9 percent) and readiness for school (17.4 percent). Three state agencies (Nebraska, Oregon, and Pennsylvania) focused such expenditures exclusively on readiness for school projects, and five state agencies (Georgia, Kansas, New Jersey, Oklahoma, and Utah) focused their expenditures exclusively on adult literacy projects. In four states (Connecticut, Indiana, Michigan, and South Carolina), over two-thirds of such expenditures were for lifelong learning projects.

*The District of Columbia Public Library functions as a state library agency and is eligible for Federal LSCA (Library Services and Construction Act) funds in this capacity. The state library agency in Hawaii is associated with the Hawaii State Public System and operates all public libraries within its jurisdiction. The state funds for aid to libraries for these two agencies are reported on the NCES Public Libraries Survey, rather than on the STLA survey, because of the unique situation of these two state agencies, and in order to eliminate duplicative reporting of these data.

†Although Alaska reported allied operations, the expenditures are not from the state library agency budget.

A study evaluating the state library survey including the comparison of data with other sources is planned for release in fall 1999.

Additional information on the state library agency survey may be obtained from Elaine Kroe, Elementary/Secondary and Libraries Studies Division, National Center for Education Statistics, 315A, 555 New Jersey Ave. N.W., Washington, DC 20208-5652 (202-219-1361).

## Survey of Library Cooperatives

A new survey of over 400 library cooperatives is moving forward with data release expected in late 1999. A planning committee was formed and met in December 1995 to work on definitions, a universe file, and survey design. A pretest was mailed in April 1997. The questionnaire was revised based on the results of the pretest in September 1997. The full-scale FY 1997 survey was mailed in March and was due in May 1998.

The survey defines a library cooperative (network, system, consortium) as "an organization that has a formal arrangement whereby library and information services are supported for the mutual benefit of participating libraries." It must meet all of the following criteria: Participant/members are primarily libraries; the organization is a U.S. not-for-profit entity which has its own budget and its own paid staff; the organization serves multiple institutions (e.g., libraries, school districts) that are not under the organization's administrative control; and the scope of the organization's activities includes support of library and information services by performing such functions as resource sharing, training, planning, and advocacy.

The survey included 55 data items and covered the following areas: Type of organization; geographic area served; whether the general public is directly served; cooperative membership; operating income; operating expenditures; capital expenditures; and cooperative services such as reference, interlibrary loan, training, consulting, Internet access, electronic services, statistics, preservation, union lists, public relations, cooperative purchasing, delivery, advocacy, and outreach programming. An E.D. TABS and data file (including a universe file) are expected to be released in late 1999. It is expected that this survey will be conducted every five years.

Additional information on the Survey of Library Cooperatives may be obtained from Rosa Fernandez, Postsecondary Studies Division, National Center for Education Statistics, Room 317, 555 New Jersey Ave. N.W., Washington, DC 20208-5652 (202-219-1358).

## Plans for Crosscutting Activities

The Library Statistics Program also sponsors activities that cut across all types of libraries. For example, NCES sponsors the attendance of librarians from all sectors at NCES training opportunities, such as the semiannual Cooperative System Fellows Program.

In 1999 NCES, with the assistance of Sierra, Inc., is enhancing its library Web site for the six surveys. Information about the surveys has been updated, and the Web site is being reorganized. Additional publications are being made available in PDF format for ease in downloading. There will be links to other Web sites.

In addition, library locators will be developed for both the Public Libraries and Academic Libraries Surveys. Customers will be able to locate data about a library in instances where they know some but not all of the identifying information about the library. For example, if one knows the city the library is in, but not its name, one will still be able to locate the library and obtain data about it. The NCES World Wide Web Home page is http://nces.ed.gov.

NCES is also developing Web-based peer analysis tools for the Academic Libraries Survey, the Public Libraries Survey, and the State Library Agencies Survey. The user will be able to customize a search for peers for a particular library using a variety of such peer-selection variables as total operating expenditures, population of the legal service area, total circulation, etc. Once the peers are selected, the user will be able to get comparative data in tabular and graphic formats. Customer feedback mechanisms will be essential to improving the quality of these products over time and will be built into the Web site.

NCES is working with constituent groups from all the surveys in planning an expanded library statistics cooperative. The goal is to facilitate work on crosscutting issues without interfering with the ability of existing constituent groups to continue their work on individual surveys. Ideas include expanding participation to add local practitioners, experts from allied professions such as publishing and technology, more data users, and possibly the media. One advantage of an expanded cooperative will be the opportunity to address crosscutting policy issues, identify and address data gaps, and encourage participation by diverse groups and all levels of government.

In support of an expanded library statistics cooperative, American Institutes for Research in 1998 initiated a review of the content and comparability of NCES's six library surveys. It is hoped that this project will lead to a Web-based matrix covering all six surveys. By topic, the customer would be able to compare definitions across surveys. This activity will be a first step in assessing the potential for a more-integrated approach to the library surveys. There will be opportunities to eliminate unnecessary duplication, and increase consistency of definitions. This will facilitate sharing and comparing information across surveys to address key policy issues.

## Dissemination of Library Statistics, Cooperative Program Reports and Data

Under its six library surveys, NCES regularly publishes E.D. TABS, which consist of tables, usually presenting state and national totals, a survey description, and data highlights. NCES also publishes separate more in-depth studies analyzing library data. Many of these publications are available in printed format and over the Internet. Edited raw data from the library surveys are made available on data diskettes, CD-ROM, and over the Internet.

## Publications

*Public Libraries in Forty-Four States and the District of Columbia: 1988; An NCES Working Paper* (November 1989). o.p.

*E.D. TABS: Academic Libraries: 1988* (September 1990). o.p.

*E.D. TABS: Public Libraries in Fifty States and the District of Columbia: 1989* (April 1991). o.p.

*E.D. TABS: Public Libraries in the U.S.: 1990* (June 1992). o.p.

*E.D. TABS: Academic Libraries: 1990* (December 1992). Government Printing Office No., 065-000-00549-2. o.p.

*Survey Report: School Library Media Centers in the United States: 1990–91* (November 1994). Government Printing Office, No. 065-000-00715-1. o.p.

*E.D. TABS: Public Libraries in the United States: 1991* (April 1993). Government Printing Office, No. 065-000-00561-1. o.p.

*E.D. TABS: Public Libraries in the United States: 1992* (August 1994). Government Printing Office, No. 065-000-00670-7. o.p.

*E.D. TABS: Academic Libraries: 1992* (November 1994). Government Printing Office, No. 065-000-00717-7. $3.75

*Data Comparability and Public Policy: New Interest in Public Library Data*; papers presented at Meetings of the American Statistical Association. Working Paper No. 94-07. National Center for Education Statistics, November 1994.

*Report on Coverage Evaluation of the Public Library Statistics Program* (June 1994). Prepared for the National Center for Education Statistics by the Governments Division, Bureau of the Census. Government Printing Office, No. 065-00-00662-6. o.p.

*Finance Data in the Public Library Statistics Program: Definitions, Internal Consistency, and Comparisons to Secondary Sources (1995).* Prepared for NCES by the Governments Division, Bureau of the Census. Government Printing Office, No 065-000-00794-9. o.p.

*Report on Evaluation of Definitions Used in the Public Library Statistics Program (1995).* Prepared for the National Center for Education Statistics by the Governments Division, Bureau of the Census. Government Printing Office, No. 065-000-00736-3. o.p.

*Staffing Data in the Public Library Statistics Program: Definitions, Internal Consistency, and Comparisons to Secondary Sources (1995).* Prepared for NCES by the Governments Division, Bureau of the Census. Government Printing Office, No. 065-000-00795-9. o.p.

*Statistical Analysis Report: Services and Resources for Children and Young Adults in Public Libraries* (August 1995). Prepared for NCES by Westat, Inc. Government Printing Office, No. 065-000-00797-5. $9.

*E.D. TABS: Public Libraries in the United States: 1993* (September 1995). Government Printing Office, No. 065-000-00800-9. $8.

*Public Library Structure and Organization in the United States.* NCES No. 96-229 (March 1996).

*E.D. TABS: State Library Agencies, Fiscal Year 1994* (June 1996). Government Printing Office No. 065-000-00878-5. $12.

*E.D. TABS: Federal Libraries and Information Centers in the United States: 1994* (July 1996).

*Statistics in Brief: Use of Public Library Services by Households in the United States: 1996* (March 1997). Government Printing Office.

*E.D. TABS: Public Libraries in the United States: FY 1994* (May 1997). Government Printing Office.

*The Status of Academic Libraries in the United States; Results form the 1990 and 1992 Academic Library Surveys* (June 1997). Prepared for NCES by American Institutes for Research.

*E.D. TABS: State Library Agencies Fiscal Year 1995* (August 1997). Government Printing Office, No. 065-000-01051-8. $14.

*Technical Report: Directory of Federal Libraries and Information Centers: 1994* (August 1997). Government Printing Office.

*Statistical Analysis Report: Distance Education in Higher Education Institutions* (October 1997). Prepared for NCES by Westat, Inc. Government Printing Office.

*Statistical Analysis Report: The Status of Federal Libraries and Information Centers in the United States: Results from the 1994 Federal Libraries and Information Centers Survey* (February 1988). Government Printing Office.

*E.D. TABS: Academic Libraries: 1994* (March 1998). Government Printing Office.

*E.D. TABS: State Library Agencies: FY 1996* (June 1998). Government Printing Office.

*Technical Report: Coverage Evaluation of the 1994 Federal Libraries and Information Centers Survey* (August 1998). Government Printing Office.

*E.D. TABS: Public Libraries in the United States: FY 1995* (August 1998). Government Printing Office.

*School Library Media Centers 1993–1994* (August 1998). Government Printing Office.

*Statistics in Brief: How Does Your Public Library Compare? Service Performance of Peer Groups* (September 1998). Government Printing Office.

*Status of Academic Libraries in the United States; Results from the 1994 Academic Library Survey with Historical Comparisons* (September 1998). Government Printing Office.

*Technical Report: Evaluation of Definitions and Analysis of Comparative Data for the School Library Statistics Program* (September 1998). Government Printing Office.

## Data Files Released on Computer Diskette

Public Libraries in Forty-Four States and the District of Columbia: 1988 (March 1990).

Public Libraries in Fifty States and the District of Columbia: 1989 (May 1990).

Academic Libraries: 1988 (October 1990).
Public Libraries Data, 1990 (July 1992).
Academic Libraries: 1990 (February 1993).

The NCES data files above are generally available on computer diskette through the U.S. Department of Education, Office of Educational Research and Improvement, National Library of Education, 555 New Jersey Ave. N.W., Washington, DC 20208-5725.

Public Library Data 1991 (November 1993). Government Printing Office.
Public Library Data 1992 (September 1994). Government Printing Office, No. 065-000-00675-8.
Academic Libraries: 1992 (November 1994). Available through the NEDRC.
Public Library Data FY 1993 on Disk (July 1995). Government Printing Office, No. 065-000-00790-8. $17.
State Library Agencies Data, FY 1994 on Disk (May 1996).
Public Libraries Data FY 1994 (June 1997). Government Printing Office, No. 065-000-01043-7. $17.
National Household Education Survey; 1991, 1993, 1995, and 1996 Surveys Data Files and Electronic Codebook (July 1997).
State Library Agencies Data, FY 1995 on Disk (September 1997).
Public Library Data, FY 1995 on Disk (June 1998). Government Printing Office, No. 065-000-01152-2.
State Library Agencies Data FY 1996 on Disk (August 1998).

The NCES data files above are generally available through the Government Printing Office.

## Internet Access

Data dissemination for the library surveys has also been broadened with electronic release of both current and back years' data and E.D. TABS on the Internet. To reach the NCES Web site, type the URL address: http://nces.ed.gov/pubsearch to view or download publications and data files.

## Ordering

To order more recent publications, write to: U.S. Department of Education, ED Pubs, P.O. Box 1398, Jessup, MD 20794-1398 or call toll-free 1-877-4-ED-Pubs.

## National Education Data Resource Center

An information service called the National Education Data Resource Center (NEDRC) is available to assist library survey customers. The NEDRC helps customers obtain NCES reports and data files through the Internet. The NEDRC also responds to requests for special tabulations on library studies and surveys. These services are free of charge. Contact the NEDRC at 1900 N. Beauregard St., Suite 200, Alexandria, Va 22311-1722, telephone 703-845-3151, fax 703-820-7465, or e-mail nedrc@pcci.com.

# Library of Congress

Washington, DC 20540
202-707-5000, World Wide Web http://www.loc.gov

Audrey Fischer
Public Affairs Specialist

The Library of Congress was established in 1800 to serve the research needs of the U.S. Congress. For nearly two centuries the library has grown both in the size of its collections (now totaling more than 115 million items) and in its mission. As the largest library in the world and the oldest federal cultural institution in the nation, the Library of Congress serves not only Congress but also government agencies, libraries around the world, and scholars and citizens in the United States and abroad. At the forefront of technology, the library now serves patrons on-site in its 22 reading rooms and at remote locations through its highly acclaimed World Wide Web site.

Planning for the library's bicentennial commemoration in the year 2000 began with the appointment of a steering committee of senior library managers under the leadership of the Librarian of Congress, the adoption of the theme "Libraries•Creativity•Liberty," and the establishment of the goal to inspire creativity in the century ahead by stimulating greater use of the Library of Congress and libraries everywhere. A bicentennial program manager was appointed to coordinate the effort. In October 1998 Congress approved a commemorative coin to mark the historic occasion in the year 2000, and a U.S. postage stamp was designed. Planning began on a number of key bicentennial initiatives such as "Gifts to the Nation" (which involves sharing the library's collections with Americans in their local communities by digitizing millions of items as part the National Digital Library effort) and "Local Legacies" (a project to document cultural traditions and events in each congressional district at the turn of the century).

In fiscal year (FY) 1998 (October 1, 1997–September 30, 1998) the library operated with a budget of $377.2 million, an increase of $15.3 million (or 4.2 percent) above FY 1997, including authority to spend $30.3 million in copyright receipts and cataloging data sales.

## Service to Congress

Serving Congress is the library's highest priority. In 1998 the library's Congressional Research Service (CRS) delivered approximately 560,000 research responses to members and committees of Congress. CRS assisted Congress in dealing with the full range of its domestic concerns, including banking and finance, campaign finance reform, clean air, congressional legal concerns, education, and patient protection legislation. In the international sphere, CRS assisted Congress on such issues as defense policy and budget, foreign policy and regional issues, and global financial crises and the international finance system.

In addition, the Law Library answered nearly 4,300 in-person reference requests from congressional users. Law Library research staff produced 710 written reports for Congress, including comprehensive multinational studies on such issues as human rights, health care, and government and finance.

The Copyright Office provided policy advice and technical assistance to Congress on important copyright-related issues. As a result, a number of key pieces of legislation were enacted, including the No Electronic Theft Act, the Digital Millennium Copyright Act, and the copyright term extension bill.

The library developed a plan for a single integrated Legislative Information System (LIS) to serve Congress, working with the Committee on House Oversight and the Senate Committee on Rules and Administration, in consultation with the House and Senate subcommittees on legislative branch appropriations. During 1998 the library updated the LIS plan and briefed congressional staff on scheduled development work. Since the initial delivery of the library's portion of the LIS on January 7, 1997, the library collaborated with House and Senate staffs to determine the most useful new search features and content to add to LIS. To ease the transition from the House legacy system to the new system, LIS was enhanced with more traditional and familiar search features. Joint planning for data exchange among the the House, the Senate, and the library occurred throughout the year, and decisions on compatible technologies were made to ensure that information would flow smoothly from all legislative branch agencies into LIS. The Legislative Information System was enhanced and more links were added to House and Senate information, increasing LIS's prominence as the central point for locating legislative information.

## Service to the Nation

The library reduced the total unprocessed arrearage by 861,548 items while keeping current with new receipts. This represented a cumulative reduction of 51.9 percent—39.7 million to less than 19.1 million—since the initial arrearage census in September 1989.

Linked to the library's arrearage reduction effort is the development of a secondary storage site to house processed materials and to provide for growth of the collection through the first part of the 21st century. In 1997 Congress authorized the Architect of the Capitol (AOC), on behalf of the library, to acquire real property and improvements in Culpeper, Virginia, for use as a National Audio-Visual Conservation Center. The library and AOC are working with the Packard Foundation, the donor of the facility, to renovate and make the new center ready for full use. The master plan for the renovation and development of the site was completed in September 1998 and approved by the library's oversight committees in December 1998. The library also continued to work closely with AOC to ensure that the first storage module at the Fort Meade, Maryland, campus will meet environmental specifications and be ready for occupancy during the middle of calendar year 2000.

Processing of print materials continued at very high levels—library staff created cataloging records for 274,890 volumes and inventory records for an additional 128,042 items. Building on the momentum generated since 1996 by the Program for Cooperative Cataloging (PCC), cooperative arrangements have continued to flourish. PCC member institutions increased by 100 during FY 1998 to a record high of 339 and once again they contributed record-breaking totals: 57,926 bibliographic records (37,559 for monographs and 20,367 for serials); 161,446 name authorities; 9,233 series authorities; 2,159 subject authorities; and 883 classification numbers.

The National Library Service for the Blind and Physically Handicapped (NLS/BPH) distributed more than 22 million items to some 769,000 readers in 1998. NLS/BPH made major advances in the development of a digital talking-book system, improved its nationwide machine-repair and recognition program (in cooperation with the telephone Pioneers of America, the Elfun Society, and other repair volunteers), and enhanced the NLS/BPH Web site to include digital files for full-text braille books.

Signed into law by President Clinton on October 21, 1998, the Legislative Branch Appropriations Act of 1999 included a provision to authorize the American Folklife Center permanently. At its annual meeting in Memphis, Tennessee, in February 1998, the North American Folk Music and Dance Alliance presented the American Folklife Center with a lifetime achievement award intended to honor members of the folk community who have made lifelong contributions to sustaining and enriching the fields of folk music and dance.

## Copyright

The Copyright Office received nearly 645,000 claims and made 558,645 registrations in 1998. During the year the office processed 6,250 documents containing 23,140 restored titles under the Copyright Restoration Provision of the GATT Uruguay Round Agreements Act. Enacted on January 1, 1996, this legislation restored the copyrights in a vast number of foreign works previously in the public domain in the United States. The office also processed 1,518 GATT registrations and 213 GATT group registrations.

The Copyright Office concluded five Copyright Arbitration Royalty Panels proceedings, setting rates for four licenses: the satellite compulsory license (17 U.S.C. 119), the mechanical license (17 U.S.C. 115), the digital performance license (17 U.S.C. 114), and the non-commercial broadcasting license (17 U.S.C. 118). The fifth proceeding determined the final distribution of the 1991 cable royalties among the claimants in the music category.

The Digital Millennium Copyright Act (DMCA) was signed into law by President Clinton on October 28, 1998. The legislation implements two 1996 World Intellectual Property Organization (WIPO) Treaties: the WIPO Copyright Treaty and the WIPO Performances and Phonograms Treaty. The DMCA also provides limitations on copyright liability relating to material online and it addresses a number of other significant copyright-related issues.

## Electronic Access

The library continued to provide Congress and the nation with a growing amount of information through its Internet-based systems. Workstations with public access to the Internet were made available in many of the library's reading rooms. During FY 1998 an average of 60 million transactions per month were recorded on the library's public electronic systems; in September 1998 the library logged a record 83 million transactions from both internal and public systems (more than double the FY 1997 monthly average).

The Library of Congress's World Wide Web site was cited for excellence throughout the year by Cybertimes (*New York Times* online), and the Library Public Relations Council presented it with an award for outstanding library public relations.

The library's American Memory Web site received the following recognition in FY 1998:

- "Best 100" list compiled jointly by *PC Magazine* and CNN
- "Best of the Web" by *eBlast, Encyclopedia Britannica*'s Internet Guide
- History Channel Hotlist
- One of "50 Great Sites for Parents and Kids" by the American Library Association's guide to quality family-friendly Web sites
- Five-Star Site by Magellan online Internet Guide
- Top 5 Percent of the Internet by Lycos
- WebCrawler Top Site
- Best of the Web by Netscape Net Guide
- Included in "Pick of the Week" fives times during the year by Yahoo! Internet Search Service
- Selected collections cited as "must see" seven times during the year by The Scout Report.

Advancements made in 1998 to increase electronic access to the library's resources included the National Digital Library Program, THOMAS, geographic information systems (GIS), the Global Legal Information Network, and several technology projects.

**National Digital Library Program**

The National Digital Library Program made significant progress during FY 1998 toward the goal of making a critical mass of Americana freely accessible by the library's bicentennial year. At year's end, more than 1.4 million Library of Congress digital files and 13,900 digital files from other collaborating institutions were available online or in digital archives. More than 2 million additional digital files from both the library's collections and other repositories were in various stages of production as part of a national collaborative effort.

During FY 1998 a total of 16 new multimedia historical collections were added to the library's World Wide Web site, including two winning collections from the Library of Congress Ameritech Competition. In the second year of the three-year nationwide competition, the program continued to provide financial and technical support to other archives and institutions in digitizing historically significant American collections. A total of 21 award winners have received support for their digitization efforts since the program's inception.

The National Digital Library Program continued to reach out to the education community with enhancements to the Learning Page and Today in History, two popular online features. In its second year, the Educators' Institute brought 50 educators from 18 states to Washington, D.C., to explore use of primary sources in education, to develop lesson plans that draw upon the library's online collections, and to share teaching ideas.

## THOMAS

Named in honor of Thomas Jefferson, THOMAS is a public database designed to make legislative information more accessible to the public. THOMAS is available 24 hours per day, free of charge to Internet users. During FY 1998 the amount of legislative information in THOMAS doubled through the addition of earlier files. THOMAS now provides continuous coverage from the 101st to the 105th Congress for the *Congressional Record* and text of legislation, and from the 103rd to 105th Congress for committee reports. Searching features in THOMAS were enhanced through a new release of the search engine and the addition of date limits. At the request of Congress, the Report of the Independent Counsel (the Starr Report) was mounted on THOMAS in September 1998, followed by two subsequent releases of testimony (monthly transactions average 9.3 million for THOMAS, but more than doubled to 19 million for the month of September). As of December 31, 1998, more than 246 million transactions had been processed by THOMAS since its inception in January 1995; more than half of these transactions occurred in FY 1998.

### Geographic Information Systems

The Geography and Map Division (G&M) is a leader in the cartographic and geographic communities through its work in geographic information systems (GIS). During the year G&M worked closely with the Congressional Research Service and the Congressional Relations Office to produce maps and geographic information for members of Congress and with the National Digital Library to digitize cartographic materials for electronic access throughout the nation. Working closely with private sector partners, G&M continued to expand the collection of large-format images available through the Internet. A second major map collection, railroad maps, was introduced on June 24, 1998. By the end of the fiscal year, 1,522 maps (4,971 images) were made available to the world through the Map Collections home page, which now averages more than 350,000 computer transactions each month.

### Global Legal Information Network

The Global Legal Information Network (GLIN) is a cooperative international network in which member nations contribute the full text of statutes and regulations to a database hosted by the library's Law Library. Twelve member countries currently participate via the Internet. In March 1998 the library put into production a new release of GLIN with expanded search capabilities and enhanced security features. At the fifth annual GLIN project directors meeting in September 1998 the library demonstrated a prototype for the input of a new category of legal information—legal writings.

**Technology Projects in Test Status**

On May 15, 1998, the library awarded a contract to Endeavor Information Systems for its Voyager integrated software system. The new system will improve automation support for bibliographic control and inventory management activities at the library through the use of a shared bibliographic database that integrates all major functional areas (such as acquisitions, cataloging, serials management, circulation, inventory control, and reference).

The Copyright Office Electronic Registration, Recordation and Deposit System (CORDS), a major new system for digital registration and deposit of copyrighted works over the Internet, uses the latest advances in networking and computer technology. CORDS is being developed by the Copyright Office in collaboration with national high-technology research and development partners (the Advanced Research Projects Agency and the Corporation for National Research Initiatives). During FY 1998 the Copyright Office drafted a cooperative agreement with UMI, a national producer of dissertation microfilm. The agreement would permit electronic registration and deposit of as many as 20,000 dissertations per year.

The Electronic Cataloging in Publication (ECIP) project enables the library to obtain texts of forthcoming publications from publishers via the Internet, catalog them entirely in an electronic environment, and transmit the completed catalog records via e-mail to the publisher for inclusion on the copyright page of the printed book. Staff cataloged 1,038 titles last year, bringing the cumulative total since the experiment's inception to more than 3,000.

## Collections

The library receives millions of pieces each year, from copyright deposits, federal agencies, purchases, exchanges, and gifts. Notable acquisitions during FY 1998 included:

- The Pamela Harriman collection of 500,000 items belonging to this diplomat and political figure
- The papers of Supreme Court Justice Ruth Bader Ginsburg covering her career before appointment to the court
- An addition of 2,000 items to the papers of Supreme Court Justice William J. Brennan
- The Martha Graham Archives, documenting the contribution of this pioneer in American dance
- Approximately 32,000 papers of poet Edna St. Vincent Millay
- Additions to the records of the National Urban League, the National Association for the Advancement of Colored People (NAACP) national office, and the NAACP Washington Bureau
- Additions to the Irving Berlin Collection and the Leonard Bernstein Archives
- Sixty drawings by political cartoonist Pat Oliphant

- Text, images, and audio files representing a full "snapshot" of the public World Wide Web donated by Brewster Kahle, president and founder of Alexa Internet
- Three rare portraits of Georgia O'Keefe by her husband, master photographer Alfred Stieglitz
- The extant collection of Russian sheet-music covers from the 1920s and 1930s
- A 19th-century Burmese manuscript on meteorology and astronomy
- The Popescu-Judetz multiformat collection of Romanian folk dance and music
- A map of Philadelphia from 1752 with the first illustration of Independence Hall
- The papers of Arab-American writer Ameen Fares Rihani.

## Publications

During 1998 the Publishing Office produced more than 40 books, calendars, CD-ROMs, and other products describing and illustrating the library's collections. Copublishing arrangements with trade publishers included *Eyes of the Nation: A Visual History of the United States* (Alfred A. Knopf), which won numerous awards and appeared on many "best of" lists; *The Library of Congress: The Art and Architecture of the Thomas Jefferson Building* (W. W. Norton & Co.); *Oliphant's Anthem: Pat Oliphant at the Library of Congress* (Andrews McMeel Publishing); and *Remembering Slavery: African Americans Talk About Their Personal Experiences of Slavery and Freedom* (The New Press).

The Publishing Office won three Washington Book Publishers Design Effectiveness Awards in 1998, all for excellence in illustrated books. The three award-winning books were *The Library of Congress: The Art and Architecture of the Thomas Jefferson Building* (which won the Best of Show award), *The African American Odyssey*, and *Eyes of the Nation*. In addition, for the first time the library won design awards in the American Association of Museums Museum Publications Design Competition. *Eyes of the Nation* won the coveted first prize for excellence in museum books and was featured in the July/August 1998 issue of *Museum News*, and *The Work of Charles and Ray Eames: A Legacy of Invention* received an honorable mention award for museum books.

The bimonthly magazine *Civilization*, which is published under a licensing agreement with the library, completed its fourth year of publication with nearly 250,000 paid subscribers who are also Library of Congress Associates.

## Exhibitions and Literary Events

The library's collections were shared with hundreds of thousands of Americans through exhibitions, special events and symposia, traveling exhibitions, and major publications.

*American Treasures of the Library of Congress*, which opened during 1997 as a permanent installation, continued to include a rotating display of "Top Treasures." The online version of the exhibition was periodically updated to capture the rotation of artifacts. Two new exhibition spaces opened during the year: the Swann Gallery of Caricature and Cartoon, and the Gershwin Room (a permanent exhibition area for materials from the library's George and Ira Gershwin Collection). Exhibition highlights included *The Thomas Jefferson Building: 'Book Palace of the American People'* in honor of the building's centennial (November 4, 1997–July 6, 1998); *African American Odyssey: A Quest for Full Citizenship* (February 5–May 2, 1998); *Monstrous Claws and Character Flaws*, the Swann Gallery's inaugural exhibition (February 25–August 22, 1998); *Religion and the Founding of the American Republic*, which explored the role of religion in the founding of the American Colonies, the shaping of American life and politics, and the formation of the American republic (June 4–August 29, 1998); *Sea to Shining Sea: An American Sampler of Children's Books from the Library of Congress* (June 25, 1998–March 6, 1999); *Zion's Call: A Library of Congress Exhibition Marking Israel's Fiftieth Year* (September 17, 1998–December 19); *The Birth of Czechoslovakia: October 1918*, which commemorated the 80th anniversary of the founding of Czechoslovakia (September 18–December 26); *Sigmund Freud: Conflict and Culture*, which explored Freud's thought and influence on 20th century culture (October 15, 1998–January 16, 1999); and *Stagestruck: Performing Arts Caricatures at the Library of Congress* (November 5, 1998–April 3, 1999). The *African American Odyssey* and *Religion and the Founding of the American Republic* exhibitions were made available to the public on the library's Web site.

In addition to presenting exhibitions within its own galleries, the library sent six exhibitions to 12 sites in 10 states: *Women Come to the Front: Journalists, Photographers, and Broadcasters During World War II*; *Cultural Landscape of the Plantation*; *Paradox of the Press*; *In Their Own Voices*; *From the Ends of the Earth*; and *Documenting America*.

*The Work of Charles and Ray Eames: A Legacy of Invention*, a collaboration between the library and the Vitra Design Museum, Weil am Rhein, Germany, presented the unparalleled Eames collections of the two institutions first at the Vitra Design Museum and then in Denmark and London. The exhibition is to open at the Library of Congress, its first U.S. venue, in May 1999.

Robert Pinsky of Boston University was appointed to a second term as poet laureate consultant in poetry, for 1998–1999.

The sixth annual Joanna Jackson Goldman Memorial Lecture was delivered on April 21, 1998, by Harvard University Professor Amartya Sen, who spoke on "Asian Values and American Priorities."

Under the terms of the National Film Preservation Act, each year the Librarian of Congress names 25 "culturally, historically, or aesthetically" significant motion pictures to the National Film Registry. Each list serves to increase public awareness of the richness of American cinema and the need for its preservation.

The following films were named to the National Film Registry in 1998, bringing the total to 250

*Bride of Frankenstein* (1935)

*The City* (1939)

*Dead Birds* (1964)

*Don't Look Back* (1967)

*Easy Rider* (1969)
*42nd Street* (1933)
*From the Manger to the Cross* (1912)
*Gun Crazy* (1949)
*The Hitch-Hiker* (1953)
*The Immigrant* (1917)
*The Last Picture Show* (1972)
*Little Miss Marker* (1934)
*The Lost World* (1925)
*Modesta* (1956)
*The Ox-Bow Incident* (1943)
*Pass the Gravy* (1928)
*Phantom of the Opera* (1925)
*Powers of Ten* (1978)
*The Public Enemy* (1931)
*Sky High* (1922)
*Steamboat Willie* (1928)
*Tacoma Narrows Bridge Collapse* (1940)
*Tootsie* (1982)
*Twelve O'Clock High* (1949)
*Westinghouse Works, 1904* (1904)

## Security

During 1998 two of the library's congressional oversight committees (House Oversight and Senate Rules and Administration) approved the comprehensive security plan that was completed at the end of FY 1997. The plan provides a framework for the security of the library's staff, visitors, facilities, collections, and other assets. At year's end the plan was being updated to reflect major physical security enhancements necessitated by recent incidents and increased threats. The library installed and activated new state-of-the-art magnetometers and increased police coverage at many strategic locations, including public entrances and exterior patrols. An additional $16.9 million to enhance the security of library staff, visitors, and facilities was included in the omnibus year-end spending bill President Clinton signed into law on October 21, 1998. These funds were part of a $106.8 million package to improve the physical security of the Capitol complex, including the House and Senate office buildings.

The library continued to implement a comprehensive computer security plan to safeguard its valuable electronic resources, and a Year 2000 plan to test, modify, or replace systems as necessary, thus ensuring that its computer systems will function properly at the turn of the century. During the year the library identified 99 mission-critical systems. As of December 31, 1998, a total of 79 systems had been renovated (fixed, but not tested), 35 had been validated (fixed, tested, but not yet in production), and 33 were implemented (fixed, tested, and certified compliant). Work began to develop contingency plans for mission-critical systems. An automated tracking system was developed and implemented for tracking and monitoring progress.

## Preservation

The library improved the preservation of its vast and diverse collections during 1998 by

- Completing the mass deacidification treatment of 80,000 additional volumes in American history using the Bookkeeper limited-production contract
- Increasing processing efficiency through the elimination of redundant keying of data, by creating an interface between the binding automation system and the library's bibliographic database
- Increasing production in binding (by 21 percent), in-house repair (by 21 percent), and boxing (by 30 percent) of library materials
- Completing the specifications for an internal text-page label that eliminates keying errors through the use of an LCCN bar code
- Establishing guidelines to assess the condition of brittle books, reformatting only those books deemed "too brittle to serve" and boxing those books considered "brittle but serviceable"

## Restoration and Renovation

The library continued to execute its multiyear plan to outfit and occupy the remaining renovated spaces of the Thomas Jefferson and Adams buildings. Major milestones included relocating the Federal Library and Information Center Committee from Market Square to newly renovated space in the John Adams building; completing renovation of the Swann Gallery, the Gershwin Room, and the Coolidge Auditorium; and completing the roof replacement project by the end of calendar year 1998. In September the American Association for State and Local History (AASLH) recognized the Library of Congress and the Office of the Architect of the Capitol as joint 1998 AASLH Award of Merit winners for the renovation and restoration of the Thomas Jefferson Building. In October the renovation of the Jefferson building also garnered a Merit Award from the Washington Chapter of the American Institute of Architects for Outstanding Achievement in Historic Resources.

## Human Resources

At year's end the library employed 4,213 permanent staff members. The library's Internal University (IU) enhanced management and work force knowledge and skills by coordinating more than 100 courses in 559 class sessions. Training courses covered facilitative leadership, computer software, and administrative management for first-line supervisors. IU formed professional partnerships with other federal training leaders to benchmark government training and build a database of successful key training programs to develop strategic links and joint ventures to maximize return on scarce training resources.

Celebrating the library's culturally diverse staff and collections remained a high priority. By the end of FY 1998, 80 percent of all staff members had attended a one-day diversity awareness training session. A new Web-based diversity training software program was implemented in a test mode in October 1998 to enable managers and supervisors to take the course at their convenience with minimal disruption in the daily work schedule. A Diversity Advisory Council, made up of representatives from each library organization, met monthly to address diversity issues and to cosponsor programs that highlight the diversity of the library's staff and collections.

The library also supported special internship programs. The Soros Foundation-Library of Congress Intern Program hosted 12 librarians and information specialists from Central and Eastern Europe and Central Asia, and the Hispanic Association of Colleges and Universities National Internship Program was offered to four students.

## Additional Sources of Information

Library of Congress telephone numbers for public information:

| | |
|---|---|
| Main switchboard (with menu) | 202-707-5000 |
| Reading room hours and locations | 202-707-6400 |
| General reference | 202-707-5522 |
| | 202-707-4210 TTY |
| Visitor information | 202-707-8000 |
| | 202-707-6200 TTY |
| Exhibition hours | 202-707-4604 |
| Research advice | 202-707-6500 |
| Sales shop | 202-707-0204 |
| Copyright information | 202-707-3000 |
| Copyright hotline (to order forms) | 202-707-9100 |

# Center for the Book

John Y. Cole

Director, The Center for the Book
Library of Congress
World Wide Web: http://lcweb.loc.gov/loc/cfbook

Since 1977, when it was established by Librarian of Congress Daniel J. Boorstin, the Center for the Book has used the prestige and the resources of the Library of Congress to stimulate public interest in books, reading, and libraries and to encourage the study of books and the printed word. With its network of 35 affiliated state centers and more than 50 national and civic organizations, it is one of the Library of Congress's most dynamic and visible educational outreach programs.

The center is a successful public-private partnership. The Library of Congress supports its four full-time positions, but the center's projects, events, and publications are funded primarily through contributions from individuals, corporations, foundations, and other government organizations.

## Highlights of 1998

- The addition of one new state—Nevada—to the center's national network of state affiliates
- The presentation of Boorstin Center for the Book Awards to the Vermont and Oklahoma state centers
- The continued use and expansion of the center's Web site (http://lcweb.loc.gov/loc/cfbook)
- The launching of the Viburnum Foundation/Center for the Book family literacy project
- The continued use of radio, especially National Public Radio, and television, particularly CBS Television, C-SPAN, and the Learning Channel, to promote books, reading, and libraries
- Sponsorship of more than 30 programs and events, at the Library of Congress and throughout the country, that promoted books, reading, and libraries.

## Themes

The Center for the Book establishes national reading-promotion themes to stimulate interest and support for reading and literacy projects that benefit all age groups. Used by state centers, national organizational partners, and hundreds of schools and libraries across the nation, each theme reminds Americans of the importance of books, reading, and libraries in today's world. The reading-promotion theme through the year 2000, "Building a Nation of Readers," was depicted in 1998 by colorful posters and bookmarks featuring the Muppets, led by Kermit the Frog and Miss Piggy. They were produced in cooperation with the Jim Henson Company and the American Library Association. "Building a Nation of

Readers" projects reinforce "Libraries-Creativity-Liberty," the theme of the Library of Congress's Bicentennial commemoration in the year 2000.

## Reading-Promotion Partners

The center's partnership program includes more than 50 civic, educational, and governmental organizations that work with the center to promote books, reading, libraries, and literacy. On March 23, 1998, representatives from most of these organizations gathered at the Library of Congress to share information about their current projects and discuss potential cooperative arrangements. During 1998 the center cosponsored projects with several of its organizational partners, including the American Institute for Graphic Arts, the American Library Association, Friends of Libraries U.S.A., International Rivers Network, the National Coalition for Literacy, the National Newspaper Association, Reading Is Fundamental, and the U.S. Department of Education.

## State Centers

When James H. Billington became Librarian of Congress in 1987, the Center for the Book had ten affiliated state centers; at the end of 1998 there were 35. The newest center, Nevada, is located at the Nevada State Library and Archives in Carson City.

Each state center works with the Library of Congress to promote books, reading, and libraries as well as the state's own literary and intellectual heritage. Each center also develops and funds its own operations and projects, using Library of Congress reading-promotion themes when appropriate and occasionally hosting Library of Congress-sponsored events and traveling exhibits. When its application is approved, a state center is granted affiliate status for three years. Renewals are for three-year periods.

On May 4, 1998, representatives from the state centers participated in an idea-sharing session at the Library of Congress. They discussed such topics as staffing, advisory boards, fund-raising, relations with other organizations, Internet sites, and programming. The highlight was the presentation of the 1998 Boorstin Center for the Book Awards to the Vermont and Oklahoma Centers for the Book. Each of these annual awards includes a cash prize of $5,000. The National Award, won by Vermont, recognizes the contribution that a state center has made to the Center for the Book's overall national program and objectives. The State Award, won by Oklahoma, recognizes a specific project. In this instance, it was the Oklahoma Book Awards program, which marks its tenth anniversary in 1999.

## Projects

In 1998 the Center for the Book began administering the Viburnum Foundation's program for supporting family literacy projects in rural public libraries. During the year the foundation made grants to 30 libraries in seven states. In September 1998 the center sponsored regional workshops in Jackson, Mississippi, and

Albuquerque, New Mexico, that provided training for representatives from the libraries and communities that received the grants.

"Letters About Literature," a student essay contest sponsored with the Weekly Reader Corporation, concluded a record-breaking year in terms of both number of entries and involvement by affiliated state centers. More than 20,000 students wrote letters to their favorite authors, and 23 state centers honored statewide winners.

With Center for the Book sponsorship, Phyllis Theroux, author of *The Book of Eulogies* (1997), presented readings in a program titled "Great American Portraits" in three cities: St. Louis, Chicago, and Hartford, Connecticut.

The center's annual "River of Words" project, an environmental art and poetry contest for young people, culminated on May 2 at the Library of Congress with an awards ceremony and display of winning artworks. The moderator was former Poet Laureate Robert Hass. The project is cosponsored by the International Rivers Network.

The Center for the Book became the Library of Congress liaison for two projects that are part of the library's bicentennial commemoration. "Favorite Poem," headed by Poet Laureate Robert Pinksy, will record citizens reciting their favorite poem for the library's Archives of Recorded Poetry and Literature. "Beyond Words: Celebrating America's Libraries" is a national photography contest, sponsored with the American Library Association, that features photographs of people of all ages using libraries.

## Outreach

The center's Web site continued to expand in coverage and use during 1998. It now includes an overview of the center's development, history, projects, and publications; a calendar of current and forthcoming events; press releases; information about state centers and organizational partners, with home page links when available; information about book arts and book history programs and organizations, nationally and internationally; and a current calendar of book and reading-promotion events throughout the United States.

In 1998 the Center for the Book continued to prepare reading lists for the Library of Congress/CBS Television "Read More About It" project. Since 1979 these 30-second messages from the Library of Congress, which direct viewers to suggested books in their local libraries and bookstores, have been telecast on more than 400 CBS Television programs. "Read More About It" lists also were prepared for digitized collections on the National Digital Library's Web site, and for the Library of Congress exhibitions "Book Palace of the American People" and "Religion and the Founding of the American Republic."

During the year C-SPAN televised many of the presentations sponsored by the Center for the Book for viewing as part of its "Booknotes" and "Book TV" programs. The center also continued its close cooperation with the Learning Channel in the production of its "Great Books" series of one-hour specials about well-known literary works.

Five issues of the newsletter *Center for the Book News* were produced in 1998. A new edition of the state center *Handbook* was published in May 1998.

The Library of Congress issued 36 press releases about center activities, and a two-page "News from the Center for the Book" appeared in each issue of the Library's *Information Bulletin*. Director John Cole provided a foreword for a book of postcards, *For the Love of Libraries*, by Diane Asseo Griliches, published by Pomegranate Books. He also made 17 presentations about the center and its activities during visits to 12 states and to France and the Netherlands.

## Events

Sponsorship of events, symposia, and lectures—at the Library of Congress and elsewhere—is an important center activity. Through such special events, the center brings diverse audiences together on behalf of books and reading and publicizes its activities nationally and locally. Examples of events at the Library of Congress include seven talks by current authors in the center's "Books & Beyond" lecture series; a symposium on the art and architecture of the library's Thomas Jefferson Building, cosponsored with the U.S. Capitol Historical Society; a program designating the Jefferson Building as a literary landmark, cosponsored with Friends of Libraries U.S.A.; a poetry program with students from the District of Columbia public schools, cosponsored with the District Lines Poetry Project; a public "Preservation Awareness Day," cosponsored with the library's Preservation Directorate; and a program with the American Library Association's Library History Round Table that celebrated 50 years of promoting library history. A program on November 4 featured novelist William Styron, his biographer James L. W. West, III, and Styron's daughter, film director Susanna, who directed the commercial film *Shadrach*. The viewing of the 90-minute film, which is based on one of Styron's short stories, concluded the event.

Information about the dozens of events sponsored by the state centers, often in cooperation with the national center, can be found in the Library of Congress *Information Bulletin*.

# Federal Library and Information Center Committee

Library of Congress, Washington, DC 20540
202-707-4800
World Wide Web: http://lcweb.loc.gov/flicc

Susan M. Tarr
Executive Director

## Highlights of the Year

During fiscal year (FY) 1998 the Federal Library and Information Center Committee (FLICC), in the words of its new mission statement, worked "to foster excellence in federal library and information services through interagency cooperation and to provide guidance and direction for FEDLINK." The FLICC Executive Board and the general membership developed this new formal mission statement and adopted it early in the year. FLICC's annual information policy forum expanded on some of the key features of this mission by exploring how the Government Performance and Results Act (GPRA) affects federal libraries and how federal librarians should approach applying its principles. FLICC also held its annual information technology update, this year focusing on equipping federal librarians with the expertise and tools to create end user training programs in their libraries and information centers.

FLICC formed two new working groups, the Awards Working Group and the Ad Hoc Library of Congress (LC) Bicentennial Working Group, and reconstituted the Preservation and Binding Working Group. Other FLICC working groups developed a Web-based, real-time information assessment of federal library information technology; created new educational initiatives in the areas of metadata, law classification and cataloging, and distance learning; issued surveys to members on fees and analyzed their responses; compiled knowledge, skills, and abilities statements for federal librarians; created three new government-wide awards; planned federal library participation in the LC Bicentennial; and continued to expand access to resources through the FLICC Web site.

In addition to supporting the membership projects, FLICC staff made substantial improvements to the FEDLINK program, improved members' use of OCLC, concluded their 18-month consultative management pilot, prepared for a replacement for the FEDLINK financial system, laid the groundwork for and began testing of a comprehensive multimedia distance-learning initiative, and executed a return from off-site offices back to the LC Capitol Hill complex. Staff also sponsored 36 seminars and workshops for 1,399 participants and conducted 103 OCLC, Internet, and related classes for 753 students.

FLICC's cooperative network, FEDLINK, continued to enhance its fiscal operations while providing its members with $53.2 million in transfer-pay services and $64.8 million in direct-pay services, saving federal agencies more than $5 million in cost avoidance and approximately $12 million more in vendor volume discounts.

FLICC managers worked to improve project planning, implementation, and staff participation through effective use of facilitative leadership (FL) techniques developed in the library's training program.

## Quarterly Membership Meetings

The first FLICC Quarterly Membership Meeting featured a visit to the "American Treasures of the Library of Congress" exhibition. Following the tour, Dorothy Fisher Weed (Department of Labor) introduced members to her department's treasures and rare books collections and Doria Grimes (NOAA) highlighted her agency's special collections.

The second Quarterly Membership Meeting was host to two guest speakers, John Cole (Center for the Book) and Gil Baldwin (GPO). Cole addressed LC's bicentennial planning that led to the formation of a FLICC Ad Hoc Working Group on the LC Bicentennial. Baldwin updated members on GPO's joint study with the National Commission on Libraries and Information Science (NCLIS) titled "Assessment of Standards for the Creation, Dissemination, and Permanent Accessibility of Electronic Government Information Products."

The third Quarterly Membership Meeting focused on federal library policy issues, including a legislative update from Glenn McLaughlin (LC-CRS), followed by a presentation from Richard Kellet (GSA) on privacy, the FOIA, and electronic FOIA.

The fourth Quarterly Membership Meeting featured LC General Counsel Elizabeth Pugh, who outlined a variety of common legal issues for federal libraries.

A fifth Quarterly Membership Meeting, held in late September, reviewed the status of government information distribution policy including a report from Fran Buckley (GPO) and Mary Alice Baish (AALL) on proposed revisions to U.S.C. Title 44 and an update by Robert Willard (NCLIS) on his commission's survey of selected electronic documents.

## Working Groups

### FLICC Ad Hoc Bicentennial LC Working Group

In honor of the Library of Congress's upcoming bicentennial celebration, a FLICC working group was formed to develop programs for the entire federal library community that will provide benefits beyond the bicentennial year. By participating in LC's bicentennial activities, federal libraries and information centers will increase recognition of their programs and link federal libraries to LC under the larger campaign to publicize the "Nation's Collections." The working group has proposed a variety of activities, including developing a tool kit comprised of a press release, a calendar of events, a poster, bookmarks, and other promotional materials that libraries and information centers can adapt for local use. The working group also hopes to sponsor a digitization competition among federal libraries and information centers to identify federal historical holdings or other collections that could be added to the library's digital collection.

### Awards Working Group

To honor the many innovative ways federal libraries, librarians, and library technicians fulfill the information demands of government, business, research, scholarly communities, and the American public, the Awards Working Group was formed in FY 1998 to inaugurate a series of three national awards for federal librarianship:

- Federal Library/Information Center of the Year: to commend a library or information center's outstanding, innovative, and sustained achievements during FY 1998 in fulfilling its organization's mission, fostering innovation in its services, and meeting the needs of its users
- Federal Librarian of the Year: to honor professional achievements during FY 1998 in the advancement of library and information sciences, the promotion and development of services in support of the agency's mission, and demonstrated professionalism as described in the Special Library Association's "Competencies for Special Librarians in the 21st Century"
- Federal Library Technician of the Year: to recognize the achievements of a federal library technician during FY 1998 for service excellence in support of the library or information center's mission, exceptional technical competency, and flexibility in adapting work methods and dealing with change

The award winners receive a certificate and a plaque honoring their contributions to the field of federal library and information service. They were to be presented at the annual FLICC Forum on Federal Information Policies in March 1999.

### Budget and Finance Working Group

The FLICC Budget and Finance Working Group began meeting in January to develop the FY 1999 FEDLINK budget and fee structure. The group also initiated and completed a survey of the full membership on changing the fee structure. The final budget approved for 1999 reduced fees for transfer-pay customers to 7.75 percent on accounts up to $300,000 and 7 percent on amounts more than $300,000. Direct-pay fees remained at fiscal year 1998 levels.

Working-group members first presented the budget proposal to FEDLINK and FLICC memberships and then mailed the proposal to all FEDLINK and FLICC members. The FLICC voting members unanimously supported the FY 1999 budget proposal.

### Education Working Group

During FY 1998 the Education Working Group developed or supported 36 programs in the areas of technology development, copyright issues, technician training, cataloging and classification, and end user training and continued the FLICC Orientation to National Libraries and Information Centers tour program.

In November 1997 the working group sponsored "End User Training and Support: A Role for Librarians," with speakers including Carol Tenopir, University of Tennessee at Knoxville; John Auditore, National Institutes of Health; Jim Bradley, U.S. Army Training and Doctrine Command; Janie Butler, LEXIS-NEXIS; Cathy Kellum, Southeastern Libraries Network; Anne Caputo, Knight Ridder Information Services; Melissa Becher, American University; and Cheryl Hunter, DTIC. Seventy-five federal librarians joined together at this program to discuss practical techniques for being effective instructional librarians.

During the winter months FLICC continued its commitment to continuing-education initiatives for librarians and library technicians education by hosting satellite downlinks to two popular teleconference series, "Soaring to . . . Excellence" and "Dancing with . . . Change," both sponsored by the College of Du Page (Glen Ellyn, Illinois).

Following the success of the 1997 program, the working group held the second annual "Federal Library Technicians Institute" in August 1998. This week-long institute continued to focus on educating library technicians. Federal and academic librarians joined FLICC professionals to discuss various areas of librarianship, including acquisitions, cataloging, reference, and automation.

The institute "Law Classification and Cataloging for Federal Librarians" provided a structured presentation for cataloging and reference librarians. Participants reviewed standards, bibliographic description, LC classifications, subject headings, and legal serials.

### Information Technology Working Group

In FY 1998 the Information Technology Working Group unveiled its new Web-based survey titled "The FLICC Information Technology Assessment for Federal Libraries and Information Centers." This assessment will help federal librarians examine how information technology is being used in their organization and glean information about other libraries' equipment and programs. The results of this informative questionnaire, accessible through the FLICC/FEDLINK Web site, allow federal librarians to assess the level of automation in their libraries by comparing their agency's use of technology with other agencies' library profiles.

To assist federal librarians in the development of metadata, descriptive data used to classify and manage electronic resources, the working group sponsored "The 1998 FLICC Information Technology Update: Metadata 101: Beyond Traditional Cataloging." This program led to the spring follow-up institute, "Metadata 201: OCLC Institute's Knowledge Access Management for Federal Librarians," where attendees spent five days applying the latest standards and guidelines in cataloging government publications on the Web.

The working group continued its series of Internet-focused brown-bag sessions in FY 1998 with two sessions on Web creation software and pricing issues between Internet and commercial databases. They also focused on ways to update federal librarians on maintenance contracts for integrated library systems and on how FEDLINK might play a role in facilitating the consortial purchasing of electronic products among federal agencies.

### Nominating Working Group

The Nominating Working Group oversaw the 1998 election process for FLICC Rotating Members and the FEDLINK Advisory Council. Librarians representing 15 federal agencies agreed to place their names in nomination for these positions.

### Personnel Working Group

The Personnel Working Group continued its efforts in developing sample knowledge, skills, and abilities (KSAs) statements to help hiring officials specify appropriate quality-ranking factors for vacancy announcements for federal librarian positions. They intend these KSAs to be used as a guide, not associated with specific grade levels nor intended to be used for classifying 1,410 positions. During FY 1998 the working group formalized KSAs for public services and systems librarians and posted them on the FLICC Web site.

### Preservation and Binding Working Group

This working group was reorganized and reformed in FY 1998, naming a new chair late in the year. The goals of the revitalized working group are to identify preservation priorities for federal libraries and information centers, discover alternative sources of funding to support these preservation efforts, and develop and disseminate preservation information and resources in an electronic format through the FLICC Web site.

## Publications and Education Office

### Publications

In FY 1998 FLICC supported an ambitious publications schedule with the departure of one permanent writer/editor in May 1998 and the arrival of another in July 1998. During the year FLICC produced 11 issues of *FEDLINK Technical Notes* (12 pages each, except for a 16-page November issue) and four issues of the *FLICC Quarterly Newsletter* (8–12 pages). FLICC also published a 36-page summary of the 1997 FLICC Forum "Clear Signals? Telecommunications, Convergence, and the Quality of Information," which was selected for public sale by the Government Printing Office. FLICC published expanded and enhanced materials to support the FEDLINK program, including the 72-page FY 1999 *FEDLINK Registration Booklet*; a 225-page complete revision of the looseleaf *FEDLINK Member Handbook*, with an index and tabs; two versions of the *FLICC/FEDLINK Education Catalog*, which was incorporated in the LCIU catalog and mailed to FEDLINK members; five FEDLINK Information Alerts; and a FLICC Awards brochure. FLICC also produced the minutes of the four FY 1998 FLICC Quarterly Meetings and bimonthly FEB meetings and all FLICC Education Program promotional and support materials, including the FLICC Forum announcement, attendee and speaker badges, press advisories, speeches and speaker remarks, and collateral materials. In addition, FLICC produced 30 FLICC Meeting Announcements to promote FLICC Education Programs; FEDLINK membership, vendor, and OCLC users' meetings; and three education institutes, along with badges, programs, certificates of completion, and other supporting materials.

FLICC and FEDLINK staff worked diligently throughout 1998 to continue to expand and update the FLICC/FEDLINK Web site. The site contains a variety of information resources, member information, links to vendors and other members, listings of membership, minutes of various FLICC governing bodies, access to account data online, event calendars, and an online registration system that is updated nightly. FLICC staff converted all publications, newsletters, announcements, alerts, member materials, and working group resources into HTML format, uploading current materials within days of their being printed. Through collaboration with the FEDLINK Network Operations staff, the FLICC Web site continues to expand and offer resources, including OCLC Usage Analysis Reports, pricing data for the FEDLINK Books Procurement Program, and many new documents, including the FY 1999 budget materials, training resources, and links to other members.

### Education

In conjunction with the Education Working Group, FLICC offered a total of 36 seminars, workshops, and lunchtime discussions to 1,399 members of the federal library and information center community. Multiday institutes covered metadata, law classification, library technician training, and HTML; one-day sessions offered theoretical and hands-on knowledge on end user training, copyright issues on the Internet, and assessing information technology in federal libraries. The "FLICC Orientations to National Libraries and Information Centers Series," comprised of tours of other federal libraries and information centers, continued in FY 1998 with visits and presentations at the National Library of Medicine, the National Library of Education, the National Agricultural Library, the Government Printing Office, the National Archives and Records Administration (Washington, D.C., and College Park, Maryland), the Defense Technical Information Center, and the National Technical Information Service. FLICC also was a host to the College of Du Page's "Dancing with . . . Change" and "Soaring to . . . Excellence," two multisession satellite downlink programs on library science issues for librarians and library technicians.

FLICC also provided organizational, promotional, and logistical support for FEDLINK meetings and events, including the FEDLINK Fall and Spring Membership Meetings; two FEDLINK OCLC Users Group meetings; a series of three vendor presentations; and a program on "How to Use FEDLINK in Fiscal Year 1999" in August 1998. FLICC continued to expand its multimedia distance-learning initiative by updating its equipment and testing new approaches for integrating titles, text, and graphics into videotape presentations. Through its arrangement with the National Library of Education for interlibrary loans to federal libraries, FLICC continued to make these educational programs available for members throughout the country and around the world.

## FEDLINK

In FY 1998 the Federal Library and Information Network gave federal agencies cost-effective access to an array of automated information retrieval services for online research, cataloging, and interlibrary loan. FEDLINK members also procured publications, technical-processing services, serials, electronic journals, CD-ROMs, books, and document delivery via LC/FEDLINK contracts with major vendors.

The FEDLINK Advisory Council (FAC) met monthly during FY 1998, except in November, June, and July. During the year, FAC approved the FY 1999 FEDLINK budget and the new FEDLINK mission statement: "To serve federal libraries and information centers as their purchasing, resource-sharing, and training consortium." FAC also voted to have its vice chair serve as the moderator for the FEDLIB listserv.

The Fall FEDLINK Membership Meeting (October 14, 1997) featured Pat McNutt, the International Trade Center Bookstore Chair and Director of Sales for the National Technical Information Service (NTIS). She described the purpose and characteristics of the new International Trade Center Bookstore at the Ronald Reagan Building. Staff also unveiled the new FLICC/FEDLINK Web site and offered attendees a virtual tour of its resources.

The guest speaker at the FEDLINK Spring Membership Meeting (April 30, 1998) was Tom Sanville, Executive Director of OhioLINK, who addressed consortial purchasing in academia. The FLICC Budget and Finance Working Group Chair presented the FY 1999 budget, and FEDLINK staff outlined consortial purchasing initiatives. The meeting concluded with a formal discussion of customer service efforts and strategies.

### FEDLINK Network Operations—OCLC Network Activity

During FY 1998 FEDLINK sponsored a spring and fall OCLC Users Group Meeting. These meetings reflected the thrust of OCLC support activities for the year and highlighted upcoming telecommunications changes as federal libraries and information centers migrate from OCLC's proprietary method and older standards to TCP/IP-based technology via the Internet, dial-up connections, and dedicated lines. Staff reported that OCLC continues to base its software enhancements on Windows-based operating systems and that its proposed prices reflect modest increases, with decreases for those libraries contributing significant amounts of cataloging.

While working with member libraries and information centers to decrease telecommunications costs by migrating to the newer technologies, the OCLC support team counseled members on the potential cost reductions associated with choosing effective cataloging and searching techniques. To maximize members' use of OCLC's Windows-based software and increase efficient use of its systems, staff developed several new training classes: "OCLC Macros," "Cataloging Shortcuts," and "Effective Strategies for Searching OCLC." Staff also contributed to a networkwide directory of course materials.

A new generic e-mail address for OCLC questions (askocfno@loc.gov) and an OCLC members' listserv greatly enhanced communication with members. In combination with the FLICC Web site, members achieved instant access to current price lists and standard usage reports that highlight administrative overhead and search-to-produce ratios, two areas that merit attention when libraries work to reduce OCLC costs.

By supporting OCLC reference products, federal libraries and information centers increased the efficiency of their migration to digital services. Staff who made site visits to member libraries emphasized using OCLC's FirstSearch and Electronic Collections Online services. Navy libraries and the Military Education Coordinating Conference (MECC) subsequently established consortial purchases of OCLC reference services, while individual libraries, such as the Army Research Lab (Adelphi, Maryland), began significant use of electronic journals via Electronic Collections Online. Several federal library participants in the

Depository Library program are also testing access to full text in ERIC via FirstSearch, a joint project of OCLC, GPO, and the National Library of Education. Another OCLC presentation, to 42 U.S. Marine Corps officers, will result in 18 new FEDLINK/OCLC members and open the door to consortial purchasing through a network of Marine Corps libraries.

FEDLINK continued its participation in activities designed to improve communication between OCLC and the other networks. FLICC Executive Director Susan Tarr chaired the Regional Network Directors Advisory Committee (RON-DAC) from July 1997 through June 1998. As chair of the Network OCLC Service Managers, FEDLINK's OCLC Program Coordinator Lynn McDonald helped establish meeting/training agendas and worked with task forces and committees to increase use of distance communication technologies between OCLC and the networks. FEDLINK staff also reviewed OCLC's newest products and documentation.

## FEDLINK Internet/Technology Program

In FY 1998 FEDLINK Network Operations (FNO) conducted an active Internet training program, continued to enhance the content of the FLICC/FEDLINK Web site, sponsored institutes on Internet technology subjects, held Internet information sessions, and consulted with members on a variety of automation topics. In the fall staff conducted three-day Internet training for the U.S. Army in Heidelberg, Germany. In the spring, staff held two Internet training sessions for LC SOROS Interns and, as part of a cooperative agreement, conducted a regional version of "Library Acquisitions and Collections Development on the World Wide Web" for federal librarians and the MINITEX Library Network. Staff also customized the Internet class "Military History Information: Finding It in the Web" for the Marine Corps.

With the assistance of other LC staff, FEDLINK initiated a new series of HTML classes designed to train federal librarians to offer their resources and expertise online. Attendees at follow-up classes, which offered additional hands-on exercises, highly rated the new classes.

During 1998 a special project conducted with the FLICC Information Technology Working Group and LC programmers resulted in an interactive Web-based survey instrument created to measure the state of automation in federal libraries and information centers. Once members complete the survey, they can download reports of how their libraries compare with other agency libraries, establish communications with other members who use similar hardware and software, and use the database as a resource when considering internal upgrades.

Throughout the year staff also provided consultation to members on ILS projects, telecommunication issues, digitizing projects, and other automation topics.

## Exhibits Program

FLICC/FEDLINK exhibited at three events in FY 1998: the Defense Technical Information Center Users' Meeting in November 1997; the American Library Association (ALA) Conference in Washington, D.C., in June 1998; and the Special Library Association (SLA) Conference in Indianapolis in June 1998. At the ALA conference, staff debuted a new promotional packet that outlines both FLICC and FEDLINK initiatives and services.

**Training Program**

The 1998 FEDLINK training program included specialized training classes and contractual arrangements for customized workshops for members. Twenty-three librarians also attended a FEDLINK Descriptive Cataloging Institute in Heidelberg, Germany, in October 1997. As part of its distance-learning efforts, staff worked with the Air Force Education and Training Command to transmit a training video to 18 of its libraries. This video, "Telecommunications and Networking Concepts," updates librarians on the latest telecommunications and networking technologies and how they can best be used for future program planning. The video was produced by the Alliance of Library Service Networks, of which FEDLINK is a member.

Other education/training events included a customized "An Introduction to MARC: Migrating from Datatrek," an on-site training program for the U.S. Court of Appeals, District of Columbia, Washington, D.C., in December 1997. Staff also facilitated a benchmarking workshop for federal librarians at the Medical Library Association's annual meeting and "Strategic Budgeting" for the Navy and Marine Corps in April 1998.

During the year staff conducted 103 OCLC, Internet, and related classes for 753 students. Fifty-two of the 103 classes were held at field sites, primarily as part of the Air Force's continuing effort to train its librarians. Besides the Heidelberg, Germany, program, FEDLINK staff held training sessions in Arizona, California, Delaware, Idaho, Kansas, Minnesota, Nebraska, New Mexico, South Carolina, Texas, Virginia, and Panama. Additional contract training, also provided through FEDLINK, included 31 OCLC Pacific Network sessions, 276 CAPCON programs, two PALINET courses, and 13 SOLINET classes.

**Procurement Services**

For serials subscription services, FY 1998 was a year of research and planning for a new statement of work, pricing structure, and evaluation criteria for a request for proposal (RFP) to establish new serials basic ordering agreements (BOAs) for the upcoming FY 1999 procurement, which will be effective for FYs 2000–2005; these BOAs will serve as the basis for competitions for more than 300 federal libraries' individual serials requirements. This new RFP will predict and anticipate changes in the serials industry that will be critical to federal libraries and information centers over the next five years. To this end, staff met with incumbent FEDLINK serials vendors, attended national meetings of serials professionals and classes on licensing, and talked with members about their experiences and plans.

The arrival of Web-based book distributors like Amazon.com has made FEDLINK books vendors operate in a more competitive environment. In FY 1998 FEDLINK assisted federal libraries and information centers as they took advantage of this new market and its better prices and services. Staff also added an expanded pricing section to the FLICC Web site so that members can compare FEDLINK publisher discounts across an array of subject, format, and source categories. With this information so readily available, librarians can apply federal contracting principles to their acquisitions work by confirming reasonable prices for orders less than $2,500; locating three potential vendor sources for orders between $2,500 and $100,000; comparing FEDLINK prices with those of outside sources; and identifying potential vendors for requests for quotations (RFQs) for larger requirements.

FEDLINK conducted just such an RFQ for the Air Force Library Program's million-dollar requirement to provide paperback book kits to libraries and detachments of Air Force personnel worldwide. Through competition, the Air Force could select a single vendor to meet its tight delivery schedule at a discount rate that reflects the volume of the order. FEDLINK also worked with the Army to help define its requirements for a similar paperback service for the Army, Navy, and Marine Corps.

Staff also worked closely with several vendors and members to take advantage of provisions in the current electronic information retrieval services BOAs that allow specialized offerings and volume-pricing plans tailored for individual customers. Negotiations with LEXIS-NEXIS, for example, secured participation in its volume bonus plan for both LC's Library Services and the Congressional Research Service. Under this fixed-price, unlimited-usage plan, these LC units will save approximately 30 percent on their online legal and current-events information.

Pricing issues remained significant during negotiations for FY 1999 BOA renewals with incumbent vendors. Through close review of the pricing proposals from FEDLINK's three largest online vendors (Dialog, LEXIS-NEXIS, and Westlaw), FNO's contracting officer's technical representative (COTR) for online services uncovered significant changes in the vendors' pricing approaches. These changes posed a serious threat to members' library and information center budgets. Staff identified specific negotiation points and alternative approaches that ultimately avoided the proposed price changes.

FEDLINK also continued its efforts to develop license agreements for electronic publications services that will meet both federal legal requirements and serve library and information center interests. The project's goals are to forestall redundant negotiations at multiple agencies and reduce the likelihood of a serious conflict between terms in the FEDLINK BOAs and those in locally negotiated licenses. FEDLINK's model license agreement was part of the open-season RFP for electronic services issued during 1998 and will serve as a basis for negotiations with incumbent vendors.

A consortial licensing task force of the FLICC Information Technology Working Group formed to further this licensing initiative and to explore opportunities for forming a consortium of FEDLINK members interested in joint acquisition of electronic journals. FEDLINK met with two publishers to discuss their consortial offerings and invited the vendors (and others) to respond to the open-season RFP. Staff also identified ways to create a consortium within current FEDLINK interagency agreements, delivery orders, and accounting procedures so that libraries and information centers can combine their funding and earn greater discounts. Navy technical libraries and other intra- and interagency groups are considering this consortial option for purchase of traditional online services, such as Dialog.

In July 1998 FEDLINK issued the RFP for electronic information retrieval services (with minor revisions) in an open season to invite new vendors to join the program. Staff reviewed proposals from 12 vendors, many of which will be added to the program for FY 1999.

After reviewing the volume of technical processing services that members continue to use, staff recommended that Contracts and Logistics (C&L) renew BOAs with the five technical processing services vendors, the Copyright Clearance Center, and the Interlibrary Loan Fee Payment Service vendor. The technical-processing COTR developed simplified procedures for specifying requirements for selecting vendors to handle small cataloging projects (less than $2,500) and continued to consult extensively with members on projects of larger size. Web versions of FEDLINK's Technical Processing Services Kit and its "Specifications" forms will debut in early FY 1999, ready for broad distribution to members.

### Streamlining Initiatives

FEDLINK's 1997 business plan calls for serious consideration of ways to streamline processes to increase efficiency and improve services to members. One of the first streamlining proposals suggested a different approach to the authorization of direct-pay purchases under FEDLINK BOAs.

Purchasing reforms instituted in the early 1990s called for all direct-pay purchase orders issued to vendors to be sent through FEDLINK for review (for current IAG status, scope of the order, procurement compliance, etc.). This process delayed the start of services for direct-pay customers and added a processing burden for the members' agency, FEDLINK and C&L. During FY 1998, LC's general counsel confirmed that this procedure was not legally required. FEDLINK decided to move with the spirit of federal procurement reform to depend on member agency contracting officers to issue orders under the simplified acquisition threshold ($100,000) in full compliance with FEDLINK BOAs. For orders more than $100,000, experience suggested that in the interest of the members and LC, FEDLINK should continue to consult and offer oversight. This revised procedure is already in place for FY 1999; members are authorized to send purchase orders for requirements less than $100,000 directly to vendors and to route orders over that threshold through FEDLINK.

By the end of FY 1998 FEDLINK engaged in a series of discussions with C&L and the LC general counsel about the application of Federal Acquisition Regulations (FAR), the Federal Acquisitions Streamlining Act (FASA), and other reform legislation to FEDLINK operations. Streamlining activities will continue into Fiscal Year 1999.

### Fiscal Operations

During FY 1998 FEDLINK processed 9,489 member service transaction requests for current and prior years, representing $53.2 million in current-year transfer pay, $3.2 million in prior-year transfer pay, $64.8 million in current-year direct pay, and $365,000 in prior-year direct pay service dollars, saving members more than $5 million in cost avoidance and approximately $12 million in volume discounts. Staff issued 56,617 invoices for payment of current and prior-year orders, incurred virtually zero net interest expense for late payment of FEDLINK vendor invoices, completed FY 1993 member service dollar refunds to close out obligations for expired appropriations, and successfully passed the Library of Congress Financial Audit of FY 1997 transactions performed by Clifton Gunderson, LLP.

FEDLINK also successfully completed steps to streamline its finance and procurement policies and procedures to enhance the efficiency of customer service operations and ensured that administrative expenditures/obligations did not exceed program fee projections. Staff also made significant progress in addressing the challenges associated with procuring a replacement financial system and maintaining SYMIN, its current system, through the year 2000, while simultaneously improving the efficiency of FEDLINK's financial processes.

### Vendor Services

Total FEDLINK vendor service dollars for FY 1998 alone comprised $53.2 million for transfer-pay customers and $64.8 million for direct-pay customers. Database retrieval services represented the largest share of service dollars, with $13.7 million and $52.4 million spent, respectively, for transfer-pay and direct-pay customers. Within this service category, online services comprised the largest procurement for transfer-pay and direct-pay customers, representing $13.3 million and $51.2 million, respectively. Publication acquisition services represented $33.2 million and $12.4 million, respectively, for transfer-pay and direct-pay customers. Within this service category, serials subscription services comprised the largest procurement for transfer-pay and direct-pay customers, representing $25.5 million and $11.9 million, respectively. Library support services represented $6.3 million for transfer-pay and zero dollars for direct-pay customers. Within this service category, bibliographic utilities constituted the largest procurement area, representing $5.1 million for transfer-pay customers.

### Accounts Receivable and Member Services

FEDLINK processed FY 1998 registrations from federal libraries, information centers and other federal offices that resulted in 695 signed FY 1998 IAGs. In addition, FEDLINK processed 2,653 IAG amendments (1,164 for FY 1998 and 1,489 for prior-year adjustments) for agencies that added, adjusted, or ended service funding. These IAGs and IAG amendments represented 9,489 individual service requests to begin, move, convert, or cancel services from FEDLINK vendors. FEDLINK executed service requests by generating 9,094 delivery orders that LC/Contracts and Logistics issued to vendors. For FY 1998 alone FEDLINK processed $53.2 million in service dollars for 2,567 transfer-pay accounts and $64.8 million in service dollars for 199 direct-pay accounts. Included in the above member service transactions are 621 member requests to move prior-year (no-year and multiyear) funds across fiscal year boundaries. These no-year and multiyear service request transactions represented an additional contracting volume of $3.5 million comprising 997 delivery orders.

The FEDLINK Fiscal Hotline responded to a variety of member questions, ranging from routine queries about IAGs, delivery orders, and account balances to complicated questions regarding FEDLINK policies and operating procedures. In addition, the FLICC Web site and e-mail contacts continued to offer FEDLINK members and vendors 24-hour access to fiscal operations. Staff continued to schedule appointments with FEDLINK member agencies and FEDLINK vendors to discuss complicated account problems; senior staff concentrated on resolving complex current and prior-year situations. FEDLINK ALIX-FS maintained current and prior-year transfer-pay accounts in FY 1998 and continued to provide members early access to their monthly balance information throughout the fiscal year. FEDLINK prepared monthly mailings that alerted individual members to unsigned IAG amendments, deficit accounts, rejected invoices, and delinquent accounts.

**Transfer-Pay Accounts-Payable Services**

For transfer-pay users, FEDLINK issued 56,617 invoices for payment during FY 1998 for both current and prior-year orders. Staff efficiently processed vendor invoices and earned $2,800 in discounts in excess of interest payment penalties levied for the late payment of invoices to FEDLINK vendors. FEDLINK continued to maintain open accounts for three prior years to pay publications service invoices ("bill laters" and "back orders") for members using books and serials services. Staff issued 91,769 statements to members (26,954 for the current year and 64,815 for prior years) and continued to generate current fiscal year statements for database retrieval service accounts on the 30th or the last working day of each month and publications and acquisitions account statements on the 15th of each month. FEDLINK issued final FY 1993 statements in support of closing obligations for expired FY 1993 appropriations. FFO issued quarterly statements for prior fiscal years, including FY 1994, and supported reconciliation of FY 1994 FEDLINK vendor services accounts.

**Financial Management**

FEDLINK completed all unfinished work associated with reconciling FY 1993 vendor obligations and payments and collaborated with LC/Financial Services to refund members' remaining account balances. This facilitated member agency compliance with statutory requirements for retiring obligations associated with FY 1993 expired appropriations.

FEDLINK also successfully passed the Library of Congress financial audit of FY 1997 transactions done by Clifton Gunderson, LLP. Staff completed the limited review of FEDLINK's automated financial system for the Library of Congress 1998 financial audit and invested time and effort to support the audit, including

- Financial systems briefings
- Documented review and analysis of financial system
- Testing and verification of account balances in the central and subsidiary financial system
- Financial statement preparation support
- Security briefings and reviews
- Research and documented responses to follow-up audit questions and findings

FEDLINK also hired a fiscal systems analyst to provide technical guidance and help systems staff address the challenges associated with procuring a replacement system and maintaining SYMIN over the next two years.

**Budget and Revenue**

During FY 1998 FEDLINK ensured that administrative expenditures and obligations did not exceed the program fee projections. As FY 1998 ended, FEDLINK service dollars fees were approximately 2 percent below the FY 1997 level for the same time period. FEDLINK earned 96 percent of its FY 1998 operating budget in fee revenues from signed IAGs.

**Financial Management Systems**

FEDLINK completed requirements for a new automated financial system that would replace the current SYMIN system. Last year FLICC executed a contract with Price Waterhouse to develop a systems requirements analysis for the replacement financial system. In its final report, Price Waterhouse recommended that FEDLINK use a public-sector customer-off-the-shelf (COTS) software package to meet its processing requirements. They concluded that a public-sector COTS software approach provides the best overall approach to meeting FEDLINK's requirements for the new financial management system. FEDLINK is now in the process of requesting proposals from GSA providers of financial management COTS software packages; FEDLINK expects the procurement to be completed during FY 1999.

Although FEDLINK is in the process of procuring a replacement SYMIN system, the new system will not be in place by the Year 2000 (Y2K). Most of the Y2K work is under way, and SYMIN is currently using database software that accommodates a four-digit year. FEDLINK continued to pursue the following initiatives to make SYMIN Y2K-compliant: migrating SYMIN from a Banyan Vines network operating system to a Windows NT network operating system and changing SYMIN tables, forms, and reports to accommodate four-character years. FEDLINK also established task orders for Y2K technical support deliverables under the LC Information Technology Service's contract with United Communications Systems (UCS).

FEDLINK made progress toward automating the IAG billing process through contract work with American Management Systems (AMS) to automate the IAG billing process. Completion of this automation effort in December 1998 will benefit FEDLINK members by significantly reducing the IAG billing turnaround time and billing operation cost.

FEDLINK successfully completed the implementation of a turnkey document imaging and archiving system for the Accounts Payable Operations to improve the retention and retrieval of accounts-payable records. Current plans entail extending the use of the system applications to Accounts Receivable and FEDLINK Contracting Operations.

# National Agricultural Library

U.S. Department of Agriculture, NAL Bldg., 10301 Baltimore Ave.,
Beltsville, MD 20705-2351
E-mail: agref@nal.usda.gov
World Wide Web: http://www.nal.usda.gov

Brian Norris
Public Affairs Officer

The National Agricultural Library (NAL) is the primary agricultural information resource for the nation and is the largest agricultural library in the world, with a collection of nearly 2.3 million volumes in print. The collection includes journals (the library receives more than 23,500 serial titles annually), audiovisuals, reports, theses, software, laser discs, and artifacts.

Established in 1862 under legislation signed by Abraham Lincoln, NAL is part of the Agricultural Research Service (ARS) of the U.S. Department of Agriculture (USDA). In addition to being a national library, NAL is the departmental library for USDA, serving USDA employees worldwide. NAL is a keystone of USDA's scientific and research activities.

As the nation's chief resource and service for agricultural information, NAL's mission is to increase the availability and use of agricultural information for researchers, educators, policy makers, farmers, consumers, and the public at large. NAL also serves a growing international clientele.

The NAL staff of about 200 includes librarians, computer specialists, administrators, information specialists, and clerical personnel. A number of volunteers, ranging from college students to retired persons, work on various programs at the library. NAL also has an active visiting-scholar program that allows scientists, researchers, professors, and students from universities around the world to work on projects of mutual interest.

NAL works closely with land grant university libraries on programs to improve access to and maintenance of the nation's agricultural knowledge.

AGRICOLA (AGRICultural OnLine Access) is NAL's bibliographic database, providing quick access to the NAL collection. AGRICOLA contains more than 3.5 million citations of agricultural literature and is available online at http://www.nal.usda.gov/ag98.

The NAL home page on the World Wide Web (http://www.nal.usda.gov) offers general and specific information on using NAL and its collection and links to agricultural information throughout the world. The home page logs an average of 650,000 hits a month.

The library maintains specialized information centers in areas of particular interest to the agricultural community. These centers provide a wide range of customized services, from responding to reference requests and developing reference publications to coordinating outreach activities and setting up dissemination networks. Subjects covered by the information centers include alternative farming systems, animal welfare, and food and nutrition, to name a few.

Some of the major NAL activities that occurred in 1998 follow.

# Highlights of the Year

## Building Renovation

NAL has undertaken a major renovation of its building because of a severe shortage of storage space for the NAL collection, a need for even more customer-friendly user areas, and a desire to "meet the new millennium with the most modern facilities possible." Construction activities have caused NAL to temporarily move some services and close some areas of the building. These disruptions will continue throughout the renovations, expected to take up to three years. While creating a somewhat hectic environment for NAL customers and staff, the library is focusing on providing customers with the same level of assistance and quality services that it has always given.

## Free Online Access to AGRICOLA

In September 1998 NAL gave the world free online access to AGRICOLA, the library's database of more than 3.5 million records of agricultural information, at http://www.nal.usda.gov/ag98. This was a major step toward NAL's goal of becoming a "library without walls," of using the burgeoning electronic information technology to make NAL's collection and expertise as widely available as possible. AGRICOLA is the backbone of the National Agricultural Library, providing access to materials in NAL's collection and at library collections throughout the country. Previously, it was available only at the library and through commercial sources by subscription.

## Microfilm Transferred to Off-site Storage

NAL completed phase one of a project to move all NAL master negative microfilm to off-site storage. The storage is in Boyers, Pennsylvania, with National Underground Storage, Inc. (NUS). The National Library of Medicine and the Smithsonian Institution also maintain storage vaults at the NUS facility. NUS constructed a vault for NAL that meets preservation level environmental standards for long-term storage of microfilm. NAL staff inventoried, bar-coded, and packed nearly 3,300 reels of master negative microfilm for transfer to the facility.

## Exchange of Information with Mexican University

NAL signed an agreement with the Biblioteca Central Magna (BCM) of the Autonomous University of Nuevo León (UANL), Mexico, to cooperate in enhancing access to agricultural and related information. The signing ceremony took place at UANL in Monterrey, Mexico, on October 29, 1998. Speaking at the ceremony, Floyd Horn, Administrator of USDA's Agricultural Research Service (ARS), praised the agreement and the history of agricultural cooperation between Mexico and the United States. ARS is NAL's parent agency. Since 1996 NAL and BCM have been exchanging agricultural materials on an informal basis, as well as working together to improve library services for their respective users, and the signing of the agreement formalized this arrangement.

**Rehousing of Special Collections**

NAL completed rehousing all but two of its manuscript collections. With detailed labeling and accession forms completed, NAL's Special Collections Section (SCS) greatly improved access to and conservation of these materials. Most of the NAL shelving used for manuscript storage and access was replaced with environmentally controlled storage. In preparation for the renovation, SCS relocated 3,000 rare books to secured areas where light, temperature, and humidity are controlled.

**Establishment of National Microfilm Archive**

NAL signed a cooperative agreement with Cornell University that names NAL as the national preservation depository and manager for archival microfilm of important state and local agricultural literature identified by the U.S. Agricultural Information Network (USAIN). Subsequently, NAL began receiving archival microfilm for cataloging and storage in an environmentally controlled space.

**Grants to Colleges**

NAL is working with Prairie View A&M University in Texas to create learning modules to incorporate the concepts of biotechnology throughout the university's curricula. This is being funded through a USDA grant to the university. Another USDA grant will allow Fort Valley State College in Georgia to work with NAL in "experimental learning in biotechnology."

**Support Continues for Egyptian Agricultural Library**

NAL staff were sent to the Egyptian National Agricultural Library (ENAL) in Cairo to provide training in advanced reference services for ENAL staff. ENAL had requested the training as part of the ten-year cooperation between NAL and the Egyptian government to create ENAL. The training consisted of customer and user services, evaluating the reference collection, making recommendations to enhance holdings, sharpening bibliographic skills, utilizing Web sites, developing bibliographic products, and promoting ENAL services. A set of recommendations was developed jointly by ENAL staff and the NAL trainers to plan for improvements in ENAL reference services.

**TEKTRAN Database**

NAL's Technology Transfer Information Center (TTIC) reported heavy use of TEKTRAN (Technology Transfer Automated Retrieval System), a database of interpretive summaries of ARS research-related articles located on the Web at http://www.nal.usda.gov/ttic/tektran/tektran.html. TEKTRAN allows researchers, industry, and the general public to read about recent ARS research on food and nutrition, crops and livestock, natural resources, and industrial products and technology. TTIC, working with the ARS Office of Technology Transfer, aided in the design, programming, implementation, and ongoing support of TEKTRAN on the

Internet. An average of 100 requests for information are received from TEK-TRAN searchers per month.

### Reference Services

NAL's Public Services Division launched a major initiative to create a new reference service model that will capitalize on the use of Web-based services and realign staff and budget with customer demand. The data-gathering phase of this effort was completed with the production of reports that investigated new models and roles for library staff and identified components to include in a new model, developed a statistical profile of current reference services and users, and analyzed the library's workload and made recommendations for selected workflow analyses. The next stage of the effort will be to create the new model for implementation during 1999.

### Electronic Document Delivery

NAL continued to encourage its patrons to send requests and receive materials electronically. Part of this effort included providing complimentary copies of Ariel software, with technical support, to more than 20 USDA regional offices and to the libraries of Historically Black Colleges and Universities (HBCUs) and Tuskegee University. Through Ariel, documents can be sent directly to a user's workstation anywhere in the world in less than a minute. Electronically submitted requests were the predominant type of document delivery requests for NAL in 1998. They accounted for 80 percent of all document delivery requests received, excluding on-site requests. Electronic delivery of materials by NAL to patrons increased 60 percent over 1997 and represented 34 percent of all delivery.

### Study of Document Delivery

NAL began a project to collate usage data based on document delivery request for 1997–1998. NAL is creating a database encompassing both bibliographic and patron details for each request. The completed database will allow the library to target the needs of NAL users and assess the development of the NAL collection.

### Agricultural Network Information Center

Representatives from U.S. and Canadian universities and agricultural organizations met at NAL to decide on the next steps in developing the Agricultural Network Information Center (AgNIC) on the World Wide Web. AgNIC (http://www.agnic.org) links worldwide agricultural information networks, providing "one-stop shopping" to anyone searching the Web for agricultural information. At the meeting, AgNIC members developed governing rules, elected an executive board and established the AgNIC Alliance Coordinating Committee. Also discussed were how to expand AgNIC coverage and ways to attract new members to the AgNIC alliance.

### Training Users to Access Electronic Resources

NAL has phased in its Electronic Media Center (EMC) so that library users can access information from NAL's electronic resources. NAL's EMC has seven customer-dedicated computers and network printers, and NAL customers can now access 30 databases, seven CD-ROMs, general Internet-based services, electronic federal depository collections, 45 electronic scientific journals, and a selection of electronic newspapers. NAL has added a significant core of current scientific literature to the resources available in the EMC. More than 170 journals in agricultural, biological, and social sciences published by Academic Press are available online at NAL with Web-based access to the International Digital Electronic Access Library (IDEAL).

Through its license agreement with Academic Press, NAL offers electronic access to the full contents of journals in the IDEAL package, commencing with 1996 issues. NAL's license authorizes access for on-site users in the library as well as for USDA employees in the Washington, D.C., area.

### Digital Preservation of Brittle Books

NAL has established procedures for digital conversion of USDA embrittled-paper publications. The library has converted collections of USDA paper publications to preservation-quality digital format. More than 24,000 pages were converted, becoming the first publications in NAL's digital archive collection. NAL is putting these images on the Internet. NAL has written a draft NAL Preservation Roll-out Plan, including program budget and organization. When reviewed and accepted by NAL management, the plan will assist the library in shaping an effective preservation program that will produce the most significant long-term benefit for the survival of NAL's permanent research collections.

### Regional Preservation Committee

NAL is a founding and active member of CIRLAP, a regional preservation committee composed of Georgetown University, Howard University, Johns Hopkins University, the Library of Congress, NAL, Smithsonian Libraries, the University of Delaware, and the University of Maryland. Preservation representatives from each institution explore collaborative programs and services, exchange information, and investigate cooperative initiatives to enhance the preservation programs of the institutions as a whole.

### Electronic Preservation Plans

NAL took the lead in 1998 in developing plans to preserve USDA electronic publications. Preservation and long-term access of these publications became an important issue due to the ephemeral nature of electronic formats. NAL is meeting with key stakeholders on this issue to develop a preservation and access plan.

### Conversion of Paper-Based Records

A milestone was reached in NAL's efforts to convert to an electronic library with the completion of a five-year project to create machine-readable and searchable catalog records for all monographs in NAL's collection. Previously, the paper-based catalog card records were only available to on-site users at NAL. When these records are loaded to AGRICOLA, NAL's online bibliographic database, information about the availability of an additional 188,000 resources in the national collection will be accessible to remote users searching AGRICOLA. Many of the records converted in the project describe historically important agricultural books, reports, and other published resources that are held only in NAL's collection.

### Food Safety Grant

The U.S. Department of Education awarded NAL's Food and Nutrition Information Center (FNIC) a $5,000 Planning Award to develop an interactive Internet site on food safety issues for high school students and teachers. The module demonstrates food safety principles for daily living and incorporates foreign-language teaching materials. The site is developed in partnership with teachers from Maryland school systems and representatives from various civic groups.

### Dietary Supplement Needs Assessment

NAL's Food and Nutrition Information Center (FNIC) is participating with the National Institutes of Health (NIH) in assessing the national need for information on dietary supplements. In May 1998 surveys were mailed to nearly 200 major U.S. nutrition, health, and medical organizations to gather information on the availability of and need for dietary supplements information resources. When compiled, the survey results will be used to coordinate existing resources and design new ones.

### *Women in Agriculture* Bibliography

Women's roles in world agriculture and rural life and their contributions worldwide are the subject of a bibliography published in 1998 by NAL's Alternative Farming Systems Information Center (AFSIC). *Women in Agriculture and Rural Life: An International Bibliography* (Special Reference Brief 98-02) was compiled by USDA's Economic Research Service and AFSIC, which produced the bibliography to coincide with the Second International Conference on Women in Agriculture held in Washington, D.C., June 28–July 2, 1998.

### Guide to Improved Animal Welfare

Information on reducing or eliminating the pain and distress of laboratory animals used in the production of antibodies is contained in a resource guide produced by NAL's Animal Welfare Information Center (AWIC) in 1998. *Information Resources for Adjuvants and Antibody Production: Comparisons and Alternative Technologies* contains 186 pages of information from journals, Web sites, researchers, and others on techniques for producing antibodies and adjuvants that seek to protect the laboratory animals in which these substances are used or produced.

### African American Bibliographies

NAL produced and made available three free bibliographies containing reference information on about 300 articles and reports related to African American sociology, economics, history, and culture. Most of the literature listed in the bibliographies is available in the NAL collection. The bibliographies are titled "African Americans in Agriculture," "African American Sociology and Economics," and "African American History and Culture."

### Screwworm Eradication Collection

NAL continued to take a lead role in documenting the history of the eradication of the screwworm parasite worldwide. The success of the international screwworm eradication program stands as a model of the positive power of agricultural research and interagency cooperation. NAL believes that developing and publicizing its Screwworm Eradication Collection will support and promote the value of agricultural research in the United States and the world.

### Food Irradiation Information on the Web

Following the approval by the Food and Drug Administration of the use of food irradiation to control bacteria in red meat in 1998, NAL made food irradiation information available on the Web through NAL's Food and Nutrition Information Center (FNIC) at http://www.nal.usda.gov/fnic/index.html.

### National Rivers Initiative

NAL's Rural Information Center (RIC) provided information services to rural communities participating in the American Heritage Rivers Initiative in 1998. The initiative supports efforts by communities along U.S. rivers to spur economic revitalization, protect natural resources and the environment, and preserve the historic and cultural heritages of river communities. The president announced the initiative in the 1997 State of the Union address and later issued an executive order directing federal agencies to establish and implement the initiative.

### Publication on Zoonoses

Diseases that can be transmitted from animals to humans were the subject of a new reference publication produced by NAL's Animal Welfare Information Center (AWIC). Such diseases are called zoonoses or zoonotic diseases. Examples are rabies, tuberculosis, anthrax, and hantavirus. AWIC developed the publication because of concerns within the medical community about such diseases, with scientists suggesting links between "mad cow disease" and its human equivalent and a strain of AIDS in monkeys recently discovered.

### Web Site on Food-Borne Illnesses

NAL began maintaining the Web site of the Foodborne Illness Education Information Center of USDA and the U.S. Food and Drug Administration. The site features food-borne illness statistics, government reports, consumer education materials, plans for controlling food-borne illnesses and a food safety index that provides links to other food safety sites. The site also includes an electronic discussion group.

### Dietary Guidelines for 2000

NAL began doing literature searches in support of the effort by the federal Center for Nutrition Policy and Promotion to develop the Dietary Guidelines for Americans that will be issued in the year 2000. The literature identified by NAL served as background to research on the new guidelines.

### Identification of Heirloom Seeds

Increased awareness throughout the agricultural world of the importance of diversity has led to increased world concern about preserving heirloom seeds, seeds of organisms that have been around for at least 50 years. In response, NAL's Alternative Farming Systems Information Center published a series of widely sought publications on the subject. These are *Vegetables and Fruits: A Guide to Heirloom Varieties and Community-Based Stewardship*, Volume 1, *Annotated Bibliography*; Volume 2, *Resource Organizations*; and Volume 3, *Historical Supplement*.

### Wheat Disease Scab in China

NAL's Plant Genome and Database Information Center and USDA's Agricultural Research Service began a critical review in 1998 of the research in breeding and selecting germ plasm resistant to wheat disease scab in China. China serves as a reservoir for genetic resistance to the pathogen wheat head scab, which has caused severe crop losses throughout the United States. The results of the review will be published in a peer-reviewed journal.

### Publication on Cover Crops

More than 5,000 copies of NAL's *Managing Cover Crops Profitably*, second edition, were reprinted and distributed by NAL as a result of large national demand for the first edition. The publication was developed by NAL's Alternative Farming Systems Information Center (AFSIC) and the Sustainable Agriculture Network, which maintains offices in AFSIC. In the publication, farmers and researchers share expertise and management techniques that will build soil by supplying organic matter through cover crops.

### Visitors Learn at NAL

NAL's Visiting Scholar, Visiting Librarian, and Short-Term Internship programs provided in-depth coverage of NAL programs for participants from throughout the world. NAL hosted visiting scholars and guests from India, China, Puerto Rico, the Omaha Tribal Library, the Nebraska Indian Community College, Historically Black Colleges and Universities, and elsewhere. Also, in a milestone for NAL, the library hosted its first tribal college library director during the year. NAL provided the director with detailed orientations on NAL programs, products, and services and on resources available from state land grant colleges and universities. In 1994 the president proclaimed that the 29 tribal colleges in the United States were members of the state land grant system. One-day NAL tours were also provided to more than 500 visitors, including groups from Brazil,

China, Egypt, Mali, Mexico, Pakistan, Puerto Rico, South Africa, South Korea, Spain, Sweden, and Turkey.

### South African Flower Exhibit

NAL hosted a free public exhibit on South African indigenous flowers, organized by the Embassy of South Africa and the U.S. National Arboretum, in its lobby in March 1998. The exhibit, "Of Flowers, Folios, and Farmers—in Celebration of the Floral Gems, Blossoming Wealth of South Africa," focused on South Africa's burgeoning flower industry and featured dried South African flower arrangements and displays highlighting the research of the Agricultural Research Council of South Africa.

### Family Care Fair

NAL's Technology Transfer Information Center and Educational Programs Unit helped organize a Child and Elder Care Fair, sponsored by USDA's Agricultural Research Service, in June 1998. At the fair, 34 organizations provided USDA employees, contractors, and cooperators with information on child- and elder-care options, government services, food and nutrition, health care, and related issues.

### County Book Fair

The NAL grounds in Beltsville, Maryland, were the site of Book Fest, the Prince George's County, Maryland, book festival. Book Fest was a community-wide literary festival that "celebrates and promotes the fun and benefits of reading." The fest featured authors, poets, and interactive literary exhibits for families. The event was sponsored by the Prince George's County government, the Prince George's County Memorial Library System, the Community Services Coalition, Journal Newspapers of Maryland, and local businesses.

# National Library of Medicine

8600 Rockville Pike, Bethesda, MD 20894
301-496-6308, 888-346-3656, fax 301-496-4450
E-mail: publicinfo@nlm.nih.gov
World Wide Web: http://www.nlm.nih.gov

Robert Mehnert
Public Information Officer

The National Library of Medicine (NLM), a part of the Department of Health and Human Services' National Institutes of Health in Bethesda, Maryland, is the world's largest library of the health sciences. NLM has two buildings with 420,000 total square feet. The older building (1962) houses the collection, public reading rooms, exhibition hall, and library staff and administrative offices. The adjacent 10-story Lister Hill Center Building (1981) contains the main computer room, auditorium, audiovisual facility, offices, and research/demonstration laboratories. At the end of 1998 the main reading room and exhibition hall were temporarily shut down for a series of facility upgrades, including the installation of additional computer terminals for online searching, a new raised floor system to accommodate telecommunications connections, and new carpeting and other enhancements to the appearance of these public areas.

## Public Access

In 1998 NLM began a formal program to encourage consumer access to health information via the NLM Web site. The library was encouraged to take this step by the public's enthusiastic response to free MEDLINE searching via the World Wide Web, which NLM began providing in 1997. MEDLINE usage has climbed from an annual rate of 7 million searches a year to more than 120 million searches. It became obvious that the audience for MEDLINE was much broader than previously suspected.

NLM's decision by to include the public among its primary audiences is a notable one. In its early days, the library was seen as a resource for the military medical establishment; it later assumed a de facto larger role in the health sciences, and in 1956 NLM was formally designated by Congress as a national resource for all health professionals. Thus, to seek to become a source of medical information for everyone is to expand significantly the library's responsibility. The decision to do so was affirmed at an extended meeting of the library's senior managers in December 1998.

The popularity of MEDLINE on the Web was not the only factor contributing to this decision. NLM has considerable experience over the past three decades in applying computers to medical information storage and retrieval. The resulting computer-based information sources are now used daily by scientists and high school students, physicians and patients, librarians and senior citizens. In addition to MEDLINE, with its 10 million references and abstracts, these databases encompass human genome information, reports and data about hazardous substances and chemical spills in various locations across the country, and a wide variety of information gathered specifically to help citizens make decisions about their health care.

## Public Library Initiative

On October 22, 1998, NLM launched a pilot project to help local librarians use the Internet to find health information pertinent to their patrons' needs. This project will provide health information to citizens without Web access and at the same time will create an experienced cadre of public librarians who can guide consumers to sources of reliable health information. The project is a cooperative one: NLM is working with members of the National Network of Libraries of Medicine (NN/LM), the American Library Association, the Medical Library Association, and the W. K. Kellogg Foundation. The participating 39 public library systems (representing several hundred individual libraries) were chosen from three NN/LM regions to represent a range of community sizes and diverse populations.

NLM, which is supplying descriptive materials and training for the project, has created a new "MEDLINEplus" information resource specifically for use by public librarians and the general public. Accessible through the NLM home page, MEDLINEplus gives Web users access to reviewed sources of health information—from NLM, the National Institutes of Health (NIH), other government agencies, and selected nongovernment organizations. The new service provides access to extensive information about 50 specific diseases and conditions (including cancer, diabetes, and alcoholism) and also has links to self-help groups, NIH consumer health information, clearinghouses, dictionaries, lists of hospitals and physicians, health information in Spanish, and clinical trials. One unique feature of MEDLINEplus is a series of preformulated MEDLINE searches on various aspects of diseases (for example, the extensive section on diabetes includes a search on "nutrition and diet"). The user need not know any searching strategy; the preformulated query does a real-time search and returns up-to-date references and abstracts. MEDLINEplus is being expanded as rapidly as possible; the 45 topics should be increased to several hundred within a year.

Other sources of useful information that will be made available through the public library project are the Human Gene Map (described later in this article), the text of NIH consensus development statements, up-to-date syntheses of cancer treatment information, and federally sponsored clinical practice guidelines. The public library project began in October 1998, and already there are reports about how useful the new site is in providing information. If the pilot project is successful, NLM may seek the resources to mount a national program.

## Communications-Related Collaborations

Under a new Partners in Information program, NLM awarded 13 contracts in September 1998 to public health agencies to help them hook up to the Internet and thus have easier access to health information. The program is a joint activity of NLM and several federal and nonfederal groups, including the Centers for Disease Control and Prevention. The awards are scattered around the United

States in rural and underserved areas, from Alaska to Vermont, and they involve information services for public health officials of all kinds who are addressing a variety of community health problems and special populations.

Another set of 14 awards, also made by NLM in the fall of 1998, is aimed at speeding life-saving treatment to those who suffer heart attacks. Working with the National Heart, Lung, and Blood Institute, the library is trying to determine whether the techniques of medical informatics can help ensure the application of known clot-dissolving agents immediately after a heart attack. Although the efficacy of these agents has been known for years, only a fraction of the 1.1 million people who suffer a heart attack each year receive such treatment. If NLM's program is successful, it would be a dramatic example of how timely information can potentially save many thousands of lives.

In the international arena, the library has always emphasized collecting and organizing the medical publications of other countries; this philosophy is reflected in the international character of MEDLINE and the other databases. It is estimated that 45 percent of all MEDLINE searches are done by and for non-U.S. health professionals. A Long Range Planning Panel on International Programs was set up by the NLM Board of Regents and, in its 1998 final report, the panel recommended that the library maintain and expand its involvement with other governments and with non-U.S. health sciences institutions. One special international program will be NLM's participation in the Multilateral Initiative on Malaria by enhancing the communications and networking capabilities of African malarial researchers. NLM's work has the potential to lessen the toll in Africa from this dread disease.

Another collaborative undertaking is Phase II of the Digital Libraries Initiative. The term "digital libraries" is used to denote the vast distributed collections of text and images available through the Internet. The goals of Phase I were to advance fundamental research and to build test-bed networks for developing and demonstrating new technologies. Supported projects in Phase II look beyond the technology and test beds and seek to apply what has been learned. NLM is contributing funds to the National Science Foundation, which is managing the program, to support projects that relate to health domains.

## Support of Research

NLM is supporting cutting-edge research that seeks to learn how the Next Generation Internet (NGI) can be used to improve health care, health education, and medical research. NLM itself depends to a great extent on the Internet to deliver health information services, and it thus has a vested interest in preserving and promoting the health of the network. The NGI initiative is a partnership among industry, academia, and government agencies that seeks to provide affordable, secure information delivery at rates thousands of times faster than today's. If we can transmit massive amounts of data quickly, and with accuracy and security, will this lower health costs, increase the quality of care, and safeguard patient privacy? In 1998 NLM supported 24 projects aimed at finding answers to these questions. These investigations (at universities, medical schools, and private companies) encompass a number of projects: telemedicine, telepresence, teleconferencing, tele-immersion, telemammography, teleradiology, and teletrauma. Several of the projects use the capabilities afforded by the Visible Human Project.

The Visible Human Project continues to command great interest in the scientific community and public media. The two data sets (which contain detailed, submillimeter, anatomical images of a man and a woman) are being used (without charge) by more than 1,000 licensees in 30 countries. Current uses of these data sets include the following: "surgical simulators" that let doctors rehearse delicate medical procedures; "recyclable cadavers" to help medical students learn about anatomy; "virtual prototyping," which creates perfectly fitted hip and knee replacements; and "virtual colonoscopy," a procedure that reduces the time, cost, and discomfort associated with a "real" colonoscopy and is expected to become an important tool in screening for colon cancer. NLM is cooperating with three other NIH institutes to fund the development of an interactive, Internet-accessible atlas of head and neck anatomy based on the Visible Human Project data sets.

A new service introduced by NLM in 1998 is Profiles in Science, a Web site that allows one to look behind the scenes of scientific findings and read the unpublished writings, letters, photographs, and lab notes of great scientists and great scientific discoveries. The first collection available is for Oswald Theodore Avery, whose research in the first half of the 20th century laid the groundwork for modern genetics and molecular biology. The new Web site, which brings together the best in archival practices with state-of-the-art technology, will be continually enriched with the papers of other great scientists of this century. The library hopes that "Profiles in Science" will kindle users' interest and appreciation scientific discoveries in biology and medicine.

## Clinical Trials Database

Also in 1998 the library was given the task of establishing a database that will contain information about clinical trials, whether federally or privately funded, for experimental treatments for serious diseases and conditions. The database will include information on the purpose of the trial (in language that nonscientific users can understand), the eligibility criteria for participating, where the clinical trial is being conducted, and how to get in touch with those conducting it. NLM is already the home of AIDSTRIALS (a database of clinical trials relating to AIDS) and HSTAT (which links to a file of NIH intramural clinical trials). Also, NLM's new MEDLINEplus service links to clinical trials (both federal and nonfederal) in a number of disease areas. The library plans to create a central search engine that will provide a uniform interface to all clinical trials and thus simplify the task of finding such information.

## Genetic Medicine

Ten years ago, in anticipation of the explosion of genomic information and the growing importance of molecular biology, Congress created the National Center for Biotechnology Information (NCBI) as part of the National Library of Medicine. By creating and maintaining immense databanks as well as sophisticated tools that allow the information to be used for making further discoveries, NCBI is making a major contribution to the Human Genome Project. Scientists in universities, research institutions, government agencies, and commercial organizations submit the results of their work to the center's highly evolved information resources so that the data will be available for use by others. As a result of the accelerating pace of research, the GenBank database of DNA sequence information is growing to vast proportions. The database now contains some 3 million sequences with a total of 2 billion base pairs, and the NCBI Web site (where GenBank is made freely available) receives some 600,000 queries per day. NCBI scientists have also collaborated with colleagues in laboratories around the world to produce the Human Gene Map, which pinpoints the chromosomal locations of almost half of all genes. This milestone in the Human Genome Project, available to all on the World Wide Web, will greatly expedite the discovery of human disease genes and, by extension, contribute to advances in detection and treatment of common illnesses.

## Basic Library Services

The library's collections constitute an unparalleled treasure for the nation. They are broad (encompassing all the health sciences) and deep (from the 11th century to the present). NLM subscribes to more than 22,000 serial publications and indexes almost 4,000 of them for MEDLINE, resulting in more than 400,000 references and citations being added to the database in an average year. In addition to NLM's online resources, extensive use is made of the library's physical collection: NLM responded to almost 700,000 requests for articles and books in 1998, by e-mail, fax, post, and on-site patrons. The library was able to handle this record workload with the help of a new interlibrary loan system called Relais, installed in 1998. Relais utilizes scanning, touch-screen, and bar code technology to process requests much faster, with less effort and paperwork, and with a higher-quality copy being delivered to the requester. Clinical emergencies are given special priority; doctors a thousand miles away have been astounded to receive a copy of an article from NLM within a half hour.

In fiscal year 1998 NLM received and processed 169,000 books, serial issues, audiovisuals, and computer-based materials. Preservation microfilming was done for 5,503 volumes (2.3 million pages). A net total of 63 journals was added to those indexed for MEDLINE (the number indexed is now 3,942).

A crucial element in delivering library services is the role played by the National Network of Libraries of Medicine. The NN/LM, with its 4,500 members, is organized through eight regions, each with a Regional Medical Library designated and supported by NLM. The regional libraries, together with 140 large academic health sciences libraries and the many hospital and other libraries in the network, provide crucial information service to scientists, health professionals, and, increasingly, the public. Working with NN/LM, NLM also has outreach programs designed to reach underserved populations, including minority and native American communities, rural areas, and senior citizens.

The director of the library is Donald A. B. Lindberg, M.D. NLM is guided in matters of policy by a board of regents consisting of 10 appointed and 11 ex officio members. Tenley E. Albright, M.D., chairs the board. In 1998 the regents welcomed three new members to four-year terms: Henry Foster, M.D., Ph.D., Senior Advisor to the President on Teen and Youth Issues; Joshua Lederberg, Ph.D., President Emeritus, Rockefeller University; and Herbert Pardes, M.D., Vice President for Health Sciences and Dean, Faculty of Medicine, College of Physicians and Surgeons, Columbia University.

**Table 1 / Selected NLM Statistics***

|  | Volume |
| --- | --- |
| Collection (book and nonbook) | 5,330,000 |
| Items cataloged | 18,800 |
| Serial titles received | 22,250 |
| Articles indexed for MEDLINE | 412,000 |
| Circulation requests processed | 694,000 |
| For interlibrary loan | 375,000 |
| For on-site users | 319,000 |
| Computerized searches (all databases) | 104,000,000 |
| Budget authority | $170,992,000 |
| Full-time staff | 577 |

* For the year ending September 30, 1998

# Educational Resources Information Center

ERIC Processing and Reference Facility
Computer Sciences Corporation
1100 West Street, Laurel, MD 20707-3598
301-497-4080, 800-799-3742, fax 301-953-0263
E-mail: ericfac@inet.ed.gov
World Wide Web: http://ericfac.piccard.csc.com

Ted Brandhorst

Director

## ERIC Program Office

### Budget

The ERIC Program Office was funded for fiscal year (FY) 1999 at essentially the same level as for FY 1998: $10,000,000.

### Clearinghouse Competition

The 16 ERIC Clearinghouse contracts were competed during the last six months of 1998. It was announced in early January 1999 that incumbents had won across the board and that there would be no change in ERIC Clearinghouse host organizations. The new five-year contracts are performance-based fixed price (FP) contracts, using "performance indicators" to ensure that certain tasks are performed to defined standards. A high level of performance can be rewarded and a low level can be penalized.

### USEIN

The United States Education Information Network (USEIN) initiative launched by the National Library of Education at a "kickoff" conference in late 1997 was further articulated by the publication in 1998 of the proceedings of that conference (see ED 414 900 in the ERIC database). USEIN's name was changed during 1998 to National Education Network (NEN).

### Year 2000 Problem

The Year 2000 (Y2K) problem became a major priority during 1998 within the Department of Education. As a consequence, ERIC required numerous reports, tests, and remedial actions on the part of its contractors. Many ERIC components were already Y2K-compliant. By the end of the year, all ERIC components could make this claim. Within the ERIC database, Publication Date is now recorded in the all-numeric format YYYY-MM-DD, ensuring both Y2K compliance and full, uncomplicated searchability.

### Limitations Imposed on Non-Reproducible Materials

Traditionally ERIC has covered the document literature and the journal article literature. About five years ago, ERIC added copyrighted, commercially published books to its coverage and more recently it added selected nonprint media.

Before books were added, the quantity of nonreproducible material accessioned by ERIC was about 3 percent. This percentage has gradually increased until in 1998 it was approaching 20 percent. This change in the "mix" of database accessions was taking place at the expense of documents and each such nonreproducible accession was also creating a "hole" in the ERIC microfiche collection. In order to protect ERIC's traditional document coverage and the integrity of the ERIC microfiche collection, the ERIC Program Office established a limit of 10 percent on nonreproducible items to be processed in 1999.

### National Clearinghouse on Educational Facilities

The National Clearinghouse on Educational Facilities (NCEF) was originally competed and awarded in 1997. In 1998, after one year of operation, the Clearinghouse contract was recompeted and awarded in May 1998 to a new contractor, the National Institute of Building Sciences (NIBS). NCEF is not an ERIC Clearinghouse per se, but is regarded as "affiliated" with ERIC because it uses ERIC to help perform its bibliographic tasks. Documents and journal articles input to ERIC by NCEF carry an "EF" Clearinghouse Accession Number prefix. (See http://www.edfacilities.org).

### CIJE Publisher

*Current Index to Journals in Education* (*CIJE*) is published by Oryx Press (Phoenix, Arizona) using data originally created by the ERIC Clearinghouses and then edited by a combination of the ERIC Facility (duplicate checking, Descriptor and Identifier validation, publisher and ISSN number for journals not regularly covered) and Oryx Press (cataloging, ISSN number for regularly covered journals).

The *Source Journal Index* (*SJI*) is the authority list of journals regularly covered by the ERIC Clearinghouses for *CIJE*. It lists journal name, publisher name and address, frequency, price, ISSN number, Clearinghouse that covers the journal, and a symbol indicating whether coverage is comprehensive or selective. The *SJI* is printed in the front of each printed issue of *CIJE*. During 1998 the *SJI* was converted to a database and loaded onto the Oryx Press Web site (http://www.oryxpress.com) where it is kept up to date and fully searchable.

Oryx Press also periodically publishes the *Thesaurus of ERIC Descriptors*. The next (14th) edition is projected as a "millennium" edition for early in the year 2000.

## ERIC Facility

### ERIC Database Size and Growth

The ERIC database consists of two files, one corresponding to the monthly abstract journal *Resources in Education* (*RIE*) and one corresponding to the monthly *Current Index to Journals in Education* (*CIJE*). *RIE* announces education-related documents and books, each with an accession number beginning ED (for educational document). *CIJE* announces education-related journal articles, each with an accession number beginning EJ (for educational journal).

Document records include a full abstract and are approximately 1,800 characters long on average. Journal article records include a brief annotation and are approximately 650 characters long on average.

Through the December 1998 issue of *RIE*, the ERIC database includes 414,563 records for documents. Through the October 1998 issue of *CIJE* (the latest issue available at this writing), ERIC includes 563,508 records for journal articles. The grand total is 978,071 bibliographic records. With approximately 2,500 additional *CIJE* records projected for the November and December 1998 issues, the *CIJE* total through 1998 will be approximately 566,000 records and the grand total through 1998 will be approximately 980,500 records.

Approximately 12,000 document records and 20,000 article records are added annually, for a total of 32,000 records per year. Overall, the ERIC database through 1998 is approximately 1,300 million bytes (1.3 gigabytes) in size and is growing at a rate of around 35 million bytes per year.

| | Number of Records | | |
|---|---|---|---|
| File | 1966–1997 | 1998 | Total |
| *Resources in Education (RIE)* | 403,324 | 11,239 (through December) | 414,563 (through December) |
| *Current Index to Journals in Education (CIJE)* | 548,446 | 15,062 (through October) | 563,508 (through October) |
| ERIC Database Total | 951,770 | 26,301 (through October) | 978,071 (through October) |

**ERIC Database Computer System**

The ERIC Database was generated throughout 1998 by the STAR database management system (offered by Cuadra Associates). The abstract journal *Resources in Education* (*RIE*) was generated during 1998 using a combination of STAR and FrameMaker composition software.

The ERIC database was distributed to vendors and other subscribers during 1998 in two formats: the old ERIC EBCDIC format that is being discontinued and the new DIALOG B format that will be used for all future distributions. About 50 percent of ERIC's database subscribers have completed conversion programs to handle ERIC data in the new DIALOG B format; the other 50 percent are still working on this transition. ERIC's goal is to cease distribution in EBCDIC by the end of 1999 (if not before). Similarly, ERIC's goal is to cease data distribution on physical reel tapes and to move to distribution by the online FTP process for all subscribers by the end of 1999 (if not before).

*ERIC Processing Manual* (*EPM*) **Revision**

The *ERIC Processing Manual* provides the rules and procedures for the ERIC Clearinghouses to use in creating the ERIC bibliographic database. It has ten sections, covering Acquisitions, Selection, Handling and Shipping, Cataloging, Abstracting, Indexing, Vocabulary Development and Maintenance (Descriptors and Identifiers), Data Entry, Database Changes, and ERIC Clearinghouse Scope of Interest Guide. The *EPM* was last produced in 1992. It is currently being revised and brought up to date to reflect a wide variety of needed additions, such as nonprint media, electronic documents and journals, the Internet and Web in acquisitions and technical processing tasks, new "levels" of reproduction release (to permit electronic page image archiving), new ERIC data fields (ISSN, ISBN, reformatted Publication Date, expanded Personal Author field, and so forth). The revised *EPM* is projected for publication by the end of 1999.

### ERIC on NISC Disc CD-ROM

The ERIC Facility distributes the ERIC database on a low-cost CD-ROM product developed by the National Information Services Company (NISC). During 1998 NISC implemented a new Windows-based retrieval program called NISC DISCover. The new program is an expanded and improved version of the previous DOS-based ROMWright retrieval system used by NISC and was implemented with the first quarter 1998 Current Disc. The Current Disc now contains both the DOS and Windows retrieval programs, permitting the user at installation time to select the appropriate program.

## ERIC Document Reproduction Service

The ERIC Document Reproduction Service (EDRS) is the document delivery arm of ERIC and handles all subscriptions for ERIC microfiche and on-demand requests for reproduced paper copy or microfiche. During 1998 the number of standing order customers (SOCs) subscribing to the total ERIC microfiche collection (about 10,000 titles on 15,000 fiche cards, for approximately $2,600 annually) rose to more than 1,000. SOCs include more than 100 overseas addresses.

EDRS prices usually increase about 3 percent annually due to increases in the cost of basic materials and labor. The table below presents prices in effect for the period January 1–December 31, 1999.

An updated order form reflecting the 1999 prices and shipping rates is now available from EDRS. The form shows a flat-fee schedule for international shipping. There are no shipping charges associated with electronic delivery.

In the summer of 1997 EDRS made the online ERIC bibliographic database available to the public on its Web site. This version of the ERIC database offers a user-friendly search template to access all ED references from 1966 forward. Users may order documents they find in their search from the same online session. The EDRS Web site also provides a quick-order feature for users who already know the document number of the material they want to order.

In response to the growing need of research institutions and their patrons for immediate access to ERIC materials, EDRS began developing a new electronic document subscription service in 1998. Features of the new service, known as E*Subscribe, will include unlimited access to the ERIC database and electronic document images from 1996 through the current *Resources in Education* (*RIE*) issue, electronic delivery in Adobe PDF format, online subscription management and administrative functions, and ordering capability for documents not yet available electronically. More than 100 institutions registered to help EDRS Beta test this new electronic subscription service. The service is expected to be available to subscribers in spring 1999. Visit the EDRS Web site (http://edrs.com) for more information.

In 1998 EDRS begin selling to the public a collection of research literature on CD-ROM from OERI's National Research and Development Centers. The collection includes bibliographic records of 8,600 center documents collected by the ERIC system from 1966–1997; the full text of 5,500 center documents collected by ERIC from 1980–1997; and Folio software for searching, viewing, and printing document images from the CD-ROM.

| Product | 1999 Prices |
| --- | --- |
| **Microfiche** | |
| Annual subscription (approximately) | $2,600.00 |
| Monthly subscription (price/fiche) | $ 0.2994 (Silver) |
| | $ 0.1463 (Diazo) |
| Back collections (1966–previous month) (price/fiche) | $ 0.1772 |
| Clearinghouse collections (price/fiche) | $ 0.3151 |
| **On-demand Documents, per title** | |
| Microfiche (MF) up to 5 fiche (5 fiche = 480 pages) | $ 1.47 |
| Each additional fiche (up to 96 pages) | $ 0.25 |
| Reproduced Paper Copies (PC) | |
| First 1–25 pages | $ 4.33 |
| Each additional 25–page increment (or part thereof) | $ 4.33 |
| **Electronic Page Images** | |
| Base price per electronic document | $ 3.50 |
| Price per page | $ 0.15 |
| Example: A 15-page document costs $5.75 ($3.50 + $2.25) | |
| **1997 Cumulative Indexes (on Microfiche)** | |
| Subject, Author, Title, Institution, Descriptor, and Identifier Indexes | $ 75.00 |

For more information, the EDRS Web site can be accessed at http://edrs. com. To reach a customer service representative, contact EDRS at 703-440-1400 or 800-443-3742, or via e-mail at Service@edrs.com

## ACCESS ERIC

ACCESS ERIC is responsible for systemwide outreach, marketing, publicity, and promotion for the ERIC system. One major outreach activity is staffing exhibits and giving presentations on ERIC at education and library conferences. In 1998 ERIC exhibited at conferences of the American Library Association, Association for Supervision and Curriculum Development, and the National School Boards Association. Presentations were given for participants in the Office of Vocational and Adult Education's National Teachers Forum and for the SOROS Fellows (librarians from Eastern Europe, Asia, and Africa).

ACCESS ERIC works closely with the ERIC Clearinghouses to produce The *ERIC Review*, a free journal on current education issues. The most recent issue (fall 1998) was produced in collaboration with the ERIC Clearinghouse on Languages and Linguistics and focused on K–12 foreign language instruction.

The Clearinghouses also provide ACCESS ERIC with material for a series of Parent Brochures, which included these titles in 1998: *Getting Online: A Friendly Guide for Parents, Students, and Teachers*; *How Can I Encourage My Young Child To Read?*; *Rights and Responsibilities of Parents of Children With Disabilities*; *What Can Parents and Teachers Do If an Adolescent Begins To Fail in School?*; *What Should Parents and Teachers Know About Bullying?*; and *Why, How, and When Should my Child Learn a Second Language?*

ACCESS ERIC maintains the ERIC systemwide Web site (http://accesseric.org:81), which provides links to all ERIC-sponsored sites as well as full-text copies of Parent Brochures, *The ERIC Review*, *All About ERIC*, and other systemwide materials. In 1998 the new ERICNews listserv provided bimonthly updates of new ERIC publications and services to more than 1,400 subscribers.

ACCESS ERIC continues to produce a number of information and referral databases and publications including the *Catalog of ERIC Clearinghouse Publications*, the *ERIC Directory of Education-Related Information Centers*, the *Directory of ERIC Resource Collections*, and the *Calendar of Education-Related Conferences*.

ACCESS ERIC also actively maintains the database for the *Education Resource Organizations Directory* available on the Department of Education's Web site (http://www.ed.gov). This directory includes information on more than 2,400 national, regional, and state organizations and is constantly being updated and expanded.

## AskERIC

AskERIC, a project of the ERIC Clearinghouse on Information and Technology, is an Internet-based reference and referral system providing question-answering, reference, and referral service to educators throughout the world. AskERIC first opened its electronic doors in November 1992 and in 1998 closed out its sixth year of operation with increased demand and increased distribution of questions throughout the ERIC system. AskERIC provides educators information with a personal touch via the Internet. People interested in education information can submit questions to AskERIC through e-mail (askeric@askeric.org) or through its Web site (www.askeric.org). In 1998 AskERIC responded to more than 40,000 Internet reference requests, an increase of 10,000 questions from last year. The AskERIC Question and Answer service spent 10 weeks above the 1,000-questions-per-week level. The AskERIC Web site also continues to gain popularity. During peak times of the year, the site receives close to 2,000,000 hits per week. The most popular feature is the lesson plan collection, followed closely by the ERIC database. In 1998 the ERIC database was expanded to cover the entire range of years (1966 to present). A lesson plan submission form and Q&A Hot Topics were also added to the Web site.

## National Parent Information Network

Since late 1993 the National Parent Information Network (NPIN), funded through the ERIC system as a special project of the ERIC Clearinghouses on

Elementary and Early Childhood Education and on Urban Education, has worked to provide education information services targeted specifically to parents. NPIN's World Wide Web site has become one of the two or three largest non-commercial collections of full-text information intended for parents on the World Wide Web. The year 1998 was marked for NPIN by new collaboration efforts, increased public awareness, research on the effectiveness of NPIN, and the continued growth of NPIN's online collection of information for parents.

NPIN collaborations this year were in two primary areas: with the Illinois Family Partnership Network leading to the development of NPIN Illinois, and with the National Parenting Education Network (NPEN).

NPIN staff continued to play a significant role in the rapid development of NPEN, a collaboration of parenting education organizations that works to advance the field of parenting education through networking and building the knowledge base on parenting education.

Increasing public awareness about the National Parenting Information Network was one of NPIN's specific goals for 1998. NPIN was represented at more than 28 conferences and meetings during the year, and also received considerable publicity from two articles published in the *New York Times* in November. In addition to publicity through the popular press, NPIN staff appeared on or were interviewed for "NBC Nightly News," ABC's "Good Morning America," Radio Free Europe, Voice of America, *Kidz Magazine*, and *Sesame Street Parent* magazine. Consequently, the NPIN World Wide Web site and the AskERIC service have seen remarkable growth over the past year. Usage of the NPIN Web site (http://ericps.crc.uiuc.edu/npin/npinhome.html) in 1998 topped 2.6 million file accesses. On an average day the ERIC Clearinghouse user services staff and AskERIC staff responded to more than 60 questions generated electronically or by the toll-free telephone number. Parenting-related questions are typically 30 percent of the total number of questions.

In addition to other Internet activities, NPIN continued to operate the PAR-ENTING-L listserv in 1998. This "virtual" parenting support group discusses a wide variety of topics that are important in the daily life of parents, such as choosing a preschool, how to talk with a teacher, balancing work and family life, and appropriate discipline for children. Increasingly, the list is being viewed as an educational resource for students in parenting education, early childhood education, and elementary education. Participants in PARENTING-L have also contributed to articles for *Parent News* as well as responding directly to students' questions to help with assignments related to parent-teacher participation.

# The Most Popular ERIC Documents Ordered From EDRS in 1998

| Title | ED Number | Clearinghouse |
|---|---|---|
| 1 Technical Issues in Performance Assessment: Setting Performance Standards | ED 379 335 | Assessment and Evaluation |
| 2 Language Planning in Preschool Education | ED 324 929 | Languages and Linguistics |
| 3 The Project Approach . . . | ED 402 068 | Elementary and Early |
| | ED 340 518 | Childhood Education |
| 4 Cross-Cutting Guidance for the Elementary and Secondary Education Act | ED 408 663 | Educational Management |
| 5 A Guide to Developing Educational Partnerships | ED 362 992 | Educational Management |
| 6 Keeping Schools Open as Community Learning Centers: Extending Learning in a Safe Drug-Free Environment Before and After School | ED 409 659 | Educational Management |
| 7 Teaching Mathematics to Limited English Proficient Students (ERIC Digest) | ED 317 086 | Languages and Linguistics |
| 8 Art Education and Human Development | ED 336 315 | Social Studies/Social Science Education |
| 9 The Online Classroom: Teaching with the Internet | ED 400 577 | Reading, English, and Communication |
| 10 101 Ways to Help Children with ADD Learn: Tips from Successful Teachers | ED 389 109 | Disabilities and Gifted Education |
| 11 When Teachers Lead | ED 366 082 | Educational Management |
| 12 Storyboarding: A Brief Description of the Process | ED 384 171 | Disabilities and Gifted Education |
| 13 Full-Day Kindergarten . . . | ED 408 046 | Elementary and Early |
| | ED 405 129 | Childhood Education |
| | ED 395 691 | |
| | ED 369 540 | |
| | ED 345 868 | |
| | ED 318 570 | |
| 14 Education and its Management: Science, Art, and Spirit | ED 340 084 | Educational Management |
| 15 Models for Integrating Human Services into the School | ED 347 244 | Urban Education |
| 16 Measurements of Personality and Leadership: Some Relationships | ED 350 694 | Educational Management |
| 17 Supports and Barriers to Teacher Leadership: Reports of Teacher Leaders | ED 408 259 | Teaching and Teacher Education |
| 18 School-to-Work Career Portfolios | ED 401 447 | Adult, Career, and Vocational Education |
| 19 Learning Without Limits: Model Distance Education Programs in Community Colleges | ED 401 969 | Community Colleges |
| 20 Block Scheduling In High Schools | ED 399 673 | Educational Management |
| 21 Guide to Quality: Even Start Family Literacy Programs | ED 393 087 | Reading, English, and Communication |
| 22 New Generation of Evidence: The Family is Critical to Student Achievement | ED 375 968 | Elementary and Early Childhood Education |
| 23 Effects of the Computerized Accelerated Reader Program on Reading Achievement | ED 363 269 | Information and Technology |
| 24 At-Risk Families & Schools: Becoming Partners | ED 342 055 | Elementary and Early Childhood Education |
| 25 Differences Between the Professional Attitudes of Full- and Part-time Faculty | ED 417 783 | Community Colleges |

# ERIC Web Sites

## ERIC Program Office

Educational Resources Information Center (ERIC)
http://www.ed.gov

## ERIC Support Contractors

ACCESS ERIC (*general information about the ERIC system and links to all other ERIC Web sites*)
http://www.accesseric.org:81

ERIC Document Reproduction Service (EDRS)
http://edrs.com

ERIC Processing & Reference Facility
http://ericfac.piccard.csc.com

Oryx Press (publisher of *Current Index to Journals in Education*)
http://www.oryxpress.com/cije

## ERIC Clearinghouses

ERIC Clearinghouse on Adult, Career, and Vocational Education
http://ericacve.org

ERIC Clearinghouse on Assessment and Evaluation
http://ericae.net

ERIC Clearinghouse for Community Colleges
http://www.gseis.ucla.edu/eric

ERIC Clearinghouse on Counseling and Student Services
http://www.uncg.edu/edu/ericass/

ERIC Clearinghouse on Disabilities and Gifted Education
http://www.cec.sped.org/ericec

ERIC Clearinghouse on Educational Management
http://eric.uoregon.edu

ERIC Clearinghouse on Elementary and Early Childhood Education
http://ericeece.org/

(NPIN [National Parent Information network]
http://npin.org/)

ERIC Clearinghouse on Higher Education
http://www.gwu.edu/~eriche/

ERIC Clearinghouse on Information & Technology
http://ericir.syr.edu/ithome

AskERIC
http://www.askeric.org

ERIC Clearinghouse on Languages and Linguistics
http://www.cal.org/ericll

ERIC Clearinghouse on Reading, English, and Communication
http://www.indiana.edu:80/~eric_rec

ERIC Clearinghouse on Rural Education and Small Schools
http://www.ael.org/eric/

ERIC Clearinghouse for Science, Mathematics, and Environmental Education
http://www.ericse.org

ERIC Clearinghouse for Social Studies/Social Science Education
http://www.indiana.edu/~ssdc/eric_chess

ERIC Clearinghouse on Teaching and Teacher Education
http://www.ericsp.org

ERIC Clearinghouse on Urban Education
http://eric-web.tc.columbia.edu

**Adjunct ERIC Clearinghouses**

Adjunct ERIC Clearinghouse for Child Care
http://niccic.org/

Adjunct ERIC Clearinghouse on Clinical Schools
http://www.aacte.org/menu2

Adjunct ERIC Clearinghouse for Consumer Education
http://www.emich.edu/public/coe/nice

Adjunct ERIC Clearinghouse on Entrepreneurship Education
http://www.celcee.edu

Adjunct ERIC Clearinghouse for International Civic Education
[None]

Adjunct ERIC Clearinghouse for United States-Japan Studies
http://www.indiana.edu/~japan

Adjunct ERIC Clearinghouse for ESL Literacy Education
http://www.cal.org/ncle

Adjunct ERIC Clearinghouse for Law-Related Education
http://www.indiana.edu/~ssdc/lre

Adjunct ERIC Clearinghouse on School Counseling Services
[None]

Adjunct ERIC Clearinghouse for Service-Learning
http://www.nicsl.coled.umn.edu

Adjunct ERIC Clearinghouse for the Test Collection
http://ericae.net/testcol

**Affiliates**

National Clearinghouse for Educational Facilities
http://www.edfacilities.org

National TRIO Clearinghouse (NTC)
http://www.trioprograms.org

# United States Government Printing Office

North Capitol and H Streets N.W., Washington, DC 20401
202-512-1991
E-mail: asherman@gpo.gov
World Wide Web: http://www.access.gpo.gov

Andrew M. Sherman
Director, Office of Congressional, Legislative, and Public Affairs

The Government Printing Office (GPO) produces or procures printed and electronic products for Congress and the agencies of the federal government and disseminates printed and electronic government information to the public through the Superintendent of Documents' sales and depository library programs. GPO also hosts a major government Web site, GPO Access, which provides free public access to major government information databases. GPO Access is located at http://www.access.gpo.gov.

GPO's central office facility is located in Washington, D.C. Nationwide, GPO maintains 14 regional printing procurement offices, six satellite procurement facilities, one field printing office, a major distribution facility in Pueblo, Colorado, 23 bookstores, and a retail sales outlet at its publications warehouse in Laurel, Maryland.

This report focuses on GPO's role as the disseminator of government information in print and electronic formats.

## Superintendent of Documents

GPO's documents programs, overseen by the Superintendent of Documents, disseminate one of the world's largest volumes of informational literature, distributing more than 65 million government publications every year in print, microform, and electronic formats.

## Library Programs

Most products produced by or through GPO are available to the American public for reference through 1,365 depository libraries located in the United States and its possessions. Depository libraries are public, academic, or other types of libraries designated by members of Congress or by law as official depositories. The Library Programs Service (LPS) administers the Federal Depository Library Program (FDLP) under the Superintendent of Documents. The mission of the FDLP is to provide equitable, efficient, timely, and dependable no-fee public access to print, microfiche, and electronic government information products within the scope of the program.

In fiscal year (FY) 1998 LPS distributed 14.4 million copies of 39,000 titles in tangible formats to depository libraries.

LPS monitors the condition of depository libraries through periodic inspection visits, self-studies, and a biennial survey. LPS also organizes continuing-education efforts for documents librarians. In 1998 the annual Federal Depository

Conference, held in the Washington, D.C., area, attracted more than 500 participants. The popular Interagency Depository Seminar, held each spring, familiarizes new depository library staff with major federal information products and services. LPS highlights for FY 1998 include

- Refining the "FDLP Electronic Collection" concept
- Developing "askLPS," an e-mail response system
- Increased distribution of tangible products, especially microfiche
- Increased cataloging output
- DOE Information Bridge partnership
- Using PURLs (persistent uniform resource locators) to improve access to Internet resources
- Continued outreach activities
- New Web applications developed by LPS staff

Many of the day-to-day administrative functions of the FDLP are handled via the FDLP Administration Web site at http://www.access.gpo.gov/su_docs/dpos/fdlppro.html. Depository libraries use this site to update their library profiles, view and download their library item selection profiles, make new selections and drop unneeded items online, and respond to the Biennial Survey of Depository Libraries. A new feature, askLPS, an e-mail response system for depository library inquiries, was instituted in 1998, and an automated claims system is planned.

Depository libraries assist users in locating government information in tangible formats, such as paper, microfiche, CD-ROM, and floppy diskettes, as well as information that is also available online and in some paid subscription services. The FDLP has made arrangements for public users to access STAT-USA, CenStats, National Climatic Data Center, and the Environmental Health Information Service at no charge to the user or the library. LPS continues to look for additional cooperative opportunities to expand the public's access to federal agency online services.

**Transition to Electronic Offerings**

During FY 1998 LPS made significant progress in its efforts to incorporate electronic government information products into the FDLP. These efforts reflect the development of a more electronic FDLP.

LPS staff continued to develop a policy defining GPO's management of the various electronic government information products made available through the FDLP as a library-like collection. The policy is documented in a paper titled "Managing the FDLP Electronic Collection: A Policy and Planning Document." This plan provides a foundation for policies and procedures and defines organizational responsibilities for managing the collection, the relationship between the collection and cataloging and locator services, and the responsibilities for current and permanent public access to information provided through the FDLP. LPS has published the plan on GPO Access at http://www.access.gpo.gov/su_docs/dpos/ecplan.html.

The FDLP Electronic Collection, which already includes more than 130,000 electronic titles, consists of several parts:

- FDLP Electronic Collection on the Web: These pages provide links to full-text resources from GPO, FDLP partner sites, and other federal government agencies. A collection of finding tools assists users in locating tangible electronic products in depository libraries, as well as products on other agency sites that GPO identifies, links to, and describes.
- DOE Information Bridge: An interagency agreement between GPO and the Department of Energy/Office of Scientific and Technical Information (DOE/OSTI) provides depository libraries and the public with electronic access to more than 26,000 reports that have been produced by DOE/OSTI since January 1996. OSTI staff introduced the depository library version of its electronic dissemination system, Information Bridge, during the April 1998 Federal Depository Conference. Since that time more than 5,000 documents have been added to the system. During its first month of operation to the depository community, Information Bridge was a "Pick of the Week" from Yahoo!, the Web navigation and indexing site. In September the Information Bridge Project Team at OSTI was selected to receive an FY 1998 DOE Information Management Quality Award for Technical Excellence. This award is designed to recognize those individuals, organizations, teams, and/or groups that have made significant quality contributions to DOE's Information Management Program.
- NTIS Pilot Project: GPO and the National Technical Information Service (NTIS) of the Department of Commerce have entered into an interagency agreement that will enable depositories to have free online access to scientific and technical documents that are currently available in electronic format from the NTIS collection. The University of California at Davis and the University of Nevada at Reno have participated in a pre-pilot test. Twenty additional libraries will take part in the pilot project in 1999.
- Electronic Content in the FDLP: Identifying and reviewing products available from government Internet sites has expanded traditional acquisitions duties. By September 1998 the Browse Electronic Titles page had more than 2,200 electronic product titles listed on the page. Weekly updates, performed each Monday, add an average of more than 30 titles a week to the Browse Electronic Titles page.

**Electronic Transition Staff**

A number of electronic collection projects involve the LPS Electronic Transition Staff (ETS), which concentrates on the issue of permanent public access for electronic government information. ETS works on creating partnerships between depository libraries, federal agencies, information-related organizations, and GPO and was instrumental in the development of the management plan for the FDLP Electronic Collection. Staff review and define LPS's responsibilities regarding Government Information Locator Service (GILS) records and are investigating all the locator services and examining how they fit with one another and the FDLP Electronic Collection Management Plan.

**LPS Web Applications**

The LPS Virtual Tour went "live" in April 1998, linked from the FDLP Administration page. The virtual tour, in words and photos, follows the order in which tangible government information products are processed in preparation for dissemination to depository libraries.

The Documents Data Miner (DDM) is a collection management tool for depository libraries. A partnership of Wichita State University, the National Institute for Aviation Research, and the FDLP, the DDM gives depository librarians, FDLP staff, and other users electronic access to various FDLP administrative information that has previously been available on a limited basis. Files from the Federal Bulletin Board downloaded into the DDM's search engine include the List of Classes of United States Government Publications, Current Item Number Selection Profiles for Depository Libraries, the Federal Depository Library Directory, and the List of Inactive or Discontinued Items.

**Cataloging and Locator Services**

LPS's mission in providing cataloging and locator services is to identify, describe, locate, and provide access to government publications and to electronic works available at agency Web sites and archives.

In FY 1998 the Cataloging Branch cataloged 29,000 pieces, including electronic works, processing most of them within two weeks of receipt or notification.

*Monthly Catalog of United States Government Publications*: GPO's cataloging records are publicly available through various media: print, CD-ROM, and online. The *Monthly Catalog of United States Government Publications* has listed more than two million bibliographic records for government information products from 1895 to the present.

The current catalog, with abbreviated records, is available on a subscription basis for $37 a year. The CD-ROM edition cumulates complete records monthly for $245 a year. More than 112,000 full cataloging records are also available online at http://www.access.gpo.gov/catalog. Each of these Web site records is linked with the names and locations of depository libraries that have selected that title, enabling users to identify the nearest depository library where that title is held. Each record also contains shelf location data for the many libraries with collections arranged according to Superintendent of Documents class numbers. Approximately 4,000 records contain links to the actual electronic texts. Records for electronic titles, including records for government agency Web sites, may be found on GPO's Web site through various locator tools. The full cataloging records are also available online through the more than 30,000 libraries worldwide that are members of the OCLC (Online Computer Library Center) network. Records are also made available to commercial vendors.

*Persistent Uniform Resource Locator*: GPO uses OCLC's freely available persistent uniform resource locator (PURL) software in cataloging electronic resources. A PURL provides a mechanism to forestall a broken uniform resource locator (URL) by providing a seamless, automatic interface to the most recent URL. The newly developed software contains features that are essential for large-scale use of PURLs, such as an integrated URL checker application, which generates a report that identifies broken links.

The PURL application is significant to the many library online catalogs that contain URLs. In this new environment, libraries with record update services will not need to update records locally when URLs change.

*Pathway Services*, which assist users in locating government information products on the Internet, continued to expand during 1998. This effort will continue until the federally funded Advanced Search Facility (ASF) is available. The ASF will create an information community architecture based in part on GILS as well as on other, related technologies.

Currently, the Pathway Indexer indexes at any given time between 150,000 and 200,000 Web pages from more than 1,600 servers. New sites are added daily.

The initial collection of sites for more than 170 topics in the subject bibliography-based Browse Topics is almost complete. Volunteers from the depository and information communities maintain more than 75 topics, with links created from topics to relevant subject bibliographies. It is the goal of the staff responsible for this site to update the topics on at least a quarterly basis.

## GPO Access

GPO Access is an online service that provides free public access to electronic government information products. GPO Access was established to provide the public with electronic access to official federal information and to assist and encourage federal agencies to make their information available electronically. The information retrieved from GPO Access may be used without restriction unless specifically noted. This service was established by the Government Printing Office Electronic Information Access Enhancement Act of 1993 (P.L. 130-40). GPO Access can be reached through GPO's home page or directly at http://www.access.gpo.gov/su_docs.

GPO Access is one of the few government information systems established by statute and the only service that provides access to information from all three branches of the federal government. GPO Access allows persons all over the world to electronically access government products and has become an invaluable resource for the public. There are more than 85,000 titles available on GPO Access servers, while GPO Access links to more than 45,000 additional titles on other official federal Web sites.

### Improvements to GPO Access Web Pages

The Superintendent of Documents GPO Access home page (http://www.access.gpo.gov/su_docs) was redesigned in 1998 to provide easier and more efficient access to GPO's online resources. This page provides access through a graphical image map, as well as a text-only interface that complies with requirements of the Americans with Disabilities Act. There is also a new "About the Superintendent of Documents" link that provides information about services available to the public through GPO's Superintendent of Documents programs.

GPO Access Web pages are designed to be intuitive to users, with easy-to-follow paths for locating and retrieving government information products. From the new home page, users follow hot links to several secondary pages; these pages allow them to access products and services quickly and conveniently through jumps to databases, locator tools, publications, and other applications. Improvements are constantly being made to the site in response to feedback GPO receives from focus group sessions, user surveys, and comments provided to the GPO Access User Support Team on a daily basis.

The free services of GPO Access fall within the following categories:

- Government information databases available for online use that provide full-text search and retrieval capabilities include regulatory materials, such as the Federal Register and Code of Federal Regulations; congressional products such as the Congressional Record and congressional bills; and business materials such as the Commerce Business Daily (CBDNet)
- Individual federal agency files available for downloading from the Federal Bulletin Board
- Tools that assist users in finding government information available either for sale or free, by keyword searching or browsing titles and topics that link to government information
- Guides to collections of federal government information available for free use at a nearby federal depository library
- User support

### Government Information Databases

GPO Access currently provides access to nearly 1,000 databases comprising more than 70 applications. Several enhancements were made to GPO Access databases in 1998.

In addition to keyword search capability, the Federal Register databases have a new point-and-click interface that allows users to browse the table of contents of the current issue in HTML or Adobe Acrobat's portable document format (PDF). Users can also browse tables of contents of 1998 back issues of the *Federal Register*.

The Code of Federal Regulations (CFR) database includes a List of Sections Affected application. This application is designed to lead users of the CFR to amendatory actions published in the *Federal Register*. Also, a new browse feature has been added for CFR titles. Users can search or browse a single CFR title for a given year or one or more CFR titles using checkboxes on the Internet.

For congressional information, a new feature enables users to retrieve a *Congressional Record* page in PDF format. Also, a limited number of House and Senate hearings are now available via GPO Access. A user has the option of searching for either House or Senate hearings or both simultaneously. An option was also added to include FY 1998 House and Senate appropriation hearings in search results.

GPO Access also met the demand for information following the release of the large volume of independent counsel's materials associated with the investigation of President Clinton. The electronic availability of these materials to the public at no cost significantly increased traffic on GPO Access for retrievals of these documents and other federal information products.

The majority of the databases available via GPO Access offer results in ASCII text and PDF formats; and in many cases, specialized search pages are available for databases that contain fields, multiple years, or some feature that makes the database unique to search. These specialized search pages allow users to build very specific searches that result in more-precise lists of search results. And the addition of browse options in several databases gives users the ability to download documents without performing a search.

### Federal Bulletin Board

Individual federal agency files are available from the Federal Bulletin Board (FBB), a free electronic bulletin board service maintained by GPO. The FBB enables federal agencies to provide immediate self-service public access to federal information in electronic form in a variety of file formats. The FBB has approximately 4,500 files with more than 15,000 distinct titles of electronic products; these products represent more than 20 federal agencies and organizations from all three branches of the government. Included in these files was the addition of the compressed text files of the Sales Products Catalog and the Monthly Catalog in USMARC format. The former is updated daily, while the latter is updated monthly. The FBB can be accessed through a link from GPO Access or directly at fedbbs.access.gpo.gov.

### Locator Tools and Access to Collections of Government Information

GPO Access provides a number of useful tools for locating government information products available not only on GPO Access but also on other agency Internet sites. These include the following:

- Monthly *Catalog of U.S. Government Publications*
- *Sales Product Catalog*, which provides information on product availability and how to purchase government products through GPO
- Government Information Locator Service (GILS)
- A variety of other tools that allow users to find government information by title, topic, or keyword search

Additionally, there are 14 federal Web sites that are now hosted by GPO Access. Web sites for the National Council on Disability, National Gambling Impact Study Commission, and the Occupational Safety and Health Review Commission were added in 1998.

GPO Access also assists users in finding collections of government information available at federal depository libraries. GPO Access search applications help users find a local depository library in their area that can provide them with tangible government information products.

### Methods of Access

GPO recognizes the various needs and technological capabilities of the public. A wide range of information dissemination technologies are supported by GPO Access, from the latest Internet client/server applications to dial-up modem access. Methods compatible with technologies to assist users affected by the

Americans with Disabilities Act are also available. People without computers can use GPO Access through public-access terminals located at federal depository libraries throughout the country. All depositories are expected to offer users access to workstations with a graphical user interface, CD-ROM capability, an Internet connection, and the ability to access government information via the World Wide Web.

**GPO Access Usage Statistics**

GPO Access is currently averaging close to 5 million searches and more than 15 million retrievals per month. Between October 1997 and September 1998, searches on GPO Access increased 21 percent while retrievals increased by 85 percent. The average trend during this time shows an increase of 108,855 searches and 723,508 retrievals per month. Whereas a search consists of a user accessing a Web page, the retrieval count consists of the actual download of information from GPO Access, which is considered a more accurate count of GPO Access usage.

The Code of Federal Regulations, Federal Register, Commerce Business Daily, and United States Code are the databases with the highest retrievals. Since December 1995 (when GPO Access was made available free to all users), the search rate on GPO Access has increased at an average of 139,669 downloads per month, while the retrieval rate has increased at an average of 413,732 downloads per month.

**GPO Access Training and Demonstrations**

GPO conducted 25 GPO Access training classes and demonstrations throughout the United States in 1998. GPO also exhibited at a number of conferences to share information about GPO Access with many individuals. An updated version of the GPO Access training booklet that is used in training classes was developed and made available both electronically and in print to GPO Access users in 1998. In addition, GPO offered "Train the Trainer" sessions, which extend opportunities to learn more about GPO Access to a wider audience.

**Recognition**

In 1998 GPO Access continued to earn recognition for outstanding service, adding to the commendations it had already received in the previous year from the Dow Jones Business Directory and the National Performance Review, among other organizations. GPO Access was selected as one of the "Best Feds on the Web" by *Government Executive* magazine, one of only 15 federal Web sites to be selected for this award and the only one selected from the legislative branch.

GPO Access was also designated as a "Site of the Week" by the Web site usbudget.com for its presentation of policy issues and detail relating to budget and appropriations. In August 1998 GPO Access was featured in the Scout Report, a weekly collection of useful Internet documents, for the second time; on this occasion, it was cited for its enhancement of the browse feature for the online Code of Federal Regulations.

### User Support

The GPO Access User Support Team averages 7,000 pieces of correspondence—phone calls, e-mails, and faxes—per month. The team has expanded its hours, providing support from 7:00 A.M. to 5:30 P.M. (Eastern Time), Monday through Friday, except federal holidays.

Questions or comments regarding the GPO Access service can be directed to the GPO Access User Support Team by e-mail at gpoaccess@gpo.gov; by toll-free telephone at 888-293-6498; by phone in the Washington, D.C., area at 202-512-1530; or by fax at 202-512-1262.

## Sales

The Superintendent of Documents' Sales Program currently offers for sale approximately 10,000 government publications on a wide array of subjects. These are sold principally by mail order and through GPO bookstores across the country. The program operates on a cost recovery basis, without the use of tax dollars.

Publications for sale include books, forms, posters, pamphlets, and maps. Subscription services for both dated periodicals and basic-and-supplement services (involving an initial volume and supplemental issues) are also offered. A growing selection of electronic information products—including CD-ROMs, computer diskettes, and magnetic tapes—are now available in the Sales Program.

U.S. Fax Watch offers customers in the United States and Canada free access to information on a variety of sales products, electronic products and services, and depository library locations. To use the service, customers call in from a touch-tone telephone, follow voice prompts to select the document they want, and then have the requested information faxed back to them in minutes. U.S. Fax Watch is available 24 hours a day, seven days a week, at 202-512-1716.

Express service, which includes priority handling and Federal Express delivery, is available for orders placed by telephone for domestic delivery. Orders placed before noon Eastern Time for in-stock publications and single-copy subscriptions will be delivered within two working days. Some quantity restrictions apply. Call the telephone order desk at 202-512-1800 for more information.

Consumer-oriented publications are also either sold or distributed at no charge through the Consumer Information Center in Pueblo, Colorado, which GPO operates on behalf of the General Services Administration.

### Sales Operations Modernized

After an extended period of modification, testing, debugging, and training, GPO's Sales Program expects to have its state-of-the-art, customer-oriented business system in place midway through 1999. The Integrated Processing System (IPS) is a computer system that will replace 18 legacy mainframe systems that were developed over the last 20 years to perform a variety of functions. IPS will integrate all these functions using one database.

IPS is being brought in to modernize Documents Sales and to improve customer service. The goal is to process all orders, inquiries, and complaints within

24 hours of receipt in the Customer Service Center. Sales hopes to accomplish this with the following:

- One central database: All transactions go into one database, eliminating duplication and giving faster order processing and real-time access to all customer, inventory, warehouse, and financial information. This will streamline the order processing and order tracking capabilities. Scanning and imaging technology will speed work from desk to desk, eliminating the paper trail.
- State-of-the-art warehouse management technology: The IPS system will automatically assign put-away locations and even prioritize the picking locations to maximize warehouse efficiency and space utilization. In addition, hand-held radio frequency bar code scanners will be used to pick the stock, further reducing paperwork and order-processing times.

IPS will bring significant improvements to GPO's Sales Program. Soon after implementation, evaluations will begin on the feasibility of extending IPS to LPS systems and other GPO systems.

**Publications of Historical Significance**

During FY 1998 the Sales Program began identifying sales titles of historical significance for the purpose of retaining them in inventory indefinitely. This ongoing process of identification will be performed with the advice of a committee of depository librarians. The goal of this effort is to ensure long-term public access to Sales Program titles of lasting historical value.

# GPO Bookstores

Publications of particular public interest are made available in GPO bookstores. In addition, to meet the information needs of all customers, any bookstore can order any government information product currently offered for sale and have it sent directly to the customer. Customers can order by phone, mail, or fax from any GPO bookstore.

GPO bookstores are located in major cities throughout the United States. Their addresses, hours, and a map are available on the GPO Web site.

# Catalogs

GPO publishes a variety of free catalogs covering hundreds of information products on a vast array of subjects. The free catalogs include

- *U.S. Government Information*: new and popular information products of interest to the general public
- *New Information*: bi-monthly listing of new titles; distributed to librarians and other information professionals

- *U.S. Government Subscriptions*: periodicals and other subscription services
- *Subject Bibliographies* (*SBs*)*: nearly 200 lists, each containing titles relating to a single subject or field of interest
- *Subject Bibliography Index*: lists all SB subject areas
- *Catalog of Information Products for Business*: GPO's largest catalog for business audiences

*U.S. Government Subscriptions* and *Subject Bibliographies* are also available from U.S. Fax Watch at 202-512-1716 and via the Web at http://www.access.gpo.gov/su_docs.

### Sales Product Catalog

The Superintendent of Documents issues the GPO *Sales Product Catalog* (*SPC*), a guide to current government information products offered for sale through the Superintendent of Documents. The fully searchable SPC database, which is updated every working day, is available online via GPO's Web site.

The SPC is also available online through DIALOG (File Code 166). DIALOG service offers online ordering, retrieval, and research capabilities.

# National Commission on Libraries and Information Science

1110 Vermont Ave. N.W., Suite 820, Washington, DC 20005-3522
202-606-9200, fax 202-606-9203
World Wide Web: http://www.nclis.gov

Robert S. Willard
Executive Director

## Highlights of the Year

On May 21, 1998, Jeanne Hurley Simon, chairperson of the National Commission on Libraries and Information Science (NCLIS), was confirmed for a second term on the commission, ending on July 19, 2002, and reappointed as chair. Commissioner Martha Gould was also appointed to a second term, ending in 2002, and continues as vice-chair. Rebecca Bingham, a retired school library administrator from Louisville, Kentucky, was appointed to the commission with a term ending in 2001; she succeeds Carol DiPrete.

Continuing commissioners are Abe Abramson, Walter Anderson, LeVar Burton, Joan Challinor, Mary Furlong, José-Marie Griffiths, Frank Lucchino, Bobby Roberts, and Joel Valdez. (The terms of Commissioners Lucchino, Roberts, and Valdez expired on July 19, 1998, but they may continue in office one year unless a successor is named earlier.) Winston Tabb continues to represent James H. Billington, the Librarian of Congress, a permanent NCLIS member. Diane Frankel, director of the Institute of Museum and Library Services, is an ex officio commissioner.

In February 1998 Acting Executive Director Jane Williams resigned from the commission staff to take a position at the University of Maryland Libraries. Commissioner Robert S. Willard assumed the role of acting executive director, and shortly thereafter was appointed executive director by the commission and resigned his commission seat. His resignation leaves a vacancy on the commission, as does the death in 1997 of Commissioner Gary Sudduth.

Long-time staff member Mary Alice Hedge retired from her position as associate executive director. Judy Russell, whose library career included a time as director of the Federal Depository Library Program, joined the NCLIS staff as deputy director.

Commissioner Roberts, director of the Central Arkansas Library System, was chosen "1997 Librarian of the Year" by the editors of *Library Journal*.

The commission adopted a strategic plan in early 1998. Under this plan, it pursued a number of ambitious projects throughout the year: a study for the Government Printing Office on electronic government information, cosponsorship with the American Library Association (ALA) of a fourth survey of public libraries and the Internet, a major hearing on "Kids and the Internet," and initial preparation for involvement in the White House Millennium Project. NCLIS also continued its role of advising on the Library Services and Technology Act (LSTA).

The NCLIS budget for fiscal year (FY) 1998 was $1,000,000, up from $897,000 for FY 1997 and the largest budget ever for NCLIS. The budget for FY 1999, which began October 1, 1998, remained at $1 million. The commission met in January, April, June, September, October, and December.

## Support for Executive and Legislative Branches

In FY 1998 the major contacts with the legislative branch concerned the proposed revision of 44 U.S.C. (S. 2288), the Wendell H. Ford Government Publications Reform Act of 1998. The commission supported S. 2288 which, in the commission's opinion, reinforced the importance of permanent public access to federal government information and provided means to improve public access to government information.

A major area of interest to the commission continues to be intellectual property, with bills to implement the 1996 treaties of the World Intellectual Property Organization (WIPO) and amend the Copyright Act to protect electronic information and databases. Although the commission did not take a formal position on any of the bills, it did support U.S. participation in the WIPO treaty.

The commission also provided information related to proposals for federally mandated use of filtering software for schools and libraries that offer children access to the Internet and receive federal funds. The commission was able to offer data from its 1998 National Survey of Public Library Outlet Internet Connectivity, sponsored by the commission and ALA. This survey contained questions about the use of Internet-content filtering software to block pornography and also about the availability of an "acceptable-use public-access Internet policy."

The commission's foremost involvement with the executive branch arose from carrying out its mission under Section 703 of Public Law 104-208, the Library Services and Technology Act. As a result of this new legislation (enacted in September 1996), NCLIS advises the Institute of Museum and Library Services (IMLS) on federal grant programs to libraries. The commission participated with the National Museum Services Board (NMSB) in drafting the guidelines by which applicants seek leadership grants from the federal government for libraries and library-museum collaborations. Commissioner Challinor also participated as an observer in the peer review of grant proposals submitted to IMLS.

NCLIS established a committee on the National Award for Library Services, a new award established by IMLS to complement awards currently made in the museum community. The committee held its first meeting in September 1998, and the initial award will be made in 2000.

NCLIS continues to work closely with officials in a variety of federal agencies to obtain information and provide timely input on national and international policies affecting library and information services. During FY 1998 commissioners and staff met with officials from the U.S. Departments of Education, Labor, Commerce, and State, as well as the Federal Communications Commission (FCC), Government Printing Office (GPO), Library of Congress (LC), National Agricultural Library, National Institute for Literacy, Office of Information and Regulatory Affairs at the Office of Management and Budget, and White House Millennium Council, among others.

## National Information Activities

On April 7–8, 1998, the commission met with the Big Twelve Plus Library Consortium at the Linda Hall Library in Kansas City, Missouri, to discuss challenges facing the nation's academic and research universities and their libraries. Commissioners were told that the cost of scholarly journals increased 148 percent from 1986 to 1996—more than three times the rate of inflation.

Recognizing the need for action at the national level, the commission established the Working Group on Issues of Journal Pricing, Publishing, and Copyright to address, as its first priority, the rapidly increasing cost of scholarly research material. The working group, chaired by Commissioner Griffiths, plans four objectives: (1) identify available and ongoing research related to the issues; (2) conduct a series of discussions in individual meetings with various stakeholder groups: publishers, authors, universities, and the library community; (3) bring the stakeholder groups together to discuss their relative positions, issues, and concerns, creating a forum for constructive dialog on those issues and concerns; and (4) produce a report with recommendations that would be widely disseminated. As part of its efforts, the working group presented a well-attended session on the topic at the annual meeting of the American Society for Information Science in October 1998.

## Library and Information Services in a Networked Environment

In June 1998 the commission launched the Assessment of Standards for the Creation, Dissemination, and Permanent Accessibility of Electronic Government Information Products. The study is a direct outgrowth of congressional concerns about the impact of electronic publishing on the ability of citizens to obtain access to government information. To assist in the data collection and analysis, a contract was awarded to Westat, Inc., a Rockville, Maryland, firm specializing in survey research.

This unprecedented study is based on a survey of 24 federal agencies in all three branches of government, sampling several hundred information products. The assessment will (1) identify medium and format standards that are the most appropriate for permanent public access, (2) assess the cost effectiveness and usefulness of various alternative medium and format standards, and (3) identify public and private medium and format standards that are, or could be, used for products throughout their entire information life cycle, not just at the dissemination for permanent public-access stage.

Data collection was to be completed by January 1999, and the contractor was to complete an analysis of the data and produce a final report that in the spring of 1999. Once the results are available, the commission will be considering the appropriate follow-on activities.

On July 16, 1998, NCLIS Chair Simon spoke at a forum on "The Internet: Empowering Older Americans," sponsored by the Senate Special Committee on Aging. Simon highlighted the positive roles of the Internet and public libraries in the lives of older Americans. During her testimony, she cited numerous examples of how the Internet empowers older Americans and how American public libraries continue to meet the challenge of helping seniors and others navigate the

Internet effectively. Commissioner Furlong served as the forum moderator and provided an overview of how older Americans use the Internet.

During 1998 the commission undertook two major initiatives in the area of library and information services to children and youth, issuing a resolution on the importance of libraries in the lives of American children and conducting a hearing on "Kids and the Internet: The Promise and the Perils."

In the resolution issued on September 8, 1998, the commission advised officials and educators at all levels, as well as community leaders, parents and other adult caregivers, confidants and role models, to utilize the vast potential of libraries in assisting youth and children to seek positive outcomes through wise use of information. The resolution emphasized that libraries can serve as a major delivery point for information on better parenting, for positive learning experiences for young children, and for redirecting troubled older children and adolescents. Senator Christopher J. Dodd (D-Conn.) commended the commission for its efforts to "lead the way" and "to mobilize resources for the purpose of curbing youth violence in this nation" and inserted the full text of the commission's resolution in the *Congressional Record*.

For some time the commission has been discussing the problems arising from public-access Internet terminals in libraries and the potential for the use of such terminals for predation by pedophiles. The commission has also expressed concerns for children and youth regarding Internet access to inappropriate materials, generally sexually explicit matter but also hate language, cult messages, and other troublesome material. Furthermore, the commission has worried about violations of privacy, especially in the case of marketing efforts that entice children to provide a wide variety of consumer information about themselves and their families. The commission recognizes that all these concerns must be balanced against the freedom of speech guaranteed by the First Amendment and the library community's aversion to censorship.

The commission held a hearing in November 1998 in order to focus attention on the enormous benefits of the Internet as well as the dangers it poses for children and to seek advice on appropriate means for libraries to protect children without denying them access to the benefits of the Internet. Testimony was received from federal and state government agencies as well as from concerned citizens, parents, public librarians, teachers, and other interested individuals and organizations.

At its subsequent December meeting, the commission reviewed the testimony. It acknowledged that individual library policies on Internet use are appropriately local issues and passed a resolution urging governing boards to put in place such Internet use policies. It also directed the staff to produce a document based on the hearing that would help libraries and their boards address the issues. A summary brochure was published in early 1999, and a full report of the hearing will be published later in the year.

## Library Statistics

In the area of library statistics, the commission continued its long partnership with the National Center for Education Statistics (NCES) while also maintaining its role in the independent statistics collection activity regarding Internet and public libraries.

Fiscal Year 1998 marked the 11th consecutive year of cooperation between the commission and NCES in implementing the Library Statistics Program (LSP). The commission serves as a liaison to the library community, organizes meetings and training workshops, supports in-state training and technical assistance, monitors trends, and advises NCES on policy matters.

The major LSP events in FY 1998 included the following: an annual training workshop and orientation for new state data coordinators, March 1998; an Integrated Postsecondary Education Data System (IPEDS) workshop, September 1998; State Library Agency Survey Steering Committee meetings, February and September 1998; a Steering Committee for Federal-State Cooperative System for public library statistics and its subcommittees, June and September 1998; and a Survey of Library Cooperatives Advisory Committee meeting, September 1998.

Earlier, in 1997, the commission initiated an assessment and planning project for the LSP that resulted in a report submitted by consultant Howard Harris: "Assessment of and Planning for NCLIS Role in Library Statistics Cooperative Program" (LSCP). The commission hosted a meeting in September 1998 to respond to the report; attendees included a variety of individuals knowledgeable about library statistics from five types of libraries surveyed by NCES: state libraries, public libraries, school libraries, academic libraries, and library cooperatives. This meeting reaffirmed the interest in the annual collection of statistics for academic libraries and called attention to the need for the more frequent and timely collection of school library and media center data, which is currently collected only once every five years.

The 1998 Helen M. Eckard Award for Exemplary Use of Federal-State Cooperative System (FSCS) Data was presented to Professor John C. Bertot, then at the University of Maryland, Baltimore County. Dr. Bertot received the FSCS data use award in recognition of his major contributions to research on public libraries, the Internet, and discounted telecommunications rates. The 1997 Keppel Award was given to 42 states and one territory, acknowledging their submission of prompt, complete, and high-quality public library data to the survey.

The first John G. Lorenz Awards were presented at the annual Chief Officers of State Library Agencies (COSLA) meeting in October 1998. This special award is named in honor of John G. Lorenz, who was coordinator of the NCLIS Library Statistics Program from 1988 to 1997. The award was presented to 24 qualifying COSLA and State Library Agency (StLA) respondents and staff for their timely and accurate submission of StLA survey data.

The fourth NCLIS study of public libraries and the Internet was conducted between April and June 1998. The 1998 National Survey of Public Library Outlet Internet Connectivity was cosponsored by NCLIS and ALA, with research conducted by John Carlo Bertot and Charles R. McClure. The survey results indicate that 83.6 percent of U.S. public library outlets (main or branch libraries, excluding bookmobiles) are now connected to the Internet and 73.3 percent of public libraries offer public Internet access. However, public Internet access is substantially lower for libraries in rural areas (67.6 percent) than for those in urban areas (84.0 percent).

Moreover, the survey results indicate that only 68.6 percent of public library outlets offer graphical public Internet access to the World Wide Web. Only 45.6 percent of the public libraries offer high-speed public Internet access (56 kbps or greater) on one or more workstations with a graphical user interface, the minimum configuration currently necessary for effective public Internet access in the view of the commission.

The 1998 survey also provided the basis for additional insights into the numbers of Internet workstations in public libraries: 31.4 percent of all library outlets do not have any graphical public access to the Internet, and at an additional 28.3 percent of library outlets only a single graphical Internet workstation is available for public access.

The commission recognizes that the advent of the discount rate for telecommunications services authorized by the Telecommunications Act of 1996, popularly known as the E-rate, and the importance of the Internet as a national resource ensure that questions about effective public Internet access will continue to be debated for the foreseeable future. The commission intends to continue to work with the wide variety of organizations, both public and private, that have a stake in defining and implementing effective public Internet access. The commission also plans to continue its support for the annual National Survey of Public Libraries and the Internet in order to track the evolving state of public Internet access and the implementation of the goals of universal service for public library Internet access.

## International Activities

The commission completed its 13th year of cooperation with the Department of State to coordinate and monitor proposals for International Contributions for Scientific, Educational and Cultural Activities (ICSECA) funds and to disburse the funds. The allocation for ICSECA, included in the State Department's International Organizations and Programs account, was formerly under International Conventions and Scientific Organizations Contributions (ICSOC). The amount for FY 1998 was $100,000, the same as in FY 1997 and up from $35,000 for FY 1996.

NCLIS was represented at the 1998 general conference of the International Federation of Library Associations and Institutions (IFLA) in Amsterdam. The commission will be an International Distinguished Partner for the 2001 IFLA conference in Boston. The commission also received approval from the Office of Management and Budget for a survey of U.S. participation in international library and archive activities and will use this baseline inventory to assess and develop its international role.

The commission has chosen an international effort as its contribution to the White House Millennium Project. NCLIS is sponsoring a Sister Libraries project, pairing American libraries with libraries in other parts of the world to encourage an exchange of professional and cultural information. Although it will begin as a millennium project, the Sister Libraries initiative is expected to continue well into the 21st century. The Internet and World Wide Web make it possible, as never before, for libraries in our country to communicate with each other and with libraries around the world. The commission is particularly interested in using this initiative as an opportunity for children to communicate with other children, both nationally and internationally, and through that contact learn from one another about their similarities and differences. The project will also introduce children to languages and cultures other than their own.

The commission continued to host or lead sessions to orient and share information with librarians and other officials visiting the United States, usually under the auspices of the U.S. Information Agency. In 1998 visitors were from South Africa and the United Kingdom.

## Publications

*Annual Report 1996–1997.* 1998, 77 pages.

Bertot, John Carlo, and Charles R. McClure, *Policy Issues and Strategies Affecting Public Libraries in the National Networked Environment: Moving Beyond Connectivity.* NCLIS, December 1997.

Bertot, John Carlo, Charles R. McClure and Patricia Diamond Fletcher. *1997 National Survey of U.S. Public Libraries and the Internet: Summary Results.* November 1997. The survey was sponsored by the American Library Association Office for Information Technology Policy in cooperation with the U.S. National Commission on Libraries and Information Science.

Harris, Howard. *Assessment of and Planning for NCLIS Role in Library Statistics Cooperative Program (LSCP).* October 1997, Rev. June 1998.

Copies of NCLIS print publications are available free in limited quantities from the NCLIS office until supplies are exhausted. Electronic versions are available on the commission's Web site. In addition, selected reports, hearing testimony, comments on various matters before Congress and the Clinton administration, news releases, and other items are on the commission's Web site.

# National Library of Education

400 Maryland Ave. S.W., Washington, DC 20202
202-205-5015, e-mail library@inet.ed.gov
World Wide Web: http://www.ed.gov

## Background

The National Library of Education (NLE) is the largest federally funded library in the world devoted solely to education. It is the hub of a national network of libraries, archives, and other information providers in the field of education. NLE serves the U.S. Department of Education's staff and other federal employees, the executive office of the president, and the United States Congress, as well as the general public.

## Mission

The mission of NLE is to ensure the improvement of educational achievement at all levels by serving as a principal center for the collection, preservation, and effective use of research and other information related to education. NLE promotes widespread access to its materials and expands access to the coverage of all education issues and subjects. The library participates with other major libraries, schools, and educational centers across the United States in providing a network of national education resources.

## Developments of 1998

NLE launched several initiatives in 1998.

The year saw the inauguration of the National Education Network (NEN), a nationwide collaborative network of publishers, education libraries, information services, and organizations dedicated to enhancing public access to education resources. NEN members will develop policies to share resources, coordinate acquisition and collection management, and create unified catalogs, guides, and other reference tools.

On the international front, NLE unveiled the new Web site (http://www.ed.gov/NLE/USNEI) of the U.S. Network for Education Information (USNEI). USNEI, an interagency and public/private partnership, provides extensive information and referral services for Americans interested in foreign educational systems or going abroad to study or teach, and residents of other countries interested in U.S. education.

NLE also started or renewed three major contract programs in 1998. The new National Clearinghouse on Educational Facilities (NCEF) contract was

*Note*: Maura Daly, Christina Dunn, Shelia Hamblin, Stephen Hunt, and Keith Stubbs contributed to this article.

awarded to provide information to local school districts and schools regarding school construction and renovation.

Another important new program is ED Pubs, a contractor service that for the first time consolidates the management and distribution of all U.S. Department of Education publications. The public can order publications and other Department of Education products through the toll-free telephone number 877-433-7827 (TTY/TDD: 877-576-7734), via fax at 301-470-1244, via e-mail at edpubs@inet.ed. gov, or online at http://www.ed.gov/pubs/edpubs.html.

In addition, the Educational Resources Information Center (ERIC) clearinghouse contracts were all renewed and several new special projects were launched, including the Gateway to Educational Materials (GEM) and the Virtual Reference Desk (VRD). GEM is a teacher-oriented service providing online lesson plans and other shared resources, while VRD is an online public reference service produced in collaboration with the White House's National Information Infrastructure initiative.

## Major Goals and Functions

A major goal of NLE is to establish and maintain a one-stop, central information and referral service, responding to telephone, mail, electronic, and other inquiries from the public on

- Programs and activities of the U.S. Department of Education
- ERIC resources and services of the 16 clearinghouses and ERIC support components (including the ERIC database of more than 980,000 bibliographic records of journal articles, research reports, curriculum and teaching guides, conference papers, and books)
- U.S. Department of Education publications
- Research in the Office of Educational Research and Improvement (OERI) Institutes
- Statistics from the National Center for Education Statistics

Referrals are made to such additional sources of information about educational issues as educational associations and foundations, the private sector, colleges and universities, libraries, and bibliographic databases. In addition, NLE aims to provide for the delivery of a full range of reference services (including specialized subject searches, search and retrieval in electronic databases, document delivery by mail and fax, interlibrary loan services, selective information dissemination, and research counseling, bibliographic instruction, and other training on subjects related to education. The library also aims to promote greater cooperation and resource sharing among libraries and archives with significant collections in education by establishing networks. The quarterly newsletter The *Open Window* and other information on the National Library of Information are available on request.

## Organizational Structure

NLE reports to the Office of the Assistant Secretary for OERI. Nine staff members work in the Office of the Director of NLE. This office is responsible for the overall management of the library, including supervising three division directors; long-range strategic planning; budgeting; assessing customer service; marketing and outreach, including writing, editing, and producing publications; and initiating and implementing special projects. NLE publications include a quarterly newsletter, a series on advances in education research, an annual report, fact sheets, monographs, brochures, posters, bookmarks, and videos.

The three divisions of NLE are Reference and Information Services (RISD), Collection Development and Technical Services (CTSD), and Resource Sharing and Cooperation (RSCD). RISD serves as NLE's "one-stop information and referral" center on education. It provides general and legislative reference and statistical and publication information services to inquiries received by phone, mail, and the Internet. In addition, RISD is responsible for interlibrary loan of NLE materials. CTSD identifies, selects, acquires, and provides bibliographic and subject access to education publications. RSCD is responsible for the development and maintenance of a national network of education and education-related technologies. In this capacity, RSCD promotes greater cooperation and resource sharing among education and library professionals, policy makers, the public, and other providers and repositories of education information in the United States; develops new information resources, such as databases, network services, user-friendly interfaces, and knowledge syntheses; and provides leadership in the effective use of technology in all aspects of NLE planning and operation. Major RSCD activities include ERIC, a distributed national information system designed to provide users with ready access to an extensive body of education-related literature, and INet, the U.S. Department of Education's public-access Internet site.

## History

The U.S. Department of Education was established by an act of Congress in 1867 for the purpose of

> collecting such statistics and facts as shall show the condition and progress of education in the several states and territories, and of diffusing information as shall aid in the establishment and maintenance of efficient school systems and otherwise promote the cause of education throughout the country." (14 Stat 434 [1867])

The prominent educator Henry Barnard was named commissioner of education. After one year of independent operation, however, the Department of Education was transferred to the Department of the Interior, where it was known as the Bureau of Education. When Barnard, who was interested in establishing an education library, resigned as commissioner in 1870, he left his own extensive private collection of books on education with the bureau. During the 70 years of its operation in the Department of the Interior, the Bureau of Education administered an independent library serving the specialized needs of its employees.

In 1939 the Bureau of Education became one of the five constituent agencies of the new Federal Security Agency, forerunner of the Department of Health, Education, and Welfare (HEW). The Bureau of Education library then became part of the Federal Security Agency library, which eventually became the HEW library.

As a result of a 1973 management study of the HEW library, which recommended decentralization of the library, the education collection was transferred to the newly established (1972) National Institute of Education (NIE). NIE agreed to maintain an educational research library in an effort to fulfill its mandate to "provide leadership in the conduct and support of scientific inquiry in the education process" (Education Amendments of 1972, U.S. Code, vol. 20, sec. 1221 a [1972]). From 1973 to 1985 the NIE Educational Research Library was the recipient of several fine education collections, including the education and library and information science collections of the HEW library, the library of the Center for Urban Education (formerly in New York City), the National Education Association library, the Community Services Administration library, and the former Central Midwest Regional Education Laboratory (CEMREL) library.

A major reorganization of OERI, which had included NIE as a component, occurred in October 1985. The name of the library was changed to the U.S. Department of Education Research Library. It operated first as part of OERI's Information Services Office, and then under OERI's Library Programs.

In March 1994 Congress authorized the establishment of the National Library of Education, with specific charges. By law, two other units in OERI—the former Education Information Branch and the former Education Information Resources Division—joined forces with the library staff to form NLE, expanding services to department employees and other clients.

## Collections

NLE's primary collections include its circulating, reference, serials, and microforms collections. The circulating collection largely includes books in the field of education published since 1965, but also includes such related areas as law, public policy, economics, urban affairs, sociology, history, philosophy, psychology, and library and information science. Current periodical holdings number more than 750 English-language journals and newsletters. The collection includes nearly all of the primary journals indexed by the *Current Index to Journals in Education* (*CIJE*) and *Education Index*. The library subscribes to eight major national newspapers and maintains back issues in microform of four national newspapers.

The microforms collection consists of more than 450,000 items, including newspapers, the *Federal Register*, the *Congressional Record*, Newsbank, the William S. Gray Collection on Reading, the Kraus Curriculum Collection, and various education and related journals. It also includes the complete microfiche collection of ERIC documents, a program funded by the U.S. Department of Education. NLE's ERIC collection also includes complete sets of the ERIC indexes and ERIC clearinghouse publications and products (bibliographies, state-of-the-art papers, reviews, and information analyses in the 16 areas of education presently covered by the ERIC system). [See the article on the Educational Resources Information Center earlier in Part 1—*Ed.*] The earliest volumes of NLE's rare books collection date to the 15th century. The collection also includes early American textbooks and books about education. This collection began with Henry Barnard's private collection of American schoolbooks, was nurtured by Commissioner John Eaton during his tenure (1870–1886), and was further enriched by several private donors. Other special collections maintained by the library are documents and archives of the former National Institute of Education and the former U.S. Office of Education (including reports, studies, manuals, and statistical publications, speeches, and policy papers).

## Online Access

NLE maintains an electronic repository of education information and provides public access through INet, an Internet-based service. INet makes information available through World Wide Web and ftp servers in an effort to make all NLE holdings accessible to the public through channels commonly used by educators.

### World Wide Web

NLE's World Wide Web server can be accessed at http://www.ed.gov/NLE. The library also maintains the U.S. Department of Education's Web server at http://www.ed.gov.

### Ftp

Ftp users can access the information at ftp.ed.gov (log on as "anonymous").

The INet World Wide Web and ftp sources are continuously updated with new press releases, grant announcements, publication summaries, full-text documents, and statistical data sets. New material on major U.S. Department of Education initiatives, such as Goal 2000, School-to-Work, Technology, Comprehensive School Reform, and Elementary and Secondary Education Act (ESEA), is added frequently. To find new items on the INet Web server, select News and Events on the left edge to display a list of recent additions.

Suggestions or questions about the Web site or ftp servers should be directed to one of the following:

| | |
|---|---|
| E-mail: | webmaster@inet.ed.gov |
| Fax: | 202-205-7759 |
| Mail: | INet Project Manager |
| | U.S. Department of Education |
| | Office of Educational Research and Improvement |
| | 400 Maryland Ave. S.W., Room 4W300 |
| | Washington, DC 20202 |

# Key NLE Telephone Numbers

| | |
|---|---|
| Library Administration | 202-401-3745 |
| Reference/Research/Statistics/Interlibrary Loan | 202-205-5015 |
| Outside Washington, D.C., area | 800-424-1616 |
| Fax | 202-205-6688 |
| Circulation | 202-205-4945 |
| Collection Development/Technical Services | 202-401-6563 |
| ACCESS ERIC | 800-LET-ERIC |

# National Association and Organization Reports

## American Library Association

50 E. Huron St., Chicago, IL 60611
312-944-6780, 800-545-2433
World Wide Web: http://www.ala.org

Ann K. Symons
President

Upholding First Amendment rights on the Internet, protecting fair use, and saving the education (or E-rate) discounts on telecommunications services were key issues for the American Library Association (ALA) during 1998.

ALA is the voice of America's libraries and the millions of people who depend on them. Its 55,573 members are primarily librarians, but members also include library trustees, publishers, and others. All types of libraries are represented—public, school, college and university and other institutional libraries, as well as special libraries serving the military, prisons, and business.

Founded in 1876, ALA is the oldest, largest, and most influential library association in the world. Its mission is to promote the highest-quality library and information services. ALA is a 501c3 charitable and educational organization. Key action areas are diversity, education and continuous learning, equity of access, intellectual freedom, and 21st century literacy.

The association encompasses 11 membership divisions focused on areas of special interest: the American Association of School Librarians (AASL), the American Library Trustee Association (ALTA), the Association for Library Collections and Technical Services (ALCTS), the Association for Library Service to Children (ALSC), the Association of College and Research Libraries (ACRL), the Association of Specialized and Cooperative Library Agencies (ASCLA), the Library Administration and Management Association, the Library and Information Technology Association (LITA), the Public Library Association (PLA), the Reference and User Services Association (RUSA), and the Young Adult Library Services Association (YALSA).

In addition to its Chicago headquarters, ALA maintains a legislative office and Office for Information Technology Policy in Washington, D.C., and an editorial office in Middletown, Connecticut, for *Choice*, a review journal for academic libraries. The association's foundation, the Fund for America's Libraries, is located at its Chicago headquarters.

## Leading the Way in Cyberspace

Amid growing concern about children's safety in cyberspace, ALA intensified its efforts to educate parents about the Internet and to provide quality online resources for children and young adults. These efforts were cited by the "Today Show," *Parade* magazine, *USA Today*, the *Washington Post*, and other media from coast to coast.

Almost a million copies of "The Librarian's Guide to Cyberspace," a brochure with safety tips and recommended sites for children, were distributed with support from America Online (AOL). ALA also joined with AOL to conduct a series of Internet Driver's Education programs at more than a dozen libraries and other locations across the country.

New and expanded Internet resources from ALA include:

- 700+ Amazing, Spectacular, Mysterious, Wonderful Web Sites for Kids and the Adults Who Care About Them (http://www.ala.org/parentspage/greatsites/), a "cybercollection" of Web sites reviewed and recommended by ALSC
- Notable Children's Web Sites (http://www.ala.org/alsc/ncwc.htm) selected by ALSC
- TEENHoopla: An Internet Guide for Teens (http://www.ala.org/teenhoopla/), a Web page with links to sites of special interest to young adults ages 12–18, developed by YALSA
- FamiliesConnect (http://www.ala.org/ICONN), a compilation of Web resources to help families guide their children's Internet use, developed as part of AASL's ICONnect technology initiative.

KidsConnect (http://www.ala.org/ICONN/kidsconn.htm), the online question-answering service for K–12 students, logged 10,937 questions during its first three years of operation. KidsConnect is operated by AASL in partnership with the Information Institute of Syracuse (Syracuse University), with funding from Microsoft Corporation.

ALA played a major role in organizing America Links Up, a public-awareness campaign sponsored by a coalition of concerned organizations to educate parents about the Internet. More than 250 school and public libraries helped launch the campaign in fall 1998 by hosting Internet "teach-ins" for parents and children.

In connection with School Library Media Month in April, students were asked to vote for their favorite Web sites as part of a special promotion sponsored by KidsConnect. The resulting list of Kids Pick Top 10 Sites included Nickelodeon, Disney, Sports Illustrated for Kids, and the Web site of the popular but controversial TV show "South Park."

*Children and the Internet: Guidelines for Developing Public Library Policy* was released by ALTA, ALSC, and PLA to help librarians and trustees set policy and develop procedures for use of the Internet.

## Equity of Access

ALA waged intensive campaigns to secure discounts on telecommunications services for libraries and to preserve fair use as part of revised copyright legislation.

Both provisions, while modified, survived. [See the article "Legislation and Regulations Affecting Libraries in 1998" in Part 2—*Ed.*]

The telecommunications discounts, known as the education rate or E-rate, are intended to promote universal access to electronic information at schools and libraries by making these connections more affordable. Commitment letters were issued at the end of the 1998 congressional session, nearly three years after the discounts were authorized as part of the revised federal Telecommunications Act of 1996. Implementation began only after much work by ALA and its education partners to withstand congressional and industry criticism of the program.

The number of public libraries offering public access to the Internet at one or more branches grew from 28 percent in 1996 to 60 percent in 1997, according to a "National Survey of U.S. Public Libraries and the Internet" sponsored by the ALA Office for Information Technology Policy and the National Commission on Libraries and Information Science (NCLIS).

The Digital Millennium Copyright Act, an updating of copyright law for cyberspace, contains significant protection for fair use as well as new provisions for digital preservation of library materials and for distance education. An overly broad database protection bill was dropped after protests by ALA and other concerned groups. A 20-year extension of the copyright term includes a limited exception for libraries, archives, and nonprofit educational institutions. These actions retained more balance between owner rights and user access as a result of work by ALA's Washington Office and its coalition partners.

Significant funding increases were enacted for library and related education programs, and a new Reading Excellence Act was enacted and funded at $260 million. Thanks to ALA legislative work, the act includes opportunities for both school and public libraries.

A poll conducted for ALA by the Gallup Organization found that Americans continue to count on their public libraries for information and entertainment. According to the poll, 66 percent of adults had used a public library at least once in the last year and 65 percent had consulted librarians. The number of library visitors was up 13 percent since a 1978 Gallup poll.

Barbara J. Ford, 1997–1998 ALA president, appointed an Outsourcing Task Force to study and advise on outsourcing, subcontracting, and privatization of library services and the impact of such practices on public service. A report will be issued in 1999.

## 21st-Century Literacy

ALA and YALSA sponsored the first Teen Read Week, October 19–25, 1998, with the message "Read for the Fun of It." Public and school libraries across the country joined in sponsoring special activities such as an Open Mike Night with readings from favorite books, visits from young-adult authors, displays, and book lists featuring teen favorites. National partners included the American Association of School Administrators, the American Booksellers Association, the National Council of Teachers of English, the National Association of Secondary School Principals, and the National Education Association.

New information literacy standards to prepare students better to live, learn, and work in the information age were released in 1998 by AASL. The standards were developed with the Association for Educational Communications and Technology. The first annual Information Power Training Institute focused on implementation of the standards.

A new position of literacy officer was approved. The person in this position will continue work with the sites in the Literacy in Libraries Across America project funded by the Lila Wallace–Reader's Digest Fund and will work to strengthen ALA's leadership and support for library literacy programs. Recognizing the critical importance of information literacy at all levels of education, ACRL announced plans for National Information Literacy Institute (http://www.ala.org/acrl/nii.html) to be held in the summer of 1999.

Popular TV talk-show host Rosie O'Donnell, singer-actress Brandy, actor Nicolas Cage, supermodel Cindy Crawford, actor Antonio Banderas, and Microsoft mogul and library benefactor Bill Gates joined the lengthy list of well-known faces on ALA posters urging children and adults to practice the most basic literacy skill: Read.

Florida became the first state to offer training in the Born to Read outreach program developed by the ALSC. The award-winning program promotes partnerships between librarians and healthcare providers to reach out with training and services to low-literate families to help them raise children who are "born to read."

## Diversity

Under Ford's leadership, ALA activities took on an international flavor. These included American delegations to bookfairs in Harare, Zimbabwe, and Guadalajara, Mexico; ALA's first Diversity Fair; an international literacy fair; and a "Local Libraries: Global Awareness" project to assist libraries in developing diversified collections and programs. The global awareness project was developed in partnership with Global Learning and the United States Information Agency (USIA).

The first 50 scholarships were awarded to graduate students of color to pursue master's degrees in library and information science as part of ALA's Spectrum initiative to increase the number of minority librarians. More than two dozen state library associations and universities contributed funds or matching scholarships in support of the Spectrum initiative.

Twelve American librarians were assigned to work in libraries in Cyprus, Russia, Vietnam, and other countries during the 11th and last year of the ALA Library Fellows Program administered by ALA and funded by USIA. The program has sent more than 147 information ambassadors to more than 90 countries since 1987.

ALA's first diversity officer was appointed to advise and consult on matters related to serving diverse populations.

## Education and Continuous Learning

ALA sponsors a wide range of educational resources and activities to promote the highest-quality library services. These include standards and policies, publications, conferences, and cultural programming to support libraries as centers for lifelong learning.

The association is recognized as the chief accrediting agency for graduate programs in library and information science. In 1998 ALA continued accreditation of 12 master's degree programs after review by the Committee on Accreditation.

YALSA issued revised competencies to reflect changing needs in library services to young adults ages 12–18.

Publications included an updated and expanded *Guidelines for Establishing Community Information and Referral Services in Public Libraries*, published by PLA, and *AAA Rated: Unscrambling the Bond Market*, published by RUSA to assist librarians in identifying correct information about the often-misunderstood bond market.

Programs for the public included "StoryLines America," developed in cooperation with libraries and public radio stations in the Southwest and Northwest. Funded by the National Endowment for the Humanities (NEH), the radio programs featured discussions of regional literature with scholars. The programs will be expanded to California and the coastal Southeast in the fall of 1999.

"From Rosie to Roosevelt: A Film History of Americans in World War II" used documentary films and books to stimulate discussion about the American experience during World War II. The project was developed by National Video Resources in partnership with the ALA Public Programs Office with major funding from NEH and support from the John D. and Catherine T. MacArthur Foundation. Twenty public libraries were selected to host the program series.

## Intellectual Freedom

ALA intensified efforts to ensure that children have a positive online experience and also developed policies and principles aimed at upholding First Amendment principles on the Internet. Examples include *Guidelines and Considerations for Developing a Public Library Internet Use Policy* (June 1998).

Amendments in the House and Senate requiring libraries and schools to install and use filtering software as a condition of receiving federal assistance were dropped, after much work by ALA, library advocates, and others to convince lawmakers that such measures were unjustified.

The 17th annual Banned Books Week (September 26–October 3, 1998) celebrated the freedom to read by pointing out that a full third of the titles on the Random House Modern Library's list of 100 best novels of the century have been targets for censors. "Most Challenged Books" as reported to the ALA Office for Intellectual Freedom in 1998 are *The Chocolate War* by Robert Cormier, *Of Mice and Men* by John Steinbeck, the Goosebump and Fear Street series by R. L. Stine, *I Know Why the Caged Bird Sings* by Maya Angelou, *It's Perfectly Normal* by Robie Harris, *The Giver* by Lois Lowry, *Always Running* by Luis Rodriguez, and *Crazy Lady* by Jane Conly.

ALA also prepared to celebrate the 30th anniversary of its Office for Intellectual Freedom and its sister organization, the Freedom to Read Foundation, in 1999.

## Conferences and Institutes

National conferences and regional institutes sponsored by ALA and its divisions provide opportunities for professional growth and renewal throughout the year. "Libraries: Global Reach. Local Touch." was the theme selected by ALA President Ford for the 117th ALA Annual Conference, held June 25–July 1, 1998, in Washington, D.C.; 24,884 librarians, exhibitors, and guests attended. The 1998 ALA Midwinter Meeting, held in New Orleans in January, drew 11,258.

PLA's seventh National Conference drew its biggest crowd—some 6,900. "Public Libraries: Vital, Valuable, Virtual" was the theme for the conference held March 10–14, 1998, in Kansas City, Missouri.

In 1997–1998 regional institutes included "Customer Service Excellence, Understanding Power and Influence: Maximizing Success for your Organization" and "Managing Educational Services: Teaching and Learning in Libraries," sponsored by LAMA.

ALCTS broadcast the Fundamentals of Acquisitions Institute as a six-hour teleconference in cooperation with the College of Library and Information Studies at the University of South Carolina. ALCTS also sponsored regional institutes, titled "Through the Arch: Electronic Serials from Acquisition to Access" and "Meeting the Challenge of Children's Materials: Acquiring, Cataloging, and Preserving for Today's Youth."

## Publishing

New editions of PLA's *Planning for Results* and AASL's *Information Power* headed up a strong front list for ALA Editions, which also included many popular new titles, such as Michael Gorman's *Our Singular Strengths*, Deborah Fritz's *Cataloging with AACR2R and USMARC*, and Shirley Duglin Kennedy's *Best Bet Internet*.

*American Libraries*, the ALA monthly membership magazine, began a weekly online edition (http://www.ala.org/alonline) in 1998. *Booklist*, the ALA review journal for public and school libraries, had another record advertising year and introduced new "Spotlight" and "Showcase" features that focus on topics of current interest. *Book Links*, a magazine that connects books, libraries, and classrooms to help make children's literature part of learning, introduced a new section, called "Beyond Boundaries," containing articles dealing with common bonds of caring.

*Library Technology Reports* published timely studies on Z39.50 clients, bibliographic utilities, and model technology plans as well as test reports on copiers and fax machines. *Reference Books Bulletin* published special issues on print and electronic reference sources.

*CHOICE*, the review journal for academic libraries published by ACRL, reviewed more than 60,000 scholarly works and research-related Web sites. The journal began the beta-test stage of an Internet-based review service in 1998; some 100 institutions worldwide are participating in the test. The new review service, ChoiceReviews.online, will be available by subscription in 1999.

## Grants

A one-year $121,559 grant was received from the Dewitt Wallace–Reader's Digest Fund for ALA's Office of Research and Statistics (ORS) to conduct a survey of how public libraries currently operate youth programs, including gathering information on types of activities, youth served, funding sources, and partnerships in the community. In conjunction with this project, ALA's Public Programs Office received $25,000 from the Lila Wallace–Reader's Digest Fund to survey cultural programming in libraries. Results of both surveys administered by ORS will be released in 1999.

The ALA Public Programs Office received $36,546 from NEH for a series of library reading and discussion programs based on biographies, titled "Lives Worth Knowing." The project, developed with the New York Council for the Humanities, offered at 35 public libraries starting in fall 1998.

Finally, the Public Programs Office received $1 million from the Lila Wallace–Reader's Digest Fund for "LIVE at the Library," a program that brings well-known authors to local libraries, and $260,545 from NEH for "Jazz Age in Paris: 1914–1940," a traveling exhibition based on a Smithsonian Institution exhibition of the same name.

## Awards

Each year ALA presents more than 100 awards and scholarships to recognize and promote excellence in such areas as children's literature, library service to the elderly, and defense of intellectual freedom.

In 1998 the association awarded its highest honor—honorary membership—to five individuals for their outstanding contributions to libraries: Bill and Melinda Gates, founders of the Gates Library Foundation; Senator Wendell B. Ford (D-Ky.) and U.S. Rep. Sidney R. Yates (D-Ill.), library legislative champions scheduled to retire at the end of the Congressional term; and K. Wayne Smith, recently retired chief of OCLC.

Judith F. Krug, director of the ALA Office for Intellectual Freedom since it was founded in 1969, received the Joseph W. Lippincott Award for distinguished service to the profession.

Karen Hesse, author of *Out of the Dust*, was awarded the 1998 Newbery Medal for the most distinguished contribution to American literature for children. The Caldecott Medal for the most distinguished American picture book went to Paul O. Zelinksy, illustrator of *Rapunzel*. The awards are presented annually by ALSC.

The 1998 Coretta Scott King Awards for the best children's books by African American authors and illustrators went to Sharon M. Draper, author of *Forged by Fire*, and Javaka Steptoe, illustrator of *In Daddy's Arms I am Tall*.

The Andrew Carnegie Medal for Excellence in Children's Video went to Tom Davenport, of Davenport Films, for "Willa: An American Snow White."

Henry Holt and Company of New York, publisher of *The Robber and Me*, was named winner of the 1998 Mildred L. Batchelder Award for the most outstanding children's book published first in another language and then in English in the United States.

Madeline L'Engle, author of *A Wrinkle in Time* and many other popular books, received the Margaret A. Edwards Award for lifetime contribution to literature for young adults. The award is sponsored by *School Library Journal* and administered by YALSA.

Russell Freedman, the author of *Lincoln: A Photobiography* and other non-fiction works for children, received the 1998 Laura Ingalls Wilder Medal for a lasting contribution to children's literature. The award is administered by ALSC.

The Pura Belpré Award, a two-part award honoring Latino writers and illustrators of children's books, was presented for the second time in 1998. The illustrator award went to Stephanie Garcia for *Snapshots from the Wedding*, written by Gary Sotto; Victor Martinez received the Belpré author award for *Parrot in the Oven: Mi Vida*. The Belpré award is administered by ALSC and REFORMA (the National Association to Promote Library Services to the Spanish Speaking).

## Leadership

Ann K. Symons, librarian at Juneau-Douglas High School in Alaska, assumed the presidency of ALA in July 1998. She selected the theme "Celebrating the Freedom to Read! Learn! Connect!" Sarah Ann Long, a past president of PLA and director of the North Suburban Library System in Wheeling, Illinois, was elected president of ALA for the 1999–2000 term. She will assume office in July 1999.

William R. Gordon became executive director of ALA on March 1, 1998. He is the 21st chief executive since Melvil Dewey created the top post of "secretary" in 1879, three years after the association was founded. Gordon previously headed the Prince George's County Memorial Library System in Hyattsville, Maryland.

Other ALA staff appointments included Ann L. O'Neill, director of the Office for Accreditation, and Lorelle Brown Swader, director of the Office for Library Personnel Resources. Sandra Rio Balderrama, formerly of the Oakland (California) Public Library, was named to the new position of ALA diversity officer.

# Association of American Publishers

71 Fifth Avenue, New York, NY 10003-3004
212-255-0200
World Wide Web: http://www.publishers.org

1718 Connecticut Ave. N.W., Washington, DC 20009
202-232-3335

Judith Platt
Director of Communications and Public Affairs

The Association of American Publishers (AAP) is the national trade association of the U.S. book-publishing industry. AAP was created in 1970 through the merger of the American Book Publishers Council, a trade publishing group, and the American Textbook Publishers Institute, a group of educational publishers. AAP's more than 200 members include most of the major commercial book publishers in the United States, as well as smaller and nonprofit publishers, university presses, and scholarly societies. AAP members publish hardcover and paperback books in every field and a range of educational materials for the elementary, secondary, postsecondary, and professional markets. Members of the association also produce computer software and electronic products and services, such as online databases and CD-ROMs. AAP's primary concerns are the protection of intellectual-property rights in all media, the defense of free expression and freedom to publish at home and abroad, the management of new technologies, development of education markets and funding for instructional materials, and the development of national and global markets for its members' products.

AAP is formally affiliated with five regional or specialized publishing groups: the Publishers Association of the South, the Rocky Mountain Book Publishers Association, the Florida Publishers Association, the Small Publishers Association of North America, and the Evangelical Christian Publishers Association.

Additional information on AAP can be found on the World Wide Web at http://www.publishers.org.

## Highlights of 1998

- Twenty-two months of AAP lobbying and hard work paid off as Congress finally enacted the Digital Millennium Copyright Act to implement the World Intellectual Property Organization (WIPO) treaties.
- Under AAP's leadership, the industry came together to create an innovative campaign to encourage reading and book buying in the 18- to 34-year-old market. "Get Caught Reading" will be launched at BookExpo '99 in Los Angeles.
- AAP's School Division played a key role in securing historic levels of instructional materials funding in California and in raising Florida's funding by $25 million.

- For the third time in two years, AAP went to court to challenge government censorship on the Internet, this time in New Mexico.
- Peter Jovanovich was elected to a two-year term as AAP chairman.
- AAP began an intensive outreach campaign to bring smaller and independent publishers into the association. Plans called for a Small and Independent Publishers Annual Meeting in early 1999.
- AAP President Pat Schroeder was on Capitol Hill for the release of a new report on the growing economic importance of the U.S. copyright industries.
- AAP intervened in a Louisiana case involving the question of a filmmaker's civil liability for a copycat crime.
- AAP announced that its 1999 Honors would go to National Public Radio.
- In cooperation with the Copyright Clearance Center, AAP began a campus copyright education program to raise awareness of copyright and permissions issues and to provide practical information on clearing permissions for course pack materials.
- In December the association filed preliminary comments with the Copyright Office on distance-learning issues, one of the key issues the 106th Congress will tackle.
- AAP protested a threat of treason charges against a prominent Swiss author and scholar, Jean Ziegler.
- President Schroeder participated in the launch of the New York "Reach Out and Read" Coalition.
- The association issued a statement on Y2K compliance in the publishing industry to aid its members in making the transition to the new millennium.
- AAP's Enabling Technologies Committee initiated a project to assess three electronic book systems.
- Publishers and librarians undertook the first survey of the library market in more than a decade.
- AAP welcomed the Evangelical Christian Publishers Association as its fifth affiliate organization.
- Charles Ellis was honored with the 1998 Curtis Benjamin Award, given for the first time at BookExpo.
- Yale University Press's *Three Thousand Years of Chinese Painting* received the R. R. Hawkins Award for the best professional/scholarly/reference work of the year.
- U.S. book sales totaled $21.3 billion in 1997, according to figures released by AAP in February.

## Government Affairs

AAP's Washington office is the industry's front line on matters of federal legislation and government policy. The Government Affairs staff keeps the AAP membership informed of developments on Capitol Hill and in the executive branch and facilitates the development of industry consensus positions on national policy issues. AAP's Government Affairs professionals serve as the industry's voice in advocating the views and concerns of American publishers on questions of national policy.

AAP cosponsored (with the McGraw-Hill Companies, the Information Industry Association, and the American Business Press) the multi-industry forum "Customer Privacy on the Web: Self-Regulation or Government Enforcement?" on March 4. The full-day forum featured a morning keynote address by presidential advisor Ira Magaziner and an afternoon address by Federal Trade Commission Chairman Robert Pitofsky. Panel discussions explored the government perspective, consumer concerns, and an overview of industry self-regulation policies, and an afternoon workshop focused on developing and implementing a workable privacy policy.

An AAP Government Affairs Council was established in 1997 to strengthen communications between the Washington Office and the AAP leadership. The council comprises individuals specially designated by AAP Board members to speak on behalf of their houses in formulating positions on legislative issues that require a rapid response. [See the article "Legislation and Regulations Affecting Publishing in 1998" in Part 2—*Ed.*]

## BookExpo America

AAP became a cosponsor of BookExpo America in 1997, giving publishers a voice for the first time in planning and strategic policy decisions for what is evolving into the premier book event of the English-speaking world.

In 1998 presentation of the prestigious Curtis Benjamin Award for Creative Publishing was moved from the AAP Annual Meeting to BookExpo. The award was given at a festive "Celebration of Books" luncheon (which also featured presentation of the Charles S. Haslam Award for Excellence in Bookselling), hosted by television newsman Peter Jennings. The popular choice for this year's Curtis Benjamin Award was Charles R. Ellis, president and CEO of John Wiley & Sons.

At BookExpo '98, AAP focused attention on the importance of reading aloud to children from the very earliest ages. In cooperation with the Institute for Civil Society, a private, non-profit foundation and think tank, AAP sponsored a literacy fair, inviting a host of organizations to display materials on their read-aloud initiatives, including "Read to Your Bunny" (American Booksellers Association), "Read Across America" (the National Education Association), "The Most Important 20 Minutes of the Day" (Association of Booksellers for Children), and "Reach Out and Read." AAP also launched a new "Designated Reader" initiative with the appearance of Theo the Lion, the star of an upcoming PBS children's reading program called *Between the Lions*. At its exhibit booth, AAP distributed thousands of "sneaker stickers" promoting reading aloud to children.

AAP's cosponsorship of BookExpo America also involves a commitment to provide educational programs, and three of these were presented at BookExpo '98. The AAP International Committee's seminar "Chain Reaction: Territorial Rights & Bookselling in the Age of Global Markets" played to a standing-room-only audience on May 29. The Professional and Scholarly Publishing Division attempted to demystify the relationship between booksellers and the STM publishing community at the May 28 seminar "Booksellers Are from Venus; Publishers Are from Mars." AAP's Freedom to Read Committee joined with the American

Booksellers Foundation for Free Expression in sponsoring a discussion of the precarious state of the First Amendment.

AAP again hosted an International Rights Center at BookExpo, giving AAP members and members of affiliated publisher organizations a central and convenient facility for meeting with international customers.

## Copyright

The Copyright Committee coordinates AAP efforts to protect and strengthen intellectual-property rights and to enhance public awareness of the importance of copyright as an incentive to creativity. The Copyright Committee works closely with the AAP Washington staff to develop and disseminate industry positions on legislation involving intellectual property rights and, through its Rights and Permissions Advisory Committee, coordinates AAP's work in the area of rights and permissions education. Charles Ellis (Wiley) chaired the committee in 1998.

In 1997 AAP joined other copyright industry groups in filing an amicus brief in the U.S. Supreme Court in *Quality King* v. *Lanza*, a case involving parallel imports. Although the case did not pertain directly to publishing, it was seen as significant because of its implications for the issue of copyright territorial exclusivity. On March 9 the Supreme Court ruled that the "first sale" doctrine applies to copyrighted products manufactured in the United States, sold overseas, and reimported into the United States without the authorization of the manufacturer. The decision has obvious implications for publishers that manufacture books in the United States and sell them overseas. AAP urged its members to examine their own business operations in light of the Supreme Court ruling.

On April 20 a three-judge panel of the U.S. Court of Appeals for the 5th Circuit (Louisiana, Texas, and Mississippi) issued a troubling decision in an important copyright case. The panel ruled that states and state employees are not subject to the jurisdiction of the federal courts in copyright infringement suits where damages are sought. The April 20 ruling means that when states or their agents infringe copyright, the only remedy available to copyright owners is injunctive relief. The case (*Chavez* v. *Arte Publico Press*) addressed the issue of whether a state's sovereign immunity rights under the 11th Amendment protect it from being sued for damages in federal court. At the heart of the case is the constitutionality of the Copyright Remedies Clarification Act (CRCA), under which states and their agents (such as universities) are subject to the full range of remedies in copyright infringement suits (including statutory damages and attorney's fees). The April 20 ruling held that CRCA (which AAP was instrumental in passing) is unconstitutional.

AAP and a group of other associations had filed an amicus brief to the Fifth Circuit out of concern that if the courts hold the states to be immune from damage suits, the absence of deterrent penalties would encourage wholesale copying of textbooks and other educational materials. In the wake of the April 20 ruling, AAP joined in asking the full Fifth Circuit to rehear the case. On October 7 the Fifth Circuit agreed to rehear the case *en banc* and vacated the April 20 ruling. AAP also joined an amicus brief in another Fifth Circuit case dealing with the same issue (*Rodriquez* v. *Texas Commission on the Arts*).

On May 7 AAP President Schroeder took part in a press event on Capitol Hill, hosted by Senators Orrin Hatch (R-Utah) and Patrick Leahy (D-Vt.), marking release of a new report on the growing importance of the copyright industries to the U.S. economy. Accounting for 3.65 percent of the U.S. gross domestic product ($278.4 billion in value added), the copyright industries, as Schroeder pointed out, "not only educate, delight, and entertain the entire world; they also put bread on the tables of more than three and a half million American households, and the number of jobs in the copyright industries will continue to grow exponentially in the new century."

The Copyright Committee oversees AAP's participation in a joint Campus Copyright Education Program with the Copyright Clearance Center. Beginning in June 1998, a campus traveler working for the program has sought, through direct on-campus visits, to raise awareness of copyright and permissions issues and to provide practical information on clearing permissions for course pack materials. Because campus stores are a frequent source of copyright information for faculty and students, the National Association of College Stores is participating in the program. At its November meeting the AAP Board voted to continue the program for the first half of 1999.

The Copyright Committee also coordinates AAP's antipiracy activities. The association works through the International Intellectual Property Alliance to enlist the help of the U.S. government in raising the level of copyright protection among its trading partners. The seriousness of the problem was underscored by the alliance's "Special 301" filing to the U.S. Trade Representative in February 1998, which estimated that the U.S. copyright industries lost in excess of $10.8 billion in 1997 as a result of piracy in 52 countries.

AAP is also waging its own antipiracy campaign by going after pirates in their own countries and bringing them into court. AAP and its member publishers joined Taiwan government officials, including representatives of Taiwan's three major political parties, and the Taipei Publishers Association at a highly publicized press conference in Taipei in September, issuing warnings about rampant copyright piracy and announcing a new crackdown involving local authorities, government agencies, and publishers to deal with the problem. The event was covered by Taiwan's major newspapers and electronic media.

Under the Technical Amendments Act passed by Congress last year, the Register of Copyrights was authorized to raise statutory copyright fees to cover "reasonable costs" of providing services and to add an adjustment for inflation. A study of costs incurred in registering original and renewal claims led the Copyright Office to publish in August a proposal to establish two alternate fee schedules to replace the single copyright registration fee (currently $20). AAP joined with music publishers, the recording industry, the motion picture industry, and software publishers in filing comments with the Copyright Office in September, noting that the proposed fee increase of 120–150 percent could have the undesirable effect of reducing the total number of registrations and thus generating less income to cover Copyright Office costs. The statement suggested that the fee increase be postponed, or at least phased in incrementally, to determine whether increased efficiencies in the electronic registration system could reduce overall costs.

The Rights and Permissions Advisory Committee sponsored several educational workshops in 1998, including a program on "Permissions in the Digital Age" in May and one on distance learning in October.

## Communications and Public Affairs

The Communications and Public Affairs Program is AAP's voice. Through regular publications, press releases and advisories, op-ed pieces, and other means, AAP expresses the views of the industry and provides up-to-the-minute information on subjects of concern to its members.

AAP's public-affairs activities include outreach and cooperative programs with such organizations as the Center for the Book in the Library of Congress; the Arts Advocacy Alliance (supporting the National Endowment for the Arts and other federal arts programs); PEN American Center and its International Freedom to Write Program (AAP was a founding member of the U.S. Rushdie Defense Committee); a host of literacy and reading-promotion efforts, including an early-childhood literacy initiative, "Reach Out and Read," President Clinton's "America Reads Challenge" and the White House "Prescription for Reading."

The association's home page on the World Wide Web (http://www.publishers.org) was totally revamped in 1998, making it more user friendly and comprehensive. For the first time in AAP history, the association's *Annual Report* (for fiscal year 1997–1998) was published online. The AAP newsletter, *AAP Monthly Report*, can also be found online, in addition to its traditional print distribution.

## Education Program

Several years ago AAP inaugurated a program to provide educational opportunities for publishing-industry personnel. The first course offered was an intensive "Introduction to Publishing," designed to give entry level employees an overview of the industry and a better understanding of the publishing process. The course has been given several times each year since its inauguration, and it continues to draw enthusiastic registrants.

AAP inaugurated a new course designed to demystify financial principles and give editors and editorial managers a new perspective on their business. The seminar, "Finance for Editors," was first presented in June 1998 and was given again in the fall.

The Annual Tax Seminar held in Washington in December featured the new Commissioner of the Internal Revenue Service as its speaker.

## Enabling Technologies

The Enabling Technologies Committee focuses on publishing in the electronic networked environment and serves as a steering committee directing AAP's efforts to promote the development of workable systems for managing copyright in the digital environment. John Conors (Harcourt Brace) chairs the committee.

The Digital Object Identifier (DOI) system, which began as a project of the AAP Enabling Technologies Committee, has evolved into an international institution under the direction of an International DOI Foundation with overall responsibility for administering the system. Norman Paskin, formerly director of information technology development for Elsevier Science, was named the International DOI Foundation's first director, effective March 1.

In 1998 the Enabling Technologies Committee established four subcommittees to deal with digital issues:

- *Y2K Compliance* will catalog the publishing industry's specific requirements for vendors and suppliers concerning Year 2000 software compliance
- *DOI* will continue monitoring developments in the DOI system and providing AAP member input to AAP President Pat Schroeder, who serves on the International DOI Foundation Board
- *Digital Content Management* will coordinate AAP member discussions with vendors and services providing content management systems
- *Metadata Project* will identify the tag sets necessary for digital content for both internal management and catalog and e-commerce descriptions

Underscoring the need for publishers and their vendors and suppliers to work together in confronting potential hurdles posed by the transition to the year 2000, AAP released a statement on December 14 on Y2K compliance. Prepared by the Enabling Technologies Committee, the statement details a list of steps for vendors and suppliers to take in order to ensure continued efficient and effective service to their clients. Publishers are encouraged to take an active stance on Y2K issues by contacting each of their vendors and suppliers directly.

In December AAP entered into a contract with Tenth Mountain Systems to provide a security assessment of three electronic book systems: Rocket eBook, SoftBook, and Peanut Press. Their report was due to the Enabling Technologies Committee early in 1999.

## Freedom to Read

Protecting intellectual freedom is a fundamental concern for AAP members and for the industry as a whole. The Freedom to Read Committee is AAP's front line in identifying and responding to free-speech issues that affect the business of book publishing. The committee performs three basic functions: early warning, intervention, and education. Serving as the association's watchdog in the area of free speech, the committee alerts the AAP membership to developments in such areas as libel, privacy, school censorship, attacks on public libraries, reporters' privilege (confidentiality of source materials), the Internet and filtering technology, sexually explicit materials, third-party liability, and efforts to punish speech that "causes harm." The Freedom to Read Committee coordinates AAP's participation (as plaintiff or friend of the court) in important First Amendment court cases and provides guidance in developing AAP's posture on legislative issues with free-speech ramifications. Through its publications, educational programs, and other activities, the committee carries the message to the industry and beyond, stressing the need for constant vigilance in defending rights guaranteed by the First Amendment. Jane Isay (Harcourt Brace) chairs the committee.

The Freedom to Read Committee works closely with allied organizations, especially the ALA's Office for Intellectual Freedom and the American Booksellers Foundation for Free Expression, and coordinates AAP participation as a member of the Media Coalition, a group of trade associations formed to fight censorship. The committee had a full agenda over the past year. Among the highlights:

- The year ended with a sense of déjà vu—another attempt by Congress to impose content-based restrictions on constitutionally protected materials on the Internet. Dubbed "CDA II," the Child Online Protection Act (COPA), which was passed by Congress in October, imposes criminal and civil penalties for "any communication for commercial purposes" via the World Wide Web that contains "harmful-to-minors" material and is available to minors. In October, two days after Congress passed COPA, the ACLU and a group of co-plaintiffs representing content providers and users of the Web challenged its constitutionality in a lawsuit filed in Philadelphia. AAP did not join as a plaintiff, choosing instead to help resurrect the broad-based Citizens Internet Empowerment Coalition (CIEC), which had successfully challenged the original CDA. At year's end AAP and other members of CIEC were looking at various options, including providing friend-of-the-court support for the ACLU, filing its own lawsuit in another jurisdiction, and mounting a comprehensive campaign to educate Congress and the public about less restrictive ways to keep inappropriate material on the Internet away from children.
- For the third time in two years, AAP went to court to challenge government censorship on the Internet, this time by the State of New Mexico. As AAP President Schroeder said when the lawsuit was filed in April, "Surely we can find better uses for tax dollars than passing and defending laws that the Supreme Court has already declared to be unconstitutional." A U.S. District Court judge apparently agreed, issuing a preliminary injunction in June.
- AAP joined with booksellers, librarians, and a host of others in supporting a legal challenge to the broad subpoena issued by independent counsel Kenneth Starr for records of Monica Lewinsky's book purchases. The subpoena was subsequently withdrawn.
- AAP was among a number of media groups asking the Louisiana Supreme Court to block a disturbing lower-court ruling that allows the makers and distributors of the film *Natural Born Killers* to be sued for damages in connection with a "copycat" crime. The Louisiana high court failed to intervene.
- AAP, the Magazine Publishers Association, and others filed an amicus brief in *Messenger* v. *Gruner & Jahr Publishing*, a case involving a publisher's editorial discretion in the use of stock photographs.
- A favorable decision was handed down in a long-standing legal challenge to the Food and Drug Administration's attempts to regulate the dissemination of constitutionally protected research materials. AAP was involved in the early stages of the case.

- In an important First Amendment victory, a federal judge in Oklahoma City ruled that the Academy Award-winning film *The Tin Drum* does not violate Oklahoma's child pornography laws. AAP formally protested the actions of Oklahoma City law enforcement officials in seizing the film.
- The committee was disappointed by an 8–1 decision by the U.S. Supreme Court upholding the constitutionality of a provision requiring the National Endowment for the Arts to take into account "general standards of decency" in awarding grants. AAP had joined People for the American Way and other groups in an amicus brief, arguing that when the government funds a program intended to encourage private speech, it may not prefer one speaker's message or viewpoint over another's.

In carrying out its educational function, the committee joined with the American Booksellers Foundation for Free Expression in presenting a First Amendment program at BookExpo America. With the ALA Office for Intellectual Freedom, the committee sponsored a highly praised panel discussion at the ALA Annual Conference in Washington, D.C., on the use of the Internet to disseminate hate speech.

Several years ago, faced with the inevitable loss of old files and archival materials and concerned about preserving its history, the committee commissioned former AAP Vice-President Richard Kleeman, who directed Freedom to Read from 1972 until 1996, to write such a history. In 1998 the committee published *The More Things Change: A Selective History of the AAP Freedom to Read Committee 1970–1996*.

The committee coordinates the publishing industry's participation in Banned Books Week: A Celebration of the Freedom to Read.

## Higher Education

AAP's Higher Education Committee continues to serve the needs and interests of AAP members who publish for the postsecondary educational market. The Higher Education Committee is chaired by June Smith (Houghton Mifflin).

The Higher Education group again coordinated AAP's participation at the National Association of College Stores' Annual Meeting and Campus Exposition, held in Indianapolis in April. The committee continues to refine and improve collection of higher education publishing statistics.

The committee published its annual *AAP College Textbook Publishers Greenbook*, a resource for college store buyers that provides a wealth of information on the college publishing industry.

## International Committee

The International Committee represents a broad cross-section of the AAP membership. Deborah Wiley (John Wiley & Sons) chairs the committee.

The committee operated an expanded International Rights and Sales Center at BookExpo '98, providing AAP members (and members of AAP's five affiliate publisher organizations) exhibiting at the show with excellent facilities for meeting their international customers.

The committee sponsored a very successful seminar on the question of territorial rights at BookExpo '98.

## International Freedom to Publish

AAP's International Freedom to Publish (IFTP) Committee defends and promotes freedom of written communication worldwide. The IFTP Committee monitors human rights issues and provides moral support and practical assistance to publishers and authors outside the United States who are denied basic freedoms. The committee carries on its work in close cooperation with other human rights groups, including Human Rights Watch and PEN American Center. William Schwalbe (Hyperion) is committee chair.

The IFTP Committee met early in the year with Judith Krug of ALA to discuss adding an international component to the annual observance of Banned Books Week, which AAP cosponsors. As a result of committee efforts, a new section was added to the *Banned Books Week Resource Guide* published by ALA calling attention to book censorship around the world by listing books that are banned in their own country but are available in the United States.

Reflecting AAP's role as a founding member of the U.S. Committee to Defend Salman Rushdie, the committee was encouraged by statements issued in September by the president and foreign minister of Iran formally disassociating their government from the death threat imposed on Rushdie almost ten years ago.

At the committee's request—after learning that the respected Swiss scholar and author Jean Ziegler might face treason charges because of a book he wrote on the complicity of Swiss banks with the Nazis during World War II—AAP President Schroeder wrote to the U.S. Ambassador to Switzerland and the International Publishers Association to seek their help.

In 1998 the IFTP Committee undertook the task of producing a brochure briefly describing the committee's history and primary achievements and discussing its ongoing work. Plans called for publication of the brochure early in 1999.

The IFTP Committee continued to voice protests on behalf of writers, journalists, and publishers who are denied basic rights of free expression. In February 1998, in letters to the president and minister of justice of Turkey, the IFTP Committee voiced strong protest over the jailing of noted Turkish writer and political scientist Haluk Gerger. Gerger was serving a ten-month sentence for an article he wrote in 1993 criticizing the Turkish army's conduct of the war in eastern Turkey. While taking no position with respect to the subject of Gerger's writings, the committee protested his punishment merely on the basis of what he has written. "This arrest, and others like it, are in violation of many international agreements to which Turkey is a signatory, including the Universal Declaration of Human Rights, the Helsinki Final Act, and the European Convention for the Protection of Human Rights and Fundamental Freedoms," the letter stated.

# Literacy

AAP is concerned with the promotion of reading and literacy in the United States. Over the years, it has lent its support to a wide variety of reading-promotion and literacy programs, working with such partners as the International Reading Association, Reading Is Fundamental, the Barbara Bush Foundation for Family Literacy, and the Center for the Book in the Library of Congress.

Several years ago AAP became involved in supporting the innovative program Reach Out and Read, which uses pediatric clinics and medical personnel to promote early-childhood literacy. The program is now operating at clinics and hospitals nationwide. In December 1998 AAP President Schroeder joined First Lady Hillary Rodham Clinton and Reach Out and Read founder Barry Zuckerman at the launch of the Reach Out and Read Coalition of Greater New York.

At the December 1 event, members of the coalition—which represents 24 area hospitals and community health centers with more than 40 Reach Out and Read programs in the five boroughs—were challenged to "prescribe" a million books by the year 2000.

AAP is involved in promoting President Clinton's America Reads Challenge and was among the organizations represented at a White House conference in the spring of 1997 at which the First Lady launched the Prescription for Reading partnership. AAP President Schroeder met with Mrs. Clinton and others at the White House in January 1998 to discuss the partnership's accomplishments in its first nine months.

Significant research activity over the past few years has created a new understanding of how the brain develops and the crucial role of early language experiences, including reading. Although most parents understand intuitively that reading to children is a positive experience, they may not be aware of the newest discoveries in neuroscience that show that reading aloud actually stimulates the growth of a baby's brain. As part of its broad initiative to encourage adults to read to children every day, AAP put together a short *Fact Sheet*, citing some of the recent research. The *Fact Sheet* has been widely distributed to AAP members and others interested in getting out the message about the importance of reading aloud to very young children.

In March 1998 Schroeder joined "The Cat in the Hat" and singer Carly Simon, in a birthday tribute to Dr. Seuss at the Children's Museum in New York City. AAP cosponsored the event, which was part of the National Education Association's nationwide literacy initiative Read Across America.

Early in 1998 AAP made contact with Professor Susan Neuman of Temple University, who had just published *Books Make a Difference: A Study of Access to Literacy*, based on a dramatic literacy intervention program called Books Aloud. Funded by the William Penn Foundation and administered by the Free Library of Philadelphia, the $2.5 million Books Aloud program inundated some 330 day care centers serving almost 18,000 economically disadvantaged children in the Delaware Valley, with new, high-quality, age-appropriate children's books, bookcases, and storage racks. Day care center staff were provided with basic training in using the books effectively. Pre- and postprogram assessments revealed significant and enduring changes in the early literacy abilities of the Books Aloud children. AAP prepared a brief summary of the Temple University study, which has been widely disseminated to member publishers.

AAP has taken the lead in bringing together a coalition comprising Temple University's Neuman, the Institute for Civil Society, and the National Association for the Education of Young Children and has established an industry advisory committee of prominent AAP-member children's publishers to explore the possibility of developing and expanding the Books Aloud model to reach children in day care centers across the country.

## Postal Committee

AAP's Postal Committee coordinates activity in the area of postal rates and regulations, monitors developments at the U.S. Postal Service and the independent Postal Rate Commission, and intervenes on the industry's behalf in formal proceedings before the commission. The committee also directs AAP lobbying activities on postal issues. Lisa Pavlock (The McGraw-Hill Companies) chairs the Postal Committee.

[A summary of proposed (but unenacted) postal-reform legislation appears in the article "Legislation and Regulations Affecting Publishing in 1998" in Part 2.—*Ed.*]

## Professional and Scholarly Publishing

The Professional and Scholarly Publishing (PSP) Division comprises AAP members who publish technical, scientific, medical, and scholarly materials, including books, journals, computer software, databases, and CD-ROM products. Professional societies and university presses play an important role in the division. Janice Kuta (Groves Dictionaries) is division chair.

PSP's 1998 Annual Meeting was held in Washington, D.C., in February. The division sponsors a prestigious awards program, open only to AAP/PSP members, to acknowledge outstanding achievements in professional, scholarly, and reference publishing. At the 22nd Annual PSP Awards banquet in Washington, the R. R. Hawkins Award for the outstanding professional/scholarly work of the year went to Yale University Press for *Three Thousand Years of Chinese Painting*. In addition, book awards were presented in 30 subject categories, in design and production, and in journal and electronic publishing.

The PSP Electronic Information Committee sponsored a seminar for publishers and librarians on "Licensing Electronic Information Products and Services." Held on the Columbia University campus, the seminar included speakers representing the full range of academic, scholarly, and STM publishing and the academic and corporate library communities.

On May 13 members of the PSP Executive Council met in New York City with a delegation of copyright officials from the People's Republic of China and academics from the Chinese Academy of Social Sciences. The discussions focused on copyright protection, with specific reference to the electronic environment. The PSP publishers described their ongoing problems with copyright infringement in China, particularly the widespread use of pirated journals by libraries that have few legitimate subscriptions.

In October the division's Journals Committee sponsored a workshop on alternative marketing methods, focusing on new ways beyond the traditional direct-mail channels that journals publishers use to reach their target audiences. Audiotapes of the workshop are available.

For the first time in more than a decade, publishers and librarians joined forces to conduct a survey of the library market, exploring the ways in which publishers and vendors market and sell products and services to the library community and assessing the effectiveness of their marketing practices. The survey, which will update surveys conducted in 1975 and 1987, is being carried out under the direction of a joint committee of AAP and the Association of Library Collections and Technical Services (a division of ALA). Three survey questionnaires were sent to libraries, vendors, and publishers in November 1998, asking each segment for its perspective on current marketing practices. Survey results will be tabulated by the Library Research Center at the University of Illinois, Urbana-Champaign, and will be published by ALA, along with an analysis comparing the results with data from the earlier surveys. Survey results will be released in a full-day program at the 1999 ALA Annual Conference. The survey is underwritten in part by the Professional and Scholarly Publishing Division.

## School Division

The School Division is concerned with publishing for the elementary and secondary school (K–12) market. The division works to enhance the role of instructional materials in the education process, to maintain categorical funding for instructional materials and increase the funds available for the purchase of these materials, and to simplify and rationalize the process of state adoptions for instructional materials. It serves as a bridge between the publishing industry and the educational community, promoting the cause of education at the national and state levels, and works closely with the AAP Washington office and an effective lobbying network in key adoption states. Buzz Ellis (Glencoe/McGraw-Hill) chairs the division.

At the 1998 School Division Annual Meeting in Austin, Texas, in January, publishers honored Bill Boyd, who had died in December 1997 after serving as AAP's Florida legislative advocate for the past 23 years, by awarding him the Mary McNulty Award.

Publicity generated by the School Division's instructional-materials survey and extensive media coverage of the textbook shortage in the Los Angeles Unified School District prompted California legislators to put forward a number of proposals to increase instructional-materials funding and to guarantee that every K–12 student is furnished with basic instructional materials in all core subjects.

In August California Governor Pete Wilson signed landmark legislation calling for the expenditure of $1 billion during the next four years for textbooks and other instructional materials aligned to the state's new academic-content standards. The governor also signed off on a 1998–1999 budget that not only fully funded the new legislation at $250 million for FY 1998–1999, but in addition allocated $172.1 million for the state's existing Instructional Materials Fund, $158.5 million for the purchase of library resources, and $71.5 million for science laboratory materials and equipment. Taken together, the 1998–1999 appropriation of $652.1 million for instructional materials, school library funding, and science resources dwarfed the preceding year's $165 million instructional-materials allocation and is far and away the largest instructional-materials appropriation ever approved by a state.

AAP's School Division played a key role in generating support for the funding initiatives. Through surveys, opinion polls, public-education efforts, and the work of its legislative advocate in Sacramento, the School Division effectively raised public awareness of the lack of adequate, up-to-date instructional materials in California and the critical importance of instructional materials in successfully implementing the rigorous new content standards.

After extensive lobbying efforts by the School Division, the Florida House and Senate passed a 1998–1999 budget that includes $184 million for the categorical funding of instructional materials, a $25 million increase over last year. Proposed language that would have required districts to purchase a textbook for every student in order to receive any funding, which AAP opposed as unrealistic and punitive, was dropped from the bill. School Division lobbying and media efforts in Florida have contributed to a remarkable 114 percent increase in instructional-materials funding in the last four years. As one of his last acts before leaving office in the fall of 1998, Florida's education commissioner submitted his 1999–2000 legislative budget request for public education, including $195 million in categorical funding for instructional materials, an $11 million (5.1 percent) increase over the previous year.

In October the School Division sponsored a seminar in Chicago on trends in school technology and the implications for K–12 publishers. Linda Roberts, director of technology for the U.S. Department of Education, was the keynote speaker.

The School Division succeeded in its efforts to gain Texas State Board of Education approval for an amendment giving publishers a "second chance" to avoid rejection from state-approved lists. The amendment adds a step to the adoption process, enabling publishers whose materials have been judged not to conform with Texas requirements to submit additional content to cover missing items. AAP had long advocated such a change.

## Trade Publishing

AAP's Trade Publishing group comprises publishers of fiction, general nonfiction, poetry, children's literature, religious materials, and reference publications in hardcover, paperback, and electronic formats. Mel Parker (Warner Books) chairs the Trade Executive Committee.

An AAP-sponsored seminar held in June focused on helping trade publishers get the most out of the $2 billion library market.

Much of the Trade Publishing Committee's attention in 1998 focused on an effort to pull together the elements of a broad, innovative, industrywide campaign to promote reading and book buying, especially to the elusive 18- to 34-year-old market. On December 7 AAP announced plans for the Get Caught Reading campaign, which will be launched at BookExpo '99 in Los Angeles and take place throughout May 1999 (which will be designated Get Caught Reading Month). The campaign is a cooperative effort and has been endorsed by every major trade publisher. A major component of the campaign will be a series of print advertisements featuring two of America's most popular celebrities (and book lovers), Rosie O'Donnell and Whoopi Goldberg. As AAP President Pat Schroeder said: "Let's face it, if a good campaign can make *milk* seem like fun, just think what we can do with something as inherently wonderful as books!"

## Administrative Committees

Two administrative committees direct and coordinate AAP member services.

### Compensation Survey Committee

This committee coordinates and supervises preparation of the *AAP Survey of Compensation and Personnel Practices in the Publishing Industry*. Published every two years, the report is available only to AAP members and is designed to provide current accurate information on prevailing compensation levels for representative management and professional positions in the book-publishing industry. No report was published in 1998.

### Lawyers Committee

The Lawyers Committee is composed of both in-house and outside counsel of AAP member companies. It meets quarterly to discuss legal issues under review in the committees and divisions.

## 1998 Annual Meeting

Reflecting the management style of its new president, the association's 1998 annual meeting was compacted into a fast-paced, information-filled 24 hours. Some of its highlights follow.

### Business Meeting

In her report to the membership, AAP President and CEO Pat Schroeder pointed out that the association's proposed operating budget of approximately $5 million represents an extraordinarily efficient use of resources. Other organizations in the content community—notably the Motion Picture Association of America (with an operating budget in excess of $50 million) and the Recording Industry Association of America (with a budget of more than $12 million)—have the advantage of powerful members and plenty of funds at their disposal, but it is AAP's work, through the efforts of its excellent staff, that is getting results on Capitol Hill, she said.

To strengthen the effective grassroots organization AAP has begun building, the new dues structure will, among other things, make it easier and more attractive for small publishers to join AAP, "to their advantage and ours," she noted.

Schroeder said it was high time for American publishers to get together in an industrywide campaign to promote books, and urged the membership to come later that day to hear a proposal for such a campaign that would be put forward by the AAP Trade Committee.

During the open discussion, Charles Ellis, President and CEO of John Wiley & Sons and a former chairman of AAP, criticized the industry's reluctance to provide adequate funding for AAP. "The dues level doesn't make sense," he said, in light of the crucial battles ahead and the need for a strong national organization to fight those battles. "What is the obligation of the industry in supporting their association and how long can we continue to undertax ourselves?" he asked.

**FY 1998–1999 Budget and New Dues Structure Approved**

The membership approved an operating budget of $5,488,600 for FY 1998–1999, with $3,758,050 allocated to Core (including the three committees serving the Trade, Higher Education, and International constituencies) and $1,730,550 allocated to the two divisions (with $1,221,300 going to the School Division and $509,250 to the Professional and Scholarly Publishing Division).

The 1998–1999 budget includes a new, simplified dues and assessments structure that provides for the reallocation of funding from the three downsized former divisions (Trade, Higher Education, International) to the major core issues identified as strategic priorities.

The new dues structure lowers core dues rates for companies with annual sales under $1 million. For AAP's larger members, the new structure establishes a cap on core dues in the amount of $300,000, indexed annually to the consumer price index, and maintains the current cap on the total that a single member can pay (in core dues and divisional assessments) to 7.5 percent of the association's expense budget for that year.

In an effort to attract smaller publishers to regular AAP membership, a new flat rate of $195 was established for houses with sales up to $1 million. Attendees at the business meeting applauded this move, noting that it makes AAP membership feasible and attractive for small publishers. AAP was urged to market the new dues structure aggressively to small publishers.

**Board Appointments**

Peter Jovanovich, President and CEO of Addison Wesley Longman, was elected to a two-year term as Chairman of the AAP Board of Directors, succeeding Richard Robinson. Other officers elected were Brian Knez (Harcourt Brace), vice-chairman; William M. Wright (Hearst Book Group), treasurer; and Kathleen Hammond (Hammond, Inc.), secretary. The membership approved three new board members: Tanis Erdmann (Reader's Digest), Robert Miller (Disney Publishing Company), and William P. Sisler (Harvard University Press).

# Association of Research Libraries

21 Dupont Circle N.W., Washington, DC 20036
202-296-2296; e-mail arlhq@arl.org
World Wide Web: http://www.arl.org

Duane E. Webster
Executive Director

The Association of Research Libraries (ARL) represents the 122 principal research libraries that serve major research institutions in the United States and Canada. ARL's mission is to shape and influence forces affecting the future of research libraries in the process of scholarly communication. ARL programs and services promote equitable access to and effective use of recorded knowledge in support of teaching, research, scholarship, and community service. The association articulates the concerns of research libraries and their institutions, forges coalitions, influences information policy development, and supports innovation and improvement in research library operations. ARL operates as a forum for the exchange of ideas and as an agent for collective action.

ARL fulfills its mission and builds its programs through a set of strategic objectives. To meet these objectives, ARL resources are organized into a framework of programs and capabilities. Annually, the ARL Board of Directors identifies priorities for the year, and ARL program staff and the association's standing committees address these priorities. The 1999 priority activities as outlined in the ARL Program Plan are to

- Intensify copyright awareness within the research and educational communities and continue copyright advocacy
- Create cost-effective models and strategies for managing global scholarly communication in partnership with other organizations
- Help research libraries, and the communities of which they are a part, move into a transformed and increasingly diverse environment through the development of human resources, programs, and products
- Ensure that research and learning will flourish through the development of advanced networking applications and Internet2

## Scholarly Communication

The Office of Scholarly Communication (OSC) undertakes activities to understand and influence the forces affecting the production, dissemination, and use of scholarly and scientific information. The office seeks to promote innovative, creative, and alternative ways of sharing scholarly findings, particularly through championing evolving electronic techniques for recording and disseminating academic and research scholarship. The office collaborates with others in the scholarly community to build common understanding of the challenges presented by electronic scholarly communication and to generate strategies for transforming the system.

The Pew Higher Education Roundtable, which was cosponsored by the Association of American Universities (AAU) and ARL in 1997, examined how the academy, in cooperation with not-for-profit publishers and scholarly societies, can take steps to manage its own intellectual property in more cost-effective ways while ensuring sustained access to scholarly research. The group agreed to five strategies that need to be undertaken to ensure future access to scholarly communication: (1) a de-emphasis on volume as a measure of quality in the review of faculty work, (2) a continued effort by libraries to shape a more coherent marketplace, (3) a well-organized campaign to teach the faculty the economics of scholarly publishing and the options they have for assigning their copyrights, (4) an investment in electronic forms of scholarly communication, and (5) the decoupling of publication and peer review for the purposes of promotion and tenure.

Several initiatives are under way in support of these recommendations. These include workshops on negotiating licenses for electronic resources, the appointment of an ARL working group to explore the feasibility of establishing a Research Library Purchasing and Negotiating Center, the development of a proposal for a joint ARL/AAU educational campaign, and the continued development of the Scholarly Publishing and Academic Resources Coalition (SPARC).

The journal crisis has had a profound effect on the market for scholarly monographs. Over the past several years, ARL has been working with the American Historical Association (AHA) on a proposal to address this issue. Now called the Historical Studies Distribution Network (HSDN), the project is designed to explore the feasibility of an electronic repository to support the dissemination and use of scholarly monographic works in historical studies.

## Scholarly Publishing and Academic Resources Coalition

Established as an initiative of the ARL Office of Scholarly Communication in the autumn of 1997 and formally launched in June 1998, SPARC is a coalition of libraries that leverages libraries' buying power to create a more competitive and cost-effective marketplace for scholarly journals. This objective is pursued via "publisher partnerships" that support lower-cost alternatives to high-priced journals and innovative models of scholarly publishing. In return for offering library-friendly pricing and policies, partnerships receive endorsement and marketing support from SPARC. Operating under the administrative, legal, and fiscal umbrella of ARL, SPARC became independent of ARL financial support and opened its membership beyond the ranks of ARL member libraries in 1998.

SPARC's most significant 1998 achievement was the creation of three publisher partnerships:

*American Chemical Society (ACS)*. SPARC and ACS agreed to a collaboration that will introduce three new reasonably priced alternative journals over a three-year period. The first of these, *Organic Letters*, will be launched in July 1999 and offer 65–70 percent of the content of a competing commercial title at about one-quarter the competitor's price. A second collaboration will be examined and announced in 1999. In 1998 SPARC also initiated discussions with ACS on author copyright policies and agreed to conduct jointly a series of focus groups in 1999 to examine the role of personal Web sites in authors' dissemination of their research.

*Royal Society of Chemistry (RSC)*. SPARC's agreement with RSC also calls for introduction of three new lower-cost journals over three years. The first of these, *PhysChemComm*, is an electronic-only title launched in fall 1998 whose cost-per-article is 20 percent of that of the key competitor.

*Evolutionary Ecology Research (EER)*. This new title has been created by the editors of a commercially published journal that had risen in price an average of 19 percent annually during the past dozen years. *EER* institutional prices will be little more than one-third the current subscription price of the competitor and will effectively compete for high-quality articles.

During 1998 partnership discussions were conducted with scores of other organizations of varying types, and a number of them offer the promise of addressing SPARC criteria and providing the basis for a partnership agreement in 1999.

At the direction of the SPARC Working Group and in response to interest demonstrated by market research, the SPARC enterprise director developed a 1998–1999 plan for membership, organization, and governance that opened SPARC participation beyond ARL ranks. The ARL Board endorsement of the plan was obtained in August 1998. Membership stood near 150 by the end of 1998.

Several library organizations have become affiliate members of SPARC:

- Association of College and Research Libraries (ACRL)
- Canadian Association of Research Libraries/Association des bibliothèques de recherche du Canada (CARL/ABRC)
- Conference of Directors of Research Libraries (Denmark)
- Council of Australian University Librarians
- Standing Conference of National and University Libraries (United Kingdom and Ireland)

For SPARC to achieve its objectives, it is essential that it establish a strong identity among the main stakeholders in the scholarly communication process: researchers, readers, academic institutions, buyers, and publishers. A valuable first step was taken during the spring of 1998 when endorsements of the SPARC concept were secured from the Association of American Universities (AAU), Association of American University Presses (AAUP), Big 12 Provosts, and National Association of State Universities and Land Grant Colleges (NASULGC).

## Federal Relations and Information Policy

The Federal Relations and Information Policy Program is designed to monitor activities resulting from legislative, regulatory, or operating practices of international and domestic government agencies and other relevant bodies on matters of concern to research libraries; prepare analysis of and response to federal information policies; influence federal action on issues related to research libraries; examine issues of importance to the development of research libraries; and develop ARL positions on issues that reflect the needs and interests of members.

Copyright and intellectual-property issues continue to be a major focus for this and other ARL programs.

In 1998 ARL actively participated in information policy debates by responding to and shaping national and international legislative initiatives that impact research libraries, including Internet2 and Next Generation Internet (NGI) initiatives, dissemination of U.S. government information, and U.S. congressional appropriations.

ARL, with others in the higher education community, worked with House and Senate staff in support of NGI funding and authorizing legislation. In addition, the ARL Executive Committee created the Internet2 Working Group to determine the best strategies for research library participation in Internet2 initiatives.

Efforts to revamp U.S. federal information dissemination policies continued throughout the year as ARL staff met with congressional and executive branch staff to discuss various proposals. ARL staff participated in numerous discussions with members of the executive and legislative branches regarding changes to Title 44, including the Inter-Association Working Group on Government Information (IAWG), comprised of representatives of library associations.

ARL participated in a U.S. Geological Survey-sponsored panel to examine issues relating to the National Land Remote Sensing Archive, specifically focusing on long-term access and preservation issues. ARL staff collaborated with members of CENDI, an STI federal-agency working group on issues relating to government information dissemination and access. ARL continues to collaborate with others in the public-interest community and with agencies in implementing the Government Information Locator Service (GILS) proposal. GILS provides a framework and common approach for federal agencies to make their information resources publicly available.

ARL worked in support of fiscal year (FY) 1999 appropriations for the National Science Foundation, the National Agricultural Library, the National Endowment for the Humanities, the Library of Congress, and the Superintendent of Documents. ARL supported the reauthorization of the Higher Education Act (HEA) and the American Folklife Center of the Library of Congress.

The ARL Geographic Information Systems (GIS) Literacy Project continues to expand and evolve. The project seeks to educate librarians and users about GIS as well as develop GIS capabilities in research libraries. Background materials related to this project, including a database of all project participants, are available on the Web at http://www.arl.org/info/gis/index.html.

## Intellectual Property and Copyright Issues

The ARL Board of Directors has identified intellectual property and copyright as a defining set of issues for the future of scholarly communications. Although these issues have been a priority for several years, activity was accelerated this year due to U.S. legislative developments. As part of the association's interest in raising library and scholarly community awareness of issues associated with copyright and intellectual-property management, several activities were undertaken to advance the ARL agenda in these critical areas.

ARL collaborated very closely with the American Association of Law Libraries (AALL), American Library Association (ALA), Medical Library Association (MLA), and Special Libraries Association (SLA) on copyright and intellectual-property issues through the Shared Legal Capability (SLC). During 1998 SLC met with members of the Clinton administration and congressional staff to discuss many proposed changes to the Copyright Act. The group submitted statements to the House and Senate regarding copyright legislation; drafted and actively supported alternative legislative proposals with others in the Digital Future Coalition (DFC); and participated in congressional negotiations on online service provider liability issues, preservation, distance education, fair use, database legislation, and term extension.

With others in the public and private sectors, ARL formed and continued to be a strong voice in the Digital Future Coalition. This coalition is comprised of a diverse constituency of library, education, legal, scholarly, consumer, and public-interest associations, hardware and software manufacturers, and telecommunications providers that share concerns with pending copyright and database legislation. They also share the belief that any copyright legislation must strike a balance between owners, users, and creators of copyrighted works.

The DFC submitted testimony to both the House and Senate on copyright-related bills. They conducted hundreds of visits to members of Congress, their staff, and senior members of the administration on copyright issues. In conjunction with ARL, ALA, and the Home Recording Rights Coalition, they launched a public-awareness campaign focused on the many dimensions of the copyright legislation.

ARL collaborated with a number of constituencies to address issues relating to the database proposal "Collections of Information Antipiracy Act" (H.R. 2652). ARL participated in numerous database forums. In addition, there have been congressional and executive branch visits and discussions. ARL, along with others in the coalition, participated in Senate-sponsored negotiations on database legislation. The negotiations were unsuccessful, but the database coalition was successful in calling for deferment of the legislation. ARL and others in the coalition also drafted an alternative bill for consideration.

A number of SLC partners participated in Uniform Commercial Code 2B (UCC2B) discussions on the licensing of information products. Several motions were drafted and considered by the drafting committee and the American Law Institute. UCC2B negotiations continued throughout the year.

ARL continues to add information to its Web site on copyright and intellectual-property rights at http://www.arl.org/info/frn/copy/copytoc.html. Recent additions include analyses of DMCA, alternative database legislation, related Comments from the Administration, distance education activities, and links to related copyright sites.

## Access and Technology

The access capability undertakes activities to support resource sharing among research libraries in the electronic environment and to improve access to research information resources. It works to strengthen cooperative cataloging programs, abstracting and indexing tools, and user access to information both on-site and remotely.

The ALA Midwinter Meeting in January 1998 marked the beginning of the five-year anniversary of the ARL North American Interlibrary Loan and Document Delivery (NAILDD) Project. Established in 1993, the NAILDD Project promotes developments to maximize access to research resources while minimizing the costs associated with such activities. The five-year status report for NAILDD highlights and salutes the responsiveness of some of the more active for-profit and not-for-profit organizations and companies to advance the project's three technical priorities. In 1998 the NAILDD Project quantified the efficiencies made possible by the application of technology and standards to library access services as identified by the ARL ILL/DD Performance Measures Study and began to identify policy and other service issues that support the use of technology and standards. Although much encouraging progress was made during the last five years, work still remains to permit library users to identify, order, and receive research materials seamlessly and cost-effectively.

Funded by the Andrew W. Mellon Foundation, the ILL/DD Performance Measures Study was completed in 1998 with the May publication of *Measuring the Performance of Interlibrary Loan Operations in North American Research and College Libraries*. The final report provides a detailed analysis of the performance of ILL/DD operations in 97 research libraries and 22 college libraries. The publication also highlights characteristics of high-performing ILL/DD operations in research libraries and presents a series of recommendations for improving local practices.

Analysis of the data provides the framework for the next phase: to enable librarians to make significant improvements in their ILL operations. This is being undertaken through two sets of activities. The first is the development of a series of workshops to assist attendees in evaluating and adapting the performance-enhancing procedures and tools for improving ILL/DD services. The workshops "From Data to Action" provide specific techniques for library managers to compare their local operations against the high-performing operations and to develop a work plan to improve their operations. Implementation of the findings of the Performance Measures Study is also being facilitated through collaboration with members of the Missouri-based MIRACL consortium to develop an institution-specific process to improve local operations. The collaboration will lead to a process other libraries may choose to follow.

The NAILDD Project convenes three groups to facilitate technical developments and sharing of information. The Developers/Implementors Group (DIG) seeks to accelerate collaboration between libraries and the more than 70 private-sector players to advance the project's three technical goals. The ILL Protocol Implementors Group (IPIG) supports the implementation of the international standard for ILL communication by more than 40 organizations in ten countries. The British Library hosted the first IPIG meeting outside North America in London in September. The Directors Forum provides an occasion for interaction between library directors and senior staff and representatives from members of the DIG and IPIG. In 1998 the forum focused on user-initiated, unmediated ILL/DD services and the findings of the ARL ILL/DD Performance Measures Study. Reports describing the 1998 NAILDD Project meetings are on the ARL Access Web page (http://www.arl.org/access/index.shtml).

# Collections

The AAU/ARL Global Resources Program, initially funded in 1997 by a three-year grant from the Andrew W. Mellon Foundation, emerged from a series of earlier activities that were focused on the state of foreign acquisitions and culminated in the 1996 publication of *Scholarship, Research Libraries, and Global Publishing*. The principal goal of the Global Resources Program—to improve access to international research materials regardless of format or location—is being addressed in a number of ways.

In 1998 the Africana Librarians Council (ALC) of the African Studies Association and the Cooperative Africana Microform Project (CAMP) of the Center for Research Libraries (CRL) began a two-year pilot project to create an electronic database of holdings information for newspapers, in all formats and languages, published in sub-Saharan Africa. Initially, the Union List of African Newspapers (ULAN) will consolidate holdings information for collections in North America, but it will later expand to include holdings in Africa, Europe, and elsewhere. ULAN will provide greatly enhanced access for researchers to this elusive but important resource. The ULAN database will be created and maintained at CRL. At present, the project has 14 participating libraries (see http://www.crl.uchicago.edu/).

The German Resources Project focuses on improving the acquisition, use, and sharing of German-language materials among North American libraries, as well as fostering collaboration with German research libraries, particularly in resource sharing and the development of digital collections. This project received funding from the Mellon Foundation in 1998 to support a series of meetings of German and North American librarians to discuss and design digital collection development agreements and means of facilitating document delivery. Four working groups have been established to address the project priorities: document delivery, bibliographic control, digital libraries, and collection development. The project is cochaired by Sarah Thomas (Cornell University) and Winston Tabb (Library of Congress) and is coordinated by Roger Brisson (Pennsylvania State University). As of December 1998 the project had 35 participating libraries, as well as five German partner libraries and one affiliated, non-ARL library (see http://lcweb.loc.gov/loc/german/).

The principal goal of the Japan Journal Access Project, which is coordinated jointly by ARL and the National Coordinating Committee on Japanese Library Resources (NCC), is to improve access to journal literature and newspapers published in Japan. A related goal is to expand awareness and availability of Japanese serials in North American libraries. Access to these materials can be made difficult by the lag in the retrospective conversion of Japanese-character-based records. With funding from the Japan-U.S. Friendship Commission, staff at Ohio State University has built the Union List of Japanese Serials and Newspapers (ULJSN), a Web database to which project participants contribute their titles. The ULJSN allows researchers to identify the location of particular titles of interest and will also be used to coordinate Japanese serials collecting in North American libraries. Efficient mechanisms for binational interlibrary lending and borrowing as well as document delivery are also being explored in this project, which has 29 participating ARL members (see http://pears.lib.ohio-state.edu).

The goals of the Latin Americanist Research Resources Project are to expand the range of materials available to Latin Americanist students and scholars; restructure access to these materials through distributed, cooperative collection development facilitated by technology; and assist libraries in containing costs through the reallocation of acquisitions funds. Initial funding for the project came from the Mellon Foundation and has been matched by contributions from the 42 participating institutions. A major project component is a searchable Web database of the tables of contents for 400 journals from Argentina, Brazil, and Mexico, through which users can request delivery of articles. Responsibility for collecting these journals and supplying articles to users is distributed among the project members. The project's distributed-resources component encourages libraries to reallocate funds to deepen collections in established areas of local emphasis. Individual participants—who each agree to devote at least 7 percent of their Latin American studies monographic budget toward acquiring more specialized research materials—select the fields. As of December 1998 the participants had collectively reallocated approximately $170,000. Six working groups and an advisory committee coordinate project activities (see http://www.arl.org/collect/grp/index.htlm#ladp).

The two-year Digital South Asia Library Project is developing an Internet-based infrastructure for intercontinental electronic document delivery to and from selected South Asia libraries. It also includes the indexing of journals and the creation of full-text electronic reference resources and finding aids to improve access to scholarly sources in English, Tamil, and Urdu. Direct delivery of scanned pages of articles will allow scholars to consult these rare publications without travel to India. Indexing records will be created for 38,000 articles in Tamil journals, 38,000 articles in Urdu journals, and 4,750 English journal articles, all published during the 19th and 20th centuries. It also includes the creation of full-text electronic versions of five titles selected from the *Official Publications of India*, one of which will be a statistical source structured as an electronic database. The project's lead institutions are Columbia University Libraries and the University of Chicago Libraries, in partnership with the Roja Muthiah Research Library in Madras, India, and the Sundarayya Vignana Kendram in Hyderabad, India, as well as the Urdu Research Library Consortium (URLC) and the South Asia Microform Project (SAMP) (see http://www.lib.uchicago.edu/LibInfo/Subjects/SouthAsia/dsal.html).

The newest Global Resources Program project, Southeast Asia Journals, is a cooperative initiative of the libraries of the Committee on Research Materials on Southeast Asia (CORMOSEA). Over a two-year period the project will create a Thai-language searchable visual database as a prototype for accessing nonroman scripts and will index colonial-era journals for the period predating the *Bibliography of Asian Studies*. Participating libraries will also work with institutions in Southeast Asia to develop a regional journal index in electronic form. Lead institutions are the University of Washington, the University of Wisconsin at Madison, Cornell University, and the Technical Information Access Center (TIAC) in Bangkok, Thailand.

Although each project addresses a particular regional need, they all focus on providing access to materials that have been previously accessible only with difficulty and on utilizing technology to ensure this access. Other Global Resources Program activities include a clearinghouse of Web links to international resources, an inventory of linkages and agreements that North American research libraries maintain with libraries and research institutes abroad, participation in efforts to recruit and train future area librarians, and opportunities for faculty and librarians to collaborate to identify future resource needs and to develop cooperative strategies to meet those needs. In this last area, the Global Resources Program is partnering with the Social Science Research Council and the American Council of Learned Societies (ACLS).

## Preservation

Strategies to accomplish ARL's preservation objectives include encouraging and strengthening broad-based participation in national preservation efforts in the United States and Canada, supporting development of preservation programs within member libraries, advocating copyright legislation that supports preservation activities in the electronic environment, supporting effective bibliographic control of preservation-related processes, encouraging development of preservation information resources, and monitoring technological developments that may have an impact on preservation goals.

The ARL Digital Initiatives Database (DID), a collaboration between the University of Illinois at Chicago and ARL, is a Web-based registry for descriptions of digital initiatives in or involving libraries. DID currently contains more than 100 library projects and includes technical features, policy choices, subject matter of the content, and contact information. Preservation data, if applicable, are included in the project descriptions. The database was designed for libraries to enter their own data about all projects both large and small in scope. In addition to links to each of the projects in the database, DID offers a list of online resources for libraries involved in digital initiatives (see http://www.arl.org/did/).

ARL member leaders and staff contributed to a series of meetings with representatives of the Modern Language Association, American Historical Association, Society of American Archivists, Council on Library and Information Resources, and others to consider issues involved in the preservation of the artifact/primary records. The group decided to commission a work that would describe, for a general campus readership, the evolution of research libraries in this country, the strategies libraries have employed in addressing preservation issues, and perspectives on preservation concerns from different segments of the scholarly community.

## Diversity

The purpose of this capability is to support and extend efforts within member institutions to promote and develop work forces that are representative of a diverse population and to foster workplace environments where all employees are valued for their uniqueness and personal contributions. These efforts include the recruitment and retention of library personnel from a variety of backgrounds, particularly those from groups traditionally underrepresented in the academic library work force, and the development of a climate in the workplace that supports and encourages library personnel to recognize and value their similarities and differences.

The pilot phase of the Leadership and Career Development (LCD) Program, made possible through a Department of Education HEA Title II-B grant, was successfully completed in July 1998. The program was designed to increase the number of librarians from underrepresented groups in positions of influence and leadership in research libraries by helping them develop the skills needed to be more competitive in the promotion process. The LCD Program consists of several components: two five-day institutes, a mentoring relationship, and research project development. Twenty directors of ARL libraries and one dean of a library and information services education program served as mentors to the LCD Program participants.

The program received strong support from the ARL membership and the library community at large. The program's success can truly be reflected in the nearly 25 percent of program participants who have been promoted internally or offered next-tier positions in other academic and research library settings. The LCD Program will be offered biannually, with the next class offered in 1999–2000.

To give visibility to and provide a mechanism for LCD Program participants to share their research project results, a new bimonthly publication series, *Leading Ideas*, was launched. *Leading Ideas* highlights trends in diversity, leadership, and career development. Topics highlighted in the first year included "Implementing Post-Masters Residency Programs," "Promotion and Tenure: The Minority Academic Librarian," and "The Shared Leadership Principle: Creating Leaders Throughout the Organization."

The Diversity Program continues to partner with allied library associations including the Association for Library and Information Science Education (ALISE), ACRL, and ALA, to further the profession's diversity efforts. One example of these partnerships at work is ARL's relationship with ALA on its Spectrum Initiative. Spectrum Initiative Scholars have been matched with participants from the Leadership and Career Development Program in a mentoring relationship.

## Office of Leadership and Management Services

Established to help research and academic libraries develop better ways of managing their human and material resources, the Office of Leadership and Management Services (OLMS) has assisted library leaders in finding more-efficient and -effective ways of meeting user needs for over 27 years. OLMS staff stay abreast of current organizational and management theory and practice, seeking concepts and techniques that are applicable to, and have the potential for contributing to, the improved effectiveness of academic and research libraries.

To assist libraries in making the transition from traditional roles to increasingly transformational roles within their institutions and globally, the OLMS Organizational Development and Consulting Program provides a wide range of consulting services, incorporating new research on effective organizational models and management and leadership practices. This program provides academic and research libraries with programs to develop workable plans for improvement in such areas as public and technical services, planning, team building, and organizational review and design. The OLMS provides on-site and telephone consultation, staff training, written reports, and other materials to aid the client library in reaching their goals and visions.

Research libraries are called upon by their institutions to rethink the deployment of their resources, both human and fiscal. The OLMS Consulting and Organizational Development Program capability has assisted these libraries in creating stronger and more flexible organizational structures in order to absorb changes in the immediate environment. Specifically, the OLMS has provided assistance in developing new organizational designs, development of strategic plans, enhancement of senior leadership team skills and programmatic reviews. Activities in 1998 focused primarily on support for strategic-planning efforts and redesigning organizational structure.

The OLMS Information Services Program maintains an active publications program comprising three principal components: the *Systems and Procedures Exchange Center (SPEC) Kits* and *Flyers*, the OLMS *Occasional Papers*, and *Transforming Libraries*. Publications are produced by ARL/OLMS staff, consultants, and guest authors from member institutions.

*SPEC Kits* organize and collect selected library documents concerning a specific area of library management. Kits are designed to illustrate alternatives and innovations used in dealing with particular issues. Documents describing both the administrative and operational aspects of the topic are included. The data-gathering process for *SPEC* was refined in 1998, and surveys are now collected via interactive Web forms.

The OLMS Training and Leadership Development Program provides support for libraries by delivering unique and dynamic learning events that actively and positively assist academic and research libraries to recognize, develop, optimize, and refine staff talents and skills. This OLMS program stays abreast of innovations in library services, library technologies, and library methods while maintaining currency with innovations and the latest research findings in the areas of organizational structure, productivity, learning, and development. The program staff, consultants, and adjunct faculty design and deliver timely, up-to-date, and focused learning events.

In 1998 the OLMS Training and Leadership Development Program was invited to contribute curriculum for two important grant proposals to support the leadership development of individuals from underrepresented groups. Both the ARL Diversity Program's Leadership and Career Development Program and the University of Minnesota Training Institute for Affirmative Action Library Science Interns and Residents were funded by the Department of Education for 1998 programs. The OLMS Training and Leadership Development Program staff took an active design and training role in both programs.

In 1998 approximately 1,200 library staff participated in OLMS Training and Leadership Development Program events. The OLMS Training and Leadership Development Program has provided specific institutes for a number of library consortia including the Washington Research Library Consortium, CIRLA, and the Boston Library Consortium. In order to assist member institutions in identifying the range of available leadership-training programs, the OLMS has developed a chart of current leadership programs in North America. This work forms a foundation for development of a planning and communication tool for academic library training programs.

## Statistics and Measurement

The Statistics and Measurement Program describes and measures the performance of research libraries and their contributions to teaching, research, scholarship, and community service. Strategies to accomplish the objectives of the program include collecting, analyzing, and publishing quantifiable information about library collections, personnel, and expenditures, as well as expenditures and indicators of the nature of research institutions; developing new ways to describe and measure traditional and networked information resources and services; developing mechanisms to assess the relationship between campus information resources and high-quality research, the teaching environment, and, in general, the success of scholars and researchers; providing customized, confidential analysis for peer comparisons; preparing workshops regarding statistics and measurement issues in research libraries; sustaining a leadership role in the testing and application of academic research library statistics for North American institutions of higher education; and collaborating with other national and international library statistics programs and accreditation agencies.

Statistical compilations produced or distributed in 1998 include: *Developing Indicators for Academic Library Performance: Ratios from the ARL Statistics 1994–95 and 1995–96*; *ARL Annual Salary Survey 1997–98*; *ARL Statistics 1996–97*; *ARL Academic Law and Medical Libraries Statistics 1996–97*; *ARL Preservation Statistics 1996–97*; *Developing Indicators for Academic Library Performance: Ratios from the ARL Statistics 1995–96 and 1996–97*; *Report on the 1996–97 ARL Supplementary Statistics*; and *Library Expenditures as a Percent of E&G Expenditures in ARL University Libraries, FY 1995–96*.

Apart from these printed publishing efforts, the program continues its strong presence in electronic publishing activities. Of special interest is the interactive electronic publication of the *ARL Statistics on the WWW*, which was completely revised by staff of the Geospatial and Statistical Data Center at the University of Virginia. The program's Web site was also revised and is updated regularly with information and data from new editions of ARL statistical publications. New pages established this year include a page for the ARL survey coordinators and a page devoted to the topic of performance measures. The performance measures site includes bibliographies and readings, descriptions and links of tools and projects for measurement, and links to organizations also working in the area of performance measures (see http://www.arl.org/stats/perfmeas).

As a result of a 1996 grant from the Council on Library and Information Resources to investigate the character and nature of research library investment in electronic resources, ARL has revised the questions in its annual Supplementary Statistics questionnaire. Institutions are asked to supply expenditures from both library and external (e.g., campus or consortia) budgets. The data provide a more accurate picture of the total institutional investment in electronic resources managed by research libraries. Analysis of the data was conducted over the summer of 1998, and a final report was prepared in December 1998. All reports are available on the Statistics Program Web site (http://www.arl.org/stats/specproj).

Three workshops on Electronic Publishing of Data Sets on the Web were held in 1998. These workshops provided another 65 individuals with the skills to develop Web services in support of data file management. Planning has begun for a revised set of workshops on user surveys in academic libraries to follow on the successful series conducted in 1996–1997.

## Office of Research and Development

The ARL Office of Research and Development consolidates the administration of grants and grant-supported projects administered by ARL. The major goal within this capability is to identify and match ARL projects that support the research library community's mission with sources of external funding. Among the projects under way in 1998 were the following:

The Global Resources Program was in the second year of funding from the Mellon Foundation. The primary goal of the project is to improve access to international research resources, regardless of format or location.

ARL organized and manages a fund for legal expertise on intellectual property and the National Information Infrastructure (NII). In addition to ARL, the ALA, AALL, MLA, and SLA have each contributed or pledged toward this Shared Legal Capability fund.

In 1997, with funding from the ALA Government Documents Round Table and the Environmental Systems Research Institute (ESRI), ARL launched a new phase of the GIS Project. In collaboration with libraries and geographers from University of Texas at Austin, ESRI, Dalhousie University Library, and the University of Maryland, ARL will help develop a Web-based introduction to GIS for library and information science schools throughout North America.

Another initiative of the office is the ARL Visiting Program Officer (VPO) Program, which provides an opportunity for a staff member in a member library to assume responsibility for carrying out part or all of a project for ARL. It provides a very visible staff development opportunity for an outstanding staff member and serves the membership as a whole by extending the capacity of ARL to undertake additional activities. Typically, the member library supports the salary of the staff person and ARL supports or seeks grant funding for travel or other project-related expenses. Depending on the nature of the project and the circumstances of the individual, a VPO may spend extended periods of time in Washington, D.C., or may complete most of the project from his or her home library. Currently, VPOs are investigating how best to use electronic means to deliver the OLMS training content to libraries and are developing a Web resource on digital library activities in ARL libraries. The ARL Web site (http://www.arl.org) reflects the scope of ARL's current agenda and suggests the range of issues where a VPO project could make a contribution.

## Communication and External Relations

The capability for Communication and External Relations is designed to acquaint ARL members with current important developments of interest to research libraries, inform the library profession of ARL's position on these issues, influence policy and decision makers within higher education and other areas related to research and scholarship, and educate academic communities about issues related to research libraries.

The ARL publications program offers a full range of timely, accurate, and informative resources to assist library and higher education communities in their efforts to improve information delivery through technology and education. Print and electronic publications are issued from ARL programs on a regular basis. ARL makes many of its titles available electronically via the Web; some are available in excerpted form for preview before purchase, and others are available in their entirety. The electronic publications catalog can be accessed via http://www.arl.org/pubscat/index.html. The ARL-Announce service provides timely information about ARL and news items about ARL member library activities. ARL sponsors more than 50 electronic discussion groups, including both private and public lists. Archives for the lists are updated monthly and made available on the ARL server.

Six issues of *ARL: A Bimonthly Newsletter of Research Library Issues and Actions* were published in 1998, including two special issues. In April the Statistics and Measurement Program sponsored one on issues in research library measurement, and in October the Office of Scholarly Communication sponsored an issue on journals and the marketplace. All newsletters are available on the Web at http://www.arl.org/newsltr/newsltr.html.

Collaboration on both a technical and policy level is documented under individual program capabilities. Activities at the executive level in the past year included collaborations with the National Humanities Alliance, NASULGC, AAU, ACLS, AAUP, the Council on Library and Information Resources, the Andrew W. Mellon Foundation, EDUCAUSE, and NINCH.

The six major presidential associations—AACC, AASCU, AAU, ACE, NAICU, and NASULGC—are exploring ways to work collaboratively in identifying and addressing key issues related to digital networking, intellectual property, and information technology. ARL provides advice and assistance in the work and discussions of this forum.

## Association Governance and Membership Activities

The May 1998 Membership Meeting was hosted by the University of Oregon at Eugene. The program theme, developed under the leadership of ARL President James G. Neal, was "The Future Network: Transforming Learning and Scholarship." The speakers examined the new intersections of technology and scholarship. They described strategies for developing advanced networks, trends in research on the impact of technology on learning, and network policy developments. Among the 143 attendees were representatives from 97 member institutions.

The October 1998 Membership Meeting sessions were held in Washington, D.C. The program focused on the theme "Confronting the Challenges of the Digital Era" and explored how libraries are managing parallel print and electronic information systems. Program sessions covered fund-raising and staffing for the digital library and the economic impact of journal publisher mergers. The 160 attendees included representatives from 111 member institutions and 18 of the Leadership and Career Development Program participants.

The site of the May 1999 meeting is Kansas City, Missouri, hosted by the Linda Hall Library and the University of Kansas. ARL President-Elect Betty G. Bengtson (University of Washington) and the Research Collections Committee are developing the program theme on special collections.

The fall Membership Meeting will take place October 13–14, 1999, in Washington, D.C., and will be followed by a SPARC Membership Meeting on October 15.

On October 16, 1998, Betty Bengtson began her term as ARL President. The board elected Kenneth Frazier Vice-President/President-Elect of the association. Three board members concluded their terms: Gloria Werner, William Crowe, and Carole Moore. Meredith Butler, Joseph A. Hewitt, and Carolynne Presser were elected to three-year terms on the ARL Board of Directors.

# Council on Library and Information Resources

1755 Massachusetts Ave. N.W., Suite 500, Washington, DC 20036
202-939-4750, fax 202-939-4765
World Wide Web: http://www.clir.org

Kathlin Smith
International Program Officer

The Council on Library and Information Resources (CLIR) marked its first anniversary as a merged organization on May 30, 1998. The merger has enabled CLIR to draw on the strengths of the predecessor organizations, the Council on Library Resources (CLR) and the Commission on Preservation and Access (CPA), to better focus on the large issues that will determine the quality and effectiveness of higher education in the future.

CLIR's mission is to identify the critical issues that affect the welfare and prospects of libraries and archives, to convene individuals and organizations in the best position to engage these issues, and to encourage institutions to work collaboratively to achieve and manage change. CLIR bases its mission on the conviction that information is a public good and of great social, intellectual, and cultural utility.

Technology, the expectations and demands of users, and dislocations in the higher education community all contribute to the rapid, fundamental changes occurring in the information agencies and divisions on college and university campuses. Four main program areas correspond to issues that CLIR has identified as being of greatest concern to decision-makers: the preservation of and access to knowledge, the effect of digital libraries on our institutions, the economics of information, and ensuring that information organizations have qualified leaders in the next generation.

## Preservation and Access

The goal of library and archival preservation activities is to ensure long-term access to information that is of enduring value. The responsibility for preservation goes far beyond the staff of a preservation and conservation department and far beyond the walls of the traditional library. Collaborative relationships between preservation experts, computer scientists and programmers, institutional managers, and private and public funders are critical for the persistence of information and the transmission of knowledge over time. CLIR's Preservation and Access program brings together the communities of experts, scholars, managers, and funders who make decisions that affect collection development and custody.

CLIR put much of its effort in 1998 into articulating to a broad audience what the challenges of preservation in the digital world are and who needs to address them. It has aimed to communicate these problems and possible solutions to everyone with whom libraries should be working. In partnership with the American Council of Learned Societies (ACLS) and with funding from the National Endowment for the Humanities (NEH), the Alfred P. Sloan Foundation, and the Xerox Foundation, CLIR produced a one-hour documentary film, *Into the Future*, that was released in January 1998 for broadcast on public television stations. CLIR developed promotional and educational materials to accompany the film and dedicated part of its Web site to information about digital preservation. CLIR staff members met with leaders in the legislative and executive branches of the federal government and with members of the computer science community to address their concerns about policy and the research and development implications of the film's message. Through a public relations campaign, CLIR communicated the message nationally in the *New York Times*, the *Washington Post*, the *Los Angeles Times*, *Business Week*, *U.S. News & World Report*, and several wire services.

The film asks what can be done to ensure the integrity of digital information over time. Taking the next step, CLIR commissioned Jeff Rothenberg, computer scientist at the RAND Corporation, to survey existing models of digital archiving. He found that migration is the only model used today. CLIR then developed a project with Cornell University to examine the risk factors of migration associated with various types of file formats. It also commissioned Rothenberg to investigate the feasibility and costs of another model of archiving—emulation—in which programs are developed to mimic obsolete hardware and software so that information stored in old formats can still be read.

The Preservation and Access program will continue to advance collaborative programs that help libraries manage the broad implications of digital technology. For example, the series of issues surrounding the scanning and conversion of analog materials to digital warrants further inquiry. Digital reformatting is often done in the name of preservation. But while scanning is an effective tool of access, it is not yet a preservation technology. CLIR issued two reports on this subject during 1998, one by Stephen Ostrow, former chief of the Library of Congress's Prints and Photographs Division, on digitizing historical collections, and another by Dan Hazen, Jeffrey Horrell, and Jan Merrill-Oldham of Harvard University on a methodology for selecting research materials for digital conversion. Both address the general issue of selection for digitization and the nature of the digital surrogate and its use in research and teaching institutions.

The program also commissioned a preliminary report on digital imaging and preservation microfilming that will outline a hybrid approach to these reformatting techniques for preservation of and access to brittle print materials. Written by Stephen Chapman of Harvard University, Paul Conway of Yale University, and Anne Kenney of Cornell University, the report summarizes what has been learned about hybrid conversion in projects conducted at Yale and Cornell. It recommends the next steps for making this approach scalable in research libraries around the country. The paper is intended to serve as the basis for discussion by a broader audience, including representatives from the commercial sector; as a result, the preliminary report appears only in electronic form on CLIR's Web site.

An unintended consequence of the growth of digital-technology applications in libraries has been the tendency to overlook problems in the care of print and media collections. Through speeches, representation at professional meetings, and publications, CLIR continues to advocate for cost-effective preservation of print and nonprint sources in their original formats. CLIR testified before a congressional committee in support of the National Endowment for the Humanities' Brittle Books program. It provided financial, organizational, and publishing support to a group funded by NEH to foster preservation nationwide.

In January 1998 CLIR launched a new bimonthly publication, *CLIR Issues*, that reports on developments within the four major program areas. *CLIR Issues* supersedes the *Commission on Preservation and Access Newsletter*. CLIR also helped sponsor the Web publication "RLG DigiNews," edited by a team of experts at Cornell University, which brings together current information in the fast-changing world of digital library technologies.

## International Program

The International Program raises awareness abroad about preservation and helps identify methods and strategies for dealing with problems of access in libraries and archives. Often the program provides modest financial resources to allow institutions to take the next steps in a preservation strategy.

The International Program maintains a broad network of institutions and individuals throughout the world, affording CLIR an overview of a growing preservation movement worldwide and allowing staff to link activities in one country to related activities in another. In 1998 the International Program launched a new quarterly publication, *Preservation and Access International Newsletter*, that reports on preservation initiatives worldwide.

CLIR's program activities in 1998 included work in South Africa, Latin America, Asia, and Europe.

### South Africa

Training in conservation and preservation management is an urgent need. There is little in-country capacity for conservation training, and preservation professionals must seek expensive training abroad. Training is needed not only in conservation practice but also in how to manage economically the preservation of large collections of endangered materials.

In the spring CLIR supported its first training activity in South Africa: a preservation workshop for South African library and archives staff members. The week-long program examined why and how paper-based records deteriorate, and it presented options for reformatting print, audio, visual, and digital materials. That workshop served as a model for a second one, in April, directed at all of Anglophone Africa, for which CLIR provided training materials.

CLIR will continue to support training activities and will sponsor a meeting of librarians and archivists from the Cape Town area to discuss regional preservation needs.

### Latin America

With CLIR support, the National Library of Venezuela completed two multiyear projects. The first was the library's contribution of more than 22,000 records of Latin American holdings in microform to the European Register of Microform

Masters (EROMM). The records represent microfilm holdings from several libraries in Venezuela and elsewhere in Latin America and in Spain. This contribution will help EROMM build a resource for scholars and preservation managers to find out if specific titles have been reformatted and how to obtain copies. The records eventually will be made available through the Research Libraries Information Network (RLIN) as part of the Research Libraries Group-EROMM record-sharing agreement.

The second project translated selected preservation literature into Spanish. This Spanish translation project was similar to an effort in Brazil in 1995–1997 that led to the publication of 52 titles in Portuguese. In 1998 CLIR helped coordinators of the Brazilian project to plan for a continuation and expansion of its translation, workshop, and data collection project.

In a separate effort, program staff concluded agreements with six countries for the distribution of the Portuguese translations in Lusophone Africa and Macao. The titles cover topics ranging from disaster preparedness to the long-term archiving of digital information. As in Brazil, the literature and other materials may form the basis for preservation workshops.

### Asia

CLIR concluded a project to sponsor the microfilming of more than 4,000 titles of Chinese-language monographs published between 1932 and 1945. The filming, done by Fudan University in Shanghai, reformatted books that were both at high risk of deterioration and of special interest to scholars of Chinese history. The project has brought a significant new body of work in the humanities and social sciences within easy reach of U.S. scholars. The microfilms are available for loan or purchase from the Center for Research Libraries. The project was supported by NEH and the Henry Luce Foundation.

### Europe

In June the National Library of Poland finished creating a system for the ongoing collection of bibliographic information about microform masters held by Polish libraries. Under contract with CLIR, the library created several thousand bibliographic records and shared them with EROMM. That information is available on RLIN, and the National Library's staff can now offer advice to other Eastern European institutions on how to establish similar nodes for collecting information about microfilm masters.

## Digital Libraries

CLIR is the administrative home for the Digital Library Federation (DLF). Begun by 15 research libraries and archives in 1995, DLF seeks to establish the necessary conditions for creating, maintaining, expanding, and preserving a distributed collection of digital materials for both scholars and the general public. Federation partners share the investment in developing the infrastructure that will allow them to bring together, or federate, the works they manage for their users.

DLF now consists of 22 libraries and other organizations participating as full partners and three institutions formally allied to DLF. The group has also forged working relationships with many institutions in the United States and abroad that have related interests in digital libraries. Directors of the partner and allied institutions serve on the DLF Steering Committee, which, with members of a Technical Architecture Committee and staff of the partner and allied institutions, works closely with the DLF director and research associate to formulate and execute a rich agenda of projects, research, and other tasks designed to help the development of digital libraries.

The activities described below reflect the work undertaken to advance the development of digital libraries.

### Discipline-Based Projects

Several projects give DLF partners a chance to contribute to the growing store of digital materials and to enhance scholarly communication for teaching and research purposes in specific disciplines. These include the following:

*Art History Image Exchange.* DLF has organized a small group of visual-resource experts (including faculty and librarians) to explore the feasibility of creating a national repository of art images. The repository would allow faculty to deposit images of art objects that they have photographed and to which they refer in their teaching. The repository would be linked to the key textbooks in the art history field and would supplement repositories available through AMICO and various commercial sources.

*Social Science Data Archives.* DLF organized an invitational workshop held in January 1999 to explore how digital libraries facilitate teaching and research in the social sciences. The workshop considered problems and emerging solutions in three areas: facilities for users to discover and retrieve relevant and related datasets; means for users to interpret and evaluate the comparability of datasets; and tools and methods of data extraction for analysis. Participants identified project activities that DLF can undertake to advance the state of the art in these three areas, with the goal of improving the use of social science databases in the undergraduate curriculum.

*Theological Digital Library.* Efforts are being made to organize a digital library of theological materials that could support the distance-learning and outreach efforts of major seminaries and divinity schools. The projected digital library will be associated with the "Houses of Workshop" initiative based in Pittsburgh and will use technology developed at Carnegie Mellon University. DLF is supporting the creation of a managing board of faculty and librarians that will serve to further define the purpose and audience of the library, criteria for selecting materials, the business plan, quality control mechanisms, and technical requirements.

## Issue-Focused Activities

### Discovery and Retrieval

*Distributed Finding Aids.* There are many ways libraries can present finding aids that are created as encoded archival descriptions. DLF is supporting research at the University of Michigan and Harvard to explore the means and costs of searching encoded finding aids that are distributed among several institutions rather than collected in a single repository.

*The Making of America, Part II.* Led by the University of California at Berkeley and including Cornell, New York Public Library, Pennsylvania State University, and Stanford University, this project focuses on the means of creating digitized versions of objects in archives and special collections. The objects are linked to encoded finding-aid descriptions and are structured to behave in standardized ways for readers.

*Workshop on Editorial Practice.* DLF seeks to enhance the editorial practices of Electronic Text Centers and others engaged in digital conversion as a form of publication. In June it sponsored a conference of leading text center staff that focused on the application of the Text Encoding Initiative (TEI) standards in library-based text-encoding projects, the ramifications of XML (extensible markup language) development on existing and future text-encoding programs, and the future governance and stability of the TEI standard.

*Linking.* With the National Information Standards Organization (NISO), the National Federation of Abstracting and Information Services (NFAIS), and the Society for Scholarly Publishing (SSP), DLF organized a workshop in February 1999 on the topic of linking digital citations and digital objects. As many solutions emerge to provide such linkages, the problem becomes more complex and of growing concern. The workshop brought together publishers, librarians, abstracting and indexing services, repositories, vendors of information services, and end users to build a shared awareness of needs and to improve understanding of the strengths and limitations of current approaches. It also sought to identify and stimulate actions needed to improve the facilities for linking citations and digital objects in the digital environment.

**Intellectual Property**

*Licensing Digital Materials.* DLF funded Ann Okerson of Yale University to develop software that will support library and publisher licensing efforts. Released as "The LIBLICENSE Guide to Digital Information Licensing Agreements," the software systematically queries librarians or producers about the details of the information to be licensed and, based on their responses, produces a draft license agreement. The draft license agreement can then be sent to information publishers or customers to serve as the basis for further negotiations for license agreements with acceptable terms.

*Access Management.* DLF is addressing the technical and other problems associated with helping users gain authorized access to networked information. The federation sponsored a planning meeting for a project that is now under way involving the libraries and information technology divisions of universities belonging to the Committee on Institutional Cooperation (CIC). The project will implement a protocol that enables one institution to accept as users of its resources users who have been authorized at other institutions.

With support from the National Science Foundation, DLF and Columbia University's Center for Research on Information Access (CRIA) sponsored a workshop in April 1998 to develop formal requirements for more-sophisticated and -versatile systems authorization than those in common use today. The report of the workshop identifies a set of themes that can guide systems designers and developers of prototype systems for information access.

### Technical Infrastructure

*Digital Library Architectures.* DLF commissioned a survey of recent literature on the systems architecture of digital libraries. It highlights selected component systems and shows how they relate to a larger architectural whole. It assesses which components are relatively well conceptualized and developed, which need further attention, and where gaps might exist in the overall conception of digital library architecture. The survey report served as the basis for a workshop of library systems staff, sponsored by the DLF Technical Architecture Committee.

*Imaging Guides.* DLF created an editorial board of experts to review the state of the art in visual resource imaging and to identify technologies and practices that can be documented and recommended to the community. The board decided to focus on documenting the science of imaging by selecting a few objective measures of image qualities—such as color, tone, and resolution—and studying how they can be controlled during the imaging process. It identified five areas in which to address these issues: setting up an imaging project, selecting a scanner, creating a scanning system, producing a digital master, and generating digital derivatives. The board produced detailed outlines of issues to be covered and commissioned authors to write the guides.

## Economics of Information

### Investment in Information Study

CLIR is developing plans for a study to explore the real costs to universities of providing information resources and the complexity of the choices institutions must make as they use their limited funds. In the past, the library budget might have been identified with the information budget. But in an age of distributed access to information from multiple wired locations, that no longer is the case. Academic information purchased or licensed through the library, through departments, and through institutes will be the focus of the study. The intent is to include all information used for research, teaching, and services.

An advisory committee of the CLIR Board is helping to shape the project. It specified three ways of measuring a university's investment in information resources: collection creation costs, access, and permanence. Three universities—two private and one public—will take part in the study. One of the private institutions will have a centralized budgetary process and the other a decentralized process. The project will involve two principal investigators—in addition to the advisory committee—a provost and an economist interested in the economics of information. An auditing team will study the three universities under the direction of the principal investigators.

The CLIR study will create models that universities can use to achieve a thorough understanding of their information budgets while moving toward unifying the management of all information resources on campuses. Administrators will learn about the role libraries can play in information management.

# Leadership

## Digital Leadership Institute

As more information has become available in electronic format, the lines of responsibility for information management on university campuses have become less distinct. Meanwhile, the instructional and scholarly uses of technology have changed teaching and research methodologies. Today digital information and communications technologies are shaping new relationships among librarians, their information technology counterparts, and faculty members. But universities are not yet organized and staffed to cope with the consequences of these remarkable changes.

To address these changes, CLIR this year established the Billy E. Frye Digital Leadership Institute in collaboration with Emory University. The Institute will train a cadre of professionals who will effect fundamental change in the way universities manage their information resources in the new digital era.

The institute will provide continuing-education opportunities for individuals who currently hold, or will one day assume, positions that make them responsible for transforming the management of scholarly information in institutions of higher education. Over the next decade, the institute will train some 600 professionals, most of them in midcareer and drawn from library and administrative staffs, computer centers, and faculties.

The institute will enroll 50 to 60 individuals each year. Their training will begin with an intensive two-week seminar on the Emory campus, followed by a year-long practicum on their home campus or in another appropriate setting. The training concludes with a summary session that reunites the participants to discuss and evaluate what they have learned. The first Frye Institute class is set for the summer of 2000. CLIR will work closely with EDUCAUSE, the Association of Research Libraries, and others to develop the institute's curriculum.

## Innovative Uses of Technology by Colleges

The College Libraries Committee (CLC), originally established to advise the Commission on Preservation and Access, is working with CLIR to study the innovative ways that college libraries use information technology to improve teaching and learning. CLC members and CLIR staff developed case studies of nine college campuses this year to identify information technology projects that have broadened the role and strengthened the leadership position of the library on campus. The case studies were not designed to identify the "best" examples of technological innovation, but to describe different approaches that have been successful in particular circumstances and to stimulate innovations on other campuses. The studies were intended to serve as the basis for a conference in March 1999 addressing leadership and innovation.

## W. K. Kellogg Foundation Project

As part of the Human Resources in Information Systems Management (HRISM) program, CLIR helped bring together disparate professional and governmental organizations to consider the social policies and strategies for providing information resources needed by a community. CLIR asked how technology can be harnessed to provide greater and better access to information for all who need it and what policies must be in place to ensure that the potential benefits are realized. CLIR continued to work with other HRISM grantees to assemble their reports and other grant products into a Web-based curriculum that schools of library and information science and training divisions of libraries can use.

In collaboration with the Benton Foundation, CLIR is creating a videotape aimed at city officials and community organizations that explains the roles of public libraries and community information networks.

### Scholarship, Instruction, and Libraries at the Turn of the Century

CLIR collaborated with the American Council of Learned Societies (ACLS) on a project that spans several of CLIR's program areas. Thirty-six scholars, librarians, and leaders of various academic enterprises were appointed to five task forces to consider changes in the process of scholarship and instruction that will result from the use of digital technology. They were asked to make recommendations to ensure that libraries continue to serve the research needs of scholars.

The results of the task force inquiry are provided in the ACLS/CLIR task force report, *Scholarship, Instruction, and Libraries at the Turn of the Century*, available in print and on CLIR's Web site in early 1999.

## Publications

In 1998 CLIR published the following:

Reports

González, Pedro. *Computerization of the Archivo General de Indias: Strategies and Results* (September 1998).

Hawkins, Brian, and Patricia Battin, eds. *The Mirage of Continuity: Reconfiguring Academic Information Resources for the 21st Century* (September 1998).

Hazen, Dan, Jeffrey Horrell, and Jan Merrill-Oldham. *Selecting Research Collections for Digitization* (August 1998).

Healy, Leigh Watson. *Library Systems: Current Developments and Future Directions* (May 1998).

Henchy, Judith. *Preservation and Archives in Vietnam* (February 1998).

Ostrow, Stephen E. *Digitizing Historical Pictorial Collections for the Internet* (February 1998).

*Council on Library and Information Resources. Annual Report 1996–1997.*

Newsletters

*CLIR Issues*, nos. 1–6 (January–December 1998).

*Preservation and Access International Newsletter*, nos. 1–4 (March–December 1998).

Research Briefs

"A Different Approach to the Evaluation of Research Libraries" (September 1998).

"Universal Service in the Digital Age: The Commercialization and Geography of U.S. Internet Access" (April 1998).

Brochure and educational materials for the film *Into the Future: On the Preservation of Knowledge in the Electronic Age* (January 1998).

## Scholarships and Awards

CLIR administers the A. R. Zipf Fellowship in Information Management, which is awarded each year to a student enrolled in graduate school, in the early stages of study, who shows exceptional promise for leadership and technical achievement in information management. Applicants must be U.S. citizens or permanent residents. For additional information, see CLIR's Web site.

In 1998 CLIR awarded the Zipf Fellowship to Maureen Mackenzie, a Ph.D. candidate in the Palmer School of Library and Information Science at Long Island University's C. W. Post campus.

# International Reports

## International Federation of Library Associations and Institutions

Box 95312, 2509 CH-The Hague, Netherlands
31-70-3-14-08-84; fax 31-70-3-83-48-27
E-mail ifla.hq@ifla.nl
World Wide Web: http://www.ifla.org

Edward J. Valauskas

Member, IFLA Professional Board

With enthusiasm and mettle, the International Federation of Library Associations and Institutions (IFLA) continues to evolve as the leading organization representing the interests of librarians and information professionals on the global stage. In 1998 IFLA brought together librarians in workshops, conferences, and other venues around the world to discuss and debate issues as far-ranging as digital information, new library architecture, and cataloging standards. Under the aegis of IFLA, librarians are charting the roles of their institutions in the ever increasing information-dependent future and are devising plans for access to diverse kinds of media in libraries, from the largest cities to the smallest hamlets in the most isolated corners of the planet.

## 64th General Conference

With some 3,300 delegates from 120 countries in attendance, the 64th IFLA General Conference (August 16–21) in Amsterdam provided plenty of professional content in the form of papers, guest lectures, exhibits, poster sessions, and other programs. During the course of the conference, participants heard 192 papers given in 213 meetings (see http://www.ifla.org/IV/ifla64/64cp.htm), visited 101 booths staffed by 495 exhibitors, and took advantage of innumerable informal opportunities to meet colleagues from nearly every continent. The opening session of the conference featured some memorable speeches, demonstrations (a living replica of Rembrandt's "Night Watch"), and an unforgettable creation by the participants of a real IFLA web created with multicolored wool skeins. One of the guest speakers at the opening session, Rick van der Ploeg, the Netherlands State Secretary of Education, Culture, and Science, remarked that "information and culture should not move along separate paths but instead lead to a square that gives access to more paths in science, education, and philosophy. This square is the library." At the conclusion of the opening session, Maria Jose

Moura was awarded the 1998 International Book Prize for her work in Portugal in developing a successful public library program.

Guest lectures at the conference looked at the history of IFLA as well as the future of information and libraries. The first lecture panel treated the relations between libraries and publishers in the next century; speakers included Dietrich Gotze of Springer Verlag, Jane Carr of the British Library, and Marianne Scott of the National Library of Canada. Herman Liebaers, Honorary President of IFLA, provided the second guest lecture, recollecting the 34th IFLA Council and General Conference in Frankfurt 30 years earlier. The last guest lecture was given by Algerian journalist Ahmed Ancer on freedom of information in Algeria.

Special exhibits in Amsterdam and elsewhere in the Netherlands provided librarians with many opportunities to visit Dutch libraries. For example, the conference coincided with the 200th anniversary of the Koninklijke Bibliotheek; a special exhibit at the Nieuwe Kerk in Amsterdam celebrated the Royal Library. Titled the "Amazing Alphabet," the exhibit demonstrated the extent of the library's collections from A for "Alles" (everything) to Z for "Zoek" (search). The exhibit was opened by Queen Beatrix during the conference, and all conference participants received a complimentary ticket to visit the exhibit during their stay.

The conference gave opportunities for IFLA's newest committees— Copyright and other Legal Matters (CLM) and Free Access to Information and Freedom of Expression (FAIFE)—to meet formally and plan future activities and programs. In addition, eight discussion groups held informal sessions on a wide array of topics, from reference work to the Internet. In other business, IFLA announced Berlin as the site for its 69th Council and General Conference in 2003. Berlin was the first site selected through a competitive bid process newly initiated by the IFLA Headquarters and Executive Board. The site of the 70th General Conference in 2004 is currently under evaluation and will be announced at the 1999 IFLA Council and General Conference in Bangkok. Other IFLA conference venues include Jerusalem in 2000, Boston in 2001, and Glasgow in 2002.

Vendor showcases were a new feature of the Amsterdam conference. Vendors were provided with opportunities to meet their customers away from the bustle of the exhibition area and discuss new products, critical professional issues, and plans for the future. The success of this new element in the conference means that vendor showcases will be an integral part of future IFLA events.

Evaluations of the conference by IFLA headquarters, in collaboration with the Royal School of Library and Information Science in Copenhagen, provided one venue for feedback on professional programs, educational opportunities, exhibits, and social events. Preliminary results from the survey indicated that most participants were very happy with the conference, selecting "meeting" or "exceeding" their professional expectations on the evaluation forms.

## IFLA and FORCE

As a result of the conference in Amsterdam, IFLA has developed a formal relationship with FORCE, a Dutch foundation working as a resource for the print handicapped in libraries in developing regions around the world. IFLA will work with the FORCE Foundation to develop projects to increase availability to products and resources for the visually handicapped.

# Membership

One measure of the success of IFLA and its programs and other activities is membership. At the end of 1998 IFLA recorded 1,602 members in four categories, including international and national associations, institutions, and personal affiliates. Thirty-eight sponsors formally support IFLA, and the organization maintains consultative status with 14 bodies. Total membership at the end of 1998 equaled 1,654, with representatives from 153 countries.

# International Presence

In addition to sponsoring the Amsterdam conference, IFLA sponsored programs, workshops, symposia, speakers, and participants in events around the world during 1998, including the following sample:

*Seminar on the Use of New Technologies*, Cape Verde, January 26–31, 1998. Sponsored by IFLA Advancement of Librarianship (ALP) Programme, 17 participants from the African Lusophone countries and elsewhere examined the ways in which new technologies could improve access to scientific and technical information in their countries. Aimed at librarians with little background in computer applications in libraries, a review was provided of library automation, CD-ROMs, the Internet, bibliographic databases, and legal issues governing electronic information.

*Regional Seminar on Bibliographic Control*, Kuala Lumpur, Malaysia, March 9–12, 1998. In conjunction with the National Library of Malaysia, the IFLA Core Programme on Universal Bibliographic Control and International MARC (UBCIM) brought together participants from Brunei, Cambodia, Indonesia, Laos, Myanmar, the Philippines, Singapore, Thailand, and Vietnam to examine issues surrounding bibliographic standards and cooperation.The seminar developed a plan of action, to encourage legal deposits of printed and other materials in national libraries, to develop national bibliographies, to create a union catalog of Malay-language materials, and to foster the use of UNIMARC among libraries.

*Expert Meeting of Educators from Library and Archives Schools in Africa*, Nairobi, Kenya, March 23–25, 1998. Given the strong interest of IFLA, the International Council on Archives, and UNESCO in preservation, a meeting was held to organize curricula on preservation and conservation in library schools in Africa. With participants from Botswana, Ghana, Kenya, Morocco, Nigeria, Senegal, South Africa, Tunisia, and Uganda, it was urged that a preservation curriculum include a strong preventive conservation element. A basic curriculum would also include information on the unique problems of preservation in African institutions.

*Seminar on the Function of Bibliographic Control in the Global Information Infrastructure*, Vilnius, Lithuania, June 17–19, 1998. With 70 participants from Belarus, Croatia, Estonia, Finland, Latvia, Lithuania, and other countries, IFLA UBCIM Core Programme organized a lively program of papers and workshops examining bibliographic control of digital information. Several strategies for providing some semblance of bibliographic control were treated, as well as the dilemmas inherent in the nature of Internet-based documents and files. The participants made a number of recommendations, including strong interest in revision of UNIMARC, greater participation of IFLA in metadata standards, and further work on the preservation of digital information.

*International Conference on National Bibliographic Services*, Copenhagen, Denmark, November 25–27, 1998. Sponsored by IFLA UBCIM Core Programme, the Copenhagen conference examined the current work of national bibliographic agencies and their future in light of new technologies and increasing bibliographic interconnectivity. The participants made a number of strong recommendations to IFLA, including a reaffirmation of legal deposit, a reassessment of the coverage of national bibliographies and their utility for users, and a plea for the use of international standards for all bibliographic work.

## Personnel

IFLA experienced two major changes in headquarters personnel in 1998. At the end of the year Leo Voogt, Secretary General of IFLA since 1992, announced that he would leave IFLA at the beginning of 1999 to become executive director of the Royal Association for the Book Trade in the Netherlands. Voogt led IFLA during a period of rapid growth and international development, assisting the organization in creating a stronger voice for librarianship around the world. The IFLA Executive Board moved quickly to find a successor and early in 1999 announced that Ross Shimmon, Chief Executive of the Library Association (Great Britain), would become IFLA's new Secretary General. In the spring of 1998 Winston Roberts, IFLA Coordinator of Professional Activities since 1990, resigned and Sjoerd Koopman was selected as his successor. Koopman came to IFLA from the PICA Library Automation Centre, where he had been head of marketing since 1995.

Paul Nauta, who retired from the post of secretary general of IFLA in 1992, died in December 1998. Nauta remained very active in IFLA after his retirement from IFLA headquarters, chairing most recently the organizing committee for the 1998 General Conference in Amsterdam.

## Conclusion

IFLA is playing a larger role in the international library community as facilitator, educator, and defender of library interests. With a growth of activities outside of Europe—in Africa, Asia, South America, and elsewhere—IFLA is providing the means for librarians in many locales to participate in the development of standards and to encourage the use of diverse tools to share information. IFLA truly is becoming the sole international representative of the library profession, speaking in many languages but with one voice on the importance of information access and distribution to all.

# Special Libraries Association

1700 Eighteenth St. N.W., Washington, DC 20009-2514
202-234-4700, fax 202-265-9317, e-mail sla@sla.org
World Wide Web: http://www.sla.org

John Crosby IV
Public Communications

Headquartered in Washington, D.C., the Special Libraries Association (SLA) is an international association representing the interests of nearly 15,000 information professionals in 60 countries. Special librarians are information resource experts who collect, analyze, evaluate, package, and disseminate information to facilitate accurate decision-making in corporate, academic, and government settings.

As of June 1998 the association had 56 regional chapters in the United States, Canada, Europe, and the Middle East; 25 divisions representing a variety of industries; and 13 special-interest caucuses.

SLA offers myriad programs and services designed to help its members serve their customers more effectively and succeed in an increasingly challenging environment of information management and technology. Association activities are developed with specific direction toward achieving SLA's strategic priorities: to ensure that SLA members have opportunities to develop professional competencies and skills; to narrow the gap between the value of the information professional and the perceived value of special librarians and information professionals among decision-makers; and to ensure the ongoing relevance of SLA to its members in the next century by managing our transition to SLA's vision of a virtual association, whereby all members will be able to access SLA services globally, equitably, and continuously.

## Computer Services and Technology

Merging and blending new and existing technologies with the association's information infrastructure in order to support strategic goals of the association is the main objective for the Computer Services and Technology department. Department staff accomplished this objective with the approval to acquire a new association management system and the development of a three-year strategic technology plan.

At its October 1997 meeting the SLA Board of Directors approved acquisition of a new association management system that is Web-enabled to support one of the association's current strategic priorities: access to association information.

This new association management system will allow members to update their membership information, register for events, and view the membership directory via the Web site 365 days a year. In addition, the system will provide staff with the ability to seamlessly blend data from the membership system with the Web, transforming the association's Web site.

The department assisted with the development of the three-year strategic technology plan. This plan accesses and aligns the association's technology infrastructure to support the strategic goals of the association. Both physical (hardware/software) and human (staff) capital were examined to ensure that the business needs of the association will be supported over the next three years.

The virtual association was expanded to incorporate new products and services. Monthly issues of *Information Outlook* are now available at www.informationoutlook.com. The database of member consultants, which was formerly accessible only through the association's Information Resources Center, is now available online to membership for direct searching at www.sla.org/consult. With the acquisition of a Citrix Winframe communications server, staff can remotely access their desktop applications and e-mail.

Computer Services continues to promote the benefits of the virtual association to members and to the association community. During DACOLT at the 1998 Winter Meeting in Washington, D.C., Computer Services provided the assembled leadership with a tour of the virtual association. The virtual tour, located at www.sla.org/membership/leader/virtual.html, showcased products and services located within the virtual association geared to support leadership needs. In addition, Computer Services presented the concept of a virtual association at a Greater Washington Society of Association Executives technology section meeting and at its technology series "Virtual Office—Working from Anywhere."

The association's virtual community was further expanded with the addition of a chat room hosting service. This new service, SLA CHAT (www.sla.org/chat), permits our international membership to converse synchronously, regardless of geographic boundaries. SLA CHAT hosts scheduled events such as the executive director's monthly chat with membership, unit board meetings, and chats with instructors of professional-development courses.

With generous three-year sponsorship by Disclosure, Inc., Computer Services continues to expand the capabilities of the association's Web site. Microsoft's software donation supports the association's virtual bookstore, where members and nonmembers can purchase books and other SLA materials using a credit card via SLA's secure socket layer technology-enabled Web site.

SLA's List Hosting service, currently sponsored by Financial Information Services (formerly Moody's Investors Group) and West Group, was expanded to provide units with an additional list for board activities. The listserv software was also upgraded to provide members with additional functionality. Also, the association's Web Hosting service was expanded to give units the ability to access secure pages using user name and password schemes.

With the implementation of these new services and technologies, in line with the association's strategic plan, the Computer Services and Technologies program will continue to enhance the association's information infrastructure to support SLA's expanding business and information requirements.

## Conferences and Meetings

Professional development and commitment to advancing their professional association were on the minds of more than 5,500 information professionals who came from around the world to Indianapolis, Indiana, June 6–11, 1998. They came to participate in SLA's 89th Annual Conference, "Leadership, Performance, Excellence: Information Professionals in the Driver's Seat."

The third annual exhibit hall ribbon-cutting ceremony opened the doors to a very exciting exhibit show—SLA's largest show ever. With more than 535 booths sponsored by approximately 400 companies, the exhibit hall was filled with the newest technologies, products, and services to help special librarians be more effective and proficient in their jobs.

Stanley Davis, this year's conference keynote speaker, spoke to a packed house about how he believes information professionals will play an expanded role in increasing the value of knowledge-based businesses. Dr. Davis's speech, "Driving Profit from Knowledge," explored ways information professionals can increase their businesses' value. Another highlight was the annual President's Reception, hosted by Judith J. Field, which drew more than 170 attendees. The money raised will go toward educational opportunities at Global 2000.

Under the guidance of Gloria Zamora, 1998 Conference Program Committee chair, SLA division program planners were responsible for implementing the program sessions. Conference attendees had the opportunity to choose from more than 500 programs, special events, continuing-education courses, meetings, and field trips to plan their personal conference itineraries. As in past years, the most popular sessions at the conference dealt with the Internet and information technology.

When not busy attending the many programs and sessions at the conference, attendees took advantage of field trips offered in and around Indianapolis. Groups visited such places as the Indianapolis 500 Motor Speedway, Eli Lilly & Company, and the Indianapolis Zoo.

## Financial and Administrative Services

The philosophy of the Financial Services program is to ensure the integrity of financial data and to establish and enforce internal controls while maintaining a high level of quality service, both internally and externally. Financial Services staff operates according to a series of detailed planning schedules and written guidelines, policies, and procedures. These policies and procedures are routinely reviewed by staff, management, leadership, and independent counsel for effectiveness and efficiency. The Financial Services staff is committed to providing the most accurate information in the most timely manner possible in order to facilitate the efficient fiscal management of all SLA programs and activities. The program staff is also committed to the cross-training of staff to increase internal controls and to accommodate periods of peak production and staff absences.

Internal operations have been streamlined by the use of lock box services, online banking, and the use of a collection agency for accounts receivable. Using the lock box services has greatly reduced the number of errors and demands on staff time, and has maximized cash flow. This service was expanded in 1998 to include the processing of credit cards. Also, upgraded banking software now allows many services to be performed in-house that previously required the aid of bank personnel. Staff continues to enhance its efforts in the areas of contingency planning, financial reporting, and cross-training.

The Financial Services staff, in conjunction with Computer Services, has developed online financial-management screens for program managers. These screens allow staff to view financial information that is pertinent to goals and objectives. In 1997 the capability to print and download this information was added to these screens. These capabilities will be further enhanced and expanded as SLA migrates to the new association management system.

The Financial Services department made a major effort in 1997 and 1998 to improve the collection of accounts receivable. The Finance Committee and Board of Directors strengthened this commitment by requiring prepayment for all SLA products and services. The staff's effort combined the use of monthly statements, dunning letters, phone calls, barring future purchases on delinquent accounts, and the use of a collection agency for those customers who still did not pay. This has greatly reduced the amount of accounts that go unpaid.

By focusing on efficiency and effectiveness, this department maintained a high level of quality service to both internal and external users. Favorable comments were received, and this positive feedback has been mirrored in reports received from outside accounting firms and association colleagues. The staff continues to search for ways to improve the value of the information it provides.

Financial Services staff continually seeks feedback from other program areas regarding the services provided, and this feedback is used to improve the effectiveness and timeliness of services provided.

The greatest opportunities for improvement still lie within the cultivation of staff. Further cross-training of staff and increasing productivity must continue so that more time can be spent developing financial tools that will assist managers and leaders in the decision-making process. The new association management system capabilities will foster increased efficiency, productivity, and effectiveness in this area.

The Administrative Services program encompasses human resources, office services, and building management; it essentially serves to support the staff members who, in turn, support the membership. The program is governed by various board-approved policies and procedures, and is reviewed semiannually by the Association Office Operations Committee (AOOC).

In 1998 a human resources audit was performed by an independent employment consulting firm. The results were favorable, and SLA was highlighted as a well-managed organization that implements sound and compliant employment practices.

Over the past few years, we have seen a significant shift in the competencies required as changes in technology place new demands on both employers and employees. From SLA's position as the employer, the strategies and activities relating to recruitment, training, compensation, and program development/delivery have certainly changed in response to new technologies. The employee also shares in the change process; employees are expected to continually revise the means by which they develop their work and perform their job responsibilities.

In the recruitment process, a desk audit and needs analysis is routinely performed when a position is being recruited. However, SLA must also be able to forecast the specific staffing requirements needed several years out. In addition, we need to know how future technologies will impact the organization, the staff position, and the delivery of the product or service. Formerly, an employer assessed an applicant's past experience as one of the major determinants of his or her qualifications or level of competency. This is no longer a sufficient means of evaluation. In addition to assessing the specific skills required, we must also assess an applicant's familiarity with technological advancements (which is often difficult to discern, especially at higher-level positions), responsiveness to change, adaptation to globalization, and so forth. The recruitment process has, therefore, become a much more complicated and time-consuming process. In response, the skills required of recruiting personnel have become much more extensive.

The trends in hiring that have been reported over the past few years remain intact: Numerous advertisements are required in various media to attract qualified personnel, the midlevel management and technical positions require greater search time, and employees are looking for greater flexibility in schedules and benefits.

In order to increase SLA's effectiveness in recruiting staff, it has initiated the following:

- Staff negotiated with two employment agencies for temporary to permanent placement without any placement fees. During the four-month trial period, the salaries are paid to the employment agencies (which is how the agencies make their profit). SLA, in turn, maximizes its hiring flexibility, minimizes its employment liabilities, reduces its employment tax liabilities, and reduces its benefits costs. We view this as a win-win situation.

- Staff continually reviews the benefits package to ensure that it offers flexibility to a diverse work force. In 1997 SLA added flexible-spending accounts that allow staff to shelter income for such items as medical expenses, qualified child care, and supplemental insurance premiums. For 1998 SLA is experimenting with and assessing a modified flexible work schedule.

With regard to the training and development of staff, SLA is challenged by both technology and diversity in the workplace. Having a membership that is educated, technologically advanced, and savvy poses challenges in meeting members' expectations. We need to focus on bridging the gap between issues relating to both associations and the profession. As new technologies are employed, SLA is faced with training the staff to gain a mastery of emerging technologies. These technologies affect both routine operations and advanced program development.

SLA requires each staff member to maintain a working knowledge of operating in a totally automated office, and each employee is expected to keep abreast of emerging technologies in developing and delivering products and services to the membership. It seems that just as one technology is fully understood and implemented, another comes along that is bigger and better and the process starts all over. Training has become a full-time, ongoing process, and staff is often working in more than one mode to accommodate technological changes.

Because SLA requires its employees to maintain and implement myriad skills and competencies, compensating the employee remains a challenge for executive and supervisory staff. They must balance the organizational expectations with qualified staff within a cost-effective compensation plan. Based on various association studies and benchmarks, SLA currently lags behind the market in compensating its employees. This provides a challenge in attracting, training, and retaining a competent, stable staff.

When planning organizational objectives, staff must determine the best means by which to administer, develop, and deliver products and services to the membership. Outsourcing is one means by which an organization or department can add to its efficiency and effectiveness. Outsourcing may be costly in dollars, but it is often more effective in the end. According to the Association Information Management Service (AIMS), associations with external professional services that represent a higher percentage of total expenses usually have a higher level of productivity. Utilizing external professional services is a good way to stretch the capabilities of staff and to meet the special and/or episodic needs of the association without a long-term staffing commitment.

SLA currently utilizes outsourcing on a limited basis in fulfilling functions related to insurance services, legal services, nonprofit postal monitoring, payroll, media relations, editing, graphic design, program planning, archiving, exhibit management, audit and financial advice and analysis, travel services, tabulation, mail services, printing, computer system analysis, training, and building maintenance. The typical ratio of outsourcing to total expenses is nearly 9 percent, whereas SLA's ratio is 6 percent. AIMS suggests an increase in specialized outsourcing as a means of enhancing the competencies of staff. SLA strives to deliver quality products and services to its membership by utilizing a balanced approach to employing competent staff and seasoned external professional services. The association has been able to move forward with its products and services in an expedient fashion, which indicates a high level of achievement.

The success of an organization is dependent largely on its operational efficiency. A major component of operational efficiency is the employment of effective, technologically advanced equipment. The AOOC, Finance Committee, and Board of Directors have supported this concept through the approval of major equipment purchases. Most recently, the board has allocated funds for the purchase of facsimile, telephone, and copying equipment, as well as the routine replacement of office furniture and minor equipment.

The Administrative Services staff has developed training schedules for each type of equipment and office service employed by the association. In addition to the up-front training for new equipment and applications, staff has developed follow-up training at six-month intervals. The interval training serves to refresh the users about equipment basics and to provide information about the more advanced features and capabilities.

The building's current assessed value is $1,435,240, with the land valued at $520,000. In order to maintain the equity in the building and a safe, pleasant work environment, the condition of the building and its operational systems must continually be inspected and reviewed. The fiscal year (FY) 1998 Association Program Plan and Budget include capital expenditures for miscellaneous projects, including upgrading a portion of the HVAC system, waterproofing and repointing, painting interior surfaces, replacing wood flooring in lobby areas, carpeting, and general office improvements.

# Fund Development

Association year 1997–1998 saw some notable successes in the Fund Development program. In the area of corporate philanthropy, the Dialog Corporation and Teltech Technical Knowledge Service generously agreed to underwrite the annual Knowledge Executive Institute. The Dialog Corporation, along with LEXIS-NEXIS, gave generous support to the new Distance Learning program by sponsoring the SLA's video conferences. Ongoing special projects continued to receive support from Disclosure, Inc., the Economist Intelligence Unit, Dun and Bradstreet, Financial Information Services (formerly Moody's Investors Group), West Group, LEXIS-NEXIS, Dow Jones & Company, the Freedom Forum, and EBSCO.

SLA's corporate supporters were also very generous with unrestricted funds in 1998, and annual giving exceeded its $50,000 goal. West Group became a member of the President's Circle for the first time, joining the H. W. Wilson Company, LEXIS-NEXIS, and the Dialog Corporation. New arrivals to the Patrons Category included Blackwell's Information Services, the Bureau of National Affairs, Teltech Technical Knowledge Service, and NERAC, Inc.

Sponsorship of the Annual Conference was also very popular this year, with ten exhibitors sponsoring events or activities for the first time. Special thanks go to LEXIS-NEXIS for an Internet Room done beautifully in Indy 500 style; to SilverPlatter for the ribbon-cutting ceremony featuring Indianapolis's own Gordon Pipers; to Chemical Abstracts Service for the tote bags; to Thomson Financial Services for sponsoring conference registration; and to West Group for sponsoring the European Commission luncheon.

The annual President's Reception at Indianapolis's famous Eiteljorg Museum, sponsored by NERAC, Inc., was very successful. This year the proceeds of this annual benefit went toward the Global 2000 conference. Current Global 2000 corporate sponsors—including H. W. Wilson, West Group, the Dialog Corporation, and Freedom Forum—were recognized and thanked by SLA President Judith Field.

The Legacy Club gained new members this year, welcoming Anne Abate, Andrew Berner, and Catherine "Kitty" Scott. Members of the club provide for the future of the Special Libraries Association through bequests, insurance policies, gifts of property, and stocks, bonds, and other financial instruments.

Members also provided support for the general fund and for SLA's special funds, such as the Scholarship Fund, which helps students get MLS degrees; the Steven I. Goldspiel Research Fund; the media and marketing plan fund; and the special programs fund. With the new ability of the Fund Development department to concentrate exclusively on fund-raising, SLA expects that association year 1998–1999 will be a banner year.

# Government Relations

The Government Relations program informs and educates government officials on issues that affect information professionals worldwide. Simultaneously, the program improves member awareness of and involvement in such policy-making activities. Staff formulates and influences government policies in these primary areas of concern:

- Copyright and intellectual property
- Access to information
- Telecommunications
- Development of the global information infrastructure
- Competitiveness for information professionals

During 1997–1998 SLA was proactive in efforts to reform the copyright laws of many nations around the globe. In coalition with other library organizations, educational groups, and corporations, SLA helped to convince the 105th Congress that its proposal to comply with international copyright treaties threatened the nature and scope of fair use in the digital world. SLA worked with the European Bureau of Library, Information and Documentation Associations (EBLIDA) to lobby the European Parliament on behalf of the European library community. SLA also coordinated with Canadian chapters to comment on their government's efforts to comply with international treaty obligations. Activities in other nations—including Australia, Japan, China, Korea, and Mexico—were also monitored and reviewed for the benefit of the membership.

SLA has promoted the interests of the membership on other copyright-related matters, including

- Database protection
- Copyright term extension
- Online service provider liability exemption
- Enforceability of shrink-wrap and "click-on" licenses

Since 1996 SLA has worked with other U.S. library organizations to develop legislation for reforming the nation's government printing and publishing policies. That legislation was developed through the hard work of this coalition and was introduced in July 1998.

The Government Relations program focused on accomplishing three internal goals:

- Improvement of the membership's awareness of and involvement with information-policy-making activities. With nearly 15,000 members, SLA possesses the power to influence public policy around the world. Grassroots communications can have a major impact on governmental decisions. Staff regularly disseminated targeted alerts for grassroots advocacy to the membership and established a telephone briefing program for members only. Internet and listserv communications served as the backbone for the program, with direct-mail efforts supplementing these efforts.
- Expanding SLA's sphere of influence on information policy to all areas of the globe. Historically, SLA has focused its government relations activities on North America. But the association's demographics have shifted to

a more global membership, and there is a growing perception of the world existing without borders. In response to these changes, SLA launched campaigns to educate members about global information policies that may impact the profession, particularly through interaction with organizations in other nations.

- Enhancing the program through the use of technology. While Internet communications have become mainstream tools for government relations, SLA seeks to develop new ideas for improving services to members. Telephone issue briefings were tested in 1998 and should be expected as a signature government relations service in the future. In coordination with Computer Services staff, targeted electronic-mail groups were used to send digital action alerts to members in specific geographic regions. Staff was enabled to focus communications where needed, and in a more systematic fashion.

The Government Relations program accomplished many of its goals by maintaining open lines of communication with other members of staff. The program focused on teaming with the Public Relations, Research, and Professional Development staff and the Executive Office in order to achieve common objectives and confront new challenges as they developed.

## Information Resources Center

SLA's Information Resources Center continues to respond to a high number of requests for information from staff, members, and nonmembers on a variety of aspects of special librarianship and association management. The majority of requests are on education and professional development, careers, salaries, and general library management.

During 1997–1998 nearly 40 percent of the IRC Web site hits were recorded for our lists of library, federal, and miscellaneous Internet joblines. The number of requests made via the Internet increased, as did IRC Web site hits, which now average over 7,500 per month. CONSULT Online—the Web version of the CONSULT database, the database of SLA member consultants—was launched in June. This enables members and the public to access the database themselves and carry out their searches.

The electronic information packets (EIPs) accessible via the IRC Web site have been updated monthly, and an average of approximately 50 resources have been added each month. New EIPs on Internet issues, Internet research tools, competitive intelligence, library costs/budgets, and library strategic plans were added during the year. All EIPs include hypertext links to Web sites of interest or full-text articles where applicable.

The Management Document Collections (MDCs) was a popular resource for both members and nonmembers. Loans of the user survey, library brochures, library marketing materials and strategic plans were the most-often-lent MDCs. The IRC staff is always seeking to enhance the collection by soliciting additional model materials from members.

The ongoing goal of the IRC is to create a "virtual IRC" and a more proactive service for members and staff. The center provides staff Internet training, new-staff orientation, and a monthly IRC Update of information and resources transferred to the IRC. By subscribing to all the SLA division listservs, IRC staff keeps environmentally aware of the concerns of members and developments in the information industry.

## Membership Development

The Membership Development program works in partnership with all other program areas to pursue membership growth through the recruitment and retention of SLA's members. In addition, the Membership Development department works closely with SLA's volunteer leaders to support the activities of the association's chapters, divisions, caucuses, and student groups. Together with SLA's data entry team, the staff maintains the membership database, including adding new and prospective members, processing renewals and address changes, and updating officer information. Further, the Membership Development program promotes and administers the SLA Scholarship program, monitors Student Group activities, works with the Affirmative Action Committee to administer SLA's Diversity Leadership Development program, and supports the activities of the Endowment Fund Grant Committee.

In the past year specific section projects included the redesign and streamlining of the membership dues invoice, the dissemination of an informative new-member packet within 10 days of a member's join date, the creation and implementation of a basic electronic new-member welcome letter, the maintenance of the membership application and a section for updating member records on SLA's Web home page, the refinement of the telemarketing program designed to encourage former association members to reinstate membership, and the provision of assistance to association leaders through monthly mailings, leadership-training sessions, and electronic communication.

The Membership Development department's retention efforts are fortified at the grassroots level. The section provided unit membership chairs with annual member rosters, bimonthly new-member reports, and deactivated member reports. In addition, Membership Chairs received monthly mailings containing membership information and tips about recruitment and retention. The Membership Chairs' listserv, maintained by the program, acts as a forum for idea sharing and problem solving among the association's volunteer leaders.

In an effort to attract students into the field of special librarianship, SLA offered a scholarship program that was created to support the activities of student members. The Membership Development department produced *The Student Union*, the student group newsletter, semiannually. Association year 1997–1998 saw the refinement of the newsletter, with the utilization of more color and the inclusion of photographs. Also, staff worked closely with the Student and Academic Relations Committee (SARC) to build a partnership with association leaders and the student members in order to increase membership retention.

Activities of the 1997–1998 Scholarship program included the disbursement of close to $30,000 in financial aid. In addition, the SARC-sponsored Certificate of Merit Program was continued to honor student groups, chapters, and divisions that demonstrated outstanding activity and/or continued commitment to promoting professional development for students within their organizations.

## Nonserial Publications

The Nonserial Publications Program (NSP) produces products that will prepare and empower the information professional in a rapidly evolving industry. In addition, the program endeavors to make a significant contribution to the literature of the information profession and to increase the influence of the professional and of the field itself. The NSP program endeavors to anticipate market demands by staying abreast of developments within the industry and producing quality titles that meet those needs.

In 1998 SLA released titles on intranets and knowledge management, two subjects that are generating a great deal of interest among special librarians. Additionally, new editions of *Special Libraries: A Guide for Management* and *Annual Salary Survey 1997* were produced.

In keeping with the initiative to move toward the virtual association, the Virtual Bookstore, which gives visitors the opportunity to browse and purchase products online, was unveiled in August 1997. This not only allows members and nonmembers access to SLA publications 24 hours a day, seven days a week; it also expands the available product information so that customers can make informed purchasing decisions.

## Professional Development

The Professional Development Program encompasses cutting-edge continuous-education (CE) activities and career services for SLA members. The program strives to help information professionals meet their potential by providing educational opportunities based on the professional and personal competencies outlined in SLA's report *Competencies for Special Librarians of the 21st Century*.

During 1997–1998, a wide variety of continuous-education programs were offered in the areas of technology, library management, strategic planning, budgeting, marketing and public relations, and general management.

The Professional Development department, in cooperation with Pace University, presented three multimedia courses in the early fall of 1997, "Creating Your Own Home Page Using HTML," "Advanced HTML," and "The Seven Keys to Highly Effective Web Sites." More than 75 students participated in these asynchronous courses, which utilized a variety of delivery platforms, including online instruction, a videotape, textbook readings, Web assignments, and an online discussion group.

In October 1997 SLA produced its fifth video conference. Cosponsored with the Dialog Corporation, the program, "Giving Users What They Really Want/Need," provided members with practical ways to differentiate between what users say they want and what they really need. The video conference reached more than 1,000 librarians at sites in the United States, Canada, and Britain.

The 1997 State-of-the-Art Institute, "Knowledge Management: A New Competitive Asset," was a sold-out event. The two-day program featured a wide variety of speakers focusing on the tools and techniques of knowledge management, real-world examples of organizations successfully managing their knowledge assets, and key issues that should be considered in implementing a knowledge management program.

The 1998 Winter Education Conference, "Building Monuments for the Future," focused on the latest developments in information technology. In addition to the nine CE courses, more than 40 vendors participated in the Technology Fair, demonstrating some of the newest information products. The "Technology and Applications" unit of the Middle Management Institute was also offered during the conference.

SLA presented its spring 1998 video conference, "Everybody Wins: Building Alliances for Greater Gains," in cooperation with LEXIS-NEXIS. The program encompassed work on the Web, workshops before and after the broadcast, a case study during the broadcast, and postconference activities with Web materials and chat rooms with each of the panelists.

SLA's 89th Annual Conference in Indianapolis featured 33 CE courses to more than 1,300 attendees. In addition, SLA presented the Knowledge Executive Institute, sponsored by the Dialog Corporation and Teltech Technical Knowledge Service, as a preconference activity. This intensive institute was developed to prepare members for advancing to knowledge executive roles within their organizations. Two MMI units, "Analytical Tools" and "Human Resources," were also offered.

A variety of career services were provided to members at the Annual Conference. SLA and Advanced Information Management (AIM) offered four job search workshops on such topics as networking and interviewing skills. Additional career services included the Employment Clearinghouse, with nearly 100 job openings posted and 100 résumés, and the Career Advisory Service, through which 18 people received career counseling from experienced members.

Some CE courses were cosponsored by various SLA units and other organizations throughout the year. Cosponsored courses are arranged through headquarters and can be offered at any location.

The self-study program was revised and reformatted during the 1997–1998 association year and was released in July 1998 in an interactive, online format. All courses are available through the SLA Web site.

## Public Relations

The primary goal of the Public Relations program is to increase awareness and appreciation of the important role special librarians play in their organizations and society. Another goal is to aid the association unit in creating ways in which the association and the profession can be represented positively in the public eye.

In the past year the department made considerable advances in the enhancement of the image of the special librarian and the association. The program's campaign to increase the value of the special librarian continued in a very positive direction. For example, a letter to the editor was published in the April issue of *Association Management* magazine—the monthly publication of the American Society of Association Executives (ASAE)—that provided testimonial for information professionals in the role of crisis communication specialists.

Relationships were further cultivated among members of the media with the placement of two in-flight airline magazines, United Airlines' *Hemispheres* and Continental Airlines' *Continental*. An opinion/editorial campaign was waged targeting large U.S. city business journals. The first piece, on knowledge management, was published in the June 19–25, 1998, issue of the *Washington Business Journal*. The *Houston Business Journal* and *Dallas Business Journal* published the same article in their July 17–23 and July 24–30 issues, respectively.

Program staff continues to focus the campaign on getting coverage of special librarians in metropolitan newspapers, major trade press, and association and business publications.

The "Public Relations Outlook" column in *Information Outlook* continues to be compiled, with more emphasis on positive articles about the profession and association members. The program relies on association members to submit items to be included in this monthly column, and unit public relations chairs are encouraged to canvas their fellow members for stories and testimonials regarding professional successes.

An annual public relations highlight is International Special Librarians Day (ISLD), the Thursday of National Library Week (an American Library Association program). This is a time for members to gain recognition for the contributions of the profession in the global sharing of information. This year's theme was "The Time Is Now!" To help members observe ISLD, a template kit was made available on the SLA Web site or mailed to those without Internet access to assist members in promoting their libraries' services.

Also, underwritten by the ISLD cosponsoring company, LEXIS-NEXIS, 3,000 pins with the event logo were distributed to members. ISLD announcements were made on National Public Radio during the weeks prior to and including the actual day.

The 1998 SLA Awards and Honors program, a function of the Public Relations program, honored 11 SLA members for outstanding service to the association and the profession at the 89th Annual Conference in Indianapolis. To stimulate member interest, the awards program was publicized via editorial coverage in information industry publications and on the SLA Web site. In addition to the association-wide awards program, Public Relations administered its awards program targeted to members who excel in promoting the profession to the general public. In this program, the Media Award and the International Special Librarians Day Award were both presented at the conference.

## Research

SLA's Research goals are to provide methodologies, data, and analyses that address significant elements of the profession. SLA supports research through a variety of activities. The association independently conducts research, works in collaboration with other organizations in conducting and sponsoring research, and funds research through the Steven I. Goldspiel Memorial Research Grant.

At its June 1998 meeting the SLA Board of Directors approved the Research Committee's nomination of Andrew Dillon as the recipient for the 1998 Steven I. Goldspiel Memorial Research Grant for his proposal "Understanding Users in Digital Environments: A Longitudinal Study of Genre Influences in Information Work." The primary objective of Dr. Dillon's project is to demonstrate how digital genres are formed in the minds of users and how such genres impact both the users' capabilities to utilize the digital resources and their ratings of such resources' usefulness. Genres are natural psychological occurrences in which the cognitive system abstracts, patterns, and automates activities so as to free up limited attentional resources. Newspaper readers have learned to recognize the purposes of an article based on its layout and position in the paper, and the same types of patterns may evolve for digital documents. In this study, users of digital resources will be tracked over a nine-month period to determine whether interaction patterns develop. The report will be available from SLA in 2000.

The 1998 Annual Salary Survey was revised considerably to reflect changes in the profession and the diversity of SLA's membership. A monograph from the survey was made available in November 1998.

In an effort to improve SLA products and services, Research staff coordinated with Membership and Professional Development program areas to hold focus groups with SLA members at the Winter Meeting and Annual Conference. The emphases of the focus groups were twofold: (1) to determine what benefits new members expect to derive from membership in SLA, and (2) to get feedback from members on the education needs of members in regard to recent technological developments. The results of the focus group sessions will be published in *Information Outlook* and on the SLA Web site.

Together with the Medical Library Association (MLA) and the Association for Library and Information Science Education (ALISE), SLA Research and Professional Development staff conducted a Library School Curriculum Project. Library and Information Science programs throughout the world were surveyed to provide a benchmark of information studies curricula and to identify competency areas better served by continuing-education programs offered through professional associations. Results were made available in late 1998.

At SLA's 1995 Research Forum, the "value of the profession" was determined to be the key area of research necessary to promote special librarians as integral components of the information society. The project report, "Studying the Value of Information Services in Special Libraries and Information Centers," was completed in December 1997 by Paul B. Kantor and Tefko Saracevic of Rutgers University. The objectives of the project were to identify and organize the dimensions of value of specific library services, to identify and test procedures for measuring the value of those services, and to develop a manual that demonstrates how to apply the research procedures at other organizations. Findings from the report were presented at the 1998 SLA Annual Conference in Indianapolis and were available from SLA in late 1998.

In June 1997 SLA's Board of Directors entered into an agreement with the Phase 5 Consulting Group, Inc. of Ottawa, Canada, and its affiliate, Information Monitor Company (IMC) of Houston, Texas, to survey SLA's global membership through a dedicated Web site accessible to respondents by password. The main purpose of the information service providers (ISP) survey is to profile the changing needs of librarians and information specialists with respect to technology and information products. The first wave of the three-year project was administered in June 1998, and summary results were available in summer 1998.

## Serial Publications

In January 1997 *Special Libraries* and *SpeciaList* were officially retired, welcoming a new four-color monthly magazine, *Information Outlook*. Now in its second year of publication, the official publication of the association continues to provide members and subscribers with even more timely, cutting-edge, and in-depth coverage of issues pertinent to information professionals working in a global environment.

During the past year *Information Outlook* included feature articles that focused on such topics as technological advances within the profession, management trends, marketing tactics for the information center, strategic positioning, benchmarking, and salary survey information. Interviews with prominent figures in the information industry were included in 1998's editorial content. These included Stanley Davis, noted educator, consultant, and author of *2020 Vision*; Nettie Seabrooks, chief operating officer for the city of Detroit; and Delano Lewis, then president and CEO of National Public Radio.

Association news found its place on the pages of *Information Outlook*. Program updates were highlighted each month in regular columns, such as "Professional Development Outlook," "Government Relations Outlook," "Money Matters," "Conference Countdown," and "Public Relations Outlook." Two new columns, "IRC Notes" and "SLA News," were added to the journal in 1998. *Information Outlook* also became accessible at its own URL in 1998. At www.informationoutlook.com, readers can get the full text of feature articles and regular columns electronically. The site also has links to SLA's "Coming Events" page and the "Online Job Search," a complete listing of available jobs for information professionals. A search engine was added as well so that users can find articles based on topic, author, or date of publication.

*Information Outlook* was recognized with an Award of Excellence in publishing for magazines. The coming years promise to be both exciting and challenging for SLA's official publication.

*Who's Who in Special Libraries*, the association's annual membership directory, contains 400 pages and continues to serve as a valuable networking tool and information resource for the membership. The 1997–1998 *Who's Who* included an expanded "Buyer's Guide," containing information on vendors of specific products and services of value to special librarians.

The publication also included chapter and division leadership and member information; member statistics; historical highlights; SLA's Bylaws, Strategic Plan, and Vision Statement; awards and honors winners; past presidents; and a schedule of future meetings and conferences. The online version of the *Who's Who* featured board information, association bylaws, unit officers, and other useful SLA information.

In 1998 the *Preliminary Conference Program* was expanded to 112 pages with a 16-page perforated "Professional Development" insert. The *Program* was again posted to the Web site, and updates to it were frequently made to ensure accurate information. The *Final Conference Program* also expanded: Included for the first time was a perforated "Tracks" insert that grouped programs according to their focus (e.g, management, technology, and so forth). Also, icons were included next to CE courses illustrating the competency (as defined in *Competencies for Special Librarians of the 21st Century*) addressed in the course. The *Final Conference Program* was posted on the Web as well.

# Trends and Issues in Library and Information Services in Canada, 1998

Ken Haycock

Mary Oh

School of Library, Archival, and Information Studies
University of British Columbia
Vancouver, British Columbia

Widespread public-sector restraint has been a constant theme during the past year, while demand for services continues to increase. Because a significant portion of materials held in Canadian libraries is produced outside of the country and is priced in U.S. dollars, the drop in value of the Canadian dollar has further challenged budgets. Across the country, there is increased cooperation to share resources and, increasingly, to address the high cost of purchasing and licensing electronic products. Although a new Copyright Act was passed in 1996, exceptions for libraries have yet to be defined, and the application of the act has varied throughout the country. Publications in electronic form add yet another dimension to ongoing copyright negotiations. Increased need for and greater initiatives in fund-raising for libraries is a major trend. Libraries are also becoming increasingly involved in the organization of Internet resources, and initiatives to connect Canadians to the Internet through libraries have presented myriad challenges as well as increased opportunities. As the trend toward digitization and electronic publishing continues, there is a greater need to adopt standards and develop best practices. The library community continues to support initiatives to ensure universal access to information.

## Initiatives in Information Technology

In June 1998 the National Library of Canada launched *Canadiana*, the national bibliography, on CD-ROM. *Canadiana* holds more than 1.4 million records from the database of monographs, serials, government publications, music scores, sound recordings, video recordings, and electronic publications. *Canadiana* also contains the National Library's name authority records and the National Archive's Carto-Canadian records.

The National Library's Virtual Canadian Union Catalogue (vCuc) pilot project was completed in March 1998. The project sought to identify and address technical issues in the use of Z39.50, a standard that allows users to perform searches in many catalogs simultaneously. The use of Z39.50 would eliminate the need to produce local or regional union catalogs and facilitate resource sharing across the country.

As more organizations take on digitization projects, the library community has taken initiatives to address such issues as the selection and planning of digital projects as well as the development of technical standards and formats. High costs, the lack of staff expertise, copyright considerations, and the need to ensure long-term access in a time of rapid technological change remain important issues that need to be addressed.

The National Library's Digital Library Infrastructure Project mandate is to develop the hardware, software, and telecommunications infrastructure to support digital library applications, as well as to manage electronic publications. The first phase focused on the acquisition and implementation of generic software that would be used to create a variety of digital library applications. The second phase will examine the use of extended relational-database management systems and full-text search software that will be used to search databases, as well as documents in SGML, PDF, XML, HTML, and ASCII formats. Phase II will also examine the need for, and a variety of ways to implement, electronic document management.

The Canadian Initiative on Digital Libraries, formed in 1997 to support communication and collaboration among libraries to address the challenges of digitization, now has more than 50 libraries of all types participating, and it is producing an information kit that will focus awareness on major issues, advocacy needs, and potential sources of funding. A project and funding framework is being developed to create a national digital collection featuring Canadian content and to encourage communities to develop digital collections showcasing local history.

The National Library recently reached the 1,000 mark in cataloging of remote-access electronic publications. It began in 1994 as the Electronic Publications Pilot Project, which sought to acquire, preserve, and make available a wide range of Canadian electronic products, as well as to create standard bibliographic records for electronic information.

## Electronic Publishing and Ensuring Access to Information

Although most government publications remain in print form, the feasibility of electronic publishing of government information is being examined. Ensuring widespread public access to government information and long-term preservation in light of rapidly changing technology are key issues in the move to electronic publishing. In June 1998 Statistics Canada announced that a number of low-demand titles were to be converted to electronic format only. The National Library is involved in major initiatives to address issues associated with this growing interest in electronic publishing.

The Task Force on the Dissemination of Government Information in Electronic Format, formed in 1996, continues efforts to ensure access to information through a network of public-access points, as well as to promote standards and best practices in publishing, managing, and organizing electronic publications. The task force seeks to ensure long-term access and preservation through rational and responsible advances in electronic publishing. The Federal Task Force on Digitization is made up of representatives from various government agencies and the National Library to develop awareness and understanding of a wide variety of digital activities and issues in federal institutions.

In 1997 Environment Canada announced its intention to charge for information previously available free through the Depository Services Program. This was met by strong opposition from the library community. The Canadian Library Association (CLA) submitted a brief titled "Access to Government Information" to the House of Commons Standing Committee on Environment and Sustainable Development, and the decision to proceed is now under consideration by the minister responsible for Environment Canada.

The high cost of telecommunications services to rural areas was the subject of another brief submitted by CLA: "Universal and Equitable Access Telecommunications to High Cost Serving Areas" was submitted to the Canadian Radio-Television and Telecommunication Commission (CRTC) in response to a series of decisions to deregulate telephone service and restructure individual telephone costs. The high cost of service provision in less-populated areas would limit competition. As increasing amounts of information appear in electronic form, high costs would present a major barrier to access in these areas. The brief recommended that communications revenues be used to form a universal-access fund that would subsidize providers in high-cost serving areas and provide discounts for libraries, schools, and community organizations to ensure a minimum level of information access for all areas.

## Libraries and the Internet

Prime Minister Jean Chretien launched the Smart Communities Initiative in June 1998 to use information technology in new and innovative ways for economic, social, and cultural development. The blue ribbon panel established by the prime minister (including Wendy Newman, president of the Canadian Association of Public Libraries) recommended that a national selection committee oversee a competitive process to support and fund the development of at least one Smart Community Project in each province, one in the North, and one in an aboriginal community by the year 2000.

A study conducted by Ekos Research Associates titled "Canadians, Public Libraries and the Information Highway" confirmed the importance of public libraries as access points to the Information Superhighway. The study was designed to help the government plan its broad goal of connecting all public libraries to the Internet and to examine how this connection will be sustained. The study found that public libraries top the list of appropriate locations for access sites for the public and that 7 out of 10 respondents believe that on-site access to the Internet is an appropriate role for public libraries. Sixty-six percent of respondents indicated that they support libraries as a resource for training on how to use the Internet and search engines. Sixty percent of respondents view public libraries as having a role in the provision of locally produced Canadian Internet content.

The Community Access Program (CAP), sponsored by Industry Canada, continued its efforts to connect Canadians to the Internet. Public libraries have played a key role as access points in the CAP, especially in rural areas. LibraryNet, another Industry Canada initiative to provide Internet access through public libraries, continues its work across the country. SchoolNet, a program sponsored by private and public partnerships to bring Internet access and support digital projects in schools and libraries, has created a number of diverse projects featuring Canadian digital content. Libraries are also playing an important and increasing role in the organization of Internet resources; an example of this is the

National Library's Canadian Information by Subject Headings, an initiative to organize Internet sites using Dewey Decimal Classification 21, which now includes 2,800 sites of Canadian interest.

## Intellectual Freedom Challenges

The British Columbia Supreme Court decided against the Surrey School Board's decision to ban from the kindergarten curriculum three books depicting same-sex parents. In its decision, the court argued that the ban was motivated by religious interests on the board and that the books were suitable for inclusion in the curriculum. The library community had spoken out against the board's decision to ban the books.

The Burlington (Ontario) Public Library obtained a legal opinion on the limitations and extent of applicability of the Criminal Code and Charter of Rights that might affect public use of the Internet and information in other electronic formats in libraries, after a highly publicized challenge to Internet access. Library systems across the country are dealing with issues of intellectual freedom and the Internet. The filtering issue is an important one—decisions are being made, compromises developed, and Internet policies approved.

The Greater Victoria (British Columbia) Public Library (GVPL) was challenged in its decision to allow the Canadian Free Speech League to book meeting rooms in its central branch. The matter received strong media interest as a number of high-profile groups argued that the organization incited hatred against ethnic and religious groups, and demonstrations were held in front of the library in June. The GVPL consulted legal authorities and with the support of the CLA and the British Columbia Library Association (BCLA) maintained that public libraries are not the proper authorities for making decisions about the legality of groups and that the use of public library facilities is not the equivalent of support of a group's ideas.

In June 1998 the Standing Senate Committee on Legal and Constitutional Affairs recommended that the Proceeds of Crime Bill (C-220), which had been passed in the House of Commons, not proceed further because of "grave reservations" by the committee about the bill's definition of "proceeds of crime" and concern over possible violations of the Charter of Rights and Freedoms. The bill states that any work that describes a criminal act by someone convicted of a crime would not be able to benefit financially from its publication. It was argued that the bill would restrict freedom of expression and discourage publishers from handling any contentious works.

## Related Issues

### Copyright

Although the new Copyright Act was passed in 1996, the regulations covering exceptions for libraries, museums, and archives have not yet been defined. Application of copyright law has varied throughout the country. Some provinces have negotiated provincewide contracts with CANCOPY, an organization that acts on behalf of artists, writers, and publishers to purchase licenses to copy published materials, while others have negotiated at the local-library level. Now that Phase II of the new Copyright Act has received royal assent, the expectation is that Phase III will follow the same pattern as I and II and extend scope of protection for copyright owners first and only at a later stage discuss limitations and exceptions for reasonable access by users. In December 1997 Canada signed two international treaties, the World Intellectual Property Organization's (WIPO) Copyright Treaty and the Performers and Phonograms Treaty, which deal with copyright law in light of new technology.

The library community's position is that copyright laws should be technology neutral, to balance protection with public interest, which is served by reasonable access to works for education, research, and private study. Technology should not detract from rights of copyright owners or legitimate public interest, and exceptions and limitations must be addressed at the same time as new protections and new sanctions are considered.

**Value of the Canadian Dollar**

The drop in value of the Canadian dollar greatly decreased its purchasing power. A significant amount of material purchased by Canadian libraries is published elsewhere and priced in U.S. dollars. The change was especially detrimental to academic libraries with large journal collections. Faxon Canada's annual price index, which measures effects of inflation on prices charged for subscriptions, reported that there was an average price inflation of 13.49 percent over 1997 prices. The report is based on analysis of 4,444 periodical titles. If the Canadian currency had been stable, the increase would have been 10.93 percent.

**Partnerships and Consortia**

The trend toward cooperation and resource sharing is most visible in the purchase and licensing of electronic resources. In Saskatchewan, libraries have developed InterLEND, a licensing consortium. The Alberta Library, a provincewide consortium to purchase and share resources, is in its second year of operation. In Nova Scotia, regional library systems have purchased a joint license for their new Web-based databases, and there are plans for further joint purchases. In Ontario, the Consortium of Ontario Libraries was formed to represent all school, college, university, and public libraries in the province in the purchase and licensing of electronic products. A Manitoba Library proposal is being developed to connect academic, school, and public libraries in the province for the sharing of resources.

Literacy programs are another area of partnership. The New Brunswick Public Library Services, the National Literacy Secretariat, and the Ministry of Education have partnered to present literacy programs for school age children. Libraries in the Yukon are also partnering with government agencies for the same purpose.

In the summer of 1998 the Canadian Institute for Science and Technical Information (CISTI) and the Science and Technology Information Center in Taipei, Taiwan, entered into an agreement to share resources, technologies, and expertise. This agreement gives Canadians access to more than 1,200 Chinese-language journals published in Taiwan, China, and Southeast Asia.

### Services to the Visually Challenged

The Canadian National Institute for the Blind (CNIB) has introduced a national information service for Canadians unable to use print. VISUNET: CANADA is a matrix of systems and services that forms a virtual library for blind and print-disabled Canadians. It integrates the CNIB's collection of material in alternate formats with resources of other libraries internationally and on the Internet. Services include access to VISUCAT, the OPAC to VISUNET, via telnet, and through CAP pilot sites, as well as partnerships with regional library systems to allow access to the CNIB Library. A pilot project in Toronto is examining a service that allows clients to read unabridged newspapers using their telephones. The CNIB is also working on VISUTEXT, a service that will provide full-text access to electronic digital media materials collected and managed by the CNIB. These are major developments to achieve information parity with sighted people, with the objective to develop a model to mainstream access in public libraries.

## Libraries by Type

### Academic Libraries

The high cost of serials—especially scientific, technical, and medical journals—continues to be of great concern. VIRTUOSO, a project funded through Industry Canada's SchoolNet Program, consists of a group of university-based publishers working cooperatively on various electronic publishing projects to keep costs of academic publishing down.

The Canadian Association of Research Libraries/Association des bibliothèques de recherche du Canada (CARL/ABRC) expressed deep concern in 1998 over the effects of the decline of the Canadian dollar against the U.S. dollar as 70 percent of books and 85 percent of journals purchased by research libraries are published outside Canada and are priced in U.S. dollars. CARL/ABRC argued that the decline of the Canadian dollar was a serious threat to research libraries, and to academic research, if these libraries are to stay in the forefront of knowledge and the international exchange of information.

CARL/ABRC submitted a brief to Industry Canada on the "Intellectual Property Protection of Databases" in January 1998. CARL/ABRC argued that the exchange of scientific and other research information must not be constrained by commercial interests that, through legislation, seek copyright protection for work contained in databases. It would be to the detriment of the communication of research if prohibitive costs result from public-domain and government information being given extra copyright life through inclusion in a commercial database. The brief maintained the principle of technological neutrality in copyright matters.

### Special Libraries

Technology is a key issue for special libraries. The CLA Special Libraries Day focused on the development of intranets, Z39.50 connections, PUSH technology, and marketing. Infopartnering is a new trend where librarians become team members and work with clients to assist them in research in their specialized areas. Infopartnering brings librarians out of the library and into the offices of the client.

The Canadian Association of Law Libraries (CALL) released the results of its 1998 Salary and Benefits Survey. Law librarians working in academic libraries made significantly more money than those in other settings. Salaries varied across geographic regions in Canada, with salaries lowest for those in the Atlantic provinces and the highest average salaries in Quebec.

CALL has released its Serials Tracking Report 1998, which documents the high cost of legal publications and the cost and licensing of CD-ROM products. Law libraries are working toward the stabilization of purchase and licensing costs.

## Health Sciences Libraries

Partnerships were a key component of major health library initiatives, to share resources and advance access to health information. Health Canada, CISTI, the Association of Canadian Medical Colleges Committee on Medical School Libraries, Canadian Health Libraries Association (CHLA), and L'ASTED are working on a concept paper for a Canadian National Health Libraries Network. The groups envision a national health knowledge network, similar to that coordinated by the National Library of Medicine in the United States, to address the needs of physicians, researchers, educators, and patients and to create technological and human networks at all levels. The hope is that new legislation would create a network of libraries funded and coordinated federally that would collect and organize information, develop technical tools, and advocate medical choices based on better information.

## Public Libraries

Public-sector restraint has had a major impact on library budgets, resulting in consideration of fees for services. The Winnipeg Public Library debated the fee issue early in the year, with the Manitoba Library Association speaking for a public library free to all. Public libraries are either developing or are actively participating in fund-raising activities. This is reflected in the growing numbers of "friends" groups across the country and the growing number of library foundations being established. Library Advocacy Now! training continues across the country as libraries see an increased need and opportunity for the promotion of public libraries. A growing trend toward amalgamations of library boards, especially in Ontario and the Atlantic provinces, has seen the creation of large, centralized library systems. The new Toronto Public Library has been a high-profile example of this trend. The impact of changes in governance and administration for public libraries as a result of these amalgamations remains to be seen. A move toward consortium buying by library systems across the country has resulted in increased savings and bargaining power. Collaboration with municipal governments in Web page developments has also been a trend, to support development of economic opportunities in the community and to develop information initiatives. The Gates Library Foundation has earmarked funds for libraries in rural and socioeconomically depressed areas, and a process to determine a funding formula is under way.

**School Libraries**

The National Library has drafted a School Library Manifesto with the hope that it will be approved at the next UNESCO General Conference in 1999. The purpose of the manifesto is to sensitize national governments, municipalities, parents, and the public at large to the goals, purposes, and crucial role of the school library in education. If adopted by UNESCO, member countries would then translate and disseminate it within their communities.

The term "broken front" has been used to describe the current state of school libraries in Canada. School board amalgamations, budget cuts, reassignments, and retirements have been common themes. The drop in value of the Canadian dollar has put further strain on reduced collections budgets. School libraries have pursued partnerships to increase buying power, but high costs and staff training issues for information technology continue to be concerns. The level of school library services in rural areas remains a concern for the school library community.

## Regional Perspectives

In British Columbia a consortium of 72 public and academic libraries has implemented a real-time Web-based interlibrary loan system called OutLOOK Online. The British Columbia Library Services Branch and the public libraries of the province have collaborated to create the Virtual Reference Desk (VRD). It is designed for quick access to electronic information through a variety of Web sites chosen and reviewed by public librarians. Links to children's and young adult sites are planned for the future. The VRD will be available through public library home pages and as of March 1998 included a test database with links to 82 Web sites accessible by subject, Dewey classification number, and keyword. The Red Cedar Awards, a children's-choice book award, were given for the first time in 1998, with more than 1,900 children voting.

The Alberta Public Library Electronic Network (APLEN) is a project designed to improve access to information for Albertans by linking all public libraries in the province by 2001. The key element is the creation of an electronic "backbone" that will provide access to a provincial database of public library resources, government information, interlibrary loan, and Internet resources. The project is a partnership between the Western Economic Partnership Agreement (WEPA) and Industry Canada through the Community Access Program. The Alberta Library continues efforts to move toward the adoption of one library card for use in any library across the province.

Libraries around the province of Saskatchewan are becoming automated and are establishing Internet access. The provincewide Library Electronic Information system allows viewing and interlibrary loan services for patrons from their local library. As of 1998 more than 150 branch libraries were linked in this system. A provincewide database-licensing project was initiated during the past year, and future buying by the consortium will include resources chosen by academic, school, and special libraries. Seamless Access is a cooperative project that seeks to link catalogs so that the user can search across the province, and also link patron files for a provincewide library card system.

In January 1998 there was a heavily publicized debate over proposed public library membership fees in Manitoba public libraries. More than 85 percent of public libraries in the province have Internet access, many through the federal Community Access Project. During the past year, interlibrary loan numbers have increased significantly, most likely through the Manitoba Public Library Information Network (MAPLIN) project that has facilitated resource sharing in rural areas by providing electronic access to library databases and catalogs. The Winnipeg Library Foundation is planning a major expansion to the downtown Winnipeg Centennial Branch Library as a millennium project, and the foundation is meeting with government and private-sector partners to raise funds.

The new Toronto Public Library opened on January 1, 1998, the result of the amalgamation of six regional library systems: Toronto, Etobicoke, East York, Scarborough, North York, York, and the Metro Reference Library. The new system has 97 branches, and the board—made up of chairs of former library region boards—continues to decide the system's structure and organization. In October 1998 the Toronto Public Library, in partnership with Atomic Energy of Canada, launched Science Net, a Web site whose goal is to provide students, educators, and the general public with access to Internet information on pure and applied sciences in English and French. The site uses the Dewey Decimal System to classify sites and makes efforts to choose only reputable and accurate information. Toronto Public Library also launched the Virtual Reference Library in 1998. Ontario launched Network 2000 with the goal of connecting public libraries by a broadband high-speed network by year 2000. Bill 109 was withdrawn after its third reading in Ontario. Strongly opposed by the Ontario Library Association, it would have given more freedom to municipal governments and withdrawn direct provincial support for libraries.

In Quebec, the passing of Bill 403 on June 18 by the Quebec National Assembly established the Grande Bibliothèque du Québec, the consolidation of the Central Montreal Public Library and the Bibliothèque Nationale du Québec. In a time of considerable public-sector restraint, the expense associated with a new library has generated considerable debate in the province. The appointment of a journalist, rather than a librarian, to head up the new library was another development.

In New Brunswick, automation remains a high priority; nearly 40 libraries in the province are now networked for access to the OPAC; the remaining libraries have the CD-ROM version of the catalog. The New Brunswick Public Library Board, the result of regional board amalgamation, has now been operating for over a year, and regional forums have been established to encourage trustees of a region to meet and share information. May 1998 saw the first meeting of the New Brunswick Library Foundation, whose purpose is to raise the profile of public libraries in the province and to raise funds. More than half of the public libraries in the province offer Internet access, and the New Brunswick Library Services Web site was launched this year. Internet training was provided for staff in public libraries through Industry Canada's Youth Employment Strategy. Twenty-five New Brunswick public libraries and 30 tutors hired by Advanced Education and Training's Priority Employment delivered the summer Literacy Program for Kids. More than 500 children, referred through the school system, participated in the program held in public libraries.

In 1998 Newfoundland gave high priority to Internet access and to automation. More than 50 libraries now have local-area networks. However, cost has been a major challenge, and the provision of technical support and training has been difficult because of the geographical distance between branches in each region. The demand for information access through the Internet has been heavy, and students hired through Industry Canada initiatives have provided training. The provincial-government initiatives for provincewide e-mail access will increase this demand. Efforts to provide resources to all regardless of geographic isolation and economic circumstances continue.

The existing funding formula for Nova Scotia's regional library boards was revised in April 1998, and recommended changes include increased funding for regional library boards over the next three years, salary increases over the same period, and supplementary funding for the Eastern Counties. Automated systems for eight of the nine regional library boards are in progress, and retrospective conversion continues. Each of the 75 fixed regional library branches have at least one Internet access terminal, and an Internet training handbook was developed through a LibraryNet grant.

The Nova Scotia Provincial Library is implementing a pilot project to provide a Government Libraries Consolidated Catalogue (GLCC) as a node in the Virtual Canadian Union Catalogue (vCuc). The Nova Scotia regional libraries have produced a strategic plan titled "Access for All." Key issues include advocacy, public relations and marketing, and bringing together all members of the library community to promote libraries. A children's choice award, the Hackmatack Award, is being developed to recognize Canadian (especially Atlantic) writing for children. The first award is planned for the year 2000. The Nova Scotia Provincial Library is developing a consortium for the purchase of databases. Regional, health, academic, and college libraries have expressed interest in joining the group. Contacts are being made with other Atlantic provinces to increase buying power of the consortium.

On Prince Edward Island (PEI), every public library now has Internet access. The three-year implementation of the provincewide automated system was completed in 1998, and the public interface was given the name AbbyCat. The CAP has identified public libraries and schools as preferred sites in 1998, and the provincial Department of Education agreed to cover the cost of connection for these sites. The Computers in Libraries Program continues to provide OPAC terminals for PEI's libraries. The system of management for the 19 rural branches in the province has been centralized and are headed up by a professional library services supervisor.

In the Yukon, there are currently nine established community libraries, with one more in development, and volunteer branches in seven smaller communities, with the central library in Whitehorse acting as the administrative center for public library services. Budgetary restraint has limited collection development, while ongoing telecommunication and maintenance costs for Internet access have been very high. Automation is a high priority because the Whitehorse library and two community libraries are mostly online and four more community library collections are slated to be automated during the next year. Through the CAP, the Yukon government, and YKnet (the local service provider), public Internet access is available in seven of the largest Yukon communities. Negotiations with

Industry Canada and the Yukon government are progressing, as access is planned for smaller communities. Literacy projects funded through the National Literacy Secretariat continue at Yukon libraries; in 1997 videos were launched, with the current focus on acquiring French materials. An initial French-language collection has been purchased for the Whitehorse Public Library through funding from Yukon French Language Services.

## Library and Information Services Education

Schools of library and information studies are reporting greater flexibility in the programs being offered. Part-time access and distance education, especially continuing education, are growing trends. Information technology continues to play an increasing role in curriculum. The trend toward contract employment and part-time employment for new graduates continues. The University of Western Ontario Graduate School of Library and Information Studies has merged with the School of Journalism to form the new Faculty of Communication, Journalism and Continuing Studies. Schools report greater attention to management, marketing, and entrepreneurship.

## Future Trends

The trend toward the formation of consortia for the purchase and licensing of electronic resources continues, as well as partnering with the public and private sectors to provide services. Public-sector restraint and the need for strong advocacy for libraries, as well as increased emphasis on fund-raising, also continue to be important concerns. As more Canadians become connected to the Internet through libraries, the library community is developing policies and practices that ensure equitable and universal access to information and the principles of intellectual freedom.

# Special Reports

## Information Age Dilemma: Filtering the Internet for Young People

Ken Haycock

Betty Chapin

David Bruce

School of Library, Archival, and Information Studies
University of British Columbia
Vancouver, British Columbia

Libraries embrace the responsibility of providing open and easy access to information to all people, regardless of age. As a result, libraries are taking the opportunity to be an important gateway to the complex collection of Internet information resources.

Americans have increasingly come to realize that it is imperative for their children to be highly skilled in new forms and uses of technology. Public and school libraries—by providing access to the Internet and supplying vital Internet education and training—are playing important roles in equipping children with this skill.

Everyone, both adults and children, will need to learn how to navigate the Internet effectively. The Internet has been called the "most innovative and exciting learning tool of this century" (American Library Association, 1997) and "the communication medium of the 21st century" (Kniffel, 1998). It makes available every kind of idea and represents a dynamic global form of communication. Today the World Wide Web, the best known Internet platform, holds more than 100 million documents, and it is estimated that thousands more are being added daily. The content on these Web sites is constantly changing because material can be added and manipulated very easily. The Internet is like a "vast library including millions of readily available and indexed publications, the content of which is as diverse as human thought" (American Civil Liberties Union, 1997).

Coping with the unique nature of this huge, diverse, and rapidly growing and evolving medium will continue to be a considerable challenge for decades to come. But while this resource greatly expands the scope of information available in a library, relatively little of its content has been selected by a librarian. It therefore has a down side; it creates problems and raises issues regarding access

*Note*: The authors express their appreciation to Ann Curry and Karen Schneider, who served as external readers for this review.

to unlawful materials and the potential exposure of children to obscene or otherwise inappropriate materials.

The fact is that there are thousands of "porn sites" on the Web at present, and dozens are added every day. This is an understandable cause for public anxiety about easy access to this new technology, and that is where the issue of filtering the Internet makes its entrance.

Internet filtering, as a control mechanism, takes place in a variety of settings. In the workplace, the Internet can be a source of distraction. As a result, some employers use filtering software to block access to sites dealing with such topics as sports, hobbies, online games, and other forms of entertainment. In the home, parents may use filtering software to prevent their children from accessing less socially acceptable information, however they define it. The types of sites that are blocked in the home depend entirely on the parents and their values and attitudes. In schools, filtering software is often used to ensure that students access only information consistent with what is being taught. In libraries, the Internet challenges librarians to reconcile professional values encouraging access to resources they have traditionally evaluated and selected while facing community values that seek to censor information and ideas that have not been reviewed. Librarians thus face diverse users and diverse community values in their quest to provide access to information.

Society often distinguishes "between what is appropriate for children and what is appropriate for adults" and "[w]hen the media cover Internet content, nearly always the potential for children to view this content is raised at least once" (Schneider, 1997). Filters are consequently used more commonly in the children's area of public libraries than in other divisions (Oder, 1997 May 1b). The use of parental consent forms by some libraries to limit Internet access for young people is also a sign of a perceived need for protection from potential litigation.

There are different types of information on the Internet that some people would like screened and that filters may screen. Depending on the configuration of the filter, drug promotion, foul language, hate literature, and violent or sexually explicit material can all be filtered. But for the most part, it is sexually explicit content that filters are intended to block in libraries, and the findings of the Internet Filter Assessment Project (TIFAP) show that this is largely in keeping with the public's wishes.

Proponents of filtering believe that the use of filters for this purpose is an effective way to protect children and others. Others call filters a quick fix at best, and believe that filters were developed for parents' use on the home computer or in business offices, but not for the library. They refer to filters used in libraries as "censorware," designed to restrict speech based on viewpoint but ultimately not having the desired effect.

The public library has a long history of advocating freedom of information and open access. This position has found its way into the mission statements of many public libraries—for example, "open access to information" (Austin Public Library, 1998), "free and open access to information" (Brooklyn Public Library, 1998), and "access to information sources throughout the nation and around the world" (Seattle Public Library, 1998).

With on-site forms of information (for example, books and videos), librarians have had control over the nature of the information to which they were providing access. With the advent of the Internet, however, it is much more difficult to control what information the library is providing. As a result, a contentious divide between librarians and certain segments of their communities can arise. While many people believe that the Internet is just one more form of information the library should make available, others believe that librarians should exert control over what can be accessed on the Web. As a result, libraries are struggling to match their open-access mission to the often more restrictive demands of their communities.

Existing and emerging groups are making position statements, publishing documents, and leading drives on both sides of the debate. For example, the American Library Association (ALA) opposes the use of any filtering software, stating that "the use of filtering software by libraries to block access to constitutionally protected speech violates the Library Bill of Rights" (ALA, 1998j). Likewise, researcher and librarian Karen Schneider is "biased toward open access" and "concerned about outsourcing decisions about what's blocked to a third, commercial party: the filter's producers" (Schneider, 1997).

On the other side of the debate are people like David Burt and his organization Filtering Facts, which describes itself as a "small nonprofit organization that promotes the use of filtering software in libraries to protect children" (Burt, 1998 March 7). Burt and Filtering Facts have set themselves up to be diametrically opposed to ALA policy by publishing such articles on their Web site (http://www.filteringfacts.org) as "Statement of Filtering Facts in Response to the American Library Association Statement to the Senate Commerce, Science and Transportation Committee, on Indecency on the Internet" (Burt, 1998 March 7), "Internet Filters and Public Library Management" (Barry, 1997), and "Why Librarians Should Filter" (Burt, 1997).

Is it possible for filtering software to legitimately claim protection against sexually explicit sites? Can filters block sexually explicit material when sites are constantly being added or are changing their names or content?

The fear of the "bad stuff" on the Internet, the common belief that filters work, and the lack of confidence in other solutions drive some libraries to use filtering software (Schneider, 1998a). Judith Krug, director of ALA's Office for Intellectual Freedom, believes that filtering is not a solution, that it only gives the public a false sense of security. "For the first time in the history of communication, you can access comments, thoughts, ideas, from anywhere, by anyone, at anytime. . . . [it] is a different medium; it's never going to be entirely safe. To attempt to make this communication medium safe means we have to unplug it" (Oder 1997 May 1b).

Some libraries have used the concept of "deselection" to explain or justify using filters to block sexually explicit material. In this view, just as libraries do not attempt to provide every book that is published, they do not need to provide access to every Web site. Using filtering software to block Web sites constitutes "deselection" of filter-blocked sites. On the other hand, if you compare providing Internet access in a library to purchasing a multivolume encyclopedia set, then isn't subjective deselection of some Web sites the same as crossing out portions of the encyclopedia that are deemed unfit? Offering access and then installing filtering software to block selected sites may be viewed as no different than removing books from the shelves—an affront to the First Amendment.

This report focuses on the professional, educational, political, and technological issues associated with filtering (blocking) access to information and ideas of any type by young people in public and school libraries.

## Filtering Software Programs

Library users want Internet access, and—with the abundance of government, educational, not-for-profit, commercial, and self-published resources available—users *need* access. Also, with more paper-based publications now available electronically through the Internet and the fact that the technology has proven to be a useful backbone for commercial databases and online catalogs, it is clear that the Internet is not going away (Schneider, 1997c). However, it is a technology that is completely different from any other with which librarians have had to deal, and as a result old library policies are proving to be inadequate. One of the proposed methods for dealing with this technology is the use of filtering software.

### How Filtering Software Works

Filtering software and services can work in a variety of ways. They can block certain types of content by using keyword or site blocking. Filters can also block by protocol or by time of day. The latter two types of blocking are usually used for security and resource allocation purposes. These are explained more fully below.

Internet filters have a predefined list of allegedly objectionable phrases, words, and letter combinations (stop words). These terms are "nearly always related to sexuality, human biology, or sexual orientation" (Schneider, 1997). Some filters, however, also include words such as "death" (CYBERsitter) or "pain" (Cyber Patrol) in their lists (Schneider, 1997). Some lists include such letter combinations as "ank," which would flag possibly objectionable words such as "spank" but also block the innocuous "bank," "Hank Aaron," and "Sherman tank." Blocking by word (also called keyword blocking, content identification, content analysis, dynamic document review, and phrase blocking) screens each incoming Web page for the phrases, words, or letter combinations that are found on its list of "stop words."

Most of the first filters relied upon this method, and filtering critics say that it is responsible for much of the bad reputation filters have acquired. This is because the method fails to take into account the context of a word's use; such words as "bottom," "breast," and "rape" have different meanings, depending on context. Many filters block "sex" as a word or as a letter combination, but this too can cause many unobjectionable Web sites to be blocked—sites, for instance, containing such words as "sextant," "sextet," and "sexton," not to mention "Sussex" and "Middlesex."

So why use this type of filtering? There are two primary reasons. First, it is far less time consuming and expensive than having someone evaluate individual sites. Second, given the rate of growth of the Internet, it is viewed (rightly or wrongly) as the only logistically feasible way to cope with the Web's rapid changes.

When a stop word is encountered, most filters will do one of the following four things: (1) stop the downloading of the file, (2) display the file but obscure the targeted term, (3) display some but not all of the file, or (4) shut down the browser or even the computer (Schneider, 1997).

Internet filters can also block by site—by far the most common approach. Such filters can either allow everything except a list of unacceptable sites (a "denial list"), or block everything except a list of acceptable sites (an "allow list"). Those who create such filtering systems review Web pages and place them into allow or denial lists, using automated tools that search the Internet for new files and flag those that have content common to the files they are attempting to categorize. Sites are usually grouped into categories that can be selected or deselected to customize the software to the user's specific needs.

Although this method is more reliable, it also has problems. Again, due to the size and rate of growth of the Internet, it is impossible to review all Web sites. Second, because software is being used to identify sites for inclusion, some files may slip by if they do not have content resembling what is being flagged. Also, some filters block at the file level, while others block at the site level. Blocking at the site level becomes a problem when a site contains some materials considered objectionable and other materials that are fully acceptable. Finally, no standards exist for the classification of sites, and a lack of standards leads to a variety of problems, all reducing the amount of control a user can exert over the filtering software. While some filters have as few as six categories (Surfwatch), others have up to 29 (WebSENSE). Also, topics can be categorized in different ways. For example, sites related to homosexuality might be placed in an area called "Sexuality/Lifestyles" (WebSENSE) or "Lifestyle" (Smart Filter), might be lumped in with "Adult" (I-Gear), or might even be sprinkled throughout the content categories (Surfwatch) (Schneider, 1997).

Protocol blocking is usually used for resource allocation and security purposes. In libraries, blocking entire portions of the Internet—such as chat rooms, newsgroups, or e-mail—ensures that Internet access is being used as the library intended. From a security standpoint, it can help prevent individuals from disseminating unsolicited information. On the Web, unless an e-mail link or a form is provided on a Web page, it is impossible to send information out. E-mail, chat rooms, and newsgroups rely on people contributing without being asked to do so. An example of where this type of filtering might be used effectively is in a school library, where the filter could be used to prevent students from disclosing to strangers information about themselves, such as their address or phone number.

Some filters that have the capability of limiting access by the time of day can combine this with the blocking by type of protocol, so that users would be allowed, for instance, to participate in a chat room discussion but not during the busiest hours of the day. One type of time filtering limits access by time-outs—in other words, a user signs on and is blocked from using the Internet after a predetermined amount of time. This feature is available through only two filtering products at present.

### Types of Filtering Software

Internet filtering can be performed in a variety of ways. Software can be loaded directly onto a specific computer (client software), for example, or an external computer (proxy server) can filter all files before they arrive at a particular computer.

Client software, not surprisingly, has advantages and disadvantages. In a library with several computers, it is possible to have different settings on each terminal—for example, one setting on the computers in the children's area and different, less restrictive settings on the computers in the rest of the library. When a library has a small number of computers, this type of filtering is economical, but the cost effectiveness diminishes as the number of stations increases. Another disadvantage is that this software requires maintenance: someone needs to ensure that the settings are correct, that users cannot tamper with the settings, and that the software is kept current by downloading regular updates provided by the manufacturer.

Normally, a request (clicking on a Web link, for example) goes from the client computer to the Internet service provider (ISP) and finally to the host computer, where the file is located. That file is then sent back along the same path and is displayed on the client computer. Remote proxy servers are third-party servers between the client and the host through which all of the traffic on an Internet connection is routed. The third party filters all of the information going in or out on an Internet connection. Generally, a subscription service tends to be cheaper than client software, particularly when a subscriber has several computers. Such a subscription also means that there is no on-site maintenance expense. A potential down side to this type of filtering concerns the proxy server's ability to manage a high volume of traffic; the server needs to be robust enough to avoid a logjam during busy periods.

Some ISPs offer filtering services for a small additional charge to their regular Internet service fees. This arrangement works just like a subscription to a proxy server. Indeed, many proxy servers are selling their services to the ISPs (Schneider, 1997). Again, the maintenance costs are minimal or nonexistent, and it tends to be inexpensive to subscribe. On the other hand, control over its configuration is sometimes very limited.

Local area network (LAN)-based software is disappearing and is now offered by only one manufacturer. This type of filtering is similar to client software but is installed on the network server instead of the individual terminals. This type of software can be troublesome because it may conflict with various other programs on the system (Schneider, 1997).

"Proxy-in-a-box" servers fall somewhere between remote proxy servers and LAN-based software. Basically, vendors install a network server on-site that then acts as a proxy server. It is not software installed on the network, like LAN-based software, nor is it a third party acting as a filter.

Schneider warns that it is important to test any product and to "ask the vendor whether you can return the product (or within what timeframe you can return it) if you are not happy with it, since you can't really test a canned solution until it is in place" (Schneider, 1997).

## The Challenges

### The Technological Challenge

Filtering the Internet has been called a "technological fix" (Oder, 1997 May 1b), but the technology does not yet exist that can selectively and successfully block inappropriate materials without also blocking valuable information. And while many feel that filtering is an easy answer, many others say there are no easy technological solutions to the problem of controversial materials on the Internet and children's exposure to them.

Librarians are concerned that the use of filtering software is delegating intellectual and technological decisions to a third party: filter software companies. A librarian-led project, the Internet Filter Assessment Project (TIFAP), attempted to tackle this concern. Its objective was to evaluate critically software for blocking or restricting Internet access.

Out of this project came some advice for those considering using filtering software:

- Librarians should first determine the library's specific filtering needs. Only by identifying features that are important to the library and involving automation and reference librarians in the selection process can the most appropriate product be chosen.
- Librarians need to test filters in the library first and then configure them to their specific needs. For instance, it is preferable if keyword or category blocking can be disabled when considered appropriate by a librarian, which eliminates the problem of arbitrary blocking of keywords and/or categories by the filtering vendor and slightly alleviates a librarian's concern regarding third-party control of library decisions.
- Librarians need to know what is being blocked. They should look for filters that provide feedback information, that allow users to "talk" to the library about blocked sites that in fact should be accessible (Schneider, 1997).
- Ideally, a filtering product for libraries should offer keyword blocking that can be disabled, the capability to determine specific categories for blocking, reports generated by category, user feedback, and local-access consideration.

But is the use of filtering software "inconsistent with the traditional functions of a librarian," as Schneider suggests (Schneider, 1998b)?

Some common problems emerge:

- Technological control usually is not in the hands of the librarian. The technology is still not available to enable filters to distinguish between users of different ages, varying levels of maturity, and individual needs, and it is unclear how it could ever reliably do so. Using filters on all library terminals necessarily limits adult access to valuable sites and "would limit access to adults and older minors to that which is suitable for a sandbox" (Peck and Symons, 1997).
- It is impossible to know exactly what is being blocked with nearly all filtering software.
- Filters often block useful sites as well as undesired ones, so users may be denied access, for instance, to information on breast cancer or gay rights.
- Library control of which site categories are blocked ranges from limited to none; some software does not allow the librarian or library user to unblock or change any settings.

- There are no agreed-upon guidelines for what should be filtered or how it should be filtered, and most librarians are not comfortable having these decisions in the hands of a third party. Vendors' definitions of the categories being blocked can be confusing, and their standards for blocking are often vague.
- Because there are millions of sites on the Internet, it is technologically impossible to prescreen all of them to determine their acceptability. In addition, many sites are added daily, and many sites change (so that what is an acceptable site one day may not be acceptable the next).

### The Political Challenge

In 1995 the National Telecommunications and Information Administration of the Department of Commerce made the following statement:

> Public libraries can play a vital role in assuring that advanced information services are universally available to all segments of the American population on an equitable basis. Just as libraries traditionally made available the marvels and imagination of the human mind to all, libraries of the future are planning to allow everyone to participate in the electronic renaissance (American Civil Liberties Union, 1997).

Accepting the opportunity to be a provider of universal Internet access, libraries now face political pressure to filter that access to protect children, and the public generally, from sexually explicit material.

Although filtering software does not have the ability to distinguish between legal and illegal materials, there are still legislative efforts to force libraries to filter the information and ideas available to users. The Communications Decency Act (CDA) was an unsuccessful attempt to legislate "safe" Internet use. Although the stated intention of the law was to protect children from materials of a sexual nature, the act's wording was so broad that it potentially deprived adults of non-sexual information in various areas of health, art, and science.

The American Library Association opposed the CDA, believing that it would have serious implications for librarians by denying the legitimate free flow of information. In addition, ALA believed that the act would have provided parents with a false sense of security for their children because its provisions would have been impossible to fairly enforce—for one reason, because the Internet is a vast, international network uncontrollable by U.S. law. Furthermore, there is the problem of defining what is "indecent" or "harmful to minors" because community and individual standards differ widely.

The CDA was struck down by the Supreme Court as a violation of free speech as guaranteed by the First Amendment, a decision that has been called the "legal birth certificate of the Internet" (Hudson, 1998, November 25). "It is true that we have repeatedly recognized the governmental interest in protecting children from harmful materials," the court stated, "but that interest does not justify an unnecessarily broad suppression of speech addressed to adults" (Hudson, 1998c).

A Loudoun County, Virginia, case in 1998 dealt specifically with public libraries. The judge, herself a librarian, ruled that the county library system violated the First Amendment with its mandatory Internet-filtering policy (the system had installed filtering software on all of its public computers, limiting the access of all of its Internet users). The decision represents a historic first application of the principles of the First Amendment to Internet access through public libraries; but despite it, many public libraries are continuing to install filtering software under community pressure.

Pointing to the Virginia case, a lawyer for the American Civil Liberties Union called most library Internet policies "constitutionally suspect" and predicted many more such lawsuits. In February 1998 U.S. Sen. John McCain (R-Ariz.) introduced Senate Bill 1619, the Internet School Filtering Act, in an attempt "to protect children from exposure to sexually explicit and other harmful material when they access the Internet in the school and in the library" (Hudson, 1998, February 20). The bill attempted to mandate filters for public and school libraries as a condition for receiving discounted telecommunications rates (E-rates).

In the last three years at least 25 states have passed or considered laws pertaining to Internet censorship, particularly in school or public libraries, but federal district courts in at least three states have ruled such laws unconstitutional.

### The Philosophical Challenge

> Filtering the Internet is contrary to the purpose of libraries and the First Amendment. You may as well remove all the naughty words from the dictionary. Free speech is a matter of faith, and it requires confidence that, exercised or otherwise, it exists in full on the Internet and in the library alike" ("Internet 'Filters' Harm Free Speech" 1998 December 3).

Bruce Taylor, president of the National Law Center for Children and Families, made this statement, which reflects the values of librarianship. Librarians have a basic philosophical problem with using filters because it is the library's mission to provide open and equal access to all materials to all users. Traditionally, the library has been the place to go for the pursuit of knowledge as well as personal discovery, and it has been the responsibility of each library user to decide what information to access.

ALA has made its position clear: "Libraries and librarians should not deny or limit access to information available via electronic resources because of its allegedly controversial content or because of the librarian's personal beliefs or fear of confrontation" (American Library Association, 1998c). But despite their individual values and the backing of their professional associations, librarians are often under considerable pressure from the public and their governing boards. One example of such public pressure occurred in Gilroy, California, in 1998. After parents found children accessing sexually explicit material at the public library, they founded an organization called KIDS (Keep the Internet Decent and Safe) and tried (unsuccessfully) to file criminal charges against the library for allowing children to download hard-core pornography.

Librarians concede that there is material on the Internet not suitable for children and offensive to many adults, but there is considerable disagreement on what libraries should do about it. There is no easy answer, and filtering should not be seen as the only answer.

## Alternatives to Filtering

Solving or reducing the problem of children encountering inappropriate materials on the Internet will require a multifaceted approach combining a variety of actions or preventative measures by librarians.

> Some policymakers suggest imposing sweeping, national approaches to deal with the problems of kids and the Internet. Others advocate a complete absence of any restrictions. We . . . believe the proper approach—indeed approaches—likely are somewhere in between . . ." (National Commission on Libraries and Information Science, 1998).

Finding alternatives to filtering can mean putting simple measures in place with which library staff, library users, and the community at large can be comfortable. The real issue should not be "to filter or not to filter," but how librarians can safely and effectively manage public access to networked information. Examples of some alternatives are:

- Privacy screens (shields around computer screens) to prevent people other than the user from viewing the screen
- Computer positioning to alleviate problems of privacy and exposure
- Time limits and guidelines regulating how and when library patrons can use the Internet
- Screen savers that cause images to vanish after a given amount of time, thereby limiting the time images can be left on an unattended screen
- Active promotion of Web sites that are recommended for adults, children, and young adults
- Bookmarking previewed sites of interest on specific topics
- Guidance courses to help Internet users think critically about sources and consider and evaluate their accuracy
- Parental-consent forms for use by children and teenagers
- Use of filters that can be deactivated by library staff for adult users
- Designated access stations for "adults only"
- Internet access in school libraries limited to school-related work
- Internet use agreements under which users can lose the privilege of Internet access for improper activity

### Education and Training

Improved education and training is a proactive, longer-term approach to Internet access problems. In part, this means educating library staff and communities to help them to understand the special characteristics of libraries and the principles of intellectual freedom.

Most librarians are skilled and effective Internet navigators, and public and school librarians in particular become Internet educators. Training library staff on effective and safe Internet use (for both adults and children), so that they then can train library users, should be given high priority.

One proactive approach is to teach parents how to use the Internet for their own needs as well as how to help their children navigate the Web.

Successful completion of an Internet seminar can be required of all users. Such seminars can emphasize evaluative skills as well as the dangers of disclosing personal information or communicating with strangers about personal matters. Parents and children can take part together, and parents can learn that they can guide their children's Internet use in the same way that they guide their reading and television viewing.

The America Links Up Campaign began in September 1998 with the purpose of helping "ensure that children have a rewarding and safe online experience" by educating parents about the Internet (Wallace, 1998). Dennis Eckart, executive director of the campaign, said, "We're answering the call from parents who want to know how to ensure that their children can reap the incredible rewards that the Internet has to offer while avoiding the risks."

This educational campaign included many local meetings, called Internet teach-ins and involving more than 250 libraries, and demonstrated a proactive approach to the problems of sexually explicit materials on the Internet through education of parents and children as a major part of a long-term solution (Wallace, 1998).

Developing library Web sites is another way that librarians can guide and educate their library users. The director of the Kansas City (Missouri) Public Library has used this analogy to describe use of the Internet in the library: "The terminals are a kind of modern-day electronic reading table. When they select our preselected links, they're taking it off the shelf; when they go beyond that, they're bringing in their own material" (Oder, 1998 October 1b). Many libraries have developed Web pages (often special children's, young-adult, and seniors pages) that provide links to the best sites as well as helpful links to other appropriate sites.

Library-initiated education of staff and users, both adults and children, is a long-term commitment requiring considerable time and resources. It is an essential component for reducing the fear surrounding the Internet and for producing thoughtful and educated users. In addition to these tools, a carefully crafted Internet acceptable-use policy promotes this commitment to education.

## Acceptable-Use Policies

Acceptable-use policies (AUPs) are by far the most commonly used method for dealing with problem sites on the Internet. Almost 85 percent of public libraries currently have an Internet acceptable-use policy, and about 12.9 percent of these libraries also use filters. Roughly another 12 percent of public libraries are currently developing such policies, and 1.5 percent of these libraries also use filters (American Library Association 1998 November b).

Upon review (in December 1998) of the Internet acceptable-use policies for several major public libraries (Brooklyn, Dallas, San Francisco, Seattle, Toronto, and Vancouver), a pattern becomes clear. In different words, they all state the same five points:

1 The Internet contains a great deal of useful and interesting information, as well as some information that may be inaccurate, unreliable, untimely, useless, unauthoritative, offensive, or even illegal.

2 The library is not responsible for any of the information on the Internet beyond that contained in the library's own pages, and it does not necessarily endorse any of the opinions expressed on the Internet, even on pages to which the library provides links.

3 Individuals are responsible for all of their activities on the Internet, including what they access.

4 Parents and guardians are responsible for all of their children's activities on the Internet, including what they access.

5 The library is not responsible for any damages occurring directly or indirectly as a result of its provision of Internet access.

Only one of the libraries surveyed, the San Francisco Public Library, states in its policy that it does not employ any kind of filtering software. Most of the libraries stated that they provide documentation for parents to help them guide their children through the Internet or that they provided a page of suitable links for children. Although all of the libraries forbade the use of the library's Internet access for activities such as attempting to gain access to restricted areas, deleting files, damaging hardware, or engaging in any illegal activities, none of the libraries restricted access to content that would be considered sexually explicit or otherwise socially unacceptable.

Norman Oder (1997 May 1b) points out that "many AUPs now forbid patrons to access or display 'pornography'." Although none of the Internet AUPs mentioned above included any such restrictions, one public library in Ventura County, California, is being sued for having such a ban. The local branch of the Libertarian Party in Ventura County has filed a complaint in federal court in Los Angeles challenging its library system's requirement that patrons who wish to use library computers must sign an Internet user's agreement, agreeing to refrain from "displaying sexually explicit sites" (Kaplan, 1998).

Despite the aforementioned controversy, a well-thought-out acceptable-use policy can be an effective alternative to filtering. Such policies—which, among other things, should include disclaiming responsibility for content, stating parents' responsibility for children's access, and warning that the Internet may contain offensive materials—will serve to help users and protect the library from parental complaints and possible legal difficulties.

Librarians need to be a strong voice in the development of these policies, working in partnership with their boards. ALA recommends that all libraries have a policy that covers access to electronic information. The ALA Interpretation of the Library Bill of Rights, "Access to Electronic Information, Services, and Networks" (Appendix A and http://www.ala.org/alaorg/oif/electacc.html), is an excellent resource for those drafting a new policy. ALA's positions on the issue of filtering are clear: It believes that freedom of expression is everyone's right and that freedom of expression encompasses freedom of speech and the right to access information. These rights extend to children. ALA suggests that each individual library "consider its mission, goals, objectives, cooperative agreements, and the needs of the entire community it serves" (American Library Association, 1998c). Its position on equity of access states that "electronic information, services, and networks provided directly or indirectly by the library should be equally, readily and equitably accessible to all library users" and that "provision of such Internet access does not imply sponsorship or endorsement" (American Library Association, 1998c).

Following the development and adoption of an acceptable-use policy, librarians need to meet with community groups and community leaders to develop understanding of the basis of the policy. Library staff meetings should also be held to discuss the policy's details and protocols.

Some libraries put their staff through "intellectual-freedom training" (Reynolds, 1997). For example, Washington State's Timberland Regional Library staff, after having received special training, were better able to deal with problems that they encountered. When complaints were lodged by a parent whose child had been exposed to nudity on the Internet, the library supported First Amendment rights and refused to limit or monitor what their users viewed on the library's Internet station. Rather than backing down on their policy and reacting with fear, the library took proactive measures. It held a staff meeting to consider the incident and establish staff procedures for coping with exposure to controversial materials. In an effort to alleviate concerns and to make customers more comfortable, the library repositioned the computer terminals in a more private location and installed privacy screens. This sensitivity to customers did not compromise the library's commitment to First Amendment rights.

Promotional materials in the form of brochures can be developed to inform customers about the library and the Internet. Educating staff and customers as well as the community might safeguard the library from future misunderstandings and problems. An acceptable-use policy will not completely protect the library or its customers, but it can help raise awareness of the issues. By enabling both children and adults to see both the potential and the possible dangers of the Internet as a new knowledge tool, the library takes one substantial step toward demonstrating commitment to access while seeking alternatives to filtering.

## Parental Responsibility

Although public librarians are naturally concerned about children being exposed to offensive materials on the Internet, the responsibility to protect children rightly rests with parents. As is true with other public library resources, restriction of a child's access to the Internet should be the responsibility of the parent or legal guardian. So the librarian's responsibility is not to protect children from inappropriate material but to provide them and their parents with the necessary training and education to enable them to do this themselves.

In an effort to encourage a "family-friendly Internet" as well as increase parental involvement, ALA developed the Web site Librarian's Guide to Cyberspace for Parents and Kids (http://www.ala.org/parentspage/greatsites/safe.html). Using this educational tool, parents and children can learn together to navigate the Internet efficiently and safely. The site offers links to more than 1,000 educational and entertainment Web sites of interest to both parents and children, as well as to other library Web sites that have been developed especially for children.

KidsConnect (http://www.ala.org/ICONN/fc-kcfaq.html) is a site designed by the American Association of School Librarians and funded by Microsoft with the goal of offering reference services to K–12 students by answering questions and helping them access information on the Internet. It is an educational site that gives students the opportunity to learn important skills that will enable them to navigate the Web successfully themselves. Likewise, FamiliesConnect (http://www.ala.org/ICONN/familiesconnect.html) is a Web site developed to educate children and parents about the Internet and to encourage them to use it together. ALA President Ann Symons, a school librarian, warns, "We must not let fear and exaggeration over the 'perils' of the Internet limit the 'promise' of this new information tool. For if we do, we stand to limit the future of our children as well" (National Commission on Libraries and Information Science, 1998).

## School Libraries

The pressures in school libraries regarding filtering are slightly different. In some cases, despite the librarian's commitment to intellectual freedom, there are conflicts with school policies and mandates. Parental pressure adds to the sensitivity surrounding the Internet. School librarians are seen to serve *in loco parentis*, so that their position and responsibility is different from that of public librarians. Some school librarians, under pressure from parents and school boards, are uncomfortable with the uncontrolled nature of the content of the Internet and question the suitability of the Internet as an information resource for children. Yet children do have First Amendment rights.

Does filtering Internet access address these concerns? One problem with filtering is that blocking access to any sites will not prepare children for the online culture of the future or for the world in which they will live (Katz, 1996). Educating children on appropriate use will give them the preparation to use the Internet to their best advantage and teach them how to avoid inappropriate sites. They need to "master those situations in a supervised way to learn how to truly protect themselves" (Katz, 1996). In this view, children need to be taught how to navigate safely for themselves.

The mission of the school library is to enable students to access and make effective use of information and ideas, including how to survive in the digital age, so that they can develop critical-thinking skills, learn to solve problems, and master safe and effective navigation. Education will provide them with the skills to protect themselves and prepare them to enter a filterless adult world.

Schools and their libraries are developing acceptable-use policies that include codes of conduct and content-neutral rules that govern how and when students can use the Internet. School libraries can also adopt a "school-related work only" policy that limits access and provides additional control of content. Schools should carefully word their AUP to provide clear instructions for parents, teachers, students, and librarians on the use of Internet terminals. Students can then assume responsibility for using the Internet in the prescribed manner or lose the privilege; parents' fears and complaints can be mitigated and the staff will be able to fall back on these established rules if necessary.

There are a variety of age-appropriate alternatives that exist to filtering in school libraries. At the primary level, because there is no educational need for the student to be actually searching the Internet, teachers and librarians can capture the sites appropriate for the topic of study and "bookmark" them for student use (there are publications and software programs to assist with this process). Students can then use preselected (prescreened) sites for their inquiry.

At the early intermediate level, students can search together with their teachers or be taught basic search strategies, such as Boolean logic. There are also search engines that screen sites for age appropriateness, for example, Yahooligans! and the Library Channel. This allows for positive selection of age-appropriate sites rather than random censorship of all information for all ages. Similarly, electronic encyclopedias allow for access to appropriate Web sites.

At the intermediate/junior level and up, schools, like public libraries, might offer "short courses" in Internet ethics—required courses on the appropriate use of the Internet. Such courses teach students how to access, evaluate, and use Internet information effectively, wisely, and safely. The following rules, in the form of a pledge, are common:

- I respect computer equipment, software, and materials
- I respect other students' work
- When I quote or copy others, I give credit
- I realize that all e-mail may be public information
- When I find something inappropriate, I exit immediately
- I don't give out my name or other personal information

Occasionally, the school may need to suspend Internet privileges to ensure compliance with the pledge.

Essential in all of this is parent education. Parents need to be assured that their child's own teacher or at least the teaching staff at the school have the competence and confidence to provide appropriate programs for young people. This can be accomplished through a school-based parent advisory council.

ICONnect (http://www.ala.org/ICONN/) is an initiative of the American Association of School Librarians to help school librarians, teachers, and students learn Internet navigation skills. Free online courses are offered at various levels of ability. This program supports the library's ongoing commitment to Internet education and integrates Internet resources into the school's curriculum.

## Communities and Compromise

Every community is unique, consisting of individuals with diverse needs, ideas, and political views. The library within each community is also unique. It follows then that each individual library or system should deal with the Internet and the issue of filters by developing its own unique vision, strategies, and policies. To accomplish this, the library must recognize community politics, listen to the needs of its public and utilize community ideas and strengths. "Your own situation is unique. Each community and library has its own character, staff, base of preexisting facilities and external context of existing and planned networks" (Fidelman, 1997). How to deal with sexually explicit material on the Internet thus needs to be tailored to the specific community and library.

Librarians, in their efforts to be community sensitive, are often caught between a rock and a hard place. On the one hand, they have a professional commitment to freedom of speech and the First Amendment; on the other hand, they sometimes face pressure from local officials or members of the community to filter Internet access. Added to that is the librarian's personal concern that children not be exposed to sexually explicit material. "Individual librarians are . . . left holding the digital bag, caught between parents, pols, reporters, the clergy, needy and curious kids, sexual opportunists" (Katz, 1997, April 7).

One librarian who has felt caught in this dilemma is Brenda Branch, Director of the Austin, Texas, Public Library. While conceding that filtering software blocks useful and important sites along with sexually explicit sites, she has made the decision to install filtering software on some computer terminals as an "interim solution" (Oder, 1997 May 1b). Texas state law makes the display of material harmful to minors a criminal offense, which exposes her and her staff to prosecution. So—while she remains supportive of ALA's position and committed to intellectual freedom and the First Amendment—under considerable pressure from the community and local government and her board and staff, she reached this compromise. Still trying to find a balance that works for her community, following that initial compromise, Branch authorized the removal of filters at one out of two workstations at each branch. Subsequent pressure from the intellectual-freedom community in Austin has resulted in the library deciding to test at two locations the disabling of filtering software at a library patron's request. Adult customers now enjoy unfiltered points of Internet access, but children are still required to use the filtered terminals. This policy is evolving in direct response to the community, and the library administration has developed the art of compromise to such a degree that both the library and the community can live with this approach.

The Austin Public Library is just one of many that have been searching for a compromise that will satisfy both the library and the community. What can other libraries learn from their experiences? Libraries should maintain unfiltered access as long as possible, while at the same time working to raise awareness and understanding in the community of the need for and value of the Internet.

## A Canadian Twist

Obscenity and child pornography are among the many illegal activities covered by the Criminal Code of Canada. The code breaks these activities into three categories: publication, distribution, and knowingly selling or exposing to public view. In a case of the latter type, it must be proven that the offender had subjective knowledge of the content and nature of the material in question (Canada: Racicot et al, 1997c). Would the library, as an Internet content provider, then be considered liable for "exposing to public view" obscene materials or child pornography? It is argued that because a level of knowledge of the material is required, prosecution is unlikely. However, this liability is a concern. By offering Internet access, Canadian libraries will also have to accept the potential liability inherent with this access. Many feel that the use of filtering software in libraries will be judged legal in Canada, unlike in the United States, where its use is being constitutionally challenged. Unlike the U.S. First Amendment, Canada's Charter of Rights and Freedoms applies only to federal government organizations, and Canadian public libraries do not fall into that arena. Thus, they do not enjoy freedom-of-expression protection. It is for that reason that Canadian public libraries are being encouraged to exercise "due diligence" in order to minimize their risk of liability for providing Internet access (Canada: Morton, 1998). Some examples of displaying due diligence are

- Establishing and posting an acceptable-use policy (possibly requiring Internet users to sign it)
- Not charging users a fee for Internet access (that would be seen as "selling" obscenity)
- Installing privacy screens
- Displaying warnings and providing pamphlets outlining possible illegal content on the Internet
- Installing filtering software on children's terminals

There are few Canadian precedents regarding the application of obscenity and hate laws to the Internet. In 1998 the Vancouver Public Library requested clarification on the library's legal position in relation to obscenity and hate literature on its Internet terminals. To avoid legal liability, the library was advised to (1) position its terminals to avoid public display, (2) maintain its current preventative steps and rendering sites containing child pornography inaccessible, and (3) provide commercial filters on some Internet terminals or filter out "criminal" sites on all terminals. The library was also informed that it was "not at risk of violating hate literature laws by providing Internet terminals to users" (Canada: Burnett, 1998).

The Canadian Library Association (CLA) maintains the position that decisions about what is illegal should be made by the courts, not librarians. CLA, in response to recommendations that libraries exercise "due diligence," disagreed with using filtering software to block Internet access. In 1998 CLA produced "Have a Safe Trip: A Parent's Guide to Safety on the Internet," an educational brochure for parents and children on using the Internet. It outlines the CLA position that parents are the only guaranteed Internet filter for children and that using blocking software may violate any one family's values and beliefs.

The Canadian Radio-Television and Telecommunications Commission (CRTC) is currently debating whether to regulate the Internet in the same way that it does television and radio. CRTC Commissioner David Colville, leading the hearings, issued this statement in December 1998: "One message we're getting from most of the parties—not all—is that the commission should not regulate the Internet . . ." (Canada: Scoffield, 1998).

But the commission is still wrestling with the problem of how to deal with children viewing sexually explicit material on the Internet without infringing on Internet service providers. Most feel that applying already present Criminal Code laws to the Internet combined with consumer pressure in the free market would be the "best shield from Internet porn." The hearings will proceed in 1999 before making any recommendations to government.

In 1998 Canadian legislators introduced bills that would restrict online material. These bills make the Internet service providers responsible for monitoring content. Technically, this monitoring is impossible because there is too much content, existing in a multitude of formats. The idea of libraries being required by law to monitor content would have a serious impact on customers' rights to privacy. To date, this legislation has not been passed, and it is unlikely that it will pass.

LibraryNet is a Canada-wide initiative funded by the federal government to facilitate the connection of all Canadian libraries to the Internet by the year 2000. The Canadian library community, through LibraryNet, is developing a Web site that will provide many links and tools to help instruct and guide Internet users. SchoolNet, a similar project, provides access and tools for schools. Through these efforts, it is hoped that all Canadians will become educated and informed Internet users.

## Summary

- Publicly supported U.S. libraries are governmental institutions and thus are subject to the First Amendment, which forbids them from restricting information based on content or viewpoint. The Internet is protected by the First Amendment, so Internet filtering in public and school libraries raises constitutional concerns about governmental restrictions on access to information.

- Libraries serve a broad and diverse community with many different ethnic backgrounds, preferences, ideas, and opinions. Materials deemed indecent by some are not viewed as indecent by others.

- Public libraries have generally taken the position that they should not restrict their community's access to information. They have taken the position that it is the responsibility of each individual and of children's parents to make those decisions. But with the growing number of public libraries now offering public access to the Internet, this philosophy "is being questioned as never before" (Reynolds, 1997).

- There are laws that prohibit the production or distribution of child pornography that apply to the Internet. Although these laws should provide a measure of protection for the library and its users, they are not able to rid the Internet of all illegal materials or all sexually explicit materials.

- Fueled by the media, there is a frenzied concern surrounding Internet access through libraries. Many fear that children will be exposed to controversial materials in public and school libraries. This fear is partly due to the novelty and complexity of the Internet medium as well as to its open and unrestricted nature. For these reasons, there exists misunderstanding and mistrust. Stemming from these public views, filtering software has found its way into the library environment.

- The issue of filtering the Internet in public and school libraries will affect every library system. At present, 73 percent of U.S. public libraries are connected to the Internet, and ALA found that 15 percent of libraries with Internet access are using filtering software to some degree (ALA, 1998 November b). The ALA survey also found that nearly every public library surveyed has or is developing a policy governing acceptable use.

- While public librarians do not serve *in loco parentis* and it is the parents' responsibility to guide their children safely on the Internet, there is much that librarians can do, and are doing, to help both parents and children in this regard. On the other hand, school librarians do serve *in loco parentis* regarding the Internet, further complicating their responsibilities.

- Producers of filtering software often do not share with the library what their software blocks, and filtering software often blocks access to more than those sites it is intended to block.

- At present, it is technologically impossible for filters to adapt to various ages, maturity levels, and backgrounds.

- The technological intervention of filters cannot completely eliminate exposure to obscene material because Web site changes and additions are made too often and too quickly.

- Limited filtering of children's access can be a compromise for libraries where the community and regional politics require it.

- Education and training will play a major part in alleviating these concerns and fears.

## Bibliography

Aguilar, R. (1996). "Site Filters Criticized." http://www.news.com/News/Item/0,4,4609,00.html.

"ALA and AOL Offer Internet Driver's Ed." (1998). *American Libraries* 29(7), 8.

American Civil Liberties Union. (1997). "Censorship in a Box: Why Blocking Software is Wrong for Public Libraries." http://www.aclu.org/issues/cyber/box.html.

American Library Association. (1991). "Free Access to Libraries for Minors: An Interpretation of the Library Bill of Rights." http://www.ala.org/oif/free_min.html

(1996 January 23). "Library Bill of Rights." http://www.ala.org/work/freedom/lbr.html.

(1996 January 24). "Access to Electronic Information, Services, and Networks: An Interpretation of the Library Bill of Rights." http://www.ala.org.

(1997). "Librarian's Guide to Cyberspace for Parents and Kids." http://www.ala.org/parentspage/greatsites/safe.html.

(1997 June 5). "Questions and Answers: Access to Electronic Information, Services, and Networks: An Interpretation of the Library Bill of Rights." http://www.ala.org.

(1997 July 2). "ALA Internet Filtering: Resolution on the Use of Internet Filters and Resolution on the Use of Filtering Software in Libraries." http://www.ala.org.

(1997 October 21). "Industry Leaders, Educators, Law Enforcement Officials and Family Advocates Meet to Discuss Child Safety in Cyberspace." http://www.ala.org/onlinesummit/summit_press971016.html.

(1997 November 20). "ALA Unveils Cybercollection of 700+ Sites for Kids." http://www.ala.org/news/cyber.html.

(1998a). "A technology initiative of the American Association of School Librarians: Get Connected to Learning Using the Internet." http://www.ala.org/aasl/filtering.html.

(1998b). "Access for Children and Young People to Videotapes and Other Nonprint Formats: An Interpretation of the Library Bill of Rights." http:www.ala.org/alaorg/oif/acc_chil.html.

(1998c). "Access to Electronic Information, Services, and Networks: An Interpretation of the Library Bill of Rights." http:www.ala.org/alaorg/oif/electacc.html.

(1998d). "ALA: Help for Public Librarians with Internet Resources." http://www.ala.org/rusa/mars/commit.html.

(1998e). "ALA-Led Coalition Challenges Communications Decency Act." http://www.ala.org/oitp/lawsuit.html.

(1998f). "First Amendment of the Bill of Rights to the United States Constitution." http://www.ala.org/alaorg/oif/first.html.

(1998g). "Guidelines and Considerations for Developing a Public Library Internet Use Policy." http://www.ala.org/oif/internet.html.

(1998h). "Internet Use Policies in Public Library Outlets." http://www.ala.org/oitp/research/survey98.pdf.

(1998i). "Librarian Declarations." http://www.ala.org/alaorg/oif/cda/krug.html.

(1998j). "Libraries and the Communications Decency Act: What You Should Know." http://www.ala.org/oitp/extramar.html.

(1998k). "Resolution on the Use of Internet Filters." http://www.ala.org/alaorg/oif/filt_res.html.

(1998l). "700+ Great Sites: Selection Criteria, How to Tell if You are Looking at a Great Web Site." http://www.ala.org/parentspage/greatsites/criteria.html.

(1998m). "700+ Great Sites: Amazing, Spectacular, Mysterious, Colorful Web Sites for Kids and the Adults who Care about Them." http://www.ala.org/parentspage/greatsites/amazing.html.

(1998n). "Statement on Internet Filtering." http://www.ala.org/alaorg/oif/filt_stm.html.

(1998o). "White House Meeting Maps a First Amendment Friendly Strategy for the Internet." http://www.ala.org/washoff/alawon/alwn659.html.

(1998 November a). "Free 'Toolkit' Available to Help Libraries Sponsor Internet 'Teach-ins'." http://www.ala.org/news/v4n6/toolkit.html.

(1998 November b). "1998 Survey ALA re: Libraries and Internet Usage." http://www.ala.org.

(1998 November 23). "Federal Mandate for Billions of Dollars for School, Library Technology Materializes; Librarians Applaud Progress." http://www.ala.org/news/v4n7/mandate.html.

(1998 November 24). "ALA President Reacts to Loudoun Internet Ruling." http://www.ala.org/news/v4n7/loudoun.html.

(1998 November 30). "Loudoun County Trustees Pull Internet Plug Instead of Filters." http://www.ala.org/alonline/news/981130.html.

(1998 December 7a). "Austin Public Library Retunes its Filtering Policy Again." http://www.ala.org/alonline/news/981207.html.

(1998 December 7b). "Internet Returns to Loudoun County Library, Filtered on Request." http://www.ala.org/alonline/news/981207.html.

(1998 December 7c). "Volusia County Council Mandates Filters Despite Lawyer's Advice." http://www.ala.org/alonline/news/981207.html.

(1998 December 14). "Loudoun Ruling Gives Florida Library Pause about Filtering." http://www.ala.org/alonline/news/981214.html.

"Austin PL Continues Fine-Tuning of Filter Policy" (1998). http://www.bookwire.com/LJDigital/leadnews.article$26784.

Austin Public Library (1998). http://www.ci.austin.tx.us/library/.

Barry, J. (1997). "Form Follows Function: Internet Filters and Public Library Management." http://www.filteringfacts.org/jud.htm.

Benton Foundation (1997). "Buildings, Books and Bytes: Libraries and Communities in the Digital Age." *Library Trends* 46, 178–223.

Bern, A. (1996). "Access to the Internet in a Central Public Library Children's Room." *Youth Services in Libraries* 9(3), 253–262.

Bertot, J. and C. McClure (1998). "Measuring Electronic Services in Public Libraries: Issues and Recommendations." *Public Libraries* 37(3), 176–180.

Billington, J. (1998). "American Public Libraries in the Information Age: Constant Purpose in Changing Times." *Libraries & Culture* 33(1), 11–16.

"Board Votes Filter Option for Internet." (1998). http://www.bookwire.com.

Braun, L. (1998). "Webwatch, Clicking on the Web." *Library Journal* 123(16), 34.

Brawner, L. (1997). "Protecting First Amendment Rights in Public Libraries." *Public Library Quarterly* 16(4), 3–7.

Brooklyn Public Library (1998). http://www.brooklynpubliclibrary.org.

Burt, D. (1997). "Why Libraries Should Filter." http://www.filteringfacts.org/whyfilt.htm.

Burt, D. (1997 May/June). "Policies for the Use of Public Internet Workstations in Public Libraries." *Public Libraries* 36(3), 156–159.

Burt, D. (1997 August). "In Defense of Filtering." *American Libraries* 28(7), 46–48.

Burt, D. (1998 January 23). "New Filtering Survey." http://www.filteringfacts. org/survey.htm.

Burt, D. (1998 March 7). "Statement of Filtering Facts in Response to the American Library Association Statement to the Senate Commerce, Science and Transportation Committee on Indecency on the Internet." http://www. filteringfacts.org/mccain.htm.

Censorware Project. (1998). "Loudoun case: Loudoun County, VA Censorware Lawsuit." http://www.censorware.org/legal/loudoun.

Champelli, L. (1997). "Understand Software That Blocks Internet Sites and Related Censorship and Safety Issues." *Internet Advocate*, http://www.monroe.lob. in.us/~lchampel/netadv4.html.

Collins, B. (1996). "Beyond Cruising: Reviewing." *Library Journal* 121(3), 122–124.

Dallas Public Library (1998). http://www.lib.ci.dallas.tx.us/.

DiMattia, S. (1997). "Ohio Medina PL Drafts Net Guidelines—Without Filters." *Library Journal* 122(8), 12.

Education and Library Networks Coalition (1998). "E-rate: Survey Finds 84 Percent of Schools and Libraries in the United States Intend to Apply for E-rate Discount." http://www.itc.org/edlinc/press/eratesurvey.html.

"Facts on Filtering." (1998). *American Libraries* 29(8), 19.

"Few Testify on Proposed IF Statement." (1998). *Library Journal* 123(13), 46–47.

Fidelman, M. (1997). "The Internet is Coming to Your Library." In "All-out Internet Access: The Cambridge Public Library Model" (pp. 1–19). Chicago: American Library Association.

Field, D. (1997). "One Library's Approach." *American Libraries* 28(10), 63.

"Filtering Bill Keeps Librarians on Defensive (1998). *Library Journal* 123(13), 45.

Filtering Facts (1998). "How Filters Really Work." http://filteringfacts.org/how-filt.htm.

"Free Speech Has Limits." (1998). http://www.archives.usatoday.com.

"Free Speech Headlines San Francisco." (1997). *Library Journal* 122(13), 36–42.

Gorman, M. (1997). "Living and Dying with 'Information': Comments on the Report 'Buildings, Books, and Bytes'." *Library Trends* 46(1), 28–35.

Horowitz, M. (1998). "Do We Need Big Mother and Big Father for the Internet?" *Chicago Tribune*, Op-ed page.

Hubbard, B., A. Sargone, R. Croneberger, and D. Iddings (1996). "Newest Members of the Net Set, Pittsburgh's Carnegie Cashes in on Community Info." *Library Journal* 121(2), 44–46.

Hudson, D. (1998). "Filtering Programs: Protecting People from Porn or Creating Constitutional Concerns?" http://www.freedomforum.org/speech/1998/2/ 20filter.asp.

Hudson, D. (1998 June 8). "Filtering Out Net Indecency: Porn Foes Look for a Technological Solution." http://www.freedomforum.org/speech/series/ cda.series.4.asp.

Hudson, D. (1998 November 25). "Decision in Library Filtering Case: Either a 'Landmark' or a 'Landmine'." http://www.freedomforum.org/speech/1998/11/25library.asp.

Hyman, K. (1996 November 1). "Sex at the Library: Film at 11." *Library Journal* 121(18), 35–36.

Hyman, K. (1997 November). "Internet Policies: Managing in the Real World." *American Libraries* 28(10), 60–61.

"Internet 'Filters' Harm Free Speech" (1998 December 3). http://www.archives.usatoday.com.

"Judge to Rule in Loudoun Case." (1998). *Library Journal* 123(18), 15.

Kafai, Y. and M. Bates (1997). Internet Web-Searching Instruction in the Elementary Classroom: Building a Foundation for Information Literacy." *School Library Media Quarterly* 25(2), 103–111.

Kaplan, C. (1998). "Library's 'Internet User's Agreement' Violates Rights, Group Says." http://www.nytimes.com/library/tech/98/04/cyber/cyber-law/03law.html.

Katz, J. (1996). "The Rights of Kids in the Digital Age." *Wired*, 120–123; 166–171.

Katz, J. (1997 March 28). "Library Wars, Part II: Screens of Hysteria, Media Rant." http://www.netizen.com/netizen/97/12/katz4a.html.

Katz, J. (1997 April 4). "Library Wars, Part III: Solutions to Confusion, Media Rant." http://www.netizen.com/netizen/97/13/index4a.html.

Katz, J. (1997 April 7). "Library Wars, Part IV: Wisdom of the Ages, Media Rant." http://www.netizen.com/netizen/97/14/katz0a.html.

"Kids Online Week Debuts" (1998). *American Libraries* 29(8), 6.

Kniffel, L. (1998). "ALA-Led Coalition Challenges Communications Decency Act." http://www.ala.org/oitp/lawsuit.html.

Llanos, M. (1998). "Libraries Forced to Rethink Net Filters: Judge Rules Against Virginia Library in Precedent-Setting Case." http://www.msnb.com.

Lynch, K. and E. Cardenas (1998). "Libraries, Parents Wary of Requiring Internet Porn Filters." http://detnews.com/1998/cyberia/9802/23/02160152.htm.

Macavinta, C. (1997 January 13). "ACLU Sues for Net Freedom." http://www.new.com/News/Item/0,4,6955,00.html.

Macavinta, C. (1997 February 13). "Boston Libraries Restrict Web Access." http://www.news.com/News/Item/0,4,7942,00.html.

Manley, W. (1997 October). "Are We Free to Talk Honestly about Intellectual Freedom?" *American Libraries* 28(9), 112.

Manley, W. (1997 November). "It's Time to Stop the Hypocrisy." *American Libraries* 28(10), 112.

Mason, M. (1997). "Sex, Kids, and the Public Library." *American Libraries* 28(6), 104–106.

Miller, L. (1998 February 11). "Schools' Net funds Could Hinge on Protecting Kids." http://archives.usatoday.com.

Miller, L. (1998 September 15). "Campaign Unfurls Safety Net for Kids." http://archives.usatoday.com.

Minow, M. (1998). "Filtering the First Amendment for Public Libraries: Background Information." http://www.best.com/~tstms/filte.html.

"More Filtering Lawsuits Looming?" (1998 December 14). http://www.bookwire. com/LJDigital/leadnews.article$26784.

Munro, K. (1997). "Filtering Utilities." http://www.zdnet.com/pcmag/features/ utility/filter/_open.htm.

National Commission on Libraries and Information Science. (1998 November 17). "NCLIS Seeks Balance and Compromise, Hearing on 'Kids and the Internet: The Promise and the Perils'." NCLIS News Release, 1–4.

"Net Screening, Telecomm Rates Highlight ALA Midwinter in DC." (1997 March 15). *Library Journal.* 122(5), 14–18.

Oder, N. (1997 May 1a). "Filtering and Its Contractions." *Library Journal* 122(8), 40–41.

Oder, N. (1997 May 1b). "Krug's Toughest Fight?" *Library Journal* 122(8), 38–41.

Oder, N. (1997 May 1c). "Ohio House Passes Bill to Filter Net." *Library Journal* 122(8), 12.

Oder, N. (1997 May 1d). "San Jose News Holds Net Policy Forum." *Library Journal* 122(8), 13.

Oder, N. (1997 June 1). "Librarians to Test Internet Filters." *Library Journal* 122(10), 13–14.

Oder, N. (1998 February 1). "Pennsylvania Study Reports Internet Essential to Libraries." *Library Journal* 123(2), 14.

Oder, N. (1998 April 1). "Intellectual Freedom Legislation: The State of the States." *Library Journal* 123(7), 54–56.

Oder, N. (1998 May 1). "Judge: Loudoun Challenge to Filtering Policy Can Proceed." *Library Journal* 123(8), 12.

Oder, N. (1998 September 1). "Congress to Address Flurry of Library-Related Bills." *Library Journal* 123(14), 110–111.

Oder, N. (1998 October 1a). "FL Library to Consider Filters." *Library Journal* 123(16), 14.

Oder, N. (1998 October 1b). "Kansas City PL Resists Filtering." *Library Journal* 123(16), 14.

Oder, N. (1998 October 1c). "Loudoun County, VA, Net Filtering Case Going to Trial?" *Library Journal* 123(16), 14.

Oder, N. (1998 November 15a). "Group Offers Tips on Disabling Filters." *Library Journal* 123(19), 16.

Oder, N. (1998 November 15b). "Loudoun Case Documents on Web." *Library Journal* 123(19), 16.

Oder, N. (1998 November 15c). "Schneider, Burt Testimony." *Library Journal* 123(19), 16.

Oram, A. (1997 May 16). "Librarians Maintain Principles in the Face of Internet Censorship." http://www.oreilly.com/people/staff/andyo/ar/library.html.

Oram, A. (1998 June 23). "Is There Anything We Can Do About Internet Porn?" http://www.oreilly.com/people/staff/andyo/ar/censor_alternatives.html.

Pasicznyuk, R. (1996). "Library Web Construction 101." Public Libraries 35(3), 168–171.

Peck, R. and A. Symons (1997 September). "Kids Have First Amendment Rights, Too." American Libraries 28(8), 64–65.

People for the American Way (1998). "Free Expression: Internet Censorship." http://www.pfaw.org/courts/index.shtml#intcensorship.

People for the American Way (1998 November 23). "Federal Court Strikes Down Loudoun County Internet Restrictions." http://www.pfaw.org/news/press//show.cgi?article=911860929.

Pickard, P. (1997). "Focus on Technology." Youth Services in Libraries 10(4), 423–425.

Raber, D. (1996). "ALA Goal 2000 and Public Libraries: Ambiguities and Possibilities." Public Libraries 35(4), 224–229.

Reynolds, T. (1997). "Unrestricted Internet Access at Public Libraries—Or Not?" http://www.wla.org/alki/jul97/whofirst.html.

Richtel, M. (1998). "Filter Used by Courts Blocks Innocuous Sites." http://www.nytimes.com/library/tech/98/06/cyber/articles/23filter.html.

Rogers, M. (1997 May 1b). "NYPL's Internet Access Under Fire." Library Journal 122(8), 13–14.

Rogers, M. (1998 May 1a). "VA to Deny Funds to Unfiltered Libraries." Library Journal 123(8), 12.

St. Lifer, E. (1996). "Libraries' Crucial Role in the 1996 Telecomm Act." Library Journal 121(5), 30–31.

St. Lifer, E. (1997). "Libraries Challenge NY's Ban on 'Indecency' Online." Library Journal 122(2), 90–91.

St. Lifer, E. (1997). "Reed Hundt Speaks to Libraries." Library Journal 122(6), 44–45.

St. Lifer, E. (1997). "Gates Speaks to Librarians." Library Journal 122(12), 44–45.

St. Lifer, E. and M. Rogers. (1997). "Will Lawsuits Put Library Telecom Discounts on Hold?" Library Journal 122(13), 12.

St. Lifer, E. (1998). "McCain Filtering Bill Draws Support Despite Misperceptions." Library Journal 123(5), 14–15.

San Francisco Public Library. (1998). http://sfpl.lib.ca.us/www/internet.html.

Schneider, K. (1997). A Practical Guide to Internet Filters. New York: Neal Schuman.

Schneider, K. (1997 September 13). "What Was TIFAP?" http://www.bluehighways.com/tifap/learn.htm.

Schneider, K. (1997 December). "TIFAP: Filter Products." http://www.bluehighways.com/tifap/products.html.

Schneider, K. (1998a). "The Internet Filter Assessment Project: A Talking Paper on Internet Filters." http://www.bluehighways.com/tifap/talker.htm.

Schneider, K. (1998b). "Mainstream Loudoun, Inc., et al. v. Board of Trustees of the Loudoun County Public Library, et al., Declaration of Karen G. Schneider." http://www.filteringfacts.org/sch-dec.html.

Schneider, K. (1998c). "Re: Schneider Declaration—Turns into Time Control Session." http://www.sunsite.berkeley.edu/Web4Lib/archive/9804/0053.html.

Seattle Public Library (1998). http://www.spl.lib.wa.us/searchnet/usepol.html.

Smith, M. (1998). "Librarianship on the Bleeding Edge: Meeting the Pressure to Filter." http://www.txla.org/pubs/tlj-2q97/smith.html.

Sternin, E. (1998). "Kids Rule! Libraries Online! Meets High Point Library." *Public Libraries* 37(4), 246–249.

"To Filter or Not to Filter: Brenda Branch and Gordon Conable Debate the Merits of Unfettered Internet Access." (1997). *American Libraries* 28(6), 100–102.

Truett, C. (1997). "Censorship and the Internet, A Stand for School Librarians: Option." *School Library Media Quarterly* 25(4), 223–227.

Turock, B. (1996). "Expert Witness: Librarians Confront the ALA Summit." *Library Journal* 121(11), 32–34.

Walter, V. (1997). "Becoming Digital: Policy Implications for Library Youth Services." *Library Trends* 45(4), 385–601. Wallace, L. (1998 November). "ALA Plays Leading Role in Internet Education Campaign." *American Libraries* 29(10), 12.

Weise, E. (1998 October 7). "The Telegraph, the Internet: Here We Go Again." *USA Today*, 8D.

**Canadian Sources**

Burnett, D. (1998, personal communication).

Campbell, B. (1998). "Universal Access, Electronic Public Space, Sustainability." *Feliciter* 44(3), 20–23.

Demirian, J. (1996). "Libraries Linking Canadians to the Internet." *Feliciter* 42(11/12), 24–25.

Hamilton, D. (1997). "Being Cool: Information Literacy." *School Libraries in Canada* 17(2), 31.

Morton, E. (1998). "Alec Szibbo—Internet Content, Libraries and Liability." *Feliciter* 44(7/8), 34–35.

Racicot, M., M. Hayes, A. Szibbo and P. Trudel. (1997 February a). Introduction in *The Cyberspace is Not a 'No Law Land,' A Study of the Issues of Liability for Content Circulating on the Internet* (pp. 24–32). Ottawa: Industry Canada.

Racicot, M., M. Hayes, A. Szibbo, and P. Trudel. (1997 February b). "Looking to the Future" in *The Cyberspace is Not a 'No Law Land,' A Study of the Issues of Liability for Content Circulating on the Internet* (pp. 289–297). Ottawa: Industry Canada.

Racicot, M., M. Hayes, A. Szibbo, and P. Trudel. (1997 February c). "Summary" in *The Cyberspace is Not a 'No Law Land,' A Study of the Issues of Liability for Content Circulating on the Internet* (pp. 1–23). Ottawa: Industry Canada.

Scoffield, H. (1998 December 10). "Free Market is Best Shield from Internet Porn, Hate." *Globe and Mail*, C1.

Schoffro, M. (1996). "SchoolNet: Electronically Linking Canada's Schools." *Feliciter* 42(5), 54–59.

Schoffro, M. (1997). "SchoolNet: Great Opportunities for School Libraries." *Feliciter* 43(5), 32–34.

Schoffro, M. and S. Boswell (1997). "The Library: Heart of the Information Society." *Feliciter* 43(6), 30–33.

Toronto Public Library (1998). http://www.tpl.toronto.on.ca/Internet/policy.htm.

"Vancouver Public Faces Angry Moms over Internet Access." (1998). *Feliciter* 44(1), 18.

Vancouver Public Library (1998). http://www.vpl.vancouver.bc.ca/.

## Appendix A
## Access to Electronic Information, Services, and Networks:
## An Interpretation of the Library Bill of Rights
(Adopted by ALA Council, January 24, 1996 [ISBN: 8389-7830-4])

## Introduction

The world is in the midst of an electronic communications revolution. Based on its constitutional, ethical, and historical heritage, American librarianship is uniquely positioned to address the broad range of information issues being raised in this revolution. In particular, librarians address intellectual freedom from a strong ethical base and an abiding commitment to the preservation of the individual's rights.

Freedom of expression is an inalienable human right and the foundation for self-government. Freedom of expression encompasses the freedom of speech and the corollary right to receive information. These rights extend to minors as well as adults. Libraries and librarians exist to facilitate the exercise of these rights by selecting, producing, providing access to, identifying, retrieving, organizing, providing instruction in the use of, and preserving recorded expression regardless of the format or technology.

The American Library Association expresses these basic principles of librarianship in its Code of Ethics and in the Library Bill of Rights and its Interpretations. These serve to guide librarians and library governing bodies in addressing issues of intellectual freedom that arise when the library provides access to electronic information, services, and networks.

Note: All World Wide Web sites were verified December 15–31, 1998.

Issues arising from the still-developing technology of computer-mediated information generation, distribution, and retrieval need to be approached and regularly reviewed in a context of constitutional principles and ALA policies so that fundamental and traditional tenets of librarianship are not swept away.

Electronic information flows across boundaries and barriers despite attempts by individuals, governments, and private entities to channel or control it. Even so, many people, for reasons of technology, infrastructure, or socioeconomic status, do not have access to electronic information.

In making decisions about how to offer access to electronic information, each library should consider its mission, goals, objectives, cooperative agreements, and the needs of the entire community it serves.

## The Rights of Users

All library system and network policies, procedures or regulations relating to electronic resources and services should be scrutinized for potential violation of user rights.

User policies should be developed according to the policies and guidelines established by the American Library Association, including "Guidelines for the Development and Implementation of Policies, Regulations, and Procedures Affecting Access to Library Materials, Services and Facilities."

Users should not be restricted or denied access for expressing or receiving constitutionally protected speech. Users' access should not be changed without due process, including, but not limited to, formal notice and a means of appeal.

Although electronic systems may include distinct property rights and security concerns, such elements may not be employed as a subterfuge to deny users' access to information. Users have the right to be free of unreasonable limitations or conditions set by libraries, librarians, system administrators, vendors, network service providers, or others. Contracts, agreements, and licenses entered into by libraries on behalf of their users should not violate this right. Users also have a right to information, training, and assistance necessary to operate the hardware and software provided by the library.

Users have both the right of confidentiality and the right of privacy. The library should uphold these rights by policy, procedure, and practice. Users should be advised, however, that because security is technically difficult to achieve, electronic transactions and files could become public.

The rights of users who are minors shall in no way be abridged.[1]

## Equity of Access

Electronic information, services, and networks provided directly or indirectly by the library should be equally, readily, and equitably accessible to all library

---

1 See "Free Access to Libraries for Minors: An Interpretation of the Library Bill of Rights," "Access to Resources and Services in the School Library Media Program: An Interpretation of the Library Bill of Rights," and "Access for Children and Young People to Videotapes and Other Non-print Formats: An Interpretation of the Library Bill of Rights," (all at http://www.ala.org/oif/).

users. American Library Association policies oppose the charging of user fees for the provision of information services by all libraries and information services that receive their major support from public funds. . . . It should be the goal of all libraries to develop policies concerning access to electronic resources in light of "Economic Barriers to Information Access: An Interpretation of the Library Bill of Rights" and "Guidelines for the Development and Implementation of Policies, Regulations and Procedures Affecting Access to Library Materials, Services and Facilities."

## Information Resources and Access

Providing connections to global information, services, and networks is not the same as selecting and purchasing material for a library collection. Determining the accuracy or authenticity of electronic information may present special problems. Some information accessed electronically may not meet a library's selection or collection development policy. It is, therefore, left to each user to determine what is appropriate. Parents and legal guardians who are concerned about their children's use of electronic resources should provide guidance to their own children.

Libraries and librarians should not deny or limit access to information available via electronic resources because of its allegedly controversial content or because of the librarian's personal beliefs or fear of confrontation. Information retrieved or utilized electronically should be considered constitutionally protected unless determined otherwise by a court with appropriate jurisdiction.

Libraries, acting within their mission and objectives, must support access to information on all subjects that serve the needs or interests of each user, regardless of the user's age or the content of the material. Libraries have an obligation to provide access to government information available in electronic format. Libraries and librarians should not deny access to information solely on the grounds that it is perceived to lack value.

In order to prevent the loss of information, and to preserve the cultural record, libraries may need to expand their selection or collection development policies to ensure preservation, in appropriate formats, of information obtained electronically.

Electronic resources provide unprecedented opportunities to expand the scope of information available to users. Libraries and librarians should provide access to information presenting all points of view. The provision of access does not imply sponsorship or endorsement. These principles pertain to electronic resources no less than they do to the more traditional sources of information in libraries.[2]

2 See "Diversity in Collection Development: an Interpretation of the Library Bill of Rights" and "Questions and Answers on Access to Electronic Information, Services and Networks: An Interpretation of the Library Bill of Rights" (at http://www.ala.org).

# Appendix B
## Internet Filtering Software Products

There are dozens of filtering software products and services available. Many products specifically designed for use in corporate settings have been omitted here. When choosing a filtering-software product, the features to consider include: keyword blocking that can be disabled, library-determined specific categories for blocking, reports generated by category, user feedback capabilities, configurable blocking, and local access consideration (Schneider 1998).

The following information comes primarily from the product or company Web sites and was current as of December 29, 1998.

The format used for each product or service is the following: Product name. Company name. Filter type. Platforms supported. Price range. Company or product Web site. Notes.

*Bess.* N2H2. Proxy server. Most platforms. $999.95, including updates. http://www.bess.net. Bess is N2H2's flagship Internet filtering service.

*Cyber Patrol.* Microsystems Software. Client. Windows, Macintosh, and LAN systems. $29.95, including a three-month subscription to the CyberNOT Block List; educational discounts available. http://www.cyberpatrol.com/. Built-in support for the PICS standard, including the SafeSurf and RSACi rating systems.

*Cyber Sentinel.* Security Software Systems. Client. Windows 95/98/NT. $29.95. http://www.securitysoft.com.

*Cyber Snoop.* Pearl Software. Client. Windows 95/NT. $29.95; educational discounts available. http://www.pearlsw.com. Places emphasis on "teaching responsible Internet usage through supervision and communication."

*CYBERsitter.* Solid Oak Software. Client. Windows 95/NT. $39.95; two users, $59.95; five users, $99.95; etc. CYBERsitter + AntiSpam, $49.95. http://www.solidoak.com/.

*GuardiaNet.* OnePlace. Proxy server. Windows 95. $59.95; 10 users $195; 25 users $345; etc.; each license allows up to four users per family; additional family members can be registered for $6.95; the annual renewal fee is $29.95 for four users; and the renewal fee for additional family members is $3.95. http://www.safekid.com.

*Gulliver's Guardian.* Gulliver Software. Client. Windows 95. $59.95; Online Edition, $39. http://www.guliver.nb.ca/index.htm.

*Hedgebuilders.* Hedgebuilders. Proxy server. No platform information provided. $60 per year; one-time set up fee, $10; for schools and churches, the first computer is free and every additional computer is $1 per month. http://www.hedge.org/. Filtering is based upon "Christian values."

*I-Gear.* URLabs. Proxy server. Solaris and Windows NT. 50 lines, $1,695; each additional 50 lines, $295. http://www.urlabs.com/public/.

*Kidz.net.* Kidz.net. Proxy server. No platform information provided. $99 per year. http://www.kidz.net/.

*Library Channel*. vImpact. Client. Windows 95/NT. No price information provided. http://www.vimpact.net/. Selects sites for visiting—a "cyber yes" list.

*Library Safe Internet System*. netFilter Technologies. Proxy server. Unix, Windows NT. Price depends on size and needs of organization. http://www.librarysafe.com. Contact information: (410) 822-8897 or info@librarysafe.com.

*Net Nanny*. Net Nanny Software International. Client. Windows 3.X/95/98. $26.95; 20 users, $199.95. http://www.netnanny.com/.

*Roadblock*. Sandhill Solutions. Client. Windows 95/NT. http://www.sandsol.com/.

*Surf Watch*. Surf Watch. Client or proxy server. Windows 3.x/95/98, Mac OS. $39.95 for Windows 95 and Mac; $49.95 for Windows 98; site licenses. http://www1.surfwatch.com/.

*Triple Exposure*. Innovative Protection Solutions. Client. Windows 3.x/95/98. $29.95; 50 users, $299; 100 users, $499; educational discounts available. http://www.ips-corp.com/tripleex.htm. This product does not prevent Web sites from being displayed, but simply keeps a detailed record of what has been displayed (including URLs, pictures, and text) and is meant to work as a deterrent more than a filter.

*WebSENSE*. NetPartners Internet Solutions. Proxy server. NT server. 25 users, $495. http://www.netpartners.com/index.html/.

*WizGuard*. WizGuard. Client or proxy server. Windows 95/98/NT. $29.99; for WizGuard Proxy Server, price is based on the number of users; 100 users, $1,799. http://www.wizguard.com/.

*X-Stop*. Log-On Data. Client or proxy server. Windows 95/98/NT. $60 per seat per year; proxy server, up to 50 seats, $695. http://www.xstop.com/.

# KALIPER: A Look at Library and Information Science Education at the Turn of a New Century

Joan C. Durrance

Professor, University of Michigan, School of Information
Chair, KALIPER Advisory Committee

Karen Pettigrew

Post-Doctoral Research Fellow
University of Michigan, School of Information
Principal Investigator, KALIPER

KALIPER—the Kellogg-ALISE Information Professions and Education Reform Project—is a ground-breaking two-year project of the Association for Library and Information Science Education (ALISE). Made possible by a grant from the W. K. Kellogg Foundation, the project is designed to analyze the nature and extent of major curricular change in library and information science (LIS) education.

The KALIPER project is perhaps the most extensive examination of the LIS curriculum since the Williamson Report, the field's first examination of education for librarianship, which was published in 1923. By the time that first report—funded by the Carnegie Corporation—was issued, the enterprise set up by Andrew Carnegie had invested millions in public library buildings. The Williamson report is credited with major changes in education of librarians, including the development of the first standards for library education (see note below, Williamson).

The KALIPER project examines library and information science education at the end of the 20th century. This project, conducted between 1998 and 2000, seeks to determine the nature and extent of major curricular change in library and information science education. It is being conducted immediately following considerable investment by the W. K. Kellogg Foundation in curricular change at several programs through its mid-1990s Human Resources for Information Systems Management (HRISM) Initiative (Marcum).

The purpose of the KALIPER project is to evaluate recent change and to document trends in library and information studies/information science curricula across North America. By analyzing and communicating advancements in curricular reform with respect to factors that affect either its content or process, ALISE seeks to help move curriculum development toward an achievement of critical mass in the field.

ALISE, a professional organization of more than 70 institutional members and more than 500 personal members in the library and information science field (including faculty members who have continuing responsibilities for curriculum renewal), is devoted to promoting excellence in research, teaching, and service for library and information science education. ALISE has already made a major commitment toward creating a context for structured curricular reform by focusing on change, innovation, and redesign at its annual conferences over a four-year period.

Several recent ALISE conferences have aimed to help prepare LIS educators to prepare librarians for the challenges they face. The 1996 ALISE conference

"Caught in the Crossfire? Conflicts and Cooperation among the Institutional Cultures of LIS Education" examined LIS education within a wide context. The 1997 conference, "Reinventing the Information Profession," examined the major challenges faced by those who seek to educate the information professional for the 21st century. In 1998 participants were challenged to consider "Transitions for Library and Information Science: Shaping the Future of Our Discipline, Profession, Organizations, and Ourselves." In 1999 "Beyond 2000: Designing Education for Library and Information Science Professionals" focuses on professionals and educators working together to develop relevant future information professionals. KALIPER builds on this extensive interest in curricular change. The results of the project will be reported at the ALISE Conference in 2000.

The KALIPER project is overseen by an advisory committee. Members include Joan C. Durrance (Chair), Professor, School of Information, University of Michigan; Leigh Estabrook, Dean, Graduate School of Library and Information Science, University of Illinois; Raymond F. von Dran, Dean, School of Information Studies, Syracuse University; Joanne Marshall, Dean, School of Information and Library Science, University of North Carolina at Chapel Hill; Thomas A. Childers, Dean, College of Information Science and Technology, Drexel University; Toni Carbo, Dean, School of Information Sciences, University of Pittsburgh; Shirley Fitzgibbons, Associate Professor, School of Library Information Science, University of Indiana (ex officio as ALISE President), Sharon J. Rogers, Executive Director, ALISE; and Karen Pettigrew, Post-Doctoral Research Fellow and Lecturer at the School of Information, University of Michigan. Pettigrew serves as the KALIPER principal investigator.

The project is being carried out by five teams of scholars, who were chosen competitively by the KALIPER advisory committee. In order to foster collaborative and continued scholarship in LIS education, the application process targeted experienced faculty as well as doctoral students and assistant professors. The teams represent 12 schools from three countries—the United States, Canada, and the United Kingdom. The five teams are:

*Scholar Team 1*: John Richardson, Professor, Department of Library and Information Science, University of California, Los Angeles (UCLA); Matthew Saxton, Ph.D. student, UCLA; Stuart Sutton, Associate Professor, School of Information Studies, Syracuse University; and Bill Gibbons, Ph.D. student, Syracuse University.

*Scholar Team 2*: Jane Robbins, Dean and Professor, School of Library and Information Studies, Florida State University; Beth Logan, Associate Professor, Florida State University; Prudence Dalrymple, Dean, Graduate School of Library and Information Science, Dominican University; and Heidi Julien, Assistant Professor, School of Library and Information Studies, Dalhousie University.

*Scholar Team 3*: Richard Cox, Associate Professor, School of Information Sciences, University of Pittsburgh; Beth Yakel, Assistant Professor, University of Pittsburgh; Jeanette Bastian, Ph.D. student, University of Pittsburgh; and David Wallace, Assistant Professor, School of Information, University of Michigan.

*Scholar Team 4*: Daniel Callison, Associate Professor, School of Library Information Science, University of Indiana; Carol Tilley, Ph.D. student, University of Indiana; Louise Robbins, Director and Associate Professor, School of Library and Information Studies, University of Wisconsin–Madison; and Pat Lawton, Ph.D. student, University of Wisconsin–Madison.

*Scholar Team 5*: Tom Wilson, Professor, Department of Information Studies, University of Sheffield; Roma Harris, Professor, Graduate School of Library and Information Science, and Vice-Provost, University of Western Ontario; Joanne Marshall, Dean, School of Information and Library Science, University of North Carolina at Chapel Hill; and Victoria Marshall, Ph.D. student, University of Western Ontario.

## Components of the KALIPER Study

The KALIPER project uses multiple approaches to examine curricular change. The project's various components permit participation in a variety of ways.

*Guidance by Blue Ribbon Committee.* The KALIPER advisory committee was formed in spring 1998. It is made up of senior faculty and administrators from several LIS programs and guides the development of the project at all stages. The committee was appointed by ALISE presidents Toni Carbo and Shirley Fitzgibbons.

*Iterative Study Design.* The principal investigator and the advisory committee developed a preliminary research design for the study, incorporating multiple data collection methods, such as content analysis, surveys, interview protocols, and focus groups. The study design is iterative and each stage builds on work completed in the previous stages. This design is revised as appropriate by the KALIPER scholars and the KALIPER advisory committee.

*Baseline Data Collection from all LIS programs* . A baseline survey of curricular change was e-mailed in late summer 1998 to all deans and directors of North American schools with an LIS program accredited by the American Library Association (ALA). Deans and directors were asked to comment on the extent to which particular factors have had an impact on their respective school's curriculum. Eighty-four percent of those contacted responded.

*Competitive Call for Participation from Junior and Senior Faculty.* The KALIPER advisory committee issued a call in summer 1998 for doctoral students and faculty to submit vitae, interest statements, and samples of writing to apply to participate as KALIPER scholars. Fifty individuals expressed interest. Twenty KALIPER junior and senior scholars were chosen in fall 1998.

*Case Study Development of Kellogg-funded HRISM Programs.* Curricular analysis of selected LIS programs began with programs that had been funded by the W. K. Kellogg Foundation HRISM Initiative. Case studies are being developed and shared by KALIPER scholars.

*Examination of a Broad Group of LIS Programs and Comparison Across Schools.* All North American LIS programs were invited to participate in this multifaceted KALIPER project. A call to deans of all LIS programs to make their curricula available for in-depth analyses by KALIPER scholars was issued in fall 1998. In all, 32 of 56 accredited schools requested that their programs be involved. Scholars began their work with these programs in January 1999 and will continue analyzing the data through fall 1999.

*Analysis of Statistics Provided by "KALIPER" Schools.* ALISE maintains a rich set of data on all LIS programs. The *Library and Information Science Education Statistical Report* is a compilation and analysis of statistical data and information about graduate library and information science programs of ALISE institutional members (Daniel and Saye). The ALISE database will be useful in this major analysis.

*Qualitative Analysis of "KALIPER" Schools.* Four teams of scholars will study patterns of change across the 32 programs, starting with themes that were initially identified by the deans. The fifth team is focusing on major changes in education for archives and records management across all North American programs. All five teams are examining such areas as curriculum review processes, identifying factors that have influenced change in particular programs, determining the rationale for current structures and the positioning of the school within the university, and so forth. They are collecting data using program Web sites, self-study reports, statistical reports submitted to ALISE, and syllabi and readings for core courses, and are conducting selected interviews.

*Exchange of Data by Scholars.* Each of the five teams has developed a method to work together via e-mail. The ALISE Web site is the vehicle for data exchange among the five teams.

*Focus Groups.* Deans and directors of schools that have invested in major curricular reform will participate in focus groups to discuss the process and content of those reforms. These focus groups will be conducted in mid-1999.

*Working Sessions.* KALIPER scholars who have been conducting most of their work over the Internet will convene periodically. During these meetings, scholars will share and analyze collected data, refine the project design, and present formal papers on patterns and factors in curricular change. The initial KALIPER retreat was held in Philadelphia in January 1999. Others will be held in July 1999 and January 2000.

## Methods and Research Questions

The methods used will result in an iterative process of reflection on curriculum reform. Through the use of multiple methods of examining change, the KALIPER project focuses on identifying models and factors that affect both the content of curriculum change and the curriculum change process.

The primary research question guiding the study of curriculum renewal with regard to curriculum content is:

- What evidence/indicators suggest that dynamic curricular changes are occurring in education for information professionals?

Related questions of a more specific nature include:

- What new courses have been added to LIS curriculum in the past three years?
- How are these new courses distinguished from other courses in terms of topics, resources, delivery, and so forth?
- In what ways have courses that cover core LIS concepts changed?

- What new perspectives can be identified in the curriculum?
- As a result of curriculum changes, which areas of study have been reduced or consolidated?

The investigation of phenomena regarding the curriculum change or transformation process will be guided by the following general research questions:

- What critical factors have affected curriculum change within schools?
- What other trends have affected the structure of the curriculum?
- How have these recent curriculum changes affected such factors as student enrollment, teaching loads, faculty hiring, and new jobs for graduates?
- How have curriculum changes at the master's LIS level affected the development of programs at other levels (for example, undergraduate, Ph.D., interdisciplinary initiatives, and so forth)?

## Components of the KALIPER project

The research questions are being investigated through a series of stages. The LIS community at large is invited to discuss the progress and results as they are reported throughout the project in different venues. The formal communication tool for the project will be the KALIPER Web site (residing on the ALISE Web site, http://www.alise.org), which will be used to disseminate work in progress, to communicate about all groups and individuals engaged in the process, and to share the analyses and reports that summarize the work.

By design, the project seeks to achieve increased involvement by a new generation of scholars, the ultimate investment in continuous renewal and change. Each team comprises junior and senior scholars who work together to gather and analyze the data. The KALIPER project will result in documentation and dissemination of the elements of curriculum reform and renewal in the LIS field, thus placing the Kellogg-HRISM developments in a broader context. The results from the KALIPER project will reach a wide audience through conference presentations, journal articles, and the ALISE Web site.

## Stage 1: Deans and Directors Survey

For Stage 1 of the KALIPER project a short questionnaire was sent by e-mail during summer 1998 to all the deans and directors of schools with an LIS program accredited by ALA. The excellent response rate, 84 percent, is an indicator of the interest among the LIS community in this study. The primary purpose of the survey was to gather baseline data regarding both the extent of curricular change within individual schools and the respondents' perceptions of the degree to which this change was affected by particular factors. The survey also served as a means for partially identifying which schools have undergone extensive curricular change of a paradigmatic nature. The preliminary results of the surveys were used to derive an initial framework that the KALIPER scholars are using to conduct in-depth analyses of curriculum-related data.

**Survey Method**

The deans and directors survey instrument was drafted by members of the KALIPER project's advisory committee during their winter 1998 meeting in Washington, D.C. Since the survey's purpose was simply to gather baseline data and was aimed toward deans and directors, the advisory committee decided the instrument should be short and conducive to being administered by e-mail.

The instrument contained 13 questions. For questions 1 through 3 deans and directors were asked to provide the names of their schools, the titles of all degrees offered, and to identify any degree changes they anticipate occurring within the schools over the next three years. For questions 4 through 13 respondents were asked to describe the extent of curricular change within their schools in terms of ten factors: vision or mission change, new relationships with other campus departments, major funding changes and shifts, market positioning, faculty changes (such as growth, new hires, and retirements), new degrees, new course content, core requirements, pre-admission requirements, and modes of delivery. Using a five-point scale, respondents were asked to rank the degree of change for each factor with regard to the past three years and what they anticipate will happen in the next three. Respondents were also asked to comment on these changes.

The questionnaire was sent by e-mail during summer 1998 to all deans and directors of 56 schools with ALA-accredited LIS programs. Respondents were informed that their individual responses would be kept confidential and that only aggregate findings would be disseminated to the LIS community at large.

## Results

The final response rate for the survey was 84 percent (47 out of 56). Nine questionnaires were received by fax, one by regular mail, and the remainder by e-mail. The following themes emerged regarding schools' current and anticipated program offerings:

*Separation of Master's Degree.* Several schools have split the traditional master's degree into two degrees—master's in library studies/science and master's in information studies/science—to facilitate greater focus on particular subject areas.

*New Degrees.* Eight schools indicated that they are implementing or exploring the possibility of offering a new bachelor's degree. Seven replied similarly for a new master's, seven for a new Ph.D., and six for post-master's or nondegree certificates. Of the nine responding schools that do not currently offer degrees beyond the MLIS or MLS, five indicated that they are considering offering new programs at either the bachelor's or Ph.D. level.

*Specialized Degrees and Areas of Concentration.* Several schools have begun offering specialized degrees or focused programs of study. These include:

- Bachelor's Level: Programs have begun to offer majors or minors in such areas as information management and technology, and information systems. LIS programs with considerable experience in offering these degrees include Drexel University, Syracuse University, and Florida State University.

- Master's Level: In addition to the general degree in library and information science, programs may also offer specialization in archives and records management, archival history, biotechnology information processing, information resource management, children's literature, communication, education specialist, educational technology, extension and distance education, fine arts, human-computer interaction, information resource management, information economics, law librarianship, management and policy, management, software engineering, and telecommunications and network management.
- Ph.D. Level: Some Ph.D. programs offer concentrations in such areas as communication, health informatics, information transfer, and print culture history.
- Certificate (nondegree) Programs: Examples of nondegree certificates being offered at the undergraduate, master's, or post-master's level include advanced study in LIS, archival administration, digital publishing, document and archival administration, information consultant, information technology sources analyst, interactive multimedia, knowledge management, legal information specialist, library administration, new media, and school librarianship.

## Factors Affecting Curriculum Change

To gauge overall change, the deans and directors were asked to state the extent to which each of ten factors had influenced change in their programs using the following five-point scale: (1) no change or effect, (2) minor change or effect, (3) moderate change or effect, (4) major change or effect, (5) fundamental change or effect.

### Vision or Mission Change

According to a majority of deans and directors, changes in their schools' vision or mission will continue to have a strong impact on curriculum changes over the next three years. While many described examining their vision or mission statements as a periodic activity, they also said it was influenced by the appointment of a new dean or director, by the scheduling of the ALA Committee on Accreditation review process, and by changes in disciplinary focus at the parent institution level. Some respondents commented on how their schools are "moving toward a conscious statewide rather than local or regional focus," and how they "hope to address the demands for information professionals in several areas beyond (but inclusive of) librarianship, archives, etc."

The theme of expanding horizons ran through several responses. As one director explained, "The school made a substantial change in its vision within the last few years and this change had substantial impact on curriculum and staffing needs. We moved from a mostly library-science-based vision to one that emphasizes the depth and breadth of the information sciences, although library science remains notably important. We are attempting to meet the professional needs of a much greater number of information agencies." Another director commented, "Basically, we're still doing the same thing (e.g., information transfer), but we are doing it in numerous new environments . . . more specifically, the electronic or network environment and in the corporate environment. How will these new environments affect the essence of what we do? It is too early to tell. But we must be very aware of the changes and (try to) keep up . . ."

## New Relationships with Other Campus Departments

Most deans and directors predicted that interdisciplinary initiatives will continue to have a strong impact on curriculum over the next three years. They described several factors as contributing to their relationships with other departments, including cross-listing courses and offering joint programs, especially doctoral programs since "they require constant monitoring of the curriculum." According to one director, the "offering of the doctorate has changed our relationship with other parts of the campus and the change is continuing as we have a greater impact on the campus culture."

New relationships with other departments were also created through cooperative use of technology and the Internet, departmental mergers (largely for the purpose of forming stronger units), joint faculty appointments, joint funding initiatives, and participation in special-interest programs in such areas as human development and aging, and environmental studies. One school, for example, said it was one of three partners in a research institute that brings together researchers from information studies, anthropology, sociology, cognitive psychology, industrial engineering, computer science, and education.

Interuniversity relationships were also facilitated through the writing of joint research or program grant proposals. One dean remarked, "A current funding initiative [will] deepen and make more complex the interrelationships with several departments." Respondents also discussed how funding programs are dictating new departmental relationships by requiring collaborative applications. An emerging theme under this question was new formal and informal relationships with departments outside the host university. Such relationships might comprise students taking a minor at a partnering university or both universities sharing the offering of particular courses. According to one respondent, "Relationships with other universities is where the true change will occur in the next five years."

The majority of respondents emphasized the need for and benefits of interdepartmental relationships. As one director explained, "Given that failure to develop substantial relationships with other campus units and lack of 'centrality' have been important variables in the decision to eliminate library science programs, we have given considerable time and effort to developing stronger relationships with the several colleges on campus." Other respondents also addressed the politics of such relationships: "Scarcity of resources forces cooperation and partnerships," explained one dean. "This, however, is dangerous because the objectives of cooperation can be seriously distorted. Partnerships based on the evolution of the field are essential. I see lots of discussions ahead with departments of communication, computer science, business, linguistics, etc. The catch, however, in those partnerships, is to find win-win situations, which is rather difficult."

While respondents were not asked to indicate which degrees were offered jointly with other departments, the survey responses suggest that such initiatives are increasing. In addition to the 18 schools (38 percent) that indicated that they offer at least one type of degree with another department, another eight schools

(17 percent) replied that such plans are in the works. Joint programs are being explored or implemented with a wide array of other disciplines: art and design, biotechnology, business administration and management, communication, computer science, economics, education, engineering, English literature, fine arts, geography, history, human ecology, journalism, Latin American studies, law, medicine, modern foreign languages, native American studies, nursing, psychology, public policy, and urban affairs.

## Major Funding Changes and Shifts

Although respondents varied in their descriptions of the extent to which funding changes and shifts affected curriculum in the past three years, a slight majority predicted a moderate to fundamental impact over the next three years. The positive nature of these effects were described by several respondents, who discussed increased funds from climbing student enrollment, new income from distance education and continuing education courses, university investment in information technology infrastructures, sponsored research (especially as a result of "new faculty with new fundable research interests" in such areas as information science and digital libraries), and seed money from external organizations for revamping curriculum.

All is not rosy across the board in LIS education. A number of respondents stressed the more turbulent nature of funding sources and identified the following negative trends: cutbacks in state and provincial funding to universities, state government implementation of matching grant systems, and university emphasis on funded projects. As one dean observed, "Downsizing, cutbacks, firing . . . this is all that we have been exposed to in the past three years. I hope the worst is gone, but I am not very optimistic for the next three years. This is getting very serious and dangerous for higher education. And it is the same with research funds." Regarding recent state legislation on fiscal autonomy for the universities, someone else remarked, "In theory, this allows the university increased flexibility in management and use of funds. There are expectations that fiscal autonomy will encourage the university to exercise entrepreneurial skills in becoming a self-supporting institution. It is too soon to realize the impact of this move; however, it will obviously have far-reaching implications for funding and fiscal management in the years to come."

## Market Positioning

While many respondents affirmed that their primary role was to educate students for positions in libraries and archives, the following three themes emerged when deans and directors discussed market positioning: revising curriculum to meet the needs of employers in corporate and technological environments (that is, "the Internet community," nonlibrary settings) due to "considerable more contact with businesses," expanding student recruitment and course delivery to other states and countries, and using professional public relations firms—as part of the curriculum review process and sometimes as part of campuswide initiatives—for conducting market analyses and for designing promotional materials and recruitment campaigns.

A majority of deans and directors felt the markets for their students will play an important role in the near future. These themes were reflected by one dean who observed, "The competition to deliver LIS education will become intense in the next five years and this will shape the curriculum." Other remarks illustrating these themes included:

- "Libraries and archives are, have been, and will be our market, but they are changing and so are our students and their positions. We are preparing students for a variety of positions in publishing, government, and art museums, for example, as well as in other nontraditional sites or types of work."
- "We must keep the core but create major openings to new markets. We are trying to do this by building on the competencies common to all information professionals, whether librarians, archivists, information specialists or others. Keeping in mind that in our field the 'core' is the organization, dissemination, and management of information in all forms and in any environment, we identified two major new markets to tackle: the electronic market and the corporate market."
- "We're aware that graduates are now quite likely to go into networking and computer technology jobs that may or may not be in library environments. By adding an undergraduate minor we must seriously consider how our markets are being repositioned."
- "We are exploring the possibility of a West Coast, European, or Asian venue for course offerings. . . . Our marketing will be increasingly national and international rather than geographically focused."
- "The university is engaged in a major marketing campaign that we are involved in. Over the next three years we will use print and electronic technologies to promote and market all our programs, particularly the new ones, by working with national professional associations, the information industry and academic units on campus."
- "A Dean's Advisory Board was established to assist with targeting markets in the so-called emerging job market, i.e., employment opportunities that require skills of information professions in electronic resources and services areas (e.g., Internet, Intranet, e-documents, business intelligence, etc.) that may reside outside of libraries, per se."
- "In the past few years the school has broadened its curriculum, augmented its faculty with appointments across many disciplines, and attracted students from an increasingly varied array of backgrounds. As a result, the school is in the process of redefining its market to include new audiences as well as strengthen its existing base. Major advertising campaigns have been mounted to reach new audiences and to inform existing constituencies."

The benefits of such campaigns were discussed by a director who anticipated that the results of his school's market analysis will result in significant market change. Another respondent described how faculty renewal, a recruitment plan, and a poster mailing raised the profile of her school. Developing new relationships with other departments, along with offering specialist degrees and certificates and distance education, hiring faculty from outside LIS, and attending professional association meetings as an exhibitor or participating in a social event, were also discussed as ways of identifying different student populations and therefore new markets (while at the same time preparing students for a changing library market).

### Faculty Change

Faculty change was another factor that respondents predicted will play an increasingly important role over the next three years. As several respondents explained, new faculty members are able to offer new courses and address the needs of undergraduate programs while existing courses are reconfigured to reflect the new faculty members' focuses. New hires (cross-disciplinary appointments, especially) also tend to bring contacts with other departments, organizations, and businesses that benefit the school and strengthen curriculum and research programs. Along these lines, new faculty "help [schools] achieve intellectual diversity and balance." While "new curricular developments influence who schools hire to fill opening positions," several respondents remarked on how increasing rates of senior faculty retirement and school degree expansion are stirring heavy competition among schools for the same junior faculty and making it difficult to stabilize departments. (This "doctoral level employee market" is one reason why schools say they are expanding Ph.D. programs.) Another theme identified among schools of all types is an increase in endowed chairs, which is largely due to contacts with external organizations.

### New Degrees

While most deans and directors felt that new degrees had (and will have) minimal impact on curriculum change within their school or department, it is important to note that several schools have expanded programs at the master's level (by focusing on particular areas or specializations, such as information economics), have added programs at the doctoral level, and have added postgraduate certificates (in such areas as document and archival administration, information technology sources analysis, and school librarianship). Several deans said their schools had created (or were creating) new programs or areas of concentration in information-related subjects at the undergraduate level. At the bachelor's level, schools are creating majors and minors in information management and technology, information systems, communications, journalism and mass media, management, and technoculture. Schools that have developed undergraduate programs indicated that such programs have had a major impact on enrollment. Drexel University College of Information Science and Technology and the Syracuse University School of Information Studies have offered bachelor's degrees for several years (Childers).

### New Course Content

As expected, the majority of respondents reported a moderate to fundamental impact of new course content on overall curriculum renewal, both with regard to the past and the next three years. Several respondents remarked on how designing new courses and revising existing ones to meet the needs of students and the market is a constant activity: "Courses always change—I've never taught a course the same way twice and I suspect most of my colleagues are the same. Course titles may not change, but content certainly does," especially in courses that "emphasize information technology or areas like reference where the resources change constantly."

While respondents identified several factors (for example, employment of new faculty and creation of cross appointments, implementation of undergraduate and doctoral programs, joint programs and cross-listed courses, and market demands, including those for students with practical experience) as affecting curriculum revision at the master's level, there is little doubt that the Internet and technology remain predominating factors. The pervasiveness of technology was remarked on by a respondent who said, "The advent of digitized information is certainly changing the way we teach and do everything," and described "integrating more and more technology into established courses." According to another director, "The effect of the Internet has [caused] massive changes in content in nearly all our courses: [as] our new curriculum goes into effect a considerable redistribution of material will take place as well as the addition of some new content."

Several respondents also commented on the rapid pace at which new courses and material are being developed. "We expect to introduce and test approximately four new courses per year," wrote one director. Among the new topics identified by respondents were advanced information technology design and analysis, advanced studies in Internet and Intranet design and development, business intelligence, case-based reasoning, communication, copyright, data mining, digital libraries, electronic commerce, information management, information policy, Intranet topologies, preservation, professional practice, and urban librarianship. Beyond emphasizing individual school needs for "more digital and Web-related courses, [and] fewer library courses per se," respondents also discussed the creation of new course content in holistic terms that reflected their schools' visions: "Current emphasis is on ways of packaging content that is more knowledge based rather than application based, thereby making more effective use of courses for multiple audiences instead of narrow ones, e.g., public libraries." The director of a school that recently implemented a new curriculum for its multistream master's program explained, "the new courses respond to the need for information professionals to manage new knowledge work environments, and to make use of the array of information technology which is rapidly changing the basis for the creation, preservation, and dissemination and use of information in digital formats. At the same time, the school emphasizes putting users in the center of information systems, and a socio-technical approach is evident throughout the curriculum."

### Core Requirements

According to a majority of deans and directors, changes in core requirements were minimal in the past three years, but such changes will assume greater importance over the next three years. Several respondents said their core was "pretty stable" having undergone major revision in recent years and they emphasized that "the core skills and values remain." Yet others described plans for extensive evaluation. Examples of core areas identified by respondents included social contexts and foundations of information, information services and sources, management of information organizations, research methods, and the representation, organization, and storage of information. While respondents uniformly commented on how they reduced (or plan to reduce) the number of core courses, schools with multiple master's programs or multistreams described the challenges of designing a core that would accommodate the needs of all students. Schools that recently implemented undergraduate and doctoral programs reported increasing the number of core courses and core course hours.

**Pre-admission Requirements**

Pre-admission requirements was another factor that respondents anticipated will play a greater role in curriculum change in the near future. Types of pre-admission requirements described by respondents included GRE scores, word-processing skills, computer and/or information literacy, industry or professional experience, and, for particular streams of study, computer programming and mathematical skills. Some respondents said they offered intensive workshops in technology and communication to incoming students or covered such skills in introductory courses. Deans and directors also said their schools had increased general admission requirements, and now require higher GRE and TOEFL scores and a higher GPA.

**Modes of Delivery**

According to the vast majority of respondents, LIS curriculum will be affected greatly by changes in modes of delivery. Responses were grouped under three themes: course scheduling times, use of electronic technology and the Internet, and interuniversity course offerings. More schools are offering courses at night and during weekends to facilitate the needs of students, particularly part-timers. As one director explained, "We have faced the reality that more adult students want alternative modes offered. So over the last several years we have increased the number of night and weekend courses offered."

The growing impact of electronic technology and the Internet on the delivery of core and continuing courses was stressed by several respondents. Interactive video conferencing (and compressed video), for example, is used to conduct distance-education courses as well as core and regular courses for which guest speakers cannot participate on-site. Beyond e-mail, Web-based tools and formats are used to maintain departmental course databases, to post course syllabi and other materials that are linked to related Web sites, to conduct course-related discussion groups, and to facilitate interaction for group projects. In the words of one respondent, "There has been a very dramatic and visible shift away from print-based course materials and traditional lecture-style teaching to more Web-based course delivery, group work, and interactive communication. [At our school] synchronous Web-enhanced interactive activities and assignments are intended to augment the classroom experience; not to replace it."

According to several deans and directors, students are comfortable with the use of information technologies (especially Web-based mechanisms) for enhancing more traditional pedagogical models, particularly in the area of distance education. One pedagogical approach adopted by a growing number of schools comprises "intensive limited residency followed by continuing electronically mediated learning and communication. Students receive the same number of classroom contact hours as do resident learners, and then receive 14 weeks of online learning." As a result of offering this approach in conjunction with varied off-site programs, schools "attract a highly qualified and internationally diverse student body."

Interuniversity course offerings also appear to be increasing. Several schools described their experiences in offering joint courses with two or more schools in different states and countries. While these initiatives require considerable coordination, the deans involved described them as successful and commented on plans for future collaborations.

## Preliminary Conclusions Based on the Deans and Directors Survey

The response of accredited LIS programs to the summer 1998 deans and directors survey was excellent, indicating a strong interest among this group of LIS leaders in helping the KALIPER project gather baseline data on curricular change. The survey's preliminary findings suggest that LIS education is at the threshold of change on several fronts, but that in-depth changes are not occurring in schools' core missions. New courses on a wide range of topics have been added and are continuing to be introduced into curricula. Some deans pointed out that while they are not considering abandoning their core constituency (that is, librarians), they are increasingly preparing their students for positions in other information professions. Some are doing this by offering new courses, others through adding undergraduate programs. Still others are moving beyond geographically based programming. It appears that some programs are developing more interdisciplinary courses and tracks, often in collaboration with other schools and departments. Joint course and program offerings with other LIS schools are also occurring. Finally, a group of deans and directors reported that within with the next three years they will be looking closely at their markets. On the negative side, directors often expressed concern over very tight budgets at a time when they see the need for major change.

## Stage 2: KALIPER Scholar Examination of Selected LIS Programs

The deans and directors survey preliminary results were used to develop an initial framework for use by the KALIPER scholars in Stage 2 of the project: in-depth analysis of curricular change in selected programs. Thirty-two programs responded to an e-mail request to all deans and directors to participate in the KALIPER study of curricular change. Each has been assigned to one of four Scholar Teams (a fifth team is examining archives and records management curricula across all schools). As part of their participation, each school is providing its respective team with access to its curriculum-related data (in both print and electronic forms), and has appointed a faculty contact person, who will serve as liaison.

The task of the KALIPER Scholars is to collect and analyze curriculum-related data from participating schools. Teams are looking both at qualitative data collected through examination of the schools' Web sites, materials provided by the program (including self-study reports and curricular materials), and quantitative data (mostly from the ALISE statistics) (Daniel and Saye). The KALIPER research teams are looking for patterns of change, starting with a look at the core courses. The teams are also planning to examine the structure of the programs they examine, the disciplines that faculty are drawn from, the types of new courses, and other curricular changes. Other changes to be examined include modes of delivery, and changes in specializations.

Given the expense of convening these teams in person, most of their work is being conducted through the use of the Internet, team e-mail, and a working Web site. Work is being coordinated by the KALIPER principal investigator, Karen Pettigrew, and the KALIPER advisory committee, led by Joan C. Durrance. The KALIPER scholars held their first in-person meeting at the 1999 ALISE Conference, a day-long retreat that focused both on sharing preliminary data collected from the first group of LIS programs examined and on making revisions in the codebook and data collection approaches. The scholars are preparing for a July 1999 retreat at the University of Michigan in Ann Arbor, where they will present reports based on their detailed examination of the 32 schools. Between summer 1999 and winter 2000, the scholars will conduct focused analyses based on specific topics identified earlier in the project. During that time the scholars will also prepare articles for a variety of publications as well as papers and presentations which will be delivered at ALISE and other conferences during 2000.

## Implications

Although the in-depth analysis of this major study is a year in the future, work so far indicates considerable change, driven by the revolution in information technology and the resulting market changes (LIS knowledge and skills are now more marketable than ever). As we come to the close of this preliminary report, it is fitting to return to the Williamson report. That report came at a time when education for librarianship was in its infancy and was extraordinarily weak. The 1923 report was highly critical of the 14 library science programs of that day. Their curricula were weak, their faculty lacked the skills needed to educate the librarians of the day adequately, and the programs themselves were badly underfunded. Major changes in education occurred as the result of that report. ALA accepted the responsibility to oversee education for librarians and then developed the association's first standards. Not long after the report, the first graduate program opened at the University of Chicago and other university-based programs designed to educate librarians were created in quick succession.

It is the aim of KALIPER scholars to determine the nature of change and to disseminate their findings to educators and librarians. Certainly the KALIPER reports issued in 2000 will prove controversial to some—there is a concern among some librarians that educators at the end of the 20th century have abandoned their roots (see the Web page http://www.ala.org/congress/). Preliminary findings of the KALIPER study indicate considerable broadening of curriculum, organizational structure, and faculty background, and show strength in diversity. They do not, however, indicate the weaknesses seen at the beginning of the century. Findings do suggest that programs that have successfully educated librarians for a century are gaining skills at educating a broader groups of information professionals. They also suggest that librarianship has not been abandoned.

## Selected Resources

American Library Association. Congress on Professional Education. http://www. ala.org/congress/

Daniel, Evelyn, and Jerry Saye, eds. *Library and Information Science Education Statistical Report.* Arlington, Va.: Association for Library and Information Science Education, 1998.

Childers, T. A. "Adventures with the 'L' Word: The Drexel Chronicle." *Library Journal* 123 (February 15, 1998): 112–113.

Estabrook, Leigh. "Rethinking Specializations." http://alexia.lis.uiuc.edu/~estabroo/special.htm

Kellogg-ALISE Information Professions and Education Reform Project (KALIPER). http://www.alise.org/kaliper_Main.htm

Marcum, Deanna B. "Transforming the Curriculum; Transforming the Profession." *American Libraries* 28 (January 1997): 35–36, 38.

Richardson, John. "The State of Library and Information Science Education." In *For the Good of the Order: Essays in Honor of Edward G. Holley*, edited by Delmus E. Williams, John M. Budd, Robert E. Martin, Barbara Moran, and Fred Roper. Westport, CT: JAI Press, 1994.

Van House, Nancy, and Stuart A. Sutton. "The Panda Syndrome: An Ecology of LIS Education." *Journal of Education for Librarianship* 37 (Spring 1996): 131–147.

Williamson, Charles Clarence. *The Williamson Reports of 1921 and 1923, Including Training for Library Work (1921) and Training for Library Service (1923).* Metuchen, NJ: Scarecrow Press, 1971.

# Copyright 1998: Recalibrating the Balance

Robert L. Oakley

Director, Law Library, and Professor of Law
Georgetown University Law Center

As history is written, 1998 will turn out to be an important year in the history of copyright law. It was a year in which major new legislation passed Congress, legislation that redefined the balance of rights between copyright owners and the users of copyrighted information. This new legislation closed the door on some of the issues that have been under discussion for several years,[1] but it opened a new door on some related issues and left others unresolved for another day.

For about 20 years, from the passage of the Copyright Act of 1976 until the middle 1990s, copyright issues did not occupy significant congressional attention. Most people involved in copyright-related industries were basically satisfied with the balance that had been struck by the 1976 act, except for a few important but specific issues.[2]

For the last several years, however, intellectual-property issues have again become important. The development of the Internet, with its capacity for the high-speed reproduction of multiple copies of copyrighted works, has made content owners worried about the potential of the Internet to facilitate widespread piracy. This fear is strong in all parts of the content community, but it is especially strong in the video and music industries. At the same time, high-level policy makers have come to see intellectual property as an international trade issue at least as much as it is a matter of author's rights. There is significant concern about international piracy, especially of software and movies, and there is a high level of interest in protecting U.S. authors and creators in overseas markets. These twin concerns of Internet development and international trade have created a new interest in finding ways to protect U.S. creativity and investment. The challenge has been to enhance the protection in a way that does not interfere with the reasonable, expected, and legitimate rights of information users, researchers, and scholars.

Responding to the concerns of content owners, legislation was passed in 1998 that meets their need for greater protection in the new environment. Throughout the legislative process, the library community worked to protect the traditional copyright balance that supports research and allows libraries to serve their users. As a result of that work, several aspects of the legislation dealt specifically with the needs and concerns of libraries. Whether, in the end, the overall balance is sufficient to meet the needs of library users will be seen as technology continues to develop and as information owners begin to rely on the new provisions of the law. Everyone involved in the process seems to believe that libraries did as well as they could. Nonetheless, some in the library community have expressed a concern that the legislation sets the stage for licensing to replace sales for many information products and for pay-per-view to replace free public access to information. They believe that the balance has been irrevocably changed.

## Term Extension

The Sonny Bono Copyright Term Extension Act was approved and became effective on October 27, 1998.[3] It extends the term of copyright protection by 20 years, creating a 20-year moratorium on any new works coming into the public domain by reason of age.[4] For newer works, created since 1978, the term of protection is now the life of the author plus 70 years. For older works, not yet in the public domain, and for corporate works, the new maximum is 95 years from the date of publication. As a result, librarians should now be aware that works published in 1922 or before are in the public domain; works published after 1923 and not already in the public domain[5] will not come into the public domain for at least 20 more years.

The term extension legislation was strongly supported by the music and movie industries. The 1920s and 1930s were a particularly fertile period in American cultural life, and the owners of some of those properties do not want them to come into the public domain. In addition, a number of European countries had begun to migrate to the longer copyright term, and it was argued that the United States needed an equivalent term in order to prevent our authors from being disadvantaged overseas. The combination of powerful industries and an overseas precedent made it difficult to resist lengthening the term.

The longer copyright term has many implications. In the creative community, it places significant barriers in the way of using these older works for the creation of newer works. The recent adaptations of the works of Jane Austen for television and the movies are examples of how older works in the public domain can be turned into something new and vital for the modern age. Other examples include the incorporation of an older work into a new multimedia work on a CD-ROM. To be sure, such new works can be created by asking permission and paying royalties; but in many cases, that is prohibitive in both time and money. The whole point of having a public domain is to encourage older works to be used in new and creative ways. Term extension slows that process down by another 20 years.

A longer copyright term also has implications for libraries, both in terms of the library's ability to serve its clientele and especially in terms of preservation. With that in mind, the act carved out an exception for nonprofit libraries, archives, and educational institutions. This provision says that during the last 20 years of the copyright term, these organizations may

> copy, distribute, display or perform a work in digital or facsimile form for purposes of preservation, scholarship, or research, *provided that* the institution has determined on the basis of reasonable investigation that (1) the work is not subject to normal commercial exploitation *and* (2) a copy or phonorecord cannot be obtained at a reasonable price *or* the copyright owner or agent provides notice through the copyright office that (1) and (2) apply.

This provision is intended to mitigate the impact of the longer term for purposes of preservation, research, and scholarship. In the process of developing this language, however, there was some disagreement over the meaning of the phrase "normal commercial exploitation." Libraries assumed that the phrase meant that the works were available in the manner in which such works are normally made available. By contrast, some publisher representatives contended that if a work had been identified as available for license, that would be sufficient to qualify. The library community felt that such an interpretation would negate the entire library exemption, because a publisher's entire backlist could be put on a list of works "available for license," whether or not the publisher actually had a copy of every work on the list. This disagreement was not resolved, and the library community expects that the plain meaning of the words will be clear. In addition, it may be hoped that the notice to be provided to the Copyright Office will preclude the wholesale identification of backlists as subject to "normal commercial exploitation" and will limit the identification of such works to those that retain some current value in the marketplace.

## Digital Millennium Copyright Act

The Digital Millennium Copyright Act[6] (DMCA) was approved by President Clinton on October 28, 1998, to implement the provisions of the World Intellectual Property Organization (WIPO) treaty that was concluded at Geneva, Switzerland, on December 20, 1996, and consented to by the Senate on October 21, 1998.

Many have felt that the treaty itself was uncontroversial. However, it should be noted that the treaty establishes what some might consider a new right for copyright owners: a "right of communication to the public."[7] This seemingly new right is not specified in U.S. law[8] and is obviously intended to encompass digital transmissions. Many commentators have felt that this provision was uncontroversial because it could be inferred from the existing rights of publication and distribution. Whether or not a communication right is inferable from the rights already specified in the statute, however, treaties are the supreme law of the land, and it should be assumed that the communication right is now among the exclusive rights accorded to copyright owners in the United States.

To implement the treaty, the DMCA included several specific sections, each of which was detailed and technical. This article will review those of greatest interest to librarians.

### Prohibition Against Circumventing Technological Protection Systems

In the Internet environment, many copyright owners have felt that technology—through systems of encryption, scrambling, or even just passwords—offered the best mechanism for the protection of their works. Accommodating that view, and as a primary means of implementing the treaty, the DMCA makes it a violation of the law to break through a system of technological protection, even if doing so is for a lawful purpose, such as to make a fair use of a work. In addition, the law bans any equipment whose primary purpose is to circumvent a technological protection measure.

The ban on circumvention does not take effect for two years. During that time, the Librarian of Congress, in consultation with the Register of Copyrights and others, is to make a determination of whether users are likely to be adversely affected in their ability to make fair uses of protected works. If the Librarian of Congress determines that users will be adversely affected, he is to identify particular classes of works that will continue to be exempt from the ban for the next three years, at which time the evaluation will be repeated. In making his evaluation, the Librarian of Congress is to consider

- The availability for use of copyrighted works
- The availability for use of works for nonprofit archival, preservation, and educational purposes
- The impact of the prohibition on criticism, comment, new reporting, teaching, scholarship, or research
- The effect circumvention has on the market for or value of copyrighted works
- Any other factors the Librarian of Congress considers appropriate

This proceeding will be important to protect the future of fair use, but it will be difficult for the library community and others to show the negative impact of encryption. First, it is always difficult to prove a negative. How do you quantify the articles that would have been written if researchers had had greater access to source material? Second, the most sophisticated systems of encryption have not yet been widely deployed and may not be deployed before the two-year period is over. Such systems will provide a mechanism for retrieval and payment for the use of individual articles. Researchers will be locked out if they choose not to pay. The pay-per-view model is very different from the model of shared access to information in a library, but it will be difficult to show a significant negative impact of a technology that is not yet in widespread use. Yet if such an impact cannot be shown, the ban will be lifted, encryption technology will be deployed, and copyright owners will have much more control over the use of their works than they have had traditionally.

*Library exception.* There is a narrow exception for libraries to the ban on circumvention. Nonprofit libraries are allowed to circumvent a technological protection measure for the limited purpose of making a good-faith determination of whether to acquire a work. When it does so, the library may not retain the copy of the work to which access has been gained any longer than necessary to make such a determination, and the library is not allowed to circumvent the technological protection if another copy is reasonably available.

## Prohibition Against Circumvention Technology

A key element in the prohibition against circumvention is the ban on the technology that would enable it to be done. If the encryption is effective and you can't get any devices to break through it, then the copyright owner can deny access to the information even for purposes that would be lawful. This law makes it essentially impossible to acquire such equipment by specifying that the manufacture, importation, sale, or trafficking in such devices is prohibited. Such a stringent provision against the availability of the technology makes one wonder about the value of the exceptions, such as the library exemption. If a library did want to decrypt a work to evaluate it for a purchase (admittedly, an unlikely scenario), how would it do that if the necessary technology is unlawful?

### Prohibition Against Altering Copyright Management Information

Encryption systems will rely on embedded copyright management information to control access to the work, to track usage, and to provide a mechanism for payment to the copyright owner. Such information consists of standard bibliographic information, including author, title, and copyright owner, as well as the names of any performers, writers, or directors who might be credited with the work. In addition, it includes any terms and conditions for the use of the work. Such terms and conditions include the cost of access, restrictions on subsequent distributions, cost of printing, limitations on printing, and payment mechanisms. These terms and conditions provide the basis to charge individual users for the use of individual articles. They set the stage and provide the means to move to a pay-per-view information environment.

In such an environment, the integrity of the copyright management information is crucial. The Digital Millennium Copyright Act makes it unlawful to remove or alter such information knowing that such change will conceal or facilitate an infringement. It also makes it a violation to provide false management information with an intent to facilitate or conceal an infringement.

### Civil and Criminal Penalties

The act provides for both civil and criminal penalties for violations of either the circumvention provisions or the copyright management information provisions of the act. In a civil case, a complaining party may obtain both temporary and permanent injunctions and either actual damages or statutory damages up to $2,500 per occurrence of circumvention and up to $25,000 per occurrence of changing or distributing false copyright management information. Where the court finds repeated violations, it may award three times these amounts as a punishment. Where it finds that such actions have been taken willfully and for purposes of commercial gain, criminal penalties may be imposed, with a fine of up to $500,000 and imprisonment for up to five years for the first offense. Libraries are exempt from the criminal portions of the act, and they may avoid civil damages if they can show that they were not aware and had no reason to believe that the acts in question constituted a violation.

### Online Service Provider Liability

Virtually all Internet users go through an online service provider (OSP) to gain access to the network. These providers range from very large companies like America Online, Microsoft, or IBM, to smaller providers, universities, and even libraries. Such organizations provide a wide range of services. At a minimum, they may simply provide a point of connection to the Internet, a wire through which the information flows. They may also provide links to other sites, indexes, and search engines. Finally, they may provide content. Such content may be created by the staff of the OSP, or it may be created under contract, by other users, or even by someone with no connection at all to the OSP. The OSP should clearly be aware of content created by its own staff and by people with whom it has contracted, but may not be aware of—in all likelihood, cannot be aware of—everything posted on the site by a user, and certainly cannot be aware of everything flowing through the site to its customers.

As content owners have become more aware of the potential for the Internet to be used for purposes of piracy or in ways that would violate their copyright, they have looked for someone or some group to be accountable, and one key link in the chain is the online service provider on whose equipment the information is stored. OSPs, on the other hand, have felt that they cannot be responsible for everything that one of their customers might do. Universities, for example, can teach students about appropriate Internet behavior, but they cannot check up on everything a student might post on the network.

With such concerns—as the Digital Millennium Copyright Act went through Congress—both sides wanted greater certainty than they were then feeling. Content owners felt that they must have some recourse, some way to stop flagrant violations of their rights when they occurred on the Internet. At the same time, online service providers felt that they could not be responsible for everything that millions of customers might do. They felt that their entire industry was threatened if they couldn't be insulated from damage claims where they had no ability to monitor or control the actions of their customers.

The DMCA addressed this issue by limiting an online service provider's exposure to monetary liability—though not the possibility of an injunction—while imposing on them a corresponding series of obligations to minimize the potential harm to copyright owners. The statute defines "service provider" quite broadly as "a provider of online services or network access" or, more technically, as "an entity offering the transmission, routing, or providing of connections for digital online communications." It is very likely that most educational institutions and many libraries would come under the first of these definitions. Therefore, they should familiarize themselves with the complex rules governing the limitation of liability and take steps to bring themselves into compliance. It should be emphasized again, however, that this provision does not insulate a library or educational institution for content that they, themselves, create and make available, but only for content created and/or stored by others over whom the OSP has no control.

The law does not require OSPs to monitor the actions of their clients. However, to take advantage of the limitation on liability, it does require the OSP to inform its users about copyright and to develop, post, and implement a policy for the termination of repeat offenders. It also requires the OSP to accommodate and not interfere with "standard" technical measures used by copyright owners to identify and protect their works (see section on copyright management information, above). In a parallel provision, copyright owners must use standard protection systems that have been developed pursuant to a broad consensus of copyright owners and service providers in an open and fair standards-setting process, that are available to anyone on reasonable terms, and that do not impose substantial costs on service providers.

If these conditions are met, the law establishes four safe harbors for online service providers, but each of these safe harbors is conditioned on a detailed series of technical requirements, most of which require the OSP to be a neutral party with no knowledge or awareness of an infringing activity. This article will highlight some of the requirements but will not endeavor to list them all. Anyone who is an online service provider and wishes to take advantage of any or all of these safe harbors should study carefully the relevant provisions of the act.

*Safe harbor for transmission and routing.* The first of the safe harbors protects an online service provider when it is simply acting as a conduit for material being sent and received by other parties. To qualify for this protection, the transmission must have been initiated by someone other than the OSP; the transmission and routing must occur by an automated process, without a selection of material by the OSP; the OSP must not select the recipients; and the material must neither be modified by the OSP nor maintained on the system for longer than is reasonably necessary.

*Safe harbor for caching.* Caching is a technique in which an OSP makes a temporary copy of Internet material requested by a user so that it can be delivered more efficiently to subsequent users. Because this technique provides greater efficiency to network services, it is very important to keep information flowing over the Internet. At the same time, because it involves the making of a copy, it has been of great concern to copyright owners. An OSP may qualify for this exemption if the cached material is created through an automated process and is transmitted to subsequent users without modification of the content. The OSP must comply with any rules on updating that are specified by the originator and may not interfere with any systems that return information to the originator. Similarly, if the originator of the material has established conditions for access, such as a password or the payment of a fee, the OSP may not allow access to users who have not complied with those conditions.

*Safe harbor for materials stored at the request of a user.* An online service provider will not be liable, under certain circumstances, for material stored at the request of a user. To qualify for this exemption, a provider must not know, or have reason to know, that the material in question is infringing. This provision allows an OSP to create space for Web pages and private chat rooms, without having to monitor each one of them. Central to this privilege, however, is a willingness and ability to remove infringing materials when notified of their presence on the OSP's system.

*Safe harbor for information-locating tools.* Finally, and perhaps of greatest significance to libraries, the law exempts OSPs from monetary liability for providing directories, indexes, hypertext links, and so forth, so long as the OSP does not know or have reason to know of infringing material on the site to which the user is referred. Again, if the OSP is notified or becomes aware of infringing material on such a site, then it must act in accordance with the law to remove the link.

## Condition on Certain Safe Harbors—Removal of Offending Material

Of the four foregoing safe harbors, three of them—for caching, for stored material, and for indexes and links—require the OSP to respond to a notice about infringing materials by expeditiously removing or disabling access to those materials. To be in a position to respond to such a request, the OSP must designate an agent to receive the notices and publicize the name of that agent both on its site and through a notice to the Copyright Office. The notice of infringement sent by a copyright owner must be signed, must identify the infringing material, and must provide sufficient information (such as a URL) for the OSP to be able to locate it. If an OSP takes down allegedly infringing material in accordance with this procedure, it may not be sued for damages by the person who put it up if the allegation turns out to be incorrect. However, the person who put the material up initially may respond with a counter-notification and have it put back unless the copyright owner continues the matter in court. The OSP must complete the notification loop by sending a copy of the counter-notification to the copyright owner who sent the original notice, so that the matter may be taken to court if that course is chosen.

## Separate Provisions Governing Nonprofit Higher-Educational Institutions

The act recognizes that principles of academic freedom create special problems for institutions of higher education and that those institutions cannot just administratively take down materials placed on the Internet by faculty members or graduate students employed to teach when those materials are placed there as part of their teaching or research activities. As a consequence, the act provides that, for purposes of the limitation on liability, faculty members and graduate students employed to teach will not be considered as "the institution." That way, the institution will not lose its exemption when it fails to take down material posted by a faculty member. To qualify for this higher level of protection, the activities in question must not involve online access to materials that were "required or recommended" within the previous three years for a course taught by the employee. In addition, the institution may not have received more than two valid notices of infringement by the faculty member or graduate student within the last three years, and the institution must provide to all users of its network informational materials promoting compliance with copyright laws.

### Library Preservation

As a significant benefit to libraries, archives, and others working to preserve our cultural heritage, the DMCA included a much needed update to the preservation sections of the Copyright Act. Since 1978 the Copyright Act has permitted libraries to make a single copy of published and unpublished works in facsimile form for purposes of preservation. The two sections differed somewhat in the purposes for which preservation copying could be done; but with these sections, Congress signaled its intention to support preservation of the historic record, even if it meant the copying of copyrighted works. Although this section was important and valuable, it became outdated.

Since the 1976 act was passed, preservation techniques have developed to include digital reproduction along with reproduction on paper and microfilm. As a result, it had become necessary to amend the law to remove the restriction to facsimile reproduction. Moreover, national standards now require preservation projects to make at least three copies of a work: an archival copy for safe, remote storage; a master from which legitimate-use copies can be made; and a copy for use.

After years of discussion, the DMCA finally did update the preservation sections of the law. Although copyright owners are very uncomfortable with libraries making any digital copies of their works without permission, the DMCA eliminated the limitation to facsimile form, thus opening the door to the use of digital formats for preservation purposes. In addition, it now permits libraries to make up to three copies of a work for preservation purposes, in accordance with national standards. It does say that for unpublished works the work may not be distributed in the digital format; and for published works, it may not be made available in that format outside the premises of the library. This limitation will hinder the library circulation of digitally reproduced materials, but it was part of the compromise necessary to reach agreement on this section.

Interestingly, this digital update to the preservation section also recognizes the problem of format obsolescence and allows libraries to reproduce published works when the format becomes obsolete, not merely when the medium deteriorates. This problem has been a serious one for libraries with collections of videotapes in older formats. Now, as the formats continue to evolve in the digital environment, this section of the law will allow libraries to migrate formats without having to buy the content over and over again.

### Database Protection: The Law That Almost Made It Through

For the last several years the producers of some databases have sought statutory protection against someone taking all or part of a database without appropriate compensation. Not only are they worried about the unauthorized user, in the electronic environment, they fear that someone could take a substantial part of a database and set up a competing product without having to make the initial investment in collecting the information. As a result, the free-rider would be able to undercut the price of the original compiler and drive them out of business.

These fears arise because neither facts[9] nor U.S. government information[10] are protectible under copyright, but some publishers have developed very large businesses by compiling such information and selling it to their clients. They believe that the lack of protection for their investment represents a major gap in U.S. intellectual-property laws and leaves them vulnerable to large-scale piracy.

An earlier attempt to create a system of *sui generis* protection for databases under copyright failed because it was overbroad, it lacked appropriate safeguards for users, and it was not clear that it would survive a constitutional challenge because it established a system of copyright for works that, by definition, did not meet the constitutional threshold of creativity for copyright.

In the 105th Congress, the proponents of protection tried a different approach: to protect databases against a misappropriation that causes harm to the market. This approach avoids the constitutional issue because it does not set up a new category for copyright. It would provide protection for investment in the compilation of information, including compilations of factual data and governmental works, as well as other kinds of compilations. The owner of the database could sue if someone extracted even a small amount of information that caused harm to its actual or even potential market. The term established for this protection was 15 years; but if the owner of the database invested significantly in its maintenance or updating, the protection could be extended essentially indefinitely.

There were a number of concerns with this bill raised by a variety of groups, including librarians, representatives of other segments of the information industry, and members of the research community, especially in science and medicine. They were concerned about the absence of a meaningful fair-use provision that would allow researchers the ability to extract modest amounts of data as needed for their research. They were concerned about the need for a definition of "harm to the market" and the need for a definition of "potential market." It seemed that even a small extraction could potentially cause some harm to the market and, therefore, be actionable. They were concerned about the impact of the legislation on free public access to government information, especially in situations where there was a de facto monopoly. Finally, they were concerned about the potential for an unlimited term of protection.

Despite all these concerns, the bill passed the House and was included in the House's version of the Digital Millennium Copyright Act. For a while, it appeared as though a very similar version would be added to the Senate version of the DMCA and passed without a hearing. As Congress was winding up its affairs, however, the Senate was persuaded to defer consideration of the database legislation and to make it a high priority for the 106th Congress.

## Also on the Agenda for 1999

### Term Extension Rules

Under the Term Extension Act, libraries may copy or use works in the last 20 years of their term of protection, provided that the work is not subject to normal commercial exploitation. A publisher may indicate that a work is still subject to normal commercial exploitation by providing a notice to the Copyright Office. Late in 1998 the Copyright Office published its interim regulations concerning this notice and requested input into the nature of the final rules. Some of the issues under consideration include the frequency of the notice requirement, the appropriate fee to be paid to the Copyright Office, and the treatment of journals or other collective works. Comments are due on these issues early in 1999, with a final rule making later in the year.

In the meantime, a lawsuit has been filed challenging the constitutionality of term extension. The plaintiff is a publisher who converts selected texts from the public domain into electronic format and makes them available over the Internet. The moratorium on new works coming into the public domain will, for the next 20 years, limit what works can be converted to those copyrighted before 1923. This publisher observes that the Constitution requires "limited" terms of protection for copyright. He then argues that the pattern of extensions of the Copyright Act makes it seem as though works from the 1920s and 1930s will never come into the public domain. At some point, he says, the term, even if it has a number, is no longer limited for any reasonable purpose and should be struck down.

### Copyright Office Study on Distance Education

As part of the Digital Millennium Copyright Act, the Copyright Office was directed to do a study within six months on "how to promote distance education through digital technologies, including interactive digital networks, while maintaining an appropriate balance between the rights of copyright owners and the needs of users of copyrighted works."

This issue arose as the DMCA was proceeding through Congress because it appeared that the existing section of the Copyright Act on distance education was designed to accommodate analog technologies, such as television, but not the exact same activity on a digital network. As part of the study, the Copyright Office must consider whether there is a need for an exemption from the exclusive rights of copyright owners for distance education through digital networks, the categories of works that might be included in such an exemption, any quantitative limits that might be appropriate, who should be able to take advantage of the exemption and who should be entitled to receive the transmitted materials, and whether or not there should be some technological measure required to protect the security of transmitted works. In addition, the Copyright Office must consider whether the availability of licenses should make a difference in the availability of the exemption.

### Study on the Impact of Encryption

As discussed in detail above, the DMCA requires the Librarian of Congress, in consultation with the Register of Copyrights and others, to perform a detailed study of the impact of technological protection systems on the availability of works for use; on the availability of works for preservation and educational purposes; on research, teaching, scholarship, news reporting and criticism; and on the market for or value of creative works. This study will be difficult to do because so much of it will be hypothetical. Nonetheless, it will be a very important study because it may lead to the widespread adoption of pay-per-view techniques for access to information, enforced by encryption systems that will otherwise keep information locked up. If those systems are deployed, then that will be the legacy of copyright developments in 1998—encryption and pay-per-view. The stage has been set.

## Notes

1. See "Copyright 1996: Fleshing Out the Issues," by Robert L. Oakley, *Bowker Annual Library and Book Trade Almanac*, 1997, 229 et seq.

2. Consider, for example, the effort to bring the United States into the Berne Convention and the effort to solve the problems created by the invention of digital recording devices.

3. P.L. 105-298 (1998).

4. Of course, new works from the U.S. government will continue to be in the public domain.

5. Such works might have come into the public domain because they did not renew their copyright at the conclusion of the first 28-year term of copyright that existed at that time. In fact, studies have shown that most works did not renew their copyright after 28 years.

6. P.L. 105-304 (1998).

7. Article 8, "Right of Communication to the Public," WIPO Copyright Treaty, adopted in Geneva, December 20, 1996, in *Copyright and Neighboring Rights: Laws and Treaties*, (WIPO, 1996– ).

8. The U.S. Copyright Act grants the owner of a work five exclusive rights: the right to reproduce a work in copies, the right to distribute copies of a work to the public, the right to prepare derivative works, the right to display a work publicly, and the right to perform a work publicly. See 17 U.S.C. 106 (1994).

9. Under *Feist* v. *Rural Telephone Co.* (499 U.S. 340 (1991)), to be protected under copyright, a work must exhibit some "modicum of originality."

10. See 17 U.S.C. 105 (1994).

# Library Networking and Cooperation in 1998

Bonnie Juergens
Executive Director
AMIGOS Bibliographic Council

Kate Nevins
Executive Director
Southeastern Library Network (SOLINET)

For this article, library networking trends in 1998 have been grouped into five major categories: (1) the broadening scope of services required of networks, (2) consortial buying of electronic information, (3) continually increasing demands on networks for training services, (4) changes in key networking and network-partnering positions, and (5) 1998 network accomplishments. The first three elements continued to be influenced in 1998 by the expanding role the Internet plays in delivering information to libraries and their patrons. Internet-based library network trends in 1998 included the continually expanding use of network Web sites to provide access to an expanding array of network services, especially to smaller and more remote library sites, and the use of the Internet for delivery of electronic databases and full texts. The roles of consortial groups, along with established regional networks, in providing electronic information to member libraries continued to expand and diversify during the year.

## Broadening Scope of Services Required of Networks

Early in 1999 the authors conducted an informal survey among individuals in leadership positions in U.S. library networks and consortial groups. Respondents were asked to identify three key 1998 trends in networking, describe three important developments in individual networks, name three key issues for networkers, and describe each network's greatest single accomplishment during the year. Eleven responses (of 20) were received. The majority of respondents referred, either directly or indirectly, to the expanding array of service demands being placed upon networks. One network director referred to this as the issue of "Greater Expectations."

Some of the services being developed or expanded include

- Electronic information license negotiation services
- Direct provision of electronic information via statewide or regional licensing
- Digitization support
- Regional Courier service
- Expansion of training programs
- Cataloging and/or resource-sharing services for small libraries
- Regional storage and delivery services

Of these developing services, it comes as no surprise, licensing support for obtaining electronic information tops the list. All respondents except one included this in one or another of the four survey questions answered. All other topics except "regional storage" were named more than once. Electronic licensing and expanded training are addressed in more detail in this report. These, and each of the other topics listed, represent a service trend to track during 1999.

The Internet continues to impact in new ways the manner in which networks offer and deliver services to their members. All OCLC-related networks support Web sites; several also support electronic lists, either one-way or interactive, for direct information delivery to the desks of staff members in member libraries. Several networks report that direct member support patterns are shifting. At AMIGOS, 1998 represented the first year in which the number of technical support questions communicated via the Internet matched the number communicated via the network's toll-free telephone service. The year also saw continuation of the trend in networks of supporting online training registration via network Web sites. Corresponding requests by members for networks to allow online ordering—with the associated commitment of sometimes large amounts of institutional funds—are being answered more slowly. The complexity of OCLC product coding and the complexities associated with purchasing technology-based services, as well as the authorization-to-commit-funds issue, combine to delay developments in this area. Some networks, such as the Michigan Library Consortium (MLC), have expanded online ordering to products that lend themselves to payment by credit card.[1] AMIGOS has established a goal to support online ordering by the end of calendar year 1999.

Network Web sites are now routinely used to provide member access to third-party electronic information services—some, as at BCR,[2] to access index or full-text databases maintained by the network, but most to access services mounted at the third-party site. Some networks, such as the Missouri Library Network Corporation (MLNC), provide links to all member Web sites and online catalogs.[3] Most networks post administrative publications, such as a general member newsletter and annual reports; many post technical publications; and a few post focused special-interest articles such as the WILS "value of libraries" summaries,[4] the MINITEX "In My Opinion" series written by Executive Director Bill DeJohn;[5] or the AMIGOS "Imaging Nuggets" series.[6] Expansion of network services on the net is a logically continuing trend for which one can envision no reduction in the next few years.

## Consortial Role in Delivering Electronic Information

It is useful for readers of this report to understand the way in which the terms "networks" and "consortial groups" are being used by the authors. "Network" tends to refer to one of the single- or multiple-state member-based cooperatives with diverse service programs that include a partnering relationship with OCLC. While "consortial group" is by definition a broader term that can include library cooperatives of any size and purpose, including OCLC-related networks, it is used here to refer to the fairly recent phenomenon of groups of libraries banding together, usually informally, to focus on negotiating discounts to license access to electronic information services. As has already been made abundantly clear, 1998 saw continued growth in electronic consortial activity. This dramatic trend has been reported in *Bowker Annual* networking reviews over the past several years[7, 8] and in 1998 was described succinctly by Tom Sanville, executive director of OhioLINK, as "consortia are playing a more dynamic role in the delivery of information."[9] The membership scope of consortia can vary significantly, from subregional or state-based multitype cooperatives to specialized multistate groups serving a specific type of library.[10] The objectives of these groups range from a focus solely on electronic database licensing to a variety of additional cooperative services, including:

- Obtaining state funding for cooperative activities
- Improving electronic access to government information
- Providing cooperative document delivery services
- Linking consortial members' OPACs
- Implementing cooperative digitization projects
- Providing library staff training[11]

Even with this wide range of objectives, consortial licensing remains perhaps the most visible action of these groups and a major reason for forming new consortia. Although the combined buying power of libraries in consortial groups can help control or reduce costs, the primary benefit of this activity is the increased availability of information to participating libraries' communities.[12]

Consortial growth was most evident in three ways in the past year: the advent of new consortial groups, enhanced funding for existing and new groups, and formalization of programs under paid administrators.

The first indicator of growing consortial strength is simply the additional consortial groups established in 1998 to provide electronic information access for their members. Examples include state-based projects such as NC Live, a cooperative North Carolina program providing services to public, independent academic, public academic, and community college libraries across the state.[13] CVL is a similar new multitype project in Kentucky. New Jersey academic libraries worked together to introduce the Virtual Academic Library Environment (VALE) project, from which member public and private academic libraries will obtain expanded access to electronic information. Funding is from the New Jersey Higher Education Technology Infrastructure Bond, a grant from the New Jersey State Library, and institutional matching funds.[14] In Indiana, the legislature provided $1 million to support the statewide virtual-library project INSPIRE (Indiana Spectrum of Information Resources). This project, under the management of INCOLSA (Indiana Cooperative Library Services Authority), provides direct access to electronic information for Indiana residents from home, office, or library.[15] Likewise, the California legislature authorized $5 million to support implementation of "a statewide networking system of resource sharing, communications, and delivery for approximately 8,000 of California's libraries."[16] Based in the California state library, this project will link California citizens through the state electronic network with libraries of all types throughout the state. Smaller groupings within states have also been initiated, such as the Estacado Library Information Network (ELIN) in New Mexico. Formed by one public and four academic libraries, ELIN will facilitate the sharing of both electronic and print resources.[17]

As noted last year, the element of competing time, dollars, and interest among multiple consortial group memberships is becoming acute for some libraries. "Increasingly, individual libraries will balance financial benefits, available terms and conditions, and loyalty or commitment to various networks when making decisions about acceptance of database offerings. While seeking to ensure that the individual library obtains the best cost-feature deal available, this can actually add to the ultimate cost of doing business as middleman networks and vendors commit exponentially more staff and management time to working through the details with individual members of the consortial groups as well as multiple consortial groups operating on behalf of the same individual libraries."[18] This trend continued unabated in 1998.

The second indicator of consortial strength and growth is the increase in funding available to some of these groups. Many states, such as Oklahoma,[19] Wyoming,[20] Pennsylvania,[21] Mississippi,[22] and Arizona,[23] along with those described above, reported funding increases for cooperatively purchased electronic resources during 1998.

The third indicator of growing consortial strength is formalization of programs under paid administrators. This is particularly evident in type-of-library consortial development at the academic/research institution level. A significant example was the Big 12 Plus Library Consortium announcement early in the year that its first executive director had been hired. Members of the Big 12 Plus, comprised of 16 public academic/research libraries in Midwestern and Southwestern states, are cooperating in obtaining electronic information and document delivery, providing distance-learning technology, and sharing collection development efforts.[24] Additional examples of consortial program staffing recruitment came from NERL, the NorthEast Research Libraries consortium,[25] and CIRLA, the Chesapeake Information and Research Library alliance.[26] Both of these recruitment efforts were delayed to early 1999, following months of careful role definition and funding decision-making among members of the consortial groups during 1998.

In addition to the licensing work of individual consortia, 1998 saw exploratory steps toward licensing across multiple consortia. Most notably, the Southeastern Library Network (SOLINET), in cooperation with more than 20 consortial groups and networks, brokered a license for the Congressional Information Service's Academic Universe. This extended access to 53 percent of academic libraries in the United States.[27] Exploration of additional "national licensing deals" with a variety of networks and consortial groups taking the lead continued as 1998 drew to a close.

As reported in last year's networking article,[28] the growth of consortial licensing has led to the establishment of the International Coalition of Library Consortia (ICOLC). Initially an informal group of librarians working on consortial issues who met to discuss licensing, the group developed into a more formal Consortium of Consortia (CoC) in 1997. In February 1998 the name was changed to the ICOLC to reflect the increasingly international scope of participants. At the end of 1998 the ICOLC membership consisted of 79 library consortia from North America, the United Kingdom, Germany, the Netherlands, and Australia. The ICOLC "serves primarily higher education institutions by facilitating discussion among consortia on issues of common interest," keeping participating consortia informed about new electronic resources, pricing practices of electronic providers and vendors, and other issues of importance to directors and governing boards of consortia. "The coalition meets with members of the information-provider community, giving them a forum to discuss their offerings and to engage in dialogue with consortial leaders."[29] The ICOLC meetings, generally held three times a year, are becoming the major forum for consortial dialogue with information providers on licensing offers and policy issues. In addition, ICOLC discussions provide a forum for consortial consideration of issues that impact the way consortial groups provide electronic information access to their members.

ICOLC has developed a number of documents providing insight and guidance to libraries and consortia engaged in database licensing. Two such important documents were released in 1998:

- "Statement of Current Perspective and Preferred Practices for the Selection and Purchase of Electronic Information" (March 1998). This statement addresses contract negotiations, pricing models, data access and archiving, system platforms, licensing terms, information content and its management, and user authentication.[30]
- "Guidelines for Statistical Measures of Usage of Web-Based Indexed, Abstracted, and Full Text Resources" (November 1998). The guidelines define "a basic set of basic use information requirements that are an integral and necessary part of any electronic product offering."[31]

Guidelines for technical issues in requests for proposals will be articulated by the ICOLC early in 1999.

There are no signs that the increase of consortial licensing activity will abate in the near future. Additional planning is under way in states not currently served by these organizations, and information providers are increasingly working with consortia to serve information consumers.

## Increasing Demands for Network Training Services

One of the trends described by respondents to the authors' informal survey about networking in 1998 was that of increasing demands for expanded network training services. One network director commented that network training, while not a hot new item, continues to serve a need that is never completely filled. "Training, training, training," said another. "Our members just can't get enough." In one case, a small state-based network is going to fund an additional full-time training position out of network reserves because the member demand for additional training is so great. The rapidly changing technology used by libraries demands access to up-to-the-minute technology information, not only concerning how to use new systems, but also how to plan for, select, negotiate for, and implement new services. A snapshot of AMIGOS's training activities during fiscal year

(FY) 1998 compared to FY 1997 describes only an 11 percent increase in the number of training sessions conducted, but a 27 percent increase in the number of trainees. These 2,131 attendees at AMIGOS's FY 1998 training sessions do not include those who attended three videoconferences hosted by AMIGOS during the same year. During FY 1998 (July 1997–June 1998), U.S. OCLC-affiliated networks conducted over 1,600 training sessions (excluding distance-learning sessions) attended by 16,000 employees of libraries.[32]

Changes in network training patterns are also being noted. One shift is in the ratio of OCLC-related training topics to non-OCLC topics. Snapshot samples from BCR, SOLINET, and AMIGOS reflect this. October 1998 saw 65 percent of BCR training for non-OCLC topics, 20 percent for marginally OCLC-related topics, and the remaining 15 percent for clear OCLC topics. In June SOLINET trained on non-OCLC topics 62 percent of the time. And in April AMIGOS trainers also found that more than half their training (52 percent) was on non-OCLC topics.[33] SOLINET also reports a major shift from a preference by members to attend scheduled regional training sessions to a preference for special-request on-site sessions. Libraries have different needs in training, and networks are responding by offering customization in content, place, and approach.

As networks continue to support technology transfer in libraries by providing training and technical support, the technology itself offers new ways to deliver education that staff in member libraries need. Network-sponsored and/or -produced videoconferences have been part of the training tool kit for the past few years, but two-way compressed-video and Web-based curricula are fairly new approaches being tested by networks for delivery of training content to broadly dispersed members. AMIGOS recently tested the use of compressed-video and has included that training methodology as a standard offering as of July 1998. Also during 1998 OCLC and affiliated networks tested the use of Internet-based NetMeeting software and have adopted it for network staff training on new OCLC products. Even as networks expand their technological infrastructure to support distance learning by member-library staff, polls of members continue to stress a preference for hands-on, on-site teacher-conducted training— but perhaps the trend will shift as distance-learning technology improves and as younger employees with different expectations come onto library staffs. Technology-based learning tools used by networks and provided to libraries by networks will be items of interest to track over the next few years.

## Changes in Key Networking and Network-Partnering Positions

The library press reported a number of changes in key network-related positions during 1998. Of particular note was the "changing of the guard" at OCLC: Jay Jordan replaced K. Wayne Smith as president and chief executive officer in May. Later in the year, OCLC senior management articulated a policy of renewed dedication to member-oriented roles and product development activities. Jordan vowed early on to get acquainted with the needs of members by making numerous library visits and described his long-term goal "to continue increasing levels of value to members."[34] Subsequent changes in high-level positions within OCLC included recruitment for vice president, member services, a critical position responsible for OCLC leadership "in the areas of OCLC's governance, professional advisory committees, and member library relations."[35] These changes are of great interest to OCLC-affiliated network managers and trustees throughout the country.

Another change at OCLC was the announcement in November that WLN and OCLC had signed a letter of intent to merge the two organizations.[36] The subsequent merger, not completed until January 1999, represents major changes overall for WLN members and the likelihood of minor shuffling among WLN member libraries in neighboring networks. Such changes in the domestic OCLC distributorship scene are also likely to influence the working relationships between OCLC and the rest of its affiliated networks.

Changes are also taking place in state library and network leadership positions. A flurry of changes in state librarian positions occurred in 1998: Alabama,[37] Connecticut,[38] New Hampshire,[39] and Wyoming[40] all recruited for new state librarians. And Marshall Keys, 10-year executive director of NELINET and highly respected as "statesman" in the library networking community, announced his retirement from networking in August.[41] He has announced that he will remain active in librarianship through consulting and speaking on library, information technology, and networking topics.

All these personnel changes in leadership positions will introduce opportunities for change in current networking partnerships and, consequently, strategic directions. Results will be of interest to follow during 1999.

## Network Accomplishments

This report will conclude with a review of "greatest single accomplishments in 1998," as reported in the authors' informal survey cited above. It is interesting to note that three respondents phrased the answer in terms of "survival." One mentioned literal network survival being accomplished by a merger; one mentioned the survival aspect of remaining financially sound while maintaining and expanding services; and one mentioned the achievement of attaining the network's 25th anniversary.

Two respondents cited accomplishments relating to ownership of network facilities and the related value to members that will ultimately result in lower expenses. Four respondents specified advances their networks made in 1998 in the provision to members of electronic information services. Two described important strategic-planning processes in place with members, and one reported a renewed focus on and commitment of resources for training as its greatest achievement in 1998.

## Conclusion

Networks continue to be tapped for an expanding array of services and in turn are tapping today's improved technologies to meet the service and training demands of members. Internet-related tools are being tapped to support and expand distribution of services, and off-the-shelf standard business technologies are being implemented to enhance productivity in internal operations. Heightened activity in licensing "deals" to obtain electronic information services continued as a key trend in 1998. Whether through consortia newly established as "buying clubs," subregional and type-of-library consortia previously established for other resource-sharing purposes, or long-standing membership in regional OCLC-affiliated networks, libraries continued to expand the avenues through which they could obtain the desired best deal. This is seen as a continually growing activity until the current volatile state of information providers settles down and/or new patterns of distribution evolve. Changes in key positions during 1998 may result in new partnership opportunities for some networks. And finally, the types of "greatest single network accomplishments" reported by an informal survey of network leaders suggest that library networking continued to thrive during the past year.

## Notes

1. Michigan Library Consortium (MLC) Web site: www.mlc.lib.mi.us.
2. Bibliographical Center for Research (BCR) Web site: www.bcr.org.
3. Missouri Library Network Corporation (MLNC) Web site: www.mlnc.org.
4. Wisconsin Interlibrary Services (WILS) web site: www.wils.wise.edu.
5. MINITEX Library Information Network Web site: othello.lib.umn.edu.
6. AMIGOS Bibliographic Council, Inc. Web site: www.amigos.org.
7. Kate Nevins and Bonnie Juergens, "Library Networking and Cooperation in 1997," *Bowker Annual Library and Book Trade Almanac*, 43rd ed. (New Providence, NJ: R. R. Bowker, 1998) p. 262.
8. David Brunell, "Library Networking and cooperation in 1996," *Bowker Annual Library and Book Trade Almanac*, 42nd ed. (New Providence, NJ: R. R. Bowker, 1997) p. 243–.
9. Tom Sanville, "A License to Deal," *Library Journal*, vol. 124, no. 3 (February 15, 1999), p. 122.
10. Alaska Department of Education Web site: http://www.educ.state.ak.us/lam/databases/survey.html.
11. ICOLC Web site: http://www.library.yale.edu/consortia/coc3vision.html.
12. Tom Sanville, op. cit., p. 122
13. North Carolina Live Web site: http://www.nclive.org/about.shtml.
14. "Company Announcements," *Library Hotline*, vol. 27, no. 49 (December 14, 1998), p. 7.
15. "Indiana's Virtual Library Plan Begins with EBSCO Contract," *Library Hotline*, vol. 27, no. 8 (March 2, 1998), p. 7.
16. "Library of CA Legislation Forms Statewide Network," *Library Hotline*, vol. 27, no. 40 (October 12, 1998), p. 1.
17. "New Mexico Library Consortium Will Share Network Resources," *Library Hotline*, vol. 27, no. 15 (April 20, 1998), p. 8.
18. Kate Nevins and Bonnie Juergens, op. cit. pp. 266–267.
19. "More State Money for Libraries Increases Online Access in Oklahoma," *Library Hotline*, vol. 27, no. 15, (April 20, 1998) p. 6.
20. "Wyoming State-Wide Database Gets Extra Funds for Upgrades," *Library Hotline*, vol. 27, no. 14 (April 13, 1998), p. 4.
21. "Pennsylvania's Record PL Funds Invested in Technology and ILL," *Library Hotline*, vol. 27, no. 19 (May 18, 1998), p. 4.

22. "Mississippi Statewide Network Licenses CARL Novelist," *Library Hotline*, vol. 27, no. 8 (March 2, 1998), p. 5.

23. "AA State Library Fund Increase Adds Electronic, Print Materials," *Library Hotline*, vol. 27, no. 26 (July 6, 1998), p. 1.

24. "People," *Library Hotline*, vol. 27, no. 8 (March 2, 1998), p. 6.

25. NorthEast Research Libraries (NERL) consortium recruitment advertisement for "Program Support Librarian" position distributed via the International Consortium of Library Consortia (ICOLC) electronic list, February 24, 1999.

26. Chesapeake Information and Research Library Alliance (CIRLA) consortium recruitment advertisement for "Executive Secretary/Program Coordinator" position distributed via the International Consortium of Library Consortia (ICOLC) electronic list, February 28, 1999

27. "Lexis-Nexis Consortia Deal Available in 53% of Colleges," *Library Hotline*, vol. 27, no. 27 (July 13, 1998), p. 2.

28. Kate Nevins and Bonnie Juergens, op. cit., p. 265.

29. "About the International Coalition of Library Consortia," http://www.library.yale.edu/consortia.

30. ICOLC Web site: http://www.library.yale.edu/consortia/statement.html.

31. ICOLC Web site: http://www.library.yale.edu/consortia/webstats.html.

32. Kate Nevins and Bonnie Juergens, "Good Neighbors: Cooperative Programs in SOLINET and AMIGOS," presentation at combined Arkansas Library Association/Southeastern Library Association Conference, Little Rock, AR, October 2, 1998.

33. Ibid.

34. "OCLC's New Prexy, Jay Jordan, Vows Greater Value to Members," *Library Hotline*, vol. 27, no. 27 (July 13, 1998), p. 7.

35. Advertisement, *Library Hotline*, vol. 27, no. 35 (September 7, 1998), p. 11.

36. "OCLC, WLN Begin Negotiations, Merger Expected by Early 1999," *Library Hotline*, vol. 27, no. 43 (November 2, 1998), p. 6.

37. Advertisement, *Library Hotline*, vol. 27, no. 29 (July 27, 1998), p. 9.

38. Advertisement, *Library Hotline*, vol. 27, no. 34 (August 31, 1998), p. 1.

39. Ibid.

40. Advertisement, *Library Hotline*, vol. 27, no. 29 (July 27, 1998), p. 12.

41. Advertisement, *Library Hotline*, vol. 27, no. 33 (August 24, 1998), p. 9.

# Part 2
# Legislation, Funding, and Grants

# Legislation

## Legislation and Regulations Affecting Libraries in 1998

### Carol C. Henderson
Executive Director, Washington Office, American Library Association

### Deirdre Herman
Communications Specialist, Washington Office, American Library Association

The 105th Congress ended with a series of events that confounded predictions. First, the president's party, which rarely gains seats in an off-year election, gained five seats in the House and lost none in the Senate. The election results prompted the resignation of Republican House Speaker Gingrich from his position and his congressional seat. Adding further confusion was the resignation of the Speaker-designate. Before the year ended the House had voted along party lines to impeach President Clinton, and the first item of business in 1999 was the Senate trial of the president for impeachment.

In negotiations late in the session, funding for library and education programs increased, and Congress dropped requirements to have libraries and schools install and use filtering and blocking software as a condition of receiving federal funds or the E-rate telecommunications discounts. E-rate commitment letters began to be sent to schools and libraries in November, almost three years after enactment.

The most significant amendments to the Copyright Act in many years were enacted as the Digital Millennium Copyright Act (updating the law for the digital environment) and the Copyright Term Extension Act (adding 20 years). The library community and others worked hard to ensure balance for users along with these new protections for proprietors.

A long-awaited Government Publications Reform Act was introduced in July but died at the end of the session. Congress passed a renewal of the Higher Education Act and a new Reading Excellence Act and passed several Internet-related bills, including the Child Online Protection Act (COPA), the Children's Online Privacy Protection Act, the Internet Tax Freedom Act, and the Next Generation Internet Research Act. The COPA legislation was immediately challenged in court.

## Funding

The Clinton administration's fiscal year (FY) 1999 budget request included major increases for some education programs and a variety of new education initiatives. Congress resisted most of these initiatives during the regular appropriations process. However, in end-of-session negotiations among a few congressional leaders and administration officials, the desire to end the session in order to campaign for the coming elections and to avoid the government shutdowns of the previous fall enabled the White House to prevail in some areas.

In late October a massive omnibus measure (H.R. 4328, P.L. 105-277)—containing eight appropriations bills, various emergency aid, and several substantial and numerous smaller authorizing bills—was passed and the 105th Congress adjourned.

The Library Services and Technology Act (LSTA) received $166.2 million for FY 1999—a $20 million increase over FY 1998—as part of the omnibus funding package. The president had requested level funding. The House Appropriations Committee had recommended level funding; the Senate Appropriations Committee approved $156,340,000.

Most LSTA funds go for grants to the states for technological innovation and outreach services in libraries; this portion of LSTA was level-funded. Library services to Native Americans received 1.75 percent of the appropriation, as the law provides. Congress put the LSTA increase in National Leadership Grants (NLGs), which received $25 million, of which $15.4 million was earmarked for specific projects. The LSTA law provides for competitive NLG awards for library education and training, library research and demonstrations, library preservation and digitization, and model library/museum projects. Language in the bill overrode the usual 3.75 percent setaside for National Leadership Grants ($5,488,000 in FY 1998). This is the first time LSTA has been subject to such specific statutory "earmarking," which increased dramatically throughout education and other programs in the omnibus package.

For ESEA VI, the innovative education strategies block grant to the states that many school libraries depend upon for materials, the administration requested zero funding. After a letter was circulated by Reps. Rod Blagojevich (D-Ill.) and Michael Castle (R- Del.), the House Labor-HHS-Education Appropriations Subcommittee recommended an increase in ESEA VI funding to $400 million from $350 million. The Senate Appropriations Committee approved $350 million, and the final omnibus package included $375 million.

The total for several elementary and secondary education technology programs was $698 million, a significant increase over the $584 million in FY 1998 but less than the $721 million the president requested. In the last-minute negotiations, the president did receive the requested $200 million for 21st-century learning centers, a program previously funded at $40 million. House and Senate Appropriations Committees had provided $60 and $76 million, respectively. Similarly, almost $1.2 billion was provided to enable schools to hire more teachers to reduce class sizes and to train teachers.

Appropriations for the Government Printing Office (GPO) and the Library of Congress were included in H.R. 4112, the FY 1999 Legislative Branch

Appropriations Bill (P.L. 105-275). GPO's Superintendent of Documents operation, which includes the Federal Depository Library Program, received level
funding of $29.3 million. This was the amount in the House bill; the Senate level
was $29.6 million; GPO had requested $30.2 million.

The Library of Congress received $391.66 million, including authority to
spend receipts of $28 million. This was an increase over the FY 1998 level of
$387.6 million but less than the library's request of $397 million. The bill also
included a permanent authorization of the American Folklife Center. Separately,
the library received authorization (H.R. 3790, P.L. 105-268) to issue commemorative coins for its bicentennial celebration in the year 2000.

The Telecommunications and Information Infrastructure Assistance
Program, administered by National Telecommunications and Information
Administration in the U.S. Department of Commerce, received $18 million, a $2
million cut. However, much deeper cuts and a proposed prohibition of all E-rate-
eligible schools and public libraries from applying for Telecommunications and
Information Infrastructure Assistance Program (TIIAP) grants were dropped. The
National Endowment for the Humanities (NEH) and the National Endowment for
the Arts (NEA) received level funding—$110.7 million for NEH and $98.5 million for NEA. (See Table 1 for details on these and other library and related program funding.)

## Government Information Programs

The Wendell H. Ford Government Publications Reform Act of 1998 (S. 2288)
was introduced on July 10 but died with congressional adjournment. At a July 29
hearing by the Senate Committee on Rules and Administration, library association witnesses testified in support of the bill on behalf of the American
Association of Law Libraries, the American Library Association, the Association
of Research Libraries, Chief Officers of State Library Agencies, the Medical
Library Association, the Special Libraries Association, and the Urban Libraries
Council. These are groups represented on the Inter-Association Working Group
that worked with congressional staff on this bill to reform Title 44 U.S.C.,
strengthen the Federal Depository Library Program, and improve public access—
work acknowledged by Sen. Ford in his introductory remarks.

## Higher Education Act Reauthorization

On October 7 President Clinton signed H.R. 6, P.L. 105-244, reauthorizing the
Higher Education Act for five years. The new act lowers interest rates for student
loans while increasing grants to needy students, establishes a new teacher-train-
ing program, continues the college work study program, and updates international education programs. In HEA Title VI, International Education Programs, a
new Technological Innovation and Cooperation Program with an electronic periodicals program exchange replaces the former Section 607 Foreign Periodicals
Program.

## Intellectual Property Issues

### Digital Millennium Copyright Act

The Digital Millennium Copyright Act (H.R. 2281) was signed into law (P.L. 105-304) on October 28. The House-Senate conference report (H. Rept. 105-796) was passed by voice vote in the Senate on October 7 and in the House on October 12. After many negotiations, this final version includes improvements to several sections of the bill of interest to librarians and users of information. The new act updates the Copyright Act for the digital environment and conforms U.S. law to the requirements of the new World Intellectual Property Organization (WIPO) treaties negotiated in Geneva in December 1996.

On August 4 the House passed its version of H.R. 2281, one substantially altered from the earlier version approved by the Judiciary Committee. It included basic access safeguards in a form similar to the version approved on July 17 by the House Commerce Committee. However, the House-passed bill also included overbroad database protection legislation strongly opposed by library and other groups (see Database Protection Legislation, below).

The Commerce Committee's markup date had been postponed several times while last-minute negotiations continued among various interests, including libraries, on how to retain fair use and other privileges for users of electronic information wrapped in technological protection measures such as encryption. The resulting agreement involving a regulatory structure to protect fair use was offered by Reps. Scott Klug (R-Wis.) and Rick Boucher (D-Va.). This version of the bill also included several provisions from the Senate-passed version, including provisions relating to online service provider liability, distance education, and library preservation activities.

The new act provides a new proprietor right by prohibiting circumvention of technological protection measures used by a copyright holder to restrict access to its material. The act also prohibits the manufacture of devices or services primarily designed to defeat technological protection measures. However, it defers the effective date of these prohibitions for two years and 18 months, respectively. During those two years and every three years thereafter, a rule-making proceeding will determine whether the anti-circumvention prohibition will adversely affect information users' ability to make noninfringing uses of particular classes of copyrighted works. This may result in a three-year waiver from the anti-circumvention prohibition for one or more classes of copyrighted works.

The act also limits the liability of online service providers under certain conditions. It updates the current Section 108 provisions to allow authorized institutions to make up to three preservation copies of an eligible copyrighted work (and removes the outdated "in facsimile form" phrase), to electronically lend those copies to other qualifying institutions, and to permit preservation, including by digital means, when the existing format in which the work has been stored becomes obsolete. It also requires a report to Congress by the Copyright Office on distance education with potential legislative recommendations.

**Table 1 / Funding for Federal Library and Related Programs, FY 1999**
(figures in thousands)

| | FY 1998 Appropriation | FY 1999 Appropriation |
|---|---|---|
| *Library Programs* | | |
| GPO Superintendent of Documents | $29,077 | $29,264 |
| Library of Congress | 376,719 [1] | 391,660 [2] |
| Library Services and Technology Act | 146,340 | 166,175 |
| National Agricultural Library | 20,508 | 20,000 |
| National Commission on Libraries and Information Science | 1,000 | 1,000 |
| National Library of Medicine (includes MLAA) | 160,885 | 181,309 |
| *Library-Related Programs* | | |
| Adult Education and Literacy | 360,551 | 385,000 |
| ESEA title I: Education for Disadvantaged | 8,012,112 | 8,357,520 |
|     Part B, Even Start | 124,000 | 135,000 |
| ESEA title II: Eisenhower professional development | | |
|     Part A, Federal activities | 23,300 | 23,300 |
|     Part B, State grants | 335,000 | 335,000 |
| ESEA title III: Educational Technology | 584,035 | 698,100 |
|     Part A, (includes Technology Literacy Challenge Fund) | 541,000 | 550,100 |
|     Part B, Star Schools | 34,000 | 45,000 |
| ESEA title VI: Innovative Education Program Strategies | | |
|     (State grants) | 350,000 | 375,000 |
| Education of Handicapped Children (State grants) | 4,831,646 | 5,124,146 |
| Educational Research | 72,567 | 82,567 |
| Educational Statistics | 59,000 | 68,000 |
| Educational Assessment | 35,471 | 40,000 |
| Goal 2000 | 491,000 | 491,000 |
| HEA title III: Institutional Development | 210,945 | 258,750 |
| HEA title IV-C: College Work-Study | 830,000 | 870,000 |
| HEA title VI: International Education | 60,351 | 67,536 |
| HEA title X-A: Postsecondary Education Improvement Fund | 25,200 | 50,000 |
| Inexpensive Book Distribution (RIF) | 12,000 | 18,000 |
| Museum Grants | 23,280 [3] | 23,405 [3] |
| NTIA Information Infrastructure Grants (TIIAP) | 20,000 | 18,000 |
| National Archives and Records Administration | 205,167 | 224,614 |
| National Endowment for the Arts | 98,000 | 98,000 |
| National Endowment for the Humanities | 110,700 | 110,700 |
| National Historical Publications and Records Commission | 5,500 | 10,000 |
| Next Generation Internet | 95,000 [4] | 67,000 [4] |
| Reading Excellence | — | 260,000 [5] |

1 Includes authority to obligate $30.3 million in receipts.

2 Includes authority to obligate $28 million in receipts.

3 Includes $1 million for joint library/museum projects under
  LSTA National Leadership Projects grants.

4 Includes funding for NGI divided among several federal agencies.

5 FY 1998 funding lapsed because authorization was not in place by July 1.

## Copyright Term Extension Act

On October 7 both the Senate and House passed a 20-year extension of the current life-plus-50-year copyright term (S. 505). The president signed the bill (P.L. 105-298) on October 27. The measure retains a limited exception for libraries, archives, and nonprofit educational institutions crafted in negotiations among interested parties in 1997.

## Database Protection Legislation

Conferees agreed to drop the Collections of Information Anti-Piracy Act from the Digital Millennium Copyright Act (H.R. 2281). The database protection measure would have had drastic negative effects on education and research and would have protected facts for the first time. Key legislators promised that the issue would be an early agenda item in the new Congress in 1999.

# Internet-Related Legislation

### Filtering and Blocking Software Requirements

An amendment by Rep. Ernest Istook, Jr. (R-Okla.) to the House Labor, Health and Human Services, and Education Appropriations bill would have required public schools and libraries to install software to protect children from obscenity as a condition of receiving federal funds from any federal agency for the acquisition or operation of computers accessible to minors and with access to the Internet.

S. 1619, a bill sponsored by Sen. John McCain (R-Ariz.), and a similar bill (H.R. 3177) by Rep. Bob Franks (R-N.J.), would have required libraries and schools that receive E-rate telecommunications discounts to install filtering software. Alternative language was proposed by Sen. Conrad Burns (R-Mont.) and others to require local Internet use policies rather than blocking or filtering software. This substitute would have been consistent with the need to have all such content and curriculum decisions made at the local level. Sen. McCain later had requirements similar to S. 1619 included as an amendment to the Commerce Department appropriations bill.

Both these funding bills were included in the omnibus package, which contained no requirements to have libraries or schools install and use filtering and blocking software as a condition of receiving federal funds or the E-rate. House-Senate negotiators on the Labor-HHS-Education Appropriations bill had agreed to drop the Istook amendment, and appropriators had also agreed to drop the McCain amendment from a commerce funding bill. However, as top congressional leaders negotiated a variety of issues, the Istook amendment was again under serious consideration for attachment to the omnibus bill. After much work by library advocates and others, the amendment was dropped.

### Child Online Protection Act

A revised version of Rep. Michael Oxley's (R-Ohio) bill (H.R. 3783) to prohibit the commercial distribution on the Web to minors of material that is "harmful to minors" was included in the omnibus package. The American Civil Liberties

Union, with other plaintiffs, filed suit to challenge this measure. On October 7 a revised version of Sen. Dan Coats's (R-Ind.) similar bill (S. 1492) was approved as an amendment to the Internet Tax Freedom Act (S. 442), with only Sen. Patrick Leahy (D-Vt.) voting against the measure. On the same date the House approved the Oxley bill by voice vote.

### Internet Tax Freedom Act

The Internet Tax Freedom Act, included in the omnibus package, provides a three-year moratorium on state or local taxation of the Internet. A "harmful-to-minors" provision denies this moratorium to those commercial providers who "knowingly and with knowledge of the character of the material" make "harmful-to-minors" material available to minors.

### Children's Online Privacy Protection Act

An amended version of the Children's Online Privacy Protection Act, S. 2326, was added to the omnibus package. Revisions in the bill respond to concerns expressed by ALA and others that the bill would interfere with children's access to information on the Internet. The bill imposes parental consent or notice before children (12 and under) could give any personally identifiable information to commercial Web sites targeted to children; however, nonprofit organizations are excluded from the scope of the bill. Both the Senate and House passed the measure separately on October 7.

### Next Generation Internet

H.R. 3332, the Next Generation Internet Research Act of 1998, was signed by the president on October 28 (P.L. 105-305). The law amends the High Performance Computing Act to authorize for two years (at a total of $67 and $75 million) research and development of advanced communication technology that will provide a basis for the Internet of the future.

## Literacy Issues

The Reading Excellence Act (H.R. 2614), a congressional revision of the administration's children's literacy initiative (America Reads), was also included as part of the omnibus package. For FY 1999, $260 million will flow to state and local educational agencies to improve the teaching of reading and to fund after-school and summer reading programs.

The purpose of the Reading Excellence Act, which amends Title II of the Elementary and Secondary Education Act, is to (1) provide children with the readiness skills they need to learn to read once they enter school; (2) to teach every child to read, no later than the third grade; (3) to improve the reading skills of students and the instructional practices for current teachers who teach reading; (4) to expand the number of high-quality family literacy programs; and (5) to provide early literacy intervention to children experiencing reading difficulties. School library media specialists are included in the definition of instructional staff. In addition, there are partnership opportunities for public libraries.

In the Workforce Investment Act (H.R. 1385, P.L. 105-220), Congress revised and renewed programs for vocational education, adult education and literacy, workforce investment, and the Jobs Corps.

## Postal Rate Case

A major postal rate case ended with new postal rates effective January 10, 1999. A typical three-pound library rate package will increase from the previous rate of $1.96 to $2.03. This is a 3.6 percent increase, compared with the 26.5 percent increase originally requested by the U.S. Postal Service. ALA entered the rate case (R97-1) as an intervenor to challenge the requested steep increases in the library postal rate that would have made the nonprofit library rate higher than the commercial book rate.

After some reconsideration of library rate issues, a final Library Rate schedule was issued in October, setting rates the same as the Special Rate (formerly the Commercial Book Rate) schedule. Both the Postal Rate Commission and the USPS Board of Governors indicated they were concerned with preserving the recognizable subclass of Library Rate mail.

## Universal Service Discounted Telecommunications Rates (E-rate)

The universal service program for schools and libraries, more commonly known as the education rate or E-rate, is part of the Telecommunications Act of 1996. As approved by the Federal Communications Commission in May 1997, the E-rate provides libraries and schools with up to $2.25 billion annually in discounts of 20 to 90 percent for telecommunications services, Internet access, and internal connections—with the deepest discounts for low-income and rural/high-cost areas.

The FCC on June 12 issued an order (FCC 98-120) to revise the program. The FCC froze collection rates at $325 million per quarter, extended the start-up phase over 18 rather than 12 months, prioritized internal connections to the neediest, and made administrative changes. The FCC action addressed the key points identified by congressional critics by cutting funding by 40 percent and making other changes.

Nevertheless, pressure from congressional critics and industry sources continued to intensify as the program prepared to launch. Hearings were held by both House and Senate commerce committees. Alternative methods of funding and administering the E-rate were proposed, such as through the federal excise tax on telephones and as a block grant administered by a federal agency. Congressional supporters of the E-rate held a rally.

Congress required audits and reviews of the program before it really began; but after being given a clean bill of health in these examinations, schools and libraries began receiving E-rate discount commitment letters in late November, almost three years after enactment of the E-rate. Procedures were also under way for the second round of applications and discounts.

# Legislation and Regulations Affecting Publishing in 1998

Allan R. Adler

Vice-President, Legal and Governmental Affairs
Association of American Publishers

In the second session of the 105th Congress, the interests of book and journal publishers were caught up in a number of legislative initiatives in the areas of intellectual-property protection, freedom of expression, new technologies, educational funding, and postal matters. This report summarizes legislation enacted during the second session, provides a brief report on significant bills that were not enacted but may reappear, and explains Association of American Publishers (AAP) activities concerning them.

## Digital Millennium Copyright Act

**H.R. 2281, enacted as Public Law 105-304, October 28, 1998**

The Digital Millennium Copyright Act (DMCA) implements two World Intellectual Property Organization (WIPO) copyright treaties adopted in December 1996 and addresses a number of nontreaty issues concerning copyright protection for works in digital formats. Passage of implementing legislation was a key political precondition for U.S. ratification of the treaties. When ratified by at least 30 nations, the treaties will effectively raise the international standards of copyright protection to those provided under U.S. law and establish the basis for applying them in the digital environment.

In broad terms, here are some of the ways in which the DMCA serves the interests of book and journal publishers in strengthening copyright protection in digital environments and the global marketplace:

- *Circumvention of technological measures.* The DMCA makes it illegal to manufacture or provide devices or services that circumvent encryption or other technological measures used to protect the rights of copyright owners in copyrighted works; in some cases, the act of circumventing such measures is itself outlawed.
- *Copyright Management Information (CMI).* The DMCA makes it illegal to knowingly alter, remove, or falsify CMI—or to knowingly traffic in copies of works linked with CMI that has been so altered, removed, or falsified—with an intent to enable or conceal copyright infringement.
- *Enforcement.* The DMCA establishes both civil and criminal penalties for violations of the prohibitions regarding circumvention and CMI.
- *Rights of copyright owners and related limitations.* The DMCA explicitly preserves, without modification, existing rights of copyright owners and the limitations on such rights, including fair use.
- *Clarification of online service provider (OSP) Liability.* The DMCA clarifies the rules concerning the liability of OSPs for copyright infringements

occurring on their systems and networks. Without changing existing law on what constitutes an infringement (or a defense to an infringement) or existing legal doctrines under which a party may be held responsible for infringing conduct by another (except with respect to universities and their faculty), the legislation allows OSPs to avoid liability for monetary damages and certain kinds of injunctive relief while providing incentives for OSPs to "take down" infringing material on their systems when they have knowledge, awareness or notice of such material.

- *Concerns of libraries and educational institutions.* The DMCA addresses concerns of potential adverse effects from the anticircumvention provisions on these entities and other users of copyrighted works, without legalizing a market in circumvention devices or creating a fair-use "right of access" to copyrighted works. The legislation also "updates" current copyright law exemptions for library preservation and replacement of copyrighted works by permitting limited use of digital technologies for such purposes and provides for a study to be done by the Copyright Office on issues regarding the "updating" of current copyright law exemptions for the use of copyrighted works in the provision of distance education.

In mid-November the Register of Copyrights published a *Federal Register* Notice of Request for Information to initiate the Distance Education Study mandated by the DMCA. AAP submitted its preliminary comments by the December deadline and expected to participate in hearings and meetings to be held by the Register of Copyrights from late January through March. The report to Congress was due in late April 1999. In November the Register of Copyrights also issued preliminary rules regarding the designation of agents by online service providers to receive notices from copyright owners of infringing activity on the OSPs' systems or networks under Title II of the DMCA.

## Sonny Bono Copyright Term Extension Act

### S. 505, enacted as Public Law 105-298, October 27, 1998

The term extension legislation, dedicated to the late songwriter-performer and congressman from California, extends the terms of copyright protection under U.S. law by an additional 20 years in order to make them equal to those provided under European law and thereby avoid competitive disadvantage to U.S. copyright owners of works distributed in Europe. The legislation had been stalled for nearly five years in Congress by an unrelated dispute over music licensing. With the incorporation in the legislation of a compromise on the latter issue, the term extension bill was quickly approved in the House and Senate.

Here are the highlights of the term extension legislation:

- *Extension of duration of copyright.* In general, the legislation extends the duration of the various terms of copyright, including that for unpublished works, by an additional 20 years; it does not, however, restore copyright protection to works that have already entered the public domain.

- *Termination rights.* The legislation provides a limited revival of termination rights (other than in works for hire) for a work subsisting in its renewal term on the effective date of the legislation (i.e., 90 days after the date of enactment) where the author or owner of the termination right has not previously exercised such right. It specifies the conditions under which the exclusive or nonexclusive grant of a transfer or license of the renewal copyright, or any right under it, executed before January 1, 1978, by any in a group of designated persons, other than by will, is subject to termination. It also specifies that the author's executor, administrator, personal representative, or trustee shall own the author's entire termination interest in the event that the author's widow or widower, children, and grandchildren are not living.

- *Use by libraries and archives.* Because of complaints from these entities that the legislation would extend copyright protection to works that otherwise would have entered the public domain, the legislation provides that, during the last 20 years of any term of copyright of a published work (i.e., the additional term added by the legislation), a library or archives (including a nonprofit educational institution that functions as such) may reproduce, distribute, display, or perform the work (including in digital form) for purposes of preservation, scholarship, or research, without the permission of the copyright owner, if it determines upon reasonable investigation that (1) the work is not subject to normal commercial exploitation, or (2) a copy or phonorecord of the work cannot be obtained at a reasonable price. In addition, the legislation provides that the copyright owner or its agent may establish that neither of these conditions applies by providing notice to the Copyright Office pursuant to regulations issued by the Register of Copyrights.

At the request of the bill's sponsors, AAP worked with the Register of Copyrights and representatives of the library, educational, and archival communities in an effort to reach consensus on an exemption provision that would, under certain conditions, permit these communities to make specified uses of copyrighted works during the extension period without having to pay or obtain permission from the rights holders. Although these negotiations did not produce a consensus compromise, the final legislation contains the Register of Copyrights' version of the near-negotiated exemption provision, which is acceptable to AAP members. In December 1998 the Copyright Office issued an interim regulation regarding the form of the notice that the copyright owner or its agent may file to inform libraries and archives (including nonprofit educational institutions functioning as such) that the conditions invoking the exemption do not apply.

## Trademark Law Treaty Implementation Act

**S. 2193, enacted as Public Law 105-330, October 30, 1998**

In June 1998, while most advocates of intellectual property rights focused their attention on legislation to implement the WIPO copyright treaties, the Senate quietly ratified the Trademark Law Treaty (TLT), an international agreement that was adopted in 1994 and signed by 35 nations for the purpose of harmonizing and simplifying the procedures for trademark registration around the world. The harmonization that TLT brings to international registration practices is particularly important to small American businesses that want to register their marks overseas but are unable to do so because of the costs and burdens of attempting to meet complicated formal requirements that differ in many countries. Through TLT's list of maximum registration requirements, such businesses will be able to secure better international protection against trademark infringement and dilution.

Shortly before its final adjournment in October, Congress passed implementing legislation to bring U.S. law into conformity with the TLT, and the president subsequently signed it into law. The main features of the legislation are as follows:

- The act amends U.S. trademark law to conform it to TLT requirements regarding application for trademark registration (or for bona fide intention to use a trademark), revival of abandoned applications, duration of registration, cancellation of registration, affidavits of continued use, renewal of registration, and recording assignment of a trademark. These amendments take effect either one year from the date of enactment or upon entry into force of the TLT with respect to the United States, whichever occurs first.
- The act also makes technical corrections to the Trademark Act and addresses the use of certification marks for promotional purposes.

The Trademark Law Treaty had already entered into force by the time of these congressional actions, with some 21 nations as parties.

## Children's Online Protection Act

**H.R. 3783, S. 1482; enacted as Title XIV of Public Law 105-277, October 21, 1998**

After a 1997 ruling by the U.S. Supreme Court in *ACLU* v. *Reno* struck down provisions of the Communications Decency Act (CDA) that prohibited online transmission of "indecent materials" to children, some members of Congress studied the court's rationale in the case and attempted to craft new legislation that would avoid the constitutional flaws of the CDA while achieving its basic purpose of using criminal law to limit the availability of sexually explicit materials to children on the Internet.

The resulting Children's Online Protection Act (COPA) was passed by the House in October and then was approved by the Senate as part of the end-of-the-session omnibus appropriations bill.

To avoid the fate of the CDA, which was held to violate First Amendment freedom-of-speech protections because its "indecent materials" restrictions were both vague and overbroad, legislators sought to give COPA a more narrow and specific scope. Thus, where the CDA made it a crime for anyone to knowingly transmit "indecent materials" to any minor by any means, the COPA offense is limited to knowing commercial distribution of more narrowly defined "harmful-to-minors" material by means of the World Wide Web. In response to the Supreme

Court's criticism of other aspects of the CDA, COPA makes the use of age verification systems a legitimate defense for commercial purveyors of pornography, lowers the "minority" standard to persons under 17 years of age, and does not restrict parental choice to make sexually explicit materials available to a minor.

The following are the main features of the new legislation:

- COPA makes it a felony under federal law for anyone to knowingly or intentionally make a communication over the World Wide Web for commercial purposes if such communication contains materials that are "harmful to minors" and is made available to any minor.

- COPA defines "harmful to minors" consistent with a combination of the Supreme Court's Ginsberg and Miller standards, which include the requirement that the material at issue "taken as a whole, lacks serious literary, artistic, political, or scientific value for minors."

- COPA provides an affirmative defense against prosecution to a defendant who, in good faith, has restricted access to such material by minors through requirement of a credit card, debit account, adult access code, or adult personal identification number; a digital certificate of age verification; or by "any other reasonable measures that are feasible under available technology."

- COPA provides an exemption from liability for telecommunications carriers, Internet access providers, and other persons who provide services that facilitate a communication made by another person without selecting or altering the content of the communication.

- COPA obligates a "provider of interactive computer service" to inform all new customers about commercially available "parental control protections" that may assist the customers in limiting access to material that is harmful to minors.

- COPA establishes a temporary Commission on Online Child Protection which, within a year of the statute's enactment, must report to Congress on its analyses, conclusions, and recommendations regarding technologies and methods to reduce access by minors to material on the Internet that is harmful to minors.

COPA was challenged on First Amendment grounds in a lawsuit brought by the ACLU in Philadelphia immediately after the new law was signed in October. The federal court issued a temporary restraining order preventing the Justice Department from enforcing the statute and at year's end was weighing a preliminary injunction request. AAP, which was a plaintiff in the successful CDA lawsuit, did not join the hurriedly filed COPA lawsuit. However, AAP's Freedom to Read Committee believes that, notwithstanding its narrower scope, COPA is no less constitutionally flawed than the CDA and plans to work with the Citizens Internet Empowerment Coalition (CIEC) to develop plans for opposing COPA and engaging the temporary commission on the study mandated by COPA. (Another potential issue is the constitutional validity of provisions in the newly enacted Internet Tax Freedom Act that exclude persons engaged in COPA conduct from the legislation's moratorium on new Internet taxes.)

## Children's Online Privacy Protection Act

**S. 2326, enacted as Title XIII of Public Law 105-277, October 21, 1998**

Apart from its application to the content of digital communications, "privacy on the Internet" has become a major public concern in connection with the collection, dissemination, and use of personally identifiable information from and about Internet users by commercial enterprises. Prodded by alarming reports in the press and from public-interest groups during the past few years, the White House and a number of individual legislators (along with the Federal Trade Commission) have been threatening to impose federal regulation if Internet entrepreneurs do not develop effective self-enforced industry standards and fair information practices to provide meaningful privacy protections for online consumers. Finally, Congress decided to act.

Passed by the Senate as an amendment to the Internet Tax Freedom Act, the Children's Online Privacy Protection Act (COPPA) was approved by Congress and enacted into law as part of the end-of-the-year omnibus appropriations legislation.

The following are the main features of the new legislation:

- COPPA requires the FTC, within a year of enactment, to issue regulations regarding unfair and deceptive acts and practices by commercial Web site operators and online service providers in connection with their online collection and use of "personal information" from and about children under 13 years of age.
- COPPA makes it unlawful for an operator of a commercial Web site or online service "directed to children"—or for any operator acting with "actual knowledge" of what it is collecting—to collect "personal information" from a child in a manner that violates the FTC regulations.
- Under the COPPA-mandated regulations, such an operator must (1) provide notice on the Web site or service of what information is collected from children, how such information is used, and the operator's disclosure practices regarding such information; (2) obtain, except in enumerated cases, "verifiable parental consent" for collection, use, or disclosure of personal information from children; (3) provide, upon request and proper identification of a parent, a description of personal information collected from the parent's child; the opportunity to refuse further use or maintenance of such information in retrievable form or future online collection of such information; and a reasonable means for the parent to obtain such information; (4) refrain from conditioning prize offers, games, or other activities on a child's disclosing more personal information than reasonably necessary to participate in such activity; and (5) establish and maintain reasonable procedures to protect the confidentiality, security, and integrity of such information.
- COPPA also permits such operators to satisfy the requirements of the mandated FTC regulations through compliance with "self-regulatory guidelines" issued by the "marketing or online industries" or "other persons" that have been approved by the FTC as meeting its regulatory requirements.

- COPPA provides for enforcement of the FTC regulations through civil actions brought by state attorneys general, as well as by the FTC.

Book publishers that are Web site operators must comply with COPPA, including where their use of technological measures and other online practices to maintain copyright protection for their products involves the collection and use of personal information from children. AAP will monitor and, as appropriate, participate in the mandated FTC rule making. COPPA becomes effective 18 months after the date of enactment, or on the date on which the FTC rules on the first "safe harbor" application if more than a year from enactment, but in no case later than 30 months after the date of enactment. Not later than five years after the effective date of its regulations, the FTC must review and report to Congress regarding the implementation of COPPA and its effects on online practices.

## Internet Tax Freedom Act

### S. 442, enacted as Title XI of Public Law 105-277, October 21, 1998

Efforts to enact a moratorium on the imposition of state and local taxes on Internet commerce, as part of a national policy against state and local regulation of such commerce, began more than two years ago. However, legislation was slowed by opposition from state and local government officials concerned about the prospective elimination of significant potential revenues and what some perceived to be the creation of an unlevel playing field between competing online and offline businesses.

Another wrinkle in dealing with the concerns of "Main Street" merchants was an effort advanced by the National Governor's Association and other state and local government officials to use the Internet tax legislation to finally address the long-simmering dispute over whether Congress should, under the Interstate Commerce Clause, give states the right to require out-of-state collection of sales and "use" taxes by mail order catalog houses that sell and deliver remotely purchased goods into a state. Other thorny issues included the length of the imposed moratorium, what kinds of taxes would be subject to the moratorium, and whether Congress should grandfather certain existing taxes.

Senate passage of the Internet tax legislation after lengthy negotiations and debate over these issues led to enactment of the Internet Tax Freedom Act as part of the end-of-the-year omnibus appropriations legislation. Highlights of the act include the following:

- For a period beginning October 1, 1998, and ending three years after the date of enactment, the act bars any state or local government from imposing "taxes on Internet access" (unless such tax was "generally imposed and actually enforced" prior to October 1) and "multiple or discriminatory taxes on electronic commerce."
- The act defines "tax" in this context as any government charge imposed for the purpose of generating government revenues, but excludes any "fee" imposed for a specific privilege, service, or benefit conferred.

- The act provides that none of its provisions affect liability or related ongoing litigation regarding taxes "accrued and enforced" before the date of enactment.

- The act excludes from the moratorium (1) persons engaged in conduct that violates the Children's Online Protection Act, and (2) Internet access providers who fail to offer their new customers "screening software" that permits the customer to limit access to Internet material that is "harmful to minors."

- The act establishes a temporary Advisory Commission on Electronic Commerce to conduct a thorough study of federal, state, local, and international taxation and tariff treatment of Internet transactions and other comparable intrastate, interstate, or international sales activities. Members of the commission must be appointed before the end of this year, and the commission's study report—including any legislative recommendations required to address its findings—must be submitted to Congress no later than 18 months after enactment. Such recommendations must be "tax and technologically neutral and apply to all forms of remote commerce" and will be included in the report only if approved by at least two-thirds of the commission's members.)

In addition to the secretary of the treasury, the secretary of commerce, and the U.S. trade representative, the commission will consist of 16 congressional appointees, including the governors of Virginia, Utah, and Washington, and top executives from Time Warner, Netscape, America Online, AT&T, MCI/Worldcom, Gateway, and Cisco Systems. AAP will track the start-up work of the commission, and will determine what level of participation by AAP (if any) in the commission's work is both necessary and sufficient to safeguard the interests of the book-publishing industry. With the expectation of substantial involvement in the study by the Multistate Tax Commission (an organization created by interstate compact to serve the interests of state governments in applying their tax laws to multistate and multinational enterprises), AAP may also consider whether to participate in one or more of the coalitions likely to emerge on behalf of the interests of commercial enterprises that engage in online transactions.

## Next Generation Internet Research Act

**H.R. 3332, enacted as Public Law 105-305, October 28, 1998**

The explosive growth in Internet traffic and its increasing importance to commerce, education, and research have highlighted the need for new technologies to increase the speed and capacity of the network. At the same time, an ongoing debate has focused on how to ensure protection of trademark rights in connection with Internet domain names, while adding new generic top-level domains (GTLDs) to allow more individuals and businesses to obtain Internet addresses that closely reflect their names and functions. (Currently, there are two classes of TLDs: generic TLDs, such as ".com," ".org," ".edu," and ".gov," and country code TLDs, such as ".us" and ".uk.")

The Clinton administration's Next Generation Internet (NGI) initiative for developing technologies that will help the Internet keep pace with increased user demands drew strong bipartisan support in the House and was passed by the Senate with no debate. Most of the official enthusiasm for the legislation focused on expectations that the NGI program will, for example, connect 100 NGI sites at 100 times the speed of today's Internet. But the legislation's mandate for a comprehensive study of trademark issues associated with the addition of new GTLDs and the establishment of related dispute resolution procedures is also viewed as a critical e-commerce measure aimed at reconciling conflicting proprietary and entrepreneurial interests with consumer interests in locating preferred brands or vendors online without confusion or deception.

The legislation's NGI program provisions identify participating federal agencies; set forth purposes, objectives, and reporting requirements; and provide funding authorization for the development program, while placing responsibility for assessing the program's success on the President's Information Technology Advisory Committee, a policy-coordinating body established by executive order two years ago.

The trademark rights/domain names study provisions require the secretary of commerce to request the National Research Council (NRC) of the National Academy of Sciences to study and, as appropriate, make recommendations regarding the effects on trademark rights of adding new GTLDs and establishing related dispute resolution procedures. An interim report to the secretary and Congress is due no later than four months after enactment, with a final report due no later than nine months after enactment.

Increasing the speed and bandwidth of the Internet will place greater emphasis on AAP's work concerning a variety of online copyright protection issues, including technological measures, copyright management information, and distance education. This is especially true because the NGI program assumes that major universities will be among the key "research partner institutions" serving as linked sites and test beds for the development of the new technologies. With respect to the domain name study, publishers obviously have as much interest in protecting their trademarks from online infringement and dilution as do other entrepreneurs. In the context of ongoing efforts to privatize the management of Internet names and addresses, the NRC's work will be important. The interim report will be released shortly before the expected March 1999 release of the results of a similar study being conducted by the World Intellectual Property Organization (WIPO); the final NRC report will then be able to take into account the conclusions and recommendations of the WIPO study. Either through its membership in the International Intellectual Property Alliance (IIPA) or on its own, AAP may want to consider participating in coalition work concerning these studies and the issues they address.

## Year 2000 Information and Readiness Disclosure Act
### S. 2392, enacted as Public Law 105-271, October 19, 1998

With zero hour rapidly approaching for the much-discussed "Year 2000 problem" (i.e., whether the internal clocks in millions of computer systems, software programs, and semiconductors will turn from year "99" to year "00"and properly read the latter as representing the year 2000 rather than the year 1900), Congress decided that it was critical for businesses and other organizations to communicate more openly with the public and each other regarding Year 2000 (Y2K) testing processes, proposed remedial solutions, and product readiness efforts. However, the fear that such disclosures could generate a variety of litigation was having a chilling effect on such open communications. Under the Y2K Disclosure Act, Congress has sought to mitigate this disincentive to disclosure through preemption of state and local liability laws regarding the requisite standard of care for the making of such disclosures.

The following are the main features of the legislation:

- The act provides that no Y2K readiness disclosure will be admissible in any civil action against the maker of the disclosure to prove the accuracy or truth of any Y2K statement in that disclosure, unless (1) it would serve as the basis for a claim of anticipatory breach, repudiation, or a similar contract claim; or (2) the court determines that the maker's use of the disclosure amounts to bad faith or fraud "or is otherwise beyond what is reasonable to achieve the purposes" of the act.

- The act provides that a maker of an allegedly false, inaccurate, or misleading Y2K statement will not be liable in any civil action on the basis of such statement, unless the claimant establishes that the statement was material and, to the extent it was not a republication of another's original statement, was made with (1) actual knowledge that it was false, inaccurate, or misleading, or (2) intent to deceive or mislead or with reckless disregard as to its accuracy.

- To the extent that such a statement was a republication, the maker of the republication will similarly not be liable, unless the republication was made (1) with actual knowledge that it was false, inaccurate, or misleading, (2) with intent to deceive or mislead, or (3) without notice that the maker has not verified its contents or that the maker is not the source of the republication and the republication is based on information supplied by another person.

- Similarly, the act provides that the maker of a Y2K statement will not be liable in an action for defamation or trade disparagement to the extent such action is based on an allegedly false, inaccurate, or misleading statement, unless the claimant establishes by clear and convincing evidence that the statement was made with knowledge that it was false or with reckless disregard as to its truth or falsity.

- With exceptions, the act provides that, in any case in which the adequacy of notice about Y2K processing is at issue (other than an action involving personal injury or serious physical damage to property), the posting of a notice by the responsible entity in a commercially reasonable manner and for a commercially reasonable duration on its Y2K Internet Web site will be deemed an adequate mechanism for providing such notice.

- With exceptions, the act provides that a Y2K statement cannot be interpreted as amending or altering a contract or warranty.

- With exceptions, the act provides a temporary antitrust exemption for conduct or communication that is solely for the purpose of correcting or avoiding a Y2K processing failure. The exemption applies only to such conduct occurring after the date of enactment and before July 14, 2001.
- The act requires the General Services Administration to establish a Y2K Web site to assist consumers and serve as a national clearinghouse for information about Y2K processing of systems, products, and services.

## Department of Education Appropriations Act
### H.R. 4274, enacted as Title III of Public Law 105-277, October 21, 1998

For months, the Labor-Health and Human Services-Education appropriations bill was stalled in both the House and Senate over a variety of fierce partisan policy and funding disputes. Finally, after intense negotiations involving both houses of Congress and the Clinton administration, the legislation became one of eight of the 13 fiscal year (FY) 1999 spending bills to be enacted as part of the end-of-the-year omnibus appropriations package.

In the end, the legislation provided a historic increase of $3.6 billion for the Department of Education to bring FY 1999 education funding to a total of $33.1 billion. Unmatched in terms of total dollars, the gain represented the same 12 percent increase that Congress had provided for FY 1998. Anticipating exit polls that would rank education as the voters' top national policy priority, Congress and the administration, as well as party leaders within Congress, argued publicly over who deserved credit for the appropriations largesse.

Once again, school technology projects received special generosity from Congress. Among the line items of possible interest to publishers as significantly affecting literacy, multimedia curricula, and distance-education programs are the following:

- $425 million for the Technology Literacy Challenge Fund, which is used to help integrate software and online learning resources, including Internet access and multimedia computers, into classroom curricula
- $385 million for adult education programs that focus on basic literacy and language skills under the Adult Education and Family Literacy Act, including $6 million for the National Institute for Literacy
- $260 million for new reading and literacy training grants under the Reading Excellence Act (see separate summary below)
- $166 million for libraries, marking a 13.6 percent increase in annual funding and including $2 million for digitization efforts to improve online access to the New York Public Library's collections
- $115 million for Technology Innovation Challenge Grants, which support the development of curriculum uses of technology, including the development of quality course content
- $75 million for the newly created Teacher Training in Technology Program, which provides grants for focused training of incoming teachers on how to use new technologies to enhance student learning

- $45 million for the Star Schools Program, reflecting a nearly one-third increase in annual funding for demonstration projects that use telecommunications technology to provide instructional programs for students and professional development activities for teachers who would not otherwise have access to them, including nearly $10 million for "a broad-based competition on utilizing distance education to improve instruction"
- $10 million for the new Learning Anytime Anywhere Partnership, the largest of a number of initiatives specifically funded in the legislation to promote distance-education programs using interactive digital networks
- $2 million for the First Book Program that makes new books available to local literacy programs

Although Congress satisfied many of the administration's goals with respect to educational spending, the legislation also includes a prohibition on federally sponsored testing that continues the FY 1998 appropriations bill's rebuff of the administration's efforts to develop and administer so-called "voluntary national testing" for fourth grade reading and eighth grade mathematics without specific congressional authorization.

The new legislation permits the National Assessment Governing Board (NAGB) to proceed with very limited test development activities, but specifically bars any pilot testing, field testing, administration, or distribution of individualized national tests that are not explicitly provided for in authorizing legislation enacted by Congress. (At present, there is no such authority for such tests.) The legislation also requires the NAGB to "clearly articulate" and report to Congress on the purpose and intended use of the proposed national tests; at the same time, it requires NAGB to respond to a September 1998 National Academy of Sciences (NAS) report that criticized the National Assessment of Educational Progress (NAEP) tests on which the proposed national tests were to be modeled. Finally, the legislation authorizes NAS to study the technical feasibility, validity, and reliability of imbedding test items from NAEP or other tests in state and district assessments of fourth grade reading and eighth grade math. Each of these reports is due by October 1999.

## Reading Excellence Act

### H.R. 2614, enacted as Title VIII of Public Law 105-277, October 21, 1998

Although Republicans and Democrats agree that illiteracy continues to be a grave national problem as we enter the 21st century, they have different ideas about how federal funds should be used to improve reading ability. This became clear in April 1997 when the Clinton administration introduced its America Reads Challenge initiative as a legislative proposal.

The administration's initiative sought appropriations to give children extra-school help in reading during afternoons, weekends, and summer vacations through the use of tutors who would be enlisted and trained to provide individualized and small-group assistance. The funds would be used to pay for 30,000 reading specialists who would train about 1 million volunteer tutors under the management of the administration's AmeriCorps program. Additional funds would pay for a Parents as First Teachers program to support parental efforts to help their children become successful readers by the end of the third grade.

But this approach was unacceptable to congressional Republicans, who preferred to focus federal resources on improving the reading ability of children by ensuring that teachers of reading have access to the best research on how reading is most effectively taught. Although they agreed to the administration's request for $260 million in appropriations to fund a major national reading initiative in FY 1999 and FY 2000, the Republicans reshaped the administration's initiative so that the funding would be used primarily to improve in-service instructional practices for teachers who teach reading. After lengthy negotiations with the administration over a House-passed version of this legislation, the Reading Excellence Act was enacted and signed into law as part of the end-of-the-year omnibus appropriations legislation.

The main features of the Act are as follows:

- The act creates a two-year competitive grant program for states to assist children having difficulty with reading, specifying the application process and approval standards by which the secretary of education may award a grant to one state educational agency in each state for the establishment of a "reading and literacy partnership."

- In awarding grants of not less than $500,000, the act requires the secretary to give priority to applications from state educational agencies that commit to changing the training and methods of teaching reading required for state certification as an elementary school teacher to reflect what it defines as "scientifically based reading research."

- Local educational agencies may apply to recipient state agencies for a subgrant, preferably as part of a partnership with one or more community-based organizations of demonstrated effectiveness in reading achievement for adults and/or children (such as a Head Start program, family literacy program, adult education program, or public library). Such subgrants must be used to advance reform of reading instruction in the neediest schools. Among other things, funding may be used to purchase curricular and other supporting materials and to promote reading programs that provide access to engaging reading material.

- The act establishes a requirement for the secretary to conduct a national assessment of funded programs, for the National Institute for Literacy to disseminate information on scientifically based reading research and subgrantee projects, and for recipient state educational agencies to evaluate the success of their subgrantees by (at a minimum) measuring the extent to which intended student beneficiaries have improved their reading skills.

- The act amends, repeals, or consolidates a number of federal educational and job-training programs and authorizes competitive grants to enable states to plan and implement statewide family literacy initiatives to coordinate or integrate existing federal, state, and local literacy resources.

# Higher Education Amendments of 1998

### H.R. 6, enacted as Public Law 105-244, October 7, 1998

The major policy and funding authorization issues for Congress in its reauthorization and revision of the Higher Education Act (HEA) focused on (1) new unified initiatives to strengthen teacher training for elementary and secondary schools, (2) improvement and expansion of financial-aid opportunities for students through increased Pell Grants and lower-interest student loans, (3) continuing support for college and university technology programs, and (4) an overall streamlining of programs through consolidation and elimination of unnecessary regulatory requirements.

Of particular interest to educational publishers, however, are the ways in which the HEA amendments, with strong support in Congress and the Clinton administration, emphasize the growth of expanded distance education opportunities for higher education. Although Congress did not go as far as the administration's proposal to treat distance education programs the same as traditional campus-based programs for purposes of Title IV funding eligibility, the legislation does the following:

- The HEA includes a five-year authorization for a new Learning Anytime Anywhere Partnerships program, through which eligible partnerships of colleges or universities, community organizations, and other public and private institutions, agencies, and organizations may apply to the secretary of education for grant funds amounting to 50 percent of the cost of a project to develop and assess model distance-learning programs or innovative educational software for postsecondary education and career-oriented lifelong learning. Congress has authorized and appropriated $10 million for this program in FY 1999.
- The HEA authorizes Distance Education Demonstration Programs that will be monitored by the secretary to test the quality and viability of expanded distance education programs for purposes of determining whether certain current statutory and regulatory requirements for such programs may be altered to afford greater access to distance education opportunities with an appropriate level of federal grant and loan support. The secretary is authorized to waive certain regulatory restrictions and requirements for the programs, which are generally limited to participation by institutions of higher education eligible for Title IV spending. The legislation, however, specifically makes the Western Governors University (solely a distance-education institution) eligible to participate, while limiting first-year participation to not more than 15 institutions, systems of institutions, or consortia of institutions; in the third year of the program, the secretary may add as many as 35 additional eligible participants. The secretary must report to Congress within 18 months of initiating the demonstration program, as well as on an annual basis thereafter regarding program evaluation and current policies that impede development and use of distance education. The statute defines "distance education" for the purposes of these programs.

The HEA amendments also include the Web-Based Education Commission Act, which establishes the commission through appointment of 14 members not later than 45 days after the date of enactment and requires its initial meeting to occur no later than 30 days after the completion of appointments. The commission is required to hold public hearings, and report to Congress and the president not later than six months after its first meeting, for the purpose of "assessing the educational software available in retail markets for secondary and postsecondary students who choose to use such software." The report shall present the commission's findings and conclusions, together with recommendations (1) for legislation and administrative actions, as deemed appropriate, and (2) "regarding the appropriate federal role in determining the quality of educational software products." The commission will terminate 90 days after its report is submitted.

## Adult Education and Family Literacy Act
### Title II of H.R. 1385, enacted as Public Law 105-220, August 7, 1998

The newly enacted Workforce Investment Act consolidates more than 50 federal employment, training, and literacy programs—including the National Literacy Act, Adult Education Act, and Job Training Partnership Act—into three block grants to the states: one for adult education and family literacy, one for disadvantaged youth, and one for adult employment and training.

Title II of the act, entitled the Adult Education and Family Literacy Act, replaces the Adult Education Act while reauthorizing the federal investment in adult education and family literacy for five more years. Although the Workforce Investment Act maximizes the integration of all three kinds of federal services for eligible individuals through a collaborative planning process at the state level, the administration, operation, funding, and reporting of adult education and family literacy remain separate.

Under the new law, family literacy programs are put on equal footing with adult basic education and English as a second language (ESL) services for purposes of state grant funding. For FY 1999 Congress has appropriated $385 million for these adult education and family literacy programs. Grants to the states are based on a formula that, in part, takes into account the number of adults age 16–61 in a state without a high school diploma or its equivalent. Organizations eligible to apply to their state agency for a grant of these funds include local education agencies, institutions of higher education, libraries, public housing authorities, community-based and volunteer literacy organizations of demonstrated effectiveness, and other public or private nonprofit organizations that can provide literacy services.

The Adult Education and Family Literacy Act also includes provisions reauthorizing the National Institute for Literacy and the Department of Education's national leadership program on literacy. Both of these programs are dedicated to advancing literacy standards and performance throughout the nation.

## Head Start Amendments of 1998

**Title I of S. 2206, enacted as Public Law 105-285, October 27, 1998**

Enacted as Title I of the Community Opportunities, Accountability, and Training and Educational Services Act of 1998, the Head Start Amendments reauthorize the highly successful Head Start Act for the five-year period from 1999 through 2003.

Since its inception as part of the Johnson administration's War on Poverty in 1964, Head Start has been one of the nation's most important programs for fighting crime and poverty through early provision of comprehensive social, educational, medical, and nutritional services for disadvantaged children. For FY 1999, Congress has appropriated $4.66 billion for Head Start programs, which are administered by the Department of Health and Human Services directly to state agency grantees.

Increasingly, family literacy services for the development of reading skills through qualified instruction built upon "scientifically based reading research" are becoming a focal point for achieving the act's purpose of promoting school readiness through enhancement of the social and cognitive development of low-income children. The legislation directs the secretary to establish "evaluation methods that measure the effectiveness and impact" of family literacy service program models and to use not less than $3 million of appropriated funds to provide technical assistance and training to Head Start agencies to improve the quality of their family literacy services.

This year, with Congress initiating requirements for "education performance standards" to measure program outcomes and ensure the school readiness of children completing Head Start programs, amendments to the act explicitly set forth additional standards to ensure that, at a minimum, participating children (among other things) "develop and demonstrate an appreciation of books." The same standard in the new legislation is part of new "professional requirements" criteria for Head Start classroom teachers.

## Non-Enacted Legislation Relevant to AAP Policy Priorities

Among the many pieces of legislation that had only limited success in working their way through Congress, but could well reappear, are the following of interest to the publishing industry:

### Database Protection Legislation

The proposed Collections of Information Antipiracy Act—a bill to protect database producers against the misappropriation of their databases—was passed by the House as a freestanding bill (H.R. 2652) last May. When it failed to generate any momentum in the Senate, House proponents revised it and passed it a second time in August as an amendment to the House version of the WIPO copyright treaty implementation legislation (H.R. 2281). However, continuing opposition to use restrictions in the legislation from the scientific, educational, and library communities, as well as some commercial enterprises, resulted in the database title being stripped from the WIPO legislation in conference, and H.R. 2652 languished as the 105th Congress ended.

This legislation was certain to return. AAP, reflecting the divided views of its members, will support the enactment of a misappropriation-based bill like H.R. 2652, provided that the legislation adequately ensures that book publishers and others can engage in transformative uses of protected databases and their contents without running afoul of its prohibitions against misappropriation.

### Encryption Legislation

Encryption—the use of complex numerical sequences to "scramble" electronic transmissions in order to preserve the confidentiality, integrity, or authenticity of communications—is a key tool for providing the privacy, security, and intellectual-property protection necessary to grow the Internet as a thriving medium for commerce, education, and entertainment. However, the government's fear that the availability of unbreakable encryption will further the activities of terrorist or other criminal enterprises has caused it to place export restrictions on the most advanced and secure forms of encryption, despite objections from U.S. industries that such restrictions hamper their ability to compete in a global marketplace where strong encryption remains available to and from foreign competitors.

Although five House committees (H.R. 695) and the Senate Commerce Committee (S. 909) approved different measures addressing export controls and restrictions on the domestic use, sale, or import of encryption technologies (including the use of mandatory key escrow systems), no consensus developed for floor consideration.

Encryption legislation is likely to be resurrected. AAP did not take a public position or actively lobby on any of the versions of legislation that were pending before Congress during 1998. However, in light of the importance of encryption for online copyright protection and electronic commerce, AAP will at least continue to monitor the debate.

### Postal Reform Legislation

Time ran out on efforts to enact comprehensive postal reform legislation in the 105th Congress. The proposed Postal Reform Act (H.R. 22) finally advanced through the House Subcommittee on the Postal Service, but it made no further progress toward enactment. In the previous Congress, AAP had testified before the subcommittee in general support of an earlier version of H.R. 22. Its testimony focused on proposed changes to the rate-making process, praising those that would provide for negotiated rate agreements, market tests for experimental new products, the institution of price caps, and a five-year cycle for rate adjustments. However, AAP expressed concerns about proposals to downgrade the significance of "content" as a rate-making criterion, distinguish between competitive and noncompetitive product categories, and provide an "exigent circumstances" exception to the five-year rate-making cycle for noncompetitive products.

Other postal bills were introduced in the 105th Congress but failed to even generate hearings. One such bill, the proposed Postal Financing Reform Act (S. 1296), was withdrawn and then reintroduced in a revised version that addressed concerns that a provision allowing the U.S. Postal Service (USPS) broad discretion to invest in equity ventures could permit USPS to buy out competitors such as UPS or Federal Express. Still, the measure went nowhere. Two other pending postal bills (S. 1107 and H.R. 198), both of which cut against the grain of H.R. 22's reform proposals by seeking to impose new restrictions on USPS activities, similarly saw no action.

It is likely that postal reform legislation will be reintroduced. If that occurs, AAP will monitor and, as appropriate, participate in the legislative process.

# Funding Programs and Grant-Making Agencies

## National Endowment for the Humanities

1100 Pennsylvania Ave. N.W., Washington, DC 20506
202-606-8400, 800-634-1121
E-mail: info@neh.fed.us
World Wide Web: http://www.neh.fed.us

### Thomas C. Phelps

> Democracy demands wisdom and vision in its citizens.
> —National Foundation on the Arts and Humanities Act of 1965

In order to "promote progress and scholarship in the humanities and the arts in the United States," Congress enacted the National Foundation on the Arts and the Humanities Act of 1965. This act established the National Endowment for the Humanities (NEH) as an independent grant-making agency of the federal government to support research, education, and public programs in the humanities. In the act, the term *humanities* includes, but is not limited to, the study of the following: language, both modern and classical; linguistics; literature; history; jurisprudence; philosophy; archaeology; comparative religion; ethics; the history, criticism, and theory of the arts; those aspects of the social sciences that have humanistic content and employ humanistic methods; and the study and application of the humanities to the human environment, with particular attention to reflecting our diverse heritage, traditions, and history and to the relevance of the humanities to the current conditions of national life.

In the words of William R. Ferris, Chair of the National Endowment for the Humanities, "There has never been a more crucial time for the presence of the humanities in civic life. We must open the doors and windows of academe and reach out to the public through teaching, preservation, research, and public programming. NEH grants and partnerships with state councils, corporations, and foundations promise to lead the way. The 1999 granting cycles offer an opportunity for individuals and institutions to accomplish their best work in the humanities fields, work that will extend far into the 21st century. The Challenge Grants initiative for public libraries will help those facilities plan long-term programming. Another initiative, planning grants for schools and libraries for the new millennium, foresees a future where entire schools are networked into the finest examples of humanities through technology. Our schools and libraries are where young minds are cultivated; our goal is to leave no one behind. These efforts, and other works of the National Endowment for the Humanities, will help the humanities endure and flourish in the future and provide all Americans with the wisdom and vision to be the best citizens of this country."

To assist with this goal of providing Americans with the means and resources for effective citizenship, NEH supports projects in three divisions: Preservation and Access, Public Programs, and Research and Education Programs. Through its Challenge Grant program, it supports institutions that in some way enhance the humanities in American life to raise needed resources. Through its Office of Enterprise, NEH works with other agencies, foundations, and corporations to bring a full complement of programs to the American people in new and dynamic ways. And through its office of Federal/State Partnerships, the endowment fosters public understanding of the humanities throughout the nation, primarily through locally developed programs aimed at general audiences. To reach this goal, NEH provides support for state humanities councils every state, the District of Columbia, Puerto Rico, the U.S. Virgin Islands, the Northern Mariana Islands, American Samoa, and Guam. (See state council addresses and telephone numbers at the end of this article, or visit the NEH home page at http://www.neh.fed.us.)

## What the Endowment Supports

NEH supports exemplary work to advance and disseminate knowledge in all disciplines of the humanities. Endowment support is intended to assist cultural and educational institutions and complement private and local efforts. In the most general terms, NEH-supported projects aid scholarship and research in the humanities, help improve humanities education, and foster a greater curiosity about and understanding of the humanities.

## Whom the Endowment Supports

NEH welcomes applications from nonprofit associations, institutions, and organizations. Applicants are encouraged to consult with NEH staff before submitting a formal proposal. Given enough lead time, staff will comment on draft proposals and assist applicants when appropriate.

## Applying for a Grant

Grant applicants are encouraged to consult with NEH staff by phone, letter, or e-mail before submitting a formal proposal. Given sufficient notice, NEH staff will comment on draft proposals and work with the applicant to submit a competitive application. Those planning to apply for NEH assistance should write to the appropriate division or office, briefly describing the proposed project and requesting guidelines and application forms. Applications and forms are available from the Public Information Office or the NEH Web site at http://www.neh.gov. The endowment does not maintain a general mailing list; instead, it responds to specific requests for publications by mail, phone, or e-mail.

# How Applications are Evaluated

Each application is assessed first by knowledgeable persons outside the agency who are asked for their judgments about the quality and significance of the proposed project. In fiscal year (FY) 1995 about 1,200 scholars, professionals in the humanities, and other experts—such as librarians, curators, and filmmakers—served on approximately 225 panels. Panelists represent a diversity of disciplinary, institutional, regional, and cultural backgrounds. In some programs the judgment of panelists is supplemented by reviews from specialists who have extensive knowledge of the specific subject or technical aspects of the application.

The advice of evaluators is assembled by the staff of the endowment, who comment on matters of fact or on significant issues that would otherwise be missing from the review. These materials are forwarded to the National Council on the Humanities, a board of 26 citizens nominated by the president of the United States and confirmed by the Senate. The National Council meets three times a year to advise the NEH chair about matters of policy and about applications. The chair, who is appointed for a four-year term by the president of the United States with consent of the Senate, takes into account the advice provided by panelists, reviewers, NEH staff, and members of the National Council, and, by law, makes the final decision about funding. A final decision can normally be expected about six months after the application deadline. Final decisions made by the chair may not be appealed, but revised submissions are encouraged and accepted.

# Grantmaking Programs

## Public Programs

The division fosters public understanding and appreciation of the humanities by supporting projects that bring significant insights of the disciplines of the humanities to general audiences of all ages through interpretive exhibitions, radio and television programs, lectures, symposia, conferences, multimedia projects, printed materials, and reading and discussion groups.

Grants support projects that lead to the study of books, new technologies, and other resources found in collections housed in libraries and archives. Projects can be in many formats, including reading and discussion programs, lectures, symposia, and interpretive exhibitions of books, manuscripts, and other library resources. Useful supplementary materials—such as publications, media components, educational programming material, and curriculum guides—also receive support through grants from this division.

The division also makes grants for the planning, scripting, and production of television and radio programs as well as for exhibitions of cultural artifacts and other resources found in the collections of museums and historical sites.

Small awards are also made for consultation grants in all programs within the Division of Public Programs. These grants are designed to enable organizations whose projects are in the early stages to confer with scholars and/or experienced programmers to help place the project on firmer humanities footing.

Eligible applicants:     Nonprofit institutions and organizations, including public television and radio stations and state humanities councils

Application deadlines:     May 17 and September 13, 1999 (consultation grants)
November 2, 1999 (planning grants only)
February 1, 2000 (planning and implementation)

Information:     202-606-8267
E-mail: publicpgms@neh.fed.us

### Preservation and Access

In this division, grants are made for projects that will create, preserve, or increase the availability of resources important for research, education, and public programming in the humanities. Projects may encompass books, journals, newspapers, manuscript and archival materials, maps, still and moving images, sound recordings, and objects of material culture held by libraries, archives, museums, historical organizations, and other repositories.

Support may be sought to preserve the intellectual content and aid bibliographic control of collections; to compile bibliographies, descriptive catalogs, and guides to cultural holdings; to create dictionaries, encyclopedias, databases, and other types of research tools and reference works; and to stabilize material-culture collections through the appropriate housing and storing of objects, improved environmental control, and the installation of security, lighting, and fire prevention systems. Applications may also be submitted for national and regional education and training projects, regional preservation field service programs, and research and demonstration projects that are intended to enhance institutional practice and the use of technology for preservation and access. Proposals may combine preservation and access activities with a single project.

Eligible applicants:     Individuals, nonprofit institutions and cultural organizations, associations, state agencies, and institutional consortia

Application deadline:     July 1, 1999

Information:     202-606-8570
E-mail: preservation@neh.fed.us

## Research and Education

Through grants to educational institutions, fellowships to scholars and teachers, and the support of significant research, this division's programs are designed to strengthen sustained, thoughtful study of the humanities at all levels of education.

### Education Development and Demonstration

Grants, including "next semester" Humanities Focus Grants, support curriculum and materials development efforts, faculty study programs within and among educational institutions, and conferences and networks of institutions. The endowment is interested in projects that help teachers use the new technologies to enhance students' understanding of the humanities.

| | |
|---|---|
| Eligible applicants: | Public and private elementary and secondary schools, school systems, colleges and universities, nonprofit academic associations, and cultural institutions, such as libraries and museums |
| Application deadlines: | Schools for the New Millennium, October 1, 1999; National Education Projects, October 15, 1999; Humanities Focus Grants, April 15, 1999 |
| Information: | 202-606-8380 |
| | E-mail: research@neh.fed.us |

### Fellowships and Stipends

Grants provide support for scholars to undertake full-time independent research and writing in the humanities. Grants are available for a maximum of one year and a minimum of six weeks of summer study.

| | |
|---|---|
| Eligible applicants: | Individuals |
| Application deadlines: | Fellowships, May 1, 1999; Summer Stipends, October 1, 1999 |
| | Faculty Graduate Study for HBCUs, March 15, 1999 |
| Information: | 202-606-8467 |
| | E-mail: research@neh.fed.us |

### Seminars and Institutes

Grants support summer seminars and national institutes in the humanities for college and school teachers. These faculty development activities are conducted at colleges and universities across the country. Those wishing to participate in seminars submit their applications to the seminar director. Lists of pending seminars and institutes are available from the program.

| | |
|---|---|
| Eligible applicants: | Individuals and institutions of higher learning |
| Application deadlines: | Participants, 1999 seminars, March 1, 1999; Directors, 2000 seminars, March 1, 1999 |
| Information: | 202-606-8463 |
| | E-mail: sem-inst@neh.fed.us |

## Challenge Grants

### Regular Challenge

Nonprofit institutions interested in developing new sources of long-term support for educational, scholarly, and preservation activities and public programs in the humanities may be assisted in these efforts by an NEH Challenge Grant. Grantees are required to raise three or four dollars in new or increased donations for every federal dollar offered. Both federal and nonfederal funds may be used to establish or increase institutional endowments and thus guarantee long-term support for a variety of humanities needs. Funds may also be used for limited direct capital expenditures where such needs are compelling and clearly related to improvements in the humanities endeavors undertaken by the institution.

| | |
|---|---|
| Eligible applicants: | Nonprofit postsecondary, educational, research, or cultural institutions and organizations, such as libraries, working within the realm of the humanities |
| Application deadline: | May 1, 1999 |
| Information: | 202-606-8309 |
| | E-mail: challenge@neh.fed.us |

## Enterprise

The Enterprise office implements endowment-wide special initiatives, creates partnerships with other federal agencies and private organizations, engages in raising funds for humanities activities, and explores other leadership opportunities for the agency.

## Federal/State Partnership

The Federal/State Partnership fosters public understanding of the humanities throughout the nation through state humanities councils in every state, the District of Columbia, Puerto Rico, the U.S. Virgin Islands, the Northern Mariana Islands, American Samoa, and Guam.

Each state council establishes its own grant guidelines and sets its own application deadlines. State humanities councils support a wide variety of projects in the humanities, including library reading programs, lectures, conferences, seminars and institutes for teachers and school administrators, media presentations, and museum and library traveling exhibitions. A list of state councils follows:

**Alabama Humanities Foundation**
2217 Tenth Ct. S.
Birmingham, AL 35205
205-930-0540

**Alaska Humanities Forum**
421 W. First Ave., No. 210
Anchorage, AK 99501
907-272-5341

**Arizona Humanities Council**
The Ellis-Shackelford House
1242 N. Central Ave.
Phoenix, AZ 85004-1887
602-257-0335

**Arkansas Humanities Council**
10816 Executive Center Dr., No. 310
Little Rock, AR 72211-4383
501-221-0091

**California Council for the Humanities**
312 Sutter St., No. 601
San Francisco, CA 94108
415-391-1474

**Colorado Endowment for the Humanities**
1623 Blake St., No. 200
Denver, CO 80202
303-573-7733

**Connecticut Humanities Council**
955 S. Main St., Suite E
Middletown CT 06547
860-685-2260

**Delaware Humanities Forum**
1812 Newport Gap Pike
Wilmington, DE 19808-6179
302-633-2400

**Humanities Council of Washington, D.C.**
1331 H Street N.W., No. 902
Washington, DC 20005
202-347-1732

**Florida Humanities Council**
1514 1/2 E. Eighth Ave.
Tampa, FL 33605-3708
813-272-3473

**Georgia Humanities Council**
50 Hurt Plaza S.E., No. 440
Atlanta, GA 30303-2915
404-523-6220

**Hawaii Committee for the Humanities**
First Hawaiian Bank Bldg.
3599 Wai'alae Ave., Rm. 23
Honolulu, HI 96816
808-732-5402

**Idaho Humanities Council**
217 W. State St.
Boise, ID 83702
208-345-5346

**Illinois Humanities Council**
203 Wabash Ave., No.#2020
Chicago, IL 60601-2417
312-422-5580

**Indiana Humanities Council**
1500 N. Delaware St.
Indianapolis, IN 46202
317-638-1500

**Iowa Humanities Board**
Oakdale Campus Northlawn
University of Iowa
Iowa City, IA 52242
319-335-4153

**Kansas Humanities Council**
112 S.W. Sixth Ave., No. 210
Topeka, KS 66603
913-357-0359

**Kentucky Humanities Council**
206 Maxwell St.
Lexington, KY 40508
606-257-5932

**Louisiana Endowment for the Humanities**
225 Baronne St., Suite 1414
New Orleans, LA 70112-1709
504-523-4352

**Maine Humanities Council**
371 Cumberland Ave.
Box 7202
Portland, ME 04112
207-773-5051

**Maryland Humanities Council**
601 N. Howard St.
Baltimore, MD 21201
410-625-4830

**Massachusetts Foundation for the Humanities**
One Woodbridge St.
South Hadley, MA 01075
413-536-1385

**Michigan Humanities Council**
119 Pere Marquette Dr., No. 3B
Lansing, MI 48912-1231
517-372-7770

**Minnesota Humanities Commission**
26 E. Ivy St.
Lower Level South
St. Paul, MN 55106-2046
612-774-0105

**Mississippi Humanities Council**
3825 Ridgewood Rd., Room 311
Jackson, MS 39211
601-982-6752

**Missouri Humanities Council**
911 Washington Ave., No. 215
St. Louis, MO 63101-1208
314-621-7705

**Montana Committee for the Humanities**
Box 8036, Hellgate Sta.
Missoula, MT 59807
406-243-6022

**Nebraska Humanities Council**
Lincoln Center Bldg., No. 225
215 Centennial Mall South
Lincoln, NE 68508
402-474-2131

Nevada Humanities Committee
1034 N. Sierra St.
Reno, NV 89507
702-784-6527

New Hampshire Humanities Council
19 Pillsbury St.
Box 2228
Concord, NH 03302-2228
603-224-4071

New Jersey Council for the Humanities
28 W. State St., Sixth fl.
Trenton, NJ 08608
609-695-4838

New Mexico Endowment for the Humanities
209 Onate Hall
University of New Mexico
Albuquerque, NM 87131
505-277-3705

New York Council for the Humanities
198 Broadway, Tenth fl.
New York, NY 10038
212-233-1131

North Carolina Humanities Council
425 Spring Garden St.
Greensboro, NC 27401
919-334-5325

North Dakota Humanities Council
2900 Broadway E., No. 3
Box 2191
Bismarck, ND 58502
701-255-3360

Ohio Humanities Council
695 Bryden Rd.
Box 06354
Columbus, OH 43206-0354
614-461-7802

Oklahoma Foundation for the Humanities
Festival Plaza
428 W. California, No. 270
Oklahoma City, OK 73102
405-235-0280

Oregon Council for the Humanities
812 S.W. Washington St., No. 225
Portland, OR 97205
503-241-0543

Pennsylvania Humanities Council
320 Walnut St., No. 305
Philadelphia, PA 19106
215-925-1005

Rhode Island Committee for the Humanities
60 Ship St.
Providence, RI 02903
401-273-2250

South Carolina Humanities Council
1308 Columbia College Dr.
Box 5287
Columbia, SC 29250
803-691-4100

South Dakota Humanities Council
Box 7050, University Sta.
Brookings, SD 57007
605-688-6113

Tennessee Humanities Council
1003 18th Ave. S.
Nashville, TN 37212
615-320-7001

Texas Council for the Humanities
Banister Place A
3809 S. Second St.
Austin, TX 78704
512-440-1991

Utah Humanities Council
350 S. 400 E., No. 110
Salt Lake City, UT 84111
801-359-9670

Vermont Council on the Humanities
17 Park St., R.R. 1, Box 7285
Morrisville, VT 05561
802-888-3183

Virginia Foundation for the Humanities
145 Ednam Dr.
Charlottesville, VA 22903-4629
804-924-3296

Washington Commission for the Humanities
615 Second Ave., No. 300
Seattle, WA 98104
206-682-1770

West Virginia Humanities Council
723 Kanawha Blvd. E., No. 800
Charleston, WV 25301
304-346-8500

**Wisconsin Humanities Council**
802 Regent St.
Madison, WI 53715
608-262-0706

**Wyoming Council for the Humanities**
Box 3643, University Sta.
Laramie, WY 82071-3643
307-766-3142

**American Samoa Humanities Council**
Box 5800
Pago Pago, AS 96799
684-633-4870

**Guam Humanities Council**
272 W. Rte. 8, No. 2A
Barrigada, Guam 96913
671-734-1713

**Commonwealth of the Northern Mariana
Islands Council for the Humanities**
AAA-3394, Box 10001
Saipan, MP 96950
670-235-4785

**Fundación Puertorriqueña de las
Humanidades**
109 San Jose St., Third fl.
Box 9023920
Old San Juan, PR 00902-3920
809-721-2087

**Virgin Islands Humanities Council**
5-6 Kongens Gade, Corbiere Complex,
Suite 200B
St. Thomas, VI 00802
809-776-4044

## Applications

Guidelines and application forms are available from the program or from the Public Information Office, National Endowment for the Humanities, 1100 Pennsylvania Ave. N.W., Washington, DC 20506, telephone 202-606-8400 or 800-634-1121, e-mail info@neh.fed.us; or from the NEH home page at http://www.neh.fed.us. For the hearing impaired, the TDD is 202-606-8282.

The Public Information Office does not maintain a general mailing list. Instead, NEH responds to specific requests for publications and guidelines.

# Institute of Museum and Library Services
# Library Programs

1100 Pennsylvania Ave. N.W., Washington, DC 20506
202-606-5227, fax 202-606-1077
World Wide Web: http://www.imls.fed.us

Diane Frankel

Director
Institute of Museum and Library Services

The Library Services and Technology Act (LSTA), Subchapter II of the Museum and Library Services Act of 1996, changed the federal administration of library programs by moving programs from the Department of Education (DOE) to the newly formed Institute of Museum and Library Services (IMLS). In 1997 staff moved from DOE to new offices at IMLS. New staff were hired, and implementation of the refocused programs began. A total of $146,340,000 was available for these programs in fiscal year (FY) 1998.

The purposes of LSTA are

- To consolidate federal library service programs
- To stimulate excellence and promote access to learning and information resources in all types of libraries for individuals of all ages
- To promote library services that provide all users access to information through state, regional, national, and international electronic networks
- To provide linkages between and among libraries
- To promote targeted library service to people of diverse geographic, cultural, and socioeconomic backgrounds, to individuals with disabilities, and to people with limited functional literacy or information skills

Within IMLS, the Office of Library Services is responsible for the administration of LSTA. It is comprised of the Division of State Programs, which administers grants to states, and the Division of Discretionary Programs, which administers the National Leadership Grant program, the Native American Library Services program, and the Native Hawaiian Library Services program.

## State-Administered Programs

LSTA sends about 90 percent of the library appropriation to the states, with a broad mandate to use technology to bring information to people in new and interesting ways. In 1997 state library administrative agencies developed and submitted to IMLS five-year state plans. The plans outlined a variety of the goals for the agencies that reflected the priorities established by LSTA for library services. The two primary priorities of LSTA are to support technology for information sharing and to support programs that make library resources more accessible to those who have difficulty using library services.

Last year IMLS began working with the Chief Officers of State Library Agencies (COSLA) organization to design a reporting system that will present a relatively complete picture of library services at the national level and help define the ultimate impact of LSTA. Annual reports will identify promising practices and exemplary programs that are funded by LSTA. They will also allow IMLS staff to track patterns in the diverse network of state programs.

On December 22, 1997, the first library program state grants were made under LSTA. Allocations totaled $135,466,990. The state allocations are based on a population-based formula, supplemented by a state minimum of $340,000. The base amount for the Pacific region "state" entities is $40,000. In December 1998 Congress appropriated $135,366,938 for FY 1999 for the state program, which was awarded based on this formula (Table 1).

*(text continues on page 343)*

**Table 1 / Funding for LSTA State Program, 1999**
Total Distributed to States: $135,366,938[1]

| State | Federal Allocation[2] | State Share[3] |
|---|---|---|
| Alabama | $2,203,656 | $1,135,217 |
| Alaska | 602,909 | 310,589 |
| Arizona | 2,305,406 | 1,187,633 |
| Arkansas | 1,428,562 | 735,926 |
| California | 14,263,331 | 7,347,777 |
| Colorado | 2,019,623 | 1,040,412 |
| Connecticut | 1,750,899 | 901,978 |
| Delaware | 655,667 | 337,768 |
| Florida | 6,662,977 | 3,432,443 |
| Georgia | 3,570,211 | 1,839,200 |
| Hawaii | 852,003 | 438,911 |
| Idaho | 862,199 | 444,163 |
| Illinois | 5,472,896 | 2,819,371 |
| Indiana | 2,870,282 | 1,478,630 |
| Iowa | 1,570,782 | 809,191 |
| Kansas | 1,459,638 | 751,935 |
| Kentucky | 2,026,302 | 1,043,853 |
| Louisiana | 2,217,729 | 1,142,466 |
| Maine | 875,928 | 451,236 |
| Maryland | 2,538,116 | 1,307,514 |
| Massachusetts | 2,979,626 | 1,534,959 |
| Michigan | 4,557,301 | 2,347,701 |
| Minnesota | 2,361,750 | 1,216,659 |
| Mississippi | 1,518,174 | 782,090 |
| Missouri | 2,670,914 | 1,375,925 |
| Montana | 719,195 | 370,494 |
| Nebraska | 1,054,917 | 543,442 |
| Nevada | 1,063,520 | 547,874 |
| New Hampshire | 846,008 | 435,822 |
| New Jersey | 3,814,694 | 1,965,145 |
| New Mexico | 1,086,364 | 559,642 |

**Table 1 / Funding for LSTA State Program, 1999** *(cont.)*
Total Distributed to States: $135,366,938[1]

| State | Federal Allocation[2] | State Share[3] |
|-------|----------------------|----------------|
| New York | 8,165,965 | 4,206,709 |
| North Carolina | 3,543,865 | 1,825,627 |
| North Dakota | 616,532 | 317,607 |
| Ohio | 5,166,749 | 2,661,659 |
| Oklahoma | 1,771,279 | 912,477 |
| Oregon | 1,739,520 | 896,116 |
| Pennsylvania | 5,526,319 | 2,846,892 |
| Rhode Island | 766,062 | 394,638 |
| South Carolina | 1,962,467 | 1,010,968 |
| South Dakota | 658,425 | 339,189 |
| Tennessee | 2,656,304 | 1,368,399 |
| Texas | 8,727,808 | 4,496,144 |
| Utah | 1,228,494 | 632,861 |
| Vermont | 594,136 | 306,070 |
| Virginia | 3,245,627 | 1,671,990 |
| Washington | 2,760,795 | 1,422,228 |
| West Virginia | 1,123,487 | 578,766 |
| Wisconsin | 2,570,645 | 1,324,272 |
| Wyoming | 547,003 | 281,789 |
| District of Columbia | 568,241 | 292,730 |
| Puerto Rico | 2,004,273 | 1,032,504 |
| American Samoa | 66,792 | 34,408 |
| Northern Marianas | 68,720 | 35,401 |
| Guam | 103,886 | 53,517 |
| Virgin Islands | 91,006 | 46,882 |
| Pacific Territories[4] | 210,959 | 108,676 |
| Total | $135,366,938 | $69,734,483 |

1 The amount available to states is based on the balance remaining after the authorized set-asides have been subtracted from the total allocation, as follows: Library allocation, FY 1999, $166,175,000; Native American Grants (1.75%), $2,908,063; National Leadership Grants (3.75%), $25,000,000; Administration (up to 3%), $2,900,000; Total available to states, $135,366,938.

2 Calculation is based on minimum set in the law (P.L. 104-208, as amended by P.L. 105-128 111 Stat 2548). Data for the Marshall Islands, Federated States of Micronesia, Puerto Rico, American Samoa, the Northern Marianas, Guam, the Virgin Islands, and Palau are, as of June 15, 1998, from the Bureau of the Census (BOC) International Data Base (at the Web site http://www.census.gov/cgi-bin/ipc/idbrank.pl). Data are also available by phone at 301-457-2419. Data for the District of Columbia and the 50 states are from BOC estimates as of July 1, 1997, which were made available by BOC on December 31, 1997. For the continental United States, BOC data can be accessed at the Web site http://www.census.gov/population/estimates/state and are also available by phone at 301-457-2419. It is important to use the most recent data available at the time distributions are made because BOC estimates sometimes change.

3 Calculated at 34 percent; the federal share is 66 percent.

4 Total allotment (including administrative costs) for Palau, the Marshall Islands, and Micronesia. Funds are awarded on a competitive basis and are administered by Pacific Resources for Education and Learning.

*(continued from page 341)*

## Discretionary Programs

In 1998 IMLS also began administering the discretionary programs of LSTA. In all, 366 grants amounting to $9,048,700* were awarded through the National Leadership Grant Program, the Native American Library Services Program, and the Native Hawaiian Library Services Grant Program.

The Native American and the Native Hawaiian Library Services Grant Programs are continuations of programs formerly administered by the Department of Education. The National Leadership Grant Program is a new grant program that expands on and replaces portions of the LSCA program for library research and demonstration and Title II-B of the Higher Education Act for education in library and information science, and adds categories of funding for the preservation or digitization of information resources and for model programs of cooperation between libraries and museums.

The FY 1999 congressional appropriation for discretionary programs includes the following:

- National Leadership Program: $9,565,000 (3.75 percent of the LSTA appropriation) for competitive programs
- Native American Library Services Program: $2,492,562 (1.5 percent of the LSTA appropriation)
- Native Hawaiian Library Services Program: $415,438 (0.25 percent of the LSTA appropriation)

### National Leadership Grant Program

In September 1998 IMLS awarded 41 grants totaling $6,487,750* for the first National Leadership Grant competition using FY 1998 funding. More than 250 applications from libraries all over the country were received. The projects funded represented the leading edge in the field of library and information science in education and training, research and demonstration, the preservation and archiving of digital media, and innovative collaborative projects between libraries and museums (Table 2).

With extensive consultation with leaders in the museum and library professions, the funding priorities for the National Leadership Grant Program were reexamined, and new priorities were developed for the 1999 grant period. Although the four categories of funding remain unchanged, the priorities were enhanced. To address a new agency-wide theme to promote education for learning in the 21st century, emphasis was added for all funding categories on the education of users of information resources. Again in 1999 IMLS is soliciting proposals that are replicable and have a national impact on the field of library science.

The FY 1999 priorities of the National Leadership Grants are as follows:

* Includes $1 million from the IMLS Office of Museum Services to supplement LSTA funding for library and museum collaborations.

- Education and training in library and information science, including graduate fellowships, traineeships, and institutes, with a new focus to train librarians to enhance people's ability to use information effectively
- Applied research and demonstration efforts that emphasize access to improved library and information resources, with a new focus on projects that enhance the ability of library users to make more effective use of information resources
- Projects that preserve unique library resources useful for the broader research community, that address the challenges of preserving and archiving digital materials, or that lead to the development of digitization standards and replicable techniques or models
- Model programs of cooperation between libraries and museums that emphasize how the community is served, how technology is used, and how education is enhanced or that help museums and libraries take a leadership role in the education of lifelong learners in the 21st century

**Native American Library Services Program**

In 1998 IMLS distributed $2,560,950 in grants to Native American tribes across the country.

The Native American Library Services Program provides opportunities for the improvement of library services to Indian tribes and Alaska native villages, the latter coming under the definition of eligible Indian tribes as recognized by the Secretary of the Interior. The program offers three types of support:

- Basic Library Services Grants, in the amount of $4,000, support core library operations on a noncompetitive basis for all eligible Indian tribes and Alaska native villages that apply for such support. IMLS awarded Basic Grants to 243 tribes in 27 states in 1998.
- Technical Assistance Grants, in the amount of $2,000, heighten the level of professional proficiency of Indian tribal library staff. It is a noncompetitive program to support assessments of Indian library service and provide advice for improvement. IMLS awarded Technical Assistance Grants to 42 tribes in 14 states in 1998.
- Enhancement Grants support new levels of Indian library service for activities specifically identified under the basic LSTA purposes. In 1998 these competitive awards ranged from $10,000 to $134,000 (Table 3).

Of the 49 applications received, IMLS awarded 12 Enhancement Grants for a total of $1,139,100.

**Native Hawaiian Library Services**

The Native Hawaiian Library Services provides opportunities for improved library services for an important part of the nation's community of library users through a single grant to a Native Hawaiian organization, as defined in section 9212 of the Native Hawaiian Education Act (20 U.S.C. 7912).

In 1998 the Native Hawaiian Library Services Grant was awarded to Alu Like, Inc. of Honolulu, a private non-profit organization serving the Native Hawaiian community, in the amount of $365,850.

### Table 2 / National Leadership Grant Awards, FY 1998

**Education and Training.** Model programs to provide education and training for the use of emerging technologies in the field of library and information science and to attract individuals from diverse cultural backgrounds to the field.

*Dominican University Graduate School of Library and Information Science, River Forest, Illinois:* $165,622 for a two-year project, in collaboration with the Chicago Public Schools Department of Libraries and Information Services, to prepare a selected group of classroom teachers for endorsement as elementary school library media specialists.

*Florida State University, Florida Resources and Environmental Analysis Center, Tallahassee:* $240,782 for a two-year project to develop a marketing research continuing-education course for librarians to prepare them to use new technologies to effectively market library services.

*Louisiana State University, School of Library and Information Science, Baton Rouge:* $43,502 for a one-year project to develop an archival training course to be offered through interactive compressed video to librarians in Arkansas and Louisiana.

*University of Maryland, College of Library and Information Services, College Park:* $94,400 for a two-year project to recruit individuals from diverse cultural backgrounds to the master's degree program in library science, focusing on part-time students and on the provision of mentoring as well as financial assistance to students.

*University of North Texas, School of Library and Information Science, Denton:* $226,791 for a two-year project, in partnership with the African American Museum in Dallas, to train library professionals in digital imaging technologies and information networks leading to Certificates of Advanced Study in digital-image management.

*University of Oklahoma, School of Library and Information Studies, Norman:* $151,416 for a two-year project to support master's degree students in the Library and Information Science Education Project to Enhance Cultural Diversity, focusing on recruitment of minority students, training in information technologies, and mentoring by peers and faculty.

**Research and Demonstration.** Model projects to enhance library services through the use of appropriate technologies and to create methods to evaluate the contributions to a community made by institutions providing access to information services.

*Duke University Library, Durham, North Carolina:* $91,188 for a one-year project to demonstrate the use of Encoded Archival Description for finding aids in conjunction with large-scale digital-imaging projects, using as a case study the collection of photographs, journals, and notebooks of documentary photographer William Gedney.

*New York Public Library:* $225,000 for a one-year project to improve electronic access to the library's rare-book, arts, and Judaica collections.

*Oregon Historical Society, Portland:* $100,000 for a two-year project to convert a program about Portland neighborhoods from a stand-alone interactive video exhibit to an interactive Web-based database and to promote its use by K–12 educators and students for researching local history.

*St. Louis Public Library:* $208,550 for a two-year project, in partnership with public libraries in Baltimore, Birmingham, Phoenix, and Seattle, to refine a case study methodology to communicate the economic benefits of services provided by large public libraries and to provide a means for libraries to estimate the direct monetary return on annual taxpayer investment.

*University at Albany, State University of New York:* $176,138 for a one-year project to develop and test a descriptive list of national core data elements, statistics, and performance measures to describe public library network uses and produce a manual describing the resulting elements, statistics, and measures and recommending data collection techniques.

*University of Michigan, Bentley Historical Library, Ann Arbor:* $17,335 for a one-year project, in partnership with the Society of American Archivists and others, to convene a meeting to finalize a formal set of Application Guidelines for Encoded Archival Description, a tool to expand access to archival materials by making finding aids effectively accessible via the Internet.

**Table 2 / National Leadership Grant Awards, FY 1998** *(cont.)*

*University of Michigan, School of Information, Ann Arbor:* $189,026 for a two-year project to investigate the role of librarians in assisting users to find community information on the Internet, using case studies of libraries in Florida, Illinois, and Pennsylvania, and to identify best practices for providing community information electronically.

*University of Pittsburgh:* $189,215 for a two-year project, in cooperation with four Chinese research libraries, to deliver digital copies of articles from Chinese-language academic journals via the Internet to researchers throughout the United States, with the goal of making the service viable as a cost-recovery operation.

*University of Wisconsin, Madison:* $172,611 for a one-year project to digitize field research materials from the university's African Studies program and to make the information accessible for teaching and research purposes via a Web-based public-domain database.

*Washington State Library, Olympia:* $114,040 for a one-year project to demonstrate the effectiveness of a Government Information Locator Service tool developed by the Washington State Library to connect people with government, in partnership with the states of Mississippi, New Hampshire, and Oregon.

**Preservation or Digitization.** Projects to preserve unique library resources of national significance, emphasizing access by researchers beyond the institution undertaking the project, and projects that address the preservation and archiving of digital media.

*Alliance Library System, Pekin, Illinois:* $101,400 for a one-year project to create a regional digital library of archival resources relating to the history of Illinois from 1818 to 1918, in collaboration with the Illinois State Historical Library and other libraries within the state.

*College of Physicians of Philadelphia:* $175,000 for a two-year project to conserve rare materials in the college's historical library.

*Cornell University, Ithaca, New York:* $200,000 for a two-year project to plan and implement an archiving solution for more than 2.5 million digital images created by Cornell in its pioneering imaging projects carried out over the last decade.

*Indiana University, Bloomington:* $166,000 for a two-year project to digitize materials in various formats from the Hoagy Carmichael jazz collection (including sound recordings, photographs, and printed and textual materials) and make them available via the Internet.

*Missouri Botanical Garden Library, St. Louis:* $225,281 for a two-year project to develop a database of plant images and associated data from the Missouri Botanical Garden's library and make it available on the institution's Web site, create a repository for plant images to which other botanical organizations can contribute, and develop a model program with software for connecting images of any type with associated data.

*Nah Tah Wahsh Library, Hannahville Indian Community, Wilson, Michigan:* $38,549 for a two-year project to provide information about the Hannahville Indian Community, the Potawatomi tribe, and the Woodland Indians of Upper Michigan—including digital copies of documents, photographs, and video and audio clips of interviews with tribal elders—via the Internet.

*Northeast Document Conservation Center, Andover, Massachusetts:* $82,300 for a two-year project to produce and disseminate an easy-to-use handbook on managing digital projects to meet the needs of libraries and museums.

*Northwestern University, Evanston, Illinois:* $108,682 for a two-year project to digitize a large collection of League of Nations publications published between 1919 and 1939 and make the materials available via the Internet.

*Rochester (New York) Institute of Technology:* $30,725 in supplemental funding for a two-year project to investigate the effects of fluctuating environments on library and archival materials.

*University of Hawaii at Manoa Library:* $100,438 for a two-year project to develop a digital library of Hawaii and Pacific Islands materials, using Hawaiian-language newspapers and historical photographs, for use as a teaching tool for Hawaiian-language immersion schools and other purposes.

*University of North Carolina, Chapel Hill:* $138,938 for a two-year project to create the full-text database The Southern Homefront, 1861–1865, consisting of an extensive collection of digitized and encoded printed works and manuscripts, maps, illustrations, and other materials documenting Southern life during the Civil War and make them available via the Internet.

*University of Virginia, Charlottesville:* $241,306 for a two-year project to digitize, identify, arrange, describe, and conserve a collection of photographs of African American educational scenes taken by photographer Jackson Davis in the South between 1915 and 1930.

**Table 2 / National Leadership Grant Awards, FY 1998** *(cont.)*

*West Virginia State Archives, Charleston*: $101,578 for a one-year project to digitize and create catalog records for a manuscript collection containing the largest known assemblage of records relating to the abolitionist John Brown and make the materials available via the Internet.

**Model Programs of Cooperation**. Projects that develop, document, and disseminate both the processes and products of model programs of cooperation between libraries and museums, with emphasis on how the community is served, technology is used, or education is enhanced.

*Arizona Department of Library, Archives and Public Records, Phoenix*: $150,545 for a one-year pilot project—in partnership with the Heard Museum and the state libraries of Colorado, New Mexico, Nevada, and Utah—to increase library, archive, and museum expertise in Indian communities and to improve access and services among tribal and other participating institutions.

*Brooklyn (New York) Children's Museum*: $297,900 for a two-year project, in partnership with the Brooklyn Museum of Art and the Brooklyn Public Library, to expand a cooperative project to increase educational services to the Brooklyn community and to develop a national model for attracting and training people from diverse backgrounds in information technology, library science, and museum programs.

*Kit Carson Historic Museums, Taos, New Mexico*: $103,833 for a two-year project—in partnership with the Zimmerman Library and Harwood Museum of the University of New Mexico and the Millicent Rogers Museum of Northern New Mexico—to establish the Southwestern Research Center of Northern New Mexico, which will make information about valuable collections available to national and international researchers.

*Children's Museum of Houston, Houston, Texas*: $194,000 for a two-year project, in partnership with the Houston Public Library System, to open a Library for Early Childhood at the Children's Museum as a resource for information on early childhood, parenting, and family learning and as a partner learning space of the Tot Spot exhibit gallery, dedicated to children 6 months to 3 years old.

*Council on Library and Information Resources, Washington, D.C.*: $72,990 for a one-year project, in partnership with the Chicago Historical Society, to host a conference on content development in the digital environment for museums, libraries, and archives.

*Florida Center for Library Automation, University of Florida, Gainesville*: $235,803 for a two-year project to create a virtual library of Florida ecological information, in partnership with the Florida Museum of Natural History and the libraries of the University of Florida, Florida International University, and Florida Atlantic University.

*IUPUI (Indiana University Purdue University at Indianapolis) University Libraries*: $290,000 for a two-year project, in partnership with the Art Museum Image Consortium (AMICO), to provide access on a trial basis to AMICO's digital-image database for the K–12 educational and public library communities in the greater Indianapolis area.

*Montana State University Libraries, Bozeman*: $138,346 for a one-year project in partnership with the Museum of the Rockies to create a database, Images of the Indian Peoples of the Northern Great Plains, which will make access to important source material on the Plains Indian cultures accessible via the Internet.

*Public Library of Charlotte and Mecklenburg County, North Carolina*: $309,484 for a two-year project, in partnership with the Mint Museum of Art, to create the program Weaving a Tale of Craft, uniting computer technology, the arts, humanities, and educational resources so the public may learn about North Carolina history and crafts.

*Rhode Island School of Design, Museum of Art, Providence*: $325,513 for a two-year partnership with the Providence Public Library for an initiative designed to expand audiences for contemporary art and interest in current issues through artists' residencies in library branches, an exhibition at the school, and a traveling Art and Text Mobile.

*University of Illinois, Urbana-Champaign*: $157,981 for a two-year project in partnership with three museums, two libraries, and three elementary schools to build a model and a test electronic database of historical information to be made available via the Internet.

*Leigh Yawkey Woodson Art Museum, Wausau, Wisconsin*: $95,542 for a two-year project in partnership with the Marathon County Public Library to link original art and literacy by focusing on extraordinary exhibitions of children's book illustrations. The exhibition, Down Under and Over Here: Children's Book Illustration from Australia and America, will showcase a model program of cooperation.

## Table 3 / Native American Library Services Program: Enhancement Grants, FY 1998

### Arctic Slope Regional Corporation
Anchorage, Alaska $100,947

For a two-year project to convert an existing boroughwide online catalog to a system supported by a statewide consortium and to train library staff in eight villages to optimize the new system's features.

### Chippewa Cree Tribe
Box Elder, Montana $134,000

For a two-year project to electronically link to the state online consortium, expand library service hours, upgrade computer resources, and create a new children's section.

### Lac Courte Oreilles Tribe
Hayward, Wisconsin $63,790

For a one-year project to develop Web access to its online catalog and library-produced databases, provide outreach services to Head Start and senior centers, and focus resources on
developing a collection of tribal materials.

### Nenana Native Village
Nenana, Alaska $10,000

For a one-year project to plan how the public library can best access the Internet, the state
network, and other electronic resources, and train both the staff and the community to effectively use them.

### Nisqually Tribe
Olympia, Washington $77,060

For a one-year project to increase access to health and community information by establishing
a Health Information Station, enhance print and electronic health resources, and employ tribal
youth pages to expand library hours.

### Northern Cheyenne Tribe
Lame Deer, Montana $127,574

For a two-year project to develop a procedural manual for converting tribal archives to a digital
format and enhance Internet and intranet tribal services.

### Pala Band of Mission Indians
Pala, California $44,820

For a one-year project to expand the collection with print and electronic resources, purchase
furnishings for a newly constructed library, and support library and educational services.

### Pilot Station Native Village
Pilot Station, Alaska $56,000

For a one-year project to support a conference convening representatives from 56 native villages to introduce them to electronic resources and to create a plan for providing ongoing
technical assistance to those villages in utilizing electronic resources.

### Pueblo of Jemez
Jemez Pueblo, New Mexico $134,000

For a two-year project to support various aspects of a tribal intergenerational learning initiative,
increase computer literacy for both library staff and tribal members, and plan a local library
consortium.

### Pueblo of Santa Clara
Espanola, New Mexico $134,000

For a two-year project to create a multimedia resource center of tribal archives, including a
mobile exhibit of cultural materials; to provide computer training courses; and to increase collections for targeted community members.

**Table 3  /  Native American Library Services Program: Enhancement Grants, FY 1998**
*(cont.)*

**Three Affiliated Tribes**

New Town, North Dakota                                      $128,067

For a two-year project to create a consortium of eight reservation libraries for the purposes of sharing of electronic and print resources, training library staff, and coordinating collection development.

**Winnebago Tribe**

Winnebago, Nebraska                                        $128,842

For a two-year project to automate card catalog records, create a Web site highlighting the tribe's collection of Native American materials, and increase access to that collection through conversion of some materials to electronic formats.

# Part 3
# Library/Information Science Education, Placement, and Salaries

# Guide to Employment Sources in the Library and Information Professions

Maxine Moore

Office for Library Personnel Resources, American Library Association

This guide updates the listing in the 1998 *Bowker Annual* with information on new services and changes in contacts and groups listed previously. The sources listed primarily give assistance in obtaining professional positions, although a few indicate assistance with paraprofessionals. The latter, however, tend to be recruited through local sources.

## General Sources of Library and Information Jobs

### Library Literature

Classified ads of library vacancies and positions wanted are carried in many of the national, regional, and state library journals and newsletters. Members of associations can sometimes list "position wanted" ads free of charge in their membership publications. Listings of positions available are regularly found in *American Libraries*, *Chronicle of Higher Education*, *College & Research Libraries News*, *Library Journal*, and *Library Hotline*. State and regional library association newsletters, state library journals, foreign library periodicals, and other types of periodicals carrying such ads are listed in later sections.

### Newspapers

The *New York Times* Sunday "Week in Review" section carries a special section of ads for librarian jobs in addition to the regular classifieds. Local newspapers, particularly the larger city Sunday editions, such as the *Washington Post*, *Los Angeles Times*, and *Chicago Tribune* often carry job vacancy listings in libraries, both professional and paraprofessional. The online versions of these newspapers also are useful.

### Internet

The many library-related electronic listservs on the Internet often post library job vacancies interspersed with other news and discussion items. A growing number of general online job-search bulletin boards exist; these may include information-related job notices along with other types of jobs. This guide includes information on electronic access where available through the individual organizations listed below. Among useful resources are "Making Short Work of the Job Search" by Marilyn Rosenthal, *Library Journal*, September 1, 1997, "Job Opportunities Glitter for Librarians Who Surf the Net" by A. Paula Azar, *American Libraries*, September 1996. "Winning Résumé" by Scott Grusky in *Internet World*, February 1996, and "Riley's Guided Tour: Job Searching on the Net" by Margaret Riley, et al, *Library Journal*, September 15, 1996, pp. 24–27 offer guidance on databases that might lead to library and information-related position listings. Some library-related job search Web links include:

- Ann's Place—Library Job Hunting Around the World http://www. uic.edu/~aerobin/libjob.html)
- Finding Library Jobs on the WWW (toltec.lib.utk.edu/~tla/nmrt/ libjobs.html)
- Job and Career Information (http://www.peachnet.edu/galileo/internet/ jobs/jobsmenu.html)
- Job Opportunities—Librarians and Library Science Net Links (http:// librarians.miningco.com/msubjobs.htm)
- Library and Information Science Jobs (http://www.fidnet.com/~map/ default4.htm)
- The Librarian's Job Search Source (http://www.zoots.com/libjob/ libjob.htm)
- Library Jobs on the Net (wings.buffalo.edu/sils/alas/usamap.html)
- The Networked Librarian Job Search Guide (pw2.netcom.com/~feridun/ nlintro/htm)

### Library Joblines

Library joblines or job "hotlines" give recorded telephone messages of job openings in a specific geographical area. Most tapes are changed once a week, although individual listings may sometimes be carried for several weeks. Although the information is fairly brief and the cost of calling is borne by the individual job seeker, a jobline provides a quick and up-to-date listing of vacancies that is not usually possible with printed listings or journal ads.

Most joblines carry listings for their state or region only, although some will occasionally accept out-of-state positions if there is room on the tape. While a few will list technician and other paraprofessional positions, the majority are for professional jobs only. When calling the joblines, one might occasionally find a time when the telephone keeps ringing without any answer; this will usually mean that the tape is being changed or there are no new jobs for that period. The classified section of *American Libraries* carries jobline numbers periodically as space permits. The following joblines are in operation:

| Jobline Sponsor | Job Seekers (To Hear Job Listings) | Employers (To Place Job Listings) |
|---|---|---|
| American Association of Law Libraries | 312-939-7877 | 53 W. Jackson Blvd., Suite 940, Chicago, IL 60604. 312-939-4764; fax 312-431-1097 |
| Arizona Department of Library, Archives and Public Records (Arizona libraries only) | 602-275-2325 | 1700 W. Washington, Phoenix, AZ 85008 |
| British Columbia Library Association (B.C. listings only) | 604-430-6411 | Jobline, 110-6545 Bonsor Ave., Burnaby, BC V51 1H3, Canada. 604-430-9633 |
| California Library Association | 916-447-5627 | 717 K St., Suite 300, Sacramento, CA 95814-3477. 916-447-8394 |
| California School Library Association | 650-697-8832 | 1499 Old Bayshore Hwy., Suite 142, Burlingame, CA 94010. 650-692-2350 |
| Cleveland (OH) Area Metropolitan Library System Job Listing Service | 216-921-4702 | CAMLS, 20600 Chagrin Blvd., Suite 500, Shaker Heights, OH 44122. |
| Colorado State Library[1] (includes paraprofessionals) | 303-866-6741 | Jobline, 201 E. Colfax, Rm. 309, Denver, CO 80203-1704. 303-866-6900; fax 303-866-6940; also via Libnet/listserv |
| Connecticut Library Association | 860-889-1200 | Box 1046, Norwich, CT 06360-1046 |
| Delaware Division of Libraries (Del., N.J., and Pa. listings) | 800-282-8696 (in-state) 302-739-4748 ext. 165 (out-of-state) | 43 S. Dupont Hwy., Dover, DE 19901 |
| Drexel University College of Info. Sci. & Tech. | 215-895-1672 215-895-1048 | College of Info. Sci. & Tech., 3141 Chestnut St., Philadelphia, PA 19104. 215-895-2478; fax 215-895-2494 |
| State Library of Florida | 904-488-5232 (in-state) | R. A. Gray Bldg., Tallahassee, FL 32399-0250. 904-487-2651 |
| Library Jobline of Illinois[2] | 312-409-5986 | Illinois Library Assn., 33 W. Grand, Suite 301, Chicago, IL 60610. 312-644-1896 ($48/2 weeks) |
| State Library of Iowa (professional jobs in Iowa; only during regular business hours) | 515-281-7574 | East 12 & Grand, Des Moines, IA 50319. 515-281-7574 |

| Jobline Sponsor | Job Seekers (To Hear Job Listings) | Employers (To Place Job Listings) |
|---|---|---|
| Kansas State Library Jobline (also includes paraprofessional and out-of-state) | 785-296-3296 | State Capitol, 300 S.W. Tenth Ave. Topeka, KS 66612-1593, fax 785-296-6650 |
| Kentucky Job Hotline | 502-564-3008 (24 hours) | Dept. for Libs. and Archives, Box 537, Frankfort, KY 40602. 502-564-8300 |
| Long Island (NY) Library Resources Council Jobline | 516-632-6658 | 516-632-6650; fax 516-632-6662 |
| Maryland Library Association | 410-685-5760 (24 hours) | 400 Cathedral St., 3rd flr., Baltimore, MD 21201. 410-727-7422 (Mon.–Fri., 9:00 A.M.–4:30 P.M.) |
| Medical Library Association Jobline | 312-553-4636 (24 hours) | 6 N. Michigan Ave., Suite 300, Chicago, IL 60602. 312-419-9094 |
| Metropolitan Washington (D.C.) Council of Governments Library Council | 202-962-3712 (24 hours) | 777 N. Capitol St. N.E., Suite 300, Washington, DC 20002. 202-962-3254 |
| Michigan Library Association | 517-694-7440 | 6810 S. Cedar, #6, Lansing, MI 48911. 517-694-6615; fax 517-694-4330 ($40/week) |
| Missouri Library Association Jobline | 573-442-6590 | 1306 Business 63 S., Suite B, Columbia, MO 65201-8404. 573-449-4627; fax 573-449-4655 |
| Mountain Plains Library Association[3] | 605-677-5757 | c/o I. D. Weeks Library, University of South Dakota, Vermillion, SD 57069. 605-677-6082; fax 605-677-5488 |
| Nebraska Job Hotline (in-state and other openings during regular business hours) | 402-471-4019 800-307-2665 (in-state) | Nebraska Library Commission, 1200 N St. 120, Lincoln, NE 68508-2023. |
| New England Library Jobline (New England jobs only) | 617-521-2815 (24 hours) | GSLIS, Simmons College, 300 The Fenway, Boston, MA 02115. Fax 617-521-3192 |
| New Jersey Library Association | 609-695-2121 | Box 1534, Trenton, NJ 08607; 609-394-8032; fax 609-394-8164 (nonmembers $50) |
| New York Library Association | 518-432-6952 800-252-6952 (in-state) | 252 Hudson Ave., Albany, NY 12210-1802. 518-432-6952 (members $15/3 months, nonmembers $25/3 months) |

| Jobline Sponsor | Job Seekers (To Hear Job Listings) | Employers (To Place Job Listings) |
|---|---|---|
| Ohio Library Council | 614-225-6999 (24 hours) | 35 E. Gay St., Suite 305, Columbus, OH 43215. 614-221-9057; fax 614-221-6234 |
| Oklahoma Department of Libraries Jobline (5:00 P.M.–8:00 A.M., 7 days a week) | 405-521-4202 | 200 N.E. 18 St., Oklahoma City, OK 73105. 405-521-2502 |
| Oregon Library Association (Northwest listings only) | 503-585-2232 | Oregon State Library, State Library Bldg., Salem, OR 97310. 503-378-4243 ext. 221 |
| Pennsylvania Cooperative Job Hotline[5] | 717-234-4646 | Pennsylvania Library Assn., 1919 N. Front St., Harrisburg, PA 17102. 717-233-3113 (weekly fee for non-members); fax 717-233-3121 |
| Pratt Institute SILS Job Hotline | 718-636-3742 | SILS, Brooklyn, NY 11205. 718-636-3702; fax 718-636-3733 |
| University of South Carolina College of Library and Information Science (no geographic restrictions) | 803-777-8443 | University of South Carolina, Columbia, SC 29208. 803-777-3887 |
| Special Libraries Association | 202-234-3632 | 1700 18th St. N.W., Washington, DC 20009. 202-234-4700 |
| Special Libraries Association, New York Chapter | 212-439-7290 | Fax 512-328-8852 |
| Special Libraries Association, San Andreas-San Francisco Bay Chapter | 415-528-7766 | 415-604-3140 |
| Special Libraries Association, Southern California Chapter | 818-795-2145 | 818-302-8966; fax 818-302-8983 |
| University of North Texas | 940-565-2445 | Box 311068, NT Station, Denton, TX 76203 |
| University of Toronto Faculty of Information Studies | 416-978-7073 | 416-978-3035; fax 416-978-5762 |
| University of Western Ontario Faculty of Communications and Open Learning | 519-661-3542 | 519-661-2111 ext. 8494; fax 519-661-3506 |

1. Weekly printed listing sent on receipt of stamps and mailing labels.
2. Cosponsored by the Special Libraries Association Illinois Chapter and the Illinois Library Association.
3. Includes listings for the states of Arizona, Colorado, Kansas, Montana, Nebraska, Nevada, North Dakota, Oklahoma, South Dakota, Utah, and Wyoming, and paid listings from out-of-region institutions—$10/week.
4. Alaska, Alberta, British Columbia, Idaho, Montana, Oregon, and Washington; includes both professional and paraprofessional jobs.
5. Sponsored by the Pennsylvania Library Association; also accepts paraprofessional out-of-state listings.

## Specialized Library Associations and Groups

**ACCESS**, 1001 Connecticut Ave. N.W., Suite 838, Washington, DC 20036, 202-785-4233, fax 202-785-4212, e-mail commjobs@aol.com, World Wide Web http://www.essential.org/access: Comprehensive national resource on employment, voluntary service, and career development in the nonprofit sector. Promotes involvement in public issues by providing specialized employment publications and services for job seekers and serves as a resource to nonprofit organizations on recruitment, diversity, and staff development.

**Advanced Information Management**, 444 Castro St., Suite 320, Mountain View, CA 94041, 415-965-7900, fax 650-965-7907, e-mail aimno.aimusa @juno.com, World Wide Web http://www.aimusa.com: Placement agency that specializes in library and information personnel. Offers work on a temporary, permanent, and contract basis for both professional librarians and paraprofessionals in the special, public, and academic library marketplace. Supplies consultants who can work with special projects in libraries or manage library development projects. Offices in Southern California (900 Wilshire Blvd., Suite 1424, Los Angeles, CA 90017, 213-489-9800, fax 213-489-9802) as well as in the San Francisco Bay Area. There is no fee to applicants.

**American Association of Law Libraries Career Hotline**, 53 W. Jackson Blvd., Suite 940, Chicago, IL 60604, 312-939-4764: The Hotline (312-939-7877) is a 24-hour-a-day recording, updated each Friday at noon. Any interested person may receive the complete Job Data Base free, by request. Ads may also be viewed on AALLNET, an Internet bulletin board (http://www.lawlib.wuacc.edu/aallnet/aallnet.html). To list a position contact AALL, Placement Assistant, fax 312-431-1097.

**American Libraries Career LEADS**, c/o *American Libraries*, 50 E. Huron St., Chicago, IL 60611: Classified job listings published in each monthly issue of *American Libraries* (*AL*) magazine, listing some 100 job openings grouped by type, plus Late Job Notices added near press time as space and time permits. Contains subsections: Positions Wanted, Librarians' Classified, joblines, and regional salary scales. Also contains ConsultantBase (see below) four times annually.

**American Libraries Career LEADS EXPRESS**, c/o Georgia Okotete, 50 E. Huron St., Chicago, IL 60611: Advance galleys (3–4 weeks) of classified job listings to be published in next issue of *AL*. Early notice of approximately 100 Positions Open sent about the 17th of each month; does not include editorial corrections and late changes as they appear in the regular AL LEADS section, but does include some Late Job Notices. For each month, send $1 check made out to AL EXPRESS, and a self-addressed, standard business-size envelope (4x9), with 55 cents postage on envelope.

**American Libraries ConsultantBase** (CBase), An *AL* service that helps match professionals offering library/information expertise with institutions seeking it. Published quarterly, CBase appears in the Career LEADS section of the January, April, June, and October issues of *AL*. Rates: $5.50/line classified, $55/inch display. Inquiries should be made to Jon Kartman, LEADS Editor, *American Libraries*, 50 E. Huron St., Chicago, IL 60611, 312-280-4211, e-mail careerleads@ALA.org.

**American Library Association, Association of College and Research Libraries**, 50 E. Huron St., Chicago, IL 60611-2795, 312-280-2513: Classified advertising appears each month in *College & Research Libraries News*. Ads appearing in the print *C&RL News* are also posted to C&RL NewsNet, an abridged electronic edition of *C&RL News* that is accessible at http://www.ala.org/acrl/c&rlnew2.html.

**American Library Association, Office for Library Personnel Resources** (OLPR), 50 E. Huron St., Chicago, IL 60611, 312-280-4281: A placement service is provided at each Annual Conference (June or July) and Midwinter Meeting (January or February). Request job seeker or employer registration forms prior to each conference. Persons not able to attend can register with the service and can also purchase job and job seeker listings sent directly from the conference site. Information included when requesting registration forms. Handouts on interviewing, preparing a résumé, and other job search information are available from OLPR.

In addition to the ALA conference placement center, ALA division national conferences usually include a placement service. See the *American Libraries* Datebook for dates of upcoming divisional conferences, since these are not held every year. ALA provides Web site job postings from *American Libraries*, C&RL NewsNet, and its conference placement services on its library education and employment menu page at http://www.ala.org.

**American Society for Information Science**, 8720 Georgia Ave., No. 501, Silver Spring, MD 20910-3602, 301-495-0900, fax 301-495-0810: An active placement service is operated at ASIS Annual Meetings (usually October; locales change). All conference attendees (both ASIS members and nonmembers), as well as ASIS members who cannot attend the conference, are eligible to use the service to list or find jobs. Job listings are also accepted from employers who cannot attend the conference. Interviews are arranged. Throughout the year, current job openings are listed in *ASIS JOBLINE*, a monthly publication sent to all members and available to non-members on request. Please check ASIS for ad rates.

**Art Libraries Society/North America** (ARLIS/NA), c/o Executive Director, 4101 Lake Boone Trail, Suite 201, Raleigh, NC 27607, 919-787-5181, fax 919-787-4916, e-mail 74517.3400@compuserve.com: Art information and visual resources curator jobs are listed in *ARLIS/NA UPDATE* (six times a year) and a job registry is maintained at ARLIS/NA headquarters. Any employer may list a job with the registry, but only members may request job information. Listings also available on the ARLIS-L listserv and Web site. Call ARLIS/NA headquarters for registration and/or published information.

**Asian/Pacific American Libraries Newsletter**, c/o Sandra Yamate, Polychrome Publishing Corp., 4509 N. Francisco, Chicago, IL 60626, 773-478-4455, fax 773-478-0786: This quarterly includes some job ads. Free to members of Asian/Pacific American Librarians Association.

**Association for Library and Information Science Education**, Box 7640, Arlington, VA 22207, 703-243-8040, fax 703-243-4551, World Wide Web http://www.alise.org: Provides placement service at annual conference (January or February) for library and information studies faculty and administrative positions.

**Association for Educational Communications and Technology**, 1025 Vermont Ave. N.W., Suite 820, Washington, DC 20005, 202-347-7834, fax 202-347-7839, e-mail aect@aect.org: AECT maintains a placement listing on the AECT Web site (www.aect.org) and provides a placement service at the annual convention, free to all registrants.

**Black Caucus Newsletter**, c/o George C. Grant, Editor, Rollins College, 1000 Holt Ave. No. 2654, Winter Park, FL 32789, 407-646-2676, fax 407-646-1515, e-mail bcnews@rollins.edu: Lists paid advertisements for vacancies. Free to members, $10/year to others. Published bimonthly by Four-G Publishers, Inc. News accepted continuously. Biographies, essays, books, and reviews of interest to members are invited.

**C. Berger And Company** (CBC), 327 E. Gundersen Dr., Carol Stream, IL 60188, 630-653-1115, 800-382-4222, fax 630-653-1691, e-mail c-berg@ dupagels.lib.ilus, World Wide Web http://www.cberger.com: CBC conducts nationwide executive searches to fill permanent positions in libraries, information centers, and related businesses at the management, supervisory, and director level. Professionals and clerks are also available from CBC as temporary workers or contract personnel for short- and long-term assignments in special, academic, and public libraries in Illinois, Indiana, Georgia, Pennsylvania, Texas, and Wisconsin. CBC also provides library and records management consulting services and direction and staff to manage projects for clients.

**Canadian Library Association**, 200 Elgin St., Suite 602, Ottawa, ON K2P 1L5, 613-232-9625: Publishes career ads in *Feliciter* magazine. CASLIS division offers job bank service in several cities. Operates Jobmart at the annual conference in June.

**Catholic Library Association**, 9009 Carter St., Allen Park, MI 48101: Personal and institutional members of the association are given free space (35 words) to advertise for jobs or to list job openings in *Catholic Library World* (four issues a year). Others may advertise. Contact advertising coordinator for rates.

**Chinese-American Librarians Association Newsletter**, c/o Lan Yang, Sterling C. Evans Library, Texas A&M University, College Station, TX 77843-5000: Job listings in newsletter issued in February, June, October. Free to members.

**Council on Library/Media Technicians, Inc.**, c/o Membership Chair Julia Ree, Box 52057, Riverside, CA 92517-3057: *COLT Newsletter* appears bimonthly in *Library Mosaics*. Personal dues: U.S. $35, foreign, $60, students $30; Institutions: U.S. $60, foreign $85.

**Gossage Regan Associates, Inc.**, 25 W. 43rd St., New York, NY 10036, 212-869-3348, fax 212-997-1127: An executive search firm specializing in the recruitment of library directors and other library/information-handling organization top management. About 50 nationwide searches have been conducted since 1983 for public, academic, and large specialized libraries in all regions. Salary limitation: $60,000 up. Library Executive Recruiters: Wayne Gossage, Joan Neumann.

**Wontawk Gossage Associates**, 25 W. 43rd St., New York, NY 10036, 212-869-3348, fax 212-997-1127, and 304 Newbury St., No. 314, Boston, MA 02115, 617-867-9209, fax 617-437-9317: Temporary/long term/temporary-to-permanent assignments in the New York/New Jersey/Connecticut and the Boston metropolitan areas in all types of libraries/information management, professional and support, all levels of responsibility, all skills. The original library temporaries firm, since 1980, as Gossage Regan. In charge: Nancy Melin Nelson, MLS; Gordon Gossage.

**Independent Educational Services**, 1101 King St., Suite 305, Alexandria, VA 22314, 800-257-5102, 703-548-9700, fax 703-548-7171, World Wide Web http://www.ies-search.org: IES is a nonprofit faculty and administrative placement agency for independent elementary and secondary schools across the country. Qualified candidates must possess an MLS degree and some experience in a school setting working with students. Jobs range from assistant librarians and interns to head librarians and rebuilding entire libraries/multimedia centers. Regional offices in Boston and San Francisco.

**Labat-Anderson, Inc.**, 8000 Westpark Dr., No. 400, McLean, VA 22102, 703-506-9600, fax 703-506-4646: One of the largest providers of library and records management services to the federal government. Supports various federal agencies in 27 states, with many positions located in the Washington, D.C., Atlanta, and San Francisco areas. Résumés and cover letters will gladly be accepted from librarians with an ALA-accredited MLS and records managers, or from applicants with library and/or records management experience, for full- and part-time employment.

**The Library Co-Op, Inc.**, 3840 Park Ave., Suite 107, Edison, NJ 08820, 732-906-1777 or 800-654-6275, fax 732-906-3562, e-mail librco@compuserve.com: The company is licensed as both a temporary and permanent employment agency and supplies consultants to work in a wide variety of information settings and functions from library moving to database management, catalog maintenance, reference, retrospective conversion, and more. Recent developments include the forming of a new division, ABCD Filing Services, and the hiring of two specialists in space planning. Another new division, LAIRD Consulting, provides a full range of automation expertise for hardware, software, LANS, and WANS.

**Library Management Systems**, Corporate Pointe, Suite 755, Culver City, CA 90230, 310-216-6436, 800-567-4669, fax 310-649-6388, e-mail lms@ix.netcom.com; and Three Bethesda Metro Center, Suite 700, Bethesda, MD 20814, 301-961-1984, fax 301-652-6240, e-mail lmsdc@ix.netcom.com: LMS has been providing library staffing, recruitment, and consulting to public and special libraries and businesses since 1983. It organizes and manages special libraries; designs and implements major projects (including retrospective conversions, automation studies, and records management); performs high-quality cataloging outsourcing; and furnishes contract staffing to all categories of information centers. LMS has a large database of librarians and library assistants on call for long- and short-term projects and provides permanent placement at all levels.

**Library Mosaics**, Box 5171, Culver City, CA 90231, 310-645-4998: *Library Mosaics* magazine is published bimonthly and will accept listings for library/media support staff positions. However, correspondence relating to jobs cannot be handled.

**Medical Library Association**, 65 E. Wacker Pl., Suite 1900, Chicago, IL 60601-7298, 312-419-9094, ext. 29; World Wide Web http://www.mlanet.org: *MLA News* (10 issues a year, June/July and November/December combined issues) lists positions wanted and positions available in its Employment Opportunities column. The position available rate is $2.80 per word. Up to 50 free words for MLA members plus $2.45 per word over 50 words. Members and nonmembers may rerun ads once in the next consecutive issue for $25. All positions available advertisements must list a minimum salary; a salary range is preferred. Positions wanted rates are $1.50 per word for nonmembers, $1.25 per word for members with 100 free words; $1.25 will be charged for each word exceeding 100. MLA

also offers a placement service at annual conference each spring. Job advertisements received for *MLA News* are posted to the MLANET Jobline.
**Music Library Association**, c/o Elisabeth H. Rebman, MLA Placement Officer, 1814 Pine Grove Ave., Colorado Springs, CO 80906-2930, 7619-475-1960, e-mail erebman@library.berkeley.edu, World Wide web http://www.musiclibraryassoc. org.se_job.htm: Monthly job list ($20/year individuals, $25 organizations), from: MLA Business Office, Box 487, Canton, MA 02021, 781-828-8450, fax 781-828-8915, e-mail acadsvc@aol.com.
**Pro Libra Associates, Inc.**, 6 Inwood Pl., Maplewood, NJ 07040, 201-762-0070, 800-262-0070, e-mail prolibra-2@mail.idt.net. A multi-service agency specializing in consulting, personnel, and project support for libraries and information centers.
**REFORMA, National Association to Promote Library Service to the Spanish-Speaking**, Box 832, Anaheim, CA 92815-0832: Those wishing to do direct mailings to the REFORMA membership of 900-plus may obtain mailing labels arranged by zip code for $100. Contact Al Milo, 714-738-6383. Job ads are also published quarterly in the *REFORMA Newsletter*. For rate information, contact Denice Adkins, 303-571-1665, fax 303-572-4787.
**Society of American Archivists**, 527 S. Wells St., 5th flr., Chicago, IL 60607-3922, fax 312-922-1452, e-mail info@archivists.org, World Wide Web http://www.archivists.org: *Archival Outlook* is sent (to members only) six times annually and contains features about the archival profession and other timely pieces on courses in archival administration, meetings, and professional opportunities (job listings). The Online Employment Bulletin is a weekly listing of professional opportunities posted on the SAA Web site. The *SAA Employment Bulletin* is a bimonthly listing of job opportunities available to members by subscription for $24 a year, and to non-members for $10 per issue. Prepayment is required.
**Special Libraries Association**, 1700 18th St. N.W., Washington, DC 20009-2508, 202-234-4700, fax 202-265-9317, e-mail sla@sla.org, World Wide Web http://www.sla.org: SLA maintains a telephone jobline, SpeciaLine, operating 24 hours a day, seven days a week, 202-234-4700, ext. 1. Most SLA chapters have employment chairs who act as referral persons for employers and job seekers. Several SLA chapters have joblines. The association's monthly magazine, *Information Outlook*, carries classified advertising. SLA offers an employment clearinghouse and career advisory service during its annual conference, held in June. SLA also provides a discount to members using the résumé evaluation service offered through Advanced Information Management. A "Guide to Career Opportunities" is a resource kit for $20 (SLA members, $15); "Getting a Job: Tips and Techniques" is free to unemployed SLA members. The SLA Job Bulletin Board, a computer listserv, is organized by Indiana University staff. Subscribe by sending the message *subscribe SLAJOB (first name, last name)* to listserv@iubvm.ucs.indiana.edu.
**TeleSec CORESTAFF**, Information Management Division, 11160 Veirs Mill Rd., Suite 414, Wheaton, MD 20902, 301-949-4097, fax 301-949-8729, e-mail telesec@clark.net: Offers many opportunities to get started in the metropolitan Washington, D.C., library market through short- and long-term assignments in federal agencies, law firms, corporations, associations, and academic institutions. Founded in 1948, TeleSec CORESTAFF has been performing library technical projects including cataloging, interlibrary loans, database design, and acquisi-

tions since the late 1960s. It also offers temporary-to-hire, full-hire, and contract positions.

**Tuft & Associates, Inc.**, 1209 Astor St., Chicago, IL 60610, 312-642-8889, fax 312-642-8883: Specialists in nationwide executive searches for administrative posts in libraries and information centers.

## State Library Agencies

In addition to the joblines mentioned previously, some state library agencies issue lists of job openings within their areas. These include: Colorado (weekly, sent on receipt of stamps and mailing labels; also available via listserv and Access Colorado Library and Information Network—ACLIN; send SASE for access); Indiana (monthly on request) 317-232-3697 or 800-451-6028 (Indiana area), e-mail ehubbard@statelib.lib.in.us; Iowa (Joblist, monthly on request), e-mail awettel@mail.lib.state.ia.us; Mississippi (Library Job Opportunities, monthly); and Nebraska.

State libraries in several states have electronic bulletin board services that list job openings. Web addresses are: Colorado http://www.aclin org (also lists out-of-state jobs); District of Columbia (Metropolitan Washington Council of Government Libraries Council) www.mwcog.org/ic/jobline.html; Florida, www.dos.state.fl.us/dlis/jobs.html; Georgia, www.public.lib.ga.us/pls/job-bank; Idaho, www.lili.org/staff/jobs. htm; Indiana, www.statelib.lib.in.us/www/ldo/posopl6.html; Iowa, www.silo.lib.ia.us; Kentucky www.kdla.state.ky.us/libserv/jobline.htm; Louisiana www.smt.state.lib.la.us/statelib.htm; Massachusetts www.mlin.lib.ma.us; Montana www.jsd.dli.state.mt.us/; Nebraska www.nlc. state.ne.us/libjob; North Carolina www.statelibrary.dcr. state.nc.us/jobs/jobs.htm (both professional and paraprofessional library positions); Texas, www.tsl. state.tx.us; Oklahoma (via modem) 405-524-4089; South Carolina, www.state. sc.us/scs/lion.html; Virginia www.vsla.edu. In Pennsylvania, the listserv is maintained by Commonwealth Libraries. Arizona offers a jobline service at the e-mail address tcorkery@lib.az.us.

On occasion, the following state library newsletters or journals will list vacancy postings: Alabama (*Cottonboll*, quarterly); Alaska (*Newspoke*, bimonthly); Arizona (*Arizona Libraries NewsWeek*); Indiana (*Focus on Indiana Libraries*, 11 times/year; Iowa (*Joblist*); Kansas (*Kansas Libraries*, monthly); Louisiana (*Library Communique*, monthly); Minnesota (*Minnesota Libraries News*, monthly); Nebraska (*NCompass*, quarterly); New Hampshire (*Granite State Libraries*, bimonthly); New Mexico (*Hitchhiker*, weekly); Tennessee (*TLA Newsletter*, bimonthly); Utah (*Directions for Utah Libraries*, monthly); and Wyoming (*Outrider*, monthly).

Many state library agencies will refer applicants informally when vacancies are known to exist, but do not have formal placement services. The following states primarily make referrals to public libraries only: Alabama, Alaska, Arizona, Arkansas, California, Louisiana, Pennsylvania, South Carolina (institutional also), Tennessee, Utah, Vermont, and Virginia. Those that refer applicants to all types of libraries are: Alaska, Delaware, Florida, Georgia, Hawaii, Idaho, Kansas, Kentucky, Maine, Maryland, Mississippi, Montana, Nebraska, Nevada (largely public and academic), New Hampshire, New Mexico, North Carolina, North Dakota, Ohio, Pennsylvania, Rhode Island, South Dakota, Vermont, West Virginia (on Pennsylvania Jobline, public, academic, special), and Wyoming. The following state libraries post library vacancy notices for all types of libraries on a bulletin board: California, Connecticut, Florida, Georgia, Hawaii, Illinois, Indiana, Iowa, Kentucky, Michigan, Montana, Nevada, New Jersey, New York, Ohio, Oklahoma, Pennsylvania, South Carolina, South Dakota, Texas, Utah, and Washington. [Addresses of the state agencies are found in Part 6 of the *Bowker Annual* and in *American Library Directory—Ed.*]

## State and Regional Library Associations

State and regional library associations will often make referrals, run ads in association newsletters, or operate a placement service at annual conferences, in addition to the joblines sponsored by some groups. Referral of applicants when jobs are known is done by the following associations: Arkansas, Delaware, Hawaii, Louisiana, Michigan, Minnesota, Nevada, Pennsylvania, South Dakota, Tennessee, and Wisconsin. Although listings are infrequent, job vacancies are placed in the following association newsletters or journals when available: Alabama (*Alabama Librarian*, 7/year); Alaska (*Newspoke*, bimonthly); Arizona (*Newsletter*, 10/year); Arkansas (*Arkansas Libraries*, 6/year); Connecticut (*Connecticut Libraries*, 11/year); Delaware (*Delaware Library Association Bulletin*, 3/year); District of Columbia (*Intercom*, 11/year); Florida (*Florida Libraries*, 6/year); Indiana (*Focus on Indiana Libraries*, 11/year); Iowa (*Catalyst*, 6/year); Kansas (*KLA Newsletter*, 6 issues/bimonthly); Minnesota (*MLA Newsletter*, 6 issues/bimonthly); Missouri (bimonthly); Mountain Plains (*MPLA Newsletter*, bimonthly, lists vacancies and position wanted ads for individuals and institutions); Nebraska (*NLAQ*); Nevada (*Highroller*, 4/year); New Hampshire (*NHLA* Newsletter, 6/year); New Jersey (*NJLA Newsletter*, 10/year); New Mexico (shares notices via state library's *Hitchhiker*, weekly); New York (*NYLA Bulletin*, 10/year; free for institutional members; $25/1 week, $40/2 weeks, others); Ohio (*ACCESS*, monthly); Oklahoma (*Oklahoma Librarian*, 6/year); Rhode Island (*RILA Bulletin*, 6/year); South Carolina (*News and Views*); South Dakota (*Book Marks*, bimonthly); Tennessee (*TLA Newsletter*); Vermont (*VLA News*, 10/year); Virginia (*Virginia Libraries*, quarterly); and West Virginia (*West Virginia Libraries*, 6/year).

The following associations have indicated some type of placement service, although it may only be held at annual conferences: Alabama, California, Connecticut, Georgia, Idaho, Indiana, Iowa, Kansas, Kentucky, Louisiana, Maryland, Massachusetts, Mountain Plains, New England, New Jersey, New York, North Carolina (biennial), Ohio, Pacific Northwest, Pennsylvania, South Dakota, Southeastern, Tennessee, Texas, Vermont, and Wyoming.

The following have indicated they have an electronic source for job postings in addition to voice joblines: California, www.cla-net.org/html/jobline.html; Illinois, www.ila.org; Kansas, www.skyways.lib.ks.us/kansas/KLA/helpwanted (no charge to list job openings); Minnesota, www.libmankato.musu.edu:2000; Missouri, www.mlnc.com/~mla; Nebraska, www.nlc.state.ne.us/libjob/

libjob.html; New Jersey Library Association, www.burlco.lib.nj.us/NJLA; Oklahoma, www.state.ok.us/~odl/fyi/jobline.htm (e-mail bpetrie@oltn.odl. state.ok.us); Pacific Northwest Library Association, e-mail listserv@wln.com or listserv@ldbsu.idbsu.edu; Texas, www.txla.org/jobline/jobline.txt; Virginia, www.vla.org; Wisconsin, www.wla.lib.wi.us/wlajob.htm.

The following associations have indicated they have no placement service at this time: Colorado, Middle Atlantic Regional Library Federation, Midwest Federation, Minnesota, Mississippi, Montana, Nebraska, Nevada, New Mexico, North Dakota, Oklahoma, Utah, and West Virginia. [State and regional association addresses are listed in Part 6 of the *Bowker Annual.—Ed.*]

## Library and Information Studies Programs

Library and information studies programs offer some type of service for their current students as well as alumni. Most schools provide job-hunting and résumé-writing seminars. Many have outside speakers representing different types of libraries or recent graduates relating career experiences. Faculty or a designated placement officer offer individual advising services or critiquing of résumés.

Of the ALA-accredited library and information studies programs, the following handle placement activities through the program: Alabama, Albany, Alberta, Buffalo (compiles annual graduate biographical listings), British Columbia, Dalhousie, Dominican, Drexel, Hawaii, Illinois, Kent State, Kentucky, Louisiana, McGill, Missouri (College of Education), Pittsburgh (Department of Library and Information Science only), Pratt, Puerto Rico, Queens, Rhode Island, Rutgers, Saint John's, South Carolina, Syracuse, Tennessee, Texas–Austin, Toronto, UCLA, Western Ontario, Wisconsin–Madison, and Wisconsin–Milwaukee.

The central university placement center handles activities for the following schools: California–Berkeley (alumni) and Emporia. However, in most cases, faculty in the library school will still do informal counseling regarding job seeking.

In some schools, the placement services are handled in a cooperative manner; in most cases the university placement center sends out credentials while the library school posts or compiles the job listings. Schools utilizing one or both sources include: Alabama, Albany, Arizona (School of Information Resources and Library Science maintains an e-mail list: jobops@listserv.arizona.edu), Buffalo, Catholic, Dominican, Florida State, Indiana, Iowa, Kent State, Long Island, Maryland, Michigan, Montreal, North Carolina–Chapel Hill, North Carolina–Greensboro, North Carolina Central, North Texas, Oklahoma, Pittsburgh, Queens, Saint John's, San Jose, Simmons, South Florida, Southern Connecticut, Southern Mississippi, Syracuse, Tennessee, Texas Woman's, Washington, Wayne State, and Wisconsin–Milwaukee. In sending out placement credentials, schools vary as to whether they distribute these free, charge a general registration fee, or request a fee for each file or credential sent out.

Those schools that have indicated they post job vacancy notices for review but do not issue printed lists are: Alabama, Alberta, Arizona, British Columbia, Buffalo, Catholic, Clark Atlanta, Dalhousie, Drexel, Florida State, Hawaii,

Illinois, Indiana, Kent State, Kentucky, Long Island, Louisiana, Maryland, McGill, Missouri, Montreal, North Carolina–Chapel Hill, North Carolina–Greensboro, North Carolina Central, Oklahoma, Pittsburgh, Puerto Rico, Queens, Rutgers, Saint John's, San Jose, Simmons, South Carolina, Southern Mississippi, Syracuse (general postings), Tennessee, Texas Woman's, Toronto, UCLA, Washington, Wayne State, Western Ontario, and Wisconsin–Madison.

In addition to job vacancy postings, some schools issue printed listings, operate joblines, have electronic access, or provide database services:

- Albany: Job Placement Bulletin free to SISP students; listserv@cnsibm. albany.edu to subscribe
- Arizona: listserv@listserv.arizona.edu to subscribe
- British Columbia: uses BCLA Jobline, 604-430-6411
- Buffalo: two job postings listservs; for alumni, sils-l@listserv.acsu.buffalo. edu, for students ubmls-l@listserv.acsu.buffalo.edu.
- California–Berkeley: weekly out-of-state job list and jobline free to all students and graduates for six months after graduation; $55 annual fee for alumni of any University of California campus; call 510-642-3283
- Clarion: http://www.clarion.edu/academic/edu-humn/nelibsci/jobs
- Dalhousie: (listserv for Atlantic Canada jobs, send message saying sub list-joblist to mailserv@ac.dal.ca
- Dominican: Placement News every two weeks, free for 6 months following graduation, $15/year for students and alumni; $25/year others
- Drexel: http://www.cis.drexel.edu/placement/placement.html
- Emporia: weekly bulletin for school, university, public jobs; separate bulletin for special; $42/6 months; Emporia graduates, $21/6 months)
- Florida State
- Hawaii
- Illinois: free online placement JOBSearch database available on campus and via access through telnet alexia.lis.uiuc.edu, login: jobs, password: Urbaign; or http://www.carousel.lis.uiuc.edu/~jobs/
- Indiana: free for one year after graduation (alumni and others may send self-addressed, stamped envelopes); or access http://www-slis.lib.indiana.edu/21stcentury
- Iowa ($15/year for registered students and alumni)
- Kentucky: http://www.uky.edu/CommInfoStudies/SLIS/jobs.htm
- Maryland: send subscribe message to listserv@umdd.umd.edu
- Michigan: http://www.si.umich.edu/jobfinder
- Missouri: http://www.coe.missouri.edu/career
- North Carolina–Chapel Hill: send subscribe message to listserv@ils.unc.edu, or see http://www.ils.unc.edu/ils/careers/resources)
- Oklahoma
- Pittsburgh: http://www.sis/pitt.edu/~lsdept/libjobs.htm

- Pratt: free to students and alumni for full-time/part-time professional positions only
- Rhode Island: monthly, $7.50/year
- Rutgers: http://www.scils.rutgers.edu or send subscribe message to listserv@scils.rutgers.edu
- Simmons: http://www.simmons.edu/gslis/jobline.html; Simmons also operates the New England Jobline (617-521-2815), which announces professional vacancies in the region
- South Carolina: http://www.libsci.sc.edu/career/job.htm)
- Southern Connecticut (http://www.scsu.ctstateu.edu/~jobline; printed listing twice a month, mailed to students and alumni free, also on gopher at scsu.ctstateu.edu
- South Florida: in cooperation with ALISE; $10/year to subscribe
- St. John's: subscribe message to listserv@maelstrom.stjohns.edu
- Syracuse: sends lists of job openings by e-mail to students
- Texas–Austin: Weekly Placement Bulletin $16/6 mos., $28/yr. by listserv, $26/6 mos., $48/yr. by mail (free to students and alumni for one year following graduation); Texas Job Weekly, $16/6 months or $28/year, or see http://www.gslis.utexas.edu/~placemnt/index.html)
- Texas Woman's: http://www.twu.edu/slis/
- Toronto: http://www.fis.utoronto.ca/news/jobsite
- Wisconsin–Madison: sends listings from Wisconsin and Minnesota to Illinois for JOBSearch
- Wisconsin–Milwaukee: send subscription message to listserv@slis.uwm.edu; selected jobs sent to students by e-mail
- Western Ontario: http://www.uwo.ca/gslis/information

Employers will often list jobs with schools only in their particular geographical area; some library schools will give information to non-alumni regarding their specific locales, but are not staffed to handle mail requests and advice is usually given in person. Schools that have indicated they will allow librarians in their areas to view listings are: Alabama, Albany, Alberta, Arizona, British Columbia, Buffalo, California–Berkeley, Catholic, Clarion, Clark Atlanta, Dalhousie, Dominican, Drexel, Emporia, Florida State, Hawaii, Illinois, Indiana, Iowa, Kent State, Kentucky, Louisiana, Maryland, McGill, Michigan, Missouri, Montreal, North Carolina–Chapel Hill, North Carolina Central, North Carolina–Greensboro, University of North Texas, Oklahoma, Pittsburgh, Pratt, Puerto Rico, Queens, Rhode Island, Rutgers, Simmons, Saint John's, San Jose, South Carolina, South Florida, Southern Connecticut, Southern Mississippi, Syracuse, Tennessee, Texas–Austin, Texas Woman's, Toronto, UCLA, Washington, Wayne State, Western Ontario, Wisconsin–Madison, and Wisconsin–Milwaukee.

A list of ALA-accredited programs with addresses and telephone numbers can be requested from ALA or found elsewhere in Part 3 of the *Bowker Annual.* Individuals interested in placement services of other library education programs should contact the schools directly.

## Federal Employment Information Sources

Consideration for employment in many federal libraries requires establishing civil service eligibility. Although the actual job search is your responsibility, the Office of Personnel Management (OPM) has developed the "USA Jobs" Web site (http://www.usajobs.opm.gov) to assist you along the way.

OPM's Career America Connection at 912-757-3000, TDD Service at 912-744-2299, is a telephone-based system that provides current worldwide federal job opportunities, salary and employee benefits information, special recruitment messages, and more. You can also record your request to have application packages, forms, and other employment-related literature mailed to you. This service is available 24 hours a day, seven days a week. Request Federal Employment Information Line fact sheet EI-42, "Federal Employment Information Sources," for a complete listing of local telephone numbers to this nationwide network.

OPM's USA Jobs, 912-757-3100 or 202-606-2700, is a computer-based bulletin board system that provides current worldwide federal job opportunities, salaries and pay rates, general and specific employment information, and more. You can also contact OPM on the Internet via Telnet at fjob.mail.opm.gov and by file transfer protocol at ftp.fjob.mail.opn.gov. Information about obtaining federal job announcement files via the Internet mail should be directed to info@fjob.mail.opm.gov. The state employment service has current federal jobs on microfiche, computer, and other formats.

USA Jobs Touch Screen Computer is a computer-based system utilizing touch-screen technology. These kiosks, found throughout the nation in OPM offices, Federal Office Buildings, and other locations, allow you to access current worldwide federal job opportunities, online information, and more.

Once you have found an opportunity that interests you, you may obtain a copy of the vacancy announcement and a complete application package by leaving your name and address in one of the automated systems or, when available, by downloading the actual announcement and any supplementary materials from FJOB. Although the federal government does not require a standard application form for most jobs, certain information is needed to evaluate your qualifications if you decide to submit any format other than the OF-612 form.

Another Web site for federal jobs is http://www.fedworld.gov/jobs/jobsearch.html.

Applicants should attempt to make personal contact directly with federal agencies in which they are interested. This is essential in the Washington, D.C., area where more than half the vacancies occur. Most librarian positions are in three agencies: Army, Navy, and Veterans Administration.

There are some "excepted" agencies that are not required to hire through the usual OPM channels. While these agencies may require the standard forms, they maintain their own employee selection policies and procedures. Government establishments with positions outside the competitive civil service include: Board of Governors of the Federal Reserve System, Central Intelligence Agency, Defense Intelligence Agency, Department of Medicine and Surgery, Federal Bureau of Investigation, Foreign Service of the United States, General Accounting Office, Library of Congress, National Science Foundation, National Security Agency, Tennessee Valley Authority, U.S. Nuclear Regulatory Commission, U.S. Postal Service, Judicial Branch of the Government,

Legislative Branch of the Government, U.S. Mission to the United Nations, World Bank and IFC, International Monetary Fund, Organization of American States, Pan American Health Organization, and United Nations Secretariat.

The Library of Congress, the world's largest and most comprehensive library, is an excepted service agency in the legislative branch and administers its own independent merit selection system. Job classifications, pay, and benefits are the same as in other federal agencies, and qualifications requirements generally correspond to those used by the U.S. Office of Personnel Management. The library does not use registers, but announces vacancies as they become available. A separate application must be submitted for each vacancy announcement. For most professional positions, announcements are widely distributed and open for a minimum period of 30 days. Qualifications requirements and ranking criteria are stated on the vacancy announcement. The Library of Congress Human Resources Operations Office is located in the James Madison Memorial Building, 101 Independence Avenue S.E., Washington, DC 20540, 202-707-5620.

## Additional General and Specialized Job Sources

**Affirmative Action Register**, 8356 Olive Blvd., St. Louis, MO 63132: The goal is to "provide female, minority, handicapped, and veteran candidates with an opportunity to learn of professional and managerial positions throughout the nation and to assist employers in implementing their Equal Opportunity Employment programs." Free distribution of a monthly bulletin is made to leading businesses, industrial and academic institutions, and over 4,000 agencies that recruit qualified minorities and women, as well as to all known female, minority, and handicapped professional organizations, placement offices, newspapers, magazines, rehabilitation facilities, and over 8,000 federal, state, and local governmental employment units with a total readership in excess of 3.5 million (audited). Individual mail subscriptions are available for $15 per year. Librarian listings are in most issues. Sent free to libraries on request.

**The Chronicle of Higher Education** (published weekly with breaks in August and December), 1255 23rd St. N.W., Suite 700, Washington, DC 20037, 202-466-1055; fax 202-296-2691: Publishes a variety of library positions each week, including administrative and faculty jobs. Job listings are searchable by specific categories, keywords, or geographic location on the Internet at http://Chronicle.com/jobs.

**Academic Resource Network On-Line Database (ARNOLD)**, 4656 W. Jefferson, Suite 140, Fort Wayne, IN 46804: This World Wide Web interactive database helps faculty, staff, and librarians to identify partners for exchange or collaborative research (http://www.arnold.snybuf.edu).

**School Libraries**: School librarians often find that the channels for locating positions in education are of more value than the usual library ones, for instance, contacting county or city school superintendent offices. Other sources include university placement offices that carry listings for a variety of school system jobs. A list of commercial teacher agencies may be obtained from the National Association of Teachers' Agencies, Dr. Eugene Alexander, CPC, CTC, Treas., c/o G. A. Agency, 524 South Ave. E., Cranford, NJ 07016-3209, 908-272-2080, fax 908-272-2080, World Wide Web http://www.jobsforteachers.com.

## Overseas

Opportunities for employment in foreign countries are limited and immigration policies of individual countries should be investigated. Employment for Americans is virtually limited to U.S. government libraries, libraries of U.S. firms doing worldwide business, and American schools abroad. Library journals from other countries will sometimes list vacancy notices. Some persons have obtained jobs by contacting foreign publishers or vendors directly. Non-U.S. government jobs usually call for foreign language fluency. *Career Opportunities for Bilinguals and Multilinguals: A Directory of Resources in Education, Employment and Business* by Vladimir F. Wertsman (Scarecrow Press, 1991, ISBN 0-8108-2439-6, $35), gives general contact names for foreign employment and business resources. "International Jobs" by Wertsman (*RQ*, Fall 1992, pp. 14–19) provides a listing of library resources for finding jobs abroad. Another source is the librarian job vacancy postings at http://bubl.ac.uk/news/jobs, a listing of U.S. and foreign jobs collected by the Bulletin Board for Libraries.

**Council for International Exchange of Scholars (CIES)**, 3007 Tilden St. N.W., Suite 5M, Washington, DC 20008-3009, 202-686-7877, e-mail cies1@ciesnet. cies.org, World Wide Web http://www.cies.org: Administers U.S. government Fulbright awards for university lecturing and advanced research abroad; usually 10–15 awards per year are made to U.S. citizens who are specialists in library or information sciences. In addition, many countries offer awards in any specialization of research or lecturing. Lecturing awards usually require university or college teaching experience. Several opportunities exist for professional librarians as well. Applications and information may be obtained, beginning in March each year, directly from CIES. Worldwide application deadline is August 1.

**Department of Defense, Dependents Schools**, Recruitment Unit, 4040 N. Fairfax Dr., Arlington, VA 22203, 703-696-3068, fax 703-696-2697, e-mail recruitment@odeddodea.edu: Overall management and operational responsibilities for the education of dependent children of active duty U.S. military personnel and Department of Defense civilians who are stationed in foreign areas. Also responsible for teacher recruitment. For complete application brochure, write to above address. The latest edition of *Overseas Opportunities for Educators* is available and provides information on educator employment opportunities in over 165 schools worldwide. The schools are operated on military installations for the children of U.S. military and civilian personnel stationed overseas.

**International Schools Services (ISS)**, Box 5910, Princeton, NJ 08543, 609-452-0990: Private, not-for-profit organization founded in 1955 to serve American schools overseas other than Department of Defense schools. These are American, international elementary and secondary schools enrolling children of business and diplomatic families living abroad. ISS services to overseas schools include recruitment and recommendation of personnel, curricular and administrative guidance, purchasing, facility planning, and more. ISS also publishes a comprehensive directory of overseas schools and a bimonthly newsletter, *NewsLinks*, for those interested in the intercultural educational community. Information regarding these publications and other services may be obtained by writing to the above address.

**Peace Corps**, 1990 K St. N.W., No. 9300, Washington, DC 20526: Volunteer opportunities exist for those holding MA/MS or BA/BS degrees in library science with one year of related work experience. Two-year tour of duty. U.S. citizens only. Living allowance, health care, transportation, and other benefits provided. Write for additional information and application or call 800-424-8580.

**Search Associates**, Box 922, Jackson, MI 49204-0922, 517-768-9250, fax 517-768-9252, e-mail JimAmbrose@compuserve.com, http://www.search-associates.com: A private organization comprised of former overseas school directors who organize about ten recruitment fairs (most occur in February) to place teachers, librarians, and administrators in about 400 independent K–12 American/international schools around the world. These accredited schools, based on the American model, serve the children of diplomats and businessmen from dozens of countries. They annually offer highly attractive personal and professional opportunities for experienced librarians.

**U.S. Information Agency (USIA)**: called U.S. Information Service (USIS) overseas, employs Information Resource Officers (librarians) on an as-needed basis. Candidates must have a master's degree in librarianship from an ALA-accredited graduate program and a minimum of four years of progressively responsible experience in adult library services, with in-depth functional experience in reference services or information resources management. A subject background in the social sciences is highly desirable, as are strong written and oral communication skills. Applicants must submit a current SF-171 (Application for Federal Employment) or OF-612 (Optional Application for Federal Employment, and the OF-306 (Declaration for Federal Employment), plus a 1,000-word autobiographical statement that should include a description of qualifications and reasons for seeking employment with USIA. U.S. citizenship is required. Benefits include overseas allowances and differentials where applicable, vacation and sick leave, health and life insurance, and a 20-year retirement program. Send application to USIA, Foreign Service Recruitment Officer for IROs, M/HRFP, Rm. 508, 401 Fourth St. S.W., Washington, DC 20547. Call 202-619-4702 for more information.

## Overseas Exchange Programs

International Exchanges: Most exchanges are handled by direct negotiation between interested parties. A few libraries have established exchange programs for their own staff. In order to facilitate exchange arrangements, the *IFLA Journal* (issued January, May, August, and October/November) lists persons wishing to exchange positions outside their own country. All listings must include the following information: full name, address, present position, qualifications (with year of obtaining), language, abilities, preferred country/city/library, and type of position. Send to International Federation of Library Associations and Institutions (IFLA) Secretariat, Box 95312, 2509 CH The Hague, Netherlands, fax 31-70-3834027, World Wide Web http://www.ifla.org.

**LIBEX Bureau for International Staff Exchange**, c/o A. J. Clark, Thomas Parry Library, University of Wales, Aberystwyth, Llanbadarn Fawr, Ceredigion SY23 3AS, Wales, 011-44-1970-622417, fax 011-44-1970-622190, e-mail parrylib@aber.ac.uk, World Wide Web http://www.aber.ac.uk/tplwww/parry.html. Assists in two-way exchanges for British librarians wishing to work abroad and for librarians from the United States, Canada, EC countries, and Commonwealth and other countries who wish to undertake exchanges.

## Using Information Skills in Nonlibrary Settings

A great deal of interest has been shown in using information skills in a variety of ways in nonlibrary settings. These jobs are not usually found through the regular library placement sources, although many library and information studies programs are trying to generate such listings for their students and alumni. Job listings that do exist may not call specifically for "librarians" by that title so that ingenuity may be needed to search out jobs where information management skills are needed. Some librarians are working on a freelance basis, offering services to businesses, alternative schools, community agencies, legislators, etc.; these opportunities are usually not found in advertisements but created by developing contacts and publicity over a period of time.

A number of information-brokering businesses have developed from individual freelance experiences. Small companies or other organizations often need "one-time" service for organizing files or collections, bibliographic research for special projects, indexing or abstracting, compilation of directories, and consulting services. Bibliographic networks and online database companies are using librarians as information managers, trainers, researchers, systems and database analysts, online services managers, etc. Jobs in this area are sometimes found in library network newsletters or data processing journals. Librarians can also be found working in law firms as litigation case supervisors (organizing and analyzing records needed for specific legal cases); with publishers as sales representatives, marketing directors, editors, and computer services experts; with community agencies as adult education coordinators, volunteer administrators, grants writers, etc.

Classifieds in *Publishers Weekly* and The *National Business Employment Weekly* may lead to information-related positions. One might also consider reading the Sunday classified ad sections in metropolitan newspapers in their entirety to locate descriptions calling for information skills but under a variety of job titles.

The *Burwell World Directory of Information Brokers, 1995–96* lists information brokers, freelance librarians, independent information specialists, and institutions that provide services for a fee. There is a minimal charge for an annual listing. The Burwell Directory Online is searchable free on the Internet at http://www.burwell.com, and a CD-ROM version is available. Burwell can be reached at Burwell Enterprises, 3724 FM 1960 West, Suite 214, Houston, TX 77068, 713-537-9051, fax 713-537-8332. Also published is a bimonthly newsletter, *Information Broker* ($40, foreign postage, $15), that includes articles by, for, and about individuals and companies in the fee-based information field, book reviews, a calendar of upcoming events, and issue-oriented articles. A bibliography and other publications on the field of information brokering are also available.

The Independent Librarians Exchange Round Table is a unit within the American Library Association that serves as a networking source for persons who own their own information businesses, are consultants, or work for companies providing support services to libraries or providing other information services outside traditional library settings. Dues are $8 in addition to ALA dues and include a newsletter, *ILERT Alert*. At the 1993 ALA Annual Conference, ILERT sponsored a program on "Jobs for Indexers," which is available on cassette ALA332 for $24 from Teach'em Inc., 160 E. Illinois St., Chicago, IL 60611, 800-224-3775.

The Association of Independent Information Professionals (AIIP) was formed in 1987 for individuals who own and operate for-profit information companies. Contact AIIP Headquarters at 212-779-1855.

A growing number of publications are addressing opportunities for librarians in the broader information arena. Among them are "You Can Take Your MLS Out of the Library," by Wilda W. Williams (*Library Journal*, Nov. 1994, pp. 43–46) and "Information Entrepreneurship: Sources for Reference Librarians," by Donna L. Gilton (*RQ*, Spring 1992, pp. 346–355). *The Information Broker's Handbook* by Sue Rugge and Alfred Glossbrenner (Blue Ridge Summit, PA: Windcrest/McGraw-Hill, 1992, 379p. ISBN 0-8306-3798-2) covers the market for information, getting started, pricing and billing, and more. *Opening New Doors: Alternative Careers for Librarians*, edited by Ellis Mount (Washington, D.C.: Special Libraries Association, 1993) provides profiles of librarians who are working outside libraries. *Extending the Librarian's Domain: A Survey of Emerging Occupation Opportunities for Librarians and Information Professionals* by Forest Woody Horton, Jr. (Washington, D.C.: Special Libraries Association, 1994) explores information job components in a variety of sectors.

*Careers in Electronic Information* by Wendy Wicks (1997, 184p.) is available for $39 and *Guide to Careers in Abstracting and Indexing* by Wendy Wicks and Ann Marie Cunningham (1992, 126p.), for $29 from the National Federation of Abstracting & Information Services, 1518 Walnut St., Philadelphia, PA 19102, 215-893-1561 (e-mail nfais@nfais.org, World Wide Web http://www.pa. utulsa.edu/nfais.html).

The American Society of Indexers, Box 39366, Phoenix, AZ 85304, 602-979-5514, fax 602-532-4088, has a number of publications that would be useful for individuals who are interested in indexing careers. The organization's Web site (http://www.well.com/user/asi) has membership and publication information.

## Temporary/Part-Time Positions

Working as a substitute librarian or in temporary positions may be considered to be an alternative career path as well as an interim step while looking for a regular job. This type of work can provide valuable contacts and experience. Organizations that hire library workers for part-time or temporary jobs include Advanced Information Management, 444 Castro St., Suite 320, Mountain View, CA 94041 (415-965-7799), or 900 Wilshire Blvd., Suite 1424, Los Angeles, CA 90017 (213-243-9236); C. Berger and Company, 327 E. Gundersen Dr., Carol Stream, IL 60188 (630-653-1115 or 800-382-4222); Gossage Regan Associates, Inc., 25 W. 43 St., New York, NY 10036 (212-869-3348) and Wontawk Gossage Associates, 304 Newbury St., Suite 304, Boston, MA 02115 (617-867-9209); Information Management Division, 1160 Veirs Mill Rd., Suite 414, Wheaton, MD 20902 (301-949-4097); The Library Co-Op, Inc., 3840 Park Ave., Suite 107,

Edison, NJ 08820 (908-906-1777 or 800-654-6275); Library Management Systems, Corporate Pointe, Suite 755, Culver City, CA 90230 (310-216-6436; 800-567-4669) and Three Bethesda Metro Center, Suite 700, Bethesda, MD 20814 (301-961-1984); and Pro Libra Associates, Inc., 6 Inwood Place, Maplewood, NJ 07040 (201-762-0070).

Part-time jobs are not always advertised, but often found by canvassing local libraries and leaving applications.

## Job Hunting in General

Wherever information needs to be organized and presented to patrons in an effective, efficient, and service-oriented fashion, the skills of librarians can be applied, whether or not they are in traditional library settings. However, it will take considerable investment of time, energy, imagination, and money on the part of an individual before a satisfying position is created or obtained, in a conventional library or another type of information service. Usually, no one method or source of job-hunting can be used alone. *Library Services for Career Planning, Job Searching, and Employment Opportunities*, edited by Byron Anderson, Haworth Press, New York (1992, 183p.) is a good source and includes bibliographical references.

Public and school library certification requirements vary from state to state; contact the state library agency for such information in a particular state. Certification requirements are summarized in *Certification of Public Librarians in the United States*, 4th ed., 1991, from the ALA Office for Library Personnel Resources. A summary of school library/media certification requirements by state is found in *Requirements for Certification of Teachers, Counselors, Librarians and Administrators for Elementary and Secondary Schools*, published annually by the University of Chicago Press. "School Library Media Certification Requirements: 1994 Update" by Patsy H. Perritt also provides a compilation in *School Library Journal*, June 1994, pp. 32–49. State supervisors of school library media services may also be contacted for information on specific states.

Civil service requirements on a local, county, or state level often add another layer of procedures to the job search. Some civil service jurisdictions require written and/or oral examinations; others assign a ranking based on a review of credentials. Jobs are usually filled from the top candidates on a qualified list of applicants. Since the exams are held only at certain time periods and a variety of jobs can be filled from a single list of applicants (e.g., all Librarian I positions regardless of type of function), it is important to check whether a library in which one is interested falls under civil service procedures.

If one wishes a position in a specific subject area or in a particular geographical location, remember those reference skills to ferret information from directories and other tools regarding local industries, schools, subject collections, etc. Directories such as the *American Library Directory*, *Subject Collections*, *Directory of Special Libraries and Information Centers*, and *Directory of Federal Libraries*, as well as state directories or directories of other special subject areas can provide a wealth of information for job seekers. "The Job Hunter's Search for Company Information" by Robert Favini (*RQ*, Winter 1991, pp. 155–161) lists general reference business sources that might be useful for librarians seeking employment in companies. Some state employment offices will include library listings as part of their Job Services department. In some cases, students have pooled resources to hire a clipping service for a specific time period in order to get classified librarian ads for a particular geographical area. Other Internet sources not mentioned elsewhere include the Association of Research Libraries at http://arl.cni.org/careers/vacancy.html and http://www.careerpath.com.

For information on other job-hunting and personnel matters, request a checklist of personnel materials available from the ALA Office for Library Personnel Resources, 50 E. Huron St., Chicago, IL 60611.

# Placements and Salaries 1997:
# Breaking the $30K Barrier

Vicki L. Gregory

Associate Professor, University of South Florida School
of Library & Information Science (SLIS), Tampa

Kathleen de la Peña McCook

Professor and Director of SLIS, University of South Florida

*Library Journal's* 47th annual Placements and Salaries Survey shows that 1997 library and information science graduates have enjoyed an improving job market. For the first time, the average beginning salary for new graduates responding to the survey broke the $30,000 barrier, coming in at $30,270, significantly up from the $29,480 reported for 1996. While a growing economy may have had some effect, part of the rise may be attributed to increased placements in academic and special libraries.

Minority graduates also scored significant salary gains when compared to statistics from the previous two years. Also, as has been the tendency for some years, those new professionals working in technologically oriented jobs garnered higher average starting salaries than those working in traditional areas such as youth services, reference, and cataloging.

Graduation rates appear steady. In 1995, 42 schools reported 4,222 graduates, while in 1996, 44 schools reported 4,136 graduates. Figures for 1997 show 46 schools reporting a total of 4,370 graduates, with women (3,385) accounting for 77.46 percent of this year's graduate pool, and men (985) representing 22.54 percent. (See Table 3 for total graduates and placements by school.)

## Job Trends

Table 1 shows the job status—both by region and in total—of those 2,151 graduates from the 41 schools who reported their job status. Out of all 1,990 graduates reporting employment in any field, 93 percent (1,850) worked in some library capacity. Of those 1,850 responding as being employed in libraries, approximately 92 percent (1,700) are in permanent or temporary professional positions, with the remaining 8 percent (149) in nonprofessional jobs.

Of those reporting, 1,540 are working in full-time permanent professional positions (83.3 percent of those employed in libraries), compared to 1,549 (80.5 percent) in 1996. The number in temporary professional positions is 160 (10.4 percent of the total in library positions), while graduates employed in nonlibrary positions account for only 6.5 percent of those who reported their job status.

 *(text continues on page 380)*

## Table 1 / Status of 1997 Graduates, Spring 1998

| Region | Number of Schools Reporting | Number of Graduates | Graduates in Library Positions | | | | Graduates in Nonlibrary Positions | Unemployed or Status Unreported |
| | | | Permanent Professional | Temporary Professional | Non-professional | Total | | |
|---|---|---|---|---|---|---|---|---|
| Northeast | 15 | 789 | 566 | 61 | 58 | 685 | 45 | 58 |
| Southeast | 11 | 525 | 373 | 34 | 40 | 447 | 42 | 36 |
| Midwest | 10 | 573 | 416 | 31 | 35 | 482 | 39 | 52 |
| Southwest/West | 4 | 253 | 176 | 33 | 14 | 223 | 14 | 16 |
| Canada | 1 | 15 | 9 | 1 | 3 | 13 | 0 | 2 |
| Total | 41 | 2,155 | 1,540 | 160 | 150 | 1,850 | 140 | 164 |

Note: Table based on survey responses from both schools and individual graduates. Figures will necessarily not be fully consistent with such of the other data reported in this study that is based only on overall reporting from schools surveyed. Only a few schools were able to provide individual survey responses from all their 1997 graduates. Tables do not always add up, individually or collectively, because both schools and individuals omitted data in some cases.

## Table 2 / Placements and Full-Time Salaries of 1997 Graduates / Summary by Region

| Region | Number of Placements | Number of Reported Salaries | | | Low | | High | | Average | | | Median | | |
| | | Women | Men | Total | Women | Men | Women | Men | Women | Men | All | Women | Men | All |
|---|---|---|---|---|---|---|---|---|---|---|---|---|---|---|
| Northeast | 530 | 400 | 98 | 498 | $13,000 | $20,000 | $70,000 | $70,000 | $31,439 | $32,076 | $31,556 | $30,000 | $30,000 | $30,000 |
| Southeast | 329 | 260 | 59 | 319 | 12,000 | 16,000 | 58,843 | 75,000 | 27,852 | 28,973 | 28,065 | 27,000 | 28,000 | 27,000 |
| Midwest | 333 | 248 | 61 | 309 | 14,000 | 21,600 | 68,000 | 82,500 | 29,473 | 32,563 | 30,075 | 28,900 | 30,000 | 29,000 |
| Southwest/West | 253 | 180 | 59 | 239 | 15,000 | 15,000 | 50,000 | 60,000 | 30,898 | 31,661 | 31,086 | 30,000 | 29,000 | 30,000 |
| Canada* | 9 | 7 | 2 | 9 | 25,000 | 25,000 | 35,000 | 35,000 | 28,750 | 30,000 | 29,375 | 25,000 | 30,000 | 27,500 |
| Combined | 1,454 | 1,095 | 279 | 1,374 | 12,000 | 16,000 | 70,000 | 82,500 | 30,044 | 31,186 | 30,270 | 29,488 | 30,000 | 29,500 |

* Reported in Canadian dollars, Canadian salary figures not included in combined averages and medians.

Table 3 / 1997 Total Graduates and Placements by School

| Schools | Graduates | | | Employed | | | Unemployed | | | Students | | | Status Unknown | | |
|---|---|---|---|---|---|---|---|---|---|---|---|---|---|---|---|
| | Women | Men | Total | Women | Men | Total | Women | Men | Total | Women | Men | Total | Women | Men | Total |
| Alabama | 62 | 14 | 76 | 49 | 12 | 61 | 0 | 0 | 0 | 0 | 0 | 0 | 12 | 3 | 15 |
| Arizona | 53 | 22 | 75 | 41 | 13 | 54 | 1 | 1 | 2 | 0 | 0 | 0 | 15 | 4 | 19 |
| California (L.A.) | 32 | 9 | 41 | 13 | 4 | 17 | 0 | 0 | 0 | 0 | 0 | 0 | 19 | 5 | 24 |
| Catholic | 101 | 38 | 139 | 52 | 18 | 70 | 0 | 0 | 0 | 0 | 0 | 0 | 49 | 20 | 69 |
| Clarion | 36 | 12 | 48 | 19 | 3 | 22 | 1 | 0 | 1 | 0 | 0 | 0 | 16 | 9 | 25 |
| Dalhousie | 20 | 6 | 26 | 12 | 3 | 15 | 0 | 0 | 0 | 0 | 0 | 0 | 8 | 3 | 11 |
| Dominican | 138 | 23 | 161 | n/a | n/a | n/a | n/a | n/a | n/a | n/a | n/a | n/a | 138 | 23 | 161 |
| Drexel | 57 | 19 | 76 | 40 | 13 | 53 | 3 | 1 | 4 | 1 | 0 | 1 | 12 | 6 | 18 |
| Emporia | 105 | 19 | 124 | 63 | 6 | 69 | 2 | 0 | 2 | 1 | 0 | 1 | 39 | 13 | 52 |
| Florida State | 113 | 30 | 143 | 29 | 6 | 35 | 6 | 0 | 6 | 2 | 0 | 2 | 76 | 24 | 100 |
| Hawaii | 32 | 7 | 39 | 20 | 4 | 24 | 5 | 2 | 7 | 5 | 1 | 6 | 2 | 0 | 2 |
| Illinois* | 80 | 40 | 120 | 47 | 25 | 72 | 0 | 0 | 0 | 0 | 0 | 0 | 33 | 15 | 48 |
| Indiana | 119 | 31 | 150 | 51 | 11 | 62 | 2 | 1 | 3 | 2 | 2 | 4 | 64 | 17 | 81 |
| Iowa | 31 | 11 | 42 | 28 | 10 | 38 | 0 | 0 | 0 | 0 | 0 | 0 | 3 | 1 | 4 |
| Kent State | 124 | 30 | 154 | 67 | 7 | 74 | n/a | n/a | n/a | n/a | n/a | n/a | 57 | 23 | 80 |
| Kentucky | 61 | 26 | 87 | 32 | 13 | 45 | 4 | 0 | 4 | 1 | 0 | 1 | 24 | 13 | 37 |
| Long Island | 116 | 18 | 134 | 60 | 10 | 70 | 3 | 1 | 4 | 53 | 7 | 60 | 0 | 0 | 0 |
| Louisiana State | 63 | 19 | 82 | 56 | 0 | 56 | 0 | 15 | 15 | 0 | 0 | 0 | 7 | 4 | 11 |
| Maryland | 73 | 27 | 100 | 40 | 6 | 46 | 3 | 7 | 10 | 5 | 2 | 7 | 25 | 12 | 37 |
| Michigan | 80 | 36 | 116 | 43 | 16 | 59 | 1 | 0 | 1 | 0 | 2 | 2 | 36 | 18 | 54 |
| Missouri | 46 | 12 | 58 | 21 | 2 | 23 | 1 | 1 | 2 | 0 | 0 | 0 | 24 | 9 | 33 |
| N.C. Central | 54 | 21 | 75 | 31 | 5 | 36 | 1 | 1 | 2 | 0 | 1 | 1 | 22 | 14 | 36 |
| N.C. Chapel Hill | 58 | 12 | 70 | 21 | 4 | 25 | 0 | 0 | 0 | 0 | 0 | 0 | 37 | 8 | 45 |
| N.C. Greensboro | 42 | 17 | 59 | 19 | 8 | 27 | 3 | 0 | 3 | 3 | 1 | 4 | 17 | 8 | 25 |

| | | | | | | | | | | | | | | | |
|---|---|---|---|---|---|---|---|---|---|---|---|---|---|---|---|
| Oklahoma | 49 | 8 | n/a | n/a | n/a | n/a | n/a | n/a | n/a | n/a | n/a | n/a | 49 | 8 | 57 |
| Pittsburgh | 91 | 32 | 57 | 36 | 8 | 44 | 2 | 1 | 3 | 0 | 0 | 0 | 53 | 23 | 76 |
| Pratt | 68 | 34 | 123 | 23 | 10 | 33 | 0 | 1 | 1 | 0 | 0 | 0 | 45 | 23 | 68 |
| Queens | 77 | 21 | 102 | 29 | 9 | 38 | 0 | 0 | 0 | 0 | 0 | 0 | 48 | 12 | 60 |
| Rhode Island | 50 | 16 | 98 | 28 | 7 | 35 | 1 | 1 | 2 | 0 | 0 | 0 | 21 | 8 | 29 |
| San Jose* | 117 | 27 | 66 | 52 | 10 | 62 | 3 | 0 | 3 | 16 | 2 | 18 | 62 | 17 | 79 |
| Simmons | 153 | 30 | 144 | 131 | 28 | 159 | 1 | 1 | 1 | 1 | 0 | 1 | 5 | 0 | 5 |
| South Carolina | 192 | 39 | 183 | 97 | 12 | 109 | 1 | 0 | 2 | 1 | 0 | 1 | 93 | 26 | 119 |
| South Florida | 96 | 35 | 231 | 40 | 7 | 47 | 1 | 0 | 1 | 0 | 0 | 0 | 54 | 28 | 82 |
| Southern Connecticut | 60 | 16 | 131 | 22 | 5 | 27 | 2 | 1 | 1 | 0 | 0 | 0 | 37 | 11 | 48 |
| Southern Mississippi | 32 | 5 | 76 | 17 | 3 | 20 | 1 | 1 | 2 | 0 | 0 | 0 | 13 | 2 | 15 |
| SUNY Albany | 86 | 28 | 37 | 36 | 13 | 49 | 2 | 1 | 2 | 0 | 0 | 0 | 49 | 14 | 63 |
| SUNY Buffalo | 51 | 28 | 114 | 32 | 11 | 43 | 2 | 0 | 2 | 0 | 0 | 0 | 17 | 17 | 34 |
| St. John's | 28 | 11 | 79 | 18 | 4 | 22 | 0 | 0 | 0 | 0 | 0 | 0 | 10 | 7 | 17 |
| Syracuse | 50 | 10 | 39 | 22 | 6 | 28 | 0 | 0 | 0 | 0 | 0 | 0 | 28 | 4 | 32 |
| Tennessee | 33 | 11 | 60 | 20 | 7 | 27 | 0 | 0 | 0 | 0 | 0 | 0 | 13 | 4 | 17 |
| Texas (Austin) | 117 | 40 | 44 | 76 | 24 | 100 | 8 | 4 | 12 | 0 | 1 | 1 | 33 | 11 | 44 |
| Texas Woman's | 61 | 3 | 157 | n/a | n/a | n/a | 3 | 0 | 3 | 1 | 0 | 1 | 57 | 3 | 60 |
| Washington | 56 | 23 | 64 | 44 | 12 | 56 | 0 | 1 | 1 | 0 | 0 | 0 | 12 | 10 | 22 |
| Wayne State | 113 | 27 | 79 | 45 | 10 | 55 | 7 | 0 | 7 | 5 | 4 | 9 | 55 | 14 | 69 |
| Wisconsin (Madison) | 40 | 18 | 140 | 33 | 14 | 47 | 3 | 1 | 4 | 3 | 2 | 5 | 1 | 1 | 2 |
| Wisconsin (Milwaukee) | 69 | 24 | 58 | 14 | 6 | 20 | 1 | 0 | 1 | 1 | 0 | 1 | 53 | 18 | 71 |
| Total | 3,385 | 985 | 4,370 | 1,669 | 405 | 2,074 | 73 | 41 | 114 | 101 | 25 | 126 | 1,543 | 513 | 2,056 |

n/a=Data not provided by school.

* Illinois and San Jose total graduate data based on the *ALISE 1998 Library and Information Science Education Statistical Report*, edited by Evelyn H. Daniel and Jerry D. Saye (in press); aggregate data were not provided by school. Note: The ALISE Statistics are based on the academic year rather than a calendar year.

## Rising Salaries

The average 1997 professional salary for starting library positions ($30,270) increased by $790 over the 1996 beginner's salary ($29,480). This 2.7 percent increase is significant compared to the 1.7 percent increase experienced in 1996, which was the second lowest increase reported for the previous ten years (see Table 5). The 1997 increase is especially heartening, in that library salaries have increased at a greater rate than the Consumer Price Index (1.57 percent).

It is not surprising to find that those positions involving heavy use of technology net higher average and median salaries, continuing a trend. To the traditional job categories used in previous *Library Journal* salary and placement surveys, several technologically oriented job categories were added this year, including database management, LAN manager, telecommunications, and webmaster (see Table 6). Those reporting jobs in database management, telecommunications, automated systems, and as webmasters, taken together, indicated salaries on average 12 percent higher than the average for all.

There has been no discernible narrowing of the gender gap for salaries; male graduates, as in 1996, still earn a median salary about $500 more than females (see Table 2). The average salary for women rose 2.8 percent, from $29,226 in 1996 to $30,044 in 1997, about the same as the 2.1 percent increase in 1996. Men's average salaries went up 2.5 percent in 1997, from $30,428 to $31,186—considerably more than the 1.1 percent increase experienced in 1996.

The overall median increased from $28,000 in 1996 to $29,500 in 1997, a hefty 5.4 percent increase. The median's growth suggests that the increase in the average is probably not the result of a few large salaries skewing the data.

In 1997 salaries for minority graduates reporting rose to $30,782 from $29,007 in 1996—a seemingly significant leap of $1,775, or 6.1 percent. However, minority salaries rose only 0.3 percent in 1996 and 1 percent in 1995, below the general rate of increase, so perhaps this is a case of making up for lost time. Also, a growing percentage of employed minority graduates (33 percent in 1997 compared with 28.53 percent in 1996) reported jobs in academic libraries, with placements of minorities in school libraries falling from 36.13 percent in 1996 to only 10 percent in 1997.

## Easier Placements?

In 1997 a total of 14 institutions reported a greater availability of jobs listed by their placement services or otherwise officially made known to their students. Nine schools saw a decrease in their listings. The reported number of available positions listed at individual schools or their placement offices ranged widely, with a median reported listing of 758 potential jobs. On a positive note, nine schools stated that in 1997 it was easier to place their graduates than during 1996, while none said it was more difficult.

Most new library and information science graduates still tend to find jobs in the same state as their library school: 64 percent in 1997, 67 percent in 1996, and

*(text continues on page 384)*

# Table 4 / Placements by Type of Organization

| Schools | Public | | | Elementary & Secondary | | | College & University | | | Special | | | Government | | | Other | | | Total | | |
|---|---|---|---|---|---|---|---|---|---|---|---|---|---|---|---|---|---|---|---|---|---|
| | Women | Men | Total | Women | Men | Total | Women | Men | Total | Women | Men | Total | Women | Men | Total | Women | Men | Total | Women | Men | Total |
| Alabama | 12 | 3 | 15 | 13 | 0 | 13 | 9 | 2 | 11 | 1 | 3 | 4 | 2 | 1 | 3 | 1 | 2 | 3 | 38 | 11 | 49 |
| California (L.A.) | 3 | 2 | 5 | 1 | 0 | 1 | 5 | 2 | 7 | 1 | 0 | 1 | 0 | 0 | 0 | 2 | 1 | 3 | 12 | 5 | 17 |
| Catholic | 2 | 2 | 4 | 6 | 0 | 6 | 8 | 5 | 13 | 22 | 7 | 29 | 3 | 1 | 4 | 2 | 1 | 3 | 43 | 15 | 58 |
| Clarion | 5 | 0 | 5 | 0 | 1 | 1 | 5 | 1 | 6 | 2 | 0 | 2 | 0 | 0 | 0 | 1 | 0 | 1 | 13 | 2 | 15 |
| Dalhousie | 2 | 0 | 2 | 2 | 0 | 2 | 2 | 0 | 2 | 1 | 0 | 1 | 3 | 0 | 3 | 3 | 2 | 5 | 13 | 2 | 15 |
| Drexel | 4 | 0 | 4 | 3 | 1 | 4 | 10 | 5 | 15 | 13 | 4 | 17 | 0 | 0 | 0 | 4 | 2 | 6 | 34 | 12 | 46 |
| Emporia | 9 | 2 | 11 | 19 | 0 | 19 | 8 | 1 | 9 | 3 | 0 | 3 | 3 | 0 | 3 | 6 | 1 | 7 | 48 | 4 | 52 |
| Florida State | 4 | 1 | 5 | 12 | 0 | 12 | 4 | 1 | 5 | 0 | 0 | 0 | 0 | 0 | 0 | 5 | 2 | 7 | 25 | 4 | 29 |
| Illinois | 10 | 3 | 13 | 7 | 0 | 7 | 18 | 13 | 31 | 6 | 2 | 8 | 1 | 1 | 2 | 1 | 4 | 5 | 44 | 23 | 67 |
| Indiana | 10 | 2 | 12 | 6 | 0 | 6 | 18 | 7 | 25 | 4 | 1 | 5 | 0 | 0 | 0 | 1 | 1 | 2 | 39 | 11 | 50 |
| Iowa | 5 | 0 | 5 | 5 | 0 | 5 | 8 | 4 | 12 | 2 | 1 | 3 | 0 | 0 | 0 | 0 | 0 | 0 | 20 | 5 | 25 |
| Kent State | 21 | 3 | 24 | 12 | 0 | 12 | 8 | 2 | 10 | 8 | 0 | 8 | 0 | 0 | 0 | 4 | 1 | 5 | 53 | 6 | 59 |
| Kentucky | 13 | 5 | 18 | 6 | 2 | 8 | 4 | 4 | 8 | 2 | 2 | 4 | 2 | 0 | 2 | 4 | 0 | 4 | 31 | 13 | 44 |
| Long Island | 14 | 3 | 17 | 22 | 2 | 24 | 6 | 1 | 7 | 4 | 1 | 5 | 0 | 0 | 0 | 5 | 1 | 6 | 51 | 8 | 59 |
| Louisiana State | 5 | 2 | 7 | 13 | 0 | 13 | 10 | 6 | 16 | 3 | 0 | 3 | 4 | 0 | 4 | 0 | 2 | 2 | 35 | 10 | 45 |
| Maryland | 2 | 0 | 2 | 1 | 0 | 1 | 4 | 0 | 4 | 4 | 0 | 4 | 6 | 2 | 8 | 3 | 1 | 4 | 20 | 3 | 23 |
| Michigan | 7 | 2 | 9 | 6 | 1 | 7 | 11 | 6 | 17 | 5 | 1 | 6 | 1 | 0 | 1 | 10 | 5 | 15 | 40 | 15 | 55 |
| Missouri | 9 | 3 | 12 | 6 | 0 | 6 | 3 | 0 | 3 | 0 | 0 | 0 | 1 | 0 | 1 | 1 | 1 | 2 | 20 | 4 | 24 |
| N.C. Central | 2 | 0 | 2 | 14 | 1 | 15 | 9 | 2 | 11 | 0 | 0 | 0 | 1 | 0 | 1 | 2 | 0 | 2 | 28 | 3 | 31 |
| N.C. Chapel Hill | 4 | 1 | 5 | 1 | 1 | 2 | 7 | 2 | 9 | 7 | 0 | 7 | 0 | 0 | 0 | 2 | 0 | 2 | 21 | 4 | 25 |
| Pittsburgh | 4 | 0 | 4 | 8 | 0 | 8 | 12 | 6 | 18 | 2 | 0 | 2 | 1 | 0 | 1 | 2 | 1 | 3 | 29 | 7 | 36 |
| Pratt | 2 | 2 | 4 | 2 | 0 | 2 | 0 | 2 | 2 | 6 | 3 | 9 | 1 | 0 | 1 | 6 | 1 | 7 | 17 | 8 | 25 |
| Queens | 11 | 2 | 13 | 3 | 0 | 3 | 0 | 2 | 2 | 4 | 2 | 6 | 0 | 0 | 0 | 0 | 0 | 0 | 18 | 6 | 24 |
| Rhode Island | 6 | 1 | 7 | 5 | 1 | 6 | 5 | 2 | 7 | 2 | 1 | 3 | 0 | 1 | 1 | 3 | 0 | 3 | 21 | 6 | 27 |

## Table 4 / Placements by Type of Organization *(cont.)*

| Schools | Public | | | Elementary & Secondary | | | College & University | | | Special | | | Government | | | Other | | | Total | | |
|---|---|---|---|---|---|---|---|---|---|---|---|---|---|---|---|---|---|---|---|---|---|
| | Women | Men | Total | Women | Men | Total | Women | Men | Total | Women | Men | Total | Women | Men | Total | Women | Men | Total | Women | Men | Total |
| San Jose | 9 | 0 | 9 | 7 | 1 | 8 | 8 | 1 | 9 | 7 | 2 | 9 | 1 | 0 | 1 | 3 | 1 | 4 | 35 | 5 | 40 |
| Simmons | 20 | 2 | 22 | 8 | 4 | 12 | 40 | 8 | 48 | 20 | 5 | 25 | 1 | 2 | 3 | 13 | 0 | 13 | 102 | 21 | 123 |
| South Carolina | 16 | 5 | 21 | 26 | 1 | 27 | 14 | 4 | 18 | 2 | 0 | 2 | 3 | 1 | 4 | 2 | 0 | 2 | 63 | 11 | 74 |
| South Florida | 16 | 2 | 18 | 11 | 0 | 11 | 8 | 4 | 12 | 0 | 0 | 0 | 0 | 0 | 0 | 0 | 0 | 0 | 35 | 6 | 41 |
| Southern Ct. | 6 | 0 | 6 | 10 | 1 | 11 | 2 | 2 | 4 | 0 | 0 | 0 | 1 | 0 | 1 | 1 | 0 | 1 | 20 | 3 | 23 |
| Southern Mississippi | 5 | 2 | 7 | 3 | 0 | 3 | 5 | 1 | 6 | 0 | 0 | 0 | 1 | 0 | 1 | 0 | 0 | 0 | 14 | 3 | 17 |
| St. John's | 3 | 3 | 6 | 5 | 0 | 5 | 3 | 0 | 3 | 5 | 0 | 5 | 0 | 0 | 0 | 0 | 1 | 1 | 16 | 4 | 20 |
| SUNY Albany | 7 | 3 | 10 | 17 | 1 | 18 | 10 | 1 | 11 | 2 | 1 | 3 | 1 | 0 | 1 | 1 | 3 | 4 | 38 | 9 | 47 |
| SUNY Buffalo | 11 | 1 | 12 | 3 | 4 | 7 | 8 | 1 | 9 | 2 | 0 | 2 | 0 | 1 | 1 | 1 | 3 | 4 | 25 | 10 | 35 |
| Syracuse | 4 | 0 | 4 | 5 | 0 | 5 | 8 | 4 | 12 | 1 | 1 | 2 | 0 | 0 | 0 | 2 | 0 | 2 | 20 | 5 | 25 |
| Tennessee | 3 | 1 | 4 | 2 | 0 | 2 | 9 | 2 | 11 | 4 | 0 | 4 | 0 | 1 | 1 | 2 | 2 | 4 | 20 | 6 | 26 |
| Texas (Austin) | 13 | 8 | 21 | 11 | 0 | 11 | 18 | 8 | 26 | 11 | 3 | 14 | 3 | 0 | 3 | 11 | 4 | 15 | 67 | 23 | 90 |
| Washington | 9 | 1 | 10 | 0 | 1 | 1 | 13 | 1 | 14 | 2 | 2 | 4 | 0 | 0 | 0 | 3 | 4 | 7 | 27 | 9 | 36 |
| Wayne State | 4 | 3 | 7 | 13 | 0 | 13 | 8 | 2 | 10 | 4 | 0 | 4 | 0 | 0 | 0 | 5 | 4 | 9 | 34 | 9 | 43 |
| Wisconsin (Madison) | 7 | 1 | 8 | 3 | 1 | 4 | 11 | 4 | 15 | 4 | 2 | 6 | 2 | 1 | 3 | 5 | 1 | 6 | 32 | 10 | 42 |
| Wisconsin (Milwaukee) | 1 | 4 | 5 | 6 | 0 | 6 | 6 | 0 | 6 | 2 | 1 | 3 | 1 | 0 | 1 | 0 | 0 | 0 | 16 | 5 | 21 |
| Total | 300 | 75 | 375 | 303 | 24 | 327 | 345 | 119 | 464 | 168 | 45 | 213 | 43 | 12 | 55 | 118 | 52 | 170 | 1,275 | 326 | 1,601 |

**Table 5 / Average Salary Index**
**Starting Library Positions, 1985–1997**

| Year | Library Schools* | Average Beginning Salary | Dollar Increase in Average Salary | Salary Index | BLS-CPI** |
|------|------------------|--------------------------|-----------------------------------|--------------|-----------|
| 1985 | 58 | $19,753 | $962 | 111.64 | 109.3 |
| 1986 | 54 | 20,874 | 1,121 | 117.98 | 110.5 |
| 1987 | 55 | 22,247 | 1,373 | 125.74 | 115.4 |
| 1988 | 51 | 23,491 | 1,244 | 132.77 | 120.5 |
| 1989 | 43 | 24,581 | 1,090 | 138.93 | 124.0 |
| 1990 | 38 | 25,306 | 725 | 143.03 | 130.7 |
| 1991 | 46 | 25,583 | 277 | 144.59 | 136.2 |
| 1992 | 41 | 26,666 | 1,083 | 150.71 | 140.5 |
| 1993 | 50 | 27,116 | 450 | 153.26 | 144.4 |
| 1994 | 43 | 28,086 | 970 | 158.74 | 148.4 |
| 1995 | 41 | 28,997 | 911 | 163.89 | 152.5 |
| 1996 | 44 | 29,480 | 483 | 166.62 | 159.1 |
| 1997 | 43 | 30,270 | 790 | 171.05 | 161.6 |

* Includes U.S. schools only.

** The U.S. Bureau of Labor Statistics' present Consumer Price Index is based on the average price data from 1982–1984 as equaling 100. The average beginning professional salary from the period was $17,693 and is used as the equivalent base of 100 for salary data.

**Table 6 / Salaries of Reporting Professionals by Area of Job Assignment**

| Assignment | Number | Percent of Total | Low Salary | High Salary | Average Salary | Median Salary |
|------------|--------|------------------|------------|-------------|----------------|---------------|
| Acquisitions | 20 | 1.6 | $20,000 | $41,000 | $30,061 | $30,000 |
| Administration | 96 | 7.8 | 16,000 | 82,500 | 32,045 | 30,084 |
| Archives | 38 | 3.1 | 15,000 | 62,000 | 28,543 | 28,000 |
| Automation/ Systems | 33 | 2.7 | 22,470 | 53,000 | 33,976 | 33,000 |
| Cataloging and Classification | 67 | 5.4 | 16,000 | 50,000 | 28,288 | 28,000 |
| Circulation | 13 | 1.1 | 17,652 | 47,000 | 28,681 | 28,000 |
| Collection Development | 20 | 1.6 | 22,620 | 39,146 | 30,928 | 30,250 |
| Database Management | 35 | 2.8 | 16,800 | 62,000 | 34,727 | 35,000 |
| Government Documents | 27 | 2.2 | 18,500 | 36,500 | 29,548 | 30,000 |
| Indexing/ Abstracting | 12 | 1.0 | 22,500 | 35,000 | 29,142 | 30,000 |
| Interlibrary Loan | 9 | 0.7 | 25,500 | 35,500 | 31,000 | 31,500 |
| LAN Manager | 6 | 0.5 | 22,000 | 38,000 | 28,767 | 28,500 |
| Media Specialist | 245 | 19.8 | 18,000 | 68,000 | 30,866 | 29,900 |
| Reference/ Info Services | 496 | 40.2 | 15,000 | 59,500 | 29,549 | 29,000 |
| Telecommunications | 3 | 0.2 | 30,000 | 42,000 | 34,000 | 30,000 |
| Youth Services | 94 | 7.6 | 15,000 | 47,000 | 27,896 | 27,780 |
| Webmaster | 21 | 1.7 | 23,000 | 47,000 | 32,542 | 30,780 |
| Total | 1,235 | 100% | $15,000 | $82,500 | $30,130 | $29,195 |

Note: Does not include those graduates who did not specify a principal job assignment.

Tables do no always add up, individually or collectively, due to omitted data on survey forms.

64 percent in 1995. An additional 15 percent on average found jobs in other states of the same region as their library school in 1997.

Table 4 reflects 1997 placements by library school and type of library. While some categories seem static, a somewhat higher proportion of graduates are taking jobs falling within the special, college and university, and other categories. For instance, from 1996 to 1997, the proportion of placements in public and in elementary/secondary libraries declined from 28 percent and 22 percent to 23 percent and 20 percent, respectively, while the percentage of total placements in college and university and in special libraries increased from 23 percent and 12 percent to 29 percent and 13 percent, respectively. Because responses were not always complete, it may be too soon to suggest a definite trend. But this factor may be contributing to the improvement in salaries.

## Graduates Talk Back

Asked about the placement process and their views on the preparation they received in library school, about 60 students responded. Some 80 percent indicated that employers sought those with technology skills for work on Internet access, electronic database searching abilities, and other computer issues. Those employers with special personnel needs (e.g., cataloging, reference) naturally emphasized skills in those areas but usually wanted to gauge the applicant's technology abilities.

Few employers apparently test graduates or make substantive inquiries in the interview process. Respondents reported that most employers continue to rely on interviews and references. About 60 percent of interviewees reported that proposed salaries were not negotiable, but others said that those with special technical skills found employers to be more flexible.

A solid plurality of respondents cited technological or computer skills as the most useful skill gained in graduate school. One graduate noted that potential employers often sought "HTML skills, which—although perhaps not a 'library' skill to the purist—appears again and again" in job postings.

Many also cited the traditional expertise relevant to cataloging, acquisitions, reference, and administration as the most useful skills from graduate school. Many mentioned in passing that "theoretical" courses they perhaps deemed insufficiently job-oriented or irrelevant during school days were much more useful on the job than anticipated.

Asked what may be missing from current curricula, several respondents cited lack of adequate training in the latest technologies, (e.g., Web page design, online systems). More notably, some 60 percent of respondents said library schools failed to teach them enough about the management and control of an institution, explaining how a library runs, the ins and outs of budgeting, and allocation of scarce resources.

How to address this perceived shortcoming? Respondents suggested not only management classes but improved or even required internship programs.

*(text continues on page 389)*

## Table 7 / Placements and Full-Time Salaries of Reporting 1997 Graduates

| Schools | Number of Placements | Salaries Women | Salaries Men | Salaries Total | Low Salary Women | Low Salary Men | High Salary Women | High Salary Men | Average Salary Women | Average Salary Men | Average Salary All | Median Salary Women | Median Salary Men | Median Salary All |
|---|---|---|---|---|---|---|---|---|---|---|---|---|---|---|
| Alabama | 44 | 32 | 9 | 41 | $17,000 | $24,000 | $47,000 | $36,000 | $27,490 | $29,333 | $27,895 | $26,200 | $30,000 | $27,000 |
| California (L.A.) | 14 | 11 | 3 | 14 | 20,000 | 32,160 | 42,000 | 34,000 | 31,183 | 32,887 | 32,436 | 33,002 | 32,500 | 32,160 |
| Catholic | 56 | 41 | 13 | 54 | 19,000 | 25,900 | 47,500 | 75,000 | 32,215 | 36,597 | 32,530 | 30,700 | 33,500 | 31,600 |
| Clarion | 15 | 13 | 1 | 14 | 15,000 | 26,000 | 35,000 | 26,000 | 21,896 | 26,000 | 22,494 | 20,000 | 26,000 | 24,000 |
| Dalhousie* | 13 | 11 | 2 | 13 | 25,000 | 25,000 | 35,000 | 35,000 | 28,750 | 30,000 | 29,375 | 25,000 | 35,000 | 27,500 |
| Drexel | 46 | 32 | 9 | 41 | 20,065 | 26,000 | 70,000 | 40,000 | 36,264 | 34,961 | 36,290 | 35,000 | 38,000 | 35,000 |
| Emporia | 51 | 43 | 3 | 46 | 16,320 | 17,107 | 47,000 | 35,622 | 30,024 | 31,541 | 30,104 | 28,200 | 29,000 | 28,200 |
| Florida State | 26 | 22 | 2 | 24 | 19,000 | 23,000 | 35,000 | 30,000 | 27,217 | 26,500 | 27,157 | 28,000 | 26,500 | 28,000 |
| Illinois | 57 | 37 | 20 | 57 | 18,000 | 24,000 | 45,000 | 42,000 | 29,976 | 31,428 | 30,453 | 29,500 | 30,000 | 30,000 |
| Indiana | 44 | 34 | 9 | 43 | 19,200 | 21,600 | 48,000 | 50,000 | 28,537 | 28,476 | 28,524 | 27,500 | 25,000 | 27,000 |
| Iowa | 20 | 17 | 2 | 19 | 24,000 | 30,000 | 34,000 | 39,000 | 28,969 | 34,500 | 29,551 | 28,800 | 34,500 | 30,000 |
| Kent State | 57 | 43 | 6 | 49 | 15,360 | 22,620 | 50,000 | 32,000 | 30,028 | 29,270 | 29,935 | 29,000 | 30,500 | 29,500 |
| Kentucky | 40 | 28 | 12 | 40 | 14,000 | 20,000 | 57,300 | 41,000 | 28,237 | 28,580 | 28,340 | 26,830 | 27,750 | 27,421 |
| Long Island | 52 | 42 | 5 | 47 | 16,800 | 27,000 | 56,000 | 40,000 | 32,909 | 31,300 | 32,765 | 32,000 | 29,000 | 31,500 |
| Louisiana State | 37 | 28 | 8 | 36 | 17,400 | 18,000 | 46,300 | 33,500 | 26,702 | 28,021 | 26,995 | 25,000 | 30,000 | 25,750 |
| Maryland | 17 | 14 | 2 | 16 | 17,850 | 32,000 | 34,000 | 51,000 | 28,489 | 41,500 | 30,933 | 30,000 | 41,500 | 31,000 |
| Michigan | 47 | 36 | 11 | 47 | 13,000 | 23,000 | 68,000 | 58,000 | 31,194 | 38,909 | 33,595 | 28,000 | 38,000 | 33,000 |
| Missouri | 25 | 19 | 4 | 23 | 18,000 | 25,000 | 37,500 | 82,500 | 27,649 | 45,025 | 30,671 | 28,000 | 36,300 | 28,000 |
| N.C. Central | 25 | 22 | 2 | 24 | 21,486 | 27,700 | 44,000 | 34,000 | 29,693 | 30,850 | 30,067 | 28,465 | 30,850 | 28,480 |
| N.C. Chapel Hill | 23 | 18 | 4 | 22 | 20,900 | 21,500 | 37,000 | 38,000 | 29,174 | 21,125 | 29,528 | 30,000 | 32,000 | 30,000 |
| Pittsburgh | 26 | 22 | 3 | 25 | 18,500 | 25,126 | 40,000 | 36,500 | 27,843 | 30,709 | 28,187 | 27,750 | 30,500 | 28,000 |

Table 7 / Placements and Full-Time Salaries of Reporting 1997 Graduates *(cont.)*

| Schools | Number of Placements | Salaries | | | Low Salary | | High Salary | | Average Salary | | | Median Salary | | |
|---|---|---|---|---|---|---|---|---|---|---|---|---|---|---|
| | | Women | Men | Total | Women | Men | Women | Men | Women | Men | All | Women | Men | All |
| Pratt | 25 | 16 | 9 | 25 | 27,000 | 24,000 | 50,000 | 70,000 | 35,703 | 36,000 | 35,849 | 35,000 | 33,000 | 35,000 |
| Queens | 27 | 21 | 6 | 27 | 13,000 | 24,000 | 44,000 | 66,000 | 31,667 | 29,267 | 33,864 | 32,000 | 34,000 | 33,000 |
| Rhode Island | 21 | 14 | 4 | 18 | 27,500 | 22,000 | 59,500 | 30,000 | 32,487 | 25,750 | 30,990 | 29,750 | 25,000 | 29,500 |
| San Jose | 32 | 27 | 4 | 31 | 22,000 | 19,000 | 47,000 | 46,000 | 33,901 | 35,750 | 33,837 | 35,000 | 39,000 | 35,000 |
| Simmons | 96 | 68 | 16 | 84 | 22,000 | 15,000 | 51,840 | 38,800 | 31,479 | 30,548 | 30,969 | 30,056 | 30,000 | 30,000 |
| South Carolina | 73 | 57 | 11 | 68 | 16,000 | 20,000 | 54,843 | 34,500 | 26,802 | 26,449 | 26,711 | 27,000 | 26,000 | 26,500 |
| South Florida | 37 | 31 | 5 | 36 | 22,000 | 23,000 | 42,500 | 32,000 | 27,547 | 27,500 | 27,541 | 25,605 | 27,500 | 26,053 |
| So. Connecticut | 17 | 15 | 2 | 17 | 24,000 | 28,000 | 60,000 | 33,100 | 32,855 | 30,550 | 32,584 | 31,500 | 30,550 | 31,500 |
| So. Mississippi | 16 | 13 | 3 | 16 | 19,500 | 15,000 | 30,000 | 28,000 | 25,825 | 21,667 | 25,045 | 26,000 | 22,000 | 25,500 |
| St. John's | 19 | 15 | 4 | 19 | 15,000 | 27,000 | 40,000 | 35,000 | 30,973 | 31,125 | 31,005 | 32,000 | 30,250 | 30,500 |
| SUNY Albany | 41 | 32 | 8 | 40 | 20,000 | 22,009 | 63,700 | 42,500 | 32,329 | 29,214 | 31,706 | 30,495 | 27,750 | 30,245 |
| SUNY Buffalo | 27 | 18 | 7 | 25 | 18,500 | 20,000 | 35,000 | 35,843 | 27,978 | 28,965 | 28,254 | 29,000 | 27,500 | 29,000 |
| Syracuse | 21 | 15 | 4 | 19 | 21,000 | 26,000 | 46,000 | 40,000 | 30,353 | 35,200 | 31,374 | 30,000 | 37,400 | 30,000 |
| Tennessee | 22 | 18 | 4 | 22 | 22,700 | 28,000 | 44,000 | 35,000 | 29,298 | 30,250 | 28,471 | 27,000 | 29,000 | 27,750 |
| Texas (Austin) | 160 | 116 | 40 | 156 | 15,000 | 16,000 | 45,000 | 45,000 | 29,430 | 27,870 | 29,090 | 30,000 | 28,325 | 29,000 |
| Washington | 31 | 21 | 9 | 30 | 19,000 | 27,000 | 50,000 | 60,000 | 31,952 | 40,500 | 35,052 | 32,500 | 38,000 | 33,600 |
| Wayne State | 31 | 24 | 5 | 29 | 17,000 | 25,000 | 62,000 | 62,000 | 32,286 | 37,000 | 32,841 | 30,000 | 32,000 | 30,000 |
| Wis. (Madison) | 33 | 23 | 3 | 26 | 18,000 | 28,000 | 40,000 | 29,007 | 28,525 | 28,536 | 28,526 | 28,500 | 28,600 | 28,550 |
| Wis. (Milwaukee) | 18 | 13 | 5 | 18 | 19,720 | 25,000 | 51,000 | 35,000 | 31,386 | 29,200 | 30,779 | 30,000 | 29,000 | 29,900 |

* Canadian salaries reported in Canadian dollars.

## Table 8 / Comparison of Salaries by Type of Organization

| | Total Placements | Salaries | | Low Salary | | High Salary | | Average Salary | | | Median Salary | | |
|---|---|---|---|---|---|---|---|---|---|---|---|---|---|
| | | Women | Men | Women | Men | Women | Men | Women | Men | All | Women | Men | All |
| **Public Libraries** | | | | | | | | | | | | | |
| Northeast | 123 | 100 | 23 | $15,360 | $22,000 | $54,843 | $34,500 | $28,421 | $28,301 | $28,398 | $29,000 | $29,000 | $29,000 |
| Southeast | 98 | 83 | 15 | 16,800 | 16,000 | 36,000 | 31,000 | 26,483 | 25,393 | 26,280 | 26,200 | 25,900 | 26,000 |
| Midwest | 91 | 71 | 20 | 15,000 | 24,000 | 47,500 | 82,500 | 26,651 | 30,432 | 27,482 | 26,000 | 27,750 | 26,000 |
| Southwest/West | 56 | 41 | 15 | 15,000 | 15,000 | 40,000 | 42,000 | 28,491 | 28,312 | 28,443 | 28,000 | 28,400 | 28,043 |
| All Public | 368 | 295 | 73 | 15,000 | 15,000 | 54,843 | 82,500 | 27,513 | 28,262 | 27,664 | 27,500 | 28,000 | 27,500 |
| **School Libraries** | | | | | | | | | | | | | |
| Northeast | 129 | 113 | 16 | 15,000 | 15,800 | 60,000 | 48,000 | 32,053 | 31,979 | 32,046 | 31,400 | 34,150 | 32,000 |
| Southeast | 87 | 85 | 2 | 15,000 | 27,700 | 44,000 | 41,000 | 29,095 | 34,350 | 29,227 | 28,543 | 34,350 | 28,543 |
| Midwest | 81 | 79 | 1 | 15,640 | 26,415 | 68,000 | 26,415 | 31,317 | 26,415 | 31,249 | 30,000 | 26,415 | 30,000 |
| Southwest/West | 32 | 28 | 4 | 24,000 | 19,000 | 49,000 | 50,000 | 31,694 | 37,375 | 32,506 | 31,982 | 40,250 | 32,500 |
| All School | 329 | 305 | 23 | 15,000 | 15,800 | 68,000 | 50,000 | 31,005 | 33,071 | 31,137 | 30,000 | 35,000 | 30,000 |
| **College/University Libraries** | | | | | | | | | | | | | |
| Northeast | 148 | 121 | 27 | 18,500 | 20,000 | 63,700 | 47,000 | 30,636 | 30,988 | 30,700 | 30,000 | 30,000 | 30,000 |
| Southeast | 103 | 73 | 30 | 19,000 | 20,000 | 37,500 | 75,000 | 27,138 | 29,666 | 27,889 | 27,000 | 28,100 | 27,000 |
| Midwest | 73 | 54 | 19 | 17,000 | 22,620 | 51,000 | 40,000 | 28,961 | 29,422 | 29,249 | 29,000 | 28,400 | 29,000 |
| Southwest/West | 48 | 38 | 10 | 15,000 | 16,000 | 41,000 | 45,000 | 29,640 | 32,764 | 30,371 | 30,000 | 34,000 | 30,000 |
| All Academic | 372 | 286 | 86 | 15,000 | 16,000 | 63,700 | 75,000 | 29,095 | 30,408 | 29,446 | 29,000 | 30,000 | 29,000 |
| **Special Libraries** | | | | | | | | | | | | | |
| Northeast | 104 | 84 | 20 | 12,000 | 22,000 | 70,000 | 66,000 | 34,100 | 33,161 | 33,929 | 32,100 | 31,000 | 32,000 |
| Southeast | 33 | 26 | 7 | 21,000 | 20,000 | 64,843 | 39,600 | 30,871 | 30,600 | 30,819 | 30,000 | 31,000 | 30,800 |
| Midwest | 36 | 28 | 8 | 15,360 | 28,000 | 57,300 | 50,000 | 34,500 | 36,986 | 35,028 | 33,000 | 38,000 | 33,500 |
| Southwest/West | 35 | 26 | 9 | 13,000 | 16,000 | 45,000 | 47,500 | 33,448 | 33,189 | 33,323 | 33,000 | 34,250 | 33,500 |
| All Special | 208 | 164 | 44 | 12,000 | 16,000 | 70,000 | 66,000 | 33,532 | 32,748 | 33,375 | 32,000 | 32,750 | 32,000 |

## Table 8 / Comparison of Salaries by Type of Organization (cont.)

| | Total Placements | Salaries | | Low Salary | | High Salary | | Average Salary | | | Median Salary | | |
|---|---|---|---|---|---|---|---|---|---|---|---|---|---|
| | | Women | Men | Women | Men | Women | Men | Women | Men | All | Women | Men | All |
| **Government Libraries** | | | | | | | | | | | | | |
| Northeast | 26 | 19 | 7 | 16,000 | 23,665 | 50,000 | 51,000 | 32,265 | 34,361 | 32,789 | 32,840 | 31,000 | 32,340 |
| Southeast | 10 | 8 | 2 | 20,000 | 24,000 | 35,000 | 26,000 | 28,200 | 25,000 | 27,489 | 31,300 | 25,000 | 26,000 |
| Midwest | 9 | 6 | 3 | 21,000 | 28,000 | 38,000 | 32,000 | 30,555 | 30,000 | 30,370 | 30,000 | 30,000 | 30,000 |
| Southwest/West | 6 | 6 | 0 | 28,000 | — | 34,500 | — | 30,340 | — | 30,340 | 30,000 | — | 30,000 |
| All Government | 51 | 39 | 12 | 16,000 | 23,665 | 50,000 | 51,000 | 30,922 | 31,470 | 31,050 | 31,150 | 30,000 | 30,700 |
| **Library Cooperatives/Networks** | | | | | | | | | | | | | |
| Northeast | 1 | 0 | 1 | — | 26,000 | — | 26,000 | — | 26,000 | 26,000 | — | 26,000 | 26,000 |
| Southeast | 1 | 1 | 0 | 25,000 | — | 25,000 | — | 25,000 | — | 25,000 | 25,000 | — | 25,000 |
| Midwest | 3 | 1 | 2 | 31,400 | 32,000 | 31,400 | 41,500 | 31,400 | 36,750 | 34,957 | 31,400 | 36,750 | 32,000 |
| Southwest/West | 0 | 0 | 0 | — | — | — | — | — | — | — | — | — | — |
| All Co-ops/Networks | 5 | 2 | 3 | 25,000 | 26,000 | 31,400 | 41,500 | 28,300 | 33,167 | 31,220 | 28,300 | 32,000 | 31,400 |
| **Vendors** | | | | | | | | | | | | | |
| Northeast | 6 | 4 | 2 | 26,500 | 27,500 | 45,000 | 70,000 | 34,800 | 59,375 | 41,821 | 30,000 | 59,375 | 45,000 |
| Southeast | 2 | 1 | 1 | 25,000 | 30,000 | 25,000 | 30,000 | 25,000 | 30,000 | 27,500 | 25,000 | 30,000 | 27,500 |
| Midwest | 5 | 4 | 1 | 22,500 | 30,000 | 30,000 | 30,000 | 28,125 | 30,000 | 28,500 | 30,000 | 30,000 | 30,000 |
| Southwest/West | 3 | 2 | 1 | 30,000 | 28,000 | 38,000 | 28,000 | 34,000 | 28,000 | 32,000 | 34,000 | 28,000 | 30,000 |
| All Vendors | 16 | 11 | 5 | 22,500 | 27,500 | 45,000 | 70,000 | 32,000 | 37,100 | 39,594 | 30,000 | 30,000 | 30,000 |
| **Other Organizations** | | | | | | | | | | | | | |
| Northeast | 43 | 33 | 10 | 16,800 | 27,000 | 55,000 | 43,000 | 32,028 | 32,500 | 32,680 | 31,250 | 35,000 | 32,000 |
| Southeast | 17 | 11 | 6 | 19,000 | 17,000 | 44,000 | 47,500 | 28,719 | 30,465 | 33,667 | 26,500 | 34,250 | 26,611 |
| Midwest | 35 | 22 | 13 | 15,000 | 21,600 | 50,000 | 62,000 | 29,637 | 38,208 | 32,821 | 29,000 | 33,000 | 31,000 |
| Southwest/West | 31 | 13 | 8 | 19,000 | 28,500 | 42,000 | 60,000 | 30,885 | 41,406 | 34,893 | 30,000 | 37,000 | 33,000 |
| All Other | 126 | 79 | 37 | 15,000 | 17,000 | 55,000 | 62,000 | 30,129 | 37,296 | 31,512 | 30,000 | 35,000 | 31,000 |

## Jobs No Longer "Traditional"

This year's survey results do not specifically group responses among so-called traditional vs. nontraditional jobs. This distinction is no longer simple. The work of librarians, especially newly minted ones, is becoming much more diversified, with many hours spent on, for example, Internet-related activities, which may not have been "traditional" but are quickly becoming the norm.

Also, many librarians and information specialists are increasingly performing librarian-type activities in settings that are not, strictly speaking, traditional libraries. We consider the distinction no longer viable—though we do list organizations and job assignments in, respectively, Tables 8 and 6.

## Using Technology More

Although graduates still tend to find jobs that do not involve extensive use of new technologies, new positions in all library areas nevertheless require more than just a modicum of technological skills and knowledge. The growing use of such technologies for personal as well as strictly job-related assignments, however, clouded the data. Many individuals reported more hours than a normal work week would encompass in searching the Web, designing Web pages, and other similar activities; this is obviously a defect of the survey. While it seems that new hires are being depended upon to work with new technologies, it is impossible to say whether in doing so they are replacing or complementing library personnel. In any case, technical competencies seem more crucial than ever to starting a library career.

# Accredited Master's Programs in Library and Information Studies

This list of graduate programs accredited by the American Library Association was issued in January 1999. The list of accredited programs is issued annually at the start of each calendar year and is available from the ALA Office for Accreditation. A list of more than 200 institutions offering both accredited and nonaccredited programs in librarianship appears in the 51st edition of *American Library Directory* (R. R. Bowker, 1998).

## Northeast: Conn., D.C., Md., Mass., N.J., N.Y., Pa., R.I.

Catholic University of America, School of Lib. and Info. Science, Washington, DC 20064. Jean Preer, Acting Dean. 202-319-5085, fax 202-219-5574, e-mail cua-slis@cua.edu. World Wide Web http://www.cua.edu/www/lsc. Admissions contact: Kevin Woods.

Clarion University of Pennsylvania, Dept. of Lib. Science, 840 Wood St., Clarion, PA 16214-1232. James T. Maccaferri, Chair. 814-226-2271, fax 814-226-2150, e-mail mccafer@mail.clarion.edu. World Wide Web http://www.clarion.edu/libsci.

Drexel University, College of Info. Science and Technology, 3141 Chestnut St., Philadelphia, PA 19104-2875. Thomas A. Childers, Interim Dean. 215-895-2474, fax 215-895-2494. World Wide Web http://www.cis.drexel.edu. Admissions contact: Anne B. Tanner. 215-895-2485, e-mail info@cis.drexel.edu.

Long Island University, Palmer School of Lib. and Info. Science, C. W. Post Campus, 720 Northern Blvd., Brookville, NY 11548-1300. Jeff Kane, Acting Dean. 516-299-2866, fax 516-299-4168, e-mail palmer @titan.liunet.edu. World Wide Web http://www.liu.edu/palmer. Admissions contact: Rosemary Chu. 516-299-2487, fax 516-299-4168.

Pratt Institute, School of Info. and Lib. Science, Info. Science Center, 200 Willoughby Ave., Brooklyn, NY 11205. S. M. Matta, Dean. 718-636-3702, fax 718-636-3733, e-mail matta@sils.pratt.edu. World Wide Web http://sils.pratt.edu.

Queens College, City University of New York, Grad. School of Lib. and Info. Studies, 65-30 Kissena Blvd., Flushing, NY 11367. Marianne Cooper, Dir. 718-997-3797, fax 718-997-3797. Admissions contact: Karen P. Smith.

Rutgers University, School of Communication, Info., and Lib. Studies, 4 Huntington St., New Brunswick, NJ 08903-1071. Gustav W. Friedrich, Dean. 732-932-7917, fax 732-932-2644, e-mail scilsmls@sclis.rutgers.edu. World Wide Web http://www.scils.rutgers.edu/lis/index.html. Admissions contact: Carol C. Kuhlthau. 732-932-7916, e-mail kuhlthau@scils.rutgers.edu.

Saint John's University, Div. of Lib. and Info. Science, 8000 Utopia Pkwy., Jamaica, NY 11439. James A. Benson, Dir. 718-990-6200, fax 718-990-2071, e-mail libis @stjohns.edu. World Wide Web http://www.stjohns.edu/academics/sjc/depts/dlis/index.html. Admissions contact: Jeanne M. Umland. 718-990-6776, fax 718-960-1677.

Simmons College, Grad. School of Lib. and Info. Science, 300 The Fenway, Boston, MA 02115-5898. James M. Matarazzo, Dean. 617-521-2800, fax 617-521-3192, e-mail gslis@simmons.edu. World Wide Web http://simmons.edu/graduate/gslis. Admissions contact: Judith Beals. 617-521-2801, e-mail jbeals@simmons.edu.

Southern Connecticut State University, School of Communication, Info., and Lib. Science, 501 Crescent St., New Haven, CT 06515. Edward C. Harris, Dean. 203-392-5781, fax 203-392-5780, e-mail libscienceit @scsu.ctstateu.edu. Admissions contact: Nancy Disbrow.

State University of New York at Albany, School of Info. Science and Policy, 135 Western Ave., Albany, NY 12222. Philip B. Eppard, Dean. 518-442-5110, fax 518-442-5367, e-mail infosci@cnsvax.albany.edu. Admissions contact: Virginia Papandrea. E-mail papand@cnsvax.albany.edu.

State University of New York at Buffalo, School of Info. and Lib. Studies, 534 Baldy Hall, Buffalo, NY 14260. George S. Bobinski, Dean. 716-645-2412, fax 716-645-3775, e-mail sils@acsu.bufalo.edu. World Wide Web http://www.sils.buffalo.edu. Admissions contact: A. Neil Yerkey. 716-645-6478.

Syracuse University, School of Info. Studies, 4-206 Center for Science and Technology, Syracuse, NY 13244-4100. Raymond F. von Dran, Dean. 315-443-2911, fax 315-443-5806, e-mail vondran@syr.edu. World Wide Web http://istweb.svr.edu.

University of Maryland, College of Lib. and Info. Services, College Park, MD 20742-4345. Ann E. Prentice, Dean. 301-405-2033, fax 301-314-9145, e-mail ap57@umail.umd.edu. Admissions contact: Diane L. Barlow. 301-405-2039, fax 301-314-9145, e-mail clisumpc@umdacc.umd.edu.

University of Pittsburgh, School of Info. Sciences, 505 IS Bldg., Pittsburgh, PA 15260. Toni Carbo, Dean. 412-624-5230, fax 412-624-5231. World Wide Web http://www.sis.pitt.edu. Admissions contact: Ninette Kay. 412-624-5146, e-mail nk@sis.pitt.edu.

University of Rhode Island, Grad. School of Lib. and Info. Studies, Rodman Hall, Kingston, RI 02881. W. Michael Havener, Dir. 401-874-2947, fax 401-874-4395. Admissions contact: C. Herbert Carson. 401-874-2947, e-mail gslis@uriacc.uri.edu.

# Southeast: Ala., Fla., Ga., Ky., La., Miss., N.C., S.C., Tenn., P.R.

Clark Atlanta University, School of Lib. and Info. Studies, 300 Trevor Arnett Hall, 223 James P. Brawley Dr., Atlanta, GA 30314. Arthur C. Gunn, Dean. 404-880-8697, fax 404-880-8977, e-mail agunn@cau.edu. Admissions contact: Doris Callahan.

Florida State University, School of Lib. and Info. Studies, Tallahassee, FL 32306-2048. Jane B. Robbins, Dean. 850-644-5775, fax 850-644-9763. World Wide Web http://www.fsu.edu/~lis. Admissions contact: Kathleen Burnett. 850-644-8106, e-mail burnett@lis.fsu.edu.

Louisiana State University, School of Lib. and Info. Science, 267 Coates Hall, Baton Rouge, LA 70803. Bert R. Boyce, Dean. 225-388-3158, fax 225-388-4581, e-mail lsslis@lsuvm.sncc.lsu.edu. World Wide Web http://adam.slis.lsu.edu. Admissions contact: Nicole Rozas.

North Carolina Central University, School of Lib. and Info. Sciences, Box 19586, Durham, NC 27707. Benjamin F. Speller, Jr., Dean. 919-560-6485, fax 919-560-6402, e-mail speller@ga.unc.edu. World Wide Web http://www.nccu.edu/slis/index.html. Admissions contact: Duane Bogenschneider, 919-560-55211, e-mail duaneb@nccu.edu.

University of Alabama, School of Lib. and Info. Studies, Box 870252, Tuscaloosa, AL 35487-0252. Joan L. Atkinson, Director. 205-348-1522, fax 205-348-3746. World Wide Web http://www.slis.ua.edu.

University of Kentucky, College of Communications and Info. Studies, School of Lib. and Info. Science, 502 King Library, Building S, Lexington, KY 40506-0039. Timothy W. Sineath, Dir. 606-257-8876, fax 606-257-4205, e-mail tsineath@pop.uky.edu. World Wide Web http://www.uky.edu/CommInfoStudies/SLIS. Admissions contact: Gloria McCowan. 606-257-3317, e-mail gmccowa@pop.uky.edu.

University of North Carolina at Chapel Hill, School of Info. and Lib. Science, 100 Manning Hall, Chapel Hill, NC 27599-3360. JoAnne G. Marshall, Dean. 919-962-8366, fax 919-962-8071, e-mail info@ils.unc.edu. World Wide Web http://www.ils.unc.edu. Admissions contact: Betty J. Kompst. E-mail kompst@ils.unc.edu.

University of North Carolina at Greensboro, Dept. of Lib. and Info. Studies, School of Education, Box 26171, Greensboro, NC 27402-6171. Keith Wright, Chair. 336-334-3477, fax 336-334-5060, e-mail teresa_hughes_holland@uncg.edu. World Wide Web http://www.uncg.edu/lis/. Admissions contact: Beatrice Kovacs. 336-334-3479, e-mail bea_kovacs@iris.uncg.edu.

University of Puerto Rico, Graduate School of Lib. and Info. Science (Escuela Graduada de Bibliotecologia y Ciencia de la Información), Box 21906, San Juan, PR 00931-1906. Consuelo Figueras, Dir. 787-763-6199, fax 787-764-2311, e-mail 73253.312@compuserv.com. Admissions contact: Migdalia Dávila. 809-764-0000, ext. 3530, e-mail m_davila@rrpad.upr.clu.edu.

University of South Carolina, College of Lib. and Info. Science, Davis College, Columbia, SC 29208. Fred W. Roper, Dean. 803-777-3858, fax 803-777-7938. World Wide Web http://www.libsci.sc.edu. Admissions contact: Nancy C. Beitz. 803-777-5067, fax 803-777-0457, e-mail nbeitz@sc.edu.

University of South Florida, School of Lib. and Info. Science, 4202 E. Fowler Ave., CIS 1040, Tampa, FL 33620-7800. Kathleen de la Peña McCook, Dir. 813-974-3520, fax 813-974-6840, e-mail pate@luna.cas.usf.edu. Admissions contact: Sonia Ramirez Wohlmuth. E-mail swohlmut@chuma.cas.usf.edu.ml.

University of Southern Mississippi, School of Lib. and Info. Science, Box 5146, Hattiesburg, MS 39406-5146. Joy M. Greiner, Dir. 601-266-4228, fax 601-266-5774, e-mail jgreiner@ocea.otr.usm.edu. World Wide Web http://www-dept.usm.edu/~slis.

University of Tennessee, School of Info. Sciences, 804 Volunteer Blvd., Knoxville, TN 37996-4330. Elizabeth Aversa, Dir. 423-974-2148, fax 423-974-4967. World Wide Web http://www.sis.utk.edu. Admissions contact: George Hoemann. 423-974-5917, e-mail hoemann@utk.edu.

# Midwest: Ill., Ind., Iowa, Kan., Mich., Mo., Ohio, Wis.

Emporia State University, School of Lib. and Info. Management, Box 4025, Emporia, KS 66801. Robert Grover, Interim Dean. 316-341-5203, fax 316-341-5233. World Wide Web http://www.slim.emporia.edu. Admissions contacts: Jean Redeker. 316-341-5734, e-mail redekerj@esumail.emporia.edu., Dan Roland, 316-341-5064, e-mail rolandda@emporia.edu.

Indiana University, School of Lib. and Info. Science, 10th St. and Jordan Ave., Bloomington, IN 47405-1801. Blaise Cronin, Dean. 812-855-2018, fax 812-855-6166, e-mail iuslis@indiana.edu. World Wide Web http://www.slis.indiana.edu. Admissions contact: Mary Krutulis. E-mail krutulis@indiana.edu.

Kent State University, School of Lib. and Info. Science, Box 5190, Kent, OH 44242-0001. Danny P. Wallace, Dir. 330-672-2782, fax 330-672-7965, e-mail wallace@slis.kent.edu. World Wide Web http://web.slis.kent.edu. Admissions Contact: Marge Hayden. E-mail slis@slis.kent.edu.

Dominican University, Grad. School of Lib. and Info. Science, 7900 W. Division St., River Forest, IL 60305. Prudence W. Dalrymple, Dean. 708-524-6845, fax 708-524-6657, e-mail gslis@email.dom.edu. World Wide Web http://www.dom.edu/academic/gslishome.html.

University of Illinois at Urbana-Champaign, Grad. School of Lib. and Info. Science, 501 E. Daniel St., Champaign, IL 61820. Leigh S. Estabrook, Dean. 217-333-3280, fax 217-244-3302. World Wide Web http://alexia.lis.uiuc.edu. Admissions contact: Carol DeVoss. 217-333-7197, e-mail devoss@alexia.lis.uiuc.edu.

University of Iowa, School of Lib. and Info. Science, Iowa City, IA 52242-1420. Padmini Srinivasan, Dir. 319-335-5707, fax 319-335-5374, e-mail padmini-srinivasan@uiowa.edu. World Wide Web http://www.uiowa.edu/~libsci. Admissions contact: Ethel Bloesch. E-mail ethel-bloesch@uiowa.edu.

University of Michigan, School of Info., 550 E. University Ave., Ann Arbor, MI 48109-1092. Gary M. Olson, Interim Dean. 734-763-2285, fax 734-764-2475, e-mail si.admissions@umich.edu. World Wide Web http://www.si.umich.edu. Admissions Contact: Cindy Tweedy.

University of Missouri–Columbia, School of Info. Science and Learning Technologies, 217 Townsend Hall, Columbia, MO 65211. John Wedman, Dir. 573-882-4546, fax 573-884-4944. World Wide Web http://tiger.coe/missouri.edu/~sislt. Admissions contact: Paula Schlager. 573-882-4546, e-mail sislt@coe.missouri.edu.

University of Wisconsin–Madison, School of Lib. and Info. Studies, 600 N. Park St., Madison, WI 53706. Louise S. Robbins, Dir. 608-263-2900, fax 608-263-4849, e-mail uw_slis@doit.wisc.edu. Admissions contact: Barbara Arnold. 608-263-2090, e-mail bjarnold@facstaff.wisc.edu.

University of Wisconsin–Milwaukee, School of Lib. and Info. Science, 2400 E. Hartford Ave., Milwaukee, WI 53211. Mohammed M. Aman, Dean. 414-229-4707, fax 414-229-4848, e-mail info@slis.uwm.edu. World Wide Web http://www.slis.uwm.edu. Admissions contact: Judy Senkevitch. 414-229-5421.

Wayne State University, Lib. and Info. Science Program, 106 Kresge Library, Detroit, MI 48202. Robert R. Powell, Interim Dir. 313-577-1825, fax 313-577-7563, e-mail info@lisp.wayne.edu. World Wide Web http://www.lisp.wayne.edu. Admissions contact: aa3805@wayne.edu.

## Southwest: Ariz., Okla., Texas.

Texas Woman's University, School of Lib. and Info. Studies, Box 425438, Denton, TX 76204-5438. Keith Swigger, Dean. 940-898-2602, fax 940-898-2611, e-mail a_swigger@twu.edu. World Wide Web http://www.twu.edu/slis.

University of Arizona, School of Info. Resources and Lib. Science, 1515 E. First St., Tucson, AZ 85719. Charles A. Seavey, Acting Dir. 520-621-3565, fax 520-621-3279, e-mail sirls@u.arizona.edu. World Wide Web http://www.sir/arizona.edu.

University of North Texas, School of Lib. and Info. Sciences, Box 311068, NT Station, Denton, TX 76203. Philip M. Turner, Dean. 940-565-2445, fax 940-565-3101, e-mail slis@unt.edu. World Wide Web http://www.unt.edu.slis. Admissions contact: Herman L. Totten. E-mail totten@lis.unt.edu.

University of Oklahoma, School of Lib. and Info. Studies, 401 W. Brooks, Norman, OK 73019-0528. June Lester, Dir. 405-325-3921, 405-325-7648, e-mail slisinfo@ou.edu. World Wide Web http://www.ou.edu/cas/slis. Admissions contact: Maggie Ryan.

University of Texas at Austin, Grad. School of Lib. and Info. Science, Austin, TX 78712-1276. Glynn Harmon, Interim Dean. 512-471-3821, fax 512-471-3971, e-mail gslis@uts.cc.utexas.edu. World Wide Web http://www.gslis.utexas.edu. Admissions contact: Ronald Wyllys. 512-471-8969, e-mail wyllys@uts.cc.utexas.edu.

## West: Calif., Hawaii, Wash.

San Jose State University, School of Lib. and Info. Science, 1 Washington Sq., San Jose, CA 95192-0029. Blanche Woolls, Dir. 408-924-2490, fax 408-924-2476, e-mail office@wahoo.sjsu.edu.

University of California at Los Angeles, Grad. School of Education and Info. Studies, Mailbox 951521, Los Angeles, CA 90095-1521. Michèle V. Cloonan, Chair. 310-825-8799, fax 310-206-3076, e-mail mcloonan@ucla.edu. World Wide Web http://dlis.gseis.ucla.edu. Admissions contact: Susan Abler. 310-825-5269, fax 310-206-6293, e-mail abler@gseis.ucla.edu.

University of Hawaii, Lib. and Info. Science Program, 2550 The Mall, Honolulu, HI 96822. Violet H. Harada, Program Chair. 808-956-7321, fax 808-956-5835, e-mail vharada@hawaii.edu.

University of Washington, Grad. School of Lib. and Info. Science, Box 352930, Seattle, WA 98195-2930. Michael B. Eisenberg, Dir. 206-543-1794, fax 206-616-3152. World Wide Web http://depts.washington.edu/~slis. Admissions contact: Dolores Potter. E-mail dpotter@u.washington.edu.

## Canada

Dalhousie University, School of Lib. and Info. Studies, Halifax, NS B3H 3J5. Bertrum H. MacDonald, Dir. 902-494-3656, fax 902-494-2451, e-mail slis@is.dal.ca. World Wide Web http://www.mgmt.dal.ca/slis. Admissions contact: Shanna Balogh. 902-494-2453, e-mail shanna@is.dal.ca.

McGill University, Grad. School of Lib. and Info. Studies, 3459 McTavish St., Montreal, PQ H3A 1Y1. Jamshid Beheshti, Dir. 514-398-4204, fax 514-398-7193, e-mail ad27@musica.mcgill.ca. World Wide Web http://www.gslis.mcgill.ca. Admissions contact: Dorothy Carruthers.

Université de Montréal, Ecole de Bibliothéconomie et des Sciences de l'Information, C.P. 6128, Succursale Centre-Ville, Montreal, PQ H3C 3J7. Gilles Deschâtelets, Dir. 514-343-6044, fax 514-343-5753, e-mail gilles.deschatelets@umontreal.ca. World Wide Web http://www.fas.umontreal.ca/EBSI/. Admissions contact: Diane Mayer. E-mail diane.mayer@umontreal.ca.

University of Alberta, School of Lib. and Info. Studies, 3-20 Rutherford S., Edmonton, AB T6G 2J4. Alvin Schrader, Dir. 403-492-4578, fax 403-492-2430, e-mail office@slis.ualberta.ca.

University of British Columbia, School of Lib., Archival, and Info. Studies, 1956 Main Mall, Vancouver, BC V6T 1Z1. Ken Haycock, Dir. 604-822-2404, fax 604-822-6006, e-mail slais@interchange.ubc.ca. World Wide Web http://www.slais.ubc.ca. Admissions contact: Lynne Lighthall. 604-822-2404, e-mail slais.admissions@ubc.ca.

University of Toronto, Faculty of Info. Studies, 140 George St., Toronto, ON M5S 3G6. Lynne C. Howarth, Dean. 416-978-8589, fax 416-978-5762. World Wide Web http://www.fis.utoronto.ca. Admissions contact: Pamela Hawes. E-mail Hawes@fis.utoronto.ca.

University of Western Ontario, Grad. Programs in Lib. and Info. Science, Middlesex College, London, ON N6A 5B7. Manjunath Pendakur, Dean. 519-661-3542, fax 519-661-3506, e-mail fimsdean@julian.uwo.ca. Admissions contact: 519-661-2111, e-mail mlisinfo@julian.uwo.ca.

# Library Scholarship Sources

For a more complete list of scholarships, fellowships, and assistantships offered for library study, see *Financial Assistance for Library and Information Studies*, published annually by the American Library Association.

American Association of Law Libraries. (1) A varying number of scholarships of a minimum of $1,000 for graduates of an accredited law school who are degree candidates in an ALA-accredited library school; (2) a varying number of scholarships of varying amounts for library school graduates working on a law degree, non-law graduates enrolled in an ALA-accredited library school, and law librarians taking a course related to law librarianship; (3) the George A. Strait Minority Stipend of $3,500 for an experienced minority librarian working toward an advanced degree to further a law library career. For information, write to: Scholarship Committee, AALL, 53 W. Jackson Blvd., Suite 940, Chicago, IL 60604.

American Library Association. (1) The Marshall Cavendish Scholarship of $3,000 for a varying number of students who have been admitted to an ALA-accredited library school. For information, write to Staff Liaison, Cavendish Scholarship Jury, ALA, 50 E. Huron St., Chicago, IL 60611; (2) The David H. Clift Scholarship of $3,000 for a varying number of students who have been admitted to an ALA-accredited library school. For information, write to: Staff Liaison, Clift Scholarship Jury, ALA, 50 E. Huron St., Chicago, IL 60611; (3) the Tom and Roberta Drewes Scholarship of $3,000 for a varying number of library support staff. For information, write to: Staff Liaison, Drewes Scholarship Jury, ALA, 50 E. Huron St., Chicago, IL 60611; (4) the Mary V. Gaver Scholarship of $3,000 to a varying number of individuals specializing in youth services. For information, write to: Staff Liaison, Gaver Scholarship Jury, ALA, 50 E. Huron St., Chicago, IL 60611; (5) the Miriam L. Hornback Scholarship of $3,000 for a varying number of ALA or library support staff. For information, write to: Staff Liaison, Hornback Scholarship Jury, ALA, 50 E. Huron St., Chicago, IL 60611; (6) the Christopher J. Hoy/ERT Scholarship of $3,000 for a varying number of students who have been admitted to an ALA-accredited library school. For information, write to: Staff Liaison, Hoy/ERT Scholarship Jury, ALA, 50 E. Huron St., Chicago, IL 60611; (7) the Tony B. Leisner Scholarship of $3,000 for a varying number of library support staff. For information, write to: Staff Liaison, Leisner Scholarship Jury, ALA, 50 E. Huron St., Chicago, IL 60611; (8) Spectrum Initiative Scholarships of $5,000 for 50 minority students admitted to an ALA-accredited library school. For information, write to: Staff Liaison, Spectrum Initiative Scholarship, ALA, 50 E. Huron St., Chicago, IL 60611.

ALA/American Association of School Librarians. The AASL School Librarians Workshop Scholarship of $2,500 for a candidate admitted to a full-time ALA-accredited MLS or school library media program. For information, write to: AASL/ALA, 50 E. Huron St., Chicago, IL 60611.

ALA/Association of College and Research Libraries and the Institute for Scientific Information. (1) The ACRL Doctoral Dissertation Fellowship of $1,000 for a student who has completed all coursework and submitted a dissertation proposal that has been accepted, in the area of academic librarianship; (2) the Samuel Lazerow Fellowship of $1,000 for research in acquisitions or technical services in an academic or research library; (3) the ACRL and Martinus Nijhoff International West European Specialist Study Grant, which pays travel expenses, room, and board for a ten-day trip to the Netherlands and two other European countries for an ALA member (selection is based on proposal outlining purpose of trip). For information, write to: Jack Briody, ACRL/ALA, 50 E. Huron St., Chicago, IL 60611.

ALA/Association for Library Service to Children. (1) The Bound to Stay Bound Books Scholarship of $6,000 each for two students who are U.S. or Canadian citizens, who have been admitted to an ALA-accredited program, and who will work with children in a library for one year after graduation; (2) the Frederic G. Melcher Scholarship of $6,000 each for two U.S. or Canadian citizens admitted to an ALA-accredited library school who will work with children in school or public libraries for one year after graduation. For information, write to: Executive Director, ALSC/ALA, 50 E. Huron St., Chicago, IL 60611.

ALA/International Relations Committee. The Bogle Pratt International Library Travel Fund grant of $1,000 for a varying number of ALA members to attend a first international conference. For information, write to: Annie Wolter, ALA/IRC, 50 E. Huron St., Chicago, IL 60611.

ALA/Library and Information Technology Association. Three LITA Scholarships in library and information technology of $2,500 each for students (two of whom are minority students) who have been admitted to an ALA-accredited program in library automation and information science. For information, write to: LITA/ALA, 50 E. Huron St., Chicago, IL 60611.

ALA/New Members Round Table. EBSCO/NMRT Scholarship of $1,000 for a U.S. or Canadian citizen who is a member of the ALA New Members Round Table. Based on financial need, professional goals, and admission to an ALA-accredited program. For information, write to: ALA Scholarship Liaison, 50 E. Huron St., Chicago, IL 60611.

ALA/Public Library Association. The New Leaders Travel Grant Study Award of up to $1,500 for a varying number of PLA members with five years or less experience. For information, write to: PLA/ALA, 50 E. Huron St., Chicago, IL 60611.

American-Scandinavian Foundation. Fellowships and grants for 25 to 30 students, in amounts from $3,000 to $15,000, for advanced study in Denmark, Finland, Iceland, Norway, or Sweden. For information, write to: Exchange Division, American-Scandinavian Foundation, 725 Park Ave., New York, NY 10021.

Association of Jewish Libraries. The May K. Simon Memorial Scholarship Fund offers a varying number of scholarships of at least $500 each for MLS students who plan to work as Judaica librarians. For information, write to: Sharona R. Wachs, Association of Jewish Libraries, 1000 Washington Ave., Albany, NY 12203.

Association for Library and Information Science Education. A varying number of research grants of up to $2,500 each for members of ALISE. For information, write to: Association for Library and Information Science Education, Box 7640, Arlington, VA 22207.

Association of Seventh-Day Adventist Librarians. The D. Glenn Hilts Scholarship of $1,000 to a member of the Seventh-Day Adventist Church in a graduate library program. For information, write to: Ms. Wisel, Association of Seventh-Day Adventist Librarians, Columbia Union College, 7600 Flower Ave., Takoma Park, MD 20912.

Beta Phi Mu. (1) The Sarah Rebecca Reed Scholarship of $1,500 for a person accepted in an ALA-accredited library program; (2) the Frank B. Sessa Scholarship of $750 for a Beta Phi Mu member for continuing education; (3) the Harold Lancour Scholarship of $1,000 for study in a foreign country related to the applicant's work or schooling; (4) the Blanche E. Woolls Scholarship for School Library Media Service of $1,000 for a person accepted in an ALA-accredited library program; (5) the Doctoral Dissertation Scholarship of $1,500 for a person who has completed course work toward a doctorate. For information, write to: F. William Summers, Executive Director, Beta Phi Mu, Florida State University, SLIS, Tallahassee, FL 32306-2100.

Canadian Association of Law Libraries. The Diana M. Priestly Scholarship of $2,500 for a student with previous law library experience or for entry to an approved Canadian law school or accredited Canadian library school. For information, write to: John Eaton, Prof., Law Library, University of Western Ontario, London, ON N6A 3K7, Canada.

Canadian Federation of University Women. The Alice E. Wilson Award of $1,000 for three Canadian citizens or permanent residents with a BA degree or equivalent accepted into a program of graduate study. For information, write to: Canadian Federation of University Women, 251 Bank St., Suite 600, Ottawa, ON K2P 1X3, Canada.

Canadian Health Libraries Association. The Student Paper Prize, a scholarship of $300 to a student or recent MLIS graduate or library technician; topic of paper must be in health or information science. For information, write to: Student Paper Prize, Canadian Health Libraries Association/ABSC, Box 94038, 3332 Yonge St., Toronto, ON M4N 3R1, Canada.

Canadian Library Association. (1) The Howard V. Phalin World Book Graduate Scholarship in Library Science of $2,500; (2) the CLA Dafoe Scholarship of $1,750; and (3) the H. W. Wilson Scholarship of $2,000. Each scholarship is given to a Canadian citizen or landed immigrant to attend an accredited Canadian library school; the Phalin scholarship can also be used for an ALA-accredited U.S. school; (4) the Library Research and Development Grant of $1,000 for a member of the Canadian Library Association, in support of theoretical and applied research in library and information science. For information, write to: CLA Membership Services Department, Scholarships and Awards Committee, 200 Elgin St., Suite 602, Ottawa, ON K2P 1L5, Canada.

Catholic Library Association. The World Book, Inc., Grant of $1,500 is divided among no more than three CLA members for workshops, institutes, etc. For information, write to: Jean R. Bostley, SSJ, Executive Director, Catholic Library Association, 100 North St., Suite 224, Pittsfield, MA 01201-5109.

Chinese American Librarians Association. (1) The Sheila Suen Lai Scholarship; (2) the C. C. Seetoo/CALA Conference Travel Scholarship. Each scholarship offers $500 to a Chinese descendant who has been accepted in an ALA-accredited program.

For information, write to: Meng Xiong Liu, Clark Library, San Jose State University, 1 Washington Sq., San Jose, CA 95192-0028.

Church and Synagogue Library Association. The Muriel Fuller Memorial Scholarship of $115 plus cost of texts for a correspondence course offered by the University of Utah Continuing Education Division. Open to CSLA members only. For information, write to: CSLA, Box 19357, Portland, OR 97280-0357.

Council on Library and Information Resources. The A. R. Zipf Fellowship in Information Management of $5,000 is awarded annually to a student enrolled in graduate school who shows exceptional promise for leadership and technical achievement. For information, write to: Council on Library and Information Resources, 1755 Massachusetts Ave. N.W., Suite 500, Washington, DC 20036.

Sandra Garvie Memorial Fund. A scholarship of $1,000 for a student pursuing a course of study in library and information science. For information, write to: Sandra Garvie Memorial Fund, c/o Director, Legal Resources Centre, Faculty of Extension, University of Alberta, 8303 112th St., Edmonton, AB T6G 2T4, Canada.

Manitoba Library Association. (1) John Edwin Bissett Memorial Fund Scholarships. Awards of varying amounts for a varying number of University of Manitoba graduates who are enrolled full-time in a master's program in library and information science; (2) Jean Thorunn Law Scholarship. An award of a varying amount for a student enrolled in a full-time master's program in library and information who has a year of library experience in Manitoba. For information, write to: Manitoba Library Association, CE Committee, 416-100 Arthur St., Winnipeg, MB R3B 1H3.

Massachusetts Black Librarians' Network. Two scholarships of at least $500 and $1,000 for a minority student entering an ALA-accredited master's program in library science, with no more than 12 semester hours toward a degree. For information, write to: Pearl Mosley, Chair,

Massachusetts Black Librarians' Network, 27 Beech Glen St., Roxbury, MA 02119.

Medical Library Association. (1) A scholarship of $2,000 for a person entering an ALA-accredited library program, with no more than one-half of the program yet to be completed; (2) a scholarship of $2,000 for a minority student for graduate study; (3) a varying number of Research, Development and Demonstration Project Grants of $100 to $1,000 for U.S. or Canadian citizens who are MLA members; (4) Continuing Education Grants of $100 to $500 for U.S. or Canadian citizens who are MLA members; (5) the Cunningham Memorial International Fellowship of $6,000 plus travel expenses for a foreign student for postgraduate study in the United States; (6) the MLA Doctoral Fellowship of $2,000 for doctoral work in medical librarianship or information science. For information, write to: Development Department, Medical Library Association, 65 E. Wacker Pl., Suite 1900, Chicago, IL 60601-7298.

Mountain Plains Library Association. (1) A varying number of grants of up to $600 each and (2) a varying number of grants of up to $150 each for MPLA members with at least two years of membership for continuing education. For information, write to: Joseph R. Edelen, Jr., MPLA Executive Secretary, I. D. Weeks Library, University of South Dakota, Vermillion, SD 57069.

REFORMA, the National Association to Promote Library Services to the Spanish-Speaking. A varying number of scholarships of $1,000 each for minority students interested in serving the Spanish-speaking community to attend an ALA-accredited school. For information, write to: Ninta Trejo, Main Library, University of Arizona, 1510 E. University, Tucson, AZ 85721.

Society of American Archivists. The Colonial Dames Awards, two grants of $1,200 each for specific types of repositories and collections. For information, write to: Debra Mills, Society of American Archivists, 600 S. Federal St., Suite 504, Chicago, IL 60605.

Southern Regional Education Board. For residents of Arkansas, Delaware, Georgia, Louisiana, Maryland, Mississippi, Oklahoma, Tennessee, Virginia, and West Virginia, a varying number of grants of varying amounts to cover in-state tuition for graduate or postgraduate study in an ALA-accredited library school. For information, write to: Academic Common Market, c/o Southern Regional Education Board, 592 Tenth St. N.W., Atlanta, GA 30318-5790.

Special Libraries Association. (1) Three $6,000 scholarships for students interested in special-library work; (2) the Plenum Scholarship of $1,000, and (3) the ISI Scholarship of $1,000, each also for students interested in special-library work; (4) the Affirmative Action Scholarship of $6,000 for minority students interested in special-library work; and (5) the Pharmaceutical Division Stipend Award of $1,200 for a student with an undergraduate degree in chemistry, life sciences, or pharmacy entering or enrolled in an ALA-accredited program. For information on the first four scholarships, write to: Scholarship Committee, Special Libraries Association, 1700 18th St. N.W., Washington, DC 20009-2508; for information on the Pharmaceutical Stipend, write to: Susan E. Katz, Awards Chair, Knoll Pharmaceuticals Science Information Center, 30 N. Jefferson St., Whippany, NJ 07981.

# Library Scholarship and Award Recipients, 1998

Library awards are listed by organization. An index listing awards alphabetically by title follows this section.

## American Association of Law Libraries (AALL)

AALL Scholarships. Offered by: AALL; Matthew Bender & Company; LEXIS-NEXIS; West Group. *Winners*: (John Johnson LEXIS-NEXIS scholarship) Mary Aldridge, Felicia Poe, Julie Stuckey; (Library Degree for Law School Graduates) Amy Hale, Iris Lee, Jennifer Lentz, Marie Mack, Joe Morris, Jennifer Murray; (Library School Graduates Attending Law School) not awarded in 1998; (Library Degree for Non-Law School Graduates) Anne Tuveson; (Library School Graduates Seeking a Non-Law Degree) Mildred Bailey; (George A. Strait Minority Stipend) Pam Fiawoo, Pauline Afuso, Kristin Nelson.

## American Library Association (ALA)

ALA Honorary Membership. Bill and Melinda Gates, Wendell H. Ford, Sidney R. Yates, K. Wayne Smith.

ALA/Information Today Library of the Future Award ($1,500). For a library, consortium, group of librarians, or support organization for innovative planning for, applications of, or development of patron training programs about information technology in a library setting. *Donor*: Information Today, Inc. *Winner*: Rowan Public Library, Rowan County, North Carolina.

Hugh C. Atkinson Memorial Award ($2,000). For outstanding achievement (including risk-taking) by academic librarians that has contributed significantly to improvements in library automation, management, and/or development or research. Offered by: ACRL, ALCTS, LAMA, and LITA divisions. *Winner*: Arnold Hirshon.

Carroll Preston Baber Research Grant (up to $7,500). For innovative research that could lead to an improvement in library services

to any specified group(s) of people. *Donor*: Eric R. Baber. *Winner*: Not awarded in 1998.

Beta Phi Mu Award ($500). For distinguished service in library education. *Donor*: Beta Phi Mu International Library Science Honorary Society. *Winner*: Elizabeth Stone.

Bogle International Library Travel Fund Award ($1,000). To ALA member(s) to attend their first international conference. *Donor*: Bogle Memorial Fund. *Winner*: Gebregeorgis Yohannes.

William Boyd Military Novel Award ($10,000). To an author for a military novel that honors the service of American veterans. *Donor*: William Young Boyd. *Winner*: Howard Bahr for *The Black Flower: A Novel of the Civil War*.

Marshall Cavendish Scholarship ($3,000). To a worthy U.S. or Canadian citizen to begin an MLS degree in an ALA-accredited program. *Winner*: Peter Espenshade.

David H. Clift Scholarship ($3,000). To a worthy U.S. or Canadian citizen to begin an MLS degree in an ALA-accredited program. *Winner*: Steven Jablonski.

Melvil Dewey Award. To an individual or group for recent creative professional achievement in library management, training, cataloging and classification, and the tools and techniques of librarianship. *Donor*: OCLC/Forest Press. *Winner*: Winston Tabb.

Tom and Roberta Drewes Scholarship ($3,000). To a library support staff person pursuing a master's degree. *Winner*: Rose Marie Allen.

EBSCO ALA Conference Sponsorships (up to $1,000). To allow librarians to attend ALA's Annual Conferences. *Donor*: EBSCO Subscription Services. *Winners*: John R. Davies, Kay Evey, Janet Foster, Mary Anne Hansen, Cathy Nelson Hartman, Sue N. Howard, Shirley Lincicum, Patricia Milheiser, Debra Rodensky, Claudia West.

Equality Award ($500). To an individual or group for an outstanding contribution that promotes equality of women and men in the library profession. *Donor*: Scarecrow Press. *Winner*: Betty J. Turock.

Freedom to Read Foundation Roll of Honor Award. *Winner*: Dorothy M. Broderick.

Elizabeth Futas Catalyst for Change Award ($1,000). To recognize and honor a librarian who invests time and talent to make positive change in the profession of librarianship. *Donor*: Elizabeth Futas Memorial Fund. *Winner*: Kathleen de la Peña McCook.

Loleta D. Fyan Public Library Research Grant (up to $10,000). For projects in public library development. *Winner*: Cindy Mediavilla, for her study "Homework Centers in Public Libraries."

Gale Research Financial Development Award ($2,500). To a library organization for a financial development project to secure new funding resources for a public or academic library. *Donor*: Gale Research Company. *Winner*: Rio (Wisconsin) Community Library.

Mary V. Gaver Scholarship ($3,000). To a library support staff member specializing in youth services. *Winner*: Elizabeth Burton.

Louise Giles Minority Scholarship ($3,000). To a worthy U.S. or Canadian minority student to begin an MLS degree in an ALA-accredited program. *Winner*: Not awarded in 1998.

Grolier Foundation Award ($1,000). For stimulation and guidance of reading by children and young people. *Donor*: Grolier Education Corporation, Inc. *Winner*: Amy M. Kellman.

Grolier National Library Week Grant ($4,000). To libraries or library associations of all types for a public awareness campaign in connection with National Library Week in the year the grant is awarded. *Donor*: Grolier Educational Corporation. *Winner*: Metronet library system, Minneapolis and St. Paul, Minnesota.

G. K. Hall Award for Library Literature ($500). For outstanding contribution to library literature issued during the three years preceding presentation. *Donor*: G. K. Hall & Company. *Winner*: Not awarded in 1998.

Mirian L. Hornback Scholarship ($3,000). To an ALA or library support staff person pursuing a master's degree in library science. *Winner*: Debora Robertson.

Paul Howard Award for Courage ($1,000). To a librarian, library board, library group, or an individual who has exhibited unusual courage for the benefit of library programs or services. *Donor*: Paul Howard. *Winner*: Not awarded in 1998.

John Ames Humphry/OCLC/Forest Press Award ($1,000). To an individual for significant contributions to international librarianship. *Donor*: OCLC/Forest Press. *Winner*: E. J. Josey.

Tony B. Leisner Scholarship ($3,000). To a library support staff member pursuing a master's degree program. *Winner*: Erik Spears.

Joseph W. Lippincott Award ($1,000). To a librarian for distinguished service to the profession. *Donor*: Joseph W. Lippincott, Jr. *Winner*: Judith Krug.

Bessie Boehm Moore Award ($1,000). Presented to a public library that has developed an outstanding and creative program for public library services to the aging. *Donor*: Bessie Boehm Moore. *Winner*: Not awarded in 1998.

Spectrum Initiative Scholarships ($5,000). Presented to 50 minority students admitted to an ALA-accredited library school. *Winners*: Alicia Antone, Margaret Auguste, Tamika Barnes, Winsome Benjamin, Tomeka Berry, Sophia Brewer, Myra Brown, Norma P. Carrion, Valerie Charbeneau, Gwen Collier, Augusto Consing, Graciela Cortez, Sandra Courtney, Jamal Cromity, Naomi Dominguez, Lisa Dunkley, Ruth Ellis-Myers, Maria Garcia, Jeffrey Gima, Alexandra Gomez, Leopoldo Gomez, Tracie Hall, Mantra Henderson, Barbara-Helen Hill, Mihoko Hosoi, Erica Johnson, Barbara Kenney, Jama Lumumba, Bie-Hwa Ma, Maynard Martinez, Michele McKenzie, Beverly Mills, Esther Nibot, Loralei Osborn, Miriam Perez, Nykia Perez, Christine Porschet, Edward Robinson-El, Shanti Satsangi, Jennie Seo, Joy Shioshita, Rubi Simon, Brent Singleton, James Soucé, Barbara Taber, Yu-Fang Tao, Brian Tirimanne, Melanie Townsend, Rita Vargas, Lee Zin Wu.

Virginia and Herbert White Award for Promoting Librarianship ($1,000). Honors a significant contribution to the public recognition and appreciation of librarianship through professional performance, teaching, and writing. *Winner*: Virginia H. Mathews.

H. W. Wilson Library Staff Development Grant ($3,500). To a library organization for a program to further its staff development goals and objectives. *Donor*: H. W. Wilson Company. *Winner*: Des Plaines (Illinois) Public Library.

Women's National Book Award Association/ Ann Heidbreder Eastman Grant ($500– $1,000). To a librarian to take a course or participate in an institute devoted to aspects of publishing as a profession or to provide reimbursement for such study completed within the past year. *Winner*: Carolyn Gutierrez.

World Book–ALA Goal Grant (up to $10,000). To ALA units for the advancement of public, academic, or school library service and librarianship through support of programs that implement the goals and priorities of ALA. *Donor*: World Book, Inc. *Winners*: American Association of School Librarians, ALA Chapter Relations Committee, ALA Intellectual Freedom Committee.

## American Association of School Librarians (AASL)

AASL ABC/CLIO Leadership Grant (up to $1,750). For planning and implementing leadership programs at state, regional, or local levels to be given to school library associations that are affiliates of AASL. *Donor*: ABC/CLIO. *Winner*: Ohio Educational Library Media Association.

AASL/Frances Henne Award ($1,250). To a school library media specialist with five or fewer years in the profession to attend an AASL regional conference or ALA Annual Conference for the first time. *Donor*: R. R. Bowker. *Winner*: Kimberly A. Grimes.

AASL/Highsmith Research Grant (up to $5,000). To conduct innovative research aimed at measuring and evaluating the impact of school library media programs on learning and education. *Donor*: The Highsmith Company. *Winners*: Joy H. McGregor, Linda L. Wolcott.

AASL Information Plus Continuing Education Scholarship ($500). To a school library media specialist, supervisor, or educator to attend an ALA or AASL continuing education event. *Donor*: Information Plus. *Winner*: Renate Hayum.

AASL Crystal Apple Award. *Winner*: Lillian N. Gerhardt.

AASL School Librarian's Workshop Scholarship ($2,500). To a full-time student preparing to become a school library media specialist at the preschool, elementary, or secondary level. *Donor*: Jay W. Toor, President, Library Learning Resources. *Winner*: Dianna H. M. Fricke.

Distinguished School Administrators Award ($2,000). For expanding the role of the library in elementary and/or secondary school education. *Donor*: Social Issues Resources Series, Inc. *Winner*: Brian Fagan.

Distinguished Service Award, AASL/Baker & Taylor ($3,000). For outstanding contributions to librarianship and school library development. *Donor*: Baker & Taylor Books. *Winner*: Bernice L. "Bunny" Yesner.

Information Technology Pathfinder Award ($1,000 to the specialist and $500 to the library). To library media specialists for innovative approaches to microcomputer applications in the school library media center. *Donor*: Follett Software Company. *Winners*: Secondary, Lynda S. Morris; Elementary, Constance Vidor.

Intellectual Freedom Award ($2,000, and $1,000 to media center of recipient's choice). To a school library media specialist who has upheld the principles of intellectual freedom. *Donor*: Social Issues Resources Series, Inc. *Winner*: Not awarded in 1998.

National School Library Media Program of the Year Award ($3,000). To school districts and a single school for excellence and innovation in outstanding library media programs. *Donor*: AASL and Encyclopedia Britannica Companies. *Winners*: Single, Hunterdon Central Regional High School, Flemington, New Jersey; Small school district, not awarded in 1998; Large school district, not awarded in 1998.

## American Library Trustee Association (ALTA)

ALTA/Gale Outstanding Trustee Conference Grant Award ($750). *Donor*: Gale Research Company. *Winners*: Margaret Pemberton, Dondi Maricle.

ALTA Literacy Award (citation). To a library trustee or an individual who, in a volunteer capacity, has made a significant contribution to addressing the illiteracy problem in the United States. *Winner*: Shirley Carver Miller.

ALTA Major Benefactors Honor Award (citation). To individual(s), families, or corporate bodies that have made major benefactions to public libraries. *Winners*: Huizence Family Foundation and Republic Industries.

Trustee Citations. To recognize public library trustees for individual service to library development on the local, state, regional, or national level. *Winners*: Wayne Coco, Jack Cole.

## Armed Forces Libraries Round Table

Armed Forces Library Certificate of Merit. To librarians or "friends" who are members of AFLRT who provide an exemplary program to an Armed Forces library. *Winners*: Joan Buntzen, Huddy B. Haller, Richard D. Hanusey.

Armed Forces Library Round Table Achievement Citation. For contributions toward development of interest in libraries and reading in armed forces library service and organizations. Candidates must be members of the Armed Forces Libraries Round Table. *Winner*: Marjorie A. Homeyard.

Armed Forces Library Round Table News-Bank Scholarship ($1,000 to the school of the recipient's choice). To members of the Armed Forces Libraries Round Table who have given exemplary service in the area of library support for off-duty education programs in the armed forces. *Donor*: NewsBank, Inc. *Winner*: Arlene Luster.

## Association for Library Collections and Technical Services (ALCTS)

Hugh C. Atkinson Memorial Award. *See under* American Library Association.

Best of LRTS Award (citation). To the author(s) of the best paper published each year in the division's official journal. *Winners*: Samuel Demas, Jennie L. Brogdon.

Blackwell's Scholarship Award ($2,000 scholarship to the U.S. or Canadian library school of the recipient's choice). To honor the author(s) of the year's outstanding monograph, article, or original paper in the field of acquisitions, collection development, and related areas of resource development in libraries. *Donor*: Blackwell/North America: *Winners*: David F. Kohl for "Resource Sharing in a Changing Ohio Environment," William Gray Potter for "Recent Trends in Statewide Academic Library Consortia."

Bowker/Ulrich's Serials Librarianship Award ($1,500). For demonstrated leadership in serials-related activities through participation in professional associations and/or library education programs, contributions to the body of serials literature, research in the area of serials, or development of tools or methods to enhance access to or management of serials. *Donor*: R. R. Bowker/Ulrich's. *Winner*: Crystal Graham.

First Step Award (Wiley Professional Development Grant) ($1,500). For librarians new to the serials field to attend ALA's Annual Conference. *Donor*: John Wiley & Sons. *Winner*: Lauren Corbett.

Leadership in Library Acquisitions Award ($1,500). For significant contributions by an outstanding leader in the field of library acquisitions. *Donor*: Harrassowitz Company. *Winner*: Christian M. Boissonnas.

Margaret Mann Citation. To a cataloger or classifier for achievement in the areas of cataloging or classification. *Winner*: John Byrum.

Esther J. Piercy Award ($1,500). To a librarian with fewer than ten years experience for contributions and leadership in the field of library collections and technical services. *Donor*: Yankee Book Peddler. *Winner*: Judith R. Ahronheim.

## Association for Library Service to Children (ALSC)

ALSC/Book Wholesalers Summer Reading Program Grant ($3,000). To an ALSC member for implementation of an outstanding public library summer reading program for children. *Donor*: Book Wholesalers, Inc. *Winner*: Rockbridge Regional Library, Lexington, Virginia.

ALSC/Econo-Clad Literature Program Award ($1,000). To an ALSC member who has developed and implemented an outstanding library program for children involving reading and the use of literature, to attend an ALA conference. *Donor*: Econo-Clad Books. *Winner*: Judith A. Rose.

May Hill Arbuthnot Honor Lecturer 1999. To invite an individual of distinction to prepare and present a paper that will be a significant contribution to the field of children's literature and that will subsequently be published in *Journal of Youth Services in Libraries*. *Winner*: Lillian N. Gerhardt.

Mildred L. Batchelder Award (citation). To an American publisher of an English-language translation of a children's book originally published in a foreign language in a foreign country. *Winner*: Henry Holt and Co. for *The Robber and Me* by Josef Holub.

Louise Seaman Bechtel Fellowship ($3,750). For librarians with 12 or more years of professional level work in children's library collections, to read and study at the Baldwin Library/George Smathers Libraries, University of Florida (must be an ALSC member with an MLS from an ALA-accredited program). *Donor*: Bechtel Fund. *Winner*: Floyd C. Dickman.

AASL/REFORMA Pura Belpré Award. See *Literary Prizes, 1998* by Gary Ink.

Bound to Stay Bound Books Scholarship ($6,000). Two awards for study in the field of library service to children toward the MLS or beyond in an ALA-accredited program. *Donor*: Bound to Stay Bound Books. *Winners*: Lisa Marie Gilgenbach, Helen M. Moore.

Caldecott Medal. See *Literary Prizes, 1998* by Gary Ink.

Andrew Carnegie Medal. To the U.S. producer of the most distinguished video for children in the previous year. *Donor*: Carnegie Corporation of New York. *Winner*: Tom

and Mimi Davenort of Davenort Films for *Willa: An American Snow White.*

Distinguished Service to ALSC Award ($1,000). To recognize significant contributions to, and an impact on, library services to children and/or ALSC. *Winner*: Spencer Shaw.

Frederic G. Melcher Scholarship ($5,000). To students entering the field of library service to children for graduate work in an ALA-accredited program. *Winners*: Karla Schmit-Benedict, Lisa Lintner-Sizemore.

John Newbery Medal. See *Literary Prizes, 1998* by Gary Ink.

Penguin Putnam Books for Young Readers Awards. To children's librarians in school or public libraries with ten or fewer years of experience to attend an ALA Annual Conference for the first time. Must be a member of ALSC. *Donor*: Penguin Putnam. *Winners*: Renee McGrath, Dorette J. Putonti, Jeanne Marie Ryan, Cheryl Space.

Laura Ingalls Wilder Medal. To an author or illustrator whose works have made a lasting contribution to children's literature. *Winner*: Russell Freedman.

## Association of College and Research Libraries (ACRL)

ACRL Academic or Research Librarian of the Year Award ($3,000). For outstanding contribution to academic and research librarianship and library development. *Donor*: Baker & Taylor. *Winner*: Alan Veaner.

ACRL EBSS Distinguished Education and Behavioral Sciences Librarian Award (citation). To an academic librarian who has made an outstanding contribution as an education and/or behavioral sciences librarian through accomplishments and service to the profession. *Winner*: Eva Kiewitt.

ACRL Doctoral Dissertation Fellowship ($1,500). To a doctoral student in the field of academic librarianship whose research has potential significance in the field. *Donor*: Institute for Scientific Information. *Winner*: Jeanine Williamson

Hugh C. Atkinson Memorial Award. *See under* American Library Association.

Miriam Dudley Bibliographic Instruction Librarian Award ($1,000). For contribution to the advancement of bibliographic instruction in a college or research institution. *Donor*: JAI Press. *Winner*: Lori Arp.

EBSCO Community College Leadership Award ($500). *Donor*: EBSCO Subscription Services. *Winner*: Bernard Fradkin.

EBSCO Community College Program Award ($500). *Donor*: EBSCO Subscription Services. *Winner*: Oakton (Illinois) Community College.

Instruction Section Innovation in Instruction Award (citation). Recognizes and honors librarians who have developed and implemented innovative approaches to instruction within their institution in the preceding two years. *Winner*: Nancy E. Adams.

Instruction Section Publication of the Year Award (citation). Recognizes an outstanding publication related to instruction in a library environment published in the preceding two years. *Winner*: Not awarded in 1998.

Marta Lange/CQ Award ($1,000). Recognizes an academic or law librarian for contributions to bibliography and information service in law or political science. *Donor*: *Congressional Quarterly*. *Winner*: Laura N. Gasaway.

Samuel Lazerow Fellowship for Research in Acquisitions or Technical Services ($1,000). To foster advances in acquisitions or technical services by providing librarians a fellowship for travel or writing in those fields. Sponsor: Institute for Scientific Information (ISI). *Winner*: Dilys E. Morris.

Katharine Kyes Leab and Daniel J. Leab American Book Prices Current Exhibition Catalog Awards (citations). For the three best catalogs published by American or Canadian institutions in conjunction with exhibitions of books and/or manuscripts. *Winners*: (Category One) *Sendak at the Rosenbach*, Rosenbach Museum and Library, Philadelphia; (Category Two) *In Praise of Aldus Manutius*, Pierpont Morgan Library, New York; (Category Three) *Garbage! the History and Politics of Trash in New York City*, New York Public Library.

Martinus Nijhoff International West European Specialist Study Grant (travel funding for up to 14 days research in Europe). Supports research pertaining to West European studies, librarianship, or the book trade. Sponsor: Martinus Nijhoff International. *Winner*: Jeffrey Garrett.

Oberly Award for Bibliography in the Agricultural Sciences. Biennially, for the best English-language bibliography in the field of agriculture or a related science in the preceding two-year period. *Donor*: Eunice R. Oberly Fund. *Winner*: Not awarded in 1998.

Rare Books & Manuscripts Librarianship Award ($1,000). For articles of superior quality published in the ACRL journal *Rare Books & Manuscripts Librarianship*. *Donor*: Christie, Manson & Woods. *Winners*: Not awarded in 1998.

K. G. Saur Award for Best *College and Research Libraries* Article ($500). To author(s) to recognize the most outstanding article published in *College and Research Libraries* during the preceding year. *Donor*: K. G. Saur. *Winners*: Jane P. Kleiner, Charles A. Hamaker.

## Association of Specialized and Cooperative Library Agencies (ASCLA)

ASCLA Exceptional Service Award. *Winner*: Steve Cooper.

ASCLA Leadership Achievement Award. To recognize leadership and achievement in the areas of consulting, multitype library cooperation, and state library development. *Winner*: Nancy Bolt.

ASCLA/National Organization on Disability Award for Library Service to People with Disabilities ($1,000). To institutions or organizations that have made the library's total service more accessible through changing physical and/or additional barriers. *Donor*: National Organization on Disability, funded by J. C. Penney. *Winner*: Decorah (Iowa) Public Library.

ASCLA Professional Achievement Award (citation). For professional achievement within the areas of consulting, networking, statewide services, and programs. *Winner*: Darrell Batson.

ASCLA Research Grant ($1,000). To stimulate researchers to look at state library services, interlibrary cooperation, networking, and services to special populations as valid areas of research interest. *Donor*: Auto-Graphics, Inc. *Winner*: Nancy Everhart.

ASCLA Service Award (citation). For outstanding service and leadership to the division. *Winner*: Not awarded in 1998.

Francis Joseph Campbell Citation. For a contribution of recognized importance to library service for the blind and physically handicapped. *Winner*: Gerald Buttars.

## Ethnic Material and Information Exchange Round Table

EMIERT/Gale Research Multicultural Award ($1,000): For outstanding achievement and leadership in serving the multicultural/multiethnic community. *Donor*: Gale Research Company. *Winner*: David Cohen.

## Exhibits Round Table

Friendly Booth Award (citation). *Cosponsor*: New Members Round Table. *Winners*: First place, Demco; second place, 3M; third place, Romance Writers of America.

Christopher J. Hoy/ERT Scholarship ($3,000). To an individual who will work toward an MLS degree in an ALA-accredited program. *Donor*: Family of Christopher Hoy. *Winner*: Paul R. Keith.

Kohlstedt Exhibit Award (citation). To companies or organizations for the best single, multiple, and island booth displays at the ALA Annual Conference. Citation. *Winners*: Watson Label Products, Barefoot Books, 3M Library Systems.

## Federal Librarians Round Table (FLRT)

Adelaide del Frate Conference Sponsor Award. To encourage library school students to become familiar with federal librarianship and ultimately seek work in federal libraries; for attendance at ALA Annual Conference and activities of the Federal Librarians Round Table. *Winner*: Not awarded in 1998.

Distinguished Service Award (citation). To honor a FLRT member for outstanding and sustained contributions to the association and to federal librarianship. *Winner*: Not awarded in 1998.

## Government Documents Round Table (GODORT)

James Bennett Childs Award. To a librarian or other individual for distinguished lifetime contributions to documents librarianship. *Winner*: Lois P. Mills.

CIS/GODORT/ALA Documents to the People Award ($2,000). To an individual, library, organization, or noncommercial group that most effectively encourages or enhances the use of government documents in library services. *Donor*: Congressional Information Service, Inc. (CIS). *Winner*: Grace York.

Bernadine Abbott Hoduski Founders Award (plaque). To recognize documents librarians who may not be known at the national level but who have made significant contributions to the field of state, international, local, or federal documents. *Winner*: Janet Fisher.

Readex/GODORT/ALA Catharine J. Reynolds Award ($2,000). Grants to documents librarians for travel and/or study in the field of documents librarianship or area of study benefitting performance as documents librarians. *Donor*: Readex Corporation. *Winner*: Not awarded in 1998.

David Rozkuszka Scholarship ($3,000). To provide financial assistance to an individual who is currently working with government documents in a library while completing a master's program in library science. *Winner*: Rosalind Lee Tedford.

## Intellectual Freedom Round Table (IFRT)

John Phillip Immroth Memorial Award for Intellectual Freedom ($500). For notable contribution to intellectual freedom fueled by personal courage. *Winner*: Rutland (Vermont) Free Library.

Eli M. Oboler Memorial Award ($1,500). Biennially, to an author of a published work in English or in English translation dealing with issues, events, questions, or controversies in the area of intellectual freedom. *Donor*: Providence Associates, Inc. *Winner*: David Rabban for *Free Speech in Its Forgotten Years.*

State and Regional Achievement Award ($1,000). To the intellectual freedom committee of a state library media association, or a state/regional coalition for the most successful and creative project during the calendar year. *Donor*: Social Issues Resource Series, Inc. (SIRS). *Winners*: Illinois Library Association, Freedom Forum.

## Library Administration and Management Association (LAMA)

AIA/ALA-LAMA Library Buildings Award (citation). A biannual award given to all types of libraries for excellence in architectural design and planning by an American architect. *Donor*: American Institute of Architects and LAMA. *Winners*: Not awarded in 1998.

Hugh C. Atkinson Memorial Award. *See under* American Library Association. Certificate of Achievement: *Winner*: Robert A. Daugherty.

John Cotton Dana Library Public Relations Awards. To libraries or library organizations of all types for public relations programs or special projects ended during the preceding year. *Donor*: H. W. Wilson Company. *Winners*: Brooklyn (New York) Public Library; Flint (Michigan) Public Library; Illinois State Library, Springfield; Multnomah County (Oregon) Library; North Kingstown (Rhode Island) Free Library; Rancho Cucamonga (California) Public Library; San Antonio (Texas) Public Library; San Francisco Public Library; Serra Cooperative Library System, San Diego.

LAMA President's Award. *Winner*: H. W. Wilson Company.

## Library and Information Technology Association (LITA)

Hugh C. Atkinson Memorial Award. *See under* American Library Association.

LITA/Gaylord Award for Achievement in Library and Information Technology ($1,000). *Donor*: Gaylord Bros., Inc. *Winner*: Ritvars Bregzis.

LITA/GEAC Scholarship in Library and Information Technology ($2,500). For work toward an MLS in an ALA-accredited program with emphasis on library automation. *Donor*: GEAC, Inc. *Winner*: Denise Wendl.

LITA/Library Hi Tech Award ($1,000). To an individual or institution for a work that shows outstanding communication for continuing education in library and information technology. *Donor*: Pierian Press. *Winner*: Michael Kaplan.

LITA/LSSI Minority Scholarship in Library and Information Science ($2,500). To encourage a qualified member of a principal minority group to work toward an MLS degree in an ALA-accredited program with emphasis on library automation. *Donor*: Library Systems & Services, Inc. *Winner*: Mantra Henderson.

LITA/OCLC Frederick G. Kilgour Award for Research in Library and Information Technology ($2,000 and expense-paid attendance at an ALA Annual Conference). To bring attention to research relevant to the development of information technologies. *Winner*: Karen Markey Drabenstott.

LITA/OCLC Minority Scholarship in Library and Information Technology ($2,500). To encourage a qualified member of a principal minority group to work toward an MLS degree in an ALA-accredited program with emphasis on library automation. *Donor*: OCLC. *Winner*: Brent Singleton.

## Library History Round Table (LHRT)

Phyllis Dain Library History Dissertation Award ($500). To the author of a dissertation treating the history of books, libraries, librarianship, or information science. *Winner*: Christine Pawley.

Justin Winsor Prize Essay ($500). To an author of an outstanding essay embodying original historical research on a significant subject of library history. *Winner*: Not awarded in 1998.

## Library Research Round Table (LRRT)

Jesse H. Shera Award for Distinguished Published Research ($500). For a research article on library and information studies published in English during the calendar year. *Winner*: Allyson Carlyle for *Fulfilling the Second Objective in the Online Catalog: Schemes for Organizing Author and Work Records into Usable Displays*.

Jesse H. Shera Award for Excellence in Doctoral Research ($500). For completed research on an unpublished paper of 10,000 words or less on library and information studies. *Winner*: Not awarded in 1998.

## Map and Geography Round Table (MAGERT)

MAGERT Honors Award (citation and cash award). To recognize outstanding contributions by a MAGERT personal member to map librarianship, MAGERT, and/or a specific MAGERT project. *Winner*: Not awarded in 1998.

## New Members Round Table (NMRT)

NMRT/EBSCO Scholarship ($1,000). To a U.S. or Canadian citizen to begin an MLS degree in an ALA-accredited program. Candidates must be members of NMRT. *Donor*: EBSCO Subscription Services. *Winners*: Sarah Price Armstrong, Christine Ann DeZelar-Tiedman, Ellen Antoinette Nelson.

NMRT/3M Professional Development Grant. To NMRT members to encourage professional development and participation in national ALA and NMRT activities. *Donor*: 3M. *Winner*: Ann Marie Pipkin.

## Public Library Association (PLA)

Advancement of Literacy Award (plaque). To a publisher, bookseller, hardware and/or software dealer, foundation, or similar group that has made a significant contribution to the advancement of adult literacy. *Donor*: *Library Journal*. *Winner*: Second Start Adult Literacy Program, Oakland, California.

Baker & Taylor Entertainment CD-ROM Grant ($2,500 worth of CD-ROMs). To promote the development of a circulating CD-ROM collection in public libraries and increase the exposure of the CD-ROM format. *Donor*: Baker & Taylor Entertain-

ment. *Winner*: Orcas Island (Washington) Public Library.

Demco Creative Merchandising Grant ($1,000 and $2,000 worth of display furniture or supplies). To a public library proposing a project for the creative display and merchandising of materials either in the library or in the community. *Donor*: Demco, Inc. *Winner*: Plaza Branch Public Library, Kansas City, Missouri.

Excellence in Small and/or Rural Public Service Award ($1,000). Honors a library serving a population of 10,000 or less that demonstrates excellence of service to its community as exemplified by an overall service program or a special program of significant accomplishment. *Donor*: EBSCO Subscription Services. *Winner*: Littleton (New Hampshire) Public Library.

Highsmith Library Innovation Award ($2,000). To recognize a public library's innovative achievement in planning and implementation of a creative program or service using technology. *Donor*: Highsmith, Inc. *Winner*: Medina County (Ohio) District Library.

Allie Beth Martin Award ($3,000). Honors a librarian who, in a public library setting, has demonstrated extraordinary range and depth of knowledge about books or other library materials and has distinguished ability to share that knowledge. *Donor*: Baker & Taylor Books. *Winner*: Pauline Druschel.

New Leaders Travel Grant (up to $1,500 each). To enhance the professional development and improve the expertise of public librarians by making their attendance at major professional development activities possible. *Donor*: GEAC, Inc. *Winners*: Linda Cannon, Patricia Crane, Roberta Johnson, Martha Walters, Renee Zurn.

NTC Career Materials Resource Grant ($500 and $2,000 worth of materials from NTC Publishing Group). To a library proposing a project for the development of a career resources collection and program for a target audience either in the library or in the community. *Donor*: NTC Publishing Group. *Winner*: Georgetown (Texas) Public Library.

Charlie Robinson Award ($1,000). Honors a public library director who, over a period of seven years, has been a risk-taker, an innovator, and/or a change agent in a public library. *Donor*: Baker & Taylor Books. *Winner*: Susan Kent.

Leonard Wertheimer Award ($1,000). To a person, group, or organization for work that enhances and promotes multilingual public library service. *Donor*: NTC Publishing Group. *Winner*: Bruggemeyer Memorial Library, Monterey Park, California.

## Publishing Committee

Carnegie Reading List Awards (amount varies). To ALA units for preparation and publication of reading lists, indexes, and other bibliographical and library aids useful in U.S. circulating libraries. *Donor*: Andrew Carnegie Fund. *Winner*: Not awarded in 1998.

## Reference and User Services Association (RUSA)

Dartmouth Medal. For creating current reference works of outstanding quality and significance. *Donor*: Dartmouth College, Hanover, New Hampshire. *Winners*: Paula E. Hyman and Deborah Dash Moore, editors, for *Jewish Women in America: A Historical Encyclopedia*.

Denali Press Award ($500). For creating reference works of outstanding quality and significance that provide information specifically about ethnic and minority groups in the United States. *Donor*: Denali Press. *Winner*: Frances Ann Day for *Latina and Latino Voices in Literature for Children and Teenagers*.

Disclosure Student Travel Award (BRASS) ($1,000). To enable a student in an ALA-accredited master's program interested in a career as a business librarian to attend an ALA Annual Conference. *Donor*: Disclosure, Inc. *Winner*: Lucrea Vinluan Dayrit.

Facts on File Grant ($2,000). To a library for imaginative programming that would make current affairs more meaningful to an adult audience. *Donor*: Facts on File, Inc. *Winner*: Loudoun County Public Library, Leesburg, Virginia.

Gale Research Award for Excellence in Business Librarianship (BRASS) ($1,000). To an individual for distinguished activities in the field of business librarianship. *Donor*: Gale Research Co. *Winner*: John Ganly.

Gale Research Award for Excellence in Reference and Adult Services. To a library or library system for developing an imaginative and unique library resource to meet patrons' reference needs ($1,000). *Donor*: Gale Research Co. *Winner*: Queens Borough Public Library, Jamaica, New York.

Genealogical Publishing Company/History Section Award ($1,000). To encourage and commend professional achievement in historical reference and research librarianship. *Donor*: The Genealogical Publishing Company. *Winner*: Judith Prowse Reid.

Margaret E. Monroe Library Adult Services Award (citation). To a librarian for impact on library service to adults. *Winner*: Jane P. Kleiner.

Isadore Gilbert Mudge–R. R. Bowker Award ($1,500). For distinguished contributions to reference librarianship. *Winner*: Beth S. Woodard.

Reference Service Press Award ($1,000). To the author of the most outstanding article published in *RQ* during the preceding two volume years. *Donor*: Reference Service Press, Inc. *Winners*: Patricia Dewdney, Gillian Michel.

John Sessions Memorial Award (plaque). To a library or library system in recognition of work with the labor community. *Donor*: AFL/CIO. *Winner*: The Institute of Industrial Relations Library, University of California–Berkeley.

Louis Shores Oryx Press Award ($1,000). To an individual, team, or organization to recognize excellence in reviewing of books and other materials for libraries. *Donor*: Oryx Press. *Winner*: Peter Jacso.

## Social Responsibilities Round Table (SRRT)

Jackie Eubanks Memorial Award ($500). To honor outstanding achievement in promoting the acquisition and use of alternative media in libraries. *Donor*: AIP Task Force. *Winner*: Chris Atton.

New Talent Award (formerly the Genesis Award) ($3,000). For an outstanding book designed to bring visibility to a black writer or artist at the beginning of his or her career. *Winner*: Not awarded in 1998.

Coretta Scott King Awards. See *Literary Prizes, 1998* by Gary Ink.

SRRT Gay, Lesbian, and Bisexual Book Awards. To authors of fiction and non-fiction books of exceptional merit relating to the gay/lesbian experience. *Donor*: SRRT Gay Book Award Committee. *Winners*: Lucy Jane Bledsoe for *Working Parts*, Adam Mastoon for *The Shared Heart: Portraits and Stories Celebrating Lesbian, Gay, and Bisexual Young People*.

## Young Adult Library Services Association (YALSA)

Alex Awards. *Winners*: David Bodanis, Rick Bragg, Rebecca Carroll, Karin Cook, Pete Hamill, Sebastian Junger, Jon Krakauer, Velma Maia Thomas, Dawn Turner Trice, Connie Willis.

Baker & Taylor Conference Grants ($1,000). To young adult librarians in public or school libraries to attend an ALA Annual Conference for the first time. Candidates must be members of YALSA and have one to ten years of library experience. *Donor*: Baker & Taylor Books. *Winner*: Shari Fesko.

Book Wholesalers, Inc./YALSA Collection Development Grant ($1,000). To YALSA members who represent a public library and work directly with young adults, for collection development materials for young adults. *Winners*: Debra L. Adams, Joy Botts.

Margaret A. Edwards Award ($1,000). To an author whose book or books have provided young adults with a window through which they can view their world and which will help them to grow and to understand themselves and their role in society. *Donor*: *School Library Journal*. *Winner*: Madeleine L'Engle.

Great Book Giveaway ($1,200 worth of books, videos, CDs and audio cassettes). *Winner*: Lisbon (Maine) High School.

Frances Henne/YALSA/VOYA Research Grant ($500 minimum). To provide seed money to an individual, institution, or group for a project to encourage research on library service to young adults. *Donor*: Voice of Youth Advocates. *Winners*: Not awarded in 1998.

## American Society for Information Science (ASIS)

ASIS Award of Merit. For an outstanding contribution to the field of information science. *Winner*: Henry Small.

ASIS Best Information Science Book. *Winner*: Robert R. Korfhage for *Information Storage and Retrieval*.

ASIS Outstanding Information Science Teacher Award ($500). *Winner*: Elisabeth Logan.

ASIS Research Award. For a systematic program of research in a single area at a level beyond the single study, recognizing contributions in the field of information science. *Winner*: Marcia J. Bates.

ASIS Special Award. To recognize long-term contributions to the advancement of information science and technology and enhancement of public access to information and discovery of mechanisms for improved transfer and utilization of knowledge. *Winner*: Herbert A. Simon.

James Cretsos Leadership Award. *Winner*: Michael Leach.

Watson Davis Award. *Winner*: Judith Watson.

ISI Citation Analysis Research Grant. *Winner*: David Dubin

ISI I.S. Doctoral Dissertation Proposal Scholarship ($1,000). *Winner*: Karla Hahn for *Electronic Journals as Innovations: A Study of Author and Editor Early Adopters*.

JASIS Paper Award. *Winner*: Howard D. White and Katherine W. McCain for *Visualizing a Discipline: An Author Co-Citation Analysis of Information Science*.

Pratt Severn Student Research Award. *Winner*: Not awarded in 1998.

UMI Doctoral Dissertation Award. *Winner*: Tomas Lipinski for *The Communication of Law in the Digital Environment: Stability and Change within the Concept of Precedent*.

## Art Libraries Society of North America (ARLIS/NA)

John Benjamins Award. To recognize research and publication in the study and analysis of periodicals in the fields of the fine arts, literature, and cross-disciplinary studies. *Winner*: Miranda Howard Haddock.

Andrew Cahan Photography Award. To encourage participation of art information professionals in the field of photography. *Winner*: Nina K. Stephenson.

Melva J. Dwyer Award. To the creators of exceptional reference or research tools relating to Canadian art and architecture. *Winner*: Loren Lerner, for *Canadian Film and Video: A Bibliography and Guide to the Literature.*

Jim and Anna Emmett Travel Award. To assist a handicapped library professional to participate in the ARLIS/NA annual conference. *Winner*: Catherine Gordon.

G. K. Hall Conference Attendance Award ($400). To encourage attendance at the annual conference by ARLIS/NA committee members, chapter officers, and moderators. *Winner*: Kathryn L. Cororan.

Howard and Beverly Joy Karno Award ($1,000). To provide financial assistance to a professional art librarian in Latin America through interaction with ARLIS/NA members and conference participation. *Cosponsor*: Howard Karno Books. *Winner*: Liliana Bandini.

David Mirvish Books/Books on Art Travel Award ($500 Canadian). To encourage art librarianship in Canada. *Winner*: Ilga Neva.

Gerd Muehsam Award. To one or more graduate students in library science programs to recognize excellence in a graduate paper or project. *Winner*: Erika Dowell for *Interdisciplinarity and New Methodologies in Art History: A Citation Analysis.*

Puvill Libros Award. To encourage professional development of European art librarians through interaction with ARLIS/NA colleagues and conference participation. *Winner*: Simon Ford.

Research Libraries Group Award. To promote participation in ARLIS/NA by supporting conference travel for an individual who has not attended an annual conference. *Winner*: Laura Graveline.

H. W. Wilson Foundation Research Award. To support research activities by ARLIS/NA members in the fields of librarianship, visual resources curatorship, and the arts. *Winner*: Nina K. Stephenson.

## Association for Library and Information Science Education (ALISE)

ALISE Doctoral Student Dissertation Awards ($400). To promote the exchange of research ideas between doctoral students and established researchers. *Winners*: Elizabeth Yakel, Mary K. Chelton.

ALISE Methodology Paper Competition ($500). To stimulate the communication of research methodology. *Winner*: Cheryl Knott Malone.

ALISE Research Paper Competition ($500). For a research paper concerning any aspect of librarianship or information studies by a member of ALISE. *Winner*: Louise S. Robbins.

ALISE Research Grant Awards (one or more grants totaling $5,000): *Winners*: John R. Richardson, Jr., Terry L. Weech.

## Association of Jewish Libraries (AJL)

AJL Bibliography Book Award. *Winner*: Sharona R. Wachs for *American Jewish Liturgies: A Bibliography of American Jewish Liturgy from the Establishment of the Press in the Colonies through 1925.*

AJL Reference Book Award. *Winners*: Paula E. Hyman and Deborah Dash Moore for *Jewish Women in America: An Historical Encyclopedia.*

Special Body of Work Citation. *Winner*: Barbara Diamond Goldin.

Sydney Taylor Children's Book Award. *Winner*: Elsa Rael for *When Zaydeh Danced on Eldridge Street.*

Sydney Taylor Manuscript Award. *Winner*: Linda Press Wulf for *Devorah.*

Sydney Taylor Older Children's Book Award. *Winner*: Nina Jaffe for *The Mysterious Visitor.*

# Beta Phi Mu

Beta Phi Mu Award. *See under* American Library Association.

Beta Phi Mu Doctoral Dissertation Award. *Winner:* Not awarded in 1998.

Harold Lancour Scholarship for Foreign Study ($1,000). For graduate study in a foreign country related to the applicant's work or schooling. *Winner:* Loss Pequeno Glazier.

Sarah Rebecca Reed Scholarship ($1,500). For study at an ALA-accredited library school. *Winner:* Ann Hemmens.

Frank B. Sessa Scholarship for Continuing Professional Education ($750). For continuing education for a Beta Phi Mu member. *Winner:* Not awarded in 1998.

E. Blanche Woolls Scholarship. For a beginning student in school library media services. *Winner:* Diana L. Saylor-Evans.

# Bibliographical Society of America (BSA)

BSA Fellowships ($1,000–$2,000). For scholars involved in bibliographical inquiry and research in the history of the book trades and in publishing history. *Winners:* Ruth B. Bottingheimer, Christine S. Haynes, David C. Hanson, Julia Boss Knapp, Maura C. Ives, Peter A. Lindenbaum, Laura Jennifer Moore, Virginia Reinburg, Shef Rogers.

# Canadian Library Association (CLA)

Olga B. Bishop Award. *Winner:* Anne Carr-Wiggin.

CLA Award for Achievement in Technical Services. *Winner:* Vancouver Public Library.

CLA Award for the Advancement of Intellectual Freedom in Canada. *Winner:* Little Sister's Book and Art Emporium.

CLA Dafoe Scholarship. *Winner:* Nadine Therese d'Entremont.

CLA/Information Today Award for Innovative Technology. *Donor:* Information Today Inc. *Winner:* Vancouver Public Library.

CLA Outstanding Service to Librarianship Award. *Donor:* R. R. Bowker. *Winner:* Ritvars Bregzis.

CLA Research and Development Grant ($1,000). *Winner:* Judith Saltman.

CLA Student Article Award. *Winner:* Kerry Anderson.

CLA/Faxon Marketing Award. *Winner:* Vancouver (British Columbia) Public Library.

OCLC/CLA Award. *Winner:* Angela Horne.

Howard V. Phalin–World Book Graduate Scholarship in Library Science. *Winner:* Ann Vanden Born.

H. W. Wilson Scholarship: *Winner:* Paul Hebbard.

# Canadian Association of College and University Libraries (CACUL)

CACUL Award for Outstanding Academic Librarian. *Winner:* William Birdsall.

CACUL Innovation Achievement Award ($1,500). *Winner:* University of Saskatchewan, Saskatoon.

CACUL/CTCL Award of Merit. *Winner:* Betty Harris.

# Canadian Association of Public Libraries (CAPL)

CAPL Outstanding Public Library Service Award. *Winner:* Frances Schwenger.

# Canadian Association of Special Libraries and Information Services (CASLIS)

CASLIS Award for Special Librarianship in Canada. *Winner:* Stephen Abram.

# Canadian Library Trustees Association (CLTA)

CLTA Achievement in Literacy Award. For an innovative literacy program by a public library board. *Donor:* ABC Canada. *Winner:* Toronto Public Library.

CLTA Merit Award for Distinguished Service as a Public Library Trustee. For outstanding leadership in the advancement of public library trusteeship and public library service in Canada. *Winner:* Hazel Thornton-Lazier.

### Canadian School Library Association (CSLA)

National Book Service Teacher-Librarian of the Year Award. *Winner*: Michelle Larose-Kuzenko, Winnipeg, Manitoba.

Margaret B. Scott Award of Merit. For the development of school libraries in Canada. *Winner*: Diana Maureen Willa Walsh, Richmond, British Columbia.

## Chinese-American Librarians Association (CALA)

CALA Scholarship. *Winner*: Hsianghui Liu-Spencer.

Sheila Suen Lai Scholarship ($500). To a student of Chinese nationality or descent pursuing full-time graduate studies for a master's degree or Ph.D. degree in an ALA-accredited library school. *Winner*: Qi Fan.

C. C. Seetoo/CALA Conference Travel Scholarship ($500). For a student to attend the ALA Annual Conference and CALKA program. *Winner*: Not awarded in 1998.

## Church and Synagogue Library Association (CSLA)

CSLA Award for Outstanding Congregational Librarian. For distinguished service to the congregation and/or community through devotion to the congregational library. *Winner*: Joe Buser.

CSLA Award for Outstanding Congregational Library. For responding in creative and innovative ways to the library's mission of reaching and serving the congregation and/or the wider community. *Winner*: First United Methodist Church Library, Pasadena, California.

CSLA Award for Outstanding Contribution to Congregational Libraries. For providing inspiration, guidance, leadership, or resources to enrich the field of church or synagogue librarianship. *Winner*: Margaret Collmus.

Helen Keating Ott Award for Outstanding Contribution to Congregational Libraries. *Winner*: Joan Hawxhurst.

Pat Tabler Memorial Scholarship Award. *Winner*: Not awarded in 1998.

Muriel Fuller Scholarship Award. *Winner*: Not awarded in 1998.

### Council on Library and Information Resources

A. R. Zipf Fellowship in Information Management. Awarded annually to a student enrolled in graduate school who shows exceptional promise for leadership and technical achievement. *Winner*: Maureen L. Mackenzie.

## Gale Research Company

ALTA/Gale Outstanding Trustee Conference Grant Award. *See under* American Library Association, American Library Trustee Association.

Gale Research Award for Excellence in Business Librarianship; and Gale Research Award for Excellence in Reference and Adult Services. *See under* American Library Association, Reference and User Services Association.

Gale Research Financial Development Award. *See under* American Library Association.

## Medical Library Association (MLA)

Estelle Brodman Award for the Academic Medical Librarian of the Year. To honor significant achievement, potential for leadership, and continuing excellence at mid-career in the area of academic health sciences librarianship. *Winner*: Ann Wood Humphries.

Cunningham Memorial International Fellowship ($3,000). A six-month grant and travel expenses in the United States and Canada for a foreign librarian. *Winner*: Anita Verhoeven.

Louise Darling Medal. For distinguished achievement in collection development in the health sciences. *Winner*: Not awarded in 1998.

Janet Doe Lectureship ($250). *Winner*: Wayne Peay.

EBSCO/MLA Annual Meeting Grant ($1,000). *Winners*: Jennifer G. Barlow, Andrea Batson.

Ida and George Eliot Prize ($200). For an essay published in any journal in the preceding calendar year that has been judged most effective in furthering medical librarianship. *Donor*: Login Brothers Books. *Winners*: E. Diane Johnson, Emma Jean McKinin, Joyce A. Mitchell, John C. Reid, Mary Ellen Sievert.

Murray Gottlieb Prize ($100). For the best unpublished essay submitted by a medical librarian on the history of some aspect of health sciences or a detailed description of a library exhibit. *Donor*: Ralph and Jo Grimes. *Winner*: Mary L. Westermann.

Joseph Leiter NLM/MLA Lectureship. *Winner*: Jean-Claude Guedon.

MLA Award for Distinguished Public Service. *Winner*: U.S. Rep. Henry Bonilla (R-Texas).

MLA Award for Excellence and Achievement in Hospital Librarianship ($500). To a member of the MLA who has made significant contributions to the profession in the area of overall distinction or leadership in hospital librarianship. *Winner*: Kay Cimpl Wagner.

MLA Doctoral Fellowship ($2,000). *Donor*: Institute for Scientific Information (ISI). *Winner*: Sharon Dezel Jenkins.

MLA Scholarship ($2,000). For graduate study in medical librarianship at an ALA-accredited library school. *Winner*: Heather B. Blunt.

MLA Scholarship for Minority Students ($2,000). *Winner*: Barbara Ferrer Kenney.

John P. McGovern Award Lectureships ($500). *Winners*: Laurie Garrett, Kenneth M. Ludmerer.

Marcia C. Noyes Award. For an outstanding contribution to medical librarianship. The award is the highest professional distinction of MLA. *Winner*: Fred W. Roper.

Rittenhouse Award ($500). For the best unpublished paper on medical librarianship submitted by a student enrolled in, or having been enrolled in, a course for credit in an ALA-accredited library school or a trainee in an internship program in medical librarianship. *Donor*: Rittenhouse Medical Bookstore. *Winner*: Charles G. Warrick.

Frank Bradway Rogers Information Advancement Award ($500). For an outstanding contribution to knowledge of health science information delivery. *Donor*: Institute for Scientific Information (ISI). *Winners*: Health Web, Julia Kelly, Elaine Russo Martin, Ellen Nagle, Patricia Redman, James Shedlock.

## K. G. Saur (Munich, Germany)

Hans-Peter Geh Grant. To enable a librarian from the former Soviet Union to attend a conference in Germany or elsewhere. *Winner*: Alevtina Choulinina, Russian State University for the Humanities.

K. G. Saur Award for Best College and Research Libraries Article. *See under* American Library Association, Association of College and Research Libraries.

## Society of American Archivists (SAA)

C. F. W. Coker Prize for finding aids. *Winner*: Encoded Archival Description Document Type Definition (EAD), developed by Berkley Finding Aid Project.

Colonial Dames Scholarship. *Winners*: Ida B. Jones, Sister Rosemary Meiman, OSU.

Council Exemplary Service Award. *Winners*: Kris Kiesling, Dennis Harrison.

Distinguished Service Award. Recognizes outstanding service and exemplary contribution to the profession. *Winner*: Master of Archival Studies Program, University of British Columbia.

Fellows Posner Prize. For an outstanding essay dealing with a facet of archival administration, history, theory, or methodology, published in the latest volume of the *American Archivist*. *Winner*: Tyler O. Walters for "Contemporary Archival Appraisal Methods and Preservation Decision-Making" (vol. 59, no. 3).

Philip M. Hamer–Elizabeth Hamer Kegan Award. For individuals and/or institutions that have increased public awareness of a specific body of documents. *Winner*: Linda A. Ries, ed., for *History of Photography in Pennsylvania*.

Oliver Wendell Holmes Award. To enable overseas archivists already in the United States or Canada for training to attend the SAA annual meeting. *Winner*: Ntombizandile ("Punky") Kwatsha.

J. Franklin Jameson Award. For an institution not directly involved in archival work that promotes greater public awareness, appreciation, and support of archival activities and programs. *Winner*: *NEWSDAY*.

Sister M. Claude Lane Award. For a significant contribution to the field of religious archives. *Winner*: Charles Nolan.

Waldo Gifford Leland Prize. For writing of superior excellence and usefulness in the field of archival history, theory, or practice. *Winners*: Minnesota Historical Society and the Hagley Museum and Library for *Records of American Business*.

Minority Student Award. Encourages minority students to consider careers in the archival profession and promotes minority participation in the Society of American Archivists with complimentary registration to the annual meeting. *Winner*: Elenita M. Tapawan.

Theodore Calvin Pease Award. For the best student paper. *Winner*: Not awarded in 1998.

Preservation Publication Award. Recognizes an outstanding work published in North America that advances the theory or the practice of preservation in archival institutions. *Winner*: Not awarded in 1998.

SAA Fellows. Highest individual distinction awarded to a limited number of members for their outstanding contribution to the archival profession. *Honored*: Karen Benedict, Richard Cameron, Luciana Duranti, Robert Sink.

## Special Libraries Association (SLA)

Mary Adeline Connor Professional Development Scholarship ($6,000). *Winner*: Not awarded in 1998.

John Cotton Dana Award. For exceptional support and encouragement of special librarianship. *Winner*: Joanne Marshall.

Dow Jones 21st Century Competencies Award. *Winner*: Eugenie E. Prime.

Steven I. Goldspiel Research Grant. *Sponsor*: Disclosure, Inc. *Winner*: Andrew Dillon for "Understanding Users in Digital Environments: A Longitudinal Study of Genre Influences in Information Work."

Hall of Fame Award. To a member of the association at or near the end of an active professional career for an extended and sustained period of distinguished service to the association. *Winner*: Winifred Sewell.

Innovations in Technology Award ($1,000). To a member of the association for innovative use and application of technology in a special library setting. *Winner*: Andrew G. Breeding.

International Special Librarians Day Award. *Winner*: Arthus Anderson.

SLA Affirmative Action Scholarship ($6,000). *Winner*: Tamika Barnes.

SLA Fellows. *Winners*: Bill Fisher, Doris S. Helfer, Eleanor A. MacLean, Donna W. Scheeder.

SLA Information Today Award for Innovations in Technology. *Winner*: Andrew Breeding.

SLA President's Award. *Winner*: Susan A. Merry.

SLA Professional Award. *Winner*: Not awarded in 1998.

SLA Public Relations Media Award. *Winner*: Roland Wilkerson.

SLA Public Relations Member Achievement Award. *Winner*: Not awarded in 1998.

SLA Student Scholarships ($6,000). For students with financial need who show potential for special librarianship. *Winners*: William Jenkins, Barbara Billings.

Rose L. Vormelker Award. *Winner*: Larry L. Wright.

H. W. Wilson Company Award. For the most outstanding article in the past year's *Information Outlook*. *Donor*: H. W. Wilson Company. *Winner*: Alison J. Head.

# Alphabetical List of Award Names

Individual award names are followed by a colon and the name of the awarding body; e.g., the Bound to Stay Bound Books Scholarship is given by ALA/ Association for Library Service to Children. Consult the preceding list of Library Scholarship and Award Recipients, 1998, which is alphabetically arranged by organization, to locate recipients and further information. Awards named for individuals are listed by surname.

AALL Scholarships: American Association of Law Libraries

AASL ABC/CLIO Leadership Grant: ALA/American Association of School Librarians

AASL/Highsmith Research Grant: ALA/American Association of School Librarians

AASL Information Plus Continuing Education Scholarship: ALA/American Association of School Librarians

AASL Crystal Apple Award: ALA/American Association of School Librarians

AASL/REFORMA Pura Belpré Award: ALA/Association for Library Service to Children

AASL School Librarians Workshop Scholarship: ALA/American Association of School Librarians

ACRL Academic or Research Librarian of the Year Award: ALA/Association of College and Research Libraries

ACRL/EBSS Distinguished Education and Behavioral Sciences Librarian Award: ALA/Association of College and Research Libraries

ACRL Doctoral Dissertation Fellowship: ALA/Association of College and Research Libraries

AJL Bibliography Book Award: Association of Jewish Libraries

AJL Reference Book Award: Association of Jewish Libraries

ALA Honorary Membership: ALA

ALA/Information Today Library of the Future Award: ALA

ALISE Doctoral Student Dissertation Awards: Association for Library and Information Science Education

ALISE Methodology Paper Competition: Association for Library and Information Science Education

ALISE Research Award: Association for Library and Information Science Education

ALISE Research Grant Award: Association for Library and Information Science Education

ALISE Research Paper Competition: Association for Library and Information Science Education

ALSC/Book Wholesalers Summer Reading Program Grant: ALA/Association for Library Service to Children

ALSC/Econo-Clad Literature Program Award: ALA/Association for Library Service to Children

ALTA/Gale Outstanding Trustee Conference Grant Award: ALA/American Library Trustee Association

ALTA Literacy Award: ALA/American Library Trustee Association

ALTA Major Benefactors Honor Awards: ALA/American Library Trustee Association

ASCLA Leadership Achievement Award: ALA/Association of Specialized and Cooperative Library Agencies

ASCLA/National Organization on Disability Award: ALA/Association of Specialized and Cooperative Library Agencies

ASCLA Professional Achievement Award: ALA/Association of Specialized and Cooperative Library Agencies

ASCLA Research Award: ALA/Association of Specialized and Cooperative Library Agencies

ASCLA Service Award: ALA/Association of Specialized and Cooperative Library Agencies

ASIS Award of Merit: American Society for Information Science

ASIS Best Information Science Book: American Society for Information Science

ASIS Doctoral Dissertation Scholarship: American Society for Information Science

ASIS Outstanding Information Science Teacher Award: American Society for Information Science

ASIS Research Award: American Society for Information Science

ASIS Special Award: American Society for Information Science

Accessibility for Attendees with Disabilities Award: ALA/Exhibits Round Table

Advancement of Literacy Award: ALA/Public Library Association

May Hill Arbuthnot Honor Lecturer: ALA/Association for Library Service to Children

Armed Forces Library Certificate of Merit: ALA/Armed Forces Libraries Round Table

Armed Forces Library Newsbank Scholarship Award: ALA/Armed Forces Libraries Round Table

Armed Forces Library Round Table Achievement Citation: ALA/Armed Forces Libraries Round Table

Hugh C. Atkinson Memorial Award: ALA

Award for the Advancement of Intellectual Freedom in Canada: Canadian Library Association

Carroll Preston Baber Research Grant: ALA

Baker & Taylor Conference Grants: ALA/Young Adult Library Services Association

Baker & Taylor Entertainment CD-ROM Grant: ALA/Public Library Association

Mildred L. Batchelder Award: ALA/Association for Library Service to Children

Louise Seaman Bechtel Fellowship: ALA/Association for Library Service to Children

John Benjamins Award: Art Libraries Society of North America

Best of LRTS Award: ALA/Association for Library Collections and Technical Services

Beta Phi Mu Award: ALA

Olga B. Bishop Award: Canadian Library Association

Blackwell's Scholarship Award: ALA/Association for Library Collections and Technical Services

Bogle International Travel Fund Award: ALA

Book Wholesalers, Inc. Collection Development Grant: ALA/Young Adult Library Services Association

Bound to Stay Bound Books Scholarship: ALA/Association for Library Service to Children

Bowker/Ulrich's Serials Librarianship Award: ALA/Association for Library Collections and Technical Services, Serials Section

William Boyd Military Novel Award: ALA

Estelle Brodman Award for the Academic Medical Librarian of the Year: Medical Library Association

BSA Fellowships: Bibliographical Society of America

CACUL Award for Outstanding Academic Librarian: Canadian Association of College and University Libraries

CACUL Innovation Achievement Award: Canadian Association of College and University Libraries

CACUL/CTCL Award of Merit: Canadian Association of College and University Libraries

Andrew Cahan Photography Award: Art Libraries Society of North America

CAPL Outstanding Public Library Service Award: Canadian Association of Public Libraries

CASLIS Award for Special Librarianship in Canada: Canadian Association of Special Libraries and Information Services

CIS/GODORT/ALA Documents to the People Award: ALA/Government Documents Round Table

CLA Award for Achievement in Technical Services: Canadian Library Association

CLA Award for the Advancement of Intellectual Freedom in Canada: Canadian Library Association

CLA Dafoe Scholarship: Canadian Library Association

CLA/Faxon Marketing Award: Canadian Library Association

CLA/Information Today Award for Innovative Technology: Canadian Library Association

CLA Outstanding Service to Librarianship Award: Canadian Library Association

CLA Research and Development Grants: Canadian Library Association

CLA Student Article Award: Canadian Library Association

CLTA Achievement in Literacy Award: Canadian Library Trustees Association

CLTA Merit Award for Distinguished Service as a Public Library Trustee: Canadian Library Trustees Association

CSLA Award for Outstanding Congregational Librarian: Church and Synagogue Library Association

CSLA Award for Outstanding Congregational Library: Church and Synagogue Library Association

CSLA Award for Outstanding Contribution to Congregational Libraries: Church and Synagogue Library Association

Francis Joseph Campbell Citation: ALA/Association of Specialized and Cooperative Library Agencies

Andrew Carnegie Medal: ALA/Association for Library Service to Children

Carnegie Reading List Awards: ALA/Publishing Committee

Marshall Cavendish Scholarship: ALA

Certificate of Achievement: ALA/Library Administration and Management Association

James Bennett Childs Award: ALA/Government Documents Round Table

David H. Clift Scholarship: ALA

C. F. W. Coker Prize: Society of American Archivists

Mary Adeline Connor Professional Development Scholarship: Special Libraries Association

James Cretsos Leadership Award: American Society for Information Science

Cunningham Memorial International Fellowship: Medical Library Association

Phyllis Dain Library History Dissertation Award: ALA/Library History Round Table

John Cotton Dana Award: Special Libraries Association

John Cotton Dana Library Public Relations Award: ALA/Library Administration and Management Association

Louise Darling Medal: Medical Library Association

Dartmouth Medal: ALA/Reference and User Services Association

Watson Davis Award: American Society for Information Science

Adelaide del Frate Conference Sponsor Award: ALA/Federal Librarians Round Table

Demco Creative Merchandising Grant: ALA/Public Library Association

Denali Press Award: ALA/Reference and User Services Association

Melvil Dewey Award: ALA

Disclosure Student Travel Award (BRASS): ALA/Reference and User Services Association

Distinguished School Administrators Award: ALA/American Association of School Librarians

Distinguished Service Award: ALA/Federal Librarians Round Table

Distinguished Service Award, AASL/Baker & Taylor: ALA/American Association of School Librarians

Distinguished Service to ALSC Award: ALA/Association for Library Service to Children

Janet Doe Lectureship: Medical Library Association

Dow Jones 21st Century Competencies Award: Special Libraries Association

Tom C. Drewes Scholarship: ALA

Miriam Dudley Bibliographic Instruction Librarian of the Year: ALA/Association of College and Research Libraries

Melva J. Dwyer Award: Art Libraries Society of North America

EBSCO ALA Conference Sponsorships: ALA

EBSCO Community College Leadership Resources Achievement Awards: ALA/Association of College and Research Libraries

EBSCO Community College Program Award: ALA/Association of College and Research Libraries

EBSCO/MLA Annual Meeting Grant: Medical Library Association

Margaret A. Edwards Award: ALA/Young Adult Library Services Association

Education Behavioral Sciences Section Library Award: ALA/Association of College and Research Libraries

Ida and George Eliot Prize: Medical Library Association

EMIERT/Gale Research Multicultural Award: ALA/Ethnic Materials and Information Exchange Round Table

Jim and Anna Emmett Travel Award: Art Libraries Society of North America.

Equality Award: ALA

Jackie Eubanks Memorial Award: ALA/Social Responsibilities Round Table

Excellence in Small and/or Rural Public Service Award: ALA/Public Library Association

Facts on File Grant: ALA/Reference and User Services Association

Federal Librarians Achievement Award: ALA/Federal Librarians Round Table

Fellows Posner Prize: Society of American Archivists

First Step Award, Serials Section/Wiley Professional Development Grant: ALA/Association for Library Collections and Technical Services

Freedom to Read Foundation Roll of Honor Awards: ALA

Friendly Booth Award: ALA/Exhibits Round Table

Elizabeth Futas Catalyst for Change Award: ALA

Loleta D. Fyan Award: ALA

Gale Research Award for Excellence in Business Librarianship (BRASS): ALA/Reference and User Services Association

Gale Research Award for Excellence in Reference and Adult Services: ALA/Reference and User Services Association

Gale Research Financial Development Award: ALA

Mary V. Gaver Scholarship: ALA

Hans-Peter Geh Grant: K. G. Saur

Genealogical Publishing Company/History Section Award: ALA/Reference and User Services Association

Louise Giles Minority Scholarship: ALA

Steven I. Goldspiel Research Grant: Special Libraries Association

Murray Gottlieb Prize: Medical Library Association

Great Book Giveaway: ALA/Young Adult Library Services Association

Grolier Foundation Award: ALA

Grolier National Library Week Grant: ALA

G. K. Hall Award for Library Literature: ALA

G. K. Hall Conference Attendance Award: Art Libraries Society of North America

Hall of Fame Award: Special Libraries Association

Philip M. Hamer–Elizabeth Hamer Kegan Award: Society of American Archivists

Frances Henne Award: ALA/American Association of School Librarians

Frances Henne/YALSA/VOYA Research Grant: ALA/Young Adult Library Services Association

Highsmith Library Innovation Award: ALA/Public Library Association

Bernadine Abbott Hoduski Founders Award: ALA/Government Documents Round Table

Oliver Wendell Holmes Award: Society of American Archivists

Miriam L. Hornback Scholarship: ALA

Paul Howard Award for Courage: ALA

Christopher J. Hoy/ERT Scholarship: ALA/Exhibits Round Table

John Ames Humphry/OCLC/Forest Press Award: ALA

John Phillip Immroth Memorial Award for Intellectual Freedom: ALA/Intellectual Freedom Round Table

Information Technology Pathfinder Award: ALA/American Association of School Librarians

Innovations in Technology Award: Special Libraries Association

Instruction Section Innovation in Instruction Award: ALA/Association of College and Research Libraries

Instruction Section Publication of the Year Award: ALA/Association of College and Research Libraries

International Special Librarians Day Award: Special Libraries Association.

ISI Citation Analysis Research Grant: American Society for Information Science

ISI I.S. Doctoral Dissertation Scholarship: American Society for Information Science

J. Franklin Jameson Award for Archival Advocacy: Society of American Archivists

JASIS Paper Award: American Society for Information Science

Howard and Beverly Joy Karno Award: Art Libraries Society of North America

Kohlstedt Exhibit Award: ALA/Exhibits Round Table

LITA/GEAC-CLSI Scholarship in Library and Information Technology: ALA/Library and Information Technology Association

LITA/Library Hi Tech Award: ALA/Library and Information Technology Association

LITA/LSSI Minority Scholarship in Library and Information Science: ALA/Library and Information Technology Association

LITA/OCLC Frederick G. Kilgour Award for Research in Library and Information Technology: ALA/Library and Information Technology Association

LITA/OCLC Minority Scholarship in Library and Information Technology: ALA/Library and Information Technology Association

Sheila Suen Lai Scholarship: Chinese-American Librarians Association

LAMA President's Award: ALA/Library Administration and Management Association

Harold Lancour Scholarship for Foreign Study: Beta Phi Mu

Marta Lange/CQ Award: ALA/Association of College and Research Libraries

Sister M. Claude Lane Award: Society of American Archivists

Samuel Lazerow Fellowship for Research in Acquisitions or Technical Services: ALA/Association of College and Research Libraries

Katharine Kyes Leab and Daniel J. Leab American Book Prices Current Exhibition Catalogue Awards: ALA/Association of College and Research Libraries

Leadership in Library Acquisitions Award: ALA/Association for Library Collections and Technical Services

Tony B. Leisner Scholarship: ALA

Joseph Leiter NLM/MLA Lectureship: Medical Library Association

Waldo Gifford Leland Prize: Society of American Archivists

Library Buildings Award: ALA/Library Administration and Management Association

Joseph W. Lippincott Award: ALA

MAGERT Honors Award: ALA/Map and Geography Round Table

MLA Award for Distinguished Public Service: Medical Library Association

MLA Award for Excellence and Achievement in Hospital Librarianship: Medical Library Association

MLA Doctoral Fellowship: Medical Library Association

MLA Scholarship: Medical Library Association

MLA Scholarship for Minority Students: Medical Library Association

John P. McGovern Award Lectureships: Medical Library Association

Margaret Mann Citation: ALA/Association for Library Collections and Technical Services

Marshall Cavendish Scholarship: ALA

Allie Beth Martin Award: ALA/Public Library Association

Frederic G. Melcher Scholarship: ALA/Association for Library Service to Children

Minority Student Award: Society of American Archivists

David Mirvish Books/Books on Art Travel Award: Art Libraries Society of North America

Margaret E. Monroe Library Adult Services Award: ALA/Reference and User Services Association

Bessie Boehm Moore Award: ALA

Isadore Gilbert Mudge–R. R. Bowker Award: ALA/Reference and User Services Association

Gerd Muehsam Award: Art Libraries Society of North America

New Talent Award: ALA/Social Responsibilities Round Table

NMRT/EBSCO Scholarship: ALA/New Members Round Table

NMRT/3M Professional Development Grant: ALA/New Members Round Table

National Book Service Teacher-Librarian of the Year Award: Canadian School Library Association

National School Library Media Program of the Year Award: ALA/American Association of School Librarians

New Leaders Travel Grant: ALA/Public Library Association

Martinus Nijhoff International West European Specialist Study Grant: ALA/Association of College and Research Libraries

Marcia C. Noyes Award: Medical Library Association

NTC Career Materials Resource Grant: ALA/Public Library Association

Oberly Award for Bibliography in the Agricultural Sciences: ALA/Association of College and Research Libraries

Eli M. Oboler Memorial Award: ALA/Intellectual Freedom Round Table

OCLC/CLA Award: Canadian Library Association

Helen Keating Ott Award for Outstanding Contribution to Congregational Libraries: Church and Synagogue Library Association

Theodore Calvin Pease Award: Society of American Archivists

Penguin Putnam Awards: ALA/Association for Library Service to Children

Howard V. Phalin–World Book Graduate Scholarship in Library Science: Canadian Library Association.

Esther J. Piercy Award: ALA/Association for Library Collections and Technical Services

Preservation Publication Award: Society of American Archivists

Pratt Severn Student Research Award: American Society for Information Science

Puvill Libros Award: Art Libraries Society of North America

Rare Books & Manuscripts Librarianship Award: ALA/Association of College and Research Libraries

Readex/GODORT/ALA Catharine J. Reynolds Award: ALA/Government Documents Round Table

Sarah Rebecca Reed Scholarship: Beta Phi Mu

Reference Service Press Award: ALA/Reference and User Services Association

Research Libraries Group Award: Art Libraries Society of North America

Rittenhouse Award: Medical Library Association

Charlie Robinson Award: ALA/Public Library Association

Frank Bradway Rogers Information Advancement Award: Medical Library Association

David Rozkuszka Scholarship: ALA/Government Documents Round Table

SAA Fellows: Society of American Archivists

SLA Affirmative Action Scholarship: Special Libraries Association

SLA Fellows: Special Libraries Association

SLA Information Today Award for Innovations in Technology: Special Libraries Association

SLA President's Award: Special Libraries Association

SLA Professional Award: Special Libraries Association

SLA Public Relations Media Award: Special Libraries Association

SLA Public Relations Member Achievement Award: Special Libraries Association

SLA Student Scholarships: Special Libraries Association

SRRT/Gay and Lesbian Task Force, Gay, Lesbian, and Bisexual Book Awards: ALA/Social Responsibilities Round Table

K. G. Saur Award for Best College and Research Libraries Article: ALA/Association of College and Research Libraries

Margaret B. Scott Award of Merit: Canadian School Library Association

C. C. Seetoo/CALA Conference Travel Scholarship: Chinese-American Librarians Association

Frank B. Sessa Scholarship for Continuing Professional Education: Beta Phi Mu

John Sessions Memorial Award: ALA/Reference and User Services Association

Jesse H. Shera Award for Distinguished Published Research: ALA/Library Research Round Table

Jesse H. Shera Award for Excellence in Doctoral Research: ALA/Library Research Round Table

Louis Shores Oryx Press Award: ALA/Reference and User Services Association

Special Body of Work Citation: Association of Jewish Libraries

State and Regional Achievement Award—Freedom to Read Foundation: ALA/Intellectual Freedom Round Table

Pat Tabler Memorial Scholarship: Church and Synagogue Library Association

Sydney Taylor Children's Book Award: Association of Jewish Libraries

Sydney Taylor Manuscript Award: Association of Jewish Libraries

Sydney Taylor Older Children's Book Award: Association of Jewish Libraries

Trustee Citations: ALA/American Library Trustee Association

UMI Doctoral Dissertation Award: American Society for Information Science

Rose L. Vormelker Award: Special Libraries Association

Leonard Wertheimer Award: ALA/Public Library Association

Virginia and Herbert White Award for Promoting Librarianship: ALA

Laura Ingalls Wilder Award: ALA/Association for Library Service to Children

H. W. Wilson Award: Special Libraries Association

H. W. Wilson Foundation Research Award: Art Libraries Society of North America

H. W. Wilson Library Staff Development Grant: ALA

H. W. Wilson Scholarship: Canadian Library Association

Justin Winsor Prize Essay: ALA/Library History Round Table

Women's National Book Award Association/Ann Heidbreder Eastman Grant: ALA

World Book ALA Goal Grants: ALA

A. R. Zipf Fellowship in Information Management: Council on Library and Information Resources.

# Part 4
# Research and Statistics

# Library Research and Statistics

## Research on Libraries and Librarianship in 1998

Mary Jo Lynch

Director, Office for Research and Statistics, American Library Association

The year 1998 was the first year of funding for research as part of the National Leadership Grants program in the Institute of Museum and Library Services (IMLS). Another article in this volume describes IMLS and the Library Services and Technology Act (LSTA), of which these grants are a part. [See "Institute of Museum and Library Services Library Programs" in Part 2—*Ed.*] That legislation provides for National Leadership Grants in four categories: education and training, research and demonstration, preservation or digitization, and model programs of cooperation between libraries and museums.

The grants program attracted 250 applicants, and grants were made to 41 for a total of $6,487,750. The news release announcing the grants lists ten in the category of research and demonstration, which is described as follows: "Model projects to enhance library services through the use of appropriate technologies and to create methods to evaluate the contributions to a community made by institutions providing access to information services." Although the descriptions in the press release are brief, it seems likely that of the ten research and demonstration grants, only three merit mention in a review of research:

- St. Louis Public Library, St. Louis, Missouri ($208,550). For a two-year project, in partnership with public libraries in Baltimore, Birmingham, Phoenix, and Seattle, to refine a case study methodology to communicate the economic benefits of services provided by large public libraries and to provide a means for libraries to estimate the direct monetary return on annual taxpayer investment.
- University at Albany, State University of New York, Albany, New York ($176,138). For a one-year project to develop and test a descriptive list of national core data elements, statistics, and performance measures to describe public library network uses and produce a manual describing the resulting elements, statistics, and measures and recommending data collection techniques.
- University of Michigan, School of Information, Ann Arbor, Michigan ($189,026). For a two-year project to investigate the role of librarians in assisting users to find community information on the Internet, using case studies of libraries in Florida, Illinois, and Pennsylvania, and to identify best practices for providing community information electronically.

A much larger source of funds for research on digital libraries was announced in February 1998. The Digital Libraries Initiative (DLI) Phase 2 is sponsored by the National Science Foundation (NSF), the Defense Advanced Research Projects Agency (DARPA), the National Library of Medicine, the Library of Congress (LC), the National Aeronautics and Space Administration (NASA), and the National Endowment for the Humanities (NEH), among others. DLI goals are to support leadership in the research fundamental to the development of next-generation digital libraries, stimulate partnerships, and understand the long-term social, behavioral, and economic implications of digital libraries.

Unlike DLI Phase 1, which was sponsored by NSF, DARPA, and NASA, DLI Phase 2 involves a much wider range of sponsors and also involves partnerships with the Smithsonian Institution and the National Archives and Records Administration. Letters of intent for the 1998 cycle were due on April 15, and full proposals were due on July 15. As of this writing (March 1, 1999), no awards have been announced. For more information, see the NSF Web site (http://www.nsf.gov/pubs/1998/nsf9863/nsf9863.htm) or the NEH Web site (http://www.neh.gov/html/guidelin/dli2.html).

## Public Libraries

The three IMLS research grants described earlier promise to result in new knowledge about public library service in the years to come. Another project in that category was announced in December 1998. The Graduate School of Library and Information Science (GSLIS) at the University of Illinois at Urbana-Champaign received a grant of $65,000 from the Lila Wallace–Reader's Digest Fund to create a national survey of literacy services in public libraries. GSLIS Dean Leigh Estabrook and consultant Debra Wilcox Johnson will lead the project, which will be carried out by the school's Library Research Center (LRC). Focus groups were conducted with library directors in the Chicago area to determine topics for the survey that will be sent to 1,500 public libraries in January. Findings will be delivered to the fund in September 1999.

Projects completed in 1998 include two from the American Library Association (ALA). At its 1998 Annual Conference in Washington, D.C., ALA announced results of eight questions sponsored by ALA in an "omnibus" survey conducted by the Gallup Organization in May 1998. Among other findings, the survey determined that 66 percent of American adults use the public library at least once a year and 90 percent believe that libraries will exist in the future despite all of the information available through computers. In October the ALA Office for Information Technology Policy (OITP) released summary results of the 1998 National Survey of Public Library Outlet Internet Connectivity conducted by John C. Bertot and Charles R. McClure. Unlike connectivity studies conducted by these two researchers in 1994, 1996, and 1997, this one focused on the approximately 16,000 library outlets—central libraries plus branches—rather than the approximately 9,000 single units and systems. Based on a sample of 2,500 outlets, the survey found that 73.3 percent offer public access to the Internet from at least one terminal. The four-page summary can be found at http://www.ala.org/oitp/research/survey98.html. A detailed final report should be available in 1999.

In 1996 this article reported on the public-opinion research contained in a report prepared by the Benton Foundation titled *Buildings, Books, and Bytes: Libraries and Communities in the Digital Age*. That research constituted the first phase of work continued in 1997 through a series of five focus groups conducted by the firm of Lake, Snell, and Perry—three in the Chicago suburb of Oak Park and two in the Baltimore suburb of Owings Mills. Participants in all groups were adults who used the public library at least "rarely." In 1998 the results of those focus groups were reported as part of a multimedia "Tool Kit for Libraries and Communities in the Digital Age" titled *The Future's in the Balance*. This tool kit contains audiotapes, videotapes, a PowerPoint presentation, and a good deal of advice on how to communicate the library's message to its public. The focus group findings are on pages 77–91 under these broad headings:

- Americans love libraries
- Libraries are about books and reading, but computers can be a value too
- Libraries are essential for children
- The librarian as an information navigator
- Younger Americans: Libraries are not a priority now, but prospects for future use are bright
- The library of the future: From bricks to bytes

The Benton project, funded by the W. K. Kellogg Foundation, is an unusual example of action research on a national scale. It was a two-year research effort designed to help public libraries explain their services to the public at a time when computers and the Internet are becoming widespread in homes, work-places, and community institutions.

Important action research at the state level was performed in 1998. As part of its effort to improve support for public libraries, the Office of Commonwealth Libraries engaged McClure and Bertot to conduct the study reported in *Public Libraries Use in Pennsylvania: Identifying Uses, Benefits, and Impacts*. Using multiple methodologies—including focus groups, site visits, user surveys, and critical-incident logs—the researchers presented an in-depth picture of who uses public libraries in Pennsylvania, why they use libraries, and how that use is beneficial to them. The full report is available on the Web at http://istweb.sjr.edu/~mcclure/padeptedumerge.pdf.

## School Libraries

Researchers needing national statistics on school libraries were pleased by the long-awaited release of data collected in the 1993–1994 academic year. *School Library Media Centers: 1993–94* was published by the National Center for Education Statistics (NCES) in August 1998. It contains more than 150 detailed tables of results from two sample surveys conducted in 1993–1994, one on school library media centers and one on school library media specialists. Plans are already under way to conduct the school library media center survey again in academic year 1999–2000.

Another event for that academic year is the Third International Forum on Research in School Librarianship to be held as part of Unleash the Power—a conference jointly sponsored by the American Association of School Librarians (AASL) and the International Association of School Librarianship (IASL) in Birmingham, Alabama, November 10–14, 1999. A brochure with full details of the call for proposals is available online at http://www.ala.org/aasl/birmingham.

AASL made another research-related announcement in 1998. Beginning in January 1999, AASL is changing the title of its online research publication from School Library Media Quarterly Online to School Library Media Research. The change was made to reflect the purpose of the online journal: original research studies that have been based on a clear methodology, analysis of data, and application of findings to the field. The primary purpose of School Library Media Research (http://www.ala.org/aasl/SLMR) will be to provide a forum for researchers at the academic level as well as field researchers in the practicing ranks to focus on the major research questions of today. The journal is more than research-based, meaning articles based only on the research of others. School Library Media Research is designed to publish original-research documents that have been extensively reviewed and judged to be of high quality. The online format allows for greater documentation and quicker linkage to other original research than can be provided through the traditional print method.

For several years advocates for school library media programs have quoted *The Impact of School Library Media Centers on Academic Achievement* (Hi Willow, 1993), a study conducted in Colorado in the early 1990s and published in 1993. This report showed a direct connection between well-trained media specialists and well-stocked media centers and higher test scores. It filled what until then had been a near vacuum of research on school libraries and academic achievement. But the data are old now and many things have changed, so the Colorado researchers found funding to do the study again—with improvements. As in the first project, the researchers will collect information from a broad sample of Colorado schools. They will look at general characteristics, such as teacher-student ratios and the number of low-income students, along with library-specific data, such as the size of collections and how closely media specialists work with students and staff. But instead of correlating this information with scores in the Iowa Test of Basic Skills, researchers this time will use Colorado's new reading and writing test, the Colorado Student Assessment Program. The new study will be called "How School Librarians Help Kids Achieve Standards." The reason for the shift is that the first study found a significant link between how much librarians participate in instruction—for instance, by collaborating with teachers—and how well students learn. But the finding was fairly general, not saying exactly which of a librarian's activities had the most impact. This time researchers will pose that question to focus groups of administrators, teachers, and students. The study will be conducted by the Library Research Service (LRS), a joint venture of the Colorado State Library and the University of Denver's Library and Information Services Program. For updates, check the LRS Web site at http://www.lrs.org. Similar projects directed by the Library Research Service are under way in Alaska and in Pennsylvania.

School library researchers who want to keep up with federally funded education research can now subscribe to a new list titled Research Bytes (http://

ResearchBytes@inet.ed.gov). This electronic list is the U.S. Department of Education's new outlet for electronic dissemination of the latest research findings from the Office of Educational Research and Improvement (OERI). Each installment will cover a variety of topics being investigated by the projects funded by OERI. The goal of Research Bytes is to share with participants the most up-to-date research findings coming out of the centers, regional labs, and field-initiated studies. This list is designed to be used by researchers and department senior staff to both inform and stimulate debate on major education issues.

## Academic Libraries

Last year this article summarized preliminary findings of the Association of Research Libraries' (ARL) two-year study of interlibrary loan and document delivery operations. The full report became available in May 1998 under the title *Measuring the Performance of Interlibrary Loan Operations in North American Research and College Libraries*. This publication reports the major findings and makes recommendations for further research and applications of the ILL/DD Performance Measure Study. Funded by the Andrew W. Mellon Foundation, the study was undertaken in collaboration with the Council on Library and Information Resources (CLIR). Mary E. Jackson, ARL Access and Delivery Services consultant, served as the principal investigator. The study identified eight interlibrary loan departments as high-performing operations and identified best practices in those departments. ARL will conduct a series of workshops based on those findings. For an executive summary of the report, see http://www.arl.org/access/illdd/execsum.shtml.

CLIR began two broad studies of academic institutions in the new information environment. Up to 12 college campuses have been chosen for the Innovative Use of Technology by Colleges Case Studies Project, which will study how these colleges are responding to the challenge of providing information services in a rapidly changing environment. CLIR staff and members of the College Libraries Committee will make site visits to the colleges and then issue a volume of case studies that illustrate the ways in which college libraries in particular have strengthened their role on campus, enhanced their information services, and improved instruction and research.

A more-complex study is under way for universities. To help universities understand in detail the full extent of their investment in information resources, CLIR intends to develop an assessment model that should be of use to many institutions. In the early stages of shaping the project, a steering committee for CLIR identified three important aspects of the problem of determining a university's investment in information sources: access (Which members of the academic community can use particular information and on what terms?), permanence (When does information become a permanent asset of the university?), and collection creation costs (What are the costs when a part of the university creates a knowledge database?).

The committee is proposing that three distinct universities figure in the pilot study, two private and one public, and that one of the private institutions have a highly centralized budgetary process and the other a decentralized process. The committee has also determined that the project must consider the following units of the university: libraries, the various schools and their departments, institutes, centers, and the academic administration. Within the libraries unit, the committee identified these types of costs as significant: collection expenses, including costs of acquiring serials, monographs, and databases; space costs; cataloging and maintenance costs; and access costs (i.e., the percentage of the network costs that should be attributed to the information budget).

The steering committee will frame the project for consideration by the CLIR Board before discussing it with a group of provosts and making such changes in the conceptualization as may then be warranted. CLIR will subsequently distribute an RFP document to a group of financial consultants with experience in higher education and, on the basis of their responses, choose one group to manage the pilot study. The eventual results are to form a kind of template that many universities can use to conduct their own studies of how they invest in information sources.

CLIR is also supporting a project in the Cornell University Library that will assess the risks associated with pursuing a particular digital preservation strategy for a number of digital object types. Under the direction of Gregory W. Lawrence, the government information librarian at Cornell, the project will survey the library's extensive digital holdings, identify the risks that attend migration of the most common file formats, develop a risk-assessment tool, and conduct a pilot test of the tool on a major file format. The risk assessment tool is also expected to be of use to other libraries in the management of their digital collections. Many university libraries have been creating or collecting digital information in a range of standard and proprietary formats, and the most pressing problem confronting managers of digital collections is now software and data format obsolescence. This CLIR project will study options for dealing with the problem.

A different kind of digitization will be studied under a $376,000 grant from the Andrew Mellon Foundation to the Milton Eisenhower Library at Johns Hopkins University to support the Comprehensive Access to Print Materials (CAPM) Project. The project will use both digital and robotics technology to improve access to hard-copy materials held in off-site storage facilities. The funding will support economic analysis and prototype development over a period of two years.

The CAPM project will operate through an online public-access catalog (OPAC), which will activate a robot to withdraw an item from the collection. The item will be scanned by a device that includes an automatic page turner after an integrated copyright management system confirms that digitization is authorized. The scanned image will be delivered to the user's computer, while the catalog record can be updated to show that a digital copy is available to future users.

The initiative will be led by Sayeed Choudhury, director of the Eisenhower Library's Digital Knowledge Center, in collaboration with faculty and graduate students in the Hopkins Whiting School of Engineering and economic researchers at the University of Colorado. Minolta, IBM, and Ameritech Library Services have contributed equipment and engineering expertise.

Last year this article noted that the National Center for Educational Statistics (NCES) had provided researchers with a new type of report on academic libraries. Instead of just displaying data at a single point in time using NCES categories (e.g., highest degree awarded), the new report made comparisons to earlier years and used the Carnegie Classification. In September 1998 a new and greatly improved version of this report was published: *The Status of Academic Libraries in the United States: Results from 1994 Academic Library Survey with Historical Comparisons* (NCES 98-311). Twice as long as the 1997 status report, this one contains 31 tables covering all topics included in the biennial Academic Library Survey plus 14 helpful figures. The report is of limited use for those working on current issues in academic libraries, but it provides very useful background data.

ALA's Association of College and Research Libraries (ACRL) took steps in 1998 to collect almost the same data annually that NCES collects biennially and to make the data available much faster. A fact sheet on the Academic Libraries Trends and Statistics Project announced that all academic libraries will be invited to participate, and results will be made available both in print and on the Web. Although original plans were to begin the project in September 1998, letters did not actually go out until January 1999. Libraries were given a code number and invited to submit their data via a Web site created by the project contractor, the University of Virginia Center for Survey Research.

## Literature Landmarks

The Spring 1998 issue of *Library Trends* (vol. 46, no. 4) was devoted entirely to qualitative research—the first such issue in the 46-year history of this key journal. Three of the nine articles were based on presentations made at Library Research Seminar I, held in Tallahassee, Florida, in November 1996, where the idea for the issue was born. Others were added to enhance the context of the seminar papers. Three of the nine articles present qualitative research and its results, two discuss related philosophies, one describes the implications of a particular line of qualitative research for public library practice, one is a bibliographic essay on methodological frameworks, one contains a discussion of teaching both quantitative and qualitative research, and one provides a commentary on how journal editors deal with the latter.

All four issues of *Library & Information Science Research* published in 1998 bore the label "20th Anniversary Volume." The first issue of the volume contained a reprint of Mel Voigt's editorial in the journal's very first issue, where Voigt asked and answered the question "Is the profession ready for a journal devoted exclusively to research?" The current editors, Peter Hernon and Candy Schwartz, then observe that Voigt and his collaborators were right to answer that question in the affirmative. In the last issue of the year, the editors summarize the first 20 volumes by listing all members of the editorial boards and all reviewers and by analyzing article authorship and content. It will probably not surprise anyone to learn that authors were 53 percent male, 77 percent from the United States, and 60 percent associated with schools of Library and Information Science. In addition, over 67 percent of the articles were by a single author and about 50 percent were about "information service activities." Of the 353 articles in the 20 years, 269 (76.2 percent) could be labeled research in that they "involved some type of data collection" (quantitative or qualitative) or "presented or refined a model, or advanced a conceptualization." After reviewing the first 20 years, Hernon and Schwartz conclude:

> *Library & Information Science Research*, reflecting the changing nature of library and information science, has published research of a generally high quality that makes contributions within and outside of the field. The initiation of a new journal in 1979 was a risk well taken—the result seems to have served the LIS community and other communities well.

## OCLC

The Online Computer Library Center (OCLC) is always mentioned in this article, both for the work done by OCLC Office of Research staff (http://www.ocle. org/oclc/research/index.htm) and for the work done elsewhere with support from OCLC. In 1998 OCLC awarded Library and Information Science Grants of up to $10,000 each to the following university researchers:

- Corrinne Jorgensen, assistant professor, University of Buffalo, State University of New York, received a grant for "The Applicability of Selected Classification Systems to Image Attributes Named by Naive Users." Dr. Jorgensen's project will analyze current indexing and classification systems in relation to recent research results concerning image attributes described by naive participants. The concrete and pragmatic goal is to provide coherently organized and easily understood information about existing image indexing and classification systems to those who are grappling with the problem of organizing large collections of images for access.
- Elaine Toms, assistant professor, Dalhousie University, Halifax, Nova Scotia, received a grant for "Genre as Interface Metaphor: Exploiting Form and Function in Digital Environments." Dr. Toms's study suggests that the form and function of a document can be defined by its genre and that each class of genre has a parsimonious set of attributes that uniquely identifies it. Furthermore, a genre can serve as an organizing metaphor to facilitate a user's recognition of and interaction with a digital document. Using two experiments, Toms will access those attributes in print form, map the discriminating cues to digital documents using XML, and assess them in digital form.
- Marcia Lei Zeng, associate professor, Kent State University, Kent, Ohio, received a grant for "Object Description on the Internet: A Study of Current Standards and Formats—Testing Existing Metadata Standards and Proposed Metadata Cores in a Digitized Historical Fashion Collection." Dr. Zeng's research will study the applicability of current metadata standards and other proposed metadata formats in object description on the Internet, using a digitized historical fashion collection as the research sample. The study will contribute to the understanding of describing non-two-dimensional and non-document-like objects on the Internet and contribute to the discussion of potential applications of current metadata standards and the elimination of abundant and overlapping efforts in metadata development.

The most important new project in the OCLC Office of Research is the Cooperative Online Resource Catalog (CORC) project, which will build a catalog of Internet resources (http://www.oclc.org/oclc/research/projects/corc/index.htm). Building on two earlier projects funded by federal grants, CORC will produce dynamically generated pages suitable for helping library users navigate their library's local resources, Web resources subscribed to by the library, and general Web resources. CORC will help with link selection, link maintenance, resource descriptions, and the creation of pages based on this information. CORC is conceived as a 12- and 18-month project with up to 100 participating libraries. It was launched at the 1999 ALA Midwinter Meeting with several presentations and workshop sessions.

## Awards that Honor Excellent Research

All active awards are listed along with the amount of the award, the URL for the award (if available), and the person(s) and project(s) that won in 1998. If the award was not given in 1998, that fact is noted. Awards by ALA units are listed first, followed by those of other agencies in alphabetical order.

### ALA/Association of College and Research Libraries

**K. G. Saur Award for Best Article in College and Research Libraries** ($500)
http://www.ala.org/acrl/saur.html
This award is not always given for research, but the 1998 winner reports on research.
*Winners*: Jean P. Kleiner and Charles A. Hamaker
*Project*: "Libraries 2000: Transforming Libraries Using Document Delivery, Needs Assessment, and Networked Resources," in *College and Research Libraries*, July 1997. The article describes several projects that were undertaken at the Louisiana State University Libraries to control journal subscription expenditures while ensuring the maintenance of a high quality of service in document delivery. The authors demonstrate that careful planning can be effectively utilized to stretch library resources in times of reduced funding and rapid change.

### ALA/Library and Information Technology Association

**Frederick G. Kilgour Award** (with OCLC) ($2,000 plus expense-paid trip to ALA Annual Conference)
*Winner*: Karen M. Drabenstott, University of Michigan, School of Information
*Rationale*: The award is made to a person doing "real-world" research in the field of library and information technology who has had an impact on the way information is published, stored, retrieved, disseminated, or managed. Dr. Drabenstott was the unanimous choice of the committee because her work epitomized the kind of work for which Frederick Kilgour is so justly honored.

### ALA/Library History Round Table

**Phyllis Dain Library History Dissertation Award** ($500)
http://www.ala.org/alaorg/ors/dain.html
*Winner*: Christine Pawley

*Project*: "Reading on the Middle Border: The Culture of Print in Osage, Iowa, 1870 to 1900." Pawley's study explores reading practices in Osage, Iowa, by analyzing primary source material on education, local newspapers, religious life, a reading club, and business affairs. It also examines public library use and correlates those findings with population demographics to highlight the interaction of print with identities of class, gender, age, ethnicity, and religion.

**Justin Winsor Prize** ($500)
http://www.ala.org/alaorg/ors/winsor.html
Not given in 1998.

### ALA/Library Research Round Table

**Jesse H. Shera Award for Distinguished Published Research** ($500)
http://www.ala.org/alaorg/ors/shera1.html
*Winner*: Allyson Carlyle
*Project*: "Fulfilling the Second Objective in the Online Catalog: Schemes for Organizing Author and Work Records into Usable Displays," published in *Library Resources and Technical Services* (vol. 41, no. 2, April 1997).

**Jesse H. Shera Award for Excellence in Doctoral Research** ($500)
http://www.ala.org/alaorg/ors/shera2.html
Not given in 1998.

### American Society for Information Science

**ASIS Research Award**
*Winner*: Marcia J. Bates, Graduate School of Education and Information Studies, University of California at Los Angeles
*Rationale*: Dr. Bates has a long and distinguished record of research on the searching of information systems, beginning with her doctoral dissertation on factors affecting subject catalog search success. Subsequently, she has examined interface design issues and developed interfaces to facilitate directed searching as well as browsing as a search technique. Many of her research contributions have explored the role of language in information retrieval. She has influenced numerous other researchers, and her key works are considered classics in the field.

**UMI Doctoral Dissertation Award**
*Winner*: Tomas A. Lipinski, doctoral student, University of Wisconsin at Milwaukee
*Project*: "The Communication of Law in the Digital Environment: Stability and Change Within the Concept of Precedent." This dissertation offers new understandings of the evolution of precedent for legal scholars and demonstrates a new domain of application to those interested in bibliometric techniques.

### Association for Library and Information Science Education

**Doctoral Dissertation Competition** ($400 for travel expenses and 1998 conference registration and membership in ALISE for 1997–1998)
*Winner 1*: Elizabeth Yakel, School of Information Science, School of Information Sciences, University of Pittsburgh
*Project*: "Record Keeping in Radiology: The Relationships Between Activities and Records in Radiological Processes"

*Winner 2*: Mary K. Chelton, Graduate School of Library and Information Studies, Queens College, City University of New York
*Project*: "Adult-Adolescent Service Encounters: The Library Context"

**Methodology Paper Competition** ($500)
*Winner*: Cheryl Knott Malone, Graduate School of Library and Information Science, University of Illinois at Urbana-Champaign
*Project*: "Reconstituting the Public Library Users of the Past: An Exploration of Nominal Record Linkage Methodology"

**Research Paper Competition** ($500)
*Winner*: Louis S. Robbins, School of Library and Information Studies, University of Wisconsin at Madison
*Project*: "Fighting McCarthyism Through Film: A Library Censorship Case Becomes a Storm Center"

## Grants that Support Research

All active grants are listed along with the amount of the grant, the URL for the grant (if available), and the person(s) and project(s) who won in 1998. If the grant was not given in 1998, that fact is noted. General ALA grants are listed first, followed by other agencies in alphabetical order.

### American Library Association

**Carroll Preston Baber Research Grant** ($7,500)
http://www.ala.org/alaorg/ors/baber99.html
Not given in 1998.

**Loleta D. Fyan Grant** ($10,000). This is not necessarily a grant for research, but a research project was selected in 1998.
http://www.ala.org/alaorg.ors/ors/fyan.html
*Winner*: Cindy Mediavilla, doctoral student, University of California at Los Angeles
*Project*: "A Study of Homework Centers in Public Libraries" will study well-established public library homework centers located throughout the United States in order to identify the elements needed to successfully organize and run a homework assistance program. It will also produce a document based on the study's findings, designed to help public library staff and administrators successfully operate local homework centers.

### American Association of School Librarians

**AASL/Highsmith Research Grant** ($5,000)
*Winner*: Joy H. McGregor, Texas Woman's University
*Project*: "Implementing Flexible Scheduling in Elementary School Libraries" explores flexible scheduling in elementary school library media centers where funding is not contingent on flexible scheduling. Data from telephone interviews with school library media specialists, their administrators, and their teachers will lead to a better understanding of how to implement flexible scheduling and deal with variables that affect implementation.

**Association of College and Research Libraries (ACRL)**

**ACRL/ISI Doctoral Dissertation Fellowship** ($1,500)
http://www.ala.org/acrl/doctoral.html
*Winner*: Jeanine M. Williamson, University of North Carolina at Chapel Hill
*Project*: "Examining Literary Studies Articles for the Possibility of Sentence Extraction: Term Occurrences and Sentence Functions"

**Samuel Lazerow Fellowship for Research in Acquisitions or Technical Services in an Academic or Research Library** ($1,000)
*Winner*: Dilys E. Morris, assistant director, technical services, Iowa State University
*Project*: "Technical Services Time and Cost Analysis: Development of Methodology to Compare Among Libraries." This project is a cooperative effort to identify and track technical services staff time and costs in different libraries to help identify areas where collaboration and greater information technology support can reduce costs and increase services. The current project expands on an earlier study at Iowa State University (ISU) and will apply the ISU model to four institutions' technical services to help create a time and cost analysis tool for a multi-institution environment. The other investigators involved in the project are Cecily Johns, associate university librarian at the University of California, Santa Barbara; Flow Wilson, associate university librarian at Vanderbilt University; Christian Boissonnas, director of central technical services at Cornell University; and Brenda Dingley, assistant director for technical services at the University of Missouri, Kansas City.

**Martinus Nijhoff West European Study Grant** (10,000 Dutch guilders)
*Winner*: Jeffrey Garrett, bibliographer, Western languages and literature, Northwestern University
*Project*: The focus of Garrett's study will be on "the fate of confiscated Bavarian monastic libraries between 1802–1814, their incorporation into collections of the Bavarian Staatsbibliothek, and the impact of these events on the founding of modern library science.

**Young Adult Library Services Association**

**Francis Henne/YALSA/VOYA Research Grant** ($500)
http://www.ala.org/yalsa/awards/hennewinner.html
Not given in 1998, but two changes were made: Student members doing research for a degree are now eligible, and the required length and detail of the proposal has been shortened.

**American Society for Information Science**

**ISI/ASIS Citation Analysis Research Grant** ($3,000)
http://www.asis.org/awards/citation.isi.htm
*Winner*: David Dubin, University of Illinois at Urbana-Champaign
*Project*: "Evaluation of Document Clustering Tendency: Citation-Based Clusters for Validation Studies." This research will contribute a better understanding of clustering in bibliographic data and of measures by which a clustering tendency can be assessed and measured. This understanding will aid and support the use of clustering algorithms in the design and deployment of information retrieval systems.

**ISI Information Science Doctoral Dissertation Proposal Scholarship** ($1,500 plus $500 toward travel or other expenses)
*Winner*: Karla Hahn, doctoral student, College of Library and Information Services, University of Maryland
*Project*: "Electronic Journals as Innovations: A Study of Author and Editor Early Adopters"

## Association for Library & Information Science Education

**Research Grant Awards** (one or more grants totaling $5,000)
http://www.alise.org/Research_grant99.html
*Winner ($3,000)*: John Richardson, Jr., University of California at Los Angeles
*Project*: "Nadezhda Konstantinovna Krupskaya (1869–1939): The Initiator of Soviet Education for Librarianship, 1917–1928"
*Winner ($2,000)*: Terry L. Weech, University of Illinois at Urbana-Champaign
*Project*: "Site Dependent and Site Independent Distance Education in Library and Information Science: A Study of Their Costs and Effectiveness"

## Medical Library Association

**ISI/MLA Doctoral Fellowship** ($2,000)
*Winner*: Sharon Dezel Jenkins, School of Library Science, University of North Texas
*Project*: Thesis on the validity and reliability of SERVPROF as a tool for judging the quality of library services provided by rural health information professionals

**Research, Development, and Demonstration Grant** ($995)
*Winner*: Mary M. Howrey, Provena Mercy Center, Aurora, Illinois
*Project*: TeenCARE Network, a participatory action research project focusing on self-directed learning and consumer health information services for Aurora teenagers and their parents via the Teen Care Network partnership and the Internet site at http://www.aurora.il.us/teencare

## Special Libraries Association

**Steven I. Goldspiel Memorial Research Grant** (up to $20,000)
http://www.sla.org/research/goldfund.html
*Winner*: Andrew Dillon, School of Library and Information Science, Indiana University
*Project*: "Understanding Users in Digital Environments: A Longitudinal Study of Genre Influences in Information Work." The primary objective of the project is to demonstrate how digital genres are formed in the minds of users and how such genres affect both the users' capabilities to utilize the digital resources and their ratings of the usefulness of such resources. Genres are natural psychological occurrences in which the cognitive system abstracts, patterns, and automates activities so as to free up limited attentional resources. As with newspapers, where readers have learned to recognize the purposes of a newspaper article based on its layout and position in the paper, the same type of patterns may evolve for digital documents. In this study, users of digital documents will be tracked over a nine-month period to determine whether interaction patterns develop.

# Assessment of the Role of School and Public Libraries in Support of Education Reform: A Status Report on the Study

Christina Dunn

Project Director and Director, Collections and Technical Services
National Library of Education
202-401-6563, e-mail christina_dunn@ed.gov

In fiscal year (FY) 1998 the U.S. Department of Education continued research, begun in FY 1994, to assess the role of school and public libraries in education reform. Westat, Inc., in cooperation with the American Library Association (ALA), is conducting the $1.3 million study, which will be completed in FY 1999. The study is funded under the Secretary's Fund for Innovation in Education.

## Background

In 1984 "Alliance for Excellence: Librarians Respond to a Nation at Risk" (U.S. Department of Education) recognized that past efforts to assess public and school libraries were outdated, calling for the nation's school and public libraries to be "assessed for their ability to respond to the urgent proposals for excellence in education and lifelong learning." The report recommended new appraisals of performance and effectiveness, as well as reevaluation of current resources. Ten years later, the U.S. Department of Education began a multiyear study to provide information on key issues that assess the capacity of school and public libraries to impact education (preschool and K–12), especially current education reform efforts.

The immediate impetus for the study was the passage of the Goal 2000: Educate America Act in 1994, which codified the National Education Goals established in 1990. The act embraces new, world-class learning standards, promotes the enrichment of course content and improved training for quality teaching and reform, encourages parental involvement, and challenges all schools to show real results. Research into how school and public libraries are responding to these Goal 2000 initiatives has the potential to shape the future role of libraries as education and information providers.

## Research Issues

Regardless of the current level and type of participation, it behooves policymakers and the library and education communities to learn more about the role of public and school libraries in supporting education in order to plan for and direct resources and to inform practice. Therefore, the time is ripe to address the recurring question, asked by librarians and educators alike: How are school and public libraries performing as education providers, and how well are they responding to the country's urgent demands for school improvement and the education and reeducation of the American work force?

The study uses a combination of quantitative and qualitative data—national surveys and case studies of selected programs—to provide a rich portrait of school and public libraries, offering current and reliable information to researchers, policymakers, and practitioners on six key issues:

- To what extent are school and public libraries contributing to education reform, and to what extent can they contribute?
- What programs and services are school and public libraries providing to meet the needs of preschool, elementary, and secondary education providers?
- How well do these services and programs meet the needs of preschool and K–12 education providers?
- Do school and public libraries have the capacity—human and information resources, technology, and facilities—to adequately respond to identified needs and support systemic reform?
- What new technologies are promoting student opportunities to learn by improving services and resources in school and public libraries?
- What can we learn from successful school and public library programs and services designed to support preschool and K–12 education? Can these programs serve as models for the improvement of all school and public libraries? What are the barriers to effective service and programs?

In addition to considering the issues above, the study gives special consideration to the issue of how school and public libraries can best serve the needs of disadvantaged and at-risk students.

## Methodology and Status of Research Activities

Two advisory bodies helped to guide the study: a steering committee of U.S. Department of Education staff, primarily those involved with research in related areas, and a national advisory panel that included educators, policymakers, and practitioners in school and public libraries who are knowledgeable about the role of school and public libraries in both formal and informal education.

*Literature Review.* A report reviewing and evaluating existing research has been completed. The purpose of the report was to provide information to refine the study's design. Documents reviewed included general discussions of issues, legislation, guidelines, and standards developed at the national and state levels; descriptions of projects and initiatives, statistical data, research studies, and survey instruments from which data were not yet available; and reports on relevant work in progress. The review provides the contextual background for the study, identifying existing useful information, pointing out problems, and indicating gaps in current knowledge regarding programs and services provided by public and school libraries that might support the National Education Goals.

*National Surveys of Public and Private Schools and Public Libraries.* Information addressing the six key issues identified above was obtained from two questionnaires, one for public and private schools and one for public libraries. Both surveys, designed to obtain data about individual libraries rather than library systems, looked at staffing, programs and services, materials and resources, and the application of technology. In addition, the public and private schools survey considered professional development for teachers and interaction with public libraries, while the public library survey addressed patronage, outreach, and interaction with schools.

The sample of libraries for the field test and main study were selected from three separate universe lists maintained by the U.S. Department of Education's National Center for Education Statistics: the Common Core of Data Public School Universe File, Private School Survey Universe File, and Public Library Universe System File. Within each group of libraries, the samples were stratified by relevant variables to ensure adequate sample sizes for key analytic subdomains and to improve the precision of national estimates.

For each of the questionnaires in the main study, sample size was approximately 1,000. (For the school questionnaire, 1,000 public and 1,000 private schools were sampled.) The overall response rate exceeded the desired 90 percent.

*Case Studies.* Ten case studies of public and school library programs, involving on-site observations and interviews, have been completed. The selected institutions represented school and public libraries in rural, suburban, and urban communities and in the major geographic regions of the country—West, Central, Southeast, and Northeast. The programs that were studied focused on technology applications, school library-public library partnerships, services to at-risk and disadvantaged children and their families, and opportunities for student (preschool and K–12) learning.

For each case study, the on-site visit looked at the type of community in which the program operated; characteristics of its public library and school systems; goals and objectives of the program; components of the program; factors leading to the development of the program; who was involved in the development and planning of the program, how they were involved and how they continue to be involved; how the program evolved over time; problems encountered in operating the program; estimated program cost; evaluation of the program; and factors a community would need to consider in adopting the program.

*Commissioned Papers.* Four commissioned papers have been completed. They examine cooperative relationships between public libraries and school library media centers (by Shirley Fitzgibbons); the effects of independent reading and school achievement (by Bernice Cullinan); public library services to young children and their families and possible effects of those services on preschool learning (by Steven Herb and Sara Willoughby-Herb); and the implications of selected school reforms for school library media services (by Gary Hartzell).

*Dissemination.* Reporting to the library and education communities will take place throughout 1999, with the first dissemination activities beginning in the spring. Presentations are scheduled for several major association annual conferences, including those of the American Library Association, the Association of Educational Communications and Technology, and the American Educational Research Association. In addition, survey and case study findings, commissioned papers, and the literature review will be made available through the U.S. Department of Education's Web site (www.edu.gov). The department also plans to publish a document for decision-makers on key findings. All reports will be made available through the U.S. Department of Education's ERIC (Educational Resources Information Center) system.

## Potential Uses of the Research

The research was designed to inform both decision-makers and the library community: library and education professionals to improve practice and government to effectively plan and target funding, exercise leadership, and develop sound, accountable policy in such areas as the initial preparation and professional development of school and public librarians, teachers, and other educators; and the development of library networks and technology applications for improving information access. Information from the study will prove useful as decision-makers and the library community work together to identify those aspects of public and school library services and programs that promote opportunities to learn, develop standards and performance requirements for public and school libraries, and help parents become more involved in the education of their children. In addition, the study will help identify the research and demonstration needs related to school and public library programs, services, and resources.

The study's combination of a national assessment of the current and evolving role of school and public libraries in support of education reform and case studies of selected programs that support the National Education Goals will help to meet the needs of a variety of users. Employing these two approaches resulted in both quantitative and qualitative data, thereby developing a more descriptive portrait of the role of school and public libraries—one that provides an in-depth look at how libraries are meeting the needs of education providers as well as a rich data collection that can be used to support model development.

# Number of Libraries in the United States, Canada, and Mexico

Statistics are from the 51st edition of the *American Library Directory* (*ALD*) 1998–1999 (R. R. Bowker, 1998). Data are exclusive of elementary and secondary school libraries.

## Libraries in the United States

| | |
|---|---|
| Public Libraries | 16,250 * |
|   Public libraries, excluding branches | 9,815 † |
|     Main public libraries that have branches | 1,302 |
|   Public library branches | 6,435 |
| Academic Libraries | 4,700 * |
|   Junior college | 1,270 |
|     Departmental | 119 |
|     Medical | 6 |
|     Religious | 3 |
|   University and college | 3,430 |
|     Departmental | 1,452 |
|     Law | 173 |
|     Medical | 213 |
|     Religious | 105 |
| Armed Forces Libraries | 363 * |
|   Air Force | 103 |
|     Medical | 12 |
|   Army | 154 |
|     Law | 1 |
|     Medical | 31 |
|   Navy | 106 |
|     Law | 1 |
|     Medical | 14 |
| Government Libraries | 1,897 * |
|   Law | 423 |
|   Medical | 224 |
| Special Libraries (excluding public, academic, armed forces, and government) | 9,898 * |
|   Law | 1,153 |
|   Medical | 1,900 |
|   Religious | 1,010 |

Total Special Libraries (including public, academic, armed forces,
and government)                                                      11,022
    Total law                                     1,750
    Total medical                                 2,388
    Total religious                               1,118
Total Libraries Counted(*)                                          33,108

## Libraries in Regions Administered by the United States

| | | |
|---|---:|---|
| Public Libraries | 28 | * |
|   Public libraries, excluding branches | 13 | † |
|     Main public libraries that have branches | 2 | |
|   Public library branches | 15 | |
| Academic Libraries | 53 | * |
|   Junior college | 7 | |
|   University and college | 46 | |
|     Departmental | 20 | |
|     Law | 2 | |
|     Medical | 1 | |
| Armed Forces Libraries | 3 | * |
|   Air Force | 1 | |
|   Army | 1 | |
|   Navy | 1 | |
| Government Libraries | 8 | * |
|   Law | 1 | |
|   Medical | 2 | |
| Special Libraries (excluding public, academic, armed forces, and government) | 17 | * |
|   Law | 4 | |
|   Medical | 5 | |
|   Religious | 1 | |
| Total Special Libraries (including public, academic, armed forces, and government) | 24 | |
|   Total law | 10 | |
|   Total medical | 8 | |
|   Total religious | 1 | |
| Total Libraries Counted(*) | 109 | |

## Libraries in Canada

| | | |
|---|---:|---|
| Public Libraries | 1,633 | * |
|   Public libraries, excluding branches | 782 | † |
|     Main public libraries that have branches | 188 | |
|   Public library branches | 851 | |

| | | |
|---|---:|---|
| Academic Libraries | 487 | * |
| Junior college | 128 | |
| Departmental | 35 | |
| Medical | 0 | |
| Religious | 2 | |
| University and college | 359 | |
| Departmental | 164 | |
| Law | 16 | |
| Medical | 15 | |
| Religious | 17 | |
| Government Libraries | 389 | * |
| Law | 23 | |
| Medical | 6 | |
| Special Libraries (excluding public, academic, armed forces, and government) | 1,422 | * |
| Law | 127 | |
| Medical | 264 | |
| Religious | 60 | |
| Total Special Libraries (including public, academic, and government) | 1,516 | |
| Total law | 166 | |
| Total medical | 285 | |
| Total religious | 103 | |
| Total Libraries Counted(*) | 3,931 | |

## Libraries in Mexico

| | | |
|---|---:|---|
| Public Libraries | 23 | * |
| Public libraries, excluding branches | 23 | † |
| Main public libraries that have branches | 0 | |
| Public library branches | 0 | |
| Academic Libraries | 310 | * |
| Junior college | 0 | |
| Departmental | 0 | |
| Medical | 0 | |
| Religious | 0 | |
| University and college | 310 | |
| Departmental | 241 | |
| Law | 0 | |
| Medical | 2 | |
| Religious | 0 | |
| Government Libraries | 9 | * |
| Law | 0 | |
| Medical | 1 | |

Special Libraries (excluding public, academic, armed forces,
and government)     29 *
    Law     0
    Medical     10
    Religious     0
Total Special Libraries (including public, academic, and government)     37
    Total law     0
    Total medical     14
    Total religious     0
Total Libraries Counted(*)     371

## Summary

| | |
|---|---|
| Total U.S. Libraries | 33,108 |
| Total Libraries Administered by the United States | 109 |
| Total Canadian Libraries | 3,931 |
| Total Mexican Libraries | 371 |
| Grand Total of Libraries Listed | 37,519 |

† Federal, state, and other statistical sources use this figure (libraries *excluding* branches) as the total for public libraries.

*Note:* Numbers followed by an asterisk are added to find "Total libraries counted" for each of the four geographic areas (United States, U.S.-administered regions, Canada, and Mexico). The sum of the four totals is the "Grand total of libraries listed" in *ALD*. For details on the count of libraries, see the preface to the 51st edition of *ALD—Ed.*

# Highlights of NCES Surveys

## Public Libraries

The following are highlights from *E.D. TABS Public Libraries in the United States: FY 1995*, released in August 1998:

### Number of Public Libraries and Their Service Outlets and Legal Basis

- There were 8,946 public libraries (administrative entities) in the 50 states and the District of Columbia in 1996.
- About 11 percent of the public libraries served nearly 71 percent of the population of legally served areas in the United States. Each of these public libraries had a legal service area population of 50,000 or more.
- A total of 1,480 public libraries (over 16 percent) had one or more branch library outlets, with a total of 7,124. The total number of central library outlets was 8,923. the total number of stationary outlets (central library outlets and branch library outlets) was 16,047. Nine percent of public libraries had one or more bookmobile outlets, with a total of 966.
- Nearly 54 percent of public libraries were part of a municipal government; nearly 12 percent were part of a county/parish; nearly 6 percent had multi-jurisdictional legal basis under an intergovernmental agreement; almost 11 percent were non-profit association or agency libraries; over 3 percent were part of a school district; and 8 percent were separate government units known as library districts. About 1 percent were combinations of academic/public libraries or school/public libraries. Over 6 percent reported their legal basis as "other."
- Over 80 percent of public libraries had a single direct-service outlet (an outlet that provides service directly to the public).
- Nearly 70 percent of public libraries were a member of a system, federation, or cooperative service, while over 28 percent were not. Over 2 percent served as the headquarters of a system, federation, or cooperative service.

### Income and Expenditures

- Nationwide total per capita* operating income for public libraries was $23.37. Of that, $18.26 was from local sources, $2.84 from state sources, $0.23 from federal sources, and $2.03 from other sources.
- Over 78 percent of public libraries' total operating income of about $5.9 billion came from local sources, over 12 percent from the state, 1 percent

---

*Per capita figures in these highlights are based on the total unduplicated population of legal service areas in the states, not on the total population of the states. Population of the legal service area means the population of those areas in the state for which a public library has been established to offer services and from which (or on behalf of which) the library derives income, plus any areas served under contract for which the library is the primary service provider. It does not include the population of unserved areas.

from federal sources, and almost 9 percent from other sources, such as gifts and donations, service fees and fines.

- Per capita operating income from local sources was under $3 for over 12 percent of public libraries, $3 to $14.99 for over 48 percent, and $15 to $29.99 for over 27 percent of public libraries. Per capita income from local sources was $30 or more for nearly 13 percent of libraries.

- Total operating expenditures for public libraries were over $5.5 billion in 1996. Of this, over 64 percent was expended for paid staff and over 15 percent for the library collection. The average U.S. per capita operating expenditure for public libraries was $21.98 The highest average per capita operating expenditure in the 50 states was $38.19 and the lowest was $9.42.

- Close to 38 percent of public libraries had operating expenditures of less than $50,000 in 1996; over 38 percent expended between $50,000 and $399,999; and close to 24 percent expended $400,000 or more.

### Staffing and Collections

- Public libraries had a total of 117,812 paid full-time-equivalent (FTE) staff.

- Nationwide, public libraries had over 711 million books and serial volumes in their collections or 2.8 volumes per capita. By state, the number of volumes per capita ranged from 1.5 to 5.2.

- Nationwide, public libraries had collections of over 25 million audio materials and 13 million video materials.

### Services

- Total nationwide circulation of public library materials was over 1.6 billion or 6.5 per capita. Highest statewide circulation per capita in the 50 states was 12.4 and the lowest was 2.8.

- Nationwide, over 10.5 million library materials were loaned by public libraries to other libraries.

- Total nationwide reference transactions in public libraries were over 284 million or 1.1 per capita.

- Total nationwide library visits to public libraries were over 1 billion or 4 per capita.

### Children's Services

- Nationwide circulation of children's materials was nearly 571 million or nearly 35 percent of total circulation. Attendance at children's programs was over 42 million.

The following are Highlights from *Statistics in Brief: Use of Public Library Services by Households in the United States: 1996*, released in July 1997:

### Public Library Use in the Past Month and Year

- About 44 percent of U.S. households included individuals who had used public library services in the month prior to the interview, and 65 percent of households had used public library services in the past year (including the past month). About one-third of households (35 percent) reported that no household members had used library services in the past year.

- When the entire past year is taken into account, households with children under 18 showed substantially higher rates of use than households without children (82 percent versus 54 percent).

**Ways of Using Public Library Services**

- The most common way of using public library services in the past month was to go to a library to borrow or drop off books or tapes (36 percent).
- Eighteen percent of households reported visiting a library for other purposes, such as a lecture or story hour or to use library equipment (the second most common form of use).
- About 14 percent of households had called a library for information during the past month.
- Only very small percentages of households reported using a computer to link to a library (4 percent), having materials mailed or delivered to their homes (2 percent), or visiting a bookmobile (2 percent).

**Purposes for Using Public Library Services**

- The highest percentage of households reported library use for enjoyment or hobbies, including borrowing books and tapes or attending activities (32 percent).
- Two other purposes for using public libraries that were commonly acknowledged by household respondents were getting information for personal use (such as information on consumer or health issues, investments, and so on; 20 percent), and using library services or materials for a school or class assignment (19 percent).
- Fewer household respondents said that household members had used public library services for the purposes of keeping up to date at a job (8 percent), getting information to help find a job (5 percent), attending a program for children (4 percent), or working with a tutor or taking a class to learn to read (1 percent).

## Academic Libraries

The following are highlights from the *E.D. TABS Academic Libraries: 1994*, released in March 1998:

**Services**

- In 1993, 3,303 of the 3,639 institutions of higher education in the United States reported that they had their own academic library.
- In fiscal year 1994, general collection circulation transactions in the nation's academic libraries at institutions of higher education totaled

183.1 million. Reserve collection circulation transactions totaled 48.4 million. For general and reference circulation transactions taken together, the median circulation was 16.6 per full-time-equivalent (FTE) student*. The median total circulation ranged from 9.5 per FTE in less than four-year institutions to 31.1 in doctorate-granting institutions.

- In 1994 academic libraries provided a total of about 8.8 million interlibrary loans to other libraries (both higher education and other types of libraries) and received about 6.3 million loans.

- Overall, the largest percentage of academic libraries (43 percent) reported having 60–79 hours of service per typical week. However, 41 percent provided 80 or more public service hours per typical week. The percent of institutions providing 80 or more public service hours ranged from 6.9 percent in less than four-year institutions to 77.8 percent in doctorate-granting institutions.

- Taken together, academic libraries reported a gate count of about 17.8 million visitors per typical week (about 1.8 visits per total FTE enrollment).

- About 2.1 million reference transactions were reported in a typical week. Over the fiscal year 1994, about 487,000 presentations to groups serving about 6.1 million were reported.

### Collections

- Taken together, the nation's 3,033 academic libraries at institutions of higher education held a total of 776.4 million volumes (books, bound serials, and government documents), representing about 422.3 million unduplicated titles at the end of FY 1994.

- The median number of volumes held per FTE student was 56.9 volumes. Median volumes held ranged from 18.4 per FTE in less than four-year institutions to 111.2 in doctorate-granting institutions.

- Of the total volumes held at the end of the year, 43.3 percent (336.6 million) were held at the 125 institutions categorized under the 1994 Carnegie classification as Research I or Research II institutions. About 54.6 percent of the volumes were at those institutions classified as either Research or Doctoral in the Carnegie classification.

- In FY 1994, the median number of volumes added to collections per FTE student was 1.6. The median number added range from .6 per FTE in less than four-year institutions to 3.1 in doctorate-granting institutions.

### Staff

- There was a total of 95,843 FTE staff working in academic libraries in 1994. Of these about 26,726 (27.9 percent) were librarians or other professional staff; 40,381 (42.1 percent) were other paid staff; 326 (0.3 per-

---

*FTE enrollment is calculated by adding one-third of part-time enrollment to full-time enrollment. Enrollment data are from the 1993–94 IPEDS Fall Enrollment Survey.

cent) were contributed services staff; and 28,411 (29.6 percent) were student assistants.

- Excluding student assistants, the institutional median number of academic library FTE staff per 1,000 FTE students was 5.9. The median ranged from 3.6 in less than four-year institutions to 9.8 in doctorate-granting institutions.

**Expenditures**

- In 1994 total operating expenditures for libraries at the 3,303 institutions of higher education totaled $4.01 billion. The three largest individual expenditure items for all academic libraries were salaries and wages, $2.02 billion (50.4 percent); current serial subscription expenditures, $690.4 million (17.2 percent); and books and bound serials, $442.5 million (11.0 percent).

## School Library Media Centers

The following are highlights from the Executive Summary of *School Library Media Centers 1993–1994,* released in August 1998:

- Library media centers are now almost universally available. In 1993–1994, 96 percent of all public schools and 80 percent of all private schools had library media centers. This compares with 50 percent of the public schools in 1950, and 44 percent of private schools in 1962.
- Out of 164,650 school library staff, 44 percent were state-certified library media specialists, 20 percent were other non-certified professional librarians, and 36 percent were other staff.
- Library media centers spent about $828 million in 1992–1993, including federal gifts and grants but not including salaries and wages. For public schools, after adjusting for differences between the two surveys, expenditures were $676 million (in 1993 dollars) in 1985 and $738 million in 1992–1993. Private school expenditures were $61 million (in 1993 dollars) in 1985 and $89 million in 1993.
- School libraries had 879 million book volumes in their collections at the end of the 1992–1993 school year, or a mean of 28.0 books per student. They also had 2.6 million serial subscriptions, 13.3 million tape and disk video materials, 42.5 million other audiovisual materials, 5.4 million microcomputer software items, and 314,000 CD-ROMs. For public schools, the mean number of books per pupil was 5.3 in 1958 and 17.8 in 1993.
- Two-thirds (67 percent) of schools with library media centers had at least one microcomputer that was supervised by library media center staff. Among those centers with staff-supervised computers, the mean number of computers was 8.9. Other equipment and services found at library media centers included a telephone (57 percent), one or more CD-ROMs for such uses as periodical indices and encyclopedias (41 percent), an automated

circulation system (32 percent), a computer with modem (31 percent), database searching with CD-ROM (28 percent), one or more video laser disks (27 percent), an automated catalog (21 percent), a connection to the Internet (11 percent), and online database searching (9 percent).

- The total number of students using library media centers per week was 42.5 million in 1985 and 32.5 million in 1993–1994 in public schools, and 5.3 million in 1985 and 3.4 million in 1993–1994 in private schools. Over the same time period, total enrollment in public schools increased from 39.4 million to 43.5 million. The mean weekly circulation per pupil per school was 1.3 in 1993–1994 in public schools, and 0.9 in 1985 and 1.2 in 1993–1994 in private schools.

- About two-thirds (65 percent) of school head librarians were regular full-time employees at the schools in which they were surveyed, while 19 percent provided library services at more than one school, and 16 percent were employed part time.

- About half (52 percent) of school head librarians reported they earned a master's degree as their highest degree, while another 8 percent reported training beyond the master's level, either as an education specialist (7 percent) or with a doctorate or first-professional degree (1 percent).

- Head librarians generally expressed positive attitudes toward their schools, the library media centers, and their own personal roles. For example, 96 percent said students believed the library media center was a desirable place to be, 95 percent said their jobs as librarians had more advantages than disadvantages, and 89 percent said the school administration's behavior toward the library media center was supportive and encouraging.

- The median base salary of school head librarians was $30,536 during the 1993–1994 academic year, and their median annual earnings from all sources was $32,000.

- In 1993 public school districts employed 51,000 full-time-equivalent (FTE) school librarians, while another 800 FTE positions were either vacant or temporarily filled by a substitute. About 150 FTE positions were abolished or withdrawn because a suitable candidate could not be found, and 450 FTE positions were lost through layoffs at the end of the last school year.

## Children, Young Adults

The following are highlights from the report *Services and Resources for Children and Young Adults in Public Libraries (1995)*:

- Sixty percent of the 18 million people entering public libraries during a typical week in fall 1993 were youth—children and young adults.

- The percentage of libraries with children's and young adult librarians has not changed since the late 1980s. Thirty-nine percent of libraries employ a children's librarian, 11 percent have a young adult librarian, and 24 percent have a youth services specialist on staff.

- Librarians report that ethnic diversity of children and young adult patrons has increased in over 40 percent of U.S. public libraries over the last five years. Seventy-six percent of public libraries currently have children's materials and 64 percent have young adult materials in languages other than English.

- Although computer technologies are among the most heavily used children's and young adult resources in public libraries, they are also among the most scarce. Only 30 percent of public libraries reported the availability of personal computers for use by children and young adults. However, 75 percent of libraries having this resource report moderate to heavy use by young adults.

- Less than half of all public libraries (40 percent) offer group programs for infants and toddlers. These programs are more prevalent now than in 1988, when only 29 percent of libraries offered group programs for infants to two-year-olds. Eighty-six percent of libraries offer group programs, such as story times, booktalks, puppetry, and crafts, for preschool and kindergarten-age children; 79 percent of libraries offer group programs for school-age children.

- Seventy-six percent of public libraries report working with schools; 66 percent work with preschools and 56 percent with day care centers.

- While almost all libraries provide reference assistance, only about 1 in 7 libraries offer homework assistance programs for children or young adults. However, fairly large percentages of libraries with homework assistance programs report moderate to heavy use by children and young adults. Sixty-four percent report moderate to heavy use by young adults.

- Librarians report that insufficient library staff is a leading barrier to increasing services and resources for both children and young adults. Sixty-five percent of librarians consider this a moderate or major barrier to increasing services for children, and 58 percent consider lack of staff a barrier to increasing services for young adults.

## State Library Agencies

The following are highlights from *E.D. TABS State Library Agencies, Fiscal Year 1996*, released in June 1998:

### Governance

- Nearly all state agencies (48 states and the District of Columbia) are located in the executive branch of government. Of these, over 65 percent are part of a larger agency, the most common being the state department of education. In two states, Arizona and Michigan, the agency reports to the legislature.

### Allied and Other Special Operations

- A total of 16 state library agencies reported having one or more operations. Allied operations most frequently linked with a state library are the state archives (10 states), the state records management service (11 states).

- Fifteen state agencies contract with libraries in their states to serve as resource or reference/information service centers. Eighteen state agencies operate a State Center for the Book*.

**Electronic Network Development**

- In all 50 states, the state library agency plans or monitors electronic network development, 42 states operate such networks, and 46 states develop network content.
- All 50 states are involved in facilitating library access to the Internet in one or more of the following ways: training library staff or consulting in the use of the Internet; providing a subsidy for Internet participation; providing equipment needed to access the Internet; providing access to directories, databases, or online catalogs; or managing gopher/Web sites, file servers, bulletin boards, or listservs.

**Library Development Services**

Services to Public Libraries

- Every state agency provides these types of services to public libraries: administration of LSCA (Library Services and Construction Act) grants, collection of library statistics, continuing education, and library planning, evaluation, and research. Nearly every state library agency provides consulting services and continuing-education programs.
- Services to public libraries provided by at least three-quarters of state agencies include administration of state aid, interlibrary loan referral services, library legislation preparation or review, literacy program support, reference referral services, state standards or guidelines, public relations or promotional campaigns, summer reading program support, and union list development.
- Over three-fifths of state agencies provide Online Computer Library Center (OCLC) Group Access Capability (GAC) to public libraries and statewide public relations or library promotion campaigns.
- Less common services to public libraries include accreditation of libraries, certification of librarians, cooperative purchasing of library materials, preservation/conservation services, and retrospective conversion of bibliographic records.

Services to Academic Libraries

- At least two-thirds of state library agencies report the following services to the academic library sector: administration of LSCA Title III grants, continuing education, interlibrary loan referral services, reference referral services, and union list development.

---

*The State Center for the Book is part of the Center for the Book program sponsored by the Library of Congress which promotes books, reading, and literacy, and is hosted or funded by the state.

- Less common services to academic libraries provided by state agencies include cooperative purchasing of library materials, literacy program support, preservation/conservation, retrospective conversion, and state standards or guidelines. No state agency accredits academic libraries; only Washington state certifies academic librarians.

### Services to School Library Media Centers

- Two-thirds of all state library agencies provide continuing education and interlibrary loan referral services and reference referral services to school library media centers (LMCs). Services to LMCs provided by at least half of state agencies include administration of LSCA Title III grants, consulting services, and union list development.
- Less common services to LMCs include administration of state aid, cooperative purchasing of library materials, and retrospective conversion. No state agency accredits LMCs or certifies LMC librarians.

### Services to Special Libraries

- Over two-thirds of state agencies serve special libraries* through administration of LSCA grants, consulting services, continuing education, interlibrary loan referral, reference referral, and union list development.
- Less common services to special libraries include administration of state aid, cooperative purchasing of library materials, and summer reading program support. Only Nebraska accredits special libraries and only Washington state certifies librarians of special libraries.

### Services to Systems

- At least three-fifths of state agencies serve library systems† through administration of LSCA grants, consulting services, continuing education, library legislation preparation or review, and library planning, evaluation, and research.
- Accreditation of systems is provided by only six states and certification of librarians by only seven states.

### Service Outlets

- State library agencies reported a total of 153 service outlets. Main or central outlets and other outlets (excluding bookmobiles) made up 47.1 percent, and bookmobiles represented 5.9 percent of the total.

---

*A library in a business firm, professional association, government agency, or other organized group; a library that is maintained by a parent organization to serve a specialized clientele; or an independent library that may provide materials or services, or both, to the public, a segment of the public, or to other libraries. Scope of collections and services are limited to the subject interests of the host or parent institution. Includes libraries in state institutions.

†A system is a group of autonomous libraries joined together by formal or informal agreements to perform various services cooperatively such as resource sharing, communications, etc. Includes multitype library systems and public library systems. Excludes multiple outlets under the same administration.

## Collections

- The number of books and serial volumes held by state library agencies totaled 22.4 million, with New York accounting for the largest collection (2.4 million). Five state agencies had book and serial volumes of over one million. In other states, these collections ranged from 500,000 to one million (12 states); 200,000 to 499,999 (10 states); 100,000 to 199,999 (10 states); 50,000 to 99,999 (6 states); and 50,000 or less (6 states). The state library agency in Maryland does not maintain a collection, and the District of Columbia does not maintain a collection in its function as a state library agency.
- The number of serial subscriptions held by state library agencies totaled over 84,000, with New York holding the largest number (over 14,300). Ten state agencies reported serial subscriptions of over 2,000. In other states, these collections ranged from 1,000 to 1,999 (6 states), 500 to 999 (18 states), 100 to 499 (13 states), and under 100 (1 state).

## Staff

- The total number of budgeted full-time-equivalent (FTE) positions in state library agencies was 3,762. Librarians with ALA-MLS degrees accounted for 1,206 of these positions, or 32.1 percent of total FTE positions. Rhode Island reported the largest percentage (57.1) of ALA-MLS librarians, and Utah reported the lowest (16.3 percent).

## Income

- State library agencies reported a total income of $847.1 million in FY 1997 (83.1 percent came from state sources, 15.4 percent from federal, and 1.5 percent from other sources).
- Of state library agency income received from state sources, over $477 million (67.8 percent) was designated for state aid to libraries. Seven states had 75 percent or more of their income from state sources set aside for state aid. Georgia had the largest percentage of state library agency income set aside for state aid (97.4 percent). Six states and the District of Columbia targeted no state funds for aid to libraries. Hawaii, Iowa, South Dakota, Vermont, Washington, and the District of Columbia reported state income only for operation of the state agency.*

## Expenditures

- State library agencies reported total expenditures of over $822.2 million. The largest percentage (83.6 percent) came from state funds, followed by federal funds (15.3 percent), and other funds (1.1 percent).

*The District of Columbia Public Library functions as a state library agency and is eligible for Federal LSCA (Library Services and Construction Act) funds in this capacity. The state library agency in Hawaii is associated with the Hawaii State Public System and operates all public libraries within its jurisdiction. The state funds for aid to libraries for these two agencies are reported on the NCES Public Libraries Survey, rather than on the STLA survey, because of the unique situation of these two state agencies, and in order to eliminate duplicative reporting of these data.

- In five states, over 90 percent of total expenditures were from state sources. These states were Georgia (94.7 percent), Massachusetts (93.5 percent), Maryland (91.9 percent), New York (92 percent), and Illinois (92.4 percent). Utah had the lowest percentage of expenditures from state sources (59.2 percent), with most of its expenditures from federal sources.
- Almost 70 percent of total state library expenditures were for aid to libraries, with the largest percentages expended on individual public libraries (53.1 percent) and public library systems (16.4 percent). Most aid-to-libraries expenditures (86.2 percent) were from state sources, and 13.6 percent were from federal sources.
- Fifteen state library agencies reported expenditures for allied operations. These expenditures totaled over $24 million and represented 2.9 percent of total expenditures by state library agencies. Of states reporting allied operations expenditures, Texas reported the highest expenditure ($3.3 million) and Vermont the lowest ($398,000).*
- Twenty-seven state library agencies reported a total of over $16.7 million in grants and contracts expenditures to assist public libraries with state education reform initiatives or the National Education Goals. The area of adult literacy accounted for the largest proportion of such expenditures (47.7 percent), followed by the areas of lifelong learning (34.9 percent) and readiness for school (17.4 percent). Three state agencies (Nebraska, Oregon, and Pennsylvania) focused such expenditures exclusively on readiness for school projects, and five state agencies (Georgia, Kansas, New Jersey, Oklahoma, and Utah) focused their expenditures exclusively on adult literacy projects. In four states (Connecticut, Indiana, Michigan, and South Carolina), over two-thirds of such expenditures were for lifelong learning projects.

[For further information about statistics collected by the National Center for Education Statistics, see the article in Part 1—*Ed.*]

---

*Although Alaska reported allied operations, the expenditures are not from the state library agency budget.

# Library Acquisition Expenditures, 1997–1998: U.S. Public, Academic, Special, and Government Libraries

The information in these tables is taken from the 51st edition of the *American Library Directory* (*ALD*) (1998–1999), published by R. R. Bowker. The tables report acquisition expenditures by public, academic, special, and government libraries.

The total number of U.S. libraries listed in the 51st edition of *ALD* is 33,108, including 16,250 public libraries, 4,700 academic libraries, 9,898 special libraries, and 1,897 government libraries.

## Understanding the Tables

*Number of libraries* includes only those U.S. libraries in *ALD* that reported annual acquisition expenditures (4,443 public libraries, 1,761 academic libraries, 1,111 special libraries, 310 government libraries). Libraries that reported annual income but not expenditures are not included in the count. Academic libraries include university, college, and junior college libraries. Special academic libraries, such as law and medical libraries, that reported acquisition expenditures separately from the institution's main library are counted as independent libraries.

The amount in the *total acquisition expenditures* column for a given state is generally greater than the sum of the categories of expenditures. This is because the total acquisition expenditures amount also includes the expenditures of libraries that did not itemize by category.

Figures in *categories of expenditure* columns represent only those libraries that itemized expenditures. Libraries that reported a total acquisition expenditure amount but did not itemize are only represented in the total acquisition expenditures column.

*Unspecified* includes monies reported as not specifically for books, periodicals, audiovisual materials and equipment, microform, preservation, other print materials, manuscripts and archives, machine-readable materials, or database fees (e.g., library materials). This column also includes monies reported for categories in combination—for example, audiovisual *and* microform. When libraries report only total acquisition expenditures without itemizing by category, the total amount is not reflected as unspecified.

Table 1 / Public Library Acquisition Expenditures

| State | Number of Libraries | Total Acquisition Expenditures | Books | Other Print Materials | Periodicals | Manuscripts & Archives | AV Materials | AV Equipment | Microform | Machine Readable Materials | Preservation | Database Fees | Unspecified |
|---|---|---|---|---|---|---|---|---|---|---|---|---|---|
| Alabama | 78 | 6,641,301 | 3,150,912 | 285,032 | 457,747 | — | 416,913 | 8,390 | 376,881 | 87,502 | 19,947 | 108,289 | 621,431 |
| Alaska | 39 | 3,410,433 | 898,350 | 216,052 | 572,227 | — | 85,764 | 45,619 | 1,000 | 19,344 | 1,465 | 35,543 | 4,707 |
| Arizona | 69 | 12,833,750 | 5,417,983 | 184,027 | 1,237,520 | — | 539,089 | 1,900 | 211,447 | 488,478 | 107,111 | 233,743 | 26,070 |
| Arkansas | 27 | 2,975,626 | 1,184,897 | 5,290 | 115,053 | — | 64,716 | 13,407 | 44,692 | 18,484 | 18,591 | 56,053 | 5,047 |
| California | 151 | 69,278,683 | 31,733,375 | 455,415 | 5,766,820 | 42,036 | 4,132,315 | 31,428 | 951,701 | 1,768,329 | 318,813 | 2,290,933 | 2,287,671 |
| Colorado | 61 | 12,308,647 | 5,154,272 | 2,284 | 777,255 | 34,000 | 575,542 | 48,817 | 106,943 | 456,942 | 14,963 | 305,881 | 391,371 |
| Connecticut | 121 | 12,251,844 | 5,166,644 | 621,640 | 785,255 | 400 | 515,643 | 37,024 | 113,340 | 135,662 | 39,304 | 334,539 | 248,256 |
| Delaware | 14 | 1,213,140 | 619,624 | 600 | 106,005 | — | 64,291 | — | 25,283 | 26,500 | — | 31,054 | — |
| District of Columbia | 2 | 8,461,351 | — | — | — | — | — | — | — | — | — | — | — |
| Florida | 108 | 41,938,860 | 20,103,309 | 32,639 | 4,050,226 | 39,285 | 2,189,341 | 106,683 | 505,648 | 1,000,086 | 117,123 | 881,247 | 545,124 |
| Georgia | 39 | 15,025,954 | 3,778,138 | 18,698 | 249,788 | 5,808 | 674,190 | 20,487 | 120,777 | 98,808 | 21,987 | 28,986 | 7,474 |
| Hawaii | 2 | 2,400,529 | 1,749,579 | 429,154 | — | — | — | — | — | — | — | — | — |
| Idaho | 46 | 2,219,582 | 1,113,560 | 19,950 | 130,587 | — | 111,187 | 7,818 | 6,750 | 16,093 | 3,779 | 106,676 | 8,768 |
| Illinois | 325 | 53,076,630 | 17,946,592 | 569,961 | 2,789,915 | 3,010 | 2,623,309 | 285,385 | 549,079 | 1,166,717 | 167,706 | 959,865 | 294,787 |
| Indiana | 157 | 30,102,818 | 14,753,284 | 69,603 | 2,082,268 | — | 3,318,833 | 81,470 | 316,138 | 520,394 | 133,095 | 292,428 | 913,671 |
| Iowa | 208 | 8,659,635 | 4,868,927 | 53,724 | 754,282 | — | 627,504 | 43,305 | 57,361 | 75,784 | 7,255 | 83,220 | 621,576 |
| Kansas | 92 | 7,428,210 | 4,982,934 | 9,912 | 928,480 | 684 | 795,452 | 9,487 | 24,794 | 57,665 | 3,392 | 117,715 | 167,857 |
| Kentucky | 60 | 8,902,684 | 2,696,897 | 4,559 | 311,216 | 911 | 381,395 | 42,661 | 29,591 | 51,826 | 8,112 | 291,496 | 120,915 |
| Louisiana | 34 | 8,435,922 | 5,419,740 | 33,429 | 865,607 | — | 397,568 | 12,908 | 140,529 | 37,138 | 21,401 | 114,934 | 3,186 |
| Maine | 98 | 2,284,652 | 1,220,219 | 3,001 | 207,917 | 1,077 | 113,035 | 2,537 | 11,073 | 12,312 | 11,469 | 36,278 | 7,952 |
| Maryland | 22 | 25,395,423 | 10,272,203 | 281,723 | 953,290 | — | 2,310,236 | 6,960 | 59,133 | 818,066 | 1,229 | 387,556 | 506,594 |
| Massachusetts | 213 | 16,207,145 | 8,180,508 | 26,277 | 1,208,043 | 1,000 | 778,808 | 29,371 | 306,991 | 328,833 | 23,120 | 404,552 | 119,714 |
| Michigan | 196 | 27,435,701 | 12,959,169 | 90,676 | 1,699,427 | 3,300 | 1,691,345 | 64,458 | 200,085 | 661,346 | 10,969 | 334,750 | 584,891 |
| Minnesota | 87 | 15,027,465 | 5,780,147 | 15,782 | 1,233,733 | — | 1,238,665 | 3,870 | 38,600 | 296,000 | 15,107 | 219,977 | 65,550 |
| Mississippi | 38 | 4,205,210 | 2,282,930 | 14,017 | 346,081 | — | 184,906 | 6,470 | 51,935 | 136,839 | 3,042 | 28,440 | 14,328 |

| | | | | | | | | | | | | | |
|---|---|---|---|---|---|---|---|---|---|---|---|---|---|
| Missouri | 76 | 18,584,749 | 10,527,598 | 40,919 | 1,706,901 | 319 | 1,636,926 | 11,665 | 593,148 | 726,899 | 22,205 | 120,517 | 316,744 |
| Montana | 44 | 1,685,846 | 741,643 | 665 | 150,358 | — | 40,670 | 700 | 2,988 | 11,084 | 5,510 | 104,823 | 33,594 |
| Nebraska | 67 | 4,517,986 | 2,126,635 | 24,398 | 173,662 | 200 | 436,897 | 21,411 | 25,855 | 70,188 | 8,334 | 349,526 | 5,845 |
| Nevada | 18 | 6,457,282 | 4,334,324 | 500 | 745,465 | — | 331,395 | 2,119 | 27,722 | 38,072 | 7,246 | 54,512 | 22,500 |
| New Hampshire | 98 | 2,690,519 | 1,208,148 | 25,938 | 151,228 | — | 91,335 | 8,170 | 45,271 | 24,773 | 8,697 | 16,722 | 11,261 |
| New Jersey | 162 | 26,533,732 | 13,990,444 | 42,084 | 2,317,661 | 6,050 | 1,361,369 | 132,730 | 231,463 | 894,454 | 44,239 | 539,733 | 766,082 |
| New Mexico | 24 | 4,279,150 | 864,014 | 33,198 | 393,539 | — | 37,429 | 10,700 | 15,376 | 58,579 | 7,000 | 11,488 | 15,672 |
| New York | 291 | 65,945,321 | 29,313,855 | 1,049,313 | 5,739,767 | 9,300 | 3,251,947 | 556,400 | 862,142 | 969,853 | 176,056 | 475,321 | 411,331 |
| North Carolina | 85 | 16,647,882 | 6,990,284 | 71,436 | 1,028,868 | 5,435 | 798,527 | 62,452 | 200,949 | 231,096 | 76,189 | 55,188 | 162,791 |
| North Dakota | 19 | 1,107,688 | 625,468 | 11,200 | 147,880 | — | 49,929 | 1,000 | 20,000 | 20,354 | 5,000 | 6,000 | 3,135 |
| Ohio | 153 | 70,577,321 | 30,666,240 | 1,001,593 | 6,001,732 | 582 | 6,705,269 | 143,340 | 906,296 | 1,064,443 | 983,247 | 2,152,947 | 577,914 |
| Oklahoma | 36 | 6,685,421 | 3,294,772 | 114,312 | 703,031 | — | 375,350 | 41,193 | 29,426 | 49,763 | 26,283 | 252,862 | 800,579 |
| Oregon | 65 | 10,359,642 | 4,896,107 | 9,632 | 996,167 | — | 875,288 | 250 | 8,952 | 461,658 | 66,528 | 50,231 | 35,835 |
| Pennsylvania | 216 | 23,308,539 | 7,655,740 | 103,034 | 1,355,713 | 2,400 | 754,428 | 52,957 | 509,178 | 208,010 | 43,402 | 270,673 | 411,593 |
| Rhode Island | 30 | 2,452,764 | 1,154,759 | 10,723 | 214,570 | — | 122,115 | 8,950 | 33,057 | 94,581 | 6,228 | 135,846 | 7,491 |
| South Carolina | 34 | 11,478,472 | 5,730,501 | 1,500 | 842,280 | — | 469,027 | 39,269 | 202,553 | 201,660 | 37,430 | 75,441 | 350,079 |
| South Dakota | 36 | 1,626,703 | 599,089 | — | 119,886 | — | 50,843 | 18,404 | 29,135 | 5,136 | 600 | 260,827 | 3,369 |
| Tennessee | 61 | 9,285,508 | 3,198,722 | 38,068 | 518,042 | 6,000 | 447,665 | 52,000 | 105,437 | 154,595 | 86,630 | 105,071 | 3,185,276 |
| Texas | 211 | 33,351,322 | 14,910,523 | 246,017 | 2,245,855 | 5,000 | 1,669,330 | 203,976 | 425,630 | 605,516 | 145,575 | 398,896 | 318,816 |
| Utah | 27 | 4,530,385 | 3,016,516 | 1,972 | 234,874 | — | 453,945 | 1,311 | 29,158 | 106,420 | 6,000 | 177,735 | 24,960 |
| Vermont | 66 | 980,203 | 435,524 | — | 48,932 | — | 20,549 | 9,178 | 1,267 | 7,520 | 3,014 | 7,520 | 3,000 |
| Virginia | 71 | 23,351,826 | 14,720,026 | 107,267 | 2,827,895 | 4,021 | 835,639 | 131,808 | 254,389 | 342,363 | 515,959 | 395,020 | 399,509 |
| Washington | 41 | 18,121,584 | 5,526,798 | 150,997 | 901,274 | 100 | 762,633 | 25,996 | 29,732 | 145,983 | 30,779 | 487,074 | 132,728 |
| West Virginia | 38 | 2,369,848 | 903,822 | 344 | 348,558 | — | 89,769 | 7,894 | 6,138 | 24,148 | 17,850 | 877 | — |
| Wisconsin | 171 | 14,460,866 | 5,468,776 | 25,874 | 835,966 | — | 835,225 | 28,788 | 90,144 | 309,286 | 26,502 | 587,333 | 823,440 |
| Wyoming | 14 | 1,574,100 | 645,311 | — | 72,395 | — | 87,575 | 50 | 19,461 | 13,334 | 2,359 | 54,652 | 1,000 |
| Pacific Islands | 1 | 80,950 | 67,679 | — | 6,875 | — | 6,396 | — | — | — | — | — | — |
| Puerto Rico | 1 | 264,188 | 235,042 | — | 7,000 | — | 14,000 | — | 7,646 | — | 500 | — | — |
| Total | 4,443 | 781,430,992 | 345,284,684 | 6,125,275 | 58,894,807 | 170,918 | 46,442,200 | 2,483,166 | 8,962,284 | 15,118,916 | 3,428,342 | 14,830,990 | 16,391,484 |
| Estimated % of Acquisition Expenditure | | | 66.64 | 1.18 | 11.37 | 0.03 | 8.96 | 0.48 | 1.73 | 2.92 | 0.66 | 2.86 | 3.16 |

# Table 2 / Academic Library Acquisition Expenditures

| State | Number of Libraries | Total Acquisition Expenditures | Books | Other Print Materials | Periodicals | Manuscripts & Archives | AV Materials | AV Equipment | Microform | Machine Readable Materials | Preservation | Database Fees | Unspecified |
|---|---|---|---|---|---|---|---|---|---|---|---|---|---|
| | | | | | | | Categories of Expenditure (Amounts in U.S. Dollars) | | | | | | |
| Alabama | 28 | 7,269,396 | 2,374,865 | 23,988 | 2,745,121 | 3,500 | 94,891 | 67,356 | 157,686 | 212,768 | 103,810 | 141,195 | 568,782 |
| Alaska | 4 | 1,303,251 | 55,041 | 5,905 | 13,523 | — | 985 | — | 4,594 | 6,179 | 925 | — | — |
| Arizona | 12 | 4,445,899 | 1,183,136 | — | 1,232,311 | — | 102,970 | 44,200 | 160,780 | 69,250 | 85,787 | 253,899 | 1,156,772 |
| Arkansas | 17 | 5,306,874 | 1,274,047 | — | 1,969,497 | — | 111,947 | 20,394 | 216,605 | 206,431 | 88,890 | 84,534 | 43,067 |
| California | 119 | 99,175,161 | 23,000,766 | 1,406,043 | 57,476,582 | 500 | 593,447 | 266,599 | 1,207,017 | 1,471,520 | 1,552,816 | 1,454,328 | 1,811,106 |
| Colorado | 24 | 11,033,056 | 2,991,862 | 92,737 | 4,807,397 | — | 168,429 | 10,573 | 232,471 | 465,769 | 275,709 | 318,326 | 103,929 |
| Connecticut | 23 | 27,079,136 | 7,088,405 | 5,737,570 | 12,236,798 | — | 246,057 | 24,932 | 155,766 | 475,577 | 494,129 | 222,783 | 74,953 |
| Delaware | 5 | 5,470,854 | 2,031,980 | 32,000 | 3,202,953 | — | 3,679 | 15,292 | 17,283 | 28,075 | 1,100 | 14,200 | 124,292 |
| District of Columbia | 10 | 14,423,622 | 2,556,578 | 30,881 | 6,252,624 | 1,737 | 63,989 | 8,902 | 104,360 | 87,585 | 132,800 | 187,160 | 1,551,416 |
| Florida | 62 | 34,947,105 | 6,169,667 | 79,658 | 8,151,070 | 2,100 | 540,310 | 203,158 | 947,510 | 938,390 | 254,770 | 349,480 | 294,000 |
| Georgia | 41 | 21,912,361 | 6,027,579 | 77,186 | 11,531,593 | 32,500 | 241,271 | 84,725 | 1,294,279 | 657,481 | 173,392 | 364,368 | 589,483 |
| Hawaii | 10 | 5,466,039 | 760,844 | 25,114 | 412,970 | — | 86,809 | 157,880 | 188,620 | 24,116 | 256,200 | 83,670 | 2,912,142 |
| Idaho | 8 | 6,235,080 | 1,530,684 | — | 3,385,107 | 500 | 46,749 | 183,500 | 40,518 | 14,000 | 174,588 | 88,437 | 541,929 |
| Illinois | 75 | 63,196,192 | 16,798,879 | 2,916,784 | 26,350,348 | 4,450 | 568,154 | 958,682 | 790,340 | 1,117,817 | 892,197 | 1,108,394 | 3,323,959 |
| Indiana | 40 | 48,592,128 | 6,582,729 | 196,633 | 11,658,245 | 7,392 | 209,607 | 61,412 | 224,450 | 583,788 | 637,770 | 462,766 | 186,085 |
| Iowa | 35 | 21,318,770 | 3,544,803 | 153,616 | 6,071,124 | 250 | 165,771 | 130,728 | 159,705 | 242,833 | 325,971 | 188,162 | 128,173 |
| Kansas | 29 | 12,529,747 | 4,276,437 | 289,024 | 6,296,565 | 2,182 | 39,762 | 30,576 | 170,677 | 449,659 | 201,786 | 68,688 | 347,009 |
| Kentucky | 31 | 18,595,834 | 4,106,178 | 23,429 | 11,181,771 | 25,900 | 133,847 | 28,117 | 327,373 | 599,722 | 334,931 | 205,601 | 586,354 |
| Louisiana | 20 | 14,877,896 | 2,973,253 | 334,100 | 8,075,793 | 26,149 | 33,266 | 118,234 | 128,464 | 149,906 | 178,045 | 104,677 | 155,443 |
| Maine | 21 | 7,535,192 | 1,919,053 | 10,658 | 4,192,073 | — | 69,777 | 19,445 | 203,655 | 247,566 | 147,562 | 70,308 | 69,368 |
| Maryland | 31 | 18,253,246 | 3,844,345 | 60,039 | 6,488,833 | — | 187,057 | 92,552 | 417,690 | 524,144 | 369,180 | 205,489 | 814,337 |
| Massachusetts | 55 | 63,464,983 | 11,052,380 | 703,321 | 19,957,605 | 2,632 | 475,196 | 301,311 | 659,078 | 1,041,569 | 999,804 | 1,260,624 | 311,152 |
| Michigan | 52 | 38,379,262 | 7,534,445 | 268,432 | 11,032,796 | 13,064 | 348,057 | 130,075 | 749,244 | 856,967 | 617,689 | 630,628 | 637,897 |
| Minnesota | 30 | 20,023,465 | 5,498,606 | 1,025,889 | 9,962,960 | 12,517 | 179,706 | 73,476 | 178,408 | 403,313 | 208,484 | 231,866 | 391,369 |
| Mississippi | 27 | 11,807,904 | 2,098,202 | — | 6,104,965 | 3,547 | 285,115 | 91,416 | 354,191 | 311,058 | 194,286 | 153,378 | 428,914 |

| | | | | | | | | | | | | | |
|---|---|---|---|---|---|---|---|---|---|---|---|---|---|
| Missouri | 45 | 24,422,154 | 5,928,439 | 50,603 | 11,236,126 | 275 | 455,762 | 108,476 | 783,072 | 1,256,616 | 595,951 | 927,774 | 451,734 |
| Montana | 12 | 724,760 | 135,370 | 300 | 206,406 | — | 3,290 | — | 2,116 | 15,203 | 5,000 | 11,192 | 9,983 |
| Nebraska | 18 | 4,858,620 | 1,433,653 | 119,217 | 2,052,653 | 1,000 | 43,203 | 119,399 | 66,126 | 96,257 | 61,894 | 91,849 | 62,719 |
| Nevada | 5 | 7,115,911 | 1,104,414 | 1,359 | 1,874,316 | 30,000 | 92,757 | 44,958 | 101,286 | 256,369 | 120,727 | 37,878 | 106,047 |
| New Hampshire | 16 | 5,035,168 | 991,851 | 150,099 | 3,207,130 | — | 42,849 | 44,394 | 112,078 | 128,654 | 69,016 | 64,006 | 76,333 |
| New Jersey | 27 | 26,537,540 | 8,023,914 | 1,132,193 | 10,754,626 | 190,815 | 297,490 | 99,000 | 783,330 | 882,713 | 150,718 | 209,897 | 1,049,817 |
| New Mexico | 16 | 7,872,132 | 2,424,097 | 5,000 | 4,461,263 | — | 48,004 | 45,450 | 197,904 | 248,369 | 235,704 | 84,725 | 38,449 |
| New York | 122 | 88,329,035 | 19,952,888 | 2,274,670 | 35,404,931 | 14,503 | 938,655 | 183,355 | 2,253,868 | 3,511,674 | 1,939,278 | 2,087,385 | 3,849,586 |
| North Carolina | 75 | 38,713,667 | 9,648,506 | 77,745 | 13,317,778 | 7,350 | 752,171 | 550,698 | 915,982 | 1,262,334 | 379,580 | 678,516 | 473,069 |
| North Dakota | 6 | 1,571,709 | 366,626 | 17,217 | 1,010,506 | — | 37,172 | 6,318 | 52,452 | 15,260 | 434 | 54,658 | 10,425 |
| Ohio | 70 | 36,444,706 | 10,331,695 | 476,432 | 17,806,747 | — | 465,755 | 209,893 | 633,982 | 873,159 | 628,457 | 432,535 | 490,303 |
| Oklahoma | 30 | 13,289,512 | 2,204,029 | 104,566 | 5,141,682 | 7,100 | 79,740 | 130,104 | 388,257 | 342,413 | 229,178 | 424,453 | 214,204 |
| Oregon | 34 | 14,202,557 | 3,766,883 | 26,531 | 6,984,977 | 500 | 157,675 | 98,473 | 391,567 | 577,446 | 200,612 | 398,257 | 197,204 |
| Pennsylvania | 109 | 67,765,090 | 15,165,512 | 804,158 | 24,773,571 | 24,850 | 683,248 | 317,953 | 1,046,722 | 2,086,567 | 1,650,142 | 1,076,919 | 1,282,238 |
| Rhode Island | 11 | 4,639,806 | 1,016,098 | 71,001 | 995,684 | 4,494 | 55,531 | 33,885 | 95,429 | 127,377 | 39,505 | 103,108 | 67,782 |
| South Carolina | 33 | 15,208,546 | 4,352,437 | 66,636 | 8,042,482 | 310 | 103,204 | 30,550 | 372,788 | 438,725 | 428,757 | 149,445 | 186,609 |
| South Dakota | 11 | 4,381,046 | 980,885 | — | 1,764,644 | — | 40,152 | 36,001 | 50,016 | 312,447 | 63,395 | 106,127 | 369,209 |
| Tennessee | 41 | 23,891,879 | 4,925,516 | 455,344 | 13,904,685 | 2,550 | 210,238 | 138,578 | 430,765 | 482,841 | 301,750 | 485,790 | 1,420,865 |
| Texas | 94 | 56,476,703 | 12,270,581 | 122,738 | 20,050,176 | 50,437 | 1,184,764 | 365,742 | 1,537,780 | 2,946,206 | 924,560 | 1,667,364 | 1,061,601 |
| Utah | 8 | 4,749,668 | 1,419,501 | 500 | 2,344,644 | 1,502 | 134,104 | 74,554 | 67,315 | 186,019 | 161,627 | 166,838 | 131,987 |
| Vermont | 18 | 7,436,122 | 2,239,338 | 500 | 3,976,448 | 700 | 84,089 | 55,046 | 162,681 | 139,273 | 118,428 | 421,401 | 21,334 |
| Virginia | 39 | 31,238,549 | 8,873,002 | 138,592 | 13,282,773 | 52,350 | 498,308 | 244,248 | 785,989 | 1,435,102 | 418,327 | 339,543 | 508,055 |
| Washington | 35 | 25,289,034 | 7,234,496 | 5,750 | 11,841,726 | 2,500 | 224,896 | 173,281 | 343,404 | 567,859 | 211,074 | 365,309 | 54,250 |
| West Virginia | 19 | 4,079,304 | 1,133,278 | 46,885 | 1,503,197 | — | 47,849 | 159,236 | 178,352 | 145,328 | 35,514 | 61,388 | 329,541 |
| Wisconsin | 45 | 15,720,348 | 4,470,255 | 33,191 | 6,552,068 | 4,300 | 399,964 | 68,405 | 567,685 | 964,245 | 261,605 | 428,610 | 644,127 |
| Wyoming | 4 | 2,986,283 | 505,865 | 17,398 | 1,975,586 | — | 19,607 | 4,044 | 2,500 | — | 71,919 | 23,876 | 309,316 |
| Pacific Islands | 3 | 861,787 | 243,721 | 1,500 | 480,781 | — | 16,350 | 12,590 | 43,210 | 32,455 | — | 21,180 | — |
| Puerto Rico | 5 | 817,745 | 331,218 | — | 344,000 | — | 57,250 | 40,000 | 20,687 | 19,207 | 4,283 | 1,100 | — |
| Virgin Islands | 1 | 56,300 | 28,000 | — | 23,000 | — | — | — | 5,000 | — | — | 300 | — |
| Totals | 1,761 | 1,117,358,134 | 258,776,832 | 19,693,132 | 466,105,230 | 534,456 | 12,170,925 | 6,518,166 | 21,483,107 | 30,535,601 | 18,010,056 | 19,174,384 | 30,568,718 |
| Estimated % of Acquisition Expenditure | | | 29.29 | 2.23 | 52.75 | 0.06 | 1.38 | 0.74 | 2.43 | 3.46 | 2.04 | 2.17 | 3.46 |

Table 3 / Special Library Acquisition Expenditures

| State | Number of Libraries | Total Acquisition Expenditures | Books | Other Print Materials | Periodicals | Manuscripts & Archives | AV Materials | AV Equipment | Microform | Machine Readable Materials | Preservation | Database Fees | Unspecified |
|---|---|---|---|---|---|---|---|---|---|---|---|---|---|
| | | | | | | | | | | Categories of Expenditure (Amounts in U.S. Dollars) | | | |
| Alabama | 5 | 84,645 | 14,000 | — | 400 | 945 | — | 500 | 31,000 | 15,000 | 1,500 | — | — |
| Alaska | 2 | 16,000 | 10,000 | — | 5,000 | — | — | — | — | — | — | — | — |
| Arizona | 24 | 1,406,285 | 168,580 | 12,700 | 304,120 | 700 | 2,225 | 2,742 | 500 | 22,895 | 12,200 | 68,813 | 3,000 |
| Arkansas | 1 | 7,100 | 5,500 | — | 1,000 | 100 | — | — | — | — | 500 | — | — |
| California | 102 | 7,248,797 | 1,286,617 | 112,354 | 2,123,106 | 4,990 | 49,701 | 1,318,388 | 55,995 | 68,344 | 58,236 | 438,922 | 31,529 |
| Colorado | 24 | 1,255,437 | 249,460 | 4,000 | 599,490 | 33,400 | 19,050 | 1,600 | 25,000 | 82,900 | 7,900 | 119,200 | 51,145 |
| Connecticut | 25 | 1,658,523 | 258,470 | 27,000 | 632,570 | — | 17,025 | 2,506 | 18,575 | 54,009 | 22,130 | 205,300 | 4,346 |
| Delaware | 3 | 228,525 | 37,000 | — | 72,000 | — | 3,500 | 18,000 | 4,500 | — | 8,700 | 22,000 | 14,000 |
| District of Columbia | 27 | 5,285,600 | 1,201,073 | 423,150 | 931,190 | — | 1,000 | 550 | 7,000 | 9,600 | 11,450 | 184,884 | 1,175,842 |
| Florida | 36 | 1,478,728 | 244,187 | 7,050 | 253,665 | 4,450 | 9,502 | 23,359 | 26,640 | 41,950 | 25,018 | 144,730 | 8,500 |
| Georgia | 22 | 1,183,261 | 255,804 | 2,000 | 360,989 | — | 21,344 | 10,000 | 9,614 | 35,000 | 16,516 | 15,828 | — |
| Hawaii | 7 | 302,037 | 38,981 | — | 131,372 | — | — | — | — | 4,200 | 177 | 12,607 | — |
| Idaho | 7 | 335,191 | 35,200 | 60,000 | 60,600 | — | — | — | — | 10,000 | 178 | — | — |
| Illinois | 74 | 5,089,750 | 1,276,797 | 215,207 | 1,107,072 | 21,465 | 39,497 | 17,209 | 75,135 | 66,100 | 25,600 | 204,870 | 71,504 |
| Indiana | 33 | 1,883,215 | 144,694 | 3,100 | 323,348 | — | 12,225 | 8,050 | 37,000 | 43,321 | 1,475 | 244,812 | 310 |
| Iowa | 22 | 1,100,882 | 490,993 | 2,000 | 252,245 | — | 7,385 | 1,000 | 2,650 | 5,650 | 11,494 | 13,857 | — |
| Kansas | 11 | 162,351 | 45,304 | 3,600 | 92,792 | 150 | — | 5,650 | 5,500 | — | 3,550 | 5,455 | — |
| Kentucky | 11 | 669,971 | 53,364 | — | 143,560 | — | 2,000 | — | 15,000 | — | 1,200 | 125 | — |
| Louisiana | 7 | 373,076 | 20,500 | 425 | 168,000 | — | 7,751 | — | — | 3,000 | — | 3,400 | — |
| Maine | 14 | 814,518 | 81,013 | 2,218 | 221,834 | — | 20,225 | 680 | — | 800 | 2,920 | 145,605 | 890 |
| Maryland | 34 | 2,913,498 | 575,738 | 64,350 | 1,050,722 | 6,550 | 12,817 | 8,000 | 89,351 | 43,265 | 38,042 | 562,259 | 5,190 |
| Massachusetts | 46 | 4,390,037 | 758,056 | 6,024 | 1,294,279 | 6,725 | 33,729 | 11,577 | 26,179 | 17,161 | 55,795 | 144,446 | 136,097 |
| Michigan | 36 | 2,999,120 | 556,749 | 10,523 | 1,363,641 | — | 24,142 | 20,715 | 14,406 | 97,553 | 1,352 | 225,343 | 36,361 |
| Minnesota | 19 | 746,600 | 234,680 | 19,000 | 104,320 | 3,900 | 8,100 | 8,200 | 10,500 | 20,500 | 5,100 | 12,600 | 8,000 |
| Mississippi | 3 | 123,828 | 8,000 | — | 112,090 | — | 200 | 100 | 238 | — | 200 | 3,000 | — |

| State | No. | | | | | | | | | | | | |
|---|---|---|---|---|---|---|---|---|---|---|---|---|---|
| Missouri | 21 | 5,064,452 | 534,400 | 1,139 | 3,062,368 | 300 | 4,505 | — | 8,300 | 48,617 | 95,103 | 918,452 | 14,466 |
| Montana | 6 | 65,138 | 11,576 | — | 18,396 | — | 573 | — | — | — | — | 2,716 | 308 |
| Nebraska | 10 | 237,238 | 22,951 | 525 | 40,800 | 2,000 | 1,025 | — | 39,102 | — | — | 390 | 8,000 |
| Nevada | 4 | 101,600 | 17,000 | 1,000 | 33,000 | — | — | — | — | — | 2,600 | — | — |
| New Hampshire | 11 | 1,041,265 | 244,058 | 4,000 | 453,870 | 5,000 | 3,100 | 15,350 | 210 | 54,800 | 16,500 | 24,764 | 33,844 |
| New Jersey | 37 | 2,622,565 | 869,080 | 2,664 | 696,114 | 3,000 | 17,374 | 8,828 | 47,464 | 119,800 | 15,150 | 85,738 | 475 |
| New Mexico | 9 | 219,050 | 77,950 | — | 97,225 | — | 2,800 | 700 | — | 500 | — | 9,250 | 145,189 |
| New York | 94 | 12,172,197 | 1,635,066 | 22,855 | 1,541,336 | 19,370 | 64,123 | 45,645 | 28,022 | 81,000 | 66,985 | 4,148,703 | — |
| North Carolina | 18 | 595,263 | 221,750 | 2,000 | 192,836 | — | 3,000 | 10,000 | — | — | 3,700 | 30,000 | 3,199 |
| North Dakota | 1 | 14,608 | 7,283 | — | 3,707 | — | — | — | — | — | 419 | — | 17,660 |
| Ohio | 45 | 4,556,393 | 1,125,602 | 20,402 | 1,243,821 | — | 25,803 | 3,569 | 70,628 | 84,035 | 22,671 | 412,243 | — |
| Oklahoma | 5 | 374,908 | 55,437 | — | 243,471 | — | 2,500 | — | 5,000 | 24,500 | 500 | 13,500 | — |
| Oregon | 11 | 284,208 | 61,297 | 1,500 | 83,125 | — | 8,279 | — | 4,000 | 9,300 | 773 | 18,100 | 24,857 |
| Pennsylvania | 59 | 4,122,756 | 602,917 | 345,000 | 1,151,594 | 59,817 | 25,056 | 8,044 | 58,825 | 84,036 | 60,913 | 89,155 | 2,842 |
| Rhode Island | 5 | 154,478 | 50,017 | — | 88,986 | — | 1,902 | — | — | 1,803 | 2,388 | 4,540 | 9,400 |
| South Carolina | 11 | 649,046 | 96,000 | 165 | 75,000 | — | 11,300 | 5,000 | 16,000 | 6,100 | 8,600 | 7,700 | — |
| South Dakota | 3 | 24,700 | 800 | — | 400 | — | — | — | — | — | — | — | 964 |
| Tennessee | 17 | 453,271 | 120,050 | 2,068 | 248,651 | 30 | 3,090 | 40 | 4,942 | 13,196 | 7,072 | 45,370 | 65,040 |
| Texas | 43 | 4,698,018 | 898,191 | 84,886 | 2,068,555 | 17,300 | 37,879 | 12,583 | 23,509 | 113,276 | 30,029 | 192,628 | — |
| Utah | 4 | 833,700 | 500,300 | — | — | — | 100 | — | 150,000 | 100,000 | 80,000 | 80,000 | 1,192 |
| Vermont | 6 | 147,713 | 8,919 | 271 | 16,087 | 2,045 | — | — | 280 | — | 2,312 | 4,469 | 24,431 |
| Virginia | 44 | 2,393,895 | 302,534 | 45,255 | 446,973 | 63,406 | 19,556 | 11,165 | 24,000 | 66,466 | 16,886 | 38,810 | 2,000 |
| Washington | 18 | 2,616,941 | 141,042 | 5,337 | 579,839 | 7,250 | 5,113 | 7,800 | 600 | 137,000 | 4,146 | 18,020 | 14,215 |
| West Virginia | 6 | 579,249 | 80,114 | 1,000 | 449,785 | — | 22,850 | 7,000 | 7,000 | — | — | 6,100 | — |
| Wisconsin | 22 | 1,166,971 | 546,221 | 18,000 | 327,579 | 4,100 | 3,589 | 15,000 | 7,050 | 77,845 | 9,550 | 27,600 | — |
| Wyoming | 3 | 78,500 | 300 | — | 200 | — | — | — | — | — | — | — | — |
| Pacific Islands | 1 | 135,893 | — | — | — | — | — | — | — | — | — | — | — |
| Puerto Rico | 2 | 471,000 | 106,800 | — | 344,200 | — | 12,000 | — | — | — | 8,000 | — | — |
| Total | 1,111 | 87,631,991 | 16,388,415 | 1,532,768 | 25,217,323 | 266,993 | 566,935 | 1,602,550 | 949,715 | 1,667,222 | 761,830 | 8,876,304 | 1,914,796 |
| Estimated % of Acquisition Expenditure | | | 27.43 | 2.57 | 42.21 | 0.45 | 0.95 | 2.68 | 1.59 | 2.79 | 1.28 | 14.86 | 3.20 |

## Table 4 / Government Library Acquisition Expenditures

| State | Number of Libraries | Total Acquisition Expenditures | Books | Other Print Materials | Periodicals | Manuscripts & Archives | AV Materials | AV Equipment | Microform | Machine Readable Materials | Preservation | Database Fees | Unspecified |
|---|---|---|---|---|---|---|---|---|---|---|---|---|---|
| | | | | | | | Categories of Expenditure (Amounts in U.S. Dollars) | | | | | | |
| Alabama | 6 | 707,960 | 331,190 | — | 124,989 | — | 11,000 | — | — | 7,453 | 9,158 | 118,510 | — |
| Alaska | 6 | 48,500 | 11,800 | 700 | 28,700 | — | 600 | 100 | 200 | 1,500 | 300 | — | 3,000 |
| Arizona | 8 | 468,799 | 233,874 | — | 8,388 | 500 | — | — | — | 3,751 | 2,223 | 2,300 | 24,247 |
| Arkansas | 2 | 386,200 | 5,000 | — | 235,200 | — | — | — | 2,000 | — | — | 144,000 | — |
| California | 34 | 7,123,626 | 1,601,813 | 172,378 | 1,018,608 | — | 84,533 | 29,528 | 136,779 | 181,946 | 175,011 | 90,949 | 13,672 |
| Colorado | 8 | 803,343 | 140,399 | 6,496 | 442,040 | — | 20,568 | 18,211 | 16,600 | 103,200 | — | 48,751 | 1,500 |
| Connecticut | 3 | 87,000 | 10,000 | — | 20,000 | 1,000 | 2,300 | 3,000 | 5,000 | 10,000 | — | — | — |
| Delaware | 1 | 89,623 | 88,673 | — | — | — | — | — | — | — | 950 | — | — |
| District of Columbia | 14 | 2,753,150 | 241,700 | 44,700 | 495,100 | 3,400 | 28,500 | 10,500 | 68,400 | 89,000 | 13,750 | 122,500 | — |
| Florida | 32 | 2,129,076 | 482,305 | 4,700 | 618,149 | 3,000 | 20,148 | — | 16,995 | 32,000 | 1,500 | 33,916 | 6,165 |
| Hawaii | 4 | 764,836 | 274,488 | 423,033 | 12,900 | 5,000 | — | — | 2,326 | 13,398 | 2,000 | 1,691 | — |
| Idaho | 2 | 291,000 | 4,000 | — | 36,000 | — | 170 | — | — | 1,100 | — | 3,000 | — |
| Illinois | 14 | 4,872,985 | 1,221,205 | — | 637,608 | — | 2,600 | 1,260 | 28,000 | 62,900 | 31,600 | 78,000 | — |
| Indiana | 4 | 133,000 | 50,000 | — | 48,000 | — | — | — | — | — | — | — | — |
| Iowa | 2 | 67,300 | 12,000 | — | 43,000 | — | 400 | 400 | — | 10,000 | 800 | 700 | — |
| Kansas | 5 | 841,862 | 261,359 | 225,056 | 253,850 | 700 | 3,000 | 6,300 | 4,800 | 5,000 | 7,593 | 17,204 | — |
| Kentucky | 3 | 564,759 | 375,169 | — | 2,950 | — | — | — | 9,895 | — | 2,700 | 7,700 | 8,863 |
| Louisiana | 4 | 3,082,100 | 17,000 | 400 | 95,000 | — | 600 | — | — | 3,000 | 300 | 12,700 | — |
| Maine | 1 | 251,156 | — | — | — | — | — | — | — | — | — | — | — |
| Maryland | 9 | 5,823,654 | 140,750 | 2,000 | 41,050 | — | 800 | 2,500 | — | 200 | 4,000 | 37,500 | — |
| Massachusetts | 10 | 2,693,235 | 1,976,424 | — | 163,373 | — | 2,000 | 1,550 | 8,046 | 550 | 1,385 | 5,000 | 4,000 |
| Michigan | 6 | 490,415 | 50,150 | 4,550 | 126,285 | — | 11,600 | 500 | 4,100 | 9,100 | — | 16,430 | 17,500 |
| Minnesota | 5 | 616,162 | 49,643 | 229,000 | 210,575 | — | — | — | 12,264 | 33,260 | 12,000 | 68,720 | — |
| Mississippi | 5 | 350,990 | 3,700 | — | — | — | — | — | — | — | — | — | — |
| Missouri | 2 | 317,000 | — | — | — | — | — | — | — | — | — | — | — |

| State | | | | | | | | | | | | | |
|---|---|---|---|---|---|---|---|---|---|---|---|---|---|
| Montana | 4 | 312,725 | 10,045 | 1,720 | 38,952 | — | — | — | 3,177 | — | 250 | 6,400 | 431 |
| Nebraska | 1 | 24,000 | — | — | — | — | — | — | — | — | — | — | — |
| Nevada | 3 | 717,941 | 495,873 | — | 21,656 | — | — | — | 4,918 | 6,340 | 4,737 | 67,659 | — |
| New Hampshire | 1 | 38,000 | 35,500 | — | 2,500 | — | — | — | — | — | — | — | — |
| New Jersey | 1 | 10,000 | 10,000 | — | — | — | — | — | — | — | — | — | — |
| New Mexico | 5 | 428,000 | 14,000 | 164,000 | 68,200 | — | — | — | 1,000 | 15,000 | 12,000 | 60,300 | — |
| New York | 20 | 2,095,438 | 749,561 | 6,300 | 607,117 | 1,100 | 9,754 | 800 | 3,725 | 15,680 | 17,300 | 6,300 | 5,210 |
| North Carolina | 4 | 672,209 | 391,455 | — | 253,130 | — | 500 | 300 | 7,130 | 11,083 | — | — | 4,546 |
| North Dakota | 1 | 53,800 | 2,000 | 27,000 | 18,500 | — | — | 800 | — | 5,500 | — | — | — |
| Ohio | 12 | 842,132 | 641,012 | 69,051 | 46,567 | — | 3,000 | — | 4,285 | 10,575 | — | 4,000 | 5,761 |
| Oklahoma | 3 | 106,738 | 2,563 | — | 100,900 | — | — | 1,000 | — | 275 | 1,000 | 1,000 | — |
| Oregon | 4 | 759,602 | 98,017 | — | 378,829 | — | 11,381 | — | — | 166,411 | — | 29,552 | 6,142 |
| Pennsylvania | 9 | 1,310,550 | 857,250 | 46,500 | 5,000 | — | — | — | — | — | 7,600 | 5,300 | — |
| Rhode Island | 1 | 72,508 | 6,109 | — | 53,277 | — | 2,968 | — | 1,307 | 3,177 | — | 2,134 | — |
| South Carolina | 4 | 209,202 | — | — | — | — | — | 500 | — | — | — | 54,355 | — |
| South Dakota | 4 | 114,318 | 26,931 | — | 69,408 | — | 7,837 | 342 | 3,200 | — | — | 800 | 800 |
| Tennessee | 4 | 239,412 | 28,618 | 200 | 83,902 | — | 6,731 | — | 6,000 | — | — | 46,746 | 24,615 |
| Texas | 5 | 295,719 | 16,815 | — | 35,798 | 117 | 1,000 | — | — | 29,000 | 20,478 | 448 | 6,480 |
| Utah | 2 | 200,854 | 26,419 | — | 128,841 | — | 6,886 | — | — | 8,821 | 5,420 | 11,268 | — |
| Vermont | 1 | 29,597 | — | — | — | — | — | — | — | — | — | — | — |
| Virginia | 7 | 561,140 | 66,275 | 500 | 183,400 | — | 1,800 | — | 7,000 | 83,500 | 3,000 | 89,700 | — |
| Washington | 8 | 1,748,660 | 14,704 | — | 31,373 | — | 11,533 | — | 4,603 | 5,180 | 11,000 | 4,750 | — |
| West Virginia | 5 | 565,900 | 343,360 | 3,260 | 73,440 | 550 | 2,762 | 1,500 | 20,500 | 1,200 | 3,500 | 34,416 | 12,042 |
| Wisconsin | 9 | 442,645 | 102,250 | 25 | 165,170 | — | 5,000 | — | 1,000 | 3,200 | — | 30,000 | — |
| Wyoming | 1 | 190,000 | 160,000 | — | 10,000 | — | — | — | 2,400 | — | — | — | — |
| Puerto Rico | 1 | 45,000 | 4,000 | — | 15,000 | — | 500 | — | — | — | — | — | 4,500 |
| Totals | 310 | 47,843,821 | 11,685,399 | 1,431,569 | 7,052,725 | 15,367 | 260,471 | 79,091 | 385,650 | 932,300 | 351,555 | 1,264,699 | 149,474 |
| Estimated % of Acquisition Expenditure | | 49.50 | 6.06 | 29.87 | 0.07 | 1.10 | 0.34 | 1.63 | 3.95 | 1.49 | 5.36 | 0.63 | |

# Price Indexes for Public and Academic Libraries

Research Associates of Washington,
1200 North Nash Street, No. 225, Arlington, VA 22209
703-243-3399

Kent Halstead

A rise in prices with the gradual loss of the dollar's value has been a continuing phenomenon in the U.S. economy. This article reports price indexes measuring this inflation for public libraries, college and university academic libraries, and school libraries. (Current data for these indexes are published annually by Research Associates of Washington. See *Inflation Measures for Schools, Colleges and Libraries, 1998 Update.*) Price indexes report the year-to-year price level of what is purchased. Dividing past expenditures per user unit by index values determines if purchasing power has been maintained. Future funding requirements to offset expected inflation may be estimated by projecting the indexes.

A price index compares the aggregate price level of a fixed market basket of goods and services in a given year with the price in the base year. To measure price change accurately, the *quality* and *quantity* of the items purchased must remain constant as defined in the base year. Weights attached to the importance of each item in the budget are changed infrequently—only when the relative *amount* of the various items purchased clearly shifts or when new items are introduced.

## Public Library Price Index

The Public Library Price Index (PLPI) is designed for a hypothetical *average* public library. The index together with its various subcomponents are reported in Tables 2 through 6. The PLPI reflects the relative year-to-year price level of the goods and services purchased by public libraries for their current operations. The budget mix shown in Table 1 is based on national and state average expenditure patterns. Individual libraries may need to tailor the weighting scheme to match their own budget compositions.

The Public Library Price Index components are described below together with sources of the price series employed.

### Personnel Compensation

PL1.0 Salaries and Wages

PL1.1 *Professional libraries*—Average salary of professional librarians at medium and large size libraries. Six positions are reported: director, deputy/associate/assistant director, department head/branch head, reference/information librarian, cataloger and/or classifier and children's and/or young adult services librarian. Source: Mary Jo Lynch, Margaret Myers, and Jeniece Guy, *ALA Survey of Librarian Salaries,* Office for Research and Statistics, American Library Association, Chicago, IL, annual.

*(text continues on page 474)*

**Table 1 / Taxonomy of Public Library Current Operations Expenditures by Object Category, 1991–1992 estimate**

| Category | Mean | Percent | Distribution |
|---|---|---|---|
| *Personnel Compensation* | | | 64.7 |
| PL1.0 Salaries and Wages | | 81.8 | |
|   PL1.1 Professional librarians | 44 | | |
|   PL1.2 Other professional and managerial staff | 6 | | |
|   PL1.3 Technical staff (copy cataloging, circulation, binding, etc.) | 43 | | |
|   PL1.4 Support staff (clerical, custodial, guard, etc.) | 7 | | |
| | 100 | | |
| PL2.0 Fringe Benefits | | 18.2 | |
| | | 100.0 | |
| *Acquisitions* | | | 15.2 |
| PL3.0 Books and Serials | | 74.0 | |
|   PL3.1 Books printed | 82 | | |
|     PL3.1a Hardcover | | | |
|     PL3.1b Trade paper | | | |
|     PL3.1c Mass market paper | | | |
|   PL3.2 Periodicals (U.S. and foreign titles) | 16 | | |
|     PL3.2a U.S. titles | | | |
|     PL3.2b Foreign titles | | | |
|   PL3.3 Other serials (newspapers, annuals, proceedings, etc.) | 2 | | |
| | 100 | | |
| PL4.0 Other Printed Materials | | 2.0 | |
| PL5.0 Non-Print Media | | 22.0 | |
|   PL5.1 Microforms (microfiche and microfilm) | 21 | | |
|   PL5.2 Audio recordings (primarily instructional and children's content) | 17 | | |
|     PL5.2a Tape cassette | | | |
|     PL5.2b Compact disk | | | |
|   PL5.3 Video (TV) recordings (primarily books & children's content) | 58 | | |
|     PL5.3a VHS Cassette | | | |
|     PL5.3b Laser disk | | | |
|   PL5.4 Graphic image individual item use | 2 | | |
|   PL5.5 Computer files (CD-ROM, floppy disks, and tape) | 2 | | |
| | 100 | | |
| PL6.0 Electronic Services | | 2.0 | |
| | | 100.0 | |
| *Operating Expenses* | | | 20.1 |
| PL7.0 Office Operations | | 27.0 | |
|   PL7.1 Office expenses | 20 | | |
|   PL7.2 Supplies and materials | 80 | | |
| | 100 | | |
| PL8.0 Contracted Services | | 38.0 | |
| PL9.0 Non-capital Equipment | | 1.0 | |
| PL10.0 Utilities | | 34.0 | |
| | | 100.0 | 100.0 |

Table 2 / Public Library Price Index and Major Component Subindexes, FY 1992 to 1997

| 1992=100 Fiscal year | Personnel Compensation | | Acquisitions | | | | Operating Expenses | | | | Public Library Price Index^ (PLPI) |
|---|---|---|---|---|---|---|---|---|---|---|---|
| | Salaries and wages (PL1.0) | Fringe benefits (PL2.0) | Books and serials (PL3.0) | Other printed materials (PL4.0) | Non-print media (PL5.0) | Electronic services (PL6.0) | Office operations (PL7.0) | Contracted services (PL8.0) | Non-capital Equipment (PL9.0) | Utilities (PL10.0) | |
| 1992 | 100.0 | 100.0 | 100.0 | 100.0 | 100.0 | 100.0 | 100.0 | 100.0 | 100.0 | 100.0 | 100.0 |
| 1993 | 102.5 | 104.8 | 101.7 | 102.9 | 75.3 | 101.9 | 99.2 | 102.6 | 101.8 | 101.5 | 101.5 |
| 1994 | 105.8 | 107.9 | 103.4 | 105.5 | 65.8 | 104.8 | 100.8 | 105.1 | 103.6 | 105.8 | 104.1 |
| 1995 | 110.5 | 110.6 | 104.7 | 107.7 | 64.8 | 108.5 | 102.6 | 107.7 | 105.7 | 103.8 | 107.2 |
| 1996 | 112.3 | 113.9 | 108.8 | 111.3 | 67.8 | 110.3 | 113.9 | 113.3 | 108.5 | 100.0 | 109.7 |
| 1997 | 114.6 | 116.1 | 115.1 | 118.5 | 69.5 | 110.3 | 113.3 | 114.1 | 110.3 | 113.7 | 113.2 |
| 1993 | 2.50% | 4.80% | 1.70% | 2.90% | -24.71% | 1.90% | -.80% | 2.60% | 1.80% | 1.50% | 1.50% |
| 1994 | 3.20% | 3.00% | 1.70% | 2.50% | -12.61% | 2.80% | 1.60% | 2.40% | 1.70% | 4.20% | 2.60% |
| 1995 | 4.40% | 2.50% | 1.20% | 2.10% | -1.41% | 3.50% | 1.70% | 2.50% | 2.10% | -1.90% | 2.90% |
| 1996 | 1.60% | 3.00% | 3.90% | 3.30% | 4.70% | 1.70% | 11.10% | 3.30% | 2.60% | -3.60% | 2.40% |
| 1997 | 2.10% | 1.90% | 5.90% | 6.50% | 2.50% | 0.00% | -0.50% | 2.60% | 1.70% | 13.70% | 3.10% |

^ PLPI weightings: See text.

Sources: See text.

# Table 3 / Public Library Price Index, Personnel Compensation, FY 1992 to 1997

| 1992=100 | Salaries and wages. | | | | | | | Fringe benefits index (PL2.0) |
| | Professional librarians | | | Other professional & managerial (PL1.2) | Technical staff (PL1.3) | Support staff (PL1.4) | Salaries & wages index* (PL1.0) | |
| Fiscal year | Medium size library~ | Large size library~ | Index^ (PL1.1) | | | | | |
|---|---|---|---|---|---|---|---|---|
| 1992 | 100.0 | 100.0 | 100.0 | 100.0 | 100.0 | 100.0 | 100.0 | 100.0 |
| 1993 | 105.0 | 99.5 | 102.3 | 102.8 | 102.7 | 102.8 | 102.5 | 104.8 |
| 1994 | 109.2 | 102.7 | 106.0 | 105.7 | 105.7 | 106.0 | 105.8 | 107.9 |
| 1995 | 115.5 | 106.9 | 111.2 | 109.5 | 110.1 | 109.1 | 110.5 | 110.6 |
| 1996 | 113.7 | 108.9 | 111.3 | 112.9 | 113.2 | 112.1 | 112.3 | 113.9 |
| 1997 | 119.2 | 112.0 | 115.6 | 115.6 | 113.6 | 113.9 | 114.6 | 116.1 |
| 1993 | 5.0% | -0.5% | 2.3% | 2.8% | 2.7% | 2.8% | 2.5% | 4.8% |
| 1994 | 4.0% | 3.2% | 3.6% | 2.8% | 2.9% | 3.1% | 3.2% | 3.0% |
| 1995 | 5.8% | 4.1% | 5.0% | 3.6% | 4.2% | 2.9% | 4.4% | 2.5% |
| 1996 | -1.6% | 1.9% | 0.1% | 3.1% | 2.8% | 2.7% | 1.6% | 3.0% |
| 1997 | 4.8% | 2.8% | 3.9% | 2.4% | 0.4% | 1.6% | 2.1% | 1.9% |

~ medium size libraries have service areas from 25,000 to 99,999 population; large libraries, 100,000 or more.

^ Professional librarian salary weights: 50% medium libraries + 50% large libraries.

* Salaries and wages index weights: 44% professional librarians + 6% other professional + 43% technical staff +7% support staff.

Sources: See text.

Table 4 / Public Library Price Index, Books and Serials, FY 1992 to 1997

Books and Serials

| Fiscal year (1992=100) | Books printed | | | | | | | Periodicals | | | | | | Other serials (newspapers) | | Books & Serials index** (PL3.0) | Other printed materials index (PL4.0) |
|---|---|---|---|---|---|---|---|---|---|---|---|---|---|---|---|---|---|
| | Hardcover | | Trade paper | | Mass market | | Books printed index* (PL3.1) | United States | | Foreign | | Periodicals index~ (PL3.2) | | Other serials | | | |
| | Price^ | Index (PL3.1a) | Price^ | Index (PL3.1b) | Price^ | Index (PL3.1c) | | Price^ | Index (PL3.2a) | Price^ | Index (PL3.2b) | | Price^^ | Index (PL3.3) | | | |
| 1992 | $12.85 | 100.0 | $7.24 | 100.0 | $2.71 | 100.0 | 100.0 | $45.17 | 100.0 | $117.71 | 100.0 | 100.0 | $222.68 | 100.0 | 100.0 | 100.0 |
| 1993 | 12.98 | 101.0 | 7.40 | 102.2 | 2.79 | 103.0 | 101.2 | 46.97 | 104.0 | 123.71 | 105.1 | 104.1 | 229.92 | 103.3 | 101.7 | 102.9 |
| 1994 | 13.16 | 102.4 | 7.59 | 104.8 | 2.85 | 105.2 | 102.7 | 47.15 | 104.4 | 133.48 | 113.4 | 105.5 | 261.91 | 117.6 | 103.4 | 105.5 |
| 1995 | 13.19 | 102.6 | 7.75 | 107.0 | 2.98 | 110.0 | 103.2 | 49.14 | 108.8 | 144.31 | 122.6 | 110.5 | 270.22 | 121.3 | 104.7 | 107.7 |
| 1996 | 13.56 | 105.5 | 8.23 | 113.7 | 3.32 | 122.5 | 106.6 | 51.58 | 114.2 | 158.67 | 134.8 | 116.7 | 300.21 | 134.8 | 108.8 | 111.3 |
| 1997 | 14.43 | 112.3 | 8.54 | 118.0 | 3.55 | 131.0 | 113.2 | 53.70 | 118.9 | 170.09 | 144.5 | 122.0 | 311.77 | 140.0 | 115.1 | 118.5 |
| 1993 | | 1.0% | | 2.2% | | 3.0% | 1.2% | | 4.0% | | 5.1% | 4.1% | | 3.3% | 1.7% | 2.9% |
| 1994 | | 1.4% | | 2.6% | | 2.2% | 1.5% | | 0.4% | | 7.9% | 1.3% | | 13.9% | 1.7% | 2.5% |
| 1995 | | 0.2% | | 2.1% | | 4.6% | 0.5% | | 4.2% | | 8.1% | 4.7% | | 3.2% | 1.2% | 2.1% |
| 1996 | | 2.8% | | 6.2% | | 11.4% | 3.3% | | 5.0% | | 10.0% | 5.6% | | 11.1% | 3.9% | 3.3% |
| 1997 | | 6.4% | | 3.8% | | 6.9% | 6.2% | | 4.1% | | 7.2% | 4.5% | | 3.9% | 5.9% | 6.5% |

^ Book and periodical prices are for calendar year. *Books printed index weights: 89.5% hardcover + 8.2% trade paper + 2.3% mass market.

~ Periodical index weights: 87.9% U.S.titles + 12.1% foreign titles.

^^Other serials prices are for calendar year.

** Books & serials index weights: 82% books + 16% periodicals + 2% other serials.

Sources: See text.

**Table 5 / Public Library Price Index, Non-Print Media and Electronic Services, FY 1992 to 1997**

| | | | | | | | Non-Print Media | | | | | | | |
|---|---|---|---|---|---|---|---|---|---|---|---|---|---|---|
| | Microforms (microfilm) | Audio recordings | | | | | Video | | | Graphic image | Computer files (CD-ROM) | | Non-print media index* | Electronic services index |
| | | Tape cassette | | Compact disc | | Audio recordings index* | VHS cassette | | Video index | | | | | |
| 1992=100 Fiscal year | Index (PL5.1) | Price^ | Index (PL5.2a) | Price^ | Index (PL5.2b) | (PL5.2) | Price^ | Index (PL5.3a) | (PL5.3) | (PL5.4) | Price^ | Index (PL5.5) | (PL5.0) | (PL6.0) |
| 1992 | 100.0 | $12.18 | 100.0 | n/a | n/a | 100.0 | $199.67 | 100.0 | 100.0 | 100.0 | $1,601 | 100.0 | 100.0 | 100.0 |
| 1993 | 104.3 | 11.73 | 96.3 | n/a | n/a | 96.3 | 112.92 | 56.6 | 56.6 | 97.3 | 1,793 | 112.0 | 75.3 | 101.9 |
| 1994 | 107.9 | 8.20 | 67.3 | $13.36 | 67.3 | 67.3 | 93.22 | 46.7 | 46.7 | 108.4 | 1,945 | 121.5 | 65.8 | 104.8 |
| 1995 | 110.6 | 8.82 | 72.4 | 14.80 | 74.6 | 73.5 | 84.19 | 42.2 | 42.2 | 111.3 | 1,913 | 119.5 | 64.8 | 108.5 |
| 1996 | 128.0 | 7.96 | 65.4 | 14.86 | 74.9 | 70.1 | 83.48 | 41.8 | 41.8 | 114.5 | 1,988 | 124.2 | 67.8 | 110.3 |
| 1997 | 132.9 | 8.13 | 66.7 | 16.43 | 82.8 | 74.8 | 82.10 | 41.1 | 41.1 | 126.5 | 2,012 | 125.7 | 69.5 | 110.3 |
| 1993 | 4.3% | | -3.7% | | | -3.7% | | -43.4% | -43.4% | -2.7% | | 12.0% | -24.7% | 1.9% |
| 1994 | 3.5% | | -30.1% | | | -30.1% | | -17.4% | -17.4% | 11.4% | | 8.5% | -12.6% | 2.8% |
| 1995 | 2.5% | | 7.6% | | 10.80% | 9.2% | | -9.7% | -9.7% | 2.7% | | -1.6% | -1.5% | 3.5% |
| 1996 | 15.7% | | -9.8% | | 0.04% | -4.6% | | -0.8% | -0.8% | 2.9% | | 3.9% | 4.7% | 1.7% |
| 1997 | 3.8% | | 2.1% | | 10.60% | 6.6% | | -1.7% | -1.7% | 10.5% | | 1.2% | 2.5% | 0.0% |

^ Prices are for immediate preceding calendar year, e.g., CY 1993 prices are reported for FY 1994.

* Audio recordings index weights: 50% tape cassette + 50% compact disk. Non-print media index weights: 21% microforms + 17% audio recordings +58% video + 2% graphic image + 2% computer files.

Sources: See text

Table 6 / Public Library Price Index, Operating Expenses, FY 1992 to 1997

| 1992=100 | Office Operations | | Office operations index^ (PL7.0) | Contracted services index (PL8.0) | Noncapital equipment index (PL9.0) | Utilities index (PL10.0) |
|---|---|---|---|---|---|---|
| Fiscal year | Office expenses (PL7.1) | Supplies and materials (PL7.2) | | | | |
| 1992 | 100.0 | 100.0 | 100.0 | 100.0 | 100.0 | 100.0 |
| 1993 | 103.1 | 98.3 | 99.2 | 102.6 | 101.8 | 101.5 |
| 1994 | 107.3 | 99.2 | 100.8 | 105.1 | 103.6 | 105.8 |
| 1995 | 111.1 | 100.4 | 102.6 | 107.7 | 105.7 | 103.8 |
| 1996 | 117.8 | 112.9 | 113.9 | 111.3 | 108.5 | 100.0 |
| 1997 | 120.0 | 111.6 | 113.3 | 114.1 | 110.3 | 113.7 |
| 1993 | 3.10% | -1.70% | -.80% | 2.60% | 1.80% | 1.50% |
| 1994 | 4.10% | 1.00% | 1.60% | 2.40% | 1.70% | 4.20% |
| 1995 | 3.50% | 1.20% | 1.70% | 2.50% | 2.10% | -1.90% |
| 1996 | 6.10% | 12.40% | 11.10% | 3.30% | 2.60% | -3.60% |
| 1997 | 1.80% | -1.20% | -0.50% | 2.60% | 1.70% | 13.70% |

^ Office operations index weights: 20% office expenses + 80% supplies and materials.
Sources: See text.

*(text continued from page 468)*

PL1.2 *Other professional and managerial staff* (systems analyst, business manager, public relations, personnel, etc.)—Employment Cost Index (ECI) for wages and salaries for state and local government workers employed in "Executive, administrative, and managerial" occupations, *Employment Cost Index*, Bureau of Labor Statistics, U.S. Department of Labor, Washington, DC.

PL1.3 *Technical staff* (copy cataloging, circulation, binding, etc.)—ECI as above for government employees in "Service" occupations.

PL1.4 *Support staff* (clerical, custodial, guard, etc.)—ECI as above for government employees in "Administrative support, including clerical" occupations.

PL2.0 Fringe Benefits

ECI as above for state and local government worker "Benefits."

### Acquisitions

PL3.0 Books and Serials

PL3.1 *Books printed*—Weighted average of sale prices (including jobber's discount) of hardcover (PL3.1a), trade paper (PL3.1b), and mass market paperback books (PL3.1c) sold to public libraries. Excludes university press publications and reference works. Source: Frank Daly, Baker & Taylor Books, Bridgewater, NJ.

PL3.2 *Periodicals*—Publisher's prices of sales of approximately 2,400 U.S. serial titles (PL3.2a) and 115 foreign serials (PL3.2b) sold to public libraries. Source: *Serials Prices*, EBSCO Subscription Services, Birmingham, AL.

PL3.3 *Other serials* (newspapers, annuals, proceedings, etc.)—Average prices of approximately 170 U.S. daily newspapers. Source: Genevieve S. Owens, University of Missouri, St. Louis, and Wilba Swearingen, Louisiana State University Medical Center. Reported by Adrian W. Alexander, "Prices of U.S. and Foreign Published Materials," in The *Bowker Annual*, R. R. Bowker, New Providence, NJ.

PL4.0 Other Printed Materials (manuscripts, documents, pamphlets, sheet music, printed material for the handicapped, etc.)

No direct price series exists for this category. The proxy price series used is the Producer Price Index for publishing pamphlets and catalogs and directories, Bureau of Labor Statistics.

PL5.0 Non-Print Media

PL5.1 *Microforms*—Producer Price Index for micropublishing in microform, including original and republished material, Bureau of Labor Statistics.

PL5.2 *Audio recordings*

PL5.2a *Tape cassette*—Cost per cassette of sound recording. Source: Dana Alessi, Baker & Taylor Books, Bridgewater, NJ. Reported by Alexander in The *Bowker Annual*, R. R. Bowker, New Providence, NJ.

PL5.2b *Compact disk*—Cost per compact disk. Source: See Alessi above.

PL5.3 *Video (TV) recordings*

PL5.3a. *VHS cassette*—Cost per video. Source: See Alessi above.

PL5.3b. *Laser disk*—No price series currently available.

PL5.4 *Graphic image* (individual use of such items as maps, photos, art work, single slides, etc.). The following proxy is used. Average median weekly earnings for the following two occupational groups: painters, sculptors, craft artists, and artist printmakers; and photographers. Source: *Employment and Earnings Series*, U.S. Bureau of Labor Statistics

PL5.5 *Computer files* (CD-ROM, floppy disks, and tape). Average price of CD-ROM disks. Source: Martha Kellogg and Theodore Kellogg, University of Rhode Island. Reported by Alexander in The *Bowker Annual*, R. R. Bowker, New Providence, NJ.

PL6.0 Electronic Services

Average price for selected digital electronic computer and telecommunications networking available to libraries. Source: This source has requested anonymity.

**Operating Expenses**

PL7.0 Office Operations

PL7.1 *Office expenses* (telephone, postage and freight, publicity and printing, travel, professional fees, automobile operating cost, etc.)—The price series used for office expenses consists of the subindex for printed materials (PL4.0) described above; Consumer Price Index values for telephone and postage; CPI values for public transportation; the IRS allowance for individual business travel as reported by Runzheimer International; and CPI values for college tuition as a proxy for professional fees.

PL7.2 *Supplies and materials*—Producer Price Index price series for office supplies, writing papers, and pens and pencils. Source: U.S. Bureau of Labor Statistics.

PL8.0 Contracted Services (outside contracts for cleaning, building and grounds maintenance, equipment rental and repair, acquisition processing, binding, auditing, legal, payroll, etc.)

Prices used for contracted services include ECI wages paid material handlers, equipment cleaners, helpers, and laborers; average weekly earnings of production or non-supervisory workers in the printing and publishing industry, and the price of printing paper, as a proxy for binding costs; ECI salaries of attorneys, directors of personnel, and accountant, for contracted consulting fees; and ECI wages of precision production, craft, and repair occupations for the costs of equipment rental and repair.

PL9.0 Non-Capital Equipment

The type of equipment generally purchased as part of current library operations is usually small and easily movable. To be classified as "equipment" rather than as "expendable utensils" or "supplies," an item generally must cost $50 or more and have a useful life of at least three years. Examples may be hand calculators, small TVs, simple cameras, tape recorders, pagers, fans, desk lamps, books, etc. Equipment purchased as an operating expenditure is usually not depreciated. Items priced for this category include PPI commodity price series for machinery and equipment, office and store machines/equipment, hand tools, cutting tools and accessories, scales and balances, electrical measuring instruments, television receivers, musical instruments, photographic equipment, sporting and athletic goods, and books and periodicals.

PL10.0 Utilities

This subindex is a composite of the Producer Price Index series for natural gas, residual fuels, and commercial electric power, and the Consumer Price Index series for water and sewerage services. Source: U.S. Bureau of Labor Statistics.

## Academic Library Price Indexes

The two academic library price indexes—the University Library Price Index (ULPI) and the College Library Price Index (CLPI)—together with their various subcomponents are reported in Tables 8–12A. The two indexes report the relative year-to-year price level of the staff salaries, acquisitions, and other goods and services purchased by university and college libraries respectively for their current operations. Universities are the 500 institutions with doctorate programs responding to the National Center for Education Statistics, U.S. Department of Education, *Academic Library Survey*. Colleges are the 1,472 responding institutions with master's and baccalaureate programs.

The composition of the library budgets involved, defined for pricing purposes, and the 1992 estimated national weighting structure are presented in Table 7. The priced components are organized in three major divisions: personnel compensation; acquisitions; and contracted services, supplies, and equipment.

The various components of the University and College Library Price Indexes are described in this section. Different weightings for components are designated in the tables "UL" for university libraries, "CL" for college libraries, and "AL" common for both types. Source citations for the acquisitions price series are listed.

### UL1.0 and CL1.0 Salaries and Wages

AL1.1 *Administrators* consists of the chief, deputy associate, and assistant librarian, e.g., important staff members having administrative responsibilities for management of the library. Administrators are priced by the head librarian salary series reported by the College and University Personnel Association (CUPA).

AL1.2 *Librarians* are all other professional library staff. Librarians are priced by the average of the median salaries for circulation/catalog, acquisition, technical service, and public service librarians reported by CUPA.

AL1.3 *Other professionals* are personnel who are not librarians in positions normally requiring at least a bachelor's degree. This group includes curators, archivists, computer specialists, budget officers, information and system specialists, subject bibliographers, and media specialists. Priced by the Higher Education Price Index (HEPI) faculty salary price series (H1.1) as a proxy.

AL1.4 *Nonprofessional staff* includes technical assistants, secretaries, and clerical, shipping, and storage personnel who are specifically assigned to the library and covered by the library budget. This category excludes general custodial and maintenance workers and student employees. This staff category is dominated by office-type workers and is priced by the HEPI clerical workers price series (H2.3) reported by the BLS Employment Cost Index.

AL1.5 *Students* are usually employed part-time for near minimum hourly wages. In some instances these wages are set by work-study program requirements of the institution's student financial aid office. The proxy price series used for student wages is the Employment Cost Index series for non-farm laborers, U.S. Bureau of Labor Statistics.

### AL2.0 Fringe Benefits

The fringe benefits price series for faculty used in the HEPI is employed in pricing fringe benefits for library personnel.

### UL3.0 and CL3.0 Books and Serials

UL3.1a *Books printed, universities.* Book acquisitions for university libraries are priced by the North American Academic Books price series reporting the average list price of approximately 60,000 titles sold to college and university libraries by four of the largest book vendors. Compiled by Stephen Bosch, University of Arizona.

CL3.1a *Books printed, colleges.* Book acquisitions for college libraries are priced by the price series for U.S. College Books representing approximately 6,300 titles compiled from book reviews appearing in *Choice* during the calendar year. Compiled by Donna Alsbury, Florida Center for Library Automation.

AL3.1b *Foreign Books.* Books with foreign titles *and* published in foreign countries are priced using U.S. book imports data. William S. Lofquist, U.S. Department of Commerce.

AL3.2a *Periodicals, U.S. titles.* U.S. periodicals are priced by the average subscription price of approximately 2,100 U.S. serial titles purchased by college and university libraries reported by EBSCO Subscription Services, Birmingham, AL.

AL3.2b *Periodicals, Foreign.* Foreign periodicals are priced by the average subscription price of approximately 600 foreign serial titles purchased by college and university libraries reported by EBSCO Subscription Services.

AL3.3 *Other Serials* (newspapers, annuals, proceedings, etc.). Average prices of approximately 170 U.S. daily newspapers. Source: Genevieve S. Owens, University of Missouri, St. Louis, and Wilba Swearingen, Louisiana State University Medical Center. Reported by Adrian W. Alexander, "Prices of U.S. and Foreign Published Materials," in The *Bowker Annual*, R. R. Bowker, New Providence, NJ.

## Other Printed Materials

These acquisitions include manuscripts, documents, pamphlets, sheet music, printed material for the handicapped, and so forth. No direct price series exists for this category. The proxy price series used is the Producer Price Index (PPI) for publishing pamphlets (PC 2731-9) and catalogs and directories (PCU2741#B), Bureau of Labor Statistics, U.S. Department of Labor.

## AL5.0 Non-Print Media

AL5.1 *Microforms.* Producer Price Index for micropublishing in microform, including original and republished material (PC 2741-597), Bureau of Labor Statistics.

AL5.2 *Audio recordings*
AL5.2a *Tape cassette*—Cost per cassette of sound recording. Source: Dana Alessi, Baker & Taylor Books, Bridgewater, NJ. Reported by Alexander in The *Bowker Annual*, R. R. Bowker, New Providence, NJ.
AL5.2b *Compact Disc*—Cost per compact disc. Source: See Alessi above.

AL5.3 *Video (TV) recordings*
PL5.3a *VHS cassette*—cost per video. Source: See Alessi above.

AL5.4 *Graphic image* (individual use of such items as maps, photos, art work, single slides, etc.). No direct price series exists for graphic image materials.

Average median weekly earnings for two related occupational groups (painters, sculptors, craft artists; artist printmakers; and photographers) is used as a proxy. these earnings series are reported in *Employment and Earnings Series*, U.S. Bureau of Labor Statistics.

AL5.5 *Computer files* (CD-ROM floppy disks, and tape). Average price of CD-ROM disks; primarily bibliographic, abstracts, and other databases of interest to academic libraries. Source: Developed from *Faxon Guide to CD-ROM* by Martha Kellogg and Theodore Kellogg, University of Rhode Island. Reported by Alexander in The *Bowker Annual*, R. R. Bowker, New Providence, NJ.

### AL6.0 Electronic Services

Average price for selected digital electronic computer and telecommunications networking available to libraries. The source of this price series has requested anonymity.

### AL7.0 Binding/Preservation

In-house maintenance of the specialized skills required for binding is increasingly being replaced by contracting out this service at all but the largest libraries. No wage series exists exclusively for binding. As a proxy, the Producer Price Index (PPI) for bookbinding and related work (PC 2789) is used. Source: Bureau of Labor Statistics, U.S. Department of Labor.

### AL8.0 Contracted Services

Services contracted by libraries include such generic categories as communications, postal service, data processing, and printing and duplication. The HEPI contracted services subcomponent (H4.0), which reports these items, is used as the price series. (In this instance the data processing component of H4.0 generally represents the library's payment for use of a central campus computer service.) However, libraries may also contract out certain specialized activities such as ongoing public access cataloging (OPAC) that are not distinctively priced in this AL8.0 component.

### AL9.0 Supplies and Materials

Office supplies, writing papers, and pens and pencils constitute the bulk of library supplies and materials and are priced by these BLS categories for the Producer Price Index, Bureau of Labor Statistics, U.S. Department of Labor.

### AL10.0 Equipment

This category is limited to small, easily movable, relatively inexpensive and short-lived items that are not carried on the books as depreciable capital equipment. Examples can include personal computers, hand calculators, projectors, fans, cameras, tape recorders, small TVs, etc. The HEPI equipment price series (H6.0) has been used for pricing.

**Table 7 / Budget Composition of University Library and College Library Current Operations by Object Category, FY 1992 Estimate**

| Category | | University Libraries Percent Distribution | | College Libraries Percent Distribution |
|---|---|---|---|---|
| *Personnel Compensation* | | | | |
| 1.0 Salaries and wages | | 43.4 | | 47.2 |
| 1.1 Administrators (head librarian) | | 10 | | 25 |
| 1.2 Librarians | | 20 | | 15 |
| 1.3 Other professionals^ | | 10 | | 5 |
| 1.4 Nonprofessional staff | | 50 | | 40 |
| 1.5 Students hourly employed | | 10 | | 15 |
| | | 100.0 | | 100.0 |
| 2.0 Fringe benefits | | 10.6 | | 11.5 |
| *Acquisitions* | | | | |
| 3.0 Books and Serials | | 28.5 | | 24.8 |
| 3.1 Books printed | | 35 | | 47 |
| 3.1a U.S. titles | 80 | | 95 | |
| 3.1b Foreign titles | 20 | | 5 | |
| 3.2 Periodicals | | 60 | | 48 |
| 3.2a U.S. titles | 80 | | 95 | |
| 3.2b Foreign titles | 20 | | 5 | |
| 3.3 Other serials (newspapers, annuals, proceedings, etc.) | | 5 | | 5 |
| | | 100.0 | | 100 |
| 4.0 Other Printed Materials* | | 1.2 | | 0.7 |
| 5.0 Non-Print Media | | 1.6 | | 3.3 |
| 5.1 Microforms (microfiche and microfilm) | | 45 | | 45 |
| 5.2 Audio recordings | | 5 | | 5 |
| 5.2a Tape cassette | | | | |
| 5.2b Compact disc (CDs) | | | | |
| 5.3 Video (TV) VHS recordings | | 15 | | 15 |
| 5.4 Graphic image individual item use~ | | 5 | | 5 |
| 5.5 Computer materials (CD-ROM, floppy disks, and tape) | | 30 | | 30 |
| | | 100.0 | | 100.0 |
| 6.0. Electronic Services^^ | | 4.0 | | 3.5 |
| *Contracted Services, Supplies, Equipment* | | | | |
| 7.0 Binding/preservation | | 1.3 | | 0.8 |
| 8.0 Services** | | 4.4 | | 3.1 |
| 9.0 Supplies and materials | | 3.1 | | 2.6 |
| 10.0 Equipment (non-capital)# | | 1.9 | | 2.5 |
| | | 100.0 | | 100 |

^ Other professional and managerial staff includes systems analyst, business manager, public relations, personnel, etc.
* Other printed materials includes manuscripts, documents, pamphlets, sheet music, printed material for the handicapped, etc.
~ Graphic image individual item use includes maps, photos, art work, single slides, etc.
^^Electronic services includes software license fees, network intra-structure costs, terminal access to the Internet, desktop computer operating budget, and subscription services.
**Contracted services includes outside contracts for communications, postal service, data processing, printing and duplication, equipment rental and repair, acquisition processing, etc.
# Relatively inexpensive items not carried on the books as depreciable capital equipment. Examples include microform and audiovisual equipment, personal computers, hand calculators, projectors, fans, cameras, tape recorders, and small TVs.
Source: Derived, in part, from data published in *Academic Libraries: 1992*, National Center for Education Statistics, USDE.

## Table 8 / University Library Price Index and Major Component Subindexes, FY 1992 to 1997

| 1992=100 Fiscal year | Personnel Compensation | | Books and serials (UL3.0) | Acquisitions | | | Binding/ preser- vation (AL7.0) | Operating Expenses | | | University Library Price Index^ ULPI |
|---|---|---|---|---|---|---|---|---|---|---|---|
| | Salaries and wages (UL1.0) | Fringe benefits (AL2.0) | | Other printed materials (AL4.0) | Non- print media (AL5.0) | Electronic services (AL6.0) | | Contracted services (AL8.0) | Supplies and material (AL9.0) | Equip- ment (AL10.0) | |
| 1992 | 100.0 | 100.0 | 100.0 | 100.0 | 100.0 | 100.0 | 100.0 | 100.0 | 100.0 | 100.0 | 100.0 |
| 1993 | 103.2 | 105.4 | 106.1 | 102.9 | 98.7 | 101.9 | 100.5 | 102.6 | 98.3 | 101.8 | 103.9 |
| 1994 | 106.5 | 110.5 | 113.1 | 105.5 | 100.8 | 104.8 | 101.2 | 106.2 | 99.2 | 103.6 | 108.2 |
| 1995 | 110.0 | 114.2 | 121.5 | 107.7 | 102.1 | 108.5 | 102.9 | 108.4 | 100.4 | 105.7 | 112.9 |
| 1996 | 113.4 | 115.8 | 131.7 | 111.3 | 110.3 | 110.3 | 107.1 | 112.4 | 112.9 | 108.5 | 118.4 |
| 1997 | 117.0 | 117.0 | 141.6 | 118.5 | 113.7 | 110.3 | 108.9 | 114.8 | 111.6 | 110.3 | 123.2 |
| 1993 | 3.2% | 5.4% | 6.1% | 2.9% | -1.3% | 1.9% | 0.5% | 2.6% | -1.7% | 1.8% | 3.9% |
| 1994 | 3.1% | 4.8% | 6.6% | 2.5% | 2.1% | 2.8% | 0.7% | 3.5% | 0.9% | 1.8% | 4.2% |
| 1995 | 3.4% | 3.4% | 7.4% | 2.1% | 1.3% | 3.5% | 1.7% | 2.1% | 1.2% | 2.0% | 4.4% |
| 1996 | 3.2% | 1.4% | 8.4% | 3.3% | 8.1% | 1.7% | 4.1% | 3.7% | 12.5% | 2.6% | 4.9% |
| 1997 | 3.1% | 1.0% | 7.5% | 6.5% | 3.1% | 0.0% | 1.7% | 2.1% | -1.2% | 1.7% | 4.0% |

^ ULPI weights: See table 3-A.

Sources: See text.

Table 9 / College Library Price Index and Major Component Subindexes, FY 1992 to 1997

| 1992=100 Fiscal year | Personnel Compensation | | Acquisitions | | | | | Operating Expenses | | | College Library Price Index^ CLPI |
|---|---|---|---|---|---|---|---|---|---|---|---|
| | Salaries and wages (CL1.0) | Fringe benefits (AL2.0) | Books and serials (CL3.0) | Other printed materials (AL4.0) | Non-print media (AL5.0) | Electronic services (AL6.0) | Binding/ preser- vation (AL7.0) | Contracted services (AL8.0) | Supplies and material (AL9.0) | Equip- ment (AL10.0) | |
| 1992 | 100.0 | 100.0 | 100.0 | 100.0 | 100.0 | 100.0 | 100.0 | 100.0 | 100.0 | 100.0 | 100.0 |
| 1993 | 103.5 | 105.4 | 107.5 | 102.9 | 98.7 | 101.9 | 100.5 | 102.6 | 98.3 | 101.8 | 104.2 |
| 1994 | 106.5 | 110.5 | 114.4 | 105.5 | 100.8 | 104.8 | 101.2 | 106.2 | 99.2 | 103.6 | 108.3 |
| 1995 | 110.0 | 114.2 | 119.4 | 107.7 | 102.1 | 108.5 | 102.9 | 108.4 | 100.4 | 105.7 | 112.0 |
| 1996 | 113.8 | 115.8 | 126.8 | 111.3 | 110.3 | 110.3 | 107.1 | 112.4 | 112.9 | 108.5 | 116.8 |
| 1997 | 117.5 | 117.0 | 136.0 | 118.5 | 113.7 | 110.3 | 108.9 | 114.8 | 111.6 | 110.3 | 121.1 |
| 1993 | 3.5% | 5.4% | 7.5% | 2.9% | -1.3% | 1.9% | 0.5% | 2.6% | -1.7% | 1.8% | 4.2% |
| 1994 | 2.9% | 4.8% | 6.4% | 2.5% | 2.1% | 2.8% | 0.7% | 3.5% | 0.9% | 1.8% | 3.9% |
| 1995 | 3.3% | 3.4% | 4.4% | 2.1% | 1.3% | 3.5% | 1.7% | 2.1% | 1.2% | 2.0% | 3.4% |
| 1996 | 3.5% | 1.4% | 6.2% | 3.3% | 8.1% | 1.7% | 4.1% | 3.7% | 12.5% | 2.6% | 4.3% |
| 1997 | 3.2% | 1.0% | 7.2% | 6.5% | 3.1% | 0.0% | 1.7% | 2.1% | -1.2% | 1.7% | 3.7% |

^ CLPI weights: See table 3-A

Sources: See text.

Table 10 / Academic Library Price Indexes, Personnel Compensation, FY 1992 to 1997

| 1992=100 Fiscal year | Administrators (head librarian) (AL1.1) | Librarians (AL1.2) | Other professional (AL1.3) | Non-professional (AL1.4) | Students hourly employed (AL1.5) | Salaries and wages indexes Universities* (UL1.0) | Colleges^ (CL1.0) | Fringe benefits index (AL2.0) |
|---|---|---|---|---|---|---|---|---|
| 1992 | 100.0 | 100.0 | 100.0 | 100.0 | 100.0 | 100.0 | 100.0 | 100.0 |
| 1993 | 105.0 | 102.6 | 102.5 | 103.2 | 102.7 | 103.2 | 103.5 | 105.4 |
| 1994 | 107.3 | 106.0 | 105.6 | 106.6 | 105.4 | 106.3 | 106.5 | 110.5 |
| 1995 | 110.6 | 110.2 | 109.3 | 110.1 | 108.5 | 110.0 | 110.0 | 114.2 |
| 1996 | 116.3 | 113.6 | 112.5 | 113.3 | 111.8 | 113.4 | 113.8 | 115.8 |
| 1997 | 120.2 | 116.5 | 115.8 | 117.0 | 115.6 | 117.0 | 117.5 | 117.0 |
| 1993 | 5.0% | 2.6% | 2.5% | 3.2% | 2.7% | 3.2% | 3.5% | 5.4% |
| 1994 | 2.2% | 3.3% | 3.0% | 3.3% | 2.6% | 3.1% | 2.9% | 4.8% |
| 1995 | 3.1% | 4.0% | 3.5% | 3.3% | 3.0% | 3.4% | 3.3% | 3.4% |
| 1996 | 5.2% | 3.1% | 2.9% | 2.9% | 3.0% | 3.2% | 3.5% | 1.4% |
| 1997 | 3.4% | 2.6% | 3.0% | 3.2% | 3.4% | 3.1% | 3.2% | 1.0% |

* University library salaries and wages index weights: 10 percent administrators, 20 percent librarians, 10 percent other professionals, 50 percent nonprofessional staff, and 10 percent students.
^ College library salaries and wages index weights: 25 percent administrators, 15 percent librarians, 5 percent other professionals, 40 percent nonprofessional staff, and 15 percent students.
Sources: See text.

**Table 11 / Academic Library Price Indexes, Books and Serials, FY 1992 to 1997**

| 1992=100 | Books printed | | | | | | Book indexes | |
| | North American | | U.S. college | | Foreign books | | | |
| Fiscal year | Price~ | Index (UL3.1a) | Price~ | Index (CL3.1a) | Price | Index (AL3.1b) | University* (UL3.1) | College^ (CL3.1) |
|---|---|---|---|---|---|---|---|---|
| 1992 | $45.84 | 100.0 | $44.55 | 100.0 | n/a | 100.0 | 100.0 | 100.0 |
| 1993 | 45.91 | 100.2 | 47.48 | 106.6 | | 98.9 | 99.9 | 106.2 |
| 1994 | 47.17 | 102.9 | 48.92 | 109.8 | | 96.7 | 101.7 | 109.2 |
| 1995 | 48.16 | 105.1 | 47.93 | 107.6 | | 105.0 | 105.0 | 107.5 |
| 1996 | 48.11 | 105.0 | 48.17 | 108.1 | | 108.3 | 105.6 | 108.1 |
| 1997 | 49.86 | 108.8 | 50.44 | 113.2 | | 106.6 | 108.3 | 112.9 |
| | | | | | | | | |
| 1993 | | 0.2% | | 6.6% | | -1.1% | -0.1% | 6.2% |
| 1994 | | 2.7% | | 3.0% | | -2.2% | 1.8% | 2.8% |
| 1995 | | 2.1% | | -2.0% | | 8.6% | 3.3% | -1.6% |
| 1996 | | -0.1% | | 0.5% | | 3.1% | 0.5% | 0.6% |
| 1997 | | 3.6% | | 4.7% | | -1.6% | 2.6% | 4.4% |

~ Prices are for previous calendar year, e.g., CY 1993 prices are reported for FY 1994.
* University library books printed index weights: 80 percent U.S. titles, 20 percent foreign titles.
^ College Library books printed index weights: 95 percent U.S. titles, 5 percent foreign titles.
Sources: See text.
n/a Not Available

**Table 11A / Academic Library Price Indexes, Books and Serials, FY 1992 to 1997**

| 1992=100 Fiscal year | Periodicals US titles Price~ | Index (AL3.2a) | Periodicals Foreign Price~ | Index (AL3.2b) | Periodical indexes University* (UL3.2) | College^ (CL3.2) | Other serials (newspapers) Price~ | Index (AL3.3) | Books and serials indexes University** (UL3.0) | College^^ (CL3.0) | Other printed materials index (AL4.0) |
|---|---|---|---|---|---|---|---|---|---|---|---|
| 1992 | $146.82 | 100.0 | $370.23 | 100.0 | 100.0 | 100.0 | $222.68 | 100.0 | 100.0 | 100.0 | 100.0 |
| 1993 | 160.03 | 109.0 | 421.32 | 113.8 | 110.0 | 109.2 | 229.92 | 103.3 | 106.1 | 107.5 | 102.9 |
| 1994 | 174.86 | 119.1 | 447.61 | 120.9 | 119.5 | 119.2 | 261.91 | 117.6 | 113.1 | 114.4 | 105.5 |
| 1995 | 192.04 | 130.8 | 489.44 | 132.2 | 131.1 | 130.9 | 270.22 | 121.3 | 121.5 | 119.4 | 107.7 |
| 1996 | 210.83 | 143.6 | 586.81 | 158.5 | 146.6 | 144.3 | 300.21 | 134.8 | 131.7 | 126.8 | 111.3 |
| 1997 | 230.80 | 157.2 | 654.56 | 176.8 | 161.1 | 158.2 | 311.77 | 140.0 | 141.6 | 136.0 | 118.5 |
| | | | | | | | | | | | |
| 1993 | | 9.0% | | 13.8% | 10.0% | 9.2% | | 3.3% | 6.1% | 7.5% | 2.9% |
| 1994 | | 9.3% | | 6.2% | 8.6% | 9.1% | | 13.9% | 6.6% | 6.4% | 2.5% |
| 1995 | | 9.8% | | 9.3% | 9.7% | 9.8% | | 3.2% | 7.4% | 4.4% | 2.1% |
| 1996 | | 9.8% | | 19.9% | 11.8% | 10.3% | | 11.1% | 8.4% | 6.2% | 3.3% |
| 1997 | | 9.5% | | 11.5% | 9.9% | 9.6% | | 3.9% | 7.5% | 7.2% | 6.5% |

~ Prices are for previous calendar year, e.g., CY 1993 prices are reported for FY 1994.
* University library periodicals index weights: 80 percent U.S. titles, 20 percent foreign titles.
^ College library periodicals index weights: 95 percent U.S. titles, 5 percent foreign titles.
** University library books and serials index weights: 35 percent books, 60 percent periodicals, 5 percent other serials.
^^College library books and serials index weights: 47 percent books, 48 percent periodicals, 5 percent other serials.
Sources: See text.

Table 12 / Academic Library Price Indexes, Non-Print Media and Electronic Services, FY 1992 to 1997

| 1992=100 Fiscal year | Microforms (microfilm) Index (AL5.1) | Audio recordings | | | | | Video | | |
|---|---|---|---|---|---|---|---|---|---|
| | | Tape cassette | | Compact disc | | Audio recordings index* (AL5.2) | VHS cassette | | Video index (AL5.3) |
| | | Price~ | Index (AL5.2a) | Price~ | Index (AL5.2b) | | Price~ | Index (AL5.3a) | |
| 1992 | 100.0 | $12.18 | 100.0 | n/a | | 100.0 | $199.67 | 100.0 | 100.0 |
| 1993 | 104.3 | 11.73 | 96.3 | n/a | | 96.3 | 112.92 | 56.6 | 56.6 |
| 1994 | 107.9 | 8.20 | 67.3 | $13.36 | 67.3 | 67.3 | 93.22 | 46.7 | 46.7 |
| 1995 | 110.6 | 8.82 | 72.4 | 14.80 | 74.6 | 73.5 | 84.19 | 42.2 | 42.2 |
| 1996 | 128.0 | 7.96 | 65.4 | 14.86 | 74.9 | 70.1 | 83.48 | 41.8 | 41.8 |
| 1997 | 132.9 | 8.13 | 66.7 | 16.43 | 82.8 | 74.8 | 82.10 | 41.1 | 41.1 |
| 1993 | 4.3% | | -3.7% | | | -3.7% | | -43.4% | -43.4% |
| 1994 | 3.5% | | -30.1% | | | -30.1% | | -17.4% | -17.4% |
| 1995 | 2.5% | | 7.6% | | 10.8% | 9.2% | | -9.7% | -9.7% |
| 1996 | 15.7% | | -9.8% | | 0.4% | -4.6% | | -0.8% | -0.8% |
| 1997 | 3.8% | | 2.1% | | 10.6% | 6.6% | | -1.7% | -1.7% |

~ Prices are for previous calendar year, e.g., CY 1993 prices are reported for FY 1994.
* Audio recordings index weights: 50 percent tape cassette, 50 percent compact disc.
Sources: See text.
n/a Not Available

**Table 12A / Academic Library Price Indexes, Non-Print Media and Electronic Services, FY 1992 to 1997**

| 1992=100 Fiscal year | Non-print Media Graphic image (AL5.4) | Computer files (CD-ROM) Price~ | Index (AL5.5) | Non-print media index# (AL5.0) | Electronic services index (AL6.0) | Total Acquisitions Indexes Univ* | College^ | All Institutions** |
|---|---|---|---|---|---|---|---|---|
| 1992 | 100.0 | $1,601 | 100.0 | 100.0 | 100.0 | 100.0 | 100.0 | 100.0 |
| 1993 | 97.3 | 1,793 | 112.0 | 98.7 | 101.9 | 105.2 | 105.9 | 105.4 |
| 1994 | 108.4 | 1,945 | 121.5 | 100.8 | 104.8 | 111.4 | 111.8 | 111.5 |
| 1995 | 111.3 | 1,961 | 122.5 | 102.1 | 108.5 | 118.7 | 116.2 | 118.0 |
| 1996 | 114.5 | 1,986 | 124.0 | 110.3 | 110.3 | 127.6 | 123.1 | 126.4 |
| 1997 | 126.5 | 2,012 | 125.7 | 113.7 | 110.3 | 136.1 | 130.6 | 134.5 |
| 1993 | -2.7% | | 12.0% | -1.3% | 1.9% | 5.2% | 5.9% | 5.4% |
| 1994 | 11.4% | | 8.5% | 2.1% | 2.8% | 5.9% | 5.6% | 5.8% |
| 1995 | 2.7% | | 0.8% | 1.3% | 3.5% | 6.6% | 4.0% | 5.8% |
| 1996 | 2.9% | | 1.3% | 8.1% | 1.7% | 7.5% | 5.9% | 7.1% |
| 1997 | 10.5% | | 1.3% | 3.1% | 0.0% | 6.6% | 6.1% | 6.5% |

~ Prices are for immediate preceding calendar year, e.g., CY 1993 prices are reported for FY 1994.
# Non-print media index weights: 45 percent microforms, 5 percent audio recordings, 15 percent video, 5 percent graphic image, 30 percent computer materials.
* University total acquisitions 1992 weights: 81 percent books, 3 percent other printed material, 5 percent non-print media, and 11 percent electronic services.
^ College total acquisitions 1992 weights: 77 percent books, 2 percent other printed material, 10 percent non-print media, and 11 percent electronic services.
** All institutions total acquisitions weights: 72 percent university acquisitions, 28 percent college acquisitions.
Sources: See text.

# State Rankings of Selected Public Library Data, 1996

| | Circulation Transactions per capita* | Reference Transactions per capita | Book Volumes per capita | ALA-MLS Librarians per 25,000 | Operating Expenditures per capita | Local Income per capita |
|---|---|---|---|---|---|---|
| Alabama | 49 | 46 | 41 | 44 | 43 | 42 |
| Alaska | 29 | 40 | 20 | 15 | 5 | 6 |
| Arizona | 27 | 21 | 45 | 27 | 28 | 25 |
| Arkansas | 47 | 48 | 38 | 49 | 49 | 46 |
| California | 39 | 18 | 48 | 23 | 32 | 28 |
| Colorado | 12 | 7 | 32 | 18 | 10 | 9 |
| Connecticut | 11 | 11 | 9 | 3 | 6 | 8 |
| Delaware | 40 | 45 | 40 | 43 | 38 | 37 |
| Dist. of Columbia † | 51 | 1 | 1 | 1 | 3 | 1 |
| Florida | 34 | 2 | 50 | 21 | 30 | 27 |
| Georgia | 43 | 35 | 47 | 25 | 42 | 45 |
| Hawaii | 30 | 30 | 24 | 12 | 34 | 51 |
| Idaho | 15 | 26 | 22 | 45 | 33 | 32 |
| Illinois | 16 | 6 | 16 | 10 | 8 | 7 |
| Indiana | 2 | 4 | 11 | 8 | 4 | 4 |
| Iowa | 10 | 32 | 13 | 28 | 29 | 26 |
| Kansas | 14 | 17 | 17 | 29 | 27 | 29 |
| Kentucky | 36 | 47 | 42 | 51 | 39 | 40 |
| Louisiana | 45 | 43 | 35 | 38 | 37 | 31 |
| Maine | 17 | 36 | 2 | 20 | 25 | 33 |
| Maryland | 8 | 10 | 26 | 2 | 11 | 17 |
| Massachusetts | 22 | 24 | 4 | 7 | 12 | 14 |
| Michigan | 37 | 28 | 29 | 13 | 21 | 21 |
| Minnesota | 5 | 9 | 28 | 22 | 13 | 11 |
| Mississippi | 50 | 49 | 46 | 46 | 51 | 49 |
| Missouri | 13 | 22 | 12 | 39 | 22 | 16 |
| Montana | 31 | 42 | 23 | 50 | 45 | 35 |
| Nebraska | 19 | 51 | 19 | 34 | 24 | 19 |
| Nevada | 38 | 38 | 36 | 35 | 18 | 15 |
| New Hampshire | 20 | 37 | 8 | 14 | 20 | 22 |
| New Jersey | 32 | 23 | 15 | 5 | 7 | 5 |
| New Mexico | 35 | 33 | 25 | 33 | 35 | 30 |
| New York | 23 | 3 | 7 | 4 | 1 | 2 |
| North Carolina | 33 | 29 | 44 | 31 | 41 | 38 |
| North Dakota | 24 | 34 | 18 | 48 | 46 | 43 |
| Ohio | 1 | 5 | 14 | 9 | 2 | 48 |
| Oklahoma | 28 | 39 | 39 | 37 | 40 | 34 |
| Oregon | 4 | 8 | 34 | 19 | 15 | 10 |
| Pennsylvania | 42 | 44 | 37 | 26 | 36 | 44 |
| Rhode Island | 26 | 31 | 10 | 6 | 14 | 20 |
| South Carolina | 44 | 20 | 49 | 24 | 44 | 39 |
| South Dakota | 9 | 12 | 6 | 41 | 26 | 18 |
| Tennessee | 48 | 27 | 51 | 42 | 48 | 47 |
| Texas | 46 | 25 | 43 | 30 | 47 | 41 |
| Utah | 6 | 15 | 31 | 36 | 23 | 23 |
| Vermont | 25 | 41 | 3 | 32 | 31 | 36 |
| Virginia | 21 | 19 | 33 | 17 | 19 | 24 |
| Washington | 3 | 16 | 27 | 11 | 9 | 3 |
| West Virginia | 41 | 50 | 30 | 47 | 50 | 50 |
| Wisconsin | 7 | 13 | 21 | 16 | 16 | 12 |
| Wyoming | 18 | 14 | 5 | 40 | 17 | 13 |

Source: U.S. Department of Education, National Center for Education Statistics, Federal-State Cooperative System (FSCS) for Public Library Data, Public Libraries Survey, Fiscal Year 1996.

* Per capita and per 1,000 population calculations are based on population of legal service area.

† The District of Columbia, while not a state, is included in the state rankings. Special care should be used in making comparisons.

# Library Buildings, 1998:
# Another Year, Another $543 Million

Bette-Lee Fox

Managing Editor, *Library Journal*

Emily J. Jones

Assistant Editor, *Library Journal*

At a time when money to build libraries may be easier to come by, libraries are still finding that cooperative projects can satisfy everyone's needs for a greater return on the dollar. Three such projects are among the 81 new buildings we are reporting this year, along with 116 additions/renovations, all completed between July 1, 1997, and June 30, 1998.

Although we are listing fewer projects (the lowest total since 1986), this year's 197 buildings cost $542.8 million. These totals are down from the 1997 figures (225 buildings, $662.1 million), but three major renovations in 1997 alone accounted for $140 million (see *Bowker Annual* 1998, pp. 457–475).

The innovative cooperative projects include two Colorado public libraries (in Fort Collins and Westminster) that combined with the Front Range Community College Library to expand services to both communities. Meanwhile, the Bellmawr Branch of the Camden (New Jersey) Public Library is the culmination of the community's need for expanded library and healthcare services, with the library sharing space with what will eventually be a regional health clinic.

Some large projects this year include the new Flushing Branch of the Queens Borough (New York) Public Library ($35.1 million)—at 76,000 square feet "the largest library in New York State"—and the City of Mountain View (California) Public Library, a 90,000-square-foot structure (including 30,000 square feet for underground parking) at a price tag of $22.3 million. The renovation of the Main Library of the Central Arkansas Library, Little Rock, spans 132,000 square feet and cost $13.8 million, while the Central Library of Rochester/Monroe County (New York), a 245,000-square-foot addition and renovation, required $26 million.

The 35 academic projects completed in fiscal year 1997 include the new Bruce T. Halle Library of Eastern Michigan University, Ypsilanti ($41 million, 273,715 square feet) and the expansion/remodeling of the Harvard Law School Library, Landell Hall ($35.9 million, 180,000 square feet).

Can the health of public libraries be equated with the cost of their buildings? If the public is willing to spend more than half a billion dollars on new structures, it undoubtedly considers libraries essential to its well-being and future.

Adapted from the December 1998 issue of *Library Journal*, which also lists architects' addresses.

Table 1 / New Public Library Buildings, 1998

| Community | Pop. ('000) | Code | Project Cost | Const. Cost | Gross Sq. Ft. | Sq. Ft. Cost | Equip. Cost | Site Cost | Other Costs | Volumes | Federal Funds | State Funds | Local Funds | Gift Funds | Architect |
|---|---|---|---|---|---|---|---|---|---|---|---|---|---|---|---|
| *Arizona* | | | | | | | | | | | | | | | |
| Phoenix | 72 | B | $2,498,550 | $1,311,441 | 13,290 | $98.68 | $271,813 | $180,000 | $735,296 | 90,000 | 0 | 0 | $2,318,550 | $180,000 | Dick & Fritsche |
| *California* | | | | | | | | | | | | | | | |
| Aliso Viejo | 33 | B | 7,580,371 | 4,381,416 | 21,500 | 203.79 | 822,178 | 1,600,000 | 776,777 | 83,000 | 0 | 0 | 7,580,371 | 0 | Jeannette & Assocs. |
| Arvin | 10 | B | 1,817,467 | 1,116,652 | 8,182 | 136.48 | 325,192 | 64,000 | 311,623 | 33,700 | 1,789,377 | 0 | 28,090 | 0 | Thirtieth St. Architects |
| Keyes | 3 | B | 99,058 | 90,181 | 2,000 | 45.09 | 4,500 | Owned | 4,377 | 12,500 | 0 | 0 | 99,058 | 0 | Frick, Frick & Jette |
| Mission Viejo | 125 | M | 11,500,000 | 5,600,000 | 27,650 | 202.53 | 1,100,000 | 2,600,000 | 2,200,000 | 160,000 | 0 | 0 | 11,000,000 | 500,000 | LPA, Inc. |
| Mountain View | 73 | M | 22,336,550 | 15,409,580 | 90,000 | 171.22 | 1,200,000 | Owned | 5,726,970 | 330,000 | 660,000 | 0 | 21,576,550 | 100,000 | Esherick, Homsey... |
| Palmdale | 117 | B | 3,202,195 | 1,532,012 | 10,050 | 152.44 | 483,926 | 166,333 | 1,019,924 | 58,150 | 0 | 0 | 3,160,920 | 41,275 | Chas. Walton Assocs. |
| Poway | 46 | B | 5,171,000 | 2,900,000 | 20,000 | 145.00 | 446,000 | 400,000 | 1,425,000 | 110,000 | 0 | 0 | 5,073,000 | 98,000 | Cardwell/Thomas |
| Salinas | 6 | B | 1,135,226 | 857,500 | 3,800 | 225.66 | 45,000 | 65,000 | 167,726 | 8,000 | 0 | 0 | 15,000 | 1,120,226 | Keeble Rhoda Todd |
| *Colorado* | | | | | | | | | | | | | | | |
| Fort Collins | 129 | B | 4,618,622 | 3,586,801 | 30,400 | 117.99 | 374,575 | Owned | 657,246 | 100,000 | 0 | 2,874,849 | 1,743,773 | 0 | Davis Partnership. |
| Lafayette | 27 | M | 5,131,905 | 3,491,898 | 28,871 | 120.95 | 850,555 | 215,000 | 574,452 | 120,000 | 0 | 0 | 4,916,905 | 226,600 | H+L/Brendle Assocs. |
| Pueblo West | 131 | B | 805,000 | 558,700 | 4,800 | 116.40 | 138,000 | 50,000 | 58,300 | 21,300 | 0 | 0 | 120,730 | 673,000 | G.V. Designs |
| Westminster | 110 | MS | 12,444,941 | 10,320,000 | 79,312 | 130.12 | 767,941 | Owned | 1,357,000 | 225,000 | 0 | 7,605,000 | 4,839,941 | 130,000 | Bennett, Wagner... |
| *Delaware* | | | | | | | | | | | | | | | |
| Millsboro | 9 | M | 829,500 | 581,000 | 5,000 | 116.20 | 10,000 | 65,716 | 172,784 | 22,693 | 0 | 230,000 | 0 | 599,500 | R. Calvin Clendaniel |
| *Florida* | | | | | | | | | | | | | | | |
| Arcadia | 27 | M | 632,829 | 516,347 | 6,889 | 74.95 | 50,743 | Owned | 65,739 | 40,000 | 80,000 | 172,000 | 380,829 | 0 | Titsch & Assocs. |
| Bartow | 15 | M | 1,918,970 | 1,609,727 | 21,800 | 73.84 | 200,000 | Owned | 109,243 | 60,000 | 400,000 | 0 | 1,378,970 | 140,000 | Educated Design |
| Jacksonville | 50 | B | 4,812,649 | 3,077,352 | 42,493 | 72.42 | 508,713 | 759,620 | 466,964 | 200,000 | 400,000 | 117,573 | 4,241,076 | 54,000 | Akel, Logan & Shafer |
| *Georgia* | | | | | | | | | | | | | | | |
| Dallas | 71 | B | 824,223 | 569,338 | 5,000 | 113.86 | 197,991 | Owned | 56,894 | 19,768 | 0 | 662,308 | 161,915 | 0 | Sterling Pettefer |
| Riverdale | 47 | B | 1,830,803 | 1,499,163 | 12,000 | 124.93 | 183,939 | Owned | 147,701 | 62,000 | 0 | 1,324,133 | 501,670 | 5,000 | Scogin Elam & Bray |
| *Illinois* | | | | | | | | | | | | | | | |
| Cordova | 1 | M | 630,316 | 504,621 | 5,684 | 88.78 | 48,590 | Owned | 77,105 | 15,000 | 250,000 | 0 | 374,816 | 5,500 | Dennis M. Kelly |
| Oakwood | 7 | M | 519,033 | 434,033 | 4,016 | 108.08 | 30,000 | Owned | 55,000 | 35,000 | 0 | 160,000 | 329,033 | 30,000 | Gary Olsen & Assocs. |

Symbol Code: B—Branch Library; BS—Branch & System Headquarters; M—Main Library; MS—Main & Branch & System Headquarters; S—System Headquarters; n/a—not available

Table 1 / New Public Library Buildings, 1998 (cont.)

| Community | Pop. ('000) | Code | Project Cost | Const. Cost | Gross Sq. Ft. | Sq. Ft. Cost | Equip. Cost | Site Cost | Other Costs | Volumes | Federal Funds | State Funds | Local Funds | Gift Funds | Architect |
|---|---|---|---|---|---|---|---|---|---|---|---|---|---|---|---|
| Philo | 2 | M | 423,000 | 361,000 | 4,000 | 90.25 | 0 | 10,000 | 52,000 | 15,000 | 0 | 150,000 | 269,000 | 4,000 | BLDD Architects |
| Port Byron | 3 | M | 776,943 | 671,056 | 6,808 | 98.57 | 18,640 | 20,127 | 67,120 | 24,620 | 250,000 | 0 | 493,364 | 33,579 | Tevis Freeman |
| Richmond | 5 | M | 833,094 | 713,776 | 18,000 | 39.65 | 56,923 | Owned | 62,395 | 67,200 | 0 | 250,000 | 583,094 | 0 | Steven M. Papesh |
| *Indiana* | | | | | | | | | | | | | | | |
| Russiaville | 7 | B | 731,458 | 553,926 | 3,642 | 152.09 | 64,638 | 46,500 | 66,394 | 31,400 | 0 | 0 | 684,958 | 46,500 | K.R. Montgomery |
| *Kentucky* | | | | | | | | | | | | | | | |
| Lexington | n/a | B | 3,157,085 | 2,551,950 | 19,838 | 128.64 | 291,907 | 261,529 | 51,699 | 110,000 | 0 | 0 | 3,143,085 | 16,000 | Brandstetter Carroll |
| South Shore | 7 | B | 714,467 | 533,237 | 5,500 | 96.96 | 50,793 | 91,650 | 38,787 | 30,000 | 0 | 300,000 | 325,467 | 89,000 | T. & O. Designers |
| *Louisiana* | | | | | | | | | | | | | | | |
| Minden | 23 | MS | 2,556,379 | 1,860,249 | 16,383 | 113.55 | 285,787 | 225,531 | 184,812 | n/a | 0 | 0 | 2,556,379 | 0 | Richard LeBlanc |
| *Maine* | | | | | | | | | | | | | | | |
| Freeport | 8 | M | 2,607,000 | 1,894,000 | 17,000 | 111.41 | 158,000 | 110,000 | 445,000 | 60,000 | 0 | 0 | 2,607,000 | 0 | Winton Scott |
| *Massachusetts* | | | | | | | | | | | | | | | |
| Abington | 14 | M | 3,600,000 | 2,344,000 | 17,800 | 131.69 | 150,000 | 761,000 | 345,000 | 72,000 | 0 | 1,344,963 | 1,685,037 | 570,000 | Tappé Assocs. |
| Carver | 11 | M | 3,528,198 | 2,685,000 | 21,000 | 127.86 | 199,183 | Owned | 644,015 | 65,000 | 0 | 1,338,662 | 2,190,256 | 0 | Architectural Resrcs. |
| Lincoln | n/a | M | 4,391,678 | 3,613,608 | 5,000 | 722.72 | 512,283 | Owned | 265,787 | 25,000 | 575,000 | 0 | 1,841,155 | 1,975,523 | James S. Thomas |
| *Minnesota* | | | | | | | | | | | | | | | |
| Oakdale | 20 | B | 1,725,218 | 1,413,395 | 10,435 | 135.45 | 91,500 | Owned | 220,323 | 25,000 | 0 | 0 | 1,725,218 | 0 | SKD Architects |
| *Missouri* | | | | | | | | | | | | | | | |
| Barnhart | 15 | B | 2,263,860 | 1,626,275 | 14,182 | 114.67 | 230,000 | 196,300 | 211,285 | 84,324 | 42,315 | 0 | 2,201,625 | 19,920 | R.L. Praprotnik |
| Florissant | 43 | B | 2,275,149 | 1,511,921 | 16,500 | 91.63 | 216,622 | 378,544 | 168,062 | 80,000 | 0 | 0 | 2,275,149 | 0 | Manske Corp. |
| Kearney | 3 | B | 1,187,125 | 846,126 | 15,000 | 56.41 | 77,561 | 190,000 | 73,438 | 100,000 | 0 | 0 | 1,187,125 | 0 | Tognascioli & Assocs. |
| Lone Jack | 1 | B | 618,388 | 514,075 | 7,500 | 68.54 | 5,608 | 46,000 | 52,705 | 50,000 | 0 | 0 | 618,388 | 0 | Tognascioli & Assocs. |
| *Montana* | | | | | | | | | | | | | | | |
| Whitefish | 10 | B | 1,125,479 | 729,289 | 9,677 | 75.36 | 200,000 | 42,500 | 153,690 | 60,000 | 0 | 0 | 217,500 | 907,979 | L'Heureux, Page... |
| *New Hampshire* | | | | | | | | | | | | | | | |
| Contoocook | 6 | M | 1,593,534 | 1,101,216 | 10,800 | 101.96 | 114,064 | 238,362 | 139,892 | 32,000 | 0 | 0 | 1,230,000 | 370,000 | Sheer McCrystal... |

Symbol Code: B—Branch Library; BS—Branch & System Headquarters; M—Main Library; MS—Main & System Headquarters; S—System Headquarters; n/a—not available

## Table 1 / New Public Library Buildings, 1998 *(cont.)*

| Community | Pop. ('000) | Code | Project Cost | Const. Cost | Gross Sq. Ft. | Sq. Ft. Cost | Equip. Cost | Site Cost | Other Costs | Volumes | Federal Funds | State Funds | Local Funds | Gift Funds | Architect |
|---|---|---|---|---|---|---|---|---|---|---|---|---|---|---|---|
| *New Jersey* | | | | | | | | | | | | | | | |
| Bellmawr | 25 | B | 1,530,097 | 1,250,597 | 12,251 | 102.08 | 200,000 | Owned | 79,500 | 46,104 | 0 | 0 | 1,530,097 | 0 | Garrison Architects |
| Marlton | 39 | B | 7,440,000 | n/a | 19,500 | n/a | 203,000 | 563,000 | n/a | 75,000 | 0 | 0 | n/a | 0 | Tarquini Organization |
| Monroe Twp. | 25 | M | 3,916,000 | 2,756,000 | 21,000 | 131.24 | 300,000 | 420,000 | 440,000 | 70,000 | 0 | 0 | 3,916,000 | 0 | Hillier Group |
| Princeton Junction | 20 | B | 3,766,000 | 3,000,000 | 23,000 | 130.43 | 385,000 | Owned | 381,000 | 88,500 | 0 | 0 | 3,766,000 | 0 | Vaughn Organization |
| *New York* | | | | | | | | | | | | | | | |
| East Northport | 37 | B | 3,953,048 | 2,950,000 | 20,000 | 147.50 | 453,048 | 100,000 | 450,000 | 120,000 | 37,048 | 13,500 | 3,737,500 | 165,000 | Beatty, Harvey |
| Flushing | 75 | B | 35,195,000 | 25,365,000 | 76,000 | 333.75 | 2,220,000 | Owned | 7,610,000 | 350,000 | 0 | 0 | 35,080,000 | 115,000 | Polshek & Partners |
| *North Carolina* | | | | | | | | | | | | | | | |
| Charlotte | 45 | B | 3,811,063 | 2,668,231 | 23,728 | 112.45 | 484,094 | 336,000 | 322,738 | 130,000 | 0 | 0 | 3,811,063 | 0 | Little & Assocs. |
| Fayetteville | 61 | B | 5,706,978 | 2,754,347 | 24,000 | 114.77 | 770,000 | 390,000 | 1,792,631 | 75,850 | 0 | 0 | 5,706,978 | 0 | Shuller, Ferris... |
| *Ohio* | | | | | | | | | | | | | | | |
| Cleveland | 26 | B | 2,388,210 | 1,947,096 | 8,400 | 231.80 | 93,000 | 80,000 | 268,114 | 18,500 | 0 | 0 | 2,388,210 | 0 | Robert P. Madison |
| Fairview Park | 18 | B | 6,659,000 | 4,309,000 | 44,000 | 97.93 | 850,000 | 817,000 | 683,000 | 150,000 | 0 | 0 | 6,659,000 | 0 | David Holzheimer |
| Millersburg | 36 | M | 2,178,994 | 1,609,349 | 16,500 | 97.54 | 198,009 | 19,795 | 351,841 | 45,000 | 500,000 | 0 | 1,175,835 | 503,159 | Beck & Tabeling |
| Owensville | 6 | BS | 1,907,176 | 1,700,619 | 16,200 | 104.98 | 52,447 | 25,000 | 129,110 | 15,500 | 0 | 0 | 1,907,176 | 0 | Harley Assocs. |
| Warren | 10 | B | 2,009,000 | 1,400,000 | 10,200 | 137.25 | 250,000 | 285,000 | 74,000 | 50,000 | 0 | 0 | 1,939,000 | 70,000 | Baker, Bednar... |
| *Oklahoma* | | | | | | | | | | | | | | | |
| Davis | 4 | B | 249,942 | 183,713 | 4,100 | 44.81 | 34,229 | 20,000 | 12,000 | 8,000 | 80,000 | 0 | 5,378 | 164,564 | Ludwig Isenberg |
| *South Carolina* | | | | | | | | | | | | | | | |
| Chapin | 8 | B | 833,821 | 655,099 | 6,540 | 100.17 | 88,677 | 40,000 | 50,045 | 30,000 | 0 | 0 | 793,821 | 40,000 | James, DuRant... |
| Charleston | 295 | MS | 20,151,000 | 12,380,000 | 148,577 | 83.33 | 2,850,000 | 1,200,000 | 3,721,000 | 570,000 | 0 | 0 | 18,816,000 | 1,335,000 | McKellar & Assoc. |
| Columbia | 26 | B | 2,726,862 | 1,950,831 | 25,400 | 76.80 | 321,721 | 300,000 | 154,310 | 135,000 | 0 | 0 | 2,726,862 | 0 | Jumper, Carter... |
| Greenville | 177 | B | 1,708,324 | 1,148,354 | 11,173 | 102.78 | 207,880 | 200,000 | 152,090 | 65,000 | 0 | 0 | 1,415,500 | 292,824 | Tarleton-Tankersley |
| Lexington | 47 | MS | 5,194,860 | 3,922,484 | 47,700 | 82.23 | 515,201 | 500,000 | 257,175 | 190,000 | 0 | 0 | 4,694,860 | 500,000 | Craig, Gaulden... |
| Richburg | 5 | B | 498,529 | 420,076 | 4,108 | 102.26 | 37,354 | 3,000 | 38,099 | 10,818 | 100,000 | 0 | 232,380 | 204,829 | James, DuRant... |
| *Tennessee* | | | | | | | | | | | | | | | |
| Athens | 45 | M | 1,936,000 | 1,524,703 | 14,000 | 108.91 | 200,000 | 50,000 | 161,297 | 75,000 | 0 | 0 | 739,500 | 1,196,500 | Brewer Ingram... |

Symbol Code: B—Branch Library; BS—Branch & System Headquarters; M—Main Library; MS—Main & System Headquarters; S—System Headquarters; n/a—not available

**Table 1 / New Public Library Buildings, 1998** *(cont.)*

| Community | Pop. ('000) | Code | Project Cost | Const. Cost | Gross Sq. Ft. | Sq. Ft. Cost | Equip. Cost | Site Cost | Other Costs | Volumes | Federal Funds | State Funds | Local Funds | Gift Funds | Architect |
|---|---|---|---|---|---|---|---|---|---|---|---|---|---|---|---|
| Dresden | 16 | M | n/a | n/a | 6,300 | n/a | n/a | n/a | n/a | 25,000 | 0 | 100,000 | 0 | n/a | Mark Lishen |
| Farragut | 22 | B | 1,696,599 | 1,283,685 | 10,100 | 127.10 | 205,000 | 60,000 | 147,914 | 50,000 | 0 | 0 | 1,636,599 | 60,000 | Goodstein & Assocs. |
| Knoxville | 12 | B | 990,510 | 897,279 | 5,315 | 168.82 | 69,835 | Owned | 23,396 | 16,000 | 0 | 0 | 990,510 | 0 | Jennifer Martella |
| Knoxville | 45 | B | 3,029,300 | 2,044,488 | 13,046 | 156.71 | 524,800 | 345,000 | 115,012 | 60,000 | 0 | 0 | 2,856,800 | 172,500 | Lewis Group |
| Memphis** | 45 | B | 1,500,000 | 612,000 | 11,300 | 54.16 | 360,000 | 462,000 (L) | 66,000 | 50,000 | 0 | 0 | 1,500,000 | 0 | Nathan, Evans... |
| Monterey | 3 | B | 216,053 | 175,705 | 2,198 | 79.94 | 28,304 | Owned | 12,044 | 10,000 | 89,874 | 58,784 | 0 | 67,395 | Wm. C. Maffett |
| *Texas* | | | | | | | | | | | | | | | |
| Austin | 20 | B | 2,915,000 | 1,134,282 | 8,110 | 139.86 | 518,300 | 800,000 | 462,418 | 40,000 | 0 | 0 | 2,915,000 | 0 | Rogers & Perry |
| Austin | 26 | B | 2,138,000 | 1,114,855 | 8,320 | 133.99 | 675,000 | Owned | 348,145 | 40,000 | 0 | 0 | 2,138,000 | 0 | Bethany Ramey |
| Beaumont | 24 | B | 1,739,336 | 1,411,377 | 11,500 | 122.73 | 161,336 | 47,000 | 119,623 | 50,000 | 970,969 | 0 | 721,367 | 47,659 | Philip Long |
| Laredo | 180 | M | 10,054,878 | 5,946,956 | 60,000 | 99.12 | 1,574,752 | 1,803,865 | 729,305 | 350,000 | 400,000 | 0 | 9,479,878 | 175,000 | Kell, Muñoz... |
| *Utah* | | | | | | | | | | | | | | | |
| Enterprise | 3 | B | 266,500 | 230,000 | 2,000 | 115.00 | 2,500 | 20,000 | 14,000 | 10,000 | 72,000 | 0 | 147,500 | 47,000 | Richardson Design |
| Morgan | 6 | M | 1,867,480 | 1,698,540 | 15,526 | 109.40 | 70,340 | Owned | 98,600 | 50,000 | 36,000 | 0 | 1,831,480 | 0 | Hart Fisher Smith |
| West Jordan | 35 | B | 2,789,919 | 2,035,283 | 18,705 | 108.81 | 333,671 | 247,940 | 173,025 | 130,000 | 0 | 0 | 2,789,919 | 0 | MHTN Architects |
| *Virginia* | | | | | | | | | | | | | | | |
| Bland | 7 | B | 560,274 | 370,270 | 5,215 | 71.00 | 67,745 | 26,000 | 96,259 | 21,700 | 0 | 150,000 | 50,000 | 360,274 | Reynolds Architects |
| *Washington* | | | | | | | | | | | | | | | |
| Airway Hgts. | 6 | B | 679,613 | 545,306 | 4,125 | 132.20 | 62,670 | Leased | 71,637 | 23,000 | 0 | 0 | 679,613 | 0 | Integrus Arch. |
| Belfair | 20 | B | 3,006,117 | 2,100,000 | 14,800 | 141.89 | 538,629 | 138,000 | 229,488 | 60,000 | 0 | 0 | 3,006,117 | 0 | Carlson Architects |
| Spokane | 43 | B | 2,026,700 | 1,318,820 | 10,600 | 124.41 | 337,570 | 235,788 | 134,522 | 50,000 | 0 | 0 | 2,026,700 | 0 | Tan-Boyle |
| *Wisconsin* | | | | | | | | | | | | | | | |
| Nekoosa | 5 | M | 824,609 | 596,581 | 9,020 | 66.14 | 94,194 | 16,000 | 117,834 | 31,000 | 0 | 0 | 70,376 | 754,233 | Stubenrauch, Inc. |
| River Falls | 11 | M | 4,685,219 | 3,606,452 | 34,142 | 105.63 | 257,310 | 500,000 | 321,457 | 74,595 | 0 | 0 | 2,985,219 | 1,700,000 | Brown Healey... |
| Two Rivers | 18 | M | 3,159,621 | 2,382,683 | 25,000 | 95.30 | 416,962 | Owned | 359,976 | 100,000 | 0 | 0 | 1,600,000 | 1,559,621 | Engberg Anderson... |
| *Wyoming* | | | | | | | | | | | | | | | |
| Pinedale | 4 | MS | 2,251,874 | 1,757,069 | 13,394 | 131.18 | 162,659 | Owned | 332,146 | 74,204 | 7,000 | 7,000 | 400,000 | 1,837,874 | Carney Architects |

Symbol Code: B—Branch Library; BS—Branch & System Headquarters; M—Main Library; MS—Main & System Headquarters; S—System Headquarters; n/a—not available

** Outlay for long-term lease included in project and site cost.

## Table 2 / Public Library Buildings, 1998: Additions and Renovations

| Community | Pop. ('000) | Code | Project Cost | Const. Cost | Gross Sq. Ft. | Sq. Ft. Cost | Equip. Cost | Site Cost | Other Costs | Volumes | Federal Funds | State Funds | Local Funds | Gift Funds | Architect |
|---|---|---|---|---|---|---|---|---|---|---|---|---|---|---|---|
| *Alabama* | | | | | | | | | | | | | | | |
| Bay Minette | 8 | MS | $1,606,119 | $1,320,419 | 12,216 | $108.09 | $180,000 | Owned | $105,700 | 70,000 | 0 | 0 | $1,606,119 | 0 | Gatlin Hudson |
| Homewood | 23 | M | 4,058,923 | 3,417,977 | 49,230 | 69.43 | 436,655 | Owned | 204,291 | 125,000 | 60,000 | 1,481 | 3,902,858 | 94,584 | Davis Architects |
| Oneonta | 31 | M | 908,234 | 481,981 | 8,000 | 60.25 | 102,896 | 267,500 | 55,857 | 45,000 | 0 | 0 | 361,914 | 546,320 | Hughes & Assocs. |
| Trussville | 14 | M | 1,563,494 | 1,054,457 | 14,288 | 73.80 | 224,415 | 95,315 | 189,307 | 52,000 | 0 | 0 | 1,536,564 | 26,930 | Joel Blackstock |
| Valley | 38 | M | 1,456,113 | 1,214,864 | 20,500 | 59.26 | 30,791 | Owned | 210,458 | 80,000 | 0 | 0 | 1,451,153 | 4,960 | Jova, Daniels, Busby |
| *Arizona* | | | | | | | | | | | | | | | |
| Greer | 1 | B | 3,165 | 3,165 | 534 | 5.93 | 0 | Leased | 0 | 3,191 | 0 | 0 | 3,165 | 0 | none |
| Mesa | 370 | MS | 3,929,152 | 2,790,224 | 76,530 | 36.46 | 809,987 | Owned | 328,941 | 300,000 | 0 | 0 | 3,929,152 | 0 | Stichler Design |
| Sanders | 1 | B | 655 | 655 | 862 | 0.76 | 0 | Leased | 0 | 8,415 | 0 | 0 | 655 | 0 | none |
| Tucson | 67 | B | 1,500,000 | 960,510 | 16,500 | 58.21 | 409,490 | Owned | 130,000 | 40,000 | 0 | 0 | 1,500,000 | 0 | Burns & Wald-Hopkins |
| Tucson | 115 | B | 1,500,000 | 953,309 | 17,000 | 56.08 | 416,691 | Owned | 130,000 | 40,000 | 0 | 0 | 1,500,000 | 0 | Burns & Wald-Hopkins |
| *Arkansas* | | | | | | | | | | | | | | | |
| Little Rock | 296 | M | 13,884,481 | 11,649,710 | 132,000 | 88.25 | 815,218 | 245,000 | 1,174,553 | 375,000 | 0 | 0 | 13,784,481 | 100,000 | Polk-Stanley-Yeary |
| *California* | | | | | | | | | | | | | | | |
| Burlingame | 36 | M | 13,300,000 | 9,600,000 | 47,000 | 204.26 | 700,000 | Owned | 3,000,000 | 275,000 | 0 | 0 | 13,100,000 | 200,000 | Group 4 |
| Los Angeles | 66 | B | 2,557,426 | 2,070,859 | 8,485 | 244.06 | 111,284 | 199,210 | 176,073 | 35,000 | 0 | 0 | 2,557,426 | 0 | City of Los Angeles |
| Point Reyes | 3 | B | 237,835 | 150,121 | 1,900 | 79.01 | 68,227 | Leased | 19,487 | 14,000 | 21,462 | 0 | 211,973 | 4,400 | Laura Natkins |
| St. Helena | 6 | M | 1,719,575 | 1,472,437 | 10,000 | 147.24 | 123,823 | Owned | 123,315 | 100,000 | 25,000 | 91,450 | 325,294 | 1,277,831 | Valley Architects |
| *Colorado* | | | | | | | | | | | | | | | |
| Montrose | 29 | MS | 6,194,138 | 4,677,078 | 39,184 | 119.36 | 408,553 | 670,000 | 438,507 | 82,000 | 113,000 | 0 | 5,565,923 | 515,215 | Patrick Davis Assocs. |
| *Connecticut* | | | | | | | | | | | | | | | |
| Branford | 27 | M | 3,971,100 | 3,257,100 | 25,100 | 129.76 | 442,100 | Owned | 271,900 | 159,000 | 0 | 350,000 | 3,164,000 | 457,100 | Buchanan Assocs. |
| Old Greenwich | 15 | M | 3,794,164 | 2,912,700 | 16,509 | 176.43 | 309,854 | Owned | 571,610 | 85,000 | 100,000 | 350,000 | 635,652 | 2,708,512 | Mark B. Thompson |
| Woodbury | 9 | M | 269,000 | 188,000 | 3,100 | 60.65 | 55,000 | Owned | 26,000 | 25,920 | 0 | 70,000 | 164,000 | 35,000 | Felix Drury |

Symbol Code: B—Branch Library; BS—Branch & System Headquarters; M—Main Library; MS—Main & System Headquarters; S—System Headquarters; n/a—not available

**Table 2 / Public Library Buildings, 1998: Additions and Renovations** *(cont.)*

| Community | Pop. ('000) | Code | Project Cost | Const. Cost | Gross Sq. Ft. | Sq. Ft. Cost | Equip. Cost | Site Cost | Other Costs | Volumes | Federal Funds | State Funds | Local Funds | Gift Funds | Architect |
|---|---|---|---|---|---|---|---|---|---|---|---|---|---|---|---|
| *Delaware* | | | | | | | | | | | | | | | |
| Claymont | 42 | M | 538,875 | 388,156 | 6,000 | 64.69 | 93,214 | Leased | 57,505 | 35,000 | 0 | 146,930 | 338,445 | 53,500 | Design Exchange |
| *Florida* | | | | | | | | | | | | | | | |
| Lake Butler | 13 | M | 124,274 | 108,493 | 3,300 | 32.88 | 6,639 | Owned | 9,142 | 30,000 | 61,399 | 0 | 62,875 | 0 | Skinner & Assocs. |
| Marco Island | 25 | B | 1,869,871 | 1,269,453 | 12,345 | 102.83 | 218,161 | Owned | 382,257 | 60,000 | 0 | 0 | 1,818,089 | 51,782 | Architectural Network |
| Merritt Island | 50 | M | 1,326,778 | 1,122,841 | 21,500 | 52.23 | 62,500 | Owned | 141,437 | 100,000 | 0 | 0 | 1,326,778 | n/a | Rood & Zwick |
| Tampa | 46 | B | 1,391,687 | 914,352 | 6,831 | 133.85 | 65,475 | 328,000 | 83,860 | 26,000 | 0 | 435,000 | 746,687 | 210,000 | Jan Abell Ken Garcia |
| Temple Terrace | 85 | M | 2,111,009 | 1,460,239 | 20,000 | 73.01 | 254,881 | 187,231 | 208,658 | 120,000 | 0 | 400,000 | 1,660,961 | 50,048 | Harvard Jolly Clees... |
| *Georgia* | | | | | | | | | | | | | | | |
| Clayton | 14 | B | 740,113 | 613,841 | 8,643 | 71.02 | 76,509 | Owned | 49,763 | 50,000 | 0 | 600,352 | 136,604 | 3,157 | Bailey Assocs. |
| Swainsboro | 21 | B | 1,109,931 | 768,101 | 6,000 | 128.02 | 277,452 | Owned | 64,378 | 44,207 | 0 | 847,732 | 217,347 | 44,852 | James W. Buckley |
| *Illinois* | | | | | | | | | | | | | | | |
| Carmi | 6 | M | 1,041,338 | 690,663 | 8,560 | 80.68 | 84,675 | 196,000 | 70,000 | 43,000 | 0 | 333,000 | 618,338 | 90,000 | Walker/Baker |
| Fairview Heights | 15 | M | 347,428 | 292,040 | 20,000 | 14.60 | 49,588 | Owned | 5,800 | n/a | 0 | 129,751 | 207,089 | 10,588 | EWR Assocs. |
| Gurnee | 49 | M | 5,896,428 | 4,105,525 | 54,000 | 76.03 | 1,176,984 | Owned | 613,919 | 211,000 | 0 | 250,000 | 5,646,428 | 0 | Frye, Gillan, Molinaro |
| Leaf River | 2 | M | 243,333 | 211,306 | 5,376 | 39.31 | 14,926 | 1 | 17,100 | 10,484 | 0 | 80,000 | 163,333 | 0 | Steven M. Papesh |
| Marion | 15 | M | 3,220,000 | 2,760,000 | 20,500 | 134.63 | 164,430 | Owned | 296,570 | n/a | 0 | 250,000 | 2,841,000 | 130,000 | Walker/Baker |
| Mascoutah | 6 | M | 981,277 | 803,363 | 12,228 | 65.70 | 24,402 | 92,880 | 60,632 | 65,000 | 0 | 225,000 | 731,583 | 24,694 | EWR Assocs. |
| Morton | 15 | M | 850,000 | 690,276 | 19,200 | 35.95 | 68,741 | Owned | 90,983 | 81,250 | 0 | 250,000 | 250,000 | 350,000 | Donald D. Westlake |
| Oak Lawn | 56 | M | 211,436 | 159,991 | 2,500 | 64.00 | 25,132 | Owned | 26,313 | n/a | 0 | 79,947 | 131,489 | 0 | Gilfillan & Callahan |
| St. Charles | 38 | M | 178,871 | 133,221 | 1,832 | 72.72 | 12,566 | Owned | 33,084 | n/a | 0 | 65,000 | 20,000 | 93,871 | Forrest Wendt |
| Tremont | 5 | M | 648,845 | 441,796 | 6,272 | 70.44 | 51,000 | 100,000 | 56,049 | 25,000 | 0 | 219,514 | 380,231 | 49,100 | Mark Misselhorn |
| *Indiana* | | | | | | | | | | | | | | | |
| Aurora | 15 | MS | 1,195,562 | 855,885 | 9,672 | 88.49 | 220,654 | Owned | 119,023 | 27,000 | 0 | 0 | 1,195,562 | 0 | HTK Architects |
| Winamac | 10 | M | 220,809 | 163,201 | n/a | n/a | 26,249 | Owned | 31,359 | 100,000 | 0 | 10,000 | 210,809 | 0 | Halstead, Thompson |

Symbol Code: B—Branch Library; BS—Branch & System Headquarters; M—Main Library; MS—Main & System Headquarters; S—System Headquarters; n/a—not available

Table 2 / Public Library Buildings, 1998: Additions and Renovations *(cont.)*

| Community | Pop. ('000) | Code | Project Cost | Const. Cost | Gross Sq. Ft. | Sq. Ft. Cost | Equip. Cost | Site Cost | Other Costs | Volumes | Federal Funds | State Funds | Local Funds | Gift Funds | Architect |
|---|---|---|---|---|---|---|---|---|---|---|---|---|---|---|---|
| *Iowa* | | | | | | | | | | | | | | | |
| Harlan | 8 | M | 401,858 | 234,907 | 4,100 | 57.29 | 115,799 | Owned | 51,152 | 52,000 | 0 | 0 | 82,000 | 319,858 | Feuert, Ramsey... |
| *Kansas* | | | | | | | | | | | | | | | |
| Lenexa | 32 | B | 3,167,730 | 2,259,157 | 17,291 | 130.65 | 615,157 | Owned | 293,416 | 76,760 | 0 | 0 | 3,167,730 | 0 | Gould Evans... |
| Newton | 18 | M | 211,621 | 169,789 | 9,830 | 17.27 | 28,076 | Owned | 13,758 | 66,000 | 31,840 | 0 | 170,585 | 9,196 | Lester Limon |
| Pittsburg | 18 | M | 3,009,791 | 2,108,440 | 27,000 | 78.09 | 282,162 | 208,415 | 410,774 | 7,382 | 0 | 0 | 2,935,083 | 74,708 | Glenn Livingood... |
| Salina | 44 | M | 1,879,586 | 1,577,065 | 39,500 | 39.93 | 160,585 | Owned | 141,936 | 230,000 | 30,000 | 0 | 1,424,586 | 425,000 | Jones-Gillam |
| *Louisiana* | | | | | | | | | | | | | | | |
| New Iberia | 2 | B | 287,540 | 252,117 | 2,100 | 120.06 | 10,000 | Owned | 25,423 | 8,000 | 0 | 0 | 287,540 | 0 | David Courville |
| Oil City | 2 | B | 107,200 | 41,344 | 1,600 | 25.84 | 15,606 | 50,250 | 0 | 6,700 | 0 | 0 | 106,950 | 250 | none |
| *Maine* | | | | | | | | | | | | | | | |
| Bangor | 33 | M | 9,562,469 | 6,983,814 | 60,000 | 116.40 | 464,307 | Owned | 2,114,348 | 500,000 | 0 | 0 | 2,844,846 | 6,717,623 | Robert A.M. Stern |
| *Maryland* | | | | | | | | | | | | | | | |
| Bel Air | 99 | M | 8,014,980 | 6,271,000 | 50,000 | 125.42 | 964,980 | Owned | 779,000 | 400,000 | 0 | 0 | 8,014,980 | n/a | Getz Taylor Koster |
| Denton | 30 | MS | 2,494,274 | 1,839,870 | 24,428 | 75.32 | 454,158 | Owned | 200,246 | 100,000 | 744,274 | 0 | 1,750,000 | 0 | Becker, Morgan... |
| *Massachusetts* | | | | | | | | | | | | | | | |
| Clarksburg | 2 | MS | 419,244 | 334,588 | 3,269 | 102.35 | 10,490 | 35,000 | 39,166 | 10,000 | 0 | 203,000 | 203,000 | 13,244 | Architecture+ |
| Duxbury | 15 | M | 6,466,423 | 4,914,792 | 39,625 | 124.03 | 667,234 | Owned | 884,397 | 140,000 | 197,608 | 2,127,801 | 3,000,000 | 1,141,014 | Galliher Baier & Best |
| Harwich | 11 | M | 3,428,834 | 2,958,036 | 20,312 | 145.63 | 0 | 125,917 | 344,881 | 65,945 | 0 | 1,326,501 | 1,673,499 | 428,834 | CBT, Inc. |
| Medfield | 16 | M | 3,260,000 | 2,810,000 | 19,200 | 146.35 | 180,000 | Owned | 270,000 | 85,000 | 0 | 1,204,234 | 2,000,000 | 55,766 | Stahl Assocs. |
| New Bedford | 97 | MS | 4,288,829 | 3,548,737 | 38,562 | 92.03 | 194,175 | Owned | 545,917 | 173,844 | 311,226 | 1,113,086 | 2,864,517 | 0 | Tappé & Assocs. |
| Salem | 100 | M | 1,635,000 | 1,235,000 | 23,100 | 53.46 | 250,000 | Owned | 150,000 | 520,000 | 0 | 0 | 0 | 1,635,000 | C&R/Rizvi, Inc. |
| Wakefield | 25 | M | 5,247,000 | 4,143,000 | 28,300 | 146.40 | 385,000 | Owned | 719,000 | 115,000 | 0 | 1,772,477 | 3,274,523 | 200,000 | CBT, Inc. |
| Warwick | 1 | M | 242,400 | 210,800 | 2,400 | 87.83 | 5,000 | Owned | 26,600 | 14,000 | 89,490 | 82,930 | 65,000 | 5,000 | Wilson Rains |
| Westminster | 7 | M | 2,109,545 | 1,747,498 | 16,000 | 109.22 | 124,647 | Owned | 237,400 | 50,000 | 0 | 817,512 | 970,000 | 356,168 | Maximilian L. Ferro |

Symbol Code: B—Branch Library; BS—Branch & System Headquarters; M—Main Library; MS—Main & System Headquarters; S—System Headquarters; n/a—not available

# Table 2 / Public Library Buildings, 1998: Additions and Renovations *(cont.)*

| Community | Pop. ('000) | Code | Project Cost | Const. Cost | Gross Sq. Ft. | Sq. Ft. Cost | Equip. Cost | Site Cost | Other Costs | Volumes | Federal Funds | State Funds | Local Funds | Gift Funds | Architect |
|---|---|---|---|---|---|---|---|---|---|---|---|---|---|---|---|
| *Minnesota* | | | | | | | | | | | | | | | |
| Duluth | 34 | B | 323,000 | 187,800 | 7,100 | 26.45 | 122,000 | Leased | 13,200 | 51,000 | 0 | 0 | 323,000 | 0 | Darryl Booker |
| Eagan | n/a | MS | 1,679,052 | 1,140,906 | 52,470 | 21.74 | 347,881 | Owned | 190,265 | n/a | 0 | 69,538 | 1,609,514 | 0 | Meyer, Scherer... |
| Minneapolis | 30 | B | 3,000,000 | 2,200,000 | 14,900 | 147.65 | 200,000 | 210,000 | 390,000 | 35,000 | 0 | 0 | 3,000,000 | 0 | Meyer, Scherer... |
| Ortonville | 4 | B | 409,500 | 385,900 | 4,700 | 82.11 | 3,600 | Owned | 20,000 | 15,000 | 0 | 158,828 | 186,936 | 63,736 | Glen L. Lindberg |
| Sauk Centre | 4 | B | 650,219 | 507,891 | 4,896 | 103.74 | 49,489 | Owned | 92,839 | n/a | 0 | 150,000 | 495,957 | 4,262 | Zuber Baker Ringdahl |
| Worthington | 19 | M | 416,874 | 384,354 | 16,872 | 22.78 | 10,862 | Owned | 21,658 | 52,600 | 147,250 | 0 | 269,624 | 0 | Vetter & Johnson |
| *New Hampshire* | | | | | | | | | | | | | | | |
| Northwood | 3 | M | 65,287 | 60,487 | 1,904 | 31.77 | 0 | Owned | 4,800 | 4,000 | 19,245 | 0 | 46,042 | 0 | Dennis Mires |
| Sullivan | 1 | M | 72,000 | 72,000 | 950 | 75.79 | 0 | Owned | 0 | n/a | 0 | 0 | 1,250 | 70,750 | none |
| *New Jersey* | | | | | | | | | | | | | | | |
| Fairview | 11 | M | 1,075,660 | 492,287 | 5,000 | 98.46 | 112,073 | 335,000 | 136,300 | 40,000 | 212,500 | 50,000 | 798,160 | 15,000 | Arcari & Iovino |
| Montclair | 38 | MS | 7,790,710 | 5,436,256 | 55,000 | 98.84 | 870,252 | Owned | 1,484,202 | 200,000 | 0 | 0 | 5,290,710 | 2,500,000 | Hillier Group |
| *New York* | | | | | | | | | | | | | | | |
| Bronx | 33 | B | 2,028,000 | 1,842,000 | 14,209 | 129.64 | 75,000 | Owned | 111,000 | 34,000 | 107,000 | 0 | 1,421,000 | 500,000 | Eric Witzler |
| Brooklyn | 15 | M | 140,000 | 90,000 | 2,500 | 36.00 | 50,000 | Owned | 0 | n/a | 0 | 0 | 140,000 | n/a | Elisabeth Martin |
| Cortland | 27 | M | 51,304 | 30,422 | 386 | 78.81 | 13,745 | Owned | 7,137 | 4,600 | 0 | 0 | 29,954 | 21,350 | Christine T. Place |
| East Hampton | 6 | M | 3,524,550 | 3,104,080 | 16,740 | 185.43 | 129,392 | Owned | 291,078 | 70,000 | 0 | 0 | 0 | 3,524,550 | Robert A.M. Stern |
| Little Genesee | 2 | M | 3,900 | 2,000 | n/a | n/a | 1,400 | Owned | 500 | n/a | 0 | 950 | 2,950 | 0 | none |
| Long Beach | 40 | M | 3,770,000 | 2,700,000 | 26,000 | 103.85 | 350,000 | 160,000 | 560,000 | 145,000 | 0 | 65,000 | 3,705,000 | 0 | Beatty Harvey |
| New Rochelle | 10 | B | 349,000 | 310,000 | 2,500 | 124.00 | 30,000 | Owned | 9,000 | 10,000 | 0 | 17,500 | | 331,500 | James Doherty |
| Oceanside | 38 | M | 4,670,000 | 3,200,000 | 30,000 | 106.67 | 370,000 | 500,000 | 600,000 | 140,000 | 0 | 70,000 | 4,600,000 | 0 | Beatty Harvey |
| Port Jefferson | 8 | M | 2,624,196 | 1,995,203 | 8,834 | 225.85 | 210,000 | 160,000 | 258,993 | 168,000 | 49,000 | 31,585 | 2,543,611 | 0 | G. Daniel Perry |
| Rochester | 713 | MS | 26,077,979 | 15,780,023 | 245,000 | 64.40 | 2,118,230 | 3,585,856 | 4,593,870 | 1,500,000 | 125,000 | 1,500,000 | 15,579,540 | 8,873,439 | R. Healy; Wm. Rawn |
| *Ohio* | | | | | | | | | | | | | | | |
| Cincinnati | 40 | B | 2,312,171 | 1,370,447 | 9,410 | 145.64 | 169,589 | 450,000 | 322,135 | n/a | 0 | 1,852,894 | 384,277 | 75,000 | Cole + Russell |

Symbol Code: B—Branch Library; BS—Branch & System Headquarters; M—Main Library; MS—Main & System Headquarters; S—System Headquarters; n/a—not available

**Table 2 / Public Library Buildings, 1998: Additions and Renovations** *(cont.)*

| Community | Pop. ('000) | Code | Project Cost | Const. Cost | Gross Sq. Ft. | Sq. Ft. Cost | Equip. Cost | Site Cost | Other Costs | Volumes | Federal Funds | State Funds | Local Funds | Gift Funds | Architect |
|---|---|---|---|---|---|---|---|---|---|---|---|---|---|---|---|
| Cincinnati | 69 | B | 2,207,770 | 1,785,209 | 12,100 | 147.54 | 118,372 | Owned | 304,189 | n/a | 0 | 2,082,409 | 125,361 | 0 | McClorey & Savage |
| Columbus | 24 | B | 1,899,130 | 1,455,743 | 22,729 | 64.05 | 204,681 | Owned | 238,706 | 114,003 | 0 | 948,365 | 948,365 | 2,400 | Design Group |
| Dayton | 20 | B | 779,474 | 602,486 | 6,087 | 98.98 | 38,860 | 60,000 | 78,128 | 50,000 | 0 | 0 | 779,474 | 0 | Edge & Tinney |
| Euclid | 53 | M | 5,000,000 | 3,875,000 | 47,370 | 81.80 | 675,000 | Owned | 450,000 | 300,000 | 0 | 0 | 5,000,000 | 0 | Meehan Architects |
| Fairview Park | 18 | B | 6,659,000 | 4,309,000 | 44,000 | 97.93 | 850,000 | 817,000 | 683,000 | 150,000 | 0 | 0 | 6,659,000 | 0 | David Holzheimer |
| Gahanna | 20 | B | 2,024,888 | 1,667,574 | 21,400 | 77.92 | 171,284 | Owned | 186,030 | 92,935 | 0 | 1,012,444 | 1,012,444 | 0 | Acock Assocs. |
| Sycamore | n/a | M | 452,000 | 387,000 | 5,984 | 64.67 | 10,000 | Owned | 55,000 | 32,000 | 0 | 0 | 282,000 | 170,000 | Rooney Clinger Murray |
| Washington Court House | 28 | M | 426,960 | 400,000 | 2,015 | 198.51 | 5,000 | Owned | 21,960 | 8,000 | 0 | 0 | 426,960 | 0 | McDonald, Cassell... |
| Westerville | 74 | MS | 7,600,000 | 5,958,139 | 71,000 | 83.92 | 768,000 | Owned | 873,861 | 410,000 | 0 | 0 | 7,600,000 | 0 | Design Group |
| *Oklahoma* | | | | | | | | | | | | | | | |
| Tulsa | 30 | B | 927,021 | 560,993 | 8,200 | 68.41 | 109,247 | 203,000 | 53,781 | 32,700 | 0 | 0 | 170,530 | 756,491 | Olsen-Coffey |
| Tulsa | 20 | B | 151,342 | 69,797 | 7,400 | 9.43 | 69,640 | Owned | 11,905 | 35,100 | 0 | 0 | 29,469 | 121,873 | Olsen-Coffey |
| *Oregon* | | | | | | | | | | | | | | | |
| Silverton | 17 | M | 1,629,768 | 1,275,422 | 17,172 | 74.27 | 206,543 | Leased | 147,803 | 140,000 | 94,451 | 0 | 15,434 | 1,519,883 | Richard P. Turi |
| *Pennsylvania* | | | | | | | | | | | | | | | |
| Dallas | 34 | M | 498,200 | 415,200 | 4,100 | 101.27 | 42,000 | Owned | 41,000 | 17,500 | 8,400 | 200,000 | 271,576 | 18,224 | Paul Rodda |
| Kutztown | 16 | M | 505,665 | 270,265 | 4,612 | 58.60 | 39,500 | 172,900 | 23,000 | 19,500 | 0 | 10,000 | 3,000 | 492,665 | Synergetics |
| Philadelphia | 10 | B | 753,000 | 615,000 | 6,500 | 94.62 | 67,000 | Owned | 71,000 | 32,550 | n/a | n/a | n/a | n/a | George Yu |
| Philadelphia | 26 | B | 554,000 | 372,000 | 6,800 | 54.71 | 118,500 | Owned | 63,500 | 16,823 | n/a | n/a | n/a | n/a | Kise, Straw, Kolodner |
| Philadelphia | 47 | B | 255,000 | 118,000 | 4,000 | 29.50 | 102,900 | Owned | 34,100 | 13,045 | n/a | n/a | n/a | n/a | Urban Consultants |
| Philadelphia | 71 | B | 786,000 | 478,000 | 14,700 | 32.52 | 230,800 | Owned | 77,200 | 98,571 | n/a | n/a | n/a | n/a | Kelly/Maiello |
| Philadelphia | 23 | B | 693,000 | 481,000 | 7,100 | 67.75 | 130,000 | Owned | 82,000 | 20,995 | n/a | n/a | n/a | n/a | Kise, Straw, Kolodner |

Symbol Code: B—Branch Library; BS—Branch & System Headquarters; M—Main Library; MS—Main & System Headquarters; S—System Headquarters; n/a—not available

**Table 2 / Public Library Buildings, 1998: Additions and Renovations** *(cont.)*

| Community | Pop. ('000) | Code | Project Cost | Const. Cost | Gross Sq. Ft. | Sq. Ft. Cost | Equip. Cost | Site Cost | Other Costs | Volumes | Federal Funds | State Funds | Local Funds | Gift Funds | Architect |
|---|---|---|---|---|---|---|---|---|---|---|---|---|---|---|---|
| Philadelphia | 33 | B | 391,000 | 260,000 | 6,000 | 43.33 | 93,000 | Owned | 38,000 | 50,384 | n/a | n/a | n/a | n/a | Urban Consultants |
| Philadelphia | 20 | B | 270,000 | 125,000 | 6,500 | 19.23 | 111,700 | Owned | 33,300 | 26,460 | n/a | n/a | n/a | n/a | Urban Consultants |
| Philadelphia | 32 | B | 1,028,000 | 794,000 | 8,800 | 90.23 | 111,800 | Owned | 122,200 | 23,617 | n/a | n/a | n/a | n/a | Kise, Straw, Kolodner |
| Philadelphia | 54 | B | 618,000 | 357,000 | 11,900 | 30.00 | 202,200 | Owned | 58,800 | 63,990 | n/a | n/a | n/a | n/a | Kelly/Maiello |
| Stroudsburg | 60 | M | 435,000 | 360,000 | 15,000 | 24.00 | 40,000 | Owned | 35,000 | 80,000 | 0 | 0 | 0 | 435,000 | Schoonover... |
| *Rhode Island* | | | | | | | | | | | | | | | |
| West Greenwich | 5 | M | 122,350 | 122,350 | 1,586 | 77.14 | 0 | Owned | 0 | 8,000 | 0 | 0 | 12,750 | 109,600 | B.R. Seelenbrandt |
| *South Dakota* | | | | | | | | | | | | | | | |
| Huron | 13 | M | 14,000 | 14,000 | 14,600 | 0.96 | 0 | Owned | 0 | n/a | 0 | 7,000 | 7,000 | 0 | none |
| *Tennessee* | | | | | | | | | | | | | | | |
| Halls | 7 | M | 53,601 | 52,912 | 960 | 55.12 | 0 | Owned | 689 | 14,662 | 0 | 0 | 53,601 | 0 | none |
| *Texas* | | | | | | | | | | | | | | | |
| Dallas | 19 | M | 2,072,000 | 1,369,314 | 46,896 | 29.20 | 429,703 | Owned | 272,983 | 61,140 | 0 | 0 | 1,000,000 | 1,072,000 | Booziotis & Co. |
| Garland | 206 | B | 659,973 | 454,569 | 8,000 | 56.81 | 143,090 | Owned | 62,314 | 40,000 | 17,048 | 0 | 642,925 | 0 | Ron Hobbs |
| Plano | 56 | B | 2,584,661 | 2,290,333 | 30,000 | 76.34 | 110,000 | Owned | 184,328 | 150,000 | 0 | 0 | 2,584,661 | 0 | Aguirre, Inc. |
| Port Isabel | 9 | M | 567,263 | 364,198 | 8,792 | 41.42 | 99,265 | 60,800 | 43,000 | 38,000 | 407,765 | 13,957 | 100,500 | 45,539 | Manuel Hinojosa |
| San Antonio | 38 | B | 494,141 | 414,761 | 9,652 | 42.97 | 35,000 | Owned | 44,380 | 37,000 | 36,000 | 0 | 458,141 | 0 | Andrew Perez |
| San Antonio | 77 | B | 503,227 | 401,679 | 12,448 | 32.27 | 51,868 | Owned | 49,680 | 60,000 | 0 | 0 | 503,227 | 0 | S.A. Partnership |
| Sweetwater | 17 | M | 330,648 | 309,472 | 9,980 | 31.03 | 0 | Owned | 21,176 | 63,237 | 100,000 | 0 | 34,000 | 196,648 | Newt Newberry |
| Wichita Falls | 106 | M | 3,997,118 | 2,910,919 | 61,500 | 47.33 | 750,834 | Owned | 335,365 | 250,000 | 0 | 0 | 3,997,118 | 0 | Dick Bundy |
| *Virginia* | | | | | | | | | | | | | | | |
| Fairfax | 92 | B | 3,847,988 | 2,982,968 | 27,745 | 143.56 | 385,000 | Owned | 480,020 | 167,000 | 0 | 0 | 3,847,988 | 0 | David Lipp |
| *Wisconsin* | | | | | | | | | | | | | | | |
| Milwaukee | 628 | M | 2,406,251 | 1,626,110 | 15,000 | 108.41 | 531,151 | Owned | 248,990 | 74,275 | 0 | 0 | 900,000 | 1,506,251 | Uihlein-Wilson |

Symbol Code: B—Branch Library; BS—Branch & System Headquarters; M—Main Library; MS—Main & System Headquarters; S—System Headquarters; n/a—not available

**Table 3 / New Academic Library Buildings, 1998**

| Name of Institution | Project Cost | Gross Area | Sq. Ft. Cost | Construction Cost | Equipment Cost | Book Capacity | Seating Capacity | Architect |
|---|---|---|---|---|---|---|---|---|
| Eastern Michigan University, Ypsilanti | $41,052,000 | 273,715 | $115.93 | $31,731,000 | $4,300,000 | 1,155,160 | 2,250 | Shepley, Bulfinch...; Giffels... |
| Wayne State University, Detroit | 33,000,000 | 300,429 | 93.20 | 28,000,000 | 4,200,000 | 100,000 | 2,700 | BEI Assocs. |
| Health Sciences and Human Services Lib., Univ. of Maryland, Baltimore | 32,000,000 | 190,000 | 121.05 | 23,000,000 | 7,000,000 | 500,000 | 900 | Perry, Dean, Rogers; |
| Science Lib., Univ. of California, Riverside | 30,471,000 | 167,134 | 150.24 | 25,111,000 | 1,747,000 | 600,000 | 1,500 | Ehrlich-Rominger; Shepley,... |
| Cleveland-Marshall College of Law Lib., Cleveland State Univ. | 16,800,000 | 110,000 | 127.27 | 14,000,000 | 1,500,000 | 532,710 | 396 | Collins Gordon Bostwick |
| Law School Lib., Boston College | 13,872,000 | 84,500 | 139.51 | 11,789,000 | 950,000 | 348,000 | 530 | Flansburgh & Assocs. |
| Augsburg College, Minneapolis | 12,500,000 | 74,000 | 124.32 | 9,200,000 | 1,390,000 | 205,000 | 640 | BWBR Architects |
| Bellarmine College, Louisville, KY | 10,000,000 | 67,585 | 101.72 | 6,875,000 | 800,000 | 200,000 | 400 | Hillier Group |
| Westminster College of Salt Lake City | 8,623,472 | 46,932 | 166.05 | 7,793,319 | 830,153 | 150,000 | 290 | Breslin Ridyard Fadero |
| Central Oregon Community College, Bend | 7,680,000 | 72,500 | 93.68 | 6,792,150 | 800,000 | 93,000 | 769 | WeGROUP Architects |
| Master's Seminary Lib., Sun Valley, CA | 6,100,000 | 35,000 | 145.71 | 5,100,000 | 1,000,000 | 200,000 | 176 | Larson Group |
| Champlain College, Burlington, VT | 5,800,000 | 29,500 | 163.00 | 4,805,000 | 500,000 | 100,000 | 326 | Truex Cullins & Partners |
| Science Research Ctr. Lib., Florida A&M University, Tallahassee | 4,561,000 | 10,369 | 335.81 | 3,482,000 | 466,030 | 10,000 | 100 | Karl Thorne Assocs. |
| Western State Univ. College of Law, Fullerton, CA | 4,145,000 | 31,000 | 125.32 | 3,885,000 | 260,000 | 400,000 | 421 | Keystone Design |
| Trinity University, San Antonio | 3,700,000 | 44,064 | 61.72 | 2,720,000 | 980,000 | 250,000 | 60 | Rehler, Vaughn & Koone |
| Univ. of Missouri Libs. Depository, Columbia | 3,000,000 | 12,400 | 225.81 | 2,800,000 | 190,500 | 1,800,000 | 0 | Peckham Guyton Albers... |
| Diehn Composers Room, Diehn Fine & Performing Arts Ctr., Old Dominion Univ., Norfolk, VA | 1,200,000 | 6,502 | 180.00 | 1,175,000 | 25,000 | 6,796 | 64 | Moseley McClintock |

**Table 4  /  Academic Library Buildings, Additions and Renovations, 1998**

| Institution | Status | Project Cost | Gross Area | Sq. Ft. Cost | Construction Cost | Equipment Cost | Book Capacity | Seating Capacity | Architect |
|---|---|---|---|---|---|---|---|---|---|
| Harvard Law School Library, Harvard University, Cambridge, MA | Total | $35,900,000 | 180,000 | $137.78 | $24,800,000 | $200,000 | 740,000 | 621 | Shepley Bulfinch... |
| | New | n/a | 2,000 | n/a | n/a | 0 | 0 | 0 | |
| | Renovated | n/a | 178,000 | n/a | n/a | 200,000 | 740,000 | 621 | |
| Green Library, Florida International Univ., Miami | Total | n/a | 325,000 | 93.57 | 30,409,206 | 3,214,715 | 1,080,750 | 2,062 | M.C. Harry & Assocs. |
| | New | n/a | 201,000 | 96.14 | 19,322,879 | 1,993,123 | 670,065 | 1,278 | |
| | Renovated | n/a | 124,000 | 89.40 | 11,086,327 | 1,221,592 | 410,685 | 784 | |
| Woodruff Library Center, Emory University, Atlanta | Total | 23,000,000 | 169,000 | 97.63 | 16,500,000 | n/a | 1,100,000 | 1,750 | Shepley Bulfinch... |
| | New | 10,500,000 | 69,000 | 118.84 | 8,200,000 | 1,500,000 | n/a | n/a | |
| | Renovated | 12,500,000 | 100,000 | 83.00 | 8,300,000 | n/a | n/a | n/a | |
| Morgan Library, Colorado State University, Fort Collins | Total | 20,637,000 | 279,193 | 57.30 | 16,000,000 | 2,400,000 | 1,400,000 | 2,400 | Luis O. Acosta; Perry Dean Rogers |
| | New | 14,637,000 | 130,567 | n/a | n/a | n/a | n/a | n/a | |
| | Renovated | 6,000,000 | 148,626 | n/a | n/a | n/a | n/a | n/a | |
| Old Dominion University Lib., Norfolk, VA | Total | 14,857,020 | 208,592 | 58.35 | 12,171,320 | 384,380 | 574,560 | 2,500 | Perry Dean Rogers |
| | New | n/a | 76,649 | n/a | n/a | n/a | n/a | n/a | |
| | Renovated | n/a | 131,943 | n/a | n/a | n/a | n/a | n/a | |
| Scheide Music Lib., Woolworth Ctr. for Musical Studies, Princeton University | Total | n/a | 55,000 | n/a | $11,500,000 | n/a | n/a | 98 | Juan Navarro Baldeweg; Wank Adams Slavin |
| | New | n/a | 34,000 | n/a | n/a | n/a | n/a | n/a | |
| | Renovated | n/a | 21,000 | n/a | n/a | n/a | n/a | n/a | |
| Morton Library, Union Theological Seminary, Richmond, VA | Total | 11,300,000 | 68,000 | 140.95 | 9,584,368 | n/a | 485,000 | 360 | Glave Firm |
| | New | n/a | 37,888 | n/a | n/a | n/a | n/a | n/a | |
| | Renovated | n/a | 30,112 | n/a | n/a | n/a | n/a | n/a | |
| Lamson Library, Plymouth (NH) State College | Total | 10,100,000 | 88,000 | 85.01 | 7,480,504 | 820,431 | 400,000 | 1,000 | Sheerr McCrystal Palson |
| | New | 5,364,362 | 33,000 | 123.25 | 4,067,214 | 307,662 | n/a | n/a | |
| | Renovated | 4,735,638 | 55,000 | 62.06 | 3,413,290 | 512,769 | n/a | n/a | |
| Mullins Library, University of Arkansas, Fayetteville | Total | n/a | 119,045 | 71.89 | 8,558,351 | n/a | n/a | 773 | AMR Architects |
| | New | n/a | 75,852 | 95.75 | 7,262,561 | n/a | n/a | 519 | |
| | Renovated | n/a | 43,193 | 30.00 | 1,295,790 | n/a | n/a | 254 | |

**Table 4 / Academic Library Buildings, Additions and Renovations, 1998 (cont.)**

| Institution | Status | Project Cost | Gross Area | Sq. Ft. Cost | Construction Cost | Equipment Cost | Book Capacity | Seating Capacity | Architect |
|---|---|---|---|---|---|---|---|---|---|
| Darling Library, Azusa Pacific University | Total | 6,700,000 | 55,000 | 100.00 | 5,500,000 | 1,200,000 | 80,000 | 250 | Winston Ko |
| | New | n/a | 9,000 | n/a | n/a | n/a | n/a | n/a | |
| | Renovated | n/a | 46,000 | n/a | n/a | n/a | n/a | n/a | |
| Hammermill Library, Mercyhurst College, Erie, PA | Total | 3,400,000 | 51,090 | 68.51 | 3,350,000 | 50,000 | 300,000 | 285 | Richard Weibel |
| | New | 1,400,000 | 8,160 | 165.44 | 1,350,000 | 50,000 | 0 | 0 | |
| | Renovated | 2,000,000 | 42,930 | 46.58 | 2,000,000 | 0 | 300,000 | 285 | |
| Science Library, Washington & Lee University, Lexington, VA | Total | 1,805,815 | 13,825 | 109.60 | 1,515,245 | 290,570 | 90,000 | 106 | Payette Assocs. |
| | New | 1,471,879 | 10,277 | 125.00 | 1,284,625 | 187,254 | n/a | 74 | |
| | Renovated | 333,936 | 3,548 | 65.00 | 230,620 | 103,316 | n/a | 32 | |
| Maki Library, Suomi College, Hancock, MI | Total | n/a | 12,100 | n/a | n/a | n/a | n/a | n/a | Hitch, Inc. |
| | New | 1,000,000 | 5,800 | 172.41 | 1,000,000 | n/a | 65,000 | n/a | |
| | Renovated | n/a | 6,300 | n/a | n/a | n/a | n/a | n/a | |

**Table 5 / Academic Library Buildings, Renovations Only, 1998**

| Institution | Project Cost | Gross Area | Sq. Ft. Cost | Construction Cost | Equipment Cost | Book Capacity | Seating Capacity | Architect |
|---|---|---|---|---|---|---|---|---|
| Eisenhower Library, Johns Hopkins Univ., Baltimore | $5,140,000 | 40,810 | $112.77 | $4,602,000 | n/a | n/a | n/a | Murphy & Dittenhafer |
| Mortola Library, Pace University, Pleasantville, NY | 308,382 | 1,085 | 139.34 | 151,182 | 157,200 | n/a | 28 | Carlton Murray |
| School of Law Lib., Washington & Lee Univ., Lexington, VA | 100,000 | 860 | 7.90 | 70,000 | 30,000 | 0 | 24 | Kirchner & Assocs. |
| Cotsen Children's Library, Princeton University | n/a | 4,600 | n/a | n/a | n/a | 23,000 | n/a | Smith-Miller & Hawkinson |
| Sterling Memorial Library, Yale University, New Haven, CT | n/a | 229,644 | n/a | n/a | n/a | 3,500,000 | 532 | Shepley Bulfinch... |

# Book Trade Research and Statistics

## Prices of U.S. and Foreign Published Materials

Stephen Bosch

Chair, ALA. ALCTS Library Materials Price Index Committee

The Library Materials Price Index Committee (LMPIC) of the American Library Association's Association for Library Collections and Technical Services (ALCTS) continues to monitor library prices for a variety of library materials and sources. As seen below, prices for library materials in general continued to increase in 1997 and 1998 at a rate much higher than the general U.S. Consumer Price Index. For 1998–1999 the CPI increased only 1.6 percent while journals again increased by more than 10 percent; prices for books were also increasing at faster rates than the CPI. Information concerning the Consumer Price Index can be found at the Bureau of Labor Statistics CPI home page at http://stats.bls.gov/cpihome.htm.

| Index | 1995 | Percent Change 1996 | 1997 | 1998/99 |
|---|---|---|---|---|
| Consumer price index (1998) | 2.9 | 3.3 | 1.7 | 1.6 |
| Periodicals | 10.8 | 9.9 | 10.3 | 10.4* |
| Serial services | 6.6 | 3.9 | 4.5 | 5.6* |
| Hardcover books | 5.6 | 6.0 | 0.4 | n.a. |
| Academic books | -0.1 | 3.6 | n.a. | n.a. |
| College books | 4.7 | 1.8 | 1.8 | 2.7 |
| Mass market paperbacks | 15.4 | 12.2 | 41.7 | n.a. |
| Trade paperbacks | 5.4 | -1.3 | 5.8 | n.a. |

\* Payment made in 1998 for 1999 receipt

n.a. = not available

### U.S. Published Materials

Tables 1 through 10 consist of average prices and price indexes for library materials published primarily in the United States. These indexes include periodicals (Table 1), serial services (Table 2), U.S. hardcover books (Table 3), North American academic books (Table 4), college books (Table 5), mass market paperback books (Table 6), trade paperback books (Table 7), daily newspapers and international newspapers (Tables 8A and 8B), nonprint media (Table 9), and CD-ROMs (Table 10).

(text continues on page 514)

**Table 1 / U.S. Periodicals: Average Prices and Price Indexes, 1997–1999**
Index Base: 1984 = 100

| Subject Area | 1984 Average Price | 1997 Average Price | 1997 Index | 1998 Average Price | 1998 Index | 1999 Average Price | 1999 Index |
|---|---|---|---|---|---|---|---|
| U.S. periodicals excluding Russian translations* | $54.97 | $181.98 | 331.1 | $200.74 | 365.2 | $221.66 | 403.2 |
| U.S. periodicals including Russian translations | 72.47 | 237.14 | 327.2 | 259.69 | 358.4 | 285.04 | 393.3 |
| Agriculture | 24.06 | 72.40 | 300.9 | 79.50 | 330.4 | 86.58 | 359.9 |
| Business and economics | 38.87 | 114.18 | 293.7 | 121.77 | 313.3 | 131.82 | 339.1 |
| Chemistry and physics | 228.90 | 957.36 | 418.2 | 1,062.49 | 464.2 | 1,189.46 | 519.6 |
| Children's periodicals | 12.21 | 23.08 | 189.0 | 24.15 | 197.8 | 24.69 | 202.2 |
| Education | 34.01 | 95.34 | 280.3 | 103.98 | 305.7 | 114.04 | 335.3 |
| Engineering | 78.70 | 273.31 | 347.3 | 306.60 | 389.6 | 338.59 | 430.2 |
| Fine and applied arts | 26.90 | 50.02 | 185.9 | 52.08 | 193.6 | 54.53 | 202.7 |
| General interest periodicals | 27.90 | 40.72 | 146.0 | 42.26 | 151.5 | 43.32 | 155.3 |
| History | 23.68 | 54.20 | 228.9 | 57.31 | 242.0 | 59.88 | 252.9 |
| Home economics | 37.15 | 98.88 | 266.2 | 100.39 | 270.2 | 108.07 | 290.9 |
| Industrial arts | 30.40 | 93.79 | 308.5 | 99.05 | 325.8 | 106.33 | 349.8 |

| | | | | | | |
|---|---|---|---|---|---|---|
| Journalism and communications | 39.25 | 98.16 | 250.1 | 104.26 | 265.6 | 108.71 | 277.0 |
| Labor and industrial relations | 29.87 | 92.28 | 308.9 | 98.99 | 331.4 | 107.74 | 360.7 |
| Law | 31.31 | 85.57 | 273.3 | 89.81 | 286.8 | 92.33 | 294.9 |
| Library and information sciences | 38.85 | 78.00 | 200.8 | 86.12 | 221.7 | 90.80 | 233.7 |
| Literature and language | 23.02 | 46.72 | 203.0 | 49.98 | 217.1 | 53.24 | 231.3 |
| Mathematics, botany, geology, general science | 106.56 | 379.84 | 356.5 | 420.36 | 394.5 | 466.61 | 437.9 |
| Medicine | 125.57 | 461.60 | 367.6 | 524.65 | 417.8 | 597.03 | 475.5 |
| Philosophy and religion | 21.94 | 48.84 | 222.6 | 51.71 | 235.7 | 54.42 | 248.0 |
| Physical education and recreation | 20.54 | 45.65 | 222.2 | 48.10 | 234.2 | 50.17 | 244.3 |
| Political science | 32.43 | 91.82 | 283.1 | 100.82 | 310.9 | 110.45 | 340.6 |
| Psychology | 69.74 | 233.90 | 335.4 | 258.91 | 371.3 | 287.91 | 412.8 |
| Russian translations | 381.86 | 1,216.51 | 318.6 | 1,311.50 | 343.5 | 1,421.31 | 372.2 |
| Sociology and anthropology | 43.87 | 137.54 | 313.5 | 151.01 | 344.2 | 166.48 | 379.5 |
| Zoology | 78.35 | 338.31 | 431.8 | 385.40 | 491.9 | 433.79 | 553.7 |
| Total number of periodicals | | | | | | |
| Excluding Russian translations | 3,731 | | 3,729 | | 3,729 | | 3,729 |
| Including Russian translations | 3,942 | | 3,939 | | 3,938 | | 3,937 |

For further comments, see *American Libraries*, May 1997, May 1998, and May 1999.

Compiled by Barbara Albee, the Faxon Company, and Brenda Dingley, University of Missouri, Kansas City.

*The category Russian translations was added in 1986.

**Table 2 / U.S. Serial Services: Average Price and Price Indexes 1997–1999**

Index Base: 1984 = 100

| Subject Area | 1984 Average Price | 1997 Average Price | 1997 Index | 1998 Average Price | 1998 Percent Increase | 1998 Index | 1999 Average Price | 1999 Percent Increase | 1999 Index |
|---|---|---|---|---|---|---|---|---|---|
| U.S. serial services* | $295.13 | $578.22 | 195.9 | $604.31 | 4.5% | 204.8 | $638.18 | 5.6% | 216.24 |
| Business | 437.07 | 751.99 | 172.1 | 781.33 | 3.9% | 178.8 | 798.73 | 2.2% | 182.75 |
| General and humanities | 196.55 | 429.12 | 218.3 | 455.78 | 6.2% | 231.9 | 492.59 | 8.1% | 250.62 |
| Law | 275.23 | 592.84 | 215.4 | 611.71 | 3.2% | 222.3 | 668.61 | 9.3% | 242.93 |
| Science and technology | 295.36 | 716.95 | 242.7 | 757.33 | 5.6% | 256.4 | 804.40 | 6.2% | 272.35 |
| Social sciences | 283.82 | 536.85 | 189.2 | 557.34 | 3.8% | 196.4 | 577.89 | 3.7% | 203.61 |
| U.S. documents | 97.37 | 151.38 | 155.5 | 162.32 | 7.2% | 166.7 | 166.57 | 2.6% | 171.07 |
| Total number of services | 1,537 | | 1,281 | | | 1,282 | | | 1,286 |

Compiled by Nancy J. Chaffin, Arizona State University (West) from data suppled by the Faxon Company, publishers' list prices, and library acquisitions records.

The definition of a serial service has been taken from *American National Standard for Library and Information Services and Related Publishing Practices-Library Materials-Criteria for Price Indexes* (ANSI Z39.20 - 1983).

* Excludes Wilson Index; excludes Russian translations as of 1988.

# Table 3 / U.S. Hardcover Books: Average Prices and Price Indexes, 1995–1998

Index Base: 1984 = 100

| Subject Area | 1984 Average Price | 1995 Volumes | 1995 Average Price | 1995 Index | 1996 Volumes | 1996 Average Price | 1996 Index | 1997 Final Volumes | 1997 Final Average Price | 1997 Final Index | 1998 Preliminary Volumes | 1998 Preliminary Average Price | 1998 Preliminary Index |
|---|---|---|---|---|---|---|---|---|---|---|---|---|---|
| Agriculture | $34.92 | 392 | $49.00 | 140.3 | 399 | $45.11 | 129.2 | 507 | $47.54 | 136.1 | 472 | $43.60 | 124.9 |
| Art | 33.03 | 1,116 | 41.23 | 124.8 | 1,070 | 53.40 | 161.7 | 870 | 46.00 | 139.3 | 873 | 43.22 | 130.8 |
| Biography | 22.53 | 1,596 | 30.01 | 133.2 | 1,829 | 31.67 | 140.6 | 1,773 | 33.50 | 148.7 | 1,625 | 33.15 | 147.1 |
| Business | 26.01 | 972 | 46.90 | 180.3 | 1,005 | 52.62 | 202.3 | 689 | 52.89 | 203.3 | 780 | 54.77 | 210.6 |
| Education | 24.47 | 610 | 43.00 | 175.7 | 652 | 47.10 | 192.5 | 453 | 45.57 | 186.2 | 451 | 49.49 | 202.2 |
| Fiction | 14.74 | 2,345 | 21.47 | 145.7 | 2,915 | 22.89 | 155.3 | 2,882 | 21.41 | 145.2 | 2,528 | 22.25 | 150.9 |
| General works | 35.61 | 1,209 | 54.11 | 152.0 | 1,181 | 68.36 | 192.0 | 1,200 | 59.39 | 166.8 | 870 | 59.65 | 167.5 |
| History | 27.53 | 1,691 | 42.19 | 153.3 | 2,028 | 45.62 | 165.7 | 2,052 | 43.51 | 158.0 | 1,854 | 43.39 | 157.6 |
| Home economics | 15.70 | 651 | 22.53 | 143.5 | 655 | 23.39 | 149.0 | 658 | 23.32 | 148.5 | 523 | 24.04 | 153.1 |
| Juvenile | 10.02 | 3,649 | 14.55 | 145.2 | 3,730 | 15.97 | 159.4 | 2,013 | 15.64 | 156.1 | 1,988 | 16.12 | 160.9 |
| Language | 22.97 | 320 | 54.89 | 239.0 | 399 | 58.81 | 256.0 | 414 | 57.95 | 252.3 | 363 | 58.52 | 254.8 |
| Law | 43.88 | 716 | 73.09 | 166.6 | 827 | 88.51 | 201.7 | 740 | 89.15 | 203.2 | 663 | 79.32 | 180.8 |
| Literature | 23.57 | 1,302 | 38.49 | 163.3 | 1,575 | 43.28 | 183.6 | 1,299 | 44.89 | 190.5 | 1,233 | 45.05 | 191.1 |
| Medicine | 40.65 | 2,035 | 75.80 | 186.5 | 2,480 | 81.48 | 200.4 | 2,088 | 85.92 | 211.4 | 1,922 | 81.77 | 201.2 |
| Music | 27.79 | 251 | 43.27 | 155.7 | 253 | 39.21 | 141.1 | 208 | 43.58 | 156.8 | 243 | 47.25 | 170.0 |
| Philosophy and psychology | 29.70 | 1,001 | 45.26 | 152.4 | 1,154 | 48.40 | 163.0 | 949 | 48.06 | 161.8 | 952 | 50.40 | 169.7 |
| Poetry and drama | 26.75 | 567 | 34.96 | 130.7 | 606 | 34.15 | 127.7 | 568 | 36.76 | 137.4 | 496 | 36.02 | 134.6 |
| Religion | 17.76 | 1,364 | 34.27 | 193.0 | 1,544 | 36.62 | 206.2 | 1,385 | 40.52 | 228.2 | 1,273 | 35.08 | 197.5 |
| Science | 46.57 | 2,095 | 93.52 | 200.8 | 2,372 | 90.63 | 194.6 | 2,242 | 78.14 | 167.8 | 2,132 | 72.39 | 155.4 |
| Sociology and economics | 33.35 | 5,145 | 55.51 | 166.4 | 5,973 | 53.82 | 161.4 | 5,081 | 55.05 | 165.1 | 5,023 | 58.36 | 175.0 |
| Sports and recreation | 20.16 | 517 | 32.14 | 159.4 | 591 | 34.71 | 172.2 | 639 | 32.35 | 160.5 | 570 | 37.21 | 184.6 |
| Technology | 45.80 | 1,454 | 88.28 | 192.8 | 1,599 | 91.60 | 200.0 | 1,559 | 89.96 | 196.4 | 1,273 | 85.47 | 186.6 |
| Travel | 21.31 | 199 | 38.30 | 179.7 | 179 | 33.92 | 159.2 | 236 | 30.58 | 143.5 | 186 | 36.59 | 171.7 |
| Total | $29.99 | 31,197 | $47.15 | 157.2 | 35,016 | $50.00 | 166.7 | 30,505 | $50.22 | 167.5 | 28,293 | $49.60 | 165.4 |

Compiled by Stephen Bosch, University of Arizona, from data supplied by the R. R. Bowker Company. Price indexes on Tables 3 and 7 are based on books recorded in the R. R. Bowker Company's Weekly Record (cumulated in the American Book Publishing Record). The 1998 preliminary figures include items listed during 1998 with an imprint date of 1998. Final data for previous years include items listed between January of that year and June of the following year with an imprint date of the specified year.

**Table 4 / North American Academic Books: Average Prices and Price Indexes 1995–1997**
(Index Base: 1989 = 100)

| Subject Area | LC Class | 1989 | | 1995 | | 1996 | | 1997 | | | |
|---|---|---|---|---|---|---|---|---|---|---|---|
| | | No. of Titles | Average Price | No. of Titles | Average Price | No. of Titles | Average Price | No. of Titles | Average Price | % Change 1996–1997 | Index |
| Agriculture | S | 897 | $45.13 | 1,230 | $67.41 | 1,173 | $56.73 | 1,107 | $62.40 | 10.0 | 138.3 |
| Anthropology | GN | 406 | 32.81 | 514 | 35.51 | 598 | 37.82 | 583 | 40.14 | 6.1 | 122.4 |
| Botany | QK | 251 | 69.02 | 204 | 82.05 | 212 | 100.21 | 200 | 94.00 | -6.2 | 136.2 |
| Business and economics | H | 5,979 | 41.67 | 6,294 | 48.65 | 6,823 | 51.07 | 6,972 | 53.15 | 4.1 | 127.6 |
| Chemistry | QD | 577 | 110.61 | 506 | 153.12 | 557 | 171.70 | 498 | 159.37 | -7.2 | 144.1 |
| Education | L | 1,685 | 29.61 | 2,200 | 35.10 | 2,506 | 38.18 | 2,291 | 39.43 | 3.3 | 133.2 |
| Engeering and technology | T | 4,569 | 64.94 | 5,076 | 74.82 | 5,630 | 78.68 | 5,974 | 82.96 | 5.4 | 127.7 |
| Fine and applied arts | M-N | 3,040 | 40.72 | 4,444 | 48.85 | 3,854 | 42.04 | 3,403 | 45.68 | 8.6 | 112.2 |
| General works | A | 333 | 134.65 | 481 | 45.16 | 141 | 91.81 | 145 | 90.37 | -1.6 | 67.1 |
| Geography | G | 396 | 47.34 | 626 | 50.78 | 724 | 53.02 | 687 | 60.40 | 13.9 | 127.6 |
| Geology | QE | 303 | 63.49 | 207 | 86.69 | 205 | 80.95 | 213 | 87.02 | 7.5 | 137.1 |
| History | C-D-E-F | 5,549 | 31.34 | 6,279 | 33.28 | 6,919 | 35.46 | 6,406 | 38.86 | 9.6 | 124.0 |
| Home economics | TX | 535 | 27.10 | 781 | 27.62 | 839 | 30.92 | 691 | 27.24 | -11.9 | 100.5 |
| Industrial arts | TT | 175 | 23.89 | 251 | 22.97 | 264 | 23.52 | 203 | 26.48 | 12.6 | 110.8 |
| Law | K | 1,252 | 51.10 | 1,455 | 59.49 | 1,609 | 62.92 | 1,479 | 66.18 | 5.2 | 129.5 |

| Subject | LC Class | | | | | | | | | | |
|---|---|---|---|---|---|---|---|---|---|---|---|
| Library and information science | Z | 857 | 44.51 | 764 | 49.95 | 820 | 56.11 | 653 | 59.06 | 5.3 | 132.7 |
| Literature and language | P | 10,812 | 24.99 | 12,285 | 29.58 | 13,369 | 30.71 | 12,717 | 33.20 | 8.1 | 132.9 |
| Mathematics and computer science | QA | 2,707 | 44.68 | 3,109 | 57.13 | 3,620 | 59.04 | 3,910 | 61.23 | 3.7 | 137.0 |
| Medicine | R | 5,028 | 58.38 | 5,707 | 66.14 | 6,665 | 67.58 | 6,446 | 70.31 | 4.0 | 120.4 |
| Military and naval science | U-V | 715 | 33.57 | 387 | 39.10 | 576 | 78.84 | 458 | 60.67 | -23.0 | 180.7 |
| Physical education and recreation | GV | 814 | 20.38 | 1,106 | 31.70 | 1,067 | 23.31 | 881 | 26.48 | 13.6 | 129.9 |
| Philosophy and religion | B | 3,518 | 29.06 | 4,537 | 36.14 | 5,005 | 41.13 | 4,755 | 41.87 | 1.8 | 144.1 |
| Physics and astronomy | QB | 1,219 | 64.59 | 1,161 | 91.73 | 1,242 | 94.10 | 1,140 | 92.21 | -2.0 | 142.8 |
| Political science | J | 1,650 | 36.76 | 1,681 | 47.83 | 2,004 | 45.57 | 2,118 | 51.76 | 13.6 | 140.8 |
| Psychology | BF | 890 | 31.97 | 1,046 | 38.71 | 1,245 | 37.00 | 1,140 | 39.46 | 6.7 | 123.4 |
| Science (general) | Q | 433 | 56.10 | 360 | 73.06 | 446 | 81.12 | 487 | 70.72 | -12.8 | 126.1 |
| Sociology | HM | 2,742 | 29.36 | 3,692 | 37.36 | 4,186 | 37.13 | 4,123 | 41.34 | 11.3 | 140.8 |
| Zoology | QH,L,P,R | 1,967 | 71.28 | 1,924 | 79.87 | 1,963 | 80.66 | 1,736 | 84.96 | 5.3 | 119.2 |
| Average for all subjects | | 59,299 | $41.69 | 68,307 | $48.11 | 74,262 | $49.86 | 71,416 | $52.68 | 5.7 | 126.4 |

Compiled by Stephen Bosch, University of Arizona, from electronic data provided by Baker and Taylor, Blackwell North America, Coutts Library Services, and Yankee Book Peddler. The data represent all titles (including hardcover, trade, and paperback books, as well as annuals) treated for all approval plan customers serviced by the four vendors. This table covers titles published or distributed in the United States and Canada during the calendar years listed.

This index does not include paperback editions. The overall average price of materials is lower than if the index consisted only of hardbound editions.

**Table 5 / U.S. College Books: Average Prices and Price Indexes, 1983, 1996, 1997, 1998**
(Index Base for all years: 1983=100. 1997 also indexed to 1996; 1998 also indexed to 1997)

| Choice Subject Categories | 1983 | | 1996 | | | 1997 | | | | 1998 | | | |
|---|---|---|---|---|---|---|---|---|---|---|---|---|---|
| | No. of Titles | Avg.Price Per Title | No. of Titles | Avg.Price Per Title | Prices Indexed to 1983 | No. of Titles | Avg.Price Per Title | Prices Indexed to 1983 | Prices Indexed to 1996 | No. of Titles | Avg.Price Per Title | Prices Indexed to 1983 | Prices Indexed to 1997 |
| General | 11 | $24.91 | 32 | $43.65 | 175.2 | 22 | $46.10 | 185.1 | 105.6 | 18 | $37.11 | 149.0 | 80.5 |
| **Humanities** | | | | | | | | | | | | | |
| Art and architecture | 40 | $24.53 | 29 | $44.04 | 179.5 | 30 | $45.45 | 185.3 | 103.2 | 36 | $45.41 | 185.1 | 99.9 |
| Communication | 372 | 40.31 | 269 | 58.36 | 144.8 | 253 | 59.34 | 147.2 | 101.7 | 304 | 52.81 | 131.0 | 89.0 |
| Language and literature | 51 | 22.22 | 77 | 42.06 | 189.3 | 64 | 45.92 | 206.7 | 109.2 | 68 | 45.33 | 204.0 | 98.7 |
| | 109 | 23.39 | 128 | 45.56 | 194.3 | 90 | 44.12 | 188.6 | 96.8 | 82 | 45.11 | 192.9 | 102.2 |
| African and Middle Eastern [4] | — | — | 13 | 40.47 | | 20 | 31.27 | | 77.3 | 34 | 35.46 | | 113.4 |
| Asian and Oceanian [4] | — | — | 8 | 38.66 | | 25 | 41.30 | | 106.8 | 35 | 41.27 | | 99.9 |
| Classical | 19 | 28.68 | 14 | 53.26 | 185.7 | 36 | 48.69 | 169.8 | 91.4 | 33 | 46.80 | 163.2 | 96.1 |
| English and American | 579 | 23.47 | 562 | 37.91 | 161.5 | 543 | 45.82 | 195.2 | 120.9 | 485 | 42.62 | 181.6 | 93.0 |
| Germanic | 53 | 20.45 | 36 | 47.64 | 233.0 | 42 | 48.78 | 238.5 | 120.4 | 33 | 43.17 | 211.1 | 88.5 |
| Romance | 93 | 20.47 | 126 | 37.66 | 184.0 | 111 | 45.04 | 220.0 | 119.6 | 100 | 42.72 | 208.7 | 94.8 |
| Slavic | 35 | 23.09 | 32 | 36.23 | 156.9 | 31 | 44.93 | 194.6 | 124.0 | 24 | 46.44 | 201.1 | 103.4 |
| Performing arts | 19 | 24.32 | 4 | 34.60 | 142.3 | 4 | 43.74 | 179.9 | 126.4 | 16 | 44.66 | 183.6 | 102.1 |
| Film | 67 | 24.81 | 83 | 42.51 | 171.3 | 82 | 43.50 | 175.3 | 102.3 | 88 | 46.86 | 188.9 | 107.7 |
| Music | 106 | 25.09 | 113 | 43.33 | 172.7 | 132 | 44.15 | 176.0 | 101.9 | 116 | 48.41 | 192.9 | 109.6 |
| Theater and dance [5] | 51 | 23.18 | 68 | 46.85 | 202.1 | 54 | 42.73 | 184.3 | 91.2 | 53 | 47.83 | 206.3 | 111.9 |
| Philosophy | 155 | 26.27 | 163 | 46.20 | 175.9 | 156 | 46.45 | 176.8 | 100.5 | 147 | 49.61 | 188.9 | 106.8 |
| Religion | 196 | 19.33 | 197 | 42.58 | 220.3 | 158 | 42.18 | 218.2 | 99.1 | 182 | 40.44 | 209.2 | 95.9 |
| **Total Humanities [6]** | 2,038 | $26.26 | 1,954 | $43.74 | 166.6 | 1,831 | $46.86 | 178.4 | 107.1 | 1,836 | $45.64 | 173.8 | 97.4 |
| **Science/Technology** | 159 | $36.11 | 81 | $46.46 | 128.7 | 85 | $39.89 | 110.5 | 85.9 | 83 | $42.83 | 118.6 | 107.4 |
| History of science/technology | 56 | 28.45 | 81 | 46.70 | 164.1 | 63 | 42.06 | 147.8 | 90.1 | 54 | 49.38 | 173.6 | 117.4 |
| Astronautics/astronomy | 18 | 27.78 | 51 | 48.42 | 174.3 | 53 | 47.94 | 172.6 | 99.0 | 40 | 50.56 | 182.0 | 105.5 |
| Biology | 145 | 39.28 | 130 | 50.66 | 129.0 | 104 | 50.34 | 128.2 | 99.4 | 107 | 49.93 | 127.1 | 99.2 |
| Botany | 23 | 31.78 | 78 | 53.07 | 167.0 | 81 | 65.08 | 204.8 | 122.6 | 95 | 68.53 | 215.6 | 105.3 |
| Zoology | 38 | 44.21 | 84 | 50.70 | 114.7 | 85 | 65.32 | 147.7 | 128.8 | 60 | 64.40 | 145.7 | 98.6 |
| Chemistry | 30 | 48.57 | 68 | 87.63 | 180.4 | 62 | 92.56 | 190.6 | 105.6 | 74 | 74.73 | 153.9 | 80.7 |
| Earth science | 42 | 35.43 | 57 | 58.81 | 166.0 | 55 | 68.04 | 192.0 | 115.7 | 48 | 71.45 | 201.7 | 105.0 |
| Engineering | 154 | 44.88 | 138 | 76.50 | 170.5 | 118 | 76.26 | 169.9 | 99.7 | 113 | 85.13 | 189.7 | 111.6 |
| Health sciences | 121 | 44.45 | 169 | 42.83 | 175.2 | 172 | 46.49 | 190.2 | 108.6 | 143 | 47.30 | 193.5 | 101.7 |
| Information/computer science | 63 | 29.48 | 62 | 43.87 | 148.8 | 82 | 48.30 | 163.8 | 110.1 | 45 | 46.70 | 158.4 | 96.7 |
| Mathematics | 44 | 32.82 | 88 | 52.83 | 161.0 | 103 | 55.03 | 167.7 | 104.2 | 142 | 53.14 | 161.9 | 96.6 |
| Physics | 38 | 34.13 | 69 | 58.46 | 171.3 | 59 | 53.59 | 157.0 | 91.7 | 57 | 62.01 | 181.7 | 115.7 |
| Sports/physical education | 61 | 18.67 | 41 | 39.04 | 209.1 | 58 | 37.08 | 198.6 | 95.0 | 38 | 40.85 | 218.8 | 110.2 |
| **Total Science/Technology** | 992 | $34.77 | 1,197 | $54.39 | 156.4 | 1,180 | $55.98 | 161.0 | 102.9 | 1,099 | $58.27 | 167.6 | 104.1 |

| Subject | No. | Avg. price | No. | Avg. price | Index | No. | Avg. price | Index | Index | No. | Avg. price | Index | Index |
|---|---|---|---|---|---|---|---|---|---|---|---|---|---|
| Social/Behavioral Sciences | 173 | $24.24 | 48 | $41.20 | 170.0 | 44 | $40.98 | 169.1 | 99.5 | 73 | $50.15 | 206.9 | 122.4 |
| Anthropology | 98 | 26.68 | 143 | 46.47 | 174.2 | 135 | 49.20 | 184.4 | 105.9 | 159 | 46.75 | 175.2 | 95.0 |
| Business management/labor | 156 | 25.01 | 146 | 44.36 | 177.4 | 152 | 45.78 | 183.1 | 103.2 | 140 | 39.80 | 159.1 | 86.9 |
| Economics | 315 | 27.60 | 275 | 54.43 | 197.2 | 257 | 50.76 | 183.9 | 93.3 | 254 | 52.18 | 189.1 | 102.8 |
| Education | 120 | 20.23 | 124 | 43.38 | 214.4 | 138 | 44.36 | 219.3 | 102.3 | 154 | 44.78 | 221.3 | 100.9 |
| History, geography/area studies | 92 | 25.58 | 58 | 48.27 | 188.7 | 46 | 43.72 | 170.9 | 90.6 | 43 | 44.14 | 172.6 | 101.0 |
| Africa | 17 | 26.94 | 37 | 48.87 | 181.4 | 46 | 45.73 | 169.8 | 93.6 | 43 | 48.63 | 180.5 | 106.3 |
| Ancient history | 46 | 31.80 | 9 | 67.94 | 213.6 | 44 | 56.09 | 176.4 | 82.6 | 32 | 56.21 | 176.7 | 106.2 |
| Asia and Oceania | 58 | 25.55 | 74 | 43.54 | 170.4 | 79 | 47.56 | 186.1 | 109.2 | 74 | 52.28 | 204.6 | 109.9 |
| Central and Eastern Europe³ | — | — | — | — | — | 19 | 46.30 | — | — | 59 | 45.90 | — | 99.1 |
| Europe³ | 285 | 29.55 | 364 | 49.94 | 169.0 | 186 | 50.24 | 170.0 | 100.6 | — | — | — | — |
| Latin America and Caribbean | 25 | 24.72 | 56 | 46.85 | 189.5 | 63 | 46.53 | 188.2 | 99.3 | 53 | 52.68 | 213.1 | 113.2 |
| Middle East and North Africa | 33 | 28.42 | 26 | 52.56 | 184.9 | 38 | 55.31 | 194.6 | 105.2 | 40 | 55.15 | 194.1 | 99.7 |
| North America | 274 | 24.42 | 402 | 37.28 | 152.7 | 388 | 37.85 | 155.0 | 101.5 | 406 | 37.89 | 155.2 | 100.1 |
| United Kingdom³ | — | — | — | — | — | 32 | 52.05 | — | — | 91 | 55.01 | — | 105.7 |
| Western Europe³ | — | — | — | — | — | 54 | 51.14 | — | — | 131 | 49.75 | — | 97.3 |
| Political science | 439 | 25.00 | — | 44.23 | 176.9 | 54 | 47.45 | 189.8 | 107.3 | 224 | 50.45 | 201.8 | 106.3 |
| Comparative politics² | — | — | 52 | 50.64 | — | 55 | 52.24 | — | 103.2 | 54 | 51.40 | — | 98.4 |
| International relations² | — | — | 183 | 46.53 | — | 175 | 50.71 | — | 109.0 | 139 | 48.88 | — | 96.4 |
| Political theory² | — | — | 142 | 43.75 | — | 131 | 45.37 | — | 103.7 | 64 | 49.67 | — | 109.5 |
| U.S. politics² | — | — | 105 | 40.88 | — | 92 | 44.04 | — | 107.7 | 168 | 48.21 | — | 109.5 |
| Psychology | 162 | 26.57 | 172 | 42.22 | 158.9 | 180 | 45.10 | 169.7 | 106.8 | 135 | 49.51 | 186.3 | 109.8 |
| Sociology | 244 | 24.38 | 218 | 45.33 | 185.9 | 216 | 41.54 | 170.4 | 91.6 | 163 | 46.92 | 192.5 | 113.0 |
| Total Social/Behavioral Sciences | 2,537 | $25.81 | 2,811 | $45.60 | 176.7 | 2,761 | $46.13 | 178.7 | 101.2 | 2,699 | $47.32 | 183.4 | 102.6 |
| Total General, Humanities, Science/Technology, Social/Behavioral Sciences (excluding Reference)⁶ | 5,578 | $27.57 | 5,994 | $46.74 | 169.5 | 5,794 | $48.37 | 175.4 | 103.5 | 5,652 | $48.87 | 177.3 | 101.0 |
| Reference | | | | | | | | | | | | | |
| General¹ | 506 | $44.75 | 648 | $84.60 | 189.1 | 397 | $78.31 | 189.1 | — | 120 | 68.53 | — | 114.5 |
| Humanities¹ | — | — | — | — | — | 47 | 59.85 | — | — | 186 | 85.92 | — | 101.4 |
| Science/Technology¹ | — | — | — | — | — | 73 | 84.74 | — | — | 75 | 109.66 | — | 102.8 |
| Social/Behavioral¹ | — | — | — | — | — | 16 | 106.64 | — | — | 206 | 98.38 | — | 112.8 |
| | | | | | | 77 | 87.24 | | | | | | |
| Total Reference | 506 | $44.75 | 648 | $84.60 | 189.1 | 610 | $79.50 | 177.7 | 94.0 | 587 | $89.77 | 200.6 | 112.9 |
| Grand Total (includes Reference)⁶ | 6,084 | $29.00 | 6,642 | $50.44 | 173.9 | 6,404 | $51.33 | 177.0 | 101.8 | 6,239 | $52.72 | 181.8 | 102.7 |

1 Began appearing as separate sections in July 1997.
2 Began appearing as separate sections in March 1988.
3 Began appearing as separate sections, replacing Europe, in July 1997.
4 Began appearing as separate sections in September 1995.
5 Separate sections for Theater and Dance combined in September 1995.
6 1983 totals include Photography (incorporated into Art and architecture in 1994), Linguistics (incorporated into Language and literature in 1985), and Non-European/Other (replaced by African and Middle Eastern and Asian and Oceanian in September 1995)

## Table 6 / U.S. Mass Market Paperback Books: Average Prices and Price Indexes, 1995–1998

Index Base: 1984 = 100

| Subject Area | 1984 Average Price | 1995 Average Price | 1995 Volumes | 1995 Index | 1996 Average Price | 1996 Volumes | 1996 Index | 1997 Final Average Price | 1997 Final Volumes | 1997 Final Index | 1998 Preliminary Average Price | 1998 Preliminary Volumes | 1998 Preliminary Index |
|---|---|---|---|---|---|---|---|---|---|---|---|---|---|
| Agriculture | $2.85 | $9.13 | 10 | 320.4 | $11.59 | 13 | 406.7 | $18.00 | 1 | 631.6 | $16.49 | 5 | 578.5 |
| Art | 8.28 | 11.24 | 12 | 135.7 | 12.00 | 8 | 144.9 | 16.45 | 20 | 198.6 | 14.26 | 17 | 172.2 |
| Biography | 4.45 | 8.08 | 39 | 181.6 | 10.12 | 38 | 227.4 | 13.73 | 43 | 308.5 | 15.97 | 74 | 358.9 |
| Business | 4.92 | 10.81 | 18 | 219.7 | 13.25 | 19 | 269.3 | 17.91 | 22 | 364.0 | 16.29 | 24 | 331.1 |
| Education | 5.15 | 12.40 | 29 | 240.8 | 10.29 | 31 | 199.8 | 14.04 | 10 | 272.6 | 16.79 | 19 | 326.1 |
| Fiction | 3.03 | 5.51 | 3,680 | 181.8 | 6.25 | 3,569 | 206.3 | 8.51 | 2,950 | 280.9 | 8.45 | 3,150 | 278.9 |
| General works | 4.58 | 19.37 | 29 | 422.9 | 9.31 | 34 | 203.3 | 13.91 | 20 | 303.7 | 10.42 | 29 | 227.5 |
| History | 3.77 | 10.06 | 24 | 266.8 | 10.92 | 17 | 289.7 | 14.71 | 25 | 390.1 | 12.57 | 30 | 333.4 |
| Home economics | 4.95 | 8.70 | 43 | 175.8 | 8.67 | 35 | 175.2 | 14.61 | 72 | 295.1 | 14.02 | 88 | 283.2 |
| Juveniles | 2.31 | 3.99 | 396 | 172.7 | 4.25 | 288 | 184.0 | 6.29 | 296 | 272.3 | 5.98 | 295 | 258.9 |
| Language | 5.56 | 9.60 | 8 | 172.7 | 7.87 | 8 | 141.5 | 8.99 | 21 | 161.7 | 10.59 | 15 | 190.5 |
| Law | 5.12 | 9.79 | 5 | 191.2 | 10.39 | 5 | 202.9 | 12.28 | 12 | 239.9 | 12.30 | 12 | 240.2 |
| Literature | 3.63 | 8.73 | 47 | 240.5 | 9.42 | 72 | 259.5 | 10.64 | 68 | 293.1 | 10.68 | 73 | 294.2 |
| Medicine | 5.01 | 8.38 | 10 | 167.3 | 8.93 | 20 | 178.2 | 11.33 | 99 | 226.1 | 13.84 | 166 | 276.2 |
| Music | 5.28 | 24.98 | 3 | 473.1 | 20.57 | 5 | 389.6 | 14.38 | 7 | 272.3 | 14.98 | 16 | 283.7 |
| Philosophy and psychology | 4.38 | 4.83 | 103 | 110.3 | 7.58 | 108 | 173.1 | 14.12 | 133 | 322.4 | 12.15 | 160 | 277.4 |
| Poetry and drama | 5.11 | 9.70 | 32 | 189.8 | 10.88 | 28 | 212.9 | 10.53 | 15 | 206.0 | 8.61 | 27 | 168.5 |
| Religion | 3.87 | 9.39 | 16 | 242.6 | 8.93 | 16 | 230.7 | 13.48 | 48 | 348.3 | 14.77 | 56 | 381.7 |
| Science | 3.55 | 11.28 | 8 | 317.7 | 12.16 | 9 | 342.5 | 15.09 | 25 | 425.1 | 14.27 | 42 | 402.0 |
| Sociology and economics | 4.42 | 9.60 | 42 | 217.2 | 9.91 | 34 | 224.2 | 16.29 | 108 | 368.6 | 14.14 | 135 | 319.9 |
| Sports and recreation | 4.06 | 8.28 | 82 | 203.9 | 8.79 | 75 | 216.5 | 14.67 | 75 | 361.2 | 14.62 | 99 | 360.1 |
| Technology | 8.61 | 11.62 | 22 | 135.0 | 11.14 | 20 | 129.4 | 12.08 | 21 | 140.3 | 13.13 | 27 | 152.5 |
| Travel | 5.86 | 13.96 | 3 | 238.2 | 9.63 | 10 | 164.3 | 15.57 | 5 | 265.7 | 11.10 | 4 | 189.4 |
| Total | $3.41 | $5.85 | 4,661 | 171.6 | $6.57 | 4,462 | 192.7 | $9.31 | 4,096 | 273.1 | $9.31 | 4,563 | 273.1 |

Compiled by Stephen Bosch, University of Arizona, from data supplied by the R. R. Bowker Company. Average prices of mass market paperbacks are based on listings of mass market titles in Bowker's *Paperbound Books in Print*.

## Table 7 / U.S. Trade (Higher Priced) Paperback Books: Average Prices and Price Indexes , 1995–1998

Index Base: 1984 = 100

| Subject Area | 1984 Average Price | 1984 Volumes | 1995 Average Price | 1995 Volumes | 1995 Index | 1996 Average Price | 1996 Volumes | 1996 Index | 1997 Final Volumes | 1997 Final Average Price | 1997 Final Index | 1998 Preliminary Volumes | 1998 Preliminary Average Price | 1998 Preliminary Index |
|---|---|---|---|---|---|---|---|---|---|---|---|---|---|---|
| Agriculture | $17.77 | 218 | $26.97 | 248 | 151.8 | $20.45 | 248 | 115.1 | 280 | $21.34 | 120.1 | 284 | $19.72 | 111.0 |
| Art | 13.12 | 874 | 20.58 | 872 | 156.9 | 21.57 | 872 | 164.4 | 728 | 22.10 | 168.4 | 643 | 23.50 | 179.1 |
| Biography | 15.09 | 813 | 16.59 | 979 | 109.9 | 17.37 | 979 | 115.1 | 902 | 17.56 | 116.4 | 766 | 17.69 | 117.3 |
| Business | 17.10 | 709 | 24.24 | 687 | 141.8 | 26.08 | 687 | 152.5 | 681 | 26.50 | 155.0 | 532 | 30.27 | 177.0 |
| Education | 12.84 | 738 | 22.96 | 832 | 178.8 | 23.76 | 832 | 185.0 | 608 | 24.98 | 194.6 | 532 | 24.79 | 193.1 |
| Fiction | 8.950 | 1,275 | 12.71 | 1,852 | 142.0 | 12.35 | 1,852 | 138.0 | 1,708 | 13.09 | 146.2 | 1,166 | 14.12 | 157.8 |
| General works | 14.32 | 1,375 | 32.99 | 1,693 | 230.4 | 34.65 | 1,693 | 242.0 | 1,546 | 38.50 | 268.9 | 1,192 | 39.80 | 277.9 |
| History | 13.49 | 1,041 | 18.48 | 1,381 | 137.0 | 20.09 | 1,381 | 148.9 | 1,165 | 19.69 | 145.9 | 941 | 20.89 | 154.9 |
| Home economics | 9.40 | 629 | 14.87 | 727 | 158.2 | 15.35 | 727 | 163.3 | 748 | 15.30 | 162.7 | 529 | 15.95 | 169.7 |
| Juveniles | 5.94 | 990 | 15.75 | 1,117 | 265.2 | 8.30 | 1,117 | 139.7 | 954 | 9.29 | 156.4 | 763 | 8.37 | 140.9 |
| Language | 11.61 | 304 | 21.58 | 427 | 185.9 | 21.17 | 427 | 182.3 | 386 | 21.94 | 189.0 | 346 | 22.79 | 196.3 |
| Law | 17.61 | 415 | 30.26 | 434 | 171.8 | 30.81 | 434 | 175.0 | 373 | 31.41 | 178.4 | 361 | 28.42 | 161.4 |
| Literature | 11.70 | 945 | 16.54 | 1,278 | 141.4 | 17.69 | 1,278 | 151.2 | 984 | 19.02 | 162.6 | 832 | 20.35 | 174.0 |
| Medicine | 15.78 | 1,092 | 27.91 | 1,577 | 176.9 | 27.37 | 1,577 | 173.4 | 1,411 | 27.46 | 174.0 | 1,273 | 27.23 | 172.6 |
| Music | 12.53 | 174 | 19.81 | 183 | 158.1 | 20.14 | 183 | 160.7 | 166 | 21.54 | 171.9 | 116 | 23.32 | 186.1 |
| Philosophy and psychology | 13.64 | 800 | 19.92 | 989 | 146.0 | 18.83 | 989 | 138.0 | 898 | 19.12 | 140.2 | 777 | 21.05 | 154.3 |
| Poetry and drama | 8.68 | 712 | 15.69 | 862 | 180.8 | 12.92 | 862 | 148.8 | 789 | 14.20 | 163.6 | 523 | 14.81 | 170.6 |
| Religion | 9.32 | 1,723 | 14.60 | 2,100 | 156.7 | 14.93 | 2,100 | 160.2 | 1,951 | 15.65 | 167.9 | 1,570 | 16.82 | 180.5 |
| Science | 16.22 | 874 | 33.42 | 1,134 | 206.0 | 32.95 | 1,134 | 203.1 | 936 | 36.42 | 224.5 | 892 | 35.49 | 218.8 |
| Sociology and economics | 17.72 | 3,321 | 23.69 | 3,983 | 133.7 | 23.47 | 3,983 | 132.4 | 3,200 | 27.29 | 154.0 | 2,767 | 24.38 | 137.6 |
| Sports and recreation | 11.40 | 900 | 16.53 | 1,028 | 145.0 | 16.33 | 1,028 | 143.2 | 779 | 17.31 | 151.9 | 607 | 18.35 | 161.0 |
| Technology | 21.11 | 827 | 38.75 | 890 | 183.6 | 39.17 | 890 | 185.6 | 821 | 37.71 | 178.6 | 556 | 32.69 | 154.9 |
| Travel | 9.88 | 480 | 16.38 | 537 | 165.8 | 16.74 | 537 | 169.4 | 517 | 16.33 | 165.2 | 432 | 16.87 | 170.7 |
| Total | $13.86 | 21,229 | $21.71 | 25,810 | 156.6 | $21.42 | 25,810 | 154.5 | 22,531 | $22.67 | 163.5 | 18,400 | $22.86 | 164.9 |

Compiled by Stephen Bosch, University of Arizona, from data supplied by the R. R. Bowker Company. Price indexes on Tables 3 and 7 are based on books recorded in the R. R. Bowker Company's Weekly Record (cumulated in the American Book Publishing Record). The 1998 preliminary figures include items listed during 1998 with an imprint date of 1998. Final data for previous years include items listed between January of that year and June of the following year with an imprint date of the specified year.

*(text continued from page 503)*

**Periodical and Serial Prices**

The LMPI Committee and the Faxon Company jointly produce the U.S. periodical price index (Table 1). The subscription prices shown are publishers' list prices, excluding publisher discount or vendor service charges. This report includes 1997, 1998, and 1999 data indexed to the base year of 1984, the new base year established last year updating the previous base of 1977. The shift in base year was needed to conform to the base period used to index the U.S. government's other national price indexes. A more extensive report, including subject breakdowns, LC (Library of Congress) class comparisons, and rankings by rate of increase and average price, was published annually in the April 15 issue of *Library Journal* through 1992, and is now published in the May issue of *American Libraries*.

Compiled by Brenda Dingley and Barbara Albee, this table shows that U.S. periodical prices, excluding Russian translations, increased by 10.4 percent from 1998 to 1999. This figure represents almost exactly the same overall rate of inflation as the 10.3 percent figure posted in 1998. Including the Russian translation category, the single-year increase was only slightly lower, at 9.8 percent. This figure is 0.3 percent higher than the rate of 9.5 percent for the entire sample in 1998. Medicine posted the highest increase of any single subject category this year (at 13.8 percent) after several consecutive years in which zoology occupied the top position. This year zoology increased at a rate of 12.6 percent, for the second-highest increase. Other subject categories that posted double-digit increases in 1999 include chemistry and physics (at 12 percent), psychology (at 11.2 percent, for the fifth consecutive year above 10 percent), mathematics, etc. (at 11 percent), engineering (at 10.4 percent), and sociology and anthropology (at 10.2 percent, the first year above 10 percent). All of these subject categories except engineering accelerated their rate of increase from last year. The library and information sciences category, which posted a double-digit increase in 1998, increased at a rate of only 5.4 percent in 1999.

U.S. serial services (Table 2), compiled by Nancy Chaffin based on data from the Faxon Company, required the replacement of several titles as publications ceased or as paper services were replaced with digital services. The replacements reflected the same subject areas, but prices were, overall, higher. Chaffin notes: "The few replacements that were made were harder to find. For these types of information sources (serial services) the logic of creating and publishing in electronic form seems to be taking hold and there is a growing number of new titles offered only in electronic form. The total number of titles in the index increased this year, but the number of U.S. documents indexed fell." A more detailed article on the topic of prices of serial services was scheduled to be published in the May 1999 *American Libraries*.

The average subscription price for 1999 U.S. serial services, excluding Wilson Index titles and Russian translations, increased an overall 5.6 percent, reflecting a small increase from the 4.5 percent increase of 1998. Business, social sciences, and U.S. documents showed decreases in their rates of inflation. Surprisingly, general and humanities, for the second straight year, increased at a rate higher than the other subject areas, joining law and science and technology as categories showing significant price increases for 1999.

The listing for Wilson Index was dropped from the serial services price index starting in 1998 at the request of Wilson Co.

## Book Prices

U.S. hardcover books (Table 3) encompasses four years: 1995, 1996, final figures for 1997, and preliminary figures for 1998. American book title costs overall remained flat, rising in 1997 to an average price of $50.22 per title, a slight increase of 0.4 percent. It is interesting to note that areas in the humanities showed the largest price increases in 1997 and other areas such as business, law, science, and technology decreased in price or showed minimal gains. This index is compiled from information published in R. R. Bowker Company's *American Book Publishing Record.*

The average price of North American academic books in 1997 (Table 4) increased by 5.7 percent in contrast to the preceding year, which showed a lower 3.6 percent increase in pricing. The data used for this index comprise titles treated by Baker and Taylor, Blackwell North America, Coutts, and Yankee Book Peddler in their approval plans during the calendar years listed. It does include paperback editions as provided by the vendors, and the recent increase in the number of these editions as part of the approval plans has clearly influenced the prices reflected in the index figures. Thus the inflation variance (hardback versus paperback editions) is much less clear than it has been in previous years. Price changes vary, as always, among subject areas, with several double-digit increases this year. However, modest increases in large publishing areas such as literature and history have driven the overall price increase for 1997.

U.S. college books (Table 5) is compiled by Donna Alsbury from reviews appearing in *Choice* during the calendar year. Hardcover prices were used when available. The table includes the past three years (1996, 1997, and 1998) and the base index year (1983). The 3.0 percent increase between 1997 and 1998 represents a continuing modest increase following the 1.8 percent increase for 1996–1997. Note that a secondary index, based on the immediate preceding year, is now a feature of this index. The humanities and general titles showed drops in the average price; price increases in the reference, science, and social science subject areas drove up the overall index. Several subject areas in the sciences and social sciences exhibited double-digit price increases during 1997–1998.

U.S. mass market paperbacks (Table 6) and U.S. trade paperbacks (Table 7) are compiled from data supplied by Bowker's *Books in Print*. Mass market paperback prices showed a sharp increase for 1997, rising from $6.57 in 1996 to $9.31, a 41 percent increase. Nearly all subject areas displayed substantial increases so the price inflation was broad in scope. The preliminary data for 1998 show that the prices are staying at the 1997 levels, so these increases may have been permanent and not a fluke for 1997. U.S. trade paperbacks increased in price from $21.42 in 1996 to $22.67 in 1997, or an increase of 6 percent. Prices in several subject areas showed double-digit increases including science, poetry and drama, juveniles, and general works. It will be necessary to monitor increases in paperback prices, as these price shifts may be in response to declining revenues from the sale of hardbound books.

**Table 8A / U.S. Daily Newspapers:**
**Average Prices and Price Indexes 1990–1999**
Index Base: 1990 = 100

| Year | No. Titles | Average Price | Percent Increase | Index |
|------|-----------|---------------|------------------|-------|
| 1990 | 165 | $189.58 | 0.0 | 100.0 |
| 1991 | 166 | 198.13 | 4.5 | 104.5 |
| 1992 | 167 | 222.68 | 12.4 | 117.5 |
| 1993 | 171 | 229.92 | 3.3 | 121.3 |
| 1994 | 171 | 261.91 | 13.9 | 138.2 |
| 1995 | 172 | 270.22 | 3.2 | 142.5 |
| 1996 | 166 | 300.21 | 11.1 | 158.4 |
| 1997 | 165 | 311.27 | 3.7 | 164.2 |
| 1998 | 163 | 316.60 | 1.7 | 167.0 |
| 1999 | 162 | 318.44 | 0.6 | 168.0 |

Compiled by Genevieve S. Owens, Williamsburg Regional Library, and Wilba Swearingen, Louisiana State University Medical Center Library, New Orleans, from data supplied by EBSCO Subscription Services. We thank Kathleen Born from EBSCO for her assistance with this project.

**Table 8B / International Newspapers:**
**Average Prices and Price Indexes 1993–1999**
Index Base: 1993 = 100

| Year | No. Titles | Average Price | Percent Increase | Index |
|------|-----------|---------------|------------------|-------|
| 1993 | 46 | $806.91 | 0.0 | 100.0 |
| 1994 | 46 | 842.01 | 4.3 | 104.3 |
| 1995 | 49 | 942.13 | 11.9 | 116.8 |
| 1996 | 50 | 992.78 | 5.4 | 123.0 |
| 1997 | 53 | 1,029.49 | 3.7 | 127.6 |
| 1998 | 52 | 1,046.72 | 1.7 | 129.7 |
| 1999 | 50 | 1,049.13 | 0.2 | 130.0 |

Compiled by Genevieve S. Owens, Williamsburg Regional Library, and Wilba Swearingen, Louisiana State University Medical Center Library, New Orleans, from data supplied by EBSCO Subscription Services. We thank Kathleen Born from EBSCO for her assistance with this project.

**Table 9 / U.S. Nonprint Media: Average Prices and Price Indexes, 1997–1998**
Index Base: 1980 = 100

| Category | 1980 Average Price | 1997 Average Price | 1997 Index | 1998 Average Price | 1998 Index |
|----------|-----|-----|-----|-----|-----|
| Videocassettes | | | | | |
| Rental cost per minute | $1.41* | $1.63 | 115.6 | $1.84 | 130.5 |
| Purchase cost per minute | 7.59 | 1.72 | 22.7 | 1.74 | 22.9 |
| Cost per video | 217.93 | 72.31 | 33.2 | 77.85 | 35.7 |
| Length per video (min.) | | 41.84 | | 44.85 | |
| Sound recordings | | | | | |
| Average cost per cassette | 9.34 | 8.31 | 89.0 | 8.20 | 87.8 |
| Average cost per CD** | 13.36 | 14.35 | 107.4 | 12.65 | 94.7 |

Compiled by Dana Alessi, Baker & Taylor, from data in *Booklist*, *Library Journal*, and *School Library Journal*.
* Rental cost per minute for 16 mm films.
** Base year for compact discs = 1993.
*Note:* The 16 mm film and filmstrip categories were discontinued due to the small number of reviews of these products.

## Newspaper Prices

U.S. daily newspapers (Table 8A) includes one fewer title than the previous year's index, reflecting the ongoing hard times of the newspaper industry as titles merge or cease altogether. Compilers Genevieve Owens and Wilba Swearingen observe that U.S. newspaper pricing continues to reflect a different dynamic than that of books and serials. Previously, pricing data suggested that increases occurred on an 18- or 24-month cycle rather than the more usual annual cycle that librarians see in other segments of the publishing industry. However, pricing for titles to be delivered in 1998 and 1999 increased 1.7 and 0.6 percent, respectively, breaking a consistent pattern of high/low price increases demonstrated since 1991. The shift from this pattern may be due to the stiff competition newspaper publishers face from other media sources, and may also be influenced by increased revenues newspapers may be receiving from electronic products that wouldn't be reflected in this price index.

A price index for international newspapers (Table 8B) appears again this year. This index is based on price information supplied by EBSCO. The increase in pricing for titles to be delivered in 1999 is a minuscule 0.2 percent. No consistent pattern of high/low price increases has been demonstrated in this index since 1993 and other factors than those impacting U.S. news publishing may be driving price changes in international newspapers. These factors may include shipping costs, currency fluctuations, or the local cost of newsprint.

## Prices of Other Media

Data for the U.S. nonprint media index (Table 9) including videocassettes and sound recordings are compiled by Dana Alessi. The U.S. Nonprint Media Index for 1998 continues the methodology used to prepare the 1997 index, utilizing a database of titles reviewed in *Booklist, Library Journal, School Library Journal,* and since 1997, *Video Librarian.* The database was created to ensure that each title is counted only once in the index. Since the review media frequently differ in price and length assigned to the reviewed media, the index assumes the higher price and the longer length.

For the first time in several years, the average cost of a video has risen significantly. This increase in cost can be attributed to several factors. First, the average length of a video has increased. This appears to be due to the proliferation of documentary videos, which usually run 60 minutes in length or more. Additionally, there was a decline in the review of children's videos, which are generally shorter. Second, after several years of lower pricing for the sell-through market, there seems to be a shift toward more rentals of higher-priced videos. Also, with the wide consumer acceptance of video as just another purchase like books or music, many producers seemed to raise prices from $19.95 to $24.95 or $24.95 to $29.95. Continuing the trend from last year, pricing within producers has become more standardized.

Sound recordings, interestingly enough, decreased in average cost per cassette—also for the first time in several years. Again, pricing among various producers is highly standardized, and it is clear that several producers set their prices by the minute. Reviews of audios continue to increase, and this year there was a significant climb in the number of audio books reviewed due to their enormous popularity. Some of the very long unabridged recordings offer great value, and this is reflected in the decreased cost. CDs also declined in cost, attributable to the ever-increasing number of CDs reviewed and the wide acceptance of CDs in the marketplace. CD pricing in particular is highly predictable and standardized.

Data for the CD-ROM price inventory (Table 10) were compiled by Martha Kellogg and Theodore Kellogg from the *Faxon Guide to CD-ROMs* and *CD-ROMs in Print*, supplemented by selected publishers' catalogs. All prices used are for single-user (non-networked) workstations at the most complete level of service, including all archival discs. Only those titles with current year price information are included in the index. A number of old familiar titles were discontinued in the CD-ROM format in this year's data as more titles are becoming available exclusively in other electronic formats.

The data indicate that CD-ROM prices were essentially unchanged over all categories for 1998. However, there were some large reductions in a few subject areas. The reductions have to do with changes in pricing arrangements for a few, very expensive CD-ROMs, in agriculture (LC class S) and in language and literature (LC class P), and the discontinuation of one expensive title in geography (LC class G). The small number of titles within each subject area makes the areas vulnerable to wide price shifts when a few expensive titles change price.

## Foreign Prices

### U.S. Purchasing Power Abroad

The U.S. dollar fell slightly against most major currencies during 1998; however the overall strength of the dollar remains high, especially against the Japanese yen. The strength of the dollar is expected to continue through 1999, although continued volatility in East Asian financial markets may inject unknown factors into the previous assumption. Uncertainty in the U.S. political arena is assumed to have caused some of the slight weakening of the dollar. During 1998 the U.S. monetary authorities didn't actively intervene in the foreign exchange markets to change the falling exchange rates. The following chart reports rates in currency per U.S. dollar based on quotations in the *Wall Street Journal* and figures from the U.S. Federal Reserve Board. Readers interested in quotations for earlier years should refer to previous volumes of the *Bowker Annual* or directly to the *Wall Street Journal*. Historical data concerning rates of exchange are also maintained at a U.S. Federal Reserve Board Web site, http://www.bog.frb.fed.us/releases/H10/hist/. Textual analysis of current trends in exchange rates can be found at http://www. federalreserve.gov/pubs/bulletin/.

|             | 12/31/94 | 12/31/95 | 12/31/96 | 12/31/97 | 12/31/98 |
|-------------|----------|----------|----------|----------|----------|
| Canada      | 1.4088   | 1.3644   | 1.3705   | 1.3567   | 1.5433   |
| France      | 5.3640   | 4.9050   | 5.1900   | 6.0190   | 5.5981   |
| U.K.        | 0.6412   | 0.6439   | 0.5839   | 0.6058   | 0.5985   |
| Germany     | 1.5525   | 1.4365   | 1.5400   | 1.7991   | 1.6698   |
| Japan       | 99.65    | 103.43   | 115.85   | 130.45   | 129.73   |
| Netherlands | 1.7391   | 1.6080   | 1.7410   | 2.0265   | 1.8816   |

(text continues on page 526)

**Table 10 / CD-ROM Price Inventory 1996–1998: Average Costs By Subject Classification**

| Classification | LC Class | Number of Titles | | | Average Price per Title | | | Percent Change | |
|---|---|---|---|---|---|---|---|---|---|
| | | 1996 | 1997 | 1998 | 1996 | 1997 | 1998 | 1996–1997 | 1997–1998 |
| General works | A | 128 | 127 | 125 | $1,805 | $1,735 | $1,499 | -4 | -14 |
| Philosophy, psychology, and religion | B | 22 | 22 | 22 | 1,153 | 1,059 | 1,062 | -8 | 0 |
| History: general and Old World | D | 7 | 7 | 7 | 786 | 777 | 777 | -1 | 0 |
| History: America | E - F | 20 | 20 | 16 | 641 | 645 | 680 | 1 | 5 |
| Geography, anthroplogy, and recreation | G | 35 | 36 | 35 | 1,884 | 1,876 | 1,383 | 0 | -26 |
| Social sciences | H | 101 | 108 | 108 | 2,196 | 2,667 | 2,776 | 21 | 4 |
| Business | HB-HJ | 118 | 122 | 118 | 3,700 | 3,298 | 3,706 | -11 | 12 |
| Political science | J | 19 | 20 | 19 | 1,297 | 1,467 | 1,558 | 13 | 6 |
| Law | K | 27 | 28 | 28 | 2,074 | 2,016 | 2,169 | -3 | 8 |
| Education | L | 30 | 30 | 32 | 921 | 958 | 1,026 | 4 | 7 |
| Music | M | 12 | 12 | 10 | 974 | 961 | 1,019 | -1 | 6 |
| Fine arts | N | 36 | 36 | 36 | 1,278 | 1,344 | 1,295 | 5 | -4 |
| Language and literature | P | 44 | 46 | 49 | 2,983 | 2,860 | 2,201 | -4 | -23 |
| Science | Q | 172 | 175 | 168 | 2,045 | 2,173 | 2,263 | 6 | 4 |
| Medicine | R | 188 | 198 | 180 | 1,404 | 1,382 | 1,445 | -2 | 5 |
| Agriculture | S | 32 | 31 | 30 | 4,139 | 3,754 | 3,261 | -9 | -13 |
| Technology | T | 72 | 79 | 77 | 2,208 | 2,119 | 2,157 | -4 | 2 |
| Military science | U - V | 25 | 28 | 26 | 1,094 | 1,061 | 1,083 | -3 | 2 |
| Bibliography, library science | Z | 72 | 73 | 67 | 1,430 | 1,525 | 1,592 | 7 | 4 |
| Totals | | 1,160 | 1,198 | 1,153 | $1,988 | $2,012 | $2,007 | 1 | 0 |

Compiled by Martha Kellogg and Theodore Kellogg, University of Rhode Island.

*Note:* In 1997, 72 titles were added and 34 removed; in 1998, 48 were added and 93 removed.

**Table 11 / British Academic Books: Average Prices and Price Indexes, 1996–1998**
(Index Base: 1985 = 100; prices listed are pounds sterling)

| Subject Area | 1985 No. of Titles | 1985 Average Price | 1996 No. of Titles | 1996 Average Price | 1996 Index | 1997 No. of Titles | 1997 Average Price | 1997 Index | 1998 No. of Titles | 1998 Average Price | 1998 Index |
|---|---|---|---|---|---|---|---|---|---|---|---|
| General works | 29 | £30.54 | 38 | £66.88 | 219.0 | 35 | £34.62 | 113.4 | 29 | £68.91 | 225.6 |
| Fine arts | 329 | 21.70 | 472 | 32.16 | 148.2 | 423 | 32.95 | 151.8 | 451 | 33.32 | 153.5 |
| Architecture | 97 | 20.68 | 203 | 32.17 | 155.6 | 150 | 37.66 | 182.1 | 145 | 29.98 | 145.0 |
| Music | 136 | 17.01 | 132 | 28.89 | 169.8 | 136 | 31.01 | 182.3 | 129 | 36.93 | 217.1 |
| Performing arts except music | 110 | 13.30 | 178 | 26.43 | 198.7 | 175 | 32.38 | 243.5 | 164 | 26.67 | 200.5 |
| Archaeology | 146 | 18.80 | 192 | 33.57 | 178.6 | 173 | 36.98 | 196.7 | 183 | 36.19 | 192.5 |
| Geography | 60 | 22.74 | 63 | 40.65 | 178.8 | 57 | 41.19 | 181.1 | 47 | 41.65 | 183.2 |
| History | 1,123 | 16.92 | 1,505 | 34.51 | 204.0 | 1,373 | 38.63 | 228.3 | 1,322 | 43.46 | 256.9 |
| Philosophy | 127 | 18.41 | 233 | 42.07 | 228.5 | 221 | 42.70 | 231.9 | 264 | 55.49 | 301.4 |
| Religion | 328 | 10.40 | 486 | 25.68 | 246.9 | 421 | 24.47 | 235.3 | 419 | 30.54 | 293.7 |
| Language | 135 | 19.37 | 218 | 41.06 | 212.0 | 193 | 42.41 | 218.9 | 164 | 50.84 | 262.5 |
| Miscellaneous humanities | 59 | 21.71 | 64 | 30.39 | 140.0 | 49 | 34.98 | 161.1 | 42 | 24.41 | 112.4 |
| Literary texts (excluding fiction) | 570 | 9.31 | 581 | 18.64 | 200.2 | 500 | 15.09 | 162.1 | 422 | 15.27 | 164.0 |
| Literary criticism | 438 | 14.82 | 579 | 36.22 | 244.4 | 491 | 36.01 | 243.0 | 527 | 38.66 | 260.9 |
| Law | 188 | 24.64 | 364 | 46.26 | 187.7 | 379 | 49.10 | 199.3 | 342 | 48.65 | 197.4 |
| Library science and book trade | 78 | 18.69 | 78 | 54.39 | 291.0 | 76 | 42.54 | 227.6 | 64 | 62.20 | 332.8 |
| Mass communications | 38 | 14.20 | 109 | 30.78 | 216.8 | 116 | 34.80 | 245.1 | 124 | 36.09 | 254.2 |
| Anthropology and ethnology | 42 | 20.71 | 90 | 39.77 | 192.0 | 62 | 41.10 | 198.5 | 78 | 45.55 | 219.9 |
| Sociology | 136 | 15.24 | 229 | 45.55 | 298.9 | 199 | 50.89 | 333.9 | 218 | 49.64 | 325.7 |
| Psychology | 107 | 19.25 | 146 | 36.60 | 190.1 | 148 | 39.12 | 203.2 | 149 | 51.03 | 265.1 |
| Economics | 334 | 20.48 | 525 | 49.67 | 242.5 | 585 | 59.99 | 292.9 | 535 | 60.24 | 294.1 |
| Political science, international relations | 314 | 15.54 | 549 | 37.06 | 238.5 | 541 | 40.31 | 259.4 | 568 | 41.60 | 267.7 |
| Miscellaneous social sciences | 20 | 26.84 | 23 | 42.75 | 159.3 | 19 | 38.55 | 143.6 | 23 | 37.23 | 138.7 |
| Military science | 83 | 17.69 | 59 | 32.92 | 186.1 | 46 | 49.14 | 277.8 | 40 | 34.31 | 194.0 |
| Sports and recreation | 44 | 11.23 | 82 | 19.97 | 177.8 | 75 | 20.03 | 178.4 | 80 | 24.33 | 216.7 |
| Social service | 56 | 12.17 | 106 | 28.45 | 233.8 | 75 | 27.20 | 223.5 | 114 | 29.83 | 245.1 |
| Education | 295 | 12.22 | 423 | 28.51 | 233.3 | 372 | 29.42 | 240.8 | 337 | 35.93 | 294.0 |
| Management and business administration | 427 | 19.55 | 594 | 44.11 | 225.6 | 599 | 38.74 | 198.2 | 606 | 42.54 | 217.6 |
| Miscellaneous applied social sciences | 13 | 9.58 | 28 | 31.58 | 329.6 | 30 | 42.20 | 440.5 | 23 | 35.22 | 367.6 |

| | | | | | | | | | | | |
|---|---|---|---|---|---|---|---|---|---|---|---|
| Criminology | 45 | 11.45 | 69 | 36.29 | 316.9 | 76 | 34.78 | 303.8 | 66 | 37.62 | 328.6 |
| Applied interdisciplinary social sciences | 254 | 14.17 | 601 | 33.50 | 236.4 | 509 | 35.96 | 253.8 | 503 | 39.87 | 281.4 |
| General science | 43 | 13.73 | 40 | 37.11 | 270.3 | 37 | 40.60 | 295.7 | 31 | 40.67 | 296.2 |
| Botany | 55 | 30.54 | 57 | 46.58 | 152.5 | 35 | 50.64 | 165.8 | 31 | 56.31 | 184.4 |
| Zoology | 85 | 25.67 | 80 | 41.48 | 161.6 | 56 | 53.14 | 207.0 | 51 | 49.91 | 194.4 |
| Human biology | 35 | 28.91 | 32 | 46.57 | 161.1 | 19 | 58.46 | 202.2 | 28 | 43.68 | 151.1 |
| Biochemistry | 26 | 33.57 | 43 | 54.39 | 162.0 | 28 | 86.64 | 258.1 | 28 | 56.01 | 166.8 |
| Miscellaneous biological sciences | 152 | 26.64 | 158 | 43.20 | 162.2 | 148 | 49.69 | 186.5 | 145 | 51.03 | 191.6 |
| Chemistry | 109 | 48.84 | 100 | 75.81 | 155.2 | 99 | 89.07 | 182.4 | 97 | 75.88 | 155.4 |
| Earth sciences | 87 | 28.94 | 117 | 59.55 | 205.8 | 95 | 56.63 | 195.7 | 93 | 62.09 | 214.5 |
| Astronomy | 43 | 20.36 | 50 | 35.33 | 173.5 | 50 | 48.61 | 238.8 | 47 | 39.94 | 196.2 |
| Physics | 76 | 26.58 | 97 | 65.99 | 248.3 | 110 | 60.58 | 227.9 | 90 | 71.76 | 270.0 |
| Mathematics | 123 | 20.20 | 170 | 37.21 | 184.2 | 177 | 39.11 | 193.6 | 149 | 40.40 | 200.0 |
| Computer sciences | 150 | 20.14 | 227 | 38.12 | 189.3 | 174 | 39.51 | 196.2 | 174 | 39.45 | 195.9 |
| Interdisciplinary technical fields | 38 | 26.14 | 68 | 42.45 | 162.4 | 49 | 39.55 | 151.3 | 52 | 54.57 | 208.8 |
| Civil engineering | 134 | 28.68 | 155 | 58.66 | 204.5 | 129 | 61.74 | 215.3 | 151 | 62.89 | 219.3 |
| Mechanical engineering | 27 | 31.73 | 45 | 57.42 | 181.0 | 36 | 77.36 | 243.8 | 47 | 64.30 | 202.6 |
| Electrical and electronic engineering | 100 | 33.12 | 112 | 52.56 | 159.0 | 104 | 58.84 | 177.7 | 85 | 53.63 | 161.9 |
| Materials science | 54 | 37.93 | 99 | 95.89 | 252.8 | 87 | 83.38 | 219.8 | 76 | 82.14 | 216.6 |
| Chemical engineering | 24 | 40.48 | 37 | 69.22 | 171.0 | 45 | 83.95 | 207.4 | 32 | 69.91 | 172.7 |
| Miscellaneous technology | 217 | 36.33 | 248 | 52.58 | 144.7 | 215 | 59.11 | 162.7 | 213 | 66.72 | 183.6 |
| Food and domestic science | 38 | 23.75 | 40 | 54.27 | 228.5 | 43 | 60.03 | 252.8 | 29 | 61.86 | 260.5 |
| Non-clinical medicine | 97 | 18.19 | 177 | 29.02 | 159.5 | 159 | 34.54 | 189.9 | 181 | 34.25 | 188.3 |
| General medicine | 73 | 21.03 | 68 | 44.43 | 211.3 | 73 | 38.85 | 184.7 | 76 | 48.30 | 229.7 |
| Internal medicine | 163 | 27.30 | 179 | 45.29 | 165.9 | 171 | 57.14 | 209.3 | 168 | 51.12 | 187.3 |
| Psychiatry and mental disorders | 71 | 17.97 | 132 | 32.00 | 178.1 | 138 | 31.98 | 178.0 | 150 | 35.51 | 197.6 |
| Surgery | 50 | 29.37 | 62 | 64.60 | 220.0 | 63 | 65.88 | 224.3 | 53 | 70.38 | 239.6 |
| Miscellaneous medicine | 292 | 22.08 | 301 | 39.16 | 177.4 | 342 | 42.34 | 191.8 | 303 | 43.80 | 198.4 |
| Dentistry | 20 | 19.39 | 22 | 50.22 | 259.0 | 16 | 34.89 | 179.9 | 20 | 44.16 | 227.7 |
| Nursing | 71 | 8.00 | 99 | 17.96 | 224.5 | 92 | 20.14 | 251.8 | 72 | 18.93 | 236.6 |
| Agriculture and forestry | 78 | 23.69 | 69 | 45.65 | 192.7 | 58 | 49.72 | 209.9 | 62 | 56.82 | 239.8 |
| Animal husbandry and veterinary medicine | 34 | 20.92 | 46 | 37.69 | 180.2 | 47 | 35.43 | 169.4 | 40 | 41.93 | 200.4 |
| Natural resources and conservation | 58 | 22.88 | 42 | 40.82 | 178.4 | 35 | 38.58 | 168.6 | 27 | 54.42 | 237.8 |
| Total, all books | 9,049 | £19.07 | 12,622 | £37.50 | 196.6 | 11,710 | £39.77 | 208.5 | 11,551 | £41.96 | 220.0 |

Compiled by Curt Holleman, Southern Methodist University, from data supplied by B. H. Blackwell and the Library and Information Statistics Unit at Loughborough University.

**Table 12 / German Academic Books: Average Prices and Price Index, 1996–1998**
(Index Base: 1989=100; prices listed are in Deutsche marks)

| Subject | LC Class | 1989 No. of Titles | 1989 Average Price | 1996 No. of Titles | 1996 Average Price | 1996 Percent increase | 1996 Index | 1997 No. of Titles | 1997 Average Price | 1997 Percent increase | 1997 Index | 1998 No. of Titles | 1998 Average Price | 1998 Percent increase | 1998 Index |
|---|---|---|---|---|---|---|---|---|---|---|---|---|---|---|---|
| Agriculture | S | 251 | DM74.99 | 335 | DM72.62 | 4.40 | 96.8 | 306 | DM76.83 | 5.80 | 102.5 | 219 | DM85.39 | 11.10 | 113.9 |
| Anthropology | GN-GT | 129 | 70.88 | 187 | 75.81 | 11.40 | 107.0 | 156 | 81.54 | 7.60 | 115.0 | 186 | 90.15 | 10.60 | 127.2 |
| Botany | QK | 83 | 109.94 | 94 | 115.01 | 7.60 | 104.6 | 74 | 108.26 | -5.90 | 98.5 | 48 | 124.31 | 14.80 | 113.1 |
| Business and economics | H-HJ | 1,308 | 86.82 | 2,560 | 74.54 | 6.30 | 85.9 | 2,432 | 78.72 | 5.60 | 90.7 | 2,146 | 73.81 | -6.20 | 85.0 |
| Chemistry | QD | 87 | 116.50 | 214 | 125.86 | -7.50 | 108.0 | 147 | 155.73 | 23.70 | 133.7 | 125 | 168.84 | 8.40 | 144.9 |
| Education | L | 426 | 41.64 | 679 | 49.83 | 8.20 | 119.7 | 572 | 50.66 | 1.70 | 121.7 | 562 | 51.40 | 1.50 | 123.5 |
| Engineering and technology | T | 906 | 79.49 | 994 | 91.60 | 1.70 | 115.2 | 823 | 127.14 | 38.80 | 160.0 | 821 | 109.52 | -13.90 | 137.8 |
| Fine and applied arts | M-N | 1,766 | 55.57 | 2,515 | 70.08 | -9.10 | 126.1 | 1,937 | 88.18 | 25.80 | 158.7 | 2,337 | 72.75 | -17.50 | 130.9 |
| General works | A | 43 | 59.63 | 58 | 166.11 | -44.90 | 278.5 | 42 | 296.5 | 78.50 | 497.2 | 46 | 120.56 | -59.30 | 202.2 |
| Geography | G-GF | 202 | 48.96 | 150 | 76.68 | -21.60 | 156.6 | 158 | 93.03 | 21.30 | 190.0 | 141 | 101.73 | 9.30 | 207.8 |
| Geology | QE | 46 | 77.10 | 76 | 79.18 | -35.00 | 102.7 | 60 | 535.79 | 576.70 | 694.9 | 59 | 103.86 | -80.60 | 134.7 |
| History | C,D,E,F | 1,064 | 62.93 | 2,194 | 67.92 | 12.10 | 107.9 | 1,837 | 74.99 | 10.40 | 119.1 | 1,994 | 77.46 | 3.30 | 123.1 |
| Law | K | 1,006 | 100.52 | 1,889 | 87.72 | -3.50 | 87.3 | 1,935 | 106.35 | 21.20 | 105.8 | 1,561 | 100.94 | -5.10 | 100.4 |
| Library and information science | Z | 118 | 94.71 | 165 | 151.38 | -54.60 | 159.8 | 145 | 221.55 | 46.30 | 233.9 | 153 | 319.66 | 44.30 | 337.5 |
| Literature and language | P | 2,395 | 52.10 | 3,689 | 62.59 | 11.00 | 120.1 | 3,750 | 67.69 | 8.10 | 129.9 | 3,731 | 67.17 | -0.80 | 128.9 |
| Mathematics and computer science | QA | 367 | 68.16 | 779 | 80.89 | -5.30 | 118.7 | 689 | 84.89 | 5.00 | 124.5 | 724 | 93.42 | 10.00 | 137.1 |
| Medicine | R | 1,410 | 82.67 | 1,849 | 93.01 | -3.50 | 112.5 | 1,643 | 88.02 | -5.40 | 106.5 | 1,508 | 98.14 | 11.50 | 118.7 |
| Military and naval science | U-V | 67 | 70.43 | 52 | 90.15 | 15.00 | 128.0 | 44 | 63.07 | -30.00 | 89.6 | 47 | 57.03 | -9.60 | 81.0 |
| Natural history | QH | 78 | 85.23 | 185 | 102.95 | 5.90 | 120.8 | 142 | 93.77 | -8.90 | 110.0 | 136 | 120.25 | 28.20 | 141.1 |
| Philosophy and religion | B | 918 | 56.91 | 1,638 | 73.46 | -0.20 | 129.1 | 1,398 | 90.38 | 23.00 | 158.8 | 1,757 | 80.43 | -11.00 | 141.3 |
| Physical education and recreation | GV | 110 | 35.65 | 149 | 39.82 | -8.50 | 111.7 | 142 | 46.68 | 17.20 | 131.0 | 147 | 42.05 | -9.90 | 118.0 |
| Physics and astronomy | QB-QC | 192 | 85.12 | 347 | 91.61 | 5.50 | 107.6 | 239 | 97.12 | 6.00 | 114.1 | 235 | 133.03 | 37.00 | 156.3 |
| Physiology | QM-QR | 163 | 124.67 | 168 | 128.73 | 13.40 | 103.3 | 153 | 114.28 | -11.20 | 91.7 | 117 | 169.11 | 48.00 | 135.6 |
| Political science | J | 482 | 50.38 | 615 | 59.63 | 5.60 | 118.4 | 571 | 62.79 | 5.30 | 124.6 | 654 | 57.44 | -8.50 | 114.0 |
| Psychology | BF | 116 | 54.95 | 220 | 58.85 | 5.30 | 107.1 | 204 | 58.97 | 0.20 | 107.3 | 211 | 62.81 | 6.50 | 114.3 |
| Science (general) | Q | 100 | 115.90 | 86 | 80.19 | 1.00 | 69.2 | 90 | 95.62 | 19.20 | 82.5 | 86 | 79.96 | -16.40 | 69.0 |
| Sociology | HM-HX | 722 | 41.52 | 1,034 | 49.75 | 9.00 | 119.8 | 1,069 | 47.85 | -3.80 | 115.3 | 1,196 | 48.32 | 1.00 | 116.4 |
| Zoology | QL | 49 | 82.74 | 91 | 100.07 | 17.70 | 120.9 | 100 | 133.58 | 33.50 | 161.4 | 86 | 109.55 | -18.00 | 132.4 |
| Total | | 14,604 | DM67.84 | 23,012 | DM74.81 | -0.80 | 110.3 | 20,858 | DM84.65 | 13.20 | 124.8 | 21,033 | DM81.08 | -4.20 | 119.5 |

Compiled by John Haar, Vanderbilt University, from approval plan data supplied by Otto Harrassowitz. Data represent a selection of materials relevant to research and documentation published in Germany. (see text for more information regarding the nature of the data). Unclassified material as well as titles in home economics and industrial arts have been excluded. The index is not adjusted for high-priced titles.

**Table 13 / German Academic Periodical Price Index, 1997–1999**
(Index Base: 1990 = 100; prices listed are in Deutsche marks)

| Subject | LC Class | 1990 Average Price | 1997 No. of Titles | 1997 Average Price | 1997 Percent Increase | 1997 Index | 1998 No. of Titles | 1998 Average Price | 1998 Percent Increase | 1998 Index | 1999 Preliminary No. of Titles | 1999 Preliminary Average Price | 1999 Preliminary Percent Increase | 1999 Preliminary Index |
|---|---|---|---|---|---|---|---|---|---|---|---|---|---|---|
| Agriculture | S | DM235.11 | 162 | DM379.09 | 14.3 | 161.2 | 162 | DM377.98 | -0.3 | 160.8 | 176 | DM373.79 | -1.1 | 159.0 |
| Anthropology | GN | 112.88 | 13 | 171.71 | 12.4 | 152.1 | 17 | 156.29 | -9.0 | 138.5 | 18 | 159.33 | 1.9 | 141.1 |
| Botany | QK | 498.79 | 17 | 847.27 | 3.2 | 169.9 | 16 | 825.07 | -2.6 | 165.4 | 16 | 887.55 | 7.6 | 177.9 |
| Business and economics | H-HJ | 153.48 | 256 | 225.16 | 3.3 | 146.7 | 259 | 230.77 | 2.5 | 150.4 | 285 | 243.32 | 6.0 | 158.5 |
| Chemistry | QD | 553.06 | 47 | 2007.13 | 38.6 | 362.9 | 56 | 2,155.55 | 7.4 | 389.7 | 57 | 2300.84 | 6.7 | 416.0 |
| Education | L | 70.86 | 58 | 91.30 | 6.6 | 128.8 | 60 | 91.53 | 0.3 | 129.2 | 64 | 93.20 | 1.8 | 131.5 |
| Engineering and technology | T-TT | 239.40 | 362 | 343.03 | 7.4 | 143.3 | 354 | 376.80 | 9.8 | 157.4 | 371 | 387.96 | 3.0 | 162.1 |
| Fine and applied arts | M-N | 84.15 | 170 | 104.75 | 3.2 | 124.5 | 169 | 108.70 | 3.8 | 129.2 | 171 | 110.97 | 2.1 | 131.9 |
| General | A | 349.37 | 72 | 386.76 | -15.5 | 110.7 | 69 | 435.91 | 12.7 | 124.8 | 76 | 412.27 | -5.4 | 118.0 |
| Geography | G | 90.42 | 24 | 150.36 | 9.9 | 166.3 | 22 | 153.05 | 1.8 | 169.3 | 23 | 149.49 | -2.3 | 165.3 |
| Geology | QE | 261.30 | 35 | 513.18 | 12.9 | 196.4 | 32 | 521.27 | 1.6 | 199.5 | 34 | 655.69 | 25.8 | 250.9 |
| History | C,D,E,F | 66.09 | 158 | 98.42 | 6.1 | 148.9 | 149 | 97.00 | -1.4 | 146.8 | 150 | 98.76 | 1.8 | 149.4 |
| Law | K | 193.88 | 152 | 314.98 | 4.6 | 162.5 | 154 | 323.26 | 2.6 | 166.7 | 161 | 328.98 | 1.8 | 169.7 |
| Library and information science | Z | 317.50 | 46 | 369.97 | -39.3 | 116.5 | 44 | 402.13 | 8.7 | 126.7 | 44 | 404.75 | 0.7 | 127.5 |
| Literature and language | P | 102.69 | 188 | 143.70 | 4.2 | 139.9 | 186 | 142.63 | -0.7 | 138.9 | 190 | 143.63 | 0.7 | 139.9 |
| Mathematics and computer science | QA | 1,064.62 | 47 | 1,404.42 | -15.6 | 131.9 | 53 | 1,295.38 | -7.8 | 121.7 | 61 | 1,176.16 | -9.2 | 110.5 |
| Medicine | R | 320.62 | 367 | 595.81 | -5.5 | 185.8 | 347 | 614.58 | 3.2 | 191.7 | 369 | 639.58 | 4.1 | 199.5 |
| Military and naval science | U-V | 86.38 | 23 | 96.14 | -4.5 | 111.3 | 23 | 99.68 | 3.7 | 115.4 | 23 | 101.13 | 1.5 | 117.1 |
| Natural history | QH | 728.36 | 55 | 1,476.30 | 8.4 | 202.7 | 53 | 1,375.24 | -6.8 | 188.8 | 54 | 1,498.16 | 8.9 | 205.7 |
| Philosophy and religion | B | 65.00 | 205 | 108.18 | 3.5 | 166.4 | 194 | 114.34 | 5.7 | 175.9 | 196 | 114.95 | 0.5 | 176.8 |
| Physical education and recreation | GV | 81.96 | 46 | 98.61 | 1.9 | 120.3 | 41 | 103.59 | 5.1 | 126.4 | 47 | 100.12 | -0.3 | 122.2 |
| Physics and astronomy | QB-QC | 684.4 | 40 | 1,470.19 | 6.6 | 214.8 | 51 | 1,899.57 | 29.2 | 277.6 | 51 | 2,105.09 | 10.8 | 307.6 |
| Physiology | QM-QR | 962.83 | 10 | 3,257.10 | 17.9 | 338.3 | 12 | 2,649.13 | -18.7 | 275.1 | 13 | 2,779.56 | 4.9 | 288.7 |
| Political science | J | 80.67 | 142 | 103.69 | -0.3 | 128.5 | 130 | 105.13 | 1.4 | 130.3 | 133 | 106.12 | 0.9 | 131.5 |
| Psychology | BF | 94.10 | 35 | 157.58 | 9.1 | 167.5 | 35 | 158.88 | 0.8 | 168.8 | 35 | 163.50 | 2.9 | 173.8 |
| Science (general) | Q | 310.54 | 30 | 490.22 | 14.1 | 157.9 | 28 | 517.91 | 5.6 | 166.8 | 30 | 510.98 | -1.3 | 164.5 |
| Sociology | HM-HX | 109.61 | 69 | 140.18 | -2.2 | 127.9 | 66 | 146.30 | 4.4 | 133.5 | 70 | 151.98 | 3.9 | 138.7 |
| Zoology | QL | 161.02 | 26 | 302.63 | 14.4 | 187.9 | 24 | 316.23 | 4.5 | 196.4 | 24 | 340.65 | 7.7 | 211.6 |
| Total | | DM228.4 | 2,857 | DM373.88 | 0.9 | 163.7 | 2,806 | DM403.69 | 8.0 | 176.7 | 2,942 | DM420.75 | 4.2 | 184.2 |

Data, supplied by Otto Harrassowitz, represent periodical and newspaper titles published in Germany. Price information for 1999 is preliminary; price data is 86% complete. Index is compiled by Steven E. Thompson, Brown University Library.

**Table 14 / Dutch (English-Language) Periodicals Price Index 1996–1999**
(Index Base: 1996=100; currency unit: DFL)

| Subject Area | LC Class | 1996 | | 1997 | | | 1998 | | | 1999 | | |
|---|---|---|---|---|---|---|---|---|---|---|---|---|
| | | No. of Titles | Average Price | No. of Titles | Average Price | Index | No. of Titles | Average Price | Index | No. of Titles | Average Price | Index |
| Agriculture | S | 36 | 1,215.10 | 37 | 1,335.84 | 109.9 | 36 | 1,559.27 | 128.3 | 36 | 1,749.35 | 144.0 |
| Botany | QK | 10 | 1,654.90 | 10 | 1,899.60 | 114.8 | 11 | 1,948.09 | 117.7 | 11 | 2,173.27 | 131.3 |
| Business and economics | H-HJ | 86 | 721.95 | 92 | 766.85 | 106.2 | 94 | 846.98 | 117.3 | 99 | 918.68 | 127.3 |
| Chemistry | QD | 32 | 4,258.83 | 32 | 4,886.74 | 114.7 | 39 | 5,319.49 | 124.9 | 40 | 5,781.60 | 135.8 |
| Education | L | 6 | 411.67 | 6 | 483.83 | 117.5 | 8 | 518.88 | 126.0 | 9 | 563.78 | 137.0 |
| Engineering and technology | T-TS | 77 | 1,526.30 | 78 | 1,725.26 | 113.0 | 79 | 2,084.85 | 136.6 | 82 | 2,292.09 | 150.2 |
| Fine and applied arts | M-N | 3 | 326.67 | 2 | 444.50 | 136.1 | 1 | 539.00 | 165.0 | 1 | 675.00 | 206.6 |
| Geography | G | 8 | 1,425.88 | 8 | 1,563.38 | 109.6 | 9 | 1,668.28 | 117.0 | 9 | 1,889.39 | 132.5 |
| Geology | QE | 25 | 1,587.60 | 26 | 1,764.78 | 111.2 | 26 | 1,956.62 | 123.2 | 26 | 2,215.83 | 139.6 |
| History | C,D,E,F | 9 | 257.00 | 9 | 290.06 | 112.9 | 12 | 312.33 | 121.5 | 12 | 332.75 | 129.5 |
| Law | K | 14 | 494.21 | 14 | 531.50 | 107.5 | 29 | 525.45 | 106.3 | 27 | 574.94 | 116.3 |
| Library and information science | Z | 6 | 262.67 | 6 | 281.83 | 107.3 | 6 | 302.83 | 115.3 | 6 | 313.67 | 119.4 |
| Literature and language | P | 35 | 348.26 | 34 | 380.32 | 109.2 | 41 | 396.34 | 113.8 | 42 | 433.76 | 124.6 |
| Mathematics and computer science | QA | 56 | 1,473.25 | 56 | 1,664.64 | 113.0 | 63 | 1,791.70 | 121.6 | 62 | 2,016.03 | 136.8 |
| Medicine | R | 62 | 1,357.47 | 63 | 1,577.76 | 116.2 | 72 | 1,705.82 | 125.7 | 75 | 1,893.45 | 139.5 |
| Military and naval science | U-V | 1 | 295.00 | 1 | 278.00 | 94.2 | 2 | 181.50 | 61.5 | 2 | 215.00 | 72.9 |
| Natural history | QH | 33 | 2,226.92 | 39 | 2,196.41 | 98.6 | 40 | 2,430.53 | 109.1 | 44 | 2,603.86 | 116.9 |
| Philosophy and religion | B,BL,BP | 33 | 407.21 | 34 | 436.97 | 107.3 | 34 | 487.62 | 119.8 | 34 | 546.38 | 134.2 |
| Physics and astronomy | QB-QC | 43 | 4,329.47 | 44 | 4,694.05 | 108.4 | 47 | 5,007.64 | 115.7 | 49 | 5,487.12 | 126.7 |
| Physiology | QM-QR | 16 | 3,568.00 | 16 | 4,071.56 | 114.1 | 17 | 4,260.00 | 119.4 | 18 | 4,653.89 | 130.4 |
| Political science | J | 4 | 428.25 | 4 | 508.25 | 118.7 | 5 | 474.20 | 110.7 | 5 | 518.40 | 121.1 |
| Psychology | BF | 4 | 925.50 | 5 | 977.00 | 105.6 | 9 | 931.11 | 100.6 | 9 | 1,037.89 | 112.1 |
| Science (general) | Q | 12 | 1,071.98 | 12 | 1,203.92 | 112.3 | 10 | 1,244.70 | 116.1 | 10 | 1,452.80 | 135.5 |
| Sociology | HM-HX | 6 | 377.33 | 5 | 448.60 | 118.9 | 3 | 457.33 | 121.2 | 4 | 409.91 | 108.6 |
| Zoology | QL | 11 | 776.21 | 10 | 992.60 | 127.9 | 10 | 1,100.00 | 141.7 | 10 | 1,252.20 | 161.3 |
| Total | | 628 | 1,560.44 | 643 | 1,734.69 | 111.2 | 703 | 1,892.15 | 121.3 | 722 | 2,092.62 | 134.1 |

No data exist for Anthropology, General works, Physical education.

*Source:* Martinus Nijhoff International, compiled by Bas Guijt and Frederick C. Lynden.

**Table 15A / Latin American Periodical Price Index, 1997–1998: Country and Region Index**

|  | Total titles w/o newspapers | Mean w/o newspapers | Index (1992=100) | Weighted mean w/o newspapers | Index (1992=100) |
|---|---|---|---|---|---|
| Argentina | 133 | $95.44 | 109 | $89.85 | 125 |
| Bolivia | 5 | 44.36 | 102 | 39.91 | 115 |
| Brazil | 261 | 77.68 | 114 | 65.95 | 89 |
| Caribbean | 43 | 36.90 | 87 | 33.39 | 85 |
| Chile | 83 | 83.24 | 135 | 79.40 | 172 |
| Colombia | 64 | 67.62 | 147 | 79.44 | 170 |
| Costa Rica | 31 | 56.08 | 215 | 56.65 | 182 |
| Cuba | 23 | 51.68 | 146 | 53.21 | 140 |
| Ecuador | 13 | 81.81 | 235 | 75.65 | 229 |
| El Salvador | 11 | 51.68 | 272 | 55.42 | 358 |
| Guatemala | 11 | 133.45 | 175 | 195.71 | 224 |
| Honduras | n.a. | n.a. | n.a. | n.a. | n.a. |
| Jamaica | 22 | 35.12 | 109 | 42.33 | 134 |
| Mexico | 199 | 78.29 | 121 | 66.14 | 116 |
| Nicaragua | 7 | 36.17 | 118 | 38.88 | 125 |
| Panama | 14 | 32.45 | 122 | 30.45 | 120 |
| Paraguay | 6 | 28.58 | 181 | 38.72 | 174 |
| Peru | 54 | 123.57 | 123 | 119.17 | 108 |
| Uruguay | 24 | 84.72 | 254 | 63.91 | 195 |
| Venezuela | 36 | 86.44 | 85 | 68.23 | 144 |
| *Region* |  |  |  |  |  |
| Caribbean | 88 | 40.32 | 109 | 42.08 | 115 |
| Central America | 74 | 60.58 | 167 | 70.59 | 171 |
| South America | 679 | 84.85 | 114 | 79.17 | 122 |
| Mexico | 199 | 78.29 | 121 | 66.14 | 116 |
| Latin America | 1,040 | 77.97 | 116 | 72.29 | 125 |

**Table 15B / Latin American Periodical Price Index, 1997–1998: Subject Index**

|  | Mean | Index 1992=100 | Weighted Mean | Index 1992=100 |
|---|---|---|---|---|
| Social sciences | $85.02 | 119 | $73.59 | 136 |
| Humanities | 53.45 | 133 | 45.87 | 126 |
| Science/technology | 66.38 | 113 | 72.50 | 129 |
| General | 96.16 | 110 | 89.02 | 96 |
| Law | 81.56 | 79 | 79.22 | 92 |
| Newspapers | 491.61 | 121 | 405.00 | 90 |
| Totals w/o newspapers | $77.97 | 93 | $72.31 | 112 |
| Total with newspapers | $103.01 | 153 | $79.51 | 137 |

Total titles with newspapers = 1,107

Total titles without newspapers = 1,042

Subscription information was provided by the Faxon Co., Library of Congress, Rio Office and the University of Texas, Austin. Index based on 1992 LAPPI mean prices. Complying with ANSI standards, 1996–1997 subscription prices were included in this year's index if no new subscription price was given. Compiled by Scott Van Jacob, University of Notre Dame.

n.a. = fewer than five subscriptions were found.

*(text continued from page 518)*

Price indexes are included for British academic books (Table 11), German academic books (Table 12), German academic periodicals (Table 13), Dutch English-language periodicals (Table 14), and Latin American periodicals (Table 15).

### British Prices

The price index for British books is compiled by Curt Holleman from information supplied by B. H. Blackwell. The average price was £41.96 in 1998, which reflects an increase of 5.5 percent over the 1997 average price of £39.77. During 1997 prices increased 6.1 percent over the 1996 average of £37.50. Holleman notes that the pound experienced an increase of 1.1 percent in 1998 in its average daily value compared to the dollar but that the output of British academic books declined by 1.4 percent. When we combine these two factors with the inflation of 5.5 percent in the cost of each British book in 1998, we find that the cost for U.S. academic libraries of maintaining a proportional collection of British books rose 5.2 percent in 1998 over 1997. It is important to note that the total sum of the number of books in the subject portion of the table doesn't equal the total number of books. Even though it has a category of General Works, Blackwell annually finds about 300 books that are unclassifiable.

### German Prices

The price index for German academic books (Table 12) is compiled by John Haar based on data supplied by Otto Harrassowitz. The index includes all German monographic publications made available for purchase to U.S. libraries during the calendar year. It also includes some German CD-ROMs and other audiovisual materials. Both mixed media and stand-alone CD prices are included in the data. The compiler notes that "these media form only a very small portion of the index" and because mixed media are implicitly reflected in book indexes he does not see the inclusion of such data as invalidating the index.

The average book price in 1998 declined by 4.2 percent. This decline follows an increase of 13.2 percent in 1997. It is important to note that the index is based not on publication year, but on deliveries made by Harrassowitz during a calendar year. Year-to-year price fluctuations are best viewed from the long-term perspective provided by the base year index, which shows an average annual price increase of about 2.2 percent since 1989.

The large price increase in 1997 (13.2 percent) was caused in part by the inclusion of several large encyclopedic sets and the overall rate of annual increases is best determined by the index factors. For 1998 the decline in the average price was driven by price changes in titles in business, engineering, arts, law, philosophy/religion, and political science. Books in these fields declined in price by an aggregate 11.3 percent. Mathematics and medicine titles experienced the highest increases.

The index for German academic periodicals (Table 13) is compiled by Steven Thompson and is based on data from Otto Harrassowitz. The preliminary data for 1999 show 22 disciplines with increases, but only geology (25.8 percent) and physics/astronomy (10.8 percent) showed double-digit rates of increase.

Overall inflation for serial titles is a modest 4.2 percent in contrast to 1998's higher increase of 8 percent. The final 1998 figures (8 percent) are slightly higher than the preliminary data reported last year (6.4 percent overall). It is difficult to discern exactly why this occurs, but the preliminary data are usually 86 percent to 87 percent complete and thus some adjustment in the final figures is inevitable.

### Dutch Prices

Dutch English-language periodicals (Table 14) is compiled by Fred Lynden based on data supplied by Martinus Nijhoff International. In past years, the data provided has varied in the number of titles included. Nijhoff continues to add titles to the data supplied; consequently, the sample shifts from year to year. This causes some unusual results in specific subject areas due to changes in the number of titles. Also, the small number of titles in some subject areas adds to the volatility of price swings in the subject area. The index is reported in Dutch guilders in order to avoid the impact of currency conversion in price changes. A further potential complication for all European Community member countries is the future adoption of a single Euro currency. This is not yet a settled issue and the LMPI Committee will monitor the situation as it pertains to library materials pricing. The 1999 overall price increase of 10.59 percent shows a slight increase over 1998's rise of 9.08 percent. Due to the small number of titles in some subjects, the price changes from year to year in some specific areas may be suspect, but overall it appears that science, technology, psychology, and philosophy all experienced double-digit inflation for 1999 and contributed to the overall 10 percent-plus increase.

### Latin American Prices

The price survey of Latin American books that was included as Table 15 in last year's report has been discontinued with the year 1997. A formal book price index is being developed and should be completed soon. This new index is based on title lists supplied by Latin American book vendors and will be published in other venues yet to be determined.

Latin American periodicals (Tables 15A and 15B), compiled by Scott Van Jacob, provides an analysis of prices quoted by the Faxon Company, the Library of Congress's Rio field office, and the University of Texas at Austin. Weighted mean prices by subject grouping continue to follow a consistent trend. Humanities journals remain the least expensive, while science, social science, law, and general titles remain much more expensive. The prices, indexed to 1992, provide data both including and excluding newspapers, recognizing that foreign newspapers have a significant influence on average price figures. From 1996–1997 to 1997–1998 the average price for all Latin American periodicals without newspapers barely increased from $72.29 to $72.31, with science and law showing the greatest increases. With newspapers included, the average price jumps from $77.95 in 1996–1997 to $79.52 in 1997–1998, a modest 2 percent gain.

## Using the Price Indexes

Librarians are encouraged to monitor both trends in the publishing industry and changes in economic conditions when preparing budget forecasts and projections. The ALA ALCTS Library Materials Price Index Committee endeavors to make information on publishing trends readily available by sponsoring the annual compilation and publication of price data contained in Tables 1–15B. The indexes cover newly published library materials and document prices and rates of price changes at the national/international level. They are useful benchmarks against which local costs may be compared, but because they reflect retail prices in the aggregate they are not a substitute for cost data that reflect the collecting patterns of individual libraries and they are not a substitute for specific cost studies.

In part, differences between local prices and those found in national indexes arise because the national indexes exclude discounts, service charges, shipping and handling fees, or other costs that the library might bear. Discrepancies may also be related to subject focus, mix of current and retrospective materials, and the portion of total library acquisitions composed of foreign imprints. Such variables can affect the average price paid by a particular library although the library's rate of price increase may not significantly differ from national price indexes. LMPIC is interested in pursuing studies correlating a particular library's costs with national prices and would appreciate being informed of any planned or ongoing studies. The committee welcomes interested parties to its meetings at the ALA Annual and Midwinter Conferences.

In addition to the tables included, the reader may wish to consult a new publication on the costs of law materials: *Price Index for Legal Publications, 1997*, prepared by Margaret Axtmann and published by the American Association of Law Libraries. In addition, Yale University Libraries has established a very useful Web page, "Price and Title Output Reports for Collection Management," at http://www.library.yale.edu/colldev.

Current members of the Library Materials Price Index Committee are Stephen Bosch (chair), Margaret Axtmann, Brenda Dingley, Martha Brogan, Wanda Dole, Mary Fugle, Beverly Harris, Bill Robnett, Penny Schroeder, and Sharon Sullivan. They are joined by consultants Barbara Albee, Dana Alessi, Donna D. Alsbury, Catherine Barr, Dave Bogart, Nancy J. Chaffin, Virginia Gilbert, Curt Holleman, John Haar, Martha H. Kellogg, Fred Lynden, Genevieve Owens, Wilba Swearingen, Steve Thompson, and Scott Van Jacob.

# Book Title Output and Average Prices: 1997 Final and 1998 Preliminary Figures

Gary Ink
Research Librarian, *Publishers Weekly*

U.S. book title output reached a final total of 65,796 titles published in 1997, according to figures compiled by R. R. Bowker. This figure represents a decrease of 2,379 titles from the all-time high of 68,175 titles achieved in 1996, and brings to an end the continuing year-to-year increases experienced since 1991. Increases for the years 1995 and 1996 were particularly dramatic, representing, respectively, the largest and second-largest year-to-year increases recorded for the past 50 years. These sharp year-to-year increases in title output occurred even though the book industry has been experiencing a simultaneous period of flat sales in most formats and subject categories. The current decline in title output reflects to a great extent the effect of these flat sales and efforts by book publishers to bring title output in line with the reality of a difficult market. Preliminary figures for 1997, as published in the 1998 *Bowker Annual*, had indicated a possible decline in title output. Preliminary figures for 1998 show a further decline.

## Output by Format and by Category

Title output in 1997 declined sharply for hardcover books and for mass market paperbacks, but showed a modest increase for trade paperbacks. Hardcover output declined by 4,511 titles, a sharp reversal from the increase of 3,819 titles recorded in 1996. Mass market paperback output (Table 3) declined by 390 titles, a sizeable increase over the 200-title decline recorded in 1996; however, 1998 preliminary figures indicate that mass market output is bouncing back. Trade paperback output (Table 2) continued to rise in 1997, to a total of 28,352 titles. While this represents an increase of 732 titles over last year's figure, it is a modest increase compared to the spectacular increase of 4,581 titles recorded in 1996. The trade paperback format remains the only format to register gains in both sales and title output in 1997.

Overall category totals (Table 1) indicate that while 11 of the 23 subject categories experienced modest growth in 1997, the remaining 12 categories experienced declines. Categories showing the largest declines are children's books (juveniles) with a decline of 1,670 titles, fiction with a decline of 610 titles, and sociology and economics with a decline of 464 titles. The large decrease in the number of juveniles titles appears to indicate an acceleration in the reaction of book publishers to the disappointing sales climate that has prevailed in this category for the past two years. Categories showing the largest increases in 1997 were science with an increase of 217 titles, agriculture with an increase of 196 titles, language with an increase of 158 titles, home economics with an increase of 146 titles, and general works with an increase of 132 titles.

*(text continues on page 531)*

# Table 1 / American Book Title Production, 1996–1998

| Category | 1996 All Hard and Paper* | 1997 Final Hard and Trade Paper | | | 1997 Final | 1998 Preliminary Hard and Trade Paper | | | 1998 Preliminary |
|---|---|---|---|---|---|---|---|---|---|
| | | Books | Editions | Total | All Hard and Paper* | Books | Editions | Total | All Hard and Paper* |
| Agriculture | 675 | 729 | 141 | 870 | 871 | 678 | 118 | 796 | 801 |
| Art | 2,033 | 1,710 | 182 | 1,892 | 1,912 | 1,495 | 173 | 1,668 | 1,685 |
| Biography | 3,007 | 2,669 | 357 | 3,026 | 3,069 | 2,295 | 288 | 2,583 | 2,657 |
| Business | 1,788 | 1,300 | 335 | 1,635 | 1,657 | 1,126 | 306 | 1,432 | 1,456 |
| Education | 1,595 | 1,210 | 218 | 1,428 | 1,438 | 1,054 | 151 | 1,205 | 1,224 |
| Fiction | 8,573 | 4,753 | 260 | 5,013 | 7,963 | 3,683 | 263 | 3,946 | 7,096 |
| General Works | 3,027 | 2,561 | 578 | 3,139 | 3,159 | 1,834 | 374 | 2,208 | 2,237 |
| History | 3,576 | 3,191 | 497 | 3,688 | 3,713 | 2,647 | 431 | 3,078 | 3,108 |
| Home Economics | 1,447 | 1,349 | 172 | 1,521 | 1,593 | 950 | 162 | 1,112 | 1,200 |
| Juveniles | 5,353 | 3,253 | 134 | 3,387 | 3,683 | 2,964 | 122 | 3,086 | 3,381 |
| Language | 898 | 793 | 242 | 1,035 | 1,056 | 685 | 140 | 825 | 840 |
| Law | 1,357 | 981 | 397 | 1,378 | 1,390 | 820 | 357 | 1,177 | 1,189 |
| Literature | 3,082 | 2,308 | 353 | 2,661 | 2,729 | 2,016 | 280 | 2,296 | 2,369 |
| Medicine | 4,223 | 3,197 | 840 | 4,037 | 4,136 | 2,741 | 769 | 3,510 | 3,676 |
| Music | 461 | 360 | 66 | 426 | 433 | 327 | 65 | 392 | 408 |
| Philosophy, Psychology | 2,333 | 1,845 | 343 | 2,188 | 2,321 | 1,662 | 282 | 1,944 | 2,104 |
| Poetry, Drama | 1,566 | 1,482 | 48 | 1,530 | 1,545 | 1,040 | 58 | 1,098 | 1,125 |
| Religion | 3,803 | 3,285 | 524 | 3,809 | 3,857 | 2,702 | 395 | 3,097 | 3,153 |
| Science | 3,725 | 3,310 | 607 | 3,917 | 3,942 | 2,864 | 526 | 3,390 | 3,432 |
| Sociology, Economics | 10,528 | 8,645 | 1,311 | 9,956 | 10,064 | 7,772 | 1,063 | 8,835 | 8,970 |
| Sports, Recreation | 1,751 | 1,388 | 228 | 1,616 | 1,691 | 1,136 | 132 | 1,268 | 1,367 |
| Technology | 2,629 | 2,279 | 465 | 2,744 | 2,765 | 1,615 | 357 | 1,972 | 1,999 |
| Travel | 745 | 577 | 227 | 804 | 809 | 446 | 202 | 648 | 652 |
| Totals | 68,175 | 53,175 | 8,525 | 61,700 | 65,796 | 44,552 | 7,014 | 51,566 | 56,129 |

* Includes mass market paperbacks (see Table 3).

Note: Figures for mass market paperbound book production are based on entries in R. R. Bowker's *Books in Print*. Other figures are from the American Book Publishing Record database. Figures under Books and Editions designate new books and new editions.

**Table 2 / Paperbacks (Excluding Mass Market), 1996–1998**

| Category | 1996 Totals | 1997 Final | | | 1998 Preliminary | | |
|---|---|---|---|---|---|---|---|
| | | Books | Editions | Totals | Books | Editions | Totals |
| Fiction | 752 | 656 | 212 | 868 | 483 | 137 | 620 |
| Nonfiction | 26,868 | 22,651 | 4,833 | 27,484 | 17,565 | 3,882 | 21,447 |
| Total | 27,620 | 23,307 | 5,045 | 28,352 | 18,048 | 4,019 | 22,067 |

**Table 3 / Mass Market Paperbacks, 1995–1998**

| Category | 1995 | 1996 | 1997 Final | 1998 Preliminary |
|---|---|---|---|---|
| Agriculture | 10 | 13 | 1 | 5 |
| Art | 12 | 8 | 20 | 17 |
| Biography | 39 | 38 | 43 | 74 |
| Business | 18 | 19 | 22 | 24 |
| Education | 29 | 31 | 10 | 19 |
| Fiction | 3,701 | 3,586 | 2,950 | 3,150 |
| General Works | 31 | 36 | 20 | 29 |
| History | 24 | 17 | 25 | 30 |
| Home Economics | 43 | 35 | 72 | 88 |
| Juveniles | 398 | 292 | 296 | 295 |
| Language | 8 | 8 | 21 | 15 |
| Law | 5 | 5 | 12 | 12 |
| Literature | 47 | 72 | 68 | 73 |
| Medicine | 10 | 20 | 99 | 166 |
| Music | 3 | 5 | 7 | 16 |
| Philosophy, Psychology | 103 | 108 | 133 | 160 |
| Poetry, Drama | 32 | 28 | 15 | 27 |
| Religion | 16 | 16 | 48 | 56 |
| Science | 8 | 9 | 25 | 42 |
| Sociology, Economics | 42 | 34 | 108 | 135 |
| Sports, Recreation | 82 | 76 | 75 | 99 |
| Technology | 22 | 20 | 21 | 27 |
| Travel | 3 | 10 | 5 | 4 |
| Total | 4,686 | 4,486 | 4,096 | 4,563 |

Mass market title output (Table 3), which recorded a drop of 200 titles in 1996, declined by a more significant 390 titles in 1997. This larger decline would appear to confirm the assumption made last year that book publishers are, indeed, reducing output in reaction to the disappointing sales experienced in this market segment over the past three years. However, preliminary 1998 figures point in the other direction, surpassing 1996's total. The largest category decreases in 1997 occurred in agriculture, education, and fiction. The following categories registered substantial growth: art, home economics, language, law, medicine, religion, science, and sociology and economics.

**Table 4 / Imported Titles, 1996–1998**
(Hard and Trade Paper Only)

| Category | 1996 Totals | 1997 Final | | | 1998 Preliminary | | |
|---|---|---|---|---|---|---|---|
| | | Books | Editions | Totals | Books | Editions | Totals |
| Agriculture | 72 | 101 | 18 | 119 | 58 | 7 | 65 |
| Art | 203 | 191 | 14 | 205 | 116 | 8 | 124 |
| Biography | 221 | 167 | 22 | 189 | 97 | 17 | 114 |
| Business | 238 | 161 | 27 | 188 | 110 | 20 | 130 |
| Education | 280 | 182 | 8 | 190 | 153 | 5 | 158 |
| Fiction | 280 | 255 | 18 | 273 | 123 | 25 | 148 |
| General works | 424 | 327 | 53 | 380 | 228 | 20 | 248 |
| History | 536 | 445 | 67 | 512 | 270 | 26 | 296 |
| Home economics | 22 | 20 | 2 | 22 | 6 | 2 | 8 |
| Juveniles | 47 | 53 | 1 | 54 | 20 | 2 | 22 |
| Language | 313 | 292 | 53 | 345 | 194 | 29 | 223 |
| Law | 264 | 250 | 46 | 296 | 183 | 40 | 223 |
| Literature | 428 | 303 | 28 | 331 | 190 | 24 | 214 |
| Medicine | 720 | 564 | 142 | 706 | 418 | 99 | 517 |
| Music | 67 | 43 | 3 | 46 | 35 | 5 | 40 |
| Philosophy, psychology | 393 | 328 | 52 | 380 | 338 | 21 | 359 |
| Poetry, drama | 231 | 184 | 12 | 196 | 84 | 9 | 93 |
| Religion | 310 | 233 | 45 | 278 | 155 | 19 | 174 |
| Science | 1,058 | 872 | 124 | 996 | 561 | 102 | 663 |
| Sociology, economics | 2,392 | 1,777 | 177 | 1,954 | 1,434 | 114 | 1,548 |
| Sports, recreation | 136 | 117 | 10 | 127 | 64 | 5 | 69 |
| Technology | 520 | 432 | 69 | 501 | 249 | 45 | 294 |
| Travel | 116 | 54 | 27 | 81 | 27 | 12 | 39 |
| Total | 9,271 | 7,351 | 1,018 | 8,369 | 5,113 | 656 | 5,769 |

**Table 5 / Translations into English, 1993–1998**

| | 1993 | 1994 | 1995 | 1996 | 1997 Final | 1998 Prelim. |
|---|---|---|---|---|---|---|
| Arabic | 23 | 17 | 36 | 25 | 13 | 23 |
| Chinese | 50 | 55 | 63 | 40 | 47 | 50 |
| Danish | 14 | 21 | 15 | 13 | 25 | 10 |
| Dutch | 35 | 39 | 50 | 55 | 61 | 41 |
| Finnish | 4 | 4 | 4 | 2 | 5 | 4 |
| French | 339 | 374 | 438 | 444 | 429 | 416 |
| German | 353 | 362 | 477 | 517 | 474 | 427 |
| Hebrew | 40 | 35 | 54 | 61 | 44 | 52 |
| Italian | 87 | 132 | 118 | 125 | 125 | 83 |
| Japanese | 59 | 50 | 58 | 78 | 66 | 36 |
| Latin | 55 | 46 | 72 | 78 | 74 | 56 |
| Norwegian | 2 | 5 | 9 | 15 | 14 | 13 |
| Russian | 133 | 137 | 100 | 141 | 114 | 103 |
| Spanish | 135 | 120 | 119 | 193 | 184 | 127 |
| Swedish | 27 | 13 | 20 | 26 | 18 | 13 |
| Turkish | 1 | 2 | 0 | 2 | 1 | 2 |
| Yiddish | 3 | 6 | 6 | 14 | 10 | 2 |
| Total | 1,360 | 1,418 | 1,639 | 1,829 | 1,704 | 1,458 |

*Note*: Total covers only the languages listed here.

**Table A / Hardcover Average Per-Volume Prices, 1995–1998**

| Category | 1995 Prices | 1996 Prices | 1997 Final Vols. | 1997 Final $ Total | 1997 Final Prices | 1998 Preliminary Vols. | 1998 Preliminary $ Total | 1998 Preliminary Prices |
|---|---|---|---|---|---|---|---|---|
| Agriculture | $49.00 | $45.11 | 507 | 24,103.70 | $47.54 | 472 | $20,580.23 | $43.60 |
| Art | 41.23 | 53.40 | 870 | 40,021.90 | 46.00 | 873 | 37,730.19 | 43.22 |
| Biography | 30.01 | 31.67 | 1,773 | 59,393.17 | 33.50 | 1,625 | 53,868.85 | 33.15 |
| Business | 46.90 | 52.62 | 689 | 36,440.67 | 52.89 | 780 | 42,722.34 | 54.77 |
| Education | 43.00 | 47.10 | 453 | 20,644.26 | 45.57 | 451 | 22,319.66 | 49.49 |
| Fiction | 21.47 | 22.89 | 2,882 | 61,694.87 | 21.41 | 2,528 | 56,241.45 | 22.25 |
| General Works | 54.11 | 68.36 | 1,200 | 71,267.60 | 59.39 | 870 | 51,892.65 | 59.65 |
| History | 42.19 | 45.62 | 2,052 | 89,273.31 | 43.51 | 1,854 | 80,446.77 | 43.39 |
| Home Economics | 22.53 | 23.39 | 658 | 15,345.20 | 23.32 | 523 | 12,575.16 | 24.04 |
| Juveniles | 14.55 | 15.97 | 2,013 | 31,478.72 | 15.64 | 1,988 | 32,050.17 | 16.12 |
| Language | 54.89 | 58.81 | 414 | 23,991.11 | 57.95 | 363 | 21,241.60 | 58.52 |
| Law | 73.09 | 88.51 | 740 | 65,968.19 | 89.15 | 663 | 52,592.37 | 79.32 |
| Literature | 38.49 | 43.28 | 1,299 | 58,311.98 | 44.89 | 1,233 | 55,544.15 | 45.05 |
| Medicine | 75.80 | 81.48 | 2,088 | 179,397.02 | 85.92 | 1,922 | 157,169.51 | 81.77 |
| Music | 43.27 | 39.21 | 208 | 9,064.26 | 43.58 | 243 | 11,482.43 | 47.25 |
| Philosophy, Psychology | 45.26 | 48.40 | 949 | 45,605.76 | 48.06 | 952 | 47,979.76 | 50.40 |
| Poetry, Drama | 34.96 | 34.15 | 568 | 20,877.98 | 36.76 | 496 | 17,864.09 | 36.02 |
| Religion | 34.27 | 36.62 | 1,385 | 56,126.28 | 40.52 | 1,273 | 44,652.36 | 35.08 |
| Science | 93.52 | 90.63 | 2,242 | 175,183.94 | 78.14 | 2,132 | 154,328.09 | 72.39 |
| Sociology, Economics | 55.51 | 53.82 | 5,081 | 279,717.21 | 55.05 | 5,023 | 293,151.96 | 58.36 |
| Sports, Recreation | 32.14 | 34.71 | 639 | 20,670.29 | 32.35 | 570 | 21,208.09 | 37.21 |
| Technology | 88.28 | 91.60 | 1,559 | 140,254.81 | 89.96 | 1,273 | 108,809.09 | 85.47 |
| Travel | 38.30 | 33.92 | 236 | 7,217.83 | 30.58 | 186 | 6,805.67 | 36.59 |
| Total | $47.15 | $50.00 | 30,505 | $1,532,050.06 | $50.22 | 28,293 | $1,403,256.64 | $49.60 |

## Price Data Shows Increases

Average book prices for 1997 showed increases for all formats. The overall average price for hardcover books (Table A) increased by 22 cents between 1996 and 1997. This small increase comes as a welcome respite to the large average price increases recorded in 1996 ($2.85) and 1995 ($2.50). The overall average price for trade paperbacks (Table C), which declined by 29 cents in 1996, showed a major increase of $1.25 between 1996 and 1997. The trade paperback format, which has been the only format experiencing strong sales growth in recent years, appears to be able to absorb this large year-on-year average price increase. The overall average price for mass market paperbacks (Table B) increased by a staggering $2.74 between 1996 and 1997. The overall average price for mass market paperbacks has continued to increase year-to-year even as sales and title output have declined, but the size of the current increase would seem to defy the conventional wisdom of the marketplace. Preliminary figures for 1998 indicate a further increase in that year.

Table A1 / Hardcover Average Per-Volume Prices—Less Than $81, 1995–1998

| Category | 1995 Prices | 1996 Prices | 1997 Final Vols. | 1997 Final $ Total | 1997 Final Prices | 1998 Preliminary Vols. | 1998 Preliminary $ Total | 1998 Preliminary Prices |
|---|---|---|---|---|---|---|---|---|
| Agriculture | $30.75 | $29.42 | 432 | $12,523.10 | $28.99 | 399 | $11,307.38 | $28.34 |
| Art | 36.10 | 38.35 | 816 | 31,121.85 | 38.14 | 823 | 32,023.34 | 38.91 |
| Biography | 27.46 | 28.18 | 1684 | 47,843.52 | 28.41 | 1,548 | 44,709.96 | 28.88 |
| Business | 38.30 | 41.15 | 602 | 24,609.68 | 40.88 | 669 | 29,176.86 | 43.61 |
| Education | 38.98 | 42.68 | 431 | 17,861.81 | 41.44 | 414 | 17,432.17 | 42.11 |
| Fiction | 20.98 | 21.26 | 2,873 | 60,296.02 | 20.99 | 2,526 | 56,006.45 | 22.17 |
| General Works | 41.63 | 44.28 | 1,006 | 42,444.52 | 42.19 | 718 | 31,664.75 | 44.10 |
| History | 37.26 | 37.77 | 1,927 | 70,046.61 | 36.35 | 1,750 | 63,879.87 | 36.50 |
| Home Economics | 22.00 | 23.13 | 654 | 14,732.20 | 22.53 | 521 | 12,350.16 | 23.70 |
| Juveniles | 14.33 | 14.76 | 2,005 | 29,151.82 | 14.54 | 1,973 | 29,458.17 | 14.93 |
| Language | 41.01 | 42.07 | 331 | 13,767.75 | 41.59 | 292 | 13,379.45 | 45.82 |
| Law | 45.08 | 46.79 | 470 | 22,473.09 | 47.82 | 465 | 21,989.89 | 47.29 |
| Literature | 36.24 | 38.36 | 1,199 | 46,596.73 | 38.86 | 1,162 | 46,917.10 | 40.38 |
| Medicine | 40.91 | 41.85 | 1,222 | 50,957.88 | 41.70 | 1,227 | 50,145.86 | 40.87 |
| Music | 40.24 | 36.52 | 197 | 8,015.56 | 40.69 | 224 | 8,694.63 | 38.82 |
| Philosophy, Psychology | 38.89 | 40.56 | 872 | 35,128.06 | 40.28 | 862 | 36,721.01 | 42.60 |
| Poetry, Drama | 30.36 | 31.77 | 534 | 16,746.58 | 31.36 | 482 | 16,290.24 | 33.80 |
| Religion | 28.92 | 30.33 | 1,278 | 38,760.03 | 30.33 | 1,202 | 36,280.56 | 30.18 |
| Science | 47.85 | 46.93 | 1,513 | 63,191.81 | 41.77 | 1,458 | 60,906.38 | 41.77 |
| Sociology, Economics | 41.33 | 43.43 | 4,592 | 199,892.06 | 43.53 | 4,405 | 197,821.05 | 44.91 |
| Sports, Recreation | 31.19 | 32.64 | 622 | 17,904.09 | 28.78 | 551 | 17,337.34 | 31.47 |
| Technology | 49.31 | 47.91 | 970 | 44,074.86 | 45.44 | 775 | 38,081.60 | 49.14 |
| Travel | 28.96 | 29.55 | 230 | 6,499.38 | 28.26 | 177 | 5,237.72 | 29.59 |
| Total | $33.29 | $34.56 | 26,460 | $914,639.01 | $34.57 | 24,623 | $877,811.94 | $35.65 |

Hardcover books recorded price decreases in 13 of the 23 subject categories for 1997. The largest decreases occurred in science with a decrease of $12.49 and general works with a decrease of $8.97. Fiction recorded a decrease of $1.48, although the overall average price remains above the $20 mark. The largest hardcover category increases occurred in music with an increase of $4.37, medicine with an increase of $4.44, and religion with an increase of $3.90. Trade paperbacks saw price increases in all subject categories except history, home economics, technology, and travel. The largest category increases were recorded in sociology and economics with an increase of $3.82, and in science with an increase of $3.47. Mass market paperbacks saw price increases in 21 of the 23 subject categories. Most of the price increases were significant. The average price for mass market fiction increased by $2.26 in 1997, while the average price for children's books (juveniles) decreased by $2.04. Figures shown here are derived from R. R. Bowker databases.

Each of the 23 standard subject groups used here represents one or more specific Dewey Decimal Classification numbers, as follows: Agriculture, 630–699, 712–719; Art, 700–711, 720–779; Biography, 920–929; Business, 650–659;

**Table B / Mass Market Paperbacks Average Per-Volume Prices, 1996–1998**

| Category | 1996 Prices | 1997 Final | | | 1998 Preliminary | | |
|---|---|---|---|---|---|---|---|
| | | Vols. | $ Total | Prices | Vols. | $ Total | Prices |
| Agriculture | $11.59 | 1 | $18.00 | $18.00 | 5 | $82.44 | $16.49 |
| Art | 12.00 | 20 | 328.93 | 16.45 | 17 | 228.12 | 14.26 |
| Biography | 10.12 | 43 | 563.04 | 13.73 | 74 | 1,165.94 | 15.97 |
| Business | 13.25 | 22 | 393.98 | 17.91 | 24 | 374.68 | 16.29 |
| Education | 10.29 | 10 | 112.29 | 14.04 | 19 | 319.09 | 16.79 |
| Fiction | 6.25 | 2,950 | 24,833.98 | 8.51 | 3,150 | 26,112.34 | 8.45 |
| General Works | 9.31 | 20 | 278.22 | 13.91 | 29 | 281.37 | 10.42 |
| History | 10.92 | 25 | 367.66 | 14.71 | 30 | 364.44 | 12.57 |
| Home Economics | 8.67 | 72 | 1,051.63 | 14.61 | 88 | 1,191.71 | 14.02 |
| Juveniles | 4.25 | 296 | 1,799.85 | 6.29 | 295 | 1,741.59 | 5.98 |
| Language | 7.87 | 21 | 161.74 | 8.99 | 15 | 158.90 | 10.59 |
| Law | 10.39 | 12 | 147.39 | 12.28 | 12 | 135.26 | 12.30 |
| Literature | 9.42 | 68 | 712.77 | 10.64 | 73 | 715.84 | 10.68 |
| Medicine | 8.93 | 99 | 1,121.62 | 11.33 | 166 | 2,283.49 | 13.84 |
| Music | 20.57 | 7 | 86.29 | 14.38 | 16 | 194.76 | 14.98 |
| Philosophy, Psychology | 7.58 | 133 | 1,849.75 | 14.12 | 160 | 1,895.40 | 12.15 |
| Poetry, Drama | 10.88 | 15 | 157.89 | 10.53 | 27 | 232.49 | 8.61 |
| Religion | 8.93 | 48 | 620.23 | 13.48 | 56 | 797.71 | 14.77 |
| Science | 12.16 | 25 | 362.13 | 15.09 | 42 | 570.71 | 14.27 |
| Sociology, Economics | 9.91 | 108 | 1,743.52 | 16.29 | 135 | 1,866.61 | 14.14 |
| Sports, Recreation | 8.79 | 75 | 1,099.92 | 14.67 | 99 | 1,388.85 | 14.62 |
| Technology | 11.14 | 21 | 253.68 | 12.08 | 27 | 341.46 | 13.13 |
| Travel | 9.63 | 5 | 77.85 | 15.57 | 4 | 44.40 | 11.10 |
| Total | $6.57 | 4,096 | $38,142.36 | $9.31 | 4,563 | $42,487.60 | $9.31 |

Education, 370–379; Fiction; General Works, 000–099; History, 900–909, 930–999; Home Economics, 640–649; Juveniles; Language, 400–499; Law, 340–349; Literature, 800–810, 813–820, 823–899; Medicine, 610–619; Music, 780–789; Philosophy, Psychology, 100–199; Poetry, Drama, 811, 812, 821, 822; Religion, 200–299; Science, 500–599; Sociology, Economics, 300–339, 350–369, 380–389; Sports, Recreation, 790–799; Technology, 600–609, 620–629, 660–699; Travel, 910–919.

Table C / Trade Paperbacks Average Per-Volume Prices, 1995–1998

| 1995 Category | 1996 Prices | Prices | 1997 Final | | | 1998 Preliminary | | |
|---|---|---|---|---|---|---|---|---|
| | | | Vols. | $ Total | Prices | Vols. | $ Total | Prices |
| Agriculture | $26.97 | $20.45 | 280 | $5,973.83 | $21.34 | 284 | $5,600.60 | $19.72 |
| Art | 20.58 | 21.57 | 728 | 16,087.13 | 22.10 | 643 | 15,112.50 | 23.50 |
| Biography | 16.59 | 17.37 | 902 | 15,840.96 | 17.56 | 766 | 13,553.50 | 17.69 |
| Business | 24.24 | 26.08 | 681 | 18,047.30 | 26.50 | 532 | 16,104.96 | 30.27 |
| Education | 22.96 | 23.76 | 608 | 15,189.46 | 24.98 | 532 | 13,190.91 | 24.79 |
| Fiction | 12.71 | 12.35 | 1,708 | 22,356.12 | 13.09 | 1,166 | 16,469.27 | 14.12 |
| General Works | 32.99 | 34.65 | 1,546 | 59,520.47 | 38.50 | 1,192 | 47,442.05 | 39.80 |
| History | 18.48 | 20.09 | 1,165 | 22,937.11 | 19.69 | 941 | 19,657.22 | 20.89 |
| Home Economics | 14.87 | 15.35 | 748 | 11,441.54 | 15.30 | 529 | 8,437.18 | 15.95 |
| Juveniles | 15.75 | 8.30 | 954 | 8,863.55 | 9.29 | 763 | 6,384.08 | 8.37 |
| Language | 21.58 | 21.17 | 386 | 8,470.53 | 21.94 | 346 | 7,886.76 | 22.79 |
| Law | 30.26 | 30.81 | 373 | 11,717.21 | 31.41 | 361 | 10,260.34 | 28.42 |
| Literature | 16.54 | 17.69 | 984 | 18,714.54 | 19.02 | 832 | 16,933.47 | 20.35 |
| Medicine | 27.91 | 27.37 | 1,411 | 38,741.50 | 27.46 | 1,273 | 34,669.54 | 27.23 |
| Music | 19.81 | 20.14 | 166 | 3,575.08 | 21.54 | 116 | 2,704.57 | 23.32 |
| Philosophy, Psychology | 19.92 | 18.83 | 898 | 17,170.19 | 19.12 | 777 | 16,356.17 | 21.05 |
| Poetry, Drama | 15.69 | 12.92 | 789 | 11,205.89 | 14.20 | 523 | 7,744.87 | 14.81 |
| Religion | 14.60 | 14.93 | 1,951 | 30,530.82 | 15.65 | 1,570 | 26,404.77 | 16.82 |
| Science | 33.42 | 32.95 | 936 | 34,086.10 | 36.42 | 892 | 31,660.97 | 35.49 |
| Sociology, Economics | 23.69 | 23.47 | 3,200 | 87,329.42 | 27.29 | 2,767 | 67,466.46 | 24.38 |
| Sports, Recreation | 16.53 | 16.33 | 779 | 13,487.80 | 17.31 | 607 | 11,138.40 | 18.35 |
| Technology | 38.75 | 39.17 | 821 | 30,956.61 | 37.71 | 556 | 18,177.57 | 32.69 |
| Travel | 16.38 | 16.74 | 517 | 8,440.54 | 16.33 | 432 | 7,286.85 | 16.87 |
| Total | $21.71 | $21.42 | 22,531 | $510,683.70 | $22.67 | 18,400 | $420,643.01 | $22.86 |

# Book Sales Statistics, 1998: AAP Preliminary Estimates

Association of American Publishers

The industry estimates shown in the following table are based on the U.S. Census of Manufactures. However, book publishing is currently being transferred to the Economic Census, also called the Census of Information. Like the Census of Manufactures, this is a five-year census conducted in years ending in "2" and "7"; 1997 was a transition census with the data being collected and processed by the same government people as in prior years, but the forthcoming output will be under the auspices of the new census. Preliminary data should be available later in 1999.

Between censuses, the Association of American Publishers (AAP) estimates are "pushed forward" by the percentage changes that are reported to the AAP statistics program, and by other industry data that are available. Some AAP data are collected in a monthly statistics program, and it is largely this material that is shown in the preliminary estimate table overleaf. More detailed data are available from, and additional publishers report to, the AAP annual statistics program, and this additional data will be incorporated into Table S1 that will be published in the AAP 1998 Industry Statistics.

Readers comparing the estimated data with census reports should be aware that the U.S. Census of Manufactures does not include data on many university presses or on other institutionally sponsored and not-for-profit publishing activities, or (under SIC 2731: Book Publishing) for the audiovisual and other media materials that are included in this table. On the other hand, AAP estimates have traditionally excluded "Sunday School" materials and certain pamphlets that are incorporated in the census data. These and other adjustments have been built into AAP's industry estimates.

As in prior reports, the estimates reflect the impact of industry expansion created by new establishments entering the field, as well as nontraditional forms of book publishing, in addition to incorporating the sales increases and decreases of established firms.

It should also be noted that the Other Sales category includes only incidental book sales, such as music, sheet sales (both domestic and export, except those to prebinders), and miscellaneous merchandise sales.

The estimates include domestic sales and export sales of U.S. product, but they do not cover indigenous activities of publishers' foreign subsidiaries.

Non-rack-size Mass Market Publishing is included in Trade—Paperbound. Prior to the 1988 AAP Industry Statistics, this was indicated as Adult Trade Paperbound. It is recognized that part of this is Juvenile (estimate: 20 percent), and adjustments have been made in this respect. AAP also notes that this area includes sales through traditional "mass market paperback channels" by publishers not generally recognized as being "mass market paperback."

Table 1 / **Estimated Book Publishing Industry Sales, 1987, 1992, 1996–98**
(Millions of Dollars)

| | 1987 | 1992 | 1996 | 1997 | % Change from 1996 | 1998 | % Change from 1997 | Compound growth rate (%) | |
|---|---|---|---|---|---|---|---|---|---|
| | | | | | | | | 1987–1998 | 1992–1998 |
| Trade (total) | 2,712.8 | 4,661.6 | 5,643.0 | 5,774.1 | 2.3 | 6,148.9 | 6.5 | 7.7 | 4.7 |
| Adult hardbound | 1,350.6 | 2,222.5 | 2,586.0 | 2,663.6 | 3.0 | 2,751.5 | 3.3 | 6.7 | 3.6 |
| Adult paperbound | 727.1 | 1,261.7 | 1,609.4 | 1,731.7 | 7.6 | 1,908.3 | 10.2 | 9.2 | 7.1 |
| Juvenile hardbound | 478.5 | 850.8 | 867.7 | 908.5 | 4.7 | 953.9 | 5.0 | 6.5 | 1.9 |
| Juvenile paperbound | 156.6 | 326.6 | 579.9 | 470.3 | -18.9 | 535.2 | 13.8 | 11.8 | 8.6 |
| Religious (total) | 638.8 | 907.1 | 1,093.4 | 1,132.7 | 3.6 | 1,178.0 | 4.0 | 5.7 | 4.5 |
| Bibles, testaments, hymnals, etc. | 177.6 | 260.1 | 294.8 | 285.4 | -3.2 | 296.0 | 3.7 | 4.8 | 2.2 |
| Other religious | 461.2 | 647.0 | 798.6 | 847.3 | 6.1 | 882.0 | 4.1 | 6.1 | 5.3 |
| Professional (total) | 2,207.3 | 3,106.7 | 3,985.0 | 4,156.4 | 4.3 | 4,418.7 | 6.3 | 6.5 | 6.0 |
| Business | 388.8 | 490.3 | 721.4 | 768.1 | 6.5 | — | — | — | — |
| Law | 780.0 | 1,128.1 | 1,429.8 | 1,502.7 | 5.1 | — | — | — | — |
| Medical | 406.5 | 622.7 | 815.8 | 856.5 | 5.0 | — | — | — | — |
| Technical, scientific, other prof'l | 632.0 | 865.6 | 1,018.0 | 1,029.1 | 1.1 | — | — | — | — |
| Book clubs | 678.7 | 742.3 | 1,091.8 | 1,143.1 | 4.7 | 1,209.4 | 5.8 | 5.4 | 8.5 |
| Mail order publications | 657.6 | 630.2 | 579.5 | 521.0 | -10.1 | 470.5 | -9.7 | -3.0 | -4.8 |
| Mass market paperback, rack-sized | 913.7 | 1,263.8 | 1,555.1 | 1,433.8 | -7.8 | 1,514.1 | 5.6 | 4.7 | 3.1 |
| University presses | 170.9 | 280.1 | 349.3 | 367.8 | 5.3 | 391.8 | 6.5 | 7.8 | 5.8 |
| Elementary and secondary text | 1,695.6 | 2,080.9 | 2,618.0 | 3,005.4 | 14.8 | 3,315.0 | 10.3 | 6.3 | 8.1 |
| College text | 1,549.5 | 2,084.1 | 2,485.8 | 2,669.7 | 7.4 | 2,888.6 | 8.2 | 5.8 | 5.6 |
| Standardized tests | 104.0 | 140.4 | 178.7 | 191.4 | 7.1 | 204.6 | 6.9 | 6.3 | 6.5 |
| Subscription reference | 437.6 | 572.3 | 706.1 | 736.5 | 4.3 | 767.4 | 4.2 | 5.2 | 5.0 |
| Other sales (incl. AV) | 423.8 | 449.0 | 493.2 | 510.0 | 3.4 | 526.3 | 3.2 | 2.0 | 2.7 |
| Total | 12,190.3 | 16,918.5 | 20,778.9 | 21,641.9 | 4.2 | 23,033.3 | 6.4 | 6.0 | 5.3 |

*Source:* Association of American Publishers

# U.S. Book Exports and Imports: 1998

Albert N. Greco

Associate Professor
Fordham University Graduate School of Business Administration

## U.S. Book Exports, 1998

Book publishing is a complex, adaptive, semi-chaotic industry, and it also happens to be a global enterprise.

While the U.S. domestic market purchased 2.4 billion book units in 1998 (up 3.24 percent over 1997's 2.32 billion) and generated $22.51 billion in revenues (up 6.51 percent over 1997's $21.13 billion), book exports make an exceptionally important contribution to an American publisher's bottom line.

U.S. publishers have sold their titles abroad for decades, with a sterling track record through the mid-1950s. After 1980, however, exports became an exceptionally crucial revenue stream as the business-of-publishing landscape changed dramatically and the U.S. domestic market began to exhibit patterns of "economic uncertainty" (Greco 1997, pp. 20–44; Asser 1989, pp. 51–59; Hayes & Abernathy 1980, pp. 67–77). These events, along with related queries, prompted many publishers to reevaluate their global plans.

- Consumer books (i.e., adult, juvenile, mass market paperbacks, religious, book club, and mail order) in the United States are "price elastic"; that is, sales are affected directly by the retail price of consumer books. Are there markets where price elasticity might not be so significant?
- After 1980, and picking up momentum after 1985, the U.S. market for media and entertainment goods and services (including consumer books) became glutted with new, seductive products and options. This included a sharp increase in book title output, feature films, prerecorded home videotapes, and cable television, along with the emergence of the Internet, satellite television, computer games, and so forth). Did media and entertainment markets exist that were not glutted?
- The amount of time available for media and entertainment increased in exceptionally small amounts, up only about 3.1 percent between 1985 and 1995. This affected the domestic market for books. Books were now in the grip of a "zero sum game"; to gain U.S. market share, books had to take media usage and expenditures away from a competing format. Were there nations were media usage was expanding at a faster pace than in the United States?

Concerned about these vexing questions, U.S. publishers created new, effective international sales forces to sell what were, in reality, exceptionally attractive products.

After all, the United States has a strong output of new fiction and nonfiction titles (about 68,000 new titles were released in 1998) as well as its impressive backlist of about 1.5 million titles. In addition, a sizable number of American authors have a global appeal—among them such top-selling novelists as John Grisham, Michael Crichton, Danielle Steele, Tom Clancy, and Stephen King—and their book sales were augmented, especially in the 1990s, by successful film adaptations of their work. Historically, export growth rates were steady in this consumer book market. Strong sales results were posted annually in the technical, scientific, and professional niches (long dominated by Americans in what is in reality a "price inelastic" niche) plus an expanding international market for U.S. textbooks (in business, medical areas, and so forth; another example of price inelasticity) (Bratland & Lofquist 1995, pp. 29–35).

In addition, some U.S. book distributors sold "out of print" books in foreign markets, which helped decrease inventory holdings that had little or no domestic market.

As the U.S. market underwent a metamorphosis, foreign markets provided a major revenue stream, especially in nations with established channels of distribution, low foreign indebtedness, low tariffs and other types of trade barriers, and mature markets with stable monetary policies and cash reserves (that could be converted into U.S. dollars to buy these books).

The United States book industry became a "positive balance of trade" industry, exporting far more books than it imported. By 1998, book publishers sold 910.3 million units abroad, generating more than $1.84 billion in revenues. U.S. Book distributors and bookstores imported 777.13 million units, accounting for more than $1.37 billion in sales, generating a positive balance of trade of $466.23 million and more than 133 million units.

Foreign book distributors and bookstore owners purchase U.S. books with U.S. dollars. So any alteration in a nation's economic underpinnings can, and usually does, have an impact on book orders, a material macroeconomic theme addressed in the published literature (Rose & Svenson 1994, pp. 1185–1216; Frankel & Rose 1996, pp. 351–366; Wyplosz 1986, pp. 167–179; Eichengreen & Bayoumi 1998, pp. 191–209; Dornbusch 1976, pp. 1161–1176; Rohatyn 1989, pp. 54–58; Blumenthal 1988, pp. 535–546; Scalapino 1988, pp. 85–89; and Hout, Porter, & Rudden 1983, pp. 7–83).

A case in point is the Asian "fiscal contagion" that first appeared in 1996 and accelerated in 1997, which undermined dozens of economies throughout the Pacific Rim, spreading ultimately to other parts of the world. This problem has been the subject of a number of studies, including Crafts (1998, pp. 1–10), Bosworth & Collins (1996, pp. 135–203), Bhattacharya, Claessens, Gosh, Hernandez & Alba (1998, pp. 1–36), and Kwack (1998, pp. 7–11).

U.S. publishers saw a softening in their export market in the summer of 1997. By 1998 a sharp downturn in U.S. book exports occurred, with a 2.89 percent decline in dollar shipments, offset slightly by a 1.45 percent decrease in unit sales. The hardest-hit categories included dictionaries and thesauruses (down 60.79 percent in dollar sales), atlases (down 17.28 percent), and art and pictorial books (down 31.12 percent). The usually strong U.S. textbook niche (immensely popular because of core market competencies in business, etc.) sustained a 10.45 percent drop in revenues, as did the almost "recession-proof" (i.e., price inelastic) technical, scientific, and professional category, which was off 1.4 percent.

**Table 1 / U.S. Exports of Books: 1998**

| Category | Value (millions of current $) | Percent change: 1997–1998 | Units (millions of copies) | Percent change, 1997–1998 |
|---|---|---|---|---|
| Dictionaries and thesauruses | $7.45 | -60.79% | 1.54 | 44.44% |
| Encyclopedias | 18.62 | -27.34 | 3.44 | -15.00 |
| Textbooks | 331.82 | -10.45 | 51.80 | -11.30 |
| Religious books | 50.56 | -5.42 | 42.14 | +11.38 |
| Technical, scientific, and professional | 541.74 | -1.40 | 73.81 | -8.78 |
| Art and pictorial books | 13.52 | -31.12 | 5.87 | -71.63 |
| Hardcover books, n.e.s. | 141.68 | -3.28 | 48.31 | -1.63 |
| Mass market paperbacks | 239.26 | +2.66 | 124.15 | +4.81 |
| Books: Flyers/circulars, 1–4 pages | 5.76 | -34.09 | 9.51 | -34.93 |
| Books: pamphlets, and brochures, 5–48 pages | 34.17 | +8.92 | 54.34 | -4.40 |
| Books: 49 or more pages | 439.10 | +4.67 | 491.80 | +3.17 |
| Music books | 15.71 | -5.42 | 3.25 | +6.45 |
| Atlases | 2.44 | -17.28 | 0.35 | -29.06 |
| Total, all books | $1,841.82 | -2.89% | 910.30 | -1.45% |

Notes: n.e.s. = Not elsewhere specified. Individual shipments are excluded from the foreign trade data if valued under $2,500. Data for individual categories may not add to totals due to statistical rounding.

Source: U.S. Department of Commerce, Bureau of the Census

While U.S. book publishers export titles to almost every nation in the world (Ingleton 1991, pp. 54–60; Kobrak & Luey 1992, pp. 1–22), 20 countries account for the vast majority of all sales with a 91.4 percent market share in 1998. Canada is the United States' most important export market for books, generating 43.85 percent of all sales ($807.58 million) and 52.23 percent of all shipped units. The U.S. Department of Commerce reported a 1.95 percent decline in dollar shipments, although there was a modest 2.33 percent increase in units sold to Canadian distributors and booksellers. The United Kingdom (with a 12.87 percent market share of U.S. exports) also purchased fewer books (down 6.82 percent), as did other traditionally important markets for U.S. books: Germany (down 16.66 percent), Singapore (down 30.79 percent), Taiwan (down 17.42 percent), the Philippines (down 47.41 percent), and India (down 30.96 percent), Overall, 15 of the top 20 countries posted declines in U.S. book exports.

The only bright spots were Australia (up 14.36 percent), New Zealand (up 14.62 percent), Mexico (up a modest 0.98 percent), the Netherlands (up 44.59 percent), and, ironically, Japan (up 10.79 percent), although it has been buffeted by a slowdown in its domestic national product and sagging exports of industrial and consumer goods.

In spite of certain macroeconomic changes, primarily addressed at stabilizing certain Asian currencies, it appears this process will take anywhere from two to three more years before real, sustained fiscal stability becomes pervasive in the Pacific Rim. The outlook is mixed for real growth in both dollar revenues and unit sales in the U.S. book export sector in 1999 or 2000.

Table 2 / U.S. Book Exports to 20 Principal Countries: 1998

| Country | Value (millions of current $) | Percent change, 1997–1998 | Units (millions of copies) | Percent change, 1997–1998 |
|---|---|---|---|---|
| Canada | $807.58 | -1.95% | 475.42 | +2.33% |
| United Kingdom | 237.06 | -6.82 | 94.02 | -2.57 |
| Australia | 157.93 | +14.36 | 71.44 | +10.93 |
| Japan | 133.28 | +10.79 | 27.77 | -9.84 |
| Mexico | 58.77 | +0.98 | 44.60 | -14.89 |
| Netherlands | 45.40 | +44.59 | 19.46 | +34.21 |
| Germany | 40.67 | -16.66 | 16.27 | -6.49 |
| Singapore | 26.54 | -30.79 | 15.97 | -19.34 |
| Taiwan | 23.70 | -17.42 | 8.25 | -6.25 |
| New Zealand | 21.32 | +14.62 | 8.16 | +13.33 |
| Hong Kong | 21.29 | -10.92 | 6.86 | +18.28 |
| Brazil | 18.20 | -31.06 | 6.61 | -37.05 |
| Korea, Republic of | 16.11 | -44.83 | 6.23 | -61.54 |
| South Africa | 15.38 | -15.49 | 7.18 | -26.73 |
| India | 12.29 | -30.96 | 5.82 | -25.38 |
| France | 11.43 | -36.85 | 3.99 | -15.11 |
| Philippines | 10.36 | -47.41 | 5.30 | -42.39 |
| Argentina | 9.50 | -12.04 | 6.63 | +0.45 |
| Italy | 9.37 | -5.35 | 3.03 | +1.00 |
| Denmark | 7.18 | -28.80 | 2.64 | +5.60 |
| Total, Top 20 countries | $1,683.36 | -3.42% | 835.65 | -1.98% |

Note: Individual shipments are excluded from the foreign trade data if valued under $2,500.

Source: U.S. Department of Commerce, Bureau of the Census

## U.S. Book Imports

Of the 13 book categories tracked by the Department of Commerce, 11 posted increases in the imported book sector in 1998. The best growth rates were recorded by religious books, up a healthy 23.91 percent, art and pictorial books, up 18.94 percent, and textbooks, up 10.48 percent. Strong tallies were also generated by mass market paperbacks (up 8.91 percent) and hardcover books (up 6.41 percent). Only music books and encyclopedias were down—by 23.73 percent and 25.93 percent, respectively (printed encyclopedias are in a "free fall" state in the U.S. market because of the incursions of electronic versions, which are often bundled with new computers).

The United Kingdom, Canada, and Hong Kong emerged as the largest sources of books imported into the United States, accounting for approximately 500 million units (about 64 percent of all imports) and $738 million (an enviable market share of more than 53 percent). The Republic of Korea experienced the largest surge in sales, up more than 50 percent over 1997. Other major nations shipping books into the U.S. market included Italy, China, Singapore, Germany, and Japan.

## Table 3 / U.S. Imports of Books: 1998

| Category | Value (millions of current $) | Percent change, 1997–1998 | Units (millions of copies) | Percent change, 1997–1998 |
|---|---|---|---|---|
| Dictionaries and thesauruses | $7.65 | +2.70% | 2.10 | -4.55% |
| Encyclopedias | 4.06 | -25.93 | 1.04 | +25.00 |
| Textbooks | 123.34 | +10.48 | 25.15 | +14.55 |
| Religious books | 62.68 | +23.91 | 38.79 | +39.07 |
| Technical, scientific, and professional | 188.73 | +3.34 | 39.99 | +16.67 |
| Art and pictorial books | 38.28 | +18.94 | 8.63 | -18.10 |
| Hardcover books, n.e.s. | 438.10 | +6.41 | 132.47 | +1.07 |
| Mass market paperbacks | 81.88 | +8.91 | 46.27 | +11.30 |
| Books: flyers/circulars, 1–4 pages | 6.15 | +12.73 | 76.29 | +53.21 |
| Books: pamphlets and brochures, 5–48 pages | 81.42 | +18.66 | 220.22 | -16.05 |
| Books: 49 or more pages | 332.3 | +2.18 | 180.98 | -9.73 |
| Music books | 4.46 | -23.73 | 2.24 | +144.44 |
| Atlases | 6.54 | +62.50 | 2.96 | +93.33 |
| Total, all books | $1,375.59 | +6.89% | 777.13 | -1.03% |

Notes: n.e.s. = Not elsewhere specified. Individual shipments are excluded from the foreign trade data if valued under $2,500. Data for individual categories may not add to totals due to statistical rounding.

Source: U.S. department of Commerce, Bureau of the Census

## Table 4 / U.S. Book Imports from 20 Principal Countries: 1998

| Country | Value (millions of current $) | Percent change, 1997–1998 | Units (millions of copies) | Percent change, 1997–1998 |
|---|---|---|---|---|
| United Kingdom | $313.87 | +10.75% | 65.27 | +5.96% |
| Canada | 224.25 | +18.53 | 310.19 | -17.50 |
| Hong Kong | 200.41 | -1.37 | 123.88 | +7.63 |
| Italy | 102.16 | +19.49 | 38.47 | +0.18 |
| China | 100.24 | +36.75 | 59.36 | +31.04 |
| Singapore | 94.72 | +2.84 | 42.76 | +12.23 |
| Germany | 63.10 | +9.74 | 12.43 | -2.89 |
| Japan | 58.65 | -11.54 | 18.93 | -8.55 |
| Spain | 37.33 | +1.72 | 11.79 | 0.00 |
| Korea, Republic of | 26.34 | +50.51 | 11.85 | +37.79 |
| France | 23.69 | -42.22 | 4.38 | -23.16 |
| Belgium | 19.43 | +29.53 | 6.62 | +20.36 |
| Netherlands | 17.56 | +25.43 | 2.58 | +43.33 |
| Mexico | 17.08 | -10.11 | 39.06 | +68.36 |
| Israel | 9.88 | +19.04 | 2.21 | +16.32 |
| Switzerland | 9.85 | +24.68 | 3.32 | +107.50 |
| Taiwan | 9.40 | -20.34 | 9.04 | -17.06 |
| Australia | 7.67 | -9.76 | 8.03 | +150.94 |
| Colombia | 6.28 | -10.29 | 6.32 | +7.12 |
| New Zealand | 1.04 | -90.88 | 0.76 | -81.00 |
| Total: Top 20 Countries | $1,342.50 | +7.54% | 777.25 | -1.87% |

Source: U.S. Department of Commerce, Bureau of the Census

Asian nations whipsawed by currency troubles (Eichengreen, Rose, & Wyplosz 1996, pp. 463–484; Engle 1993, pp. 35–50) targeted the United States because of the vastness of its consumer market and the strength of the dollar, a marketing strategy likely to followed well into 1999 and 2000.

## Major U.S. Book Export-Import Issues

U.S. book exports have increased since 1970, growing from a modest $174.9 million to a robust $1.84 billion in 1998. Since 1995 the U.S. book publishing industry has generated an impressive $2.195 billion surplus in exports ($7.3 billion) over imports ($5.1 billion).

However, an analysis of recent data revealed that the pivotal gap between exports and imports shifted, with a $599.1 million positive balance of trade between exports and imports in 1997 but only $466.23 million in 1998. This pattern of uneven growth was evident throughout the 1990s. There was also a fairly sharp downward shift in the ratio between exports and imports in 1990 (1.65) and 1998 (1.34). This ratio is a significant indicator of the growth and strength of the export sector, and a downward spiral in the export-import ratio must be viewed with some concern.

U.S. book industry shipments and exports also revealed uneven export growth patterns, vacillating between 9.1 percent in 1995 and 8.2 percent in 1998.

A review of business economic forecasts released by the Federal Reserve Bank of Philadelphia, along with econometric projections from the Commerce Department, indicated that the United States should continue to experience low levels of inflation (pegged at 2.3 percent annually through 2003 by the Commerce Department) and strong economic growth in both 1999 and 2000. It also appears that the Asian contagion abated slightly in 1998. These positive econo-

### Table 5 / U.S. Trade in Books: 1970–1998
(in millions of current dollars)

| Year | U.S. Book Exports | U.S. Book Imports | Ratio, U.S. Book Exports/imports |
|------|-------------------|-------------------|----------------------------------|
| 1970 | $174.9 | $92.0 | 1.90 |
| 1975 | 269.3 | 147.6 | 1.82 |
| 1980 | 518.9 | 306.5 | 1.69 |
| 1985 | 591.2 | 564.2 | 1.05 |
| 1990 | 1,415.1 | 855.1 | 1.65 |
| 1995 | 1,779.5 | 1,184.5 | 1.50 |
| 1996 | 1,775.6 | 1,240.1 | 1.43 |
| 1997 | 1,896.6 | 1,297.5 | 1.46 |
| 1998 | 1,841.82 | 1,375.59 | 1.34 |

Source: U.S. Department of Commerce, Bureau of the Census. Due to changes in the classification of U.S. traded products and what constitutes products classified as "books," data prior to 1990 are not strictly comparable to data beginning in 1990.

metric drivers prompted some book industry observers to predict an increase in U.S. exports in 1999 and 2000.

However, far too many nagging concerns remain regarding U.S. exports, especially related to the important Pacific Rim as well as the nations affected by fiscal developments in that region.

Some trade barriers still exist in certain nations, primarily in China. The Republic of Korea, Thailand, Indonesia, and other nations in the Pacific Rim sustained economic losses related to widespread capital flows out of these nations and the impact of unrestricted lending. Their exchange rates fell in relation to the U.S. dollar, impacting lending agreements, liquidity of lending, and existing debts pegged to the U.S. dollar. Interest rates surged, as did requests for multi-billion-dollar bailouts from the International Monetary Fund to shore up the faith and stability of certain key currencies. Grand plans for satellite systems and expanding megaprojects stalled.

In reality, assuming that emerging economies would continue to post high growth rates in exports and gross domestic products, along with very high rates of capital accumulation (often in double digits), is an exceptionally flawed strategy. Pacific Rim growth was premised, to a substantial degree, on increasing their exports (with a concomitant policy of many Rim nations to provide preferential financing and tax incentives) to garner hard currencies to purchase foreign goods and services. This macroeconomic strategy worked, with high degrees of macro-economic stability evident throughout the Rim, for a number of years.

However, any downward shift in exports out of the Pacific Rim could trigger economic instability, including cuts in both their imports and gross domestic product, which is precisely what occurred. The end results were disheartening. The massive construction projects, automobile plants, and condominiums-hotels-office buildings that dot the Pacific Rim's landscape are, in many instances, standing idle. In addition, nonperforming loan rates continue to increase, indicators of an overheated economy, plagued with far too many external and internal problems, that just ran out of gas.

On the positive side, the influx of imports seems to have created jobs in the United States, helping to fuel its expanding economy; and the unsettled economic conditions in the Pacific Rim just might be a cooling off economies that were running the risk of "overheating."

It is abundantly evident, however, that if U.S. publishers want to achieve impressive export tallies in the next two years they must refocus their efforts to understand more completely the relationship between economic downturns (Krugman 1999, 56–74) and currency conversion problems. The major U.S. book industry trade associations should consider creating a division or a task force to monitor foreign economic conditions, paralleling their very successful efforts to track book adoptions on the state level.

The U.S. book industry is preoccupied with selling and marketing (which is totally understandable), not with analyzing foreign macroeconomic conditions in a structured manner. However, if the U.S. book industry continues to operate as it has in the past, and pays little or no attention to foreign economic and currency issues, U.S. book exports might continue to languish in 1999, 2000, and possibly beyond.

**Table 6 / U.S. Book Industry Shipments Compared to U.S. Book Exports: 1970–1998**
(in millions of dollars)

| Year | Total Shipments, U.S. Book Industry | U.S. Book Exports | Exports as a Percent of Total Shipments |
|------|------|------|------|
| 1970 | $2,434.2 | $174.9 | 7.2% |
| 1975 | 3,536.5 | 269.3 | 7.6 |
| 1980 | 6,114.4 | 518.9 | 8.5 |
| 1985 | 10,165.7 | 591.2 | 5.8 |
| 1990 | 14,982.6 | 1,415.1 | 9.4 |
| 1995 | 19,471.0 | 1,779.5 | 9.1 |
| 1996 | 20,285.7 | 1,775.6 | 8.8 |
| 1997 | 21,131.9 | 1,896.6 | 9.0 |
| 1998 | 22,507.0 | 1,841.8 | 8.2 |

Sources: U.S. Department of Commerce, Bureau of the Census; and the Book Industry Study Group, Inc. (BISG). BISG's totals were used for shipments beginning in 1985 through 1998. Commerce totals were used for 1970–1980. Due to changes in the classification of U.S. traded products and what constitutes products classified as "books," data prior to 1990 are not strictly comparable to data beginning in 1990

# Notes

Asser, P. N. (1989). "Consolidation, Internationalization, and the Future of Publishing: A Scenario." *Book Research Quarterly*, vol. 5 (Fall), pp. 51–59.

Bhattacharya, A., S. Claessens, S. Gosh, L. Hernandez, and P. Alba. "Volatility And Contagion in a Financially Integrated World: Lessons from East Asia's Recent Experience." Working Paper. Washington: World Bank (May): pp. 1–36.

Blumenthal, W. M. (1988). "The World Economy and Technological Change." *Foreign Affairs*, vol. 66, pp. 535–546.

Bosworth, B. P. and S. M. Collins (1996). "Economic Growth in East Asia: Accumulation Versus Assimilation." Brookings Papers on Economic Activity, vol. 2, pp. 135–203.

Bratland, R. M. and W. S. Lofquist (1995). "Economic Outlook for the U.S. Printing and Publishing Industry." *Publishing Research Quarterly*, 11 (Summer), pp. 29–35.

Crafts, N. (1998). "East Asian Growth Before and After the Crisis." Working Paper 98/137. Washington: International Monetary Fund (October), pp. 1–10.

Dornbusch, R. (1976). "Expectations and Exchange Rate Dynamics." *Journal of Political Economy*, vol. 84, pp. 1161–1176.

Eichengreen, B. and T. Bayoumi (1998). "Exchange Rate Volatility and Intervention: Implications of the Theory of Optimum Currency Areas." *Journal of International Economics,* vol. 45, pp. 191–209.

Eichengreen, B., A. Rose, and C. Wyplosz (1996). "Contagious Currency Crises: First Tests." *Scandinavian Journal of Economics*, vol. 98, pp. 463–484.

Engle, C. (1993). "Real Exchange Rates and Relative Prices." *Journal of Monetary Economics*, vol. 32, pp. 35–50.

Frankel, J. and A. Rose (1996). "Currency Crashes in Emerging Markets: An Empirical Treatment." *Journal of International Economics*, vol. 41, pp. 351–366.

Greco, A. N. (1997). *The Book Publishing Industry*. Boston: Allyn & Bacon.

Hayes, R. H. and W. J. Abernathy (1980). "Managing Our Way to Economic Decline." *Harvard Business Review*, vol. 58 (July-August), pp. 67–77.

Hout, T. M., M. Porter, and E. Rudden (1983). "How Global Companies Win Out," in Hammermesh, R. G., ed., *Strategic Management*. New York: John Wiley & Sons.

Ingleton, N. (1991). "Selling American Books in Japan." *Publishing Research Quarterly*, vol. 7 (Spring), pp. 54–60.

Kobak, F. and B. Luey (1992). *The Structure of International Publishing in the 1990s*. New Brunswick, NJ: Transaction.

Krugman, P. (1999). "The Return of Depression Economics." *Foreign Affairs*, vol. 78, pp. 56–74.

Kwack, S. (1998). "The Financial Crisis in Korea: Causes and Cure." Seminar Series, No. 1998–1999. Washington: International Monetary Fund (June): pp. 7–11.

Meese, R. and K. Rogoff (1993). "Empirical Exchange Rate Models of the Seventies." *Journal of International Economics*, vol. 14, pp. 3–24.

Rose, A. and L. Svenson (1994). "European Exchange Rate Credibility Before the Fall." *European Economic Review*, vol. 38, pp. 1185–1216.

Rohatyn, F. (1989). "America's Economic Dependence." *Foreign Affairs*, vol. 69, pp. 54–58.

Scalapino, R. A. (1988). "Asia's Future." *Foreign Affairs*, vol. 66, pp. 85–89.

Wyplosz, C. (1986). "Capital Controls and Balance of Payments Crises." *Journal of International Money and Finance*, vol. 5, pp. 167–179.

# International Book Title Output: 1990–1996

Albert N. Greco

Associate Professor
Fordham University Graduate School of Business Administration

## Title Output Research

Title output has long been viewed as a significant barometer of intellectual activity in a nation. After all, books educate, inform, and entertain. They spread literacy and provide readers with an inexpensive mechanism to expand their horizons and increase their understanding of distant locations and conflicting theories about a wide variety of topics. Books are a powerful means to transmit ideas—a fact that has concerned tyrants and dictators since the days of Gutenberg.

Researchers seeking to discern changing patterns in fiction and nonfiction, to interpret a nation's "liberal" or "conservative" viewpoint, and to comprehend completely the economic structure and development of a nation's book publishing industry rely extensively on title output statistics. Unfortunately, this type of analysis is an exceedingly difficult task.

While UNESCO's *Statistical Yearbook 1998* (UNESCO Publishing and Bernan Press, 1998) contains rather detailed tables, researchers confront a plethora of problems with these tallies, including:

- Data methodology and collection problems: How detailed are a country's title output surveys? Are both hardcover and paper titles included? Are all book categories (trade, textbook, professional, and so forth) included in the surveys? Are electronic versions of a book included in the totals? Are electronic or paper surveys utilized? What types of follow-up procedures are employed to capture unreported or underreported data?

- Data collection lags: How often are title output surveys conducted? How often do governments report national data to UNESCO?

- Missing data: Why do some nations (especially some of the "advanced" industrial countries—Japan, Belgium, the Netherlands and France, among others) not report data on certain years?

- Discrepancies in the data: Why do some national title output reports differ significantly from UNESCO's tallies? Why do some nations report incredibly large annual increases in title output, followed by sharp declines? Are these spikes the result of faulty data collecting in certain years rather than just a surge in titles?

- Missing data on certain countries: Some nations are never included in the UNESCO studies. Is this because they are developing nations with fragile publishing infrastructures generating exceptionally small numbers of books each year? Is it because certain nations annually import sizable numbers of titles and are not counted by UNESCO? Are the costs associated with conducting this type of title output beyond the means of certain nations?

## Title Output, 1990–1996

In spite of these methodological issues and queries, the UNESCO data provides researchers with the best and most usable framework and overview of book title output. The results for 1990–1996 (the most recent data released by UNESCO) revealed uneven patterns of growth and decline.

While the United Kingdom issued more titles in 1995 (101,764) than any other nation, China's performance in 1996 was stunning, topping 110,283 titles (up 12.41 percent), easily surpassing the United Kingdom (107,263 titles, up 5.4 percent) as the global leader. Other nations that posted sizable increases in title output include Romania (30.49 percent), Poland (18.27 percent), Iran (15.67 percent), the Czech Republic (13.9 percent), the United States (9.89 percent), Argentina (8.09 percent), Russia (7.77 percent), Sweden (6.27 percent), Turkey (4.32 percent), the Ukraine (3.78 percent), Italy (2.3 percent), and India (2.23 percent). These small increases were affected in all likelihood by the global economic malaise triggered by the Asian fiscal "contagion."

On the down side, a large cohort of nations reported declines (in some instances, steep declines) in title output, due in some part to the impact of the Asian fiscal crisis and the resulting economic slowdown. The Republic of Korea's totals were off 14.99 percent, as were Malaysia (down 9.62 percent), Norway (5.02 percent), Spain (4.41 percent), Germany (3.58 percent), Finland (2.89 percent), Hungary (2.35 percent), Austria (2.02 percent), and Denmark (1.01 percent).

Table 1, *International Title Output: 1990–1996*, reveals the patterns of book title growth and reduction for the 47 major nations reporting at least a minimum of 3,000 titles in 1996 (with the exception of the Philippines, which was added to the totals). Nations on this list for the first time include South Africa, Mexico, Sri Lanka, Venezuela, Bulgaria, Yugoslavia, Slovakia, Slovenia, Lithuania, Greece, and Belarus.

## International Book Title Outlook

The outlook for title output for 1999 and 2000 remains "cautiously optimistic." While a fairly large number of new countries made the international list for the first time—an indicator of robust growth—the impact of the Asian "contagion" remains cloudy at best. It is likely that it will take several more years before substantive macroeconomic weaknesses (associated with or impacted by the "contagion") are corrected, stimulating positively the book publishing industry in certain nations; and all of these economic factors have a direct bearing on both the intellectual vigor and financial health of book publishing establishments (and, concomitantly, on title output) in many nations.

Table 1 / International Book Title Output: 1990–1996

| Country | 1990 | 1991 | 1992 | 1993 | 1994 | 1995 | 1996 |
|---|---|---|---|---|---|---|---|
| United Kingdom | n.a. | n.a. | 86,573 | n.a. | 95,015 | 101,764 | 107,263 |
| China | 73,923 | 90,156 | n.a. | 92,972 | 100,951 | 98,987 | 110,283 |
| Germany | 61,015 | 67,890 | 67,277 | 67,206 | 70,643 | 74,174 | 71,515 |
| United States | 46,743 | 48,146 | 49,276 | 49,757 | 51,863 | 62,039 | 68,175 |
| Spain | 36,239 | 39,082 | 41,816 | 40758 | 44261 | 48,467 | 46,330 |
| France | 41,720 | 43,682 | 45,379 | 41,234 | 45,311 | 34,766 | n.a. |
| Korea, Republic of | 39,330 | 29,432 | 27,889 | 30,861 | 34,204 | 35,864 | 30,487 |
| Japan | n.a. | n.a. | 35,496 | n.a. | n.a. | n.a. | 56,221 |
| Italy | 25,068 | 27,751 | 29,351 | 30,110 | 32,673 | 34,470 | 35,236 |
| Netherlands | 13,691 | 11,613 | 15,997 | 34,067 | n.a. | n.a. | n.a. |
| Russia | n.a. | 34,050 | 28,716 | 29,017 | 30,390 | 33,623 | 36,237 |
| Brazil | n.a. | n.a. | 27,557 | 20,141 | 21,574 | n.a. | n.a. |
| Canada* | 8,291 | 8,722 | 9,192 | 9,501 | 10,257 | 10,620 | 11,400 |
| India | 13,937 | 14,438 | 15,778 | 12,768 | 11,460 | 11,643 | 11,903 |
| Switzerland | 13,839 | 14,886 | 14,663 | 14,870 | 15,378 | 15,771 | 15,371 |
| Belgium | 12,157 | 13,913 | n.a. | n.a. | n.a. | n.a. | n.a. |
| Sweden | 12,034 | 11,866 | 12,812 | 12,895 | 13,822 | 12,700 | 13,496 |
| Finland | 10,153 | 11,208 | 11,033 | 11,785 | 12,539 | 13,494 | 13104 |
| Denmark | 11,082 | 10,198 | 11,761 | 11,492 | 11,973 | 12,478 | 12,352 |
| Poland | 10,242 | 10,688 | 10,727 | 9,788 | 10,874 | 11,925 | 14,104 |
| Australia | n.a. | n.a. | n.a. | n.a. | 10,835 | n.a. | n.a. |
| Iran | n.a. | 5,018 | 6,822 | n.a. | 10,753 | 13,031 | 15,073 |
| Hungary | 8,322 | 8,133 | 8,536 | 9,170 | 10,108 | 9,314 | 9,193 |
| Serbia | 9,797 | 4,049 | 2,618 | n.a. | n.a. | n.a. | n.a. |
| Czech Republic | 8,585 | 9,362 | 6,743 | 8,203 | 9,309 | 8,994 | 10,244 |
| Argentina | 4,915 | 6,092 | 5,628 | n.a. | 9,065 | 9,113 | 9,850 |
| Austria | 3,740 | 6,505 | 4,986 | 5,628 | 7,987 | 8,222 | 8,056 |
| Thailand | 7,783 | 7,676 | 7,626 | n.a. | n.a. | n.a. | 8,142 |
| Philippines | n.a. | n.a. | n.a. | n.a. | 1,233 | 1,229 | 927 |
| Norway | 3,712 | 3,884 | 4,881 | 4,943 | 6,946 | 7,265 | 6,900 |
| Ukraine | 7,046 | 5,857 | 4,410 | 5,002 | 4,882 | 6,225 | 6,460 |
| Portugal | 6,150 | 6,430 | 6,462 | 6,089 | 6,667 | n.a. | 7,868 |
| Turkey | 6,291 | 6,365 | 6,549 | 5,978 | 4,473 | 6,275 | 6,546 |
| Malaysia | n.a. | 3,748 | n.a. | 3,799 | 4,050 | 6,465 | 5,843 |
| Indonesia | 1,518 | 1,774 | 6,303 | n.a. | n.a. | n.a. | 4,018 |
| Romania | 2,178 | 2,914 | 3,662 | 6,130 | 4,074 | 5,517 | 7,158 |
| Mexico | n.a. | n.a. | n.a. | n.a. | n.a. | n.a. | 6,183 |
| South Africa | n.a. | n.a. | n.a. | n.a. | n.a. | 4,574 | 5,418 |
| Yugoslavia | n.a. | n.a. | n.a. | n.a. | 2,799 | 3,531 | 5,367 |
| Bulgaria | n.a. | n.a. | n.a. | n.a. | 5,925 | 5,400 | 4,840 |

**Table 1 / International Book Title Output: 1990–1996** *(cont'd)*

| Country | 1990 | 1991 | 1992 | 1993 | 1994 | 1995 | 1996 |
|---------|------|------|------|------|------|------|------|
| Greece | n.a. | n.a. | n.a. | n.a. | n.a. | 4,134 | 4,225 |
| Sri Lanka | n.a. | n.a. | n.a. | n.a. | 2,929 | 3,933 | 4,115 |
| Slovakia | n.a. | n.a. | n.a. | n.a. | 3,481 | n.a. | 3,800 |
| Belarus | n.a. | n.a. | n.a. | n.a. | 3,346 | 3,205 | 3,809 |
| Lithuania | n.a. | n.a. | n.a. | n.a. | 2,885 | 3,164 | 3,645 |
| Venezuela | n.a. | n.a. | n.a. | n.a. | 3,660 | 4,225 | 3,468 |
| Slovenia | n.a. | n.a. | n.a. | n.a. | 2,906 | 3,194 | 3,441 |

*Note*: n.a. = not available

\* Source: *UNESCO Statistical Yearbook, 1998*, with the following exception: title output for Canada obtained from *Profile of Book Publishing and Exclusive Agency in Canada*, Canadian Culture, Tourism & the Center for Education Statistics. UNESCO figures for Canada for 1994, 1995, and 1996 were 21,701, 17,931, and 19,900, respectively.

# Number of Book Outlets in the United States and Canada

The *American Book Trade Directory* has been published by R. R. Bowker since 1915. Revised annually, it features lists of booksellers, wholesalers, periodicals, reference tools, and other information about the U.S. and Canadian book markets. The data shown in Table 1, the most current available, are from the 1998–1999 edition of the directory.

The 30,125 stores of various types shown are located throughout the United States, Canada, and regions administered by the United States. "General" bookstores stock trade books and children's books in a general variety of subjects. "College" stores carry college-level textbooks. "Educational" outlets handle school textbooks up to and including the high school level. "Mail order" outlets sell general trade books by mail and are not book clubs; all others operating by mail are classified according to the kinds of books carried. "Antiquarian" dealers sell old and rare books. Stores handling secondhand books are classified as "used." "Paperback" stores have more than 80 percent of their stock in paperbound books. Stores with paperback departments are listed under the appropriate major classification ("general," "department store," "stationer," etc.). Bookstores with at least 50 percent of their stock on a particular subject are classified by subject.

## Table 1 / Bookstores in the United States and Canada, 1998

| Category | United States | Canada |
|---|---|---|
| Antiquarian General | 1,463 | 89 |
| Antiquarian Mail Order | 593 | 14 |
| Antiquarian Specialized | 260 | 6 |
| Art Supply Store | 60 | 2 |
| College General | 3,238 | 161 |
| College Specialized | 133 | 11 |
| Comics | 258 | 25 |
| Computer Software | 405 | 0 |
| Cooking | 151 | 6 |
| Department Store | 1,825 | 64 |
| Educational* | 266 | 45 |
| Federal Sites† | 259 | 1 |
| Foreign Language* | 128 | 32 |
| General | 6,236 | 673 |
| Gift Shop | 381 | 13 |
| Juvenile* | 367 | 35 |
| Mail Order General | 387 | 18 |
| Mail Order Specialized | 830 | 24 |
| Metaphysics, New Age, and Occult | 297 | 22 |
| Museum Store and Art Gallery | 539 | 37 |
| Nature and Natural History | 148 | 7 |
| Newsdealer | 119 | 7 |
| Office Supply | 50 | 15 |
| Other§ | 4,304 | 526 |
| Paperback‡ | 319 | 15 |
| Religious* | 3,990 | 232 |
| Self Help/Development | 62 | 13 |
| Stationer | 17 | 20 |
| Toy Store | 109 | 7 |
| Used* | 836 | 75 |
| Totals | 27,930 | 2,195 |

\* Includes Mail Order Shops for this topic, which are not counted elsewhere in this survey.

† National Historic Sites, National Monuments, and National Parks.

‡ Includes Mail Order. Excludes used paperback bookstores, stationers, drugstores, or wholesalers handling paperbacks.

§ Stores specializing in subjects or services other than those covered in this survey.

# Book Review Media Statistics

Compiled by the staff of The *Bowker Annual*

## Number of Books Reviewed by Major Book-Reviewing Publications, 1997–1998

| | Adult | | Juvenile | | Young Adult | | Total | |
|---|---|---|---|---|---|---|---|---|
| | 1997 | 1998 | 1997 | 1998 | 1997 | 1998 | 1997 | 1998 |
| *Booklist*[1] | 4,308 | 4,206 | 2,429 | 2,277 | 832 | 879 | 7,569 | 7,362 |
| *Bulletin of the Center for Children's Books*[2] | — | — | 800 | 853 | — | — | 800 | 853 |
| *Chicago Sun Times*[1] | n.a. | 800 | n.a. | 125 | — | — | n.a. | 925 |
| *Chicago Tribune* | 884 | 728 | 29 | 53 | — | 9 | 913 | 790 |
| *Choice*[3] | 6,788 | 6,252 | — | — | — | — | 6,788 | 6,252 |
| *Horn Book Magazine* | 9 | 2 | 274 | 259 | 78 | 67 | 361 | 328 |
| *Horn Book Guide*[4] | — | — | 3,312 | 3,659 | — | — | 3,312 | 3,659 |
| *Kirkus Reviews*[4] | n.a. | 3,261 | n.a. | 1,227 | — | — | n.a. | 4,488 |
| *Library Journal*[5] | 5,955 | 5,723 | — | — | — | — | 5,955 | 5,723 |
| *Los Angeles Times*[4] | 1,760 | 1,950 | 110 | 200 | — | — | 1,870 | 2,150 |
| *New York Review of Books* | 410 | 473 | — | — | — | — | 410 | 473 |
| *New York Times Sunday Book Review*[4] | 1,900 | 1,857 | 300 | 286 | — | — | 2,200 | 2,143 |
| *Publishers Weekly* | 4,800 | 5,576 | 1,800 | 2,076 | — | — | 6,600 | 7,652 |
| *Rapport* (formerly *West Coast Review of Books*) | 714 | 624 | — | — | — | — | 714 | 624 |
| *School Library Journal*[6] | 289 | 269 | 1,653 | 1,637 | 1,353 | 1,410 | 3,662 | 3,615 |
| *Washington Post Book World* | 1,362 | 1,400 | 40 | 40 | 23 | 25 | 1,425 | 1,465 |

n.a.=not available

1 All figures are for a 12-month period from September 1 to August 31; 1998 figures are for September 1, 1997–August 31, 1998 (vol. 94). Some YA books are included in the juvenile total, and the YA total includes reviews of adult books that are appropriate for young adults.

2 All figures are for 12-month period beginning September and ending July/August.

3 All books reviewed in *Choice* are scholarly publications intended for undergraduate libraries.

4 Juvenile figures include young adult titles.

5 This includes 131 reviews in roundups. In addition, *LJ* reviewed 62 magazines, 405 audio books, 393 videos, 728 books in "Prepub Alert," 455 books in "Collection Development," 194 Web sites, and 200 CD-ROMs.

6 Total includes 135 "Curriculum Connectors," 60 December holiday books, 49 books in Spanish, 119 reference books, and 18 books in "At-a-Glance."

# Part 5
# Reference Information

# Bibliographies

## The Librarian's Bookshelf

Cathleen Bourdon, MLS

Executive Director, Reference and User Services Association
American Library Association

Librarians continue to grapple with the issues of providing appropriate Internet access to children and adults. Publishers have responded with an outpouring of helpful titles, and many are included here. Most of the books in this selective bibliography have been published since 1995; a few earlier titles are retained because of their continuing importance.

## General Works

*Alternative Library Literature, 1996/1997: A Biennial Anthology.* Ed. By Sanford Berman and James P. Danky. McFarland, 1996. Paper $35.

*American Library Directory, 1998–99.* 2v. Bowker, 1998. $259.95.

*The Bowker Annual Library and Book Trade Almanac, 1999.* Bowker, 1999. $185.

*Concise Dictionary of Library and Information Science.* By Stella Keenan. Bowker-Saur, 1996. $45.

*Encyclopedia of Library and Information Science.* 62v. to date. Marcel Dekker, 1968–. $100/v.

*The International Encyclopedia of Information and Library Science.* Ed. by John Feather and Paul Sturges. Routledge, 1997. $160.

*The Librarian's Companion: A Handbook of Thousands of Facts on Libraries/Librarians, Books/Newspapers, Publishers/Booksellers.* 2nd ed. By Vladimir F. Wertsman. Greenwood Press, 1996. $65.

*Librarians' Thesaurus: A Concise Guide to Library and Information Terms.* By Mary Ellen Soper and others. American Library Association, 1990. Paper $25.

*Library and Information Science Annual.* Vol. 6. Ed. by Bohdan S. Wynar. Libraries Unlimited, 1998. $65.

*Library Literature.* H. W. Wilson, 1921. Also available online and on CD-ROM, 1984–. Indexes periodicals in librarianship.

Library Reference Center. http://www.epnet.com. Indexes 30 periodicals in librarianship for the past five years.

*Library Technology Reports.* American Library Association, 1965–. Bi-monthly. $225.

*The Whole Library Handbook: Current Data, Professional Advice, and Curiosa about Libraries and Library Services.* 2nd ed. Comp. by George Eberhart. American Library Association, 1995. Paper $30.

## Academic Libraries

*ACRL University Library Statistics, 1996–1997.* Association of College and Research Libraries/American Library Association, 1998. $80.

*ARL Statistics.* Association of Research Libraries. Annual. 1964–. $70.

*The Academic Library Director: Reflections on a Position in Transition.* Ed. by Frank D'Andraia. Haworth, 1997. Paper $39.95.

*The Academic Library: Its Context, Its Purposes, and Its Operation.* By John M. Budd. Libraries Unlimited, 1998. Paper $35.

*The Challenge and Practice of Academic Accreditation: A Sourcebook for Library Administrators.* Ed. by Edward G. Garten. Greenwood Press, 1995. $69.50.

*CLIP* (College Library Information Packet) *Notes.* Association of College and Research Libraries/American Library Association, 1980–. Most recent volume is No. 26, 1997. $28.50.

*Constancy and Change in the Worklife of Research University Librarians.* By Rebecca Watson-Boone. Association of College and Research Libraries/American Library Association, 1998. Paper $30.

*Creating the Agile Library: A Management Guide for Librarians.* Ed. by Lorraine J. Haricombe and T. J. Lusher. Greenwood Press, 1998. $49.95.

*Electronic Services in Academic Libraries.* Ed. by Mary Jo Lynch. American Library Association, 1996. Paper $6. A statistical survey.

*The Gateway Library: Reinventing Academic Libraries.* By Caroline M. Kent and Laura Farwell. American Library Association, 1997. Paper $35.

*Measuring Academic Library Performance: A Practical Approach.* By Nancy Van House, Beth Weil, and Charles McClure. American Library Association, 1990. Paper $36. Accompanying diskette with data collection and analysis forms. $60.

*Outsourcing Library Operations in Academic Libraries: An Overview of Issues and Outcomes.* By Claire-Lise Benaud and Sever Bordeianu. Libraries Unlimited, 1998. $40.

*Preparing for Accreditation: A Handbook for Academic Librarians.* By Patricia Ann Sacks and Sara Lou Whildin. American Library Association, 1993. Paper $18.

*Recreating the Academic Library: Breaking Virtual Ground.* Ed. by Cheryl LaGuardia. Neal-Schuman, 1998. Paper $59.95.

*Restructuring Academic Libraries: Organizational Development in the Wake of Technological Change.* Ed. by Charles Schwartz. Association of College and Research Libraries/American Library Association, 1997. Paper $28.

*SPEC Kits.* Association of Research Libraries. 1973–. 10/yr. $280.

*Tenure and Promotion for Academic Librarians: A Guidebook with Advice and Vignettes.* By Carol W. Cubberly. McFarland, 1996. $32.50.

## Administration and Personnel

*The ABCs of Collaborative Change: The Manager's Guide to Library Renewal.* By Kerry David Carson, Paula Phillips Carson, and Joyce Schouest Phillips. American Library Association, 1997. Paper $35.

*The ALA Library Personnel Companion: New Strategies in Human Resources.* Ed. by Jeniece Guy. American Library Association, 1997. Paper $25.

*Avoiding Liability Risk: An Attorney's Advice to Library Trustees and Others.* By Renee Rubin. American Library Association, 1994. Paper $15.

*Budgeting for Information Access: Resource Management for Connected Libraries.* By Murray Martin and Milton Wolf. American Library Association, 1998. Paper $35.

*Charging and Collecting Fees and Fines: A Handbook for Libraries.* By Murray S. Martin and Betsy Parks. Neal-Schuman, 1998. Paper $49.95.

*Complete Guide to Performance Standards for Library Personnel.* By Carole E. Goodson. Neal-Schuman, 1997. Paper $49.95.

*Costing and Pricing in the Digital Age: A Practical Guide for Information Services.* By Herbert Snyder and Elisabeth Davenport. Neal-Schuman, 1997. Paper $45.

*Evaluating Library Staff: A Performance Appraisal System.* By Patricia Belcastro. American Library Association, 1998. Paper $35.

*Getting Political: An Action Guide for Librarians and Library Supporters.* By Anne M. Turner. Neal-Schuman, 1997. Paper $39.95.

*Library Personnel Administration.* By Lowell Martin. Scarecrow Press, 1994. $31.

*Library Public Relations, Promotions and Communications: A How-to-Do-It Manual.* By Lisa Wolfe. Neal-Schuman, 1997. Paper $39.95.

*Library Security and Safety Handbook: Prevention, Policies and Procedures.* By Bruce A. Shuman. American Library Association, 1998. Paper $38.

*Managing Overdues: A How-To-Do-It Manual for Librarians.* Ed. by Patsy J. Hansel. Neal-Schuman, 1998. Paper $39.95.

*Managing Student Library Employees: A Workshop for Supervisors.* By Michael and Jane Kathman. Library Solutions Press, 1995. Paper $45. An accompanying diskette contains presentation slides.

*Moving Library Collections: A Management Handbook.* By Elizabeth Chamberlain Habich. Greenwood Press, 1998. $79.50

*Organizational Structure of Libraries* Rev. ed. by Lowell A. Martin. Scarecrow Press, 1996. $39.50.

*Practical Help for New Supervisors.* 3rd ed. Ed. by Joan Giesecke. American Library Association, 1997. Paper $22.

*Scenario Planning for Libraries.* Ed. by Joan Giesecke. American Library Association, 1998. Paper $30.

*Strategic Planning for Multitype Library Cooperatives: A Planning Process.* By Nancy M. Bolt and Sandra S. Stephan. Association of Specialized and Cooperative Library Agencies/American Library Association, 1998. Paper $28.

*Technology and Management in Library and Information Services.* By F. W. Lancaster and Beth Sandore. University of Illinois, Urbana-Champaign, 1997. $39.95.

*Total Quality Management in Information Services.* By Guy St. Clair. Bowker-Saur, 1996. $45.

## Bibliographic Instruction

*Designs for Active Learning: A Sourcebook of Classroom Strategies for Information Education.* Ed. by Gail Gradowski, Loanne Snavely, and Paula Dempsey. Association of College and Research Libraries/American Library Association, 1998. Paper with diskette $35.

*Evaluating Library Instruction: Sample Questions, Forms, and Strategies for Practical Use.* Ed. by Diana Shonrock. American Library Association, 1995. Paper $34.

*Student Learning in the Information Age.* By Patricia Senn Breivik. Oryx Press, 1997. $34.95.

*Teaching Electronic Literacy: A Concepts-based Approach for School Library Media Specialists.* By Kathleen Craver. Greenwood Press, 1997. $39.95.

*Teaching Library Skills in Grades K through 6: A How-to-Do-It Manual.* By Catharyn Roach and JoAnne Moore. Neal-Schuman, 1993. Paper $35.

*Teaching Library Skills in Middle and High School: A How-to-Do-It Manual.* By Linda J. Garrett and JoAnne Moore. Neal-Schuman, 1993. Paper $35.

*Teaching the New Library: A How-to-Do-It Manual.* By Michael Blake and others from the Electronic Teaching Center for the Harvard College Libraries. Neal-Schuman, 1996. Paper $45.

## Cataloging and Classification

*ArtMARC Sourcebook: Cataloging Art, Architecture and Their Visual Images.* Ed. By Linda McRae and Lynda S. White. American Library Association, 1998. Paper $75.

*The Bibliographic Record and Information Technology.* 3rd ed. By Ronald Hagler. American Library Association, 1997. Paper $45.

*Cataloging and Classification: Trends, Transformations, Teaching and Training.* Ed. by James Sheearer and Alan Thomas. Haworth, 1997. Paper $19.95.

*Cataloging Correctly for Kids: An Introduction to the Tools.* 3rd ed. Ed. by Sharon Zuiderveld. American Library Association, 1997. Paper $18.

*Cataloging with AACR and MARC for Books, Computer Files, Serials, Sound Recordings and Video Recordings.* By Debra A. Fritz. American Library Association, 1997. Paper $60.

*Dewey Decimal Classification, 21st Edition: A Study Manual and Number Building Guide.* By Mona L. Scott. Libraries Unlimited, 1998. $47.50.

*Immroth's Guide to the Library of Congress Classification.* 4th ed. By Lois Mai Chan. Libraries Unlimited, 1990. $42.50.

*Introduction to Cataloging and classification.* 8th ed. By Arlene G. Taylor and Bohdan S. Wynar. Libraries Unlimited, 1991. $47.50.

*Library of Congress Subject Headings: Principles and Application.* 3rd ed. By Lois Mai Chan. Libraries Unlimited, 1995. $46.

*Standard Cataloging for School and Public Libraries.* 2nd ed. By Sheila S. Intner and Jean Weihs. Libraries Unlimited, 1996. $32.50.

*SUPERLCSS on CD-ROM.* Gale, 1999. $3,400. The text of the Library of Congress classification schedules.

## Children's and Young Adult Services and Materials

*African-American Voices in Young Adult Literature: Tradition, Transition, Transformation.* By Karen Patricia Smith. Scarecrow, 1994. $47.50.

*Against Borders: Promoting Books for a Multicultural World.* By Hazel Rochman. Booklist/American Library Association, 1993. Paper $25.

*Bibliotherapy with Young People: Librarians and Mental Health Professionals Working Together.* By Beth and Carol Doll. Libraries Unlimited, 1997. Paper $23.

*Building a Special Collection of Children's Literature in Your Library.* Ed. by Doleres Blythe Jones. American Library Association, 1997. Paper $40.

The Center for the Study of Books in Spanish for Children and Adolescents at California State University, San Marcos Web site: http://www.csusm.edu/campus_centers/csb. Lists recommended books in Spanish for youth published worldwide.

*Connecting Young Adults and Libraries: A How-to-Do-It Manual.* 2nd ed. By Patrick Jones. Neal-Schuman, 1998. Paper $45.

*Excellence in Library Services to Young Adults: The Nation's Top Programs.* 2nd ed. By Mary K. Chelton. American Library Association, 1997. Paper $22.

*The Frugal Youth Cybrarian: Bargain Computing for Kids.* By Calvin Ross. American Library Association, 1997. Paper $25.

*Inviting Children's Authors and Illustrators: A How-to-Do-It Manual for School and Public Librarians.* By Kathy East. Neal-Schuman, 1995. Paper $32.50.

*Learning Environments for Young Children: Rethinking Library Space and Services.* By Sandra Feinberg, Joan F. Kuchner, and Sari Feldman. American Library Association, 1998. Paper $35.

*Managing Children's Services in the Public Library.* 2nd ed. By Adele M. Fasick. Libraries Unlimited, 1998. $34.50.

*Output Measures and More: Planning and Evaluating Public Library Services for Young Adults.* By Virginia A. Walter. American Library Association, 1995. Paper $25.

*Output Measures for Public Library Service to Children: A Manual of Standardized Procedures.* By Virginia A. Walter. American Library Association, 1992. Paper $25.

*School Library Journal's Best: A Reader for Children's, Young Adult and School Librarians.* Ed. by Lillian N. Gerhardt, Marilyn L. Miller, and Thomas W. Downen. Neal-Schuman, 1997. Paper $39.95.

*Serious About Series: Evaluations and Annotations of Teen Fiction in Paperback Series.* By Silk Makowski. Scarecrow Press, 1998. Paper $26.50.

*Story: From Fireplace to Cyberspace: Connecting Children and Narrative.* Ed. by Betsy Hearne, Janice M. Del Nego, Christine Jenkins, and Deborah Stevenson. GSLIS, University of Illinois, 1998. Paper $21.95

*VOYA Reader Two: Articles from Voices of Youth Advocate.* Ed. by Dorothy M. Broderick and Mary K. Chelton. Scarecrow Press, 1998. Paper $24.50.

## Collection Development

*Collection Development: Access in the Virtual Library.* Ed. by Maureen Pastine. Haworth Press, 1997. $49.95

*Collection Development & Finance: A Guide to Strategic Library-Materials Budgeting.* By Murray S. Martin. American Library Association, 1995. Paper $30.

*Collection Management for the 21st Century: A Handbook for Librarians.* Ed. by G. E. Gorman and Ruth H. Miller. Greenwood Press, 1997. $75.

*Developing Christian Fiction Collections for Children and Adults: Selection Criteria and a Core Collection.* By Barbara J. Walker. Neal-Schuman, 1998. Paper $35.

*Fiction Acquisition/Fiction Management: Education and Training.* Ed. by Georgine N. Olson. Haworth Press, 1998. $29.95.

*Guide for Training Collection Development Librarians.* Ed. by Susan Fales. American Library Association, 1996. Paper $15.

*Guide to Cooperative Collection Development.* Ed. by Bart Harloe. American Library Association, 1994. Paper $15.

*Guide for Written Collection Policy Statements.* 2nd ed. Ed. by Joanne S. Anderson. American Library Association, 1996. Paper $15.

*Recruiting, Educating, and Training Librarians for Collection Development.* Ed. by Peggy Johnson and Sheila S. Intner. Greenwood Press, 1994. $55.

*Weeding Library Collections: Library Weeding Methods.* 4th ed. By Stanley J. Slote. Libraries Unlimited, 1997. $55.

## Copyright

*The Copyright Primer for Librarians and Educators.* 2nd ed. By Janis H. Bruwelheide. American Library Association, 1995. Paper $25.

*Does Your Project Have a Copyright Problem? A Decision-Making Guide for Librarians.* By Mary Brandt-Jensen. McFarland, 1996. Paper $25.

*Growing Pains: Adapting Copyright for Libraries, Education and Society.* By Laura N. Gasaway. Rothman, 1997. $75.

*Plagiarism, Copyright Violation and Other Thefts of Intellectual Property: An Annotated Bibliography with a Lengthy Introduction.* By Judy Anderson. McFarland, 1998. Paper $38.

*Technology and Copyright Law: A Guidebook for the Library, Research and Teaching Professions.* By Arlene Bielefield and Lawrence Cheesemen. Neal-Schuman, 1997. Paper $49.95.

## Customer Service

*Assessing Service Quality: Satisfying the Expectations of Library Customers.* By Peter Hernon and Ellen Altman. American Library Association, 1998. Paper $40.

*Customer Service: A How-to-Do-It Manual for Librarians.* By Suzanne Walters. Neal-Schuman, 1994. Paper $39.95.

*Customer Service and Innovation in Libraries.* By Glenn Miller. Highsmith Press, 1996. Paper $18.

*Customer Service Excellence: A Concise Guide for Librarians.* By Darlene E. Weingand. American Library Association, 1997. Paper $27.

*Patron Behavior in Libraries: A Handbook of Positive Approaches to Negative Situations.* Ed. by Beth McNeil and Denise J. Johnson. American Library Association, 1995. Paper $25.

## Education for Librarianship

*The Closing of American Library Schools: Problems and Opportunities.* By Larry J. Ostler, Therrin C. Dahlin, and J. D. Willardson. Greenwood Press, 1995. $55.

*Education for the Library/Information Profession: Strategies for the Mid-1990s.* Ed. by Patricia Reeling. McFarland, 1993. Paper $19.95.

## The Electronic Library

"Books, Bricks and Bytes." *Daedalus*, vol. 125, no. 4, Fall 1996. $10.95. Prominent librarians write about the future of the library in this issue of *Daedalus* totally devoted to the topic.

*Buildings, Books, and Bytes: Libraries and Communities in the Digital Age.* The Benton Foundation, 1996. http://www.benton.org/Library/Kellogg/home.html.

Interviews with the public about their views of libraries show that they have trouble figuring out where libraries fit in the new digital world.

*Digitizing Historical Pictorial Collections for the Internet.* By Stephen E. Ostrow. Council on Library and Information Resources, 1998. Paper $20.

*Economics of Digital Information: Collection, Storage and Delivery.* Ed. by Sul H. Lee. Haworth Press, 1997. $29.95.

*Finding Common Ground: Creating the Library of the Future Without Diminishing the Library of the Past.* Ed. by Cheryl LaGuardia and Barbara A. Mitchell. Neal-Schuman, 1998. Paper $75.

*Future Libraries: Dreams, Madness, and Reality.* By Walt Crawford and Michael Gorman. American Library Association, 1995. Paper $28. Deflates the overblown "virtual" library concept.

*Ink Into Bits: A Web of Converging Media.* By Charles T. Meadow. Scarecrow Press, 1998. Paper $24.50.

*A Nation of Opportunity: Realizing the Promise of the Information Superhighway.* By the National Information Infrastructure Advisory Council. The Benton Foundation, 1996. http://www.benton.org/Library/KickStart/nation.home.html.

*The National Electronic Library: A Guide to the Future for Library Managers.* Ed. by Gary M. Pitkin. Greenwood Press, 1996. $55.

*Scholarly Journals at the Crossroads: A Subversive Proposal for Electronic Publishing.* Ed. by Ann Okerson and James J. O'Donnell. Association of Research Libraries, 1995. Paper $20.

## Evaluation of Library Services

*Descriptive Statistical Techniques for Librarians.* By Arthur W. Hafner. American Library Association, 1997. Paper $55.

*The TELL IT! Manual: The Complete Program for Evaluating Library Performance.* By Douglas Zweizig, Debra Wilcox Johnson, and Jane Robbins. American Library Association, 1996. Paper $30.

## Fund-Raising

*The Big Book of Library Grant Money 1998–1999: Profiles of Private and Corporate Foundations and Direct Corporate Givers Receptive to Library Grant Proposals.* By the Taft Group. American Library Association, 1998. Paper $235.

*Friends of Libraries Sourcebook.* 3rd ed. Ed. by Sandy Dolnick. American Library Association, 1996. Paper $32.

*Fundraising and Friend-Raising on the Web.* By Adam Corson-Finnerty and Laura Blanchard. American Library Association, 1998. Paper $50.

*Library Fundraising: Models for Success.* Ed. by Dwight Burlingame. American Library Association, 1995. Paper $25.

*Organizing Friends Groups: A How-to-Do-It Manual for Librarians.* By Mark Y. Herring. Neal-Schuman, 1992. Paper $39.95.

*Recognizing Fundraising Opportunities.* 11-minute video. Library Video Network, 1998. $99.

## Government Documents

*Guide to Popular U.S. Government Publications.* By Frank W. Hoffman and Richard J. Wood. Libraries Unlimited, 1998. $38.50.

*International Information: Documents, Publications and Electronic Information of International Governmental Organizations.* 2nd ed. Ed. by Peter I. Hajnal. Libraries Unlimited, 1997. $105.

*Management of Government Information Resources in Libraries.* Ed. by Diane H. Smith. Libraries Unlimited, 1993. $40.

*Neal-Schuman Guide to Finding Legal and Regulatory Information on the Internet.* By Yvonne J. Chandler. Neal-Schuman, 1997. Paper $125.

*Subject Guide to U.S. Government Reference Sources.* 2nd ed. By Gayle J. Hardy and Judith Schiek Robinson. Libraries Unlimited, 1996. $45.

## Intellectual Freedom

*Banned Books Resource Guide.* Office for Intellectual Freedom/American Library Association, 1999. Paper $20.

*Banned in the U.S.A.: A Reference Guide to Book Censorship in Schools and Public Libraries.* By Herbert N. Foerstel. Greenwood Press, 1994. $45.

*Hit List: Frequently Challenged Books for Young Adults.* By Donna R. Pistolis. American Library Association, 1996. $22.

*Hit List: Frequently Challenged Books for Children.* By Merri M. Monks and Donna Reidy Pistolis. American Library Association, 1996. $22.

*Intellectual Freedom Manual.* 5th ed. ALA Office for Intellectual Freedom. American Library Association, 1996. Paper $35.

## Interlibrary Loan, Document Delivery, and Resource Sharing

*The Economics of Access versus Ownership.* Ed. by Bruce R. Kingma. Haworth Press, 1996. $29.95.

*The Future of Resource Sharing.* Ed. by Shirley K. Baker and Mary E. Jackson. Haworth Press, 1995. $49.95.

*Interlibrary Loan/Document Delivery and Customer Satisfaction.* Ed. by Pat Weaver-Meyers, Wilbur Stolt and Yem Fong. Haworth, 1997. Paper $19.95.

*Interlibrary Loan Policies Directory.* 5th ed. Ed. by Leslie R. Morris. Neal-Schuman, 1995. Paper $135.

*Interlibrary Loan Practices Handbook.* 2nd ed. By Virginia Boucher. American Library Association, 1996. Paper $45.

## The Internet

*Authoritative Guide to Web Search Engines.* By Susan Maze, David Moxley and Donna J. Smith. Neal-Schuman, 1997. Paper $49.95.

*Basic Internet for Busy Librarians: A Quick Course for Catching Up.* By Laura K. Murray. American Library Association, 1998. Paper $25.

*Best Bet Internet: Reference and Research When You Don't Have Time to Mess Around.* By Shirley Duglin Kennedy. American Library Association, 1997. Paper $35.

*Children and the Internet: Guidelines for Developing Public Library Policy.* American Library Association, 1998. Paper $22.

*Coyle's Information Highway Handbook: A Practical File on the New Information Order.* By Karen Coyle. American Library Association, 1997. Paper $30.

*Cybrarian's Guide to Developing Successful Internet Programs and Services.* By Diane and Michael Kovacs. Neal Schuman, 1997. Paper $59.95.

*The Cybrarian's Manual.* Ed. by Pat Ensor. American Library Association, 1996. Paper $30. Excerpts from this book are on the Web at http://www.ala.org/editions/cyberlib.net.

*Designing Web Interfaces to Library Services and Resources.* By Kristen L. Garlock and Sherry Piontek. American Library Association, 1998. Paper $32.

*Internet Access and Use: Metropolitan Public Libraries, Sample Internet Policies.* 2v. Urban Libraries Council, 1997. Paper $50.

*Internet Issues and Applications, 1997–98.* Ed. by Bert J. Dempsey and Paul Jones. Scarecrow Press, 1998. $22.50.

*Linking People to the Global Networked Society: Evaluation of the Online at PA Libraries Project: Public Access to the Internet Through Public Libraries.* By Charles R. McClure and John Carlo Bertot. ERIC, 1998. Study revealed that having access to the Internet at public libraries contributes to economic development in rural areas.

*More Internet Troubleshooter: New Help for the Logged-On and Lost.* By Nancy R. John and Edward J. Valauskas. American Library Association, 1998. Paper $36.

*The 1998 National Survey of U.S. Public Library Outlet Internet Connectivity.* By John Carlo Bertot and Charles R. McClure. National Commission on Libraries and Information Science/American Library Association, 1998. http://www.ala.org/oitp/research/survey98.html

*Neal-Schuman Complete Internet Companion for Librarians.* 2nd ed. By Allen C. Benson. Neal-Schuman, 1997. Paper $65.

*A Practical Guide to Internet Filters.* By Karen Schneider. Neal-Schuman, 1997. Paper $49.95.

*Searching Smart on the World Wide Web: Tools and Techniques for Getting Quality Results.* By Cheryl Gould. Library Solutions, 1998. Paper $40.

*World Wide Web Troubleshooter: Help for the Ensnared and Entangled.* By Nancy R. John and Edward J. Valauskas. American Library Association, 1998. Paper $36.

## Librarians and Librarianship

*The ALA Survey of Librarian Salaries 1998.* Ed. by Mary Jo Lynch. American Library Association, 1998. Paper $55.

*ARL Annual Salary Survey, 1997–98.* Association of Research Libraries, 1997. Paper $70.

*Dewey Decimal System Defeats Truman: Library Cartoons.* By Scott McCullar. McFarland, 1998. Paper $22.95.

*Ethics, Information and Technology: Readings.* Ed. by Richard N. Stichler and Robert Hauptman. McFarland, 1997. $39.95.

*Information Brokering: A How-To-Do-It Manual.* By Florence Mason and Chris Doson. Neal-Schuman, 1998. Paper $39.95.

*Librarians in Fiction: A Critical Bibliography.* By Grant Burns. McFarland, 1998. Paper $25.

*Librarianship and the Information Paradigm.* By Richard Apostle and Boris Raymond. Scarecrow Press, 1997. $32.

*The Manley Art of Librarianship.* By Will Manley. McFarland, 1993. $23.95. Other humorous books by Manley include *The Truth About Reference Librarians* and *The Truth About Catalogers.*

*Me? A Librarian?* 10-minute video. Ohio Library Council, 1997. $20.

*Our Singular Strengths: Meditations for Librarians.* By Michael Gorman. American Library Association, 1997. Paper $20.

*What Else You Can Do With a Library Degree: Career Options for the '90s and Beyond.* Ed. by Betty-Carol Sellen. Neal-Schuman, 1997. Paper $29.95.

*Writing Resumes That Work: A How-To-Do-It Manual for Librarians.* By Robert R. Newlen. Neal-Schuman, 1998. Paper and disk $55.

## Library Automation

*Automating Media Centers and Small Libraries: A Microcomputer-Based Approach.* By Dania Meghabghab. Libraries Unlimited, 1997. Paper $30.

*Automating Small Libraries.* By James Swan. Highsmith Press, 1996. Paper $18.

*Directory of Library Automation Software, Systems, and Services.* Ed. by Pamela Cibbarelli. Information Today, 1998. Paper $89. Published biennially.

*Improving Online Public Access Catalogs.* By Martha M. Lee and Sara Shatford Layne. American Library Association, 1998. Paper $48.

*Library Systems: Current Developments and Future Directions.* By Leigh Watson Healy. Council on Library and Information Resources, 1998. Paper $25.

*Local Area Networking for the Small Library: A How-to-Do-It Manual.* 2nd. ed. By Norman Howden. Neal-Schuman, 1997. Paper $39.95.

*Planning for Automation.* 2nd. ed. By John Cohn, Ann Kelsey, and Keith Fiels. Neal-Schuman, 1997. Paper $49.95.

*Securing PCs and Data in Libraries and Schools: A Handbook with Menuing, Antivirus and Other Protective Software.* By Allen C. Benson. Neal-Schuman, 1998. Paper with CD-ROM $125.

*The Systems Librarian: Designing Roles, Defining Skills.* By Thomas C. Wilson. American Library Association, 1998. Paper $38.

## Library Buildings and Space Planning

*Checklist of Building Design Considerations.* 3rd ed. By William W. Sannwald. American Library Association, 1996. Paper $30.

*Determining Your Public Library's Future Size: A Needs Assessment and Planning Model.* By Lee B. Brawner and Donald K.

Beck, Jr. American Library Association, 1996. $30.

*The Evolution of the American Academic Library Building.* By David Kaser. Scarecrow Press, 1996. $36.

*Financing Public Library Buildings.* By Richard B. Hall. Neal-Schuman, 1994. Paper $65.

*Library Buildings, Equipment, and the ADA: Compliance Issues and Solutions.* By Susan E. Cirilolo and Robert E. Danford. American Library Association, 1996. Paper $25.

*Planning Library Interiors: The Selection of Furnishings for the 21st Century.* 2nd. ed. By Carol Brown. Oryx Press, 1994. Paper $29.95.

## Library History

*Carnegie Libraries Across America: A Public Legacy.* By Theodore Jones. Wiley, 1997. $29.95.

*Cuneiform to Computer: A History of Reference Sources.* By Bill Katz. Scarecrow Press, 1998. $46.

*Enrichment: A History of the Public Library in the United States in the Twentieth Century.* By Lowell A. Martin. Scarecrow Press, 1998. $35.

*The Evolution of the Book.* By Frederick G. Kilgour. Oxford University Press, 1998. $35.

*History of Libraries in the Western World.* 4th ed. By Michael H. Harris. Scarecrow Press, 1995. $41.50.

*Irrepressible Reformer: A Biography of Melvil Dewey.* By Wayne A. Wiegand. American Library Association, 1996. Paper $35.

*The Library of Congress: The Art and Architecture of the Thomas Jefferson Building.* Ed. by John Y. Cole and Henry Hope Reed. W. W. Norton, 1998. $60.

*Libraries and Philanthropy.* Ed. by Donald G. Davis, Jr. Graduate School of Library and Information Science, University of Texas at Austin, 1996. $25.

*OCLC 1967–1997: Thirty Years of Furthering Access to the World's Information.* Ed. by K. Wayne Smith. Haworth, 1998. Paper $19.95.

*The Story of Libraries From the Invention of Writing to the Computer Age.* By Fred Lerner. Continuum, 1998. $24.94.

## Nonprint Materials

*Cataloging of Audiovisual Materials and Other Special Materials.* 4th ed. By Nancy B. Olson. Media Marketing Group, 1998. Paper $75.

*Developing and Managing Video Collections in Libraries: A How-to-Do-It Manual for Public Libraries.* By Sally Mason-Robinson. Neal-Schuman, 1996. Paper $39.95.

*Finding and Using Educational Videos: A How-To-Do-It Manual.* By Barbara Stein, Gary Treadway, and Lauralee Ingram. Neal-Schuman, 1998. Paper $35.

*A Library Manager's Guide to the Physical Processing of Nonprint Materials.* By Karen C. Driessen and Sheila A. Smyth. Greenwood Press, 1995. $65.

## Preservation

*Advances in Preservation and Access.* v.2. Ed. by Barbra Buckner Higginbotham. Information Today, 1995. $49.50.

*Book Repair: A How-to-Do-It Manual for Librarians.* By Kenneth Lavender and Scott Stockton. Neal Schuman, 1992. Paper $39.95.

*Disaster Response and Planning for Libraries.* By Miriam B. Kahn. American Library Association, 1998. Paper $38.

*Emergency Response and Salvage Wheel.* National Task Force on Emergency Response, 1997. $5.95. A two-sided cardboard wheel with tips for quick action in an emergency.

*New Tools for Preservation: Assessing Long-Term Environmental Effects on Library and Archives Conditions.* By James M. Reilly, Douglas W. Nishimura, and Edward Zinn. Commission on Preservation and Access, 1995. Paper $10.

*Preservation Microfilming: A Guide for Librarians and Archivists.* 2nd ed. Ed. by Lisa L. Fox. American Library Association, 1996. $70.

*Preserving Digital Information.* By Donald Waters and John Garrett. Commission on Preservation and Access. 1996. Paper $15.

*Storage Guide for Color Photographic Materials.* By James M. Reilly. New York State Library, 1998. Paper $20.

## Public Libraries

*Civic Space/Cyberspace: The American Public Library in the Information Age.* By R. Kathleen Molz and Phyllis Dain. MIT Press, 1998. $30.

*Collecting and Using Public Library Statistics.* By Mark L. Smith. Neal-Schuman, 1995. Paper $45.

*The Library Trustee: A Practical Guidebook.* 5th ed. By Virginia G. Young. American Library Association, 1995. $37.

*Model Policies for Small and Medium Public Libraries.* By Jeanette Larson and Hermon Totten. Neal-Schuman, 1998. Paper $45.

*New Measures for the New Library: A Social Audit of Public Libraries.* By Rebecca Linley and Bob Usherwood. University of Sheffield, United Kingdom, 1998. Paper £20.

*Planning for Results: A Public Library Transformation Process.* By Ethel Himmel and William James Wilson, with the ReVision Committee of the Public Library Association. American Library Association, 1998. Paper $40.

*Policy Issues and Strategies Affecting Public Libraries in the National Networked Environment: Moving Beyond Connectivity.* By John Carlo Bertot and Charles R. McClure. National Commission on Libraries and Information Science, 1998. Paper free.

*Public Librarian's Human Resources Handbook.* By David A. Baldwin. Libraries Unlimited, 1998. Paper $30.

*Public Library Data Service Statistical Report.* Public Library Association/ALA, 1998. Paper $75.

*The Public Library Effectiveness Study: The Complete Report.* By Nancy A. Van House and Thomas A. Childers. American Library Association, 1993. Paper $25.

*Sample Evaluations of Public Library Directors.* Ed. by Sharon Saulman. American Library Trustee Association/American Library Association, 1997. Paper $23.

*Strategic Management for Public Libraries: A Handbook.* By Robert M. Hayes and Virginia A. Walter. Greenwood Press, 1996. $65.

*What's Good? Describing Your Public Library's Effectiveness.* By Thomas A. Childers and Nancy A. Van House. American Library Association, 1993. Paper $25.

*Why Adults Use the Public Library: A Research Perspective.* By Maurice P. Marchant. Libraries Unlimited, 1994. Paper $24.

*Winning Library Referenda Campaigns: A How-to-Do-It Manual.* By Richard B. Hall. Neal-Schuman, 1995. Paper $49.95.

## Reference and Readers' Advisory

*ALA's Guide to Best Reading.* American Library Association, 1998. Kit $29.95. Camera-ready lists of the year's best books for children, teens and adults.

*Delivering Web Reference Service to Young People.* By Walter Minkel and Roxanne Hsu Feldman. American Library Association, 1998. Paper $32.

*Developing Readers' Advisory Services: Concepts and Commitments.* Ed. by Kathleen de la Peña and others. Neal-Schuman, 1993. Paper $35.

*Introduction to Reference Work.* 7th ed. 2v. By William A. Katz. McGraw-Hill, 1996. $57.75.

*Readers' Advisory Service in the Public Library.* 2nd ed. By Joyce G. Saricks and Nancy Brown. American Library Association, 1997. Paper $22.

*The Reference Assessment Manual.* Comp. by the Evaluation of Reference & Adult Services Committee of RASD/ALA. Pierian Press, 1995. Paper $35. A disk with copies of assessment instruments is also available at $15.

*Reference and Collection Development on the Internet: A How-to-Do-It Manual.* By Elizabeth Thomsen. Neal-Schuman, 1996. Paper $45.

*The Reference Interview as a Creative Art.* By Elaine and Edward Jennerich. Libraries Unlimited, 1997. $26.50

*Reference Sources on the Internet: Off the Shelf and Onto the Web.* Ed. by Karen R. Diaz. Haworth, 1997. $49.95

*Rethinking Reference in Academic Libraries.* Ed. by Anne G. Lipow. Library Solutions Press, 1993. Paper $32.

*Where to Find What: A Handbook to Reference Service.* 4th ed. By James M. Hillard. Scarecrow Press, 1999. $45.

## School Libraries/Media Centers

*Acquiring and Organizing Curriculum Materials: A Guide and Directory of Resources.* By Gary A. Lare. Scarecrow Press, 1997. Paper $32.

*Developing a Vision: Strategic Planning and the Library Media Specialist.* By John D. Crowley. Greenwood Press, 1994. $35.

*Information Power: Building Partnerships for Learning.* American Library Association, 1998. Paper $35.

*Internet for Active Learners: Curriculum-Based Strategies for K–12.* By Pam Berger. American Library Association, 1998. Paper $35.

*Operating and Evaluating School Library Media Programs: A Handbook for Administrators and Librarians.* By Bernice L. Yesner and Hilda L. Jay. Neal-Schuman, 1998. Paper $39.95.

*New Steps to Service: Common-Sense Advice for the School Library Media Specialist.* By Ann M. Wasman. American Library Association, 1998. Paper $20.

*Reading Fun: Quick and Easy Activities for the School Library Media Center.* By Mona Kerby. Scarecrow Press, 1997. $19.50.

*The School Library Media Specialist as Manager: A Book of Case Studies.* By Amy G. Job and Mary Kay W. Schnare. Scarecrow Press, 1997. Paper $24.95.

*Serving Linguistically and Culturally Diverse Students: Strategies for the School Library Media Specialist.* By Melvina A. Dame. Neal-Schuman, 1993. Paper $25.

*Special Events Programs in School Library Media Centers.* By Marcia Trotta. Greenwood Press, 1997. $35.

*The Virtual School Library: Gateways to the Information Superhighway.* Ed. by Carol Collier Kuhlthau. Libraries Unlimited, 1996. Paper $24.

## Serials

*Guide to Performance Evaluation of Serials Vendors.* Association for Library Collections and Technical Services/American Library Association, 1997. Paper $15.

*International Subscription Agents.* 6th ed. By Lenore Rae Wilkas. American Library Association, 1993. Paper $35.

*Management of Serials in Libraries.* By Thomas E. Nisonger. Libraries Unlimited, 1998. $55.

*Serials Cataloging at the Turn of the Century.* Ed. by Jeanne M. K. Boydston, James W. Williams, and Jim Cole. Haworth, 1997. $39.95.

*Serials Cataloging Handbook.* By Carol Liheng and Winnie S. Chan. American Library Association, 1998. Paper $75.

## Services for Special Groups

*American Indian Library Services in Perspective.* By Elizabeth Rockefeller-MacArthur. McFarland, 1998. $29.50.

*Choosing and Using Books with Adult New Readers.* By Marguerite Crowley Weibel. Neal-Schuman, 1996. Paper $39.95.

*Information Services for People with Developmental Disabilities: The Library Manager's Handbook.* Ed. by Linda Lucas Walling and Marilyn M. Irwin. Greenwood Press, 1995. $69.95.

*The Librarian's Guide to Homeschooling Resources.* By Susan G. Scheps. American Library Association, 1998. Paper $25.

*Libraries Inside: A Practical Guide for Prison Librarians.* Ed. by Rhea Joyce Rubin and Daniel Suvak. McFarland, 1995. $41.50.

*Literacy, Access and Libraries Among the Language Minority Population.* Ed. by

Rebecca Constantino. Scarecrow Press, 1998. $36.

*Literacy is for Everyone: Making Library Activities Accessible for Children with Disabilities.* National Lekotek Center, 1998. Paper $49.95.

*Poor People and Library Services.* Ed. by Karen M. Venturella. McFarland, 1998. Paper $26.50.

*Preparing Staff to Serve Patrons with Disabilities: A How-to-Do-It Manual for Librarians.* By Courtney Deines-Jones and Connie Van Fleet. Neal-Schuman, 1995. Paper $39.95.

*Serving Print Disabled Library Patrons: A Textbook.* Ed. by Bruce Edward Massis. McFarland, 1996. $42.50.

*Serving Latino Communities: A How-To-Do-It Manual for Librarians.* By Camila Alire and Orlando Archibeque. Neal-Schuman, 1998. Paper $35.

*Universal Access: Electronic Resources in Libraries.* By Sheryl Burgstahler, Dan Comden, and Beth Fraser. American Library Association, 1998. Binder/video $75.

## Technical Services

*Directory of Library Technical Services Homepages.* By Barbara Stewart. Neal-Shuman, 1997. Paper $55.

*Guide to Managing Approval Plans.* Ed. by Susan Flood. American Library Association, 1998. Paper $18.

*Guide to Technical Services Resources.* Ed. by Peggy Johnson. American Library Association, 1994. $65.

*Outsourcing Library Technical Services: A How-to-Do-It Manual for Librarians.* By Arnold Hirshon and Barbara Winters. Neal-Schuman, 1996. $49.95. (Sample RFPs are available on diskette for $25 via *Outsourcing Technical Services: Ready-to-Import RFP Specifications Disk.*)

*Outsourcing Library Technical Services Operations: Practices in Public, Academic and Special Libraries.* Ed. by Karen A. Wilson and Marylou Colver. American Library Association, 1997. Paper $38.

*Planning and Implementing Technical Services Workstations.* Ed. by Michael Kaplan. American Library Association, 1997. Paper $32.

*Technical Services Today and Tomorrow.* 2nd ed. Ed. by Michael Gorman. Libraries Unlimited, 1998. $38.50.

*Understanding the Business of Library Acquisitions.* 2nd ed. Ed. by Karen A. Schmidt. American Library Association, 1998. Paper $48.

## Volunteers

*Library Volunteers—Worth the Effort! A Program Manager's Guide.* By Sally Gardner Reed. McFarland, 1994. Paper $27.50.

*Recruiting and Managing Volunteers in Libraries: A How-to-Do-It Manual for Librarians.* By Bonnie F. McCune and Charleszine "Terry" Nelson. Neal-Schuman, 1995. Paper $39.95.

## Periodicals and Periodical Indexes

*Acquisitions Librarian*
*Advanced Technology Libraries*
*Against the Grain*
*American Libraries*
*American Society for Information Science Journal*
*Behavioral and Social Sciences Librarian*
*Book Links*
*Book Report: Journal for Junior and Senior High School Librarians*
*Booklist*
*The Bottom Line*
*Cataloging and Classification Quarterly*
*CHOICE*
*College and Research Libraries*
*Collection Management*
*Community and Junior College Libraries*
*Computers in Libraries*
*The Electronic Library*
*Government Information Quarterly*
*Journal of Academic Librarianship*
*Journal of Information Ethics*
*Journal of Interlibrary Loan, Document Delivery and Information Supply*
*Journal of Library Administration*
*Journal of Youth Services in Libraries*
*Knowledge Quest*
*Law Library Journal*
*Legal Reference Services Quarterly*

*Libraries & Culture*
*Library Administration and Management*
*Library and Information Science Research (LIBRES)*
*Library Issues: Briefings for Faculty and Academic Administrators* (also on the Web by subscription at http://www.netpubs intl.com/LI.html)
*Library Hi-Tech*
*Library Journal*
*The Library Quarterly*
*Library Resources and Technical Services*
*Library Talk: The Magazine for Elementary School Librarians*
*Library Trends*
*MLS: Marketing Library Services*
*Medical Reference Services Quarterly*
*MultiCultural Review*
*MultiMedia Schools*
*Music Library Association Notes*
*Music Reference Services Quarterly*
*The One-Person Library*
*Online & CD-ROM Review*

*Online–Offline: Themes and Resources*
*Public and Access Services Quarterly*
*Public Libraries*
*Public Library Quarterly*
*Rare Books and Manuscripts Librarianship*
*Reference and User Services Quarterly* (formerly *RQ*)
*Reference Librarian*
*Reference Services Review*
*Resource Sharing & Information Networks*
*Rural Libraries*
*School Library Journal*
*Science & Technology Libraries*
*Searcher: The Magazine for Database Professionals*
*Serials Librarian*
*Serials Review*
*Special Libraries*
*Technical Services Quarterly*
*Technicalities*
*Video Librarian*
*Voice of Youth Advocates (VOYA)*

# Ready Reference

## Publishers' Toll-Free Telephone Numbers

Publishers' toll-free numbers continue to play an important role in ordering, verification, and customer service. This year's list comes from *Literary Market Place* (R. R. Bowker) and includes distributors and regional toll-free numbers, where applicable. The list is not comprehensive, and toll-free numbers are subject to change. Readers may want to call for toll-free directory assistance (800-555-1212).

| Publisher/Distributor | Toll-Free No. |
| --- | --- |
| A D D Warehouse, Plantation, FL | 800-233-9273 |
| A D P Hollander, Plymouth, MN | 800-761-9266 |
| A-R Editions Inc., Madison, WI | 800-736-0070 |
| Abacus, Grand Rapids, MI | 800-451-4319 |
| Abbeville Publishing Group, New York, NY | 800-ART-BOOK |
| ABC-CLIO, Santa Barbara, CA | 800-422-2546; 800-368-6868 |
| Abdo & Daughters Publishing, Minneapolis, MN | 800-458-8399 |
| ABELexpress, Carnegie, PA | 800-542-9001 |
| Aberdeen Group, Addison, IL | 800-837-0870 |
| Abingdon Press, Nashville, TN | 800-251-3320 |
| ABI Professional Publications, Arlington, VA | 800-551-7776 |
| Harry N Abrams Inc., New York, NY | 800-345-1359 |
| Academic Press, San Diego, CA | (cust serv) 800-321-5068 |
| Academic Therapy Publications, Novato, CA | 800-422-7249 |
| Academy Chicago Publishers, Chicago, IL | 800-248-READ |
| Academy of Producer Insurance Studies Inc., Austin, TX | 800-526-2777 |
| Access Publishers Network, Grawn, MI | 800-345-0096 |
| Acres USA, Metairie, LA | 800-355-5313 |
| ACS Publications, San Diego, CA | (orders only) 800-888-9983 |
| ACTA Publications, Chicago, IL | 800-397-2282 |
| Action Direct, Miami, FL | 800-472-2388 |
| ACU Press, Abilene, TX | 800-444-4228 |
| Adams-Blake Publishing, Fair Oaks, CA | 800-368-ADAM |
| Adams Media Corp., Holbrook, MA | 800-872-5627 |
| ADDAX Publishing Group, Lenexa, KS | 800-598-5550 |
| Addicus Books Inc., Omaha, NE | 800-352-2873 |
| Addison Wesley Longman Inc. (Corporate Headquarters), Reading, MA (orders only) (school serv team) | 800-552-2259 |

| Publisher/Distributor | Toll-Free No. |
|---|---|
| (college serv team) | 800-322-1377 |
| (college sales) | 800-552-2499 |
| (trade & agency) | 800-358-4566 |
| (corporate & professional) | 800-822-6339 |
| Adi, Gaia, Esalen Publications Inc., Los Angeles, CA | 800-652-8574 |
| (order fulfillment) | 800-263-1991 |
| Adirondack Mountain Club, Lake George, NY | 800-395-8080 |
| Advantage Publishers Group, San Diego, CA | 800-284-3580 |
| Adventure Publications, Cambridge, MN | 800-678-7006 |
| Aegean Park Press, Laguna Hills, CA | 800-736-3587 |
| Aegis Publishing Group Ltd., Newport, RI | 800-828-6961 |
| AEI Press, Washington, DC | 800-223-2336 |
| African American Images, Chicago, IL | 800-552-1991 |
| Afton Publishing, Andover, NJ | 888-238-6665 |
| Agora Inc., Baltimore, MD | 800-433-1528 |
| Agreka Books, Sandy, UT | 800-360-5284 |
| Ahsahta Press, Boise, ID | 800-992-TEXT |
| AIMS Education Foundation, Fresno, CA | 888-733-2467 |
| Airmont Publishing Co. Inc., New York, NY | 800-223-5251 |
| Alba House, Staten Island, NY | 800-343-ALBA |
| Alban Institute Inc., Bethesda, MD | 800-486-1318 |
| Alef Design Group, Los Angeles, CA | 800-845-0662 |
| Alfred Publishing Co. Inc., Van Nuys, CA | 800-292-6122 |
| ALI-ABA Committee on Continuing Professional Education, Philadelphia, PA | 800-CLE-NEWS |
| Allied Health Publications, National City, CA | 800-221-7374 |
| Allworth Press, New York, NY | 800-491-2808 |
| Allyn & Bacon, Needham Heights, MA | 800-223-1360 |
| Almanac Publishing Inc., Washington, DC | 888-825-6262 |
| ALPHA Publications of America Inc., Tucson, AZ | 800-528-3494 |
| Alpine Publications Inc., Loveland, CO (orders only) | 800-777-7257 |
| Alyson Publications Inc., Los Angeles, CA | 800-525-9766 |
| AMACOM Books, New York, NY (orders) | 800-538-4761 |
| Frank Amato Publications Inc., Portland, OR | 800-541-9498 |
| Amboy Associates, San Diego, CA | 800-448-4023 |
| America West Pubs, Carson City, NV | 800-729-4130 |
| American Academy of Orthopaedic Surgeons, Rosemont, IL | 800-626-6726 |
| American Academy of Pediatrics, Elk Grove Village, IL | 800-433-9016 |
| American Alliance for Health, Physical Education, Recreation & Dance, Reston, VA | 800-213-7193 |
| American Association for Vocational Instructional Materials, Winterville, GA | 800-228-4689 |
| American Association of Cereal Chemists, St. Paul, MN | 800-328-7560 |
| American Association of Community Colleges (AACC), Washington, DC | 800-250-6557 |
| American Association of Engineering Societies, Washington, DC | 888-400-2237 |

| Publisher/Distributor | Toll-Free No. |
|---|---|
| American Bankers Association, Washington, DC | 800-338-0626 |
| American Bible Society, New York, NY | (orders only) 800-322-4253 |
| American Chemical Society, Washington, DC | 800-227-9919 |
| American College of Physician Executives, Tampa, FL | 800-562-8088 |
| American Correctional Association, Lanham, MD | 800-222-5646 |
| American Council on Education, Washington, DC | 800-279-6799, ext. 642 |
| American Counseling Association, Alexandria, VA | 800-422-2648 |
| American Diabetes Association, Alexandria, VA | 800-232-6733 |
| American Eagle Publications Inc., Show Low, AZ | 800-719-4957 |
| American Federation of Arts, New York, NY | 800-AFA-0270 |
| American Federation of Astrologers Inc., Tempe, AZ | 888-301-7630 |
| American Foundation for the Blind (AFB Press), New York, NY | 800-232-3044 |
| American Geophysical Union, Washington, DC | 800-966-2481 |
| American Guidance Service Inc., Circle Pines, MN | 800-328-2560 |
| American Health Publishing Co., Dallas, TX | 800-736-7323 |
| American Historical Press, Sun Valley, CA | 800-550-5750 |
| American Institute of Aeronautics & Astronautics, Reston, VA | 800-639-2422 |
| American Institute of Certified Public Accountants, Jersey City, NJ | 800-862-4272 |
| American Institute of Chemical Engineers (AIChE), New York, NY | 800-242-4363 |
| American Law Institute, Philadelphia, PA | 800-CLE-NEWS |
| American Library Association (ALA), Chicago, IL | 800-545-2433 |
| American Map Corp., Maspeth, NY | 800-432-MAPS |
| American Marketing Association, Chicago, IL | 800-262-1150 |
| American Mathematical Society, Providence, RI | 800-321-4267 |
| American Medical Association, Chicago, IL | 800-621-8335 |
| American Nurses Publishing, Washington, DC | 800-637-0323 |
| American Occupational Therapy Association Inc., Bethesda, MD | 800-877-1383 |
| American Phytopathological Society, St. Paul, MN | 800-328-7560 |
| American Printing House for the Blind Inc., Louisville, KY | (cust serv) 800-223-1839 |
| | (sales & marketing) 800-572-0844 |
| American Psychiatric Press Inc., Washington, DC | 800-368-5777 |
| American Psychological Association, Washington, DC | 800-374-2721 |
| American Showcase Inc., New York, NY | 800-894-7469 |
| American Society for Nondestructive Testing, Columbus, OH | 800-222-2768 |
| American Society of Civil Engineers, Reston, VA | 800-548-2723 |
| American Society of Mechanical Engineers (ASME), New York, NY | (cust serv) 800-843-2763 |
| American Technical Publishers Inc., Homewood, IL | 800-323-3471 |
| Amirah Publishing, Flushing, NY | 800-337-4287 |
| Amon Carter Museum, Fort Worth, TX | 800-573-1933 |
| Amsco School Publications Inc., New York, NY | 800-969-8398 |
| Analytic Press, Hillsdale, NJ | (orders only) 800-926-6579 |
| Ancestry Inc., Orem, UT | 800-262-3787 |
| Anderson Publishing Co., Cincinnati, OH | 800-582-7295 |
| Andrews McMeel Publishing, Kansas City, MO | 800-826-4216 |
| Andrews University Press, Berrien Springs, MI | (Visa & Mastercard) 800-467-6369 |

| Publisher/Distributor | Toll-Free No. |
|---|---|
| Angelus Press, Kansas City, MO | 800-966-7337 |
| Annabooks, San Diego, CA | 800-462-1042 |
| Ann Arbor Press Inc., Chelsea, MI | 800-858-5299 |
| Anness Publishing Inc., New York, NY | 800-354-9657 |
| Annual Reviews Inc., Palo Alto, CA | 800-523-8635 |
| ANR Publications University of California, Oakland, CA | 800-994-8849 |
| Antioch Publishing, Yellow Springs, OH | 800-543-1515 |
| Antique Collectors Club Ltd., Wappingers Falls, NY | 800-252-5231 |
| Antique Publications, Marietta, OH | 800-533-3433 |
| Antique Trader Books, Norfolk, VA | 800-480-5168 |
| AOCS Press, Champaign, IL | 800-336-AOCS |
| APDG, Fuquay-Varina, NC | 800-227-9681 |
| Apex Press, New York, NY | 800-316-2739 |
| Applause Theatre Book Publishers, New York, NY | 800-798-7787 |
| Applied Therapeutics Inc., Vancouver, WA | (US) 800-345-0247 |
| Aqua Quest Publications Inc., Locust Valley, NY | 800-933-8989 |
| Ardis Publishers, Dana Point, CA | (orders) 800-877-7133 |
| ARE Press, Virginia Beach, VA | 800-723-1112 |
| Ariel Press, Alpharetta, GA | 800-336-7769 |
| Arion Press, San Francisco, CA | 800-550-7737 |
| Armenian Reference Books Co., Glendale, CA | 888-504-2550 |
| Arrow Map Inc., Bridgewater, MA | 800-343-7500 |
| Artabras Inc., New York, NY | 800-ART-BOOK |
| Artech House Inc., Norwood, MA | 800-225-9977 |
| Arte Publico Press, Houston, TX | 800-633-ARTE |
| ASCP Press, Chicago, IL | 800-621-4142 |
| Ashgate Publishing Co., Brookfield, VT | 800-535-9544 |
| Aslan Publishing, Fairfield, CT | 800-786-5427 |
| ASM International, Materials Park, OH | 800-336-5152 |
| ASM Press, Washington, DC | 800-546-2416 |
| Aspen Publishers Inc., Gaithersburg, MD | (orders) 800-638-8437 |
| Association for Computing Machinery, New York, NY | 800-342-6626 |
| Association for Supervision & Curriculum Development, Alexandria, VA | 800-933-2723 |
| Association for the Advancement of Medical Instrumentation, Arlington, VA | 800-332-2264 |
| Association of College & Research Libraries, Chicago, IL | 800-545-2433 |
| Association of Specialized & Cooperative Library Agencies (ASCLA), Chicago, IL | 800-545-2433 |
| Astronomical Society of the Pacific, San Francisco, CA | (orders only) 800-335-2624 |
| Atlantic Publishing Inc., Ocala, FL | 800-555-4037 |
| ATL Press, Shrewsbury, MA | 800-835-7543 |
| Augsburg Fortress Publishers, Publishing House of the Evangelical Lutheran Church in America, Minneapolis, MN | 800-426-0115 |
| | (orders) 800-328-4648 |
| | (permissions) 800-421-0239 |

| Publisher/Distributor | Toll-Free No. |
|---|---|
| August House Publishers Inc., Little Rock, AR | 800-284-8784 |
| Augustinian Press, Villanova, PA | 800-871-9404 |
| Austin & Winfield Publishers Inc., Bethesda, MD | 800-99-AUSTIN |
| Ave Maria Press, Notre Dame, IN | 800-282-1865 |
| Avery Publishing Group Inc., Wayne, NJ | 800-548-5757 |
| Aviation Heritage Inc., Destin, FL | 800-748-9308 |
| Avon Books, New York, NY | 800-238-0658 |
| Avotaynu Inc., Bergenfield, NJ | 800-286-8296 |
| Back to the Bible, Lincoln, NE | 800-759-2425 |
| Baha'i Publishing Trust, Wilmette, IL | 800-999-9019 |
| Baker Books, Grand Rapids, MI | 800-877-2665 |
| Balcony Publishing Inc., Austin, TX | 800-777-7949 |
| Ballantine Publishing Group Ballantine/Del Rey/Fawcett/House of Collectibles/Ivy/One World, New York, NY | 800-638-6460 |
| Banner of Truth, Carlisle, PA | 800-263-8085 |
| Bantam Books, New York, NY | 800-223-6834 |
| Bantam Doubleday Dell Books for Young Readers, New York, NY | 800-223-6834 |
| Bantam Doubleday Dell Publishing Group Inc., New York, NY | 800-223-6834 |
| Baptist Spanish Publishing House (dba Casa Bautista de Publicaciones), El Paso, TX (orders & cust serv) | 800-755-5958 |
| Barcelona Publishers/Pathway Book Service, Gilsum, NH | 800-345-6665 |
| Barnes & Noble Books (Imports & Reprints), Lanham, MD | 800-462-6420 |
| Barricade Books Inc., New York, NY | 800-592-6657 |
| Barron's Educational Series Inc., Hauppauge, NY | 800-645-3476 |
| Basic Books, New York, NY (orders) | 800-242-7737 |
| Battelle Press, Columbus, OH | 800-451-3543 |
| Bay Books & Tapes Inc., San Francisco, CA | 800-231-4944 |
| Baywood Publishing Co. Inc., Amityville, NY | 800-638-7819 |
| Beacham Publishing Corp., Osprey, FL | 800-466-9644 |
| Beacon Hill Press of Kansas City, Kansas City, MO | 800-877-0700 |
| Bear & Co. Inc., Santa Fe, NM | 800-932-3277 |
| Peter Bedrick Books Inc., New York, NY | 800-788-3123 |
| Thomas T Beeler Publisher, Hampton Falls, NH | 800-251-8726 |
| Beeman Jorgensen Inc., Indianapolis, IN | 800-553-5319 |
| Beginning Press, Seattle, WA | 800-831-4088 |
| Frederic C Beil Publisher Inc., Savannah, GA | 800-829-8406 |
| Bellerophon Books, Santa Barbara, CA | 800-253-9943 |
| Bell Springs Publishing, Willits, CA | 800-515-8050 |
| R Bemis Publishing Ltd., Marietta, GA | 800-497-6663 |
| Matthew Bender & Co. Inc., New York, NY (outside NY) | 800-227-5158 |
| | (NY) 800-722-3288 |
| Benefactory, Fairfield, CT | 800-729-7251 |
| John Benjamins Publishing Co., Erdenheim, PA | 800-562-5666 |
| Robert Bentley Publishers, Cambridge, MA | 800-423-4595 |
| R J Berg & Co., Publishers, Indianapolis, IN | 800-638-3909 |
| Berkeley Hills Books, Berkeley, CA | 888-848-7303 |

| Publisher/Distributor | Toll-Free No. |
|---|---|
| Berkshire House Publishers, Lee, MA | 800-321-8526 |
| Berlitz Publishing Co. Inc., Princeton, NJ | 800-923-7548 |
| Bernan Associates, Lanham, MD | 800-274-4888 |
| Bess Press, Honolulu, HI | 800-910-2377 |
| Best Publishing Co., Flagstaff, AZ | 800-468-1055 |
| Bethany House Publishers, Minneapolis, MN | 800-328-6109 |
| Bethel Publishing Co., Elkhart, IN | 800-348-7657 |
| Bethlehem Books, Minto, ND | 800-757-6831 |
| Betterway Books, Cincinnati, OH | 800-289-0963 |
| Beverage Marketing Corp., Mingo Junction, OH | 800-332-6222 |
| Beverly Publishing Co., Houston, TX | 800-955-2665 |
| Beyond Words Publishing Inc., Hillsboro, OR | 800-284-9673 |
| Bhaktivedanta Book Publishing Inc., Los Angeles, CA | 800-927-4152 |
| Biblical Archaeology Society, Washington, DC | 800-221-4644 |
| Biblo & Tannen Booksellers & Publishers Inc., Cheshire, CT | (voice & fax) 800-272-8778 |
| Binford & Mort, Hillsboro, OR | 888-221-4514 |
| Birkhauser Boston, Cambridge, MA | 800-777-4643 |
| George T Bisel Co., Philadelphia, PA | 800-247-3526 |
| Bisk Publishing Co., Tampa, FL | 800-874-7877 |
| Black Belt Publishing LLC, Montgomery, AL | 800-959-3245 |
| Blackbirch Press Inc., Woodbridge, CT | 800-831-9183 |
| Black Diamond Book Publishing, Los Angeles, CA | 800-444-2524 |
| Blacksmith Corporation, Chino Valley, AZ | 800-531-2665 |
| John F Blair, Publisher, Winston-Salem, NC | 800-222-9796 |
| Bloomberg Press, Princeton, NJ | 800-388-2749 |
| Blue Dolphin Publishing Inc., Nevada City, CA | 800-643-0765 |
| Blue Dove Press, San Diego, CA | (orders) 800-691-1008 |
| Blue Moon Books Inc., New York, NY | 800-535-0007 |
| Blue Mountain Press Inc., Boulder, CO | 800-525-0642 |
| Blue Note Publications, Cape Canaveral, FL | 800-624-0401 |
| Blue Poppy Press Inc., Boulder, CO | 800-487-9296 |
| Bluestar Communication Corp., Woodside, CA | 800-625-8378 |
| Bluestocking Press, Placerville, CA | 800-959-8586 |
| Blushing Rose Publishing, San Anselmo, CA | 800-898-2263 |
| BNA Books, Washington, DC | 800-960-1220 |
| Bob Jones University Press, Greenville, SC | 800-845-5731 |
| Bold Strummer Ltd., Westport, CT | 800-375-3786 |
| Bonus Books Inc., Chicago, IL | 800-225-3775 |
| BookPartners Inc., Wilsonville, OR | 800-895-7323 |
| Book Peddlers, Minnetonka, MN | 800-255-3379 |
| Book Publishing Co., Summertown, TN | 888-260-8458 |
| Book Sales Inc., Edison, NJ | 800-526-7257 |
| Book Tech Inc., Winchester, MA | 800-650-7229 |
| Book World Inc./Blue Star Productions, Sun Lakes, AZ | 888-472-2665 |
| BookWorld Press Inc., Sarasota, FL | 800-444-2524 |

| Publisher/Distributor | Toll-Free No. |
|---|---|
| Thomas Bouregy & Co. Inc., New York, NY | 800-223-5251 |
| R R Bowker, New Providence, NJ | 800-521-8110 |
| | (sales) 888-269-5372 |
| Boyds Mills Press, Honesdale, PA | 800-949-7777 |
| Boynton/Cook Publishers Inc., Portsmouth, NH | (orders) 800-793-2154 |
| Boys Town Press, Boys Town, NE | 800-282-6657 |
| William K Bradford Publishing Co. Inc., Acton, MA | 800-421-2009 |
| Brady Publishing, Indianapolis, IN | 800-545-5914 |
| Brain Sync, Ashland, OR | 800-984-7962 |
| Branden Publishing Co. Inc., | |
| Brookline Village, MA | (Mastercard & Visa) 800-537-7335 |
| Brassey's Inc., Dulles, VA | 800-775-2518 |
| Breakaway Books, New York, NY | 800-548-4348 |
| Breakthrough Publications, Ossining, NY | 800-824-5000 |
| Brethren Press, Elgin, IL | 800-323-8039 |
| Brewers Publications, Boulder, CO | (US & Canada) 888-822-6273 |
| Bridge Learning Systems Inc., American Canyon, CA | 800-487-9868 |
| Bridge-Logos Publishers, North Brunswick, NJ | 800-631-5802 |
| Bridge Publications Inc., Los Angeles, CA | 800-722-1733 |
| | (CA) 800-843-7389 |
| Brighton Publications, New Brigton, MN | 800-536-2665 |
| Brill Academic Publishers Inc., Boston, MA | 800-962-4406 |
| Bristol Publishing Enterprises Inc., San Leandro, CA | 800-346-4889 |
| Broadman & Holman Publishers, Nashville, TN | 800-251-3225 |
| Broadway Books, New York, NY | 888-290-2929 |
| Broadway Press, Louisville, KY | 800-869-6372 |
| Paul H Brookes Publishing Co., Baltimore, MD | 800-638-3775 |
| Brookings Institution, Washington, DC | 800-275-1447 |
| Brookline Books Inc., Cambridge, MA | 800-666-2665 |
| Brooks/Cole Publishing Co., Pacific Grove, CA | 800-354-9706 |
| Brunner/Mazel Publishing, Levittown, PA | 800-821-8312 |
| Building News, Needham, MA | 800-873-6397 |
| Bull Publishing Co., Palo Alto, CA | 800-676-2855 |
| Burrelle's Information Services, Livingston, NJ | 800-876-3342 |
| Business & Legal Reports Inc., Madison, CT | 800-727-5257 |
| Business Research Services Inc., Washington, DC | 800-845-8420 |
| Butte Publications Inc., Hillsboro, OR | 800-330-9791 |
| Butterworth-Heinemann, Woburn, MA | 800-366-2665 |
| C & T Publishing Inc., Lafayette, CA | 800-284-1114 |
| Calyx Books, Corvallis, OR | 888-336-2665 |
| Cambridge Educational, Charleston, WV | 800-468-4227 |
| Cambridge University Press, New York, NY | 800-221-4512 |
| Camden Court Publishers Inc., Midvale, UT | (orders only) 888-481-6230 |
| Cameron & Co., San Francisco, CA | 800-779-5582 |
| Career Press Inc., Franklin Lakes, NJ | 800-CAREER-1 |
| Career Publishing Inc., Orange, CA | 800-854-4014 |

| Publisher/Distributor | Toll-Free No. |
|---|---|
| William Carey Library, Pasadena, CA | 800-647-7466 |
| Carolrhoda Books Inc., Minneapolis, MN | 800-328-4929 |
| Carroll Press, New York, NY | 800-366-7086 |
| CarTech Inc., North Branch, MN | 800-551-4754 |
| CAS, Columbus, OH | 800-848-6538 |
| Cassell Academic, Herndon, VA | 800-561-7704 |
| Castle Books Inc., Edison, NJ | (orders) 800-526-7257 |
| CAT Publishing, Redding, CA | 800-767-0511 |
| Catbird Press, North Haven, CT | 800-360-2391 |
| Catholic News Publishing Co. Inc., New Rochelle, NY | 800-433-7771 |
| Caxton Printers Ltd., Caldwell, ID | 800-657-6465 |
| Cedar Fort Inc./C F T Distribution, Springville, UT | 800-759-2665 |
| Cedco Publishing Co., San Rafael, CA | 800-227-6162 |
| CEF Press, Warrenton, MO | 800-748-7710 |
| Celestial Arts, Berkeley, CA | 800-841-BOOK |
| Center for Futures Education Inc., Grove City, PA | 800-966-2554 |
| Center for Healthcare Information, Irvine, CA | 800-627-2244 |
| Central Conference of American Rabbis/CCAR Press, New York, NY | 800-935-CCAR |
| Chain Store Guide, Tampa, FL | 800-927-9292 |
| Chalice Press, St Louis, MO | 800-366-3383 |
| Chandler House Press, Worcester, MA | 800-642-6657 |
| Richard Chang Associates Inc., Irvine, CA | 800-756-8096 |
| Chaosium Inc., Oakland, CA | 800-213-1489 |
| Chariot Victor Publishing, Colorado Springs, CO | 800-437-4337 |
| CharismaLife Publishers, Lake Mary, FL | 800-451-4598 |
| Charles River Media, Rockland, MA | 800-382-8505 |
| Chartwell Books Inc., Edison, NJ | (orders) 800-526-7257 |
| Chatelaine Press, Burke, VA | 800-249-9527 |
| Chatsworth Press, Chatsworth, CA | (US) 800-262-7367 |
|  | (Canada) 800-272-7367 |
| Cheever Publishing Inc., Bloomington, IL | 800-787-8444 |
| Chelsea Green Publishing Co., White River Junction, VT | 800-639-4099 |
| Chelsea House Publishers, Broomall, PA | 800-848-BOOK |
| Chelsea Publishing Co. Inc., Providence, RI | 800-821-4267 |
| Chemical Publishing Co. Inc., New York, NY | 800-786-3659 |
| Cherokee Publishing Co., Marietta, GA | 800-653-3952 |
| Chess Combination Inc., Bridgeport, CT | 800-354-4083 |
| Chess Digest Inc., Grand Prairie, TX | 800-462-3548 |
| Chicago Review Press, Chicago, IL | 800-888-4741 |
| Chicago Spectrum Press, Louisville, KY | 800-594-5190 |
| Child's Play, Auburn, ME | 800-472-0099 |
| Chitra Publications, Montrose, PA | 800-628-8244 |
| Chivers North America Inc., Hampton, NH | 800-621-0182 |
| Chockstone Press Inc., Helena, MT | 800-582-2665 |
| Chosen Books, Grand Rapids, MI | 800-877-2665 |

| Publisher/Distributor | Toll-Free No. |
|---|---|
| Christendom Press, Front Royal, VA | 800-877-5456 |
| Christian Literature Crusade Inc., Fort Washington, PA | (orders) 800-659-1240 |
| Christian Publications Inc., Camp Hill, PA | 800-233-4443 |
| Christian Schools International, Grand Rapids, MI | 800-635-8288 |
| Christian Science Publishing Society, Boston, MA | 800-288-7090 |
| Christopher Gordon Publishers Inc., Norwood, MA | 800-934-8322 |
| Chronicle Books, San Francisco, CA | (orders) 800-722-6657 |
| Chronicle Guidance Publications Inc., Moravia, NY | 800-622-7284 |
| Chronimed Publishing, Minnetonka, MN | 800-848-2793 |
| Church Growth Institute, Forest, VA | (orders only) 800-553-GROW |
| Churchill Livingstone, Philadelphia, PA | 800-553-5426 |
| Cinco Puntos Press, El Paso, TX | 800-566-9072 |
| Citadel Press, Secaucus, NJ | (cust serv) 800-866-1966 |
| Clarity Press Inc., Atlanta, GA | (COD or credit card orders only) 800-533-0301 |
| Clark City Press, Livingston, MT | 800-835-0814 |
| Clark Publishing Inc., Topeka, KS | 800-845-1916 |
| Clarkson Potter Publishers, New York, NY | 800-526-4264 |
| Clear Light Publishers, Santa Fe, NM | 800-253-2747 |
| Cleis Press, San Francisco, CA | 800-780-2279 |
| Cliffs Notes Inc., Lincoln, NE | 800-228-4078 |
| Close Up Publishing, Alexandria, VA | 800-765-3131 |
| Clymer Publications, Overland Park, KS | 800-262-1954 |
| Cold Spring Harbor Laboratory Press, Cold Spring Harbor, NY | 800-843-4388 |
| Cole Publishing Group Inc., Santa Rosa, CA | 800-959-2717 |
| Collector Books, Paducah, KY | 800-626-5420 |
| Collectors Press Inc., Portland, OR | 800-423-1848 |
| College Press Publishing Co., Joplin, MO | 800-289-3300 |
| Colonial Press, Birmingham, AL | 800-264-7541 |
| Colonial Williamsburg Foundation, Williamsburg, VA | 800-HISTORY |
| Colorado Railroad Museum, Golden, CO | 800-365-6263 |
| Columba Publishing Co., Akron, OH | 800-999-7491 |
| Columbia Books Inc., Washington, DC | 888-265-0600 |
| Columbia University Press, New York, NY | 800-944-8648 |
| Combined Publishing, Conshohocken, PA | 800-418-6065 |
| Comex Systems Inc., Mendham, NJ | 800-543-6959 |
| Common Courage Press, Monroe, ME | 800-497-3207 |
| Commune-A-Key Publishing Inc., Salt Lake City, UT | 800-983-0600 |
| Communication Publications & Resources, Alexandria, VA | 800-888-2084 |
| Communication Skill Builders, San Antonio, TX | 800-211-8378; 800-228-0752 |
| Commuters Library, Falls Church, VA | 800-643-0295 |
| Compact Clinicals, Kansas City, MO | 800-408-8830 |
| Competency Press, White Plains, NY | 800-603-3779 |
| Comprehensive Health Education Foundation (CHEF), Seattle, WA | 800-323-2433 |
| Conari Press, Berkeley, CA | 800-685-9595 |
| Conciliar Press, Ben Lomond, CA | 800-967-7377 |
| Concordia Publishing House, St Louis, MO | 800-325-3040 |

| Publisher/Distributor | Toll-Free No. |
| --- | --- |
| Congressional Information Service Inc., Bethesda, MD | 800-638-8380 |
| Congressional Quarterly Books, Washington, DC | 800-638-1710 |
| Continuing Education Press, Portland, OR | 800-547-8887, ext. 4891 |
| Continuum Publishing Group, New York, NY | 800-561-7704 |
| Conway Greene Publishing Co., South Euclid, OH | 800-977-2665 |
| Copley Publishing Group, Acton, MA | 800-562-2147 |
| Cornell Maritime Press Inc., Centreville, MD | 800-638-7641 |
| CorpTech (Corporate Technology Information Services Inc.), Woburn, MA | 800-333-8036 |
| Cortina Learning International Inc., Wilton, CT | 800-245-2145 |
| Cottonwood Press Inc., Fort Collins, CO | 800-864-4297 |
| Council for Exceptional Children, Reston, VA | 800-232-7323 |
| Council Oak Books LLC, Tulsa, OK | 800-247-8850 |
| Council of State Governments, Lexington, KY | 800-800-1910 |
| Countryman Press, Woodstock, VT | 800-245-4151 |
| Countrysport Press, Selma, AL | 800-367-4114 |
| Course Technology, Cambridge, MA | 800-648-7450 |
| Covenant Communications Inc., American Fork, UT | 800-662-9545 |
| Covered Bridge Press, North Attleboro, MA (New England only) | 800-752-3769 |
| Cowles Creative Publishing Inc., Minnetonka, MN | 800-328-0590 |
| Cowley Publications, Boston, MA | 800-225-1534 |
| CQ Staff Directories Inc., Alexandria, VA | 800-252-1722 |
| Crabtree Publishing Co., New York, NY | 800-387-7650 |
| Craftsman Book Co., Carlsbad, CA | 800-829-8123 |
| Crane Hill Publishers, Birmingham, AL | 800-841-2682 |
| CRC Publications, Grand Rapids, MI | 800-333-8300 |
| Creative Arts Book Co., Berkeley, CA | 800-848-7789 |
| Creative Co., Mankato, MN | 800-445-6209 |
| Creative Homeowner Press, Upper Saddle River, NJ | 800-631-7795 |
| Creative Teaching Press/Youngheart Music, Cypress, CA | 800-444-4287 |
| CRICKET: Magazine For Children, Peru, IL (orders) | 800-BUG PALS |
| Crisp Publications Inc., Menlo Park, CA | 800-442-7477 |
| Cross Cultural Publications Inc., South Bend, IN | 800-273-6526 |
| Crossing Press, Freedom, CA | 800-777-1048 |
| Crossroad Publishing Co. Inc., New York, NY | 800-395-0690 |
| Crystal Clarity Publishers, Nevada City, CA | 800-424-1055 |
| Crystal Productions, Glenview, IL | 800-255-8629 |
| Cumberland House Publishing Inc., Nashville, TN | 888-439-2665 |
| Curiosity Canyon Press, Agoura Hills, CA | 800-613-1182 |
| Current Clinical Strategies Publishing, Laguna Hills, CA | 800-331-8227 |
| Current Medicine, Philadelphia, PA | 800-427-1796 |
| Da Capo Press Inc., New York, NY | 800-221-9369 |
| Dame Publications Inc., Houston, TX | 800-364-9757 |
| Dandy Lion Publications, San Luis Obispo, CA | 800-776-8032 |
| John Daniel & Co., Publishers, Santa Barbara, CA | 800-662-8351 |
| Dark Horse Comics, Milwaukie, OR | 800-862-0052 |

| Publisher/Distributor | Toll-Free No. |
|---|---|
| Dartnell Publishers, Chicago, IL | 800-621-5463 |
| Database Publishing Co., Anaheim, CA | 800-888-8434 |
| DATA Business Publishing, Englewood, CO | 800-447-4666 |
| Data Research Inc., Eagan, MN | 800-365-4900 |
| Data Trace Publishing Co., Towson, MD | (orders only) 800-342-0454 |
| Davies-Black Publishing, Palo Alto, CA | 800-624-1765 |
| F A Davis Co., Philadelphia, PA | 800-523-4049 |
| Davis Publications Inc. (MA), Worcester, MA | 800-533-2847 |
| Dawbert Press, Duxbury, MA | 800-93-DAWBERT |
| DAW Books Inc., New York, NY | 800-526-0275 |
| Dawn Horse Press, Middletown, CA | 800-524-4941 |
| Dawn Publications, Nevada City, CA | 800-545-7475 |
| Dawn Sign Press, San Diego, CA | 800-549-5350 |
| Day Star Publications, Wheeling, IL | 800-743-7700 |
| DBI Books, Iola, WI | 888-457-2873 |
| DBS Productions, Charlottesville, VA | 800-745-1581 |
| DC Comics, New York, NY | (distribution) 800-759-0190 |
| DDC Publishing, New York, NY | 800-528-3897 |
| Ivan R Dee Publisher, Chicago, IL | (orders) 800-634-0226 |
| John Deere Publishing, Moline, IL | 800-522-7448 |
| Dell Publishing, New York, NY | 800-223-6834 |
| Delmar Publishers, Albany, NY | (NY) 800-347-7707 |
| Delta Systems Co. Inc., McHenry, IL | 800-323-8270 |
| Demos Medical Publishing, New York, NY | 800-532-8663 |
| T S Denison & Co. Inc., Minneapolis, MN | 800-328-3831 |
| Derrydale Press Inc., Lyon, MS | 800-443-6753 |
| Deseret Book Co., Salt Lake City, UT | 800-453-3876 |
| Design Image Group, Burr Ridge, IL | 800-563-5455 |
| Destiny Image, Shippensburg, PA | (orders only) 800-722-6774 |
| Developmental Studies Center, Oakland, CA | 800-666-7270 |
| De Vorss & Co. Inc., Marina Del Rey, CA | 800-843-5743; (CA) 800-331-4719 |
| Dharma Publishing, Berkeley, CA | 800-873-4276 |
| Diablo Press Inc., Emeryville, CA | 800-488-2665 |
| Diamond Communications Inc., South Bend, IN | 800-480-3717 |
| Diamond Farm Book Publishers, Alexandria Bay, NY | 800-481-1353 |
| DIANE Publishing Co., Upland, PA | 800-782-3833 |
| Dimensions for Living, Nashville, TN | 800-281-3320 |
| Discipleship Publications International (DPI), Woburn, MA | 888-DPI-Book |
| Discovery Enterprises Ltd., Carlisle, MA | 800-729-1720 |
| Discovery House Publishers, Grand Rapids, MI | 800-653-8333 |
| Dissertation.com, Parkland, FL | 800-636-8329 |
| Distributed Art Publishers (DAP), New York, NY | 800-338-2665 |
| Diversity Press, Idabel, OK | 800-642-0779 |
| Dog-Eared Publications, Middleton, WI | 888-364-3277 |
| Doheny Publications Inc., Edmonds, WA | 888-436-4369 |
| Dominie Press Inc., Carlsbad, CA | 800-232-4570 |

| Publisher/Distributor | Toll-Free No. |
|---|---|
| Donning Co./Publishers, Virginia Beach, VA | 800-296-8572 |
| Doral Publishing, Wilsonville, OR | (orders) 800-633-5385 |
| Dorset House Publishing Co. Inc., New York, NY | 800-DHBOOKS |
| Doubleday, New York, NY | 800-223-6834; (sales) 800-223-5780 |
| Douglas Charles Press, North Attleboro, MA | (New England only) 800-752-3769 |
| Dover Publications Inc., Mineola, NY | (orders) 800-223-3130 |
| Down East Books, Camden, ME | 800-766-1670 |
| Dramatic Publishing Co., Woodstock, IL | 800-448-7469 |
| Dryden Press, Fort Worth, TX | 800-447-9479 |
| Dual Dolphin Publishing Inc., Winter Springs, FL | 800-336-5746 |
| Dufour Editions Inc., Chester Springs, PA | 800-869-5677 |
| Duke Press, Loveland, CO | 800-621-1544 |
| Dun & Bradstreet, Murray Hill, NJ | 800-526-0651 |
| Duquesne University Press, Pittsburgh, PA | 800-666-2211 |
| Dushkin/McGraw-Hill, Guilford, CT | (cust serv) 800-338-3987 |
| Dustbooks, Paradise, CA | 800-477-6110 |
| E M C Corp., St. Paul, MN | 800-328-1452 |
| E M Press Inc., Manassas, VA | 800-727-4630 |
| Eagle's View Publishing, Liberty, UT | (orders over $100) 800-547-3364 |
| Eakin Press, Austin, TX | 800-880-8642 |
| Eastland Press, Vista, CA | 800-453-3278 |
| East View Publications, Minneapolis, MN | 800-477-1005 |
| Eckankar, Minneapolis, MN | (orders only) 800-327-5113 |
| ECS Learning Systems Inc., San Antonio, TX | 800-688-3224 |
| ECS Publishing, Boston, MA | 800-777-1919 |
| EDC Publishing, Tulsa, OK | 800-475-4522 |
| Nellie Edge Resources Inc., Salem, OR | 800-523-4594 |
| Editorial Bautista Independiente, Sebring, FL | 800-398-7187 |
| Editorial Betania/Caribe, Miami, FL | 800-322-7423 |
| Editorial Caribe, Nashville, TN | 800-322-7423 |
| Editorial Portavoz, Grand Rapids, MI | 800-733-2607 |
| Editorial Unilit, Miami, FL | 800-767-7726 |
| Educational Impressions Inc., Hawthorne, NJ | 800-451-7450 |
| Educational Insights Inc., Carson, CA | 800-933-3277 |
| Educational Ministries Inc., Prescott, AZ | 800-221-0910 |
| Educational Technology Publications, Englewood Cliffs, NJ | (US & Canada, orders only) 800-952-BOOK |
| Educators Progress Service Inc., Randolph, WI | 888-951-4469 |
| Educators Publishing Service Inc., Cambridge, MA | 800-225-5750 |
| Edupress, San Clemente, CA | 800-835-7978 |
| Edward Elgar Publishing Inc., Northampton, MA | (orders) 800-390-3149 |
| Wm B Eerdmans Publishing Co., Grand Rapids, MI | 800-253-7521 |
| Elysium Growth Press, Los Angeles, CA | 800-350-2020 |
| Emanuel Publishing Corp., Larchmont, NY | 800-362-6835 |
| Emerald Books, Lynnwood, WA | 800-922-2143 |
| EMIS Inc., Durant, OK | 800-225-0694 |

| Publisher/Distributor | Toll-Free No. |
| --- | --- |
| Encore Performance Publishing, Orem, UT | 800-927-1605 |
| Encyclopaedia Britannica Educational Corp., Chicago, IL | 800-554-9862 |
| Encyclopaedia Britannica Inc., Chicago, IL | 800-323-1229 |
| Energeia Publishing Inc., Salem, OR | 800-639-6048 |
| Engineering & Management Press, Norcross, GA | 800-494-0460 |
| Engineering Information Inc. (EI), Hoboken, NJ | 800-221-1044 |
| Engineering Press, Austin, TX | 800-800-1651 |
| EPM Publications Inc., McLean, VA | 800-289-2339 |
| ERIC Clearinghouse on Higher Education, Washington, DC | 800-773-ERIC, ext.13 |
| ERIC Clearinghouse on Reading, English & Communication, Bloomington, IN | 800-759-4723 |
| ETC Publications, Palm Springs, CA | 800-382-7869 |
| ETR Associates, Santa Cruz, CA | 800-321-4407 |
| Eurotique Press Inc., West Palm Beach, FL | 800-547-4326 |
| Evangel Publishing House, Nappanee, IN | 800-253-9315 |
| Evan-Moor Educational Publishers, Monterey, CA | 800-777-4362 |
| Evanston Publishing Inc., Louisville, KY | 800-594-5190 |
| Everyday Learning Corp., Chicago, IL | 800-382-7670 |
| Exley Giftbooks, New York, NY | 800-423-9539 |
| Explorers Guide Publishing, Rhinelander, WI | 800-487-6029 |
| F C & A Publishing, Peachtree City, GA | 800-226-8024 |
| F J H Music Co. Inc., North Miami Beach, FL | 800-262-8744 |
| Faber & Faber Inc., Winchester, MA | (NY) 800-666-2211 |
| (outside NY, CUP services orders only) | 607-666-2211 |
| Factor Press, Mobile, AL | (orders only) 800-304-0077 |
| Facts On File Inc., New York, NY | 800-322-8755 |
| Fairchild Books, New York, NY | 800-932-4724 |
| Fairview Press, Minneapolis, MN | 800-544-8207 |
| Faith & Fellowship Press, Fergus Falls, MN | 800-332-9232 |
| Faith & Life Press, Newton, KS | 800-743-2484 |
| Falcon Publishing Inc., Helena, MT | 800-582-2665 |
| Fantagraphics Books, Seattle, WA | 800-657-1100 |
| W D Farmer Residence Designer Inc., Atlanta, GA | 800-225-7526; (GA) 800-221-7526 |
| Faxon Co., Westwood, MA | 800-999-3594 |
| Federal Publications Inc., Washington, DC | 800-922-4330 |
| Philipp Feldheim Inc., Nanuet, NY | 800-237-7149 |
| Fell Publishers, Hollywood, FL | 800-771-FELL |
| Ferguson Publishing Co., Chicago, IL | 800-306-9941 |
| Financial Executives Research Foundation Inc., Morristown, NJ | 800-680-FERF |
| Finley-Greene Publications Inc., Island Park, NY | 800-431-1131 |
| Firebird Publications Inc., Rockville, MD | 800-854-9595 |
| Fire Engineering Books & Videos, Saddle Brook, NJ | 800-752-9768 |
| Firefly Books Ltd., Buffalo, NY | 800-387-5085 |
| Fisher Books, Tucson, AZ | 800-255-1514 |
| Fisherman Library, Point Pleasant, NJ | 800-553-4745 |

| Publisher/Distributor | Toll-Free No. |
|---|---|
| Fitzroy Dearborn Publishers, Chicago, IL | 800-850-8102 |
| Flatiron Publishing Inc., New York, NY | 800-LIBRARY |
| Flower Valley Press Inc., Gaithersburg, MD | 800-735-5197 |
| Focus on the Family Publishing, Colorado Springs, CO | 800-232-6459 |
| Focus Publishing, Bemidji, MN | 800-913-6287 |
| Focus Publishing/R Pullins Co. Inc., Newburyport, MA | (orders) 800-848-7236 |
| Fodor's Travel Publications Inc., New York, NY | 800-733-3000; 800-533-6478 |
| Foghorn Press, Petaluma, CA | 800-FOGHORN |
| Fondo de Cultura Economica USA Inc., San Diego, CA | 800-532-3872 |
| Fordham University Press, Bronx, NY | 800-247-6553 |
| Forest House Publishing Co. Inc. & HTS Books, Lake Forest, IL | 800-394-READ |
| Forest of Peace Publishing Inc., Leavenworth, KS | 800-659-3227 |
| Forward Movement Publications, Cincinnati, OH | 800-543-1813 |
| Walter Foster Publishing Inc., Laguna Hills, CA | 800-426-0099 |
| Foundation Center, New York, NY | 800-424-9836 |
| Foundation for Economic Education Inc., Irvington-on-Hudson, NY | 800-452-3518 |
| Franciscan University Press, Steubenville, OH | 800-783-6357 |
| Franklin Library, Franklin Center, PA | 800-843-6468 |
| Fraser Publishing Co., Burlington, VT | 800-253-0900 |
| Free Spirit Publishing Inc., Minneapolis, MN | 800-735-7323 |
| Friends United Press, Richmond, IN | 800-537-8839 |
| Frog Ltd., Berkeley, CA | (book orders only) 800-337-2665 |
| Front Row Experience, Byron, CA | (voice & fax) 800-524-9091 |
| Fulcrum Publishing Inc., Golden, CO | 800-992-2908 |
| Futura Publishing Co. Inc., Armonk, NY | 800-877-8761 |
| Future Horizons Inc., Arlington, TX | 800-489-0727 |
| G W Medical Publishing Inc., St. Louis, MO | 800-600-0330 |
| P Gaines Co., Oak Park, IL | 800-578-3853 |
| Gale, Detroit, MI | (cust serv) 800-877-GALE |
| | (editorial) 800-347-GALE |
| Gallopade Publishing Group, Peachtree City, GA | 800-536-2GET |
| Gareth Stevens Inc., Milwaukee, WI | 800-341-3569 |
| Garrett Educational Corp., Ada, OK | 800-654-9366 |
| Garrett Publishing Inc., Deerfield Beach, FL | (book orders) 800-333-2069 |
| Gateways Books & Tapes, Nevada City, CA | 800-869-0658 |
| Gaunt Inc., Holmes Beach, FL | 800-942-8683 |
| Gayot/Gault Millau Inc., Los Angeles, CA | 800-LE BEST 1 |
| Thomas Geale Publications Inc., Montara, CA | 800-554-5457 |
| Gefen Books, Hewlett, NY | 800-477-5257 |
| GemStone Press, Woodstock, VT | 800-962-4544 |
| Genealogical Publishing Co. Inc., Baltimore, MD | 800-296-6687 |
| Genesis Press Inc., Columbus, MS | 888-463-4461 |
| Geological Society of America (GSA), Boulder, CO | 800-472-1988 |
| Georgetown University Press, Washington, DC | 800-246-9606 |
| GeoSystems Global Corp., Mountville, PA | 800-626-4655 |
| Gessler Publishing Co. Inc., Roanoke, VA | 800-456-5825 |

| Publisher/Distributor | Toll-Free No. |
| --- | --- |
| Gibbs Smith Publisher, Layton, UT | 800-748-5439 |
| C R Gibson Co., Norwalk, CT | 800-243-6004 |
| Giga Information Group, Norwell, MA | 800-874-9980 |
| Gleim Publications Inc., Gainesville, FL | 800-87-GLEIM |
| Glenbridge Publishing Ltd., Lakewood, CO | 800-986-4135 |
| Glencoe/McGraw-Hill, Westerville, OH | 800-848-1567 |
| Glenlake Publishing Co. Ltd., Chicago, IL | 800-537-5920 |
| Peter Glenn Publications, New York, NY | 888-332-6700 |
| Global Travel Publishers Inc., Fort Lauderdale, FL | 800-882-9453 |
| Globe Pequot Press, Old Saybrook, CT | 800-243-0495 |
| Gold Book, Atlanta, GA | 800-842-6848 |
| Golden Aura Publishing, Philadelphia, PA | 800-979-8642 |
| Golden Books Family Entertainment, New York, NY | (cust serv) 800-558-5972 |
| Golden Educational Center, Redding, CA | 800-800-1791 |
| Golden West Publishers, Phoenix, AZ | 800-658-5830 |
| Gold Horse Publishing Inc., Annapolis, MD | 800-966-DOLL |
| Goodheart-Willcox Publisher, Tinley Park, IL | 800-323-0440 |
| Goofy Foot Press, West Hollywood, CA | 800-310-PLAY |
| Goosefoot Acres Press, Cleveland Heights, OH | 800-697-4858 |
| Gospel Publishing House, Springfield, MO | 800-641-4310 |
| Gould Publications Inc., Longwood, FL | 800-847-6502 |
| Government Research Service, Topeka, KS | 800-346-6898 |
| Grafco Productions Inc., Marietta, GA | 888-656-1500 |
| Grail Foundation Press, Gambier, OH | 800-427-9217 |
| Donald M Grant Publisher Inc., Hampton Falls, NH | 800-476-0510 |
| Grapevine Publications Inc., Corvallis, OR | 800-338-4331 |
| Graphic Arts Center Publishing Co., Portland, OR | 800-452-3032 |
| Graphic Arts Publishing Inc., Livonia, NY | 800-724-9476 |
| Graphic Arts Technical Foundation (GATF), Sewickley, PA | 800-910-GATF |
| Graphic Learning, Waterbury, CT | 800-874-0029 |
| Grayson Bernard Publishers, Bloomington, IN | 800-925-7853 |
| Great Quotations Inc., Glendale Heights, IL | 800-354-4889 |
| Greenhaven Press Inc., San Diego, CA | 800-231-5163 |
| Warren H Green Inc., St. Louis, MO | 800-537-0655 |
| Greenwillow Books, New York, NY | 800-631-1199 |
| Greenwood Publishing Group Inc., Westport, CT | (orders) 800-225-5800 |
| Grey House Publishing Inc., Lakeville, CT | 800-562-2139 |
| Griffin Publishing, Glendale, CA | 800-472-9741 |
| Grolier Educational, Danbury, CT | 800-243-7256 |
| Group Publishing Inc., Loveland, CO | 800-447-1070 |
| Grove's Dictionaries Inc., New York, NY | 800-221-2123 |
| Grove/Atlantic Inc., New York, NY | 800-521-0178 |
| Gryphon Editions, New York, NY | 800-633-8911 |
| Gryphon House Inc., Beltsville, MD | 800-638-0928 |
| Guild, Madison, WI | 800-969-1556 |
| Guilford Press, New York, NY | (orders) 800-365-7006 |

| Publisher/Distributor | Toll-Free No. |
|---|---|
| Gulf Publishing Co., Book Division, Houston, TX | (TX) 800-392-4390; (all other except AK & HI) 800-231-6275 |
| H C I A Inc., Baltimore, MD | 800-568-3282 |
| H D I Publishers, Houston, TX | 800-321-7037 |
| Hachai Publications Inc., Brooklyn, NY | 800-50-HACHAI |
| Hagstrom Map Co. Inc., Maspeth, NY | 800-432-MAPS |
| Half Halt Press Inc., Boonsboro, MD | 800-822-9635 |
| Hambleton Hill Publishing Inc., Nashville, TN | 800-327-5113 |
| Alexander Hamilton Institute, Ramsey, NJ | 800-879-2441 |
| Hammond Inc., Maplewood, NJ | 800-526-4953 |
| Hampton-Brown Co. Inc., Carmel, CA | 800-933-3510 |
| Hampton Press Inc., Cresskill, NJ | 800-894-8955 |
| Hampton Roads Publishing Co. Inc., Charlottesville, VA | (orders) 800-766-8009 |
| Hancock House Publishers, Blaine, WA | 800-938-1114 |
| Hanley & Belfus Inc., Philadelphia, PA | 800-962-1892 |
| Hanser-Gardner Publications, Cincinnati, OH | 800-950-8977 |
| Harcourt Brace & Co., Orlando, FL | (cust serv) 800-225-5425 |
| Harcourt Brace College Publishers, Fort Worth, TX | (cust serv) 800-782-4479 |
| Harcourt Brace Legal & Professional Publications, Chicago, IL | (orders) 800-787-8717 |
| Harcourt Brace Professional Publishing, San Diego, CA | 800-831-7799 |
| Harcourt Brace School Publishers, Orlando, FL | (cust serv) 800-225-5425 |
| Harmonie Park Press, Warren, MI | 800-886-3080 |
| HarperCollins Publishers, New York, NY | 800-242-7737; (PA) 800-982-4377 |
| Harris InfoSource, Twinsburg, OH | 800-888-5900 |
| Harrison House Publishers, Tulsa, OK | 800-888-4126 |
| Hartley & Marks Publishers Inc., Point Roberts, WA | 800-277-5887 |
| Harvard Business School Press, Boston, MA | 888-500-1016 |
| Harvard Common Press, Boston, MA | 888-657-3755 |
| Harvard University Press, Cambridge, MA | (orders, US & Canada) 800-448-2242 |
| Harvest House Publishers Inc., Eugene, OR | 800-547-8979 |
| Hasbro Inc., Pawtucket, RI | 800-242-7276 |
| Hatherleigh Press, New York, NY | 800-367-2550 |
| Haworth Press Inc., Binghamton, NY | 800-342-9678 |
| Hay House Inc., Carlsbad, CA | (orders) 800-654-5126 |
| Haynes Manuals Inc., Newbury Park, CA | 800-442-9637 |
| Hazelden Publishing & Education, Center City, MN | 800-328-9000 |
| HB Trade Division, San Diego Office, San Diego, CA | (cust serv) 800-543-1918 |
| Health Communications Inc., Deerfield Beach, FL | (cust serv) 800-851-9100 (order entry) 800-441-5569 |
| Health for Life, Marina del Rey, CA | 800-874-5339 |
| Health Information Network Inc., San Ramon, CA | 800-446-1947 |
| Health Leadership Associates Inc., Potomac, MD | 800-435-4775 |
| Health Press, Santa Fe, NM | 800-643-BOOK |
| Health Professions Press, Baltimore, MD | 888-337-8808 |
| Health Science, Santa Barbara, CA | 800-446-1990 |
| Healthy Healing Publications, Carmel Valley, CA | 800-736-6015 |

| Publisher/Distributor | Toll-Free No. |
|---|---|
| Heartland Samplers Inc., Minneapolis, MN | 800-999-2233 |
| Hearts & Tummies Cookbook Co., Wever, IA | 800-571-BOOK |
| Heartsfire Books, Sante Fe, NM | 800-988-5170 |
| William S Hein & Co. Inc., Buffalo, NY | 800-828-7571 |
| Heinemann, Westport, CT | 800-541-2086 |
| Heinle & Heinle ITP Publishers, Boston, MA | 800-237-0053 |
| Hemingway Western Studies Series, Boise, ID | 800-992 TEXT |
| Hendrickson Publishers Inc., Peabody, MA | 800-358-3111 |
| Herald Press, Scottdale, PA | 800-245-7894 |
| Herald Publishing House, Independence, MO | 800-767-8181 |
| Heritage Books Inc., Bowie, MD | 800-398-7709 |
| Heritage Foundation, Washington, DC | 800-544-4843 |
| Heritage House, Indianapolis, IN | 800-419-0200 |
| Hewitt Homeschooling Resources, Washougal, WA | 800-348-1750 |
| High Mountain Press, Santa Fe, NM | 800-4-ONWORD; 800-466-9673 |
| High-Lonsome Books, Silver City, NM | 800-380-7323 |
| Highsmith Press LLC, Fort Atkinson, WI | 800-558-2110 |
| Hill & Wang, New York, NY | (orders, cust serv) 800-631-8571 |
| Hillsdale College Press, Hillsdale, MI | 800-437-2268 |
| Hi-Time Publishing, Milwaukee, WI | 800-558-2292 |
| Hi Willow Research & Publishing, San Jose, CA | 800-873-3043 |
| Hobar Publications, Minneapolis, MN | 800-846-7027 |
| Hogrefe & Huber Publishers, Kirkland, WA | 800-228-3749 |
| Hohm Press, Prescott, AZ | 800-381-2700 |
| Hollywood Creative Directory, Santa Monica, CA | (outside LA) 800-815-0503 |
| Holmes & Meier Publishers Inc., New York, NY | (orders only) 800-698-7781 |
| Henry Holt & Co. Inc., New York, NY | 800-488-5233 |
| Holt, Rinehart & Winston, Austin, TX | (cust serv) 800-225-5425 |
| Holt, Rinehart & Winston, Fort Worth, TX | 800-447-9479 |
| Home Builder Press, Washington, DC | 800-223-2665 |
| Home Planners LLC, Tucson, AZ | 800-322-6797 |
| Homestyles Publishing & Marketing Inc., St. Paul, MN | 888-626-2026 |
| Honor Books, Tulsa, OK | 800-678-2126 |
| Hoover Institution Press, Stanford, CA | 800-935-2882 |
| Hoover's Inc., Austin, TX | (orders only) 800-486-8666 |
| Hope Publishing Co., Carol Stream, IL | 800-323-1049 |
| Horizon Books, Camp Hill, PA | 800-233-4443 |
| Horizon Publishers & Distributors Inc., Bountiful, UT | 800-453-0812 |
| Houghton Mifflin Co., Boston, MA | (trade books) 800-225-3362 |
|  | (textbooks) 800-733-2828 |
|  | (college texts) 800-225-1464 |
| Howard Publishing, West Monroe, LA | 800-858-4109 |
| Howell Press Inc., Charlottesville, VA | 800-868-4512 |
| Humanics Publishing Group, Atlanta, GA | 800-874-8844 |
| Human Kinetics Inc., Champaign, IL | 800-747-4457 |
| Human Resource Development Press, Amherst, MA | 800-822-2801 |

| Publisher/Distributor | Toll-Free No. |
|---|---|
| Hunter House Inc., Publishers, Alameda, CA | 800-266-5592 |
| Huntington Press Publishing, Las Vegas, NV | 800-244-2224 |
| Hyperion, New York, NY | (orders) 800-343-9204 |
| I O P Publishing Inc., Philadelphia, PA | 800-358-4677 |
| IBC USA (Publications) Inc., Ashland, MA | 800-343-5413 |
| IBFD Publications USA Inc. (International Bureau of Fiscal Documentation), Valatie, NY | 800-299-6330 |
| Iconografix Inc., Hudson, WI | (orders only) 800-289-3504 |
| ICS Press, Oakland, CA | 800-326-0263 |
| Ideals Children's Books, Nashville, TN | 800-327-5113 |
| IDG Books Worldwide Inc., Foster City, CA | 800-762-2974 |
| IEEE Computer Society Press, Los Alamitos, CA | 800-272-6657 |
| Ignatius Press, San Francisco, CA | (orders only) 800-651-1531 |
| Images from Past Inc., Bennington, VT | 888-442-3204 |
| Imaginart Press, Bisbee, AZ | 800-828-1376 |
| Imperius Publishing, Marina Del Rey, CA | 800-444-8211 |
| Incentive Publications Inc., Nashville, TN | 800-421-2830 |
| Index Publishing Group Inc., San Diego, CA | 800-546-6707 |
| Indiana Historical Society, Indianapolis, IN | (orders only) 800-447-1830 |
| Indiana University Press, Bloomington, IN | (orders only) 800-842-6796 |
| Industrial Press Inc., New York, NY | 888-528-7852 |
| Industrial Text Co., Marietta, GA | 800-752-8398 |
| InfoBooks, Santa Monica, CA | 800-669-0409 |
| Information Guides, Hermosa Beach, CA | 800-347-3257 |
| Information Plus, Wylie, TX | 800-463-6757 |
| Inner Traditions International Ltd., Rochester, VT | 800-246-8648 |
| Innisfree Press Inc., Philadelphia, PA | (nontrade orders) 800-367-5872 |
| | (trade orders) 800-283-3572 |
| Innovanna Publishing Co. Inc., Sugar Land, TX | 800-577-9810 |
| Insiders' Publishing Inc., Manteo, NC | 800-765-2665 |
| Institute for International Economics, Washington, DC | 800-229-3266 |
| Institute for Language Study, Wilton, CT | 800-245-2145 |
| Institute for Research & Education, Minneapolis, MN | 800-372-7775 |
| Institute of Private Investigative Studies Inc., Phoenix, AZ | 800-Need-A-PI |
| Interarts/GeoSystems, Mountville, PA | 800-626-4655 |
| Interchange Inc., Saint Louis Park, MN | 800-669-6208 |
| Intercollegiate Studies Institute Inc. (ISI), Wilmington, DE | 800-652-4600 |
| Intercultural Press Inc., Yarmouth, ME | 800-370-2665 |
| International Chess Enterprises (ICE), Seattle, WA | 800-26-CHESS |
| International Foundation of Employee Benefit Plans, Brookfield, WI | 888-33-IFEBP |
| International Learning Works, Durango, CO | 800-344-0451 |
| International Risk Management Institute Inc., Dallas, TX | 800-827-4242 |
| International Scholars Publications, Bethesda, MD | 800-55-PUBLISH |
| International Society for Technology in Education, Eugene, OR | (orders only) 800-336-5191 |
| International Wealth Success Inc., Merrick, NY | 800-323-0548 |

| Publisher/Distributor | Toll-Free No. |
|---|---|
| Interstate Publishers Inc., Danville, IL | 800-843-4774 |
| Inter Trade Corp., Norcross, GA | 800-653-7363 |
| InterVarsity Press, Downers Grove, IL | 800-843-7225 |
| Interweave Press, Loveland, CO | 800-272-2193 |
| Iowa State University Press, Ames, IA | (orders only) 800-862-6657 |
| Irish American Book Co., Niwot, CO | 800-452-7115 |
| Irwin/McGraw-Hill, Burr Ridge, IL | (cust serv) 800-338-3987 |
| Island Press, Washington, DC | 800-828-1302 |
| J & B Editions Inc., Richmond, VA | 800-266-5480 |
| Jalmar Press, Carson, CA | 800-662-9662 |
| Jameson Books Inc., Ottawa, IL | 800-426-1357 |
| Jane's Information Group, Alexandria, VA | 800-243-3852 |
| January Productions Inc., Hawthorne, NJ | 800-451-7450 |
| Jason Aronson Inc., Northvale, NJ | (orders) 800-782-0015 |
| Jewish Lights Publishing, Woodstock, VT | 800-962-4544 |
| Jewish Publication Society, Philadelphia, PA | 800-234-3151 |
| JIST Works Inc., Indianapolis, IN | 800-648-5478, ext. 2130 |
| Johns Hopkins University Press, Baltimore, MD | 800-537-5487 |
| Johnson Institute, Minneapolis, MN | 800-231-5165 |
| Jones & Bartlett Publishers Inc., Sudbury, MA | 800-832-0034 |
| Jones Publishing Inc., Iola, WI | 800-331-0038 |
| Joy Publishing, Fountain Valley, CA | 800-454-8228 |
| Judaica Press Inc., Brooklyn, NY | 800-972-6701 |
| Judson Press, Valley Forge, PA | 800-458-3766 |
| Kaeden Corp., Rocky River, OH | 800-890-7323 |
| Kaleidoscope Press, Edgewood, WA | 800-977-7323 (code 6673) |
| Kalimat Press, Los Angeles, CA | 800-788-4067 |
| Kalmbach Publishing Co., Waukesha, WI | 800-558-1544 |
| Kar-Ben Copies Inc., Rockville, MD | 800-4-KARBEN |
| Kaye Wood Inc., West Branch, MI | 800-248-5293 |
| KC Publications Inc., Las Vegas, NV | 800-626-9673 |
| Keats Publishing Inc., New Canaan, CT | 800-858-7014 |
| J. J. Keller & Associates, Inc., Neenah, WI | 800-327-6868 |
| Kendall/Hunt Publishing Co., Dubuque, IA | (orders only) 800-228-0810 |
| Kennedy Publications, Fitzwilliam, NH | 800-531-0007 |
| Kenneth Hagin Ministries Inc., Broken Arrow, OK | (orders only) 888-258-0999 |
| Kensington Publishing Corp., New York, NY | 800-221-2647 |
| Kent State University Press, Kent, OH | (orders) 800-247-6553 |
| Key Curriculum Press, Berkeley, CA | 800-338-7638 |
| Kidsbooks Inc., Chicago, IL | 800-515-KIDS |
| Kids Can Press Ltd., Buffalo, NY | 800-265-0884 |
| Kirkbride Bible Co. Inc., Indianapolis, IN | 800-428-4385 |
| Kitchen Cupboard Cookbooks, Boise, ID | 800-878-4532 |
| Kitchen Sink Press, Northampton, MA | 800-365-SINK |
| Neil A Kjos Music Co., San Diego, CA | 800-854-1592 |
| Kluwer Law International (KLI), Cambridge, MA | 800-577-8118 |

| Publisher/Distributor | Toll-Free No. |
|---|---|
| Alfred A Knopf Inc., New York, NY | 800-638-6460 |
| Knopf Publishing Group, New York, NY | 800-638-6460 |
| Kodansha America Inc., New York, NY | 800-788-6262 |
| Krause Publications, Iola, WI | 800-258-0929 |
| Kregel Publications, Grand Rapids, MI | 800-733-2607 |
| Kumarian Press Inc., West Hartford, CT | (orders only) 800-289-2664 |
| LADYBUG: Magazine for Children, Peru, IL | (orders) 800-BUG PALS |
| Lakewood Publications, Minneapolis, MN | 800-328-4329 |
| LAMA Books, Hayward, CA | 888-452-6244 |
| Langenscheidt Publishers Inc., Maspeth, NY | 800-432-MAPS |
| LangMarc Publishing, San Antonio, TX | 800-864-1648 |
| Larousse Kingfisher Chambers Inc., New York, NY | 800-497-1657 |
| Larson Publications, Burdett, NY | 800-828-2197 |
| Laughing Owl Publishing Inc., Grand Bay, AL | 800-313-7412 (access code 71) |
| Laureate Press, Bangor, ME | 800-946-2727 |
| Lawbook Exchange Ltd., Union, NJ | 800-422-6686 |
| Lawrence Erlbaum Associates Inc., Mahwah, NJ | (orders only) 800-9-BOOKS-9 |
| LDA Publishers, Bayside, NY | 888-388-9887 |
| Leadership Publishers Inc., Des Moines, IA | 800-814-3757 |
| Leading Edge Reports, Commack, NY | 800-866-4648 |
| Learning Connection, Frostproof, FL | 800-338-2282 |
| Learning Links Inc., New Hyde Park, NY | 800-724-2616 |
| Learning Publications Inc., Holmes Beach, FL | (orders) 800-222-1525 |
| Learning Resources Network (LERN), Manhattan, KS | (orders only) 800-678-5376 |
| Learn Quickly, Solana Beach, CA | 888-LRN-FAST |
| Lectorum, New York, NY | 800-345-5946 |
| Legacy Publishing Group, Clinton, MA | 800-322-3866 |
| Leisure Arts Inc., Little Rock, AR | 800-643-8030 |
| Leisure Books, New York, NY | (order dept) 800-481-9191 |
| Hal Leonard Corp., Milwaukee, WI | 800-524-4425 |
| Lerner Publications Co., Minneapolis, MN | 800-328-4929 |
| Lexis Law Publishing, Charlottesville, VA | 800-446-3410 |
| Liberty Fund Inc., Indianapolis, IN | 800-955-8335 |
| Libraries Unlimited Inc., Englewood, CO | 800-237-6124 |
| Library Research Associates Inc., Monroe, NY | 800-914-3379 |
| Lickle Publishing Inc., West Palm Beach, FL | 888-454-2553 |
| Mary Ann Liebert Inc., Larchmont, NY | 800-654-3237 |
| Lifetime Books Inc., Hollywood, FL | 800-771-3355 |
| Liguori Publications, Liguori, MO | 800-464-2555 |
| Lincoln Institute of Land Policy, Cambridge, MA | 800-LAND-USE |
| LinguiSystems Inc., East Moline, IL | 800-PRO-IDEA |
| Linton Day Publishing Co., Stone Mountain, GA | 800-549-6757 |
| Lippincott-Raven Publishers, Philadelphia, PA | (MD) 800-638-3030 |
| Listen & Live Audio Inc., Roseland, NJ | 800-653-9400 |
| Literacy & Evangelism International, Tulsa, OK | 800-266-7139 |
| Little, Brown and Company Inc., Boston, MA | 800-759-0190 |

| Publisher/Distributor | Toll-Free No. |
|---|---|
| Littlefield, Adams Quality Paperbacks, Lanham, MD | 800-462-6420 |
| Little Tiger Press, Waukesha, WI | 800-541-2205 |
| Liturgical Press, Collegeville, MN | 800-858-5450 |
| Liturgy Training Publications, Chicago, IL (US & Canada only) | 800-933-1800 |
| Living Language, New York, NY (orders) | 800-733-3000 |
| Llewellyn Publications, St Paul, MN | 800-843-6666 |
| Loizeaux Brothers Inc., Neptune, NJ | 800-526-2796 |
| Lone Eagle Publishing Co., Los Angeles, CA | 800-345-6257 |
| Lonely Planet Publications, Oakland, CA (orders) | 800-275-8555 |
| Longstreet Press, Marietta, GA | 800-927-1488 |
| Loompanics Unlimited, Port Townsend, WA | 800-380-2230 |
| Looseleaf Law Publications Inc., Flushing, NY | 800-647-5547 |
| Lost Classics Book Co., Lake Wales, FL | 888-611-2665 |
| Lothrop, Lee & Shepard Books, New York, NY | 800-843-9389 |
| Lotus Light Publications, Twin Lakes, WI (orders only) | 800-824-6396 |
| Loyola Press, Chicago, IL | 800-621-1008 |
| Lucent Books Inc., San Diego, CA | 800-231-5163 |
| Lyle Stuart, Secaucus, NJ (cust serv) | 800-866-1966 |
| Lyons Press, New York, NY | 800-836-0510 |
| Lyrick Publishing, Allen, TX | 800-418-2371 |
| Macalester Park Publishing Co., Minneapolis, MN | 800-407-9078 |
| Macmillan Computer Publishing USA, Indianapolis, IN | 800-545-5914 |
| Macmillan Digital Publishing USA, Indianapolis, IN | 800-545-5914 |
| Macmillan Publishing USA, Indianapolis, IN | 800-545-5914 |
| MacMurray & Beck, Denver, CO | 800-774-3777 |
| Madison Books Inc., Lanham, MD | 800-462-6420 |
| Madison House Publishers, Madison, WI | 800-604-1776 |
| Mage Publishers Inc., Washington, DC | 800-962-0922 |
| Maharishi University of Management Press, Fairfield, IA | 800-831-6523 |
| Many Cultures Publishing, San Francisco, CA | 800-484-4173, ext. 1073 |
| MapEasy Inc., Amagansett, NY | 888-627-3279 |
| Marcel Dekker Inc., New York, NY (outside NY) | 800-228-1160 |
| MAR CO Products Inc., Warminster, PA | 800-448-2197 |
| MARC Publications, Monrovia, CA (US only) | 800-777-7752 |
| Market Data Retrieval, Shelton, CT | 800-333-8802 |
| Marketing Directions Inc., Avon, CT | 800-562-4357 |
| Markowski International Publishers, Hummelstown, PA | 800-566-0534 |
| Marlor Press Inc., St. Paul, MN | 800-669-4908 |
| Marlton Publishers, Severn, MD | 800-859-1073 |
| Marquette University Press, Milwaukee, WI | 800-247-6553 |
| Marshall & Swift, Los Angeles, CA | 800-544-2678 |
| MarshMedia, Kansas City, MO | 800-821-3303 |
| Marsilio Publishers Corp., New York, NY | 800-992-9685 |
| Martingale & Co., Bothell, WA | 800-426-3126 |
| Massachusetts Continuing Legal Education, Inc., Boston, MA | 800-966-6253 |
| Mathematical Association of America, Washington, DC (orders) | 800-331-1622 |

| Publisher/Distributor | Toll-Free No. |
|---|---|
| Maverick Publications Inc., Bend, OR | 800-800-4831 |
| Mayfield Publishing Co., Mountain View, CA | 800-433-1279 |
| MBI Publishing Co., Osceola, WI | 800-458-0454 |
| McBooks Press, Ithaca, NY | 888-266-5711 |
| McClanahan Publishing House Inc., Kuttawa, KY | 800-544-6959 |
| McCormack's Guides Inc., Martinez, CA | 800-222-3602 |
| McCutchan Publishing Corp., Berkeley, CA | 800-227-1540 |
| McDonald & Woodward Publishing Co., Granville, OH | 800-233-8787 |
| McFarland & Co. Inc. Publishers, Jefferson, NC | (orders only) 800-253-2187 |
| McGraw-Hill College, Boston, MA | (cust serv) 800-338-3987 |
| McGraw-Hill Higher Education, Burr Ridge, IL | (cust serv) 800-338-3987 |
| McPherson & Co., Kingston, NY | 800-613-8219 |
| MDRT Center for Productivity, Park Ridge, IL | 800-879-6378 |
| Meadowbrook Press Inc., Minnetonka, MN | 800-338-2232 |
| R S Means Co. Inc., Kingston, MA | 800-448-8182 |
| MedBooks, Richardson, TX | 800-443-7397 |
| Media & Methods, Philadelphia, PA | 800-555-5657 |
| Media Associates, Wilton, CA | (orders) 800-373-1897 |
| Medical Economics, Montvale, NJ | 800-442-6657 |
| Medical Physics Publishing Corp., Madison, WI | 800-442-5778 |
| Medicode, Salt Lake City, UT | 800-999-4600 |
| Mega Media Press, San Diego, CA | 800-803-9416 |
| Mel Bay Publications Inc., Pacific, MO | 800-863-5229 |
| Menasha Ridge Press Inc., Birmingham, AL | 800-247-9437 |
| Mercer University Press, Macon, GA | (outside GA) 800-637-2378, ext. 2880 |
|  | (GA) 800-342-0841, ext. 2880 |
| Meriwether Publishing Ltd./Contemporary Drama Service, Colorado Springs, CO | 800-937-5297 |
| Merlyn's Pen: Stories by American Students, East Greenwich, RI | 800-247-2027 |
| Merriam-Webster Inc., Springfield, MA | (orders & cust serv) 800-828-1880 |
| Merritt Publishing, Santa Monica, CA | 800-638-7597 |
| Merryant Publishers Inc., Vashon, WA | 800-228-8958 |
| Merry Thoughts Inc., Bedford Hills, NY | 800-637-7459 |
| Mesorah Publications Ltd., Brooklyn, NY | 800-637-6724 |
| Metal Bulletin Inc., New York, NY | 800-METAL-25 |
| Metamorphous Press, Portland, OR | 800-937-7771 |
| MGI Management Institute Inc., White Plains, NY | 800-932-0191 |
| Michelin Travel Publications, Greenville, SC | 800-423-0485; 800-223-0987 |
| MicroMash, Englewood, CO | 800-272-7277 |
| Microsoft Press, Redmond, WA | 800-MSPRESS |
| MidWest Plan Service, Ames, IA | 800-562-3618 |
| Midwest Traditions Inc., Shorewood, WI | 800-736-9189 |
| Milady Publishing, Albany, NY | 800-998-7498 |
| Milkweed Editions, Minneapolis, MN | 800-520-6455 |
| Millbrook Press Inc., Brookfield, CT | 800-462-4703 |
| Millennium Publishing Group, Monterey, CA | 800-524-6826 |
| Miller Freeman Inc., San Francisco, CA | (orders only) 800-848-5594 |

| Publisher/Distributor | Toll-Free No. |
|---|---|
| Milliken Publishing Co., St. Louis, MO | 800-325-4136 |
| Minerals, Metals & Materials Society (TMS), Warrendale, PA | 800-759-4867 |
| Ministry Publications, Scottsdale, AZ | 800-573-4105 |
| Minnesota Historical Society Press, St. Paul, MN | 800-647-7827 |
| Missouri Archaeolgical Society, Columbia, MO | (MO only) 800-472-3223 |
| Mitchell Lane Publishers Inc., Elkton, MD | 800-814-5484 |
| MIT Press, Cambridge, MA | (orders only) 800-356-0343 |
| MMB Music Inc., St. Louis, MO | 800-543-3771 |
| Momentum Books Ltd., Troy, MI | 800-758-1870 |
| Monday Morning Books Inc., Palo Alto, CA | 800-255-6049 |
| Mondo Publishing, Greenvale, NY | 800-242-3650 |
| Money Market Directories Inc., Charlottesville, VA | 800-446-2810 |
| Monthly Review Press, New York, NY | 800-670-9499 |
| Moody Press, Chicago, IL | 800-678-8812 |
| Moon Travel Handbooks, Chico, CA | 800-345-5473 |
| Morehouse Publishing Co., Harrisburg, PA | (orders only) 800-877-0012 |
| Morgan Kaufmann Publishers Inc., San Francisco, CA | 800-745-7323 |
| Morgan Quitno Corp., Lawrence, KS | 800-457-0742 |
| Morningside Bookshop, Dayton, OH | 800-648-9710 |
| Morrow Junior Books, New York, NY | 800-843-9389 |
| Morton Publishing Co., Englewood, CO | 800-384-3777 |
| Mosaic Press, Buffalo, NY | 800-387-8992 |
| Mosaic Press, Cincinnati, OH | 800-932-4044 |
| Mosby, St. Louis, MO | 800-325-4177 |
| Mountaineers Books, Seattle, WA | 800-553-4453 |
| Mountain Press Publishing Co., Missoula, MT | 800-234-5308 |
| Andrew Mowbray Inc. Publishers, Lincoln, RI | 800-999-4697 |
| Moyer Bell, Wakefield, RI | 888-789-1945 |
| Moznaim Publishing Corp., Brooklyn, NY | 800-364-5118 |
| John Muir Publications Inc., Santa Fe, NM | 800-285-4078 |
| Mulberry Paperback Books, New York, NY | 800-843-9389 |
| Multicultural Publications, Akron, OH | 800-238-0297 |
| Multnomah Publishers Inc., Sisters, OR | 800-929-0910 |
| Municipal Analysis Services Inc., Austin, TX | 800-488-3932 |
| Mike Murach & Associates Inc., Fresno, CA | 800-221-5528 |
| Museum of New Mexico Press, Santa Fe, NM | (orders) 800-249-7737 |
| Music Sales Corp., New York, NY | 800-431-7187 |
| Mustang Publishing Co. Inc., Memphis, TN | 800-250-8713 |
| NAFSA: Association of International Educators, Washington, DC | 800-836-4994 |
| Naiad Press Inc., Tallahassee, FL | (order desk only) 800-533-1973 |
| Nancy Renfro Studios Inc., Austin, TX | 800-933-5512 |
| NAPSAC Reproductions, Marble Hill, MO | 800-758-8629 |
| Narwhal Press Inc., Charleston, SC | 800-981-1943 |
| National Academy Press, Washington, DC | 800-624-6242 |
| National Archives & Records Administration, Washington, DC | (orders) 800-234-8861 |

| Publisher/Distributor | Toll-Free No. |
|---|---|
| National Association of Broadcasters, Washington, DC | 800-368-5644 |
| National Association of Secondary School Principals, Reston, VA | 800-253-7746 |
| National Association of Social Workers (NASW), Washington, DC | 800-638-8799 |
| National Braille Press, Boston, MA | 800-548-7323 |
| National Center for Non-profit Boards, Washington, DC | 800-883-6262 |
| National Council of Teachers of English (NCTE), Urbana, IL | 800-369-6283 |
| National Council on Radiation Protection & Measurements (NCRP), Bethesda, MD | 800-229-2652 |
| National Geographic Society, Washington, DC | 800-638-4077 |
| National Golf Foundation, Jupiter, FL | 800-733-6006 |
| National Information Center for Educational Media, Albuquerque, NM | 800-926-8328 |
| National Institute for Trial Advocacy, Notre Dame, IN | 800-225-6482 |
| National Learning Corp., Syosset, NY | 800-645-6337 |
| National Museum of Women in the Arts, Washington, DC | 800-222-7270 |
| National Notary Association, Chatsworth, CA | 800-876-6827 |
| National School Services, Wheeling, IL | 800-262-4511 |
| National Science Teachers Association (NSTA), Arlington, VA | (sales) 800-722-NSTA |
| National Textbook Co. (NTC), Lincolnwood, IL | (orders only) 800-323-4900 |
| National Underwriter Co., Cincinnati, OH | 800-543-0874 |
| Naturegraph Publishers Inc., Happy Camp, CA | 800-390-5353 |
| Naval Institute Press, Annapolis, MD | 800-233-8764 |
| NavPress Publishing Group, Colorado Springs, CO | 800-366-7788 |
| NBM Publishing Inc., New York, NY | 800-886-1223 |
| Nebbadoon Press, Etna, NH | 800-500-9086 |
| Neibauer Press, Warminster, PA | 800-322-6203 |
| Thomas Nelson Inc., Nashville, TN | 800-251-4000 |
| Nelson Information, Port Chester, NY | 800-333-6357 |
| NelsonWord Publishing Group, Nashville, TN | 800-251-4000 |
| New City Press, Hyde Park, NY | (orders only) 800-462-5980 |
| New Dimensions in Education, Waterbury, CT | 800-227-9120 |
| New Directions Publishing Corp., New York, NY | (PA) 800-233-4830 |
| New Editions International Ltd., Sedona, AZ | 800-777-4751 |
| New Harbinger Publications Inc., Oakland, CA | (orders only) 800-748-6273 |
| New Horizon Press, Far Hills, NJ | (orders only) 800-533-7978 |
| New Leaf Press Inc., Green Forest, AR | 800-643-9535 |
| NewLife Publications, Orlando, FL | 800-235-7255 |
| Newmarket Press, New York, NY | 800-669-3903 |
| New Press, New York, NY | (orders) 800-233-4830 |
| New Readers Press, Syracuse, NY | 800-448-8878 |
| New Rivers Press, Minneapolis, MN | 800-339-2011 |
| New Victoria Publishers, Norwich, VT | 800-326-5297 |
| New World Library, Novato, CA | (retail orders) 800-227-3900, ext. 902 |
| New York Academy of Sciences, New York, NY | 800-843-6927 |

| Publisher/Distributor | Toll-Free No. |
|---|---|
| New York State Bar Association, Albany, NY | 800-582-2452 |
| New York University Press, New York, NY | (orders) 800-996-6987 |
| Nightingale-Conant, Niles, IL | 800-572-2770 |
| Nightshade Press, Troy, ME | (book orders only) 800-497-9258 |
| Nilgiri Press, Tomales, CA | 800-475-2369 |
| Nolo Press, Berkeley, CA | 800-992-6656 |
| Nolo Press Occidental, Occidental, CA | 800-464-5502 |
| Norman Publishing, San Francisco, CA | 800-544-9359 |
| North Atlantic Books, Berkeley, CA | (book orders) 800-337-2665 |
| North Country Press, Unity, ME | 800-722-2169 |
| Northland Publishing Co., Flagstaff, AZ | 800-346-3257 |
| North Light Books, Cincinnati, OH | 800-289-0963 |
| Northmont Publishing Co., West Bloomfield, MI | 800-472-3485 |
| North River Press Inc., Great Barrington, MA | 800-486-2665 |
| North South Books, New York, NY | 800-282-8257 |
| Northwestern University Press, Evanston, IL | (orders only) 800-621-2736 |
| W W Norton & Company Inc., New York, NY | (orders & cust serv) 800-233-4830 |
| Jeffrey Norton Publishers Inc., Guilford, CT | 800-243-1234 |
| Nova Press, Los Angeles, CA | 800-949-6175 |
| NTC/Contemporary Publishing Group, Lincolnwood, IL | 800-323-4900 |
| Nystrom, Chicago, IL | 800-621-8086 |
| OAG Worldwide, Oak Brook, IL | 800-323-3537 |
| Oasis Press/Hellgate Press, Central Point, OR | 800-228-2275 |
| Ocean View Books, Denver, CO | 800-848-6222 |
| Ohara Publications Inc., Valencia, CA | 800-423-2874 |
| Ohio State University Foreign Language Publications, Columbus, OH | 800-678-6999 |
| Ohio State University Press, Columbus, OH | 800-437-4439 |
| Ohio University Press, Athens, OH | 800-621-2736 |
| Old Books Publishing Co., Earlysville, VA | 888-651-8520 |
| Oliver Press Inc., Minneapolis, MN | 800-8-OLIVER |
| Omnibus Press, New York, NY | 800-431-7187 |
| Omnigraphics Inc., Detroit, MI | 800-234-1340 |
| One-Off CD Shop Washington Inc., White Plains, MD | 800-678-8760 |
| OneOnOne Computer Training, Addison, IL | 800-424-8668 |
| Online Press Inc./Quick Course Books, Bellevue, WA | 800-854-3344 |
| Open Court Publishing Co., Peru, IL | 800-435-6850 |
| Open Horizons Publishing Co., Fairfield, IA | 800-796-6130 |
| Optical Society of America, Washington, DC | 800-582-0416 |
| Opus Communications, Marblehead, MA | 800-650-6787 |
| Orbis Books, Maryknoll, NY | (orders) 800-258-5838 |
| Orca Book Publishers, Custer, WA | 800-210-5277 |
| Orchard Books, New York, NY | 800-433-3411 |
| Order of the Cross, La Grange, IL | (voice & fax) 800-611-1361 |
| Oregon Catholic Press, Portland, OR | 800-548-8749 |
| O'Reilly & Associates Inc., Sebastopol, CA | 800-998-9938 |

| Publisher/Distributor | Toll-Free No. |
|---|---|
| Organization for Economic Cooperation & Development, OECD Washington, Washington, DC | 800-456-6323 |
| Orion Research Corp., Scottsdale, AZ | 800-844-0759 |
| Oryx Press, Phoenix, AZ | 800-279-6799 |
| Osborne/McGraw-Hill, Berkeley, CA | 800-227-0900 |
| Other Press LLC, New York, NY | 877-THE OTHER; 877-843-6843 |
| Oughten House Foundation, Livermore, CA | 888-ORDER-IT |
| Our Sunday Visitor Publishing, Huntington, IN | (orders) 800-348-2440 |
| Out There Press, Ashville, NC | 800-579-4458 |
| Overmountain Press, Johnson City, TN | 800-992-2691 |
| Richard C Owen Publishers Inc., Katonah, NY | 800-336-5588 |
| Oxbridge Communications Inc., New York, NY | 800-955-0231 |
| Oxford University Press Inc., New York, NY | (orders) 800-451-7556 |
| Oxmoor House Inc., Birmingham, AL | 800-633-4910 |
| Ozark Publishing Inc., Prairie Grove, AR | 800-321-5671 |
| P & R Publishing Co., Phillipsburg, NJ | 800-631-0094 |
| P P I Publishing, Kettering, OH | 800-773-6825 |
| P S M J Resources Inc., Newton, MA | 800-537-7765 |
| Pacific Press Publishing Association, Nampa, ID | 800-447-7377 |
| Paladin Press, Boulder, CO | 800-392-2400 |
| Palm Island Press, Key West, FL | 800-763-4345 |
| Panoptic Enterprises, Burke, VA | 800-594-4766 |
| Pantheon Books/Schocken Books, New York, NY | 800-638-6460 |
| Papier-Mache Press, Watsonville, CA | 800-776-1956 |
| Paraclete Press, Orleans, MA | 800-451-5006 |
| Paradigm Publications, Brookline, MA | 800-873-3946 |
| Paradigm Publishing Inc., St. Paul, MN | 800-328-1452 |
| Paradise Cay Publications, Arcata, CA | 800-736-4509 |
| Para Publishing, Santa Barbara, CA | 800-PARAPUB |
| Parenting Press Inc., Seattle, WA | 800-99-BOOKS |
| Parker Publications Division, Carlsbad, CA | 800-452-9873 |
| Parlay International, Emeryville, CA | 800-457-2752 |
| Parthenon Publishing Group Inc., Pearl River, NY | 800-735-4744 |
| Passage Press, Sandy, UT | 800-873-0075 |
| Passport Books, Lincolnwood, IL | (orders only) 800-323-4900 |
| Pastoral Press, Laurel, MD | 800-976-9669 |
| Pathfinder Publishing of California, Ventura, CA | 800-977-2282 |
| Path Press Inc., Chicago, IL | 800-548-2600 |
| Pathway Books, Golden Valley, MN | 800-958-3375 |
| Pathways Publishing, Hudson, MA | 888-333-7284 |
| Patrice Press, Tucson, AZ | 800-367-9242 |
| Patrick's Press Inc., Columbus, GA | 800-654-1052 |
| Pauline Books & Media, Boston, MA | (orders only) 800-876-4463 |
| PBC International Inc., Glen Cove, NY | 800-527-2826 |
| Peachtree Publishers Ltd., Atlanta, GA | 800-241-0113 |
| Pearce-Evetts Publishing, Greenville, SC | 800-842-9571 |

| Publisher/Distributor | Toll-Free No. |
|---|---|
| T H Peek Publisher, Palo Alto, CA | 800-962-9245 |
| Peer-to-Peer Communications, San Jose, CA | 800-420-2677 |
| Pelican Publishing Co. Inc., Gretna, LA | 800-843-1724; 888-5PELICAN |
| Penbrooke Publishing, Tulsa, OK | 888-493-2665 |
| Pencil Point Press Inc., Fairfield, NJ | 800-356-1299 |
| Penfield Press, Iowa City, IA | 800-728-9998 |
| Pennsylvania Historical & Museum Commission, Harrisburg, PA | 800-747-7790 |
| Pennsylvania State University Press, University Park, PA | 800-326-9180 |
| PennWell Books, Tulsa, OK | 800-752-9764 |
| Pentrex Pub, Pasadena, CA | (continental US only) 800-950-9333 |
| People's Medical Society, Allentown, PA | 800-624-8773 |
| Peradam Press, Santa Barbara, CA | 800-241-8689 |
| Per Annum Inc., New York, NY | 800-548-1108 |
| Perfection Learning Corp., Des Moines, IA | 800-762-2999 |
| Peter Pauper Press Inc., White Plains, NY | 800-833-2311 |
| Peterson's, Princeton, NJ | 800-338-3282 |
| Petroleum Extension Service Petex, Austin, TX | 800-687-4132 |
| Pfeifer-Hamilton Publishers, Duluth, MN | 800-247-6789 |
| Phi Delta Kappa Educational Foundation, Bloomington, IN | 800-766-1156 |
| Philosophy Documentation Center, Bowling Green, OH | 800-444-2419 |
| Phoenix Learning Resources, New York, NY | 800-221-1274 |
| Phoenix Publishing, Lansing, MI | 800-345-0325 |
| Phoenix Society for Burn Survivors, Nashua, NH | 800-888-BURN |
| Pictorial Histories Publishing Co., Missoula, MT | 888-763-8350 |
| Picture Me Books, Akron, OH | 800-762-6775 |
| Pieces of Learning, Dayton, OH | 800-729-5137 |
| Pierian Press, Ann Arbor, MI | 800-678-2435 |
| Pilgrim Press/United Church Press, Cleveland, OH | 800-537-3394 |
| Pilot Books, Greenport, NY | 800-79PILOT |
| Pineapple Press Inc., Sarasota, FL | (orders) 800-746-3275 |
| Pitspopany Press, New York, NY | 800-232-2931 |
| Planetary Publications, Boulder Creek, CA | 800-372-3100 |
| Planning/Communications, River Forest, IL | 888-366-5200 |
| Plays Inc., Boston, MA | 888-273-8214 |
| Pleasant Co. Publications, Middleton, WI | 800-845-0005 |
| Plenum Publishing Corp., New York, NY | 800-221-9369 |
| Plough Publishing House, Farmington, PA | 800-521-8011 |
| Police Executive Research Forum, Washington, DC (publication orders only) | 888-202-4563 |
| Polyscience Publications Inc., Champlain, NY | 800-840-5870 |
| Pomegranate Communications, Rohnert Park, CA | 800-227-1428 |
| Popular Culture Ink, Ann Arbor, MI | 800-678-8828 |
| Popular Press, Bowling Green, OH | 800-515-5118 |
| Practising Law Institute, New York, NY | 800-260-4754 |
| Prakken Publications Inc., Ann Arbor, MI | (orders only) 800-530-9673 |
| Precept Press, Chicago, IL | 800-225-3775 |

| Publisher/Distributor | Toll-Free No. |
|---|---|
| PREP Publishing, Fayetteville, NC | 800-533-2814 |
| Preservation Press Inc., Swedesboro, NJ | 888-233-0911 |
| Presidio Press, Novato, CA | 800-966-5179 |
| Primedia Special Interest Publications, Peoria, IL | 800-521-2885 |
| Princeton Architectural Press, New York, NY | 800-722-6657 |
| Princeton Book Co. Publishers, Hightstown, NJ | 800-220-7149 |
| Princeton University Press, Princeton, NJ | 800-777-4726 |
| Printers Shopper, Chula Vista, CA | 800-854-2911 |
| Productivity Press Inc., Portland, OR | 800-394-6868 |
| PRO-ED, Austin, TX | 800-897-3202 |
| Professional Education Group Inc., Minnetonka, MN | 800-229-2531 |
| Professional Publications Inc., Belmont, CA | 800-426-1178 |
| Professional Publishing, Burr Ridge, IL | 800-2McGraw |
| Professional Resource Exchange Inc., Sarasota, FL | 800-443-3364 |
| Professional Tax & Business Publications, Columbia, SC | 800-829-8087 |
| Pro Lingua Associates, Brattleboro, VT | 800-366-4775 |
| Prometheus Books, Amherst, NY | 800-421-0351 |
| Providence House Publishers, Franklin, TN | 800-321-5692 |
| Pruett Publishing Co., Boulder, CO | 800-247-8224 |
| PST Inc., Redmond, WA | 800-284-7043 |
| Psychological Assessment Resources Inc. (PAR), Lutz, FL | 800-331-8378 |
| Psychological Corp., San Antonio, TX | (cust serv) 800-211-8378 |
| PT Publications, West Palm Beach, FL | 800-547-4326 |
| Public Utilities Reports Inc., Vienna, VA | 800-368-5001 |
| PuraVida Publishing, Mountlake Terrace, WA | 888-670-1346 |
| Purdue University Press, West Lafayette, IN | 800-933-9637 |
| Purple Mountain Press Ltd., Fleischmanns, NY | 800-325-2665 |
| Quail Ridge Press, Brandon, MS | 800-343-1583 |
| Quality Education Data, Denver, CO | 800-525-5811 |
| Quality Medical Publishing Inc., St. Louis, MO | 800-423-6865 |
| Quality Press, Milwaukee, WI | 800-248-1946 |
| Quality Resources, New York, NY | 800-247-8519 |
| Quintessence Publishing Co. Inc., Carol Stream, IL | 800-621-0387 |
| Quixote Press, Wever, IA | 800-571-BOOK |
| Race Point Press, Provincetown, MA | 800-446-5544 |
| Ragged Edge Press, Shippensburg, PA | 888-WHT-MANE |
| Rainbow Books Inc., Highland City, FL | 800-356-9315; 888-613-BOOK |
| Rainbow Publishers, San Diego, CA | 800-323-7337 |
| Rainbow Studies International, El Reno, OK | 800-242-5348 |
| Raintree/Steck-Vaughn Publishers, Austin, TX | 800-531-5015 |
| Rand McNally, Skokie, IL | 800-333-0136 |
| Random House Inc., New York, NY | 800-726-0600 |
| Rayve Productions Inc., Windsor, CA | 800-852-4890 |
| RCL Resources for Christian Living, Allen, TX | 800-527-5030 |
| Reader's Digest Association Inc., Pleasantville, NY | 800-431-1726 |
| Reader's Digest USA, Pleasantville, NY | 800-431-1726 |

| Publisher/Distributor | Toll-Free No. |
|---|---|
| Reader's Digest USA Select Editions, Pleasantville, NY | 800-431-1726 |
| Record Research Inc., Menomonee Falls, WI | 800-827-9810 |
| Redbird Productions, Hastings, MN | 800-950-6898 |
| Red Crane Books Inc., Santa Fe, NM | 800-922-3392 |
| Redleaf Press, St. Paul, MN | 800-423-8309 |
| Regal Books, Ventura, CA | (orders) 800-446-7735 |
| Regnery Publishing Inc., Washington, DC | 800-462-6420 |
| Regular Baptist Press, Schaumburg, IL | 888-588-1600 |
| | (orders only) 800-727-4440 |
| Rei America Inc., Miami, FL | 800-726-5337 |
| Renaissance Media, Los Angeles, CA | 800-266-2834 |
| Research Press, Champaign, IL | 800-519-2707 |
| Resurrection Press Ltd., Williston Park, NY | 800-892-6657 |
| Retail Reporting Corp., New York, NY | 800-251-4545 |
| Fleming H Revell, Grand Rapids, MI | 800-877-2665 |
| Review & Herald Publishing Association, Hagerstown, MD | 800-234-7630 |
| Rip Off Press Inc., Auburn, CA | 800-468-2669 |
| Rising Sun Publishing, Marietta, GA | 800-524-2813 |
| Riverside Publishing Co., Itasca, IL | 800-767-8420 |
| | (orders) 800-323-9540 |
| Rizzoli International Publications Inc., New York, NY | (orders & cust serv) 800-221-7945 |
| Roberts Rinehart Publishers, Niwot, CO | 800-352-1985 |
| Rockbridge Publishing Co., Berryville, VA | 800-473-3943 |
| Rock Hill Press, Bala Cynwyd, PA | 888-ROCKHILL |
| Rocky River Publishers, Shepherdstown, WV | 800-343-0686 |
| Rodale Press Inc., Emmaus, PA | 800-848-4735 |
| Rosen Publishing Group Inc., New York, NY | 800-237-9932 |
| Ross Books, Berkeley, CA | 800-367-0930 |
| Norman Ross Publishing Inc., New York, NY | 800-648-8850 |
| Fred B Rothman & Co., Littleton, CO | 800-457-1986 |
| Roth Publishing Inc., Great Neck, NY | 800-899-ROTH |
| Rough Notes Co. Inc., Carmel, IN | 800-428-4384 |
| H M Rowe Co., Baltimore, MD | 800-638-6026 |
| Rowman & Littlefield Publishers Inc., Lanham, MD | 800-462-6420 |
| Royal House Publishing Co. Inc., Beverly Hills, CA | 800-277-5535 |
| Rudi Publishing, San Francisco, CA | (orders only) 800-999-6901 |
| Rudra Press, Portland, OR | 800-876-7798 |
| Runestone Press, Minneapolis, MN | 800-328-4929 |
| Running Press Book Publishers, Philadelphia, PA | (orders) 800-345-5359 |
| Russell Meerdink Co. Ltd., Neenah, WI | 800-635-6499 |
| Russell Sage Foundation, New York, NY | 800-666-2211 |
| Rutgers University Press, Piscataway, NJ | (orders only) 800-446-9323 |
| Rutledge Books Inc., Bethel, CT | 800-278-8533 |
| Rutledge Hill Press, Nashville, TN | 800-234-4234 |
| William H Sadlier Inc., New York, NY | 800-221-5175 |

| Publisher/Distributor | Toll-Free No. |
|---|---|
| Sagamore Publishing Inc., Champaign, IL | (orders) 800-327-5557 |
| Saint Anthony Messenger Press, Cincinnati, OH | 800-488-0488 |
| Saint Anthony Publishing Inc., Reston, VA | 800-632-0123 |
| Saint Augustine's Press Inc., South Bend, IN | 888-997-4994 |
| Saint Bede's Publications, Petersham, MA | (orders) 800-507-1000 |
| Saint James Press, Detroit, MI | 800-345-0392 |
| Saint Martin's Press Inc., New York, NY | 800-221-7945 |
| Saint Mary's Press, Winona, MN | 800-533-8095 |
| Saint Nectarios Press, Seattle, WA | 800-643-4233 |
| Salem Press Inc., Englewood Cliffs, NJ | 800-221-1592 |
| Howard W Sams & Co., Indianapolis, IN | 800-428-7267 |
| J S Sanders & Co. Inc., Nashville, TN | 800-350-1101 |
| Sandlapper Publishing Inc., Orangeburg, SC | (orders only) 800-849-7263 |
| Santa Monica Press LLC, Santa Monica, CA | 800-784-9553 |
| Santillana USA Publishing Co. Inc., Miami, FL | 800-245-8584 |
| Sarpedon Publishers, Rockville Centre, NY | 800-207-8045 |
| Sasquatch Books, Seattle, WA | 800-775-0817 |
| W B Saunders Company, Philadelphia, PA | (cust serv) 800-545-2522 |
| Savage Press, Superior, WI | 800-732-3867 |
| Scarborough House, Lanham, MD | 800-462-6420 |
| Scarecrow Press Inc., Lanham, MD | 800-462-6420 |
| Scepter Publishers, Princeton, NJ | 800-322-8773 |
| Schaffer Frank Publications Inc., Torrance, CA | (cust serv) 800-421-5565 |
| Scholarly Resources Inc., Wilmington, DE | 800-772-8937 |
| Schonfeld & Associates Inc., Lincolnshire, IL | 800-205-0030 |
| School Zone Publishing Co., Grand Haven, MI | 800-253-0564 |
| Schwann Publications, Woodland, CA | 800-845-8444 |
| Arthur Schwartz & Co. Inc./Woodstock Book, Woodstock, NY | 800-669-9080 |
| Scott & Daughters Publishing Inc., Los Angeles, CA | 800-547-2688 |
| Scott Publications, Livonia, MI | 800-458-8237 |
| Scott Publishing Co., Sidney, OH | 800-572-6885 |
| Scurlock Publishing Co. Inc., Texarkana, TX | 800-228-6389 |
| Seal Press, Seattle, WA | (orders) 800-754-0271 |
| Search Resources, Houston, TX | 800-460-4673 |
| SeedSowers, Sargent, GA | 800-228-2665 |
| SelectiveHouse Publishers Inc., Gaithersburg, MD | (orders only) 888-256-6399 |
| Self-Counsel Press Inc., Bellingham, WA | 800-663-3007 |
| Seven Locks Press Inc., Santa Ana, CA | 800-354-5348 |
| Severn House Publishers Inc., New York, NY | 800-830-3044 |
| M E Sharpe Inc., Armonk, NY | 800-541-6563 |
| Harold Shaw Publishers, Wheaton, IL | 800-SHAW-PUB |
| Sheed & Ward, Kansas City, MO | 800-444-8910 |
| | (cust serv) 800-333-7373 |
| Sheep Meadow Press, Bronx, NY | 800-972-4491 |
| Shelter Publications Inc., Bolinas, CA | 800-307-0131 |
| Shen's Books, Arcadia, CA | 800-456-6660 |

| Publisher/Distributor | Toll-Free No. |
|---|---|
| Sherman Asher Publishing, Santa Fe, NM | (orders) 888-984-2686 |
| Sidran Press, Lutherville, MD | 888-825-8249 |
| Sierra Press, Mariposa, CA | 800-745-2631 |
| Signature Books Inc., Salt Lake City, UT | (orders) 800-356-5687 |
| Sigo Press, Gloucester, MA | 800-338-0446 |
| SIGS Books & Multimedia, New York, NY | (orders only) 800-871-7447 |
| Silver Moon Press, New York, NY | 800-874-3320 |
| Silver Pixel Press, Rochester, NY | 800-394-3686 |
| Simon & Schuster, New York, NY | (cust serv) 800-223-2348 |
| | (orders) 800-223-2336 |
| Simon & Schuster Trade Division, New York, NY | (cust serv) 800-223-2348 |
| | (orders) 800-223-2336 |
| Simpler Gifts Press, San Diego, CA | 800-688-1209 |
| Singular Publishing Group Inc., San Diego, CA | 800-521-8545 |
| Six Strings Music Publishing, Torrance, CA | 800-784-0203 |
| Skidmore-Roth Publishing Inc., Englewood, CO | 800-825-3150 |
| SkillPath Publications, Mission, KS | 800-873-7545 |
| Skylight Training & Publishing Inc., Arlington Heights, IL | 800-348-4474 |
| Sky Publishing Corp., Cambridge, MA | 800-253-0245 |
| Slack Incorporated, Thorofare, NJ | 800-257-8290 |
| Smith & Kraus Inc. Publishers, North Stratford, NH | 800-895-4331 |
| Smithmark Publishers, New York, NY | 800-645-9990 |
| M Lee Smith Publishers LLC, Brentwood, TN | 800-274-6774 |
| Smithsonian Institution Press, Washington, DC | 800-762-4612 |
| Smithsonian Press/Smithsonian Productions, Washington, DC | 800-782-4612 |
| Smyth & Helwys Publishing Inc., Macon, GA | 800-747-3016; 800-568-1248 |
| Snow Lion Publications Inc., Ithaca, NY | 800-950-0313 |
| Society for Industrial & Applied Mathematics, Philadelphia, PA | 800-447-SIAM |
| Society for Mining, Metallurgy & Exploration Inc., Littleton, CO | 800-763-3132 |
| Society of Manufacturing Engineers, Dearborn, MI | 800-733-4SME |
| Solano Press Books, Point Arena, CA | 800-931-9373 |
| Soli Deo Gloria Publications, Morgan, PA | 888-266-5734 |
| Solitaire Publishing, Tampa, FL | 800-226-0286 |
| Sophia Institute Press, Manchester, NH | 800-888-9344 |
| Sopris West, Longmont, CO | 800-547-6747 |
| Soundprints, Norwalk, CT | 800-228-7839 |
| South Carolina Bar, Columbia, SC | (SC only) 800-768-7787 |
| Southern Illinois University Press, Carbondale, IL | 800-346-2680 |
| Southern Institute Press, Indian Rocks Beach, FL | 800-633-4891 |
| South-Western Educational Publishing, Cincinnati, OH | 800-543-0487 |
| Space Link Books, New York, NY | 800-444-2524 |
| Specialty Press Publishers & Wholesalers, North Branch, MN | 800-895-4585 |
| Spider, Peru, IL | (orders) 800-BUG PALS |
| Spinsters Ink, Duluth, MN | 800-301-6860 |
| SPIRAL Books, Bedford, NH | 800-SPIRALL |
| Spizzirri Publishing Inc., Rapid City, SD | 800-325-9819; (fax) 800-322-9819 |

| Publisher/Distributor | Toll-Free No. |
|---|---|
| Sports Publishing Inc., Champaign, IL | 800-327-5557 |
| Springer-Verlag New York Inc., New York, NY | 800-SPRINGER |
| Springhouse Corp., Springhouse, PA | 800-346-7844 |
| Squarebooks Inc., Santa Rosa, CA | 800-345-6699 |
| Stackpole Books, Mechanicsburg, PA | 800-732-3669 |
| STA-Kris Inc., Marshalltown, IA | 800-369-5676 |
| Stalsby-Wilson Press, Rockville, MD | 800-642-3228 |
| Standard Publishing Co., Cincinnati, OH | 800-543-1301 |
| ST Publications Book Division, Cincinnati, OH | 800-925-1110 |
| Starburst Publishers, Lancaster, PA | (orders only) 800-441-1456 |
| Starlite Inc., St. Petersburg, FL | 800-577-2929 |
| State House Press, Austin, TX | 800-421-3378 |
| State University of New York Press, Albany, NY | 800-666-2211 |
| Steck-Vaughn Co., Austin, TX | 800-531-5015; (fax orders) 800-699-9459 |
| Stemmer House Publishers Inc., Owings Mills, MD | 800-676-7511 |
| Stenhouse Publishers, York, ME | (sales) 800-988-9812 |
| Sterling House Publisher, Pittsburgh, PA | 800-898-7886 |
| Sterling Publishing Co. Inc., New York, NY | 800-367-9692 |
| Stillpoint Publishing, Walpole, NH | 800-847-4014 |
| Stoeger Publishing Co., Wayne, NJ | 800-631-0722 |
| Stone Bridge Press, Berkeley, CA | 800-947-7271 |
| Storey Books, Pownal, VT | 800-793-9396 |
| Story Press, Cincinnati, OH | 800-289-0963 |
| Strang Communications Co./Creation House, Lake Mary, FL | 800-283-8494; (Canada) 800-665-1468 |
| Studio 4 Productions, Northridge, CA | 888-PUBLISH |
| Studio Press, Soulsbyville, CA | 800-445-7160 |
| SubGenius Foundation Inc., Dallas, TX | 888-669-2323 |
| Sulzburger & Graham Publishing Co. Ltd., New York, NY | 800-366-7086 |
| Summers Press Inc., Austin, TX | 800-743-6491 |
| Summit Publications, Indianapolis, IN | 800-419-0200 |
| Summit Publishing Group, Arlington, TX | 800-875-3346 |
| Summit University Press, Corwin Springs, MT | 800-245-5445 |
| Summy-Birchard Inc., Miami, FL | 800-327-7643 |
| Sunbelt Books, El Cajon, CA | 800-626-6579 |
| Sundance Publishing L P, Littleton, MA | 800-245-3388 |
| Sunflower University Press, Manhattan, KS | 800-258-1232 |
| Sunset Books, Menlo Park, CA | 800-227-7346; (CA) 800-321-0372 |
| SuperPuppy Press, Escondido, CA | 800-342-7877 |
| Surrey Books Inc., Chicago, IL | 800-326-4430 |
| Swedenborg Foundation Inc., West Chester, PA | (cust serv) 800-355-3222 |
| SYBEX Inc., Alameda, CA | 800-227-2346 |
| Syracuse University Press, Syracuse, NY | (orders only) 800-365-8929 |
| T L C Genealogy, Miami Beach, FL | 800-858-8558 |
| TAFT Group, Detroit, MI | 800-877-8238 |
| Tapestry Press Ltd., Acton, MA | 800-535-2007 |

| Publisher/Distributor | Toll-Free No. |
|---|---|
| Taschen America, New York, NY | 888-TASCHEN |
| Taunton Press Inc., Newtown, CT | 800-283-7252; (orders) 800-888-8286 |
| Taylor & Francis Publishers Inc., Philadelphia, PA | 800-821-8312 |
| Taylor Publishing Co., Dallas, TX | (voice & fax) 800-677-2800 |
| Teacher Created Materials Inc., Westminster, CA | 800-662-4321 |
| Teacher Ideas Press, Englewood, CO | 800-237-6124 |
| Teacher's Discovery, Auburn Hills, MI | 800-832-2437 |
| Teachers Friend Publications Inc., Riverside, CA | 800-343-9680 |
| Teaching Strategies, Washington, DC | 800-637-3652 |
| Teach Me Tapes Inc., Minnetonka, MN | 800-456-4656 |
| Technical Association of the Pulp & Paper Industry (TAPPI), Atlanta, GA | 800-332-8686 |
| Technology Training Systems Inc., Aurora, CO | 800-676-8871 |
| Technomic Publishing Co. Inc., Lancaster, PA | 800-233-9936 |
| Templegate Publishers, Springfield, IL | 800-367-4844 |
| Temple University Press, Philadelphia, PA | 800-447-1656 |
| Ten Speed Press, Berkeley, CA | 800-841-BOOK |
| te Neues Publishing Co., New York, NY | 800-352-0305 |
| Tesla Book Co., Chula Vista, CA | 800-398-2056 |
| Tetrahedron Publishing Group, Rockport, MA | 800-336-9266 |
| Tetra Press, Blacksburg, VA | 800-526-0650 |
| Texas A&M University Press, College Station, TX | (orders) 800-826-8911 |
| Texas Instruments Data Book Marketing, Dallas, TX | 800-336-5236 |
| Texas Tech University Press, Lubbock, TX | 800-832-4042 |
| Texas Western Press, El Paso, TX | 800-488-3789 (4UTEP-TWP) |
| TFH Publications Inc., Neptune, NJ | 800-631-2188 |
| Thames & Hudson, New York, NY | 800-233-4830 |
| Theosophical Publishing House, Wheaton, IL | 800-669-9425 |
| Theta Reports, Rocky Hill, CT | 800-995-1550 |
| Thieme Medical Publishers Inc., New York, NY | 800-782-3488 |
| Thinkers Press, Davenport, IA | 800-397-7117 |
| Thinking Publications, Eau Claire, WI | 800-225-4769 |
| Third World Press, Chicago, IL | 800-785-1498 |
| Thomas Publications, Gettysburg, PA | 800-840-6782 |
| Charles C Thomas Publisher Ltd., Springfield, IL | 800-258-8980 |
| Thomas Reed Publications Inc., Boston, MA | 800-995-4995 |
| Thomson Financial Publishing, Skokie, IL | 800-321-3373 |
| Thorndike Press, Thorndike, ME | 800-223-6121 |
| Threshold Books, Putney, VT | 888-638-5384 |
| Tiare Publications, Lake Geneva, WI | 800-420-0579 |
| Tide-mark Press, East Hartford, CT | 800-338-2508 |
| Tidewater Publishers, Centreville, MD | 800-638-7641 |
| Timber Press Inc., Portland, OR | 800-327-5680 |
| Time Being Books-Poetry in Sight & Sound, St. Louis, MO | 800-331-6605 |
| Time Life Inc., Alexandria, VA | 800-621-7026 |
| Timeless Books, Spokane, WA | 800-251-9273 |

| Publisher/Distributor | Toll-Free No. |
|---|---|
| Times Books, New York, NY | 800-733-3000 |
| Todd Publications, Nyack, NY | 800-747-1056 |
| TODTRI Book Publishers, New York, NY | 800-241-4477 |
| Torah Aura Productions, Los Angeles, CA | 800-238-6724 |
| Tor Books, New York, NY | (cust serv) 800-221-7945 |
| Tower Publishing Co., Standish, ME | 800-969-8693 |
| Tracks Publishing, Chula Vista, CA | 800-443-3570 |
| Traders Press Inc., Greenville, SC | 800-927-8222 |
| Tradery House, Memphis, TN | 800-727-1034 |
| Trafalgar Square, North Pomfret, VT | 800-423-4525 |
| Trafton Publishing, Cary, NC | 800-356-9315 |
| Trails Illustrated/National Geographic Maps, Evergreen, CO | 800-962-1643 |
| Trakker Maps Inc., Miami, FL | 800-327-3108; (FL) 800-432-1730 |
| Transaction Publishers, Piscataway, NJ | 888-999-6778 |
| Transnational Publishers Inc., Ardsley, NY | (orders only) 800-914-8186 |
| Transportation Technical Service Inc., Fredericksburg, VA | 888-ONLY-TTS |
| Travelers' Tales Inc., Sebastopol, CA | 800-998-9938 |
| Treasure Publishing, Fort Collins, CO | 800-284-0158 |
| Treehaus Communications Inc., Loveland, OH | (orders) 800-638-4287 |
| Tricycle Press, Berkeley, CA | 800-841-2665 |
| Trinity Press International, Harrisburg, PA | 800-877-0012 |
| TripBuilder Inc., New York, NY | 800-525-9745 |
| TriQuarterly Books, Evanston, IL | (orders only) 800-621-2736 |
| Triumph Books, Chicago, IL | 800-335-5323 |
| Troll Communications LLC, Mahwah, NJ | 800-526-5289 |
| Turtle Point Press, Chappaqua, NY | 800-453-2992 |
| Charles E Tuttle Co. Inc., Boston, MA | (cust serv) 800-526-2778 |
| Twenty-Third Publications Inc., Mystic, CT | 800-321-0411 |
| Twin Sisters Productions Inc., Akron, OH | 800-248-8946 |
| 2 13 61 Publications Inc., Los Angeles, CA | 800-992-1361 |
| Two Thousand Three Associates, New Smyrna Beach, FL | 800-598-5256 |
| Tyndale House Publishers Inc., Wheaton, IL | 800-323-9400 |
| Type & Archetype Press, Gladwyne, PA | 800-IHS-TYPE |
| UAHC Press, New York, NY | 888-489-UAHC (8242) |
| ULI-Urban Land Institute, Washington, DC | 800-462-1254 |
| Ulysses Press, Berkeley, CA | 800-377-2542 |
| UMI, Ann Arbor, MI | 800-521-0600 |
| Unarius Academy of Science Publications, El Cajon, CA | 800-475-7062 |
| UNI Press, Campo, CA | 888-463-8654 |
| Unicor Medical Inc., Montgomery, AL | 800-825-7421 |
| Unique Publications Books & Videos, Burbank, CA | 800-332-3330 |
| United Methodist Publishing House, Nashville, TN | 800-251-3320 |
| United Nations Publications, New York, NY | 800-253-9646 |
| United Seabears Corp., Culver City, CA | 800-421-3388 |
| United States Holocaust Memorial Museum, Washington, DC | (orders) 800-259-9998 |
| United States Institute of Peace Press, Herndon, VA | (cust serv) 800-868-8064 |

| Publisher/Distributor | Toll-Free No. |
| --- | --- |
| United States Pharmacopoeial, Rockville, MD | 800-227-8772 |
| United States Tennis Association, White Plains, NY | 800-223-0456 |
| Universal Radio Research, Reynoldsburg, OH | 800-431-3939 |
| Universal Reference Publications, Boca Raton, FL | 800-377-7551 |
| University Museum of Archaeology & Anthropology, Philadelphia, PA | 800-306-1941 |
| University of Alabama Press, Tuscaloosa, AL | (orders only) 800-825-9980 |
| University of Alaska Press, Fairbanks, AK | (US only) 888-252-6657 |
| University of Arizona Press, Tucson, AZ | (orders) 800-426-3797 |
| University of Arkansas Press, Fayetteville, AR | 800-626-0090 |
| University of California Press, Berkeley, CA | 800-822-6657 |
| University of Chicago Press, Chicago, IL | (orders) 800-621-2736 |
| University of Denver Center for Teaching International Relations Publications, Denver, CO | 800-967-2847 |
| University of Georgia Press, Athens, GA | (orders only) 800-266-5842 |
| University of Hawaii Press, Honolulu, HI | 888-UHPRESS |
| University of Idaho Press, Moscow, ID | 800-847-7377 |
| University of Illinois Press, Champaign, IL | (orders) 800-545-4703 |
| University of Iowa Press, Iowa City, IA | (orders only) 800-235-2665 |
| University of Missouri Press, Columbia, MO | 800-828-1894 |
| University of Nebraska Press, Lincoln, NE | (orders) 800-755-1105 |
| University of New Mexico Press, Albuquerque, NM | (orders only) 800-249-7737 |
| University of North Carolina Press, Chapel Hill, NC | (orders only) 800-848-6224 |
| University of Notre Dame Press, Notre Dame, IN | 800-621-2736 |
| University of Oklahoma Press, Norman, OK | (orders) 800-627-7377 |
| University of Oregon ERIC Clearinghouse on Educational Management, Eugene, OR | 800-438-8841 |
| University of Pennsylvania Press, Philadelphia, PA (orders & cust service only) | 800-445-9880 |
| University of Pittsburgh Press, Pittsburgh, PA | 800-666-2211 |
| University of Tennessee Press, Knoxville, TN (warehouse, continental US except IL) | 800-621-2736 |
| University of the South Press, Sewanee, TN | 800-367-1179 |
| University of Utah Press, Salt Lake City, UT | 800-773-6672 |
| University of Washington Press, Seattle, WA | 800-441-4115 |
| University of Wisconsin Press, Madison, WI | 800-829-9559 |
| University Press of America Inc., Lanham, MD | 800-462-6420 |
| University Press of Colorado, Niwot, CO | 800-268-6044 |
| University Press of Florida, Gainesville, FL | (sales only) 800-226-3822 |
| University Press of Kentucky, Lexington, KY | 800-666-2211 |
| University Press of Mississippi, Jackson, MS | 800-737-7788 |
| University Press of New England, Hanover, NH | (orders only) 800-421-1561 |
| University Publications of America, Bethesda, MD | 800-692-6300 |
| University Publishing Group, Frederick, MD | 800-654-8188 |
| Upper Room Books, Nashville, TN | 800-972-0433 |
| USA Gymnastics, Indianapolis, IN | 800-4-USAGYM |
| US Catholic Conference, Washington, DC | 800-235-8722 |

| Publisher/Distributor | Toll-Free No. |
|---|---|
| US Games Systems Inc., Stamford, CT | 800-544-2637 (800-54GAMES) |
| Utah Geological Survey, Salt Lake City, UT | 888-UTAH-MAP |
| Utah State University Press, Logan, UT | 800-239-9974 |
| Vandamere Press, Arlington, VA | 800-551-7776 |
| VanDam Inc., New York, NY | 800-UNFOLDS |
| Vanderbilt University Press, Nashville, TN | (orders only) 800-937-5557 |
| Vanderplas Publications, San Francisco, CA | 800-468-8233 |
| Vestal Press Ltd., Lanham, MD | 800-462-6420 |
| VGM Career Horizons, Lincolnwood, IL | (orders only) 800-323-4900 |
| Virgil Hensley Publishing, Tulsa, OK | 800-288-8520 |
| Visible Ink Press, Detroit, MI | 800-776-6265 |
| Vista Publishing Inc., Long Branch, NJ | 800-634-2498 |
| Visual Education Association, Springfield, OH | (US) 800-243-7070 |
| Vital Issues Press, Lafayette, LA | 800-749-4009 |
| Volcano Press Inc., Volcano, CA | 800-879-9636 |
| Volt Directory Marketing, Ltd., Huntingdon Valley, PA | 800-897-2491 |
| Voyageur Press, Stillwater, MN | 800-888-9653 |
| Wadsworth Publishing Co., Belmont, CA | 800-354-9706 |
| George Wahr Publishing Co., Ann Arbor, MI | 800-805-2497 |
| Waite Group Press, Corte Madera, CA | 800-368-9369 |
| J Weston Walch Publisher, Portland, ME | 800-341-6094 |
| Waldman House Press, Minneapolis, MN | 888-700-PEEF |
| Walker & Co., New York, NY | 800-AT-WALKER |
| Wallace Homestead Book Co., Iola, WI | 888-457-2873 |
| Walnut Creek CDROM, Concord, CA | 800-786-9907 |
| Warner Bros Publications Inc., Miami, FL | 800-468-5010 |
| Warner Press Church of God Publications, Anderson, IN | 800-741-7721 |
| Warren, Gorham & Lamont, New York, NY | 800-922-0066 |
| Warren Publishing House, Everett, WA | 800-421-5565 |
| Washington State University Press, Pullman, WA | 800-354-7360 |
| Waterfront Books, Burlington, VT | (orders) 800-639-6063 |
| Watson-Guptill Publications, New York, NY | 800-451-1741 |
| Waverly, Inc., Baltimore, MD | 800-882-0483 |
| Wayne State University Press, Detroit, MI | 800-978-7327 |
| WCB/McGraw-Hill, Burr Ridge, IL | (cust serv) 800-338-3987 |
| Weatherhill Inc., New York, NY | 800-788-7323 |
| Weil Publishing Co. Inc., Augusta, ME | 800-877-WEIL |
| Samuel Weiser Inc., York Beach, ME | 800-423-7087 |
| Wellspring, York, PA | 800-533-3561 |
| Wesleyan University Press, Middletown, CT | 800-421-1561 |
| Westcliffe Publishers Inc., Englewood, CO | 800-523-3692 |
| Western Psychological Services, Los Angeles, CA | (US & Canada) 800-648-8857 |
| West Group, Independence, OH | 800-362-4500 |
| West Group, Rochester, NY | 800-527-0430 |
| Westminster John Knox Press, Louisville, KY | 800-227-2872 |
| WH&O International, Wellesley, MA | 800-553-6678 |

| Publisher/Distributor | Toll-Free No. |
|---|---|
| Wheatherstone Press, Portland, OR | 800-980-0077 |
| Whispering Coyote Press, Dallas, TX | 800-929-6104 |
| White Cliffs Media Inc. c/o Pathway, Gilsum, NH | 800-359-3210 |
| White Cloud Press, Ashland, OR | 800-380-8286 |
| Whitehorse Press, North Conway, NH | 800-531-1133 |
| White Mane Publishing Co. Inc., Shippensburg, PA | 888-WHT-MANE |
| White Wolf Publishing, Clarkston, GA | 800-454-WOLF |
| Albert Whitman & Co., Morton Grove, IL | 800-255-7675 |
| Whittier Publications Inc., Long Beach, NY | 800-897-TEXT |
| Whole Person Associates Inc., Duluth, MN | 800-247-6789 |
| Wichita Eagle & Beacon Publishing Co., Wichita, KS | 800-492-4043 |
| Wide World of Maps Inc., Phoenix, AZ | 800-279-7654 |
| Wilderness Adventures Press, Gallatin Gateway, MT | 800-925-3339 |
| Wilderness Press, Berkeley, CA | 800-443-7227 |
| John Wiley & Sons Inc., New York, NY | 800-CALL WILEY |
| Williams & Wilkins, Baltimore, MD | 800-638-0672 |
| Williamson Publishing Co., Charlotte, VT | 800-234-8791 |
| Willow Creek Press, Minocqua, WI | 800-850-9453 |
| H W Wilson Co., Bronx, NY | 800-367-6770 |
| Wimmer Companies/Cookbook Distribution, Memphis, TN | 800-727-1034 |
| Windsor Books, Babylon, NY | 800-321-5934 |
| Windward Publishing Inc., Miami, FL | 800-330-6232 |
| Wine Appreciation Guild Ltd., South San Francisco, CA | 800-231-9463 |
| Win Publications!, Tulsa, OK | 800-749-4597 |
| Winston-Derek Publishers Group Inc., Nashville, TN | 800-826-1888 |
| Wintergreen/Orchard House Inc., Itasca, IL | 800-323-9540 |
| Winters Publishing, Greensburg, IN | 800-457-3230 |
| Wisconsin Dept of Public Instruction, Madison, WI | 800-243-8782 |
| WJ Fantasy Inc., Bridgeport, CT | 800-ABC-PLAY |
| Woodbine House, Bethesda, MD | 800-843-7323 |
| Woodbridge Press Publishing Co., Santa Barbara, CA | 800-237-6053 |
| Woodford Press, San Francisco, CA | 800-359-3373 |
| Woodholme House Publishers, Baltimore, MD | 800-488-0051 |
| Woodland Books, Pleasant Grove, UT | 800-777-2665 |
| Wordware Publishing Inc., Plano, TX | 800-229-4949 |
| Workman Publishing Company Inc., New York, NY | 800-722-7202 |
| World Book Educational Products, Chicago, IL | 800-967-5325 |
| World Book Inc., Chicago, IL | 800-255-1750 |
| World Book Publishing, Chicago, IL | 800-255-1750 |
| World Book School and Library, Chicago, IL | (US) 800-975-3250 |
| | (Canada) 800-837-5365 |
| World Book Trade, Chicago, IL | (US) 800-255-1750, ext. 2238 |
| World Citizens, Mill Valley, CA | (orders only) 800-247-6553 |
| World Eagle, Littleton, MA | 800-854-8273 |
| World Information Technologies Inc., Northport, NY | 800-WORLD-INFO |
| World Leisure Corp., Boston, MA | 800-292-1966 |

| Publisher/Distributor | Toll-Free No. |
|---|---|
| World Music Press, Danbury, CT | 800-810-2040 |
| World Resources Institute, Washington, DC | 800-822-0504 |
| World Scientific Publishing Co. Inc., River Edge, NJ | 800-227-7562 |
| Worldtariff, San Francisco, CA | 800-556-9334 |
| Wright Group, Bothell, WA (training dept) 800-523-2371; | 800-345-6073 |
| Writer Inc., Boston, MA | 888-273-8214 |
| Writer's Digest Books, Cincinnati, OH | 800-289-0963 |
| Write Way Publishing, Aurora, CO | 800-680-1493 |
| Writings of Mary Baker Eddy/Publisher, Boston, MA | 800-288-7090 |
| Wrox Press Inc., Chicago, IL | 800-814-4527 |
| Wyndham Hall Press, Bristol, IN | 888-947-2665 |
| Wyrick & Co., Charleston, SC | 800-227-5898 |
| Yale University Press, New Haven, CT | 800-YUP-READ |
| Yardbird Books, Airville, PA | (sales) 800-622-6044 |
| YMAA Publication Center, Roslindale, MA | 800-669-8892 |
| York Press Inc., Timonium, MD | 800-962-2763 |
| Young People's Press Inc. (YPPI), San Diego, CA | 800-231-9774 |
| Yucca Tree Press, Las Cruces, NM | 800-383-6183 |
| YWAM Publishing, Seattle, WA | 800-922-2143 |
| Zagat Survey, New York, NY | 800-333-3421 |
| Zaner-Bloser Inc., Columbus, OH | 800-421-3018 |
| Zondervan Publishing House, Grand Rapids, MI | (cust serv) 800-727-1309 |

# How to Obtain an ISBN

Emery Koltay

Director Emeritus
United States ISBN Agency

The International Standard Book Numbering (ISBN) system was introduced into the United Kingdom by J. Whitaker & Sons Ltd., in 1967 and into the United States in 1968, by the R. R. Bowker Company. The Technical Committee on Documentation of the International Organization for Standardization (ISO TC 46) defines the scope of the standard as follows:

> . . . the purpose of this standard is to coordinate and standardize the use of identifying numbers so that each ISBN is unique to a title, edition of a book, or monographic publication published, or produced, by a specific publisher, or producer. Also, the standard specifies the construction of the ISBN and the location of the printing on the publication.
>
> Books and other monographic publications may include printed books and pamphlets (in various bindings), mixed media publications, other similar media including educational films/videos and transparencies, books on cassettes, microcomputer software, electronic publications, microform publications, braille publications and maps. Serial publications and music sound recordings are specifically excluded, as they are covered by other identification systems. [ISO Standard 2108]

The ISBN is used by publishers, distributors, wholesalers, bookstores, and libraries, among others, in 116 countries to expedite such operations as order fulfillment, electronic point-of-sale checkout, inventory control, returns processing, circulation/location control, file maintenance and update, library union lists, and royalty payments.

## Construction of an ISBN

An ISBN consists of 10 digits separated into the following parts:

1 Group identifier: national, geographic, language, or other convenient group
2 Publisher or producer identifier
3 Title identifier
4 Check digit

When an ISBN is written or printed, it should be preceded by the letters *ISBN,* and each part should be separated by a space or hyphen. In the United States, the hyphen is used for separation, as in the following example: ISBN 1-879500-01-9. In this example, 1 is the group identifier, 879500 is the publisher identifier, 01 is the title identifier, and 9 is the check digit. The group of English-speaking countries, which includes the United States, Australia, Canada, New Zealand, and the United Kingdom, uses the group identifiers 0 and 1.

## The ISBN Organization

The administration of the ISBN system is carried out at three levels—through the International ISBN Agency in Berlin, Germany; the national agencies; and the publishing houses themselves. Responsible for assigning country prefixes and for coordinating the worldwide implementation of the system, the International ISBN Agency in Berlin has an advisory panel that represents the International Organization for Standardization (ISO), publishers, and libraries. The International ISBN Agency publishes the *Publishers International ISBN Directory,* which is distributed in the United States by R. R. Bowker. As the publisher of *Books in Print,* with its extensive and varied database of publishers' addresses, R. R. Bowker was the obvious place to initiate the ISBN system and to provide the service to the U.S. publishing industry. To date, the U.S. ISBN Agency has entered more than 95,630 publishers into the system.

## ISBN Assignment Procedure

Assignment of ISBNs is a shared endeavor between the U.S. ISBN Agency and the publisher. The publisher is provided with an application form, an Advance Book Information (ABI) form, and an instruction sheet. After an application is received and verified by the agency, an ISBN publisher prefix is assigned, along with a computer-generated block of ISBNs. The publisher then has the responsibility to assign an ISBN to each title, to keep an accurate record of the numbers assigned by entering each title in the ISBN Log Book, and to report each title to the *Books in Print* database. One of the responsibilities of the ISBN Agency is to validate assigned ISBNs and to retain a record of all ISBNs in circulation.

ISBN implementation is very much market-driven. Wholesalers and distributors, such as Baker & Taylor, Brodart, and Ingram, as well as such large retail chains as Waldenbooks and B. Dalton recognize and enforce the ISBN system by requiring all new publishers to register with the ISBN Agency before accepting their books for sale. Also, the ISBN is a mandatory bibliographic element in the International Standard Bibliographical Description (ISBD). The Library of Congress Cataloging in Publication (CIP) Division directs publishers to the agency to obtain their ISBN prefixes.

## Location and Display of the ISBN

On books, pamphlets, and other printed material, the ISBN shall be on the verso of the title leaf or, if this is not possible, at the foot of the title leaf itself. It should also appear at the foot of the outside back cover if practicable and at the foot of the back of the jacket if the book has one (the lower right-hand corner is recommended). If neither of these alternatives is possible, then the number shall be printed in some other prominent position on the outside. The ISBN shall also appear on any accompanying promotional materials following the provisions for location according to the format of the material.

On other monographic publications, the ISBN shall appear on the title or credit frames and any labels permanently affixed to the publication. If the publication is issued in a container that is an integral part of the publication, the ISBN shall be displayed on the label. If it is not possible to place the ISBN on the item or its label, then the number should be displayed on the bottom or the back of the container, box, sleeve, or frame. It should also appear on any accompanying material, including each component of a multitype publication.

## Printing of ISBN in Machine-Readable Coding

In the last few years, much work has been done on machine-readable representations of the ISBN, and now all books should carry ISBNs in bar code. The rapid worldwide extension of bar code scanning has brought into prominence the 1980 agreement between the International Article Numbering, formerly the European Article Numbering (EAN), Association and the International ISBN Agency that translates the ISBN into an ISBN Bookland EAN bar code.

All ISBN Bookland EAN bar codes start with a national identifier (00–09 representing the United States), *except* those on books and periodicals. The agreement replaces the usual national identifier with a special "ISBN Bookland" identifier represented by the digits 978 for books (see Figure 1) and 977 for periodicals. The 978 ISBN Bookland/EAN prefix is followed by the first nine digits of the ISBN. The check digit of the ISBN is dropped and replaced by a check digit calculated according to the EAN rules.

**Figure 1  /**    Printing the ISBN in Bookland/EAN Symbology

ISBN 1 - 879500 - 01 - 9

9   781879   500013

The following is an example of the conversion of the ISBN to ISBN Bookland/EAN:

| | |
|---|---|
| ISBN | 1-879500-01-9 |
| ISBN without check digit | 1-879500-01 |
| Adding EAN flag | 978187950001 |
| EAN with EAN check digit | 9781879500013 |

## Five-Digit Add-On Code

In the United States, a five-digit add-on code is used for additional information. In the publishing industry, this code can be used for price information or some other specific coding. The lead digit of the five-digit add-on has been designated a currency identifier, when the add-on is used for price. Number 5 is the code for the U.S. dollar; 6 denotes the Canadian dollar; 1 the British pound; 3 the Australian dollar; and 4 the New Zealand dollar. Publishers that do not want to indicate price in the add-on should print the code 90000 (see Figure 2).

**Figure 2** / Printing the ISBN Bookland/EAN Number in Bar Code with the Five-Digit Add-On Code

978 = ISBN Bookland/EAN prefix
5 + Code for U.S. $
0995 = $9.95

90000 means no information
in the add-on code

## Reporting the Title and the ISBN

After the publisher reports a title to the ISBN Agency, the number is validated and the title is listed in the many R. R. Bowker hard-copy and electronic publications, including *Books in Print, Forthcoming Books, Paperbound Books in Print, Books in Print Supplement, Books Out of Print, Books in Print Online, Books in Print Plus-CD ROM, Children's Books in Print, Subject Guide to Children's Books in Print, On Cassette: A Comprehensive Bibliography of Spoken Word Audiocassettes, Variety's Complete Home Video Directory, Software Encyclopedia, Software for Schools,* and other specialized publications.

For an ISBN application form and additional information, write to United States ISBN Agency, R. R. Bowker Company, 121 Chanlon Rd., New Providence, NJ 07974, or call 908-665-6770. The e-mail address is ISBN-SAN@bowker.com. The ISBN Web site is at http://www.bowker.com/standards/.

# How to Obtain an ISSN

National Serials Data Program
Library of Congress

Two decades ago, the rapid increase in the production and dissemination of information and an intensified desire to exchange information about serials in computerized form among different systems and organizations made it increasingly clear that a means to identify serial publications at an international level was needed. The International Standard Serial Number (ISSN) was developed and has become the internationally accepted code for identifying serial publications. The number itself has no significance other than as a brief, unique, and unambiguous identifier. It is an international standard, ISO 3297, as well as a U.S. standard, ANSI/NISO Z39.9. The ISSN consists of eight digits in arabic numerals 0 to 9, except for the last, or check, digit, which can be an X. The numbers appear as two groups of four digits separated by a hyphen and preceded by the letters ISSN—for example, ISSN 1234-5679.

The ISSN is not self-assigned by publishers. Administration of the ISSN is coordinated through the ISSN Network, an intergovernmental organization within the UNESCO/UNISIST program. The network consists of national and regional centers, coordinated by the ISSN International Centre, located in Paris. Centers have the responsibility to register serials published in their respective countries.

Because serials are generally known and cited by title, assignment of the ISSN is inseparably linked to the key title, a standardized form of the title derived from information in the serial issue. Only one ISSN can be assigned to a title; if the title changes, a new ISSN must be assigned. Centers responsible for assigning ISSNs also construct the key title and create an associated bibliographic record.

The ISSN International Centre handles ISSN assignments for international organizations and for countries that do not have a national center. It also maintains and distributes the collective ISSN database that contains bibliographic records corresponding to each ISSN assignment as reported by the rest of the network. The database contains more than 900,000 ISSNs.

In the United States, the National Serials Data Program at the Library of Congress is responsible for assigning and maintaining the ISSNs for all U.S. serial titles. Publishers wishing to have an ISSN assigned can either request an application form from or send a current issue of the publication to the program and ask for an assignment. Assignment of the ISSN is free, and there is no charge for its use.

The ISSN is used all over the world by serial publishers to distinguish similar titles from each other. It is used by subscription services and libraries to manage files for orders, claims, and back issues. It is used in automated check-in systems by libraries that wish to process receipts more quickly. Copyright centers use the ISSN as a means to collect and disseminate royalties. It is also used as an identification code by postal services and legal deposit services. The ISSN is included as a verification element in interlibrary lending activities and for union catalogs as a collocating device. In recent years, the ISSN has been incorporated into bar codes for optical recognition of serial publications and into the standards for the identification of issues and articles in serial publications.

For further information about the ISSN or the ISSN Network, U.S. libraries and publishers should contact the National Serials Data Program, Library of Congress, Washington, DC 20540-4160 (202-707-6452; fax 202-707-6333; e-mail issn@loc.gov). Non-U.S. parties should contact the ISSN International Centre, 20 rue Bachaumont, 75002 Paris, France (telephone: (33 1) 44-88-22-20; fax (33 1) 40-26-32-43; e-mail issnic@issn.org).

ISSN application forms and instructions for obtaining an ISSN are also available via the Library of Congress World Wide Web Site, http://lcweb.loc.gov/issn.

# How to Obtain an SAN

Emery Koltay

Director Emeritus
United States ISBN/SAN Agency

SAN stands for Standard Address Number. It is a unique identification code for addresses of organizations that are involved in or served by the book industry, and that engage in repeated transactions with other members within this group. For purposes of this standard, the book industry includes book publishers, book wholesalers, book distributors, book retailers, college bookstores, libraries, library binders, and serial vendors. Schools, school systems, technical institutes, colleges, and universities are not members of this industry, but are served by it and therefore included in the SAN system.

The purpose of SAN is to facilitate communications among these organizations, of which there are several hundreds of thousands, that engage in a large volume of separate transactions with one another. These transactions include purchases of books by book dealers, wholesalers, schools, colleges, and libraries from publishers and wholesalers; payments for all such purchases; and other communications between participants. The objective of this standard is to establish an identification code system by assigning each address within the industry a discrete code to be used for positive identification for all book and serial buying and selling transactions.

Many organizations have similar names and multiple addresses, making identification of the correct contact point difficult and subject to error. In many cases, the physical movement of materials takes place between addresses that differ from the addresses to be used for the financial transactions. In such instances, there is ample opportunity for confusion and errors. Without identification by SAN, a complex record-keeping system would have to be instituted to avoid introducing errors. In addition, it is expected that problems with the current numbering system such as errors in billing, shipping, payments, and returns, will be significantly reduced by using the SAN system. SAN will also eliminate one step in the order fulfillment process: the "look-up procedure" used to assign account numbers. Previously a store or library dealing with 50 different publishers was assigned a different account number by each of the suppliers. SAN solved this problem. If a publisher indicates its SAN on its stationery and ordering documents, vendors to whom it sends transactions do not have to look up the account number, but can proceed immediately to process orders by SAN.

Libraries are involved in many of the same transactions as are book dealers, such as ordering and paying for books, charging and paying for various services to other libraries. Keeping records of transactions, whether these involve buying, selling, lending, or donations, entails similar operations that require a SAN. Having the SAN on all stationery will speed up order fulfillment and eliminate errors in shipping, billing, and crediting; this, in turn, means savings in both time and money.

## History

Development of the Standard Address Number began in 1968 when Russell Reynolds, general manager of the National Association of College Stores (NACS), approached the R. R. Bowker Company and suggested that a "Standard Account Number" system be implemented in the book industry. The first draft of a standard was prepared by an American National Standards Institute (ANSI) Committee Z39 subcommittee, which was co-chaired by Russell Reynolds and Emery Koltay. After Z39 members proposed changes, the current version of the standard was approved by NACS on December 17, 1979.

The chairperson of the ANSI Z39 Subcommittee 30, which developed the approved standard, was Herbert W. Bell, former senior vice president of McGraw-Hill Book Company. The subcommittee comprised the following representatives from publishing companies, distributors, wholesalers, libraries, national cooperative online systems, schools, and school systems: Herbert W. Bell (chair), McGraw-Hill Book Company; Richard E. Bates, Holt, Rinehart and Winston; Thomas G. Brady, The Baker & Taylor Companies, Paul J. Fasana, New York Public Library; Emery I. Koltay, R. R. Bowker Company; Joan McGreevey, New York University Book Centers; Pauline F. Micciche, OCLC, Inc.; Sandra K. Paul, SKP Associates; David Gray Remington, Library of Congress; Frank Sanders, Hammond Public School System; and Peter P. Chirimbes (alternate), Stamford Board of Education.

## Format

SAN consists of six digits plus a seventh *Modulus 11* check digit; a hyphen follows the third digit (XXX-XXXX) to facilitate transcription. The hyphen is to be used in print form, but need not be entered or retained in computer systems. Printed on documents, the Standard Address Number should be preceded by the identifier "SAN" to avoid confusion with other numerical codes (SAN XXX-XXXX).

## Check Digit Calculation

The check digit is based on *Modulus 11*, and can be derived as follows:

1. Write the digits of the basic number. $\qquad$ 2 3 4 5 6 7
2. Write the constant weighting factors associated with each position by the basic number. $\qquad$ 7 6 5 4 3 2
3. Multiply each digit by its associated weighting factor. $\qquad$ 14 18 20 20 18 14
4. Add the products of the multiplications. $\qquad$ $14 + 18 + 20 + 20 + 18 + 14 = 104$
5. Divide the sum by *Modulus 11* to find the remainder. $\qquad$ $104 \div 11 = 9$ plus a remainder of 5
6. Subtract the remainder from the *Modulus 11* to generate the required check digit. If there is no remainder, generate a check digit of zero. If the check digit is 10,

generate a check digit of X to represent 10,
since the use of 10 would require an extra digit. $11 - 5 = 6$

7. Append the check digit to create the standard
seven-digit Standard Address Number. SAN 234-5676

## SAN Assignment

The R. R. Bowker Company accepted responsibility for being the central administrative agency for SAN, and in that capacity assigns SANs to identify uniquely the addresses of organizations. No SANs can be reassigned; in the event that an organization should cease to exist, for example, its SAN would cease to be in circulation entirely. If an organization using SAN should move or change its name with no change in ownership, its SAN would remain the same, and only the name or address would be updated to reflect the change.

SAN should be used in all transactions; it is recommended that the SAN be imprinted on stationery, letterheads, order and invoice forms, checks, and all other documents used in executing various book transactions. The SAN should always be printed on a separate line above the name and address of the organization, preferably in the upper left-hand corner of the stationery to avoid confusion with other numerical codes pertaining to the organization, such as telephone number, zip code, and the like.

## SAN Functions and Suffixes

The SAN is strictly a Standard Address Number, becoming functional only in applications determined by the user; these may include activities such as purchasing, billing, shipping, receiving, paying, crediting, and refunding. Every department that has an independent function within an organization could have a SAN for its own identification. Users may choose to assign a suffix (a separate field) to its own SAN strictly for internal use. Faculty members ordering books through a library acquisitions department, for example, may not have their own separate SAN, but may be assigned a suffix by the library. There is no standardized provision for placement of suffixes. Existing numbering systems do not have suffixes to take care of the "subset" type addresses. The SAN does not standardize this part of the address. For the implementation of SAN, it is suggested that wherever applicable the four-position suffix be used. This four-position suffix makes available 10,000 numbers, ranging from 0000 to 9999, and will accommodate all existing subset numbering presently in use.

For example, there are various ways to incorporate SAN in an order fulfillment system. Firms just beginning to assign account numbers to their customers will have no conversion problems and will simply use SAN as the numbering system. Firms that already have an existing number system can convert either on a step-by-step basis by adopting SANs whenever orders or payments are processed on the account, or by converting the whole file by using the SAN listing provided by the SAN Agency. Using the step-by-step conversion, firms may adopt SANs as customers provide them on their forms, orders, payments, and returns.

For additional information or suggestions, please write to Diana Fumando, SAN Coordinator, ISBN/SAN Agency, R. R. Bowker Company, 121 Chanlon Rd., New Providence, NJ 07974, call 908-771-7755, or fax 908-665-2895. The e-mail address is ISBN-SAN@bowker.com. The SAN Web site is at http://www.bowker.com/standards/.

# Distinguished Books

## Best Books of 1998

The Notable Books Council of the Reference and User Services Association (RUSA), a division of the American Library Association, selected these titles for their significant contribution to the expansion of knowledge or for the pleasure they can provide to readers.

### Fiction

Anderson, Scott. *Triage*. Scribner, $23 (0-684-84695-0).

Anthony, Patricia. *Flanders*. Ace, $23.95 (0-441-00528-4).

Barrett, Andrea. *The Voyage of the Narwhal*. W. W. Norton, $24.95 (0-393-04632-X).

Borge, Jorge Luis. *Collected Fictions*. Translated by Andrew Hurley. Viking, $35 (0-670-84970-7).

Byers, Michael. *The Coast of Good Intentions*. Houghton/Mariner, paper, $12 (0-395-89170-1).

Danticat, Edwidge. *The Farming of Bones*. Soho, $23 (1-56947-126-6).

Hornby, Nick. *About a Boy*. Penguin/Riverhead, $22.95 (1-57322-087-6).

McDermott, Alice. *Charming Billy*. Farrar, $22 (0-374-12080-3).

Moore, Lorrie. *Birds of America*. Knopf, $23 (0-679-44597-8).

Roth, Philip. *I Married a Communist*. Houghton Mifflin, $26 (0-395-93346-3).

Vakil, Ardashir. *Beach Boy*. Scribner, $22 (0-684-85299-3).

### Nonfiction

Ackroyd, Peter. *The Life of Thomas More*. Doubleday, $30 (0-385-47709-0).

Berg, A. Scott. *Lindbergh*. Putnam, $30 (0-399-14449-8).

Branch, Taylor. *Pillar of Fire: America in the King Years, 1963–65*. Simon & Schuster, $30 (0-684-80819-6).

Chernow, Ron. *Titan: The Life of John D. Rockfeller, Sr.*. Random, $30 (0-679-43808-4).

Clapp, Nicholas. *The Road to Ubar: Finding the Atlantis of the Sands*. Houghton Mifflin, $24 (0-395-87596-X).

Gorney, Cynthia. *Articles of Faith: A Frontline History of the Abortion Wars*. Simon & Schuster, $27.50 (0-684-80904-4).

Hochschild, Adam. *King Leopold's Ghost: A Story of Greed, Terror, and Heroism in Colonial Africa*. Houghton Mifflin, $26 (0-395-75924-2).

Kinder, Gary. *Ship of Gold in the Deep Blue Sea*. Atlantic Monthly, $27.50 (0-87113-464-0).

Nasar, Sylvia. *A Beautiful Mind*. Simon & Schuster, $25 (0-684-81906-6).

Suskind, Ron. *A Hope in the Unseen: An American Odyssey from the Inner City to the Ivy League*. Broadway, $25 (0-7679-0125-8).

### Poetry

Doty, Mark. *Sweet Machine*. HarperFlamingo, paper, $12 (0-06-095256-3).

Hall, Donald. *Without*. Houghton Mifflin, $22 (0-395-88408-X).

Hughes, Ted. *Tales from Ovid*. Farrar, $25 (0-374-22841-8).

Matthews, William. *After All: Last Poems*. Houghton Mifflin, $20 (0-395-91340-3).

# Best Young Adult Books

Each January a committee of the Young Adult Library Services Association (YALSA), a division of the American Library Association, compiles a list of best books published for young adults in the preceding 16 months, selected for their proven or potential appeal to the personal reading taste of the young adult.

Abelove, Joan. *Go and Come Back.* DK Ink.

Alabisco, Vincent, ed. *Flash! The Associated Press Covers the World.* Harry N. Abrams.

Arnoldi, Katherine. *The Amazing True Story of a Teenage Single Mom.* Hyperion.

Bauer, Joan. *Rules of the Road.* Putnam.

Bennett, Cherie. *Life in the Fat Lane.* Delacorte.

Blackwood, Gary. *The Shakespeare Stealer.* Dutton.

Bolden, Tonya, ed. *33 Things Every Girl Should Know.* Crown.

Burgess, Melvin. *Smack.* Holt.

Clinton, Catherine. *I, Too, Sing America: African American Poetry.* Houghton Mifflin.

Colman, Penny. *Corpses, Coffins, and Crypts: A History.* Holt.

Cormier, Robert. *Heroes.* Delacorte.

Dessen, Sarah. *Someone Like You.* Viking.

Farrell, Jeanette. *Invisible Enemies: Stories of Infectious Diseases.* Farrar, Straus & Giroux.

Ferris, Jean. *Love Among the Walnuts.* Harcourt Brace.

Flake, Sharon G. *The Skin I'm In.* Hyperion.

Fleischman, Paul. *Whirligig.* Holt.

Fletcher, Susan. *Shadow Spinner.* Atheneum.

Freedman, Russell. *Martha Graham: A Dancer's Life.* Clarion.

Griffin, Adele. *The Other Shepards.* Hyperion.

Haddix, Margaret. *Among the Hidden.* Simon & Schuster.

Hardman, Ric Lynden. *Sunshine Rider: The First Vegetarian Western.* Delacorte.

Helfer, Ralph. *Modoc.* Harper Collins.

Hesser, Terry Spencer. *Kissing Doorknobs.* Delacorte.

Hill, Ernest. *A Life for a Life.* Simon & Schuster.

Hobbs, Will. *The Maze.* Morrow.

Holt, Kimberly Willis. *My Louisiana Sky.* Holt.

Jimenez, Francisco. *The Circuit: Stories from the Life of a Migrant Child.* University of New Mexico Press.

Johnson, Angela. *Heaven.* Simon & Schuster.

Koller, Jackie French. *The Falcon.* Atheneum.

Larson, Gary. *There's a Hair in My Dirt: A Worm's Story.* HarperCollins.

Lawrence, Iain. *The Wreckers.* Delacorte.

Laxalt, Robert. *Dust Devils.* University of Nevada Press.

Lester, Julius. *From Slave Ship to Freedom Road.* Dial Books.

Lobel, Anita. *No Pretty Pictures: A Child of War.* Greenwillow.

McCaughrean, Geraldine. *The Pirate's Son.* Scholastic.

McKee, Tim/Blackshaw, Anne. *No More Strangers Now: Young Voices from a New South Africa.* DK.

McKissack, Patricia. *Young, Black, and Determined: A Biography.* Holiday House.

Marrin, Albert. *Commander-in-Chief.* Dutton.

Mastoon, Adam. *The Shared Heart.* Morrow.

Matcheck, Diane. *The Sacrifice.* Farrar, Straus & Giroux.

Mikaelson, Ben. *Petey.* Hyperion.

Napoli, Donna Jo. *Sirena.* Scholastic.

Newth, Mette. *The Dark Light.* Farrar, Straus & Giroux.

Nicholson, Joy. *Tribes of Palos Verdes.* St. Martin's Press.

Nye, Naomi Shihab. *The Space Between Our Footsteps.* Simon & Schuster.

Paulsen, Gary. *Soldier's Heart.* Delacorte.

Peck, Richard. *A Long Way from Chicago.* Dial.

Peck, Richard. *Strays Like Us.* Dial.

Philip, Neil. *War and the Pity of War*. Clarion.

Porter, Tracey. *Treasures in the Dust*. HarperCollins.

Potok, Chaim. *Zebra and Other Stories*. Knopf.

Quarles, Heather. *A Door Near Here*. Delacorte.

Ritter, John H. *Choosing Up Sides*. Philomel.

Rottman, S. L. *Hero*. Peachtree.

Rowling, J. K. *Harry Potter and the Sorcerer's Stone*. Scholastic Press/Levine.

Sachar, Louis. *Holes*. Farrar, Straus & Giroux.

Salisbury, Graham. *Jungle Dogs*. Delacorte.

Silvey, Anita, selector. *Help Wanted: Short Stories About Young People Working*. Little, Brown.

Spinelli, Jerry. *Knots in My Yo-yo String*. Knopf.

Springer, Nancy. *I Am Mordred*. Philomel.

Sweeney, Joyce. *Spirit Window*. Delacorte.

Thomas, Jane Resh. *Behind the Mask: The Life of Queen Elizabeth I*. Clarion.

Thomas, Velma Maia. *Lest We Forget: The Passage from Africa to Slavery and Emancipation*. Crown.

Turner, Ann. *A Lion's Hunger: Poems of First Love*. Marshall Cavendish.

Walter, Virginia. *Making Up Megaboy*. DK Ink.

Weaver, Will. *Hard Ball*. Harper.

Werlin, Nancy. *The Killer's Cousin*. Delacorte.

Willis, Connie. *To Say Nothing of the Dog*. Bantam.

Wilson, Diane. *I Rode a Horse of Milk White Jade*. Orchard.

Woodson, Jacqueline. *If You Come Softly*. Putnam.

Yolen, Jane, and Bruce Coville. *Armageddon Summer*. Harcourt Brace.

# Notable Children's Videos

These titles are selected by a committee of the Association for Library Service to Children (ALSC), a division of the American Library Association. Recommendations are based on originality, creativity, and suitability for young children. The members select materials that respect both children's intelligence and imagination, exhibit venturesome creativity, and encourage the interests of users.

*Chrysanthemum*. 15 min. Produced by Weston Woods, distributed by Scholastic. $60. Ages 3–10.

*Dance Lexie, Dance*. 15 min. Produced by Tim Loane, distributed by Cinema Guild. $59.95. Ages 8–12.

*Elmopalooza!* 30 min. Produced by Children's Television Workshop, distributed by Sony Wonder. $12.98. All ages.

*The First Christmas*. 21 min. Produced by Billy Budd Films Inc. Age 5 and up.

*Good Night, Gorilla*. 8 min. Produced by Weston Woods, distributed by Scholastic. Ages 4–8.

*Kristen's Fairy House*. 39 min. Produced and distributed by Great White Dog Picture Co. $19.95. Ages 7–11.

*Land Snails and Their Life Cycle*. 12 min. Produced and distributed by Klaudiusz Jankowski Productions. $80. Age 9 and up.

*Oceans in Motion*. 24 min. Produced and distributed by National Geographic. $99. Age 7 and up.

*Sheep Crossing*. 27 min. Produced and distributed by Great White Dog Picture Co. $14.95. All ages.

*Smoking: Truth or Dare*. 52 min. Produced by Arnold Shapiro, distributed by AIMS. Age 10 and up.

# Best Children's Books

A list of notable children's books is selected each year by the Notable Children's Books Committee of the Association for Library Service to Children (ALSC), a division of the American Library Association. Recommended titles are selected by children's librarians and educators based on originality, creativity, and suitability for children. [See "Literary Prizes, 1998" in Part 6 for Caldecott, Newbery, and other award winners.—*Ed.*].

## Books for Younger Readers

Alda, Arlene. *Arlene Alda's 1 2 3*. Tricycle Press.

Babbitt, Natalie. *Ouch! A Tale from Grimm*. Illus. by Fred Marcellino. HarperCollins/Michael di Capua Books.

Banks, Kate. *And If the Moon Could Talk*. Illus. by Georg Hallensleben. Farrar, Straus & Giroux/Frances Foster.

Feiffer, Jules. *I Lost My Bear*. Morrow Junior Books.

Fleming, Denise. *Mama Cat Has Three Kittens*. Holt.

Heap, Sue. *Cowboy Baby*. Candlewick Press.

Hurd, Thatcher. *Zoom City*. HarperFestival.

Krensky, Stephen. *How Santa Got His Job*. Illus. by S. D. Schindler. Simon & Schuster.

Kvasnosky, Laura McGee. *Zelda and Ivy*. Candlewick Press

Rathmann, Peggy. *10 Minutes Till Bedtime*. Putnam.

San Souci, Robert D. *Cendrillon: A Caribbean Cinderella*. Illus. by Brian Pinkney. Simon & Schuster

Shannon, David. *No, David!* Scholastic/The Blue Sky Press.

Shulevitz, Uri. *Snow*. Farrar, Straus & Giroux.

Sis, Peter. *Fire Truck*. Greenwillow.

Steig, William. *Pete's a Pizza*. HarperCollins/Michael di Capua Books.

Stuve-Bodeen, Stephanie. *Elizabeti's Doll*. Illus. by Christy Hale. Lee & Low Books.

Winter, Jeanette. *My Name Is Georgia*. Harcourt Brace/Silver Whistle.

## Books for Middle Readers

Carlson, Laurie. *Boss of the Plains: The Hat that Won the West*. Illus. by Holly Meade. DK Ink.

Deem, James M. *Bodies From the Bog*. Houghton Mifflin.

Enzensberger, Hans Magnus. *The Number Devil: A Mathematical Adventure*. Translated by Michael Henry Heim. Holt/Metropolitan.

Fleischman, Sid. *Bandit's Moon*. Greenwillow.

Gantos, Jack. *Joey Pigza Swallowed the Key*. Farrar, Straus & Giroux.

Gerstein, Mordicai. *The Wild Boy*. Farrar, Straus & Giroux/Frances Foster.

Gollub, Matthew. *Cool Melons—Turn to Frogs: The Life and Poems of Issa*. Illus. by Kazuko G. Stone. Lee & Low Books.

Greenberg, Jan, and Sandra Jordan. *Chuck Close, Up Close*. DK Ink.

McCully, Emily Arnold. *Beautiful Warrior: The Legend of the Nun's Kung Fu*. Scholastic/Arthur A. Levine.

Martin, Jacqueline Briggs. *Snowflake Bentley*. Illus. by Mary Azarian. Houghton Mifflin.

Morgenstern, Susie Hoch. *Secret Letters from 0-10*. Translated by Gill Rosner. Viking.

Pinkney, Andrea Davis. *Duke Ellington: The Piano Prince and His Orchestra*. Illus. by Brian Pinkney. Hyperion.

Poole, Josephine. *Joan of Arc*. Illus. by Angela Barrett. Knopf.

Rowling, J. K. *Harry Potter and the Sorcer-er's Stone*. Illus. by Mary Grandpre. Scholastic/Arthur A. Levine.

Santiago, Chiori. *Home to Medicine Mountain*. Illus. by Judith Lowry. Children's Book Press.

Schwartz, David M. *G Is for Googol: A Math Alphabet Book*. Illus. by Marissa Moss. Tricycle Press.

Stanley, Diane. *Joan of Arc*. Morrow Junior Books.

Thomas, Joyce Carol. *I Have Heard of a Land*. Illus. by Floyd Cooper. Harper-Collins/Joanna Cotler.

## Books for Older Readers

Abelove, Joan. *Go and Come Back*. DK Ink.

Armstrong, Jennifer. *Shipwreck at the Bottom of the World: The Extraordinary True Story of Shackleton and the Endurance*. Crown.

Bauer, Joan. *Rules of the Road*. Putnam.

Blackwood, Gary. *The Shakespeare Stealer*. Dutton.

Fletcher, Susan. *Shadow Spinner*. Atheneum/Jean Karl.

Freedman, Russell. *Martha Graham: A Dancer's Life*. Clarion.

Griffin, Adele. *The Other Shepards*. Hyperion.

Holt, Kimberly Willis. *My Louisiana Sky*. Holt.

Lobel, Anita. *No Pretty Pictures: A Child of War*. Greenwillow.

McCaughrean, Geraldine. *The Pirate's Son*. Scholastic.

McKee, Tim. *No More Strangers Now: Young Voices from a New South Africa*. Photographs by Anne Blackshaw. DK Ink.

Murphy, Jim. *Gone-a-Whaling: The Lure of the Sea and the Hunt for the Great Whale*. Clarion.

Partridge, Elizabeth. *Restless Spirit: The Life and Work of Dorothea Lange*. Viking.

Peck, Richard. *A Long Way from Chicago: A Novel in Stories*. Dial.

Rabinovici, Schoschana. *Thanks to My Mother*. Translated by James Skofield. Dial.

Sachar, Louis. *Holes*. Farrar, Straus & Giroux/Frances Foster.

Walter, Virginia. *Making Up Megaboy*. Illus. by Katrina Roeckelein. DK Ink/Richard Jackson.

Wolff, Virginia Euwer. *Bat 6*. Scholastic.

## Books for All Ages

Browne, Anthony. *Voices in the Park*. DK Ink.

Burleigh, Robert. *Home Run*. Illus. by Mike Wimmer. Harcourt Brace.

Florian, Douglas. *Insectlopedia*. Harcourt Brace.

Guthrie, Woody. *This Land Is Your Land*. Illus. by Kathy Jakobsen. Little, Brown.

Igus, Toyomi. *I See the Rhythm*. Illus. by Michele Wood. Children's Book Press.

Marcus, Leonard. *A Caldecott Celebration: Six Artists Share Their Paths to the Caldecott Medal*. Walker.

Sis, Peter. *Tibet: Through the Red Box*. Farrar, Straus & Giroux/Frances Foster.

Van Lann, Nancy. *With a Whoop and a Holler: A Bushel of Lore from Way Down South*. Illus. by Scott Cook. Atheneum/Anne Schwartz.

Weitzman, Jacqueline Preiss. *You Can't Take a Balloon in the Metropolitan Museum*. Illus. by Robin Preiss Glasser. Dial.

Wick, Walter. *Walter Wick's Optical Tricks*. Scholastic/Cartwheel Books.

# Notable Recordings for Children

This list of notable recordings for children was selected by the Association for Library Service to Children (ALSC), a division of the American Library Association. Recommended titles, many of which are recorded books, are chosen by children's librarians and educators on the basis of their originality, creativity, and suitability. Selections are cassettes unless otherwise indicated.

"Autumnsongs." Performed by John McCutcheon. 44 min. Rounder Records. $9.98. CD, $14.98.

"Back on Broadway." Performed by the Broadway Kids. 42 min. Lightyear Entertainment. $9.98. CD, $15.98.

"Ben's Trumpet." Performed by Charles Turner and jazz musicians. 6.5 minutes. Live Oak Media. Book and cassette, $15.95.

"The Best Christmas Pageant Ever." Performed by C. J. Critt. Recorded Books Inc. 2 hours. 2 cassettes, $18.

"Chrysanthemum." Performed by Meryl Streep. 14 min. Weston Woods Studios Inc. Book and cassette, $12.95.

"Door in the Wall." Performed by Roger Rees. 3 hours. Bantam Doubleday Dell Audio Publishing. 2 cassettes, $16.99.

"Eleanor Roosevelt." Performed by Barbara Caruso. Recorded Books Inc. 3 hours, 45 min. 3 cassettes, $26.

"Elmopalooza!" Performed by Sesame Street characters and various artists. Sony Wonder. 40 min. $9.98. CD, $13.98.

"40 Winks." Performed by Jessica Harper. Alacazam! 38 min. $9.98. CD, $11.98.

"Freak the Mighty." Performed by Elden Henson. Listening Library Inc. 3 hours, 16 min. 2 cassettes, $16.98.

"The Gardener." Performed by Bonnie Kelly-Young. Live Oak Media. 11 min. Book and cassette, $22.95.

"The Great Fire." Performed by John McDonough. Recorded Books Inc. 3 hours. 3 cassettes, $26.

"If Fish Could Sing . . . " Performed by Teresa Doyle. Bedlam Records. 38 min. $9.98. CD, $13.98.

"In My Hometown." Performed by Tom Chapin. Sony Wonder. 40 min. $9.98. CD, $13.98.

"Jacob Have I Loved." Performed by Christina Moore. Recorded Books Inc. 5.75 hours. 4 cassettes, $34.

"Jazz-A-Ma-Tazz." Performed by Hayes Greenfield and others. Baby Music Boom Inc. 47 min. $10.98. CD, $15.98.

"John Henry." Performed by Samuel L. Jackson. Weston Woods Studios Inc. 18 min. Book and cassette, $12.95.

"Joyful Noise." Performed by B. Caruso, J. MCDonough, C. Moore, and J. Woodman. Recorded Books Inc. 20 min. $10.

"Leon's Story." Performed by Graham Brown. Recorded Books Inc. 1.25 hours. $10.

"Moorchild." Performed by Virginia Leishman. Recorded Books Inc. 6 hours. 5 cassettes, $42.

"Norwegian Tales of Enchantment." Performed by Judith Simundson. Makoche Recording Co. 63 min. CD, $15.95.

"Rascal." Performed by Jim Weiss. Listening Library Inc. 4 hours 41 min. 3 cassettes, $23.98.

"Rudy and the Roller Skate." Performed by Dan Keding. Turtle Creek Recordings. 1 hour. $10.

"Running Out of Time." Performed by Kimberly Schraf. Listening Library Inc. 5 hours 23 min. 4 cassettes, $29.98.

"Sarny: A Life Remembered." Performed by Lynne Thigpen. Recorded Books Inc. 4.25 hours. 3 cassettes, $26.

"The Silver Chair." BBC Radio Dramatization. Bantam Doubleday Dell Audio Publishing. 3 hours. 2 cassettes, $16.99.

"Swingin' in the Rain." Performed by Maria Muldaur. Music for Little People. 41 min. $9.98. CD, $15.98.

"Under the Green Corn Moon: Native American Lullabies." Performed by various Native American artists. Silver Wave Records. 50 min. $9.98. CD, $15.98.

"Under the Mango Tree: Stories from Spanish Speaking Countries." Performed by Elida Guardia Bonet. Zarati Press. 72 min. $12.

"World Tales, Live at Bennington College." Performed by Tim Jennings and Leanne Ponder. Eastern Coyote. 1 hour. $10. CD, $15.

# Notable Software and Web Sites for Children

These lists are chosen by committees of the Association for Library Service to Children (ALSC), a division of the American Library Association.

## Software

*Carmen Sandiego Math Detective.* Broderbund Software Inc. Windows 95/Power Macintosh. $34.95. Age 9 and up.

*Dr. Seuss Kindergarten.* Broderbund Software Inc. Window 95/98. $19.95. Ages 4–6.

*Dr. Seuss Preschool.* Broderbund Software Inc. Windows 95/98. $19.95. Ages 4–6.

*Encarta 99.* Microsoft Corp. Windows 95/98 (Mac version available by Web download). $69.95.

## Web Sites

At the Tomb of Tutankhamen
http://www.nationalgeographic.com/egypt/
index.html

Audrey Wood's Website
http://www.audreywood.com

Bill Nye the Science Guy's Nye Labs Online
http://www.nyelabs.com/flash_go.html

FunBrain.com
http://www.funbrain.com/

Kids' Castle
http://www.kidscastle.si.edu

Kinetic City Cyber Club
http://www.kineticcity.com

The Moonlit Road
http://www.themoonlitroad.com/
welcome001.html

National Zoo (Washington, DC)
http://www.si.edu/natzoo/

Redwall: The Brian Jacques Home Page
http://www.redwall.org/dave/jacques.html

Salem
http://www.nationalgeographic.com/
features/97/salem/

SchoolHouse Rock
http://genxtvland.simplenet.com/
SchoolHouseRock/index-hi.shtml

UNICEF Voices of Youth
http://www.unicef.org/voy/

Yuckiest Site on the Internet
http://www.nj.com/yucky/index.html

Zoom Dinosaurs
http://www.zoomdinosaurs.com/

# Quick Picks for Reluctant Young Adult Readers

The Young Adult Library Services Association (YALSA), a division of the American Library Association, annually chooses a list of outstanding titles that will stimulate the interest of reluctant teen readers. The list is intended for the teenager who, for whatever reason, does not like to read.

## Nonfiction

Alabiso, Vincent, Kelly Smith Tunney, and Chuck Zoelle. *Flash! The Associated Press Covers the World.* 200p. Harry N. Abrams Inc. $39.95. 0-8109-1974-5. Hardcover.

Arnoldi, Katherine. *The Amazing "True" Story of a Teenage Single Mom.* 192p. Hyperion. $16. 0-7868-6420-6. Hardcover.

Ash, Russell. *The Top 10 of Everything: 1998.* 256p. DK Publishing Inc. $17.95. 0-7894-2082-1. Paperback. $24.95. 0-7894-2199-2. Hardcover.

Ballard, Robert D., and Rick Archbold. *Ghost Liners: Exploring the World's Greatest Lost Ships.* 62p. Little, Brown/Madison Press. $18.95. 0-316-08020-9. Hardcover.

Boitano, Brian, and Suzanne Harper. *Boitano's Edge: Inside the Real World of Figure Skating.* 97p. Simon & Schuster. $25. 0-689-81915-3. Hardcover.

Deem, James M. *Bodies from the Bog.* 42p. Houghton Mifflin. $16. 0-395-85784-8. Hardcover.

Elffers, Joost. *Play with Your Food.* 109p. Stewart Tabori & Chang. $24.95. 1-55678-638-8. Hardcover.

Guzzetti, Paula. *Jim Carrey.* 63p. Dillon Press. $22. 0-382-39730-4. Library Binding. $10. 0-382-39731-2. Paperback.

Hamilton, Jake. *Special Effects in Film and Television.* 63p. DK. $17.95. 0-7894-2813-X. Hardcover.

Jacobs, Thomas A. *What Are My Rights?* 198p. Free Spirit. $14.95. 1-57542-028-7. Paperback.

Jenkins, Martin. *Informania: Vampires.* 88p. Candlewick Press. $15.99. 0-7636-0315-5. Spiral bound.

Kilcher, Jewel. *A Night Without Armor: Poems.* 139p. HarperCollins. $15. 0-06-019198-8. Hardcover.

Kahl, Jonathan. *National Audubon Society First Field Guide: Weather.* 157p. Scholastic. $10.95. 0-590-05488-0. Paperback. $17.95. 0-590-05469-4. Hardcover.

Masoff, Joy. *Fire!* 47p. Scholastic. $16.95. 0-590-97872-1. Hardcover. 0-590-97585-4. Paperback.

Maynard, Christopher. *Informania: Sharks.* 92p. Candlewick Press. $14.99. 0-7636-0328-7. Spiral bound.

Newson, Lesley. *Devastation: The World's Worst Natural Disasters.* 159p. DK. $24.95. 0-7894-3518-7. Hardcover.

Packer, Alex J. *How Rude! The Teenager's Guide to Good Manners, Proper Behavior and Not Grossing People Out.* 448p. Free Spirit. $19.95. 1-57542-024-4. Paperback.

Paulsen, Gary. *My Life in Dog Years.* 137p. Delacorte. $15.95. 0-385-32570-3. Hardcover.

Pfetzer, Mark, and Jack Galvin. *Within Reach: My Everest Story.* 160p. Dutton. $16.99. 0-525-46089-6. Hardcover.

Pratt, Jane. *Beyond Beauty.* 159p. Clarkson Potter. $30. 0-609-80148-1. Paperback.

Reynolds, David West. *Star Wars: Incredible Cross-Sections.* 32p. DK $19.95. 0-7894-3480-6. Hardcover.

Reynolds, David West. *Star Wars: The Visual Dictionary.* 64p. DK $19.95. 0-7894-3481-4. Hardcover.

*Rolling Stone: The Complete Covers 1967–1997.* 273p. Abrams. $39.95. 0-8109-3797-2. Hardcover.

Squires, K. M. *NSYNC: The Official Book.* 80p. Bantam Doubleday Dell. $9.95. 0-440-41636-1. Paperback.

Tanaka, Shelley. *Lost Temple of the Aztecs.* 47p. Hyperion. $16.95. 0-7858-0441-6. Hardcover.

Turner, Ann. *A Lion's Hunger: Poems of First Love.* 47p. Marshall Cavendish. $14.95. 0-7614-5035-1. Hardcover.

Wick, Walter. *Optical Tricks.* 41p. Scholastic. $13.95. 0-590-22227-9. Hardcover.

Williams, Stanley "Tookie." *Life in Prison.* 80p. Morrow. $15. 0-688-15589-8. Hardcover.

# Fiction

Bauer, Joan. *Rules of the Road.* 201p. Putnam. $15.99. 0-399-23140-4. Hardcover.

Block, Francesca Lia. *I Was a Teenage Fairy.* 160p. HarperCollins. $14.95. 0-06-027748-3. Hardcover. $14.89. 0-06-027748-3. Library Binding.

Butts, Nancy. *The Door in the Lake.* 157p. Front Street Books. $15.95. 1-686910-27-8. Hardcover.

Conford, Ellen. *Crush.* 138p. HarperCollins. $14.95. 0-06-025414-9. Hardcover. $14.89. 0-06-025415-7. Library Binding. $4.95. 0-06-440778-0. Paperback.

Cormier, Robert. *Heroes.* 135p. Delacorte. $15.95. 0-385-32590-8. Hardcover.

Cray, Jordan. *Gemini7.* (Book 1 of the danger.com series). 202p. Aladdin Paperbacks. $0.99. 0-689-81432-1. Paperback.

Danziger, Paula, and Ann M. Martin. *P.S. Longer Letter Later.* 234p. Scholastic. $15.95. 0-590-21310-5. Hardcover.

Dessen, Sarah. *Someone Like You.* 281p. Viking. $15.99. 0-670-87778-6. Hardcover.

Ewing, Lynne. *Party Girl.* 110p. Knopf. $16. 0-679-89285-0. Hardcover. 0-679-99285-5. Library Binding.

Ferris, Jean. *Bad.* 192p. Farrar, Straus & Giroux. $16. 0-374-30479-3. Hardcover.

Flake, Sharon G. *The Skin I'm In.* 171p. Hyperion. $14.95. 0-7868-0444-0. Hardcover. $15.49. 0-7868-2392-5. Library Binding.

Fraustino, Lisa Rowe, ed. *Dirty Laundry: Stories About Family Secrets.* Hardcover. 181p. Viking. $16.99. 0-670-87911-8.

Glovach, Linda. *Beauty Queen.* 176p. HarperCollins. $14.95. 0-06-205161-X. Hardcover.

Grant, Cynthia D. *The White Horse.* 157p. Atheneum/Simon & Schuster. $16. 0-689-82127-1. Hardcover.

Hautman, Pete. *Stone Cold.* 163p. Simon & Schuster. $16. 0-689-81759-2. Hardcover.

Hesser, Terry Spencer. *Kissing Doorknobs.* 149p. Delacorte. $15.95. 0-385-32329-8.

Hobbs, Will. *The Maze.* 198p. Morrow. $15. 0-688-15092-6. Hardcover.

Hoh, Diane. *Titanic: The Long Night.* 371p. Scholastic. $4.99. 0-590-33123-X. Paperback.

Kaye, Marilyn. *Amy Number Seven: Replica Series.* 202p. Bantam. $0.99. 0-553-49238-1. Paperback.

Kaye, Marilyn. *Last on Earth Book One: The Vanishing.* 174p. Avon. $4.99. 0-380-79832-8. Paperback.

Kerven, Rosalind. *King Arthur.* Eyewitness Classics Series. 64p. DK. $14.95. 0-7894-2887-3. Hardcover.

Larson, Gary. *There's a Hair in My Dirt.* HarperCollins. $15.95. 0-06-019104-X. Hardcover.

Lawrence, Iain. *The Wreckers.* 196p. Delacorte. $15.95. 0-385-432535-5. Hardcover.

Lerangis, Peter. *Last Stop: Watchers.* 159p. Apple/Scholastic. $3.99. 0-590-10996-0. Paperback.

Lott, Bret. *The Hunt Club.* 243p. Villard Books. $23. 0-375-59914-6. Hardcover.

Martin, Ann M. *Amalia: California Diaries #4.* Scholastic. $3.99. 0-590-29838-0. Paperback.

McDaniel, Lurlene. *Till Death Do Us Part.* 214p. Bantam. $4.50. 0-553-57085-4. Paperback.

Myers, Anna. *Ethan Between Us.* 153p. Walker. $15.95. 0-8027-8670-7. Hardcover.

Nixon, Joan Lowery. *The Haunting.* 184p. Delacorte. $15.95. 0-385-32247-X. Hardcover.

Paulsen, Gary. *Soldier's Heart.* 106p. Delacorte. $15.95. 0-385-32498-7. Hardcover.

Paulsen, Gary. *The Transall Saga.* 248p. Delacorte. $15.95. 0-385-43196-1. Hardcover.

Pierce, Tamora. *Tris's Book.* 256p. Scholastic. $15.95. 0-590-55357-7. Hardcover.

Preston, Richard. *The Cobra Event.* 404p. Random House. $25.95. 0-679-45714-3. Hardcover. Ballantine. $7.99. 0-345-40997-3. Paperback.

Pullman, Philip. *Clockwork.* Scholastic/Arthur A. Levine. $14.95. 0-590-12999-6. Hardcover.

*Read For Your Life: Tales of Survival.* 160p. Millbrook Press. $22.40. 0-7613-0362-6. Library Binding. 0-7613-0344-8. Paperback.

Rottman, S. L. *Rough Waters*. 179p. Peachtree. $14.95. 1-56145-172-X.

Sachar, Louis. *Holes*. 233p. Farrar, Straus & Giroux. $16. 0-374-332655. Hardcover.

Saul, John. *The Presence*. 338p. Fawcett. $25. 0-449-91055-5. Hardcover. $7.99. 0-449-00241-1. Paperback.

Sleator, William. *The Boxes*. 196p. Dutton. 0-525-46012-8. Hardcover.

Smith, Roland. *Sasquatch*. 188p. Hyperion. $15.95. 0-7868-0368-1. $16.49. 0-7868-2315-1. Library Binding.

Soto, Gary. *Petty Crimes*. 157p. Harcourt Brace. $16. 0-15-201658-9. Hardcover.

Vande Velde, Vivian. *Ghost of a Hanged Man*. 95p. Marshall Cavendish. $14.95. 0-7614-5015-7. Hardcover.

Warner, Sally. *Sort of Forever*. 136p. Knopf. $16. 0-679-88648-6. Hardcover. $17.99. 0-679-98648-0. Library Binding.

Werlin, Nancy. *The Killer's Cousin*. 227p. Delacorte. 0-385-32560-6. Hardcover.

Yolen, Jane, and Bruce Coville. *Armageddon Summer*. 272p. Harcourt Brace. $17. 0-15-201767-4. Hardcover.

Zindel, Paul. *Reef of Death*. 177p. Harper-Collins. $15.95. 0-06-024728-2. $15.89. 0-06-024733-9. Library Binding.

# Bestsellers of 1998

## Hardcover Bestsellers: The Name Makes the Game

Daisy Maryles
Executive Editor, *Publishers Weekly*

If one had to pick a single word that best describes the 1998 crop of bestsellers, it would be "predictable." Second choice would be "commercial," and third—you'd need three words here—"name-brand recognition."

Looking at fiction's top 30, almost all the authors are repeaters and many claimed the same positions as in previous years. John Grisham is again in the number one spot (his place on these year-end lists since 1994), and Danielle Steel again takes three of the top 10. Tom Clancy, Stephen King, Patricia Cornwell, Sidney Sheldon, Anne Rice, and Mary Higgins Clark dominate the top 15—which they have done many, many times. Two names new to this roster are Toni Morrison and Wally Lamb, but here, too, the reason is predictable—both were Oprah Book Club picks.

While some of the first fiction from 1997—*Cold Mountain* and *Memoirs of a Geisha*—continued to shine on the 1998 weekly charts, only two first novels published last year enjoyed sales of 100,000 or more and only one, *Numbered Account* by Christopher Reich, actually made the weekly lists. There was more contemporary women's fiction among the books that sold over 100,000 and a greater number of romance authors moved successfully from paperback to hardcover. Mysteries, suspense, and thrillers are plentiful on this year-end list; here, too, many of the names—James Patterson, Sue Grafton, Dean Koontz, Ken Follett, to mention just a few—are recognized denizens of these annual charts.

Predictable, commercial, and having the right name also characterize 1998's nonfiction bestsellers. Even the new author names on these lists are writing about familiar categories. Business, diet, and self-help titles are prominent on the top 30 and plentiful among the top sellers with sales of more than 100,000. Books with spiritual and religious messages also abound, from evangelical Christians (Max Lucado, T.D. Jakes) to more New Age authors (James Van Praagh, Neale Donald Walsch).

There are five books in the top 30 that carried over from 1996 and 1997, four of them among the top 15. Two went out the publishers' doors with modest first printings in the low five-figure range. Frank McCourt's *Angela's Ashes* (Scribner) now boasts total sales of about 2.5 million with a little over 500,000 rung up in 1998. Mitch Albom's *Tuesdays with Morrie* (Doubleday) is in its 15th month and is still on the top third of *PW*'s weekly lists.

Retrospectives on the 20th century were popular, but the titles that went to the top were written by well-known TV newscasters Tom Brokaw and Peter Jennings. Check out the authors of the top-selling nonfiction. A good portion of them are by celebrities from entertainment and sports arenas—Jimmy Buffett, Michael Jordan, Emeril Lagasse, Cokie Roberts, and Steve Martin, to name just a few. And books about Princess Diana and the Clinton White House also racked up big numbers—expect more on these topics in the 1999 lineup.

Adapted from *Publishers Weekly*, March 29, 1999

# Publishers Weekly 1998 Bestsellers

## FICTION

1. **The Street Lawyer** by John Grisham. Doubleday (2/98) \*\*2,550,000
2. **Rainbow Six** by Tom Clancy. Putnam (8/98) 2,000,000
3. **Bag of Bones** by Stephen King. Scribner (9/98) 1,496,520
4. **A Man in Full** by Tom Wolfe. Farrar, Straus & Giroux (11/98) 1,260,000
5. **Mirror Image** by Danielle Steel. Delacorte (11/98) 1,187,877
6. **The Long Road Home** by Danielle Steel. Delacorte (4/98) 1,161,229
7. **The Klone and I** by Danielle Steel. Delacorte (6/98) 1,152,681
8. **Point of Origin** by Patricia Cornwell. Putnam (7/98) 1,000,000
9. **Paradise** by Toni Morrison. Knopf (1/98) 804,862
10. **All Through the Night** by Mary Higgins Clark. S&S (10/98) \*\*775,000
11. **I Know This Much Is True** by Wally Lamb. HarperCollins/ReganBooks (5/98) 756,051
12. **Tell Me Your Dreams** by Sidney Sheldon. Morrow (8/98) 690,441
13. **The Vampire Armand** by Anne Rice. Knopf (10/98) 660,780
14. **The Loop** by Nicholas Evans. Delacorte (9/98) 649,087
15. **You Belong to Me** by Mary Higgins Clark. S&S (4/98) \*\*600,000

## NONFICTION

1. **The 9 Steps to Financial Freedom:** by Suze Orman. Crown (4/97) \*1,470,865
2. **The Greatest Generation** by Tom Brokaw. Random House (12/98) 1,423,863
3. **Sugar Busters!** by H. Leighton Steward, Morrison C. Bethea, Sam S. Andrews and Luis A. Balart. Ballantine (5/98) 1,201,000
4. **Tuesdays with Morrie** by Mitch Albom. Doubleday (8/97) \* \*\*1,150,000
5. **The Guinness Book of Records 1999**. Guinness Media (11/98) 714,000
6. **Talking to Heaven** by James Van Praagh. Dutton (11/97) \*696,816
7. **Something More: Excavating Your Authentic Self** by Sarah Ban Breathnach. Warner (10/98) 682,958
8. **In the Meantime** by Iyanla Vanzant. S&S (1/98) 649,503
9. **A Pirate Looks at Fifty** by Jimmy Buffett. Random House (6/98) 605,982
10. **If Life Is a Game These Are the Rules** by Cherie Carter-Scott, Ph.D. Broadway Books (9/98) 530,561
11. **Angela's Ashes** by Frank McCourt. Scribner (9/96) \*500,000
12. **For the Love of the Game: My Story** by Michael Jordan. Crown (10/98) 502,288
13. **The Day Diana Died** by Christopher Andersen. Morrow (8/98) 490,705
14. **The Century** by Peter Jennings and Todd Brewster. Doubleday (11/98) \*\*475,000
15. **Eat Right 4 Your Type** by Peter J. D'Adamo. Putnam (1/97) \*460,808

---

Note: Rankings are determined by sales figures provided by publishers; the numbers generally reflect reports of copies "shipped and billed" in calendar year 1998 and publishers were instructed to adjust sales figures to include returns through February 10, 1999. Publishers did not at that time know what their total returns would be—indeed, the majority of returns occur after that cut-off date—so none of these figures should be regarded as final net sales. (Dates in parentheses indicate month and year of publication.)

\*Sales figures reflect books sold only in calendar year 1998.

\*\*Sales figures were submitted to *PW* in confidence, for use in placing titles on the lists. Numbers shown are rounded down to the nearest 25,000 to indicate relationship to sales figures of other titles.

## What It Took to Score

The number of fiction titles with 1998 sales of more than 100,000 set a record: 101 books compared to 1997's 100. Consider that in 1990 there were only 54 hardcover novels that sold more than 100,000. In nonfiction, the 105 books with sales passing the 100,000 mark was considerably lower than the record-holding 1997 total of 128.

For the 1997 bestsellers, we noted that nonfiction bestseller sales outpaced fiction for the first time in five years. That was a blip rather than a trend. In 1998 fiction sales for top sellers were way ahead of nonfiction. Eight novels sold more than one million copies, with two hitting the two-million-or-more level; in nonfiction, four books hit that mark. Twelve more works of fiction went over the 500,000 mark, while only eight more nonfiction books did the same. In fiction, it took sales of more than 600,000 copies to make the top 15; in nonfiction 400,000-plus was enough.

Another trend noted in last year's feature was that the number of books with sales of more than 100,000 that did not make *PW*'s weekly charts or monthly religious lists was increasing. This trend reversed itself in 1998. In fiction, 22 books reporting sales of more than 100,000 did not make the charts, down from the record 25 set in 1997. In nonfiction, the 1998 figure is 39, less than the tally of 60 for 1997. And in both fiction and nonfiction, about half of the no-shows were among books with sales of less than 125,000.

## Same Old Disclaimer

As always, all our calculations are based on shipped-and-billed figures supplied by publishers for new books issued in 1998 and 1997 (a few books published earlier that continued their tenure on this year's bestseller charts are also included). These figures reflect only 1998 domestic trade sales—publishers were specifically instructed not to include book club and overseas transactions. We also asked publishers to take into account returns through February 10. All sales figures in these pages should not be considered final net sales. For many of the books, especially those published in the latter half of last year, returns are still to be calculated. Some books appear on our lists without sales figures; these figures were supplied for ranking purposes only.

## The Fiction Runners-Up

This second tier of bestsellers includes a number of books with long tenure on the weekly charts. Nicholas Sparks had a 28-week run. Judy Blume's first adult novel in 20 years was on the weekly charts 24 times. Poetry from 24-year-old singer Jewel Kilcher hit the right note; it has been on the list 22 times. And an eagerly awaited new novel by John Irving was on the charts for 21 weeks.

16. *Message in a Bottle* by Nicholas Sparks (Warner, 605,831)
17. *When the Wind Blows* by James Patterson (Little, Brown, 553,142)
18. *Summer Sisters* by Judy Blume (Delacorte, 549,136)

19. *Black and Blue* by Anna Quindlen (Random House, 529,104)
20. *Soul Harvest* by Jerry B. Jenkins and Tim LaHaye (Tyndale House, 509,799)
21. *The Locket* by Richard Paul Evans (Simon & Schuster)
22. *Pandora* by Anne Rice (Knopf, 453,892)
23. *The Path of Daggers* by Robert Jordan (Tor, 449,128)
24. *A Night Without Armor* by Jewel Kilcher (HarperCollins, 432,198)
25. *Memoirs of a Geisha* by Arthur Golden (Knopf, with sales of 425,677 in 1998 in addition to 100,000-plus sold in 1997)
26. *The Simple Truth* by David Baldacci (Warner, 410,185)
27. *N Is for Noose* by Sue Grafton (Henry Holt, 400,110)
28. *Seize the Night* by Dean Koontz (Bantam, 400,000)
29. *A Widow for One Year* by John Irving (Random House, 343,730)
30. *The Hammer of Eden* by Ken Follett (Crown, 342,833)

## 300,000+ Fiction Didn't Place

This year, for the first time, nine fiction titles with reported sales of more than 300,000 did not make a top-30 list. Only one of these books—*The Present, a Malory Holiday Novel* by Johanna Lindsey (Avon) did not land on *PW*'s weekly charts. Judith McNaught's *Night Whispers* (Pocket) had a two-week run.

All the other 300,000-plus players were on the weekly charts for more than a month, with Helen Fielding's *Bridget Jones's Diary* (Viking) enjoying the longest '98 tenure (16 weeks); Barbara Kingsolver's *The Poisonwood Bible* (HarperFlamingo) was on the list for 10 weeks with an additional 13 weeks so far in '99. The other 300,000-plus are *The Reef* by Nora Roberts (Putnam); *Secret Prey* by John Sandford (Putnam); *Homeport* by Nora Roberts (Putnam); *Toxin* by Robin Cook (Putnam); and *Fear Nothing* by Dean Koontz (Bantam).

## Fiction's 200,000+ Group

Considering the large number of books with sales of more than 300,000 that did not make a top 30 chart, it's no surprise that the more-than-200,000 group was smaller in 1998—14, compared with 21 in 1997 and 18 in 1996. There were two books in this group that never landed on a weekly chart—*Blessing* by Jude Deveraux (Pocket) and *Critical Mass* by Steve Martini (Putnam). Three other books had only a week or two on the charts—*The Most Wanted* by Jacquelyn Mitchard (Viking), *Flight of Eagles* by Jack Higgins (Putnam), and *The Target* by Catherine Coulter (Putnam).

All the other bestsellers in this group were on the *PW* weekly charts for more than one month, with Charles Frazier's first novel, *Cold Mountain* (Atlantic Monthly), clocking an astounding 60 weeks from June 1997 through last summer (total hardcover sales top 1.6 million). The other 200,000-plus titles are *Billy Straight* by Jonathan Kellerman (Random), *Unspeakable* by Sandra Brown

(Warner), *No Safe Place* by Richard North Patterson (Knopf), *Welcome to the World, Baby Girl!* by Fannie Flagg (Random), *The First Eagle* by Tony Hillerman (HC), *The Last Full Measure* by Jeff Shaara (Ballantine), *The Investigators* by W.E.B. Griffin (Putnam), and *Field of Thirteen* by Dick Francis (Putnam).

## At Fiction's 150,000+ Level

There were 11 works of fiction with sales of more than 150,000 that did not make it onto the year's top-30, two fewer than on the 1997 year-end list. Three did not land on the weekly charts at all: *The Return Journey* by Maeve Binchy (Delacorte), *The Jewels of Tessa Kent* by Judith Krantz (Crown), and *The Emperor's New Clothes: An All-Star Illustrated Retelling of the Classic Fairy Tale by Hans Christian Andersen* by the Starbright Foundation (Harcourt Brace).

The eight that did show on the weekly charts are *Moon Music* by Faye Kellerman (Morrow), *The Cat Who Sang for the Birds* by Lilian Jackson Braun (Putnam), *Singing in the Comeback Choir* by Bebe Moore Campbell (Putnam), *Guilty Pleasures* by Lawrence Sanders (Putnam), *There's a Hair in My Dirt* by Gary Larson (HC), *Monument Rock* by Louis L'Amour (Bantam), *The Eleventh Commandment* by Jeffrey Archer (HC), and *Low Country* by Anne Rivers Siddons (HC).

## Looking at the 125,000+ Group

This group includes 14 books that didn't make a top-30 list, one less than in 1997. All but four landed on the weekly lists.

Out of the 10 that made the charts, two titles tied for the longest run, eight weeks each—*Patchwork Planet* by Anne Tyler (Knopf) and *Blood Work* by Michael Connelly (LB). Other titles with appearances on the charts are *Day of Confession* by Allan Folsom (LB), *Sudden Mischief* by Robert B. Parker (Putnam), *Coast Road* by Barbara Delinsky (S&S), *Sharp Edges* by Jayne Ann Krentz (Pocket), *By the Light of My Father's Smile* by Alice Walker (Random), *Orchid Beach* by Stuart Woods (HC), *Thrill!* by Jackie Collins (S&S), and *Trouble in Paradise* by Robert B. Parker (Putnam).

The four that did not make an appearance on the weekly lists are *Legacy of Silence* by Belva Plain (Delacorte), *Fortunes of War* by Stephen Coonts (St. Martin's), *Flash* by Jayne Ann Krentz (Pocket), and *Secret Warriors* by W.E.B. Griffin (Putnam).

## At the 100,000+ Level

Last year, 23 novels sold more than 100,000 copies, two more than in 1997. Twelve of these never made it onto our weekly charts. Of the 11 that made a showing, the best run was *Numbered Account* by Christopher Reich (Delacorte), a first novel.

In ranked order, the 100,000-plus titles that made the weekly charts are *Cities of the Plain* by Cormac McCarthy (Knopf), *Star Wars: Vision of the Future* by Timothy Zahn (Bantam), *The Hundred Days* by Patrick O'Brian

(Norton), *Master Harper of Pern* by Anne McCaffrey (Del Rey), *Miracle Cure* by Michael Palmer (Bantam), *Cuba Libre* by Elmore Leonard (Delacorte), *Damascus Gate* by Robert Stone (Houghton Mifflin), *An Instance of the Fingerpost* by Iain Pears (Riverhead), *Charming Billy* by Alice McDermott (FS&G), and *With This Ring* by Amanda Quick (Bantam).

The 11 no-shows on *PW*'s lists are *The Christmas Cross* by Max Lucado (Word), *On the Occasion of My Last Afternoon* by Kaye Gibbons (Putnam), *Red White and Blue* by Susan Isaacs (HC), *Sunset Limited* by James Lee Burke (Doubleday), *Bloodstream* by Tess Gerritsen (Pocket), *Jade Island* by Elizabeth Lowell (Avon), *The First Horseman* by John Case (Ballantine), *American Dreams* by John Jakes (Dutton), *Rogue Warrior: Seal Force Alpha* by Richard Marcinko and John Weisman (Pocket), *Cavedweller* by Dorothy Allison (Dutton), *Firebird* by Janice Graham (Putnam), and *Genuine Lies* by Nora Roberts (Bantam).

## The Nonfiction Runners-Up

All books in this group except for *Best Friends* made it onto the weekly charts or the monthly religion lists. But only one, *A Walk in the Woods,* had a run of more than 20 weeks. Danielle Steel took the nonfiction route in *His Bright Light,* in which she tells of the tragic death of her son, Nick Traina.

16. *The Death of Outrage: Bill Clinton and the Assault on American Ideals* by William J. Bennett (Free Press, 407,747)
17. *The Millionaire Next Door* by Dr. Thomas Stanley and Dr. William Danko (Longstreet Press, 392,112 in '98; total sales are 1,011,345)
18. *Emeril's TV Dinners* by Emeril Lagasse (Morrow, 380,328)
19. *The Lady, Her Lover, and Her Lord* by Bishop T.D. Jakes (Putnam, 350,237)
20. *Conversations with God, Book 3* by Neale Donald Walsch (Hampton Roads, 349,351)
21. *The Ten Commandments* by Laura Schlessinger and Stewart Vogel (HarperCollins/Cliff Street, 338,585)
22. *His Bright Light* by Danielle Steel (Delacorte, 318,973)
23. *We Are Our Mother's Daughters* by Cokie Roberts (Morrow, 317,514)
24. *Just Like Jesus* by Max Lucado (Word, 309,852)
25. *The Breast Cancer Prevention Diet* by Dr. Bob Arnot (Little, Brown, 296,423)
26. *Blind Man's Bluff* by Sherry Sontag and Christopher Drew (Public Affairs, 289,685)
27. *A Walk in the Woods* by Bill Bryson (Broadway Books, 281,253)
28. *Best Friends* by Sharon Wolmuth and Carol Saline (Doubleday)
29. *Mars and Venus Starting Over* by John Gray (HarperCollins, 264,869)
30. *Joy of Cooking* by Irma S. Rombauer, Marion Rombauer Becker, and Ethan Becker (Scribner, 261,191 in 1998; total sales are 1,511,191).

## The 200,000+ NF Players

There was a significant falloff in the number of books with sales of 200,000 copies or more that did not make a top 30 list. The 1998 figure is 14, compared with 26 in 1997. The majority of the books in this group made it onto the weekly bestselling charts. Four of them had double-digit tenure. These were *The Gifts of the Jews* by Thomas Cahill (DD/Talese, nine weeks on the 1998 charts); *A Monk Swimming* by Malachy McCourt (Hyperion, with a 14-week tenure), *The Professor and the Madman* by Simon Winchester (HC, 15 weeks), and *Marilu Henner's Total Health Makeover* by Marilu Henner and Laura Morton (HC, 13 weeks).

Other bestsellers with sales of more than 200,000 that did not make it to the top-30 1998 list but did enjoy time on the weekly charts or monthly religion list are *Pure Drivel* by Steve Martin (Hyperion), *Still Me* by Christopher Reeve (Random), *The Weigh Down Diet* by Gwen Shamblin (Doubleday), *We Interrupt This Broadcast* by Joe Garner (Sourcebooks), and *Lindbergh* by A. Scott Berg (Putnam).

Of the five books with sales of more than 200,000 that did not make the weekly charts, the two Meredith titles are the kind that benefit by nontraditional sales. The other three authors have all been on the charts with earlier titles that have covered the same ground or themes. The titles are *The Home Depot Outdoor Projects 1-2-3* edited by Ben Allen (Meredith), *Kids Are Punny 2* by Rosie O'Donnell (Warner), *101 Full-Size Quilt Blocks and Borders* by Better Homes and Gardens editors (Meredith), *The Victors* by Stephen Ambrose (S&S), and *Charles Kuralt's American Moments* by Charles Kuralt, edited by Peter Freundlich (S&S).

## 150,000+ Group in Nonfiction

There were 17 books with sales of more than 150,000 that did not make the year's top-30 bestsellers, a bit lower than the 1997 record-breaker of 21 titles. Only six of these books never landed on *PW*'s weekly charts or monthly religion charts; that's a strong contrast to the 1997 numbers when 17 out of the 21 never landed on the charts.

The six books that did not make the charts are *Journey to Beloved* by Oprah Winfrey (Hyperion), *The Anti-Aging Zone* by Barry Sears (HC/ReganBooks), *Dear Socks, Dear Buddy* by Hillary Rodham Clinton (S&S), *Everything and a Kite* by Ray Romano (Bantam), *Barbie: Four Decades of Fashion, Fantasy, and Fun* by Marco Tosa (Abrams), and *Kids Say the Darndest Things* by Bill Cosby (Bantam).

Three of the books with sales of more than 150,000 were holdovers from previous years: *The Man Who Listens to Horses* by Monty Roberts (Random), which had a 37-week tenure on *PW*'s weekly charts; *Don't Worry, Make Money* by Richard Carlson (Hyperion), which had a 20-week run; and *Suzanne Somers' Eat Great, Lose Weight* by Suzanne Somers (Crown), which was on the charts for about a month. Two books—*Final Dawn over Jerusalem* by John Hagee

(Nelson) and *What's So Amazing About Grace?* by Philip Yancey (Zondervan)—
were fixtures on the monthly religion charts.

Most of the other books landed on the charts for less than a month except for
*Titan: The Life of John D. Rockefeller, Sr.* by Ron Chernow (Random) and *And
the Horse He Rode In on: The People v. Kenneth Starr* by James Carville (S&S),
which had runs of nine weeks and six weeks, respectively. The four with shorter
runs are *The Joy of Work* by Scott Adams (HarperBusiness), *Working with
Emotional Intelligence* by Daniel Goleman (Bantam), *Just Jackie: Her Private
Years* by Edward Klein (Ballantine), and *Ship of Gold in the Deep Blue Sea* by
Gary Kinder (Atlantic Monthly).

## The 125,000+ Nonfiction Group

This group includes 18 titles that did not make our top-30 list, matching the 1996
record and three less than 1997's 15.

A larger number of books than usual at this sales level had some presence on
*PW*'s weekly charts or monthly religion lists. *The Long Hard Road Out of Hell*
by Marilyn Manson (HC) racked up nine weeks, and *Spin Cycle: Inside the
Clinton Propaganda Machine* by Howard Kurtz (Free Press) had a seven-week
run. Both *Seven from Heaven* by Bobbi and Kenny McCaughey (Nelson) and
*Don't Know Much About the Bible* by Kenneth C. Davis (Morrow/Eagle Brook)
had impressive runs on the religion charts.

Bestsellers in this 125,000-plus group that were on *PW*'s charts for a month
or less are *The Rape of Nanking: The Forgotten Holocaust of World War II* by
Iris Change (Basic), *High Crimes and Misdemeanors: The Case Against Bill
Clinton* by Ann Coulter (Regnery), *Eat the Rich: A Treatise on Economics* by
P.J. O'Rourke (Atlantic Monthly), *Great Political Wit of the 20th Century* by
Bob Dole (DD/Talese), and *Death of a Princess: The Investigation* by Thomas
Sancton and Scott MacLeod (St. Martin's).

The eight that did not make a weekly *PW* slot are *Children's Book of
America* by William J. Bennett (S&S), *The Wonder of Boys* by Michael Gurian
(Tarcher); *Who Moved My Cheese?* by Spencer Johnson (Putnam), *Oprah
Winfrey Speaks* by Janet Lowe (Wiley), *The Roaring 2000s* by Harry Dent
(S&S), *The 21 Irrefutable Laws of Leadership* by John Maxwell (Nelson), *The
Millennium Bug* by Michael S. Hyatt (Regnery), and *New Baking Book* by Better
Homes and Gardens editors (Meredith).

## Nonfiction's 100,000+ List

In 1998, 26 additional hardcovers sold more than 100,000. The figure is just one
higher than in 1997 and lower than the 31 with more than 100,000 sales in 1996.
This is also the group with the largest number of titles that never made *PW*'s
weekly lists. In fact, only five books landed on those charts, and one—*The
Perfect Storm* by Sebastian Junger (Norton)—was a holdover from 1997. One
book, *Titanic: Legacy of the World's Greatest Ocean Liner* by Susan Wels (Time
Life), had a three-week run; *Dave Barry Turns 50* by Dave Barry (Crown) and *I
Think I'm Outta Here* by Carroll O'Connor (Pocket) each had a two-week run;

and Bill Bradley's *Values of the Game* (Artisan) landed for a week. *Amazing Grace* by Kathleen Norris (Riverhead) was a regular on *PW*'s monthly religion charts.

The 20 that did not show on the 1998 charts are: *Diana: The Secret Years* by Simone Simmons (Ballantine), *The Spirit of America* by Thomas Kinkade (Nelson), *How to Cook Everything* by Mark Bittman (Macmillan), *King of the World: Muhammad Ali and the Rise of an American Hero* by David Remnick (Random), *Shakespeare: The Invention of the Human* by Harold Bloom (Riverhead), *Cook Right 4 Your Type* by Peter D'Adamo (Putnam), *Work in Progress* by Michael Eisner (Random), *The Good Life* by Tony Bennett with Will Friedwald (Pocket), *Simplify Your Christmas* by Elaine St. James (Andrews McMeel), *Understanding Men's Passages* by Gail Sheehy (Random), *Newman's Own Cookbook* by Paul Newman and A.E. Hotchner (S&S), *Bill Gates Speaks* by Janet Lowe (Wiley), *Fresh Wind, Fresh Fire* by Jim Cymbala (Zondervan), *Winning Every Day* by Lou Holtz (HarperBusiness), *Diana: Portrait of a Princess* by Jayne Fincher (S&S Editions), *The Pie and Pastry Bible* by Rose Levy Beranbaum (Scribner), *Reach for the Summit* by Pat Summitt with Sally Jenkins (Broadway Books), *Believe* with illustrations by Mary Engelbreit (Andrews McMeel), *Never Be Lied to Again* by David J. Lieberman (St. Martin's), and *Joseph—Great Lives Series* by Charles Swindoll (Word).

## Paperback Bestsellers: 'Soup' and Oprah over the Top

### Mark Rotella

Associate Editor, *Publishers Weekly*

Although the past year has seen a few changes in paperback sales patterns, several categories—and factors that influence sales in those categories—have remained constant. Not surprisingly, Oprah, that bookseller extraordinaire, continues to influence fiction on the trade paper list. Her picks in 1998 included Alice Hoffman's *Here on Earth*, Edwidge Danticat's *Breath, Eyes, Memory*, Chris Bohjalian's *Midwives,* and Billie Letts's *Where the Heart Is.*

Ever more, Health Communications continues to fill the upper ranks with chicken soup for a wide variety of souls. The publisher's 12 titles have focused on kids, teenagers, women, country music fans, and pet lovers, with combined sales totaling more than 10 million copies. Readers in great numbers are following Richard Carlson's advice: his *Don't Sweat the Small Stuff* just passed the 100-week mark on our list. (But small stuff it's clearly not, as sales to date exceed five million copies.) With a third more self-help than last year, it seems likely that chicken soup consumption will remain up and deodorant sales down.

Many more publishers are reporting their computer book sales, including IDG, Macmillan and Coriolis. Books on Windows 98 and 95 figure highly, as do titles on how to master Microsoft's MCSE exams.

While mass market figures reflect the customary dominant presence of such staples as John Grisham, Danielle Steel, Nora Roberts, and Patricia Cornwell, there were more sightings of nonfiction titles. Of note are Jon Krakauer's *Into*

*Thin Air*, Robert Atkins's *Dr. Atkins' New Diet Revolution*, and *Protein Power* by Michael and Mary Dan Eades.

Both trade paperback and mass market figures reflect originals, reprints or dual editions published in 1997 or 1998 for which publishers have billed and shipped at least 50,000 copies (for trade paperbacks) or one million copies (for mass market) in 1998. They do not always reflect net sales. Titles released in 1997 are marked by an asterisk.

## Trade Paperbacks
### 1 Million+

*Don't Sweat the Small Stuff . . . And It's All Small Stuff*. Richard Carlson, Ph.D. Orig. Hyperion (3,626,470)

*Divine Secrets of the Ya-Ya Sisterhood*. Rebecca Wells. Rep. HarperPerennial (1,771,340)

*Chicken Soup for the Teenage Soul*. Jack Canfield, Mark Victor Hansen, et al. Orig. Health Communications (1,743,000)

*Don't Sweat the Small Stuff with Your Family*. Richard Carlson, Ph.D. Orig. Hyperion (1,450,201)

*Chicken Soup for the Kid's Soul*. Jack Canfield, Mark Victor Hansen, et al. Orig. Health Communications (1,337,980)

*Chicken Soup for the Pet Lover's Soul*. Jack Canfield, Mark Victor Hansen, et al. Orig. Health Communications (1,232,261)

*Chicken Soup for the Mother's Soul*. Jack Canfield, Mark Victor Hansen, et al. Orig. Health Communications (1,210,948)

*A 2nd Helping of Chicken Soup for the Woman's Soul*. Jack Canfield, Mark Victor Hansen, et al. Orig. Health Communications (1,155,058)

*Here on Earth*. Alice Hoffman. Rep. Berkley (1,050,000)

### 500,000+

*Prescription for Nutritional Healing: A Practical A-Z Reference to Drug-Free Remedies Using Vitamins, Minerals, Herbs & Food Supplements*. James F. Balch, M.D., and Phyllis A. Balch, C.N.C. Orig. Avery (974,486)

*Midwives*. Chris Bohjalian. Rep. Vintage (898,000)

*Cold Mountain*. Charles Frazier. Rep. Vintage (838,000)

*James Cameron's Titanic*. Ed W. Marsh. Dual. HarperPerennial (822,566)

*A 5th Portion of Chicken Soup for the Soul*. Jack Canfield and Mark Victor Hansen. Orig. Health Communications (822,026)

*Where the Heart Is*. Billie Letts. Rep. Warner (770,561)

*What Looks Like Crazy on an Ordinary Day*. Pearl Cleage. Rep. Avon (743,318)

*Beloved*. Toni Morrison. Tie-In/Rep. Plume (680,736)

*Chicken Soup for the Christian Soul*. Jack Canfield and Mark Victor Hansen. Orig. Health Communications (675,420)

*One Day My Soul Just Opened Up*. Iyanla Vanzant. Orig. Fireside (665,742)

*Windows 98 for Dummies*. Andy Rathbone. Orig. IDG (648,000)

*The Elusive Flame*. Kathleen E. Woodiwiss. Orig. Avon (624,355)

*Little Altars Everywhere*. Rebecca Wells. Rep. HarperPerennial (609,758)

*Windows 95 for Dummies, 2nd ed.* Andy Rathbone. Orig. IDG (609,000)

*Chicken Soup for the Teenage Soul Journal*. Jack Canfield, Mark Victor Hansen, and Kimberly Kirberger. Orig. Health Communications (590,212)

*Chicken Soup for the Country Soul*. Jack Canfield, Mark Victor Hansen, and Ron Camacho. Orig. Health Communications (535,519)

*A Civil Action*. Jonathan Harr. Tie-In/Rep. Vintage (505,400)

### 100,000+

*I'm Not Anti-Business, I'm Anti-Idiot*. Scott Adams. Orig. Andrews McMeel (480,010)

*Breath, Eyes, Memory—Oprah Book Club Edition*. Edwidge Danticat. Rep. Vintage (458,600)

*Color of Water*. James McBride. Rep. Riverhead (450,000)

*Anatomy of the Spirit: The Seven Stages of Power and Healing.* Caroline Myss, Ph.D. Rep. Crown/Three Rivers (435,930)

*Under the Tuscan Sun.* Frances Mayes. Rep. Broadway (435,761)

The Millionaire Next Door. Thomas J. Stanley, Ph.D., and William D. Danko, Ph.D. Rep. Pocket

Don't Worry, Make Money. Richard Carlson. Ph.D. Rep. Hyperion (428,164)

Eight Weeks to Optimum Health. Dr. Andrew Weil. Rep. Fawcett (425,000)

*Into the Wild.* Jon Krakauer. Rep. Anchor (410,961)

Leonardo DiCaprio. Mark Bego. Orig. Andrews McMeel (408,910)

The Death of Outrage: Bill Clinton and the Assault on American Ideals. William J. Bennett. Orig. Free Press (407,797)

Dr. Atkins New Carbohydrate Gram Counter. Robert Atkins, M.D. Rep. M. Evans (403,765)

Journey to Cubeville. Scott Adams. Orig. Andrews McMeel (395,760)

The Seven Habits of Highly Effective Teens. Sean Covey. Orig. Fireside (386,723)

*The Lost Boy.* Dave Pelzer. Orig. Health Communications (380,673)

Internet for Dummies, 5th ed. John R. Levine. Orig. IDG (374,000)

Out to Canaan. Jan Karon. Rep. Penguin (350,000)

Citizen Soldiers. Stephen Ambrose. Rep. Touchstone (343,000)

*Undaunted Courage.* Stephen Ambrose. Rep. Touchstone (322,000)

Nicolae: The Rise of the Anti Christ. Jerry B. Jenkins and Tim LaHaye. Orig. Tyndale House (316,854)

Brain Droppings. George Carlin. Rep. Hyperion (296,245)

The Starr Report. Kenneth W. Starr. Orig. Public Affairs (282,345)

Caring for Baby: Birth to Five. Reissue. American Academy of Pediatrics. Bantam (280,000)

The Simpsons: A Complete Guide to Our Favorite Family. Matt Groening. Orig. HarperPerennial (278,024)

The Yogi Book. Yogi Berra. Orig. Workman (275,464)

Women's Bodies, Women's Wisdom. Chris Northrup. Reissue. Bantam (270,000)

Microsoft Office 97 for Windows for Dummies. Roger C. Parker. Orig. IDG (237,000)

Why People Don't Heal and How They Can. Caroline Myss, Ph.D. Rep. Crown/Three Rivers (224,733)

Fear and Loathing. Hunter S. Thompson. Tie-In/Rep. Vintage (224,000)

Windows 95 for Dummies Quick Reference, 3rd ed. Greg Harvey. Orig. IDG (222,000)

Personal History. Katharine Graham. Rep. Vintage (219,000)

Dr. Atkins' New Diet Revolution. Robert C. Atkins, M.D. Rep. Avon (216,840)

Adventures of a Psychic. Sylvia Brown and Antoinette. Rep. Hay House (201,000)

The Shunning. Beverly Lewis. Orig. Bethany House (198,245)

Windows 95 Simplified. Ruth Maran. Orig. IDG (197,000)

The Bible Code. Michael Drosnin. Rep. Touchstone (191,000)

A 4th Course of Chicken Soup for the Soul. Jack Canfield, Mark Victor Hansen, et al. Orig. Health Communications (187,033)

Small Miracles. Yitta Halberstam and Judith Leventhal. Orig. Adams Media (184,763)

Internet for Dummies Quick Reference, 4th ed. John R. Levine. Orig. IDG (182,000)

Into the Storm: A Study in Command. Tom Clancy with Gen. Frederick Franks, Jr. Rep. Berkley (180,000)

The Confession. Beverly Lewis. Orig. Bethany House (179,812)

Complete Idiot's Guide to Windows 98. Paul McFedries. Orig. Macmillan/Que (178,721)

The Reckoning. Beverly Lewis. Orig. Bethany House (178,418)

Virtues of Aging. Jimmy Carter. Orig. Ballantine/Library of Contemporary Thought (178,000)

South Park: A Sticky Forms Adventure. Rich Dahm, Sean Lafluer, and Ben Karlin. Orig. Pocket

*Emotional Intelligence.* Daniel Goleman. Rep. Bantam (175,000)

Backtalk. Audrey Ricker. Orig. Fireside (174,000)

Seven Habits of Highly Effective Families. S. Covey. Rep. Golden (172,431)

Violin. Anne Rice. Rep. Ballantine (172,000)

*The Simpsons Guide to Springfield.* Matt Groening. Orig. HarperPerennial (171,414)

*Success Is a Choice.* Rick Pitino. Rep. Broadway (168,615)

*WIN 98 for Dummies Quick Reference.* Greg Harvey. Orig. IDG (168,000)

*\*The Motley Fool Investment Guide.* Tom and David Gardner. Rep. Fireside (165,967)

*Easy Windows 98.* Shelley O'Hara. Orig. Macmillan/Que (165,694)

*\*Chocolate for a Woman's Soul.* Kay Allenbaugh. Orig. Fireside (165,000)

*The Evidence: Starr Report.* Edited by Phil Kuntz. Orig. Pocket

*AOL for Dummies, 4th ed.* John Kaufeld. Orig. IDG (163,000)

*Microsoft Windows 98 Resource Kit.* Microsoft Corp. Orig. Microsoft (162,000)

*Strong Women Stay Young.* Miriam Nelson. Rep. Bantam (160,000)

*Success for Dummies.* Zig Ziglar. Orig. IDG (157,000)

*Practical Feng Shui.* Simon Brown. Orig. Sterling (155,503)

*\*First Things First.* Stephen Covey. Orig. Fireside (153,402)

*Small Miracles II.* Yitta Halberstam and Judith Leventhal. Orig. Adams Media (152,519)

*Dr. Atkin's New Diet Cookbook.* Robert Atkins, M.D. Rep. M. Evans (152,293)

*No Island of Sanity.* Vincent Bugliosi. Orig. Ballantine/Library of Contemporary Thought (150,000)

*Wait Till Next Year.* Doris Kearns Goodwin. Rep. Touchstone (150,000)

*The Milk Mustache Book.* Jay Schulberg. Orig. Ballantine (150,000)

*Windows 98 Simplified.* Ruth Maran. Orig. IDG (149,000)

*\*The Celestine Prophecy.* James Redfield. Rep. Warner (147,563)

*\*Dr. Atkins Quick and Easy New Diet Cookbook.* Robert Atkins. Orig. Fireside (146,000)

*Brave New World Classics.* Aldous Huxley. Rep. HarperPerennial (141,607)

*\*Complete Idiot's Guide to Windows 95, 2nd ed.* Paul McFedries. Orig. Macmillan/Que (139,269)

*\*Chicken Soup for Little Souls.* Jack Canfield and Mark Victor Hansen. Orig. Health Communications (137,169)

*PCs for Dummies, 5th ed.* Dan Gookin. Orig. IDG (136,000)

*Underworld.* Don DeLillo. Rep. Scribner. (135,000)

*\*When Angels Speak.* Martha Williamson. Orig. Fireside (131,000)

*\*Top Secret Restaurant Recipes.* Todd Wilbur. Orig. Plume (130,470)

*Timequake.* Kurt Vonnegut, Jr. Rep. Berkley (130,000)

*All Over but the Shoutin'.* Rick Bragg. Rep. Vintage (130,000)

*Death of a Princess.* Thomas Sancton and Scott MacLeod. Orig. St. Martin's (129,591)

*Die Broke.* Stephen M. Pollan. Rep. HarperBusiness (129,155)

*\*Succulent Wild Women.* Sark. Orig. Fireside (128,000)

*Upgrading & Repairing PCS, 10th Anniversary Edition.* Scott Mueller. Orig. Macmillan/Que (127,470)

*Networking Essentials, 2nd ed.* Rep. Microsoft (125,951)

*\*Microsoft Office 97 Professional 6-in-1, 2nd Edition.* Faithe Wempen. Orig. Macmillan/Que (125,709)

*Children Learn What They Live.* Dorothy Law Nolte and Rachel Harris. Orig. Workman (125,060)

*The First Coming—Tiger Woods: Mastery or Martyr?* John Feinstein. Orig. Ballantine/Library of Contemporary Thought (125,000)

*The Rape of Nanking.* Iris Chang. Rep. Penguin (125,000)

*Spin Cycle: Inside the Clinton Propaganda Machine.* Howard Kurtz. Orig. Free Press (125,000)

*Using Windows 98.* Kathy Ivens, Don Child and Robert Mcgregor. Orig. Macmillan/Que (124,348)

*Le Divorce.* Diane Johnson. Rep. Plume (123,144)

*Naked.* David Sedaris. Rep. Little, Brown (121,926)

*Teach Yourself Windows 95 Visually.* Ruth Maran. Orig. IDG (121,000)

*Word 97 for Windows for Dummies.* Dan Gookin. Orig. IDG (121,000)

*American Pastoral.* Philip Roth. Rep. Vintage (121,000)

*Garfield 20th Anniversary Edition.* Jim Davis. Orig. Ballantine (120,000)

*Teach Yourself Windows 98 Visually.* Ruth Maran. Orig. IDG (117,000)

*Tomorrow's Dream.* Janette Oke and T. Davis Bunn. Orig. Bethany House (112,068)

*Wobegon Boy.* Garrison Keillor. Rep. Penguin (112,000)

*365 WWJD.* Nick Harrison. Orig. Harper San Francisco (108,500)

*PCs for Dummies, 6th ed.* Dan Gookin. Orig. IDG (106,000)

*Tyra's Beauty Inside and Out.* Tyra Banks. Orig. HarperPerennial (105,644)

*Against the Gods: The Remarkable Story of Risk.* Peter Bernstein. Rep. Wiley (105,000)

*Dogs Never Lie About Love: Reflections on the Emotional World of Dogs.* Jeffrey Moussaieff Masson. Rep. Crown/Three Rivers (103,564)

*\*101 Nights of Great Romance.* Laura Corn. Orig. Park Avenue (102,471)

*Welcome to Jasorassic Park.* Bill Amend. Orig. Andrews McMeel (101,917)

*Never Be Lied to Again.* David Lieberman. Orig. St. Martin's (101,652)

*The Starr Evidence.* Kenneth W. Starr. Orig. Public Affairs (101,233)

*Garfield Throws His Weight Around.* Jim Davis. Orig. Ballantine (101,000)

*Camp Foxtrot.* Bill Amend. Orig. Andrews McMeel (100,500)

*Americans at War.* Stephen Ambrose. Rep. Berkley (100,000)

*Andrew Weil Omnibus.* Andrew Weil. Orig. Ballantine (100,000)

## 75,000+

*10 Stupid Things Men Do to Mess Up Their Lives.* Laura Schlessinger. Rep. Harper-Collins/Cliff St. (99,641)

*Billions and Billions.* Carl Sagan. Rep. Ballantine (98,000)

*Spice World: The Movie.* Edited by Sue Carswell. Orig. Crown/Three Rivers (96,426)

*\*Kitchen Table Wisdom.* Rachel Remen. Rep. Riverhead (95,000)

*\*Buffy the Vampire Slayer: The Watcher's Guide.* Christopher Golden, Nancy Holder, Keith R.A. DeCandido, and Joss Whedon. Orig. Pocket

*\*1001 Ways to Energize Employees.* Bob Nelson. Orig. Workman (94,241)

*Special Edition Using Windows 98.* Ed Bott and Ron Person. Orig. Macmillan/Que (94,231)

*The Path to Love: Spiritual Strategies for Healing.* Deepak Chopra. Rep. Crown/Three Rivers (92,883)

*The Dilbert Future.* Scott Adams. Rep. HarperBusiness (92,555)

*Power of Birthdays, Stars & Numbers.* Saffi Crawford and Gerald Sullivan. Orig. Ballantine (90,000)

*The Road Less Traveled and Beyond.* M. Scott Peck. Rep. Touchstone (90,000)

*Dating for Dummies.* Joy Brown. Orig. IDG (90,000)

*\*Upgrading & Repairing PCs, 8th ed.* Scott Mueller. Orig. Macmillan/Que (88,054)

*Computers Simplified, 3rd ed.* Ruth Maran. Orig. IDG (88,000)

*The End of the Age.* Pat Robertson. Reissue. Word (87,448)

*The Bodacious Book of Succulence.* Sark. Orig. Fireside (87,000)

*Excel 97 for Windows For Dummies.* Greg Harvey. Orig. IDG (87,000)

*Decorating for the Holidays: Recipes, Gifts, Decorations, and Entertaining Ideas for the Holidays.* Editors of Martha Stewart Living. Orig. Clarkson Potter (86,884)

*\*The Little Giant: Encyclopedia of the Zodiac.* Diagram Group. Rep. Sterling (85,765)

*Living the Simple Life.* Elaine St. James. Rep. Hyperion (80,532)

*Running Microsoft Windows 98.* Craig Stinson. Orig. Microsoft (84,443)

*The Reader.* Bernhard Schlink. Rep. Vintage (84,000)

*Easy Internet, 3rd ed.* Joe Kraynak. Orig. Macmillan/Que (82,978)

*Access 97 for Windows for Dummies.* John Kaufeld. Orig. IDG (82,000)

*\*Special Edition Using Microsoft Office 97.* Jim Boyce. Orig. Macmillan/Que (80,727)

*Unlimited Access.* Gary Aldrich. Rep. Regnery (80,090)

*Even the Stars Look Lonesome.* Maya Angelou. Rep. Bantam (80,000)

*Windows 98 Secrets.* Brian Livingston. Orig. IDG (79,000)

*More Windows 98 for Dummies.* Andy Rathbone. Orig. IDG (79,000)

*Chasing Cezanne.* Peter Mayle. Rep. Vintage (77,700)

*Internet & WWW Simplified, 2nd ed.* Ruth Maran. Orig. IDG (77,000)

*St. John's Wort: Nature's Blues Buster.* Hyla Cass, M.D. Orig. Avery (76,707)

*The World's Best-Kept Diet Secrets.* Diane Irons. Orig. Sourcebooks (76,474)

*Microsoft Windows 98 At a Glance.* Jerry Joyce and Marianne Moon. Orig. Microsoft (76,055)

*Master Windows 95 Visually.* Ruth Maran. Orig. IDG (76,000)

*\*The Color Books: 11,261 Color Combinations for Your Home.* Orig. Chronicle (75,615)

*New Father Book.* Better Homes & Gardens. Orig. Meredith (75,096)

*Team Rodent: How Disney Devours the World.* Carl Hiaasen. Orig. Ballantine/ Library of Contemporary Thought (75,000)

*A Cup of Tea.* Amy Ephron. Rep. Ballantine (75,000)

*Star Wars Essential Guide to Planets.* Edited by Daniel Wallace. Orig. Del Rey (75,000)

*Light of Falling Stars.* J. Robert Lennon. Rep. Riverhead (75,000)

**50,000+**

*Ragtime.* E.L. Doctorow. Tie-In/ Rep. (74,900)

*\*Don't Pee on My Leg & Tell Me It's Raining.* Judy Sheindlin. Rep. HarperPerennial (74,774)

*In the House: MTV's the Real World: Seattle.* James Solomon. Orig. Pocket

*The New Birth Order Book.* Dr. Kevin Leman. Orig. Revell/Baker (73,287)

*\*Wizard and Glass.* Stephen King. Orig. Plume (72,760)

*\*Special Edition Using Microsoft Word 97.* Bill Carmada. Orig. Macmillan/Que (73,159)

*How Reading Changed My Life.* Anna Quindlen. Orig. Ballantine/Library of Contemporary Thought (72,000)

*Slowing Down to the Speed of Life.* Richard Carlson and Joe Bailey. Rep. Harper San Francisco (72,000)

*\*Manifest Your Destiny.* Wayne Dyer. Rep. HarperPerennial (71,836)

*Top Secret Recipes Lite.* Todd Wilbur. Orig. Plume (71,508)

*The Tribble Handbook.* Terry J. Erdman. Orig. Pocket

*If This World Were Mine.* E. Lynn Harris. Rep. Anchor (71,461)

*The Complete Idiot's Guide to Learning Spanish on Your Own.* Gail Stein and Marc Einsohn. Orig. Macmillan (71,000)

*Living Somewhere Between Estrogen and Death.* Barbara Johnson. Orig. Word (70,953)

*The Tenth Insight.* James Redfield. Rep. Warner (70,602)

*Slowing Down to the Speed of Life.* Richard Carlson. Rep. Harper San Francisco (70,398)

*Seinfeld: The Totally Unauthorized Tribute (Not That There's Anything Wrong with That).* David Wild. Orig. Crown/Three Rivers (70,153)

*News Is a Verb.* Pete Hamill. Orig. Ballantine/Library of Contemporary Thought (70,000)

*Brief History of Time.* Stephen Hawking. Reissue. Bantam (70,000)

*Windows 98 6-in-1.* Jennifer Fulton, Jane Calabria, and Dorothy Burke. Orig. Macmillan/Que (69,482)

*Leonardo.* Victoria Looseleaf. Orig. Ballantine (69,000)

*Becoming a Woman of Grace.* Cynthia Heald. Orig. Thomas Nelson (68,974)

*The Motley Fool Investment Workbook.* Tom and David Gardner. Orig. Fireside (68,841)

*Java in a Nutshell, 2nd ed.* David Flanagan. Orig. O'Reilly (68,483)

*The Tender Years.* Janette Oke. Orig. Bethany House (68, 273)

*Master Windows 98 Visually.* Ruth Maran. Orig. IDG (68,000)

*Black Boy Classics Edition.* Richard Wright. Rep. HarperPerennial (67,940)

*Case for Christ: A Journalist's Personal Investigation of the Evidence of Jesus.* Lee Strobel. Dual. Zondervan (67,926)

*The Barbecue! Bible.* Steven Raichlen. Orig. Workman (67,852)

*The Weight of Water.* Anita Shreve. Rep. Little, Brown (67,704)

*HTML 4: Visual QuickStart Guide.* Liz Castro. Rep. Peachpit (67,577)

*\*Special Edition Using Microsoft Excel 97.* Bruce Hallberg et al. Orig. Macmillan/Que (67,575)

*The Horse Whisperer Companion.* Nicholas Evans. Orig. Delta/DTP (67,437)

*Miracles Cures.* Jean Carper. Rep. Harper-Perennial (67,271)

*The World's Best-Kept Beauty Secrets.* Diane Irons. Orig. Sourcebooks (67,247)

*Easy Windows 95, 2nd ed.* Sue Plumlye. Orig. Que (67,017)

*Our Bodies, Ourselves for the New Century.* Boston Women's Health Book Collective. Orig. Touchstone (67,000)

*Ginkgo: A Practical Guide.* Georges Halpern, M.D. Orig. Avery (66,594)

*Angels.* Billy Graham. Reissue. Word (66,249)

*The Dark Side of Camelot.* Seymour Hersh. Rep. Little, Brown (66,073)

*How Computers Work, 4th ed.* Ron White. Orig. (65,334)

*Complete Idiot's Guide to PCs, 6th ed.* Joe Kraynak. Orig. Macmillan (64,577)

*Special Edition Using Access 97, 2nd ed.* Roger Jennings. Orig. Macmillan/Que (64,162

*Sosa! Sosa!* P.J. Duncan. Orig. Fireside (64,000)

*The Complete Idiot's Guide to Making Money on Wall Street, 2nd ed.* Christy and Robert Heady. Orig. Macmillan (64,000)

*Finding Your Way Home.* Melody Beattie. Orig. Harper San Francisco (63,900)

*Complete Guide to Flower Gardening.* Better Homes and Gardens. Orig. Meredith (63,847)

*Resumes that Knock 'em Dead, 3rd ed.* Martin Yate. Reprint. Adams Media (63,413)

*1-2-3 Magic.* Thomas Phelan. Orig. Child Management (63,055)

*Flyy Girl.* Omar Tyree. Rep. Scribner (63,000)

*Hole in the Wall Gang Cookbook.* Paul Newman. Orig. Fireside (63,000)

*Networking for Dummies, 3rd ed.* Doug Lowe. Orig. IDG (62,000)

*Computers Simplified, 4th ed.* Ruth Maran. Orig. IDG (62,000)

*Photography for Dummies.* Russell Hart. Orig. IDG (62,000)

*Mason & Dixon.* Thomas Pynchon. Rep. Holt (62,000)

*Their Eyes Were Watching God.* Zora Neale Hurston. Rep. HarperPerennial (61,900)

*MCSE Core Four Exam Cram 4 Pack.* Ed Tittel, Kurt Hudson and J. Michael Stewart. Rep. Coriolis

*101 Things God Can't Do.* Maisie Sparks. Orig. Thomas Nelson (61,627)

*Love Coupons.* Gregory J.P. Godek. Orig. Sourcebooks (61,519)

*Been There Should've Done That: 505 Tips for Making the Most of College.* Suzette Tyler. Orig. Front Porch (61,489)

*Miracles Happen When You Pray: True Stories of the Remarkable Power of Prayer.* Quin Sherrer. Orig. Zondervan (61,468)

*What Is Scientology?* L. Ron Hubbard. Rep. Bridge (61,290)

*Creating Web Pages for Dummies, 3rd ed.* Bud E. Smith. Orig. IDG (61,000)

*AOL for Dummies Quick Reference, 2nd ed.* John Kaufeld. Orig. IDG (61,000)

*Sams Teach Yourself Visual Basic 5 in 24 Hours.* Greg Perry. Orig. Macmillan/Sams (60,298)

*Sams Teach Yourself Linux in 24 Hours.* Bill Ball. Orig. Macmillan/Sams (60,165)

*Smoothies.* Mary Corpening Barber, Sara Corpening and Lori Lynn Narlock. Orig. Chronicle (60,134)

*More Windows 95 for Dummies.* Any Rathbone. Orig. IDG (60,000)

*Mutual Funds for Dummies, 2nd ed.* Eric Tyson. Orig. IDG (60,000)

*Animals as Teachers and Healers.* Susan Chernak McElroy. Rep. Ballantine (60,000)

*Woe Is I: The Grammarphobe's Guide to Better English.* Patricia O'Conner. Rep. Riverhead (60,000)

*The Odyssey: Homer.* Trans. by Robert Fagles. Rep. Penguin (60,000)

*Healthy Crockery Cookery.* Mable Hoffman. Orig. Perigee/HPBooks (60,000)

*The Complete Idiot's Guide to Losing Weight.* Susan McQuillan and Edward Saltzman. Orig. Macmillan (60,000)

*Business Writers Book of Lists.* Mary Devries. Orig. Perigee/HPBooks (60,000)

*The Girlfriend's Guide to Surviving the First Year of Motherhood.* Vicki Iovine. Orig. Perigee/HPBooks (60,000)

*What Your First Grader Needs to Know.* E.D. Hirsch. Rep. Delta/DTP (59,992)

*Dr. Bob's Revolutionary Weight Control Program.* Dr. Bob Arnot. Rep. Little, Brown (59,780)

*Holidays on Ice.* David Sedaris. Rep. Little, Brown (59,707)

*The New Strategic Selling.* Stephen E. Heiman and Diane Sanchez. Rep. Warner (59,424)

*\*How Computers Work, Deluxe Edition.* Ron White. Macmillan/Ziff-Davis (59,239)

*\*Ten Minute Guide to Windows 95, 2nd ed.* Sue Plumley. Orig. Macmillan/Que (59,127)

*\*Weddings for Dummies.* Marcy Blum and Laura Fischler Kaiser. Orig. IDG (59,000)

*Microsoft Office 97 for Windows for Dummies, Quick Reference.* Doug Lowe. Orig. IDG (59,000)

*The Straight Man.* Richard Russo. Rep. Vintage (59,000)

*American Sphinx.* Joseph J. Ellis. Rep. Vintage (59,000)

*NUTS!: Southwest Airlines' Crazy Recipe for Business and Personal Success.* Jackie and Kevin Freiberg. Rep. Broadway (58,463)

*Macs for Dummies, 5th ed.* David Pogue. Orig. IDG (58,000)

*Touched by an Angel: My Dinner with Andrew.* Martha Williamson. Orig. Thomas Nelson (57,984)

*Race for the Record.* Lee R. Schreiber. Orig. HarperEntertainment (57,879)

*NightWatch: A Practical Guide to Viewing the Universe.* Terence Dickinson. Reissue. Firefly (57,530)

*Buy Wholesale by Mail '99.* The Print Project. Orig. HarperResource (57,220)

*Poetry Under Oath.* Tom Simon. Orig. Workman (57,018)

*HTML 4 for Dummies.* Ed Tittel. Orig. IDG (57,000)

*The Thin Red Line.* James Jones. Reissue. Delta/DTP (56,882)

*Peter Norton's Complete Guide to Windows 95, 1998 Edition.* Peter Norton and John Mueller. Orig. Macmillan/Sams (56,791)

*\*MCSE NT Server 4 Exam Cram.* Ed Tittel, Kurt Hudson, and J. Michael Stewart. Rep. Coriolis

*\*Alias Grace.* Margaret Atwood. Rep. Anchor (56,462)

*Sam's Teach Yourself Visual Basic 6 in 24 Hours.* Greg Perry. Orig. Macmillan/Sams (56,393)

*Cloister Walk.* Kathleen Norris. Rep. Riverhead (56,000)

*Programming Perl, 2nd ed.* Larry Wall. Orig. O'Reilly (56,264)

*HTML: The Definitive Guide, 2nd ed.* Chuck Musciano. Orig. O'Reilly (55,998)

*\*WWJD Spiritual Challenge Journal: A 30-Day Faith-in-Action Adventure for Students.* Mike Yaconelli. Orig. Zondervan (55,856)

*Sam's Teach Yourself the Internet in 10 Minutes.* Paul Cassel. Origx. Macmillan/ Sams (55,804)

*\*I Love You, Mom.* Edited by Gary Morris. Orig. Blue Mountain (55,673)

*Sam's Teach Yourself Windows 95 in 10 Minutes.* Dick Oliver. Orig. Macmillan/Sams (55,635)

*MCSE TCP/IP Exam Cram.* Ed Tittel, Kurt Hudson, and J. Michael Stewart. Rep. Coriolis

*Book of God: The Bible as a Novel.* Walter Wangerin, Jr. Rep. Zondervan (53,551)

*\*Weight Training for Dummies.* Lize Neporent and Suzanne Schlosberg. Orig. IDG (55,000)

*Blackstone Chronicles.* John Saul. Orig. Fawcett (55,000)

*The Complete Idiot's Guide to a Healthy Relationship.* Dr. Judy Kuriansky. Orig. Macmillan (55,000)

*Naked Came the Manatee.* Carl Hiaasen. Rep. Ballantine (55,000)

*\*To My Child.* Edited by Gary Morris. Orig. Blue Mountain (54,970)

*\*MCSE Networking Essentials Exam Cram.* Ed Tittel, Kurt Hudson, and J. Michael Stewart. Rep. Coriolis

*\*Essential Guide to Prescription Drugs.* James Rybacki. Rep. HarperResource (54,433)

*Two Brothers: The Lawman & the Gunslinger.* Linda Lael Miller. Orig. Pocket

*The Simpsons Comics on Parade.* Matt Groening. Orig. HarperPerennial (53,492)

*Quicken 99 for Windows for Dummies.* Stephen L. Nelson. Orig. IDG (53,000)

*Road Rules Journals.* Alison Pollet. Orig. Pocket

*Middle Age Spread.* Lynn Johnston. Orig. Andrews McMeel (52,879)

*I Want to Believe.* Any Meisler. Orig. HarperEntertainment (52,551)

*The Little iMac Book.* Robin Williams. Orig. Peachpit (52,294)

*Mistress of Spices.* Chitra Divakaruni. Rep. Anchor (52,250)

*Cover Letters That Knock 'em Dead, 3rd ed.* Martin Yate. Rep. Adams Media (52,117)

*Organizing from the Inside Out.* Julie Morgenstem. Orig. Holt (52,073)

*All the Birds of North America.* Jack Griggs. Orig. HarperResource (52,012)

*Teach Yourself Office 97 Visually.* Ruth Maran. Orig. IDG (52,000)

*Word for Windows 95 for Dummies.* Dan Gookin. Orig. IDG (52,000)

*Office 97 Simplified.* Ruth Maran. Orig. IDG (52,000)

*\*Oscar & Lucinda.* Peter Carey. Rep. Vintage (51,900)

*On Writing Well, 6th ed.* William Zinsser. Rep. HarperResource (51,885)

*Palm Pilot: The Ultimate Guide.* David Pogue. Orig. O'Reilly (51,855)

*Java Script: The Definitive Guide.* David Flanagan. Orig. O'Reilly (51,622)

*Sam's Teach Yourself Windows 95 in 10 Minutes.* Sue Plumley. Orig. Macmillan/Sams (51,576)

*Crooked Little Hearts.* by Anne Lamont. Rep. Anchor (51,516)

*Sam's Teach Yourself Office 97 in 10 Minutes.* Nancy Warner. Orig. Macmillan/Sams (51,471)

*Microsoft Windows NT Workstation 4.0 Resource Kit.* Microsoft Corp. Rep. Microsoft (51,457)

*How to Use Windows 98.* Doug Hergert. Orig. Macmillan/Ziff-Davis (51,431)

*Wine Spectator's Ultimate Guide to Buying Wine.* Orig. Running Press (51,396)

*\*Ten Minute Guide to Lotus Notes 4.6.* Dorothy Burke. Orig. Macmillan/Que (51,291)

*The Complete Idiot's Guide to Vitamins & Minerals.* Alan Pressman and Sheila Buff. Orig. Macmillan (51,000)

*Club Dumas.* Arturo Pérez-Reverte. Rep. Vintage (51,000)

*The Complete Idiot's Guide to Beanie Babies.* Carol Turkington and Holly Stowen. Orig. Macmillan (51,000)

*\*Eiger Dreams.* John Krakauer. Rep. Anchor (50,994)

*\*How to Use the World Wide Web, 2nd Edition.* Wayne Ause, Kathy Ivens, and Scott Arpajian. Orig. Macmillan/Que (50,965)

*Awakening the Buddha Within: Eight Steps to Enlightenment.* Lama Surya Das. Rep. Broadway (50,872)

*Unstoppable.* Cynthia Kersey. Orig. Sourcebooks (50,495)

*\*The Real Vitamin & Mineral Book: Using Supplements for Optimum Health, 2nd Edition.* Shari Lieberman and Nancy Bruning. Orig. Avery (50,452)

*Anam Cara.* John O'Donahue. Rep. HarperCollins/Cliff Street (50,348)

*The Good Book.* Peter Gomes. Rep. Avon (50,241)

*\*Rapture of Canaan.* Sheri Reynolds. Rep. Berkley (50,000)

*There Are No Accidents.* Robert Hopcke. Rep. Riverhead (50,000)

*Complete Guide to Prescription and Non-Prescription Drugs.* H. Winter Griffith. Orig. Perigee/HPBooks (50,000)

*A Man on the Moon.* Andrew Chaikin. Tie-In/Rep. Penguin (50,000)

*The Only Way I Know.* Cal Ripkin, Jr. Rep. Penguin (50,000)

*Cod.* Mark Kurlansky. Rep. Penguin (50,000)

*The Complete Idiot's Guide to Choosing, Training & Raising a Dog.* Sarah Hodgson. Orig. Macmillan (50,000)

*Ranch of Dreams.* Cleveland Amory. Rep. Penguin (50,000)

*The Complete Idiot's Guide to Starting Your Own Business, 2nd ed.* Ed Paulsen and Marcia Layton. Orig. Macmillan (50,000)

*Teach Yourself Microsoft Windows 98.* Al Stevens. Orig. IDG (50,000)

*The Complete Idiot's Guide to Learning French on Your Own.* Gail Stein. Orig. Macmillan (50,000)

*The Complete Idiot's Guide to Organizing Your Life.* Georgene Lockwood. Orig. Macmillan (50,000)

## Almanacs, Atlases and Annuals

*The World Almanac and Book of Facts 1999.* Robert Famighetti. Orig. World Almanac (1,321,405)

*The Ernst & Young Tax Guide 1998.* Orig. Wiley (450,000)

*The World Almanac and Book of Facts 1998.* Robert Famighetti. Orig. World Almanac (316,228)

*The Old Farmer's Almanac 1999.* Robert B. Thomas. Orig. Yankee Publishing (263,998)

*The Best American Short Stories 1998.* Edited by Garrison Keillor. Orig. Houghton Mifflin (141,036)

*Taxes for Dummies, '99 Edition.* Eric Tyson and David J. Silverman. Orig. IDG (137,000)

*The Unofficial Guide to Walt Disney World.* Bob Sehlinger. Orig. Macmillan (131,000)

*Birnbaum's Walt Disney World 1998.* Birnbaum Travel Guides. Orig. Hyperion (119,647)

*Birnbaum's Walt Disney World 1999.* Birnbaum Travel Guides. Orig. Hyperion (113,839)

*American Express '99 Tax Guide.* American Express. Orig. HarperCollins (101,338)

*Knock 'em Dead 1998.* Martin Yate. Orig. Adams Media (98,473)

*H&R Block 1999 Income Tax Guide.* H&R Block. Orig. Fireside (95,000)

*Places Rated Almanac.* David Savageau. Orig. Macmillan (92,000)

*The World Almanac for Kids 1999.* Elaine Israel. Orig. Yankee Publishing (87,435)

*Kovels' Antiques & Collectibles Price List 1999.* Ralph and Terry Kovel. Orig. Crown/Three Rivers (74,178)

*The 1998 ESPN/Information Please Sports Almanac.* Orig. Hyperion (70,260)

*1999 Blackbook Guide: Coins.* Marc Hudgeons. Orig. House of Collectibles (70,000)

*The New York Times Almanac 1999.* Edited by John W. Wright. Orig. Penguin (70,000)

*1999 Sports Illustrated Almanac. Sports Illustrated.* Orig. Little, Brown (60,584)

*Magical Almanac.* Orig. Llewellyn (56,812)

*The Best American Mystery Stories 1998.* Edited by Sue Grafton. Orig. Houghton Mifflin (55,324)

*Price Guide to Baseball Cards '99.* Edited by James Beckett. Orig. House of Collectibles (55,000)

*Europe on $50 a Day.* Beth Reiber. Orig. Macmillan (55,000)

*The Witches' Almanac.* Edited by Elizabeth Pepper and John Wilcock. Orig. Witches' Almanac (51,803)

*The Best American Essays 1998.* Edited by Cynthia Ozick. Orig. Houghton Mifflin (51,649)

*Europe Through the Back Door 1998.* Rick Steves. Orig. John Muir (51,159)

*Frommer's Hawaii.* Jocelyn Fuji. Orig. Macmillan (50,900)

## Mass Market

### 2 Million+

*The Partner.* John Grisham. Rep. Dell/Island (4,862,401)

*The Ghost.* Danielle Steel. Rep. Dell (2,764,713)

*The Ranch.* Danielle Steel. Rep. Dell (2,630,464)

*Special Delivery.* Danielle Steel. Rep. Dell (2,203,756)

*Unnatural Exposure.* Patricia Cornwell. Rep. Berkley (2,200,000)

*Pretend You Don't See Her.* Mary Higgins Clark. Rep. Pocket (2,100,000)

*Power Plays: ruthless.com.* Tom Clancy. Orig. Berkley (2,100,000)

*Rising Tides.* Nora Roberts. Orig. Jove (2,000,000)

### 1 Million+

*Wizard and Glass.* Stephen King. Rep. Signet (1,950,000)

*Dr. Atkins' New Diet Revolution.* Robert C. Atkins, M.D. Rep. Avon (1,798,550)

*Into Thin Air.* Jon Krakauer. Rep. Anchor (1,759,977)

*Tom Clancy's Op-Center V.* Created by Tom Clancy and Steve Pieczenik. Orig. Berkley (1,750,000)

*The Notebook.* Nicholas Sparks. Rep. Warner Vision (1,677,496)

*Fear Nothing.* Dean Koontz. Rep. Bantam (1,650,000)

*Sanctuary.* Nora Roberts. Rep. Jove (1,600,000)

*Small Town Girl.* Lavyrle Spencer. Rep. Jove (1,535,000)

*Butterfly.* V.C. Andrews. Orig. Pocket

*Crystal.* V.C. Andrews. Orig. Pocket

*The Best Laid Plans.* Sidney Sheldon. Rep. Warner (1,414,761)

*The Perfect Storm.* Sebastian Junger. Rep. HarperPerennial (1,406,804)

*M Is for Malice.* Sue Grafton. Rep. Fawcett (1,403,000)

*Chromosome 6.* Robin Cook. Rep. Berkley (1,400,000)

*Brooke.* V.C. Andrews. Orig. Pocket

*Raven.* V.C. Andrews. Orig. Pocket

*Music in the Night.* V.C. Andrews. Dual. Pocket

*Cat & Mouse.* James Patterson. Rep. Warner (1,305,227)

*The Maze.* Catherine Coulter. Rep. Jove (1,300,000)

*Night Crew.* John Sandford. Rep. Berkley (1,300,000)

*Survival of the Fittest.* Jonathan Kellerman. Rep. Bantam (1,300,000)

*Runaways.* V.C. Andrews. Dual. Pocket

*All I Need Is You.* Johanna Lindsey. Rep. Avon (1,207,575)

*She's Come Undone.* Wally Lamb. Rep. Pocket

*\*Protein Power.* Michael R. Eades, M.D., and Mary Dan Eades, M.D. Rep. Bantam (1,200,000)

*Fat Tuesday.* Sandra Brown. Rep. Warner Vision (1,196,732)

*Public Secrets.* Nora Roberts. Rep. Bantam (1,175,000)

*Secrecy.* Belva Plain. Rep. Dell (1,144,954)

*Angel of Darkness.* Caleb Carr. Rep. Ballantine (1,140,000)

*Evening Class.* Maeve Binchy. Rep. Dell (1,112,365)

*The Servant of the Bones.* Anne Rice. Rep. Ballantine (1,105,000)

*Petals on the River.* Kathleen E. Woodiwiss. Rep. Avon. (1,102,425)

*Homecoming.* Belva Plain. Rep. Dell (1,094,133)

*Flood Tide.* Clive Cussler. Rep. Pocket

*The Winner.* David Baldacci. Rep. Warner Vision (1,046,618)

*Come the Spring.* Julie Garwood. Rep. Pocket

*Angel for Emily.* Jude Deveraux. Orig. Pocket

*Up Island.* Anne Rivers Siddons. Rep. HarperPaperbacks (1,014,590)

*Power of a Woman.* Barbara Taylor Bradford. Rep. HarperPaperbacks (1,008,186)

*The Cobra Event.* Richard Preston. Rep. Ballantine (1,000,000)

*The Presence.* John Saul. Rep. Fawcett (1,000,000)

*Critical Judgment.* Michael Palmer. Rep. Bantam (1,000,000)

*A Thin Dark Line.* Tami Hoag. Rep. Bantam (1,000,000)

*And Then You Die.* Iris Johansen. Rep. Bantam (1,000,000)

*Detective.* Arthur Hailey. Rep. Berkley (1,000,000)

# Children's Bestsellers: Licensed Tie-ins Make Registers Ring

## Diane Roback
### Senior Editor, Children's Books, *Publishers Weekly*

Children's book sales held their own in 1998, with dips in some segments of the market balanced by increases in others. Hardcover frontlist did not perform as well as the previous year; in 1997, 150 titles sold more than 75,000 copies, compared to 117 in 1998. And 32 titles sold more than 200,000 copies last year, down from 39 the year before.

A major factor for the decline was a slowdown of sales at Golden Books. In 1997, eight of the top ten hardcover frontlist titles were published by Golden, for a total of 2,706,260 copies sold. In comparison, only one Golden title landed in 1998's top ten (a tie-in to Disney's *Mulan*, with sales of 436,042).

TV licenses *Blue's Clues* and *Teletubbies*, newly translated into books last year, made strong showings on our lists, with *Blue's Clues* titles nabbing the number one and number two hardcover frontlist spots. Strong non-series sellers included *If You Give a Pig a Pancake* (the second follow-up to the very successful *If You Give a Mouse a Cookie*); *The 20th-Century Children's Book Treasury*, an anthology that performed very well over the holiday season; and *Today I Feel Silly*, the latest picture book by Jamie Lee Curtis.

The category of hardcover backlist showed some gains: 23 titles sold more than 300,000 copies, compared to 17 in 1997, and 117 titles sold more than 125,000 copies, vs. only 85 the previous year. Backlist perennials like Pooh, Barney and various Disney titles are still going strong, as are board-book editions of favorite picture books (*Goodnight Moon, Guess How Much I Love You* and *Brown Bear, Brown Bear, What Do You See?*).

As for paperback frontlist, overall sales were down slightly compared to the preceding year. In 1998, 92 titles sold more than 125,000 copies, compared to 100 in 1997, and 25 titles sold more than 300,000 copies, vs. 22 in 1997. The Animorphs have invaded: 12 Animorphs titles sold more than 300,000 copies each last year (the series debuted in 1996). The Goosebumps series was much less of a force; 1997 had shown a dramatic decline in sales compared to the year before, and that trend continued. The bestselling Goosebumps title of 1996 sold 2,140,000 copies, compared to 886,000 copies for 1997's topselling title, and just 267,000 in 1998.

Paperback backlist, though, showed a comeback over the previous year's levels: 91 titles sold over the 125,000 mark in 1998, compared to 77 in 1997. There were some dramatic jumps in sales (*The Giver* rose from 302,059 copies to 644,560, and *Shiloh* increased from 262,344 copies to 520,726, thanks to a summer reading campaign by Bantam Doubleday Dell, while other books showed more modest gains (*Where the Wild Things Are* went from 201,843 copies to 233,510, and *Hatchet* rose from 210,094 copies to 233,579). *Love You Forever*, a staple of backlist bestseller lists, had remarkably steady sales: 625,463 copies in 1998 and 626,489 copies the year before.

Adapted from *Publishers Weekly*, March 29, 1999

For this roundup, publishers were asked to supply trade figures only, reflecting returns as of February 1, 1999. Since figures do not include total returns, they consequently do not represent net sales. Some books appear on our lists without sales figures; these figures were supplied for ranking purposes only.

## Hardcover Frontlist

### 300,000+

1. *Blue's Clues: The Shape Detective.* Simon Spotlight (488,753)
2. *Blue's Clues: Blue's #1 Picnic.* Simon Spotlight (470,532)
3. *Barney's Twinkle, Twinkle Little Star.* Lyrick/Barney (444,948)
4. *Disney's Mulan.* Golden (436,042)
5. *If You Give a Pig a Pancake.* Laura Numeroff, illus. by Felicia Bond. HarperCollins/Geringer (419,021)
6. *A Bug's Life: Classic Storybook.* Disney/Mouseworks (375,000)
7. *Blue's Clues: Blue's Big Birthday.* Simon Spotlight (366,159)
8. *The 20th-Century Children's Book Treasury.* Edited by Janet Schulman. Knopf (348,219)
9. *Teletubbies: The Magic String.* Scholastic (345,000)
10. *Teletubbies Play Hide-and-Seek.* Scholastic (343,000)
11. *Blue's Clues: Lights On! Lights Off!* Simon Spotlight (341,382)
12. *The Little Puffy Cloud (Teletubbies).* Scholastic (336,000)
13. *Today I Feel Silly & Other Moods That Make My Day.* Jamie Lee Curtis, illus. by Laura Cornell. HarperCollins/Cotler (324,559)
14. *Blue's Clues: Blue's Felt Friends.* Simon Spotlight (320,092)
15. *Mulan Classic Storybook.* Disney/MouseWorks (300,000)
16. *Disney's Christmas Friendly Tales: Santa Pooh.* Disney/MouseWorks (300,000)

### 200,000+

17. *Mickey: Disney's Friendly Tales.* Disney/MouseWorks (298,826)
18. *Rudolph the Red-Nosed Reindeer.* Golden (287,350)
19. *Teletubbies Like to Dance!* Scholastic (287,000)
20. *Pooh: King of the Beasties.* Golden (284,192)
21. *Here Come the Teletubbies.* Scholastic (269,000)
22. *Dear America: Titanic Voyage.* Ellen Emerson White. Scholastic (260,000)
23. *Animorphs: Hork-Bajir Chronicles.* K.A. Applegate. Scholastic (259,000)
24. *I Spy Gold Challenger!* Jean Marzollo, illus. by Walter Wick. Scholastic (258,000)
25. *The Cheerios Play Book.* Lee Wade. Little Simon (256,392)
26. *Hooray for Diffendoofer Day!* Jack Prelutsky, illus. by Lane Smith. Knopf (242,500)

27. *Minnie: Disney's Friendly Tales.* Disney/MouseWorks (232,218)
28. *Donald Duck: Disney's Friendly Tales.* Disney/MouseWorks (221,669)
29. *The Night Before Christmas.* Jan Brett. Putnam (220,921)
30. *Goofy: Disney's Friendly Tales.* Disney/MouseWorks (220,334)
31. *The Prince of Egypt Classic Storybook.* Jane Yolen. Dutton/DreamWorks (207,259)
32. *Disney Storybook Collection.* Disney (200,000)

**100,000+**

33. *Barney's Baby Farm Animals.* Lyrick/Barney (198,163)
34. *Barney's Animal Homes.* Lyrick/Barney (190,938)
35. *101 Dalmatians: Rainbow Puppies.* Golden (184,148)
36. *The Legend of Candy Cane.* Lori Walburg, illus. by James Bernardin. Zondervan (184,023)
37. *Wait for Elmo.* Molly Cross, illus. by Joe Mathieu. Random House (183,611)
38. *Barney's Adventure Hunt.* Lyrick/Barney (181,888)
39. *Squids Will Be Squids.* Jon Scieszka, illus. by Lane Smith. Viking (179,804)
40. *Simba Pride's Classic Storybook.* Disney/MouseWorks (175,000)
41. *Happy Days.* Disney/MouseWorks (175,000)
42. *A Bug's Life: Seek and See.* Disney/MouseWorks (175,000)
43. *I Spy Little Animals Board Book.* Jean Marzollo, illus. by Walter Wick. Scholastic (166,000)
44. *Look-Alikes.* Joan Steiner. Little, Brown (165,280)
45. *Arthur Counts.* Marc Brown. Random House (159,256)
46. *The Christmas Candle.* Richard Paul Evans, illus. by Jacob Collins. S&S (157,129)
47. *Barney: A Very Musical Day.* Golden (152,638)
48. *Better Homes and Gardens New Junior Cookbook.* Meredith (152,493)
49. *Breakfast Time: The Tank Engine Storybook.* Rev. W. Awdry, illus. by Owain Bell. Random House (149,222)
50. *The New Way Things Work.* David Macaulay. Houghton Mifflin/Lorraine (146,018)
51. *Arthur Decks the Halls.* Marc Brown. Random House (145,238)
52. *Babe: Looking for Dash.* Molly Kates, illus. by Jan Gerardi. Random House (143,488)
53. *Richard Scarry's Little Counting Book.* Richard Scarry. Random House (142,769)
54. *Trucks.* Harry McNaught. Random House (140,029)
55. *The Snowman's Song.* Mallory Clare, illus. by Jean Hirashima. Random House (138,569)

56. *The Berenstain Bears Get the Don't Haftas.* Stan and Jan Berenstain. Random House (138,545)

57. *Richard Scarry's ABC.* Richard Scarry. Random House (136,584)

58. *Harry Potter and the Sorcerer's Stone.* J.K. Rowling. Scholastic/ Levine (136,000)

59. *Arthur Goes on the Farm.* Marc Brown. Random House (134,709)

60. *Fruit Troop: Gladys Grape.* Melody Carlson. Multnomah (133,679)

61. *The Berenstain Bears Get the Screamies.* Stan and Jan Berenstain. Random House (131,885)

62. *It's Almost Christmas, Rudolph!* Golden (131,745)

63. *West to the Land of Plenty.* Jim Murphy. Scholastic (130,000)

64. *A Bug's Life: Where Are the Bugs?* Disney/MouseWorks (130,000)

65. *Guess How Much I Love You Pop-Up.* Sam McBratney, illus. by Anita Jeram. Candlewick (128,366)

66. *Nursery Rhymes of Winnie the Pooh.* Disney (125,000)

67. *ABC Disney Pop-Up.* Robert Sabuda. Disney (125,000)

68. *Barney and Twinken.* Lyrick/Barney (124,541)

69. *Disney's Mickey and Friends: Mickey Goes to the Airport.* Golden (123,767)

70. *Dear America: Dreams in the Golden Country.* Kathryn Lasky. Scholastic (123,000)

71. *I Love You As Much (board book).* Laura Krauss Melmed, illus. by Henri Sorensen. Morrow/Tupelo (120,521)

72. *Arthur's Boo Boo Book.* Marc Brown. Random House (120, 251)

73. *Time for School, Little Dinosaur.* Gail Herman, illus. by Norman Gorbaty. Random House (120,198)

74. *A Bug's Life: Red Bug, Blue Bug.* Disney/MouseWorks (120,000)

75. *Three Little Kittens.* Lilian Obligado. Random House (119, 882)

76. *Pippa Mouse's House.* Betty Boegehold, illus. by Julie Durrell. Random House (117,204)

77. *Bambi.* Golden (114,910)

78. *Curious George's ABC.* H.A. Rey. Houghton Mifflin (111,817)

79. *Fruit Troop: Strawberry Sam.* Melody Carlson. Multnomah (111,177)

80. *I Spy Little Wheels Board Book.* Jean Marzollo, illus. by Walter Wick. Scholastic (111,000)

81. *Wheels on the Bus (board book).* Raffi, illus. by Sylvie Kantorovitz Wickstrom. Crown (109,245)

82. *Sing with Me... My Name Is Ernie.* Golden (108,909)

83. *American Heritage Children's Dictionary.* Houghton Mifflin (108,783)

84. *Are You My Mother? (board book).* P.D. Eastman. Random House (106,114)

85. *Fruit Troop: Penny Pear.* Melody Carlson. Multnomah (105,214)

86. *Curious George and the Bunny.* H.A. Rey. Houghton Mifflin (104,805)

87. *Dear America: Standing in the Light.* Mary Pope Osborne. Scholastic (103,000)
88. *Hand, Hand, Finger, Thumb.* Al Perkins, illus. by Eric Gurney. Random House (102,585)
89. *Marlfox.* Brian Jacques. Philomel (101,332)
90. *Disney's Family Story Collection.* Disney (100,000)
91. *Pooh Says Boo!* Disney/MouseWorks (100,000)
92. *Winnie the Pooh's Christmas Tree Holiday Board Book.* Disney/Mouse-Works (100,000)
93. *Pooh's Five Little Honeypots.* Disney/MouseWorks (100,000)
94. *Pooh's Red Blue & Pooh Shapes, Too!* Disney/MouseWorks (100,000)

**75,000+**

95. *Curious George's Are You Curious?* H.A. Rey. Houghton Mifflin (99,793)
96. *Barney's Storybook Treasury.* Lyrick/Barney (98,946)
97. *Dear America: A Line in the Sand.* Sherry Garland. Scholastic (98,000)
98. *Miss Spider's ABC Book.* David Kirk. Scholastic (98,000)
99. *The Rainbow Fish and the Big Blue Whale.* Marcus Pfister. North-South (96,371)
100. *Rudolph the Red-Nosed Reindeer.* Golden (95,505)
101. *Disney's A Bug's Life: Dot's Great Big World.* Golden (95,178)
102. *My Many Colored Days (board book).* Dr. Seuss, illus. by Steve Johnson and Lou Fancher. Knopf (91,368)
103. *Disney's Simba's Pride: Kiara's Colors.* Golden (89,595)
104. *When Mama Comes Home Tonight.* Eileen Spinelli, illus. by Jane Dyer. S&S (89,065)
105. *Stop, Train, Stop!* Rev. W. Awdry, illus. by Owain Bell. Random House (83,495)
106. *Pooh's First Clock.* A.A. Milne. Dutton (82,879)
107. *The Long Patrol.* Brian Jacques. Philomel (82,451)
108. *Miss Fannie's Hat.* Jan Karon, illus. by Toni Goffe. Augsburg (82,136)
109. *Picture That! Bible Storybook.* Zondervan (80,615)
110. *Wake Up, Groundhog!* Golden (80,047)
111. *Arthur's Baby (board book).* Marc Brown. Little, Brown (79,748)
112. *Arthur's Helpful Bedtime Stories.* Marc Brown. Random House (76,389)
113. *Mary's First Christmas.* Walter Wangerin Jr., illus. by Timothy Ladwig. Zondervan (75,762)
114. *Disney's Pooh's 123.* Disney/ MouseWorks (75,000)
115. *Winnie the Pooh's Spookable Halloween.* Disney/MouseWorks (75,000)
116. *Mickey's Christmas Candy Holiday Board Book.* Disney/MouseWorks (75,000)
117. *Simba's Faces.* Disney/MouseWorks (75,000)

# Hardcover Backlist
**300,000+**

1. *Pooh's Friendly Tale.* Disney/ MouseWorks, 1997 (710,393)
2. *Tigger's Friendly Tale.* Disney/ MouseWorks, 1997 (653,871)
3. *Disney: Thank You, Pooh!* Golden, 1996 (628,870)
4. *Eeyore's Friendly Tale.* Disney/ MouseWorks, 1997 (540,614)
5. *Barney: Sharing Is Caring.* Golden, 1996 (532,811)
6. *Piglet's Friendly Tale.* Disney/ MouseWorks, 1997 (530,200)
7. *Pooh: The Grand and Wonderful Day.* Golden, 1995 (506,866)
8. *Goodnight Moon (board book).* Margaret Wise Brown, illus. by Clement Hurd. HarperFestival, 1991 (417,973)
9. *Barbie: The Special Sleepover.* Golden, 1997 (392,925)
10. *Disney's Lion King: Way to Go, Simba!* Golden, 1996 (391,719)
11. *My First Little Mother Goose.* Illus. by Lucinda McQueen. Golden, 1996 (391,719)
12. *Scholastic Children's Dictionary.* Scholastic, 1996 (367,000)
13. *Disney: Pooh's Grand Adventure: The Search for Christopher Robin.* Golden, 1997 (363,848)
14. *Brown Bear, Brown Bear, What Do You See? (board book).* Bill Martin Jr., illus. by Eric Carle. Holt, 1996 (355,845)
15. *Pooh: The Sweetest Christmas.* Golden, 1996 (349,732)
16. *Disney: Baby Mickey's Book of Shapes.* Golden, 1986 (348, 307)
17. *Disney's 101 Dalmatians.* Golden, 1996 (336,072)
18. *Disney's Winnie the Pooh and the Honey Tree.* Golden, 1994 (335,228)
19. *The Many Adventures of Winnie the Pooh.* Disney, 1997 (334,033)
20. *Green Eggs & Ham.* Dr. Seuss. Random House, 1966 (333,425)
21. *The Night Before Christmas.* Clement C. Moore, illus. by Christian Birmingham. Running Press/ Courage, 1995 (327,539)
22. *Oh, the Places You'll Go!* Dr. Seuss. Random House, 1990 (313,779)
23. *Barney: Catch the Hat!* Golden, 1997 (309,529)

**200,000+**

24. *Sesame Street: Count to Ten.* Golden, 1986 (294,082)
25. *Disney's Pooh and the Dragon.* Golden, 1997 (279,968)
26. *The Three Bears.* Golden, 1983 (277,686)
27. *Tickle Me: My Name Is Elmo.* Golden, 1993 (277,567)
28. *Pooh: The Very Best Easter Bunny.* Golden, 1997 (275,846)
29. *Pat the Bunny.* Dorothy Kunhardt. Golden, 1940 (273,200)
30. *Polar Bear, Polar Bear, What Do You Hear? (board book).* Bill Martin Jr., illus. by Eric Carle. Holt, 1997 (267,025)
31. *The Wheels on the Bus.* Illus. by R.W. Alley. Golden, 1992 (251,258)

32. *Where the Sidewalk Ends.* Shel Silverstein. HarperCollins, 1974 (249,817)

33. *Noah's Ark.* Golden, 1997 (249,368)

34. *Sesame Street: Shake a Leg!* Golden, 1991 (247,950)

35. *The Giving Tree.* Shel Silverstein. HarperCollins, 1964 (247,899)

36. *Falling Up.* Shel Silverstein. HarperCollins, 1996 (247,248)

37. *The Cat in the Hat.* Dr. Seuss. Random House, 1966 (210,607)

38. *Guess How Much I Love You (board book).* Sam McBratney, illus. by Anita Jeram. Candlewick, 1995 (245,127)

39. *Pooh: Trick or Treat!* Golden, 1991 (236,977)

40. *Pooh: I Can Share Too!* Golden, 1997 (236,960)

41. *Sesame Street: Another Monster at the End of This Book.* Golden, 1996 (234,774)

42. *Baby Animals on the Farm.* Golden, 1990 (231,655)

43. *A Day with Barney.* Lyrick/Barney, 1994 (230,719)

44. *The Very Hungry Caterpillar (board book).* Eric Carle. Philomel, 1994 (230,169)

45. *Barney's Number Friends.* Lyrick/Barney, 1996 (228,952)

46. *Moo, Baa, La La La (board book).* Sandra Boynton. Little Simon, 1995 (226,395)

47. *Butterfly Kisses.* Bob Carlisle et al. Golden, 1997 (223,091)

48. *My First Counting Book.* Golden, 1996 (216,804)

49. *Elmo's Twelve Days of Christmas.* Golden, 1996 (216,304)

50. *The Going to Bed Book (board book).* Sandra Boynton. Little Simon, 1995 (209,770)

51. *Elmo's Guessing Game.* Golden, 1994 (205,190)

52. *The Three Little Pigs.* Golden, 1996 (200,368)

**125,000+**

53. *The Little Engine That Could.* Watty Piper. Grosset & Dunlap, 1930 (199,596)

54. *I Spy Christmas.* Jean Marzollo, illus. by Walter Wick. Scholastic, 1992 (199,000)

55. *Disney's 101 Dalmatians.* Golden, 1997 (197,117)

56. *Dr. Seuss' ABC (board book).* Dr. Seuss. Random House, 1996 (194,356)

57. *The Little Golden Picture Dictionary.* Golden, 1981 (191,694)

58. *Arthur Goes to School.* Marc Brown. Random House, 1995 (190,899)

59. *Mr. Brown Can Moo: Can You?* Dr. Seuss. Random House, 1996 (190,274)

60. *Sesame Street: Zip! Pop! Hop! And Other Fun Words to Say.* Golden, 1996 (189,522)

61. *Olive, the Other Reindeer.* J.otto Seibold and Vivian Walsh. Chronicle, 1997 (189,000)

62. *The Fuzzy Duckling.* Jane Werner, illus. by Alice and Martin Provensen. Golden, 1949 (187,603)
63. *Disney: Bambi and the Butterfly.* Golden, 1982 (187,285)
64. *I Spy Super Challenger.* Jean Marzollo, illus.by Walter Wick. Scholastic, 1997 (184,000)
65. *Disney: Pooh Has Ears.* Golden, 1995 (183,702)
66. *Bedtime for Baby Bop.* Lyrick/Barney, 1996 (183,468)
67. *Fuzzy Yellow Ducklings.* Matthew Van Fleet. Dial, 1995 (179,825)
68. *I Spy Little Book.* Jean Marzollo, illus. by Walter Wick. Scholastic, 1997 (179,000)
69. *Barney Goes to the Zoo.* Lyrick/ Barney, 1993 (173,888)
70. *Barbie and the Scavenger Hunt.* Golden, 1996 (171,137)
71. *Pooh: All Year Long.* Golden, 1981 (171,017)
72. *Elmo Loves You.* Golden, 1997 (170,841)
73. *A to Z (board book).* Sandra Boynton. Little Simon, 1995 (170,123)
74. *The Poky Little Puppy.* Janette Sebring Lowrey, illus. by Gustaf Tenggren. Golden, 1942 (167,398)
75. *A Light in the Attic.* Shel Silverstein. HarperCollins, 1981 (165,483)
76. *Barney Plays Nose to Toes.* Lyrick/Barney, 1996 (164,304)
77. *Barney: The Best Christmas Eve!* Golden, 1997 (163,899)
78. *If You Give a Mouse a Cookie.* Laura Numeroff, illus. by Felicia Bond. HarperCollins/Geringer, 1985 (163,369)
79. *Barney's Alphabet Soup.* Lyrick/ Barney, 1997 (162,469)
80. *Time for Bed (board book).* Mem Fox. Harcourt/Red Wagon, 1997 (157,373)
81. *The Complete Adventures of Curious George.* Margret and H.A. Rey. Houghton Mifflin, 1995 (156,698)
82. *Hop on Pop.* Dr. Seuss. Random House, 1966 (156,028)
83. *Where the Wild Things Are.* Maurice Sendak. HarperCollins, 1963 (155,589)
84. *The Polar Express.* Chris Van Allsburg. Houghton Mifflin, 1985 (155,272)
85. *Disney's The Lion King.* Golden, 1994 (153,409)
86. *Barney: A Very Musical Day.* Golden, 1996 (152,638)
87. *I Spy School Days.* Jean Marzollo, illus. by Walter Wick. Scholastic, 1995 (152,000)
88. *Pooh: Eeyore, Be Happy!* Golden, 1991 (151,245)
89. *Sesame Street: Big Bird's Busy Day.* Golden, 1993 (149,929)
90. *My Little Golden Book About God.* Golden, 1975 (149,686)
91. *I Spy Spooky Night.* Jean Marzollo, illus. by Walter Wick. Scholastic, 1995 (149,000)
92. *Are You My Mother?* P.D. Eastman. Random House, 1960 (148,993)
93. *My Little People Farm.* Reader's Digest, 1997 (145,987)

94. *Barney's This Little Piggy*. Lyrick/Barney, 1997 (143,301)

95. *Opposites (board book)*. Eric Carle. Little Simon, 1995 (142,060)

96. *I Spy Fun House*. Jean Marzollo, illus. by Walter Wick. Scholastic, 1993 (142,000)

97. *Prayers for Children*. Illus. by Peter Alvarado. Golden, 1974 (141,398)

98. *Pooh: Guess Who?* Golden, 1996 (141,209)

99. *I Spy Fantasy*. Jean Marzollo, illus. by Walter Wick. Scholastic, 1994 (141,000)

100. *What Would Jesus Do?* Helen Haidle. Multnomah, 1997 (138,458)

101. *I Spy*. Jean Marzollo, illus. by Walter Wick. Scholastic, 1992 (137,000)

102. *Barney's Farm Animals*. Lyrick/ Barney, 1993 (136,286)

103. *How the Grinch Stole Christmas*. Dr. Seuss. Random House, 1966 (135,766)

104. *Barney's Color Surprise*. Lyrick/ Barney, 1993 (135,538)

105. *Dr. Seuss' ABC Book*. Dr. Seuss. Random House, 1966 (135,264)

106. *Good Night, Gorilla (board book)*. Peggy Rathmann. Dutton, 1996 (133,133)

107. *The Rainbow Fish*. Marcus Pfister. North-South, 1992 (133,350)

108. *Pooh: Happy Easter*. Golden, 1996 (133,055)

109. *Barnyard Dance! (board book)*. Sandra Boynton. Workman, 1993 (133,000)

110. *Where's Arthur's Gerbil?* Marc Brown. Random House, 1997 (131,648)

111. *The Complete Tales of Winnie-the-Pooh*. A.A. Milne. Dutton, 1996 (130,634)

112. *My Little People School Bus*. Reader's Digest, 1997 (130,611)

113. *The Mitten (board book)*. Jan Brett. Putnam, 1996 (128,326)

114. *The Very Quiet Cricket (board book)*. Eric Carle. Philomel, 1997 (127,042)

115. *Dear America: Across the Wide and Lonesome Prairie*. Kristina Gregory. Scholastic, 1997 (126,000)

116. *Seussisms*. Dr. Seuss. Random House, 1997 (125,699)

117. *Inside the Titanic*. Hugh Brewster, illus. by Ken Marschall. Little, Brown, 1997 (125,318)

## Paperback Frontlist

### 300,000+

1. *Chicken Soup for the Kid's Soul*. Jack Canfield, Mark Victor Hansen, Patty Hansen, and Irene Dunlap. Health Communications (1,325,991)

2. *Leonardo: A Scrapbook in Words and Pictures*. Grace Catalano. Dell (586,065)

3. *Disney's A Bug's Life*. Golden (581,474)

4. *Barney's Great Adventure*. Lyrick/ Barney (512,331)

5. *Blue's Clues: Blue and the Color Detectives.* Simon Spotlight (477,408)
6. *Blue's Clues: Blue Skidoos to the Farm.* Simon Spotlight (406,453)
7. *Nickelodeon: The Rugrats Movie.* Cathy East Dubowski and Mark Dubowski. Pocket/Minstrel
8. *In the Time of Dinosaurs (Animorphs Megamorphs #2).* K.A. Applegate. Scholastic (364,000)
9. *Pooh's Pumpkin.* Disney (350,000)
10. *Arthur Tricks the Tooth Fairy.* Marc Brown. Random House (346,900)
11. *The Threat (Animorphs #21).* K.A. Applegate. Scholastic (339,000)
12. *The Pretender (Animorphs #23).* K.A. Applegate. Scholastic (339,000)
13. *The Escape (Animorphs #15).* K.A. Applegate. Scholastic (334,000)
14. *The Discovery (Animorphs #20).* K.A. Applegate. Scholastic (333,000)
15. *The Suspicion (Animorphs #24).* K.A. Applegate. Scholastic (333,000)
16. *The Solution (Animorphs #22).* K.A. Applegate. Scholastic (330,000)
17. *The Departure (Animorphs #19).* K.A. Applegate. Scholastic (329,000)
18. *The Warning (Animorphs #16).* K.A. Applegate. Scholastic (321,000)
19. *The Decision (Animorphs #18).* K.A. Applegate. Scholastic (317,000)
20. *The Extreme (Animorphs #25).* K.A. Applegate. Scholastic (315,000)
21. *Barney's Alphabet Fun.* Lyrick/Barney (311,016)
22. *The Underground (Animorphs #17).* K.A. Applegate Scholastic (309,000)
23. *Barney Goes to the Farm.* Lyrick/Barney (302,139)
24. *Disney's Mulan.* Disney (300,846)
25. *Disney's The Parent Trap.* Disney (300,000)

## 200,000+

26. *Teletubbies: Four Happy Teletubbies.* Scholastic (298,000)
27. *\*N SYNC: The Official Book.* \*N SYNC, with K.M. Squires. Dell (290,390)
28. *Zac Hanson: Totally Zac!* Matt Netter. Pocket/Archway
29. *Teletubbies: Tubby Custard Mess.* Scholastic (284,000)
30. *Teletubbies: Go, Po, Go!* Scholastic (282,000)
31. *Leonardo DiCaprio: A Biography.* Nancy Krulik. Pocket/Archway
32. *Disney's Simba's Pride.* Golden (274,100)
33. *Barney's The Chase Is On!* Lyrick/Barney (271,832)
34. *Teletubbies: Dipsy Dances.* Scholastic (269,000)
35. *Disney's A Bug's Life: The Big Rescue.* Golden (267,340)
36. *Bride of the Living Dummy (Goosebumps 2000 #2).* R.L. Stine. Scholastic (267,000)
37. *A Bug's Life.* Disney (260,000)
38. *Disney's First Reader: Flik's Perfect Gift.* Disney (260,000)
39. *Creature Teacher (GB 2000 #3).* R.L. Stine. Scholastic (259,000)
40. *The Rugrats' Joke Book.* David Lewman. Simon Spotlight (258,273)

41. *The Rugrats Movie: Tommy's New Playmate.* Simon Spotlight (254,127)
42. *The Rugrats Movie Storybook.* Simon Spotlight (240,500)
43. *Isaac Hanson: Totally Ike!* Nancy Krulik. Pocket/Archway
44. *Redwall.* Brian Jacques. Berkley/ Ace (240,000)
45. *The Rugrats Movie: The Rugrats vs. the Monkeys.* Simon Spotlight (236,403)
46. *Invasion of the Body Squeezers Pt. 1 (GB 2000 #40).* R.L. Stine. Scholastic (231,000)
47. *The Care & Keeping of You: The Body Book for Girls.* Valerie Schaefer, illus. by Norm Bendell. Pleasant Co. (222,410)
48. *Rugrats: Where the Sharks Are.* Duncan Maxfield, illus. by George Ulrich. Simon Spotlight (218,391)
49. *Belle Prater's Boy.* Ruth White. Dell/ Yearling (212,227)
50. *Rugrats Jungle Trek.* Simon Spotlight (211,068)
51. *Invasion of the Body Squeezers, Pt. II (GB 2000 #5).* R.L. Stine. Scholastic (204,000)
52. *\*N SYNC: Tearin' Up the Charts.* Matt Netter. Pocket/Archway
53. *The Heart and Soul of Nick Carter: Secrets Only a Mother Knows.* Jane Carter. Onyx (200,000)

**150,000+**

54. *The Vanishings (Left Behind—The Kids #1).* Jerry B. Jenkins and Tim LaHaye. Tyndale (194,464)
55. *I Am Your Evil Twin (GB 2000 #6).* R.L. Stine. Scholastic (193,000)
56. *Taylor Hanson: Totally Taylor!* Nancy Krulik. Pocket/Archway
57. *Blue's Clues: Blue's Bubbly Tub.* Simon Spotlight (184,060)
58. *Prince of Egypt: Moses in Egypt.* Lynne Reid Banks. Puffin/DreamWorks (173,572)
59. *Fright Camp (GB 2000 #8).* R.L. Stine. Scholastic (163,000)
60. *Revenge R Us (GB 2000 #7).* R.L. Stine. Scholastic (162,000)
61. *Arthur's Mystery Envelope (Arthur Chapter Books #1).* Marc Brown. Little, Brown (159,543)
62. *Pocket Flyers Paper Airplane Book.* Ken Blackburn and Jeff Lammers. Workman (153,924)
63. *Zac Attack: Hanson's Little Brother.* Tracey West. Scholastic (153,000)
64. *Hanson: The Ultimate Hanson Trivia Book.* Matt Netter. Pocket/ Archway
65. *Happy Birthday, Josefina!* Valerie Tripp, illus. by Jean Paul Tibbles. Pleasant Co. (151,835)

**125,000+**

66. *Rugrats Vacation!* Simon Spotlight (148,674)
67. *Josefina Saves the Day.* Valerie Tripp, illus. by Jean Paul Tibbles. Pleasant Co. (148,019)

68. *Lovin' Leo: Your Leonardo DiCaprio Scrapbook.* Stephanie Scott. Scholastic (148,000)

69. *Barney's Happy Valentine's Day.* Lyrick/Barney (147,810)

70. *More Games & Giggles.* Jeanette Ryan Wall, illus. by Paul Meisel. Pleasant Co.(145,472)

71. *Second Chance (Left Behind—The Kids #2).* Jerry Jenkins and Tim LaHaye. Tyndale (145,402)

72. *Are You Terrified Yet? (GB 2000 #9).* R.L. Stine. Scholastic (145,000)

73. *The Rugrats Movie: Hang on to Your Diapers, Babies, We're Going In!* Simon Spotlight (144,798)

74. *Changes for Josefina.* Valerie Tripp, illus by Jean Paul Tibbles. Pleasant Co. (142,322)

75. *Rugrats: Tommy Catches a Cold.* Simon Spotlight (139,157)

76. *The Case of the Ballet Bandit (The New Adventures of Mary-Kate and Ashley #1).* Laura O'Neil. Scholastic (136,000)

77. *Godzilla.* H.B. Gilmour. Scholastic (136,000)

78. *Through the Flames (Left Behind—The Kids #3).* Jerry Jenkins and Tim LaHaye. Tyndale (132,661)

79. *Titanic: The Long Night.* Diane Hoh. Scholastic (132,000)

80. *The View from Saturday.* E.L. Konigsburg. Aladdin (131,393)

81. *Arthur and the Scare-Your-Pants-Off Club (Arthur Chapter Books #2).* Marc Brown. Little, Brown (131,290)

82. *Headless Halloween (GB 2000 #10).* R.L. Stine. Scholastic (131,000)

83. *Facing the Future (Left Behind—The Kids #4).* Jerry Jenkins and Tim LaHaye. Tyndale (130,418)

84. *Brian's Winter.* Gary Paulsen. Dell/Laurel-Leaf (128,809)

85. *Ella Enchanted.* Gail Carson Levine. HarperTrophy (128,357)

86. *The Maltese Dog (Wishbone Mysteries #6).* Lyrick/Big Red Chair (127,634)

87. *Arthur Makes the Team (Arthur Chapter Books #3).* Marc Brown. Little, Brown (127,065)

88. *Rugrats: The Bestest Mom.* Simon Spotlight (126,871)

89. *The Stolen Trophy. (Wishbone Mysteries #5).* Lyrick/Big Red Chair (126,649)

90. *Star Wars: Young Jedi Knights: Trouble on Cloud City.* Kevin Anderson and Rebecca Moesta. Berkley/ Jam (126,000)

91. *Moneymakers: Good Cents.* Ingrid Roper, illus. by Susan Synarski. Pleasant Co. (125,146)

92. *Wringer.* Jerry Spinelli. HarperCollins/Cotler (125,016)

93. *Mark McGwire: A Biography.* Jonathan Hall. Pocket/Archway

94. *Most Wanted: Holiday Hunks.* Pocket/ Archway

95. *Sammy Sosa: A Biography.* Bill Gutman. Pocket/Archway

96. *My Life Is a Three Ring Circus (Full House Michelle #20).* Cathy East Dubowski. Pocket/Minstrel

97. *All that Glitters (Sabrina, the Teenage Witch #12)*. Ray Garton. Pocket/-Archway

98. *Buffy the Vampire Slayer: The Angel Chronicles, Vol. 1.* Nancy Holder. Pocket/Archway

## Paperback Backlist

**200,000+**

1. *Leonardo DiCaprio: A Modern-Day Romeo.* Grace Catalano. Dell, 1997 (734,696)
2. *The Giver.* Lois Lowry. Dell/Laurel-Leaf, 1994 (644,560)
3. *Love You Forever.* Robert Munsch, illus. by Sheila McGraw. Firefly, 1986 (625,463)
4. *Shiloh.* Phyllis Reynolds Naylor. Dell/Yearling, 1992 (520,726)
5. *Number the Stars.* Lois Lowry. Dell/Yearling, 1990 (463,294)
6. *The Outsiders.* S.E. Hinton. Puffin, 1997 (370,392)
7. *The Sign of the Beaver.* Elizabeth Speare. Dell/Yearling, 1984 (296,218)
8. *Charlotte's Web.* E.B. White, illus. by Garth Williams. HarperTrophy, 1974 (271,269)
9. *Where the Red Fern Grows.* Wilson Rawls. Bantam, 1984 (270,709)
10. *Charlie and the Chocolate Factory.* Roald Dahl. Puffin, 1988 (247,926)
11. *A Wrinkle in Time.* Madeleine L'Engle. Dell/Laurel-Leaf, 1976 (247,912)
12. *Island of the Blue Dolphins.* Scott O'Dell. Dell/Yearling, 1978 (239,998)
13. *The Lion, the Witch & the Wardrobe.* C.S. Lewis. HarperTrophy, 1994 (238,755)
14. *Hatchet.* Gary Paulsen. Aladdin, 1996 (233,579)
15. *Where the Wild Things Are.* Maurice Sendak. HarperTrophy, 1963 (233,501)
16. *Freckle Juice.* Judy Blume. Dell/Yearling, 1978 (228,527)
17. *Little Critter: Just Me and My Dad.* Mercer Mayer. Golden, 1994 (221,584)
18. *Bridge to Terabithia.* Katherine Paterson. HarperTrophy, 1987 (217,475)
19. *Little Critter: The New Potty.* Mercer Mayer. Golden, 1992 (204,420)
20. *Goodnight Moon.* Margaret Wise Brown, illus. by Clement Hurd. Harper-Trophy, 1977 (204,098)
21. *Little House in the Big Woods.* Laura Ingalls Wilder, illus. by Garth Williams. HarperTrophy, 1971 (200,893)

**150,000+**

22. *Barney's Trick or Treat.* Lyrick/ Barney, 1997 (198,994)
23. *Arthur's Birthday.* Marc Brown. Little, Brown, 1991 (196,795)
24. *The Egypt Game.* Zilpha Keatley Snyder. Dell/Yearling, 1985 (193,498)
25. *On My Honor.* Marion Dane Bauer. Dell/Yearling, 1987 (193,463)

26. *Barney's Book of Hugs.* Lyrick/ Barney, 1997 (192,792)
27. *The M&M's Brand Chocolate Candies Counting Book.* Barbara McGrath. Charlesbridge, 1994 (188,490)
28. *Sesame Street Babies: Peekaboo!* Golden, 1994 (178,531)
29. *Barney's Christmas Wishes.* Lyrick/Barney, 1997 (178,161)
30. *Barney's Christmas Surprise.* Lyrick/Barney, 1996 (177,822)
31. *Barney's Easter Egg Hunt.* Lyrick/Barney, 1996 (177,235)
32. *Barney & Baby Bop Go to School.* Lyrick/Barney, 1997 (176,949)
33. *Maniac Magee.* Jerry Spinelli. HarperTrophy, 1992 (174,295)
34. *Stone Fox.* John Reynolds Gardiner. HarperTrophy, 1983 (171,885)
35. *Little House on the Prairie.* Laura Ingalls Wilder, illus. by Garth Williams. HarperTrophy, 1983 (170,994)
36. *Sarah Plain and Tall.* Patricia MacLachlan. HarperTrophy, 1987 (164,449)
37. *Pooh: Just Be Nice . . . and Get Ready for Bed!* Golden, 1996 (164,007)
38. *The Care & Keeping of Friends.* Illus. by Nadine Bernard Westcott. Pleasant Co., 1996 (162,015)
39. *Madeline.* Ludwig Bemelmans. Puffin, 1977 (161,219)
40. *The Chocolate Touch.* Patrick Catling. Dell/Yearling, 1984 (160,040)
41. *The Haunted Clubhouse (Wishbone Mysteries #2).* Lyrick/Big Red Chair, 1997 (159,800)
42. *Barbie: Dance, Ballerina.* Golden, 1997 (158,271)
43. *Tales of a Fourth Grade Nothing.* Judy Blume. Dell/Yearling, 1976 (155,728)
44. *Barney's Big Balloon.* Lyrick/Barney, 1995 (154,493)
45. *Kids' U.S. Road Atlas.* Rand McNally, 1992 (153,746)
46. *Games & Giggles.* Illus. by Paul Meisel. Pleasant Co., 1995 (153,618)
47. *The Invasion (Animorphs #1).* K.A. Applegate. Scholastic, 1996 (152,000)
48. *Tuck Everlasting.* Natalie Babbitt. FSG/Sunburst, 1985 (151,801)
49. *How to Eat Fried Worms.* Thomas Rockwell. Dell/Yearling, 1953 (151,533)
50. *Chocolate Fever.* Robert Kimmel Smith. Dell/Yearling, 1978 (151,297)

## 125,000+

51. *Sesame Street: Babies: Look at Me!* Golden, 1994 (149,605)
52. *Little Critter: Going to the Dentist.* Mercer Mayer. Golden, 1990 (147,138)
53. *Oops! The Manners Guide for Girls.* Nancy Holyoke, illus. by Debbie Tilley. Pleasant Co., 1997 (145,933)
54. *Are We There Yet?* Rand McNally, 1996 (145,573)
55. *Riddle of the Wayward Books (Wishbone Mysteries #3).* Lyrick/Big Red Chair, 1997 (145,379)
56. *Barney's Halloween Party.* Lyrick/Barney, 1996 (144,805)

57. *Barney Goes to the Dentist.* Lyrick/Barney, 1997 (144,182)
58. *Exploring the Titanic.* Robert D. Ballard. Scholastic, 1993 (144,000)
59. *Groom Your Room.* Pleasant Co., 1997 (143,008)
60. *The Cricket in Times Square.* George Selden. Dell/Yearling, 1970 (141,822)
61. *Sesame Street: My Name Is Elmo.* Golden, 1993 (140,943)
62. *Julie of the Wolves.* Jean Craighead George. HarperTrophy, 1974 (140,684)
63. *Little Critter: All By Myself.* Mercer Mayer. Golden, 1983 (140,669)
64. *Tale of the Missing Mascot (Wishbone Mysteries #4).* Lyrick/Big Red Chair, 1997 (139,874)
65. *The Pigman.* Paul Zindel. Bantam, 1978 (139,223)
66. *Titanic Crossing.* Barbara Williams. Scholastic, 1997 (139,000)
67. *My Side of the Mountain.* Jean Craighead George. Puffin, 1991 (138,356)
68. *Little Critter: I Was So Mad.* Mercer Mayer. Golden, 1983 (138,194)
69. *A Wrinkle in Time.* Madeleine L'Engle. Dell/Yearling, 1973 (138,008)
70. *Little Critter: Just Go to Bed!* Mercer Mayer. Golden, 1983 (137,728)
71. *Roll of Thunder, Hear My Cry.* Mildred Taylor. Puffin, 1991 (137,577)
72. *Arthur's Family Vacation.* Marc Brown. Little, Brown, 1995 (137,558)
73. *Rugrats: Reptar to the Rescue!* Simon Spotlight, 1997 (136,598)
74. *Dear Barbie: Let's Share.* Golden, 1997 (136,149)
75. *The Magican's Nephew.* C.S. Lewis. HarperTrophy, 1994 (135,392)
76. *Disney's Pooh: Just Be Nice . . . and Say You're Sorry.* Golden, 1997 (135,196)
77. *Barney & BJ Go to the Firestation.* Lyrick/Barney, 1997 (133,908)
78. *Rugrats Blast Off!* Simon Spotlight, 1997 (133,452)
79. *The River.* Gary Paulsen. Dell/ Yearling, 1993 (132,840)
80. *The Boxcar Children.* Gertrude Chandler Warner. Albert Whitman, 1989 (132,012)
81. *Little Critter: Just Me in the Tub.* Gina and Mercer Mayer. Golden, 1994 (130,849)
82. *Walk Two Moons.* Sharon Creech. HarperTrophy, 1996 (130,177)
83. *Little Critter: I Just Forgot!* Mercer Mayer. Golden, 1990 (129,972)
84. *The Grouchy Ladybug.* Eric Carle. HarperTrophy, 1996 (128,880)
85. *The Face on the Milk Carton.* Caroline B. Cooney. Dell/Laurel-Leaf, 1991 (128,658)
86. *Arthur's Halloween.* Marc Brown. Little, Brown, 1983 (128,583)
87. *Meet Josefina.* Valerie Tripp, illus. by Jean Paul Tibbles. Pleasant Co., 1997 (128,401)
88. *Pooh: Oh, Bother, Someone's Messy.* Golden, 1992 (127,091)
89. *Rugrats: Stormy Weather.* Simon Spotlight, 1997 (127,037)
90. *The Treasure of Skeleton Reef (Wishbone Mysteries #1).* Lyrick/Big Red Chair, 1997 (125,726)
91. *Island of the Blue Dolphins.* Scott O'Dell. Dell/Yearling, 1978 (125,278)

# Literary Prizes, 1998

## Gary Ink
### Research Librarian, *Publishers Weekly*

ABBY Awards. To honor titles that members have most enjoyed handselling in the past year. *Offered by*: American Booksellers Association. *Winners*: (adult) Charles Frazier for *Cold Mountain* (Atlantic Monthly); (children's) Jan Brett for *The Hat* (Putnam).

Academy of American Poets. Poetry Fellowship. For distinguished poetic achievement. *Offered by*: Academy of American Poets. *Winner*: Charles Simic.

J. R. Ackerley Award (United Kingdom). For autobiography. *Offered by*: PEN UK. *Winner*: Kathryn Fitzherbert for *True to Both My Selves* (Virago).

Jane Addams Children's Book Award. For a book promoting the cause of peace, social justice, and world community. *Offered by*: Women's International League for Peace and Freedom and the Jane Addams Peace Association. *Winner*: Naomi Shihab Nye for *Habibi* (Simon & Schuster); (picture book) Betsy Hearne and Bethanne Andersen for *To Seven Brave Women* (Greenwillow).

American Academy of Arts and Letters Award of Merit for Fiction. *Offered by*: American Academy of Arts and Letters. *Winner*: Thom Gunn.

American Academy of Arts and Letters Awards in Literature. *Offered by*: American Academy of Arts and Letters. *Winners*: (poetry) Edward Hirsch, Mary Ruefle, Gjertrud Schnackenberg; (fiction) Albert Guerard, Bradford Morrow; (memoir) Annie Dillard; (translation) Edward Snow.

Hans Christian Andersen Awards. *Offered by*: International Board on Books for Young People (IBBY). *Winners*: (author) Katherine Paterson (United States); (illustrator) Tomi Ungerer (France).

Mildred L. Batchelder Award. For an American publisher of a children's book originally published in a foreign language in a foreign country, and subsequently published in English in the United States.

*Offered by*: American Library Association, Association for Library Service to Children. *Winner*: Henry Holt for *The Robber and Me* by Josef Holub, translated by Elizabeth Crawford.

James Beard Foundation Book Awards. For cookbooks. *Offered by*: James Beard Foundation. *Winners*: (cookbook of the year) Madeleine Kamman for *The New Making of a Cook* (Morrow); (Cookbook Hall of Fame) Maida Heatter for *Maida Heatter's Book of Great Desserts* (Random House); (baking and desserts) Charlie van Over for *The Best Bread Ever* (Broadway Books); (entertaining) Linda West Eckhardt and Katherine West DeFoyd for *Entertaining 101* (Doubleday); (food of the Americas) Anya von Bremzen for *Fiesta* (Doubleday); (food of the Mediterranean) Marcella Hazen for *Marcella Cucina* (HarperCollins); (food reference and technique) Shirley O. Corriher for *Cookwise* (Morrow); (general) Madeleine Kamman for *The New Making of a Cook* (Morrow); (healthy focus) Melanie Barnard et al for *American Medical Association Family Health Cookbook*; (international) Georgeanne Brennan for *The Food and Flavors of Haute Provence* (Chronicle Books); (single subject) Rebecca Wood for *The Splendid Grain* (Morrow); (vegetarian) Deborah Madison for *Vegetarian Cooking for Everyone* (Broadway Books); (wine and spirits) Clive Coates for *Cote D'Or* (Univ. of California); (writing on food) Mark Kurlansky for *Cod* (Walker); (food photography) John Torode and Sarah Francis for *The Mezzo Cookbook* with John Torode, photographed by Diana Miller and James Murphy (SOMA Books).

Before Columbus Foundation American Book Awards. For literary achievement by people of various ethnic backgrounds. *Offered by*: Before Columbus Foundation. *Winners*: (poetry) Allison Adelle Hedge for *Dog Road Woman* (Coffee House Press); Brenda Marie Osbey for *All Saints*

(Louisiana State Univ.); John A. Williams for *Safari West* (Hochelaga Press); (fiction) Sandra Benitez for *Bitter Grounds* (Hyperion); Don DeLillo for *Underworld* (Scribner); Nora Okja Keller for *Comfort Woman* (Viking); Nancy Rawles for *Love Like Gumbo* (Fjord Press); (nonfiction) Jim Barnes for *On Native Ground* (Univ. of Oklahoma); Thomas Lynch for *The Undertaking* (Norton); (editor/publisher award) Douglas Messerli; (lifetime achievement award) Paul Metcalf.

Pura Belpré Award. To honor Latino writers and illustrators. *Offered by*: American Library Association, Association for Library Service to Children. *Winners*: (Writer) Victor Martinez for *Parrot in the Oven: Mi Vida* (HarperCollins); (Illustrator) Stephanie Garcia for *Snapshots from the Wedding*, written by Gary Soto (Putnam).

Curtis Benjamin Award for Creative Publishing. *Offered by*: Association of American Publishers. *Winner*: Charles R. Ellis.

James Tait Black Memorial Prizes (United Kingdom). For the best biography and the best novel of the year. *Offered by*: University of Edinburgh. *Winners*: (biography) R. F. Foster for *W. B. Yeats: A Life, Vol 1: The Apprentice Mage 1865–1914* (Oxford); (fiction) Andrew Miller for *Ingenious Pain* (Sceptre).

Booker Prize for Fiction (United Kingdom). *Offered by*: Book Trust and Booker PLC. *Winner*: Ian McEwan for *Amsterdam* (Cape).

Boston Globe-Horn Book Awards. For excellence in children's literature. Offered by: The *Boston Globe* and The *Horn Book*. *Winners*: (fiction) Francisco Jimenez for *The Circuit* (Univ. of New Mexico); (nonfiction) Leon Walter Tillage for *Leon's Story*, illus. by Susan L. Roth (Farrar, Straus & Giroux); (picture book) Kate Banks for *And If the Moon Could Talk* illus. by Georg Hallensleben (Farrar, Straus & Giroux).

Witter Bynner Prize for Poetry. To support the work of young poets. *Offered by*: American Academy of Arts and Letters. *Winner*: Elizabeth Spires.

Caldecott Medal. For the artist of the most distinguished picture book. *Offered by*:

R. R. Bowker Company. *Winner*: Paul O. Zelinsky for *Rapunzel* (Dutton).

California Book Awards. To provide recognition and encouragement to California authors. *Offered by*: Commonwealth Club of California. *Winners*: Gold Medals: (fiction) Diane Johnson for *Le Divorce* (Dutton); (nonfiction) Jared Diamond for *Guns, Germs and Steel* (Norton); Silver Medals: (fiction) Molly Giles for *Creek Walk and Other Stories* (Papier-Mache Press); (first work of fiction) Steve Lattimore for *Circumnavigation* (Houghton Mifflin); (nonfiction) Peter Ostwald for *Glenn Gould* (Norton); (Californiana) Kevin Starr for *The Dream Endures* (Oxford); (poetry) Lawrence Ferlinghetti for *A Far Rockaway of the Heart* (New Directions); Amy Gerstler for *Crown of Weeds* (Penguin); (juvenile) Robert San Souci for *The Hired Hand* (Dial); (notable contribution to publishing) Harry Greene for *Snakes* (Univ. of California).

John W. Campbell Award for Best New Writer. For science fiction writing. *Offered by*: Center for the Study of Science Fiction. *Winner*: Mary Doria Russell.

John W. Campbell Memorial Award. For outstanding science fiction writing. *Offered by*: Center for the Study of Science Fiction. *Winner*: Joe Haldeman.

Carnegie Medal (United Kingdom). For the outstanding children's book of the year. Offered by: The Library Association. *Winner*: Tim Bowler for *River Boy* (Oxford).

Cholmondeley Awards (United Kingdom). For contributions to poetry. *Offered by*: Society of Authors. *Winners*: Robert Minhinnick, Roger McGough, Anne Ridler, Ken Smith.

Arthur C. Clarke Award (United Kingdom). For the best science fiction novel of the year. *Offered by*: British Science Fiction Association. *Winner*: Mary Doria Russell for *The Sparrow* (Black Swan).

Commonwealth Writers Prize (United Kingdom). *Offered by*: Commonwealth Institute. *Winners*: Peter Carey for *Jack Maggs* (Faber); (first work) Tim Wynveen for *Angel Falls* (Key Porter).

Thomas Cook/*Daily Telegraph* Travel Book Award (United Kingdom). *Offered by*:

Book Trust. *Winner*: Tim Macintosh-Smith for *Yemen* (John Murray).

Stephen Crane Award for First Fiction. *Offered by*: Book-of-the-Month Club. *Winner*: Thomas Moran for *The Man In the Box* (Riverhead).

Crime Writers' Association Awards (United Kingdom). For the best crime fiction of the year. *Offered by*: Crime Writers' Association. *Winners*: (Gold Dagger) James Lee Burke for *Sunset Limited* (Orion); (Silver Dagger) Nicholas Blincoe for *Manchester Slingback* (Picador).

Alice Fay Di Castagnola Award. For a work in progress to recognize a poet at a critical stage in his or her work. *Offered by*: Poetry Society of America. *Winner*: Gloria Vando for *Shadows and Supposes*.

Philip K. Dick Award. For a distinguished paperback original published in the United States. *Offered by*: Norwescon. *Winner*: Stepan Chapman for *The Troika* (Ministry of Whimsy Press).

John Dos Passos Prize for Literature. To a writer who has a substantial body of significant publication, and whose work demonstrates an intense and original exploration of specifically American themes, an experimental quality, and a whole range of literary forms. *Offered by*: Longwood College. *Winner*: E. Annie Proulx.

T. S. Eliot Award for Creative Writing. To authors of abiding importance whose works affirm the moral principles of Western Civilization. *Offered by*: Ingersoll Foundation. *Winner*: Madison Jones.

T. S. Eliot Prize (United Kingdom). For poetry. *Offered by*: Poetry Book Society. *Winner*: Don Paterson for *God's Gift to Women* (Faber).

Encore Award (United Kingdom). For a second novel. *Offered by*: Society of Authors. *Winners*: Timothy O'Grady and Steve Pyke for *I Could Read the Sky* (Harvill); Alan Warner for *These Demented Lands* (Cape).

Norma Farber First Book Award. For a first book of poetry. *Offered by*: Poetry Society of America. *Winner*: Rebecca Reynolds for *Daughter of the Hangnail* (New Issues Press).

Forward Poetry Prizes (United Kingdom). *Offered by*: The *Forward*. *Winners*: (best collection) Ted Hughes for *Birthday Letters* (Faber); (best first collection) Paul Farley for *The Boy From the Chemist Is Here to See You* (Picador).

Frost Medal for Distinguished Achievement. To recognize achievement in poetry over a lifetime. *Offered by*: Poetry Society of America. *Winner*: Stanley Kunitz.

Lionel Gelber Prize. For important nonfiction works pertaining to foreign affairs and global issues. *Offered by*: Lionel Gelber Foundation. *Winner*: Robert Kinloch Massie for *Loosing the Bonds* (Doubleday).

Kate Greenaway Medal (United Kingdom). For children's book illustration. *Offered by*: The Library Association. *Winner*: P. J. Lynch for *When Jessie Came Across the Sea* (Candlewick).

Eric Gregory Trust Awards (United Kingdom). For poets under the age of 30. Offered by: Society of Authors. *Winners*: Mark Goodwin, Joanne Limburg, Patrick McGuinness, Christiana Whitehead, Kona Macphee, Frances Williams, Esther Morgan.

*Guardian* Children's Fiction Prize (United Kingdom). For recognition of a children's novel by a British or Commonwealth writer. *Offered by*: The *Guardian*. *Winner*: Henrietta Branford for *Fire, Bed and Bone* (Walker Books).

*Guardian* Fiction Prize (United Kingdom). For recognition of a novel by a British or Commonwealth writer. *Offered by*: The *Guardian*. *Winner*: Jackie Kay for *Trumpet* (Picador).

Guggenheim Literary Fellowships. For unusually distinguished achievement in the past and exceptional promise for future accomplishment. *Offered by*: Guggenheim Memorial Foundation. *Winners*: (poetry) Bei Dao, Anne Carson, Marie Howe, Dionisio D. Martinez, Campbell McGrath, Susan Wood, Baron Wormser; (fiction) David Gates, Francisco Goldman, Julie Hecht, A. M. Homes, Elizabeth McCracken, Janet Peery, Kate Wheeler.

O. B. Hardison, Jr. Poetry Prize. To a U.S. poet who has published at least one book within the past five years, has made important contributions as a teacher, and is committed to furthering the understanding of poetry. *Offered by*: Folger Shakespeare Library. *Winner*: Heather McHugh.

Heartland Prize. To recognize an outstanding work of fiction about people and places in America's heartland. *Offered by*: *Chicago Tribune*. *Winner*: Jane Hamilton for *The Short History of a Prince* (Random House).

Drue Heinz Literature Prize. To recognize and encourage writing of short fiction. *Offered by*: Drue Heinz Foundation and University of Pittsburgh. *Winner*: Barbara Croft for *Necessary Fictions* (Univ. of Pittsburgh).

Peggy V. Helmerich Distinguished Author Award. To a nationally acclaimed writer for a body of work and contributions to American literature and letters. *Offered by*: Tulsa Library Trust. *Winner*: E. L. Doctorow.

Ernest Hemingway Foundation Award. For a distinguished work of first fiction by an American. *Offered by*: PEN New England. *Winner*: Charlotte Bacon for *A Private State* (Univ. of Massachusetts).

IMPAC Dublin Literary Award (Ireland). For a book of high literary merit written in English or translated into English. *Offered by*: IMPAC Corp. and the City of Dublin. *Winner*: Herta Muller for *The Land of Green Plains* (Metropolitan Books).

Rona Jaffe Writers' Awards. To identify and support women writers of exceptional talent in the early stages of their careers. *Offered by*: Rona Jaffe Foundation. *Winners*: (fiction) Lan Samantha Chang, Stephanie Gunn, Marjorie Sandor; (poetry) Jody Bolz, Ellen Hinsey, Larissa Szporluk; (creative nonfiction) Marilyn Abildskov, Megan Foss.

Sue Kaufman Prize for First Fiction. *Offered by*: American Academy of Arts and Letters. *Winner*: Charles Frazier for *Cold Mountain* (Atlantic Monthly).

Coretta Scott King Awards. For works that promote the cause of peace and brotherhood. *Offered by*: American Library Association, Social Responsibilities Round Table. *Winners*: (author award) Sharon M. Draper for *Forged by Fire* (Atheneum); (illustrator award) Javaka Steptoe for *In Daddy's Arms I Am Tall* (Lee & Low).

Robert Kirsch Award. To a living author whose residence or focus is the American West and whose contributions to American letters clearly merit body-of-work recognition. *Offered by*: *Los Angeles Times*. *Winner*: Ray Bradbury.

Gregory Kolovakos Award. For a sustained contribution over time to Hispanic literature in English translation. *Offered by*: PEN American Center. *Winner*: Johannes Wilbert.

Harold Morton Landon Translation Award. For a book of verse translated into English by a single translator. *Offered by*: Academy of American Poets. *Winner*: Louis Simpson for *Modern Poets of France: A Bilingual Anthology* (Story Line Press).

Lannan Literary Awards. To recognize both established and emerging writers of poetry, fiction, and nonfiction. *Offered by*: Lannan Foundation. *Winners*: (poetry) Frank Bidart, Jon Davis, Mary Oliver; (fiction) J. M. Coetzee, Lydia Davis, Stuart Dybeck, Lois Ann Yamanaka; (nonfiction) Chet Raymo, Lawrence Wechsler, Howard Zimm; (lifetime achievement) John Barth.

James Laughlin Award. To support the publication of a second book of poetry. Offered by: Academy of American Poets. *Winner*: Sandra Alcosser for *Except by Nature* (Greywolf Press).

Ruth Lilly Poetry Fellowships. To help aspiring writers to continue their study and practice of poetry. *Offered by*: Modern Poetry Association. *Winners*: Robin Cooper-Stone, Christine Stewart.

Ruth Lilly Poetry Prize. To a United States poet whose accomplishments warrant extraordinary recognition. *Offered by*: Modern Poetry Association. *Winner*: W. S. Merwin.

Locus Awards. For science fiction writing. *Offered by*: Locus Publications. *Winners*: (science fiction novel) Dan Simmons for *The Rise of Endymion* (Bantam); (fantasy novel) Tim Powers for *Earthquake Weather* (Tor); (first novel) Ian R. MacLeod for *The Great Wheel* (Harcourt Brace); (nonfiction) John Clute et al eds., *The Encyclopedia of Fantasy* (St. Martin's); (art book) Vincent Di Fate for *Infinite Words* (Penguin Studio); (collection) Harlan Ellison for *Slippage* (Houghton Mifflin); (anthology) Gardner Dozois, ed., *The Year's Best*

*Science Fiction: Fourteenth Annual Collection* (St. Martin's).

*Los Angeles Times* Book Prizes. To honor literary excellence. *Winners*: (fiction) James Carlos Blake for *In the Rogue Blood* (Avon); (poetry) Charles Wright for *Reading In the Dark* (Knopf); (history) Orlando Figes for *A People's Tragedy* (Viking); (biography) Sam Tanenhaus for *Whittaker Chambers* (Random House); (science and technology) Steven Pinker for *How the Mind Works* (Norton); (current interest) Anne Fadiman for *The Spirit Catches You and You Fall Down* (Farrar, Straus & Giroux); (Art Seidenbaum Award for First Fiction) Carolyn Ferrell for *Don't Erase Me* (Houghton Mifflin).

McKitterick Prize (United Kingdom). For a first novel by a writer over the age of 40. *Offered by*: Society of Authors. *Winner*: Eli Gottlieb for *The Boy Who Went Away* (Cape).

Lenore Marshall Poetry Prize. For an outstanding book of poems published in the United States. *Offered by*: Academy of American Poets and The *Nation*. *Winner*: Mark Jarman for *Questions for Ecclesiastes* (Story Line).

Somerset Maugham Awards (United Kingdom). For young British writers to gain experience in foreign countries. *Offered by*: Society of Authors. *Winners*: Rachel Cusk for *Country Life* (Picador); Jonathan Rendall for *This Bloody Mary* (Faber); Kate Summerscale for *The Queen of Whale Cay* (Fourth Estate); Robert Twigger for *Angry White Pyjamas* (Indigo).

Addison Metcalf Award for Literature. To a young writer of great promise. *Offered by*: American Academy of Arts and Letters. *Winner*: Rick Moody.

National Arts Club Medal of Honor for Literature. *Offered by*: National Arts Club. *Winner*: Grace Paley.

National Book Awards. *Offered by*: National Book Foundation. *Winners*: (fiction) Alice McDermott for *Charming Billy* (Farrar, Straus & Giroux); (nonfiction) Edward Ball for *Slaves in the Family* (Farrar, Straus & Giroux); (poetry) Gerald Stern for *This Time* (Norton); (children's) Louis Sachar for *Holes* (Farrar, Straus & Giroux).

National Book Critics Circle Awards. *Offered by*: National Book Critics Circle. *Winners*: (fiction) Penelope Fitzgerald for *The Blue Flower* (Mariner); (criticism) Mario Vargas Llosa for *Making Waves* (Farrar, Straus & Giroux); (biography/autobiography) James Tobin for *Ernie Pyle's War* (Free Press); (general nonfiction) Anne Fadiman for *The Spirit Catches You and You Fall Down* (Farrar, Straus & Giroux); (poetry) Charles Wright for *Black Zodiac* (Farrar, Straus & Giroux).

National Book Foundation Medal for Distinguished Contribution to American Letters. *Offered by*: National Book Foundation. *Winner*: John Updike.

Nebula Awards. For the best science fiction writing. *Offered by*: Science Fiction Writers of America. *Winners*: (best novel) Vonda N. McIntyre for *The Moon and the Sun* (Pocket Books); (grand master) Poul Anderson.

Neustadt International Prize for Literature. *Offered by*: University of Oklahoma and *World Literature Today*. *Winner*: Nuruddin Farah.

John Newbery Medal. For the most distinguished contribution to literature for children. *Donor*: American Library Association, Association for Library Service to Children. *Medal Contributed by*: Daniel Melcher. *Winner*: Karen Hesse for *Out of the Dust* (Scholastic).

Nobel Prize in Literature. For the total literary output of a distinguished career. *Offered by:* Swedish Academy. *Winner*: Jose Saramago.

Flannery O'Connor Awards for Short Fiction. *Offered by*: PEN American Center. *Winners*: Mary Clyde for *Survival Rates* (Univ. of Georgia); Frank Soos for *Unified Field Theory* (Univ. of Georgia).

Scott O'Dell Award for Historical Fiction. For children's or young adult fiction set in the Americas and published by a U.S. publisher. *Offered by: Bulletin of the Center for Children's Books*, University of Chicago. *Winner*: Karen Hesse for *Out of the Dust* (Scholastic).

Orange Prize for Fiction (United Kingdom). For the best novel written by a woman and published in the United Kingdom. *Offered by*: Orange PLC. *Winner*: Carol Shields for *Larry's Party* (Viking).

PEN Award for Poetry in Translation. *Offered by*: PEN American Center. *Winner*: Eamon Grennan for *Selected Poems by Giacomo Leopardi* (Princeton Univ.).

PEN/Martha Albrand Award for the Art of the Memoir. *Offered by*: PEN American Center. *Winner*: Peter Balakian for *Black Dog of Fate* (Syracuse Univ.).

PEN/Martha Albrand Award for First Nonfiction. *Offered by*: PEN American Center. *Winner*: Serge Schmemann for *Echoes of a Native Land* (Knopf).

PEN/Book-of-the-Month Club Translation Award. *Offered by*: PEN American Center. *Winner*: Peter Constantine for *Six Early Stories by Thomas Mann* (Sun & Moon Press).

PEN/Faulkner Award for Fiction. To honor the best work of fiction published by an American. *Offered by*: PEN American Center. *Winner*: Rafi Zabor for *The Bear Comes Home* (Norton).

PEN/Malamud Award for Excellence in Short Fiction. To an author who has demonstrated long-term excellence in short fiction. *Offered by*: PEN Faulkner Foundation. *Winner*: Alice Munro.

PEN/Newman's Own First Amendment Award. To recognize extraordinary actions in defense of freedom of expression. *Offered by*: PEN American Center and Newman's Own. *Winner*: Terrilyn Simpson.

PEN/Spielvogel-Diamonstein Essay Award. *Offered by*: PEN American Center. *Winner*: Adam Hochschild for Finding the Trapdoor (Syracuse Univ.).

PEN/Voelcker Award for Poetry. *Offered by*: PEN American Center. *Winner*: C. K. Williams.

Edgar Allan Poe Awards. For outstanding mystery, crime, and suspense writing. Offered by: Mystery Writers of America. *Winners*: (novel) James Lee Burke for *Cimarron* (Hyperion); (first novel) Joseph Canon for *Los Alamos* (Broadway Books); (original paperback) Laura Lippman for *Charm City* (Avon); (fact crime) Richard Firstman and Jamie Talan for *The Death of Innocents* (Bantam); (critical/biographical) Natalie Henever Kaufman and Carol Mc-

Ginniss McKay for *G Is for Grafton* (Henry Holt); (children's book) Barbara Brooks Wallace for *Sparrows in the Scullery* (Atheneum); (young adult) Will Hobbs for *Ghost Canoe* (Morrow); (Grand Master) Barbara Mertz.

Poets' Prize. For the best book of poetry published in the United States in the previous year. *Offered by*: Nicholas Roerich Museum. *Winners*: Sydney Lea, Leon Stokesbury.

Renato Poggioli Translation Award. To assist a translator of Italian whose work in progress is especially outstanding. *Offered by*: PEN American Center. *Winner*: Minna Proctor for *Stories by Federigo Tozzi*.

Premio Aztlan. To a Chicano or Chicana fiction writer who has published no more than two books. *Offered by*: Rudolfo and Patricia Anaya and the University of New Mexico. *Winner*: Pat Mora.

Pulitzer Prizes in Letters. To honor distinguished work by American writers, dealing preferably with American themes. *Offered by*: Columbia University, Graduate School of Journalism. *Winners*: (fiction) Philip Roth for *American Pastoral* (Houghton Mifflin); (history) Edward J. Larson for *Summer for the Gods* (Basic Books); (biography) Katharine Graham for *Personal History* (Knopf); (general nonfiction) Jared Diamond for *Guns, Germs and Steel* (Norton); (poetry) Charles Wright for *Black Zodiac* (Farrar, Straus & Giroux).

Raiziss/de Palchi Book Prize. For a published translation of Italian poetry into English. *Offered by*: Academy of American Poets. *Winner*: Michael Palma for *The Man I Pretend to Be: The Colloquies and Selected Poems of Guido Gozzano* (Princeton Univ.).

Rea Award for the Short Story. To honor a living writer who has made a significant contribution to the short story as an art form. *Offered by*: Dungannon Foundation. *Winner*: John Edgar Wideman.

Rhone-Poulenc Science Book Award (United Kingdom). *Offered by*: Rhone-Poulenc. *Winner*: Jared Diamond for *Guns, Germs and Steel* (Cape).

John Llewellyn Rhys Memorial Award (United Kingdom). *Offered by*: The *Mail on Sunday*.

*Winner*: Phil Whitaker for *Eclipse of the Sun* (Phoenix).

Romance Writers of America RITA Awards. For excellence in the romance genre. *Offered by*: Romance Writers of America. *Winners*: (traditional) Lucy Gordon for *His Brother's Child* (Harlequin); (short contemporary) Jennifer Greene for *Nobody's Princess* (Silhouette); (long contemporary) Ruth Wind for *Reckless* (Silhouette); (contemporary single) Susan Elizabeth Phillips for *Nobody's Baby But Mine* (Avon); (suspense/gothic) Ingrid Weaver for *On the Way to a Wedding* (Silhouette); (paranormal) Justine Dare for *Fire Hawk* (Topaz); (inspirational) Melody Carlson for *Homeward* (Multnomah); (Regency) Jean R. Ewing for *Love's Reward* (Zebra); (short historical) Barbara Samuel for *Heart of a Knight* (HarperPaperbacks); (long historical) Maggie Osborne for *The Promise of Jenny Jones* (Warner); (first book) Elizabeth Boyle for *Brazen Angel* (Dell); (favorite book) Susan Elizabeth Phillips for *Nobody's Baby But Mine* (Avon).

Richard and Hinda Rosenthal Foundation Award. For a work of fiction that is a considerable literary achievement though not necessarily a commercial success. *Offered by*: American Academy of Arts and Letters. *Winner*: Joseph Skibell for *Blessing on the Moon* (Algonquin Books).

Juan Rulfo International Latin American and Caribbean Prize for Literature (Mexico). To a writer of poetry, novels, short stories, drama, or essays who is a native of Latin America or the Caribbean, and who writes in Spanish, Portuguese, or English. *Offered by*: Juan Rulfo Award Committee. *Winner*: Olga Orozco.

Sagittarius Prize (United Kingdom). For a first novel by a writer over the age of 60. *Offered by*: Society of Authors. *Winner*: A. Sivanandan for *When Memory Dies* (Arcadia Books).

Shelley Memorial Award. To a poet living in the United States who is chosen on the basis of genius and need. *Offered by*: Poetry Society of America. *Winner*: Eleanor Ross Taylor.

Smarties Book Prizes (United Kingdom). To encourage high standards and to stimulate interest in books for children. *Offered by*: Book Trust and Nestle Rowntree. *Winners*: (ages 9–11) J. K. Rowling for *Harry Potter and the Chamber of Secrets* (Bloomsbury); (ages 6–8) Harry Horse for *Last of the Gold Diggers* (Puffin); (ages 0–5) Sue Heap for *Cowboy Baby* (Walker).

W. H. Smith Literary Award (United Kingdom). For a significant contribution to literature. *Offered by*: W. H. Smith. *Winner*: Ted Hughes for *Tales from Ovid* (Faber).

Agnes Lynch Starrett Poetry Prize. For a first book of poetry. *Offered by*: University of Pittsburgh. *Winner*: Richard Blanco for *City of a Hundred Fires* (Univ. of Pittsburgh).

Mildred and Harold Strauss Living Award. To free writers from the obligation to earn a living other than through their writing. *Offered by*: American Academy of Arts and Letters. *Winners*: Marilynne Robinson, W. D. Wetherell.

Tanning Prize. For outstanding and proven mastery in the art of poetry. *Offered by*: Academy of American Poets. *Winner*: Anthony Hecht.

Templeton Prize for Progress in Religion. *Offered by*: Templeton Foundation. *Winner*: Sigmund Sternberg.

Betty Trask Awards (United Kingdom). For works of a romantic or traditional nature by writers under the age of 35. *Offered by*: Society of Authors. *Winners*: Kiran Desai for *Hullabaloo in the Guava Orchard* (Faber); Nick Earls for *Zigzag Street* (Macmillan); Phil Whitaker for *Eclipse of the Sun* (Weidenfeld); Gail Anderson-Dargatz for *Cure for Death by Lightning* (Little, Brown); Tobias Hill for *Underground* (unpublished).

Kate Frost Tufts Discovery Award. For a first or very early book of poetry by an emerging poet. *Offered by*: Claremont Graduate School. *Winner*: Charles Harper Webb for *Reading the Water* (Northeastern Univ.).

Kingsley Tufts Poetry Award. For a book of poetry by a mid-career poet. *Offered by*: Claremont Graduate School. *Winner*: John L. Koethe for *Falling Water* (HarperCollins).

Harold D. Vursell Memorial Award. To a writer for the quality of his or her prose. *Offered by*: American Academy of Arts and Letters. *Winner*: Howard Bahr for *The Black Flower* (Henry Holt).

Lila Wallace-Reader's Digest Fund Writer's Awards. *Offered by*: Lila Wallace Foundation. *Winners*: Lydia Davis, Jim Grimsley, Kimiko Hahn, Joy Harjo, Grace Paley, Ishmael Reed, Arthur Sze.

Whitbread Book of the Year (United Kingdom). *Offered by*: Booksellers Association of Great Britain. *Winner*: Ted Hughes for *Tales from Ovid* (Faber).

Whitbread Children's Book of the Year (United Kingdom). *Offered by*: Booksellers Association of Great Britain. *Winner*: Andrew Norriss for *Aquila* (Hamish Hamilton).

William Allen White Children's Book Award. *Offered by*: Emporia State University. *Winner*: Barbara Park for *Mick Harte Was Here* (Knopf).

Whiting Writers Awards. For outstanding talent and promise. *Offered by*: Mrs. Giles Whiting Foundation. *Winners*: Michael Byers, Nancy Eimers, Daniel Hall, W. David Hancock, James Kimbrell, Ralph Lombregalia, D. J. Waldie, Anthony Walton, Charles Harper Webb, Greg Williamson.

Walt Whitman Award. For poetry. *Offered by*: Academy of American Poets. *Winner*: Jan Heller Levi for *Once I Gazed at You in Wonder* (Louisiana State Univ.).

Laura Ingalls Wilder Medal. For a substantial and lasting contribution to children's literature. *Offered by*: American Library Association, Association for Library Service to Children. *Winner*: Russell Freedman.

William Carlos Williams Award. For the best book of poetry published by a small, nonprofit, or university press. *Offered by*: Poetry Society of America. *Winner*: John Balaban for *Locusts at the Edge of Summer* (Copper Canyon).

Robert H. Winner Memorial Award. For a poem or sequence of poems characterized by a delight in language and the possibilities of ordinary life. *Offered by*: Poetry Society of America. *Winner*: Natasha Saje.

L. L. Winship Award. For a book of fiction, poetry, or nonfiction by a New England author or with a New England topic or setting. *Offered by*: PEN New England. *Winner*: Anita Shreve for *The Weight of Water* (Little, Brown).

World Fantasy Convention Awards. For outstanding fantasy writing. *Offered by*: World Fantasy Convention. *Winners*: (novel) Jeffrey Ford for *The Physiognomy* (Avon); (anthology) Nicola Griffith and Stephen Pagel, eds. for *Bending the Landscape: Fantasy* (White Wolf Borealis); (collection) Brian McNaughton for *The Throne of Bones* (Terminal Fright); (special award: professional) John Clute and John Grant, eds. for *The Encyclopedia of Fantasy* (St. Martin's); (lifetime achievement) Edward L. Ferman.

World Science Fiction Convention Hugo Awards. For outstanding science fiction writing. *Offered by*: World Science Fiction Convention. *Winners*: (best novel) Joe Haldeman for *Forever Peace* (Ace); (best related book) John Clute and John Grant, eds. for *The Encyclopedia of Fantasy* (St. Martin's).

Morton Dauwen Zabel Award in Poetry. *Offered by*: American Academy of Arts and Letters. *Winner*: Yusef Komunyakaa.

# Part 6
# Directory of Organizations

# Directory of Library and Related Organizations

## Networks, Consortia, and Other Cooperative Library Organizations

This list is taken from the 1997–1998 edition of *American Library Directory* (R. R. Bowker), which includes additional information on member libraries and primary functions of each organization.

### United States

#### Alabama

Alabama Health Libraries Association, Inc. (ALHeLa), Univ. S. Alabama, Medical Center Lib., 2451 Fillingim St., Mobile 36617. SAN 372-8218. Tel. 334-471-7855, fax 334-471-7857. *Pres.* Jie Li.

American Gas Association-Library Services (AGA-LSC), c/o Alabama Gas Corp., 605 21st St. N., Birmingham 35203-2707. SAN 371-0890. Tel. 205-326-8436, fax 205-326-2619, e-mail cbaker@go1.energen.com. *Chair* Calvin Baker.

Jefferson County Hospital Librarians Association, Brookwood Medical Center, 2010 Brookwood Medical Center Dr., Birmingham 35209. SAN 371-2168. Tel. 205-877-1131, fax 205-877-1189. *Coord.* Lucy Moor.

Library Management Network, Inc., 110 Johnston St. S.E., Decatur 35601. SAN 322-3906. Tel. 256-308-2529, fax 256-308-2533, e-mail charlotte@lmn.lib.al.us. *System Coord.* Charlotte Moncrief.

Marine Environmental Sciences Consortium, Dauphin Island Sea Lab, 101 Bienville Blvd., Dauphin Island 36528. SAN 322-0001. Tel. 334-861-2141, fax 334-861-4646, e-mail cmallon@disl.org. *Dir.* George Crozier; *Libn.* Connie Mallon.

Network of Alabama Academic Libraries, c/o Alabama Commission on Higher Education, Box 302000, Montgomery 36130-2000. SAN 322-4570. Tel. 334-242-2211, fax 334-242-0270. *Dir.* Sue O. Medina.

#### Alaska

Alaska Library Network (ALN), 344 W. Third Ave., Suite 125, Anchorage 99501. SAN 371-0688. Tel. 907-269-6570, fax 907-269-6580, e-mail aslanc@muskox.alaska.edu. *In Charge* Mary Jennings.

#### Arizona

Maricopa County Community College District, 2411 W. 14th St., Tempe 85281-6942. SAN 322-0060. Tel. 602-731-8774, fax 602-731-8787, e-mail jenkins@dist.maricopa.edu. *Coord. Lib. Technical Svcs.* Vince Jenkins.

#### Arkansas

Arkansas Area Health Education Center Consortium (AHEC), Sparks Regional Medical Center, 1311 South I St., Box 17006, Fort Smith 72917-7006. SAN 329-3734. Tel. 501-441-5337, fax 501-441-5339, e-mail grace@sparks.org. *Regional Health Sciences Libn.* Grace Anderson.

Arkansas' Independent Colleges & Universities, formerly Independent College Fund of Arkansas, One Riverfront Pl., Suite 610, North Little Rock 72114. SAN 322-0079. Tel. 501-378-0843, fax 501-374-1523, e-mail kdietz@alltel.net. *Pres.* E. Kearney Dietz.

Northeast Arkansas Hospital Library Consortium, 223 E. Jackson, Jonesboro 72401. SAN 329-529X. Tel. 870-972-1290, fax 870-931-0839. *Dir.* Karen Crosser.

South Arkansas Film Coop., 202 E. Third St., Malvern 72104. SAN 321-5938. Tel. 501-332-5442, fax 501-332-6679. *Coord.* Tammy Carter; *Project Dir.* Mary Cheatham.

## California

Area Wide Library Network (AWLNET), 2420 Mariposa St., Fresno 93721. SAN 322-0087. Tel. 559-488-3229. *Dir. Info. Svcs.* Sharon Vandercook.

Bay Area Library & Information Network (BAYNET), 672 Prentiss St., San Francisco 94110-6130. SAN 371-0610. Tel. 415-826-2464, e-mail rosef@exploritorium.edu. *Pres.* Jo Falcon.

Central Association of Libraries (CAL), 605 N. El Dorado St., Stockton 95202-1999. SAN 322-0125. Tel. 209-937-8649, fax 209-937-8292. *Systems Dir.* Darla Gunning.

Consortium for Distance Learning, 3841 N. Freeway Blvd., Suite 200, Sacramento 95834-1948. SAN 329-4412. Tel. 916-565-0188, fax 916-565-0189, e-mail cdl@calweb.com. *Exec. Dir.* Jerome Thompson; *Operations Mgr.* Sandra Scott-Smith.

Consumer Health Information Program & Services (CHIPS), County of Los Angeles Public Library, 151 E. Carson St., Carson 90745. SAN 372-8110. Tel. 310-830-0909, fax 310-834-4097. *Libn.* Scott A. Willis; *Aide* Mona Porotesano.

The Dialog Corporation, PLC, formerly Knight-Ridder Corporation, Inc., 2440 El Camino Real, Mountain View 94040. SAN 322-0176. Tel. 650-254-7000, fax 650-254-8093. *Pres.* Dan Wagner; *Exec. V.P.* Jeff Galt.

Hewlett-Packard Library Information Network, 1501 Page Mill Rd., Palo Alto 94304. SAN 375-0019. Tel. 650-857-3091, 857-6620, fax 650-852-8187, e-mail eugenie_prime@hp.com. *Chair* Eugenie Prime.

Kaiser Permanente Library System—Southern California Region (KPLS), Health Sciences Lib., 4647 Zion Ave., San Diego 92120. SAN 372-8153. Tel. 619-528-7323, fax 619-528-3444. *Dir.* Sheila Latus.

Metropolitan Cooperative Library System (MCLS), 3675 E. Huntington Dr., Suite 100, Pasadena 91107. SAN 371-3865. Tel. 626-683-8244, fax 626-683-8097, e-mail mclshg@mclsys.org. *Exec. Dir.* Barbara Custen.

National Network of Libraries Of Medicine—Pacific Southwest Region (PSRML), Louise Darling Biomedical Library, 12-077 Center for Health Sciences, Box 951798, Los Angeles 90095-1798. SAN 372-8234. Tel. 800-338-7657, fax 310-825-5389. *Dir.* Alison Bunting; *Assoc. Dir.* Beryl Glitz.

Northern California Association of Law Libraries (NOCALL), 601 Van Ness Ave. No. E3-840, Box 109, San Francisco 94102. SAN 323-5777. Tel. 916-653-8001, fax 916-653-0952. *Pres.* Mary Ann Parker.

Northern California Consortium of Psychology Libraries (NCCPL), California School of Professional Psychology, 1005 Atlantic, Alameda 94501. SAN 371-9006. Tel. 510-523-2300, ext. 185, fax 510-523-5943, e-mail pgsp@itsa.ucsf.edu. *Chair* Alan Schut.

Northern California & Nevada Medical Library Group, 2140 Shattuck Ave., Box 2105, Berkeley 94704. SAN 329-4617. Tel. 916-733-8822, fax 916-733-3879. *Pres.* Andrea Woodruff.

OCLC Pacific, 9227 Haven Ave., Suite 260, Rancho Cucamonga 91730. SAN 370-0747. Tel. 909-941-4220, fax 909-948-9803. *Dir.* Mary Ann Nash; *Acting Dir.* Pamela Bailey.

Peninsula Libraries Automated Network (PLAN), 25 Tower Rd., San Mateo 94402-4000. SAN 371-5035. Tel. 650-358-6704, fax 650-358-6706. *Database Mgr.* Susan Yasar.

Performing Arts Libraries Network of Greater Los Angeles (PALNET), Autry Museum of Western Heritage, 4700 Western Heritageway, Los Angeles 90027. SAN 371-3997. Tel. 323-667-2000, ext. 271, fax

323-660-5721. *Chair, Special Collections Libn,. and Archivist* Sharon Johnson.

Research Libraries Group, Inc. (RLG), 1200 Villa St., Mountain View 94041-1100. SAN 322-0206. Tel. 800-537-7546, fax 650-964-0943, e-mail bl.ric@rlg.stanford. edu. *Pres.* James Michalko.

San Bernardino, Inyo, Riverside Counties United Library Services (SIRCULS), 3581 Mission Inn Ave., Box 468, Riverside 92502. SAN 322-0222. Tel. 909-369-7995, fax 909-784-1158, e-mail sirculs@ inlandlib.org. *Exec. Dir.* Kathleen F. Aaron; *Reference Libn.* Cecelia Mestas-Holm.

San Diego & Imperial Counties College Learning Resources Cooperative (SDICC-CL), formerly Learning Resources Cooperative, Palomar College, 1140 W. Mission Rd., San Marcos 92069. SAN 375-006X. Tel. 760-744-1150, ext. 2848, fax 760-761-3500, e-mail jconte@swc.cc.ca.us. *Pres.* George Mozes.

San Francisco Biomedical Library Network (SFBLN), H M Fishbon Memorial Lib., USCF-Mount Zion, UCSF Standard Health Care, 1600 Divisadero St., A116, San Francisco 94115. SAN 371-2125. Tel. 415-885-7378, fax 415-776-0689. *Coord.* Gail Sorrough.

Santa Clarita Interlibrary Network (SCIL-NET), 24700 McBean Pkwy., Santa Clarita 91355. SAN 371-8964. Tel. 805-253-7885, fax 805-254-4561. *Coord.* Frederick B. Gardner; *Recorder* Judy Trapenberg.

Serra Cooperative Library System, 5555 Overland Ave., Bldg. 15, San Diego 92123. SAN 372-8129. Tel. 619-694-3600, fax 619-495-5905, e-mail serrahq@electriciti. com. *System Coord.* Susan Swisher.

The Smerc Library, 101 Twin Dolphin Dr., Redwood City 94065-1064. SAN 322-0265. Tel. 650-802-5655, fax 650-802-5665. *Educ. Svc. Mgr.* Karol Thomas; *Electronic Reference. Svcs. Coord.* Carol Quigley.

Southnet, c/o Silicon Valley Library System, 180 W. San Carlos St., San Jose 95113. SAN 322-4260. Tel. 408-294-2345, fax 408-295-7388, e-mail sbcl@netcom.com. *Asst. Systems Dir.* Susan Holmer.

Substance Abuse Librarians & Information Specialists (SALIS), Box 9513, Berkeley 94709-0513. SAN 372-4042. Tel. 510-642-5208, fax 510-642-7175. *Exec. Dir.* Andrea Mitchell; *Chair* Barbara Seitz Demartinez.

Total Interlibrary Exchange (TIE), 4882 McGrath St., Suite 230, Ventura 93003-7721. SAN 322-0311. Tel. 805-922-6966, ext. 3475, fax 805-642-9095, e-mail tieweb@rain.org. *Pres.* Marcia Frasier.

## Colorado

Arkansas Valley Regional Library Service System (AVRLSS), 635 W. Corona, Suite 113, Pueblo 81004. SAN 371-5094. Tel. 719-542-2156, fax 719-542-3155, e-mail dmorris@uscolo.edu. *Dir.* Donna Jones Morris; *Chair* Tim Baublits.

Bibliographical Center for Research, Rocky Mountain Region, Inc., 14394 E. Evans Ave., Aurora 80014-1478. SAN 322-0338. Tel. 303-751-6277 ext. 117, fax 303-751-9787. *Exec. Dir.* David H. Brunell.

Central Colorado Library System (CCLS), 4350 Wadsworth Blvd., Suite 340, Wheat Ridge 80033-4638. SAN 371-3970. Tel. 303-422-1150, fax 303-431-9752, e-mail kenomoto@qadas.com. *Dir.* Gordon C. Barhydt; *Deputy Dir.* Judy Zelenski.

Colorado Alliance of Research Libraries, 3801 E. Florida Ave., Suite 515, Denver 80210. SAN 322-3760. Tel. 303-759-3399, fax 303-759-3363. *Exec. Dir.* Alan Charnes.

Colorado Association of Law Libraries, Box 13363, Denver 80201. SAN 322-4325. Tel. 303-492-7312, fax 303-295-3040. *Acting Pres. and V.P.* Georgia Briscoe.

Colorado Council of Medical Librarians (CCML), Box 101058, Denver 80210-1058. SAN 370-0755. Tel. 303-315-6435, fax 303-315-0294, e-mail pat.nelson@ uchsc.edu. *Pres.* Pat Nelson.

Colorado Library Resource Sharing & Information Access Board, c/o Colorado State Library, 201 E. Colfax, Denver 80203-1799. SAN 322-3868. Tel. 303-866-6900, fax 303-866-6940. *Coord.* Susan Fayed.

High Plains Regional Library Service System, 800 Eighth Ave., Suite 341, Greeley 80631. SAN 371-0505. Tel. 970-356-4357, fax 970-353-4355, e-mail bhager@

csn.net. *Dir.* Nancy Knepel; *Chair* Linda Clements.

Peaks & Valleys Library Consortium, c/o Arkansas Valley Regional Lib. Svc. System, 635 W. Corona Ave., Suite 113, Pueblo 81004. SAN 328-8684. Tel. 719-542-2156, 546-4197, fax 719-546-4484. *Secy.* Carol Ann Smith.

Southwest Regional Library Service System (SWRLSS), PO Drawer B, Durango 81302. SAN 371-0815. Tel. 970-247-4782, fax 970-247-5087. *Dir.* S. Jane Ulrich; *Technical Svc. Resource-Sharing Mgr.* Judith M. Griffiths.

## Connecticut

Capitol Area Health Consortium, 270 Farmington Ave., Suite 352, Farmington 06032-1909. SAN 322-0370. Tel. 860-676-1110, fax 860-676-1303. *Pres.* Robert Boardman; *V.P.* Karen Goodman.

Capitol Region Library Council, 599 Matianuck Ave., Windsor 06095-3567. SAN 322-0389. Tel. 860-298-5319, fax 860-298-5328, e-mail office@crlc.org. *Exec. Dir.* Dency Sargent; *Regional Projects Coord.* Patricia Copes.

Council of State Library Agencies in the Northeast (COSLINE), Connecticut State Library, 231 Capitol Ave., Hartford 06106. SAN 322-0451. Tel. 860-566-4301, 207-287-5600 (Maine), fax 860-566-8940. *Pres.* Kendall Wiggin.

CTW Library Consortium, Olin Memorial Library, Wesleyan Univ., Middletown 06457-6065. SAN 329-4587. Tel. 860-685-3889, fax 860-685-2661, e-mail ahagyard@ wesleyan. *Dir.* Alan E. Hagyard; *Applications Programmer* Mary Wilson.

Eastern Connecticut Libraries (ECL), Franklin Commons, 106 Rte. 32, Franklin 06254. SAN 322-0478. Tel. 860-885-2760, fax 860-885-2757, e-mail pholloway@ecl.org. *Dir.* Patricia Holloway; *Asst. Dir.* Sandra Brooks.

Hartford Consortium for Higher Education, 260 Girard Ave., Hartford 06105. SAN 322-0443. Tel. 860-236-1203, fax 860-233-9723. *Exec. Dir.* Rosanne Druckman.

LEAP (Library Exchange Aids Patrons), 110 Washington Ave., North Haven 06473.

SAN 322-4082. Tel. 203-239-1411, fax 203-239-9458. *Chair* Lois Baldini.

Libraries Online, Inc. (LION), 123 Broad St., Middletown 06457. SAN 322-3922. Tel. 860-347-1704, fax 860-346-3707. *Pres.* Edward Murray; *Exec. Dir.* William F. Edge, Jr.

National Network of Libraries of Medicine New England Region (NN-LM N.E. Region), University of Connecticut Health Center, 263 Farmington Ave., Farmington 06030-5370. SAN 372-5448. Tel. 860-679-4500, fax 860-679-1305. *Dir.* Ralph D. Arcari; *Assoc. Dir.* John Stey.

Northwestern Connecticut Health Science Libraries, Charlotte Hungerford Hospital, Torrington 06790. SAN 329-5257. Tel. 860-496-6689, fax 860-496-6631. *Coord.* Jackie Rorke.

Southern Connecticut Library Council, 2911 Dixwell Ave., Suite 201, Hamden 06518-3130. SAN 322-0486. Tel. 203-288-5757, fax 203-287-0757, e-mail office@sclc.org. *Dir.* Michael Golrick; *Project Dirs.* Sue Eisner, Susan Muro.

Western Connecticut Library Council, Inc., 530 Middlebury Rd., Suite 210B, Box 1284, Middlebury 06762. SAN 322-0494. Tel. 203-577-4010, fax 203-577-4015, e-mail abarney@wclc.org. *Exec. Dir.* Anita R. Barney.

## Delaware

Central Delaware Library Consortium, Dover Public Library, 45 S. State St., Dover 19901. SAN 329-3696. Tel. 302-736-7030, fax 302-736-5087. *Pres.* Robert S. Wetherall.

Delaware Library Consortium (DLC), Delaware Academy of Medicine, 1925 Lovering Ave., Wilmington 19806. SAN 329-3718. Tel. 302-656-6398, fax 302-656-0470. *Pres.* Gail P. Gill.

Libraries in the New Castle County System (LINCS), Box 128, Odessa 19730. SAN 329-4889. Tel. 302-378-8838, fax 302-378-7803. *Pres.* Lynda Whitehead.

Sussex Help Organization for Resources Exchange (SHORE), Box 589, Georgetown 19947. SAN 322-4333. Tel. 302-855-7890, fax 302-855-7895. *Pres.* Mary Brittingham.

Wilmington Area Biomedical Library Consortium (WABLC), Christiana Care Health System, Box 6001, Newark 19718. SAN 322-0508. Tel. 302-733-1116, fax 302-733-1365, e-mail ccw@christianacare.org. *Pres.* Christine Chastain-Warheit.

## District of Columbia

Capcon Library Network, 1990 M St. N.W., Suite 200, Washington 20036-3430. SAN 321-5954. Tel. 202-331-5771, fax 202-331-5788, e-mail capcon@capcon.net. *Exec. Dir.* Robert A. Drescher.

Coalition for Christian Colleges & Universities, 329 Eighth St. N.E., Washington 20002. SAN 322-0524. Tel. 202-546-8713, fax 202-546-8913. *Pres.* Robert C. Andringa.

Educational Resources Information Center (ERIC), U.S. Dept. Education, Office of Educ. Resources and Improvement, National Lib. of Educ. (NLE), 555 New Jersey Ave. N.W., Washington 20208-5721. SAN 322-0567. Tel. 202-401-6014, fax 202-219-1817, e-mail enic@inet.ed.gov. *Dir.* Dr. Keith Stubbs.

Educause, c/o 1112 16th St. N.W., Suite 600, Washington 20036. SAN 371-487X. Tel. 202-872-4200, fax 202-872-4318. *Pres.* Brian Hawkins; *Publications Mgr.* Jeff Hansen.

Fedlink (Federal Library & Information Network), c/o Federal Library & Information Center Committee, Library of Congress, Washington 20540-5110. SAN 322-0761. Tel. 202-707-4800, fax 202-707-4818, e-mail flicc@loc.gov. *Exec. Dir.* Susan M. Tarr; *Network Coord.* Milton Megee.

National Library Service for the Blind & Physically Handicapped, Library of Congress (NLS), 1291 Taylor St. N.W., Washington 20542. SAN 370-5870. Tel. 202-707-5100, fax 202-707-0712, e-mail nls@loc.gov. *Dir.* Frank Kurt Cylke; *Asst. to the Dir.* Marvine R. Wanamaker.

Transportation Research Information Services (TRIS), 2101 Constitution Ave. N.W., Washington 20418. SAN 370-582X. Tel. 202-334-3250, fax 202-334-3495. *Dir.* Jerome T. Maddock.

Veterans Affairs Library Network (VAL-NET), Library Division Programs Office, 810 Vermont Ave. N.W., Washington 20420. SAN 322-0834. Tel. 202-273-8694, fax 202-273-9386, e-mail wendy. carter@hq.med.va.gov. *Dir. Lib. Programs* Wendy N. Carter.

Washington Theological Consortium, 487 Michigan Ave. N.E., Washington 20017-1585. SAN 322-0842. Tel. 202-832-2675, fax 202-526-0818, e-mail wtconsort@aol. com. *Exec. Dir.* John Crossin.

## Florida

Central Florida Library Cooperative (CFLC), 431 E. Horatio Ave., Suite 230, Maitland 32751. SAN 371-9014. Tel. 407-644-9050, fax 407-644-7023. *Exec. Dir.* Marta Westall.

Florida Library Information Network, c/o Bureau of Lib. and Network Services, State Lib. of Florida, R A Gray Bldg., Tallahassee 32399-0250. SAN 322-0869. Tel. 850-487-2651, fax 850-488-2746, e-mail library@mail.dos.state.fl.us. *Chief, Bureau Lib. and Network Services.* Debra Sears.

Miami Health Sciences Library Consortium (MHSLC), KBI/IDM (142D), 1201 N.W. 16th St., Miami 33125-1673. SAN 371-0734. Tel. 305-324-3187, fax 305-324-3118, e-mail harker.susan@miami.va.gov. Susan Harker.

Palm Beach Health Sciences Library Consortium (PBHSLC), c/o Good Samaritan Medical Center Medical Library, Box 3166, West Palm Beach 33402. SAN 370-0380. Tel. 561-650-6315, fax 561-650-6417. *Chair* Karen Bledsoe.

Panhandle Library Access Network (PLAN), 5 Miracle Strip Loop, Suite 2, Panama City Beach 32407-3850. SAN 370-047X. Tel. 850-233-9051, fax 850-235-2286, e-mail Internet: jaskows@firnvx.firn.edu; Bitnet: jaskows@firnvx. *Exec. Dir.* William P. Conniff; *Lib. Resources Specialist* Carol A. DeMent.

Sangamon Valley Academic Library Consortium, Blackburn College, Lumpkin Library, 700 College Ave., Carlinvile 62626. SAN 322-4406. Tel. 217-854-3231, fax 217-854-8564, e-mail cscha@gorilla.blackburn.

edu. *Chair* Carol Schaefer; *Secy.-Treas.* Susan Full.

Southeast Florida Library Information Network, Inc. (SEFLIN), 100 S. Andrews Ave., Fort Lauderdale 33301. SAN 370-0666. Tel. 954-357-7345, fax 954-357-6998, e-mail currye@mail.seflin.org. *Exec. Dir.* Elizabeth Curry; *Pres.* Donald Riggs.

Tampa Bay Library Consortium, Inc., 1202 Tech Blvd., Suite 202, Tampa 33619. SAN 322-371X. Tel. 813-622-8252, fax 813-628-4425. *Exec. Dir.* Diane Solomon; *Pres.* Joe Stines.

Tampa Bay Medical Library Network (TABAMLN), Lakeland Regional Medical Center, 1324 Lakeland Hills Blvd., Lakeland 33805. SAN 322-0885. Tel. 941-687-1176, fax 941-687-1488. *Pres.* Jan Booker.

## Georgia

Atlanta Health Science Libraries Consortium, Shepherd Center, 2020 Peachtree Rd., Atlanta 30309. SAN 322-0893. Tel. 404-350-7473, fax 404-350-7736, e-mail pat_herndon@shepherd.org. *Pres.* Pat Herndon.

Biomedical Media, 1440 Clifton Rd. N.E., Rm. 113, Atlanta 30322. SAN 322-0931. Tel. 404-727-9797, fax 404-727-9798. *Dir.* Chuck Bogle; *Business Mgr.* Marilane Bond.

Georgia Health Sciences Library Association (GHSLA), University Hospital, 1350 Walton Way, Augusta 30901. SAN 372-8307. Tel. 706-774-5078, fax 706-774-8672. *Pres.* Donna Trainor.

Georgia Interactive Network for Medical Information (GaIN), c/o Medical Lib., School of Medicine, Mercer Univ., 1550 College St., Macon 31207. SAN 370-0577. Tel. 912-752-2515, fax 912-752-2051, e-mail rankin.ja@gain.mercer.edu. *Dir.* Jocelyn A. Rankin.

Georgia Online Database (GOLD), c/o Public Lib. Services, 1800 Century Pl. N.E., Suite 150, Atlanta 30345-4304. SAN 322-094X. Tel. 404-982-3560, fax 404-982-3563. *Acting Dir.* David Singleton.

Health Science Libraries of Central Georgia (HSLCG), c/o J Rankin Medical Lib.,

School of Medicine, Mercer Univ., 1550 College St., Macon 31207. SAN 371-5051. Tel. 912-752-2515, fax 912-752-2051, e-mail rankin.ja@gain.mercer.edu. *In Charge* Michael Shadix.

South Georgia Associated Libraries, 208 Gloucester St., Brunswick 31520-7007. SAN 322-0966. Tel. 912-267-1212, fax 912-267-9597. *Pres.* Tena Roberts; *Secy.-Treas.* Jim Darby.

Southeastern Library Network (SOLINET), 1438 W. Peachtree St. N.W., Suite 200, Atlanta 30309-2955. SAN 322-0974. Tel. 404-892-0943, fax 404-892-7879, e-mail mrichard@mail.solinet.net. *Exec. Dir.* Kate Nevins.

SWGHSLC, Colquitt Regional Medical Center, Health Sciences Lib. , Moultrie 31776. SAN 372-8072. Tel. 912-890-3460, fax 912-891-9345. *Medical Libn.* Susan Statom.

University Center in Georgia, Inc., 50 Hurt Plaza, Suite 465, Atlanta 30303-2923. SAN 322-0990. Tel. 404-651-2668, fax 404-651-1797. *Pres.* Michael Gerber.

## Hawaii

Hawaii-Pacific Chapter of the Medical Library Association (HIPAC-MLA), 1221 Punchbowl St., Honolulu 96813. SAN 371-3946. Tel. 808-536-9302, fax 808-524-6956. *Chair* Carolyn Ching.

## Idaho

Boise Valley Health Sciences Library Consortium (BVHSLC), Health Sciences Library, Saint Alphonsus Regional Medical Center, Boise 83706. SAN 371-0807. Tel. 208-367-3993, fax 208-367-2702. *Contact* Judy Balcerzak.

Canyon Owyhee Library Group, 203 E. Idaho Ave., Homedale 83628. SAN 375-006X. Tel. 208-337-4613, fax 208-337-4933, e-mail stokes@sd370.k12.id.us. *Chair* Ned Stokes.

Catalyst, c/o Boise State University, Albertsons Library, Box 46, Boise 83707-0046. SAN 375-0078. Tel. 208-426-4024, fax 208-426-1394. *Contact* Timothy A. Brown.

Cooperative Information Network (CIN), 8385 N. Government Way, Hayden 83835-9280. SAN 323-7656. Tel. 208-772-5612, fax 208-772-2498, e-mail jhartung@cin. kcl.org. *Contact* John Hartung.

Eastern Idaho Library System, 457 Broadway, Idaho Falls 83402. SAN 323-7699. Tel. 208-529-1450, fax 208-529-1467. *Contact* Paul Holland.

Gooding County Library Consortium, c/o Gooding High School, 1050 Seventh Ave. W., Gooding 83330. SAN 375-0094. Tel. 208-934-4831, fax 208-934-4347, e-mail senators@northrim.com. *Contact* Cora Caldwell.

Grangeville Cooperative Network, c/o Grangeville Centennial Library, 215 W. North St., Grangeville 83530-1729. SAN 375-0108. Tel. 208-983-0951, fax 208-983-2336, e-mail granglib@lcsc.edu. *Contact* Linda Ruthruff.

Idaho Health Information Association (IHIA), Columbia Eastern Idaho Regional Medical Center, Health Information Access Center, Box 2077, Idaho Falls 83403. SAN 371-5078. Tel. 208-529-6077, fax 208-529-7014. *Pres.* Kathy Nelson.

Lynx, c/o Boise Public Library, 715 Capitol Blvd., Boise 83702-7195. SAN 375-0086. Tel. 208-384-4238, fax 208-384-4025, e-mail lmelton@ci.boise.id.us. *Contact* Marilyn Poertner.

Palouse Area Library Information Services (PALIS), c/o Latah County Free Lib. District, 110 S. Jefferson, Moscow 83843-2833. SAN 375-0132. Tel. 208-882-3925, fax 208-882-5098, e-mail lkeenan@norby. latah.lib.id.us. *Contact* Lori Keenan.

Southeast Idaho Document Delivery Network, c/o American Falls District Library, 308 Roosevelt St., American Falls 83211-1219. SAN 375-0140. Tel. 208-226-2335, fax 208-226-2303. *Contact* Margaret McNamara.

Valnet, Lewis Clark State College Library, 500 Eighth Ave., Lewiston 83501. SAN 323-7672. Tel. 208-799-2227, fax 208-799-2831. *Contact* Paul Krause.

## Illinois

A Consortium of Midwest Community Colleges, Colleges & Universities, 1011 Lake St., Suite 434, Oak Park 60301. SAN 329-5583. Tel. 708-848-4844, fax 708-848-

4888, e-mail jberry@aakton.edu. *Exec. Dir.* John W. Berry; *Business Mgr.* Lisa A. Sikova.

Alliance Library System, 845 Brenkman Dr., Pekin 61554. SAN 371-0637. Tel. 309-353-4110, fax 309-353-8281. *Exec. Dir.* Valerie J. Wilford.

American Theological Library Association (ATLA), 820 Church St., Suite 400, Evanston 60201-5613. SAN 371-9022. Tel. 847-869-7788, fax 847-869-8513, e-mail atla@atla.com. *Exec. Dir.* Dennis A. Norlin; *Dir. Memb. Svcs.* Karen L. Whittlesey.

Areawide Hospital Library Consortium of Southwestern Illinois (AHLC), c/o Saint Elizabeth Hospital Health Science, 211 S. Third St., Belleville 62222. SAN 322-1016. Tel. 618-234-2120 ext. 1181, fax 618-234-0408, e-mail campese@apci.net, campese@exl.com. *Coord.* Michael Campese.

Association of Chicago Theological Schools (ACTS), McCormick Seminary, 5555 S. Woodlawn Ave., Chicago 60637. SAN 370-0658. Tel. 773-947-6300, fax 773-288-2612, e-mail nfisher@nwv.edu. *Pres.* Cynthia Campbell.

Capital Area Consortium, Saint Mary's Hospital Health Sciences Library, 1800 E. Lakeshore Dr., Decatur 62521-3883. SAN 322-1024. Tel. 217-464-2182, fax 217-429-2925. *Coord.* Laura Brosamer.

Center for Research Libraries, 6050 S. Kenwood, Chicago 60637-2804. SAN 322-1032. Tel. 773-955-4545, fax 773-955-4339, e-mail simpson@uhuru.uchicago. edu. *Pres.* Donald B. Simpson.

Chicago Library System (CLS), 224 S. Michigan, Suite 400, Chicago 60604. SAN 372-8188. Tel. 312-341-8500, fax 312-341-1985, e-mail calabrese@chilibsys.org. *Exec. Dir.* Alice Calabrese.

Chicago & South Consortium, Saint Joseph Medical Center, Health Science Library, 333 N. Madison Ave., Joliet 60435. SAN 322-1067. Tel. 815-725-7133 ext. 3530, fax 815-725-9459. *Coord.* Virginia Gale.

Consortium of Museum Libraries in the Chicago Area, c/o Morton Arboretum, Sterling Morton Lib., 4100 Illinois Rte. 53, Lisle 60532-1293. SAN 371-392X. Tel. 630-719-2427, fax 630-719-7950.

*Chair* Michael T. Stieber; *Secy.* Nancy Pajeau.

Council of Directors Of State University Libraries of Illinois (CODSULI), Southern Illinois University, Medical Library, Box 19625, Springfield 62795-9625. SAN 322-1083. Tel. 217-782-2658, fax 217-782-0988, e-mail cfakl@eiu.edu. *Dir.* Connie Poole.

East Central Illinois Consortium, Carle Foundation Hospital Library, 611 W. Park St., Urbana 61801. SAN 322-1040. Tel. 217-383-3011, fax 217-383-3452. *Coord.* Anita Johnson.

Fox Valley Health Science Library Consortium, Central DuPage Hospital Medical Library, 25 N. Winfield Rd., Winfield 60190. SAN 329-3831. Tel. 630-681-4535, fax 630-682-0028, e-mail gloria_sullivan@cdh.org. *Coord.* Gloria Sullivan.

Heart of Illinois Library Consortium, Carl Sanburg College, Bromenn Healthcare, Galesburg 61401. SAN 322-1113. Tel. 309-341-5106, fax 309-344-3526, e-mail ttucker@clarkstar.lib.il.us. *Coord.* Mary Evans.

Illinois Health Libraries Consortium, c/o Meat Industry Info. Center, National Cattleman's Beef Assn., 444 N. Michigan Ave., Chicago 60611. SAN 322-113X. Tel. 312-670-9272, fax 312-467-9729. *Coord.* William D. Siarny, Jr.

Illinois Library Computer Systems Office (ILCSO), Univ. of Illinois, 205 Johnstowne Centre, 502 E. John St., Champaign 61820. SAN 322-3736. Tel. 217-244-7593, fax 217-244-7596, e-mail oncall@listserv.ilcso.uiuc.edu. *Dir.* Kristine Hammerstrand; *Lib. System Coords.* Mary Ellen Farrell, Mary Sutherland.

Illinois Library & Information Network (ILLINET), c/o Illinois State Library, 300 S. Second St., Springfield 62701-1796. SAN 322-1148. Tel. 217-782-2994, fax 217-785-4326. *Dir.* Bridget L. Lamont; *Asst. Dir. for Lib. Development and Grants and Programs* Patricia Norris.

Judaica Library Network of Metropolitan Chicago (JLNMC), 618 Washington Ave., Wilmette 60091. SAN 370-0615. Tel. 847-251-0782, e-mail wolfecg@interaccess.com. *Pres.* Margaret Burka.

Libras, Inc., Dominican University, River Forest 60305. SAN 322-1172. Tel. 708-524-6875 ext. 6889, fax 708-366-5360, e-mail czange@mail.judson-il.edu. *Pres.* Sonja Terry.

Metropolitan Consortium of Chicago, Webster Library, Evanston Hospital, 2650 Ridge Ave., Chicago 60201. SAN 322-1180. Tel. 847-570-2664, e-mail libsch@interaccess.com. *Coord.* Dalia Kleinmuntz.

National Network of Libraries Of Medicine, c/o Library of the Health Sciences, University of Illinois at Chicago, 1750 W. Polk St., Chicago 60612-7223. SAN 322-1202. Tel. 312-996-2464, fax 312-996-2226. Jean Sayre.

Office of Educational Services, K 80, Office of Educational Svcs., K80, Univ. of Illinois at Springfield, Box 19243, Springfield 62794-9423. SAN 371-5108. Fax 217-786-6036, e-mail iscc@uis.edu. *Dir.* Rebecca Woodhull; *Libn.* Susie Shackleton.

Private Academic Libraries of Illinois (PALI), c/o Concordia Univ. Library, 7400 Augusta St., River Forest 60305-1499. SAN 370-050X. Tel. 708-209-3050, fax 708-209-3175, e-mail crflatzkehr@curf.edu. *Pres.* Henry R. Latzke.

Quad Cities Libraries in Cooperation (QUADLINC), Box 125, Coal Valley 61240. SAN 373-093X. Tel. 309-799-3155, fax 309-799-5103, e-mail mstewart@libb.rbls.lib.il.us. *Mgr. Automation Svcs.* Mary Anne Stewart.

Quad City Area Biomedical Consortium, Perlmutter Library, 855 Hospital Rd., Silvis 61282. SAN 322-435X. Tel. 309-792-4360, fax 309-792-4362. *Coord.* Barbara Tharp.

River Bend Library System (RBLS), Box 125, Coal Valley 61240. SAN 371-0653. Tel. 309-799-3155, fax 309-799-7916, e-mail jhutchin@libby.rbls.lib.il.us. *Coord.* Judy Hutchinson.

Shabbona Consortium, c/o Illinois Valley Community Hospital, 925 West St., Peru 61354. SAN 329-5133. Tel. 815-223-3300 ext. 502, fax 815-223-3394. *Contact* Sheila Brolley.

Upstate Consortium, c/o Menbota Community Hospital, 1315 Memorial Dr., Menbota

61342. SAN 329-3793. Tel. 815-539-7461 ext. 305. *Coord.* Janet Lane.

## Indiana

American Zoo & Aquarium Association (AZA-LSIG), Indianapolis 200, 1200 W. Washington St., Indianapolis 46222. SAN 373-0891. Tel. 317-630-5110, fax 317-630-5114. *Chair* Suzanne Braun.

Central Indiana Health Science Libraries Consortium, Saint Vincent Hospital & Health Care Center, Garceau Lib., 2001 W. 86th St., Indianapolis 46260. SAN 322-1245. Tel. 317-338-2095, fax 317-338-6516, e-mail lshass@stvincent.org; lhass@iquest.net. *Pres.* Louise S. Hass.

Collegiate Consortium Western Indiana, c/o Cunningham Memorial Library, Indiana State University, Terre Haute 47809. SAN 329-4439. Tel. 812-237-3700, fax 812-237-3376. *Assoc. V.P. Info. Svcs. and Dean of Libs.* Ellen Watson.

Evansville Area Library Consortium, 3700 Washington Ave., Evansville 47750. SAN 322-1261. Tel. 812-485-4151, fax 812-485-7564. *Coord.* E. Jane Saltzman.

Indiana Cooperative Library Services Authority (INCOLSA), 6202 Morenci Trail, Indianapolis 46268-2536. SAN 322-1296. Tel. 317-298-6570, fax 317-328-2380. *Exec. Dir.* Millard Johnson.

Indiana State Data Center, Indiana State Library, 140 N. Senate Ave., Indianapolis 46204-2296. SAN 322-1318. Tel. 317-232-3733, fax 317-232-3728, e-mail sandrews@statelib.lib.in.us. *Libn.* Cynthia Saint Martin & Ronald Sharpe; *Coord.* Sylvia Andrews.

Northeast Indiana Health Science Libraries Consortium (NEIHSL), Lutheran Center for Health Svcs., Health Sciences Lib., 3024 Fairfield Ave., Fort Wayne 46807. SAN 373-1383. Tel. 219-434-7691, fax 219-434-7695, e-mail avenlc@cris.com. *Coord.* Lauralee Aven.

Northwest Indiana Health Science Library Consortium, c/o N.W. Center for Medical Education, Indiana University School of Medicine, 3400 Broadway, Gary 46408-1197. SAN 322-1350. Tel. 219-980-6852, fax 219-980-6566, e-mail fyoung@iunhaw1. iun.indiana.edu. *Coord.* Felicia Young.

Society of Indiana Archivists, University Archives, 201 Bryan Hall, Indiana University, Bloomington 47405. SAN 329-5508. Tel. 812-855-5897, fax 812-855-8104. *Asst. to Pres.* Philip Bantin.

Wabash Valley Health Science Library Consortium, Indiana State University, Cunningham Memorial Library, Terre Haute 47809. SAN 371-3903. Tel. 812-237-2540, fax 812-237-8028, e-mail libbirk@cml.indstate.edu. *Medical Libn. & Consortium Coord.* Evelyn J. Vail.

## Iowa

Bi-state Academic Libraries (BI-SAL), c/o Marycrest International Univ., Davenport 52804. SAN 322-1393. Tel. 319-326-9255.

Consortium of College & University Media Centers, Instructional Technology Center, Iowa State Univ., 121 Pearson Hall, Ames 50011-2203. SAN 322-1091. Tel. 515-294-1811, fax 515-294-8089, e-mail ccumc@ccumc.org. *Exec. Dir.* Don A. Rieck.

Dubuque (Iowa) Area Library Information Consortium, c/o Divine Word College Seminary, 102 Jacoby Dr., Epworth 52045. SAN 322-1407. Tel. 319-876-3353 ext. 207, fax 319-876-3407. *Pres.* Dan Boice.

Iowa Private Academic Library Consortium (IPAL), c/o Buena Vista University Library, 610 W. Fourth St., Storm Lake 50588. SAN 329-5311. Tel. 712-749-2127, fax 712-749-2059, e-mail proberts@keller.clarke.edu. *Dir.* Jim Kennedy.

Linn County Library Consortium, Stewart Memorial Library, Coe College, Cedar Rapids 52402. SAN 322-4597. Tel. 319-399-8023, fax 319-399-8019. *Pres.* Richard Doyle; *V.P.* Margaret White.

Polk County Biomedical Consortium, c/o Mercy Hospital Medical Library, 400 University Ave., Des Moines 50314. SAN 322-1431. Tel. 515-247-4189, fax 515-643-8809, e-mail celtic@netins.net. *Coord.* Pat Styles.

Sioux City Library Cooperative (SCLC), c/o Sioux City Public Library, 529 Pierce St., Sioux City 51101-1203. SAN 329-4722. Tel. 712-255-2933 ext. 251, fax 712-279-6432. *Agent* Betsy J. Thompson.

State of Iowa Libraries Online Interlibrary Loan (SILO-ILL), State Library of Iowa, E. 12th & Grand, Des Moines 50319. SAN 322-1415. Tel. 515-281-4105, fax 515-281-6191. *State Libn.* Sharman B. Smith.

Tri-college Cooperative Effort, Loras College, c/o Wahlert Memorial Library, 1450 Alta Vista, Dubuque 52004-0178. SAN 322-1466. Tel. 319-588-7164, fax 319-588-7292, e-mail klein@loras.edu. *Dir.* Robert Klein; *Dirs.* Paul Roberts, Joel Samuels.

## Kansas

Associated Colleges of Central Kansas, 210 S. Main St., McPherson 67460. SAN 322-1474. Tel. 316-241-5150, fax 316-241-5153. *Dir.* Donna Zerger.

Dodge City Library Consortium, c/o Dodge City, 1001 Second Ave., Dodge City 67801. SAN 322-4368. Tel. 316-225-0243, fax 316-225-0252. *Pres.* Patty Collins.

Kansas Library Network Board, State Capital, Rm. 343N, 300 S.W. Tenth, Topeka 66612-1593. SAN 329-5621. Tel. 785-296-3875, fax 785-296-6650, e-mail mpiper@ink.org. *Exec. Dir.* Eric Hansen.

## Kentucky

Association of Independent Kentucky Colleges & Universities, 484 Chenault Rd., Frankfort 40601. SAN 322-1490. Tel. 502-695-5007, fax 502-695-5057, e-mail gary@mail.aikcu.org. *Pres.* Gary S. Cox.

Eastern Kentucky Health Science Information Network (EKHSIN), c/o Camden-Carroll Library, Morehead State University, Morehead 40351. SAN 370-0631. Tel. 606-783-2610, fax 606-783-5311. *Coord.* William J. DeBord.

Kentuckiana Metroversity, Inc., 3113 Lexington Rd., Louisville 40206. SAN 322-1504. Tel. 502-897-3374, fax 502-895-1647. *Exec. Dir.* Jack Will.

Kentucky Health Science Libraries Consortium, VA Medical Center, Lib. Svcs. 142D, 800 Zorn Ave., Louisville 40206-1499. SAN 370-0623. Tel. 502-894-6240, fax 502-894-6134. *Pres.* Jim Kastner.

Kentucky Library Information Center (KLIC), Kentucky Dept. for Libraries & Archives,

300 Coffee Tree Rd., Box 537, Frankfort 40602-0537. SAN 322-1512. Tel. 502-564-8300, fax 502-564-5773. *Branch Mgr. Network Development* Linda Sherrow.

Kentucky Library Network, Inc., 300 Coffee Tree Rd., Box 537, Frankfort 40602. SAN 371-2184. Tel. 502-564-8300, fax 502-564-5773. *Pres.* William DeBord.

Southern Kentucky (AHEC), formerly Bluegrass Medical Librarians, Health Sciences Lib., Southern Kyahec, 305 Estill St., Berea 40404. SAN 371-3881. Fax 606-986-0534, e-mail skahec@skn.net. *Pres.* Kelly Bickery.

State Assisted Academic Library Council of Kentucky (SAALCK), c/o Steely Library, Northern Kentucky University, Highland Heights 41099. SAN 371-2222. Tel. 606-572-5483, fax 606-572-6181, e-mail winner@nku.edu. *Chair & Pres.* Marian C. Winner.

Theological Education Association of Mid America (TEAM-A), c/o Southern Baptist Theological Seminary, 2825 Lexington Rd., Louisville 40280-0294. SAN 322-1547. Tel. 502-897-4807, fax 502-897-4600. *Dir.* Ronald F. Deering.

## Louisiana

Baton Rouge Hospital Library Consortium, Earl K Long Hospital, 5825 Airline Hwy., Baton Rouge 70805. SAN 329-4714. Tel. 504-358-1089, fax 504-358-1240, e-mail estanl@mail.ekl.lsvmc.edu. *Pres.* Eileen H. Stanley.

Health Sciences Library Association of Louisiana Medical Library, Children's Hospital, 200 Henry Clay Ave., New Orleans 70118. SAN 375-0035. Tel. 504-896-9264, fax 504-896-3932, e-mail estanley@chmcat.cem.lsu.edu. *Chair* Lauren Clement Leboeuf.

Lasernet, State Library of Louisiana, Box 131, Baton Rouge 70821. SAN 371-6880. Tel. 225-342-4923, 342-3389, fax 225-219-4804. *Deputy Asst. Libn.* Michael R. McKann; *Automation Consultant* Sara Taffae.

Louisiana Government Information Network (LaGIN), c/o State Library of Louisiana, Box 131, Baton Rouge 70821. SAN 329-5036. Tel. 225-342-4914, fax 225-342-

3547, e-mail jsmith@pelican.state.lib.la.
us. *Coord.* Judith D. Smith.
New Orleans Educational Telecommunications Consortium, 2 Canal St., Suite 2038,
New Orleans 70130. SAN 329-5214. Tel.
504-524-0350, fax 504-524-0327. *Chair*
Gregory M. St. L. O'Brien; *Exec. Dir.*
Robert J. Lucas.

## Maine

Health Science Library Information Consortium (HSLIC), USVAM ROC, Box 3395,
Togus 04330. SAN 322-1601. Tel. 207-
743-5933 ext. 323, fax 207-973-8233,
e-mail brunjes@saturn.caps.maine.edu.
*Chair* Cindy White.

## Maryland

District of Columbia Health Sciences Information Network (DOCHSIN), Shady Grove
Adventist Hospital Library, 9901 Medical
Center Dr., Rockville 20850. SAN 323-
9918. Tel. 301-279-6101, fax 301-279-
6500. *Pres.* Janice Lester.
ERIC Processing & Reference Facility, 1100
West St., 2nd flr, Laurel 20707-3598. SAN
322-161X. Tel. 301-497-4080, fax 301-
953-0263, e-mail tbrandho@inet.ed.gov.
*Dir.* Ted Brandhorst.
Library Video Network (LVN), 320 York
Rd., Towson 21204. SAN 375-5320. Tel.
410-887-2090, fax 410-887-6103, e-mail
inlib@mail.bcpl.lib.md.us. *Production
Mgr.* Jeff Lifton.
Maryland Association of Health Science
Librarians (MAHSL), Saint Agnes Healthcare, 900 Caton Ave., Baltimore 21229.
SAN 377-5070. Tel. 410-368-3123. *Pres.*
Joanne Sullivan.
Maryland Interlibrary Organization (MILO),
c/o Enoch Pratt Free Library, 400 Cathedral St., Baltimore 21201-4484. SAN 343-
8600. Tel. 410-396-5498, fax 410-396-
5837, e-mail pwallace@mail.pratt.lib.md.
us. *Mgr.* Sharon A. Smith.
Metropolitan Area Collection Development
Consortium (MCDAC), c/o Carrol County
Public Lib., 15 Airport Dr., Westminster
21157. SAN 323-9748. Tel. 410-876-
6008, fax 410-876-3002, e-mail nhaile@
ccpl.carr.org. *Coord.* Nancy Haile.

National Library of Medicine, MEDLARS,
8600 Rockville Pike, Bethesda 20894.
SAN 322-1652. Tel. 301-402-1076, fax
301-496-0822, e-mail mms@nlm.nih.gov.
*MEDLARS Mgt. Section* Carolyn Tilley.
National Network of Libraries of Medicine,
Univ. Md Health Scis & Human Svcs.
Lib., 601 W. Lombard St., Baltimore
21201-1583. SAN 322-1644. Tel. 410-
706-2855, fax 410-706-0099, e-mail Internet: fmeakin@umab.umd.edu. *Exec. Dir.*
Janice Kelly; *RML Dir.* Frieda Weise.
National Network of Libraries of Medicine
(NN-LM), Nat Lib. of Medicine, 8600
Rockville Pike, Rm. B1E03, Bethesda
20894. SAN 373-0905. Tel. 301-496-
4777, fax 301-480-1467, e-mail blyon@
nlm.nih.gov. *Head* Becky Lyon.
Regional Alcohol and Drug Abuse Resource
Network (RADAR), National Clearinghouse Alcohol & Drug Info., Box 2345,
Rockville 20847-2345. SAN 377-5569.
Tel. 301-468-2600. *Dir.* John Noble.
Washington Research Library Consortium
(WRLC), 901 Commerce Dr., Upper Marlboro 20774. SAN 373-0883. Tel. 301-390-
2031, fax 301-390-2020. *Exec. Dir.* Lizanne
Payne.

## Massachusetts

Automated Bristol Library Exchange (ABLE,
Inc), 547 W. Grove St., Box 4, Middleboro
02346. SAN 378-0074. Tel. 508-946-
8600, fax 508-946-8605. *Exec. Dir.* Deborah K. Conrad; *Pres.* Margaret Bentley.
Boston Area Music Libraries (BAML), Music
Library, Wellesley College, Wellesley
02140. SAN 322-4392. Tel. 781-283-
2076, fax 781-283-3687, e-mail dgilbert@
wellesley.edu. *Coord.* David Gilbert.
Boston Biomedical Library Consortium
(BBLC), c/o Paul E. Woodard Health Sciences Library, New England Baptist Hospital, 125 Parker Hill Ave., Boston 02120.
SAN 322-1725. Tel. 617-754-5155, fax
617-754-6414, e-mail lllnebh@world.std.
com. *Chair* Leonard L. Levin.
Boston Library Consortium, 700 Boylston
St., Rm. 317, Boston 02117. SAN 322-
1733. Tel. 617-262-0380, fax 617-262-
0163, e-mail hstevens@bpl.org. *Exec. Dir.*
Hannah M. Stevens.

Boston Theological Institute Library Program, 45 Francis Ave., Cambridge 02138. SAN 322-1741. Tel. 617-495-5780, 527-4880, fax 617-495-9489, e-mail putney@harvarda.harvard.edu. *Lib. Coord.* Clifford Putney.

C W Mars (Central-Western Massachusetts Automated Resource Sharing), One Sunset Lane, Paxton 01612-1197. SAN 322-3973. Tel. 508-755-3323, fax 508-755-3721, e-mail jkuklins@cwmars.org. *Exec. Dir.* Joan Kuklinski; *Mgr. Lib. Applications* Gale E. Eckerson.

Cape Libraries Automated Materials Sharing (CLAMS), 270 Communication Way, Unit 4E-4F, Hyannis 02601. SAN 370-579X. Tel. 508-790-4399, fax 508-771-4533, e-mail mgrace@clams.lib.ma.us; dtustin@clams.lib.ma.us. *Pres.* Debra DeJonker-Berry; *Exec. Dir.* Monica Grace.

Catholic Library Association, 100 North St., Suite 224, Pittsfield 01201-5109. SAN 329-1030. Tel. 413-443-2252, fax 413-442-2252, e-mail cla@vgernet.net. *Exec. Dir.* Jean R. Bostley.

Central Massachusetts Consortium of Health Related Libraries (CMCHRL), c/o The Medical Lib., Univ. Mass. Memorial Healthcare, 119 Belmont St., Worcester 01605. SAN 371-2133. *Pres.* Andy Dzaugis.

Consortium for Information Resources, Emerson Hospital, Old Rd. to Nine Acre Corner, Concord 01742. SAN 322-4503. Tel. 978-287-3090, fax 978-287-3651. *Pres.* Nancy Callander.

Cooperating Libraries of Greater Springfield (CLGS), c/o Hatch Library, Bay Path College, 588 Longmeadow St., Longmeadow 01106. SAN 322-1768. Tel. 413-565-1284, fax 413-567-8345. *Chair* Jay Schafer; *Treas.* F. Knowlton Utley.

Corporate Library Group (CLG), 50 Nagog Park, AK02-3/E10, Acton 01720. SAN 370-0534. Tel. 978-264-6500, fax 978-264-7724. *Mgr.* Mary Lee Kennedy.

Corporate Library Network Group, 50 Nagog Park, Acton 01720. SAN 377-5097. Tel. 978-264-7914. *Dir.* Mary Lee Kennedy.

Fenway Libraries Online (FLO), Wentworth Institute Technology, 550 Huntington Ave., Boston 02115. SAN 373-9112. Tel. 617-442-2384, fax 617-442-1519. *Network Dir.* Jamie Ingram; *Technician & User Support* Stephanie Norris.

Fenway Library Consortium, Simmons College, 300 The Fenway, Boston 02115. SAN 327-9766. Tel. 617-521-2754, fax 617-521-3093, e-mail ecl_maz@flo.org. *Coord.* Harvey Varnet.

Massachusetts Health Sciences Libraries Network (MAHSLIN), c/o New England Regional Primate Center, Harvard Medical School, Box 9102, Southborough 01772-9102. SAN 372-8293. Tel. 508-624-8028, fax 508-460-1209, e-mail sfingold@warren.med.harvard.edu. *Pres.* Sydney Ann Fingold.

Merrimac Interlibrary Cooperative, c/o J V Fletcher Library, 50 Main St., Westford 01886. SAN 329-4234. Tel. 508-692-5555, fax 508-692-4418, e-mail jefferso@mvlc.lib.ma.us. *Co-Chairs* Sue Jefferson, Nanette Eichell.

Merrimack Valley Library Consortium, 21 Canal St., Lawrence 01840. SAN 322-4384. Tel. 978-687-5300, fax 978-687-5312, e-mail manson@mvlc.lib.ma.us. *Pres.* Sue Ellen Holmes; *Exec. Dir.* Bill Manson.

Minuteman Library Network, 4 California Ave., 5th flr, Framingham 01701. SAN 322-4252. Tel. 508-879-8575, fax 508-879-5470, e-mail ccaro.@mln.lib.ma.us. *Exec. Dir.* Carol B. Caro; *Bibliog. Svc.* Allison Powers.

NELINET, Inc., 2 Newton Executive Park, Newton 02162. SAN 322-1822. Tel. 617-969-0400, fax 617-332-9634, e-mail admin@nelinet.org. *Exec. Dir.* Marshall Keys.

New England Law Library Consortium, Inc., Harvard Law School Library, Langdell Hall, Cambridge 02138. SAN 322-4244. Tel. 617-496-2121, 508-428-5342, fax 617-428-7623, e-mail klaiber@law.harvard.edu. *Exec. Dir.* Diane Klaiber.

North of Boston Library Exchange, Inc. (NOBLE), 26 Cherry Hill Dr., Danvers 01923. SAN 322-4023. Tel. 978-777-8844, fax 978-750-8472. *Exec. Dir.* Ronald A. Gagnon; *Member Svcs. Mgr.* Elizabeth B. Thomsen.

Northeast Consortium of Colleges & Universities in Massachusetts (NECCUM), c/o Gordon College, 255 Grapevine Rd., Wenham 01984. SAN 371-0602. Tel. 978-927-2300 ext. 4068, fax 978-524-3708, e-mail macleod@hope.gordonc.edu. *Coord.* Stephen MacLeod.

Northeastern Consortium for Health Information (NECHI), Tewksbury State Hospital, 365 E. St., Tewksbury 01876. SAN 322-1857. Tel. 978-741-6762, 851-7321 ext. 2255, e-mail glynn@noblenet.org. *Chair* Chris Young.

Sails, Inc., 547 W. Groves St., Box 4, Middleboro 02346. SAN 378-0058. Tel. 508-946-8600, fax 508-946-8605. *Exec. Dir.* Deborah K. Conrad; *Pres.* Mary Jane Pillsbury.

Southeastern Automated Libraries, Inc. (SEAL), 547 W. Grove St., Box 4, Middleboro 02346. SAN 371-5000. Tel. 508-946-8600, fax 508-946-8605. *Exec. Dir.* Deborah K. Conrad; *Coord. User Svcs.* Barbara Bonville.

Southeastern Massachusetts Consortium of Health Science Libraries (SEMCO), South Shore Hospital, 55 Fogg Rd., South Weymouth 02190. SAN 322-1873. Tel. 781-340-8528, fax 781-331-0834, e-mail ubh0341@slh.org. *Chair* Cathy McCarthy.

Southeastern Massachusetts Cooperating Libraries (SMCL), c/o Wheaton College, Madeleine Clark Wallace Library, Norton 02766-0849. SAN 322-1865. Tel. 508-285-8225, fax 508-286-8275, e-mail pdeekle@wheatonma.edu. *Chair* Peter Deekle.

West of Boston Network (WEBNET), Horn Library-Babson College, Babson Park 02157. SAN 371-5019. Tel. 781-239-4308, fax 781-239-5226, e-mail benzer@babson.edu. *System Admin.* Susan Benzer; *Pres.* Hope Tillman.

Western Massachusetts Health Information Consortium, c/o Holyoke Hospital Medical Lib., 575 Beech St., Holyoke 01040. SAN 329-4579. Tel. 413-534-2500 ext. 5282, fax 413-534-2710, e-mail mcaraker@mail.map.com. *Pres.* Mary Caraker.

Worcester Area Cooperating Libraries, c/o Worcester State College Learning Resources Center, Rm. 221, 486 Chandler St., Worcester 01602-2597. SAN 322-1881. Tel. 508-754-3964, 793-8000 ext. 8544, fax 508-929-8198, e-mail gwood@worc.mass.edu. *Coord.* Gladys Wood.

## Michigan

Berrien Library Consortium, c/o Lake Michigan College Library, 2755 E. Napier Ave., Benton Harbor 49022-1899. SAN 322-4678. Tel. 616-927-8605, fax 616-927-6656. *Pres.* Diane Baker; *Treas.* Cynthia Helms.

Capital Area Library Network Inc. (CALNET), 4061 Holt Rd., Holt 48842. SAN 370-5927. Tel. 517-699-1657, fax 517-699-4859, e-mail aholt@isd.ingham.k12.mi.us. *Contact Person* Ann C. Holt; *Chair* Rita J. Echt.

Council on Resource Development (CORD), Oakland County Library, 1200 N. Telegraph Rd., Pontiac 48341. SAN 374-6119. Tel. 248-858-0380, fax 248-452-9145. *Chair* Phyllis Jose.

Detroit Area Consortium of Catholic Colleges, c/o Sacred Heart Seminary, 2701 Chicago Blvd., Detroit 48206. SAN 329-482X. Tel. 313-883-8500, fax 313-868-6440. *Rector & Pres.* Allen H. Vigneron.

Detroit Associated Libraries Region of Cooperation (DALROC), Detroit Public Library, 5201 Woodward Ave., Detroit 48202. SAN 371-0831. Tel. 313-833-4835, fax 313-832-0877. *Chair Board* Patrice Merritt; *Regional Contact* James Lawrence.

Kalamazoo Consortium for Higher Education (KCHE), Kalamazoo College, 1200 Academy St., Kalamazoo 49006. SAN 329-4994. Tel. 616-337-7220, fax 616-337-7305. *Pres.* James F. Jones, Jr.; *Admin. Coord.* Margie Flynn.

Lakeland Area Library Network (LAKENET), 4138 Three Mile N.W., Grand Rapids 49544-1134. SAN 371-0696. Tel. 616-559-5253, fax 616-559-4329.

Library Cooperative of Macomb (LCM), 16480 Hall Rd., Clinton Township 48038. SAN 373-9082. Tel. 810-286-5750, fax 810-286-8951, e-mail turgeont@lcm.macomb.lib.mi.us. *Acting Dir.* Tammy L. Turgeon.

Michigan Association of Consumer Health Information Specialists (MACHIS), Bronson Methodist Hospital, Health Sciences Library, 252 E. Lovell St., Box B, Kalamazoo 49007. SAN 375-0043. Tel. 616-341-8627, fax 616-341-8828, e-mail dhummel @bw.brhn.org. *Chair* Marge Kars.

Michigan Health Sciences Libraries Association (MHSLA), c/o Spectrum Health-Downtown Campus, 100 Michigan Ave. N.E., Grand Rapids 49503. SAN 323-987X. Tel. 616-391-1655, fax 616-391-3527, e-mail dianehummel@spectrumhealth.org. *Pres.* Diane Hummel.

Michigan Library Consortium (MLC), 6810 S. Cedar St., Suite 8, Lansing 48911. SAN 322-192X. Tel. 517-694-4242, fax 517-694-9303. *Exec. Dir.* Randy Dykhuis.

Northland Interlibrary System (NILS), 316 E. Chisholm St., Alpena 49707. SAN 329-4773. Tel. 517-356-1622, fax 517-354-3939, e-mail cawleyr@northland.lib.mi.us. *Dir.* Rebecca E. Cawley.

Southeastern Michigan League of Libraries (SEMLOL), c/o Wayne State University, Undergraduate Library, 5150 Anthony Wayne Dr., Detroit 48202. SAN 322-4481. Tel. 313-577-6630, fax 313-577-5265. *Chair* Lynn Sutton.

Southern Michigan Region of Cooperation (SMROC), 415 S. Superior, Suite A, Albion 49224-2135. SAN 371-3857. Tel. 517-629-9469, fax 517-629-3812. *Fiscal Agent* James C. Seidl.

Southwest Michigan Library Cooperative (SMLC), 305 Oak St., Paw Paw 49079. SAN 371-5027. Tel. 616-657-4698, fax 616-657-4494. *Dir.* Alida L. Geppert.

The Library Network, 13331 Reeck Rd., Southgate 48195. SAN 370-596X. Tel. 313-281-3830, fax 313-281-1905, 281-1817, e-mail hrc@tlnlib.mi.us. *Dir.* Harry Courtright; *Deputy Dir.* Eileen M. Palmer.

UMI Information Store, Inc., 300 N. Zeeb Rd., Box 1346, Ann Arbor 48106-1346. SAN 374-7913. Tel. 734-761-4700, fax 734-761-1032. *Mgr. Customer Svc. & Product Info.* Cheri Marken.

Upper Peninsula of Michigan Health Science Library Consortium, c/o Marquette General Hospital, 420 W. Magnetic, Marquette 49855. SAN 329-4803. Tel. 906-225-3429, fax 906-225-3524. *Chair* Kenneth Nelson.

Upper Peninsula Region of Library Cooperation, Inc., 1615 Presque Isle Ave., Marquette 49855. SAN 329-5540. Tel. 906-228-7697, fax 906-228-5627. *Pres.* Ken Nelson; *Treas.* Suzanne Dees.

## Minnesota

Arrowhead Health Sciences Library Network, Library—Saint Luke's Hospital, Duluth 55805. SAN 322-1954. Tel. 218-726-5320, fax 218-726-5181, e-mail droberts@slhduluth.com. *Coord.* Doreen Roberts.

Capital Area Library Consortium (CALCO), c/o Minnesota Dept of Transportation, Library MS155, 395 John Ireland Blvd., Saint Paul 55155. SAN 374-6127. Tel. 612-296-1741, fax 612-297-2354. *Pres.* Dennis Skradie.

Central Minnesota Libraries Exchange (CMLE), c/o Learning Resources, Rm. 61, Saint Cloud State University, Saint Cloud 56301-4498. SAN 322-3779. Tel. 320-255-2950, fax 320-654-5131, e-mail ppeterson@stcloudstate.edu. *Dir.* Patricia E. Peterson.

Community Health Science Library, c/o Saint Francis Medical Center, 415 Oak St., Breckenridge 56520. SAN 370-0585. Tel. 218-643-7516, fax 218-643-7487. Carla Lobaasen.

Cooperating Libraries in Consortium (CLIC), 1619 Dayton Ave., Suite 204A, Saint Paul 55104. SAN 322-1970. Tel. 651-644-3878, fax 651-644-6258, e-mail olsonc@macalester.edu. *Exec. Dir.* Chris Olson; *Computer Systems Specialist* Steve Waage.

Metronet, 2324 University Ave. W., Suite 116, Saint Paul 55114. SAN 322-1989. Tel. 651-646-0475, fax 651-646-0657. *Dir.* Mary Treacy.

Metropolitan Library Service Agency (MELSA), 570 Asbury St., Suite 201, Saint Paul 55104-1849. SAN 371-5124. Tel. 612-645-5731, fax 612-649-3169, e-mail melsa@gopher.melsa.lib.mn.us. *Exec. Dir.* James Wroblewski.

Minitex Library Information Network, c/o S-33 Wilson Lib., Univ. of Minn., 309 19th Ave. S., Minneapolis 55455-0414. SAN 322-1997. Tel. 612-624-4002, fax 612-624-4508, e-mail w_dejo@tc.umn.edu.

*Dir.* William DeJohn; *Asst. Dirs.* Becky Ringwelski, Mary Parker.

Minnesota Department of Human Services Library DHS Library & Resource Center, 444 Lafayette, Saint Paul 55155-3820. SAN 371-0750. Tel. 612-297-8708, fax 612-282-5340, e-mail kate.o.nelson@state. mn.us. *Dir. & Coord.* Kate Nelson.

Minnesota Theological Library Association (MTLA), c/o Luther Seminary Library, 2375 Como Ave., Saint Paul 55108. SAN 322-1962. Tel. 612-641-3202, fax 612-641-3280, e-mail twalker@luthersem.edu. *Co-Pres.* Sandy Oslund, Pam Jervis; *Dir. Learning Resources* Tom Walker.

North Country Library Cooperative, Olcott Plaza, 820 Ninth St. N., Suite 110, Virginia 55792-2298. SAN 322-3795. Tel. 218-741-1907, fax 218-741-1907, e-mail nclcmn@northernnet.com. *Dir.* Linda J. Wadman.

Northern Lights Library Network, 318 17th Ave. E., Box 845, Alexandria 56308-0845. SAN 322-2004. Tel. 320-762-1032, fax 320-762-1032. *Dir.* Joan B. Larson.

SMILE (Southcentral Minnesota Inter-Library Exchange), 110 S. Broad, Box 3031, Mankato 56002-3031. SAN 321-3358. Tel. 507-625-7555, fax 507-625-4049, e-mail llowry@tds.lib.mn.us. *Dir.* Lucy Lowry; *Contact* Kate Tohal.

Southeast Library System (SELS), 107 W. Frontage Rd., Hwy. 52 N., Rochester 55901. SAN 322-3981. Tel. 507-288-5513, fax 507-288-8697. *Admin.* Ann Hutton.

Southwest Area Multi-county Multi-type Interlibrary Exchange (SAMMIE), BA 282 Southwest State University Library, Marshall 56258. SAN 322-2039. Tel. 507-532-9013, fax 507-532-2039. *Coord.* Robin Chaney.

Twin Cities Biomedical Consortium, c/o Health East Saint Joseph's Hospital Library, 69 W. Exchange St., Saint Paul 55102. SAN 322-2055. Tel. 651-232-3193, fax 651-232-3296. *Chair* Karen Brudvig.

Valley Medical Network, Lake Region Hospital Library, 712 S. Cascade St., Fergus Falls 56537. SAN 329-4730. Tel. 218-736-8158, fax 218-736-8723. *Pres.* Connie Schulz.

Waseca Interlibrary Resource Exchange (WIRE), c/o Waseca High School, 1717 Second St. N.W., Waseca 56093. SAN 370-0593. Tel. 507-835-5470 ext. 218, fax 507-835-1724, e-mail tlouganl@platec.net. *Dir.* Les Tlougan.

West Group, Box 64526, Saint Paul 55164-0526. SAN 322-4031. Tel. 612-687-7000, fax 612-687-5614. *Contact* Jennifer Goldbluff.

## Mississippi

Central Mississippi Consortium of Medical Libraries (CMCML), Medical Center U.S. Dept. of Veterans Affairs, 1500 E. Woodrow Wilson Dr., Jackson 39216. SAN 372-8099. Tel. 601-362-4471, 362-5378, 362-1680. *Chair* Rose Anne Tucker; *V.Chair* Wanda King.

Central Mississippi Library Council (CMLC), c/o Hinds Community College Library, Raymond 39154-9799. SAN 372-8250. Tel. 601-857-3255, fax 601-857-3293. *Chair* Tom Henderson; *Secy.* Rachel Smith.

Mississippi Biomedical Library Consortium, c/o College of Veterinary Medicine, Miss. State Univ., Box 9825, Mississippi State 39762. SAN 371-070X. Tel. 601-325-1240, fax 601-325-1141, e-mail kinkus@ cvm.msstate.edu. *Pres.* Jane Kinkus.

## Missouri

Kansas City Library Network, Inc., University of Missouri Dental Library, 650 E. 25th St., Kansas City 64108. SAN 322-2098. Tel. 816-235-2030, fax 816-235-2157.

Kansas City Metropolitan Library & Information Network, 15624 E. 24th Hwy., Independence 64050. SAN 322-2101. Tel. 816-521-7257, fax 816-461-0966, e-mail sburton@kcmlin.org. *Exec. Dir.* Susan Burton.

Kansas City Regional Council for Higher Education, Park College, 8700 N.W. River Park Dr., No 40, Parkville 64152-3795. SAN 322-211X. Tel. 816-741-2816, fax 816-741-1296, e-mail kcrche@aol or rondoering@aol; michmangus@aol. *Pres.* Ron Doering.

Missouri Library Network Corporation, 8045 Big Bend Blvd., Suite 202, Saint Louis

63119-2714. SAN 322-466X. Tel. 314-918-7222, fax 314-918-7727, e-mail mlnc@mlnc.com. *Dir.* Susan Singleton.

Philsom-Philnet-Bacs Network, c/o Washington University, Bernard Becker Medical Library, 660 S. Euclid Ave., Saint Louis 63110. SAN 322-2187. Tel. 314-362-2778, fax 314-362-0190, e-mail monikar@msnotes.wustl.edu. *Mgr.* Russ Monika.

Saint Louis Medical Librarians Consortia (SLML), c/o Washington University, Bernard Becker Medical Library, 660 S. Euclid Ave., Saint Louis 63110. SAN 375-0027. Tel. 314-362-2778, fax 314-362-0190, e-mail monikar@msnotes.wustl.edu. *Chair* Russ Monika.

Saint Louis Regional Library Network, 9425 Big Bend, Saint Louis 63119. SAN 322-2209. Tel. 314-965-1305, fax 314-965-4443. *Admin.* Bernyce Christiansen.

## Nebraska

Eastern Library System (ELS), 11929 Elm St., Suite 12, Omaha 68144. SAN 371-506X. Tel. 402-330-7884, fax 402-330-1859, e-mail ktooker@nde.unl.edu. *Admin.* Kathleen Tooker; *Board Pres.* Ruth Rasmussen.

ICON, formerly Information Consortium, 5302 S. 75th St., Ralston 68127. SAN 372-8102. Tel. 402-398-6092, fax 402-398-6923. *Chair* Ken Oyer.

Lincoln Health Sciences Library Group (LHSLG), Univ. of Nebraska, 219 North Love Library, Lincoln 68588-0410. SAN 329-5001. Tel. 402-472-2554, fax 402-472-5131. *Treas.* Joan Latta Konescky.

Meridian Library System, 3423 Second Ave., Suite 301, Kearney 68847. SAN 325-3554. Tel. 308-234-2087, fax 308-234-4040, e-mail sosenga@nol.org. *Pres.* Mary Neben; *Admin.* Sharon Osenga.

Mid-America Law School Library Consortium (MALSLC), c/o Klutznick Law Library, Creighton Univ. School of Law, Omaha 68178-0001. SAN 371-6813. Tel. 402-280-2251, fax 402-280-2244, e-mail andrus@culaw.creighton.edu. *Chair* Kay L. Andrus.

National Network of Libraries Of Medicine—Midcontinental Region (NN-LM-MR), c/o 986706 Nebraska Medical Center,

Omaha 68198-6706. SAN 322-225X. Tel. 402-559-4326, fax 402-559-5482, e-mail pmullaly@unmcvm.unmc.edu. *Dir.* Nancy N. Woelfl; *Assoc. Dir.* Rebecca Satterthwaite.

Nebase, c/o Nebraska Library Commission, 1200 N. St., Suite 120, Lincoln 68508-2023. SAN 322-2268. Tel. 402-471-4031, fax 402-471-2083. *Dir.* Jo Budler; *Network Svcs. Staff Asst.* Jeannette Powell.

Northeast Library System, 2813 13th St., Columbus 68601. SAN 329-5524. Tel. 402-564-1586. *Admin.* Carol Speicher.

Southeast Nebraska Library System, 5730 R St., Suite C-1, Lincoln 68505. SAN 322-4732. Tel. 402-467-6188, fax 402-467-6196, e-mail bealey@nol.org. *Admin.* Brenda Ealey; *Admin. Asst.* Sara Schott.

Western Council of State Libraries, Inc., Nevada State Lib. & Archives, 100 N. Stewart St., Carson City 89701. SAN 322-2314. Tel. 702-687-8315, fax 702-687-8311. *Pres.* Jim Sheppke.

## Nevada

Information Nevada, Interlibrary Loan Dept., Nevada State Library & Archives, Capitol Complex, Carson City 89710-0001. SAN 322-2276. Tel. 702-687-8325, fax 702-687-8330, e-mail akelley@clan.lib.nv.us. *Dir.* Joan Kerschner; *ILL Mgr.* Annie Kelley.

Nevada Medical Library Group (NMLG), Barton Memorial Hospital Library, 2170 S. Ave., Box 9578, South Lake Tahoe 89520. SAN 370-0445. Tel. 530-542-3000 ext. 2903, fax 530-543-0239, e-mail kanton@oakweb.com. *Chair* Laurie Anton.

## New Hampshire

Carroll County Library Cooperative, Box 240, Madison 03849. SAN 371-8999. Tel. 603-367-8545. *Pres.* Carolyn Busell.

Hillstown Cooperative, 3 Meetinghouse Rd., Bedford 03110. SAN 371-3873. Tel. 603-472-2300, fax 603-472-2978. *Chair* Frances M. Wiggin; *Secy.* Sarah Chapman.

Librarians of the Upper Valley Coop. (LUV Coop.), Enfield Public Library, Main St., Box 1030, Enfield 03748-1030. SAN 371-6856. Tel. 603-632-7145. *Secy.* Marjorie Carr; *Treas.* Patricia Hand.

Merri-Hill-Rock Library Cooperative, c/o Griffin F P Library, 22 Hooksett Rd., Box 308, Auburn 03032. SAN 329-5338. Tel. 603-483-5374, e-mail hailstones@juno. com. *Chair* Edith B. Cummings.

New Hampshire College & University Council, Libraries Committee, 116 S. River Rd., D4, Bedford 03110. SAN 322-2322. Tel. 603-669-3432, fax 603-623-8182. *Exec. Dir.* Thomas R. Horgan.

North Country Consortium (NCC), Gale Medical Library, Littleton Regional Hospital, 262 Cottage St., Littleton 03561. SAN 370-0410. Tel. 603-444-7731 ext. 164, fax 603-444-7491. *Coord.* Linda L. Ford.

Nubanusit Library Cooperative, c/o Peterborough Town Library, 2 Concord, Peterborough 03458. SAN 322-4600. Tel. 603-924-8040, fax 603-924-8041. *Contact* Ann Geisel.

Scrooge & Marley Cooperative, 310 Central St., Franklin 03235. SAN 329-515X. Tel. 603-934-2911. *Chair* Randy Brough.

Seacoast Coop. Libraries, North Hampton Public Library, 235 Atlantic Ave., North Hampton 03862. SAN 322-4619. Tel. 603-964-6326, fax 603-964-1107. *Contact* Pam Schwotzer.

**New Jersey**

Bergen County Cooperative Library System, 810 Main St., Hackensack 07601. SAN 322-4546. Tel. 201-489-1904, fax 201-489-4215. *Exec. Dir.* Robert W. White; *Mgr. Computer Svcs.* Brian DeSantis.

Bergen Passaic Health Sciences Library Consortium, c/o Englewood Hospital & Medical Center, 350 Engle St., Englewood 07631. SAN 371-0904. Tel. 201-894-3069, fax 201-894-9049, e-mail yoga@csnet.net. *ILL Coord. & Board Rep.* Lia Sabbagh.

Central Jersey Health Science Libraries Association, Saint Francis Medical Center Medical Library, 601 Hamilton Ave., Trenton 08629. SAN 370-0712. Tel. 609-599-5068, fax 609-599-5773. *Dir.* Donna Barlow; *Technical Info. Specialist* Joan O'Donnell.

Central Jersey Regional Library Cooperative—Region V, 4400 Rte. 9 S., Freehold 07728-1383. SAN 370-5102. Tel. 732-

409-6484, fax 732-409-6492. *Dir.* Connie S. Paul.

Cosmopolitan Biomedical Library Consortium, Medical Library, East Orange General Hospital, 300 Central Ave., East Orange 07019. SAN 322-4414. Tel. 973-266-8519. *Pres.* Peggy Dreker.

Dow Jones Interactive, Box 300, Princeton 08543-0300. SAN 322-404X. Tel. 609-520-4679, fax 609-520-4775. *In Charge* Pat Rodeawald.

Health Sciences Library Association of New Jersey (HSLANJ), NJ Hospital Association, 760 Alexander Rd., Princeton 08543-0001. SAN 370-0488. Tel. 609-566-6800, fax 609-566-6380, e-mail skica@umdnj. edu. *Pres.* Open.

Highlands Regional Library Cooperative, 31 Fairmount Ave., Box 486, Chester 07930. SAN 329-4609. Tel. 908-879-2442, fax 908-879-8812, e-mail cnersinger@interactive.net or bcarroll@interactive.net. *Exec. Dir.* Carol A. Nersinger; *Program Coord.* Barbara A. Carroll.

Infolink Eastern New Jersey Regional Library Cooperative, Inc., 44 Stelton Rd., Suite 330, Piscataway 08854. SAN 371-5116. Tel. 732-752-7720, 973-673-2343, fax 732-752-7785, 973-673-2710, e-mail glr@infolink.org. *Exec. Dir.* Charles Edwin Dowlin; *Programs & Svcs. Coord.* Cheryl O'Connor.

LMX Automation Consortium, 1030 Saint George, Suite 203, Avenel 07001. SAN 329-448X. Tel. 732-750-2525, fax 732-750-9392. *Exec. Dir.* Ellen Parravano.

Lucent Technologies Global Library Network, 600 Mountain Ave., Rm. 3A-426, Murray Hill 07974. SAN 329-5400. Tel. 908-582-4840, fax 908-582-3146, e-mail libnet@library.lucent.com. *Managing Dir.* Nancy J. Miller.

Monmouth-Ocean Biomedical Information Consortium (MOBIC), Community Medical Center, 99 Hwy. 37 W., Toms River 08755. SAN 329-5389. Tel. 732-240-8117, fax 732-240-8354. *Dir.* Reina Reisler.

Morris Automated Information Network (MAIN), Box 900, Morristown 07963-0900. SAN 322-4058. Tel. 973-989-6112, fax 973-989-6109, e-mail mainhelp@main.morris.org. *Network Admin. & Div. Head* Ellen Sleeter.

Morris-Union Federation, 214 Main St., Chatham 07928. SAN 310-2629. Tel. 973-635-0603, fax 973-635-7827. *Treas.* Diane R. O'Brien.

New Jersey Academic Library Network, c/o The College of New Jersey, Roscoe L West Library, 2000 Pennington Rd., Box 7718, Ewing 08628-0718. SAN 329-4927. Tel. 609-771-2332, fax 609-637-5177, e-mail mbiggs@tcnj.edu. *Chair* Mary Biggs.

New Jersey Health Sciences Library Network (NJHSN), Mountainside Hospital, Health Sciences Library, Montclair 07042. SAN 371-4829. Tel. 973-429-6240, fax 973-680-7850. *Chair* Patricia Regenberg.

New Jersey Library Network, Library Development Bureau, 185 W. State St., CN-520, Trenton 08625-0520. SAN 372-8161. Tel. 609-984-3293, fax 609-984-7898. *Svc. Coord.* Marilyn R. Veldof.

Society for Cooperative Healthcare & Related Education (SCHARE), UMDNJ, 1776 Raritan Rd., Scotch Plains 07076. SAN 371-0718. Tel. 908-889-6410, fax 908-889-2487. *Chair* Eden Trinidad; *Coord.* Anne Calhoun.

South Jersey Regional Library Cooperative, Paint Works Corporate Center, 10 Foster Ave., Suite F-3, Gibbsboro 08026. SAN 329-4625. Tel. 609-346-1222, fax 609-346-2839. *Exec. Dir.* Karen Hyman; *Program Development Coord.* Katherine Schalk-Greene.

### New Mexico

New Mexico Consortium of Academic Libraries, Dean's Office, University New Mexico, Albuquerque 87131-1466. SAN 371-6872. Fax 505-277-7288, e-mail ctownley@lib.nmsu.edu. *Dean* Bob Migneault.

New Mexico Consortium of Biomedical & Hospital Libraries, c/o Lovelace Medical Library, 5400 Gibson Blvd. S.E., Albuquerque 87108. SAN 322-449X. Tel. 505-262-7158, fax 505-262-7897. *Contact* Peg Fletcher.

### New York

Academic Libraries of Brooklyn, Polytechnic University Bern Dibner Library, 5 Metro-tech Center, Brooklyn 11201. SAN 322-2411. Tel. 718-260-3109, fax 715-260-3756, e-mail jrichman@duke.poly.edu. *Convener.* Jana Richman.

American Film & Video Association, Cornell Univ. Resource Center, 8 Business & Technology Park, Ithaca 14850. SAN 377-5860. Tel. 607-255-2090, fax 607-255-9946, e-mail dist_cent@cce.cornell.edu. *AV Libn.* Richard Gray.

Associated Colleges of the Saint Lawrence Valley, 200 Merritt Hall, State University of New York at Potsdam, Potsdam 13676-2299. SAN 322-242X. Tel. 315-267-3331, fax 315-267-2389, e-mail larranaj@potsdam.edu. *Exec. Dir.* Anneke J. Larrance.

Brooklyn-Queens-Staten Island Health Sciences Librarians (BQSI), Saint John's Episcopal Hospital, South Shore Div. Medical Library, 327 Beach 19th St., Far Rockaway 11691. SAN 370-0828. Tel. 718-869-7699, fax 718-869-8528, e-mail sjeh2@metgate.metro.org. *Pres.* Kalpana Desai.

Capital District Library Council for Reference & Research Resources, 28 Essex St., Albany 12206. SAN 322-2446. Tel. 518-438-2500, fax 518-438-2872, e-mail cdlc@cdlc.org. *Exec. Dir.* Jean K. Sheviak; *Program Svcs.* J. James Mancuso.

Central New York Library Resources Council (CLRC), 3049 E. Genesee St., Syracuse 13224-1690. SAN 322-2454. Tel. 315-446-5446, fax 315-446-5590, e-mail washburn@clrc.org. *Exec. Dir.* Keith E. Washburn; *Asst. Dir.* Jeannette Smithee.

Consortium of Foundation Libraries, c/o Carnegie Corporation of New York, 437 Madison Ave., 27th flr, New York 10022. SAN 322-2462. Tel. 212-207-6245, fax 212-754-4073, e-mail lgusts@email.cfr.org. *Chair* Ron Sexton.

Council of Archives & Research Libraries in Jewish Studies (CARLJS), 330 Seventh Ave., 21st flr, New York 10001. SAN 371-053X. Tel. 212-629-0500 ext. 205, fax 212-629-0508, e-mail nsjc@jewishculture.org. *Pres.* Michael Grunberger; *Dir. Cultural Svcs.* Jerome Chanes.

Educational Film Library Association, c/o AV Resource Center, Cornell Univ., Business & Technology Park, Ithaca 14850.

SAN 371-0874. Tel. 607-255-2090, fax 607-255-9946. *AV Sales* Rich Gray; *AV Technician* Gerry KIalk.

Health Information Libraries of Westchester (HILOW), NY Medical College, Medical Science Lib., Basic Sciences Bldg., Valhalla 10595. SAN 371-0823. Tel. 914-437-3121, fax 914-437-3002. *Pres.* Mary Jo Russell.

Library Consortium of Health Institutions in Buffalo, 155 Abbott Hall, SUNY at Buffalo, 3435 Main St., Buffalo 14214. SAN 329-367X. Tel. 716-829-2903, fax 716-829-2211. *Exec. Dir.* Martin E. Mutka.

Long Island Library Resources Council, Melville Library Bldg., Suite E5310, Stony Brook 11794-3399. SAN 322-2489. Tel. 516-632-6650, fax 516-632-6662, e-mail director@lilrc.org. *Dir.* Herbert Biblo; *Asst. Dir.* Judith Neufeld.

Manhattan-Bronx Health Sciences Libraries Group, c/o KPR Medical Library, 333 E. 38th St., New York 10016. SAN 322-4465. Tel. 212-856-8721, fax 212-856-8884. *Pres.* Penny Klein.

Medical Library Center of New York, 5 E. 102nd St., 7th flr, New York 10029. SAN 322-3957. Tel. 212-427-1630, fax 212-860-3496, 876-6697, e-mail mlcny@metgate. metro.org. *Dir.* Lois Weinstein.

Medical & Scientific Libraries of Long Island (MEDLI), c/o Palmer School of Lib. & Info. Sciences, C W Post Campus, Long Island Univ., Brookville 11548. SAN 322-4309. Tel. 516-299-2866, fax 516-299-4168, e-mail westerma@titan.liunet.edu. *Pres.* Ludmila Tsytlenok.

Metropolitan New York Library Council (METRO), formerly New York Metropolitan Reference & Research Library Agency, 57 E. 11th St., 4th flr, New York 10003-4605. SAN 322-2500. Tel. 212-228-2320, fax 212-228-2598, e-mail hiebing@metgate. metro.org. *Exec. Dir.* Dottie Hiebing.

Middle Atlantic Region National Network of Libraries of Medicine, New York Academy of Medicine, 1216 Fifth Ave., New York 10029-5293. SAN 322-2497. Tel. 212-822-7396, fax 212-534-7042, e-mail rml@nyam.org. *Acting Dir.* Mary Mylenki.

New York State Interlibrary Loan Network (NYSILL), c/o New York State Library,

Albany 12230. SAN 322-2519. Tel. 518-474-5129, fax 518-474-5786, e-mail ill@unixII.nysed.gov. *Dir.* Elizabeth Lane; *Principal Libn.* J. Van der Veer Judd.

North Country Reference & Research Resources Council, 7 Commerce Lane, Canton 13617. SAN 322-2527. Tel. 315-386-4569, fax 315-379-9553, e-mail info@northnet.org. *Exec. Dir.* John J. Hammond; *Systems Mgr.* Tom Blauvelt.

Northeast Foreign Law Cooperative Group, Fordham University, 140 W. 62nd, New York 10023. SAN 375-0000. Tel. 212-636-6913, fax 212-977-2662, e-mail vessien@law.fordham.edu. *Libn.* Victor Essien.

Research Library Association of South Manhattan, New York Univ. Bobst Lib., 70 Washington Sq. S., New York 10012. SAN 372-8080. Tel. 212-998-2566, fax 212-995-4583, e-mail grant@is.nyu.edu. *Coord.* Joan Grant.

Rochester Regional Library Council (RRLC), 390 Packetts Landing, Box 66160, Fairport 14450. SAN 322-2535. Tel. 716-223-7570, fax 716-223-7712, e-mail rrlc@rrlc. rochestr.lib.ny.us. *Dir.* Kathleen M. Miller.

South Central Regional Library Council, 215 N. Cayuga St., Ithaca 14850. SAN 322-2543. Tel. 607-273-9106, fax 607-272-0740, e-mail scrlc@lakenet.org. *Exec. Dir.* Jean Currie.

Southeastern New York Library Resources Council, 220 Rte. 299, Box 879, Highland 12528. SAN 322-2551. Tel. 914-691-2734, fax 914-691-6987, e-mail shaloiko@senylbc.org or starr@senylrc.org. *Exec. Dir.* John L. Shaloiko; *Asst. Dir.* Karen Starr.

State University of New York-OCLC Library Network (SUNY-OCLC), System Admin, State University Plaza, Albany 12246. SAN 322-256X. Tel. 518-443-5444, fax 518-432-4346, e-mail sunyoclc@slscva. sysaom.suny.edu. *Dir.* Mary-Alice Lynch.

United Nations System Consortium, c/o Dag Hammarskjold Library, Rm. L-166A, United Nations, Rm. L-166A, New York 10017. SAN 377-855X. Tel. 212-963-5142, fax 212-963-2608, e-mail cherifm@un.org. *Coord.* Mary F. Cherif.

Western New York Library Resources Council, 4455 Genesee St., Box 400, Buffalo 14225-0400. SAN 322-2578. Tel. 716-633-0705, fax 716-633-1736. *Exec. Dir.* Gail M. Staines.

## North Carolina

Association of Southeastern Research Libraries, University of Memphis Libraries, Memphis 38152-6500. SAN 322-1555. Tel. 901-678-2201, fax 901-678-8218, e-mail channing@lib.wfu.edu. *Chair* Lester J. Pourciau.

Cape Fear Health Sciences Information Consortium, Southeastern Regional Medical Center, 300 W. 27th St., Lumberton 28359. SAN 322-3930. Tel. 910-671-5000, fax 910-671-4143. *Dir.* Cathy McGinnis.

Microcomputer Users Group for Libraries in North Carolina (MUGLNC), Rowan Public Library, Box 4039, Salisbury 28145-4039. SAN 322-4449. Tel. 704-638-3009, fax 704-638-3013, e-mail whites@co. rowan.nc.us. *Pres.* Suzanne White; *Treas.* Barbara Thompson.

Mid-Carolina Academic Library Network (MID-CAL), Methodist College, Davis Memorial Library, 5400 Ramsey St., Fayetteville 28311. SAN 371-3989. Tel. 910-630-7122, fax 910-630-7119, e-mail gregory@ecsvax.uncecs.edu. *Chair* Susan Pulsipher.

NC Area Health Education Centers, Health Sciences Library, CB 7585, University of North Carolina, Chapel Hill 27599-7585. SAN 323-9950. Tel. 919-962-0700, fax 919-966-5592. *Network Coord.* Diana C. McDuffee.

North Carolina Community College System, 200 W. Jones St., Raleigh 27603-1379. SAN 322-2594. Tel. 919-733-7051, fax 919-733-0680. *Dir.* Pamela B. Doyle; *Coord. Lib. Info. Technology* Grant Pair.

North Carolina Library & Information Network, 109 E. Jones St., Raleigh 27601-2807. SAN 329-3092. Tel. 919-733-2570, fax 919-733-8748, e-mail netinfo@ncsl. dcr.state.nc.us. *Dir.* Sandra M. Cooper.

Northwest AHEC Library at Salisbury, c/o Rowan Regional Medical Center, 612 Mocksville Ave., Salisbury 28144. SAN 322-4589. Tel. 704-638-1069, fax 704-636-5050. *Contact* Nancy Stine.

Northwest AHEC Library Information Network, Northwest Area Health Education Center, Wake Forest Univ. School of Medicine, Medical Center Blvd., Winston-Salem 27157-1060. SAN 322-4716. Tel. 336-713-7015, fax 336-713-7028, e-mail bladner@bgsm.edu. *Network Coord.* Betty Ladner.

Resources for Health Information Consortium (ReHI), c/o Wake Medical Center Medical Library, 3024 Newbern Ave., Suite G01, Raleigh 27610. SAN 329-3777. Tel. 919-250-8529, fax 919-250-8836. *Assoc. Dir.* Beverly Richardson.

Triangle Research Libraries Network, Wilson Library, CB No 3940, Chapel Hill 27514-8890. SAN 329-5362. Tel. 919-962-8022, fax 919-962-4452, e-mail david-carlson@ unc.edu. *Exec. Dir.* Jordan M. Scepanski.

Unifour Consortium of Health Care & Educational Institutions, c/o Northwest AHEC Library at Hickory, Catawba Memorial Hospital, 810 Fairgrove Church Rd., Hickory 28602. SAN 322-4708. Tel. 828-326-3662, fax 828-326-2464, e-mail klmartin@ med.unc.edu. *Dir.* Karen Lee Martinez.

Western North Carolina Library Network (WNCLN), D Hiden Ramsey Library, One University Heights, Univ. of North Carolina at Asheville, Asheville 28804-3299. SAN 376-7205. Tel. 828-232-5095, fax 828-251-6012, e-mail reichelml@appstate.edu or moulrh@appstate.edu. *Chair* Mary Reichel; *Exec. Dir. & Network Libn.* Richard Moul.

## North Dakota

Dakota West Cooperating Libraries (DWCL), 3315 University Dr., Bismarck 58504. SAN 373-1391. Tel. 701-255-3285, fax 701-255-1844. *Chair* Charlene Weis; *Secy.-Treas.* Kelly Steckler.

Tri-college University Libraries Consortium, 209 Engineering Technology, North Dakota State University, Fargo 58105. SAN 322-2047. Tel. 701-231-8170, fax 701-231-7205. *Coord.* Richard Bovard; *Provost, Tri College Univ.* Jean Strandness.

## Ohio

Central Ohio Hospital Library Consortium, Prior Health Sciences Lib., 376 W. Tenth

Ave., Columbus 43210. SAN 371-084X.
Tel. 614-292-4891, fax 614-566-6949,
e-mail cohsla@lists.acs.ohio-state.edu.
*Archival Rec.* Jo Yeoh; *Pres.* Barbara Van
Brimmer.

Cleveland Area Metropolitan Library System
(CAMLS), 20600 Chagrin Blvd., Suite
500, Shaker Heights 44122-5334. SAN
322-2632. Tel. 216-921-3900, fax 216-
921-7220. *Exec. Dir.* Michael G. Snyder;
*Continuing Educ. Dir.* Terri Pasadja.

Columbus Area Library & Information Council of Ohio (CALICO), c/o Westerville
Public Library, 126 S. State St., Westerville 43081. SAN 371-683X. Tel. 614-882-
7277, fax 614-882-5369. *Treas.* Norma
Ekleberry.

Consortium of Popular Culture Collections in
the Midwest (CPCCM), c/o Popular Culture Library, Bowling Green State University, Bowling Green 43403-0600. SAN
370-5811. Tel. 419-372-2450, fax 419-
372-7996, e-mail bmccall@epic.bgsu.edu.
*Chair* Jeanne Somers.

Greater Cincinnati Library Consortium, 3333
Vine St., Suite 605, Cincinnati 45220-
2214. SAN 322-2675. Tel. 513-751-4422,
fax 513-751-0463, e-mail gclc@one.net.
*Exec. Dir.* Martha J. McDonald.

Health Science Librarians of Northwest Ohio
(HSLNO), Raymon H Mulford Lib. Bldg.,
Rm. 0409, Medical College of Ohio, 3045
Arlington Ave., Toledo 43614-5805. SAN
377-5801. Tel. 419-381-4220. *Pres.* Mar-
lene Porter.

MOLO Regional Library System, 1260 Mon-
roe Ave., New Philadelphia 44663-4147.
SAN 322-2705. Tel. 330-364-8535, fax
330-364-8537, e-mail molo@tusco.net.
*PGM Coord.* Christina Hopkins; *Exec.
Dir.* Renee Croft.

NEOUCOM Council of Associated Hospital
Librarians, Ocasek Regional Medical Info.
Center, Box 95, Rootstown 44272-0095.
SAN 370-0526. Tel. 330-325-6611, fax
330-325-0522, e-mail lsc@neoucom.cdu.
*Dir. & Chief Medical Libn.* Larry S. Ellis.

NOLA Regional Library System, 4445 Ma-
honing Ave. N.W., Warren 44483. SAN
322-2713. Tel. 330-847-7744, fax 330-
847-7704. *Dir.* Millie Fry.

Northwest Library District (NORWELD),
181 1/2 S. Main St., Bowling Green 43402.

SAN 322-273X. Tel. 419-352-2903, fax
419-353-8310. *Dir.* Allan Gray.

OCLC Online Computer Library Center, Inc.,
6565 Frantz Rd., Dublin 43017-3395.
SAN 322-2748. Tel. 614-764-6000, fax
614-764-6096, e-mail oclc@oclc.org.
*Pres.* Robert L. Jordan.

Ohio Library & Information Network (Ohio-
LINK), Ohio Library Info. Network, 2455
N. Star Rd., Columbus 43221. SAN 374-
8014. Tel. 614-728-3600, fax 614-728-
3610, e-mail info@ohiolink.edu. *Exec.
Dir.* Thomas J. Sanville; *Dir. Lib. Systems*
Anita I. Cook.

Ohio Network of American History Research
Centers, Ohio Historical Society Archives/
Library, 1982 Velma Ave., Columbus
43211-2497. SAN 323-9624. Tel. 614-
297-2501, fax 614-297-2546, e-mail
gparkins@winslo.ohio.gov. *Archivist*
George Parkinson.

Ohio Valley Area Libraries (OVAL), 252 W.
13th St., Wellston 45692-2299. SAN 322-
2756. Tel. 740-384-2103, fax 740-384-
2106, e-mail ovalrls@oplin.lib.oh.us or
andersen@oplin.lib.oh.us. *Dir.* Eric S.
Anderson; *Clerk-Treas.* Regina Ghearing.

Ohio-Kentucky Coop. Libraries, Box 647,
Cedarville 45314. SAN 325-3570. Tel.
937-766-7842, 766-2955, fax 937-766-
2337. *Ed.* Janice Bosma; *Asst. Ed.* Kelly
Hellwig.

Ohionet, 1500 W. Lane Ave., Columbus
43221-3975. SAN 322-2764. Tel. 614-
486-2966, fax 614-486-1527. *Exec. Dir.*
Michael P. Butler; *Mgr. Computer Svcs.*
Chad Barrie.

Southwestern Ohio Council for Higher Education, 3171 Research Blvd., Suite 141,
Dayton 45420-4014. SAN 322-2659. Tel.
937-259-1370, fax 937-259-1380, e-mail
soche@soche.org. *Exec. Dir.* Tamara Yea-
ger; *Chair Lib. Council* Jennilou Grotevant.

## Oklahoma

Greater Oklahoma Area Health Sciences
Library Consortium (GOAL), 12101 N.
MacArthur Blvd., Suite 251, LRC 6420
S.E. 15th, Oklahoma City 73162-1800.
SAN 329-3858. Tel. 405-271-6085, fax
405-271-1926, e-mail sheri-greenwood@
ouhsc.edu. *Pres.* Sheri Greenwood.

Metropolitan Libraries Network of Central Oklahoma Inc. (MetroNetwork), Box 250, Oklahoma City 73101-0250. SAN 372-8137. Tel. 405-231-8602, 733-7323, fax 405-236-5219. *Chair* Sharon Saulmon.

Oklahoma Health Sciences Library Association (OHSLA), University of Oklahoma—HSC Bird Health Science Library, Box 26901, Oklahoma City 73190. SAN 375-0051. Tel. 271-2672, fax 405-271-3297, e-mail jwilkers@rex.vokhsc.edu. *Pres.* Judy Wilkerson.

## Oregon

Chemeketa Cooperative Regional Library Service, c/o Chemeketa Community College, 4000 Lancaster Dr. N.E., Salem 97309-7070. SAN 322-2837. Tel. 503-399-5105, fax 503-399-5214, e-mail cocl@chemek.cc.or.us. *Coord.* Linda Cochrane.

Coos County Library Service District, Extended Service Office, Tioga 104, 1988 Newmark, Coos Bay 97420. SAN 322-4279. Tel. 541-888-7260, fax 541-888-7285. *Extended Svcs. Dir.* Mary Jane Fisher.

Library Information Network of Clackamas County, 16239 S.E. McLoughlin Blvd., Suite 208, Oak Grove 97267. SAN 322-2845. Tel. 503-655-8550, fax 503-655-8555, e-mail joannar@lincc.lib.or.us. *Network Admin.* Joanna Rood; *Systems Libn.* Jeff Ring.

Northwest Association of Private Colleges & Universities (NAPCU), c/o Murdock Learning Resource Center, 416 N. Meridian St., Newberg 97132-2698. SAN 375-5312. Tel. 503-554-2411, fax 503-554-3599. *Pres.* Merrill Johnson; *Treas.* Nancy Hoover.

Orbis, 1299 Univ. Ore, Eugene 97403-1299. SAN 377-8096. Tel. 541-346-3049, fax 541-346-3485, e-mail libsys@oregon.uoregon.edu. *Chair* Victoria Hanawalt; *Head Lib. Systems* John F. Helmer.

Oregon Health Sciences Libraries Association (OHSLA), Sacred Heart Medical Center Professional Library Services, 1255 Hilyard St., Eugene 97401. SAN 371-2176. Tel. 541-686-6837, fax 541-686-7391. *Pres.* Beverly Schriver.

Portland Area Health Sciences Librarians, c/o Legacy Emanuel Library, 2801 N. Gantenbein, Portland 97227. SAN 371-0912. Tel.

503-413-2558, fax 503-413-2544, e-mail wittend@ohsu.edu. Cindy Muller.

Southern Oregon Library Federation, c/o Klamath County Library, 126 S. Third St., Klamath Falls 97601. SAN 322-2861. Tel. 541-882-8894, fax 541-882-6166. *Pres.* Andy Swanson.

Washington County Cooperative Library Services, 17880 S.W. Blanton St., Box 5129, Aloha 97006. SAN 322-287X. Tel. 503-642-1544, fax 503-591-0445. *Mgr.* Eva Calcagno.

## Pennsylvania

Associated College Libraries of Central Pennsylvania, c/o Lehman Memorial Library, Shippensburg University, Shippensburg 17257-2299. SAN 322-2888. Tel. 717-532-1473, fax 717-532-1389, e-mail bhl@ship.edu. *Pres.* Berkley Laite; *Treas.* Scott Anderson.

Association of Vision Science Librarians (AVSL), Medical Library, Wills Eye Hospital, 900 Walnut St., Philadelphia 19107. SAN 370-0569. Tel. 215-928-3288, fax 215-928-7247, e-mail freeman@indiana.edu. *Chair* Judith Schaeffer Young.

Basic Health Sciences Library Network, Latrobe Area Hospital Health Sciences Library, 121 W. Second Ave., Latrobe 15650-1096. SAN 371-4888. Tel. 724-537-1275, fax 724-537-1890. *Chair* Marilyn Daniels.

Berks County Library Association (BCLA), Sixth & Spruce, Reading 19612-6052. SAN 371-0866. Tel. 610-378-6418, fax 610-320-9775. *Treas.* Margaret Hsieh.

Berks County Public Libraries (BCPLS), Agricultural Center, Box 520, Leesport 19533. SAN 371-8972. Tel. 610-378-5260, fax 610-378-1525, e-mail bcpl@epix.net. *Admin.* Julie Rinehart; *Extended Svcs. Libn.* Susan Harvard.

Central Pennsylvania Consortium, c/o Franklin & Marshall College, Box 3003, Lancaster 17604-3003. SAN 322-2896. Tel. 717-291-3919, fax 717-399-4455, e-mail cpc_dfg@fandm.edu. *Exec. Asst.* Molly Seidel.

Central Pennsylvania Health Science Library Association (CPHSLA), Harrisburg Central Hospital, Pouch A, Harrisburg 17051.

SAN 375-5290. Tel. 717-271-8198, fax 717-772-7653, e-mail srobishaw@smpp. geisinger.edu. *Pres.* Martha Ruff.

Consortium for Health Information & Library Services, One Medical Center Blvd., Upland 19013-3995. SAN 322-290X. Tel. 610-447-6163, fax 610-447-6164, e-mail ch1@hslc.org. *Exec. Dir.* Barbara R. Devlin.

Cooperating Hospital Libraries of the Lehigh Valley Area, Muhlenberg Hospital Center, 2545 Schoenersville Rd., Bethlehem 18017-7384. SAN 371-0858. Tel. 610-861-2237, fax 610-861-0711. *Libn.* Nancy Romich.

Delaware Valley Information Consortium, c/o The Devereux Foundation Behavioral Healthcare Library, Box 638, Villanova 19085. SAN 329-3912. Tel. 610-542-3051, fax 610-542-3092, e-mail nlong@ wista.wistar.upenn.edu. *Coord.* Rachel Roth.

Eastern Mennonite Associated Libraries & Archives (EMALA), 2215 Millstream Rd., Lancaster 17602. SAN 372-8226. Tel. 717-393-9745, fax 717-393-8751. *Chair* Joel D. Alderfer; *Secy.* Lloyd Zeager.

Erie Area Health Information Library Cooperative (EAHILC), Northwest Medical Center Medical Library, One Spruce St., Franklin 16323. SAN 371-0564. Tel. 814-437-7000, fax 814-437-5023, e-mail scott@hslc.org. *Chair* Ann L. Lucas.

Greater Philadelphia Law Library Association (GPLLA), Box 335, Philadelphia 19105. SAN 373-1375. Tel. 215-898-9013, fax 215-898-6619, e-mail gplla-l@hslc.org. *Pres.* Merle J. Slyhoff.

Health Information Library Network of Northeastern Pennsylvania, c/o Wyoming Valley Health Care System, Inc, Library Services, Wilkes-Barre 18764. SAN 322-2934. Tel. 717-552-1175, fax 717-552-1183. *Chair* Rosemarie Taylor.

Health Sciences Libraries Consortium, 3600 Market St., Suite 550, Philadelphia 19104-2646. SAN 323-9780. Tel. 215-222-1532, fax 215-222-0416, e-mail info@hslc.org. *Exec. Dir.* Joseph C. Scorza; *Assoc. Dir.* Alan C. Simon.

Interlibrary Delivery Service of Pennsylvania, 471 Park Lane, State College 16803-3208. SAN 322-2942. Tel. 814-238-0254, fax 814-238-9686, e-mail janph2@aol. com. *Admin. Dir.* Janet C. Phillips.

Laurel Highlands Health Sciences Library Consortium, Owen Library, Rm. 209, University of Pittsburgh, Johnstown 15904. SAN 322-2950. Tel. 814-269-7280, fax 814-266-8230. *Dir.* Heather W. Brice.

Lehigh Valley Association of Independent Colleges, Inc., 119 W. Greenwich St., Bethlehem 18018-2307. SAN 322-2969. Tel. 610-882-5275, fax 610-882-5515. *Exec. Dir.* Galen C. Godbey.

Mid-Atlantic Law Library Cooperative (MALLCO), c/o Allegheny County Law Library, 921 City/County Bldg., Pittsburgh 15219. SAN 371-0645. Tel. 412-350-5353, fax 412-350-5889. *Dir.* Joel Fishman.

NIEU Consortium, 1200 Line St., Archbald 18403. SAN 372-817X. Tel. 717-876-9268, fax 717-876-8663. *IMS Dir.* Robert Carpenter; *Program Coord.* Rose Bennett.

Northeastern Pennsylvania Bibliographic Center, c/o Marywood University Library, Scranton 18509-1598. SAN 322-2993. Tel. 717-348-6260, fax 717-961-4769, e-mail chs@ac.marywood.edu. *Dir.* Catherine H. Schappert.

Northwest Interlibrary Cooperative of Pennsylvania (NICOP), Erie County Public Library, 160 E. Front St., Erie 16507-1554. SAN 370-5862. Tel. 814-451-6920, fax 814-451-6907, e-mail tonyk@gator. ecls.lib.pa.us. *Chair* Tony Keck.

PALINET & Union Library Catalogue of Pennsylvania, 3401 Market St., Suite 262, Philadelphia 19104. SAN 322-3000. Tel. 215-382-7031, fax 215-382-0022, e-mail palinet@palinet.org. *Exec. Dir.* James E. Rush; *Dir. Operations.* Carolyn Dearnaley.

Pennsylvania Citizens for Better Libraries (PCBL), 806 West St., Homestead 15120. SAN 372-8285. Tel. 412-461-1322, fax 412-461-1250. *Chief Exec. Officer* Sharon A. Alberts.

Pennsylvania Community College Library Consortium, c/o Community College of Philadelphia, 1700 Spring Garden St., Philadelphia 19130. SAN 329-3939. Tel. 215-751-8384, fax 215-751-8762, e-mail jjohnson@ccp.cc.pa.us. *Exec. Dir. Lib.-Learning Resources* Joan E. Johnson.

Pennsylvania Library Association, 1919 N. Front St., Harrisburg 17102. SAN 372-8145. Tel. 717-233-3113, fax 717-233-3121. *Exec. Dir.* Glenn R. Miller; *Pres.* Barbara P. Casini.

Philadelphia Area Consortium of Special Collections Libraries (PACSCL), Dept. of Special Collections, Univ. of Pennsylvania Library, 3420 Walnut, Philadelphia 19104-6206. SAN 370-7504. Tel. 215-898-7552, fax 215-573-9079. *Pres.* Eric Pumory.

Pittsburgh Council on Higher Education (PCHE), Box 954, Pittsburgh 15230-0954. SAN 322-3019. Tel. 412-536-1206, fax 412-536-1199, e-mail hunterb@pitt.edu. *Exec. Dir.* Janet Sherer.

Southeastern Pennsylvania Theological Library Association (SEPTLA), c/o Saint Charles Borromeo Seminary, Ryan Memorial Lib., 100 E. Wynnewood Rd., Wynnewood 19096-3012. SAN 371-0793. Tel. 610-667-3394, fax 610-664-7913, e-mail ebasemlib@ebts.edu or stcthelib@hslc.org. *Pres.* Darren Poley.

State System of Higher Education Libraries Council (SSHELCO), c/o F H Green Library, West Chester Univ. of Pennsylvania, West Chester 19383. SAN 322-2918. Tel. 610-436-2643, fax 610-436-2251. *Chair* Frank Q. Helms.

Susquehanna Library Cooperative, Susquehanna Health System, Learning Resources Center, 777 Rural Ave., Williamsport 17701. SAN 322-3051. Tel. 570-321-2266, fax 570-321-2271, e-mail srobishaw@smpp.geisinger.edu. *Pres.* Michael Heyd; *Treas.* Brian Bunnett.

Tri-County Library Consortium, c/o New Castle Public Lib., 207 E. North St., New Castle 16101. SAN 322-306X. Tel. 724-658-6659, fax 724-658-9012. *Dir.* Susan E. Walls.

Tri-State College Library Cooperative (TCLC), c/o Rosemont College Library, 1400 Montgomery Ave., Rosemont 19010-1699. SAN 322-3078. Tel. 610-525-0796, fax 610-525-1939, e-mail tclc@hslc.org. *Coord.* Ellen Gasiewski.

## Rhode Island

Association of Rhode Island Health Sciences Libraries (ARIHSL), c/o Providence College, River Ave. at Eaton St., Providence 02918. SAN 371-0742. Tel. 401-865-2631, fax 401-865-2823, e-mail jschustr@providence.edu. *Pres.* Janice Schuster.

Consortium of Rhode Island Academic & Research Libraries (CRIARL), Box 40041, Providence 02940-0041. SAN 322-3086. Tel. 401-232-6298, fax 401-232-6126, e-mail mmoroney@bryant.edu. *Pres.* Mary Moroney.

Cooperating Libraries Automated Network (CLAN), c/o Providence Public Library, 225 Washington St., Providence 02903. SAN 329-4560. Tel. 401-455-8044, 455-8085, 732-7687 (Exec. Dir.), fax 401-455-8080, e-mail peterbt@ids.net. *Chair* Tom Channahan; *V. Chair.* Mary Ellen Hardiman.

Rhode Island Library Network (RHILINET), c/o Office of Library & Info. Services, One Capitol Hill, 4th fl., Providence 02908-5870. SAN 371-6821. Tel. 401-222-2726, fax 401-222-4195. *Chief Info. Officer* Barbara Weaver; *Lib. Program Mgr. & Deputy Dir.* Dorothy Frechette.

## South Carolina

Catawba-Wateree Area Health Education Consortium, 1228 Colonial Commons, Box 2049, Lancaster 29721. SAN 329-3971. Tel. 803-286-4121, fax 803-286-4165. *Libn.* Tonia Harris.

Charleston Academic Libraries Consortium, College of Charleston, Robert Scott Small Lib., Charleston 29424. SAN 371-0769. Tel. 843-953-5530, fax 843-953-8019. *Chair* David Cohen.

Columbia Area Medical Librarians' Association (CAMLA), Professional Library, 1800 Colonial Dr., Box 202, Columbia 29202. SAN 372-9400. Tel. 803-898-1735, fax 803-898-1712. *Coord.* Neeta N. Shah.

South Carolina AHEC, c/o Medical Univ. of South Carolina, 171 Ashley Ave., Charleston 29425. SAN 329-3998. Tel. 843-792-4431, fax 843-792-4430. *Exec. Dir.* Sabra C. Slaughter; *Allied Health-Pharmacy Program Dir.* Beth Kennedy.

South Carolina State Library, South Carolina Library Network, 1500 Senate St., Box 11469, Columbia 29211-1469. SAN 322-4198. Tel. 803-734-8666, fax 803-734-8676, e-mail lea@leo.scsl.state.sc.us. *State*

*Libn.* James B. Johnson, Jr.; *Dir. Network Svcs.* Lea Walsh.

Upper Savannah AHEC Medical Library, Self Memorial Hospital, 1325 Spring St., Greenwood 29646. SAN 329-4110. Tel. 864-227-4851, fax 864-227-4838, e-mail libform@ais.ais-gurd.com. *Libn.* Thomas Hill; *Head Board Dir.* Stoney Abercrombie.

## South Dakota

South Dakota Library Network (SDLN), University Sta., Box 9672, Spearfish 57799-9672. SAN 371-2117. Tel. 605-642-6835, fax 605-642-6298. *Operations Dir.* Gary Johnson.

## Tennessee

Association of Memphis Area Health Science Libraries (AMAHSL), c/o Univ. of Tennessee Health Scis Lib., 877 Madison Ave., Memphis 38163. SAN 323-9802. Tel. 901-726-8862, fax 901-726-8807, e-mail gjackson@utmem1.utmem.edu. *Pres.* Gwen Jackson.

Consortium of Southern Biomedical Libraries (CONBLS), Meharry Medical College, 1005 Dr. D B Todd Blvd., Nashville 37208. SAN 370-7717. Tel. 615-327-6728, fax 615-321-2932. *Treas.* Cheryl Hamberg.

Knoxville Area Health Sciences Library Consortium (KAHSLC), c/o Hodges Lib., Univ. of Tenn, 1015 Volunteer Blvd., Knoxville 37996-1000. SAN 371-0556. Tel. 423-974-4700, fax 423-974-9424, e-mail njcook@usit.net. *Pres.* Lana Dixon.

Mid-Tennessee Health Science Librarians Association, VA Medical Center, Murfreesboro 37129. SAN 329-5028. Tel. 615-867-6142, fax 615-867-5778, e-mail alovvorn@stthomas.org. *Pres.* Pamela Howell.

Tennessee Health Science Library Association (THeSLA), Holston Valley Medical Center Health Sciences Library, Box 238, Kingsport 37662. SAN 371-0726. Tel. 423-224-6870, fax 423-224-6014, e-mail forbeseh@ctrvax.vanderbilt.edu. *Pres.* Patsy Ellis.

Tri-cities Area Health Sciences Libraries Consortium, East Tenn State Univ., James H Quillen College of Medicine, Medical Library, Box 70693, Johnson City 37614-0693. SAN 329-4099. Tel. 423-439-6252, fax 423-439-7025, e-mail fisherj@medserv. etsu-tn.edu. *Pres.* Annis Evans.

West Tennessee Academic Library Consortium, Univ. of Tenn—Paul Mead Library, Lane Ave., Martin 38301. SAN 322-3175. Tel. 901-587-7070, fax 901-423-4931. *Chair* Joel Stowers.

## Texas

Abilene Library Consortium, 241 Pine St., Suite 15C, Abilene 79699-9208. SAN 322-4694. Tel. 915-672-7081, fax 915-672-7084, e-mail robert.gillette@alc.org. *Systems Mgr.* Robert Gillette.

Alliance for Higher Education Alliance, Suite 250, LB 107, 17103 Preston Rd., Dallas 75248-1332. SAN 322-3337. Tel. 972-713-8170, fax 972-713-8209. *Pres.* Allan Watson.

AMIGOS Bibliographic Council, Inc., 12200 Park Central Dr., Suite 500, Dallas 75251. SAN 322-3191. Tel. 972-851-8000, fax 972-991-6061, e-mail amigos@amigos. org. *Exec. Dir.* Bonnie Juergens; *Dir. Business Svc.* Barry Breen.

APLIC International Census Network, c/o Population Research Center (PRC), 1800 Main Bldg., Univ. Texas, Austin 78712. SAN 370-0690. Tel. 512-471-8335, fax 512-471-4886. *Dir.* Gera Draaijer; *Libn.* Diane Fisher.

Council of Research & Academic Libraries (CORAL), Box 290236, San Antonio 78280-1636. SAN 322-3213. Tel. 210-536-2651, fax 210-536-2902, e-mail goff@ alhr.brooks.af.mil. *Pres.* Marilyn Goff.

Del Norte Biosciences Library Consortium, c/o Reference Dept. Library, Univ. of Texas at El Paso, 500 W. Univ., El Paso 79968. SAN 322-3302. Tel. 915-747-6714, fax 915-747-5327, e-mail emoreno @utep.edu. *Pres.* Esperanza A. Moreno.

Forest Trail Library Consortium, Inc. (FTLC), 222 W. Cotton St., Longview 75601. SAN 374-6283. Tel. 903-237-1340, fax 903-237-1327. *Pres.* Jerry McCulley; *V.P.-Pres. Elect* David King.

Harrington Library Consortium, Box 447, Amarillo 79178. SAN 329-546X. Tel.

806-371-5135, fax 806-345-5678, e-mail roseann@hlc.actx.edu. *Exec. Dir.* Roseann Perez.

Health Library Information Network, John Peter Smith Hospital Library, 1500 S. Main St., Fort Worth 76104. SAN 322-3299. Tel. 817-921-3431 ext. 5088, fax 817-923-0718. *Chair* Leslie Herman.

Health Oriented Libraries of San Antonio (HOLSA), 59 MDW/MSIL, 2200 Bergquist Dr., Suite 1, Lakeland AFB 78236-5300. SAN 373-5907. Tel. 210-292-7204, fax 210-292-7030. *Pres.* Rita Smith.

Houston Area Research Library Consortium (HARLiC), c/o Houston Public Library, 500 McKinney St., Houston 77002. SAN 322-3329. Tel. 713-247-2700, fax 713-247-1266, e-mail dudley-yates@tamu.edu. *Board of Dirs.* Barbara Gubbins.

National Network of Libraries of Medicine—South Central Region, c/o HAM-TMC Library, 1133 M D Anderson Blvd., Houston 77030-2809. SAN 322-3353. Tel. 713-799-7880, fax 713-790-7030, e-mail ruicham@library.tmc.edu. *Dir.* Naomi Broering; *Network Coord.* Ruicha Mishra.

Northeast Texas Library System (NETLS), 625 Austin, Garland 75040-6365. SAN 370-5943. Tel. 972-205-2566, fax 972-205-2767, e-mail dgf@onramp.net. *Dir.* Claire Bausch; *Coord.* Dale Fleeger.

Piasano Consortium, Victoria College, Univ. of Houston, Victoria Library, 2602 N. Ben Jordan, Victoria 77901-5699. SAN 329-4943. Tel. 512-573-3291, 576-3151, fax 512-788-6227, e-mail dahlstromj@jadc. vic.uh.edu. *Coord.* Joe F. Dahlstrom.

South Central Academic Medical Libraries Consortium (SCAMeL), c/o Lewis Lib./ UNTHSC, 3500 Camp Bowie Blvd., Fort Worth 76107. SAN 372-8269. Tel. 817-735-2380, fax 817-735-5158. *Chair* Richard C. Wood.

Texas Council of State University Librarians, Univ. of Texas—Health Science Center at San Antonio, 7703 Floyd Curl Dr., San Antonio 78284-7940. SAN 322-337X. Tel. 210-567-2400, fax 210-567-2490, e-mail bowden@uthscsa.edu. *Contact* Virginia M. Bowden.

Texnet, Box 12927, Austin 78711. SAN 322-3396. Tel. 512-463-5406, fax 512-463-8800. *Mgr.* Rebecca Linton.

## Utah

Forest Service Library Network, formerly FS-INFO, Rocky Mountain Research Sta., 324 25th St., Ogden 84401. SAN 322-032X. Tel. 801-625-5445, fax 801-625-5129, e-mail library/rmrs_ogden@fs.fed. us. *Coord.* Carol A. Ayer.

Utah Academic Library Consortium (UALC), Marriott Library, University of Utah, Salt Lake City 84112-0860. SAN 322-3418. Tel. 801-581-8558, fax 801-585-3464. *Chair* Sarah Michalak.

Utah Health Sciences Library Consortium, c/o Eccles Health Science Library, University of Utah, Salt Lake City 84112. SAN 376-2246. Tel. 801-581-8771, fax 801-581-3632. *Chair* Kathleen McCloskey.

## Vermont

Health Science Libraries of New Hampshire & Vermont (HSL-NH-VT), c/o Archivist, Dana Medical Lib., University of Vermont, Burlington 05401. SAN 371-6864. Tel. 802-656-8765. *Pres.* Rebecca Mueller.

North Atlantic Health Sciences Libraries, Inc. (NAHSL), Univ. of Vermont, Charles A Dana Medical Library, Gwen Bldg., Burlington 05405. SAN 371-0599. Tel. 802-656-4396, fax 802-656-0762, e-mail bob.sekerak@vtmednet.org. *Chair* Bob Sekerak.

Vermont Resource Sharing Network, c/o Vermont Dept of Libraries, 109 State St., Montpelier 05609-0601. SAN 322-3426. Tel. 802-828-3261, fax 802-828-2199, e-mail mzunder@dol.state.vt.us. *Dir., Lib. & Info. Svcs.* Marjorie Zunder.

## Virgin Islands

VILINET (Virgin Islands Library & Information Network), c/o Division of Libraries, Museums & Archives, 23 Dronningens Gade, Saint Thomas 00802. SAN 322-3639. Tel. 340-774-3407, fax 340-775-1887.

## Virginia

American Indian Higher Education Consortium (AIHEC), c/o AIHEC, 121 Oronoco St., Alexandria 22314. SAN 329-4056. Tel. 703-838-0400, fax 703-838-0388, e-mail aihec@aol.com. *Pres.* Janine Pease.

Defense Technical Information Center, 8725 John J Kingman Rd., Suite 0944, Fort Belvoir 22060-6218. SAN 322-3442. Tel. 703-767-9100, fax 703-767-9183. *Admin.* Kurt N. Molholm.

Interlibrary Users Association (IUA), c/o Litton PRC, 1500 PRC Dr., McLean 22102. SAN 322-1628. Tel. 703-556-1166, fax 703-556-1174, e-mail kopp_barbara@prc.com. *Pres.* Barbara Kopp; *V.P.* Nancy Minter.

Lynchburg Area Library Cooperative, Bedford Public Library, 321 N. Bridge St., Bedford 24523. SAN 322-3450. Tel. 540-586-8911, fax 540-586-7280, e-mail dunn@lynchburg.edu. *Chair* Steve Preston; *Vice-Chair* Claire Meissener.

Lynchburg Information Online Network, c/o Knight-Capron Library, Lynchburg College, Lynchburg 24501. SAN 374-6097. Tel. 804-381-6311, fax 804-381-6310. *Project Dir.* John G. Jaffe; *System Admin.* Marjorie Freeman.

NASA Libraries' Information System— NASA Galaxie, NASA Langley Research Center, MS 185—Technical Library, Hampton 23681-0001. SAN 322-0788. Tel. 757-864-2392, fax 757-864-2375, e-mail rridgeway@sti.nasa.gov. *Project Mgr.* Nancy Kaplan.

Richmond Academic Library Consortium (RALC), J Tyler Community College, 13101 Jefferson Davis Hwy., Chester 23831. SAN 371-3938. Tel. 804-796-4066, fax 804-796-4238, e-mail estephens@vsu.edu. *Pres.* Gary Graham.

Richmond Area Film-Video Cooperative, Richard Bland College Library, 11301 Johnson Rd., Petersburg 23805. SAN 322-3469. Tel. 804-862-6226, fax 804-862-6125, e-mail nchenaul@vcu.edu. *Chair* Virginia Cherry.

Southside Virginia Library Network (SVLN), Longwood College, 201 High St., Farmville 23909-1897. SAN 372-8242. Tel. 804-395-2633, fax 804-395-2453. *Dir.* Calvin J. Boyer; *Head Tech. Svcs.* Rebecca R. Laine.

Southwestern Virginia Health Information Librarians (SWVAHILI), Danville Regional Medical Center, 142 S. Main St., Danville 24541. SAN 323-9527. Tel. 804-799-4418, fax 804-799-2255. *Chair* Ann Duesing; *Secy. & Treas.* Claire Meisner.

United States Army Training & Doctrine Command (TRADOC), ATBO-FL, Bldg. 5A, Rm. 102, Fort Monroe 23651-5000. SAN 322-418X. Tel. 757-727-4096, fax 757-728-5300. *Dir.* Janet Scheitle; *Systems Analysts* James Bradley, Alexandra Campbell.

Virginia Independent College & University Library Assoc., c/o Mary Helen Cochran Library, Sweet Briar College, Sweet Briar 24595. SAN 374-6089. Tel. 804-381-6139, fax 804-381-6173. *Chair* John Jankey.

Virginia Library & Information Network (VLIN), c/o The Library of Virginia, 800 E. Broad St., Richmond 23219-8000. SAN 373-0921. Tel. 804-692-3774, fax 804-692-3771. *State Libn.* Nolan T. Yelich.

Virginia Tidewater Consortium for Higher Education, 5215 Hampton Blvd., William Spong Hall, Rm. 129, Norfolk 23529-0293. SAN 329-5486. Tel. 757-683-3183, fax 757-683-4515, e-mail lgdotolo@aol.com. *Pres.* Lawrence G. Dotolo.

## Washington

Consortium for Automated Library Services (CALS), The Evergreen State College Library L2300, Olympia 98505. SAN 329-4528. Tel. 360-866-6000 ext. 6260, fax 360-866-6790, e-mail metcalfs@elwha.evergreen.edu. *Systems Mgr.* Steven A. Metcalf.

Council on Botanical Horticultural Libraries, 2525 S. 336th St., Box 3798, Federal Way 98063-3798. SAN 371-0521. Tel. 253-927-6960, fax 253-838-4686. *Contact* Mrs. George Harrison.

Inland Northwest Health Sciences Libraries (INWHSL), Box 10283, Spokane 99209-0283. SAN 370-5099. Tel. 509-324-7344, fax 509-324-7349, e-mail rpringle@wsu. edu. *Chair* Kathy Schwanz.

Inland Northwest Library Automation Network (INLAN), Foley Center, Gonzaga University, Spokane 99258. SAN 375-0124. Tel. 509-328-4220 ext. 6110, fax 509-323-5855. *Contact* Robert Burr.

National Network of Libraries Of Medicine—Pacific Northwest Region (NN-LM PNR), University of Washington, Box 357155, Seattle 98195-7155. SAN 322-3485. Tel. 206-543-8262, fax 206-543-2469, e-mail nnlm@u.washington.edu. *Dir.* Sherrilynne S. Fuller.

WLN, Box 3888, Lacey 98509-3888. SAN 322-3507. Tel. 360-923-4000, fax 360-923-4009, e-mail info@wln.com. *Pres. & Chief Exec. Officer* Paul McCarthy; *Dir. Lib. Svcs.* Sharon West.

## West Virginia

Consortium of South Eastern Law Libraries (COSELL), Hugh F MacMillan Law Lib., Emory Univ. School of Law, 1301 Clifton Rd., Atlanta 30322. SAN 372-8277. Tel. 404-627-6720, fax 404-727-5361. *Chair* Rosalie Sanderson.

East Central Colleges, Box AJ, Bethany 26032-1434. SAN 322-2667. Tel. 304-829-7812, fax 304-829-7546. *Exec. Dir.* Preston W. Forbes.

Huntington Health Science Library Consortium, Marshall University Health Science Libraries, 1600 Medical Center Dr., Suite 2400, Huntington 25701-3655. SAN 322-4295. Tel. 304-691-1753, fax 304-691-1766. *Chair* Edward Dzierzak.

Mountain States Consortium, c/o Alderson Broaddus College, Philippi 26416. SAN 329-4765. Tel. 304-457-1700, fax 304-457-6239. *Treas.* Stephen Markwood.

Southern West Virginia Library Automation Corporation, 221 N. Kanawha St., Box 1876, Beckley 25802. SAN 322-421X. Tel. 304-255-0511, fax 304-255-9161, e-mail gunsaulj@raleigh.lib.wv.us. *Pres.* Judy Gunsaulis; *Systems Mgr.* Margaret Thompson.

## Wisconsin

Council of Wisconsin Libraries, Inc. (COWL), 728 State St., Rm. 464, Madison 53706-1494. SAN 322-3523. Tel. 608-263-4962, fax 608-262-6067, e-mail schneid@doit. wisc.edu. *Dir.* Kathryn Schneider Michaelis.

Fox River Valley Area Library Consortium, Moraine Park Technical College, 235 N. National Ave., Fond Du Lac 54935. SAN 322-3531. Tel. 920-924-3112, fax 920-924-3117, e-mail cpettit@moraine.tecwi. us. *Coord.* Charlene Pettit.

Fox Valley Library Council (FVLC), c/o Owls, Fox Valley Library Council, 225 N. Oneida St., Appleton 54911. SAN 323-9640. Tel. 920-832-6190, fax 920-832-6422. *Pres.* Edie Phillips.

Library Council of Metropolitan Milwaukee, Inc., 814 W. Wisconsin Ave., Milwaukee 53233-2309. SAN 322-354X. Tel. 414-271-8470, fax 414-286-2794, e-mail ricec@vms.csd.mu.edu. *Exec. Dir.* Corliss Rice.

North East Wisconsin Intertype Libraries, Inc. (NEWIL), c/o Nicolet Federated Library System, 515 Pine St., Green Bay 54301. SAN 322-3574. Tel. 920-448-4412, fax 920-448-4420, e-mail tdhowe@ mail.wiscnet.net. *Coord.* Terrie Howe.

Northwestern Wisconsin Health Science Library Consortium, Wausau Hospital, 333 Pine Ridge Blvd., Wausau 54401. SAN 377-5801. Tel. 715-847-2184, fax 715-847-2183. *Coord.* Jan Kraus.

South Central Wisconsin Health Science Library Cooperative, c/o FAMHS Medical Library, 611 Sherman Ave. E., Fort Atkinson 53538. SAN 322-4686. Tel. 920-568-5194, fax 920-568-5059, e-mail carrie. garity@famhs.org. *Rep.* Carrie Garity.

Southeastern Wisconsin Health Science Library Consortium, Convenant Healthcare Systems Library, 5000 W. Chambers, Milwaukee 53210. SAN 322-3582. Tel. 414-447-2194, fax 414-447-2128. *Presiding Officer* Sunja Shaikh.

Southeastern Wisconsin Information Technology Exchange, Inc. (SWITCH), 6801 N. Yates Rd., Milwaukee 53217-3985. SAN 371-3962. Tel. 414-351-2423, fax 414-228-4146, e-mail jfri@switchinc.org. *Exec. Dir.* Jack Fritts; *Operations Mgr.* Bill Topritzhofer.

Wisconsin Area Research Center Network ARC Network, State Historical Society of Wisconsin, 816 State St., Madison 53706.

SAN 373-0875. Tel. 608-264-6480, fax 608-264-6486, e-mail archives.reference @ccmail.adp.wisc.edu. *State Archivist* Peter Gottlieb; *Reference* Harold Miller.
Wisconsin Interlibrary Services (WILS), 728 State St., Rm. 464, Madison 53706-1494. SAN 322-3612. Tel. 608-263-4962, fax 608-292-6067, e-mail schneid@doit.wisc. edu or cbradley@doit.wisc.edu. *Dir.* Kathryn Schneider Michaelis; *Asst. Dir.* Mary Williamson.
Wisconsin Valley Library Service (WVLS), 300 N. First St., Wausau 54403. SAN 371-3911. Tel. 715-261-7250, fax 715-261-7259, e-mail eldred@wisvalley.lib.wi.us. *Dir.* Heather Ann Eldred; *Admin. Asst.* Marla Sepnafski.

## Wyoming

Health Sciences Information Network, University of Wyoming Libraries (HSIN), Univ. of Wyoming, 104 Coe Library, Box 3334, Laramie 82071-3334. SAN 371-4861. Tel. 307-766-6537, fax 307-766-3062, e-mail henning@uwyo.edu. *Coord.* Mary M. Henning.
WYLD Network, c/o Wyoming State Library, Supreme Court & State Library Bldg., Cheyenne 82002-0060. SAN 371-0661. Tel. 307-777-7281, fax 307-777-6289. *State Libn.* Lesley Boughton; *WYLD Program Mgr.* Corky Walters.

## Canada

### Alberta

Alberta Association of College Librarians (AACL), Alberta Vocational College, 201 Main St. S.E., Slave Lake, Alberta P0G 2A3. SAN 370-0763. Tel. 403-849-8671, fax 403-849-2570, e-mail lloydp@admin. gmcc.ab.ca. *Chair* Geoff Owens.
Alberta Government Libraries Council (AGLC), c/o Alberta Legislature Library, 216 Legislature Bldg., 10800-97th Ave., Edmonton T5K 2B6. SAN 370-0372. Tel. 403-422-5085, fax 403-427-5688, e-mail sperry@assembly.ab.ca. *Chair* Christina Andrews; *Chair* Sandra Perry.
Northern Alberta Health Libraries Association (NAHLA), 11620 168 St. N.W., Ed-

monton T5M 4A6. SAN 370-5951. Tel. 403-453-0534, fax 403-482-4459, e-mail lmychaj@nurses.ab.ca. *Pres.* Lorraine Mychajlunon.

### British Columbia

British Columbia College & Institute Library Services, Langara College Library, 100 W. 49th Ave., Vancouver V5Y 2Z6. SAN 329-6970. Tel. 604-323-5237, fax 604-323-5544. *Contact* Atsuko Barbour.
Media Exchange Cooperative (MEC), Vancouver Community College, 250 W. Pender St., Vancouver V6B 1S9. SAN 329-6954. Tel. 604-443-8346, fax 604-443-8329, e-mail pbutler@vcc.bc.ca. *Chair* Phyllis Butler.

### Manitoba

Manitoba Government Libraries Council (MGLC), 360-1395 Ellice Ave., Winnipeg R3G 3P2. SAN 371-6848. Tel. 204-239-3162, fax 204-945-8427, e-mail mlavergne @em.gov.mb.ca. *Chair* Linda Petriuk.
Manitoba Library Consortium, Inc. (MLCI), Industrial Technology Centre, 1329 Niakwa Rd. E., Winnipeg R2J 3T4. SAN 372-820X. Tel. 204-945-1413, fax 204-945-1784. *Chair* Betty Dearth.

### New Brunswick

Maritimes Health Libraries Association (MHLA-ABSM), c/o IWK Grace Health Center, 5850-5980 University Ave., Halifax B3H 4N1. SAN 370-0836. Tel. 902-420-6729, fax 902-420-3122. *Pres.* Darlene Chapman.

### Nova Scotia

NOVANET, 6080 Young St., Suite 601, Halifax B3K 5L2. SAN 372-4050. Tel. 902-453-2451 ext. 2461, fax 902-453-2369, e-mail novanet@ac.dal.ca. *Mgr. Info. Systems* Scott W. Nickerson.

### Ontario

Bibliocentre, 80 Cowdray Ct., Scarborough M1S 4N1. SAN 322-3663. Tel. 416-289-5151, fax 416-299-4841, e-mail falt@ cencol.on.ca. *Dir.* Annetta Protain.

Canadian Agriculture Library System, Sir John Carling Bldg., 930 Carling Ave., Ottawa K1A 0C5. SAN 377-5054. Tel. 613-759-7068, fax 613-759-6627, e-mail cal-bca@em.agr.ca. *Dir.* Victor Desroches.

Canadian Association of Research Libraries-Association des Bibliothèques de Recherche du Canada (CARL-ABRC), University of Ottawa Morisset Hall, Rm. 239, 65 University St., Ottawa K1N 9A5. SAN 323-9721. Tel. 613-562-5800 ext. 3652, fax 613-562-5195, e-mail carl@uottawa.ca. *Exec. Dir.* Timothy Mark.

Canadian Health Libraries Association (CHLA-ABSC), Office of Secretariat, 3332 Yonge St., Box 94038, Toronto M4N 3R1. SAN 370-0720. Tel. 416-485-0377, fax 416-485-6877. *Pres.* Marthe Brideau.

Hamilton & District Health Library Network, c/o Saint Josephs Hospital, 50 Charlton Ave. E., Hamilton L8N 4A6. SAN 370-5846. Tel. 905-522-1155 ext. 3410, fax 905-521-6111, e-mail marge@fhs.mcmaster. ca. *Network Coord.* Jean Maragno.

Health Science Information Consortium of Toronto, c/o Gerstein Science Info. Center, Univ. of Toronto, 7 King's College Circle, Toronto M5S 1A5. SAN 370-5080. Tel. 416-978-6359, fax 416-971-2637, e-mail scottl@library.utoronto.ca. *Exec. Dir.* Laurie Scott.

Information Network for Ontario Ministry of Citizenship, Culture & Recreation: Cultural Partnerships Branch, 77 Bloor St. W., 3rd flr, Toronto M7A 2R9. SAN 329-5605. Tel. 416-314-7342, fax 416-314-7635. *Dir.* Michael Langford.

Kingston Area Health Libraries Association (KAHLA), c/o Belleville General Hospital Library, 265 Dundas St. E., Belleville K8N 1E2. SAN 370-0674. Tel. 613-969-7400 ext. 2540, fax 613-968-8234, e-mail cmartin@bgh.on.ca. *Pres.* Cheryl Martin.

Ontario Council of University Libraries (OCUL), Stauffer Library, Queen's University, 101 Union St., Kingston K7L 5C4. SAN 371-9413. Tel. 705-675-1151, fax 613-545-6362, e-mail jgarnett@library. laurentian.ca. *Chair* Paul Weins.

Ontario Health Libraries Association (OHLA), The Library, Sarnia General Hospital, 220 N. Mitton St., Sarnia N7T 6H6. SAN 370-0739. Tel. 519-464-4500 ext. 5251, fax 519-464-4511, e-mail jcampbell@ebtech. net. *Pres.* Jill Campbell.

QL Systems Limited, One Gore St., Box 2080, Kingston K7L 5J8. SAN 322-368X. Tel. 613-549-4611, fax 613-548-4260, e-mail hlawford@qlsys.ca. *Pres.* Hugh Lawford.

Shared Library Services (SLS), South Huron Hospital, Shared Library Services, 24 Huron St. W., Exeter N0M 1S2. SAN 323-9500. Tel. 519-235-2700 ext. 249, fax 519-235-3405, e-mail lwilcox@julian. uwo.ca. *Dir.* Linda Wilcox.

Sheridan Park Association, Library & Information Science Committee (SPA-LISC), 2275 Speakman Dr., Mississauga L5K 1B1. SAN 370-0437. Tel. 905-823-6160, fax 905-823-6160. *Contact* Cindy Smith.

Toronto Health Libraries Association (THLA), Box 94056, Toronto M4N 3R1. SAN 323-9853. Tel. 416-485-0377, fax 416-485-6877. *Pres.* Karen Smith.

Toronto Public Library Systems, formerly Disability Resource Library Network, c/o North York Central Library, 5120 Yonge St., North York M2N 5N9. SAN 323-9837. Tel. 416-395-5591, fax 416-395-5594. *Contact* Joanne Bar.

Toronto School of Theology, 47 Queen's Park Crescent E., Toronto M5S 2C3. SAN 322-452X. Tel. 416-978-4039, fax 416-978-7821, e-mail fox@library.utoronto.ca. *Chair Lib. Committee* Douglas Fox.

Wellington Waterloo Dufferin (WWD) Health Library Network, c/o Library, University of Guelph, Guelph N1G 2W1. SAN 370-0496. Tel. 519-824-4120 ext. 4214, fax 519-826-7941, e-mail dhull@uoguelph.ca. *Coord.* David Hull.

## Quebec

Association des Bibliothèques de la Sante Affiliées a L'Université De Montréal (ABSAUM), c/o Health Library, Box 6128, Sta. Downtown, University of Montreal, Montreal H3C 3J7. SAN 370-5838. Tel. 514-343-6826, fax 514-343-2350. *Secy.* Danielle Tardif.

Canadian Heritage Information Network (CHIN), 15 Eddy St., 4th flr, Hull K1A 0M5. SAN 329-3076. Tel. 819-994-1200, fax 819-994-9555, e-mail service@chin.qc.ca. *Dir. Gen.* Lyn Elliot Sherwood.

McGill Medical & Health Libraries Association (MMAHLA), c/o Royal Victoria Hospital, Women's Pavillion Library, 687 Pine Ave. W., Rm. F4-24, Montreal H3A 1A1. SAN 374-6100. Tel. 514-842-1231 ext. 4738, fax 514-843-1678. *Co-Chairs* Lynda Dickson, Irene Shanefield.

Montreal Health Libraries Association (MHLA), 2365 Côte de Liesse, Montreal H4N 2M7. SAN 323-9608. Tel. 514-333-2057, fax 514-331-6387. *Pres.* Donna Gibson; *V.P.* Sean DeNora.

**Saskatchewan**

Saskatchewan Government Libraries Council (SGLC), c/o Saskatchewan Agriculture & Food Library, 3085 Albert St., Regina S4S 0B1. SAN 323-956X. Tel. 306-787-5151, fax 306-787-0216. *Chair* Helene Stewart.

# National Library and Information-Industry Associations, United States and Canada

## American Association of Law Libraries

Executive Director, Roger Parent
53 W. Jackson Blvd., Suite 940, Chicago, IL 60604
312-939-4764, fax 312-431-1097
World Wide Web http://www.aallnet.org

## Object

The American Association of Law Libraries (AALL) is established for educational and scientific purposes. It shall be conducted as a nonprofit corporation to promote and enhance the value of law libraries to the public, the legal community, and the world; to foster the profession of law librarianship; to provide leadership in the field of legal information; and to foster a spirit of cooperation among the members of the profession. Established 1906.

## Membership

Memb. 5,000. Persons officially connected with a law library or with a law section of a state or general library, separately maintained. Associate membership available for others. Dues (Indiv., Indiv. Assoc., and Inst.) $133; (Inst. Assoc.) $256 times the number of members; (Retired) $32.50; (Student) $30; (SIS Memb.) $12 each per year. Year. July 1 –June 30.

## Officers

*Pres.* James S. Heller, College of William & Mary, Marshall-Whythe Law Lib., S. Henry St., Williamsburg, VA 23187-8795. Tel. 757-221-3252, fax 757-221-3051, e-mail jshell@facstaff.wm.edu; *V.P.* Margaret Maes Axtmann, Univ. of Minnesota Law Lib., 229 19th Ave. S., Minneapolis, MN 55455. Tel. 612-625-4301, fax 612-625-3478, e-mail maxtm@maroon.tc.umn.edu; *Past Pres.* Judith Meadows, State Law Lib. of Montana, Justice Bldg., 215 N. Sanders, Helena, MT

59620-3004. Tel. 406-444-3660, fax 406-444-3603, e-mail jmeadows@mt.gov; *Secy.* Susan P. Siebers, Katten Muchin and Zavis, 525 W. Monroe St., Suite 1600, Chicago, IL 60661-3693. Tel. 312-902-5675, fax 312-902-1626, e-mail ssiebers@kmz.com; *Treas.* Janis L. Johnston, Kresge Lib., Notre Dame Law School, Box 535, Notre Dame, IN 46556-0535. Tel. 219-631-5922, fax 219-631-6371, e-mail janis.l.johnson.1@nd.edu.

## Executive Board

Mark Folmsbee (2000), e-mail zzfolm@acc.wuacc.edu; Ruth A. Fraley, e-mail rfraley@worldnet.att.net; Nancy P. Johnson (1999), e-mail lawnpj@gsusgi2.gsu.edu; Frank Y. Liu, e-mail liu@mail.cc.duq.edu; Kathleen S. Martin (1999), e-mail mart7131@mlb.com; Heather B. Simmons (2000), e-mail Lnusgmb. qz31dc@gmeds.com.

## Committee Chairpersons

Annual Meeting Program Selection. Timothy L. Coggins.
Awards. Sandra Marz.
Bylaws. Janice Snyder Anderson.
Call for Papers. Denise Kay Russell.
Citation Format. Marcia J. Koslov.
Copyright. Anne Klinefelter.
Diversity. Susanna Marlowe.
Executive Board Finance and Budget. Janis L. Johnston.
Executive Board Governance. Susan P. Siebers.
Executive Board Strategic Planning. Nancy P. Johnson.
Government Relations. Darcy Kirk.
Grants. Carol Watson.

Index to Foreign Legal Periodicals (Advisory). Timothy G. Kearley.
Indexing Periodical Literature (Advisory). Sandra Lee Braber-Grove.
Information Technology and Implementation (Ad Hoc Working Group). Timothy L. Coggins.
Law Library Journal and AALL Spectrum (Advisory). Ruth Levor.
Local Arrangements (Advisory). Aleta Benjamin.
Mentoring and Retention. Gayle Lynn-Nelson.
Nominations. Gail Warren.
Placement. Nancy L. Strohmeyer.
Preservation. Gail Warren.
Professional Development. Mary A. Hotchkiss.
Public Relations. Carol Bredemeyer.
Publications Policy. Barbara Bintiff.
Recruitment. Ann T. Fessenden.
Relations with Information Vendors. Frank G. Houdek.
Research. Richard A. Leiter.
Scholarships. John D. Edwards.

## Special-Interest Section Chairpersons

Academic Law Libraries. Ed Edmonds.
Computing Services. Ken Hirsh.
Foreign, Comparative, and International Law. Maria Smolka-Day.
Government Documents. Charlene Cain.
Legal History and Rare Books. Laura Bedard.
Legal Information Services to the Public. Patricia Court McKenzie.
Micrographics and Audiovisual. John Pedini.
Online Bibliographic Services. Jack Bissett.
Private Law Libraries. Glen Gustafson.
Research Instruction and Patron Services. Celeste Feather.
SIS Council. Gail Warren.
Social Responsibility. Karen Westwood.
State Court and County Law Libraries. Jean Holcomb.
Technical Services. Joseph Thomas.

# American Library Association

Executive Director, William R. Gordon
50 E. Huron St., Chicago, IL 60611
800-545-2433, 312-280-3215, fax 312-944-3897
World Wide Web http://www.ala.org

## Object

The mission of the American Library Association (ALA) is to provide leadership for the development, promotion, and improvement of library and information services and the profession of librarianship in order to enhance learning and ensure access to information for all. Founded 1876.

## Membership

Memb. (Indiv.) 54,008; (Inst.) 3,190; (Total) 57,198. Any person, library, or other organization interested in library service and librarians. Dues (Indiv.) 1st year, $50; 2nd year, $75, 3rd year and later, $100; (Trustee and Assoc. Memb.) $45; (Student) $25; (Foreign Indiv.)

$60; (Other) $35; (Inst.) $70 and up, depending on operating expenses of institution.

## Officers (1998–1999)

*Pres.* Ann K. Symons, Libn., Juneau-Douglas H.S., 10014 Crazy Horse Dr., Juneau, AK 99801. Tel. 907-463-1947, fax 907-463-1932, e-mail symons@alaska.net; *Pres.-Elect* Sarah Ann Long, North Suburban Lib. System, 200 W. Dundee Rd., Wheeling, IL 60090-2799. Tel 847-459-1300, ext. 125, fax 847-459-0391, e-mail slong@nslsilus.org; *Immediate Past Pres.* Barbara J. Ford, Chicago Public Lib., Harold Washington Lib. Center, 400 S. State St., Chicago, IL 60605. Tel. 312-747-4070, fax 312-747-4077, e-mail bford@chipublib.org; *Treas.* Bruce E. Daniels, 4418

Eagle Village Rd., Manlius, NY 13104. Tel. 315-682-2645, fax 315-682-3583, e-mail bd3ALA@aol.com; *Exec. Dir.* William R. Gordon, ALA Headquarters, 50 E. Huron St., Chicago, IL 60611. Tel. 312-280-3215, fax 312-944-3897, e-mail wgordon@ala.org.

## Executive Board

Liz Bishoff (2002); Charles M. Brown (1999); Julie Cummins (2002); Martin J. Gomez (2001); James G. Neal (2000); Robert R. Newlen (2000); Sally G. Reed (2001); Patricia H. Smith (1999).

## Endowment Trustees

Bernard A. Margolis (1998); Patricia Glass Schuman, Rick J. Schwieterman; *Exec. Board Liaison* Bruce E. Daniels; *Staff Liaison* Gregory L. Calloway.

## Divisions

See the separate entries that follow: American Assn. of School Libns.; American Lib. Trustee Assn.; Assn. for Lib. Collections and Technical Services; Assn. for Lib. Service to Children; Assn. of College and Research Libs.; Assn. of Specialized and Cooperative Lib. Agencies; Lib. Admin. and Management Assn.; Lib. and Info. Technology Assn.; Public Lib. Assn.; Reference and User Services Assn.; Young Adult Lib. Services Assn.

## Publications

*ALA Handbook of Organization* (ann.).
*American Libraries* (11 per year; membs.; organizations $60; foreign $70; single copy $6).
*Book Links* (6 per year; U.S. $24.95; foreign $29.95; single copy $5).
*Booklist* (22 per year; U.S. and possessions $69.50; foreign $85; single copy $4.50).
*Choice* (11 per year; U.S. $185; foreign $210; single copy $24).

## Round Table Chairpersons

(ALA staff liaison is given in parentheses.)
Armed Forces Libraries. Katherine Gillen (Patricia May).
Continuing Library Education Network and Exchange. Judy Card (Lorelle R. Swader).
Ethnic Materials and Information Exchange. Tamiye T. Meehan (Satia Orange).
Exhibits. Jon Malinowski (Diedre Ross).
Federal Librarians. Andrea Gruhl (Patricia May).
Government Documents. Kathy E. Tezla (Patricia May).
Intellectual Freedom. Carlyn A. Caywood (Don Wood).
International Relations. Lucinda Covert-Vail (Michael Dowling).
Library History. David M. Hovde (Mary Jo Lynch).
Library Instruction. Catherine Gale Burrow (Mary Jo Lynch).
Library Research. Helen R. Tibbo (Mary Jo Lynch).
Map and Geography. David Y. Allen (Danielle M. Alderson).
New Members. Linda M. Golian (Gerald G. Hodges).
Social Responsibilities. Wendy M. Thomas (Satia Orange).
Staff Organizations. Leon S. Bey (Lorelle R. Swader).
Support Staff Interests. Paulette A. Feld (Lorelle R. Swader).
Video. Rebecca S. Albitz (Irene Wood).

## Committee Chairpersons

Accreditation (Standing). James C. Baughman (Ann L. O'Neill).
American Libraries Advisory (Standing). Camila A. Alire (Leonard Kniffel).
Appointments (Standing). Sarah Ann Long (Elizabeth Dreazen).
Awards (Standing). Judith R. Farley (Cheryl Malden).
Budget Analysis and Review (Standing). Mary Elizabeth Wendt (Gregory Calloway).

Chapter Relations (Standing). Juliana G. Huiskamp (Gerald G. Hodges).

Committee on Committees (Elected Council Committee). Sarah Ann Long (Elizabeth Dreazen).

Conference Committee (Standing). Mary Ann Rupert (Mary W. Ghikas, Diedre Ross).

Constitution and Bylaws (Standing). Nancy A. Davenport (Linda Mays).

Council Orientation (Standing). Elizabeth E. Bingham (Lois Ann Gregory-Wood).

Council Formats (Task Force on). Juliana G. Huiskamp (Lois Ann Gregory-Wood).

Education (Standing). Connie J. Van Fleet (Lorelle R. Swader).

Election (Standing). Judith M. Baker (Ernest Martin).

Information Technology Policy Advisory. Nancy M. Bolt (Frederick Weingarten).

Intellectual Freedom (Standing). Steven L. Herb (Judith F. Krug).

International Relations (Standing). Patricia Glass Schuman (Michael Dowling).

Legislation (Standing). Nancy C. Kranich (Carol C. Henderson).

Library Personnel Resources (Standing). Julie B. Todaro (Lorelle R. Swader).

Literacy and Outreach (Standing). Carla J. Stoffle (Satia Orange).

Membership (Standing). Marianne Hartzell (Gerald G. Hodges).

Minority Concerns and Cultural Diversity (Standing). Joseph R. Diaz (Satia Orange).

Nominating, 1999 Election (Special). Mary E. (Molly) Raphael (Elizabeth Dreazen).

Organization (Standing). Thomas Kirk (Lois Ann Gregory-Wood).

Pay Equity (Standing). Tami Echavarria (Lorelle R. Swader).

Policy Monitoring (Standing). Donald J. Sager (Lois Ann Gregory-Wood).

Professional Ethics (Standing). Charles Harmon (Judith F. Krug).

Public Awareness Advisory (Standing). Wayne Coco (Linda K. Wallace).

Publishing (Standing). James R. Rettig (Donald Chatham).

Research and Statistics (Standing). Peggy D. Rudd (Mary Jo Lynch).

Resolutions. Kenton L. Oliver (Kathryn Osen).

Spectrum Initiative Advisory. Carla Hayden (Sandra Balderrama).

Standards (Standing) Sarah M. Pritchard (Mary Jo Lynch).

Status of Women in Librarianship (Standing). Theresa A. Tobin (Lorelle R. Swader).

## Joint Committee Chairpersons

American Association of Law Libraries/ American Correctional Association– ASCLA Committee on Institution Libraries (joint). Thea B. Chesley (ACA); To be appointed (ASCLA).

American Federation of Labor/Congress of Industrial Organizations–ALA, Library Service to Labor Groups, RUSA. John N. Schact (ALA); Anthony Sarmiento (AFL/ CIO).

Anglo-American Cataloguing Rules Fund. William R. Gordon (ALA); Vicki L. Whitmell (Canadian Lib. Assn.); Ross Shimmon (Library Assn.).

Anglo-American Cataloguing Rules, Joint Steering Committee for Revision of. Brian E. C. Schottlaender (ALA), Ralph W. Manning (Canadian Commission on Cataloguing), Margaret Stewart (National Lib. of Canada), Ann Huthwaite (Australian Commission on Cataloguing), Sue M. Brown (British Lib.), Barbara B. Tillett (Lib. of Congress).

Association of American Publishers–ALA. Ann K. Symons (ALA); To be appointed (AAP).

Association of American Publishers–ALCTS. Robert P. Holley (ALCTS); Rebecca Seger (AAP).

Children's Book Council–ALA. Mary Rinato Berman (ALA); Lauren L. Wohl (CBC).

Society of American Archivists–ALA (Joint Committee on Library-Archives Relationships). Samuel Boldrick (ALA); William E. Brown, Jr. (SAA).

# American Library Association
# American Association of School Librarians

Executive Director, Julie A. Walker
50 E. Huron St., Chicago, IL 60611
312-280-4381, 800-545-2433 ext. 4386, fax 312-664-7459

## Object

The American Association of School Librarians (AASL) is interested in the general improvement and extension of library media services for children and young people. AASL has specific responsibility for planning a program of study and service for the improvement and extension of library media services in elementary and secondary schools as a means of strengthening the educational program; evaluation, selection, interpretation, and utilization of media as they are used in the context of the school program; stimulation of continuous study and research in the library field and establishing criteria of evaluation; synthesis of the activities of all units of the American Library Association in areas of mutual concern; representation and interpretation of the need for the function of school libraries to other educational and lay groups; stimulation of professional growth, improvement of the status of school librarians, and encouragement of participation by members in appropriate type-of-activity divisions; conducting activities and projects for improvement and extension of service in the school library when such projects are beyond the scope of type-of-activity divisions, after specific approval by the ALA Council. Established in 1951 as a separate division of ALA.

## Membership

Memb. 7,425. Open to all libraries, school library media specialists, interested individuals, and business firms with requisite membership in ALA.

## Officers (1998–1999)

*Pres.* Sharon Coatney, Oak Hill School, 10200 N. 124 St., Overland Park, KS 66216.

Tel. 913-681-4325, fax 913-681-4329, e-mail sharonc@unicom.net; *Pres.-Elect* M. Ellen Jay, Damascus Elementary School, 10201 Bethesda Church Rd., Damascus, MD 20872-1799. Tel. 301-253-7080, fax 301-253-8717, e-mail mejay@umd5.umd.edu; *Treas./Financial Officer* Nancy Zimmerman, School of Lib. and Info. Science, SUNY–Buffalo, Buffalo, NY 14051. Tel. 716-645-2412, fax 716-645-3775, e-mail npz@acsu.buffalo.edu; *Past Pres.* Ken Haycock, 831-1956 Main Mall, University of British Columbia, Vancouver, BC V6T 1Z1, Canada. Tel. 604-822-4991, fax 604-822-6006, e-mail haycock@unixg.ubc.ca.

## Board of Directors

Officers; Christine A. Allen, Augie Beasley, Susan Bryan, Jody Charter, Jean Donham, Margaret A. Hallisey, Judith King, Mary McClintock, Vivian Melton, Antoinette Negro, Frances R. Roscello, Deborah Roberts Stone, Joie Taylor, Sharyn van Epps, Idella Washington, Barbara Weathers, Julie A. Walker (ex officio).

## Publications

*Knowledge Quest* (5/yr.; memb.; nonmemb. $40). *Eds.* Nancy L. Teger, e-mail tegern@gate.net; Debbie Abilock, e-mail debbie@neuva.pvt.k12.ca.us.

School Library Media Research (nonsubscription electronic publication available to memb. and nonmemb. at http://www.ala.org/assl/SLMR). *Ed.* Daniel Callison, School of Lib. and Info. Sciences, 10th and Jordan, Indiana Univ., Bloomington, IN 47405. E-mail callison@indiana.edu.

## Committee Chairpersons

AASL/ACRL Task Force on the Educational Role of Libraries. Janet Nichols.

AASL/Highsmith Research Grant. Roma McConkey.

American Univ. Press. Deborah Lawton.

Annual Conference. Barbara Herrin.

Awards. Janice Ostrom.

Bylaws and Organization. Jacqueline Morris.

Distinguished School Administrators Award. Carolyn Cain.

Distinguished Service Award. Carol Kroll.

Frances Henne Award. Sharyn Van Epps.

ICONnect Task Force. Pam Berger.

Information Plus Continuing Education Scholarship. Antoinette Negro.

Information Technology Pathfinder Award. Clara Hoover.

Intellectual Freedom Award. Beth Welsh.

Knowledge Quest Editorial Board. Nancy Teger, Debbie Abilock.

Legislation. Bob Saffold.

National Conference, Birmingham 1999. Carolyn Hayes, Connie Mitchell.

Nominating, 1999 Election. Ruth Toor.

National School Library Media Program of the Year. Ann C. Weeks.

Presidential Task Force for Coordinating the Implementation of the New National Guidelines and Standards. Carolyn Giambra.

Publications. Drucie Raines.

Research/Statistics. June Kahler Berry.

School Librarians Workshop Scholarship. Jane Robertson

SLMR Electronic Editorial Board. Daniel Callison.

Task Force on Competencies for Library Media Specialists in the 21st Century. Ken Haycock.

Teaching for Learning Task Force. Barbara Stripling.

## American Library Association
## American Library Trustee Association

Executive Director, Susan Roman
50 E. Huron St., Chicago, IL 60611-2795
312-280-2161, 800-545-2433 ext. 2161, fax 312-280-3257

## Object

The American Library Trustee Association (ALTA) is interested in the development of effective library service for all people in all types of communities and in all types of libraries; it follows that its members are concerned, as policymakers, with organizational patterns of service, with the development of competent personnel, the provision of adequate financing, the passage of suitable legislation, and the encouragement of citizen support for libraries. ALTA recognizes that responsibility for professional action in these fields has been assigned to other divisions of ALA; its specific responsibilities as a division, therefore, are

1. A continuing and comprehensive educational program to enable library trustees to discharge their grave responsibilities in a manner best fitted to benefit the public and the libraries they represent.

2. Continuous study and review of the activities of library trustees.

3. Cooperation with other units within ALA concerning their activities relating to trustees.

4. Encouraging participation of trustees in other appropriate divisions of ALA.

5. Representation and interpretation of the activities of library trustees in contacts outside the library profession,

particularly with national organizations and governmental agencies.

6. Promotion of strong state and regional trustee organizations.

7. Efforts to secure and support adequate library funding.

8. Promulgation and dissemination of recommended library policy.

9. Assuring equal access of information to all segments of the population.

10. Encouraging participation of trustees in trustee/library activities, at local, state, regional, and national levels.

Organized 1890. Became an ALA division in 1961.

## Membership

Memb. 1,566. Open to all interested persons and organizations. For dues and membership year, see ALA entry.

## Officers (1998–1999)

*Pres.* Ruth Newell-Minor; *1st V.P./Pres.-Elect* Patricia Fisher; *Past Pres.* Clifford Dietrich; *Councilor* Judith Baker.

## Board of Directors

Officers; *Trustee Voice Ed.* Kerry Ward (1999); *Regional V.P.s* To be appointed; *ex officio* Susan Roman.

## Staff

*Exec. Dir.* Susan Roman; *Deputy Exec. Dir.* Kerry Ward; *Admin. Secy.* Dollester Thorp-Hawkins.

## Publication

*Trustee Voice* (q.; memb.). *Ed.* Kerry Ward.

# American Library Association
# Association for Library Collections and Technical Services

Executive Director, Karen Muller
50 E. Huron St., Chicago, IL 60611
800-545-2433 ext. 5031, fax 312-280-5033
E-mail kmuller@ala.org

## Object

The Association for Library Collections and Technical Services (ALCTS) is responsible for the following activities: acquisition, identification, cataloging, classification, and preservation of library materials; the development and coordination of the country's library resources; and those areas of selection and evaluation involved in the acquisition of library materials and pertinent to the development of library resources. ALCTS has specific responsibility for:

1. Continuous study and review of the activities assigned to the division

2. Conduct of activities and projects within its area of responsibility

3. Syntheses of activities of all units within ALA that have a bearing on the type of activity represented

4. Representation and interpretation of its type of activity in contacts outside the profession

5. Stimulation of the development of librarians engaged in its type of activity, and stimulation of participation by

members in appropriate type-of-library divisions

6. Planning and development of programs of study and research for the type of activity for the total profession

ALCTS will provide its members, other ALA divisions and members, and the library and information community with leadership and a program for action on the access to, and identification, acquisition, description, organization, preservation, and dissemination of information resources in a dynamic collaborative environment. In addition, ALCTS provides forums for discussion, research, and development and opportunities for learning in all of these areas. To achieve this mission, ALCTS has the following organizational goals:

1. To promote the role of the library and information science in an information society

2. To provide its members with opportunities for information exchange

3. To promote innovative and effective library education and training, to foster the recruitment of individuals with diverse qualities to library work, and to provide continuing education for librarians and library practitioners

4. To develop, support, review, and promote standards to meet library and information needs

5. To provide opportunities for members to participate through research and publications and professional growth

6. To manage the association effectively and efficiently

Established 1957; renamed 1988.

## Membership

Memb. 4,984. Any member of the American Library Association may elect membership in this division according to the provisions of the bylaws.

## Officers (July 1998–July 1999)

*Pres.* Sheila S. Intner, Professor, Simmons College, 300 The Fenway, Boston, MA 02115. Tel. 617-521-2790, fax 617-521-3192, e-mail sintner@simmons.edu; *Pres.-Elect* Peggy Johnson, Asst. Univ. Libn., Univ. of Minnesota, 309 19th Ave. S., Minneapolis, MN 55455. Tel. 612-624-2312, fax 612-626-9353, e-mail m-john@tc.umn.edu; *Past Pres.* Janet Swan Hill, Assoc. Dir., Norlin Lib., Univ. of Colorado, Boulder, CO 80309-0184. Tel. 303-492-3797, fax 303-492-0494, e-mail hilljs@colorado.edu.

Address correspondence to the executive director.

## Directors

Officers; Exec. Dir.; *Div. Councilor* Alexander Bloss; *CRG Rep.* Helen I Reed; *Dirs.* Alice J. Allen, Barbara Berger, Shirley F. Coleman, Karen D. Darling, Olivia M. A. Madison, Judith F. Niles, John J. Reimer, Karen A. Schmidt, Lynn F. Sipe, Dale S. Swensen, Paul J. Weiss.

## Publications

*ALCTS Network News* (irreg.; free). *Ed.* Karen Muller. Subscribe via listproc@ala.org "subscribe an2 [yourname]."

*ALCTS Newsletter* (6 per year; memb.; nonmemb. $25). *Ed.* Dale S. Swensen, Lee Lib., Brigham Young Univ., Provo, UT 84602.

*Library Resources and Technical Services* (q.; memb.; nonmemb. $55). *Ed.* Jennifer A. Younger, Univ. of Notre Dame Libs., Notre Dame, IN 46556. Tel. 219-631-7792.

## Section Chairpersons

Acquisitions. Judith F. Niles.
Cataloging and Classification. Paul J. Weiss.
Collection Management and Development. Lynn F. Sipe.
Preservation and Reformatting. Barbara Berger.
Serials. Karen D. Darling.

## Committee Chairpersons

Hugh C. Atkinson Memorial Award. William A. Gosling.

Association of American Publishers/ALCTS Joint Committee. Robert P. Holley, Marsha S. Clark.

Best of *LRTS*. Carol J. Fleishauer.

Blackwell's Scholarship Award. Janet G. Padway.

Budget and Finance. Olivia M. A. Madison.

Catalog Form and Function. Patrick F. Callahan.

Commercial Technical Services. Karen H. Wilhoit.

Duplicates Exchange Union. Rebecca House Stankowski.

Education. Lynne C. Howarth.

Electronic communications. Eleanor I. Cook.

Fund-raising. Karen L. Horny.

International Relations. Marjorie E. Bloss.

Leadership Development. William A. Garrison.

Legislation. Lynn F. Sipe.

Library Materials Price Index. Stephen J. Bosch.

*LRTS* Editorial Board. Jennifer A. Younger.

MARBI. Bruce Johnson.

Media Resources. E. Ann Caldwell.

Membership. Beverley Geer.

Networked Resources and Metadata. Ann M. Sandberg-Fox.

Nominating. Pamela M. Bluh.

Organization and Bylaws. Janet Swan Hill, October R. Ivins.

Esther J. Piercy Award Jury. Sally C. Tseng.

Planning. Shirley F. Coleman.

Publications. Kerry A. Keck.

Publisher/Vendor Library Relations. Susan A. Davis.

Research and Statistics. Cynthia M. Coulter.

## Discussion Groups

Authority Control in the Online Environment. Rebecca J. Dean.

Automated Acquisitions/In-Process Control Systems. Patricia A. Adams.

Computer Files. Elizabeth Allerton, Greta G. de Groat.

Creative Ideas in Technical Services. Richard Baumgarten, Kuang-Hwei Lee-Smeltzer.

MARC Formats. William W. Jones, Jr.

Newspaper. Robert C. Dowd.

Out of Print. Ned O. Kraft.

Pre-Order and Pre-Catalog Searching. Phelix B. Hanible.

Retrospective Conversion. Donna J. Cappelle-Cook, Karen Joan Davis.

Role of the Professional in Academic Research Technical Scholarly Communications. Betty H. Day, Diane K. Karvey.

Serials Automation. Maria Michelle Sitko, Lianhong-Zhou.

Technical Services Administrators of Medium-Sized Research Libraries. James L. Huesmann.

Technical Services Directors of Large Research Libraries. Catherine C. A. Tierney.

Technical Services in Public Libraries. Ross W. McLachlan.

Technical Services Workstations. Louise M. Ratliff.

# American Library Association
## Association for Library Service to Children

Executive Director, Susan Roman
50 E. Huron St., Chicago, IL 60611
312-280-2163, 800-545-2433 ext. 2163
E-mail sroman@ala.org
World Wide Web http://www.ala.org/alsc

## Object

Interested in the improvement and extension of library services to children in all types of libraries. Responsible for the evaluation and selection of book and nonbook materials for, and the improvement of techniques of, library services to children from preschool through the eighth grade or junior high school age, when such materials or techniques are intended for use in more than one type of library. Founded 1901.

## Membership

Memb. 3,609. Open to anyone interested in library services to children. For information on dues, see ALA entry.

Address correspondence to the executive director.

## Officers

*Pres.* Leslie Edmonds Holt; *V.P./Pres.-Elect* Caroline Ward; *Past Pres.* Elizabeth Watson.

## Directors

Clara Nalli Bohrer, Eliza Dresang, Barbara Genco, Sylvia A. Mavrogenes, Marie Orlando, Sue McCleaf Nespeca, Cynthia K. Richey, Grace Ruth, Kathy Toon; *Divisional Counselor* Eliza Dresang; *Staff Liaison* Susan Roman.

## Publications

*Journal of Youth Services in Libraries* (*JOYS*) (q.; memb.; nonmemb. $40; foreign $50).

*Eds.* Betty Carter, Keith Swigger, School of Lib. and Info. Studies, Texas Woman's Univ., Box 425438, Denton, TX 76204-5438.

## Committee Chairpersons

### Priority Group I: Child Advocacy

Consultant. Jean B. Gaffney.
Intellectual Freedom.
International Relations.
Legislation.
Library Service to Children with Special Needs.
Preschool Services and Parent Education.
Preschool Services Discussion Group.
Public Library-School Partnership Discussion Group.
Social Issues DIscussion Group.

### Priority Group II: Evaluation of Media

Consultant. Judith F. Davie.
Notable Children's Books.
Notable Children's Recordings.
Notable Children's Videos.
Notable Children's Web Sites.
Notable Computer Software for Children.

### Priority Group III: Professional Awards and Scholarships

Consultant. Hilda Weeks Kuter.
Arbuthnot Honor Lecture.
Louise Seaman Bechtel Fellowship.
Distinguished Service Award.
Econo-Clad Literature Program Award.
Penguin Putnam Books for Young Readers Award.
Scholarships: Melcher and Bound to Stay Bound.

### Priority Group IV: Organizational Support

Consultant. Carole Fiore.
Local Arrangements.
Membership.
Nominating.
Organization and Bylaws.
Planning and Budget.
Preconference Planning.

### Priority Group V: Projects and Research

Collections of Children's Books for Adult Research (Discussion Group).

National Planning of Special Collections.
National Reading Program.
Oral Record Project (Advisory Committee).
Publications.
Research and Development.

### Priority Group VI: Award Committees

Consultant. Jan Moltzan.
Mildred L. Batchelder Award Selection.
Pura Belpré Award.
Caldecott Award.
Carnegie Award.
Newbery Award.
Wilder Award.

# American Library Association
## Association of College and Research Libraries

Executive Director, Althea H. Jenkins
50 E. Huron St., Chicago, IL 60611-2795
312-280-3248, 800-545-2433 ext. 3248, fax 312-280-2520
E-mail ajenkins@ala.org

## Object

The Association of College and Research Libraries (ACRL) provides leadership for development, promotion, and improvement of academic and research library resources and services to facilitate learning, research, and the scholarly communication process. ACRL promotes the highest level of professional excellence for librarians and library personnel in order to serve the users of academic and research libraries. Founded 1938.

## Membership

Memb. 10,616. For information on dues, see ALA entry.

## Officers

*Pres.* Maureen Sullivan, Organizational Development Consultant, 3696 Thomas Point Rd., Annapolis, MD 21403-5026. Tel. 410-268-3539, fax 410-268-3810, e-mail maureen@

arl.org; *Past Pres.* W. Lee Hisle, Assoc. V.P. for Learning Resource Services, Austin Community College, 1212 Rio Grande Ave., Austin, TX 78701. Tel. 512-223-3069, fax 512-495-7431; *Pres.-Elect* Larry Hardesty, College Libn., Abell Lib., Austin College, 900 N. Grand Ave., Suite 6L, Sherman, TX 75090-4440. Tel. 903-813-2490, fax 903-813-2297, e-mail lhardesty@austinc.edu; *Budget and Finance Chair* Cathy Henderson, Univ. of Texas, Box 7219, Austin, TX 78713-7219. Tel. 512-471-9119, fax 512-471-2899, e-mail c.henderson@mail.utexas.edu; *ACRL Councilor* Helen H. Spalding, Associate Director of Libs., Univ. of Missouri, Kansas City (postal address: 600 Roman Rd., Kansas City, MO 65113-2037). Tel. 816-235-1558, fax 816-333-5584, e-mail spaldinh@umkc.edu.

## Board of Directors

Officers; William E. Brown, Jr., Paul E. Dumont, Barbara Baxter Jenkins, Linda S. Muroi, Carol Pfeiffer, Dana C. Rooks, Mary Lee Sweat.

## Publications

*Choice* (11 per year; $185; foreign $210). *Ed.* Irving Rockwood.

*College & Research Libraries* (6 per year; memb.; nonmemb. $55). *Ed.* Donald E. Riggs.

*College and Research Libraries News* (11 per year; memb.; nonmemb. $40). *Ed.* Mary Ellen Kyger Davis.

*Publications in Librarianship* (formerly *ACRL Monograph Series*) (occasional). *Ed.* John M. Budd.

*Rare Books and Manuscripts Librarianship* (2 per year; $30). *Ed.* Sidney E. Berger.

List of other publications available through the ACRL office, ALA, 50 E. Huron St., Chicago, IL 60611-2795; or call 312-280-2517.

## Committee and Task Force Chairpersons

Academic Libraries: Trends & Statistics. William Miller.

Academic Librarian Status. Lara A. Bushallow.

Academic or Research Librarian of the Year Award. James F. Williams, II.

Appointments (1998). Lynn K. Chmelir.

Hugh C. Atkinson Memorial Award. William A. Gosling.

Budget and Finance. Cathy Henderson.

Bylaws. William F. Louden.

*Choice* Editorial Board. Richard AmRhein.

Colleagues. William Miller, Betsy Wilson.

*College and Research Libraries* Editorial Board. Donald E. Riggs.

*College and Research Libraries News* Editorial Board. Gary B. Thompson.

Conference Program Planning, New Orleans (1999). Maureen Sullivan.

Copyright. Julia C. Blixrud.

Council of Liaisons. Althea H. Jenkins.

Doctoral Dissertation Fellowship. William Gray Potter.

Equal Access to Software Information Advisory Committee. Tom McNulty.

Government Relations. Carolyn Gray.

Institute for Information Literacy. Cerise Oberman.

Intellectual Freedom. Lawrence A. Miller.

International Relations. Connie E. Costantino.

Samuel Lazerow Fellowship. Cynthia Gozzi.

Leadership Development. Jane Hedberg.

Media Resources. Kristine R. Brancolini.

Membership. Ray Metz.

National Conference Executive Committee, Detroit, 1999. Charles E. Beard.

New Publications Advisory. James R. Cubit.

Nominations (1999). Micheline E. Jedrey.

Orientation. W. Lee Hisle.

Professional Development. Lee C. Ketcham Van Orsdel.

Professional Enhancement. Joan Reyes.

Publications. Brian Coutts.

*Publications in Librarianship* Editorial Board. John M. Budd.

Racial and Ethnic Diversity. Mae Schreiber.

*Rare Books and Manuscripts Librarianship* Editorial Board. Sidney E. Berger.

Research. Rebecca L. Schreiner-Robles.

K. G. Saur Award for Best *College and Research Libraries* Article. William G. Jones.

Standards and Accreditation. Barton Lessin.

Statistics. Jan Kemp.

## Discussion Group Chairpersons

Alliances for New Directions in Teaching/Learning. Mari Miller.

Austrian Studies. Faye Christenberry.

Canadian Studies. Pam Hays, Margaret S. Brill.

Criminal Justice/Criminology. Mary Jane Brustman.

Development Officers. Margaret Gordon.

Electronic Library Development. Steven Bischof.

Electronic Reserves. Lorre Smith.

Electronic Text Centers. Michael Seadle.

Exhibits and Displays. Michael M. Miller.

Fee-Based Information Service Centers in Academic Libraries. Gail Etschmaier.

Heads of Public Services. Wendy Starkweather.

Home Economics/Human Ecology Librarians. Priscilla Geahigan.

Library Science Librarians. Cathy Rentschler.

Medium-Sized Libraries. Jeanne G. Sohn, Charlotte Slocum.

MLA International Bibliography. Faye Christenberry.

Personnel Administrators and Staff Development Officers. William Gentz, Peter Devlin.
Philosophical, Religious, and Theological Studies. Barbara L. Berman.
Popular Cultures. Diane Kachmar.
Public Relations in Academic Libraries. Barbara Kile.
Research. Darrell L. Jenkins.
Sports and Recreation. Mila C. Su.
Team-Based Organizations. Janet S. Fore.
Undergraduate Librarians. Mark Watson.

## Section Chairpersons

Afro-American Studies Librarians. Sylverna V. Ford.
Anthropology and Sociology. Christina Smith.
Arts. Judy Harvey Sahak.
Asian, African, and Middle Eastern. David Hirsch.

College Librarians. Carolyn A. Sheehy.
Community and Junior College Libraries. Cary Sowell.
Distance Learning. Robert P. Morrison.
Educational and Behavioral Sciences. Janice M. Wilson.
English and American Literature. Robert W. Melton.
Instruction. Mary Jane Petrowski.
Law and Political Science. Paula J. Popma.
Rare Books and Manuscripts. Richard W. Oram.
Science and Technology. Billie Joy Reinhart.
Slavic and East European. Tatiana Goerner Barr.
University Libraries. Maureen Pastine.
Western European Specialists. Stephen Lehmann.
Woman's Studies. Kristin H. Gerhard.

# American Library Association
# Association of Specialized and Cooperative Library Agencies

Executive Director, Cathleen Bourdon
50 E. Huron St., Chicago, IL 60611
312-280-4395, 800-545-2433 ext. 4396, fax 312-944-8085

## Object

To represent state library agencies, specialized library agencies, and multitype library cooperatives. Within the interest of these types of library organizations, the Association of Specialized and Cooperative Library Agencies (ASCLA) has specific responsibility for

1. Development and evaluation of goals and plans for state library agencies, specialized library agencies, and multitype library cooperatives to facilitate the implementation, improvement, and extension of library activities designed to foster improved user services, coordinating such activities with other appropriate ALA units.

2. Representation and interpretation of the role, functions, and services of state library agencies, specialized library agencies, and multitype library cooperatives within and outside the profession, including contact with national organizations and government agencies.

3. Development of policies, studies, and activities in matters affecting state library agencies, specialized library agencies, and multitype library cooperatives relating to (a) state and local library legislation, (b) state grants-in-aid and appropriations, and (c) relationships among state, federal, regional, and local governments, coordinating such activities with other appropriate ALA units.

4. Establishment, evaluation, and promotion of standards and service guidelines relating to the concerns of this association.

5. Identifying the interests and needs of all persons, encouraging the creation of services to meet these needs within the areas of concern of the association, and promoting the use of these services provided by state library agencies, specialized library agencies, and multitype library cooperatives.

6. Stimulating the professional growth and promoting the specialized training and continuing education of library personnel at all levels of concern of this association and encouraging membership participation in appropriate type-of-activity divisions within ALA.

7. Assisting in the coordination of activities of other units within ALA that have a bearing on the concerns of this association.

8. Granting recognition for outstanding library service within the areas of concern of this association.

9. Acting as a clearinghouse for the exchange of information and encouraging the development of materials, publications, and research within the areas of concern of this association.

## Membership

Memb. 1,420.

## Board of Directors (1998–1999)

*Pres.* John M. Day (2000); *Pres.-Elect* Barbara H. Will (2001); *Past Pres.* Nancy M. Bolt (1999); *Dirs.-at-Large* Amy L. Kellerstrass (1999), Stephen Prine (2000), Rhea J. Rubin (1999), Rod Wagner (2000); *ex officio* Frederick Duda (2001), Donna Z. Pontau (1999).

## Executive Staff

*Exec. Dir.* Cathleen Bourdon; *Deputy Exec. Dir.* Lillian Lewis.

## Publications

*Interface* (q.; memb.; nonmemb. $20). *Ed.* Frederick Duda, Talking Book Service, 4884 Kestral Park Circle, Sarasota, FL 34231-3369. Tel. 941-742-5914, fax 941-751-7098.

## Committee Chairpersons

American Correctional Association/ASCLA Joint Committee on Institution Libraries. Thea Chesley, Tim Brown.

Awards. H. Neil Kelley.

Budget and Finance. John Day.

Conference Program Coordination. Diane Solomon.

Guidelines for Library Service for People with Developmental Disabilities. Marilyn Irwin.

Legislation. Barbara Will.

Library Personnel and Education. Amy Kellerstrass.

Membership Promotion. Marjorie MacKenzie.

Organization and Bylaws. Donna Pontau.

Planning. Nancy Bolt.

Publications. Tina Roose.

Research. Ruth Kowal.

Standards Review. Ethel Himmell.

# American Library Association
## Library Administration and Management Association

Executive Director, Karen Muller
50 E. Huron St., Chicago, IL 60611
312-280-5031, 800-545-2433 ext. 5031, fax 312-280-3257
E-mail kmuller@ala.org

## Object

The Library Administration and Management Association (LAMA) provides an organizational framework for encouraging the study of administrative theory, for improving the practice of administration in libraries, and for identifying and fostering administrative skill. Toward these ends, the division is responsible for all elements of general administration that are common to more than one type of library. These may include organizational structure, financial administration, personnel management and training, buildings and equipment, and public relations. LAMA meets this responsibility in the following ways:

1. Study and review of activities assigned to the division with due regard for changing developments in these activities.

2. Initiating and overseeing activities and projects appropriate to the division, including activities involving bibliography compilation, publication, study, and review of professional literature within the scope of the division.

3. Synthesizing the activities of other ALA units which have a bearing upon the responsibilities or work of the division.

4. Representing and interpreting library administrative activities in contacts outside the library profession.

5. Aiding the professional development of librarians engaged in administration and encouraging their participation in appropriate type-of-library divisions.

6. Planning and developing programs of study and research in library administrative problems which are most needed by the profession.

Established 1957.

## Membership

Memb. 4,996.

## Officers (July 1998–July 1999)

*Pres.* Thomas L. Wilding; *Pres.-Elect* Carol L. Anderson; *Past Pres.* Charles E. Kratz, Jr.; *Div. Councilor* Judith A. Adams-Volpe; *Dirs.-at-Large* Deborah J. Leather, Rebecca R. Martin; *Section Chairs* Janice H. Dost, Charles A. Hansen, Mary M. Harrison, Sarah C. Michalak, Rita A. Scherrei, Virginia Steel, Barbara Simpson, Joyce G. Taylor; *ex officio* Emily Batista, Kathryn Hamell Carpenter, Sharon E. Clark, Patricia Conor Hodapp, Melissa A. Laning, Claudia J. Morner, Catherine L. Murray-Rust, Maria Otero-Boisvert, Phyllis W. Trammell, Desiree Webber, *Exec. Dir.* Karen Muller.

Address correspondence to the executive director.

## Publications

*Library Administration and Management* (q.; memb.; nonmemb. $55; foreign $65). *Ed.* Barbara G. Preece.

LEADS from LAMA (approx. weekly; free through Internet. *Ed.* Elizabeth Dreazen. To subscribe, send to listproc@ala.org the message *subscribe lamaleads [first name last name]*.

## Committee Chairpersons

Budget and Finance. John Vasi.

Certified Public Library Administrator Certification, LAMA/PLA/ASCLA. Robert H. Rohlf.

Council of LAMA Affiliates. Barbara Simpson.

Cultural Diversity. Janice D. Simmons-Welburn.
Editorial Advisory Board. Mary Augusta Thomas.
Education. Philip Tramdack.
Governmental Affairs. Janice Feye-Stukas.
Membership. Ann Williams.
Nominating, 1999 Elections. Elizabeth C. Habich.
Organization. Sharon E. Clark.
Leadership Development. Kate W. Ragsdale.
Program. J. Linda Williams.
Publications. Joan R. Giesecke.
Recognition of Achievement. Louise S. McAulay.
Small Libraries Publications Series. Anders C. Dahlgren.
Special Conferences and Programs. Paul M. Anderson.

## Section Chairpersons

Buildings and Equipment. Sarah C. Michalak.

Fund-Raising and Financial Development. Mary M. Harrison.
Library Organization and Management. Joyce G. Taylor.
Personnel Administration. Janice H. Dost.
Public Relations. Charles A. Hansen.
Statistics. Rita A. Scherrei.
Systems and Services. Virginia Steel.

## Discussion Groups

Assistants-to-the-Director. Theresa Liedtka.
Diversity Officers. Joseph R. Diaz.
Library Storage. Catherine L. Murray-Rust, Judith A. Scalf.
Middle Management. Alberta Walker.
Total Quality Management. Larry Nash White.
Women Administrators. Cheryl C. Kugler.

# American Library Association
# Library and Information Technology Association

Executive Director, Jacqueline Mundell
50 E. Huron St., Chicago, IL 60611
312-280-4270, 800-545-2433

## Object

The Library and Information Technology Association (LITA) envisions a world in which the complete spectrum of information technology is available to everyone—in libraries, at work, and at home. To move toward this goal, LITA provides a forum for discussion, an environment for learning, and a program for actions on many aspects of information technology for both practitioners and managers.

LITA is concerned with the planning, development, design, application, and integration of technologies within the library and information environment, with the impact of emerging technologies on library service, and with the effect of automated technologies on people.

LITA's strategic goals include providing opportunities for professional growth and performance in areas of information technology, influencing national and international initiatives relating to information and access, influencing the development of technical standards, and developing services and products needed and valued by its members.

## Membership

Memb. 5,000.

## Officers (1998–1999)

*Pres.* Barbra B. Higginbotham; *V.P./Pres.-Elect* Michael Gorman; *Past Pres.* Linda D. Miller.

# Directors

Officers; Pat Ensor (2000), Susan Harrison (2001), Susan Jacobson (2001), Karen J. Starr (2000), Kathleen A. Wakefield (1999), Flo Wilson (1999); *Councilor* Tamara Miller (2000); *Bylaws and Organization* Sara L. Randall (2000); *Exec. Dir.* Jacqueline Mundell.

# Publications

*Information Technology and Libraries* (q.; memb.; nonmemb. $50; single copy $15). *Ed.* James J. Kopp. For information or to send manuscripts, contact the editor.
LITA Newsletter (q.; electronic only, at http://www.lita.org). *Ed.* Martin Kalfatovic.

# Committee Chairpersons

Committee Chair Coordinators. Linda Robinson-Barr, Kate Wakefield.
Hugh C. Atkinson Memorial Award. William A. Gosling.
Budget Review. Linda D. Miller.
Bylaws and Organization. Sara L. Randall.
Education. D. Russell Bailey.
Executive. Barbra B. Higginbotham.
Information Technology and Libraries. Dan K. Marmion.
International Relations. John R. James.
Leadership Development. Bonnie S. Postlethwaite.
Legislation and Regulation. Nancy K. Roderer.
LITA/Gaylord Award. Fred I. Gertler.
LITA/Geac Scholarship. Nancy H. Evans.
LITA/Library Hi Tech Award. Charles Husbands.
LITA National Forum, 1999. Pat Ensor.
LITA Newsletter (Subcommittee). Martin A. Kalfatovic.
LITA/OCLC Kilgour Award. Michael Gorman.
LITA/OCLC and LITA/LSSI Minority Scholarships. Marietta A. Plank.
Machine-Readable Form of Bibliographic Information (MARBI). Bruce Johnson.
Membership. Sue Kopp.
Nominating. Colby M. Riggs.
Program Planning. Lynne D. Lysiak.
Publications. Thomas C. Wilson.
Regional Institutes. Howard Spivak.
Research. Kathleen M. Herick.

Strategic Initiatives Planning Group. Michael Gorman.
Technical Standards for Library Automation (TESLA). Jennie L. McKee.
Technology and Access. To be announced.
Top Technology Trends Committee. Pat Ensor.
Telecommunications Electronic Reviews (TER) Board. Thomas C. Wilson.
Web Editorial Board. Mary M. Deane.

# Interest Group Chairpersons

Interest Group Coordinator. Mary Ann Van Cura.
Authority Control in the Online Environment (LITA/ALCTS). Rebecca J. Dean.
Customized Applications for Library Microcomputers (CALM). Stephen Westman.
Distance Learning. Susan Logue.
Distributed Systems and Networks. Marvin Biewalski.
Electronic Publishing/Electronic Journals. James Campbell.
Emerging Technologies. Martin Halbert.
Geographic Information Systems (GIS). Diane K. Harvey.
Human/Machine Interface. John W. Forys, Jr.
Imagineering. Richard Kuster.
Intelligent and Knowledge-Based Systems. Schott Burright.
Internet Resources. Sandy Colby.
Library Consortia/Automated Systems. Anne T. Gilliland.
MARC Formats (LITA/ALCTS). William Jones.
Microcomputer Users. Karen Davis.
Online Catalogs. Karen Davis.
Programmer/Analyst. Philip Boyer.
Retrospective Conversion (LITA/ALCTS). Karen J. Davis.
Secure Systems and Services. Thomas Klinger.
Serials Automation (LITA/ALCTS). Liana Zhou.
Technical Issues of Digital Data. Debra Shapiro.
Technical Services Workstations (LITA/ALCTS). Louise M. Ratliff.
Technology and the Arts. Debra Shapiro.
Telecommunications. Peter Burslem.
Vendor/User. Linda Bills.

# American Library Association
## Public Library Association

Executive Director, Greta K. Southard
50 E. Huron St., Chicago, IL 60611
312-280-5752, 800-545-2433 ext. 5752, fax 312-280-5029
E-mail pla@ala.org

## Object

The Public Library Association (PLA) has specific responsibility for

1. Conducting and sponsoring research about how the public library can respond to changing social needs and technical developments.
2. Developing and disseminating materials useful to public libraries in interpreting public library services and needs.
3. Conducting continuing education for public librarians by programming at national and regional conferences, by publications such as the newsletter, and by other delivery means.
4. Establishing, evaluating, and promoting goals, guidelines, and standards for public libraries.
5. Maintaining liaison with relevant national agencies and organizations engaged in public administration and human services, such as the National Association of Counties, the Municipal League, and the Commission on Post-Secondary Education.
6. Maintaining liaison with other divisions and units of ALA and other library organizations, such as the Association of American Library Schools and the Urban Libraries Council.
7. Defining the role of the public library in service to a wide range of user and potential user groups.
8. Promoting and interpreting the public library to a changing society through legislative programs and other appropriate means.
9. Identifying legislation to improve and to equalize support of public libraries.

PLA enhances the development and effectiveness of public librarians and public library services. This mission positions PLA to

- Focus its efforts on serving the needs of its members
- Address issues that affect public libraries
- Promote and protect the profession
- Commit to quality public library services that benefit the general public

To carry out its mission, PLA will identify and pursue specific goals. These goals will drive PLA's structure, governance, staffing, and budgeting, and will serve as the basis for all evaluations of achievement and performance. The following broad goals and strategies were established for PLA in 1997 for accomplishment by the year 2000:

1. PLA will provide market-driven, mission-focused programs and services delivered in a variety of formats.
2. PLA will have increased its members and diversified its leadership.
3. PLA will have maximized its fiscal resources to enable the full implementation of its goals and to take full advantage of strategic opportunities.
4. PLA will be recognized as a positive, contemporary champion of public librarians and public libraries.
5. PLA will have demonstrated its leadership in developing and promoting sound public policies affecting public libraries.
6. PLA will have implemented, evaluated, and refined its structure and governance.
7. PLA will have the facilities, technology, staff, and systems required to achieve its mission.

## Membership

Memb. 8,500+. Open to all ALA members interested in the improvement and expansion of public library services to all ages in various types of communities.

## Officers (1998–1999)

*Pres.* Christine L. Hage, Clinton-Macomb Public Lib., 43245 Garfield, Clinton Township, MI 48038. Tel. 810-228-7810, fax 810-228-9093, e-mail hagec@metronet.lib.mi.us; *V.P./Pres.-Elect* Harriet Henderson, Montgomery Conty Dept. of Libs., 99 Maryland Ave., Rockville, MD 20850. Tel. 301-271-3804, fax 301-271-3934, e-mail hendch@co.mo.md.us; *Past Pres.* Ginnie Cooper, Multnomah County Lib., Lib. Assn. of Portland, 205 N.E. Russell St., Portland, OR 97212. Tel. 503-248-5403, fax 503-248-5441, e-mail ginniec@nethost.multnomah.lib.or.us.

## Publication

*Public Libraries* (bi-m.; memb.; nonmemb. $50; foreign $60; single copy $10). *Managing Ed.* Kathleen Hughes, PLA, 50 E. Huron St., Chicago, IL 60611.

## Cluster Chairpersons

Issues and Concerns Steering Committee. Barbara Webb.
Library Development Steering Committee. Catharine Cook.
Library Services Steering Committee. Carol G. Walters.

## Committee Chairs

### Issues and Concerns Cluster

Intellectual Freedom. Bruce S. Farrar.
Legislation. David Macksam.

Library Confidentialty Task Force. Elaine McConnell.
Recruitment of Public Librarians. Christie Brandau.
Research and Statistics. Diane Mayo.
Workload Measures and Staffing Patterns. Hampton Auld.

### Library Development Cluster

Branch Libraries. Miriam L. Morris.
Marketing Public Libraries. Tim Grimes.
Medium-Sized Libraries. Jo K. Potter.
Metropolitan Libraries. Diane J. Chrisman.
Public Library Systems. Carol Sheffer.
Resource Allocation. June Garcia.
Technology in Public Libraries. William H. Ptacek.

### Library Services Cluster

Adult Lifelong Learning Services. Lorraine Sano Jackson.
Audiovisual. James Massey.
Basic Education and Literacy Services. Margaret Smith.
Cataloging Needs of Public Libraries. Margaret Shen.
Collection Management. Deborah Pawlik.
Community Information, Development, Support, and Education. Patricia Hollander, Donna Reed.
Community Information Service Technology. Donna Reed, Louise Sevold.
Continuing and Independent Learning Services. Caryl Mobley.
Internal Revenue Service. Elizabeth Bingham.
Job and Career Information Services. Frances Roehm.
Publishers Liaison. Penny Pace-Cannon, Buff Hirko.
Services to Business. Don Barlow.
Services to Multicultural Populations. Fred Gitner.
2000 National Conference. Fran C. Freimarck.
2000 National Conference (Local Arrangements). Lois Kilkka.
2000 National Conference (Program). Claudia B. Sumler.

# American Library Association
# Reference and User Services Association

Executive Director, Cathleen Bourdon
50 E. Huron St., Chicago, IL 60611
312-944-6780, 800-545-2433 ext. 4398, fax 312-944-8085
E-mail rusa@ala.org
World Wide Web http://www.ala.org/rusa

## Object

The Reference and User Services Association (RUSA) is responsible for stimulating and supporting in every type of library the delivery of reference/information services to all groups, regardless of age, and of general library services and materials to adults. This involves facilitating the development and conduct of direct service to library users, the development of programs and guidelines for service to meet the needs of these users, and assisting libraries in reaching potential users.

The specific responsibilities of RUSA are

1. Conduct of activities and projects within the division's areas of responsibility.
2. Encouragement of the development of librarians engaged in these activities and stimulation of participation by members of appropriate type-of-library divisions.
3. Synthesis of the activities of all units within the American Library Association that have a bearing on the type of activities represented by the division.
4. Representation and interpretation of the division's activities in contacts outside the profession.
5. Planning and development of programs of study and research in these areas for the total profession.
6. Continuous study and review of the division's activities.

## Membership

Memb. 4,835. For information on dues, see ALA entry.

## Officers (June 1998–June 1999)

*Pres.* Jo Bell Whitlarch; *Pres.-Elect* Peggy A. Seiden; *Secy.* Ruth A. Carr.

## Directors and Other Members

Karen J. Chapman, Elaine Lyon, David Niall, Carol M. Tobin, Bernard F. Pasqualini, Rebecca Whitaker; *Councilor* Pam Sieving; *Past Pres.* Caroline Long; *Ed., RUSA Update* Beth Woodard; *Ed., RUSQ* Gail Schlachter; *Exec. Dir.* Cathleen Bourdon.

Address correspondence to the executive director.

## Publications

*RUSA Update* (q.; memb.; nonmemb. $20).
*RUSQ* (q.; memb; nonmemb. $50).

## Section Chairpersons

Business Reference and Services. William R. Taylor.
Collection Development and Evaluation. Georgianna S. Miles.
History. Martha L. Henderson.
Machine-Assisted Reference. Lise M. Dyckman.
Management and Operation of User Services. Linda L. Thompson.

## Committee Chairpersons

Access to Information. Harriet Gottfried.
AFL/CIO Joint Committee on Library Services to Labor Groups. John N. Schacht.
Awards Coordinating. Candace R. Benefiel.
Conference Program. W. Michael Havener.

Conference Program Coordinating. Janice Simons-Welburn.

Dartmouth Medal. Richard Bleiler.

Denali Press Award. Lisa Pillow.

Facts on File Grant. Christine Bulson.

Gale Research Award for Excellence in Reference and Adult Services. Joanne Harrar.

Membership. Joyce C. Wright.

Margaret E. Monroe Library Adult Services Award. Ann Coder.

Isadore Gilbert Mudge/R. R. Bowker Award. Susan G. Miller.

Nominating. Marilyn K. Von Seggern.

Organization. Laryne J. Dallas.

Planning and Finance. Caroline Long.

Publications. Geraldine King.

Reference Services Press Award. Marian Shemberg.

John Sessions Memorial Award. Carol H. Krismann.

Louis Shores/Oryx Press Award. Hope H. Yelich.

Standards and Guidelines. Sarah Sartain Jane.

# American Library Association
# Young Adult Library Services Association

Executive Director, Julie A. Walker
50 E. Huron St., Chicago, IL 60611
312-280-4390, 800-545-2433 ext. 4390, fax 312-664-7459
E-mail yalsa@ala.org

## Object

In every library in the nation, quality library service to young adults is provided by a staff that understands and respects the unique informational, educational, and recreational needs of teenagers. Equal access to information, services, and materials is recognized as a right, not a privilege. Young adults are actively involved in the library decision-making process. The library staff collaborates and cooperates with other youth-serving agencies to provide a holistic, community-wide network of activities and services that support healthy youth development. To ensure that this vision becomes a reality, the Young Adult Library Services Association (YALSA), a division of the American Library Association (ALA)

1. Advocates extensive and developmentally appropriate library and information services for young adults, ages 12 to 18

2. Promotes reading and supports the literacy movement

3. Advocates the use of information and communications technologies to provide effective library service

4. Supports equality of access to the full range of library materials and services, including existing and emerging information and communications technologies, for young adults

5. Provides education and professional development to enable its members to serve as effective advocates for young people

6. Fosters collaboration and partnerships among its individual members with the library community and other groups involved in providing library and information services to young adults

7. Influences public policy by demonstrating the importance of providing library and information services that meet the unique needs and interests of young adults

8. Encourages research and is in the vanguard of new thinking concerning the

provision of library and information services for youth

# Membership

Memb. 2,200. Open to anyone interested in library services and materials for young adults. For information on dues, see ALA entry.

# Officers (July 1998–July 1999)

*Pres.* Joel Shoemaker, 3101 Raven St., Iowa City, IA 52245. Tel. 319-339-6823, fax 319-339-5735, e-mail shoemaker@Iowa-city.k12.Ia.us; *V.P/Pres.-Elect* Jana Fine, Clearwater Public Lib., 100 N. Osceola Ave., Clearwater, FL 33755. Tel. 727-462-6800 ext. 252, fax 727-298-0095, e-mail janafine01@sprynet.com; *Past Pres.* Michael Cart. E-mail mrmcart @aol.com; *Councilor* Pamela Spencer. E-mail pgspencer@erols.com.

# Directors

Officers; Betty Acerra (2001), Mary Arnold (1999), Audra Caplan (2000), Rosemary Chance (2000), Phyllis Fisher (1999), Carol Sipos (2001); Ex officio: *Chair, Budget and Finance* Elizabeth O'Donnell; *Chair, Organization and Bylaws* Daphne Daly; *Chair, Strategic Planning* Patricia Muller.

# Publications

*Journal of Youth Services in Libraries* (q.; memb.; nonmemb. $40; foreign $50). *Eds.* Donald J. Kenney, Linda J. Wilson.
*Voices: Newsletter of the Young Adult Services Association* (s. ann.; memb.). *Ed.* Jana Fine.

# Committee Chairpersons

Adult Books for Young Adults Project. Bonnie Kunzel

ALSC/YALSA JOYS Editorial (Advisory). Betty Carter, Keith Swigger.
Best Books for Young Adults (1999). Carol Fox.
Best Books for Young Adults (2000). Suzanne Manczuk.
Best Young Adult Book Award Feasibility Task Force. Michael Cart.
Budget and Finance. Elizabeth O'Donnell.
Division Promotion. Ellen Duffy.
Education. Cyndi Giorgis.
Margaret A. Edwards Award 1999. Jana Fine.
Margaret A. Edwards Award 2000. Joan Atkinson.
Intellectual Freedom. Christine Allen.
Legislation. Bill Stack.
Media Selection and Usage. Stephen Crowley.
Membership. Susan Raboy.
National Organizations Serving the Young Adult (liaison). Dale McNeill.
Nominating (1999). Charles Harmon.
Nominating (2000). Judy Nelson.
Organization and Bylaws. Daphne Daly.
Outreach to Young Adults with Special Needs. Jeff Katz.
Outstanding Books for the College Bound. Donald Kenney.
Oversight. Patricia Muller.
Popular Paperbacks for Young Adults. Nancy Reich, Lora Bruggerman.
President's Program, 1999. Audra Caplan, Judy Sasges
Program Planning Clearinghouse and Evaluation. Connie Bush.
Publications. Kathy Latrobe.
Publishers Liaison. Joyce Valenza.
Quick Picks for Reluctant Young Adult Readers. Diana Herald, Mary Long.
Research. Gloria Walty.
Selected Films and Videos for Young Adults. Ranae Pierce.
Serving Young Adults in Large Urban Populations Discussion Group. Susan Raboy.
Strategic Planning. Patricia Muller.
Teaching Young Adult Literature Discussion Group. Mary Cissell.
Technology for Young Adults. Michael Hackwelder.
Webmaster, YALSA Web site. Linda Braun.
Youth Participation. Ali Turner.

# American Merchant Marine Library Association

(An affiliate of United Seamen's Service)
Executive Director, Roger T. Korner
One World Trade Center, Suite 2161, New York, NY 10048
212-775-1038

## Object

Provides ship and shore library service for American-flag merchant vessels, the Military Sealift Command, the U.S. Coast Guard, and other waterborne operations of the U.S. government. Established 1921.

## Officers (1998–1999)

*Pres.* Talmage E. Simpkins; *Chair, Exec. Committee* Edward Morgan; *V.P.s* John M. Bowers, Capt. Timothy E. Brown, James Capo, Ernest Corrado, Remo DiFiore, John Halas, Ren, Lioeanjie, George E. Murphy, S. Nakanishi, Capt. Gregorio Oca, Michael Sacco, John J. Sweeney; *Secy.* Lillian Rabins; *Treas.* William D. Potts; *Exec. Dir.* Roger T. Korner.

# American Society for Information Science

Executive Director, Richard B. Hill
8720 Georgia Ave., Suite 501, Silver Spring, MD 20910
301-495-0900, fax 301-495-0810, e-mail ASIS@asis.org

## Object

The American Society for Information Science (ASIS) provides a forum for the discussion, publication, and critical analysis of work dealing with the design, management, and use of information, information systems, and information technology.

## Membership

Memb. (Indiv.) 3,700; (Student) 600; (Inst.) 200. Dues (Indiv.) $115; (Student) $30; (Inst.) $425 and $650.

## Officers

*Pres.* Candy Schwartz, Simmons College; *Pres.-Elect* Eugene Garfield, Institute for Scientific Information; *Treas.* George D. Ryerson, Chemical Abstracts Service; *Past Pres.* Michael K. Buckland, Univ. of California.

Address correspondence to the executive director.

## Board of Directors

*Dirs.-at-Large* Samantha Kelly Hastings, Julie M. Hurd, Ray R. Larson, Merri Beth Lavagnino, Gary J. Marchionini, Pat Molholt, Victor Rosenberg, Ellen L. Sleeter; *Deputy Dirs.* Michael Stallings, Douglas Kaylor; *Exec. Dir.* Richard B. Hill.

## Publications

*Advances in Classification Research*, Vols. 1–7. *Eds.* Barbara Kwasnik, Raya Fidel.

Available from Information Today, 143 Old Marlton Pike, Medford, NJ 08055.

*Annual Review of Information Science and Technology.* Available from Information Today, 143 Old Marlton Pike, Medford, NJ 08055.

*ASIS Thesaurus of Information Science and Librarianship.* Available from Information Today, 143 Old Marlton Pike, Medford, NJ 08055.

*Bulletin of the American Society for Information Science.* Available from ASIS.

*Challenges in Indexing Electronic Texts and Images.* Eds. Raya Fidel, Trudi Bellardo (Hahn), Edie M. Rasmussen, and Philip J. Smith. Available from Information Today, 143 Old Marlton Pike, Medford, NJ 08055.

*Electronic Publishing: Applications and Implications.* Eds. Elisabeth Logan and Myke Gluck. Available from Information Today, 143 Old Marlton Pike, Medford, NJ 08055.

*Entertainment Technology and the Information Business.* Thomas E. Kinney. Available from ASIS.

*From Print to Electronic: The Transformation of Scientific Communication.* Susan Y. Crawford, Julie M. Hurd, and Ann C. Weller. Available from Information Today, 143 Old Marlton Pike, Medford, NJ 08055.

*Historical Studies in Information Science.* Eds. Trudi Bellardo Hahn and Michael Buckland. Available from Information Today, 143 Old Marlton Pike, Medford, NJ 08055.

*Information Management for the Intelligent Organization: The Art of Environmental Scanning.* Chun Wei Choo. Available from ASIS.

*Interfaces for Information Retrieval and Online Systems: The State of the Art.* Ed. Martin Dillon. Available from Greenwood Press, 88 Post Rd. W., Westport, CT 06881.

*Journal of the American Society for Information Science.* Available from John Wiley and Sons, 605 Third Ave., New York, NY 10016.

*Proceedings of the ASIS Annual Meetings.* Available from Information Today, 143 Old Marlton Pike, Medford, NJ 08055.

*Scholarly Publishing: The Electronic Frontier.* Eds. Robin P. Peek and Gregory B. Newby. Available from MIT Press, Cambridge, Massachusetts.

*Studies in Multimedia.* Eds. Susan Stone and Michael Buckland. Based on the Proceedings of the 1991 ASIS Mid-Year Meeting. Available from Information Today, 143 Old Marlton Pike, Medford, NJ 08055.

## Committee Chairpersons

Awards and Honors. Jay Trolley.

Budget and Finance. George Ryerson.

Constitution and Bylaws. Shirley Lincicum.

Education. Beth Logan.

Membership. Roberta Horowitz.

Standards. Kurt Kopp.

# American Theological Library Association

820 Church St., Suite 400, Evanston, IL 60201-5613
880-665-2852, 847-869-7788, fax 847-869-8513
E-mail atla@atla.com; World Wide Web http://www.atla.com

## Object

To bring its members into close working relationships with each other, to support theological and religious librarianship, to improve theological libraries, and to interpret the role of such libraries in theological education, developing and implementing standards of library service, promoting research and experimental projects, encouraging cooperative programs that make resources more available, publishing and disseminating literature and research tools and aids, cooperating with organizations having similar aims, and otherwise supporting and aiding theological education. Founded 1946.

## Membership

Memb. (Inst.) 240; (Indiv.) 550. Membership is open to persons engaged in professional library or bibliographical work in theological or religious fields and others who are interested in the work of theological librarianship. Dues (Inst.) $75 to $750, based on total library expenditure; (Indiv.) $15 to $150, based on salary scale. Year. Sept. 1–Aug. 31.

## Officers

*Pres.* Milton J. (Joe) Coalter, Ernest Miller White Lib., Louisville Presbyterian Theological Seminary, 1044 Alta Vista Rd., Louisville, KY 40205. Tel. 502-894-3411 ext. 471, e-mail jcoalter@lpts.edu.; *V.P.* Dorothy G. Thomason, Union Theological Seminary in Virginia, 3401 Brok Rd., Richmond, VA 23227. Tel. 804-278-4314, fax 804-278-4375, e-mail thomason@utsva.edu; *Secy.* Christopher Brennan, Ambrose Swasey Lib.,

Colgate Rochester Divinity School, 1100 S. Goodman St., Rochester, NY 14620. Tel. 716-271-1320, fax 716-271-2166, e-mail crbn@uhura.cc.rochester.edu.

## Board of Directors

Officers; Cass Armstrong, Michael P. Boddy, Christoper P. Brennan, Bruce Eldevik, D. William Faupel, M. Patrick Graham, Bill Hook, Alan D. Krieger, Melody Mazuk, Eileen K. Saner, *Exec. Dir.* Dennis A. Norlin; *Dir. of Finance* To be appointed; *Dir. of Member Services* Karen L. Whittlesey.

## Publications

ATLA Indexes in MARC Format (semi-ann.).
ATLA Religion database on CD-ROM, 1949–.
Biblical Studies on CD-ROM (ann.).
Catholic Periodical and Literature Index on CD-ROM (ann.).
*Index to Book Reviews in Religion* (ann.).
*Newsletter* (q.; memb.; nonmemb. $45). *Ed.* Margaret Tacke.
Old Testment Abstracts on CD-ROM (ann.).
*Proceedings* (ann.; memb.; nonmemb. $40). *Ed.* Margaret Tacke.
*Religion Index One: Periodicals* (semi-ann.).
*Religion Index Two: Multi-Author Works* (ann.).
Religion Indexes: RIO/RIT/IBRR 1975– on CD-ROM.
*Research in Ministry: An Index to Doctor of Ministry Project Reports* (ann.).
South African Theological Bibliography on CD-ROM (ann.).
Zeitschrifteninhaltsdienst Theologie on CD-ROM (ann.).

## Committee Chairpersons and Other Officials

Annual Conference. Christine Wenderoth.
Archivist. Boyd Reese.
Collection Evaluation and Development. Andrew Kadel.
College and University. Elizabeth Leahy.
Education. James Pakala.
Judaica. Suzanne Smailes.
NISO Representative. Myron Chace.

Nominating. David Bundy.
OCLC Theological User Group. Linda Umoh.
Online Reference Resource. Charles Willard.
Oral History. Alice Kendrick.
Preservation. Myron Chace.
Public Services. Anne Womack.
Publication. William Miller.
Special Collections. Andrea Lamb.
Technical Services. Lynn Berg.
Technology. William Hook.
World Christianity. Paul Staehrenberg.

# Archivists and Librarians in the History of the Health Sciences

President, Elaine M. Challacombe
Curator, Owen H. Wangensteen
Historical Library of Biology and Medicine
University of Minnesota
568 Diehl Hall, 505 Essex St. S.E., Minneapolis, MN 55455
612-626-6881

## Object

This association is established exclusively for educational purposes to serve the professional interests of librarians, archivists, and other specialists actively engaged in the librarianship of the history of the health sciences by promoting the exchange of information and by improving the standards of service.

## Membership

Memb. (Voting) 200. Dues $15, membs.; outside U.S. and Canada, $16.

## Officers (May 1998–May 2000)

*Pres.* Elaine M. Challacombe, Curator, Owen H. Wangensteen Historical Lib. of Biology and Medicine, Univ. of Minnesota, 568 Diehl Hall, 505 Essex St. S.E., Minneapolis, MN 55455. Tel. 612-626-6881, fax 612-626-2454, e-mail e-chal@tc.umn.edu; *Secy.-Treas.* Elizabeth Ihrig, Bakken Lib. of Electricity, 3537 Zenith Ave. S., Minneapolis, MN 55416. Tel. 612-927-6508, e-mail ihrig@bakkenmuseum.org.

## Publication

*Watermark* (q.; memb.; nonmemb. $16). *Ed.* Lilli Sentz, New York Academy of Medicine, 1216 Fifth Ave., New York, NY 10029-5293. Tel. 212-822-7313, e-mail Isentz@nyam.org.

# ARMA International
## (Association of Records Managers and Administrators)

Executive Director/CEO, Peter R. Hermann, CAE
4200 Somerset Dr., Suite 215, Prairie Village, KS 66208
800-422-2762, 913-341-3808, fax 913-341-3742
E-mail phermann@arma.org, World Wide Web http://www.arma.org/hq

## Object

To advance the practice of records and information management as a discipline and a profession; to organize and promote programs of research, education, training, and networking within that profession; to support the enhancement of professionalism of the membership; and to promote cooperative endeavors with related professional groups.

## Membership

Membership application is available through ARMA headquarters. Annual dues are $100 for international affiliation. Chapter dues vary from city to city. Membership categories are chapter member ($100 plus chapter dues), student member ($15), and unaffiliated member.

## Officers (1998–1999)

*Pres.* Christine M. Ardern, Canadian Imperial Bank of Commerce, Commerce Ct. N., Seventh flr., Toronto, ON M5L 1A2, Canada. Tel. 416-980-7966, fax 416-861-3666, e-mail ardern@CIBC.CA. *Immediate Past Pres. and Chair of the Board* Robert Nawrucki, 10287 Cedar Ridge Dr., Manassas, VA 22110. Tel. 703-361-3879, fax 703-257-5459; *Pres.-Elect* Tad C. Howington, Lower Colorado River Authority, 3701 Lake Austin Blvd., Austin, TX 78703. Tel. 512-473-4047, fax 512-473-3561, e-mail thowing@lcra.org; *Treas.* Juanita M. Skillman, Fremont Comp., 500 N. Brand Blvd., Suite 1150, Glendale, CA 91203-3392. Tel. 818-552-3860, fax 818-549-4568; *Region Directors* Region I, H. Larry Eiring; Region II, Timothy W. Hughes; Region III, Jack R. Ingle; Region IV, Cheryl L. Pederson; Region V, Susan A. Hubbard; Region VI, Terrence J. Coan; Region VII, Paul J. Singleton; Region VIII, Gisele L. Crawford; Region IX, Rosalie C. Stremple; Region X, David P. McDermott; Region XI, Phyllis W. Parker; Region XII, Hella Jean Bartolo.

## Publication

*Information Management Journal.* Ed. J. Michael Pemberton, Assoc. Professor, School of Info. Sciences, Univ. of Tennessee at Knoxville, 804 Volunteer Blvd., Knoxville, TN 37996-4330, e-mail jpembert@utkux.utcc.utk.edu.

## Committee Chairpersons

Awards. Christine M. Ardern, Canadian Imperial Bank of Commerce, Commerce Ct. N., Seventh flr., Toronto, ON M5L 1A2, Canada. Tel. 416-980-7966, fax 416-861-3666.

Canadian Legislative and Regulatory Affairs (CLARA). Raphael Thierrin, 4515 45 St. S.W., Calgary, AB T3E 6K7. Tel. 403-686-3310, fax 403-686-0075.

Education Development. Carol E. B. Choksy, IRAD Strategic Consulting, Inc., 4103 Golden Grove Rd., Greenwood, IN 46143. Tel. 317-535-7117, fax 317-535-7784.

Financial Planning. Juanita M. Skillman, Fremont Comp., 500 N. Brand Blvd., Suite 1150, Glendale, CA 91203-3392. Tel. 818-552-3860, fax 818-549-4568.

Industry Specific Program. Nyoakee B. Salway, Occidental Petroleum Corp. 10889 Wilshire Blvd., Suite 920, Los Angeles, CA 90024. Tel. 310-443-6219, fax 310-443-6340.

Electronic Records Management. Robert Meagher, CONDOR Consulting, Inc., 130 Albert St., Suite 419, Ottawa, ON K1P 5G4, Canada. Tel. 613-233-4962 ext. 23, fax 613-233-4249.
International Relations. Hella Jean Bartolo, Sunshine House, 60 Stella Maris St., Silema SLM12, Malta. Tel. 35-624-7480, fax 35-624-3051, e-mail hella@waldonet. net.mt.
Publications Coordination. Jean K. Brown, Univ. Archives, Univ. of Delaware, Pear-

son Hall, Newark, DE 19716. Tel. 302-831-2750, fax 302-831-6903.
Strategic Planning. Tad C. Howington, Lower Colorado River Authority, 3701 Lake Austin Blvd., Austin, TX 78703. Tel. 512-473-4047, fax 512-473-3561.
U.S. Government Relations. Keith C. S. Siu, 5285 Kilauea Ave., Honolulu, HI 96816-5612. Tel. 808-734-7056, fax 808-538-5309.

# Art Libraries Society of North America

Executive Director, Ashley Prather
4101 Lake Boone Trail, Suite 201
Raleigh, NC 27607-7506
800-892-7547, 919-787-5181, fax 919-787-4916
E-mail arlisna@olsonmgmt.com, World Wide Web http://www.lib.duke.edu/lilly/arlis

## Object

To foster excellence in art librarianship and visual resources curatorship for the advancement of the visual arts. Established 1972.

## Membership

Memb. 1,325. Dues (Inst.) $1,000; (Indiv.) $65; (Business Affiliate) $100; (Student) $40; (Retired/ Unemployed) $50; (Sustaining) $250; (Sponsor) $500; (Overseas) basic plus $25. Year. Jan. 1–Dec. 31. Membership is open and encouraged for all those interested in visual librarianship, whether they be professional librarians, students, library assistants, art book publishers, art book dealers, art historians, archivists, architects, slide and photograph curators, or retired associates in these fields.

## Officers (1998–1999)

*Pres.* Mary E. Graham, Arizona State Museum Lib., Univ. of Arizona, Tucson, AZ 85721-0026. Tel. 520-621-4695, fax 520-621-2976, e-mail megraham@u.arizona.edu;

*V.P./Pres.-Elect* Kathryn M. Wayne, Fine Arts Libn., 308F Doe Lib., Univ. of California, Berkeley, CA 94720. Tel. 510-643-2809, fax 510-643-2155, e-mail kwayne@library. bereley.edu; *Past Pres.* Roger Lawson, National Gallery of Art Lib., Sixth St. and Constitution Ave. N.W., Washington, DC 20565. Tel. 202-842-6529, fax 202-408-8530, e-mail r-lawson@nga.gov; *Secy.* Jeanne Brown, Architecture Studies Lib., Univ. of Nevada–Las Vegas, Box 45-4049, Las Vegas, NV 89154-4049. Tel. 702-895-4369, fax 702-895-1975, e-mail jeanneb@nevada.edu; *Treas.* Katharine R. (Kitty) Chibnik, Avery Architectural and Fine Arts Lib., Columbia Univ., 1172 Amsterdam Ave., Mail Code 0301, New York, NY 10027. Tel. 212-854-3506, fax 212-854-8904, e-mail chibnik@ columbia.edu.

Address correspondence to the executive director.

## Executive Board

Officers; *Regional Reps.* (Northeast) Margaret N. Webster, (South) Lee R. Sorenson, (Midwest) Jane A. Carlin, (West) Lorna Corbetta-Noyes, (Canada) Marilyn Berger.

## Publications

*ARLIS/NA Update* (bi-m.; memb.).
*Art Documentation* (semi-ann.; memb., subsc.).
*Handbook and List of Members* (ann.; memb.).
Occasional Papers (price varies).
Miscellaneous others (request current list from headquarters).

## Committees

Awards.
Cataloging (Advisory).
Collection Development.
Conference.
Development.
Diversity.
Finance.
International Relations.
Membership.
Gerd Muehsam Award.

Nominating.
North American Relations.
Professional Development.
Public Policy.
Publications.
Research.
Standards.
Technology Education.
Technology Relations.
Travel Awards.
George Wittenborn Award.

## Chapters

Arizona; Canada (National); Central Plains; D.C.-Maryland-Virginia; Delaware Valley; Michigan; Midstates; Montreal-Ottawa-Quebec; Mountain West; New England; New Jersey; New York; Northern California; Northwest; Ohio Valley; Ontario; Southeast; Southern California; Texas; Twin Cities; Western New York.

# Asian/Pacific American Librarians Association

President, Soon J. Jung
Head of Cataloging, Newport Beach Public Library
1000 Avocado Ave., Newport Beach, CA 92660
Tel. 714-717-3824, fax 714-640-5681
E-mail sjung@city.newport-beach.ca.us.

## Object

To provide a forum for discussing problems and concerns of Asian/Pacific American librarians; to provide a forum for the exchange of ideas by Asian/Pacific American librarians and other librarians; to support and encourage library services to Asian/Pacific American communities; to recruit and support Asian/Pacific American librarians in the library/information science professions; to seek funding for scholarships in library/information science programs for Asian/Pacific Americans; and to provide a vehicle whereby Asian/Pacific American librarians can cooperate with other associations and organizations having similar or allied interests.

Founded 1980; incorporated 1981; affiliated with the American Library Association 1982.

## Membership

Open to all librarians and information specialists of Asian/Pacific descent working in U.S. libraries and information centers and other related organizations and to others who support the goals and purposes of APALA. Asian/Pacific Americans are defined as those who consider themselves Asian/Pacific Americans. They may be Americans of Asian/Pacific descent, Asian/Pacific people with the status of permanent residency, or Asian/Pacific people living in the United

States. Dues (Inst.) $25; (Indiv.) $10; (Students/Unemployed Librarians) $5.

## Officers (July 1998–June 1999)

*Pres.* Soon J. Jung, Head of Cataloging, Newport Beach Public Lib., 1000 Avocado Ave., Newport Beach, CA 92660. Tel. 714-717-3824, fax 714-640-5681, e-mail sjung@city.newport-beach.ca.us. *V.P./Pres.-Elect* Patricia Mei-Yung Wong, Supervising Libn., South Branch, Berkeley Public Lib., 1901 Russell St., Berkeley, CA 94703. Tel. 510-644-6860, fax 510-549-3054, e-mail kaiming@ix.netcom.com; *Past Pres.* Abdulfazal M. Fazle Kabir, Associate Professor, School of Lib. and Info. Studies, Clark Atlanta Univ., 223 James P. Brawley Dr. S.W., Atlanta, GA 30314-4391. Tel. 404-880-8701, fax 404-880-8977, e-mail akabir@cau.edu; *Secy.* Tokiko Yamamoto Bazzell, 7525 Muolea Pl., Honolulu, HI 96825. Tel. 808-395-6279, e-mail tbazzell@capaccess.org; *Treas.* Rama Vishwanatham, Lib. of the Health Sciences M/C 763, 1750 Polk St., Chicago, IL 60612. Tel. 312-996-8993, fax 312-996-1899, e-mail rama@uic.edu.

## Publication

*APALA Newsletter* (q.). *Ed.* Sandra Yamate, Polychrome Publishing Corp., 4509 N. Francisco Ave., Chicago, IL 60625. Tel. 773-478-4455, fax 773-478-0786.

## Committee Chairpersons

Constitution and Bylaws. Lourdes Collantes.
Membership and Recruitment. Katherine Wong.
Newsletter and Publications. Sandra Yamate.
Nominations. Abulfazal M. F. Kabir.
Program and Local Arrangement. Patricia Mei-Yung Wong.

# Association for Information and Image Management

President, John F. Mancini
1100 Wayne Ave., Suite 1100, Silver Spring, MD 20910
301-587-8202, fax 301-587-2711
E-mail aiim@aiim.org, World Wide Web http://www.aiim.org

## Object

The mission of the Association for Information and Image Management is to be the leading global association bringing together the users of document technologies with the providers of that technology. Our focus is on helping corporate and institutional users understand these technologies and how they can be applied to improve critical business processes.

## Officers

*Chair* David S. Silver, Kofax Image Products, 3 Jenner St., Irvine, CA 92618. *V. Chair* John A. O'Connell, Staffware PLC, Staffware House, 3 The Switchback, Gardener Rd., Maidenhead, Berkshire SL6 7RJ, United Kingdom; *Treas.* Robert F. Smallwood, IMERGE Consulting, 201 St. Charles Ave., Suite 2511, New Orleans, LA 70170.

## Publication

*INFORM* (10 per year; memb.). *Ed.* Bryant Duhon.

# Association for Library and Information Science Education

Executive Director, Sharon J. Rogers
Box 7640, Arlington, VA 22207
703-243-8040, fax 703-243-4551, e-mail sroger7@ibm.net
World Wide Web http://www.alise.org

## Object

The Association for Library and Information Science Education (ALISE) is an association devoted to the advancement of knowledge and learning in the interdisciplinary field of information studies. Established 1915.

## Membership

Memb. 500. Dues (Inst.) for ALA-accredited programs, sliding scale; (International Affiliate Inst.) $125; (Indiv.) $90 or $50. Year. July–June. Any library/information science school with a program accredited by the ALA Committee on Accreditation may become an institutional member. Any school that offers a graduate degree in librarianship or a cognate field but whose program is not accredited by the ALA Committee on Accreditation may become an institutional member at the lower rate. Any school outside the United States and Canada offering a program comparable to that of institutional membership may become an international affiliate institutional member. Any faculty member, administrator, librarian, researcher, or other individual employed full time may become a personal member. Any retired or part-time faculty member, student, or other individual employed less than full time may become a personal member at the lower rate.

## Officers (1998–1999)

*Pres.* Shirley Fitzgibbons, Indiana Univ. E-mail Fitzgibbons@indiana.edu; *Past Pres.* Toni Carbo, Univ. of Pittsburgh. E-mail carbo@sis.pitt.edu; *Secy.-Treas.* Lynne C. Howarth, Univ. of Toronto. E-mail howarth @fis.toronto.edu.

## Directors

Officers; Carol Kuhlthau, Rutgers Univ. (2000). E-mail kuhlthau@scils.rutgers.edu; Danny P. Wallace, Kent State Univ. E-mail wallace@slis.kent.edu; Louis S. Robbins, Univ. of Wisconsin–Madison. E-mail LRobbins@ macc.wisc.edu; *Co-Eds.* Joseph Mika (2001), Wayne State Univ. E-mail jmika@cms.cc. wayne.edu; Ronald W. Powell (2001), Wayne State Univ. E-mail rpowell@cms.cc. wayne.edu; *Exec. Dir.* Sharon J. Rogers. E-mail Sroger7@ibm.net; *Parliamentarian* Norman Horrocks.

## Publications

*ALISE Library and Information Science Education Statistical Report* (ann.; $65).
*Journal of Education for Library and Information Science* (4 per year; $78; foreign $88).
*Membership Directory* (ann.; $55).

## Committee Chairpersons

Awards and Honors. Fred Roper, South Carolina Univ.
Conference Planning. Toni Carbo, Univ. of Pittsburgh.
Editorial Board. Ann Prentice, Univ. of Maryland.
Government Relations. Ann Prentice, Univ. of Maryland.
International Relations. Blanche Woolls, San Jose State Univ.
LIS Education Statistical Report Project. Evelyn Daniel and Jerry Saye, Univ. of North Carolina.
Membership. Ken Haycock, Univ. of British Columbia.
Nominating. Charles Curran, South Carolina Univ.

Organization and Bylaws. Norman Horrocks, Dalhousie Univ.

Recruitment. Ling Hwey Jen, Univ. of Kentucky.

Research. M. Della Neumann, Univ. of Maryland.

Tellers. Sibyl Moses, Catholic Univ.

# Association of Academic Health Sciences Libraries

2150 N. 107, Suite 205, Seattle, WA 98133
206-367-8704, fax 206-367-8777
E-mail sbinc@halcyon.com

## Object

To promote—in cooperation with educational institutions, other educational associations, government agencies, and other nonprofit organizations—the common interests of academic health sciences libraries located in the United States and elsewhere, through publications, research, and discussion of problems of mutual interest and concern, and to advance the efficient and effective operation of academic health sciences libraries for the benefit of faculty, students, administrators, and practitioners.

## Membership

Memb. 135. Dues $500. Regular membership is available to nonprofit educational institutions operating a school of health sciences that has full or provisional accreditation by the Association of American Medical Colleges. Regular members shall be represented by the chief administrative officer of the member institution's health sciences library. Associate membership (and nonvoting representation) is available at $200 to organizations having an interest in the purposes and activities of the association.

# Association of Jewish Libraries

15 E. 26 St., Rm. 1034, New York, NY 10010
212-725-5359, fax 212-678-8998

## Object

To promote the improvement of library services and professional standards in all Jewish libraries and collections of Judaica; to serve as a center of dissemination of Jewish library information and guidance; to encourage the establishment of Jewish libraries and collections of Judaica; to promote publication of literature that will be of assistance to Jewish librarianship; and to encourage people to enter the field of librarianship. Organized in 1965 from the merger of the Jewish Librarians Association and the Jewish Library Association.

## Membership

Memb. 1,100. Dues $35; (Foreign) $60; (Student/Retired) $25; Year. July 1–June 30.

## Officers (June 1998–June 2000)

*Pres.* David Gilner, Hebrew Union College, 3101 Clifton Ave., Cincinnati, OH 45220; *Past Pres.* Esther Nussbaum, Ramaz Upper School Lib., 60 E. 78 St., New York, NY 10021; *V.P./Pres.-Elect* Toby Rossner, Bureau of Jewish Education of Rhode Island,

130 Sessions St., Providence, RI 02906; *V.P., Memb.* Shoshanah Seidman, 9056 Tamaroa Terrace, Skokie, IL 60076; *Treas.* Leah Adler, Yeshiva Univ., 500 W. 185 St., New York, NY 10033; *Recording Secy.* Frances Wolf, Congregation Beth Shalom, 9400 Wornall Rd., Kansas City, MO 64114; *Corresponding Secy.* Elizabeth Stabler, 92nd St. YM-YWHA, 1395 Lexington Ave., New York, NY 10128; *Publications V.P.* Laurel S. Wolfson, Hebrew Union College, 3101 Clifton Ave., Cincinnati, OH 45220.

Address correspondence to the association.

## Publications

*AJL Newsletter* (q.). *General Ed.* Nancy Sack, Northwestern Univ. Lib., 1935 Sheridan Rd., Evanston, IL 60208.
*Judaica Librarianship* (irreg.). *Ed.* Bella Hass Weinberg, Div. of Lib. and Info. Science, Saint John's Univ., 8000 Utopia Pkwy., Jamaica, NY 11439.

## Division Presidents

Research and Special Library. Rick Burke.
Synagogue, School, and Center Libraries. Cheryl Banks.

# Association of Research Libraries

Executive Director, Duane E. Webster
21 Dupont Circle N.W., Suite 800, Washington, DC 20036
202-296-2296, fax 202-872-0884
E-mail arlhq@arl.org, World Wide Web http://www.arl.org

## Object

The mission of the Association of Research Libraries (ARL) is to shape and influence forces affecting the future of research libraries in the process of scholarly communication. ARL's programs and services promote equitable access to and effective use of recorded knowledge in support of teaching, research, scholarship, and community service. The association articulates the concerns of research libraries and their institutions, forges coalitions, influences information policy development, and supports innovation and improvement in research library operations. ARL is a not-for-profit membership organization comprising the libraries of North American research institutions and operates as a forum for the exchange of ideas and as an agent for collective action.

## Membership

Memb. 122. Membership is institutional. Dues $15,550.

## Officers (Oct. 1998–Oct. 1999)

*Pres.* Betty Bengtson, Univ. of Washington; *Past Pres.* James Neal, Dir. of Libs., Johns Hopkins Univ.; *Pres.-Elect* Ken Frazier, Dir. of Libs., Univ. of Wisconsin.

## Board of Directors

Shirley K. Baker, Washington Univ. (St. Louis); Betty G. Bengtson, Univ. of Washington; Scott Bennett, Yale Univ.; Meredith Butler, SUNY–Albany; Kenneth Frazier, Univ. of Wisconsin; Joseph A. Hewitt, Univ. of North Carolina; Paula Kaufmann, Univ. of Tennesee; James G. Neal, Johns Hopkins Univ.; William G. Potter, Univ. of Georgia; Carolynne Pressar, Univ. of Manitoba; Carla Stoffle, Univ. of Arizona.

## Publications

*ARL: A Bimonthly Newsletter of Research Li-*

*braries Issues and Actions* (bi-m.; memb. $25; nonmemb. $50).

*ARL Academic Law and Medical Library Statistics* (ann.; memb. $35; nonmemb. $65).

*ARL Annual Salary Survey* (ann.; memb. $35; nonmemb. $65).

*ARL Preservation Statistics* (ann.; memb. $35; nonmemb. $65).

*ARL Statistics* (ann.; memb. $35; nonmemb. $65).

*Developing Indicators for Academic Library Performance: Ratios from the ARL Statistics 1993–94 and 1994–95* (ann.; memb. $25; nonmemb. $50).

*Leading Ideas* (bi-m.; $35)

*Proceedings of the ARL Membership Meetings* (2 per yr.; memb. $45; nonmemb. $70).

*Systems and Procedures Exchange Center (SPEC): Kits and Flyers* (10 per year; kits memb. $185, nonmemb. $280; flyers $50).

# Committee and Work Group Chairpersons

Access to Information Resources. Shirley Baker, Washington Univ., St. Louis.

Copyright Issues (Working Group). James G. Neal, Johns Hopkins Univ.

Diversity. Nancy Baker, Washington State Univ.

Information Policies. Fred Heath, Texas A&M Univ.

Leadership and Management of Research Library Resources. Paul Kobulnicky, Univ. of Connecticut.

Preservation of Research Library Materials. Meredith Butler, SUNY Albany.

Research Collections. Joe A. Hewitt, Univ. of North Carolina at Chapel Hill.

Scholarly Communication. Elaine F. Sloan, Columbia Univ.

SPARC (Working Group). Kenneth Frazier, Univ. of Wisconsin.

Statistics and Measurement. William J. Studer, Ohio State Univ.

# ARL Membership

## Nonuniversity Libraries

Boston Public Lib., Canada Inst. for Scientific and Technical Info., Center for Research Libs., Linda Hall Lib., Lib. of Congress, National Agricultural Lib., National Lib. of Canada, National Lib. of Medicine, New York Public Lib., New York State Lib., Smithsonian Institution Libs.

## University Libraries

Alabama, Alberta, Arizona, Arizona State, Auburn, Boston, Brigham Young, British Columbia, Brown, California (Berkeley), California (Davis), California (Irvine), California (Los Angeles), California (Riverside), California (San Diego), California (Santa Barbara), Case Western Reserve, Chicago, Cincinnati, Colorado, Colorado State, Columbia, Connecticut, Cornell, Dartmouth, Delaware, Duke, Emory, Florida, Florida State, Georgetown, Georgia, Georgia Inst. of Technology, Guelph, Harvard, Hawaii, Houston, Howard, Illinois (Chicago), Illinois (Urbana), Indiana, Iowa, Iowa State, Johns Hopkins, Kansas, Kent State, Kentucky, Laval, Louisiana State, McGill, McMaster, Manitoba, Maryland, Massachusetts, Massachusetts Inst. of Technology, Miami (Florida), Michigan, Michigan State, Minnesota, Missouri, Nebraska (Lincoln), New Mexico, New York, North Carolina, North Carolina State, Northwestern, Notre Dame, Ohio, Ohio State, Oklahoma, Oklahoma State, Oregon, Pennsylvania, Pennsylvania State, Pittsburgh, Princeton, Purdue, Queen's (Kingston, ON, Canada), Rice, Rochester, Rutgers, Saskatchewan, South Carolina, Southern California, Southern Illinois, Stanford, SUNY (Albany), SUNY (Buffalo), SUNY (Stony Brook), Syracuse, Temple, Tennessee, Texas, Texas A&M, Texas Tech, Toronto, Tulane, Utah, Vanderbilt, Virginia, Virginia Polytechnic, George Washington, Washington, Washington (St. Louis, Mo.), Washington State, Waterloo, Wayne State, Western Ontario, Wisconsin, Yale, York.

# Association of Vision Science Librarians

Chair, Judith Schaeffer Young, Wills Eye Hospital, Medical Lib., 900 Walnut St.,
Philadelphia, PA 19107
215-928-3288, e-mail young@hslc.org

## Object

To foster collective and individual acquisition and dissemination of vision science information, to improve services for all persons seeking such information, and to develop standards for libraries to which members are attached. Founded 1968.

## Membership

Memb. (U.S.) 60; (Foreign) 15.

## Publications

*Guidelines for Vision Science Libraries.*
*Opening Day Book Collection–Visual Science.*
*Ph.D. Theses in Physiological Optics* (irreg.).
*Standards for Vision Science Libraries.*
*Union List of Vision-Related Serials* (irreg.).

## Meetings

Annual meeting held in December in connection with the American Academy of Optometry; midyear mini-meeting with the Medical Library Association.

# Beta Phi Mu
# (International Library and Information Studies Honor Society)

Executive Director, F. William Summers
School of Information Studies, Florida State University,
Tallahassee, FL 32306-2100
850-644-3907, fax 850-644-6253
E-mail beta_phi_mu@lis.fsu.edu

## Object

To recognize high scholarship in the study of librarianship and to sponsor appropriate professional and scholarly projects. Founded at the University of Illinois in 1948.

## Membership

Memb. 23,000. Open to graduates of library school programs accredited by the American Library Association who fulfill the following requirements: complete the course requirements leading to a fifth year or other advanced degree in librarianship with a scholastic average of 3.75 where A equals 4 points (this provision shall also apply to planned programs of advanced study beyond the fifth year that do not culminate in a degree but that require full-time study for one or more academic years) and in the top 25 percent of their class; receive a letter of recommendation from their respective library schools attesting to their demonstrated fitness for successful professional careers.

## Officers

*Pres.* Marion T. Reid, Dean of Lib. Services, California State Univ. at San Marcos, 820 Los Vallecitos Blvd., San Marcos, CA 92096-0001. Tel. 619-750-4330, fax 619-750-3287, e-mail mreid@mailhost1.csusm.edu; *V.P./ Pres.-Elect* Barbara Immroth, Graduate

School of Lib. and Info. Science, Univ. of Texas at Austin, Austin, TX 78712-1276. Tel. 512-471-3875, fax 512-471-3971, e-mail immroth@uts.cc.utexas.edu; *Past Pres.* Elfreda A. Chatman, School of Info. Studies, Florida State Univ., Tallahassee, FL 32306-2100. Tel. 850-644-8104, fax 850-644-6253, e-mail chatman@lis.fsu.edu; *Treas.* Sondra Taylor-Furbee, State Lib. of Florida, 500 S. Bronough St., Tallahassee, FL 32399; *Exec. Dir.* F. William Summers, School of Info. Studies, Florida State Univ., Tallahassee, FL 32306-2100. Tel. 850-644-8111, fax 850-644-6253, e-mail Beta_Phi_Mu@lis.fsu.edu.

## Directors

Lois Pausch (1999), Onva K. Boshears (1999), Anna Perrault (2000), Jane Robbins (2000), *Dir.-at-Large* Emily Melton (2000).

## Publications

Beta Phi Mu Monograph Series. Book-length scholarly works based on original research in subjects of interest to library and information professionals. Available from Greenwood Press, 88 Post Rd. W., Box 5007, Westport, CT 06881-9990.

Chapbook Series. Limited editions on topics of interest to information professionals. Call Beta Phi Mu for availability.

*Newsletter.* (2 per year). *Ed.* Mary Upshaw Rhodes.

## Chapters

*Alpha.* Univ. of Illinois, Grad. School of Lib. and Info. Science, Urbana, IL 61801; *Beta.* (Inactive). Univ. of Southern California, School of Lib. Science, Univ. Park, Los Angeles, CA 90007; *Gamma.* Florida State Univ., School of Lib. and Info. Studies, Tallahassee, FL 32306; *Delta* (Inactive). Loughborough College of Further Education, School of Libnshp, Loughborough, England; *Epsilon.* Univ. of North Carolina, School of Lib. Science, Chapel Hill, NC 27599; *Zeta.* Atlanta Univ., School of Lib. and Info. Studies, Atlanta, GA 30314; *Theta.* Pratt Inst., Grad.

School of Lib. and Info. Science, Brooklyn, NY 11205; *Iota.* Catholic Univ. of America, School of Lib. and Info. Science, Washington, DC 20064; Univ. of Maryland, College of Lib. and Info. Services, College Park, MD 20742; *Kappa.* (Inactive). Western Michigan Univ., School of Libnshp., Kalamazoo, MI 49008; *Lambda.* Univ. of Oklahoma, School of Lib. Science, Norman, OK 73019; *Mu.* Univ. of Michigan, School of Lib. Science, Ann Arbor, MI 48109; *Nu.* (Inactive); *Xi.* Univ. of Hawaii, Grad. School of Lib. Studies, Honolulu, HI 96822; *Omicron.* Rutgers Univ., Grad. School of Lib. and Info. Studies, New Brunswick, NJ 08903; *Pi.* Univ. of Pittsburgh, School of Lib. and Info. Science, Pittsburgh, PA 15260; *Rho.* Kent State Univ., School of Lib. Science, Kent, OH 44242; *Sigma.* Drexel Univ., School of Lib. and Info. Science, Philadelphia, PA 19104; *Tau.* (Inactive). State Univ. of New York at Geneseo, School of Lib. and Info. Science, Geneseo, NY 14454; *Upsilon.* (Inactive). Univ. of Kentucky, College of Lib. Science, Lexington, KY 40506; *Phi.* Univ. of Denver, Grad. School of Libnshp. and Info. Mgt., Denver, CO 80208; *Chi.* Indiana Univ., School of Lib. and Info. Science, Bloomington, IN 47401; *Psi.* Univ. of Missouri at Columbia, School of Lib. and Info. Sciences, Columbia, MO 65211; *Omega.* (Inactive). San Jose State Univ., Div. of Lib. Science, San Jose, CA 95192; *Beta Alpha.* Queens College, City College of New York, Grad. School of Lib. and Info. Studies, Flushing, NY 11367; *Beta Beta.* Simmons College, Grad. School of Lib. and Info. Science, Boston, MA 02115; *Beta Delta.* State Univ. of New York at Buffalo, School of Info. and Lib. Studies, Buffalo, NY 14260; *Beta Epsilon.* Emporia State Univ., School of Lib. Science, Emporia, KS 66801; *Beta Zeta.* Louisiana State Univ., Grad. School of Lib. Science, Baton Rouge, LA 70803; *Beta Eta.* Univ. of Texas at Austin, Grad. School of Lib. and Info. Science, Austin, TX 78712; *Beta Theta.* (Inactive). Brigham Young Univ., School of Lib. and Info. Science, Provo, UT 84602; *Beta Iota.* Univ. of Rhode Island, Grad. Lib. School, Kingston, RI 02881; *Beta Kappa.* Univ. of Alabama, Grad. School of Lib. Service, University, AL 35486; *Beta Lambda.* North

Texas State Univ., School of Lib. and Info. Science, Denton, TX 76203; Texas Woman's Univ., School of Lib. Science, Denton, TX 76204; *Beta Mu.* Long Island Univ., Palmer Grad. Lib. School, C. W. Post Center, Greenvale, NY 11548; *Beta Nu.* Saint John's Univ., Div. of Lib. and Info. Science, Jamaica, NY 11439. *Beta Xi.* North Carolina Central Univ., School of Lib. Science, Durham, NC 27707; *Beta Omicron.* (Inactive). Univ. of Tennessee at Knoxville, Grad. School of Lib. and Info. Science, Knoxville, TN 37916; *Beta Pi.* Univ. of Arizona, Grad. Lib. School, Tucson, AZ 85721; *Beta Rho.* Univ. of Wisconsin at Milwaukee, School of Lib. Science, Milwaukee, WI 53201; *Beta Sigma.* (Inactive). Clarion State College, School of Lib. Science, Clarion, PA 16214; *Beta Tau.* Wayne State Univ., Div. of Lib. Science, Detroit, MI 48202; *Beta Upsilon.* (Inactive). Alabama A & M Univ., School of Lib. Media, Normal, AL 35762; *Beta Phi.* Univ. of South Florida, Grad. Dept. of Lib., Media, and Info. Studies, Tampa, FL 33647; *Beta Psi.* Univ. of Southern Mississippi, School of Lib. Service, Hattiesburg, MS 39406; *Beta Omega.* Univ. of South Carolina, College of Libnshp., Columbia, SC 29208; *Beta Beta Alpha.* Univ. of California at Los Angeles, Grad. School of Lib. and Info. Science, Los Angeles, CA 90024; *Beta Beta Gamma.* Rosary College, Grad. School of Lib. and Info. Science, River Forest, IL 60305; *Beta Beta Delta.* Univ. of Cologne, Germany; *Beta Beta Epsilon.* Univ. of Wisconsin at Madison, Lib. School, Madison, WI 53706; *Beta Beta Zeta.* Univ. of North Carolina at Greensboro, Dept. of Lib. Science and Educational Technology, Greensboro, NC 27412; *Beta Beta Theta.* Univ. of Iowa, School of Lib. and Info. Science, Iowa City, IA 52242; *Beta Beta Iota.* State Univ. of New York, Univ. at Albany, School of Info. Science and Policy, Albany, NY 12222; *Pi Lambda Sigma.* Syracuse Univ., School of Info. Studies, Syracuse, NY 13210.

# Bibliographical Society of America

Executive Secretary, Michèle E. Randall
Box 1537, Lenox Hill Station, New York, NY 10021
212-452-2500, fax 212-452-2710, e-mail bsa@bibsocamer.org
World Wide Web: http://www.cla.sc.edu/engl/bsa

## Object

To promote bibliographical research and to issue bibliographical publications. Organized 1904.

## Membership

Memb. 1,200. Dues $50.

## Officers

*Pres.* Roger E. Stoddard; *V.P.* Hope Mayo; *Treas.* R. Dyke Benjamin; *Secy.* Nancy Burkett.

## Council

T. Anna Lou Ashby (2001), Kimball Brooker (2000), Peter S. Graham (2001), James N. Green (1999), Robert H. Hirst (2000), Trevor Howard-Hill (2000), Leslie Morris (1999), William Reese (2001), Fred Schreiber (1998), Alice Schreyer (1998), William P. Stoneman (2001), Michael Winship (1999), Elizabeth Witherell (2000), David S. Zeidberg (1999).

## Publication

*Papers* (q.; memb.). *Ed.* Trevor Howard-Hill, Dept. of English, Univ. of South Carolina, Columbia, SC 29208. Tel./fax 803-777-7046, e-mail rahayes@vm.sc.edu.

## Committee Chairpersons

Bibliographical Projects. Michael Winship.
Delegate to American Council of Learned

Societies. Marcus McCorison.
Finance. Daniel D. Chabris.
Publications. Anna Lou Ashby, James N. Green.

# Canadian Association for Information Science
# (Association Canadienne des Sciences de l'Information)

140 Saint George St., Toronto, ON M5S 3G6, Canada
416-978-8876

## Object

To bring together individuals and organizations concerned with the production, manipulation, storage, retrieval, and dissemination of information, with emphasis on the application of modern technologies in these areas. The Canadian Association for Information Science (CAIS) is dedicated to enhancing the activity of the information transfer process; utilizing the vehicles of research, development, application, and education; and serving as a forum for dialogue and exchange of ideas concerned with the theory and practice of all factors involved in the communication of information.

## Membership

Institutions and individuals interested in information science and involved in the gathering, organization, and dissemination of information (computer scientists, documentalists, information scientists, librarians, journalists, sociologists, psychologists, linguists, administrators, etc.) can become members of CAIS. Dues (Inst.) $165; (Personal) $75; (Student) $40.

## Publication

*Canadian Journal of Information and Library Science* (q.; $95; outside Canada $110).

# Canadian Library Association

Executive Director, Vicki Whitmell
200 Elgin St., Ottawa, ON K2P 1L5, Canada
613-232-8837, fax 613-563-9895
E-mail Whitmell@istar.ca

## Object

To provide leadership in the promotion, development, and support of library and information services in Canada for the benefit of association members, the profession, and Canadian society. Offers library school scholarship and book awards; carries on international liaison with other library associations; makes representation to government and official commissions; offers professional development programs; and supports intellectual freedom. Founded in 1946, CLA is a nonprofit voluntary organization governed by an elected executive council.

## Membership

Memb. (Indiv.) 4,000; (Inst.) 1,000. Open to individuals, institutions, and groups interested in librarianship and in library and information services. Dues (Indiv.) $175; (Inst.) $300. Year. Anniversary date renewal.

## Officers

*Pres.* Sydney Jones, Dir., Lib. Operations, Metro Toronto Reference Lib., 789 Yonge St., Toronto, ON M4W 2G8. Tel. 416-393-7214, fax 416-393-7229, e-mail syd@mtrl. toronto.on.ca; *V.P./Pres.-Elect* Lorraine McQueen, Univ. Libn., Univ. Lib., Acadia Univ., 50 Acadia St., Wolfville, NS B0P 1X0. Tel. 902-585-1510, fax 905-585-1748, e-mail lorraine.mcqueen@acadia.ca; *Treas.* Ruth Reedman, Libn., Canadian Wheat Board, Box 816, 423 Main St., Winnipeg, MB R3C 2P5. Tel. 204-983-3437, fax 204-983-4031, e-mail ruth_reedman@cwb.ca; *Past Pres.* Paul Whitney, Chief Libn., Burnaby Public Lib., 6100 Willingdon Ave., Burnaby, BC V5H 4N5. Tel 604-436-5431, fax 604-436-2961, e-mail pwhitnea@sfu.ca.

## Publication

*Feliciter* (6 per year; newsletter).

## Division Representatives

Canadian Association of College and University Libraries (CACUL). Melody C. Burton, Head of Access Services, Queen's Univ., Stauffer Lib., Kingston, ON K7L 5C4.

Canadian Association of Public Libraries (CAPL). Wendy J. Newman, Brantford Public Lib. 173 Colborne St., Brantford, ON N3T 2G8. Tel. 519-756-2223, fax 519-756-4979, e-mail wnewman@brantford. library.on.ca.

Canadian Association of Special Libraries and Information Services (CASLIS). Claudette Cloutier, Science Liaison Libn., Univ. of Calgary, MLB 331-C, 2500 University Dr. NW, Calgary, AB T2N 1N4. E-mail cloutier@ucalgary.ca.

Canadian Library Trustees' Association (CLTA). Gary Archibald, Box 2680, R.R. 2, Yarmouth, NS B5A 4A6.

Canadian School Library Association (CSLA). Anne M. Gauer, Concordia Univ., Lib. Studies, 1455 Blvd. de Maissoneuve W., Montreal, PQ H3G 1M8. Tel. 514-848-2453, fax 514-848-4520, e-mail ang@ alcor.concordia.ca.

# Catholic Library Association

Executive Director, Jean R. Bostley, SSJ
100 North St., Suite 224, Pittsfield, MA 01201-5109
413-443-2252, fax 413-442-2252, e-mail cla@vgernet.net
World Wide Web http://www.cathla.org

## Object

The promotion and encouragement of Catholic literature and library work through cooperation, publications, education, and information. Founded 1921.

## Membership

Memb. 1,500. Dues $45–$500. Year. July–June.

## Officers (1997–1999)

*Pres.* Julanne M. Good, St. Louis Public Lib., 5005 Jamieson Ave., St. Louis, MO 63109-3027. Tel. 314-832-2319, e-mail bopeep@ inlink.com; *V.P./Pres.-Elect* Rev. Bonaventure Hayes, OFM, Christ the King Seminary, 711 Knox Rd., East Aurora, NY 1452-0607. Tel. 716-652-8940, fax 716-652-8903.

Address correspondence to the executive director.

## Executive Board

Officers; Nicholas Falco, 1256 Pelham Pkwy., Bronx, NY 10461; Mary E. Gallagher, SSJ, College of Our Lady of the Elms, 291 Springfield St., Chicopee, MA 01013; Barbara Anne Kilpatrick, RSM, Saint Vincent de Paul School, Nashville, TN 37212-4202; Mary Agnes Casey, SSJ, Jersey City Public Lib., Jersey City, NJ 07921; Linda B. Gonzales, Sacred Heart School of Theology, Box 429, Hales Corners, WI 53130-0429; Sally Anne Thompson, Orangedale School Lib., 7015 E. San Miguel, Paradise Valley, AZ 85253; H. Warren Willis, 5209 Rayland Dr., Bethesda, MD 20814-1427.

## Publications

*Catholic Library World* (q.; memb.; nonmemb. $60). *Ed.* Allen Gruenke.
*Catholic Periodical and Literature Index* (q.; $400 calendar year; abridged ed., $100 calendar year; CPL on CD-ROM, inquire. *Ed.* Barry C. Hopkins.

## Section Chairpersons

Academic Libraries/Library Education. William R. Brace.
Archives. H. Warren Willis.
Children's Libraries. Rosemarie Anthony, OP

High School Libraries. Patricia Ann Berger, IHM.
Parish/Community Libraries. Phyllis Petre.

## Round Table Chairpersons

Bibliographic Instruction. To be appointed.
Cataloging and Classification. To be appointed.
Preservation of American Catholic Materials. To be appointed.

## Committee Chairpersons

*Catholic Library World* Editorial. Mary E. Gallagher, SSJ.
*Catholic Periodical and Literature Index.* Rev. Bonaventure Hayes, OFM.
Constitution and Bylaws. H. Warren Willis.
Elections. Bert A. Thompson.
Finance. Rev. Bonaventure Hayes, OFM.
Grant Development. Jean R. Bostley, SSJ.
Membership Development. To be appointed.
Nominations. Paul J. Ostendorf, FSC.
Publications. Nicholas Falco.
Scholarship. Kathleen O'Leary.

## Special Appointments

American Friends of the Vatican Library Board. Jean R. Bostley, SSJ.
Convention Program Coordinator. Jean R. Bostley, SSJ.
Parliamentarian. Rev. Joseph P. Browne, CSC.

# Chief Officers of State Library Agencies

167 W. Main Street, Suite 600, Lexington, KY 40507
606-231-1925, fax 606-231-1928

## Object

To provide a means of cooperative action among its state and territorial members to strengthen the work of the respective state and territorial agencies, and to provide a continuing mechanism for dealing with the problems faced by the heads of these agencies, which are responsible for state and territorial library development.

## Membership

Chief Officers of State Library Agencies (COSLA) is an independent organization of the men and women who head the state and territorial agencies responsible for library development. Its membership consists solely of the top library officers of the 50 states, the District of Columbia, and the territories, variously designated as state librarian, director, commissioner, or executive secretary.

## Officers (1999–2001)

*Pres.* C. Ray Ewick, Dir., State Lib., 140 N. Senate Ave., Indianapolis, IN 46204. Tel. 317-232-3692, fax 317-232-3728, e-mail ewick@statelib.lib.in.us; *V.P./Pres.-Elect* Keith Fiels, Dir., Bd. of Lib. Commissioners, 648 Beacon St., Boston, MA 02215. Tel. 617-267-9400, fax 617-421-9833, e-mail kfiels@state.ma.us; *Secy.* GladysAnn Wells, Dir., Dept. of Libs., Archives and Public Records, State Capital, Rm. 200, 1700 W. Washington, Phoenix, AZ 85007. Tel. 602-542-4035, fax 602-542-4972, e-mail gawells@dlapr.lib.az.us; *Treas.* Duane Johnson, State Libn., State Lib., Capital, 3rd fl., Topeka, KS 66612. Tel. 913-296-3296, fax 913-296-6650, e-mail duanej@ink.org.

## Directors

Officers; Immediate Past Pres. Sara Parker, State Libn., State Lib. Box 387, 600 W. Main St., Jefferson City, MO 65102-0387. Tel. 573-751-2751, fax 573-751-3612, e-mail sparker@mail.state.mo.us; Michael Lucas, State Libn., State Lib., 65 S. Front St., Columbus, OH 43215-4163. Tel. 614-644-6863, fax 614-466-3584, e-mail mlucas@mail.slonet.ohio.gov; Jim Scheppke, State Libn., State Lib., 250 Winter St. N.E., Salem, OR 97310-0640. Tel. 503-378-4367, fax 503-588-7119, e-mail jim.b.scheppke@state.or.us.

# Chinese-American Librarians Association

Executive Director, Amy Seetoo
E-mail adseetoo@umich.edu

## Object

To enhance communications among Chinese-American librarians as well as between Chinese-American librarians and other librarians; to serve as a forum for discussion of mutual problems and professional concerns among Chinese-American librarians; to promote Sino-American librarianship and library services; and to provide a vehicle whereby Chinese-American librarians may cooperate with other associations and organizations having similar or allied interest.

## Membership

Memb. 770. Open to everyone who is interested in the association's goals and activities. Dues (Regular) $15; (Student/Nonsalaried) $7.50; (Inst.) $45; (Permanent) $200.

## Officers

*Pres.* Linna Yu. E-mail linnay@queenslib.ny.us; *V.P./Pres.-Elect* Ling Hwey Jeng. E-mail lhjeng00@ukcc.uky.edu; *Treas.* Ming Li.

## Publications

*Journal of Library and Information Science*, (2 per year; memb.; nonmemb. $15). *Ed.* Mengxiong Liu.
*Membership Directory* (memb.).
*Newsletter* (3 per year; memb.; nonmemb. $10). *Ed.* Lan Yang.

## Committee Chairpersons

Constitution and Bylaws. Sha-Li Zhang.
Finance. Susan Tsui.

International Relations. Priscilla Yu.
Membership. Margaret Feng.
Public Relations/Fund-Raising. Linda Tse, Elizabeth Hsu.
Publications. Lena Yang.
Scholarship. Mengxiong Liu.
Long-Range Planning (task force). Connie Wu.

## Chapter Presidents

California. Yulan Chou ychou.
Florida. Shixing Wen swen.
Greater Mid-Atlantic. Tsai-Hong Miller.
Midwest. Marian Chou MChou
Northeast. Theresa Huang.
Southwest. Cloris Yue Yue.

# Church and Synagogue Library Association

Box 19357, Portland, OR 97280-0357
503-244-6919, 800-542-2752, fax 503-977-3734
e-mail CSLA@worldaccessnet.com
World Wide Web http://www.worldaccessnet.com/~CSLA

## Object

To act as a unifying core for the many existing church and synagogue libraries; to provide the opportunity for a mutual sharing of practices and problems; to inspire and encourage a sense of purpose and mission among church and synagogue librarians; to study and guide the development of church and synagogue librarianship toward recognition as a formal branch of the library profession. Founded 1967.

## Membership

Memb. 1,900. Dues (Inst.) $120; (Affiliated) $75; (Church/Synagogue) $45; (Indiv.) $25. Year. July–June.

## Officers (July 1998–June 1999)

*Pres.* Barbara Mall, 5137 Oven Bird Green, Columbia, MD 21004; *1st V.P.* Alrene Hall, 10715 Mahaffey Rd., Tomball, TX 77375; *2nd V.P.* Russell Newburn, 12590 Beeson St., Alliance, OH 44601; *Treas.* Marilyn Demeter, 3145 Corydon Rd., Cleveland Heights, OH 44118; *Administrator* Judith Janzen; *Financial Asst.* J. Robert Waggoner,

413 Robindale Ave., Dearborn, MI 48128; *Publications Ed.* Karen Bota, 490 N. Fox Hills Dr., No. 1, Bloomfield Hills, MI 48304; *Book Review Ed.* Charles Snyder, 213 Lawn Ave., Sellersville, PA 18960.

## Executive Board

Officers; committee chairpersons.

## Publications

*Bibliographies* (1–5; price varies).
*Church and Synagogue Libraries* (bi-mo.; memb.; nonmemb. $35; Canada $45). *Ed.* Karen Bota.
*CSLA Guides* (1–17; price varies).

## Committee Chairpersons

Awards. Evelyn Pockrass.
Conference. Barbara May.
Finance and Fund-raising. Beth Hodgson.
Library Services. Catherine Bishop.
Nominations and Elections. Beverley Manning.
Personnel. Lois Ward.
Publications. Carol Campbell.

# Coalition for Networked Information

Executive Director, Clifford A. Lynch
21 Dupont Circle, Suite 800, Washington, DC 20036
202-296-5098, fax 202-872-0884
E-mail info@cni.org, World Wide Web http://www.cni.org

## Mission

The Coalition for Networked Information (CNI) is an organization created to advance the transformative promise of networked information technology for the advancement of scholarly communication and the enrichment of intellectual productivity. The coalition was founded in 1990 by the Association of Research Libraries, CAUSE, and Educom. In 1998 CAUSE and Educom merged to create a new organization, Educause. In establishing CNI, these sponsor organizations recognized the need to broaden the community's thinking beyond issues of network connectivity and bandwidth to encompass networked information content and applications. Reaping the benefits of the Internet for scholarship, research, and education demands new partnerships, new institutional roles, and new technologies and infrastructure. The coalition seeks to further these collaborations, to explore these new roles, and to catalyze the development and deployment of the necessary technology base.

## Membership

Memb. 198. Membership is institutional. Dues $4,900. Year. July–June.

## Officers (July 1998–June 1999)

Duane Webster, Exec. Dir., Association of Research Libraries; Brian Hawkins, Pres., Educause.

## Steering Committee

Richard West, California State Univ.; William Graves, COLLEGIS Research Institute; Marin Runkle, Univ. of Chicago; Miriam Drake, Georgia Institute of Technology; Susan Foster, Univ. of Delaware; Sharon Hogan, Univ. of Illinois, Chicago.

## Publications

CNI-Announce (subscribe by e-mail to LISTPROC@CNI.ORG)

# Council of Planning Librarians

101 N. Wacker Dr., Suite CM 190, Chicago, IL 60606
312-409-3349, fax 312-263-7417

## Object

To provide a special interest group in the field of city and regional planning for libraries and librarians, faculty, professional planners, university, government, and private planning organizations; to provide an opportunity for exchange among those interested in problems of library organization and research and in the dissemination of information about city and regional planning; to sponsor programs of service to the planning profession and librarianship; to advise on library organization for new planning programs; and to aid and support administrators, faculty, and librarians in their efforts to educate the public and their appointed or elected representatives to the necessity for strong library programs in support of planning. Founded 1960.

## Membership

Memb. 142. Open to any individual or institution that supports the purpose of the council, upon written application and payment of dues to the membership office, 101 N. Wacker Dr., Suite CM 190, Chicago, IL 60606. Dues (Inst.) $55; (Indiv.) $35; Year. July 1–June 30.

## Officers and Board (1998–1999)

*Pres.* Jan Horah, Jack Brause Lib., Real Estate Inst., New York Univ., 11 W. 42 St., Suite 510, New York, NY 10036-8002. Tel. 212-790-1629, fax 202-790-1684, e-mail horah@is.nyu.edu; *V.P./Pres.-Elect* Elizabeth R. Cardman, Univ. Archives, 19 Main Lib., Univ. of Illinois at Urbana-Champaign, 1408 W. Gregory Dr., Urbana, IL 61801. Tel. 217-333-0798, e-mail ecardman@uiuc.edu; *Past Pres.* Julia M. Gelfand, Univ. Lib., Univ. of California at Irvine, Box 19557, Irvine, CA 92713. Tel. 714-824-4971, e-mail jgelfand@uci.edu; *Member-at-Large* Priscilla Yu, Library, Univ. of Illinois, 1301 W. Gregory Dr., Urbana, IL 61801-3608. Tel. 317-333-0424, e-mail p-U2@uiuc.ed; *Secy./Treas.* Deborah Sommer, Environmental Design Lib., 210 Wurster Hall, Univ. of California, Berkeley, CA 94720. Tel. 510-642-4819, e-mail dsommer@library.berkeley.edu.

## Publications

CPLFYI-L. Electronic Discussion List. Contact Marilyn Myers at iadmxm@asuvm.inre.asu.edu.

# Council on Library and Information Resources

1755 Massachusetts Ave. N.W., Suite 500, Washington, DC 20036-2124
202-939-4750, fax 202-939-4765
World Wide Web http://www.clir.org

## Object

In 1997 the Council on Library Resources (CLR) and the Commission on Preservation and Access (CPA) merged and became the Council on Library and Information Resources (CLIR). The mission of the council is to identify and define the key emerging issues related to the welfare of libraries and the constituencies they serve, convene the leaders who can influence change, and promote collaboration among the institutions and organizations that can achieve change. The council's interests embrace the entire range of information resources and services from traditional library and archival materials to emerging digital formats. It assumes a particular interest in helping institutions cope with the accelerating pace of change associated with the transition into the digital environment. The council pursues this mission out of the conviction that information is a public good and has great social utility.

The term library is construed to embrace its traditional meanings and purposes and to encompass any and all information agencies and organizations that are involved in gathering, cataloging, storing, preserving, and distributing information and in helping users meet their information requirements.

While maintaining appropriate collaboration and liaison with other institutions and organizations, the council operates independently of any particular institutional or vested interests.

Through the composition of its board, it brings the broadest possible perspective to bear upon defining and establishing the priority of the issues with which it is concerned.

## Membership of Board

The council's membership and board of directors are limited to 18 members.

## Officers

*Chair* Stanley Chodorow; *V. Chair* Marilyn Gell Mason; *Pres.* Deanna B. Marcum. E-mail dmarcum@CLIR.org; *Secy.* David B.

Gracy, II; *Treas.* Dan Tonkery.
Address correspondence to headquarters.

## Publications

*Annual Report.*
*CLIR Issues.*
*Preservation and Access International Newsletter.*
Various program publications.

# Federal Library and Information Center Committee

Executive Director, Susan M. Tarr
Library of Congress, Washington, DC 20540-4930
202-707-4800
World Wide Web http://lcweb.loc.gov/flicc

## Object

The committee makes recommendations on federal library and information policies, programs, and procedures to federal agencies and to others concerned with libraries and information centers. The committee coordinates cooperative activities and services among federal libraries and information centers and serves as a forum to consider issues and policies that affect federal libraries and information centers, needs and priorities in providing information services to the government and to the nation at large, and efficient and cost-effective use of federal library and information resources and services. Furthermore, the committee promotes improved access to information, continued development and use of the Federal Library and Information Network (FEDLINK), research and development in the application of new technologies to federal libraries and information centers, improvements in the management of federal libraries and information centers, and relevant education opportunities. Founded 1965.

## Membership

Libn. of Congress, Dir. of the National Agricultural Lib., Dir. of the National Lib. of Medicine, Dir. of the National Lib. of Educa-

tion, representatives from each of the other executive departments, and representatives from each of the following agencies: National Aeronautics and Space Admin., National Science Foundation, Smithsonian Institution, U.S. Supreme Court, U.S. Info. Agency, National Archives and Records Admin., Admin. Offices of the U.S. Courts, Defense Technical Info. Center, Government Printing Office, National Technical Info. Service (Dept. of Commerce), and Office of Scientific and Technical Info. (Dept. of Energy), Exec. Office of the President, Dept. of the Army, Dept. of the Navy, Dept. of the Air Force, and chairperson of the FEDLINK Advisory Council. Fifteen additional voting member agencies shall be selected on a rotating basis by the voting members of FEDLINK. These rotating members will serve a three-year term. One representative from each of the following agencies is invited as an observer to committee meetings: General Accounting Office, General Services Admin., Joint Committee on Printing, National Commission on Libs. and Info. Science, Office of Mgt. and Budget, Office of Personnel Mgt., and Lib. of Congress U.S. Copyright Office.

## Officers

*Chair* James H. Billington, Libn. of Congress; *Chair Designate* Winston Tabb, Assoc.

Libn. for Lib. Services, Lib. of Congress; *Exec. Dir.* Susan M. Tarr, Federal Lib. and Info. Center Committee, Lib. of Congress.

Address correspondence to the executive director.

## Publications

*Annual FLICC Forum on Federal Information Policies* (summary and papers).
*FEDLINK Technical Notes* (m.).
*FLICC Newsletter* (q.).

# Federal Publishers Committee

Chairperson, Glenn W. King
Bureau of the Census, Washington, DC 20233
301-457-1171, fax 301-457-4707
E-mail glenn.w.king.@ccmail.census.gov

## Object

To foster and promote effective management of data development and dissemination in the federal government through exchange of information, and to act as a focal point for federal agency publishing.

## Membership

Memb. 700. Membership is available to persons involved in publishing and dissemination in federal government departments, agencies, and corporations, as well as independent organizations concerned with federal government publishing and dissemination. Some key federal government organizations represented are the Joint Committee on Printing, Government Printing Office, National Technical Info. Service, National Commission on Libs. and Info. Science, and the Lib. of Congress. Meetings are held monthly during business hours.

## Officers

*Chair* Glenn W. King; *V. Chair, Programs* Sandra Smith; *V. Chair, Roundtables* June Malina; *Secy.* Marilyn Marbrook.

## Roundtable Leaders

Marketing and Promotion. John Ward.
Subscriptions and Periodicals. Nancy Nicoletti.

# Lutheran Church Library Association

Executive Director, Leanna D. Kloempken
122 W. Franklin Ave., No. 604, Minneapolis, MN 55404
612-870-3623, fax 612-870-0170
E-mail lclahq@aol.com

## Object

To promote the growth of church libraries by publishing a quarterly journal, *Lutheran Libraries*; furnishing book lists; assisting member libraries with technical problems; and providing workshops and meetings for mutual encouragement, guidance, and exchange of ideas among members. Founded 1958.

## Membership

Memb. 1,800 churches, 250 personal. Dues (1999) $28, $40, $55, $70, $75, $100, $500, $1,000.

## Officers (1998–1999)

*Pres.* Willis Erickson; *V.P.* Jeanette Johnson; *Secy.* Dorothy Anderson; *Treas.* Diane Erickson.
Address correspondence to the executive director.

## Directors

Doris Engstrom, Jan Koski, Betsy Papp, Henrietta Pruissen, Sue Ellen Golke, Ruth Scholye.

## Publication

*Lutheran Libraries* (q.; memb.; nonmemb. $25).

## Board Chairpersons

Advisory. Rolf Aaseng.
Finance. L. Edwin Wang.
Library Services. Betty Le Dell.
Publications. Rod Olson.
Telecommunications. Chuck Mann

# Medical Library Association

Executive Director, Carla Funk
65 E. Wacker Pl., Suite 1900, Chicago, IL 60601
312-419-9094, fax 312-419-8950
E-mail info@mlahq.org; World Wide Web http://mlanet.org

## Object

The major purposes of the Medical Library Association (MLA) are to foster medical and allied scientific libraries, to promote the educational and professional growth of health science librarians, and to exchange medical literature among the members. Through its programs and publications, MLA encourages professional development of its membership, whose foremost concern is dissemination of health sciences information for those in research, education, and patient care. Founded 1898; incorporated 1934.

## Membership

Memb. (Inst.) 1,300; (Indiv.) 3,800. Institutional members are medical and allied scientific libraries. Individual members are people who are (or were at the time membership was established) engaged in professional library or bibliographic work in medical and allied scientific libraries or people who are interested in medical or allied scientific libraries.

Dues (Student) $25; (Emeritus) $40; (Intro.) $75; (Indiv.) $110; (Sustaining) $345; and (Inst.) $175_$410, based on the number of the library's periodical subscriptions. Members may be affiliated with one or more of MLA's 23 special-interest sections and 14 regional chapters.

## Officers

*Pres.* Jacqueline Donaldson Doyle, Samaritan Health System, 1111 E. McDowell Rd., Box 2989, Phoenix, AZ 85062-2989; *Pres.-Elect* Frieda O. Weise, Univ. of Maryland–Baltimore Health Sciences and Human Services Lib., 601 W. Lombard St., Balimore, MD 21201; *Past Pres.* Rachael K. Anderson, Arizona Health Sciences Lib., 1501 N. Campbell Ave., Tucson, AZ 85724.

## Directors

Rosalind F. Dudden (2001), Suzanne F. Gertsheim (2001), Elaine Russo Martl1in (1999),

James Shedlock (1999), Diane Schwartz (2000), Bernie Todd Smith (2000), Patricia L. Thibodeau (1999), Mary Joan Tooey (2001), Linda A. Watson (1999).

## Publications

*Bulletin of the Medical Library Association* (q.; $136).
*Directory of the Medical Library Association* ($150).
*MLA News* (10 per year; $48.50).
Miscellaneous (request current list from association headquarters).

## Committee Chairpersons

Awards. Karen Curtis.
Books (Panel). Kellie N. Kaneshiro.
Bulletin Editorial Board. J. Michael Homan.
Bylaws. Elaine C. Johnston.
Continuing Education. Penny Coppernell-Blach.
Credentialing. Patricia Rodgers.
Governmental Relations. Marianne Puckett.
Grants and Scholarships. Susan London.
Health Sciences Library Technicians. Marcia I. Batchelor.

Joseph Leiter NLM/MLA Lectureship. Suzanne F. Gertsheim.
Membership. Craig Haynes.
National Program (1998). Frieda O. Weise
National Program (1999). Mark E. Funk.
National Program (2000). Brett A. Kirkpatrick.
Oral History. Virginia Matson-Carden.
Professional Recognition (Review Panel). Alan Carr.
Publications. Janice Swiatek.
Publishing and Information Industries Relations. Ruth H. Maniken.
Status and Economic Interests. Kathleen Cimpl Wagner.

## Ad Hoc Committee and Task Force Charges

Centennial Coordinating. June H. Fulton.
Executive. Naomi C. Broering.
Joint MLA/AAHSLD Legislative (Task Force). Marianne Puckett.
Research Policy Implementation. Joanne G. Marshall.
Professional Development. Carol G. Jenkins.
Role of Information Professionals in the 21st Century. Wayne P. Peay.

# Music Library Association

Box 487, Canton, MA 02021
617-828-8450, fax 617-828-8915
E-mail adadsvc@aol.com

## Object

To promote the establishment, growth, and use of music libraries; to encourage the collection of music and musical literature in libraries; to further studies in musical bibliography; to increase efficiency in music library service and administration; and to promote the profession of music librarianship. Founded 1931.

## Membership

Memb. 2,000. Dues (Inst.) $90; (Indiv.) $75; (Retired) $45; (Student) $35. Year. Sept. 1–Aug. 31.

## Officers

*Pres.* Paula D. Matthews, George and Helen Ladd Lib., Bates College, Lewiston, ME

04240. Tel. 207-786-6266, fax 207-786-6055, e-mail pmatthew@abacus.bates.edu; *Past Pres.* Diane Parr Walker, Office of the Libn., Alderman Lib., Univ. of Virginia, Charlottesville, VA 22903-2498. Tel. 804-924-4606, fax 804-924-1431, e-mail dpw@poe.acc.virginia.edu; *Rec. Secy.* Roberta Chodacki, Music Lib., East Carolina Univ., Greenville, NC 27858-4353. Tel. 252-328-1239, fax 252-328-1243, e-mail chodackir@mail.ecu.edu; *Treas.* Laura Gayle Green, Miller Nichols Lib., Univ. of Missouri–Kansas City, 5100 Rockill Rd., Kansas City, MO 64110. Tel. 816-235-1679, fax 816-333-5584, e-mail greenlg@umkc.edu. *Exec. Secy.* Bonna J. Boettcher, Music Lib. and Sound Recording Archives, William T. Jerome Lib., 3rd fl., Bowling Green State Univ., Bowling Green, OH 43403-0179. Tel. 419-372-9929, fax 419-372-7996, e-mail bboettc@bgnet.bgsu.edu.

## Members-at-Large

Leslie Bennett, Univ. of Oregon; Robert Curtis, Tulane Univ.; Bonnie Jo Dopp, Univ. of Maryland; Jim Farrington, Sibley Music Lib./Eastman School of Music; Edwin A. (Ned) Quist, Peabody Conservatory of Music; Brad Short, Washington Univ.

## Special Officers

*Advertising Mgr.* Susan Dearborn, 1572 Massachusetts Ave., No. 57, Cambridge, MA 02138. Tel. 617-876-0934; *Business Mgr. Academic Services*, c/o Music Library Assn., Box 487, Canton, MA 02021. Tel. 781-828-8450, fax 781-828-8915, e-mail acadsvc@aol.com; *Convention Mgr.* Don L. Roberts, Northwestern Univ. Music Lib. 1935 Sheridan Rd., Evanston, IL 60208-2300. Tel. 847-491-3434, fax 847-491-8306, e-mail droberts@nwu.edu; *Asst. Convention Mgr.* Susan H,. Hitchens, 1961 School House La., Aurora, IL 60504. Tel./fax 630-892-4524, e-mail susadorm@ameritech.net; *Placement* To be appointed; *Publicity* To be appointed.

## Publications

*MLA Index and Bibliography Series* (irreg.; price varies).
*MLA Newsletter* (q.; memb.).
*MLA Technical Reports* (irreg.; price varies).
*Music Cataloging Bulletin* (mo.; $25).
*Notes* (q.; indiv. $70; inst. $80).

## Committee and Roundtable Chairpersons

Administration. Deborah Pierce, Univ. of Washington.
Bibliographic Control. Linda Barnhart, Univ. of California–San Diego.
Development. Laura Dankner, Loyola Univ.
Education. Lois Kuyper-Rushing, Louisiana State Univ.
Finance. Edwin A. (Ned) Quist, Peabody Conservatory of Music.
Legislation. Lenore Coral, Cornell Univ.
Membership. Geraldine Ostrove, Lib. of Congress.
Nominating, November 1999 ballot. To be appointed.
Preservation. To be appointed.
Public Libraries. Jeannette Casey, Chicago Public Lib.
Publications. Nancy Nuzzo, SUNY Buffalo.
Reference Sharing and Collection Development. William Coscarelli, Univ. of Georgia.

# National Association of Government Archives and Records Administrators

Executive Director, Bruce W. Dearstyne
48 Howard St., Albany, NY 12207
518-463-8644, fax 518-463-8656
E-mail nagara@caphill.com

## Object

Founded in 1984, the association is successor to the National Association of State Archives and Records Administrators, which had been established in 1974. NAGARA is a growing nationwide association of local, state, and federal archivists and records administrators, and others interested in improved care and management of government records. NAGARA promotes public awareness of government records and archives management programs, encourages interchange of information among government archives and records management agencies, develops and implements professional standards of government records and archival administration, and encourages study and research into records management problems and issues.

## Membership

Most NAGARA members are federal, state, and local archival and records management agencies.

## Officers

*Pres.* Roy Turnbaugh, Oregon State Archives; *V.P.* Jeanne Young, Board of Governors of the Federal Reserve System; *Secy.* Gerald G. Newborg, State Historical Society of North Dakota; *Treas.* Jim Berberich, Florida Bureau of Archives and Records Management.

## Directors

J. Wesley Chaffin, Moore & VanAllen, PLLC, Charlotte, NC; Terry Ellis, Salt Lake County (UT) Records Management and Archives; Diane LeBlanc, National Archives and Records Admin., Northeast Region; Robert Martin, Texas State Lib. and Archives Commission; Michael Miller, National Archives and Records Admin.; David Olson, North Carolina Division of Archives and History.

## Publications

*Clearinghouse* (q.; memb.).
*Crosswords* (q.; memb.).
*Government Records* Issues (series).
*Preservation Needs in State Archives* (report).
*Program Reporting Guidelines for Government Records Programs.*

# National Federation of Abstracting and Information Services

Executive Director, Richard T. Kaser
1518 Walnut St., Philadelphia, PA 19102
215-893-1561, fax 215-893-1564
E-mail nfais@nfais.org

## Object

NFAIS is an international, not-for-profit membership organization comprising leading information producers, distributors, and corporate users of secondary information. Its purpose is to serve the information community through education, research, and publication. Founded 1958.

## Membership

Memb. 60+. Full membership (regular and government) is open to organizations that, as a substantial part of their activity, produce secondary information services for external use. Secondary information products are compilations containing printed or electronic summaries of, or references to, multiple sources of publicly available information. For example, organizations that assemble bibliographic citations, abstracts, indexes, and data are all secondary information services.

Associate membership is available to organizations that operate or manage online information services, networks, in-house information centers, and libraries; conduct research or development work in information science or systems; are otherwise involved in the generation, promotion, or distribution of secondary information products under contract; or publish primary information sources. Members pay dues annually based on the fiscal year of July 1–June 30. Dues are assessed based on the member's revenue derived from information-related activities.

## Officers (1998–1999)

*Pres.* James E. Lohr; *Past Pres.* John Anderson; *Pres.-Elect* Gladys Cotter; *Secy.* Sheldon Kotzin; *Treas.* Brian Sweet.

## Directors

Brian Earle, Marjorie Hlava, Taissa Kusma, George Lewicky, Jim McGinty, R. Paul Ryan, Brian Sweet, Michael Tansey.

## Staff

*Exec. Dir.* Richard T. Kaser; *Asst. Dir.* Marian H. Gloninger; *Office Mgr.* Wendy McMillan; *Customer Service* Margaret Manson.

## Publications

*Automated Support to Indexing* (1992; memb. $50; nonmemb. $75).

*Beyond Boolean* (1996; memb. $50; nonmemb. $75).

*Careers in Electronic Information* (1997; memb. $29; nonmemb. $39).

*Changing Roles in Information Distribution* (1994; memb. $50; nonmemb. $75).

*Computer Support to Indexing* (1998; mem. $175; nonmemb. $235).

*Developing New Markets for Information Products* (1993; memb. $50; nonmemb. $75).

*Document Delivery in an Electronic Age* (1995; memb. $50, nonmemb. $75).

*Flexible Workstyles in the Information Industry* (1993; memb. $50; nonmemb. $75).

*Government Information and Policy: Changing Roles in a New Administration* (1994; memb. $50; nonmemb. $75).
*Guide to Careers in Abstracting and Indexing* (1992; memb. $25; nonmemb. $35).
*Guide to Database Distribution*, 2nd ed., (1994; memb. $100; nonmemb. $175).
*Impacts of Changing Production Technolo-* *gies* (1995; memb. $50, nonmemb. $75).
*NFAIS Member Directory and Guide to Leading Information Companies* (1996; memb. $25, nonmemb. $35).
*NFAIS Newsletter* (mo.; North America $120; elsewhere $135).
*Partnering in the Information Industry* (1996; memb. $50, nonmemb. $75).

# National Information Standards Organization

Executive Director, Patricia R. Harris
4733 Bethesda Ave., Suite 300, Bethesda, MD 20814
301-654-2512, fax 301-654-1721
E-mail nisohq@niso.org, World Wide Web http://www.niso.org

## Object

To develop technical standards used in libraries, publishing, and information services. Experts from the information field volunteer to lend their expertise in the development and writing of NISO standards. The standards are approved by the consensus of NISO's voting membership, which consists of 70 voting members representing libraries, government, associations, and private businesses and organizations. NISO is supported by its membership and corporate grants. Formerly a committee of the American National Standards Institute (ANSI), NISO, formed in 1939, was incorporated in 1983 as a nonprofit educational organization. NISO is accredited by ANSI and serves as the U.S. Technical Advisory Group to ISO/TC 46.

## Membership

Memb. 65. Open to any organization, association, government agency, or company willing to participate in and having substantial concern for the development of NISO standards.

## Officers

*Chair* Joel H. Baron, Publisher, The *New England Journal of Medicine*, 1440 Main St., Waltham, MA 02154; *Past Chair* Michael J. McGill, Chief Info. Officer, Univ. of Michigan Medical Center, 4251 Plymouth Rd., Suite 3300, Ann Arbor, MI 48105; *V. Chair/Chair-Elect* Donald J. Muccino, Exec. V.P./COO, Online Computer Library Center, 6565 Frantz Rd., Dublin, OH 43017-0702; *Exec. Dir./Secy.* Patricia R. Harris, NISO, 4733 Bethesda Ave., Suite 300, Bethesda, MD 20814; *Treas.* Michael J. Mellinger, Pres., Data Research Assoc., Inc., 1276 N. Warson Rd., St. Louis, MO 63132.

## Publications

*Information Standards Quarterly* (q.; $78; foreign $120).
NISO published standards are available from NISO Press Fulfillment, Box 338, Oxon Hill, MD 20750-0338. Tel. 301-567-9522, 800-282-6476, fax 301-567-9553, e-mail nisohq@niso.org.
NISO Press catalogs and the *NISO Annual Report* are available on request.

# REFORMA
## (National Association to Promote Library Services to Latinos and the Spanish Speaking)

President, Jacqueline Ayala
Box 88756, Los Angeles, CA 90009-8756
E-mail jayala@earthlink.net

## Object

Promoting library services to the Spanish-speaking for more than 28 years, REFORMA, an ALA affiliate, works in a number of areas: to promote the development of library collections to include Spanish-language and Latino-oriented materials; the recruitment of more bilingual and bicultural professionals and support staff; the development of library services and programs that meet the needs of the Latino community; the establishment of a national network among individuals who share our goals; the education of the U.S. Latino population in regard to the availability and types of library services; and lobbying efforts to preserve existing library resource centers serving the interest of Latinos.

## Membership

Memb. 900. Any person who is supportive of the goals and objectives of REFORMA.

## Officers

*Pres.* Jacqueline Ayala, Box 88756, Los Angeles, CA 90009-8756. Tel. 310-282-6279, fax 310-827-9187, e-mail jayala@earthlink.net; *V.P./Pres.-Elect* Toni Bissessar, Brooklyn Public Lib., Multilingual Center, Grand Army Plaza, Brooklyn, NY 11239. E-mail tbissessar@BrooklynPublicLibrary.org; *Past Pres.* Sandra Balderrama, American Library Association, 50 E. Huron St., Chicago, IL 60611. E-mail sbalderr@ala.org; *Treas.* Rene Amaya, East Los Angeles Public Lib., 4801 E. Third St., Los Angeles, CA 90033. Tel. 213-264-0155, fax 213-264-

5465; *Secy.* Vivian Pisano, San Francisco Public Lib., Civic Center, San Francisco, CA 94102. Tel. 415-557-4340, e-mail Vpisano@sfpl.lib.ca.us; *Newsletter Ed.* Denice Adkins; *Archivist* Salvador Guerena; *Membership Coordinator* Al Milo.

## Publications

*REFORMA Newsletter* (q.; memb.). *Ed.* Denice Adkins, Byers Branch Lib., 675 Santa Fe Dr., Denver, CO 80204. Tel. 303-571-1665, e-mail Denice@u.arizona.edu.

## Committees

Children's and Young Adult Service. Pamela Martin-Diaz.
Information Technology. Carlos Rodriguez.
Librarian-of-the-Year Award. Mario Gonzalez.
Nominations. Ben Ocon.
Organizational Development. Paola Ferate.
Public Relations. Brigida Campos.
Scholarship. Ninfa Trejo.
Pura Belpr, Award. Yolanda Bonitch.
Education. Camila Alire.
RNC II (National Conference). Susana Hinojosa.
Finance. Sandra Balderrama.

## Meetings

General membership and board meetings take place at the American Library Association's Midwinter meeting and Annual Conference. The second REFORMA National Conference will take place Aug. 3–6, 2000, in Tucson, Arizona.

# Research Libraries Group, Inc.

Manager of Corporate Communications, Jennifer Hartzell
1200 Villa St., Mountain View, CA 94041-1100
650-691-2207, fax 650-964-0943
E-mail jlh@notes.rlg.org, World Wide Web http://www.rlg.org

## Object

The Research Libraries Group, Inc. (RLG) is a not-for-profit membership corporation of approximately 160 universities, archives, historical societies, national libraries, and other institutions devoted to improving access to information that supports research and learning. RLG exists to support its members in containing costs, improving local services, and contributing to international collective access to scholarly materials. For its members, RLG develops and operates cooperative programs to manage, preserve, and extend access to research library, museum, and archival holdings. For both its members and for nonmember institutions and individuals worldwide, RLG develops and operates databases and software to serve an array of information access and management needs. CitaDel, Eureka, Marcadia, RLIN, and Zephyr are registered trademarks of the Research Libraries Group, Inc. Ariel is a registered trademark of the Ariel Corporation used by RLG under license.

## Membership

Memb. c. 160. Membership is open to any nonprofit institution with an educational, cultural, or scientific mission. There are two membership categories: general and special. General members are institutions that serve a clientele of more than 5,000 faculty, academic staff, research staff, professional staff, students, fellows, or members. Special members serve a similar clientele of 5,000 or fewer.

## Directors

RLG has a 19-member board of directors, comprising 12 directors elected from and by RLG's member institutions, up to six at-large directors elected by the board itself, and the president. Theirs is the overall responsibility for the organization's governance and for ensuring that it faithfully fulfills its purpose and goals. Annual board elections are held in the spring. In 1999 the board's chair is Martin Runkle, Director, Univ. of Chicago Lib. For a current list of directors, see the Web site http://www.rlg.org/boardbio.html.

## Staff

*Pres.* James Michalko; *V.P.* John W. Haeger; *Dir., Integrated Information Services* Susan Yoder; *Dir., Member Programs and Initiatives* Linda West; *Dir., Customer and Operations Support* Jack Grantham; *Dir., Computer Development* David Richards; *Dir., Finance and Administration* Molly Singer.

## Publications

*Research Libraries Group News* (3 per year; 16-page news magazine).
*RLG DigiNews* (bi-m.; Web-based newsletter to help keep pace with preservation uses of digitization.)
*RLG Focus* (bi-m.; eight-page user services newsletter).
For informational, research, and user publications, see the Web site http://www.rlg.org/pub.html, or contact RLG.

# Society for Scholarly Publishing

Executive Directors, Francine Butler, Jerry Bowman
10200 W. 44 Ave., Suite 304, Wheat Ridge, CO 80033
303-422-3914, fax 303-422-8894
E-mail ssp@resourcenter.com

## Object

To draw together individuals involved in the process of scholarly publishing. This process requires successful interaction of the many functions performed within the scholarly community. The Society for Scholarly Publishing (SSP) provides the leadership for such interaction by creating opportunities for the exchange of information and opinions among scholars, editors, publishers, librarians, printers, booksellers, and all others engaged in scholarly publishing.

## Executive Committee (1998–1999)

*Pres.* Frederick Bowes, III, Bowes & Assoc., Box 1637, Buxbury, MA 02331-1637; *Pres.-Elect* Kathleen Case, American College of Physicians, 190 N. Independence Mall W., Philadelphia, PA 19106; *Secy.-Treas.* Patricia Sabosik, Elsevier Science, 655 Ave. of the Americas, New York, NY 10010-5107; *Past Pres.* Janice Fleming, Cadmus Journal Services, 940 Elkridge Landing Rd., Linthicum, MD 21090-2908.

## Membership

Memb. 900. Open to all with an interest in the scholarly publishing process and dissemination of information. There are four categories of membership: individual ($85), contributing ($500), sustaining ($1,000), and sponsoring ($1,500). Year. Jan. 1–Dec. 31.

## Meetings

An annual meeting is conducted in June. The location changes each year. Additionally, SSP conducts several seminars throughout the year.

## Publications

*Scholarly Publishing Today* (q.; memb., nonmemb. $70)

*SSP Bulletin* (q.; newsletter)

## Object

To promote sound principles of archival economy and to facilitate cooperation among archivists and archival agencies. Founded 1936.

## Membership

Memb. 3,400. Dues (Indiv.) $65–$170, graduated according to salary; (Assoc.) $65, domestic; (Student) $40, with a two-year maximum on membership; (Inst.) $210; (Sustaining) $410.

## Officers (1998–1999)

*Pres.* Luciana Duranti; *V.P.* Thomas Hickerson; *Treas.* Robert Sink.

## Council

Valerie Browne, Dennis Harrison, Fynnette Eaton, Anne Gilliland-Swetland, Peter Hirtle, Karen Jefferson, Jan Kenamore, Helen Tibbo, Wilda Logan Willis.

## Staff

*Exec. Dir.* Susan E. Fox; *Meetings/Memb.*

*Coord.* Bernice E. Brack; *Publications Dir.* Teresa Brinati; *Publications Asst.* Troy Sturdivant; *Dir. of Finance* Carroll Dendler; *Educ. Dir.* Joan Sander.

## Publications

*American Archivist* (q.; $75; foreign $90). *Ed.* Philip Eppard; *Managing Ed.* Teresa Brinati. Books for review and related correspondence should be addressed to the managing editor.

*Archival Outlook* (bi-m.; memb.). *Ed.* Teresa Brinati.

# Software and Information Industry Association

1730 M St. N.W., Suite 700, Washington, DC 20036-4510
202-452-1600, fax 202-223-8756
World Wide Web: http://www.siia.net

## Membership

Memb. 1,500 companies. Formed January 1, 1999, through the merger of the Software Publishers Association (SPA) and the Information Industry Association (IIA). Open to companies involved in the creation, distribution, and use of software information products, services, and technologies. For details on membership and dues, see the SIIA Web site.

## Staff

*Pres.* Kenneth Wasch; *V.P., Marketing and Communications* Sheri Robey; *V.P., Program Development and CTO* Lauren Looney-Hall; *V.P., Government Affairs* David Byer.

## Board of Directors

Robert E. Aber, NASDAQ; Mauro Ballabeni, MicroBusiness Italiana SRL; Graham Beachum, II, Parnassus Associates International; Herb Brinberg, Parnassus Associates International; James E. Coane, N2K, Inc.; Dan Cooperman, Oracle Corporation; Glenn Goldberg, McGraw-Hill Companies; Larry Gross, Cendent Software; Brian Hall, West Group, representing Thomson Corporation; Kathy Hurley, The Learning Company, SkillsBank Division; Ted Johnson, Visio Corporation; Roberta Katz, Netscape; John Laing; Gail Littlejohn, LEXIS-NEXIS, representing Reed Elsevier, Inc.; Kirk Loevner; Dorothea Coccali Palsho, Dow Jones; Becky Ranninger, Symantec; Joel Ronning, Digital River; Steve Solazzo, IBM; David W. Turner, Reuters America Holdings, Inc.; Cheryl Vedoe, Post Communications; Ron Verni, Peachtree Software; Ken Wasch, SIIA.

# Special Libraries Association

Executive Director, David R. Bender
1700 18th St. N.W., Washington, DC 20009-2514
202-234-4700, fax 202-265-9317
E-mail sla@sla.org, World Wide Web http://www.sla.org

## Object

To advance the leadership role of special librarians in putting knowledge to work in the information and knowledge-based society. The association offers myriad programs and services designed to help its members serve their customers more effectively and succeed in an increasingly challenging environment of information management and technology.

## Membership

Memb. 14,500. Dues (Sustaining) $500; (Indiv.) $125; (Student) $35. Year. July–June.

## Officers (July 1998–June 1999)

*Pres.* L. Susan Hayes; *Pres.-Elect* Susan S. DiMattia; *Past Pres.* Judith J. Field; *Treas.* Richard Wallace; *Chapter Cabinet Chair* Anne K. Abate; *Chapter Cabinet Chair-Elect* Sandy Spurlock; *Div. Cabinet Chair* Richard P. Hulser; *Div. Chapter Chair-Elect* Joan E. Gervino.

## Directors

Officers; Stephen Abram (1999), Monica M. Ertel (2000), Cynthia V. Hill (2000), Sharyn Ladner (1999), Sandy Moltz (2001), Wilda B. Newman (2001).

## Publications

*Information Outlook* (mo.) (memb., nonmemb. $65/yr.) *Ed.* Susan Broughton.

## Committee Chairpersons

Affirmative Action. Andrea Greer.
Association Office Operations. Suzi Hayes.
Bylaws. Betty Eddison.
Cataloging. Dorothy McGarry.
Committees. Jim Tchobanoff.
Conference Plan (2000). Lynne McCay.
Consultation Service. Barbara Best-Nichols.
Copyright. Lolly Gasaway.
Finance. Dick Wallace.
Government Relations. Barb Spiegleman.
Innovations in Technology Award. Roberta Brody.
International Relations. Marydee Ojala.
Networking. Gail Stahl.
Nominating, 2000 Election. Liz Bibby.
Professional Development. Carol Ginsberg.
Public Relations. Mary Marshall.
Research. Doris Helfer.
SLA Endowment Fund Grants. Nettie Seaberry.
SLA Scholarship. Thomas Moothart.
Strategic Planning. Monica Ertel.
Student Relations. Barbara Semonche.
Technical Standards. Marje Hlava.
H. W. Wilson Award. Nancy Wilmes.

# Theatre Library Association

c/o The Shubert Archive, 149 W. 45th St., New York, NY 10036
212-944-3895, fax 212-944-4139
World Wide Web
http://www.brown.edu/Facilities/University_Library/beyond/TLA/TLA.html

## Object

To further the interests of collecting, preserving, and using theater, cinema, and performing-arts materials in libraries, museums, and private collections. Founded 1937.

## Membership

Memb. 500. Dues (Indiv./Inst.) $30. Year. Jan. 1–Dec. 31.

## Officers

*Pres.* Susan Brady, Yale Univ.; *V.P.* Ken Winkler, New York Lib. for the Performing Arts; *Exec. Secy.* Maryann Chach, Shubert Archive; *Treas.* Paul Newman, private collector.

## Executive Board

Lorraine A. Brown, Nena Couch, Rosemary Cullen, Camille Croce Dee, Annette Fern, B. Donald Grose, Mary Ann Jensen, Stephen B. Johnson, Brigitte J. Kueppers, Martha S. LoMonaco, Melissa M. Miller, Susan L. Peters; *Ex officio* Maryann Chach, Madeleine Nichols, Nancy L. Stokes; *Honorary* Paul Myers; *Historian* Louis A. Rachow.

## Publications

*Broadside* (q.; memb.). *Ed.* Nancy L. Stokes.
*Performing Arts Resources* (ann.; memb.).

## Committee Chairpersons

Awards. Richard Wall.
Membership. Geraldine Duclow.
Nominations. To be appointed.
Program and Special Events. Kevin Winkler.

# Urban Libraries Council

President, Eleanor Jo (Joey) Rodger
1603 Orrington Ave., Suite 1080, Evanston, IL 60201
847-866-9999, fax 847-866-9989
E-mail ulc@gpl.glenview.lib.il.us; World Wide Web http://www.clpgh.org/ulc/

## Object

To identify and make known the problems relating to urban libraries serving cities of 50,000 or more individuals, located in a Standard Metropolitan Statistical Area; to provide information on state and federal legislation affecting urban library programs and systems; to facilitate the exchange of ideas and programs of member libraries and other libraries; to develop programs that enable libraries to act as a focus of community development and to supply the informational needs of the new urban populations; to conduct research and educational programs that will benefit urban libraries and to solicit and accept grants, contributions, and donations essential to their implementation.

ULC currently receives most of its funding from membership dues. Future projects will involve the solicitation of grant funding. ULC is a 501(c)(3) not-for-profit corporation based in the state of Illinois.

## Membership

Membership is open to public libraries serving populations of 50,000 or more located in a Standard Metropolitan Statistical Area and to corporations specializing in library-related materials and services. Dues are based on the size of the organization's operating budget, according to the following schedule: under $2 million, $1,000; $2 million to $5 million, $1,250; $5 million to $10 million, $1,500; $10 million to $15 million, $2,000; over $15 million, $2,500. In addition, ULC member libraries may choose Sustaining or Contributing status (Sustaining, $10,000; Contributing, $5,000).

## Officers (1998–1999)

*Chair* Andrew Blau, John and Mary Markle Foundation, 75 Rockefeller Plaza, Suite 1800, New York, NY 10019. Tel. 212-489-6655, fax 212-765-9690, e-mail andrew_blau@markle.org; *V. Chair/Chair Elect* Susan Kent, Los Angeles Public Lib., 630 W. Fifth St., Los Angeles, CA 90071. Tel. 213-228-7516, fax 213-228-7519, e-mail skent@lapl.org; *Secy./Treas.* Elliot Shelkrot, Free Lib. of Philadelphia, 1901 Vine St., Philadelphia, PA 19103-1189. Tel. 215-686-5300, fax 215-686-5368, e-mail shelkrote@Library.Phila.Gov.

Officers serve one-year terms, members of the executive board two-year terms. New officers are elected and take office at the summer annual meeting of the council.

## Executive Board

Dan Bradbury. E-mail dan@kcpl.lib.mo.us; Steven A. Coulter. E-mail coult@pactell.net; Mary Doty. Tel. 612-332-7853; Jim Fish. E-mail jfish@mail.bcpl.lib.md.us; Sally Freeman Frasier. E-mail sfra5354@aol.com; Toni Garvey. E-mail tgarvey@ci.phoenix.az.us; Frances Hunter. E-mail fran@cua3.csuohio.edu; Marilyn Jackson. Tel. 612-922-1521; G. Victor Johnson. E-mail Vic-Johnson@Checkers-LLP.COM; Betty Jane Narver. E-mail bjnarver@u.washington.edu; Dianne Sautter. Tel. 312-527-1000; Michael (Mickey) Schott. Tel. 210-696-5177; Edward M. Szynaka. E-mail eds@imcpl.lib.in.us; Eleanor Jo (Joey) Rodger. E-mail ejr@gpl.glenview.lib.il.us.

## Key Staff

*Pres.* Eleanor Jo Rodger; *V.P., Admin. and Program* Bridget A. Bradley; *Project Dir.* Marybeth Schroeder; *Admin. Assistants* Shanice Davis, Sandra Marcelin, Sara Murphy.

## Publications

Frequent Fast Facts Surveys: *Fund Raising and Financial Development Survey Results* (1993); *Staffing Survey Results* (1993); *Collection Development Survey Results* (1994); *Library Security Survey Results* (1994); *Public Libraries and Private Fund Raising: Opportunities and Issues* (1994); *Off Site Survey Results* (1995); *Governance and Funding of Urban Public Libraries Survey Results* (1997); *Internet Access and Use Survey Results* (1997).

*Urban Libraries Exchange* (mo.; memb.).

# State, Provincial, and Regional Library Associations

The associations in this section are organized under three headings: United States, Canada, and Regional. Both the United States and Canada are represented under Regional associations.

## United States

### Alabama

Memb. 1,200. Term of Office. Apr. 1998–Apr. 1999. Publication. *The Alabama Librarian* (q.). *Pres.* Nancy Simms Donahoo, North Shelby County Lib.; *Secy.* Jane Garrett, 3533 Honeysuckle Rd., Montgomery 36109; *Treas.* Donna Fitch, 2917 Dublin Dr., Helena 35080; *Exec. Dir.* Barbara Black, 400 S. Union St., Suite 255, Montgomery 36104. Tel. 334-262-5210, fax 334-834-6398.

Address correspondence to the executive director.

### Alaska

Memb. 359. Publication. *Newspoke* (bi-mo.). *Pres.* Charlotte Glover. E-mail charg@muskox.alaska.edu; *V.P.* Bill Smith. E-mail whsakla@juno.com; *Secy.* Judy Green. E-mail afjfg@uaa.alaska.edu; *Treas.* Debbie Kalvez. E-mail ffdhk@auroura.alaska.edu; *Exec. Secy.* Bob Anderl. E-mail boba@muskox.alaska.edu. Association e-mail akla@alaska.net, fax 907-479-4784.

Address correspondence to the secretary, Alaska Library Association, Box 81084, Fairbanks 99708.

### Arizona

Memb. 1,200. Term of Office. Nov. 1998–Dec. 1999. Publication. *AzLA Newsletter* (mo.). Articles for the newsletter should be sent to the attention of the newsletter editor. *Pres.* Caryl Major, 1357 E. Sheena Dr., Phoenix, AZ 85022. Tel. 602-548-1405, 602-942-0126, e-mail cmajor1015@aol.com; *Treas.* Sharon Laser, Scottsdale Public Lib., 3839 Civic Center Blvd., Scottsdale 85251. Tel. 602-994-2692, fax 602-994-7993; *Exec. Secy.* Jean Johnson, 14449 N. 73 St., Scottsdale 85260-3133. Tel. 602-998-1954, fax 602-998-7838, e-mail meetmore@aol.com.

Address correspondence to the executive secretary.

### Arkansas

Memb. 603. Term of Office. Jan.–Dec. 1999. Publication. *Arkansas Libraries* (bi-mo.). *Pres.* Mary Furlough, Layman Public Lib., 2801 Orange St., North Little Rock 72114; *Exec. Dir.* Jennifer Coleman, Arkansas Lib. Assn., 9 Shackleford Plaza, Suite 1, Little Rock 72211. Tel. 501-228-0775, fax 501-228-5535.

Address correspondence to the executive director.

### California

Memb. 2,500. Term of Office. Nov. 1998–Nov. 1999. Publication. *California Libraries* (mo., except July/Aug., Nov./Dec.). *Pres.* Anne Campbell, National City Public Lib.; *V.P./Pres.-Elect* Linda Crowe; *Exec. Dir.* Mary Sue Ferrell, California Lib. Assn., 717 K St., Suite 300, Sacramento 95814. Tel. 916-447-8541, fax 916-447-8394, e-mail info@cla-net.org. Organization World Wide Web site http://www.cla-net.org.

Address correspondence to the executive director.

### Colorado

Memb. 995. Term of Office. Oct. 1998–Oct. 1999. Publication. *Colorado Libraries* (q.). *Ed.* Nancy Carter, Univ. of Colorado, Campus Box 184, Boulder 80309. *Pres.* James LaRue, Douglas Public Lib. District, 961 S. Plum Creek Blvd. Castle Rock 80104. Tel. 303-688-8752, e-mail jlarue@csn.net; *V.P./Pres.-Elect* Eloise May, Arapahoe Lib. District, 2305 E. Arapahoe Rd., No. 112, Littleton 80122-1583. Tel. 303-798-2444, e-mail emay@ald.lib.co.us; *Treas.*

George Jaramillo, Univ. of Northern Colorado, Greeley 80634; *Exec. Dir.* Kim Enomoto. Address correspondence to the executive director at 4350 Wadsworth Blvd., Suite 340, Wheat Ridge 80033. Tel. 303-422-1150, fax 303-431-9752, e-mail CLA2000@info.jeffer son.lib.co.us.

## Connecticut

Memb. 1,100. Term of Office. July 1998–June 1999. Publication. *Connecticut Libraries* (11 per year). *Ed.* David Kapp, 4 Llynwood Dr., Bolton 06040. Tel. 203-647-0697.

*Pres.* Michael Moran, Asnuntuck Community Technical College, Enfield 06082. Tel. 860-253-3171; *V.P./Pres.-Elect* Michael Golacik, Southern Connecticut Lib. Council, Hamden 06518-3130. Tel. 203-288-5757; *Treas.* Nora Bird, Gateway Community Technical College, North Haven 06473. Tel. 203-789-7064; *Administrator* Karen Zoller, Connecticut Lib. Assn., Franklin Commons, 106 Rte. 32, Franklin 06254. Tel. 860-885-2758, e-mail kzoller@connix.com.

Address correspondence to the administrator.

## Delaware

Memb. 300. Term of Office. Apr. 1999–Apr. 2000. Publication. *DLA Bulletin* (3 per year).

*Pres.* David Burdash, Wilmington Institute Lib., Wilmington. Tel. 302-571-7400; *Treas.* Paula Davino, Dover Public Lib. Tel. 302-736-7030.

Address correspondence to the association, Box 816, Dover 19903-0816.

## District of Columbia

Memb. 600. Term of Office. Aug. 1999–Aug. 2000. Publication. *CAPCON Alert* (mo.).

*Pres.* Robert Drescher, 1990 M Street N.W., Suite 200, Washington 20036. Tel. 202-331-5771, fax 202-331-5788, e-mail drescher@capcon.net.

Address correspondence to the association, 1990 M Street, N.W., Suite 200, Washington 20036.

## Florida

Memb. (Indiv.) 1,400; (In-state Inst.) 93. Term of Office. July 1998–June 1999. Publication. *Florida Libraries* (bi-mo.).

*Pres.* Mary Jane Little, St. Johns County Public Lib., 1960 N. Ponce de Leon Blvd., St. Augustine 32084. Tel. 904-823-2651, voice mail 904-823-2623, fax 904-823-2656, e-mail mjlittle@co.ct-johns.fl.us; *V.P./Pres.-Elect* Madison Mosley, Jr., Charles A. Dana Law Lib., Stetson Univ. College of Law, 1401 61st St. S., St. Petersburg 33707. Tel 27-562-7827, fax 727-345-8973, e-mail mosley@law.stetson.edu; *Secy.* Sandra Newell, State Lib. of Florida, 500 S. Bronough St., Tallahassee 32399. Tel. 850-487-2651, fax 850-488-2746, e-mail snewell@mail. cos.state.fl.us; *Treas.* Ruth O'Donnell, 3509 Trillium Ct., Tallahassee 32312. Tel. 850-668-6911, fax 850-894-5652, e-mail odonnellr@ worldnet.att.net. *Exec. Secy.* Marjorie Stealey, Florida Lib. Assn., 1133 W. Morse Blvd., Suite 201, Winter Park 32789. Tel. 407-647-8839 ext. 225, fax 407-629-2502, e-mail mjs@crowsegal.com.

Address correspondence to the executive secretary.

## Georgia

Memb. 1,100. Term of Office. Oct. 1998–Oct. 1999. Publication. *Georgia Library Quarterly.* *Ed.* Susan Cooley, Sara Hightower Regional Lib., 203 Riverside Pkwy., Rome 30161. Tel. 706-236-4621.

*Pres.* Ann Hamilton, Assoc. Univ. Libn., Zach S. Henderson Lib., Georgia Southern Univ., Box 807 4, Statesboro 30460-8074. Tel. 912-681-5115, fax 912-681-0093, e-mail ahamilton@gasou.edu; *1st V. P./Pres.-Elect,* Mike Seigler, Dir., Smyrna Public Lib., 100 Village Green Circle, Smyrna, 30080-3478. Tel. 770 431-2860, fax 770-431-2862, e-mail mseigler@bellsouth.et; *2nd V.P.* Julie White Walker, Asst. Dir., Athens Regional Lib. System, 2025 Baxter St., Athens 30606. Tel. 706-613-3650, fax 706-613-3660, e-mail jwalker@mail.clarke.public.lib.ga.us; *Secy.* Diana Ray Tope, Dir., Cherokee Regional Lib., 305 South Duke St., Lafayette 30728-2936. Tel. 706-638-2992, fax 706-638-4059, e-mail dtope@mail.walker.public.lib.ga.us; *Treas.* Gordon Baker, Media Center Dir., Eagle's Landing H.S., 301 Tunis Rd., McDonough 30253. Tel. 770-954-9515, fax 770 914 9789, e-mail GordonBaker@mail.clayton. edu; *Past Pres.* Alan Kaye, Dir., Roddenbery Memorial Lib., 320 North Broad St., Cairo 31728-2199. Tel. 912-377-3632, fax 912-377-7204, e-mail akaye@mail.grady.public. lib.ga.us; *ALA Councillor* Ralph E. Russell, 8160 Willow Tree Way, Alpharetta 30202. E-mail r1933@mindspring.com.

Address correspondence to the president.

## Hawaii

Memb. 450. Publications. *HLA Newsletter* (q.); *HLA Journal* (ann.); *HLA Membership Directory* (ann.).

Address correspondence to the association, Box 4441, Honolulu 96812-4441.

## Idaho

Memb. 500. Term of Office. Oct. 1998–Oct. 1999. Publication. *Idaho Librarian* (q.). *Ed.* Christine DeZelar-Tiedman, Univ. of Idaho Lib., Moscow 83844-2350. Tel. 208-885-2509, e-mail chrisd@belle.lib.uidaho.edu.

*Pres.* Dawn Wittman, Rte. 1, Box 47, Cul de Sac, Idaho 83524. Tel. 208-843-2960; *1st V.P.* Ron Force, Univ. of Idaho Lib., Moscow, Idaho 83844. Tel. 208-885-6534; *Treas.* Sandi Shropshire, F. M. Oboler Lib., Idaho State Univ., Box 8089, Pocatello 83209. Tel. 208-236-2671.

Address correspondence to the president.

## Illinois

Memb. 3,000. Term of Office. July 1998–July 1999. Publication. *ILA Reporter* (bi-mo.).

*Pres.* Pamela Gaitskill, Prairie State College, 202 S. Halsted St., Chicago Heights 60411-8226. Tel. 708-709-3551, fax 708-709-3940, e-mail pgaitskill@prairie.cc.il.us; *V.P./Pres.-Elect* Carolyn Anthony, Skokie Public Lib., 5215 Oakton St., Skokie 60077-3680. Tel. 847-673-7774, fax 847-673-7797, e-mail anthc@skokie.lib.il.us; *Treas.* Susan K. Herring, Peoria Public Lib., 107 N.E. Monroe St., Peoria 61602-1070. Tel. 309-

672-8835, fax 309-674-0116, e-mail sherring @darkstar.rsa.lib.il.us; *Exec. Dir.* Robert P. Doyle, 33 W. Grand Ave., Suite 301, Chicago 60610. Tel. 312-644-1896, fax 312-644-1899, e-mail doyle@ila.org. Organization World Wide Web site http://www.ila. org.

Address correspondence to the executive director.

## Indiana

Memb. (Indiv.) 4,000; (Inst.) 300. Term of Office. May 1998–May 1999. Publications. *Focus on Indiana Libraries* (11 per year), *Indiana Libraries* (s. ann.). *Ed.* Patricia Tallman.

*Pres.* Charr Skirvin, Plainfield Public Lib., 1120 Stafford Rd., Plainfield 46168. Tel 317-839-6602, fax 317-839-4044, e-mail cskirvin@ plainfield.lib.in.us; *1st V.P.* Patricia Kantner, Purdue Univ. Libs., 1310 Northwestern Ave., W. Lafayette 47906-2263. Tel. 765-494-2812, fax 765-494-0156, e-mail kantner@ purdue.edu; *Secy.* Sara Anne Hook, IU School of Dentistry Lib., 1121 W. Michigan St., Indianapolis 46202. Tel. 317-274-5208, fax 317-278-1256, e-mail sahook@iupui.edu; *Treas.* Connie Patsiner, IVAN, 6201 LaPaz Trail, Suite 280, Indianapolis 46268. Tel./fax 317-329-9163, e-mailiaudio@indy.edu; *Past Pres.* Steven Schmidt, 50 S. Butler Ave., Indianapolis 46219. Tel. 317-274-0470, fax 317-274-0492, e-mail schmidt@iupui. edu.

Address correspondence to the Indiana Lib. Federation, 6408 Carrolton Ave., Indianapolis 46220. Tel. 317-257-2040, fax 317-257-1393, e-mail ilf@indy.net.

## Iowa

Memb. 1,700. Term of Office. Jan.–Dec. Publication. *The Catalyst* (bi-mo.). *Ed.* Naomi Stovall.

*Pres.* Mary Wegner, Central Iowa Health Systems, 1200 Pleasant, Des Moines 50300. *V.P.* Carol French Johnson, Cedar Falls Public Lib., 524 Main, Cedar Falls 50613.

Address correspondence to the association, 505 Fifth Ave., Suite 823, Des Moines 50309. Tel. 515-243-2172, fax 515-243-0614, e-mail ialib@mcleoduse.net.

## Kansas

Memb. 1,200. Term of Office. July 1998–June 1999. Publications. *KLA Newsletter* (q.); *KLA Membership Directory* (ann.).

*Exec. Secy.* Leroy Gattin, South Central Kansas Lib. System, 901 N. Main St., Hutchinson 67501. Tel. 316-663-5441 ext. 110, fax 316-6 63-9506, e-mail lgatt@hplsck.org; *Secy.* Judith Edelsetin, Manhattan Public Lib., 629 Poyntz, Manhattan 66502. Tel. 316-283-2890, fax 316-283-2916; *Treas.* Marcella Ratzlaff, Hutchinson Public Lib., 901 N. Main St., Hutchinson 67501. Tel. 316-663-5441.

Address correspondence to the executive secretary.

## Kentucky

Memb. 1,900. Term of Office. Oct. 1998–Oct. 1999. Publication. *Kentucky Libraries* (q.).

*Pres.* Carol Brinkman. Tel. 502-852-1008; *V.P./Pres.-Elect* Carolyn Tassie. Tel. 606-233-8225; *Secy.* Linda Smith. Tel. 606-885-3612; *Exec. Secy.* Tom Underwood, 1501 Twilight Trail, Frankfort 40601. Tel. 502-223-5322.

Address correspondence to the executive secretary.

## Louisiana

Memb. (Indiv.) 1,500; (Inst.) 60. Term of Office. July 1998–June 1999. Publication. *LLA Bulletin* (q.). *Ed.* Mary Cosper Le Boeuf, 424 Roussell St., Houma 70360. Tel. 504-876-5861, fax 504-876-5864, e-mail ter@pelican.state.lib.la.us.

*Pres.* Idella Washington, 2001 Leon C. Simon, New Orleans 70122. Tel. 504-286-2611; *1st V.P./Pres.-Elect* Paige Hanchy, 301 W. Claude St., Lake Charles 70605. Tel. 318-475-8798, e-mail paige@grok.calcasieu.lib.la.us; *Exec. Secy.* Christy Chandler. Tel. 504-342-4928.

Address correspondence to the association, Box 3058, Baton Rouge 70821. Tel. 504-342-4928, fax 504-342-3547, e-mail lla@pelican.state.lib. la.us.

## Maine

Memb. 900. Term of Office. (Pres., V.P.) spring 1998–spring 2000. Publications. *Maine Entry* (q.); *Maine Memo* (mo.).

*Pres.* Elizabeth Moran, Camden Public Lib., Camden 04843. Tel. 207-236-3440; *V.P.* Jay Scherma, Thomas Memorial Lib., 6 Scott Dyer Rd., Cape Elizabeth. Tel. 207-799-1720; *Secy.* Elizabeth Breault, Abbott Memorial Lib., 1 Church St., Dexter 14930. Tel. 207-924-7292; *Treas.* Robert Filgate, McArthur Public Lib., Biddeford 04005. Tel. 207-284-4181.

Address correspondence to the association, 60 Community Dr., Augusta 04330. Tel. 207-623-8428, fax 207-626-5947.

## Maryland

Memb. 1,300. Term of Office. July 1999–July 2000. Publication. *The Crab.*

*Pres.* Mary Baykan, Washington County Free Lib., 100 S. Potomac St., Hagerstown 21740. Tel. 301-739-3250, fax 301-739-5839.

Address correspondence to the association, 400 Cathedral St., Baltimore 21201-4401. Tel. 410-727-7422, fax 410-625-9594, e-mail mla@mail.pratt.lib.md.us

## Massachusetts

Memb. (Indiv.) 950; (Inst.) 100. Term of Office. July 1999–June 2000. Publication. *Bay State Libraries* (10 per year).

*Pres.* Dierdre Hanley, Reading Public Lib., 64 Middlesex Ave., Reading 01867. Tel. 781-942-9110; *Treas.* Cynthia Roach, Southeastern Massachusetts Lib. System, 10 Riverside Dr., Lakeville 02347. Tel. 508-923-3531; *Exec. Secy.* Barry Blaisdell, Massachusetts Lib. Assn., Countryside Offices, 707 Turnpike St., North Andover 01845. Tel. 508-923-3531, e-mail masslib@world.std.com.

Address correspondence to the executive secretary.

## Michigan

Memb. (Indiv.) 2,200; (Inst.) 375. Term of Office. July 1998–June 1999. Publication. *Michigan Librarian Newsletter* (10 per year).

*Pres.* Nancy Bujold, Rochester Hills Public Lib., 306 Ferndale, Rochester 48334; *Treas.* Tom Genson, Grand Rapids Public Lib., 60 Library Plaza N.E., Grand Rapids 49503; *Exec. Dir.* Marianne Hartzell, Michigan Lib. Assn., 6810 S. Cedar St., Suite 6, Lansing 48911. Tel. 517-694-6615.

Address correspondence to the executive director.

## Minnesota

Memb. 1,094. Term of Office. (Pres., Pres.-Elect) Jan.–Dec. 1999; (Treas.) Jan. 1998–Dec. 1999; (Secy.) Jan. 1999–Dec. 2000. Publication. *MLA Newsletter* (6 per year).

*Pres.* Beth Kelly, Duluth Public Lib., 520 Superior St., Duluth 55802; *Pres.-Elect* Joan Larson, Northern Lights Lib. Network, Box 845, Alexandria 56308; *ALA Chapter Councillor* Gretchen Marie Wronka, Hennepin County Lib., 12601 Ridgedale Dr., Minnetonka 55343; *Secy.* Zona Meyer, Hamline Law Lib., 1536 Hewitt, St. Paul 55104; *Treas.* Donald Kelsey, Univ. of Minnesota, Twin Cities; *Exec. Dir.* William R. Brady, 2324 University Ave. W., Suite 103, Saint Paul 55114. Tel. 651-641-0982, fax 651-641-1035, e-mail mla@mr.net.

Address correspondence to the executive director.

## Mississippi

Memb. 700. Term of Office. Jan.–Dec. 1999. Publication. *Mississippi Libraries* (q.).

*Pres.* Susanna Turner, 305 Edgewood Dr., Starkville 39759. Tel. 601-325-8391; *Exec. Secy.* Mary Julia Anderson, Box 20448, Jackson 39289-1448. Tel. 601-352-3917.

Address correspondence to the executive secretary.

## Missouri

Memb. 1,000. Term of Office. Oct. 1998–Oct. 1999. Publication. *MO INFO* (bi-mo.). *Ed.* Jean Ann McCartney.

*Pres.* Elinor Barrett, Daniel Boone Regional Lib., 100 W. Broadway, Columbia 65203-1267. Tel. 573-443-3161; *V.P./Pres.-Elect* Molly Lawson, Central Missouri State Univ., Warrensburg 64093-5020. Tel. 660-543-

8780; *Past Pres.* Elizabeth Ader, Univ. of Missouri Kansas City Lib., 5100 Rockhill Rd., Kansas City 64110-2499. Tel. 816-235-1530; *Treas.* Robert Almony, Ellis Lib., Univ. of Missouri, Columbia 65201-5249. Tel. 573-882-4701; *Secy.* Anitra Steele, Mid-Continent Public Lib., 15616 E. 24 Hwy., Independence 65200. Tel. 816-836-5200; *ALA Councillor* June De Weese, Head of Access Services, Ellis Lib., Univ. of Missouri, Columbia 65201-5149. Tel. 573-882-7315, fax 573-882-8044, e-mail elsjune@mizzou1.missouri.edu; *Exec. Dir.* Jean Ann McCartney, Missouri Lib. Assn., 1306 Business 63 S., Suite B, Columbia 65201. Tel. 573-449-4627, fax 573-449-4655, e-mail jmccartn@mail.more.net.

Address correspondence to the executive director.

## Montana

Memb. 700. Term of Office. July 1998–June 1999. Publication. *Montana Library Focus* (bi-mo.). *Ed.* Dee Ann Redman, Box 505 Helena 59624.

*Pres.* Bill Cochran, Parmly Billings Lib., 510 N. Broadway, Billings 59101. Tel. 406-657-8292, fax 406-657-8293, e-mail cochran@billings.lib.mt.us; *V.P./Pres.-Elect* Bruce Newell, Lewis & Clark Lib., 120 S. Last Chance, Helena 59601.Tel.406-447-1690, fax 406-447-1687, e-mail bnewell@mtlib.org; *Secy./Treas.* Alice Meister, Bozeman Public Lib., 220 E. Lamme, Bozeman 59715. Tel. 406-582-2401, fax 406-582-2424, e-mail ameister@mtlib.org; *Admin. Asst.* John Thomas, Box 505, Helena 596 24-0505. Tel. 406-442-9446.

Address correspondence to the administrative assistant.

## Nebraska

Memb. 1,000. Term of Office. Oct. 1998–Oct. 1999. Publication. *NLA Quarterly* (q.).

*Pres.* Jeanne Saathoff, Kearney Public Lib., Kearney; *Exec. Dir.* Margaret Harding, Box 98, Crete 68333. Tel. 402-826-2636, e-mail ghl2521@navix.net.

Address correspondence to the executive director.

## Nevada

Memb. 400. Term of Office. Jan.–Dec. 1999. Publication. *Nevada Libraries* (q.).

*Pres.* Bonnie Buckley, Nevada State Lib. and Archives. Tel. 702-687-8324, e-mail bjbuckle@clan.lib.nv.us; *V.P./Pres.-Elect* Richard Lee. Tel. 702-256-1111, e-mail richardl@lvccld.lib.nv.us; *Treas.* Susan Antipa. Tel. 702-887-2244 ext. 1016, e-mail smantipa@clan.lib.nv.us; *Exec. Secy.* Nadine Phinney. Tel. 702-674-7606, fax 702-673-7273, e-mail nphinney@fs.scs.unr.edu.

Address correspondence to the executive secretary.

## New Hampshire

Memb. 700. Publication. *NHLA Newsletter* (bi-mo.).

*Pres.* John Brisbin, Manchester City Lib., 405 Pine St., Manchester 03104-6199. Tel. 603-624-6550; *Secy.* Lindalee Lambert, Box 367, West Ossipee 03890. Tel. 603-539-4606.

## New Jersey

Memb. 1,700. Term of Office. July 1998–June 1999. Publications. *New Jersey Libraries* (q.); *New Jersey Libraries Newsletter* (mo.).

*Pres.* Cynthia Czesak, Clifton Lib., 292 Piaget Ave., Clifton 07011; *Pres.-Elect* Joseph Keenan, Elizabeth Public Lib., 11 S. Broad St., Elizabeth 07202; *Treas.* John Hurley, Woodbridge Public Lib., George Frederick Plaza, Woodbridge 07095; *Exec. Dir.* Patricia Tumulty, New Jersey Lib. Assn., 4 W. Lafayette St., Trenton 08608. Tel. 609-394-8032.

Address correspondence to the executive director, Box 1534, Trenton 08607.

## New Mexico

Memb. 550. Term of Office. Apr. 1999–Apr. 2000. Publication. *New Mexico Library Association Newsletter* (6 per year). *Ed.* Jackie Shane. Tel. 505-277-5410, e-mail jshane@unm.edu.

*Pres.* Charlene Greenwood, 3540 Haines Ave. N.E., Albuquerque 87106; Tel. 505-256-1379; *Admin. Svcs.* Linda O'Connell,

Box 26074, Albuquerque 87125. Tel. 505-899-3516, e-mail nmla@rt66.com.

Address correspondence to the association, Box 26074, Albuquerque 87125.

## New York

Memb. 3,000. Term of Office. Oct. 1998–Nov. 1999. Publication. *NYLA Bulletin* (10 per year). *Ed.* Paul Girsdansky.

*Pres.* Nancy Zimmerman, Asst. Professor, School of Info. and Lib. Studies, 534 Baldy Hall, Box 601020, Buffalo 14260. E-mail npz@acsu.buffalo.edu; *Exec. Dir.* Susan Lehman Keitel, New York Lib. Assn., 252 Hudson Ave., Albany 12210. Tel. 518-432-6952, e-mail nyla.skeitel@pobox.com.

Address correspondence to the executive director.

## North Carolina

Memb. 2,200. Term of Office. Oct. 1997–Oct. 1999. Publication. *North Carolina Libraries* (q.). *Ed.* Frances Bradburn, Media and Technology, N.C. Dept. of Public Instruction, 301 N. Wilmington St., Raleigh 27601-2825.

*Pres.* Beverley Gass, Guilford Technical Community College, Box 309, Jamestown 27282-0309. Tel. 910-334-4822 ext. 2434, fax 910-841-4350; *V.P./Pres.-Elect* Al Jones, Dir. of Lib. Service, Catawba College, 2300 W. Innes St., Salisbury, NC 28144. Tel. 704-637-4449; *Secy.* Elizabeth Jackson, West Lake Elementary School, 207 Glen Bonnie La., Cary, NC 27511. Tel. 919-380-8232; *Treas.* Diane Kester, Dept. of Lib. Services Educ. and Technology, East Carolina Univ., 105 Longview Dr., Goldsboro, NC 27534. Tel. 919-328-6621.

Address correspondence to NCLA, 109 E. Jones St., No. 27, Raleigh, NC 27601-1023.

## North Dakota

Memb. (Indiv.) 367; (Inst.) 18. Term of Office. Oct. 1998–Sept. 1999. Publication. *The Good Stuff* (q.). *Ed.* Ellen Kotrba, ODIN, Box 7085, Grand Forks 58202-7085. Tel. 701-777-2166.

*Pres.* Barb Knight, UND Medical Lib., Box 9002, Grand Forks 58202-9002. Tel. 701-777-2166; *Secy.* Phyllis Bratton, Raugust

Lib., 6070 College La., Jamestown 58405-0002. Tel. 701-252-3467; *Treas.* Donna Maston, Bismarck Public Lib., 515 N. Fifth St., Bismarck 58501. Tel. 701-222-6414.

Address correspondence to the president.

## Ohio

Memb. 3,090. Term of Office. Jan.–Dec. Publications. *Access* (mo.); *Ohio Libraries* (q.).

*Chair* Terry Casey, 249 Overbrook Dr., Columbus 43214; *Secy.* Jack Carlson, 2904 Green Vista Dr., Fairborn 45324; *Exec. Secy.* Frances Haley.

Address correspondence to the association, 35 E. Gay St., Suite 305, Columbus 43215. Tel. 614-221-9057.

## Oklahoma

Memb. (Indiv.) 1,050; (Inst.) 60. Term of Office. July 1998–June 1999. Publication. *Oklahoma Librarian* (bi-mo.).

*Pres.* Deborah Engel, Pioneer Lib. System, 225 N. Webster, Norman 73069. Tel. 405-321-1481; *Secy.* Gary Phillips, Oklahoma Dept. of Libs., 200 N.E. 18th St., Oklahoma City 73105. Tel. 405-521-2502; *Treas.* John Augelli, Stillwater Public Lib., 1107 S. Duck, Stillwater 74074. Tel. 405-372-3633; *Exec. Dir.* Kay Boies, 300 Hardy Dr., Edmond 73013. Tel./fax 405-348-0506, e-mail kboies @ionet.net.

Address correspondence to the executive director.

## Oregon

Memb. (Indiv.) 1,000. Publications. *OLA Hotline* (bi-w.), *OLA Quarterly.*

*Pres.* Sara Charleton, Tillamook County Lib. Tel. 503-842-4792; *Secy.* Anne Van Sickle, McMinnville Public Lib., 225 N. Adams St., McMinnville 97128. Tel. 503-434-7433.

Address correspondence to the secretary.

## Pennsylvania

Memb. 1,500. Term of Office. Jan.–Dec. 1999. Publication. *PaLA Bulletin* (mo.).

*Pres.* Barbara P. Casini, Memorial Lib. of Radnor Township, 114 W. Wayne Ave., Wayne, PA 19087. Tel. 610-687-1124, e-mail casini@ hslc.org; *1st V.P.* David J. Roberts, Wissahickon Valley Public Lib., 713 Stradone Rd., Bala Cynwyd, PA 19004. Tel. 215-643-1320, e-mail droberts@mciunix.mciu.k12,pa. us; *Exec. Dir.* Glenn R. Miller, Pennsylvania Lib. Assn., 1919 N. Front St., Harrisburg 17102. Tel. 717-233-3113, e-mail plassn@hslc.org.

Address correspondence to the executive director.

## Rhode Island

Memb. (Indiv.) 341; (Inst.) 59. Term of Office. June 1999–June 2001. Publication. *Rhode Island Library Association Bulletin. Ed.* Frank Iacono.

*Pres.* Kathy Ellen Bullard, Woonsocket Harris Public Lib., 303 Clinton St., Woonsocket 02895. Tel. 401-769-9044, fax 401-767-4140, e-mail kathybd@lori.state.ri.us; *Secy.* Derryl Johnson, Marian Mohr Memorial Lib., 1 Memorial Drive, Johnston 02919; Tel. 401-231-4980, fax 401-231-4984.

Address correspondence to the secretary.

## South Carolina

Memb. 800. Term of Office. Jan.–Dec. 1999. Publication. *News and Views.*

*Pres.* Betsey Carter, The Citadel, Charleston. Tel. 843-953-6844, fax 843-953-5190, e-mail cartere@citadel.edu; *V.P.* Norman Belk, Greenville County Lib. Tel. 864-242-3000 ext. 238, fax 864-235-8375, e-mail Nbelk@infoave.net; *2nd V.P.* Thomas Shepley, South Carolina State Lib. Tel. 803-734-8666, fax 803-734-8676, e-mail thomas@ leo.scsl.state.sc.us; *Secy.* Nonie Price, CLIS, Univ. of South Carolina. Tel. 803-777-0513, fax 803-777-7938, e-mail nprice@sc.edu; *Treas.* Maureen Harris, Clemson Univ. Tel. 864-656-5174, fax 864-656-2025, e-mail maureen@clemson.edu; *Exec. Secy.* Drucie Raines, South Carolina Lib. Assn., Box 219, Goose Creek 29445. Tel. 803-764-3668, fax 803-824-2690, e-mail scla@charleston.net.

Address correspondence to the executive secretary.

## South Dakota

Memb. (Indiv.) 432; (Inst.) 55. Term of Office. Oct. 1998–Oct. 1999. Publication. *Book Marks* (bi-mo.).

*Pres.* Mike Mullin, Watertown Regional Lib., Watertown 57201. Tel. 605-882-6226, fax 605-882-6221, e-mail mmullin@sdln.net; *Secy.* Jane Goettsch, Siouxland Libs., Ronning Branch, 3100 E. 49 St., Sioux Falls 57103. Tel. 605-367-4607; *Treas.* Ann Eichinger, South Dakota State Lib., 800 Governors Dr., Pierre 57501; *ALA Councillor* Ethelle Bean, Karl E. Mundt Lib., Dakota State Univ., Madison 57042; *MPLA Rep.* Colleen Kirby, E. Y. Berry Lib., Black Hills State Univ., Spearfish 57783. Tel. 605-642-6361.

Address correspondence to Ann Smith, Exec. Secy., SDLA, c/o Mikkelsen Lib., Augustana College, Sioux Falls 57197. Tel. 605-336-4921, fax 605-336-5442, e-mail asmith@inst.augie.edu.

## Tennessee

Memb. 934. Term of Office. July 1998–July 1999. Publications. *Tennessee Librarian* (q.), *TLA Newsletter* (bi-mo.).

*Pres.* Martha Earl, Preston Medical Lib., Univ. of Tennessee at Knoxville, 1924 Alcoa Hwy., Knoxville 37920. Tel. 423-544-6616; *V.P./Pres.-Elect* Charles A. Sherrill, Tennessee State Lib. and Archives, 403 7th Ave. N., Nashville 37243-0312. Tel. 615-741-2764; *Treas.* Katherine Sleighter, S. Cheatham Public Lib., Box 310, Kingston Springs 37082-0310. Tel. 615-952-4752; *Past Pres.* Annelle R. Huggins, Univ. Libs., Univ. of Memphis, Campus Box 526500, Memphis 39152-6500. Tel. 901-678-4482; *Exec. Secy.* Betty Nance, Box 158417, Nashville 37215-8417. Tel. 615-207-8316, fax 615-269-1807, e-mail nancebo@dlu.edu.

Address correspondence to the executive secretary.

## Texas

Memb. 7,200. Term of Office. Apr. 1998–Apr. 1999. Publications. *Texas Library Journal*; (q.); *TLACast* (9 per year).

*Pres.* JoAnne Moore; *Exec. Dir.* Patricia Smith, TLA, 3355 Bee Cave Rd., Suite 401, Austin 78746-6763. Tel. 512-328-1518, fax 512-328-8852, e-mail pats@txla.org.

Address correspondence to the executive director.

## Utah

Memb. 650. Term of Office. May 1998–May 1999. Publication. *UTAH Libraries News* (bi-mo.).

*Pres.* Larry Ostler; *Treas./Exec. Secy.* Christopher Anderson. Tel. 801-273-8150.

Address correspondence to the executive secretary, Box 711789, Salt Lake City 84171-1789.

## Vermont

Memb. 450. Publication. *VLA News* (10 per year).

*Pres.* Hilari Farrington, Stowe Free Lib., Box 1029, Stowe 05672. Tel. 802-253-6145; *Secy.* Kathy Naftaly, Rutland Free Lib., 10 Court St., Rutland 05701. Tel. 802-773-1860; *ALA Councillor* Melissa Malcolm, Mount Abraham Union H.S., 7 Airport Dr., Bristol 05443. Tel. 802-453-2333; *NELA Rep.* Pamela Murphy, Hartness Lib., Vermont Technical College, Randolph Center 05060. Tel. 802-728-1236.

Address correspondence to the president.

## Virginia

Memb. 1,500+. Term of Office. Jan.–Dec. 1999. Publications. *Virginia Libraries* (q.), *Ed.* Cy Dillon; *VLA Newsletter* (10 per year), *Ed.* Mary Hansbrough, 2505 Gloucester Dr., Blacksburg 24060.

*Pres.* Sandra Heinemann, Hampden-Sydney College Lib., Box 122, Hampden-Sydney 23943. Tel. 804-223-8271; *V.P./Pres.-Elect* Carolyn Barkley, Virginia Beach Public Lib., Virginia Beach 23452. Tel. 757-431-3072; *2nd V.P.* Stella Pool, Jefferson Madison Regional Lib., 201 E. Market St., Charlottesville 23902. Tel. 804-979-7151; *Secy.* Nancy Newins, McGraw Page Lib., Randolph Macon College, Ashland, VA 23005. Tel. 804-752-4718; *Treas.* Terry Sumey, Box 770, Stuarts Draft 24477. Tel. 540-337-2630;

*Past Pres.* Thomas Hehman, Bedford Public Lib. Tel. 540-586-8911; *Exec. Dir.* Linda Hahne, Box 8277, Norfolk 23503-0277. Tel. 757-583-0041, fax 757-583-5041, e-mail hahne@bellatlantic.net. Organization World Wide Web site http://www.vla.org.

Address correspondence to the executive director.

## Washington

Memb. 1,200. Term of Office. Apr. 1999–Apr. 2001. Publications. *ALKI* (3 per year), *WLA Link* (5 per year); World Wide Web site http://www.wla.org.

*Pres.* Cynthia Cunningham; *V.P./Pres.-Elect* To be announced; *Treas.* To be announced; *Secy.* Carol Gill Schuyler; *Assn. Coord.* Gail E. Willis.

Address correspondence to the association office, 4016 1st Ave. N.E., Seattle 98105-6502. Tel. 206-545-1529, fax 206-545-1543, e-mail wasla@wla.org.

## West Virginia

Memb. 700. Term of Office. Dec. 1998–Nov. 1999. Publication. *West Virginia Libraries* (6 per year). *Eds.* Denise Ash, Box 149, Spencer 25276. Tel. 304-927-1770; Sue Eichelberger, West Virginia Lib. Commission, 1900 Kanawha Blvd. E., Charleston 25305. Tel. 304-558-2531.

*Pres.* Betty Gunnoe, Martinsburg Public Lib., 101 W. King St., Martinsburg 25401. Tel. 304-267-8933, fax 304-267-9720, e-mail gunnoeb@martin.lib.wv.us; *Past Pres.* Judy Duncan, Saint Albans Public Lib., 602 Fourth St., Saint Albans 25177-2820. Tel. 304-722-4244, fax 304-722-4276, e-mail duncanj@wvlc.wvnet.edu; *1st V.P./Pres.-Elect* Pam Coyle, South Charleston Public Lib., 312 Fourth Ave., South Charleston 25303-1297. tel. 304-744-6561, fax 304-744-8808, e-mail coyle@scpl.wvnet.edu; *2nd V.P.* Dottie Thomas, Ohio County Public Lib., 52 16th St., Wheeling 25003. Tel. 304-232-0244, fax 304-232-6848, e-mail thomasd@weirton.lib.wv.us; *Treas.* R. David Childers, West Virginia Lib. Commission, Cultural Center, 1900 Kanawha Blvd. E., Charleston 25305. Tel. 304-558-2041, fax 304-558-2044, e-mail childers@wvlc.wvnet.edu; *Secy.* Linda Lind-

sey, Richwood Public Lib., 8 White Ave., Richwood 26261-1338. Tel./fax 304-846-6222, e-mail lindseyl@wvlc.wvnet.edu; *ALA Councillor* Joseph Barnes, Scarborough Lib., Shepherd College, Shepherdstown 25443. Tel. 304-876-5312, fax 304-876-0731, e-mail jbarnes@shepherd.evnet.edu.

Address correspondence to the president.

## Wisconsin

Memb. 2,100. Term of Office. Jan.–Dec. 1999. Publication. *WLA Newsletter* (bi-mo.).

*Pres.* Jane Pearlmutter. Tel. 608-262-6398; *Exec. Dir.* Lisa Strand. Tel. 608-245-3640, fax 608-245-3646.

Address correspondence to the executive director.

## Wyoming

Memb. (Indiv.) 425; (Inst.) 21. Term of Office. Oct. 1998–Oct. 1999.

*Pres.* Keith Cottam, Univ. of Wyoming Libs., Box 3334, Laramie 82071. Tel. 307-766-3279. *Past Pres.* Mary Jayne Jordan, Sundance Jr. High, Box 850, Sundance 82729. Tel. 307-283-1007; *V.P./Pres.-Elect* Vickie Hoff; *Exec. Secy.* Laura Grott, Box 1387, Cheyenne 82003. Tel. 307-632-7622, fax 307-638-3469.

Address correspondence to the executive secretary.

## Guam

Memb. 75. Publication. *Guam Library Association News* (mo. during school year).

Address correspondence to the association, Box 20981 GMF, Guam 96921.

# Canada

## Alberta

Memb. 500. Term of Office. May 1998–Apr. 1999. Publication. *Letter of the LAA* (5 per year). World Wide Web site http://www.laa.ab.ca.

*Pres.* Barbara Bulat, Idylwyide Branch, Edmonton Public Lib., 8310 88 Ave., Edmonton T6C 1L1. Tel. 403-496-1808, fax 403-496-7092, e-mail bbulat@publib.edmonton.

ab.ca; *Exec. Dir.* Christine Sheppard, 80 Baker Crescent N.W., Calgary T2L 1R4. Tel. 403-284-5832, fax 403-282-6646, e-mail shepparc@cadvision.com.

Address correspondence to the executive director.

## British Columbia

Memb. 750. Term of Office. Apr. 1998–May 1999. Publication. *BCLA Reporter.* Ed. Ted Benson.

*Pres.* Greg Buss; *V.P./Pres.-Elect* Sybil Harrison; *Exec. Dir.* Michael Burris.

Address correspondence to the association, 150-900 Howe St., Vancouver V6Z 2M4. Tel. 604-683-5354, fax 604-609-0707, e-mail bcla@interchange.ubc.ca.

## Manitoba

Memb. 494. Term of Office. May 1998–May 1999. Publication. *Newsline* (mo.).

*Pres.* Jo Ann Brewster; *V.P./Pres.-Elect* Sheila Andrich.

Address correspondence to the association, 606-100 Arthur St., Winnipeg R3B 1H3. Tel. 204-943-4567, fax 204-942-1555.

## Ontario

Memb. 3,800+. Term of Office. Jan. 1999–Jan. 2000. Publications. *Access* (q.); *Teacher-Librarian* (q.); *Inside OLA* (q.). World Wide Web site http://www.accessola.org.

*Pres.* June Wilson, Ministry of Transportation Lib. Tel. 905-704-2011; *Treas.* Charlotte Meissner, Oakville Public Lib. Tel. 905-815-2042.

Address correspondence to the association, 100 Lombard St., Suite 303, Toronto M5C 1M3. Tel. 416-363-3388, fax 416-941-9581, e-mail info@acc essola.com.

## Quebec

Memb. (Indiv.) 140; (Inst.) 26; (Commercial) 3. Term of Office. June 1999–May 2000. Publication. *ABQ/QLA Bulletin* (3 per year).

*Pres.* Rennie MacLeod; *Exec. Secy.* Pat Fortin, Box 1095, Pointe Claire H95 4H9. Tel. 514-630-4875, e-mail abqla.qc.ca.

Address correspondence to the executive secretary.

## Saskatchewan

Memb. 225. Term of Office. June 1998–May 1999. Publication. *Forum* (5 per year). World Wide Web page http://www.lib.sk.ca/sla/.

*Pres.* Ken Vaughan; *Exec. Dir.* Judith Silverthorne, Box 3388, Regina S4P 3H1. Tel. 306-780-9413, fax 306-780-9447, e-mail sla@pleis.lib.sk.ca.

Address correspondence to the executive director.

# Regional

## Atlantic Provinces: N.B., Nfld., N.S., P.E.I.

Memb. (Indiv.) 196; (Inst.) 20. Term of Office. May 1998–May 1999. Publications. *APLA Bulletin* (bi-mo.), *Ed.* John Neilson; *Membership Directory and Handbook* (ann.).

*Pres.* Francesco Lai; *V.P./Pres.-Elect* Peter Webster; *V. P., Nova Scotia* Cathy Chisholm; *V.P., Prince Edward Island* Moira Davidson; *V.P. New Brunswick* Charlotte Dionne; *V.P., Newfoundland* Stephen Field; *V.P., Memb.* Barbara McDonald; *Secy.* Suzanne Sexty. Tel. 709-737-7427; *Treas.* Elaine MacLean.

Address correspondence to Atlantic Provinces Lib. Assn., c/o School of Lib. and Info. Studies, Dalhousie Univ., Halifax, NS B3H 4H8.

## Mountain Plains: Ariz., Colo., Kan., Mont., Neb., Nev., N.Dak., N.M., Okla., S.Dak., Utah, Wyo.

Memb. 920. Term of Office. One year. Publications. *MPLA Newsletter* (bi-mo.), *Ed. and Adv. Mgr.* Heidi M. Nickisch, I. D. Weeks Lib., Univ. of South Dakota, Vermillion, SD 57069. Tel. 605-677-6088, e-mail nickisch@usd.edu; *Membership Directory* (ann.).

*Pres.* Roann Masterson, Univ. of Mary, 7500 University Dr., Bismarck, ND 58504-9652. Tel. 701-255-7500 ext. 447, fax 701-255-7690, e-mail r.masterson@mail.cdln.lib.nd.us; *V.P./Pres.-Elect* Marilyn Hinshaw, Eastern Oklahoma District Lib. System, 814 W. Okmulgee, Muskogee, OK 74401. Tel. 918-683-2846, fax 918-683-0436, e-mail mhinshaw@esk.lib.ok.us; *Exec. Secy.* Joe Edelen, I. D. Weeks Lib., Univ. of South

Dakota, Vermillion, SD 57069. Tel. 605-677-6082, fax 605-677-6082, e-mail jedelen@usd.edu.

Address correspondence to the executive secretary.

### New England: Conn., Maine, Mass., N.H., R.I., Vt.

Memb. (Indiv.) 1,300; (Inst.) 100. Term of Office. One year (Treas., Dirs., and Secy, two years). Publication. *New England Libraries* (bi-mo.). *Ed.* Debra Covell, New England Lib. Assn., 707 Turnpike St., North Andover 01845. Tel. 978-685-5966.

*Exec. Secy.* Barry Blaisdell, New England Lib. Assn., 707 Turnpike St., North Andover, MA 01845. Tel. 508-685-5966, e-mail info@nelib.org

Address correspondence to the executive secretary.

### Pacific Northwest: Alaska, Idaho, Mont., Oreg., Wash., Alberta, B.C.

Memb. (Active) 550; (Subscribers) 100. Term of Office. Aug. 1998–Aug. 1999. Publication. *PNLA Quarterly. Ed.* Sue Samson, Mansfield Lib., Univ. of Montana, Missoula, MT 59812-1195. Tel. 406-243-4335, fax 406-243-2060, e-mail ss@selway.umt.edu.

*Pres.* Andrew Johnson, Government Publications Div., Univ. of Washington Lib., Box 352900, Seattle WA 98195-2900. Tel. 206-543-9156; fax 206-685-8049, e-mail afj@u.washington.edu; *1st V.P./Pres.-Elect* Karen Labuik, Marigold Lib. System, 710 2nd St., Strathmore, AB T1P 1K4. Tel. 403-934-5334; *2nd V.P..* Christine Sheppard, Lib. Assoc. of Alberta, 80 Baker Crescent N.W. Calgary, AB T2L 1R4. Tel. 403-284-5818; *Secy.* Colleen Bell, Knight Lib., 1299 U. of Oregon, Eugene, OR 97403-1299. Tel. 541-346-1817; *Treas.* Monica Weyhe, State Dept. of Administration, 118 Troy Ave., Juneau, AK 99801. Tel. 907-465-6989.

Address correspondence to the president, Pacific Northwest Lib. Assn.

### Southeastern: Ala., Ark., Fla., Ga., Ky., La., Miss., N.C., S.C., Tenn., Va., W.Va.

Memb. 700. Term of Office. Oct. 1998–Oct. 2000. Publication. *The Southeastern Librarian* (q.).

*Pres.* Frances N. Coleman, 2403 Maple Dr., Starkville, MS 39759; *V.P./Pres.-Elect* Barry Baker, 318 Prestwick Ct., Oviedo, FL 32765; *Secy.* Ellen Johnson, Univ. of Central Arkansas, 31 Forest Ct., Conway, AR 72032; *Treas.* William McRee, Stow South Carolina Historical Room, Greenville County Lib., 300 College St., Greenville, SC 29601-2086.

Address correspondence to the president or executive secretary, SELA Administrative Services, SOLINET, 1438 W. Peachtree St. N.W., Atlanta, GA 30309-2955. Tel. 404-892-0943.

# State and Provincial Library Agencies

The state library administrative agency in each of the U.S. states will have the latest information on its state plan for the use of federal funds under the Library Services and Technology Act. The directors and addresses of these state agencies are listed below.

### Alabama

Dir., Alabama Public Lib. Service, 6030 Monticello Dr., Montgomery 36130-2001. Tel. 334-213-3900, fax 334-213-3993.

### Alaska

Karen R. Crane, Dir., Div. of Libs., Archives, and Museums, Alaska Dept. of Educ., Box 110571, Juneau 99811-0571. Tel. 907-465-2910, fax 907-465-2151, e-mail karen_crane@educ.state.ak.us.

### Arizona

GladysAnn Wells, Dir., Dept. of Libs., Archives, and Public Records, State Capitol, 1700 W. Washington, Rm. 200, Phoenix 85007-2896. Tel. 602-542-4035, fax 602-542-4972, e-mail gawells@ dlapr.lib.az.us.

### Arkansas

John A. (Pat) Murphey, Jr., State Libn., Arkansas State Lib., One Capitol Mall, Little Rock 72201-1081. Tel. 501-682-1526, fax 501-682-1899, e-mail jmurphey @comp.uark.edu.

### California

Kevin Starr, State Libn., California State Lib., Box 942837, Sacramento 94237-0001. Tel. 916-654-0174, fax 916-654-0064, e-mail kstarr@library.ca.gov.

### Colorado

Nancy Bolt, Dep. State Libn. and Asst. Commissioner, Colorado State Lib., 201 E. Colfax Ave., Rm. 309, Denver 80203. Tel. 303-866-6733, fax 303-866-6940, e-mail nbolt@csn.net.

### Connecticut

Ken Wiggin, Interim State Libn., Connecticut State Lib., 231 Capitol Ave., Hartford 06106. Tel. 806-566-4301, fax 806-566-8940, e-mail kwiggin@csl.ctstateu.edu.

### Delaware

Tom W. Sloan, State Libn. and Div. Dir., Div. of Libs., 43 S. DuPont Hwy., Dover 19901. Tel. 302-739-4748, fax 302-739-6787, e-mail tsloan@lib.de.us.

### District of Columbia

Mary E. (Molly) Raphael, Dir. and State Libn., Dist. of Columbia Public Lib., 901 G St. N.W., Suite 400, Washington 20001. Tel. 202-727-1101, fax 202-727-1129, e-mail mraphael@rapgroup.com.

### Florida

Barratt Wilkins, State Libn., State Lib. of Florida, R. A. Gray Bldg., Tallahassee 32399-0250. Tel. 904-487-2651, fax 904-488-2746, e-mail bwilkins@mail.dos.state.fl.us.

### Georgia

David Singleton, Dir., Div. of Public Lib. Services, 1800 Century Pl. N.E., Atlanta 30345-4304. Tel. 404-982-3560, fax 404-982-3563.

### Hawaii

Virginia Lowell, State Libn., Hawaii State Public Lib. System, 465 S. King St., Rm. B1, Honolulu 96813. Tel. 808-586-3704, fax 808-586-3715.

## Idaho

Charles A. Bolles, State Libn., Idaho State Lib., 325 W. State St., Boise 83702-6072. Tel. 208-334-2150, fax 208-334-4016, e-mail cbolles@isl.state.id.us.

## Illinois

Bridget L. Lamont, Dir., Illinois State Lib., 300 S. Second St., Springfield 62701-1796. Tel. 217-782-2994, fax 217-785-4326, e-mail blamont@library.sos.state.il.us.

## Indiana

C. Ray Ewick, Dir., Indiana State Lib., 140 N. Senate Ave., Indianapolis 46204-2296. Tel. 317-232-3692, fax 317-232-3728, e-mail ewick@statelib.lib.in.us.

## Iowa

Sharman B. Smith, State Libn., State Lib. of Iowa, E. 12 and Grand, Des Moines 50319. Tel. 515-281-4105, fax 515-281-6191, e-mail ssmith@mail.lib.state.ia.us.

## Kansas

Duane F. Johnson, State Libn., Kansas State Lib., State Capiton, 3rd fl., Topeka 66612. Tel. 785-296-3296, fax 913-296-6650, e-mail duanej@ink.org.

## Kentucky

James A. Nelson, State Libn./Commissioner, Kentucky Dept. for Libs. and Archives, 300 Coffee Tree Rd., Box 537, Frankfort 40602-0537. Tel. 502-564-8300, fax 502-564-5773, e-mail jnelson@ctr.kdla.state.ky.us.

## Louisiana

Thomas F. Jaques, State Libn., State Lib. of Louisiana, Box 131, Baton Rouge 70821-0131. Tel. 504-342-4923, fax 504-342-3547, e-mail tjaques@pelican.state.lib.la.us.

## Maine

J. Gary Nichols, State Libn., Maine State Lib., LMA Bldg., 64 State House Sta., Augusta 04333-0064. Tel. 207-287-5600, fax 207-287-5615, e-mail gary.nichols@state.me.us.

## Maryland

J. Maurice Travillian, Asst. State Superintendent for Libs., Div. of Lib. Development and Services, Maryland State Dept. of Educ., 200 W. Baltimore St., Baltimore 21201-2595. Tel. 410-767-0435, fax 410-333-2507, e-mail mj54@umail.umd.ed.

## Massachusetts

Keith Fields, Dir., Massachusetts Board of Lib. Commissioners, 648 Beacon St., Boston 02215. Tel. 617-267-9400, fax 617-421-9833, e-mail kfiels@state.ma.us.

## Michigan

George M. Needham, State Libn., Lib. of Michigan, 717 W. Allegan St., Box 30007, Lansing 48909-9945. Tel. 517-373-1580, fax 517-373-4480, e-mail gneedham@libofmich.lib.mi.us.

## Minnesota

Joyce Swonger, Dir., Office of Lib. Development and Services, Minnesota Dept. of Educ., 440 Capitol Sq. Bldg., 550 Cedar St., Saint Paul 55101. Tel. 612-296-0909, fax 612-296-5418, e-mail joyce.swonger@state.mn.us.

## Mississippi

John Pritchard, Exec. Dir., Mississippi Lib. Commission, Box 387, 1221 Ellis Ave., Box 10700, Jackson 39289-0700. Tel. 601-359-1036, fax 601-354-4181, e-mail japritchard@mlc.lib.ms.us.

## Missouri

Sara Parker, State Libn., Missouri State Lib., 600 W. Main, Box 387, Jefferson City 65102-0387. Tel. 573-751-2751, fax 573-751-3612, e-mail sparker@mail.sos.state. mo.us.

## Montana

Karen Strege, State Libn., Montana State Lib., 1515 E. Sixth Ave., Helena 59620-1800. Tel. 406-444-3115, fax 406-444-5612, e-mail kstrege@msl.mt.gov.

## Nebraska

Rod Wagner, Dir., Nebraska Lib. Commission, The Atrium, 1200 N St., Suite 120, Lincoln 68508-2023. Tel. 402-471-4001, fax 402-471-2083, e-mail rwagner@neon. nlc.state.ne.us.

## Nevada

Joan G. Kerschner, Dir., Dept. of Museums, Libs. and Arts, 100 N. Stewart St., Carson City 89701. Tel. 702-687-8315, fax 702-687-8311, e-mail jgkersch@clan.lib.nv.us.

## New Hampshire

Michael York, Administrator of Lib. Operations, New Hampshire State Lib., 20 Park St., Concord 03301-6314. Tel. 603-271-2393, fax 603-271-6826, e-mail myork@finch.nhsl.lib.nh.us.

## New Jersey

John H. Livingstone, Jr., State Libn., New Jersey State Lib., 185 W. State St., CN520, Trenton 08625-0520. Tel. 609-292-6200, fax 609-292-2746, e-mail jaliving@njsl. tesc.edu.

## New Mexico

Benjamin Wakashige, State Libn., New Mexico State Lib., Aquisitions Section, 1209 Camino Carlos Rey, Santa Fe 87505. Tel. 505-827-3804, fax 505-827-3888, e-mail ben@stlib.state.nm.us.

## New York

Janet M. Welch, State Libn./Asst. Commissioner for Libs., New York State Lib., Cultural Education Center, Albany 12230. Tel. 518-474-5930, fax 518-486-2152, e-mail jwelch2@mail.nysed.gov.

## North Carolina

Sandra M. Cooper, State Libn., State Lib. of North Carolina, Dept. of Cultural Resources, 109 E. Jones St., Raleigh 27601-2807. Tel. 919-733-2570, fax 919-733-8748, e-mail scooper@hal.dcr.state.nc.us.

## North Dakota

Michael Jaugstetter, State Libn., North Dakota State Lib., Capitol Grounds, 604 E. Boulevard Ave., Bismarck 58505-0800. Tel. 701-328-2492, fax 701-328-2040, e-mail mjaugstetter@ranch.state.nd.us.

## Ohio

Michael Lucas, State Libn., State Lib. of Ohio, 65 S. Front St., Columbus 43215-4163. Tel. 614-644-6863, fax 614-466-3584, e-mail mlucas@mail.slonet.hio.gov.

## Oklahoma

Robert L. Clark, Jr., State Libn., Oklahoma Dept. of Libs., 200 N.E. 18 St., Oklahoma City 73105. Tel. 405-521-2502, fax 405-525-7804, e-mail bclark@oltn.odl.state. ok.us.

## Oregon

Jim Scheppke, State Libn., Oregon State Lib., State Lib. Bldg., 250 Winter St. N.E., Salem 97310-0640. Tel. 503-378-4367, fax 503-588-7119, e-mail jim.b.scheppke @state.or.us.

## Pennsylvania

Gary D. Wolfe, Dep. Secy. and Commissioner of Libs., Pennsylvania Dept. of Educ., Box 1601, Harrisburg 17105. Tel. 717-787-2646, fax 717-772-3265, e-mail wolfe@hslc.org.

## Rhode Island

Barbara Weaver, Chief Information Officer, Office of Lib. and Info. Services, Rhode Island Dept. of Administration, 1 Capitol Hill, Providence 02908-5870. Tel. 401-222-4444, fax 401-222-4260, e-mail barbwr @lorl.state.ri.us.

## South Carolina

James B. Johnson, Dir., South Carolina State Lib., 1500 Senate St., Box 11469, Columbia 29211. Tel. 803-734-8666, fax 803-734-8676, e-mail jim@leo.scsl.state.sc.us.

## South Dakota

Jane Kolbe, State Libn., South Dakota State Lib., 800 Governors Dr., Pierre 57501-2294. Tel. 605-773-3131, fax 605-773-5502, e-mail janeK@stlib.state.sd.us.

## Tennessee

Edwin S. Gleaves, State Libn./Archivist, Tennessee State Lib. and Archives, 403 Seventh Ave. N., Nashville 37243-0312. Tel. 615-741-7996, fax 615-741-6471, e-mail egleaves@mail.state.tn.us.

## Texas

Robert S. Martin, Dir./State Libn., Texas State Lib. and Archives Commission, Box 12927, Austin 78711-2927. Tel. 512-463-5460, fax 512-463-5436, e-mail robert. martin@tsl.state.tx.us.

## Utah

Amy Owen, Dir., State Lib., 2150 S. 300 W., Suite 16, Salt Lake City 84115. Tel. 801-468-6770, fax 801-468-6767, e-mail aowen @inter.state.lib.ut.us.

## Vermont

Sybil Brigham McShane, State Libn., Vermont Dept. of Libs., 109 State St., Montpelier 05609-0601. Tel. 802-828-3265, fax 802-828-2199, e-mail smcshane@dol. state.vt.us.

## Virginia

Nolan T. Yelich, State Libn., Lib. of Virginia, 800 E. Broad St., Richmond 23219-3491. Tel. 804-692-3535, fax 804-692-3594, e-mail nyelich@leo.vsla.edu.

## Washington

Nancy L. Zussy, State Libn., Washington State Lib., Box 42460, Olympia 98504-2460. Tel. 360-753-2915, fax 360-586-7575, e-mail nzussy@statelib.wa.gov.

## West Virginia

David Price, Exec. Dir., West Virginia Lib. Commission, 1900 Kanawha Blvd. E., Charleston 25305-0620. Tel. 304-558-2041, fax 304-558-2044, e-mail priced@ wvlc.wvnet.edu.

## Wisconsin

Calvin Potter, Asst. Superintendent, Div. for Libs. and Community Learning, 125 S. Webster St., Box 7841, Madison 53707-7841. Tel. 608-266-2205, fax 608-267-1052, e-mail pottecj@mail.state.wi.us.

## Wyoming

Jerry Krois, Interim State Libn., State Lib. Div., Dept. of Administration and Info., Supreme Court and State Lib. Bldg., Cheyenne 82002-0060. Tel. 307-777-7283, fax 307-777-6289, e-mail jkrols@ missc.state.wy.us.

## American Samoa

Emma F. C. Penn, Program Dir., Office of Lib. Services, Box 1329, Pago Pago 96799. Tel. 684-633-1181.

## Guam

Christine K. Scott-Smith, Dir./Territorial Libn., Nieves M. Flores Memorial Lib., 254 Martyr St., Agana 96910-0254. Tel. 671-472-8264, fax 671-477-9777, e-mail csctsmth@kuentos.guam.net.

## Northern Mariana Islands

Paul J. Steere, Dir., Joeten-Kiyu Public Lib., Box 1092, Commonwealth of the Northern Mariana Islands, Saipan 96950. Tel. 670-235-7322, fax 670-235-7550, e-mail psteere @saipan.com; William Matson, Federal Programs Coordinator, Dept. of Educ., Commonwealth of the Northern Mariana Islands, Saipan 96950. Tel. 670-322-6405, fax 670-322-4056.

## Palau (Republic of)

Masa-Aki N. Emeschiol, Federal Grants Coord., Ministry of Educ., Box 189, Koror 96940. Tel. 680-488-2570, ext. 1003, fax 680-488-2830, e-mail emesiocm@prel. hawaii.edu.; Fermina Salvador, Libn., Palau Public Lib., Box 189, Koror 96940. Tel. 680-488-2973, fax 680-488-3310.

## Puerto Rico

Victor Fajardo, Secy., Dept. of Educ., P.I. Box 190759, San Juan 00919-0759. Tel. 809-753-2062, fax 809-250-0275.

## Virgin Islands

Jeannette Allis Bastian, Dir. and Territorial Libn., Div. of Libs., Archives and Museums, 23 Dronningens Gade, Saint Thomas 00802. Tel. 809-774-3407, fax 809-775-1887, e-mail jbastia@icarus.lis.pitt.edu.

# Canada

## Alberta

Punch Jackson, Mgr. Libs. Section, Arts & Libs. Branch, 901 Standard Life Center, 10405 Jasper Ave., Edmonton T5J 4R7. Tel. 403-427-6315, fax 403-422-9132.

## British Columbia

Barbara Greeniaus, Dir., Lib. Services Branch, Ministry of Municipal Affairs and Housing, Box 9490 Stn. Prov. Govt., Victoria V8W 9N7. Tel. 250-356-1791, fax 250-953-3225, e-mail bgreeniaus@hq. marh.gov.bc.ca.

## Manitoba

Sylvia Nicholson, Dir., Manitoba Culture, Heritage, and Citizenship, Public Lib. Services, Unit 200, 1525 First St., Brandon R7A 7A1. Tel. 204-726-6864, fax 204-726-6868.

## New Brunswick

Jocelyne Thompson, Acting Provincial Libn., New Brunswick Lib. Service, Box 6000, Fredericton E3B 5H1. Tel. 506-453-2354, fax 506-453-2416, e-mail jocelyne.thompson @gov.nb.ca.

## Newfoundland

Judy Anderson, Acting Provincial Dir., Provincial Information and Library Resources Board, Arts and Culture Centre, Allandale Rd., St. John's A1B 3A3. Tel. 709-737-3964, fax 709-737-3009, World Wide Web http://www.publib.nf.ca/.

## Northwest Territories

Suliang Feng, Territorial Libn., Northwest Territories Lib. Services, Rm. 207, 2nd fl., Wright Centre, 62 Woodland Dr., Hay River X0E 1G1. Tel. 867-874-6531, fax 867-874-3321, e-mail suliang@gov.nt.ca.

## Nova Scotia

Marion L. Pape, Provincial Libn., Nova Scotia Provincial Lib., 3770 Kempt Rd., Halifax B3K 4X8. Tel. 902-424-2457, fax 902-424-0633, e-mail mpape@nshpl. library.ns.ca.

## Ontario

Michael Langford, Dir., Cultural Partnerships Branch, Ontario Government Ministry of Citizenship, Culture, and Recreation, 77 Bloor St. W., 3rd fl., Toronto M7A 2R9. Tel. 416-314-7342, fax 416-314-7635, e-mail Michael.Langford@mczcr.gov.on.ca.

## Prince Edward Island

Harry Holman, Dir., P.E.I. Provincial Lib., Red Head Rd., Box 7500, Morell C0A 1S0. Tel. 902-961-7320, fax 902-961-7322, e-mail plshq@gov.pe.ca.ca.

## Quebec

Denis Delangie, Dir., Direction des politiques et de la coordination des programmes, 225 Grande Allée Est, Bloc C, 2e étage, Quebec G1R 5G5. Tel. 418-644-0485, fax 418-643-4080, e-mail patrimoi@mail. mccq.gouv.gc.ca, or Denis_Delangie@ MCC.gouv.qc.ca.

## Saskatchewan

Maureen Woods, Provincial Libn., Saskatchewan Provincial Lib., 1352 Winnipeg St., Regina S4P 3V7. Tel. 306-787-2976, fax 306-787-2029, e-mail srp.adm@provlib. lib.sk.ca.

## Yukon Territory

Linda R. Johnson, Dir., Dept. of Educ., Libs., and Archives, Box 2703, Whitehorse Y1A 2C6. Tel. 867-667-5309, fax 867-393-6253, e-mail Linda.Johnson@gov.yk.ca.

# State School Library Media Associations

## Alabama

Children's and School Libns. Div., Alabama Lib. Assn. Memb. 650. Publication. *The Alabama Librarian* (q.).

*Exec. Dir.* Missy Mathis, 400 S. Union St., Suite 140, Montgomery 36104. Tel. 334-262-5210, fax 334-262-5255, e-mail alala@mindspring.com. World Wide Web http://davisref.samford.edu/alala/alala.htm.

Address correspondence to the executive director.

## Alaska

Alaska Assn. of School Libns.

*Pres.* Janet Madsen. E-mail hadleyj@ves.ssd.k12.ak.us; *Secy.* Linda Thibodeau. E-mail thibodel@jsd.k12.ak.us; *Treas.* Jane Meacham. E-mail janem@muskox.alaska.edu; *Alaska School Lib. Media Coord.* Della Matthis, 344 W. Third Ave., Suite 125, Anchorage 99501-2337. E-mail dellam@muskox.alaska.edu.

## Arizona

School Lib. Media Div., Arizona Lib. Assn. Memb. 500. Term of Office. Nov. 1998–Dec. 1999. Publication. *AZLA Newsletter.*

*Pres.* Gail Scheck, Curtis O. Greenfield School, 7009 S. 10th St., Phoenix 85040. Tel. 602-232-4240, fax 602-243-4973. *Pres.-Elect* Paul Kreamer. Tel. 520-733-8027.

Address correspondence to the president.

## Arkansas

Arkansas Assn. of School Libns. and Media Educators. Term of Office. Jan.–Dec. 1999.

*Chair* Lucy Lyon, Little Rock School District, 3001 S. Pulaski, Little Rock 72206. Tel. 501-324-0577, e-mail LMLYON@LRSDADA. LRSD.k12.ar.us; *V. Chair* Loveida Ingram, Jacksonville H.S., 2400 Linda La., Jacksonville 72000. Tel. 501-982-2128; *Secy.-Treas.* Carol Ann Hart, Forrest City School District, 467 Victoria St., Forrest City 72335. Tel. 870-633-1464, e-mail hartc@fcsd.grsc.k12.ar.us.

Address correspondence to the chairperson.

## California

California School Lib. Assn. Memb. 2,200. Term of Office. Pres, V.P., Secy., Oct. 1998–Nov. 1999; Treas., Oct. 1999–Nov. 2001. Publication. *Journal of the CSLA* (2 per year). *Ed.* Leslie Farmer.

*Pres.* Betty Silva, Fairfield H.S. Lib., 205 E. Atlantic, Fairfield 94533. Tel. 707-422-8672; *Pres.-Elect* Marylin Robertson, Los Angeles Unified School Dist., 1320 W. Third St., Los Angeles 90017. Tel. 213-625-5548; *Secy.* Claudette McLinn, Los Angeles Unified School Dist., 1320 W. Third St., Los Angeles 90017. Tel. 213-625-6481. *Treas.* Harmon Skyles, Box 2433, Hellendale 92342-2433. Tel. 760-952-3288; *Business Office Secy.* Nancy D. Kohn, CSLA, 1499 Old Bayshore Hwy., Suite 142, Burlingame 94010. Tel. 650-692-2350, fax 650 -692-4956.

Address correspondence to the business office secretary.

## Colorado

Colorado Educational Media Assn. Memb. 450. Term of Office. Feb. 1998–Feb. 1999. Publication. *The Medium* (6 per year).

*Pres.* Sandy Martinez; *Pres.-Elect* Joan Arrowsmith; *Secy.* Cathy Foutch; *Exec. Secy.* Heidi Baker.

Address correspondence to the executive secretary, Box 22814, Wellshire Sta., Denver 80222. Tel. 303-292-5434, e-mail cemacolorado@juno.com.

## Connecticut

Connecticut Educational Media Assn. Memb. 550. Term of Office. May 1998–May 1999. Publications. *CEMA Update* (q.); *CEMA Gram* (mo.).

*Pres.* Frances Nadeau, 440 Matthews St., Bristol 06010. Tel. 203-589-0813; *V.P.* Irene Kwidzinski, 293 Pumpkin Hill Rd., New Milford 06776. Tel. 203-355-0762; *Secy.* Linda Robinson, 24 Willowbrook Rd., Storrs 06268; *Treas.* Wendell Rector, 4 Woodbury Pl., Woodbury 06798. Tel. 203-263-2707; *Admin.*

*Secy.* Anne Weimann, 25 Elmwood Ave., Trumbull 06611. Tel. 203-372-2260.

Address correspondence to the administrative secretary.

## Delaware

Delaware School Lib. Media Assn., Div. of Delaware Lib. Assn. Memb. 115. Term of Office. Apr. 1998–Apr. 1999. Publications. *DSLMA Newsletter* (irreg.); column in *DLA Bulletin* (3 per year).

*Pres.* Susan Cushwa, Middletown H.S. Appoquinimink, 504 S. Broad St., Middletown. Tel. 302-378-5290, e-mail scushwa@dpi1.k12.state.de.us.

Address correspondence to the president.

## District of Columbia

District of Columbia Assn. of School Libns. Memb. 93. Term of Office. Jan. 1998–Jan. 1999. Publication. *Newsletter* (4 per year).

*Pres.* Lydia Jenkins; *Rec. Secy.* Olivia Hardison; *Treas.* Mary Minnis; *Financial Secy.* Connie Lawson; *Corres. Secy.* Sharon Sorrels, Banneker H.S., 800 Euclid St. N.W., Washington 20001.

## Florida

Florida Assn. for Media in Education. Memb. 1,450. Term of Office. Nov. 1998–Oct. 1999. Publication. *Florida Media Quarterly.* Ed. William H. Taylor, 2991 Foxcroft Dr., Tallahassee 32308. Tel. 850-668-1564.

*Pres.* Sandra Nelson, 1816 Southeast First St., Cape Coral 33990. Tel. 941-335-1446, fax 941-337-8654, e-mail nelson_s@popmailo.firm.edu; *V.P.* Chuck St. Louis, 7203 Broughton, Sarasota 34243. Tel. 941-741-3470 ext. 204, fax 941-741-3480, e-mail st.louisc@gate.net; *Assn. Exec.* Louise Costello, Box 70577, Fort Lauderdale 33307. Tel./fax 954-566-1312, e-mail costell@mail.firn.edu.

Address correspondence to the the association executive.

## Georgia

School Lib. Media Div., Georgia Lib. Assn. Memb. 217. Term of Office. Oct. 1998–Oct. 1999.

*Chair* Lydia Piper, Wilkinson Gardens Elementary School, 1918 Tubman Home Rd., Augusta 30906. Tel. 706-481-1621; *Chair-Elect.* Diane Barton, Lincoln County Elementary School, Lincolnton 30817. Tel. 706-359-3449.

## Hawaii

Hawaii Assn. of School Libns. Memb. 250. Term of Office. June 1998–May 1999. Publications. *HASL Newsletter* (4 per year). World Wide Web http://www.k12.hi.us/~hasl.

*Pres.* Donna Shiroma. E-mail dshiroma@kalama.doe.hawaii.edu; *1st V.P., Programming* Carolyn Kirio. E-mail ckirio@makani.k12.hi.us; *V.P., Membership* Irmalee Choo. E-mail ichoo@hekili.

Address correspondence to the association, Box 235019, Honolulu 96823.

## Idaho

Educational Media Div., Idaho Lib. Assn. Memb. 125. Term of Office. Oct. 1998–Oct. 1999. Publication. Column in *The Idaho Librarian* (q.).

*Chair* Marlene Earnest, Vallivue H.S., 1407 Homedale Rd., Caldwell 83605. E-mail mearnest@sd139.k12.id.us.

Address correspondence to the chairperson.

## Illinois

Illinois School Lib. Media Assn. Memb. 1,100. Term of Office. July 1998–June 1998. Publications. *ISLMA News* (5 per year), *ISLMA Membership Directory* (ann.).

*Pres.* Donna Lutkehaus, R.R. 21, Box 29, Bloomington 61704. Tel. 309-828-0958, e-mail dmlucky@ice.net; *Pres.-Elect* Kenneth Hawley, 135 Dover Dr., Decatur 62521. Tel. 217-424-8857, e-mail khawley@cam.k12.il.us; *Exec. Secy.* Kay Maynard, Box 598, Canton 61520. Tel. 309-649-0911, fax 309-647-0140, e-mail ISLMA@aol.com.

Address correspondence to the executive secretary.

## Indiana

Assn. for Indiana Media Educators. Memb. 1,013. Term of Office. May 1998–Apr. 1999. Publications. *Focus* (11 per year).

*Pres.* Jackie Carrigan, Plainfield Community Schools, 709 Stafford Rd., Plainfield 46168. Tel. 317-838-3556, fax 317-838-3671, e-mail jcarrigan@plainfield.k 12.in.us; *Past Pres.* Nancy McGriff, South Central Schools, 9808 S. 600 W., Union Mills 46382. Tel. 219-767-2263, fax 219-767-2260; *Exec. Dir., Indiana Lib. Federation* Linda D. Kolb.

Address correspondence to the federation executive office, 6408 Carrolton Ave., Indianapolis 46220. Tel. 317-257-2040, fax 317-257-1393, e-mail ilf@indy.net.

## Iowa

Iowa Educational Media Assn. Memb. 500. Term of Office. Mar. 1998–Mar. 1999. Publication. *Iowa Media Message* (4 per year). *Ed.* Karen Lampe, Green Valley AEA, 1405 N. Lincoln, Creston 50801.

*Pres.* Laura Pratt; *Pres.-Elect* Mary Cameron; *Secy.* Jen Buckingham; *Treas.* Rick Valley; *Exec. Secy.* Paula Behrendt, 2306 6th, Harlan 51537. Tel./fax 712-755-5918, e-mail paulab@harlannet.com.

Address correspondence to the executive secretary.

## Kansas

Kansas Assn. of School Libns. Memb. 700. Term of Office. Aug. 1998–July 1999. Publication. *KASL Newsletter* (s. ann.).

*Pres.* Sue Buhler, 620 Illinois, Pratt 67124. Tel. 316-672-7752; *Exec. Secy.* Judith Eller, 5201 N. St. Clair, Wichita 67204. Tel. 316-838-6395, e-mail judyelibr@aol.com.

Address correspondence to the executive secretary.

## Kentucky

Kentucky School Media Assn. Memb. 620. Term of Office. Oct. 1998–Oct. 1999. Publication. *KSMA Newsletter* (q.).

*Pres.* Emmalee Hill, Twenhofel Middle School, 11800 Taylor Mills Rd., Independence 41051. Tel. 606-356-0183, fax 606-356-1137, e-mail ehill@kenton.k12.ky.us; *Pres.-Elect* Susan Melcher, Hawthorne Elementary, 2301 Clarendon Ave., Louisville 40205. Tel. 502-485-8263; *Secy.* Margaret Roberts, Scott County H.S., 1080 Long Lick Pike, Georgetown 40324. Tel. 502-863-4131

ext. 1292, fax 502-867-0544, e-mail mroberts @scott.k12.ky.us; *Treas.* Becky Stephens, Burkhead Elementary, 521 Charlemagne Blvd., Elizabethtown 42701. Tel. 502-769-5983, fax 502-737-0989, e-mail bstephen@ hardon.k12.ky.us.

Address correspondence to the president.

## Louisiana

Louisiana Assn. of School Libns. Memb. 420. Term of Office. July 1998–June 1999.

*Pres.* Catherine M. Brooks, 6123 Hagerstown Dr., Baton Rouge 70817. Tel. 225-387-2328, e-mail cbrooks54@worldnet.att.net; *1st V.P.* Barbara Burney, 3805 Rushmore Dr., Shreveport 71119. Tel. 318-631-8131; *Secy.* Susan Cheshire, 16446 Centurion Ave., Baton Rouge 70816. Tel. 225-272-2268.

Address correspondence to the association, c/o Louisiana Lib. Assn., Box 3058, Baton Rouge 70821.

## Maine

Maine School Lib. Assn. Memb. 350. Term of Office. May 1999–May 2000. Publication. *Maine Entry* (with the Maine Lib. Assn.; q.).

*Pres.* Sylvia K. Norton, Freeport H.S. Lib., 30 Holbrook St., Freeport 04032. Tel. 207-865-4706, e-mail sylvian@saturn.caps.maine. edu; *1st V.P.* Suzan J. Nelson, Portland H.S., 284 Cumberland Ave., Portland 04101. Tel. 207-874-8250, e-mail sjnelson@saturn. caps.maine.edu; *Secy.* Nancy B. Grant, Penquis Valley H.S., 35 W. Main St., Milo 04463. Tel. 207-943-7346.

Address correspondence to the president.

## Maryland

Maryland Educational Media Organization. Term of Office. July 1998–June 1999. Publication. *MEMORANDOM.*

*Pres.* Linda Williams; *Secy.* Jayne Moore, 25943 Fox Grape Rd., Greensboro 21639.

Address correspondence to the association, Box 21127, Baltimore 21228.

## Massachusetts

Massachusetts School Lib. Media Assn. Memb. 700. Term of Office. June 1998–May 1999. Publication. *Media Forum* (q.).

*Pres.* Doris Smith. Tel. 781-275-7606, e-mail dorsmith@tiac.net; *Pres.-Elect* Rita Fontinha. Tel. 508-543-1643, e-mail ritaf@massed.net; *Secy.* Carolann Costello. Tel. 508-841-8821, e-mail cacostello@shrewsbury.k12.ma.us; *Admin. Asst.* Sue Rebello, MSLMA, Box 25, Three Rivers 01080-0025. Tel./fax 413-283-6675.

Address correspondence to the administrative assistant.

## Michigan

Michigan Assn. for Media in Education. Memb. 1,400. Term of Office. Jan.–Dec. 1999. Publications. *Media Spectrum* (3 per year); *MAME Newsletter* (4 per year). World Wide Web http://www.mame.gen.mi.us.

*Pres.* Dee Gwaltney, South Redford Public Schools, 26255 Schoolcraft, Redford 48239. Tel. 313-535-4000; *Pres.-Elect* Cyndi Phillip, Grand Haven Pub. Schools, 1415 Beech Tree, Grand Haven 49417. Tel. 616-850-5400; *V.P. for Regions/Special Interest Groups* Marsha Lambert, Marshall Pub. Schools, 100 E. Green St., Marshall 49068. Tel. 616-781-1294; *Secy.* Kathleen Nist, Algonac Community Schools, 5200 Taft Rd., Algonac 48001. Tel. 810-794-4911; *Treas.* Susan Luse Thornton, Napoleon Community Schools, Box 308, Napoleon 49261. Tel. 517-536-8637; *Past Pres.* Ruth Lumpkins, Grand Rapids Public Schools, 1440 Davis N.W., Grand Rapids 49504. Tel. 616-771-2595; *Exec. Dir.* Burton H. Brooks, 6810 S. Cedar St., Suite 8, Lansing 48911. Tel. 517-699-1717, fax 616-842-9195, e-mail bhbrooks@aol.com.

Address correspondence to the executive director.

## Minnesota

Minnesota Educational Media Organization. Memb. 750. Term of Office. (Pres.) Aug. 1998–Aug. 1999. Publications. *Minnesota Media*; *ImMEDIAte*; *MEMOrandum.*

*Co-Pres.* Judy Arnold, 13301 Maple Knoll Way, Maple Grove 55369. E-mail judy.arnold@fridley.k12.mn.us; Lars Steltzner, 15998 Putnam Blvd. S., Afton 55001. E-mail lsteltzner@vc.k12.mn.us; *Co-Pres.-Elect* Al Edwards, 2824 The Narrows Dr. S.W., Alexandria 56308; Leslie Erickson, 1396 Summit Ave., Saint Paul 55105-2218; *Secy.* Virjean Griensewic, 304 Stoltzman Rd., Mankato 56001; *Treas.* Sybil Solting, 502 Second Ave. S.E., Box 154, Mapleton 56065. Tel. 507-524-3917, e-mail 2135mrhs@informns.k12.mn.us; *Admin. Asst.* Evie Funk, 331 Wedgewood La. N., Plymouth 56467.

## Mississippi

School Section, Mississippi Lib. Assn. Memb. 1,300.

*Chair* Florence Box; *Secy.* Robert McKay.

Address correspondence to the association, c/o Mississippi Lib. Assn., Box 20448, Jackson 39289-1448.

## Missouri

Missouri Assn. of School Libns. Memb. 1099. Term of Office. June 1998–May 1999. Publication. *Media Horizons* (ann.).

*Pres.* Kay Rebstock, Central Middle School, New Madrid 63869. Tel. 573-688-2176; *1st V.P./Pres.-Elect* Brenda Steffens; *2nd V.P.* Dale Guthrie; *Secy.* Jane Rainey; *Treas.* Marianne Fues.

Address correspondence to the association, 1552 Rue Riviera, Bonne Terre 63628-9349. Tel./fax 573-358-1053, e-mail masloffice@aol.com.

## Montana

Montana School Lib. Media Div., Montana Lib. Assn. Memb. 215. Term of Office. July 1998–June 1999. Publication. *FOCUS* (published by Montana Lib. Assn.) (q.).

*Chair* Arlene Garvey, 1030 W. Gold, Butte 59701. Tel. 406-782-5995; *Chair-Elect.* Lynn McKinney, Arrowhead Elementary School, 2510 38th St. W., Billings 59102. Tel. 406-655-3131, fax 406-655-3143. *Admin. Asst.* John Thomas, Box 505, Helena 59624-0505.

Address correspondence to the chairperson.

## Nebraska

Nebraska Educational Media. Assn. Memb. 350. Term of Office. July 1999–June 2000. Publication. *NEMA News* (q.).

*Pres.* Sue Divan, West Kearney High School—Youth Rehabilitation and Treatment Center, 2802 30th St., Kearney 68847. Tel. 308-865-5313, e-mail sdivan@genie.esu10.k12.ne.us; *Past Pres.* Joie Taylor, 2301 31st St., Columbus 68601. Tel. 402-564-1781, fax 402-563-7003, e-mail jtaylor@gilligan.esu7.k12.ne.us; *Pres.-Elect.* Marilyn Scahill, Dodge Elementary School, 641 South Oak St., Grand Island 68801. Phone 308-385-5889, fax 402-694-5026, e-mail mscahill@genie.esu10.k12.ne.us; *Secy.* Deb Grove, Papillion-LaVista High School, 402 E. Centennial Rd., Papillion 68046-2078, Tel. 402-339-0405, fax 402-339-6929, e-mail dgrove@esu3.esu3.k12.ne.us, *Treas.* Deborah Smith, Pleasanton Public School, 303 West Church St., Box 190, Pleasanton 68866. Tel. 308-388-2041, fax 308-388-5502, e-mail dsmith@genie.esu10.k12.ne.us; *Exec. Secy.* Phyllis Brunken, ESU #7, 2657 44th Avenue, Columbus 68601, Tel. 402-564-5753, fax 402-563-1121, e-mail pbrunke@gilligan.esu7.k12.ne.us.

Address correspondence to the executive secretary.

### Nevada

Nevada School and Children's Lib. Section, Nevada Lib. Assn. Memb. 120.

*Chair* Ida McBride, Nevada Youth Training Center, 100 Youth Center Rd., Elko 89803. Tel. 775-738-5907 ext. 244, fax 775-753-7514; *Exec. Secy.* Nadine Phinney, Truckee Meadows Community College Lib., 7000 Dandini Blvd., Reno 89512. Tel. 775-674-7606, fax 775-673-7273.

### New Hampshire

New Hampshire Educational Media Assn., Box 418, Concord 03302-0418. Memb. 265. Term of Office. June 1998–June 1999. Publications. *On line* (5 per year). *Ed.* Nancy J. Keane, Rundlett Middle School, 144 South St., Concord 03301. Tel. 603-225-0862, fax 603-226-3288.

*Pres.* Jeanette Lizotte, Bow H.S., 32 White Rock Hill Rd., Bow 03304. Tel. 603-228-2210, fax 603-228-2212, e-mail jlizotte@bow.k12.nh.us; *Past Pres.* Kay Klein, Peter Woodbury Elementary School, 180 Country Rd., Bedford 03110. E-mail kay@kleins.

mv.com; *Pres.-Elect* Nancy Keane, Rundlett Middle School 144 South St., Concord 03301. E-mail nancy.keane@rundlett.concord.k12.nh.us; *Treas.* Jeffrey Kent, Broken Ground School, Portsmouth St., Concord 03301. Tel. 603-225-0825, fax 603-225-0869, e-mail jeff.kent@bg.concord.k12.nh.us.

Address correspondence to the president.

### New Jersey

Educational Media Assn. of New Jersey. Memb. 1,100. Term of Office. June 1999–June 2000. Publications. *Bookmark* (mo.); *Emanations* (s. ann.). World Wide Web http://www.emanj.org.

*Pres.* Villy Ghandi, Lakeside Middle School, 316 Lakeside Ave., Pompton Lakes 07442. Tel. 973-835-6221, e-mail villy@cybertnex.net; *Pres.-Elect* Connie Hitchcock, Clark Mills School, Gordons Corner Rd., Englishtown 07726-3798. Tel. 732-446-8124, e-mail Cahitchco@aol.com; *V.P.* Jackie Gould, Clearview Regional H.S., 625 Breakneck Rd., Box 2000, Mullica Hill 08062. Tel. 609-223-2723, e-mail jegould@snip.net; *Past Pres.* Nina Kemps, Horace Mann Elementary School, 150 Walt Whitman Blvd., Cherry Hill 08003. E-mail nkeps@recom.com.

Address correspondence to the president, president-elect, or vice president.

### New Mexico

[See "New Mexico" under "State, Provincial, and Regional Library Associations" earlier in Part 6—*Ed.*].

### New York

School Lib. Media Section, New York Lib. Assn., 252 Hudson St., Albany 12210. Tel. 518-432-6952, 800-252-6952. Memb. 950. Term of Office. Oct. 1998–Oct. 1999. Publications. *SLMSGram* (q.); participates in *NYLA Bulletin* (mo. except July and Aug.).

*Pres.* Christie Frost-Wendlowsky, SCT BOCES, 459, Philo Rd., Bldg. 11, Elmira 14903. Tel. 607-739-3581 ext. 2703; *V.P./Pres.-Elect* Ellen Rubin, 29 Queen Anne La., Wappingers Falls 12590; *Past Pres.* Eva Effron, Box 336, West Islip 11795-0336;

*Treas.* Sue Norkeliunas, Box 98, Hyde Park 12538. *Secy.* Rosina Alaimo, 540 Ashland Ave., Buffalo 14222.

Address correspondence to the president or secretary.

## North Carolina

North Carolina Assn. of School Libns. Memb. 800. Term of Office. Oct. 1997–Oct. 1999.

*Chair* Melinda Ratchford, Gaston County Schools, 366 W. Garrison Blvd., Gastonia 28054. Tel. 704-866-6251, e-mail meleis@aol.com; *Chair-Elect* Karen Gavigan, Burlington Day School, 1615 Greenwood Terrace, Burlington 27215. Tel. 336-228-0296, e-mail kpwg@aol.com.

Address correspondence to the chairperson.

## North Dakota

School Lib. and Youth Services Section, North Dakota Lib. Assn. Memb. 108. Term of Office. Sept. 1998–Sept. 1999. Publication. *The Good Stuff* (q).

*Pres.* Paulette Nelson, Minot Public Lib., 516 Second Ave. S.W., Minot 58701-3792. Fax 701-852-2595, e-mail pnelson@minotpl.ndak.net; *V.P./Pres.-Elect* Darlene Fairaizl, Box 551, Mandan 58554. Tel. 701-663-9859; *Past Pres.* Marvia Boettcher, Bismarck Public Lib., 515 5th St. N., Bismarck 58501. Tel. 701-222-6412, fax 701-221-6854, e-mail m.boettcher@mail.cdln.lib.nd.us.

Address correspondence to the president.

## Ohio

Ohio Educational Lib. Media Assn. Memb. 1,300. Publication. *Ohio Media Spectrum.*

*Exec. Dir.* Ann Hanning, 1631 N.W. Professional Plaza, Columbus 43220. Tel. 614-326-1460, fax 614-459-2087, e-mail oelma@mec.ohio.gov.

Address correspondence to the executive director.

## Oklahoma

Oklahoma Assn. of School Lib. Media Specialists. Memb. 3,005. Term of Office. July 1998–June 1999. Publication. *Oklahoma Librarian.*

*Chair* Carol Fox, State of Oklahoma Dept. of Libs., 200 N.E. 18 St., Oklahoma City 73105. E-mail cfox@oltn.odl.state.ok.us; *Chair-Elect* Janet Coontz, Glenwood Elementary, 824 N. Oakwood, Enid 73703; *Secy.* Lori Bradley, Yukon Public Schools, 2800 Mustang Rd., Yukon 73099. Tel. 405-354-4852, e-mail gmbdog@aol.com; *Treas.* Vicki Stewart, Bartlesville Public Schools, 801 S.E. 13, Bartlesville 74003. Tel. 918-337-6204, e-mail vickis4476@aol.com; *AASL Delegate* Bettie Estes Rickner, 12400 S. Mustang Rd., Mustang 73064. E-mail ber@ionet.net.

Address correspondence to the chairperson.

## Oregon

Oregon Educational Media Assn. Memb. 600. Term of Office. Aug. 1998–July 1999. Publication. *INTERCHANGE.*

*Pres.* Patty Sorensen; *Pres.-Elect* Sheryl Steinke; *Exec. Dir.* Jim Hayden, Box 277, Terrebonne 97760. Tel./fax 541-923-0675.

Address correspondence to the executive director.

## Pennsylvania

Pennsylvania School Libns. Assn. Term of Office. July 1998–June 2000. Publication. *Learning and Media* (4 per year).

*Pres.* Lin Carvell, 1419 Hillcrest Rd., Lancaster 17603. Tel. 717-397-9383; *Past Pres.* Peggy Benjamin, R.R. 6, Box 6362, Moscow 18444. Tel. 717-842-7201, fax 717-842-7026.

Address correspondence to the president.

## Rhode Island

Rhode Island Educational Media Assn. Memb. 398. Term of Office. June 1998–May 2000. Publication. *RIEMA Newsletter* (q.) and *REIMA Flash* (q.) *Ed.* Barbara Ashby, 22 Winthrope Dr., Barrington 02806. E-mail gjwl@aol.com.

*Pres.* Marykay W. Schnare, 11 Nelson St., Providence 02908. Tel. 401-331-2059, e-mail ritoy@aol.com; *V.P.* Donna Ouellette, 22 Chapel St., Lincoln 02865. Tel. 401-723-7443, e-mail donnaoe@dsl.rhilinet.gov; *Secy.* Susan Peckham, 68 Sefton Dr., Cranston

02905. Tel. 401-785-0987, e-mail nshst004@llwsbe.wsbe.org; *Treas.* Livia Giroux, 333 Potters Ave., Warwick 02886. Tel. 401-738-5666.

Address correspondence to the association, Box 762, Portsmouth 02871.

## South Carolina

South Carolina Assn. of School Libns. Memb. 1,100. Term of Office. June 1998–May 1999. Publication. *Media Center Messenger* (5 per year).

*Pres.* Olivia Padgett, Bells Elementary School, 12088 Bells Highway, Ruffin 29475. Tel. 843-866-2417, fax 843-866-7361, e-mail opadgett@lowcountry.com; *Pres.-Elect* Penny Hayne, Lake Murray Elementary School, 1531 Three Dog Rd., Chapin 29036. Tel. 803-732-8151, e-mail phayne@lex5. k12.sc.us; *Secy.* Kwamine Simpson, Media Specialist, Lower Richland H.S., 7717 Burdell Dr., Columbia 29709. Tel. 803-783-9172; *Treas.* Sue Waddell, Lakeview Middle School, 3801 Old Buncombe Rd., Greenville 29609. Tel. 864-294-4361, fax 864-294-4236, e-mail lakeview@greenville.k12.sc.

Address correspondence to the secretary.

## South Dakota

South Dakota School Lib. Media Assn., Section of the South Dakota Lib. Assn. and South Dakota Education Assn. Memb. 146. Term of Office. Oct. 1998–Oct. 1999.

*Pres.* Peggy Morris, Redfield Public School, Redfield 57469; *Pres.-Elect* Bev Birkeland, Box 55, Faith 57626; *Secy.-Treas.* Linda Demery, Faulkton School, Box 161, Faulkton 57438.

Address correspondence to the secretary-treasurer.

## Tennessee

Tennessee Assn. of School Libns. (affiliated with the Tennessee Education Assn.). Memb. 450. Term of Office. Jan. 1999–Dec. 1999. Publication. *Footnotes* (q.).

*Pres.* Mary J. Smith, 8707 Bradley Creek Rd., Lascassas 37085; *V.P./Pres.-Elect* Sherry Ball, 7721 Sevilla Rd., Powell 37849. Tel.

423-947-5726, e-mail slball2@aol.com; *Secy.* Margaret Moore, 1403 N. Tennessee Blvd., Murfreesboro 37130. Tel. 615-890-6602, e-mail moorem@mail.rcs.tn.k12.tn.us; *Treas.* Carol Burr, 2523 Stinson Rd., Nashville 37214. Tel. 615-883-7395, e-mail BURRC@ten-nash.ten.k12.tn.us.

Address correspondence to the president.

## Texas

Texas Assn. of School Libns. (Div. of Texas Lib. Assn.). Memb. 3,686. Term of Office. Apr. 1999–Apr. 2000. Publication. *Media Matters* (3 per year).

*Chair* Vicki M. Krebsbach, 21045 Crescent Oaks, San Antonio 78258. Tel. 210-497-6200, fax 210-497-6204.

Address correspondence to the association, 3355 Bee Cave Rd., Suite 401, Austin 78746. Tel. 512-328-1518, fax 512-328-8852, e-mail tla@txla.org.

## Utah

Utah Educational Lib. Media Assn. Memb. 393. Term of Office. Mar. 1999–Feb. 2000. Publication. *UELMA Newsletter* (4 per year).

*Pres.* Ann Olsen, Box Elder Junior H.S., 18 South 500 E., Brigham City 84302. Tel. 435-734-4880, fax 435-734-4885, e-mail be0779ao@m.k12.ut.us; *Pres.-Elect.* Dennis Morgan, Riverview Junior H.S., 751 W. Tripp La., Murray 84123. Tel. 801-264-7406, e-mail dmorgan@rjh.mury.k12.ut.us; *Secy.* Marlo Johnson, Jim Bridger Elementary School, 5368 Cyclamen Way, West Jordan 84084. Tel. 801-964-5935. *Exec. Dir.* Larry Jeppesen, Cedar Ridge Middle School, 65 N. 200 W., Hyde Park 84318. Tel. 435-563-6229, fax 435-563-3914, e-mail ljeppese@crms.cache.k12.ut.us.

Address correspondence to the executive director.

## Vermont

Vermont Educational Media Assn. Memb. 203. Term of Office. May 1998–May 1999. Publication. *VEMA News* (q.).

*Pres.* Merlyn Miller, Burrand Burton Seminary, Seminary Ave., Manchester 05254.

Tel. 802-362-1775, fax 802-362-0574, e-mail mmiller@sovern.net; *Pres.-Elect* Melissa Malcolm, Mt. Abraham Union H.S., 7 Airport Dr., Bristol 05443. Tel. 802-453-2333, fax 802-453-4359, e-mail mmalcolm@mtabe.k12.vt.us.

Address correspondence to the president.

## Virginia

Virginia Educational Media Assn. Memb. 1,450. Term of Office. (Pres. and Pres.-Elect) Oct. 1998–Oct. 1999 (other offices two years in alternating years). Publication. *Mediagram* (q.). *Pres.* Ann Martin, 5039 Bonnie Brae Rd., Richmond 23234. Tel. 804-378-2420; *Pres.-Elect* Linda Owen, Box 88, Walkerton 23177. Tel. 804-343-6550; *Exec. Mgr.* Jean Remler. Tel./fax 703-764-0719, e-mail jremler@pen.k12.va.us.

Address correspondence to the association, Box 2744, Fairfax 22031-2744.

## Washington

Washington Lib. Media Assn. Memb. 1,200. Term of Office. Oct. 1998–Oct. 1999. Publications. *The Medium* (3 per year); *The Message* (2 per year). *Ed.* Mary Lou Gregory, 711 Spruce St., Hoquiam 98550. Tel. 206-533-4897. *Pres.* Judy Carlson. Tel. 253-566-5710, fax 253-566-5626, e-mail jcarlson@halcyon.com; *V.P.* Paul M. Christensen. Tel. 360-598-8423, fax 360-598-8406, e-mail nkviking@esd224.wednet.edu; *Treas.* Barbara J. Baker. Tel. 425-823-0836, fax 425-821-5254, e-mail denmother@worldnet.att.net; *Secy.* Jennifer G. Larson. Tel. 425-888-1921, fax 425-888-1934, e-mail jennifer_larson@snogvalerie.wednet.edu.

Address correspondence to the president.

## West Virginia

West Virginia Technology, Education, and Media Specialists (WVTEAMS). Memb. 150. Term of Office. July 1998–July 1999. *Pres.* June Geiger, 1444 Sunset Lane, Glendale 26038. Tel. 304-843-4444, fax 304-843-4419, e-mail jgeiger@access.k12.wv.us; *Secy.* Brenda Bleigh, Box 167, Burnsville 26335. Tel. 304-853-2523, fax 304-853-2431, e-mail bbleigh@access.k12.wv.us.

Address correspondence to the president.

## Wisconsin

Wisconsin Educational Media Assn. Memb. 1,122. Term of Office. Apr. 1999–Apr. 2000. Publications. *Dispatch* (7 per year); *Wisconsin Ideas in Media* (ann.). *Pres.* Sherry Freiberg, Fond du Lac School Dist., 72 S. Portland St., Fond du Lac 54935. Tel. 920-929-2780, e-mail freibergs@fond dulac.k12.wi.us; *Past Pres.* Helen Adams, Rosholt H.S., 346 W. Randolph St., Rosholt 54473. Tel. 715-677-4541, e-mail hadams@coredcs.com.

Address correspondence to the president.

## Wyoming

Section of School Library Media Personnel, Wyoming Lib. Assn. Memb. 91. Term of Office. Oct. 1998–Oct. 1999. Publication. *WLA Newsletter*; *SSLMP Newsletter*. *Chair* Jan Segerstrom, Jackson Hole Middle School, Box 568, Jackson, Wyoming 83001. Tel. 307-733-3019, fax 307-733-4254, e-mail jasegerstrom@teton1.k12.wy.us; *Chair-Elect* Alice Hild Farris, Central H.S., 5500 Education Dr., Cheyenne 82009. Tel. 307-771-2680, fax 307-771-2699, e-mail afarris@will.state.wy.us.

Address correspondence to the chairperson.

# International Library Associations

## International Association of Agricultural Information Specialists

c/o J. van der Burg, President
Boeslaan 55, 6703 ER Wageningen, Netherlands
Tel./fax 31-317-422820

### Object

The association facilitates professional development of and communication among members of the agricultural information community worldwide. Its goal is to enhance access to and use of agriculture-related information resources. To further this mission, it will promote the agricultural information profession, support professional development activities, foster collaboration, and provide a platform for information exchange. Founded 1955.

### Membership

Memb. 600+. Dues (Inst.) US$90; (Indiv.) $35.

### Officers

*Pres.* J. van der Burg, Boeslaan 55, 6703 ER Wageningen, Netherlands; *Senior V.P.* Syed Salim Agha, Dept. of Lib. and Info. Science, International Islamic Univ., Malaysia (postal address: Box 70, Jalan Sultan, 467000 Petaling Jaya, Selangor Darul Ehsan, Malaysia); *Secy.-Treas.* Margot Bellamy, c/o CAB International, Wallingford, Oxon, OX10 8DE, United Kingdom. Tel. 44-1491-832111, fax 44-1491-833508.

### Publications

*Quarterly Bulletin of the IAALD* (memb.).
*World Directory of Agricultural Information Resource Centres.*

## International Association of Law Libraries

Box 5709, Washington, DC 20016-1309
804-924-3384, fax 804-924-7239

### Object

IALL is a worldwide organization of librarians, libraries, and other persons or institutions concerned with the acquisition and use of legal information emanating from sources other than their jurisdictions, and from multinational and international organizations.

IALL's basic purpose is to facilitate the work of librarians who must acquire, process, organize, and provide access to foreign legal materials. IALL has no local chapters but maintains liaison with national law library associations in many countries and regions of the world.

### Membership

More than 500 members in more than 50 countries on five continents.

### Officers

*Pres.* Larry Wenger (USA); *1st V.P.* Roberta Shaffer (USA); *2nd V.P.* Holger Knudsen (Germany); *Secy.* Marie-Louise H. Bernal (USA); *Treas.* Gloria F. Chao (USA).

## Board Members

Joan A. Brathwaite (Barbados); Jacqueline Elliott (Australia); Gabriel Frossard (Switzerland); Brit S. M. Kjölstad (Switzerland); Ann Morrison (Canada); Harald Müller (Germany); Lisbeth Rasmussen (Denmark); Jules Winterton (United Kingdom).

## Publications

*International Journal of Legal Information* (3 per year; US$55 for individuals; $80 for institutions).

## Committee Chairpersons

Communications. Richard A. Danner (USA).

# International Association of Music Libraries, Archives and Documentation Centres (IAML)

c/o Alison Hall, Secretary-General
Cataloging Dept., Carleton University Library
1125 Colonel By Drive, Ottawa, ON K15 5B6, Canada
Fax 613-520-3583

## Object

To promote the activities of music libraries, archives, and documentation centers and to strengthen the cooperation among them; to promote the availability of all publications and documents relating to music and further their bibliographical control; to encourage the development of standards in all areas that concern the association; and to support the protection and preservation of musical documents of the past and the present.

## Membership

Memb. 2,000.

## Board Members (1998–2001)

*Pres.* Pamela Thompson, Royal College of Music Lib., Prince Consort Rd., London SW7 2BS, England; *Past Pres.* Veslemîy Heintz, Statens Musikbibliotek, Box 16326, S-103 26 Stockholm, Sweden; *V.P.s* Massimo Gentili-Tedeschi, Ufficio Ricerca Fondi Musicali, Via Conservatorio 12, I-20122 Milano, Italy; Joachim Jaenecke, Staasbibliothek zu Berlin, Preussischer Kulturbesitz, Tiergarten, Potsdamer Strasse 33, D-10785 Berlin, Germany; John Roberts, Music Lib., 240 Morrison Hall, Univ. of California–Berkeley, Berkeley, CA 94720; Kirsten Voss-Eliasson, Herlev Bibliotekeme, Bygaden 70, DK-2730 Herlev, Denmark; *Secy.-Gen.* Alison Hall, Cataloging Dept., Carleton Univ. Lib., 1125 Colonel By Dr., Ottawa ON K1S 5B6; *Treas.* Martie Severt, Muziekcentrum van de Omroep, Postbus 125, NL-1200 AC Hilversum, Netherlands.

## Publication

*Fontes Artis Musicae* (4 per year; memb.). *Ed.* Susan T. Sommer, New York Public Lib. for the Performing Arts, 111 Amsterdam Ave., New York, NY 10023-7498.

## Professional Branches

Archives and Documentation Centres. Inger Enquist, Statens Musikbibliotek, Box 16326, S-10326 Stockholm, Sweden.

Broadcasting and Orchestra Libraries. Kauko Karjalainen, Yleisradio Oy, Box 76, FIN-00024 Yleisradio, Finland.

Libraries in Music Teaching Institutions. Federica Riva, Conservatorio di Musica G. Verdi, Via del Conservatorio 12, I-20122 Milano, Italy.

Public Libraries. Kirsten Voss-Eliassen, Herlev Bibliotekeme, Bygaden 70, DK-2730, Denmark.

Research Libraries. Ann Kersting, Music- und Theaterabteilung, Stadt- und Universitatsbibliothek, Bockenheimer Landstr. 134-138, D-60325 Frankfurt, Germany.

# International Association of School Librarianship

Ken Haycock, Executive Director
Box 34069, Dept. 300, Seattle, WA 98124-1069
604-925-0266, fax 604-925-0566, e-mail iasl@rockland.com
World Wide Web http://www.hi.is/~anne/iasl.html

## Object

The objectives of the International Association of School Librarianship are to advocate the development of school libraries throughout all countries; to encourage the integration of school library programs into the instructional and curriculum development of the school; to promote the professional preparation and continuing education of school library personnel; to foster a sense of community among school librarians in all parts of the world; to foster and extend relationships between school librarians and other professionals connected with children and youth; to foster research in the field of school librarianship and the integration of its conclusions with pertinent knowledge from related fields; to promote the publication and dissemination of information about successful advocacy and program initiatives in school librarianship; to share information about programs and materials for children and youth throughout the international community; and to initiate and coordinate activities, conferences, and other projects in the field of school librarianship and information services. Founded 1971.

## Membership

Memb. 850.

## Officers and Executive Board

*Pres.* Blanche Woolls, USA; *V.P.s* Peter Genco, USA; Rebecca Knuth, USA; Ross Todd, Australia; *Financial Officer* Kathy Lemaire, United Kingdom; *Deputy Exec. Dir.* Lynne Lighthall; *Dirs.* Allison Kaplan, North America; Mary Jamil Fasheh, North Africa/Middle East; Isabel Gomez, Latin America; James Henri, Australia/Pacific Ocean Islands; Mieko Nagakura, East Asia; Monica Milsson, Europe; Sandra Olen, Africa–Sub-Sahara; Cherrell Shelley-Robinson, Caribbean; Diljit Singh, Asia.

## Publications

*Annual Proceedings of the International Association of School Librarianship: An Author and Subject Index to Contributed Papers, 1972–1984*; $10.

*Books and Borrowers*; $15.

*Connections: School Library Associations and Contact People Worldwide*; $15.

*Indicators of Quality for School Library Media Programs*; $15.

*School Librarianship: International Perspectives and Issues*; $35.

*Sustaining the Vision: A Collection of Articles and Papers on Research in School Librarianship*; $35.

IASL *Worldwide Directory*; $15.

## U.S. Association Members

American Assn. of School Libns.; American Lib. Assn.; Illinois School Lib. Media Assn.; International Reading Assn.; International School Service; Louisiana Assn. of School Libns.; Michigan Assn. for Media in Education; Washington Lib. Media Assn.

# International Association of Technological University Libraries

c/o President, Nancy Fjällbrant, Chalmers University of Technology Library
412 96 Gothenburg, Sweden
46 31 7723754, fax 46 31 168494, e-mail nancyf@lib.chalmers.se

## Object

To provide a forum where library directors can meet to exchange views on matters of current significance in the libraries of universities of science and technology. Research projects identified as being of sufficient interest may be followed through by working parties or study groups.

## Membership

Ordinary, official observer, sustaining, and nonvoting associate. Membership fee is US$117 per year ($307 for three years, $487 for five years). Memb. 207 (in 43 countries).

## Officers and Executives

Pres. Nancy Fjällbrant, Chalmers University of Technology Library, 412 96 Gothenburg, Sweden. Tel. 46 31 7723754, fax 46 31 168494, e-mail nancyf@lib.chalmers.se; *1st V.P.* Michael Breaks, Heriot-Watt Univ. Lib., Edinburgh, Scotland. Tel. 44-131-451-3570, fax 44-131-451-31654, e-mail m.l.breaks@hw.ac.uk; *Secy.* Sinikka Koskiala, Helsinki Univ. of Technology Lib., Box 7000, FIN-02015 HUT, Finland. Tel. 358-9-4514112, fax 358-9-4514132, e-mail Sinikka.Koskiala@hut.fi; *Treas.* Leo Waaijers, Delft Univ. of Technology Lib., Postbus 98, 2600 MG Delft, Netherlands. Tel. 3115-785-656, fax 3115-158-759, e-mail Waaijers@library.tudelft.nl; *Membs.* Gaynor Austen, Australia; Egbert D. Gerryts, South Africa; *North American Regional Group Chair* Richard P. Widdicombe, USA; *Ed.* Nancy Fjällbrant, Sweden.

## Publications

*IATUL News* (q.).
*IATUL Proceedings* (ann.).

# International Council on Archives

Joan van Albada, Secretary General
60 Rue des Francs-Bourgeois, F-75002
Paris, France
33-1-4027-6306, fax 33-1-4272-2065, e-mail 100640.54@compuserve.com
World Wide Web http://www.archives.ca/ICA/

## Object

To establish, maintain, and strengthen relations among archivists of all lands, and among all professional and other agencies or institutions concerned with the custody, organization, or administration of archives, public or private, wherever located. Established 1948.

## Membership

Memb. 1,574 (representing 176 countries and territories). Dues (Indiv.) $80 or $125; (Inst.) $125; (Archives Assns.) $125 or $275; (Central Archives Directorates) $275 or $150 minimum, computed on the basis of GNP and GNP per capita.

## Officers

*Secy.-Gen.* Joan van Albada; *Deputy Secy.-Gen.* George P. MacKenzie.

## Publications

*Archivum* (ann.; memb. or subscription to K. G. Saur Verlag, Ortlerstr. 8, Postfach 70 16 20, 81-316 Munich, Germany).

*Guide to the Sources of the History of Nations* (Latin American Series, 12 vols. pub.; African Series, 18 vols. pub.; Asian Series, 28 vols. pub.), North Africa, Asia, and Oceania: 15 vols. pub.; other guides, 3 vols. pub.

*ICA Bulletin* (s. ann.; memb.).

*Janus* (s. ann.; memb.)

List of other publications available from the secretariat.

# International Federation for Information and Documentation (FID)

J. Stephen Parker, Executive Director
Box 90402, 2509 LK The Hague, Netherlands
31 70 314 0671, fax 314 0667, e-mail fid@python.konbib.nl

## Object

To promote, through international cooperation, research in and development of information science, information management, and documentation, which includes inter alia the organization, storage, retrieval, repackaging, dissemination, value adding, and evaluation of information, however recorded, in the fields of science, technology, industry, social sciences, arts, and humanities.

## Program

FID devotes much of its attention to corporate information; industrial, business, and finance information; information policy research; the application of information technology; information service management; the marketing of information systems and services; content analysis, for example, in the design of database systems; linking information and human resources; and the repackaging of information for specific user audiences.

The following commissions, committees, and groups have been established to execute FID's program of activities: *Regional Commissions*: Commission for Western, Eastern and Southern Africa (FID/CAF), Commission for Asia and Oceania (FID/CAO), Commission for Latin America (FID/CLA), Commission for the Caribbean and North America (FID/CNA), Commission for Northern Africa and the Near East (FID/NANE), Regional Organization for Europe (FID/ROE); *Committees*: Classification Research for Knowledge Organization, Education and Training, Fundamental Theory of Information, Information for Industry, Information Policies and Programmes, Intellectual Property Issues; *Special Interest Groups*: Archives and Records Management; Banking, Finance, and Insurance Information; Environmental Information; Business; Intelligence; Roles, Careers, and Development of the Modern Information Professional; Safety Control and Risk Management.

## Publications

*FID Annual Report* (ann.).

*FID Directory* (bienn.).

*FID Bulletin* (bi.-mo.) with quarterly inserts *Document Delivery Survey* and *ET Newsletter*.

*FID Publications List* (irreg.).

*International Forum on Information and Documentation* (q.).

Proceedings of congresses; directories; bibliographies on information science, documentation, education and training, and classification research.

# International Federation of Film Archives (FIAF)

Secretariat, Rue Defacqz 1, 1000 Brussels, Belgium
(32-2) 538-3065, fax (32-2) 534-4774, e-mail info@fiafnet.org
World Wide Web http://www.cinema.ucla.edu/FIAF/fiaf.html

## Object

Founded in 1938, FIAF brings together institutions dedicated to rescuing films both as cultural heritage and as historical documents. FIAF is a collaborative association of the world's leading film archives whose purpose has always been to ensure the proper preservation and showing of motion pictures. More than 100 archives in more than 60 countries collect, restore, and exhibit films and cinema documentation spanning the entire history of film.

FIAF seeks to promote film culture and facilitate historical research, to help create new archives around the world, to foster training and expertise in film preservation, to encourage the collection and preservation of documents and other cinema-related materials, to develop cooperation between archives, and to ensure the international availability of films and cinema documents.

## Officers

*Pres.* Michelle Aubert; *Secy.-Gen.* Roger Smither; *Treas.* Mary Lea Bandy; *Members* Iván Trujillo Bolio, Gabrielle Claes, Steve Ricci, Vittorio Boanini, Paolo Cherchi Usai, Nelly V. Cruz Rodriguez, Hervé Dumont, Clyde Jeavons, Peter Konlechner, José Maria Prado.

Address correspondence to Christian Dimitriu, Senior Administrator, c/o the Secretariat.

## Publications

*Journal of Film Preservation.*
International Filmarchive CD-ROM.

For other FIAF publications, see the Web site http://www.cinema.ucla.edu/FIAF/english/book.html.

# International Federation of Library Associations and Institutions (IFLA)

Box 95312, 2509 CH The Hague, Netherlands
31-70-3140884, fax 31-70-3834027
E-mail IFLA@IFLA.org, World Wide Web http://www.IFLA.org

## Object

To promote international understanding, cooperation, discussion, research, and development in all fields of library activity, including bibliography, information services, and the education of library personnel, and to provide a body through which librarianship can be represented in matters of international interest. Founded 1927.

## Membership

Memb. (Lib. Assns.) 158; (Inst.) 1,118; (Aff.) 321; Sponsors: 38.

## Officers and Executive Board

*Pres.* Christine Deschamps, Bibliothèque de l'Université Paris, V–René Descartes, Paris, France; *1st V.P.* Ekaterina U. Genieva, M. I. Rudomino All-Russia State Lib. of Foreign Literature, Moscow, Russia; *Treas.* Derek Law, King's College London Lib., London, United Kingdom; *Exec. Board* Nancy John, Univ. of Illinois at Chicago; Klaus-Dieter Lehmann, Die Deutsche Bibliothek, Frankfurt am Main, Germany; Beixin Sun, National Lib. of China, Beijing, China; Børge Sørensen, Copenhagen Public Libs., Copenhagen, Denmark; *Ex officio memb.* Sissel Nilsen, Baerum Public Lib., Oslo, Norway;

*Secy.-Gen.* Ross Shimmon; *Coord. Professional Activities* Sjoerd M. J. Koopman; *IFLA Office for Universal Bibliographic Control and International MARC Program Dir.* Kurt Nowak; *Program Officer* Marie-France Plassard, c/o Deutsche Bibliothek, Frankfurt am Main, Germany; *IFLA International Program for UAP Program Dir.* Graham Cornish, c/o British Lib. Document Supply Centre, Boston Spa, Wetherby, West Yorkshire, England; *IFLA Office for Preservation and Conservation Program Dir.* M. T. Varlamoff, c/o Bibliothèque Nationale de France, Paris; *IFLA Office for University Dataflow and Telecommunications Program Dir.* Leigh Swain, c/o National Lib. of Canada, Ottawa, Canada; *IFLA Office for the Advancement of Librarianship in the Third World Program Dir.* Birgitta Bergdahl, c/o Uppsala Univ. Lib., Uppsala, Sweden; *IFLA Office for International Lending Dir.* Graham Cornish.

## Publications

*IFLA Directory* (bienn.).

*IFLA Council Report 1995–1997*
*IFLA Journal* (6 per year).
*IFLA Professional Reports.*
*IFLA Publications Series.*
*International Cataloguing and Bibliographic Control* (q.).
*PAC Newsletter.*
*UAP Newsletter* (s. ann.).
UDT Digest (electronic).

## American Membership

American Assn. of Law Libs.; American Lib. Assn.; Art Libs. Society of North America; Assn. for Lib. and Info. Science Education; Assn. of Research Libs.; International Assn. of Law Libs.; International Assn. of School Libns.; Medical Lib. Assn.; Special Libs. Assn. *Institutional Membs.* There are 141 libraries and related institutions that are institutional members or consultative bodies and sponsors of IFLA in the United States (out of a total of 1,070), and 84 personal affiliates (out of a total of 321).

# International Organization for Standardization (ISO)

ISO Central Secretariat, 1 rue de Varembé, Case Postale 56, CH-1211 Geneva 20
Switzerland
41-22-749-0111, fax 41-22-733-3430, e-mail central@iso.ch

## Object

Worldwide federation of national standards bodies, founded in 1947, at present comprising some 130 members, one in each country. The object of ISO is to promote the development of standardization and related activities in the world with a view to facilitating international exchange of goods and services, and to developing cooperation in the spheres of intellectual, scientific, technological, and economic activity. The scope of ISO covers international standardization in all fields except electrical and electronic engineering standardization, which is the responsibility of the International Electrotechnical Commission (IEC). The results of ISO technical work are published as International Standards.

## Officers

*Pres.* Liew Mun Leong, Singapore; *V.P. (Policy)* A. Aoki, Japan; *V.P. (Technical Management)* J. Kean, Canada; *Secy.-Gen.* L. D. Eicher.

## Technical Work

The technical work of ISO is carried out by some 180 technical committees. These include:

*ISO/TC 46–Information and documentation* (Secretariat, Deutsches Institut für Normung, 10772 Berlin, Germany). Scope: Standardization of practices relating to libraries, documentation and information centers, indexing and abstracting services, archives, information science, and publishing.

*ISO/TC 37–Terminology (principles and coordination)* (Secretariat, Österreiches Normungsinstitut, Heinestr. 38, Postfach 130, A–1021 Vienna, Austria). Scope: Standardization of methods for creating, compiling, and coordinating terminologies.

*ISO/IEC JTC 1–Information technology* (Secretariat, American National Standards Institute, 11 W. 42 St., 13th fl., New York, NY 10036). Scope: Standardization in the field of information technology.

## Publications

*ISO Annual Report.*
*ISO Bulletin* (mo.).
*ISO Catalogue* (ann.).
*ISO International Standards.*
*ISO 9000 News* (bi-mo.).
*ISO Memento* (ann.).
ISO Online information service on World Wide Web (http://www.iso.ch/).

# Foreign Library Associations

The following list of regional and national library associations around the world is a selective one. A more complete list can be found in *International Literary Market Place* (R. R. Bowker).

## Regional

### Africa

Standing Conference of African Univ. Libs., c/o E. Bejide Bankole, Editor, African Journal of Academic Librarianship, Box 46, Univ. of Lagos, Akoka, Yaba, Lagos, Nigeria. Tel. 1-524968.

### The Americas

Asociación de Bibliotecas Universitarias, de Investigación e Institucionales del Caribe (Assn. of Caribbean Univ., Research and Institutional Libs.), Box 23317, San Juan 00931, Puerto Rico. Tel. 787-764-0000, fax 787-763-5685. *Exec. Secy.* Oneida R. Ortiz.

Seminar on the Acquisition of Latin American Lib. Materials, c/o *Exec. Secy.* Sharon A. Moynahan, General Lib., Univ. of New Mexico, Albuquerque, NM 87131-1466. Tel. 505-277-5102, fax 505-277-0646.

### Asia

Congress of Southeast Asian Libns. IV (CONSAL IV), c/o Serafin D. Quiason, National Historic Institute of the Philippines, T. M. Kalaw St., 100 Ermita, Box 2926, Manila, Philippines. Tel./fax 2-590646.

### The Commonwealth

Commonwealth Lib. Assn., c/o *Exec. Secy.* Norma Amenu-Kpodo, Box 144, Mona, Kingston 7, Jamaica. Tel. 876-927-2123, fax 876-927-1926. *Pres.* Elizabeth Watson; *Exec. Secy.* Norma Amenu-Kpodo.

Standing Conference on Lib. Materials on Africa, Univ. of London, Institute of Commonwealth Studies, Thornhaugh St., Russell Square, London WC1H 0XG, England. Tel. 171-580-5876, ext. 2304, fax 171-

636-2834, e-mail rt4@soas.ac.uk. *Chair* J. Pinfold.

### Europe

Ligue des Bibliothèques Européennes de Recherche (LIBER) (Assn. of European Research Libs.), c/o H.-A. Koch, Universität Bremen, Postfach 330440, 28334 Bremen, Germany. Tel. 421-218-3361.

## National

### Argentina

Asociación de Bibliotecarios Graduados de la República Argentina (Assn. of Graduate Libns. of Argentina), Corrientes 1642, 1° piso, Of. 22-2° cuerpo, 1042 Buenos Aires. Tel./fax 1-382-4821, 384-8095. *Pres.* Ana María Peruchena Zimmermann; *Exec. Secy.* Rosa Emma Monfasani.

### Australia

Australian Council of Libs. and Info. Services, Box 202, Queen Victoria Terrace, Kingston, ACT 2600. Tel. 6-262-1244, fax 6-273-4493. *Pres.* Derek Whitehead; *Exec. Officer* Gordon Bower.

Australian Lib. and Info. Assn., Box E 441, Queen Victoria Terrace, Kingston, ACT 2600. Tel. 6-285-1877, fax 6-282-2249.

Australian Society of Archivists, Box 83, O'Connor, ACT 2602. Tel. 7-3875-8705, fax 7-3875-8764, e-mail shicks@gil. com.au. *Pres.* Kathryn Dan; *Secy.* Fiona Burn.

Council of Australian State Libs., c/o State Lib. of Queensland, Queensland Cultural Centre, South Brisbane, Qld. Tel. 7-3840-7666, fax 7-3846-2421. *Chair* D. H. Stephens.

## Austria

Österreichische Gesellschaft für Dokumentation und Information (Austrian Society for Documentation and Info.), c/o TermNet, Simmeringer Hauptstr. 24, A-1110 Vienna. Tel. 1-7404-0280, fax 1-7404-0281. *Pres.* Gerhard Richter.

Vereinigung Österreichischer Bibliothekarinnen und Bibliothekare (Assn.of Austrian Libns.), A-1082, Vienna. Tel. 1-4000-84936, 1-4000-7219, e-mail post@m09magwieu. gv.at. *Pres.* Herwig Würtz; *Secy.* Ruth Lotter.

## Bangladesh

Lib. Assn. of Bangladesh, c/o Bangladesh Central Public Institute of Library & Information Sciences, Library Bldg., Shahbagh, Ramna, Dacca 1000. Tel. 2-504-269, e-mail msik@bangla.net. *Pres.* M. Shamsul Islam Khan; *Gen. Secy.* Kh Fazlur Rahman.

## Barbados

Lib. Assn. of Barbados, Box 827E, Bridgetown. *Pres.* Shirley Yearwood; *Secy.* Hazelyn Devonish.

## Belgium

Archives et Bibliothèques de Belgique/ Archief-en Bibliotheekwezen in België (Archives and Libs. of Belgium), 4 Blvd. de l'Empereur, B-1000 Brussels. Tel. 2-519-5351, fax 2-519-5533. *Gen. Secy.* Wim De Vos.

Association Belge de Documentation/Belgische Vereniging voor Documentatie (Belgian Assn. for Documentation), Chausee de Wavre 1683, Waversesteenweg, B-1160 Brussels. Tel. 2-675-5862, fax 2-672-7446, e-mail abd@synec-doc.be. *Pres.* Evelyne Luetkens; *Secy.* Vincent Maes.

Association Professionnelle des Bibliothécaires et Documentalistes, 7 rue des Marronniers, 5651 Thy-Le Chateau, Brussels. *Pres.* Jean Claude Trefois; *Secy.* Angelique Matlioli.

Vlaamse Vereniging voor Bibliotheek-, Archief-, en Documentatiewezen (Flemish Assn. of Libns., Archivists, and Documentalists), Waterloostraat 11, 2600 Berchem,

Antwerp. Tel. 3-281-4457, fax 3-218-8077, e-mail ms.vvbad@innet.be. *Pres.* Erwin Pairon; *Exec. Dir.* Marc Storms.

## Belize

Belize Lib. Assn., c/o Central Lib., Bliss Inst., Box 287, Belize City. Tel. 2-7267. *Pres.* H. W. Young; *Secy.* Robert Hulse.

## Bolivia

Asociación Boliviana de Bibliotecarios (Bolivian Lib. Assn.), c/o Biblioteca y Archivo Nacional, Calle Bolivar, Sucre.

## Bosnia and Herzegovina

Drustvo bibliotekara Bosne i Hercegovine (Libns. Society of Bosnia and Herzegovina), Obala v Stepe 42, 71000 Sarajevo. Tel. 71-283245. *Pres.* Neda Cukac.

## Botswana

Botswana Lib. Assn., Box 1310, Gaborone. Tel. 31-355-2295, fax 31-357291. *Chair* F. M. Lamusse; *Secy.* A. M. Mbangiwa.

## Brazil

Associação dos Arquivistas Brasileiros (Assn. of Brazilian Archivists), Rua da Candelária, 9-Sala 1004, Centro, Rio de Janeiro RJ 20091-020. Tel./fax 21-233-7142. *Pres.* Lia Temporal Malcher; *Secy.* Laura Regina Xavier.

## Brunei

Persatuan Perpustakaan Kebangsaan Negara Brunei (National Lib. Assn. of Brunei), c/o Language and Literature Bureau Lib., Jalan Elizabeth II, Bandar Seri Begawan. Tel. 2-235501.

## Bulgaria

Sajuz na Bibliotechnite i Informazionnite Rabotnitzi (Union of Libns. and Info. Officers), Pl. Slavejkov 4, Rm. 609, Box 269, 1000 Sofia. Tel. 2-864264. *Pres.* Maria Kapitanova-Iordandva.

## Cameroon

Association des Bibliothécaires, Archivistes, Documentalistes et Muséographes du Cameroon (Assn. of Libns., Archivists, Documentalists and Museum Curators of Cameroon), Université de Yaounde, Bibliothèque Universitaire, B.P. 337, Yaounde. Tel. 220744.

## Canada

Bibliographical Society of Canada/La Société Bibliographique du Canada, Box 575, Postal Sta. P, Toronto, ON M5S 2T1. World Wide Web: http://www.library. utoronto.ca/~bsc.

Canadian Assn. for Info. Science/Association Canadienne de Sciences de l'Information, c/o CAIS Secretariat, Univ. of Toronto, 140 Saint George St., Toronto, ON M5S 3G6. Tel. 416-978-8876, fax 416-971-1399, e-mail caisasst@fis.utoronto.ca.

Canadian Council of Lib. Schools/Conseil Canadien des Ecoles de Bibliothéconomie, c/o Faculty of Info. Studies, Univ. of Toronto, 140 Saint George St., Toronto M5S 3G6. Tel. 416-978-3202, fax 416-978-5762.

Canadian Lib. Assn., c/o Exec. Dir. Vicki Whitmell, 200 Elgin St., Suite 602, Ottawa, ON K2P 1L5. Tel. 613-232-8837, fax 613-563-9895, e-mail whitmell@istar.ca. (For detailed information on the Canadian Lib. Assn. and its divisions, see "National Library and Information-Industry Associations, United States and Canada"; for information on the library associations of the provinces of Canada, see "State, Pro-vincial, and Regional Library Associations.")

## Chile

Colegio de Bibliotecarios de Chile AG (Chilean Lib. Assn.), Diagonal Paraguay 383, Depto 122 Torre 11, Santiago 3741. Tel. 2-222-5652, e-mail cdb@interaccesses.cl. Pres. Esmerelda Ramos Ramos; Secy. Monica Nunez.

## China

China Society for Lib. Science, 39 Bai Shi Qiao Rd., Beijing 100081. Tel. 10-684-15566, ext. 5563, fax 10-684-19271. Secy.-Gen. Liu Xiangsheng.

## Colombia

Asociación Colombiana de Bibliotecarios (Colombian Lib. Assn.), Calle 10, No. 3-16, Apdo. Aéreo 30883, Bogotá.

## Costa Rica

Asociación Costarricense de Bibliotecarios (Costa Rican Assn. of Libns.), Apdo. 3308, San José. Secy.-Gen. Nelly Kopper.

## Croatia

Hrvatsko Bibliotekarsko Drustvo (Croation Lib. Assn.), Ulica Hrvatske bratske zajednice b b, 10000 Zagreb. Tel. 41-616-4111, fax 41-611-64186. Pres. Dubravka Kunstek; Secy. Dunja Gabriel.

## Cuba

Lib. Assn. of Cuba, Biblioteca Nacional José Martí, Apdo. 6881, Ave. de Independencia e/20 de Mayo y Aranguren, Plaza de la Revolución, Havana. Tel. 7-708-277. Dir. Marta Terry González.

## Cyprus

Kypriakos Synthesmos Vivliothicarion (Lib. Assn. of Cyprus), Box 1039, Nicosia. Pres. Costas D. Stephanov; Secy. Paris G. Rossos.

## Czech Republic

Svaz Knihovníkua Informačních Pracovníkú Ceské Republiky (Assn. of Lib. and Info. Professionals of the Czech Republic), Klementinum 190, c/o Národní Knihovna, 110 01 Prague 1. Tel./fax 2-2166-3295, e-mail burget@mondia.cz. Pres. Jarmila Burgetová.

Ústřední knihovnícká rada CR (Central Lib. Council of the Czech Republic), Valdštejnské nám. 4, 11811 Prague 1. Tel. 2-531-225, fax 2-532-185. Pres. Jaroslav Vyčichlo; Secy. Adolf Knoll.

# Denmark

Arkivforeningen (Archives Society), c/o Landsarkivet for Sjaelland, jagtvej 10, 2200 Copenhagen K K. Tel. 3139-3520, fax 3315-3239. *Pres.* Tyge Krogh; *Secy.* Charlotte Steinmark.

Bibliotekarforbundet (Union of Libns.), Lindevangs Allé 2, DK-2000 Frederiksberg. Tel. 3888-2233, fax 3888-3201. *Pres.* Anja Rasmussen; *V.P.* Flemming Faarup.

Danmarks Biblioteksforening (Danish Lib. Assn.), Telegrafvej 5, DK-2750 Ballerup. Tel. 4468-1466, fax 4468-1103. *Dir.* Jens Thorhauge.

Danmarks Forskningsbiblioteksforening (Danish Research Lib. Assn.), Campusvej 55, 5230 Odense M. Tel. Tel. 66-15-67-68, fax 66-15-81-62. *Pres.* Mette Stockmarr; *Secy.* D. Skovgaard.

Danmarks Skolebiblioteksforening (Assn. of Danish School Libns.), Mariavej 1, Sdr Bjert, 6091 Bjert. Tel. 755-7101, fax 4239-4349. *Chair* Gert Larsen.

# Dominican Republic

Asociación Dominicana de Bibliotecarios (Dominican Assn. of Libns.), c/o Biblioteca Nacional, Plaza de la Cultura, Cesar Nicolás Penson 91, Santo Domingo. Tel. 809-688-4086. *Pres.* Prospero J. Mella-Chavier; *Secy.-Gen.* V. Regús.

# Ecuador

Asociación Ecuatoriana de Bibliotecarios (Ecuadoran Lib. Assn.), c/o Casa de la Cultura Ecuatoriana Benjamín Carrión, Apdo. 67, Ave. 6 de Diciembre 794, Quito. Tel. 2-528-840, 02-263-474. *Pres.* Eulalia Galarza.

# Egypt

Egyptian Assn. for Lib. and Info. Science, c/o Dept. of Archives, Librarianship and Info. Science, Faculty of Arts, Univ. of Cairo, Cairo. Tel. 2-567-6365, fax 2-572-9659. *Pres.* S. Khalifa; *Secy.* Hosam El-Din.

# El Salvador

Asociación de Bibliotecarios de El Salvador (El Salvador Lib. Assn.), c/o Biblioteca Nacional, 8A Avda. Norte y Calle Delgado, San Salvador. Tel. 216-312.

Asociación General de Archivistas de El Salvador (Assn. of Archivists of El Salvador), Archivo General de la Nación, Palacio Nacional, San Salvador. Tel. 229-418.

# Ethiopia

Ye Ethiopia Betemetshaft Serategnoch Mahber (Ethiopian Lib. Assn.), Box 30530, Addis Ababa. Tel. 1-110-844, fax 1-552-544. *Pres.* Mulugeta Hunde; *Secy.* Girma Makonnen.

# Fiji

Fiji Lib. Assn., Govt. Bldgs., Box 2292, Suva. *Secy.* E. Qica.

# Finland

Suomen Kirjastoseura (Finnish Lib. Assn.), Kansakouluk 10 A 19, FIN-00100 Helsinki. Tel. 0-694-1844, fax 0-694-1859, e-mail fla@fla.fi. *Pres.* Kaarina Dromberg; *Secy.-Gen.* Tuula Haavisto.

# France

Association des Archivistes Français (Assn. of French Archivists), 60 Rue des Francs-Bourgeois, F-75141 Paris cedex 3. Tel. 1-4027-6000. *Pres.* Jean-Luc Eichenlaub; *Secy.* Jean LePottier.

Association des Bibliothécaires Français (Assn. of French Libns.), 7 Rue des Lions-Saint-Paul, F-75004 Paris. Tel. 1-4887-9787, fax 4887-9713. *Pres.* Claudine Belayche; *Gen. Secy.* Marie-Martine Tomiteh.

Association des Professionnels de l'Information et de la Documentation (French Assn. of Info. and Documentation Professionals), 25 Rue Claude Tillier, F-75012 Paris. Tel. 1-4372-2525, fax 1-4372-3041, e-mail adbs@adbs.fr. *Pres.* Florence Wilhelm.

# Germany

Arbeitsgemeinschaft der Spezialbibliotheken (Assn. of Special Libs.), OAR La Eckl, Universitatsbibliothek, Karlsruhe, Postfach 6920, 76049, Karlsruhe. Tel. 721-608-3101, fax 721-608-4886. *Chair* Wolfrudolf Laux; *Secretariat Dir.* Marianne Schwarzer.

Deutsche Gesellschaft für Dokumentation (German Society for Documentation), Ostbahnhofstr. 13, 60314 Frankfurt-am-Main 1. Tel. 69-430-313, fax 69-490-9096. *Pres.* Joachim-Felix Leonard.

Deutscher Bibliotheksverband eV (German Lib. Assn.), Alt-Moabit 101A, 10559 Berlin. Tel. 30-3907-7274, fax 30-393-8011, e-mail dbv@dbi-berlin.de. *Pres.* Christof Eichert.

Verein der Bibliothekare an Öffentlichen Bibliotheken (Assn. of Libns. at Public Libs.), Postfach 1324, 72703 Reutlingen. Tel. 7121-36999, fax 7121-300-433. *Pres.* Konrad Umlauf; *Secy.* Katharina Boulanger.

Verein der Diplom-Bibliothekare an Wissenschaftlichen Bibliotheken (Assn. of Certified Libns. at Academic Libs.), c/o BIOst, Bibliothek, Lindenbornstre 22, 50823 Cologne. Tel. 221-574-7161, fax 221-574-7110. *Chair* Marianne Saule.

Verein Deutscher Archivare (Assn. of German Archivists), Westphälisches Archivamt, 48133 Münster. Tel. 251-591-3886, fax 251-591-269. *Chair* Norbert Reimann.

Verein Deutscher Bibliothekare (Assn. of German Libns.), Krummer Timpen 3-5, 48143 Munsten. Tel. 251-832-4032, fax 251-832-8398. *Pres.* Klaus Hilgemann; *Secy.* Lydia Jungnickel.

# Ghana

Ghana Lib. Assn., Box 4105, Accra. Tel. 2-668-731. *Pres.* E. S. Asiedo; *Secy.* A. W. K. Insaidoo.

# Great Britain

*See* United Kingdom.

# Greece

Enosis Hellinon Bibliothekarion (Greek Lib. Assn.), Themistocleus 73, 10683 Athens. Tel. 1-322-6625. *Pres.* K. Xatzopoulou; *Gen. Secy.* E. Kalogeraky.

# Guyana

Guyana Lib. Assn., c/o National Lib., Church St. & Ave. of the Republic, Georgetown. Tel. 2-62690, 2-62699. *Pres.* Hetty London; *Secy.* Jean Harripersaud.

# Honduras

Asociación de Bibliotecarios y Archiveros de Honduras (Assn. of Libns. and Archivists of Honduras), 11a Calle, 1a y 2a Avdas. No. 105, Comayagüela DC, Tegucigalpa. *Pres.* Fransisca de Escoto Espinoza; *Secy.-Gen.* Juan Angel R. Ayes.

# Hungary

Magyar Könyvtárosok Egyesülete (Assn. of Hungarian Libns.), Szabó Ervin tér 1, H-1088 Budapest. Tel./fax 1-118-2050. *Pres.* Tibor Horváth; *Secy.* István Papp.

# Iceland

Bókavardafélag Islands (Icelandic Lib. Assn.), Box 1497, 121 Reykjavik. Tel. 354-1-564-2050, fax 354-1-564-3877. *Pres.* H. A. Hardarson; *Secy.* A. Agnarsdottir.

# India

Indian Assn. of Special Libs. and Info. Centres, P-291, CIT Scheme 6M, Kankurgachi, Calcutta 700054. Tel. 33-349651.

Indian Lib. Assn., c/o Dr. Mukerjee Nagar, A/40-41, Flat 201, Ansal Bldg., Delhi 110009. Tel. 11-711-7743. *Pres.* P. S. G. Kumar.

# Indonesia

Ikatan Pustakawan Indonesia (Indonesian Lib. Assn.), Jalan Merdeka Selatan No. 11, Box 274, Jakarta, Pusat. Tel. 21-375-718, fax 21-310-3554. *Pres.* S. Kartosdono.

# Iraq

Iraqi Lib. Assn., c/o National Lib., Bab-el-Muaddum, Baghdad. *Dir.* Abdul Hameed Al-Alawchi.

# Ireland

Cumann Leabharlann Na h-Eireann (Lib. Assn. of Ireland), 53 Upper Mount St., Dublin. Tel. 1-661-9000, fax 1-676-1628, e-mail laisec@iol.ie. *Pres.* L. Ronayne; *Hon. Secy.* Brendan Teeling.

# Israel

Israel Libns. and Info. Specialists Assn., Box 238, 17 Strauss St., 91001 Jerusalem. *Pres.* Benjamin Schachter.
Israel Society of Special Libs. and Info. Centers, 31 Habarzel St., Ramat Ha Hayal, 69710 Tel Aviv. Tel. 3-648-0592. *Chair* Liliane Frenkiel.

# Italy

Associazione Italiana Biblioteche (Italian Lib. Assn.), C.P. 2461, I-00100 Rome A-D. Tel. 6-446-3532, fax 6-444-1139, e-mail aib.italia@agora.stm.it. *Pres.* Rossella Caffo; *Secy.* Luca Bellingeri.

# Ivory Coast (Côte d'Ivoire)

Association pour le Développement de la Documentation des Bibliothèques et Archives de la Côte d'Ivoire (Assn. for the Development of Documentation Libs. and Archives of the Ivory Coast), c/o Bibliothèque Nationale, B.P. V 180, Abidjan. Tel. 225-213-872. *Dir.* Ambroise Agnero; *Secy.-Gen.* Cangah Guy.

# Jamaica

Jamaica Lib. Assn., Box 58, Kingston 5. *Pres.* P. Kerr; *Secy.* F. Salmon.

# Japan

Joho Kagaku Gijutsu Ky kai (Info. Science and Technology Assn.), Sasaki Bldg., 5-7 Koisikawa 2, Bunkyo-ku, Tokyo. *Pres.* T. Gondoh; *Gen. Mgr.* Yukio Ichikawa.
Nihon Toshokan Kyokai (Japan Lib. Assn.), c/o *Secy.-Gen.* Reiko Sakagawa, 1-10 Taishido, 1-chome, Setagaya-ku, Tokyo 154. Tel. 3-3410-6411, fax 3-3421-7588.
Senmon Toshokan Kyogikai (Japan Special Libs. Assn.), c/o National Diet Lib., 10-1 Nagata-cho, 1-chome, Chiyoda-ku, Tokyo 100. Tel. 3-3581-2331, fax 3-3597-9104.

*Pres.* Kousaku Inaba; *Exec. Dir.* Fumihisa Nakagawa.

# Jordan

Jordan Lib. Assn., Box 6289, Amman. Tel. 6-629-412. *Pres.* Anwar Akroush; *Secy.* Yousra Abu Ajamieh.

# Kenya

Kenya Lib. Assn., Box 46031, Nairobi. Tel. 2-214-917, fax 2-36-885, e-mail jwere@ken.healthnet.org. *Chair* Jacinta Were; *Secy.* Alice Bulogosi.

# Korea (Republic of)

Korean Lib. Assn., 60-1 Panpo Dong, Seocho-ku, Seoul. Tel. 2-535-4868, fax 2-535-5616, e-mail klanet@kol.co.kr. *Pres.* Chal Sakong; *Exec. Dir.* Ho Jo Won.

# Laos

Association des Bibliothécaires Laotiens (Assn. of Laotian Libns.), c/o Direction de la Bibliothèque Nationale, Ministry of Education, B.P. 704, Vientiane. *Dir.* Somthong.

# Latvia

Lib. Assn. of Latvia, Latvian National Lib., Kr. Barona iela 14, 1423 Riga. Tel. 132-728-98-74, fax 132-728-08-51. *Pres.* Aldis Abele.

# Lebanon

Lebanese Lib. Assn., c/o American Univ. of Beirut, Univ. Lib./Gifts and Exchange, Box 113/5367, Beirut. Tel. 1-340740, ext. 2603. *Pres.* Rafi' Ma'rouf; *Exec. Secy.* Linda Sadaka.

# Lesotho

Lesotho Lib. Assn., Private Bag A26, Maseru. *Chair* E. M. Nthunya; *Secy.* M. M. Moshoeshoe-Chadzingwa.

# Lithuania

Lithuanian Librarians Assn., Didzioji str 10, 2001 Vilnius. Tel. 2-611-875, fax 2-221-1324.

## Malawi

Malawi Lib. Assn., Box 429, Zomba. Tel. 50-522-222, fax 50-523-225. *Chair* Joseph J. Uta; *Secy.* Vote D. Somba.

## Malaysia

Persatuan Perpustakaan Malaysia (Lib. Assn. of Malaysia), Box 12545, 50782 Kuala Lumpur. Tel. 3-756-6516. *Pres.* Chew Wing Foong; *Secy.* Leni Abdul Latif.

## Mali

Association Malienne des Bibliothécaires, Archivistes et Documentalistes (Mali Assn. of Libns., Archivists, and Documentalists), c/o Bibliothèque Nationale du Mali, Ave.
Kasse Keita, B.P. 159, Bamako. Tel. 224963. *Dir.* Mamadou Konoba Keita.

## Malta

Ghaqda Bibljotekarji/Lib. Assn. (Malta), c/o Univ. Lib., Msida MSD 06. *Secy.* Marion Borg.

## Mauritania

Association Mauritanienne des Bibliothécaires, Archivistes et Documentalistes (Mauritanian Assn. of Libns., Archivists, and Documentalists), c/o Bibliothèque Nationale, B.P. 20, Nouakchott. *Pres.* O. Diouwara; *Secy.* Sid'Ahmed Fall dit Dah.

## Mauritius

Mauritius Lib. Assn., c/o The British Council, Royal Rd., Box 11, Rose Hill. Tel. 541-602, fax 549-553. *Pres.* K. Appadoo; *Secy.* S. Rughoo.

## Mexico

Asociación Mexicana de Bibliotecarios (Mexican Assn. of Libns.), Apdo. 27-651, Admin. de Correos 27, México D.F. 06760. Tel./fax 5-575-1135, e-mail ambac@solar.sar.net. *Pres.* Elsa M. Ramirez Leyva; *Secy.* Jose L. Almanza Morales.

## Myanmar

Myanmar Lib. Assn., c/o National Lib., Strand Rd., Yangon. *Chief Libn.* U Khin Maung Tin.

## Nepal

Nepal Lib. Assn., c/o National Lib., Harihar Bhawan, Pulchowk Lib., Box 2773, Kathmandu. Tel. 1-521-132. *Libn.* Shusila Dwivedi.

## The Netherlands

Nederlandse Vereniging van Bibliothecarissen, Documentalisten en Literatuur Onderzoekers (Netherlands Libns. Society), NVB-Verenigingsbureau, Plompetorengracht 11, NL-3512 CA Utrecht. Tel. 30-231-1263, fax 30-231-1830, e-mail nvbinfo@worldaccess.nl. *Pres.* H. C. Kooyman-Tibbles; *Secy.* R. Tichelaar.

UKB (Universiteitsbibliotheek Vriji Universiteit) (Assn. of the Univ. Libs., the Royal Lib., and the Lib. of the Royal Netherlands Academy of Arts and Sciences), De Boelelaan 1103, NL-1081 HV Amsterdam. Tel. 44-45140, fax 44-45259. *Pres.* A. C. Klugkist; *Libn.* J. H. de Swart.

## New Zealand

New Zealand Lib. and Info. Assn., Level 6, Old Wool House, 139-141 Featherston St., Box 12-212, Wellington. Tel. 4-473-5834, fax 4-499-1480, e-mail nzlia@netlink.co.nz.

## Nicaragua

Asociación Nicaraguense de Bibliotecarios y Profesionales a Fines (Nicaraguan Assn. of Libns.), Apdo. Postal 3257, Managua. *Exec. Secy.* Susana Morales Hernández.

## Nigeria

Nigerian Lib. Assn., c/o National Lib. of Nigeria, 4 Wesley St., PMB 12626, Lagos. Tel. 1-263-1716, fax 1-616404. *Pres.* A. O. Banjo; *Secy.* D. D. Bwayili.

## Norway

Arkivarforeningen (Assn. of Archivists), c/o Riksarkivet, Folke Bernadottes Vei 21, Postboks 10, N-0807 Oslo. Tel. 22-022-600, fax 22-237-489.

Norsk Bibliotekforening (Norwegian Lib. Assn.), Malerhaugveien 20, N-0661 Oslo. Tel. 2-268-8550, fax 2-267-2368. *Dir.* Berit Aaker.

Norsk Fagbibliotekforening (Norwegian Assn. of Special Libs.), c/o Technical Univ. Lib. of Norway, Chemistry Branch Lib., N-7034 Trondheim 6. Tel. 7-359-4188, fax 7-359-5103. *Chair* Else-Margrethe Bredland.

## Pakistan

Pakistan Lib. Assn., c/o Pakistan Inst. of Development Economics, Univ. Campus, Box 1091, Islamabad. Tel. 51-921-4041, fax 51-921-0886, e-mail arshad%pide@sdnpk.undp.org. *Pres.* Azmat Ullah Bhatti; *Secy.-Gen.* Hafiz Khubaib Ahmad.

## Panama

Asociación Panameña de Bibliotecarios (Panama Lib. Assn.), c/o Biblioteca Interamericana Simón Bolívar, Estafeta Universítaria, Panama City. *Pres.* Bexie Rodríguez de León.

## Paraguay

Asociación de Bibliotecarios del Paraguay (Assn. of Paraguayan Libns.), Casilla de Correo 1505, Asunción. *Secy.* Mafalda Cabrerar.

## Peru

Asociación de Archiveros del Perú (Peruvian Assn. of Archivists), Archivo Central Slaverry 2020 Jesús Mario, Universidad del Pacifico, Lima 11. *Pres.* José Luis Abanto Arrelucea.

Asociación Peruana de Bibliotecarios (Peruvian Assn of Libns.), Bellavista 561 Miraflores, Apdo. 995, Lima 18. Tel. 14-474869. *Pres.* Martha Fernandez de Lopez; *Secy.* Luzmila Tello de Medina.

## Philippines

Assn. of Special Libs. of the Philippines, Rm. 301, National Lib. Bldg., T. M. Kalaw St., Manila. Tel. 2-590177. *Pres.* Zenaida F. Lucas; *Secy.* Socorro G. Elevera.

Bibliographical Society of the Philippines, National Lib. of the Philippines, T. M. Kalaw St., 1000 Ermita, Box 2926, Manila. Tel. 2-583252, fax 2-502329. *Secy.-Treas.* Leticia R. Maloles.

Philippine Libns. Assn., c/o National Lib. of the Philippines, Rm. 301, T. M. Kalaw St., Manila. Tel. 2-590177. *Pres.* Antonio M. Sontos; *Secy.* Rosemarie Rosali.

## Poland

Stowarzyszenie Bibliotekarzy Polskich (Polish Libns. Assn.), Ul. Konopczynskiego 5/7, 00950 Warsaw. Tel. 22-275296. *Chair* Stanislaw Czajka; *Secy.-Gen.* Dariusz Kuzminski.

## Portugal

Associação Portuguesa de Bibliotecários, Arquivistas e Documentalistas (Portuguese Assn. of Libns., Archivists, and Documentalists), R. Morais Soares, 43C-1 DTD, 1900 Lisbon. Tel. 1-815-4479, fax 1-815-4508, e-mail badbn@telepac.pt. *Pres.* António Pina Falcao.

## Puerto Rico

Sociedad de Bibliotecarios de Puerto Rico (Society of Libns. of Puerto Rico), Apdo. 22898, Universidad de Puerto Rico Sta., San Juan 00931. Tel. 787-764-0000. *Pres.* Aura Jiménez de Panepinto; *Secy.* Olga L. Hernández.

## Romania

Asociatüia Bibliotecarilor din Bibliotecile Publice-România (Assn. of Public Libns. of Romania), Strada Ion Ghica 4, Sector 3, 79708 Bucharest. Tel. 1-614-2434, fax 1-312-3381, e-mail bnr@ul.ici.ro. *Pres.* Gheorghe-Iosif Bercan; *Secy.* Georgeta Clinca.

## Russia

Lib. Council, State V. I. Lenin Lib., Prospect Kalinina 3, Moscow 101000. Tel. 95-202-4656. *Exec. Secy.* G. A. Semenova.

## Senegal

Association Sénégalaise des Bibliothécaires, Archivistes et Documentalistes (Senegalese Assn. of Libns., Archivists and Documentalists), BP 3252, Dakar. Tel. 246-981, fax 242-379. *Pres.* Mariétou Diongue Diop; *Secy.* Emmanuel Kabou.

## Sierra Leone

Sierra Leone Assn. of Archivists, Libns., and Info. Scientists, c/o Sierra Leone Lib. Board, Box 326, Freetown. *Pres.* Deanna Thomas.

## Singapore

Lib. Assn. of Singapore, c/o Bukit Merah Central, Box 0693, Singapore 9115. *Hon. Secy.* Siti Hanifah Mustapha.

## Slovenia

Zveza Bibliotekarskih Drustev Slovenije (Lib. Assn. of Slovenia), Turjaska 1, 61000 Ljubljana. Tel. 61-125-50-14, fax 61-125-92-57. *Pres.* Nada Cesnovar; *Secy.* Stanislav Bahor.

## South Africa

African Lib. Assn. of South Africa, c/o Lib., Univ. of the North, Private Bag X1106, Sovenga 0727. Tel. 1521-689111. *Secy. and Treas.* A. N. Kambule.

## Spain

Asociación Española de Archiveros, Bibliotecarios, Museólogos y Documentalistas (Spanish Assn. of Archivists, Libns., Curators and Documentalists), Recoletos 5, 28001 Madrid. Tel. 1-575-1727. *Pres.* Julia M. Rodrigez Barrero.

## Sri Lanka

Sri Lanka Lib. Assn., Professional Center, 275/75 Bauddhaloka Mawatha, Colombo 7. Tel. 1-589103, e-mail postmast@slla. ac.lk. *Pres.* Harrison Perera; *Secy.* Wilfred Ranasinghe.

## Swaziland

Swaziland Lib. Assn., Box 2309, Mbabane. Tel. 43101. *Chair* L. Dlamini; *Secy.* P. Muswazi.

## Sweden

Svenska Arkivsamfundet (Swedish Assn. of Archivists), c/o Riksarkivet, Box 12541, S-10229 Stockholm. Tel. 8-737-6350, fax 8-657-9564, e-mail anna-christina.ulfsparre@riksarkivet.ra.se. *Pres.* Anna Christina Ulfsparre.

Sveriges Allmänna Biblioteksförening (Swedish Lib. Assn.), Box 3127, S-103 62 Stockholm. Tel. 8-241-020, 8-723-0082, fax 8-723-0083, e-mail yvla.mannerheim@bbl.sab.se; World Wide Web: http://www.sab.e/. *Secy.-Gen.* Christina Stenberg.

Swedish School of Lib. and Info. Science Lib., Box 874, S-50115 Boras. Tel. 33-164-000, fax 33-111-053. *Exec. Secy.* Staffan Lööf.

## Switzerland

Association des Bibliothèques et Bibliothécaires Suisses/Vereinigung Schweizerischer Bibliothekare/Associazione dei Bibliotecari Svizzeri (Assn. of Swiss Libns.), Effingerstr. 35, CH-3008 Berne. Tel. 31-382-4240, fax 31-382-4648, e-mail bbs@bbs.ch, World Wide Web http://www.bbs.ch. *Secy.* Alain Huber.

Schweizerische Vereinigung für Dokumentation/Association Suisse de Documentation (Swiss Assn. of Documentation), Schmidgasse 4, Postfach 601, CH-6301, Zug. Tel. 41-726-4505, fax 41-726-4509. *Pres.* S. Holláander; *Secy.* H. Schweuk.

Vereinigung Schweizerischer Archivare (Assn. of Swiss Archivists), Archivstr. 24,

CH-3003 Berne. Tel. 31-618989. *Secy.* Bernard Truffer.

## Taiwan

Lib. Assn. of China, c/o National Central Lib., 20 Chungshan S Rd., Taipei. Tel. 2-331-2475, fax 2-382-0747, e-mail lac@ msg.ncl.edu.tu. *Pres.* James S. C. Hu; *Secy.-Gen.* Teresa Wang Chang.

## Tanzania

Tanzania Lib. Assn., Box 2645, Dar es Salaam. Tel. 51-402-6121. *Chair* T. E. Mlaki; *Secy.* A. Ngaiza.

## Thailand

Thai Lib. Assn., 273 Vibhavadee Rangsit Rd., Phayathai, Bangkok 10400. Tel. 2-271-2084. *Pres.* K. Chavallt; *Secy.* Karnmanee Suckcharoen.

## Trinidad and Tobago

Lib. Assn. of Trinidad and Tobago, Box 1275, Port of Spain. Tel. 868-624-5075, e-mail latt@fm1.wow.net. *Pres.* Esahack Mohammed; *Secy.* Shamin Renwick.

## Tunisia

Association Tunisienne des Documentalistes, Bibliothécaires et Archivistes (Tunisian Assn. of Documentalists, Libns., and Archivists), B.P. 380, 1015 Tunis. *Pres.* Ahmed Ksibi.

## Turkey

Türk Küüphaneciler Dernegi (Turkish Libns. Assn.), Elgün Sok-8/8, 06440 Yenisehir, Ankara. Tel. 312-230-1325, fax 312-232-0453. *Pres.* A. Berberoglu; *Secy.* A. Kaygusuz.

## Uganda

Uganda Lib. Assn., Box 5894, Kampala. Tel. 141-285001, ext. 4. *Chair* P. Birungi; *Secy.* L. M. Ssengero.

## Ukraine

Ukrainian Lib. Assn., 14 Chyhorin St., Kyiv 252042, Ukraine. Tel. 380-44-268-2263, fax 380-44-295-8296. *Pres.* Valentyna S. Pashkova.

## United Kingdom

ASLIB (The Assn. for Info. Management), Information House, 20-24 Old St., London EC1V 9AP, England. Tel. 171-253-4488, fax 171-430-0514, e-mail aslib@aslib. co.uk. *Dir.* R. B. Bowes.

Bibliographical Society, c/o The Welcome Institute, Victoria & Albert Museum, 183 Euston Rd., London SW7 2RL, England. Tel. 171-611-7244, fax 171-611-8703, e-mail d.pearson@welcome.ac.uk. *Hon. Secy.* David Pearson.

The Lib. Assn., 7 Ridgmount St., London WC1E 7AE, England. Tel. 171-636-7543, fax 171-436-7218, e-mail info@la-hq. org.uk. *Chief Exec.* Ross Shimmon.

School Lib. Assn., Liden Lib., Barrington Close, Liden, Swindon, Wiltshire SN3 6HF, England. Tel. 1793-537-374, e-mail info@sla.org.uk. *Pres.* Frank N. Hogg; *Exec. Secy.* Kathy Lemaire.

Scottish Lib. Assn., 1 John St., Hamilton ML3 7EU, Scotland. Tel. 1698-458-888, fax 1698-458-899, e-mail sctlb@leapfrog. almac.co.uk. *Dir.* Robert Craig.

Society of Archivists, Information House, 20-24 Old St., London, EC1V 9AP, England. Tel. 171-253-5087, fax 171-253-3942. *Exec. Secy.* P. S. Cleary.

Standing Conference of National and Univ. Libs., 102 Euston St., London NW1 2HA, England. Tel. 171-387-0317, fax 171-383-3197. *Exec. Secy.* A. J. C. Bainton.

Welsh Lib. Assn., c/o Publications Office, College of Wales, Llanbadarn Fawr, Aberystwyth, Dyfed SY23 3AS, Wales. Tel. 1970-622-174, fax 1970-622-190, e-mail a.m.w.green@swansea.ac.uk. *Exec. Officer* Glyn Collins.

## Uruguay

Agrupación Bibliotecológica del Uruguay (Uruguayan Lib. and Archive Science

Assn.), Cerro Largo 1666, 11200 Montevideo. Tel. 2-405-740. *Pres.* Luis Alberto Musso.

Asociación de Bibliocólogos del Uruguay, Eduardo V Haedo 2255, CC 1315, 11200 Montevideo. Tel. 2-499-989.

## Vatican City

Biblioteca Apostolica Vaticana, 00120 Vatican City, Rome. Tel. 6-698-83302, fax 6-698-84795, e-mail Libr@librsbk.vatlib.it. *Prefect* Don Raffaele Farina.

## Venezuela

Colegio de Bibliotecólogos y Archivólogos de Venezuela (Assn. of Venezuelan Libns.

and Archivists), Apdo. 6283, Caracas. Tel. 2-572-1858. *Pres.* Elsi Jimenez de Diaz.

## Vietnam

Hôi Thu-Viên Viet Nam (Vietnamese Lib. Assn.), National Lib. of Viet Nam, 31 Trang Thi, 10000 Hanoi. Tel. 4-52643.

## Zambia

*Zambia Lib. Assn., Box 32839, Lusaka.* Chair C. Zulu; *Hon. Secy.* W. C. Mulalami.

## Zimbabwe

Zimbabwe Lib. Assn., Box 3133, Harare. *Chair* Driden Kunaka; *Hon. Secy.* Albert Masheka.

# Directory of Book Trade and Related Organizations

## Book Trade Associations, United States and Canada

For more extensive information on the associations listed in this section, see the annual edition of *Literary Market Place* (R. R. Bowker).

American Booksellers Assn. Inc., 828 S. Broadway, Tarrytown, NY 10591. Tel. 800-637-0037, 914-591-2665, fax 914-591-2720; *Pres.* Richard Howorth, Square Books, Oxford, MS 38665; *V.P.* Neal Coonerty, Bookshop Santa Cruz, Santa Cruz, CA 95060; *Secy.* Roxanne Coady, R. J. Julia Booksellers, Madison, CT 06443; *Treas.* Norman Laurila, A Different Light Bookstore, New York, NY 10011; *Chief Exec. Officer* Avin Mark Domnitz.

American Institute of Graphic Arts, 164 Fifth Ave., New York, NY 10010. Tel. 212-807-1990, fax 212-807-1799, e-mail aiga@aiga.org. *Exec. Dir.* Richard Grefe.

American Literary Translators Association (ALTA), Univ. of Texas–Dallas, Box 830688, Richardson, TX 75083-0688. Tel. 214-690-2093, fax 214-705-6303.

American Medical Publishers Assn., 14 Fort Hill Rd., Huntington, NY 11734. Tel./fax 516-423-0075, World Wide Web http://www.am-pa.com. *Pres.* Jack Farrell; *Exec. Dir.* Jill Rudansky, e-mail jillrudansky-ampa@msn.com.

American Printing History Assn., Box 4922, Grand Central Sta., New York, NY 10163-4922. *Pres.* Anne Anninger; *Exec. Secy.* Stephen Crook.

American Society of Indexers, Inc., Box 39366, Phoenix, AZ85069-9366. Tel. 602-979-5514, fax 602-530-4088, e-mail info@ASindexing.org, World Wide Web http://www.ASindexing.org.

American Society of Journalists and Authors, 1501 Broadway, Suite 302, New York, NY 10036. Tel. 212-997-0947, fax 212-768-7414, e-mail ASJA@compuserve.com, World Wide Web http://www.asja.org. *Exec. Dir.* Alexandra Cantor Owens.

American Society of Media Photographers, 14 Washington Rd., Suite 502, Princeton Junction, NJ 08550-1033. Tel. 609-799-8300, fax 609-799-2233. *Pres.* Les Riess; *Exec. Dir.* Richard Weisgrau.

American Society of Picture Professionals, Inc., 409 S. Washington St., Alexandria, VA 22314. Tel./fax 703-299-0219. *Exec. Dir.* Cathy Sachs; *National Pres.* Richard Pasley. Tel. 617-864-8386.

American Translators Assn., 1800 Diagonal Rd., Suite 220, Alexandria, VA 22314-2840. Tel. 703-683-6100, fax 703-683-6122, e-mail ata@atanet.org. *Pres.* Muriel Jerome-O'Keeffe; *Pres.-Elect* Ann Mac-Farlane; *Secy.* Eric McMillan; *Treas.* Monique-Paule Tubb; *Exec. Dir.* Walter W. Bacak, Jr.

Antiquarian Booksellers Assn. of America, 20 W. 44 St., Fourth fl., New York, NY 10036-6604. Tel. 212-944-8291, fax 212-944-8293, e-mail abaa@panix.com, World Wide Web http://www.abaa-booknet.com; *Exec. Dir.* Liane Wade.

Assn. of American Publishers, 71 Fifth Ave., New York, NY 10003. Tel. 212-255-0200. *Pres./CEO* Patricia S. Schroeder; *Exec. V.P.* Thomas D. McKee; *V.P.s* Richard F.

Blake, Barbara Meredith; *Washington Office* 1718 Connecticut Ave. N.W., Washington, DC 20009. Tel. 202-232-3335; *V.P.s* Allan Adler, Carol Risher; *Dir.* Judith Platt; *Chair* Peter Jovanovich, Pearson Education; *V. Chair* Brian J. Knez, Harcourt Brace & Co.; *Treas.* William M. Wright, Hearst Book Group; *Secy.* Kathleen D. Hammond, Hammond, Inc.

Assn. of American Univ. Presses, 71 W. 23 St., Suite 901, New York, NY 10010. Tel. 212-989-1010. *Pres.* Robert Faherty; *Exec. Dir.* Peter Givler; *Assoc. Exec. Dir.* Hollis Holmes. Address correspondence to the executive director.

Assn. of Authors' Representatives, Inc., 10 Astor Place, Third fl., New York, NY 10003. Tel. 212-353-3709, World Wide Web http://aar-online.org. *Pres.* Jean Naggar; *Admin. Secy.* Ginger Knowlton.

Assn. of Canadian Publishers, 110 Eglinton Ave. W., Suite 401, Toronto, ON M4R 1A3. Tel. 416-487-6116, fax 416-487-8815. *Exec. Dir.* Paul Davidson. Address correspondence to the executive director.

Assn. of Jewish Book Publishers, c/o Jewish Lights Publishing, Box 237, Woodstock, VT 05091. Tel. 802-457-4000, fax 802-457-4004. *Pres.* Stuart M. Matlins. Address correspondence to the president.

Assn. of Graphic Communications, 330 Seventh Ave., New York, NY 10001. Tel. 212-279-2100, fax 212-279-5381, e-mail BD@AGCcomm.org, World Wide Web http://www.agcomm.org. *Pres.* William A. Dirzulaitis; *Dir. Ed.* Pam Suett; *Dir. Exhibits* Carl Gessman.

Book Industry Study Group, Inc., 160 Fifth Ave., New York, NY 10010. Tel. 212-929-1393, fax 212-989-7542, World Wide Web http://www.bisg.org. *Chair* Kent Freeman; *V. Chair* Robert Severud; *Treas.* Seymour Turk; *Secy.* Richard W. Hunt; *Managing Agent* SKP Assocs. Address correspondence to William Raggio.

Book Manufacturers Institute, 65 William St., Suite 300, Wellesley, MA 02481-3800. Tel. 781-239-0103, fax 781-239-0106. *Pres.* Mark Bawden, Bawden Printing Co.; *Exec. V.P.* Stephen P. Snyder. Address correspondence to the executive vice president.

Book Publicists of Southern California, 6464 Sunset Blvd., Suite 580, Hollywood, CA 90028. Tel. 213-461-3921, fax 213-461-0917. *Pres.* Barbara Gaughen-Muller; *V.P.* Ernest Weckbaugh; *Secy.* Jeanne Baird; *Treas.* Lynn Walford.

Book Publishers of Texas Association, 3404 S. Ravinia Dr., Dallas, TX 75233. Tel. 214-330-8759, fax 214-330-9795.

Bookbuilders of Boston, Inc., 27 Wellington Dr., Westwood, MA 02090. Tel. 617-266-3335, fax 781-326-2975, World Wide Web http://www.bbboston.org; *Pres.* Meredith White, BookCrafters; *1st V.P.* Andrew Van Sprang, Courier; *2nd V.P.* Katie Tarlin, D. B. Hess; *Treas.* John Walsh, Harvard Univ. Press; *Auditor* Doug Buitenhuys, Plymouth Color; *Secy.* Joni McDonald, UUA.

Bookbuilders West, Box 7046, San Francisco, CA 94120-9727. Tel. 415-273-5790, jobs bank 415-643-8600, World Wide Web http://www.bookbuilders.org; *Pres.* Leslie Austin; *V.P.* Stephen Thomas, Edwards Brothers, Inc.; *Secy.* Karen Richardson, Convert It!; *Treas.* Paul Butzler, Paul Butzler Publishing Management.

Canadian Booksellers Assn., 301 Donlands Ave., Toronto, ON M4J 3R8. Tel. 416-467-7883, fax 416-467-7886, e-mail enquiries@cbabook.org, World Wide Web http://www.cbabook.org. *Exec. Dir.* Sheryl M. McKean, ext. 225; *Ed., Canadian Bookseller* Jennifer Carham, ext. 230.

Canadian ISBN Agency, c/o Acquisitions and Bibliographic Services Branch, National Library of Canada, 395 Wellington St., Ottawa, ON K1A 0N4. Tel. 819-994-6872, fax 819-953-8508.

Canadian Printing Industries Association, 75 Albert St., Suite 906, Ottawa, ON K1P 5E7. Tel. 613-236-7208, fax 613-236-8169.

Catholic Book Publishers Assn. Inc., 2 Park Ave., Manhasset, NY 11030. Tel. 516-869-0122, fax 516-627-1381, e-mail cbpa1@aol.com, World Wide Web http://cbpa.org; *Pres.* John A. Thomas; *V.P.* Bernadette Price; *Secy.* John G. Powers; *Treas.* Gregory F. Augustine Pierce; *Exec. Dir.* Charles A. Roth.

CBA (International Network of Christian Stores and Their Suppliers), Box 200, Colorado Springs, CO 80901. Tel. 719-576-7880, fax 719-576-9240, e-mail dgore@cba-intl.org. *Pres. and CEO* William R.

Anderson; *V.P. and COO* Dorothy Gore; *Chair* Winston Maddox; *Secy.* Rick Brown; *Treas.* John Constance.

Chicago Book Clinic, 825 Green Bay Rd., Suite 270, Wilmett, IL 60091. Tel. 847-256-8448, fax 847-256-8954, e-mail kgboyer@ix.netcom.com, www.chicagobookclinic.org. *Pres.* Elizabeth O'Connor; *Exec. Dir.* Kevin G. Boyer.

Children's Book Council, Inc., 568 Broadway, New York, NY 10012. Tel. 212-966-1990, e-mail staff@CBCbooks.org, World Wide Web http://www.cbcbooks.org. *Pres.* Paula Quint; *Dir., Marketing and Publicity* JoAnn Sabatino.

Copyright Society of the USA, 1133 Avenue of the Americas, New York, NY 10036. Tel. 212-354-6401, fax 212-354-2847, e-mail info@csusa.org. *Pres.* Michael J. Pollack; *V.P.* Robert J. Bernstein; *Secy.* Phillip M. Cowan; *Treas.* Maria A. Danzilo.

Council of Literary Magazines & Presses, 154 Christopher St., Suite 3C, New York, NY 10014. Tel. 212-741-9110, fax 212-741-9112.

Educational Paperback Assn., *Pres.* Robert J. Laronga; *V.P.* Fred Johnson; *Treas.* Bill Hanlon; *Exec. Secy.* Marilyn Abel, Box 1399, East Hampton, NY 11937. Tel. 212-879-6850.

Educational Press Association of America (EdPress), c/o Rowan College of New Jersey, Glassboro, NJ 08028-1773. Tel. 609-863-7349, fax 609-863-5012.

Evangelical Christian Publishers Assn., 1969 E. Broadway Rd., Suite 2, Tempe, AZ 85282. Tel. 602-966-3998, fax 602-966-1944, e-mail dross@ecpa.org. *Pres.* Doug Ross.

Friendship Press, 475 Riverside Dr., Suite 860, New York, NY 10115. Tel. 212-870-2585, fax 212-870-2550, World Wide Web http://www.nccusa.org

Graphic Artists Guild Inc., 90 John St., Suite 403, New York, NY 10038. Tel. 212-791-3400, fax 212-792-0333, e-mail execdir@gag.org, World Wide Web http://www.gag.org. *Exec. Dir.* Paul Basista. Address correspondence to the executive director.

Great Lakes Booksellers Assn., c/o *Exec. Dir.* Jim Dana, Box 901, 509 Lafayette, Grand Haven, MI 49417. Tel. 616-847-2460, fax 616-842-0051, e-mail glba@books-glba.org,

World Wide Web http://www.books-glba.org. *Pres.* Terry Whittaker, Viewpoint Books, Columbus, IN 47201.

Guild of Book Workers, 521 Fifth Ave., New York, NY 10175. Tel. 212-292-4444. *Pres.* Karen Crisalli. E-mail karenc5071@aol.com.

International Association of Printing House Craftsmen, Inc. (IAPHC), 7042 Brooklyn Blvd., Minneapolis, MN 55429. Tel. 612-560-1620, 800-466-4274, fax 612-560-1350. *Chair* Jeanann Georgianna; *V. Chair* Anthony Sarubbi; *Office Admin.* Teresa Sherwood; *CEO* Kevin Keane.

International Copyright Information Center, c/o Assn. of American Publishers, 70 F Street N.W., Washington, DC 20001. Tel. 202-232-3335 ext. 228, fax 202-745-0694, e-mail crisher@publishers.org. *Dir.* Carol Risher.

International Standard Book Numbering U.S. Agency, 121 Chanlon Rd., New Providence, NJ 07974. Tel. 908-665-6700, fax 908-665-2895, e-mail ISBN-SAN@bowker.com, World Wide Web http://www.bowker.com/standards/. *Chair* Charles Halpin; *Dir.* Doreen Gravesande; *Dir. Emeritus* Emery I. Koltay; *Industrial Relations Mgr.* Don Riseborough; *SAN Mgr.* Diana Fumando.

Jewish Book Council, 15 E. 26 St., 10th fl., New York, NY 10010. Tel. 212-532-4949 ext. 297, fax 212-481-4174. *Pres.* Moshe Dworkin; *Exec. Dir.* Carolyn Starman Hessel.

Library Binding Institute, 7401 Metro Blvd., Suite 325, Edina, MN 55439-3631. Tel. 612-835-4707, fax 612-835-4780, e-mail 71035.3504@compuserve.com. *Exec. Dir.* Sally Moyer.

Magazine Publishers of America, Inc., 919 Third Ave., 22nd fl., New York, NY 10022. Tel. 212-872-3700, fax 212-888-4217, e-mail mpa@magazine.org

Metropolitan Lithographers Assn., 950 Third Ave., Suite 1500, New York, NY 10022. Tel. 212-838-8480, fax 212-644-1936. *Pres.* Frank Stillo.

Midwest Independent Publishers Assn., Box 581432, Minneapolis, MN 55458-1432. Tel. 612-917-0021, e-mail dshidell@aol.com, World Wide Web http://www.mipa.org; *Pres.* Doug Shidell.

Miniature Book Society, Inc., c/o *Pres.* Arthur A. Keir, 506 Buell Ave., Joliet, IL 60435. Tel./fax 815-726-1286; *V.P.* Paul Devenyi, 50 grange Mill Crescent, Toronto, ON M3B 2J2. Tel. 416-445-2038, fax 416-444-0246; *Secy.* Evron Collins, 2008 Boone Ct., Bowling Green, OH 43402. Tel. 419-352-8735; *Treas.* Mark Palcovic, 620 Clinton Springs Ave., Cincinnati, OH 45229-1325. Tel. 513-861-3554, fax 513-556-2113.

Minnesota Book Publishers Roundtable. *Pres.* Sid Farrar, Milkweed Press, 430 First Ave. N., No. 668, Minneapolis, MN 55401. Tel. 612-332-3192 ext. 105, fax 612-332-6248, e-mail sidfarrar@milkweed.org; *V.P.* Katherine Werner, Consortium Book Sales and Distribution, 1045 Westgate Drive, St. Paul, MN 55114. Tel. 651-221-9035, fax 651-221-0124, e-mail kwerner@cbsd.com; *Secy.-Treas.* Brad Vogt, Bradley & Assoc., 40214 Wallaby Rd., Rice, MN 56367. Tel. 320-249-9806, fax 320-656-9520, e-mail bvogt@cloudnet.com. Association Web site: http://www.publishersroundtable.org. Address correspondence to the secretary-treasurer.

Mountains and Plains Booksellers Assn., 19 Old Town Sq., Suite 238, Fort Collins, CO 80524. Tel. 970-484-5856, fax 970-407-1479, e-mail lknudser@mountainsplains.org, World Wide Web http://www.mountains plains.org. *Exec. Dir.* Lisa Knudsen; *Pres.* Gayle Shanks; *Treas.* Tracey Ballast.

National Assn. of College Stores, 500 E. Lorain St., Oberlin, OH 44074-1294. Tel. 440-775-7777, fax 440-775-4769, e-mail jbuchs @nacs.org, World Wide Web http://www. nacs.org. *Pres./Treas.* Bob McCampbell; *Exec. Dir.* Brian Cartier; *Public Relations Dir.* Jerry L. Buchs. Address correspondence to the public relations director.

National Association of Independent Publishers, Box 430, Highland City, FL 33846. Tel./fax 813-648-4420, e-mail NAIP@ aol.com.

National Association of Printers & Lithographers, 780 Palisade Ave., Teaneck, NJ 07666. Tel. 201-342-0700, fax 201-692-1862, e-mail napl@napl.org.

National Coalition Against Censorship (NCAC), 275 Seventh Ave., 20th fl., New York, NY 10001. Tel. 212-807-6222, fax 212-807-6245.

National Directory Publishing Association, Box 19107, George Mason Sta., Alexandria, VA 22320. Tel. 703-329-8206, fax 703-960-9618.

National Ministries Unit, National Council of Churches, 475 Riverside Dr., New York, NY 10115. Tel. 212-870-2227, e-mail news@ncccusa.org. *Dir.* Staccato Powell.

New Atlantic Independent Booksellers Assn., 108 S. 13 St., Philadelphia, PA 19107. Tel. 215-732-5207, fax 215-735-2670, e-mail naiba@ix.netcom.com, World Wide Web http://www.naiba.com. *Pres.* Fern Jaffe; *V.P.* Gerry Dooley; *Secy.* John Bennett; *Treas.* David Dashner; *Exec. Dir.* Larry Robin.

New England Booksellers Assn., 847 Massachusetts Ave., Cambridge, MA 02139. Tel. 617-576-3070, fax 617-576-3091, e-mail neba@neba.org. *Pres.* Fran Keilty; *V.P.* Susan Avery; *Treas.* Sarah Zacks; *Exec. Dir.* Wayne A. Drugan.

New Mexico Book League, 8632 Horacio Place N.E., Albuquerque, NM 87111. Tel. 505-299-8940, fax 505-294-8032. *Ed., Book Talk* Carol A. Myers.

New York, New Jersey Booksellers Assn., 397 Arbuckle Ave., Cedarhurst, NY 11516. Tel. 516-295-1004.

North American Bookdealers Exchange, Box 606, Cottage Grove, OR 97424. Tel. 503-942-7455, fax 541-942-7455.

Northern California Independent Booksellers Assn., 5643 Paradise Dr., Suite 12, Corte Madera, CA 94925. Tel. 415-927-3937, fax 415-927-3971, e-mail office@ nciba.com, World Wide Web http://www. nciba.com; *Exec. Dir.* Hut Landon.

Pacific Northwest Booksellers Assn., 317 W. Broadway, Suite 214, Eugene, OR 97401-2890. Tel. 541-683-4363, fax 541-683-3910, e-mail pnba@rio.com. *Pres.* Megan Scott, Scott's Bookstore, 121 Freeway Dr., Mt. Vernon WA 98273-5816; *Exec. Dir.* Thom Chambliss.

PEN American Center, Div. of International PEN, 568 Broadway, New York, NY 10012. Tel. 212-334-1660, fax 212-334-2181.

Periodical and Book Assn. of America, Inc., 475 Park Ave. S., Eighth fl., New York,

NY 10016. Tel. 212-689-4952, fax 212-545-8328, e-mail PBAA@aol.com *Pres.* Will Michalopoulos, Consumer Reports; *V.P.s* Robert Bruno, Buena Vista Publishing; Gerald Cohen, Total Publisher Services; Kathi Robold, Scientific American; *Treas.* Edward Handi, LFP; *Secy.* Gary Michelson, Consumer Reports; *Exec. Dir.* Richard T. Browne; *Asst. Exec. Dir.* Keith E. Furman; *Legal Counsel* Lee Feltman; *Advisers to the Pres.* Marcia Orovitz, Times Mirror Magazines; Mary C. McEvoy, McEvoy Associates.

Periodical Wholesalers of North American and Periodical Marketers of Canada, 1007-175 Bloor St. E., South Tower, Toronto, ON M4W 3R8. Tel. 416-968-7218, fax 416-968-6182. *Pres.* Ray Argyle.

Philadelphia Book Clinic, c/o *Secy.* Thomas Colaiezzi, 136 Chester Ave., Yeadon, PA 19050-3831. Tel. 610-259-7022, fax 610-394-9886. *Treas.* Robert Pigeon.

Publishers Marketing Assn., 627 Aviation Way, Manhattan Beach, CA 90266. Tel. 310-372-2732, fax 310-374-3342, e-mail info@pma-online.org, World Wide Web http://www.pma-online.org. *Exec. Dir.* Jan Nathan.

Research and Engineering Council of the Graphic Arts Industry, Inc., Box 639, Chadds Ford, PA 19317. Tel. 610-388-7394, fax 610-388-2708. *Pres.* James Henderson; *Exec. V.P./Secy.* Ted Ringman; *Exec. V.P./Treas.* Edmund Funk; *Managing Dir.* Ronald Mihills.

Rocky Mountain Book Publishers Assn., Box 19013, Boulder, CO 80308. Tel. 303-499-9540, fax 303-499-9584, e-mail rmbpa@aol.com.

Romance Writers of America, 3707 F.M. 1960 W., Suite 555, Houston, TX 77068. Tel. 281-440-6885, fax 281-440-7510, e-mail info@rwanational.com. *Pres.* Jo Ann Ferguson; *V.P.* Debra Dixon; *Secy.* Claudia Yates; *Treas.* Monica Caltabiano; *Exec. Sec.* Allison Kelley; *Communications Mgr.* Charis McEachern; *Special Projects Coord.* Janet Johnson.

Science-Fiction and Fantasy Writers of America, Inc., Box 171, Unity, Maine 04988-0171. Tel./fax 207-861-8078, e-mail execdir@sfwa.org. *Pres.* Robert J. Sawyer; *V.P.* Paul Levinson; *Secy.* Michael A. Burstein; *Treas.* Ian Randal Strock; *Exec. Dir.* Sharon Lee.

Small Press Center, 20 W. 44 St., New York, NY 10036. Tel. 212-764-7021, fax 212-354-5365.

Small Publishers Assn. of North America (SPAN), Box 1306, Buena Vista, CO 81211-1306. Tel. 719-395-4790, fax 719-395-8374, e-mail span@spannet.org. World Wide Web http://www.SPANnet.org; *Exec. Dir.* Marilyn Ross.

Society of Children's Book Writers & Illustrators (SCBWI), 22736 Vanowen St., Suite 106, West Hills, CA 91307. Tel. 818-888-8760

Society of Illustrators (SI), 128 E. 63 St., New York, NY 10021. Tel. 212-838-2560, fax 212-838-2561.

Society of National Association Publications (SNAP), 1650 Tysons Blvd., Suite 200, McLean, VA 22102. Tel. 703-506-3285, fax 703-506-3266, e-mail ajoly@snaponline.org. *Pres.* Matt Towan; *V.P.* Robert Mahaffey; *Treas.* Michael Springer.

Technical Assn. of the Pulp and Paper Industry, Technology Park/Atlanta, Box 105113, Atlanta, GA 30348-5113. Tel. 770-446-1400, fax 770-446-6947. *Exec. Dir.* W. H. Gross.

West Coast Book People Assn., 27 McNear Dr., San Rafael, CA 94901. *Exec. Dir.* Frank G. Goodall. Tel. 415-459-1227, fax 415-459-1227, e-mail goodall27@aol.com.

Western Writers of America, Inc., 1012 Fair St., Franklin, TN 37064. World Wide Web http://www.imt.net/~geison/wwahome.html. *Pres.* Preston Lewis, 3408 62nd St., Lubbock, TX 79413. E-mail lijpl@ttacs.ttu.edu.

Women's National Book Assn., 160 Fifth Ave., New York, NY 10010. Tel. 212-675-7805, fax 212-989-7542, e-mail skpassoc@internetmci.com; *Pres.* Diane Ullius; *V.P.* Nancy Stewart; *Secy.* Grace Houghton; *Treas.* Margaret Auer; *Past Pres.* Donna Paz. *Chapters in*: Binghamton, Boston, Dallas, Detroit, Los Angeles, Nashville, New York, San Francisco, Washington, D.C.

# International and Foreign Book Trade Associations

For Canadian book trade associations, see the preceding section, "Book Trade Associations, United States and Canada." For a more extensive list of book trade organizations outside the United States and Canada, with more detailed information, consult *International Literary Market Place* (R. R. Bowker), which also provides extensive lists of major bookstores and publishers in each country.

## International

Afro-Asian Book Council, 4835/24 Ansari Rd., Daryaganj, New Delhi 110-002, India. Tel. 11-326-1487, fax 11-326-7437. *Chair* Dato Jaji Jumaat; *Secy.-Gen.* Asang Machwe; *Dir.* Abul Hasan.

Centre Régional pour la Promotion du Livre en Afrique (Regional Center for Book Promotion in Africa), Box 1646, Yaoundé, Cameroon. Tel. 22-4782/2936. *Secy.* William Moutchia.

Centro Régional para el Fomento del Libro en América Latina y el Caribe (CERLALC) (Regional Center for Book Promotion in Latin America and the Caribbean), Calle 70, No. 9-52, Apdo. Aeréo 57348, Santafé de Bogotá 2, Colombia. Tel. 1-321-7501, fax 1-321-7503. *Dir.* Carmen Barvo.

Federation of European Publishers, Ave. de Tervueren 204, B-1150, Brussels, Belgium. Tel. 2-736-3616, fax 2-736-1987. *Pres.* Volker Schwarz; *Secy. Gen.* Mechtild Von Alemann.

International Board on Books for Young People (IBBY), Nonnenweg 12, Postfach, CH-4003 Basel, Switzerland. Tel. 61-272-2917, fax 61-272-2757. *Dir.* Leena Maissen.

International Booksellers Federation, Boulevard Lambermont 140 BTE 1, B1030 Brussels, Belgium. Tel./fax 2-242-0957, e-mail eurobooks@skynet.be. *Pres.* Yvonne Steinberger; *Gen. Secy.* Christiane Vuidar.

International Group of Scientific, Technical and Medical Publishers (STM), Keizersgracht 462, 1016 GE Amsterdam, Netherlands. Tel. 20-225214, fax 20-381566. *Secy.* Lex Lefebvre.

International League of Antiquarian Booksellers, 400 Summit Ave., St. Paul, MN 55102. Tel. 800-441-00076, 612-290-0700, fax 612-290-0646, e-mail rulon@ winternet.com. *Secy. Gen.* Rob Rulon-Miller.

International Publishers Assn. (Union Internationale des Editeurs), Ave. Miremont 3, CH-1206 Geneva, Switzerland. Tel. 22-346-3018, fax 22-347-5717, e-mail secretariat @ipa-uie.org. *Pres.* Alain Gründ; *Secy.-Gen.* J. Alexis Koutchoumow.

## National

### Argentina

Cámara Argentina de Publicaciones (Argentine Publications Assn.), Lavalle 437, 6 D-Edif Adriático, 6 piso, 1047 Buenos Aires. Tel./fax 01-394-2892. *Pres.* Bautista Leoncio Tello.

Cámara Argentina del Libro (Argentine Book Assn.), Avda. Belgrano 1580, 6 piso, 1093 Buenos Aires. Tel. 1-381-9277, fax 1-381-9253. *Dir.* Norberto J. Pou.

Fundación El Libro (Book Foundation), Avda. Cordoba 744 PB Dto. 1, 1054 Buenos Aires. Tel. 322-2225, fax 325-5681, e-mail fund@libro.satlink.net. *Pres.* Jorge Navelro; *Dir.* Marta V. Diaz.

### Australia

Australian and New Zealand Assn. of Antiquarian Booksellers, Box 279, Cammeray, NSW 2062. Tel. 3-826-1779, fax 3-521-3412. *Secy.* Nicholas Dawes.

Australian Booksellers Assn., 136 Rundle Mall, Adelaide, SA 5000. Tel. 3-966-37-888, fax 3-966-37-557. *Pres.* Tim Peach; *Exec. Dir.* Celia Pollock.

Australian Publishers Assn., Suite 59, 89 Jones St., Ultimo, Sydney, N.S.W. 2007. Tel. 2-9281-9788, fax 2-9281-1073, e-mail ape@magna.com.au. *Pres.* Sandy Grant; *Exec. Dir.* Susan Blackwell.

National Book Council, 71 Collins St., Melbourne, Vic. 3000. Tel. 3-663-8043, fax 3-663-8658. *Pres.* Michael G. Zifcak; *Exec. Dir.* Thomas Shapcott.

## Austria

Hauptverband des Österreichischen Buchhandels (Austrian Publishers and Booksellers Assn.), Grünangergasse 4, A-1010 Vienna. Tel. 1-512-1535, fax 1-512-8482. *Pres..* Anton C. Hilscher.
Verband der Antiquare Österreichs (Austrian Antiquarian Booksellers Assn.), Grünangergasse 4, A-1010 Vienna. Tel. 1-512-1535, fax 1-512-8482, e-mail hbv-wein@austrobook.co.at. *Pres.* Hansjörg Krug.

## Belarus

National Book Chamber of Belarus, 31a Very Khoruzhey St., 220002 Minsk. Tel./fax 172-769-396, e-mail palata@palata.belpakminsk.by. *Contact* Anatolij Voronko.

## Belgium

Vereniging ter Bevordering van het Vlaamse Boekwezen (Assn. for the Promotion of Dutch Language Books/Books from Flanders), Hof ter Schrieclaan 17, 2600 Berchem/Antwerp. Tel. 3-230-8923, fax 3-281-2240. *Pres.* Luc Demeester; *Gen. Secy.* Wim de Mont.
Vlaamse Boekverkopersbond (Flemish Booksellers Assn.), Hof ter Schrieclaan 17, 2600 Berchem/Antwerp. Tel. 3-230-8923, fax 3-281-2240. *Pres.* Luc Vander Velpen; *Gen. Secy.* Carlo Van Baelen.

## Bolivia

Cámara Boliviana del Libro (Bolivian Booksellers Assn.), Casilla 682, Avda. 20 de Octubre 2005, Edificio Las Palmas, Planta Baja, La Paz. Tel. 2-327-039, fax 2-391-817. *Pres.* Rolando S. Condori; *Secy.* Teresa G. de Alvarez.

## Brazil

Associação Brasileira do Livro (Brazilian Booksellers Assn.), Ave. 13 de Maio, 16, 20031 Rio de Janeiro. Tel. 21-240-9115. *Pres.* Ernesto Zahar.
Associação Nacional de Livrarias (National Assn. of Bookstores), Ave. Ipiranga 1267, 10 andar, 01039-907 São Paulo SP. Tel. 11-225-8277, fax 11-229-7463. *Pres.* Eduardo Yasuda.
Cámara Brasileira do Livro (Brazilian Book Assn.), Av. Ipiranga 1267, 10 andar, 01039-907 São Paulo. Tel. 11-220-7855, fax 11-229-7463. *Gen. Mgr.* Aloysio T. Costa.
Sindicato Nacional dos Editores de Livros (Brazilian Publishers Assn.), SDS, Edif Venancio VI, Loja 9/17, 70000 Brasilia, Brazil. Tel. 21-233-6481, fax 21-253-8502. *Pres.* Sérgio Abreu da Cruz Machado; *Exec. Secy.* Henrique Maltese.

## Chile

Cámara Chilena del Libro AG (Chilean Assn. of Publishers, Distributors and Booksellers), Avda. Libertador Bernardo O'Higgins 1370, Of. 501, 13526 Santiago. Tel. 2-698-9519, fax 2-698-9226, e-mail camlibro@reuna.cl. *Exec. Secy.* Carlos Franz.

## Colombia

Cámara Colombiana del Libro (Colombian Book Assn.), Carrera 17A, No. 37-27, Apdo. Aereo 8998, Santafé de Bogotá. Tel. 1-245-1940, 232-7550, 288-6188, fax 1-287-3320.

## Cuba

Cámara Cubano del Libro (Cuban Book Assn.), Calle 15 N 604 entre B y C, Vedado, La Habana CP 10400. Tel. 7-36034, fax 537-338-212, e-mail cclfilh@ceniai.cu. *Pres.* José A. Robert Gasset.

## Cyprus

Cyprus Booksellers Assn., Box 1455, Nicosia 1509. Tel. 2-449500, fax 2-367433. *Secy.* Socrates Heracleous.

## Czech Republic

Svaz ceskych knihkupcu a nakladetelu (Czech Publishers and Booksellers Assn.), Jana

Masaryka 56, 120 00 Prague 2. Tel./fax 2-2423-9003-0150, e-mail book@login.cz.

### Denmark

Den Danske Boghandlerforening (Danish Booksellers Assn.), Siljangade 6, DK-2300 Copenhagen S. Tel. 3154-2255, fax 3157-2422. *Pres.* Hanne Madsen.

Danske Forlaeggerforening (Danish Publishers Assn.), Kobmagergade 11/13, DK-1150 Copenhagen K. Tel. 45-3315-6688, fax 45-3315-6588, e-mail publassn@webpartner.dk. *Dir.* Erik V. Krustrup.

### Ecuador

Cámara Ecuatoriana del Libro, Núcleo de Pichincha, Guayaquil 1629, piso 4, Casilla No. 3329, Quito. Tel. 2-212-226, fax 2-566-340, e-mail abyayala@abyayala.org.ec. *Contact* Claudio Mena Villamar.

### Egypt

General Egyptian Book Organization, Box 1660, Corniche El-Nile-Boulaq, Cairo. Tel. 2-775-371, 775-649, fax 2-754-213. *Chair* Ezz El Dine Ismail.

### Estonia

Estonian Publishers Assn., Box 3366, EE0090 Tallinn. Tel. 2-650-5592, fax 2-650-5590. *Dir.* A. Tarvis.

### Finland

Kirja-ja Paperikauppojen Liitto ry (Finnish Booksellers and Stationers Assn.), Eerikinkatu 15-17 D 43-44, 00100 Helsinki. Tel. 694-4866, fax 694-4900, e-mail kpl@kplry.pp.fi. *Chief Exec.* Olli Eräkivi.

Suomen Kustannusyhdistys ry (Finnish Book Publishers Assn.), Box 177, FIN-00121 Helsinki. Tel. 9-2287-7250, fax 9-612-1226, e-mail finnpubl@skyry.pp.fi. *Dir.* Veikko Sonninen.

### France

Cercle de la Librairie (Circle of Professionals of the Book Trade), 35 Rue Grégoire-de-Tours, F-75006 Paris. Tel. 1-44-41-28-00, fax 1-44-41-28-65. *Pres.* Charles Henri Flammarion.

Fédération Française des Syndicats de Libraires-FFSL (French Booksellers Assn.), 43 Rue de Châteaudun, F-75009 Paris. Tel. 1-42-82-00-03, fax 1-42-82-10-51. *Pres.* Jean-Luc Dewas.

France Edition, 35 Rue Grégoire-de-Tours, F-75006 Paris. Tel. 1-44-41-13-13, fax 1-46-34-63-83. *Chair* Bernard Foulon. *New York Branch* French Publishers Agency, 853 Broadway, New York, NY 10003-4703. Tel. 212-254-4520, fax 212-979-6229.

Syndicat National de la Librairie Ancienne et Moderne (National Assn. of Antiquarians and Modern Booksellers), 4 Rue Gît-le-Coeur, F-75006 Paris. Tel. 1-43-29-46-38, fax 1-43-25-41-63. *Pres.* Jean-Etienne Huret.

Syndicat National de l'Edition (National Union of Publishers), 115 Blvd. Saint-Germain, F-75006 Paris. Tel. 1-441-4050, fax 1-441-4077. *Pres.* Serge Eyrolles; *Deputy Gen.* Jean Sarzana.

Union des Libraires de France, 40 Rue Grégoire-de-Tours, F-75006 Paris. Tel. 1-43-29-88-79, fax 1-46-33-65-27. *Pres.* Eric Hardin; *Gen. Delegate* Marie-Dominique Doumenc.

### Germany

Börsenverein des Deutschen Buchhandels e.V. (Stock Exchange of German Booksellers), Postfach 100442, 60004 Frankfurt-am-Main. Tel. 69-130-6311, fax 69-130-6300. *Gen. Mgr.* Hans-Karl von Kupsch.

Bundesverband der Deutschen Versandbuchhändler e.V. (National Federation of German Mail-Order Booksellers), An der Ringkirche 6, 65197 Wiesbaden. Tel. 611-44-9091, fax 611-48451. *Mgrs.* Stefan Rutkowsky, Kornelia Wahl.

Verband Deutscher Antiquare e.V. (German Antiquarian Booksellers Assn.), Kreuzgasse 2-4, Postfach 10-10-20, 50450 Cologne. Tel./fax 221-92-54-82-82; *Pres.* Jochen Granier; *V.P.* Inge Utzt.

# Ghana

Ghana Book Development Council, Box M430, Accra. Tel. 21-22-9178, fax 21-22-0271. *Deputy Exec. Dir.* Annor Nimako.

# Great Britain

See United Kingdom

# Greece

Book Publishers Assn., Themistocleous 73, 10683 Athens. Tel./fax 1-330-1956. *Pres.* Magda Kotzia.
Hellenic Federation of Publishers and Booksellers, Themistocleous 73, 10683 Athens. Tel. 1-330-0924, fax 1-330-1617. *Pres.* Georgios Dardanos.

# Hungary

Magyar Könyvkiadók és Könyvterjesztök Egyesülése (Assn. of Hungarian Publishers and Booksellers), Vörösmarty tér 1, 1051 Budapest (mail: PB 130, 1367 Budapest). Tel. 1-117-6222. *Pres.* István Bart; *Secy.-Gen.* Péter Zentai.

# Iceland

Félag Islenskra Bókaútgefenda (Icelandic Publishers Assn.), Sudurlandsbraut 4A, 108 Reykjavik. Tel. 553-8020, fax 588-8668.*Chair* Olafur Ragnarsson; *Gen. Mgr.* Vilborg Hardardóttir.

# India

Federation of Indian Publishers, Federation House, 18/1-C Institutional Area, JNU Rd., Aruna Asaf Ali Marg, New Delhi 110067. Tel. 11-696-4847, 685-2263, fax 11-686-4054. *Pres.* Shri R. C. Govil; *Exec. Secy.* S. K. Ghai.

# Indonesia

Ikatan Penerbit Indonesia (Assn. of Indonesian Book Publishers), Jl. Kalipasir 32, Jakarta 10330. Tel. 21-314-1907, fax 21-314-1433. *Pres.* Rozali Usman; *Secy. Gen.* Setia Dharma Majidd.

# Ireland

CLÉ: The Irish Book Publishers Assn., The Writers Centre, 19 Parnell Sq., Dublin 1. Tel. 1-872-9090, fax 1-872-2035. *Contact* Orla Martin.

# Israel

Book and Printing Center, Israel Export Institute, 29 Hamered St., Box 50084, Tel Aviv 68125. Tel. 3-514-2910, fax 3-514-2815. *Dir.* Corine Knafo.
Book Publishers Assn. of Israel, Box 20123, Tel Aviv 61201. Tel. 3-561-4121, fax 3-561-1996. *Managing Dir.* Amnon Ben-Shmuel.

# Italy

Associazione Italiana Editori (Italian Publishers Assn.), Via delle Erbe 2, 20121 Milan. Tel. 2-86-46-3091, fax 2-89-01-0863.
Associazione Librai Antiquari d'Italia (Antiquarian Booksellers Assn. of Italy), Via Jacopo Nardi 6, I-50132 Florence. Tel./fax (55) 24-3253, e-mail alai@dada.it. *Pres.* Vittorio Soave; *Secy.* Francesco Scala.

# Jamaica

Booksellers Assn. of Jamaica, c/o Novelty Training Co. Ltd., Box 80, Kingston. Tel. 876-922-5883, fax 876-922-4743. *Pres.* Keith Shervington.

# Japan

Japan Book Importers Assn., Chiyoda Kaikan 21-4, Nihonbashi 1-chome, Chuo-ku, Tokyo 103. Tel. 3-32-71-6901, fax 3-32-71-6920. *Chair* Nobuo Suzuki.
Japan Book Publishers Assn., 6 Fukuromachi, Shinjuku-ku, Tokyo 162. Tel. 3-32-68-1301, fax 3-32-68-1196. *Pres.* Takao Watanabe; *Exec. Dir.* Toshikazu Gomi.

# Kenya

Kenya Publishers Assn., c/o Phoenix Publishers Ltd., Box 18650, Nairobi. Tel. 2-22-2309, 22-3262, fax 2-33-9875. *Secy.* Stanley Irura.

## Korea (Republic of)

Korean Publishers Assn., 105-2 Sagan-dong, Jongro-gu, Seoul 110-190. Tel. 2-735-2701, fax 2-738-5414, e-mail kpasibf@soback.kornet.nm.kr. *Pres.* Na Choon Ho; *Secy.-Gen.* Jong-Jin Jung.

## Latvia

Latvian Book Publishers Assn., Aspazijas Bulvaris 24, 1050 Riga. Tel. 2-722-5843, fax 2-783-0518.

## Lithuania

Lithuanian Publishers Assn., K Sirvydo 6, 2600 Vilnius. Tel. 2-628-945, fax 2-619-696. *Pres.* Vincas Akelis.

## Mexico

Cámara Nacional de la Industria Editorial Mexicana (Mexican Publishers' Assn.), Holanda No. 13, CP 04120 Mexico 21. Tel. 5-688-2221, fax 5-604-3147. *Pres.* A. H. Gayosso, J. C. Cramerez.

## The Netherlands

Koninklijke Vereeniging ter Bevordering van de Belangen des Boekhandels (Royal Dutch Book Trade Assn.), Postbus 15007, 1001 MA Amsterdam. Tel. 20-624-0212, fax 20-620-8871. *Secy.* M. van Vollenhoven-Nagel.

Nederlandsche Vereeniging van Antiquaren (Netherlands Assn. of Antiquarian Booksellers), Postbus 664, 1000 AR Amsterdam. Tel. 20-627-2285, fax 20-625-8970, e-mail a.gerits@inter.nl.net. *Pres.* F. W. Kuyper; *Secy.* A. Gerits.

Nederlandse Boekverkopersbond (Dutch Booksellers Assn.), Postbus 90731, 2509 LS The Hague. Tel. 70-324-4395, fax 70-324-4411. *Pres.* W. Karssen; *Exec. Secy.* A. C. Doeser.

Nederlandse Uitgeversbond (Royal Dutch Publishers Assn.), Postbus 12040, 1100 AA Amsterdam. Tel. 20-430-9150, fax 20-430-9179, e-mail r.vrijuitgeversverbond.nl. *Pres.* Henk J. L. Vonhoff; *Secy.* R. M. Vrij.

## New Zealand

Book Publishers Assn. of New Zealand, Box 101, 271 North Shore Mail, Auckland. Tel. 9-309-2561, fax 9-309-7798.

Booksellers New Zealand, Box 11-377, Wellington. Tel. 4-472-8678, fax 4-472-8628. *Chair* Brian Phillips; *Chief Exec.* Jo Breese.

## Nigeria

Nigerian Publishers Assn., GPO Box 3541, Dugbe, Ibadan. Tel. 22-411-557. *Pres.* V. Nwankwo.

## Norway

Norske Bokhandlerforening (Norwegian Booksellers Assn.), Øvre Vollgate 15, 0158 Oslo. Tel. 22-396800, fax 22-356810. *Dir.* Einar J. Einarsson.

Norske Forleggerforening (Norwegian Publishers Assn.), Øvre Vollgate 15, N-0158 Oslo 1. Tel. 22-421-355, fax 22-333830, e-mail dnf@forleggerforeningen.no. *Dir.* Paul Martens Røthe.

## Pakistan

National Book Council of Pakistan, Block 14D, 1st fl., Al-Markaz F/8,, Box 1610, Islamabad. Tel. 51-853-581. *Dir. Gen.* Rafiq Ahmad.

## Paraguay

Cámara Paraguaya de Editores, Libreros y Asociados (Paraguayan Publishers Assn.), Ayolas 129, Asunción. Tel./fax 21-497-325. *Dir.* Alejandro Gatti.

## Peru

Cámara Peruana del Libro (Peruvian Publishers Assn.), Apdo Postal 10253, Lima 1. Tel. 14-715152. *Pres.* Julio César Flores Rodriguez; *Exec. Dir.* Loyda Moran Bustamente.

## Philippines

Philippine Educational Publishers Assn., 84 P Florentino St., 3008 Quezon City. Tel.

2-968-316, fax 2-921-3788. *Pres.* D. D. Buhain.

## Poland

Polskie Towarzystwo Wydawców Ksiazek (Polish Society of Book Editors), ul. Mazowiecka 2/4, 00-048 Warsaw. Tel./fax 22-826-0735. *Pres.* Janusz Fogler; *Gen. Secy.* Donat Chruscicki.

Stowarzyszenie Ksiegarzy Polskich (Assn. of Polish Booksellers), ul. Mokotowska 4/6, 00-641 Warsaw. Tel. 22-252-874. *Pres.* Tadeusz Hussak.

## Portugal

Associação Portuguesa de Editores e Livreiros (Portuguese Assn. of Publishers and Booksellers), Largo de Andaluz, 16-7 Esq., 1000 Lisbon. Tel. 1-556-241, fax 1-315-3553. *Pres.* Francisco Espadinha; *Secy. Gen.* Jorge de Carvalho Sá Borges.

## Russia

All-Union Book Chamber, Kremlevskaja nab 1/9, 121019 Moscow. Tel. 95-20271, 95-20272, fax 95-202-3992. *Dir.-Gen.* Yuri Torsuev.

Publishers Assn., 44B Hertsen Str., 121069 Moscow. Tel. 95-202-1174, fax 95-202-3989. *Contact* M. Shishigin.

## Singapore

Singapore Book Publishers Assn., 86, Marine Parade Centre, No. 03-213, Singapore 440086. Tel. 344-7801, fax 447-0897. *Pres.* K. P. Sivan; *V.P.* Wu Cheng Tan.

## Slovenia

Zdruzenje Zaloznikov in Knjigotrzcev Slovenije Gospodarska Zbornica Slovenije (Assn. of Publishers and Booksellers of Slovenia), c 41, 1504 Ljubljana. Tel./fax 61-342-398. *Contact* Joze Korinsek.

## South Africa

Associated Booksellers of Southern Africa, Box 870, Bellville 7530. Tel. 21-951-

6611, fax 21-951-4903. *Pres.* M. Hargraves; *Secy.* R. Stoltenkamp.

Publishers Assn. of South Africa, Box 116, 7946 St. James. Tel. 21-788-6470, fax 21-788-6469. *Chair* Basil Van Rooyen.

## Spain

Federación de Gremios de Editores de España (Federation of Spanish Publishers Assns.), Juan Ramón Jiménez, 45-9 Izda, 28036 Madrid. Tel. 1-350-9105, fax 1-345-4351. *Pres.* Pere Vincens; *Secy.* Ana Molto.

## Sri Lanka

Sri Lanka Assn. of Publishers, 112 S. Mahinda Mawatha, Colombo 10. Tel. 1-695-773, fax 1-696-653. *Pres.* Dayawansa Jayakody.

## Sudan

Sudanese Publishers Assn., H. Q. Al Ikhwa Bldg., Flat 7, 7th fl., Box 2771, Khartoum. Tel. 249-11-75051, 79180.

## Suriname

Publishers Assn. Suriname, Domineestr. 26, Box 1841, Paramaribo. Tel. 472-545, fax 410-563. *Mgr.* E. Hogenboom.

## Sweden

Svenska Förläggareföreningen (Swedish Publishers Assn.), Drottninggatan 97, S-11360 Stockholm. Tel. 8-736-1940, fax 8-736-1944. *Dir.* Kristina Ahlinder.

## Switzerland

Schweizerischer Buchhändler- und Verleger-Verband (Swiss German-Language Booksellers and Publishers Assn.), Baumackerstr. 42, 8050 Zurich. Tel. 1-312-5343, fax 1-318-6462, e-mail sbvv@dm.krinfo.ch. *Secy.* Egon Räz.

Societa Editori della Svizzera Italiana (Publishers Assn. for Italian-Speaking Switzerland), Via San Gottardo 50, 6900 Lugano. Tel. 91-232-271, fax 91-232-805. *Pres.* Alfonso Pezzati.

Société des Libraires et Editeurs de la Suisse Romande (Assn. of Swiss French-Lan-

guage Booksellers and Publishers), 2 Ave.
Agassiz, 1001 Lausanne. Tel. 21-319-
7111, fax 21-319-7910. *Contact* Philippe
Schibli.

## Thailand

Publishers and Booksellers Assn. of Thailand, 320 Lat Phrao 94-aphat Pracha-u-thit
Rd., Bangkok 10310. Tel. 2-255-93348,
fax 2-253-81499.

## Uganda

Uganda Publishers and Booksellers Assn.,
Box 7732, Plot 2C Kampala Rd., Kam-
pala. Tel. 41-259-163, fax 41-251-160.
*Contact* Martin Okia.

## United Kingdom

Antiquarian Booksellers Assn., 154 Buckingham Palace Rd., London W1V 9PA, England. Tel. 171-730-9273, fax 171-439-
3119. *Administrators* Philippa Gibson;
Deborah Stratford.

Assn. of Learned and Professional Society
Publishers, Sentosa Hill Rd., Fairlight,
Hastings, E. Sussex TN35 4AE, England.
Tel. 1424-812-353, fax 181-663-3583,
e-mail donovan@alpsp.demon.co.uk.
*Secy.-Gen.* B. T. Donovan.

Book Trust, 45 E. Hill, Wandsworth, London
SW18 2QZ. Tel. 181-516-2977, fax 181-
516-2978.

Book Trust Scotland, Scottish Book Centre,
137 Dundee St., Edinburgh EH11 1BG,
Scotland. Tel. 131-229-3663, fax 131-228-
4293.

Booksellers Assn. of Great Britain and Ireland, Minster House, 272 Vauxhall Bridge
Rd., London SW1V 1BA, England. Tel.
171-834-5477, fax 171-834-8812, e-mail

100437.2261@compuserve.com. *Chief
Exec.* Tim Godfray.

Educational Publishers Council, 19 Bedford
Sq., London WC1B 3HJ, England. Tel.
171-580-6321, fax 171-636-5375. *Dir.*
John R. M. Davies.

Publishers Assn., 19 Bedford Sq., London
WC1B 3HJ, England. Tel. 171-580-6321,
fax 171-636-5375. *Pres.* Trevor Glover;
*Chief Exec.* Ronnie Williams; *Secy.* Mandy
Knight.

Scottish Publishers Assn., Scottish Book
Centre, 137 Dundee St., Edinburgh EH11
1BG, Scotland. Tel. 131-228-6866, fax
131-228-3220. *Dir.* Lorraine Fannin;
*Chair* Mike Miller.

Welsh Books Council (Cyngor Llyfrau Cym-
ru), Castell Brychan, Aberystwyth, Ceredigion, SY23 2JB, Wales. Tel. 1970-624-
151, fax 1970-625-385. *Dir.* Gwerfyl
Pierce Jones.

## Uruguay

Cámara Uruguaya del Libro (Uruguayan
Publishers Assn.), Juan D. Jackson 1118,
11200 Montevideo. Tel. 2-241-5732, fax
2-241-1860.

## Venezuela

Cámara Venezolana del Libro (Venezuelan
Publishers Assn.), Ave. Andrés Bello,
Torre Oeste, 11 piso, Of. 112-0, Apdo.
51858, Caracas 1050-A. Tel. 2-793-1347,
fax 2-793-1368. *Secy.* M. P. Vargas.

## Zambia

Booksellers and Publishers Assn. of Zambia,
Box 31838, Lusaka. Tel. 1-225-195, fax 1-
225-282; *Exec. Dir.* Basil Mbewe.

# National Information Standards
# Organization (NISO) Standards

**Information Storage and Retrieval**

| | |
|---|---|
| Z39.2-1994* | Information Interchange Format |
| Z39.47-1993 (R 1998) | Extended Latin Alphabet Coded Character Set for Bibliographic Use (ANSEL) |
| Z39.50-1995 | Information Retrieval (Z39.50) Application Service Definition and Protocol Specification |
| Z39.53-1994* | Codes for the Representation of Languages for Information Interchange |
| Z39.63-1989* | Interlibrary Loan Data Elements |
| Z39.64-1989 (R 1995) | East Asian Character Code for Bibliographic Use |
| Z39.76-1996 | Data Elements for Binding Library Materials |
| NISO/ANSI/ISO 3166 | Codes for the Representation of Names of Countries |
| NISO/ANSI/ISO 23950 | Information Retrieval (Z39.50); Application Service Service Definition and Protocol Specification |

**Library Management**

| | |
|---|---|
| Z39.7-1995 | Library Statistics |
| Z39.20-1999 | Criteria for Price Indexes for Print Library Materials |
| Z39.71-1999 | Holdings Statements for Bibliographic Items |
| Z39.73-1994* | Single-Tier Steel Bracket Library Shelving |

**Preservation and Storage**

| | |
|---|---|
| Z39.32-1996 | Information on Microfiche Headers |
| Z39.48-1992 (R 1997) | Permanence of Paper for Publications and Documents in Libraries and Archives |
| Z39.62-1993* | Eye-Legible Information on Microfilm Leaders And Trailers and on Containers of Processed Microfilm on Open Reels |
| Z39.66-1992 (R 1998) | Durable Hard-Cover Binding for Books |
| Z39.74-1996 | Guides to Accompany Microform Sets |

## Publishing

| | |
|---|---|
| Z39.9-1992* | International Standard Serial Numbering (ISSN) |
| Z39.14-1997 | Guidelines for Abstracts |
| Z39.18-1995 | Scientific and Technical Reports—Elements, Organization, and Design |
| Z39.19-1993 | Guidelines for the Construction, Format, and Management of Monolingual Thesauri |
| Z39.22-1989* | Proof Corrections |
| Z39.23-1997 | Standard Technical Report Number Format and Creation |
| Z39.26-1997 | Micropublishing Product Information |
| Z39.41-1997 | Printed Information on Spines |
| Z39.43-1993* | Standard Address Number (SAN) for the Publishing Industry |
| Z39.56-1996 | Serial Item and Contribution Identifier (SICI) |
| Z39.67-1993* | Computer Software Description |
| NISO/ANSI/ISO 12083* | Electronic Manuscript Preparation and Markup |

## In Development

Bibliographic References
Book Item and Contribution Identifier
Circulation Interchange Protocol
Digital Talking Book Features List
Dublin Core Metadata Element Set
Environmental Conditions for Exhibiting Library and Archival Materials
Library Binding
Preservation Product Information
Standard Format for Downloading Records
Syntax for Digital Object Identifiers
Title Pages of Conference Proceedings

## NISO Technical Reports

| | |
|---|---|
| TR-01-1995 | Environmental Guidelines for the Storage of Paper Records |
| TR-02-1997 | Guidelines for Indexes and Related Information Retrieval Devices |
| TR-03-1999 | A Guide to Alphanumeric Arrangement and Sorting |

*This standard is being reviewed by NISO's Standards Development Committee or is under revision. For further information, please contact NISO, 4733 Bethesda Ave., Suite 300, Bethesda, MD 20814. Tel. 301-654-2512, fax 301-654-1721, e-mail nisohq@cni.org, World Wide Web http://www.niso.org.

# Calendar, 1999–2003

The list below contains information on association meetings or promotional events that are, for the most part, national or international in scope. State and regional library association meetings are also included. To confirm the starting or ending date of a meeting, which may change after the *Bowker Annual* has gone to press, contact the association directly. Addresses of library and book trade associations are listed in Part 6 of this volume. For information on additional book trade and promotional events, see the *Exhibits Directory*, published annually by Contemporary Books, 180 N. Michigan Ave., Chicago, IL 60601; *Literary Market Place* and *International Literary Market Place*, published by R. R. Bowker; and the "Calendar" section in each issue of *Publishers Weekly* and *Library Journal*.

## 1999

### May

| | | |
|---|---|---|
| 1 | Women's National Book Assn. | Los Angeles, CA |
| 1–2 | Chief Officers of State Library Agencies (COSLA) | Washington, DC |
| 1–3 | American Booksellers Assn. | Los Angeles, CA |
| 1–3 | BookExpo America | Los Angeles, CA |
| 1–3 | West Coast Book People Assn. | Los Angeles, CA |
| 2–4 | Book Manufacturers' Institute | Orlando, FL |
| 2–7 | International Reading Assn. | San Diego, CA |
| 7 | Delaware Library Assn. | Middletown, DE |
| 4–7 | Florida Library Assn. | Saint Augustine, FL |
| 5–6 | Archivists and Librarians in the History of the Health Sciences | New Brunswick, NJ |
| 6–8 | Mid-Atlantic Regional Archives Conference | State College, PA |
| 10–11 | New Hampshire Library Assn. | Manchester, NH |
| 10–11 | New Hampshire Educational Media Assn. | Manchester, NH |
| 11–14 | Assn. of Research Libraries | Kansas City, MO |
| 12–14 | Utah Library Assn. | Cedar City, UT |
| 13–17 | Warsaw International Book Fair | Warsaw, Poland |
| 14–20 | Medical Library Assn. | Chicago, IL |
| 13–15 | Research and Engineering Council of the Graphic Arts Industry | Lake Geneva, WI |
| 13–15 | Saskatchewan Library Assn. | Waskesieu, SK |
| 14–20 | Medical Library Assn. | Chicago, IL |

**May 1999** *(cont.)*

| | | |
|---|---|---|
| 16–18 | Maine Libraries Conference | Orono, ME |
| 17–18 | Virginia Library Assn. Paraprofessional Forum | Richmond, VA |
| 17–22 | International Assn. of Technological Univ. Libraries | Chania, Crete |
| 18 | Assn. of Graphic Communications | New York, NY |
| 18–20 | Conference on Integrated Online Library Systems | New York, NY |
| 19–21 | Maryland Library Assn. | Hagerstown, MD |
| 19–22 | Internet World Brazil '99 | Sao Paulo, Brazil |
| 20–21 | Japan Medical Library Assn. | Fukuoka, Japan |
| 21–23 | Michigan Assn. for Media in Education | Mackinac Island, MI |
| 24–26 | American Society for Information Science (ASIS) | Pasadena, CA |
| 24–26 | Maine Library Assn. | Orono, ME |
| 26–27 | Vermont Library Conference | Killington, VT |
| 26–28 | Florida Records Management Assn. | St. Petersburg, FL |
| 27–30 | Atlantic Provinces Library Assn. | Saint John, NB |
| 29–6/6 | World Book Fair | Singapore |
| 30–6/2 | Canadian Assn. of Law Libraries | Banff, AB |

**June**

| | | |
|---|---|---|
| 4–9 | Assn. for Media and Technology in Education in Canada | Ottawa, ON |
| 5–10 | Council of Planning Librarians | Minneapolis, MN |
| 5–10 | Special Libraries Assn. | Minneapolis, MN |
| 7–9 | Society of National Assn. Publishers | Bethesda, MD |
| 7–10 | Scottish Library Assn. | Peebles, Scotland |
| 8–11 | Assn. of Christian Librarians | Cleveland, TN |
| 8–11 | International Information Management Congress '99 | Amsterdam, Netherlands |
| 8–12 | American Theological Library Assn. | Chicago, IL |
| 9–11 | Society for Scholarly Publishing | Boston, MA |
| 9–13 | American Society of Indexers | Indianapolis, IN |
| 10–12 | International Communications Industries Assn. | Orlando, FL |
| 13–15 | Canadian Assn. of Research Libraries | Toronto, ON |
| 13–16 | Montana Library Assn. | Big Sky, MT |
| 13–16 | Mountain Plains Library Assn. | Big Sky, MT |
| 15–19 | Canadian Booksellers Assn. | Toronto, ON |
| 16–20 | Canadian Assn. of Special Libraries | Toronto, ON |
| 17–20 | Canadian Library Assn. | Toronto, ON |
| 20–23 | Assn. of American University Presses | Austin, TX |
| 20–23 | Assn. of Jewish Libraries | Boca Raton, FL |
| 20–23 | Women in Scholarly Publishing | Austin, TX |

| | | |
|---|---|---|
| 22–24 | International Society for Technology in Education | Atlantic City, NJ |
| 24–7/1 | American Library Assn. | New Orleans, LA |
| 24–30 | Asian/Pacific American Librarians Assn. | New Orleans, LA |
| 25 | Beta Phi Mu | New Orleans, LA |
| 27–1/7 | Western Writers of America | Rapid City, SD |
| 30–7/2 | National Education Assn. | Orlando, FL |

**July**

| | | |
|---|---|---|
| 1–3 | The Library Assn. | Manchester, England |
| 5–9 | Children's Literature Assn. | Calgary, AB |
| 8–10 | Canadian Education Assn. | Victoria, BC |
| 10–15 | Christian Booksellers Assn. | Orlando, FL |
| 14–17 | National Assn. of Government Archives and Records Administrators | Columbus, OH |
| 17–22 | American Assn. of Law Libraries | Washington, DC |
| 19–22 | Black Caucus, American Library Assn. | Las Vegas, NV |
| 19–22 | National Conference of African American Librarians | Las Vegas, NV |
| 19–24 | International Assn. of Music Libraries, Archives, and Documentation Centres (IAML) | Wellington, New Zealand |
| 23–29 | Society of American Archivists | Pittsburgh, PA |
| 25–27 | Church and Synagogue Library Assn. | Orlando, FL |
| 28–8/1 | Romance Writers of America | Chicago, IL |

**August**

| | | |
|---|---|---|
| 11–15 | Pacific Northwest Library Assn. | Calgary, AB |
| 12–16 | Miniature Book Society Conclave | Koblenz, Germany |
| 19–28 | International Federation of Library Assns. and Institutions (IFLA) | Bangkok, Thailand |
| 23–29 | Society of American Archivists | Pittsburgh, PA |

**September**

| | | |
|---|---|---|
| 1–6 | Moscow International Book Fair | Moscow, Russia |
| 8–10 | Conservation Conference, British Museum | London, England |
| 12–16 | International Assn. of Law Libraries | Melbourne, Australia |
| 15–17 | British Library Conference | London, England |
| 16–19 | Göteborg Book Fair | Göteborg, Sweden |
| 17–18 | Kentucky School Media Assn. | Covington, KY |
| 21–24 | North Carolina Library Assn. | Winston Salem, NC |
| 23–25 | North Dakota Assn. of School Librarians | Fargo, ND |
| 23–25 | North Dakota Library Assn. | Fargo, ND |
| 23–26 | Mountain Plains Booksellers Assn. | Denver, CO |
| 24–26 | New Atlantic Independent Booksellers Assn. Trade Show | Philadelphia, PA |

**September 1999** *(cont.)*

| | | |
|---|---|---|
| 24–26 | Pacific Northwest Booksellers Assn. | Spokane, WA |
| 26–28 | New England Library Assn. | Manchester, NH |
| 26–10/2 | International Council on Archives | Budapest, Hungary |
| 29–10/1 | Idaho Library Assn. | Boise, ID |
| 29–10/1 | Minnesota Library Assn. | Duluth, MN |
| 29–10/1 | Ohio Library Council | Cincinnati, OH |
| 29–10/2 | Pennsylvania Library Assn. | Pittsburgh, PA |

**October**

| | | |
|---|---|---|
| 1–3 | New England Booksellers Assn. | Providence, RI |
| 1–3 | Northern California Independent Booksellers Assn. Trade Show | Oakland, CA |
| 1–3 | Southeast Booksellers Assn. Trade Show | Greensboro, NC |
| 5–9 | LIBER '99 | Madrid, Spain |
| 6–9 | Idaho Library Assn. | Boise, ID |
| 6–9 | South Dakota Library Assn. | Watertown, SD |
| 7–9 | Minnesota Educational Media Organization | Mankato, MN |
| 7–9 | Washington Library Media Assn. | Spokane, WA |
| 7–11 | Colorado Library Assn. | Snowmass, CO |
| 8–10 | Great Lakes Booksellers Assn. Fall Trade Show | Lansing, MI |
| 8–10 | Oregon Educational Media Assn. | Wilsonville, OR |
| 8–10 | Southern Festival of Books | Nashville, TN |
| 12–15 | Assn. of Research Libraries | Washington, DC |
| 12–17 | Literacy Volunteers of America | San Antonio, TX |
| 13–15 | Iowa Library Assn. | Dubuque, IA |
| 13–16 | Wyoming Library Assn. | Cheyenne, WY |
| 13–17 | Kentucky Library Assn. | Louisville, KY |
| 13–18 | Frankfurt Book Fair | Frankfurt am Main, Germany |
| 16–19 | Illinois Library Assn. | Chicago, IL |
| 17–20 | ARMA International | Cincinnati, OH |
| 18 | Graph Expo '99 | Chicago, IL |
| 19–22 | Wisconsin Library Assn. | La Crosse, WI |
| 20–22 | Georgia Library Assn. | Jekyll Island, GA |
| 20–22 | Georgia Library Media Assn. | Jekyll Island, GA |
| 20–22 | Mississippi Library Assn. | Hattiesburg, MS |
| 20–22 | Nebraska Educational Media Assn. | Lincoln, NE |
| 20–22 | Nebraska Library Assn. | Lincoln, NE |
| 21–23 | Tennessee Assn. of School Librarians | Nashville, TN |
| 21–23 | West Virginia Library Assn. | Shepherdstown, WV |
| 22–23 | Evangelical Church Library Assn. | Wheaton, IL |
| 23–27 | Chief Officers of State Library Agencies | Indianapolis, IN |
| 24–25 | Connecticut Educational Media Assn. | Cromwell, CT |
| 24–26 | Assn. of Academic Health Sciences Libraries | Washington, DC |
| 24–26 | Illinois Library Assn. | Chicago, IL |

| 24–26 | New Jersey Educational Media Assn. | Long Branch, NJ |
| 26–29 | EDUCOM '99 | Long Beach, CA |
| 27–28 | Florida Assn. for Media in Education | Orlando, FL |
| 27–29 | Michigan Library Assn. | Grand Traverse, MI |
| 27–29 | Nebraska Educational Media Assn. | Lincoln, NE |
| 27–29 | Nebraska Library Assn. | Lincoln, NE |
| 27–30 | Michigan Assn. for Media in Education | Grand Rapids, MI |
| 27–30 | Virginia Educational Media Assn. | Hot Springs, VA |
| 27–30 | Virginia Library Assn. | Hot Springs, VA |
| 27–31 | New York Library Assn. | Buffalo, NY |
| 28–30 | Illinois School Library Media Assn. | Decatur, IL |
| 28–30 | Virginia Library Assn. | Hot Spring, VA |

## November

| 1–4 | American Society for Information Science (ASIS) | Washington, DC |
| 2–5 | Michigan Library Assn. | Dearborn, MI |
| 3–4 | Computer and Communications Show | Hartford, CT |
| 3–5 | Ohio Educational Library Media Assn. | Columbus, OH |
| 3–7 | American Translators Assn. | St. Louis, MO |
| 4–6 | Virginia Educational Media Assn. | Williamsburg, VA |
| 6–7 | San Francisco Bay Area Book Festival | San Francisco, CA |
| 6–10 | American Medical Informatics Assn. | Washington, DC |
| 6–10 | Evangelical Christian Publishers Assn. | Palm Springs, CA |
| 7–10 | Book Manufacturers' Institute | Scottsdale, AZ |
| 7–10 | Periodical Wholesalers of North America | New York, NY |
| 10–14 | American Assn. of School Librarians | Birmingham, AL |
| 10–14 | International Assn. of School Librarianship | Birmingham, AL |
| 12–14 | International Antiquarian Book Fair | Hamburg, Germany |
| 13–16 | California Library Assn. | Palm Springs, CA |
| 17–19 | Arizona Library Assn. | Phoenix, AZ |
| 18–23 | Montreal Book Show | Montreal, PQ |
| 20 | Hawaii Library Assn. | Honolulu, HI |

## December

| 1–4 | South Carolina Library Assn. | Hilton Head, SC |
| 4–6 | Assn. of Vision Science Librarians | Seattle, WA |
| 7–9 | Online Information '99 | London, England |
| 27–30 | Modern Language Assn. of America | Chicago, IL |

# 2000

## January

| 11–14 | Assn. for Library and Information Science Education (ALISE) | San Antonio, TX |
| 14–19 | American Library Assn. Midwinter Meeting | San Antonio, TX |

**February**

\*    Colorado Educational Media Assn.   Colorado Springs, CO

**March**

9–11  Assn. for Indiana Media Educators   Indianapolis, IN
16–23  Art Libraries Society of North America  Pittsburgh, PA
28–4/1  Public Library Assn.      Charlotte, NC

**April**

5–7   Kansas Library Assn.      Wichita, KS
13–15  Iowa Educational Media Assn.   Council Bluffs, IA
17–19  Connecticut Library Assn.    Cromwell, CT
22–26  Evangelical Christian Publishers Assn. Scottsdale, AZ
25–28  Catholic Library Assn.     Baltimore, MD
26–29  Montana Library Assn.     Billings, MT
\*    FIAF–International Federation of Film
     Archives         London, England

**May**

5–11   Medical Library Assn.     Vancouver, BC

**June**

10–15  Special Libraries Assn.     Philadelphia, PA
\*    Western Writers of America   Kerrville, TX

**July**

6–13   American Library Assn.     Chicago, IL
15–20  American Assn. of Law Libraries   Philadelphia, PA
23–25  Church and Synagogue Library Assn.  Kansas City, KS

**August**

3–6   REFORMA National Conference   Tucson, AZ
5–12   International Assn. of Music Libraries,
     Archives, and Documentation Centres
     (IAML)         Edinburgh, Scotland
28–9/3  Society of American Archivists   Denver, CO

**September**

20–24  American Translators Assn.    Orlando, FL

**October**

2–6   Michigan Library Assn.     Detroit, MI
4–6   Idaho Library Assn.      Lewiston, ID
5–7   Minnesota Educational Media Organization Duluth, MN
7–10   Arkansas Library Assn.     Springdale, AR

| | | |
|---|---|---|
| 11–13 | Minnesota Library Assn. | Minneapolis/ Saint Paul, MN |
| 16–22 | Global 2000 (Special Libraries Assn.) | Brighton, England |
| 18–20 | Iowa Library Assn. | Ames, IA |
| 22–25 | ARMA International | Las Vegas, NV |
| 24–28 | Alabama Library Assn. | Mobile, AL |
| 24–28 | Southeastern Library Assn. | Mobile, AL |
| 25–27 | Mountain Plains Library Assn. | Omaha, NE |
| 25–27 | Nebraska Educational Media Assn. | Omaha, NE |
| 25–27 | Nebraska Library Assn. | Omaha, NE |

**November**

| | | |
|---|---|---|
| 2–4 | Illinois School Library Media Assn. | Lincolnshire, IL |
| 11–14 | California Library Assn. | Santa Clara, CA |

# 2001

**January**

| | | |
|---|---|---|
| 12–17 | American Library Assn. Midwinter Meeting | Washington, DC |

**March**

| | | |
|---|---|---|
| * | Assn. for Indiana Media Educators | Indianapolis, IN |

**April**

| | | |
|---|---|---|
| 4–6 | Kansas Library Assn. | Topeka, KS |
| 17–20 | Catholic Library Assn. | Milwaukee, WI |
| 25–28 | Montana Library Assn. | Kalispell, MT |
| 28–5/2 | Evangelical Christian Publishers Assn. | Hilton Head, SC |

**June**

| | | |
|---|---|---|
| 9–14 | Special Libraries Assn. | San Antonio, TX |
| 14–21 | American Library Assn. | San Francisco, CA |
| * | Western Writers of America | Idaho Falls, ID |

**July**

| | | |
|---|---|---|
| 8–14 | International Assn. of Music Libraries, Archives, and Documentation Centres (IAML) | Perigueux, France |

**August**

| | | |
|---|---|---|
| 26–9/2 | Society of American Archivists | Washington, DC |

**September**

| | | |
|---|---|---|
| 30–10/3 | ARMA International | Montreal, PQ |

**October**

| | | |
|---|---|---|
| 10–12 | Iowa Library Assn. | Davenport, IA |
| 31–11/4 | American Translators Assn. | Los Angeles, CA |

**November**

| | | |
|---|---|---|
| 6–9 | Michigan Library Assn. | Lansing, MI |

## 2002

**March**

| | | |
|---|---|---|
| * | Assn. for Indiana Media Educators | Indianapolis, IN |

**April**

| | | |
|---|---|---|
| 24–27 | Montana Library Assn. | Great Falls, MT |

**June**

| | | |
|---|---|---|
| 8–13 | Special Libraries Assn. | Los Angeles, CA |

**August**

| | | |
|---|---|---|
| 4–9 | International Assn. of Music Libraries, Archives, and Documentation Centres (IAML) | Los Angeles, CA |
| 19–25 | Society of American Archivists | Birmingham, AL |

**September**

| | | |
|---|---|---|
| 29–10/2 | ARMA International | New Orleans, LA |

**October**

| | | |
|---|---|---|
| 29–11/1 | Michigan Library Assn. | Grand Rapids, MI |

## 2003

**October**

| | | |
|---|---|---|
| 19–22 | ARMA International | Boston, MA |

* To be determined

# Acronyms

AALL. American Association of Law
  Libraries
AAP. Association of American Publishers
AAR. Association of Authors'
  Representatives
AASL. American Association of School
  Librarians
ACLIN. Access Colorado Library
  Information Network
ACLU. American Civil Liberties Union
ACRL. Association of College and Research
  Libraries
AECT. Association of Educational
  Communications and Technology
AGRIS. Agricultural Science and
  Technology Database
AJL. Association of Jewish Libraries
ALA. American Library Association
ALCTS. Association for Library Collections
  and Technical Services
ALISE. Association for Library and
  Information Science Education
ALS. Academic Libraries Survey
ALSC. Association for Library Service to
  Children
ALTA. American Library Trustee
  Association
AMMLA. American Merchant Marine
  Library Association
AOL. America Online
APALA. Asian/Pacific American Librarians
  Association
APLEN. Alberta Public Library Electronic
  Network
ARL. Association of Research Libraries
ARLIS/NA. Art Libraries Society of North
  America
ARMA. ARMA International (Association of
  Records Managers and Administrators)

ASCLA. Association of Specialized and
  Cooperative Library Agencies
ASIS. American Society for Information
  Science
ATLA. American Theological Library
  Association
ATPA. American Technology Preeminence
  Act
AUPs. Internet, acceptable-use policies

## B

BEA. BookExpo America
BSA. Bibliographical Society of America

## C

CACUL. Canadian Association of College
  and University Libraries
CAIS. Canadian Association for Information
  Science
CALA. Chinese-American Librarians
  Association
CALL. Canadian Association of Law
  Libraries
CAPL. Canadian Association of Public
  Libraries
CASLIS. Canadian Association of Special
  Libraries and Information Services
CD-ROM. Compact Disc Read-Only
  Memory
CDA. Communications Decency Act
CIEC. Citizens Internet Empowerment
  Coalition
CIPS. National Archives and Records
  Administration, Centers Information
  Processing System
CISTI. Canadian Institute for Scientific and
  Technical Information

CLA. Canadian Library Association;
Catholic Library Association
CLTA. Canadian Library Trustees
Association
CNIB. Canadian National Institute for the
Blind
COPA. Child Online Protection Act
COPPA. Children's Online Privacy
Protection Act
CORDS. Library of Congress, Copyright
Office Electronic Registration,
Recordation and Deposit System
COSLA. Chief Officers of State Library
Agencies
CPL. Council of Planning Librarians
CRCA. Copyright Remedies Clarification
Act
CRS. Library of Congress, Congressional
Research Service
CRTC. Canadian Radio-Television and
Telecommunications Commission
CSLA. Canadian School Library Association;
Church and Synagogue Library
Association

**D**

DDM. Federal depository libraries,
Documents Data Miner
DFC. Digital Future Coalition
DLF. Digital Library Foundation
DMCA. Digital Millennium Copyright Act
DOE. Education, U.S. Department of

**E**

EAR. National Technical Information
Service, U.S. Export Administration
Regulations
ECIP. Library of Congress, Electronic
Cataloging in Publication
EDB. Energy Science and Technology
EDRS. Educational Resources Information
Center, ERIC Document Reproduction
Service
EMC. National Agricultural Library,
Electronic Media Center
EMIERT. American Library Association,
Ethnic and Multicultural Information
Exchange Round Table
ENAL. Egyptial National Agricultural
Library

ERIC. Educational Resources Information
Center
EROMM. European Register of Microform
Masters

**F**

FBB. GPO Access, Federal Bulletin Board
FBIS. Foreign Broadcast Information Service
FDLP. Government Printing Office, Federal
Depository Library Program
FEDRIP. National Technical Information
Service, Federal Research in Progress
Database
FIAF. International Federation of Film
Archives
FID. International Federation for Information
and Documentation
FLICC. Federal Library and Information
Center Committee
FLRT. American Library Association,
Federal Librarians Round Table
FNIC. Food and Nutrition Information
Center
FPC. Federal Publishers Committee
FSCS. Federal-State Cooperative System for
Public Library Data

**G**

GLIN. Global Legal Information Network
GODORT. American Library Association,
Government Documents Round Table
GPO. Government Printing Office
GPRA. Government Performance and
Results Act

**H**

HEA. Higher Education Act

**I**

IALL. International Association of Law
Libraries
IAML. International Association of Music
Libraries, Archives and Documentation
Centres
IASL. International Association of School
Librarianship

IATUL. International Association of Technological University Libraries

ICOLC. International Coalition of Library Consortia

ICSECA. International Contributions for Scientific, Educational and Cultural Activities

IFLA. International Federation of Library Associations and Institutions

IFRT. American Library Association, Intellectual Freedom Round Table

ILL. Interlibrary loan

IMLS. Institute of Museum and Library Services

IPS. Integrated Processing System

IRC. Special Libraries Association, Information Resources Center

ISBN. International Standard Book Number

ISLD. International Special Librarians Day

ISO. International Organization for Standardization

ISSN. International Standard Serial Number

## L

LAMA. Library Administration and Management Association

LHRT. American Library Association, Library History Round Table

LIS. Library of Congress, Legislative Information System

LIS. Library/information science

LITA. Library and Information Technology Association

*LJ. Library Journal*

LPS. Government Printing Office (GPO), Library Programs Service

LRRT. American Library Association, Library Research Round Table

LSCA. Library Services and Construction Act

LSP. National Center for Education Statistics, Library Statistics Program

LSSI. Library Systems and Services, Inc.

LSTA. Library Services and Technology Act

## M

MAGERT. American Library Association, Map and Geography Round Table

MLA. Medical Library Association; Music Library Association

## N

NAC. National Audiovisual Center

NAGARA. National Association of Government Archives and Records Administrators

NAILDD. North American Interlibrary Loan and Document Delivery (NAILDD) Project

NAL. National Agricultural Library

NARA. National Archives and Records Administration

NCBI. National Center for Biotechnology Information

NCEF. National Clearinghouse on Educational Facilities

NCES. National Center for Education Statistics

NCLIS. National Commission on Libraries and Information Science

NDLF. National Digital Library Federation

NEA. National Endowment for the Arts

NEDRC. National Education Data Resource Center

NEH. National Endowment for the Humanities

NEN. National Education Network

NFAIS. National Federation of Abstracting and Information Services

NGI. Next Generation Internet

NIOSH. National Institute for Occupational Safety and Health

NISO. National Information Standards Organization

NLC. National Library of Canada

NLE. National Library of Education

NLM. National Library of Medicine

NMAM. National Institute for Occupational Safety and Health, Manual of analytical Methods

NMRT. American Library Association, New Members Round Table

NN/LM. National Network of Libraries of Medicine

NPG. National Institute for Occupational Safety and Health, NIOSH Pocket Guide to Chemical Hazards

NPIN. National Parent Information Network

NTIS. National Technical Information Service

NUS. National Underground Storage, Inc.

## O

OCLC. Online Computer Library Center
OSP. Online service provider

## P

PDQ. United States Information Agency,
    library programs, Public Diplomacy Query
    database
PLA. Public Library Association
PURL. Computer software, persistent uni-
    form resource locator
*PW. Publishers Weekly*

## R

RASD. American Library Association,
    Reference and Adult Services Division.
    *See new name* Reference and User
    Services Association
RCLS. Riverside County (California) Library
    System
RIC. National Agricultural Library, Rural
    Information Center
RLG. Research Libraries Group
RTECS. Registry of Toxic Effects of
    Chemical Substances
RUSA. Reference and User Services
    Association

## S

SAA. Society of American Archivists
SAN. Standard Address Number

SASS. Schools and Staffing Survey
SLA. Special Libraries Association
*SLJ. School Library Journal*
SPARC. Scholarly Publishing & Academic
    Resources Coalition
SRRT. American Library Association, Social
    Responsibilities Round Table
SSP. Society for Scholarly Publishing
STLA. State Library Agencies Survey

## T

TIFAP. Internet Filter Assessment Project
TIIAP. Telecommunications and Information
    Infrastructure Assistance Program
TLA. Theatre Library Association

## U

ULAN. Africa; Union List of African
    Newspapers
ULC. Urban Libraries Council
USEIN. United States Education Information
    Network, *see new name* National
    Education Network
USIA. United States Information Agency
USIS. United States Information Service,
    *overseas name for* United States
    Information Agency
USPS. Postal Service, U.S.

## Y

YALSA. Young Adult Library Services
    Association

# Index of Organizations

Please note that this index includes cross-references to the Subject Index. Many additional organizations can be found in Part 6 under the following headings: Networks, Consortia, and Cooperative Library Organizations; National Library and Information-Industry Associations, United States and Canada; State, Provincial, and Regional Library Associations; State and Provincial Library Agencies; State School Library Media Associations; International Library Associations; Foreign Library Associations; Book Trade Associations, United States and Canada; International and Foreign Book Trade Associations

## A

Access Colorado Library Information Network (ACLIN), 13

AGRICOLA (Agricultural OnLine Access), 38–39, 103, 104

Agricultural Network Information Center (AgNIC), 106

Agriculture, U.S. Department of (USDA) *see* National Agricultural Library

AGRIS (Agricultural Science and Technology database), 39

Alberta Public Library Electronic Network (APLEN), 230

America Online (AOL), 154

American Association of Law Libraries (AALL), 704–705

awards, 399

American Association of School Librarians (AASL), 11, 708–709

awards, 401

grants, 437

ICONnect, 249

KidsConnect, 248

American Civil Liberties Union (ACLU), 10

American Library Association (ALA), 153–159, 242, 705–725

"Access to Electronic Information, Services and Networks", 246–247

Armed Forces Libraries Round Table awards, 402

awards, 159–160, 399–409, 435, 436

Banned Books Week, 157

Born to Read, 156

conferences, 158, 428

E–rate, activities related to, 154–155

Ethnic Material and Information Exchange Round Table (EMIERT) awards, 405

Exhibits Round Table awards, 405

Federal Librarians Round Table award, 405

filtering software, position on, 10, 157, 237

Government Documents Round Table (GODORT) awards, 405

grants, 159, 437

*Information Power: Building Partnerships for Learning*, 11

Intellectual Freedom Round Table award (IFRT), 405–406

KidsConnect, 154

Library History Round Table (LHRT) awards, 406, 435–436

Library Research Round Table (LRRT) awards, 406–407, 436

Map and Geography Round Table (MAGERT) awards, 407

minority librarians, efforts to increase, 156

National Survey of Public Library Outlet Internet Connectivity, 428

New Members Round Table (NMRT) awards, 407

notable books list, 619–627

personnel, 160

Publishing Committee awards, 408

Reference and Adult Services Division (RASD), *see* Reference and User Services Association

# Subject Index

Please note that many cross-references refer to entries listed in the Index of Organizations.

## M

McElderry, Margaret, 13
Machine-readable materials
  acquisition expenditures
    academic libraries, 462–463(table)
    government libraries, 466–467(table)
    public libraries, 460–461(table)
    special libraries, 464–465(table)
Maine
  library associations, 766
  networks and cooperative library organiza-
    tions, 683
  school library media associations, 782
Maryland
  Book Fest, 111
  library associations, 766
  networks and cooperative library organiza-
    tions, 683
  school library media associations, 782
Massachusetts
  library associations, 766
  networks and cooperative library organiza-
    tions, 683–685
  school library media associations, 782–783
Media services, *see* School library media
  centers and services
Medical libraries, *see* Archivists and Librarians in the History of the Health Sciences; Association of Academic
  Health Sciences Librarians; Medical
  Library Association; National Library
  of Medicine
Mexico
  libraries, number of, 446–447
  NAL/Mexican University information
    exchange, 104
Michigan
  library associations, 766
  networks and cooperative library organiza-
    tions, 685–686
  school library media associations, 783
Microforms
  acquisition expenditures
    academic libraries, 462–463(table), 478
    government libraries, 466–467(table)
    public libraries, 460–461(table)
    special libraries, 464–465(table)
  archives, 104, 105
  prices and price indexes, 473(table),
    480(table), 486(table)

  *See also* Association for Information and
    Image Management; Association of
    Research Libraries; European Register
    of Microform Masters
Minnesota
  library associations, 767
  networks and cooperative library organiza-
    tions, 686–687
  school library media associations, 783
Minorities
  scholarships, 156
  *See also* African Americans; American
    Libraries Association, Ethnic Material
    and Information Exchange Round
    Table; Native Americans, library and
    information services to
Mississippi
  library associations, 767
  networks and cooperative library organiza-
    tions, 687
  school library media associations, 783
Missouri
  library associations, 767
  networks and cooperative library organiza-
    tions, 687–688
  school library media associations, 783
Montana
  library associations, 767
  school library media associations, 783
Muppets, 85–86
Music
  libraries, *see* International Association of
    Music Libraries, Archives and Docu-
    mentation Centres; Music Library
    Association

## N

National Digital Library Program, 77–78
National Film Preservation Act, 8
National Household Education Survey, 54
National Information Standards Organiza-
  tion, Z39 standards, 819–820
Native Americans, library and information
  services to; LSTA Native American
  Library Services Program, 343,
  348–349(table)
  bibliography for librarians, 567–568
*Natural Born Killers*, 168
Nebraska
  library associations, 767